MW01623271

# THE TRÈS RICHES HEURES OF JEAN, DUKE OF BERRY

# THE TRÈS RICHES HEURES
## OF JEAN, DUKE OF BERRY

## THE MASTERPIECE OF MEDIEVAL ILLUMINATION

Edited by Mathieu Deldicque

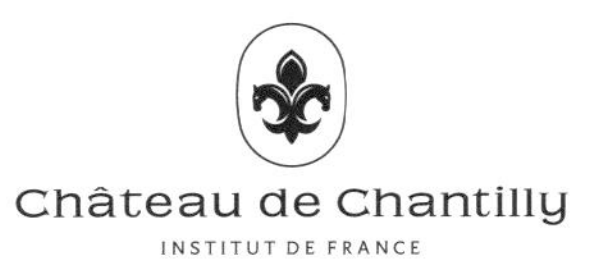


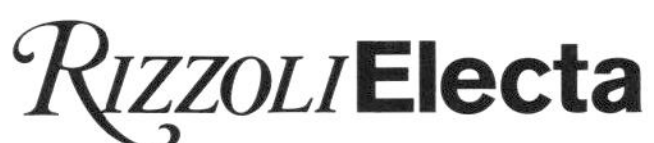

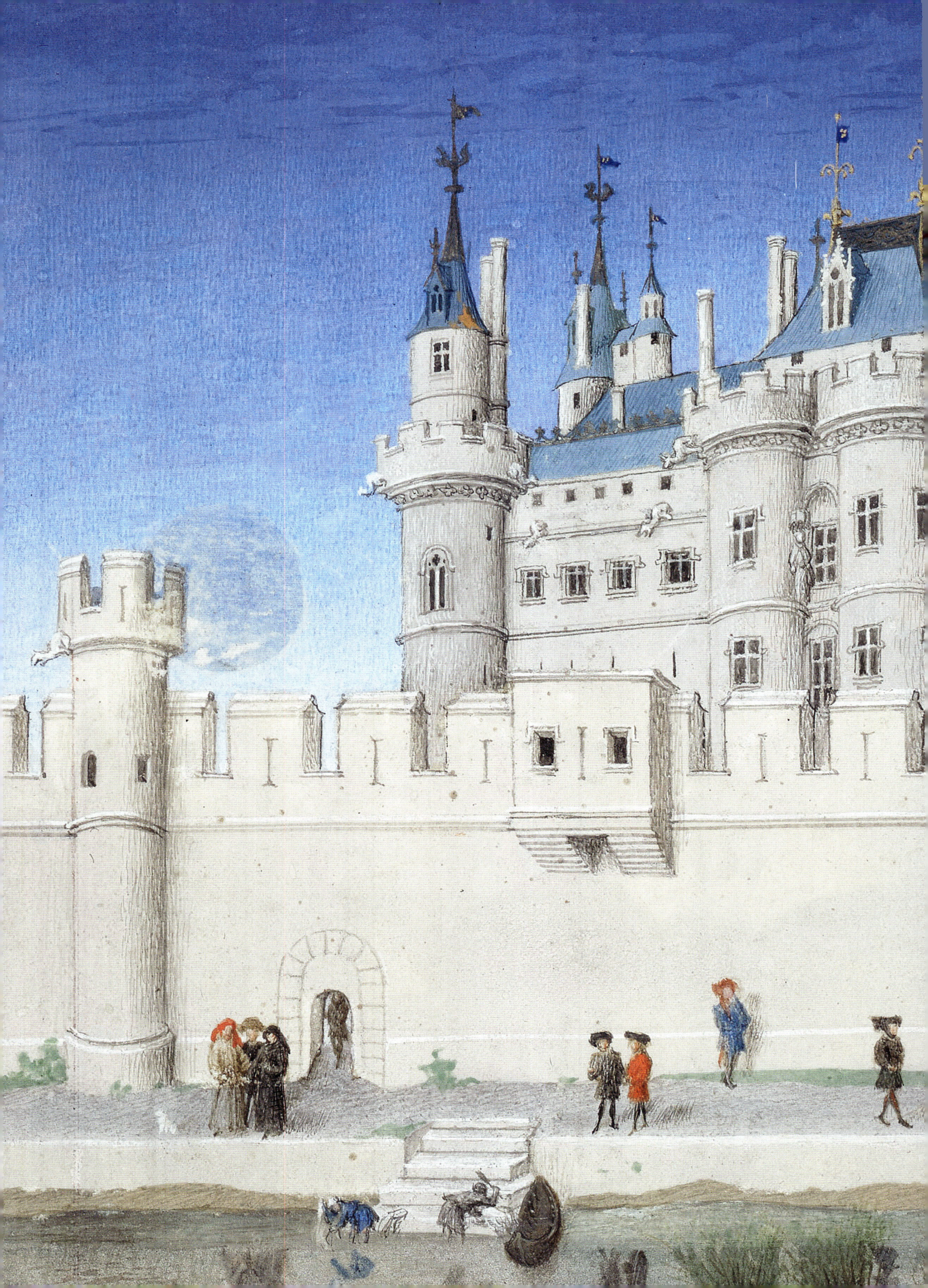

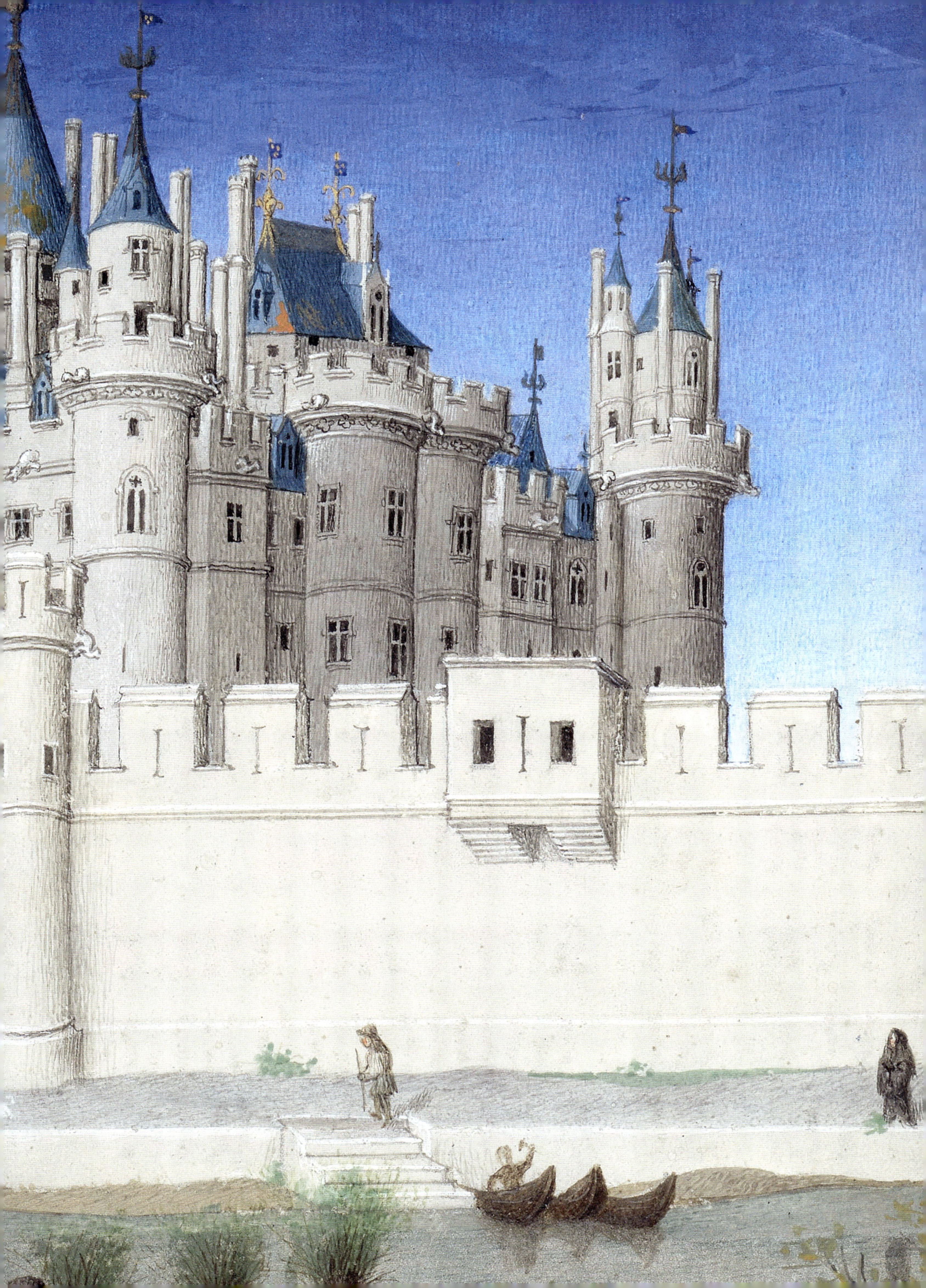

# Forewords

The exhibition *Les Très Riches Heures du duc de Berry* reveals both an absolute masterpiece and, through it, the apogee of a golden age of princely patronage. One of the most fruitful and innovative periods in the art of the Middle Ages flourished at the courts of the brothers of King Charles V—the dukes of Berry, Burgundy, and Anjou. The result of the meeting between the audacious vision of a patron and the inventiveness of exceptional artists, the *Très Riches Heures* stands out as a high point of the art that blossomed in a France at the crossroads of diverse inspirations—a symbol of a prosperous and interconnected Europe. The book was a daring commission given to the three Van Lymborch brothers, nephews of the painter Johan Maelwael, by the Duke of Berry towards the end of his life, around 1411. But its creation continued well beyond the duke's death; it was only completed around 1485—a remarkable act of endurance that bears witness to the power of the initial design.

Today, bringing together works that belonged to the Duke of Berry—paintings, sculptures, manuscripts (in particular, all his books of hours), gold and silver objects, and pieces of embroidery—makes it possible for us to gauge the scale of his ambitions, the creative energy of the workshops he inspired, and the movement of artistic ideas across Europe. Above all, this exhibition is a unique opportunity to admire twenty-six leaves and their miniatures from the *Très Riches Heures* as well as two illuminated pages that will be changed every two weeks, thus revealing one of the highlights of medieval illumination in all its splendor, as never seen before.

But what else could be revealed about such a famous work, reproduced over and over again, so familiar to us that we think we know it without ever having really looked at it? One of the great merits of this exhibition is that it shows the manuscript in a different light, partly unbound, in light of the discoveries made by restorers and the analyses carried out by the Centre de Recherche et de Restauration des Musées de France (C2RMF). These interventions shed light on the abundance of techniques and materials used and, by drawing attention to the finer details, make it possible to identify the hands of the various artists who worked on the manuscript.

Supported by leading scientific collaborations with, among others, the Bibliothèque nationale de France, the Musée du Berry, and the Bibliothèque municipale de Bourges, this exhibition has been awarded the label "Exposition d'intérêt national" (exhibition of national interest) by the French Ministry of Culture. This label recognizes its scholarly ambition, the scope of its discoveries, and the exceptional collection of works it makes available to the public. This accompanying catalog reproduces all the works on display, enriched with analyses and new findings, offering a major contribution to the historiography of the manuscript.

We wish to thank and congratulate all those who have worked to make this project a success, in particular its leaders, Mathieu Deldicque, curator and director of the Musée Condé, and Marie-Pierre Dion, general curator of the museum's library.

**Bertrand Gaume**
Prefect of the North and the Hauts-de-France region

Previous pages: Van Lymborch brothers, *Très Riches Heures*, fol. 10v: October, detail

To say that the Duke of Aumale, who donated the Musée Condé to the Institut de France, showed flair in amassing his art collection is an understatement. It is still something of a surprise to learn that he established the most important museum of ancient art in France after the Louvre in Paris. Integrated into this museum is an equally exceptional library, one of our country's richest, where illuminated manuscripts are like the ancestors of the later paintings on display nearby. Among these manuscripts, one in particular has been the source of many dreams and fantasies. It is the most famous in the world, the one that is used to provide illustrations whenever the Middle Ages are mentioned. Its name alone is enough to fire the imagination: the *Très Riches Heures du duc de Berry* (The Très Riches Heures of Jean, Duke of Berry).

A masterpiece that is as famous as it is inaccessible, this work is more than a mere book. It is a world unto itself, a manuscript commissioned by a brilliant patron of the arts who entrusted three young illuminators with the task of realizing his bibliophilic dream, in the evening of his life. Sadly, all four breathed their last only a few months apart, in 1416, leaving it to other patrons and other renowned miniaturists to complete, over the course of much of the fifteenth century, a work that instantly became an inspiring icon. We owe it to the Duke of Aumale not only to have grasped the importance of this treasure when he acquired it in 1856, but also to have immediately ensured it was studied and promoted.

It is the destiny of the most incredible of manuscripts that this exhibition and its catalog honor, under the leadership of Mathieu Deldicque, assisted by Marie-Pierre Dion. I am grateful to them both for their efforts to look after this admirable work of art, to preserve it and to showcase it in such an exceptional manner. For it is a truly historic event that we are celebrating here. The *Très Riches Heures* was in need of restoration, as experts had long agreed. The curators of the Musée Condé took every possible precaution and asked the best specialists to carry out preliminary analyses and determine a careful approach to any restoration. This operation involved, among other things, removing the binding from the first two quires—those of the famous calendar—which will enable visitors to the Château de Chantilly to see all the miniatures of the twelve months in this landmark exhibition. Indeed, for the first time since the death of the Duke of Berry and the dispersal of his collection, all his books of hours are reunited here, temporarily, around the *Très Riches Heures*. The exhibition has benefited from many other exceptional loans that make it possible to place the manuscript in context, and I wish to thank all the lenders, who Mathieu Deldicque was able to convince of the historical nature of this event. I also wish to acknowledge the numerous and generous patrons of this truly unique project. This catalog bears lasting witness to this undertaking, thanks to the contributions of many scholars. After the exhibition, the restored and rebound manuscript will be returned to the storerooms of the library of the Musée Condé—for a long time. We can be sure that interest in the library and its precious Cabinet des livres, which is itself in need of restoration, will remain strong: it is one of the greatest treasures of humanity.

**Xavier Darcos**
Chancellor, Institut de France

## JEAN, DUKE OF BERRY



## THE VAN LYMBORCH BROTHERS

## THE OTHER DECORATION CAMPAIGNS



## REDISCOVERY & RECOGNITION



## ANALYSES & RESTORATION

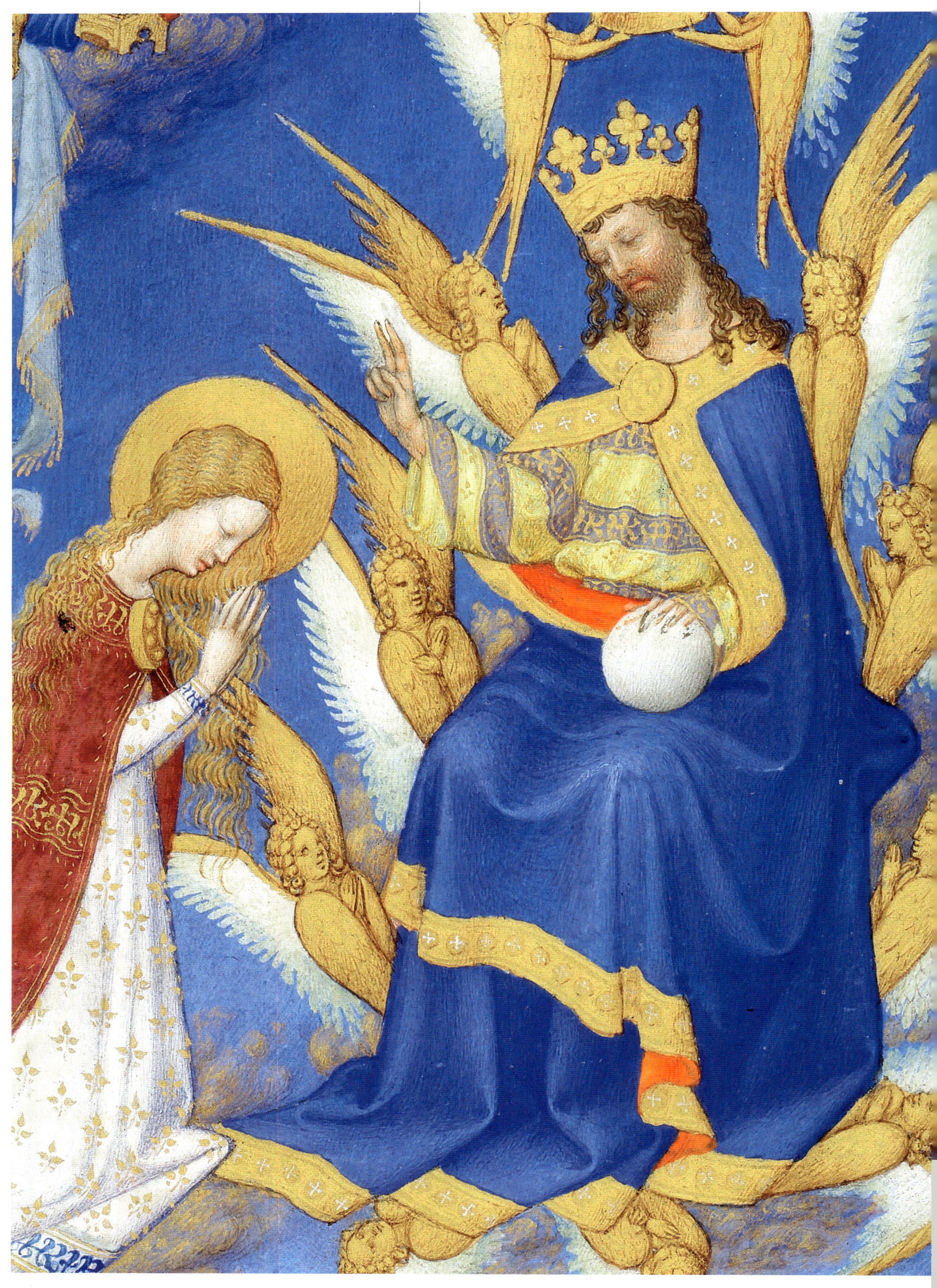

# “This book occupies a significant place in the history of art; I dare say it has no rival.”

– Henri d’Orléans, Duke of Aumale

Van Lymborch brothers, *Très Riches Heures*, fol. 60v: The Coronation of the Virgin, detail

# Introduction

Mathieu Deldicque

At the start of this work, it's only fitting to remember the words of Henri d'Orléans, Duke of Aumale, who discovered the *Très Riches Heures* in 1856. While writing the catalog of his manuscripts—works that would soon make up the exceptional collection of the library of the Musée Condé—the duke was full of praise for one of his most amazing acquisitions: "This book occupies a significant place in the history of art; I dare say it has no rival."[1] Aware of the magnitude of this monument of illumination, the prince congratulated himself on a more than opportune purchase and shared "several indications" about Jean of Berry, the book's fate, its decoration, and the buildings illustrated in its calendar, leaving it to future scholars to compose the magnum opus devoted to this most prodigious of manuscripts.

"These *Heures* deserve a complete description, a thorough critique; others will accomplish this task," wrote the Duke of Aumale. It was high time to fulfill his wish. Shown to visitors to the Musée Condé twice over the past hundred years, in special exhibitions in 1956 and 2004, the *Très Riches Heures* was patiently waiting for its own hour to come. It was in 2012 that the idea of such an exhibition took root. I was then a trainee curator at the Musée Condé, and a new space designed specifically for the manuscript, the Jeu de Paume, had just been inaugurated. Exposure to this fascinating yet intimidating masterpiece led to the gradual conception of a plan: a major study and exhibition that would make this manuscript and it alone—not its first patron nor its artists—the center of attention. The aim would be to demonstrate why this work, whose evocative title of *Très Riches Heures* was discovered in 1881 by Léopold Delisle in the 1416 estate inventory of the Duke of Berry, was, despite its state of incompleteness, so much admired, so widely studied, and such a source of inspiration to the greatest artists of the time, from its inception to the early sixteenth century. The subject of countless reproductions since the time of the Duke of Aumale, this manuscript largely shaped the view we have of the medieval landscape—enchanting castles, sumptuous lords, beautiful ladies, workers laboring on the land throughout the seasons—via the images of its calendar that have been used and reused right up to the present day.

Since its reappearance in the 1850s, this fabulous work has inevitably been the subject of ongoing research. Following the essential studies of Léopold Delisle and Paul Durrieu, the great work of Millard Meiss on the Van Lymborch brothers and illumination at the time of the Duke of Berry remains unsurpassed.[2] Others have followed in their footsteps and added their own stone to this scholarly edifice. Luciano Bellosi was the first to identify the contribution of Barthélemy d'Eyck to the calendar.[3] Drawing on these studies, Raymond Cazelles, curator of the Musée Condé, published several monographs in the twentieth century,[4] which were only updated at the beginning of the twenty-first century, when interest in the manuscript was rekindled with the exhibition at Chantilly,[5] the release of a CD-ROM accompanying a new digitization of the manuscript (and again in 2020), and studies by Patricia Stirnemann and Inès Villela-Petit.[6] Meanwhile, the art of the Van Lymborch brothers and their great masterpieces have been the subject of several comprehensive studies published between 2005 and 2017,[7] and even prompted the establishment of the Maelwael Van Lymborch Foundation (based in Nijmegen, the brothers' birthplace, and dedicated to researching, promoting, and preserving their legacy) and a series of multidisciplinary studies.[8] But academic interest aside, the appeal of the *Très Riches Heures* lies in the very special aura that makes it *the* absolute manuscript, the Holy Grail of anyone with an interest in the Middle Ages. Umberto Eco, who was often inspired by the medieval world, confided in the preface to Raymond Cazelles's book that the miniatures of the *Très Riches Heures* were "one of the paths that enabled [him] to approach the Middle Ages,"[9] a sentiment shared by many that explains the fascination and desire aroused by this masterpiece. A largely frustrated desire, however: As Christopher de Hamel notes mischievously, it is "easier to meet the Pope or the President of the US than to hold the *Très Riches Heures*."[10]

In the past, however, the manuscript was widely consulted, perhaps too much, since it still bears the traces of such handlings. These increasingly visible marks of time gradually convinced me that it was necessary to carry out a restoration. Marie-Pierre Dion's appointment as head of the Musée Condé's library and archives in 2019 further strengthened my conviction. The backgrounds of the first quires showed inelegant stains; the parchment was disintegrating at the folds; the stitching was weakening at the joints; the margins of the calendar, the most admired pages, were soiled; above all, some flaking of the pictorial layer could be observed, notably on one of the famous double pages of the manuscript. After an initial appraisal carried out by the manuscripts department of the Bibliothèque nationale de France in early 2022, the need for comprehensive preliminary studies became apparent. French heritage conservator Coralie Barbe and her team then carried out the first true material analysis of the manuscript. This study was complemented by two analytical investigations—the first ever!—undertaken by the Centre de Recherche et de Restauration des Musées de France (C2RMF) in 2022 and 2023, coordinated by Élisabeth Ravaud. A wealth of new and diverse imaging, covering a considerable number of pages of the manuscript, was gathered. The relocation of the manuscript to the C2RMF at the Palais du Louvre (itself illustrated in the month of October) in 2023 was an ideal opportunity to physically compare it with the only painting currently attributed to the Van Lymborch brothers, *Man of Sorrows* (Musée du Louvre), and thus confirm this recent attribution, as explained in this volume.

While these investigations greatly advanced our knowledge of the *Très Riches Heures du duc de Berry*, the other studies confirmed that the manuscript was indeed in need of restoration. But working on the Mona Lisa of manuscripts is no light matter. The results of various analyses and our discussions with Coralie Barbe led us to take cautious but resolute decisions. To do nothing was to take a risk; to unbind the entire manuscript in order to be able to bind it again after carrying out the restoration work, even if its stitching had already been changed in the early twentieth century, was to expose ourselves to the possibility of no longer being able to replace the body of the work in its eighteenth-century binding. The decision was made to unbind the two quires of the calendar, the most damaged, a prudent solution that was to be accompanied by campaigns to fix the paint flakes that were falling off, and other necessary interventions described in this catalog.

This restoration offered a unique opportunity to show visitors to Chantilly the manuscript almost stripped bare, a state it had not been in since the fifteenth century, before it was first bound. The famous miniatures of the calendar could be displayed on their own, before being returned to the book's binding. This truly exceptional event was an invitation to examine the manuscript once again from start to finish, to capitalize on the countless studies about it, and to renew our approach to it on the basis of previously unpublished information gathered during the preparation of this project.

Of course, to take an interest in the *Très Riches Heures du duc de Berry* is also to look beyond the miracle of their creation, extraordinary though it was. The fruit of a meeting between the greatest patron of the arts of the late French Middle Ages and three brothers who revolutionized the art of illumination, the manuscript is one of the founding works of the history of Western art. It represents a veritable paradox: It was born in an era that, although troubled by the Hundred Years' War, fratricidal conflicts between princely factions, popular revolts, political assassinations, the Great Schism, and many other scourges, provided a wealth of resources when it came to artistic creation.

This wildly ambitious book was the result of a meeting between, on the one hand, an elderly man eager to pass on the memory of an intense political life and a consuming passion for the arts and also to push experimentation even further, within his very last book of hours, and, on the other, young prodigies ready to show all the audacity they were capable of. Despite the death of these four figures in 1416, leaving the work unfinished, the manuscript was already worthy of every superlative. A world unto itself, the *Très Riches Heures* is a melting pot of iconographies, styles, and references that reach far beyond what is usually found in a book of hours. A cathedral-like book, the *Très Riches Heures* was not only ornamented by a reliable team, renewed three times, of scribes and illuminators headed by the Van Lymborch brothers, but completed by two other illumination campaigns carried out during the fifteenth century by two of the greatest artists in the field, Barthélemy d'Eyck and then Jean Colombe. It took more than seventy years to complete the decoration of the manuscript—as long as it takes to finish a cathedral!

Before we step into this monument to illumination, let us point out that the essays gathered here, the reflection of a multidisciplinary approach, are only the beginning of the revival of the rich history of the most fabulous of manuscripts.

1 Aumale 1900–11, I, 59–71.
2 Meiss 1968 and 1974a.
3 Bellosi 1975.
4 Longnon and Cazelles 1969a; Cazelles and Rathofer 1984.
5 Chantilly 2004.
6 See, among others, Stirnemann and Villela-Petit 2013.
7 Nijmegen 2005; Los Angeles and New York 2008–10; Paris 2012; Amsterdam 2017–18.
8 *Maelwael Van Lymborch Studies*, I, 2018 and II, 2022.
9 Cazelles 1988a, 7.
10 De Hamel 2016, 2.

**Paul, Johan, and Herman Van Lymborch**
Breviary Master of John the Fearless
Pseudo-Jacquemart (Jeannin Petit?)
Egerton Master
Haincelin de Haguenau (Bedford Master)
Master of the KL of January
Master of the KL of August
Master of the Saracen
Pierre Gilbert and his workshop
**Barthélemy d'Eyck**
**Jean Colombe**
and an assistant (Jacquelin de Montluçon or Philibert Colombe?)

# TRÈS RICHES HEURES DU DUC DE BERRY

Paris and Bourges, c. 1411–16 (Van Lymborch brothers)
Anjou, c. 1446 (Barthélemy d'Eyck)
Bourges, c. 1485 (Jean Colombe)
Parchment, 206 folios, 290 × 210 mm
(Chantilly, Bibliothèque du musée Condé, ms. 65)

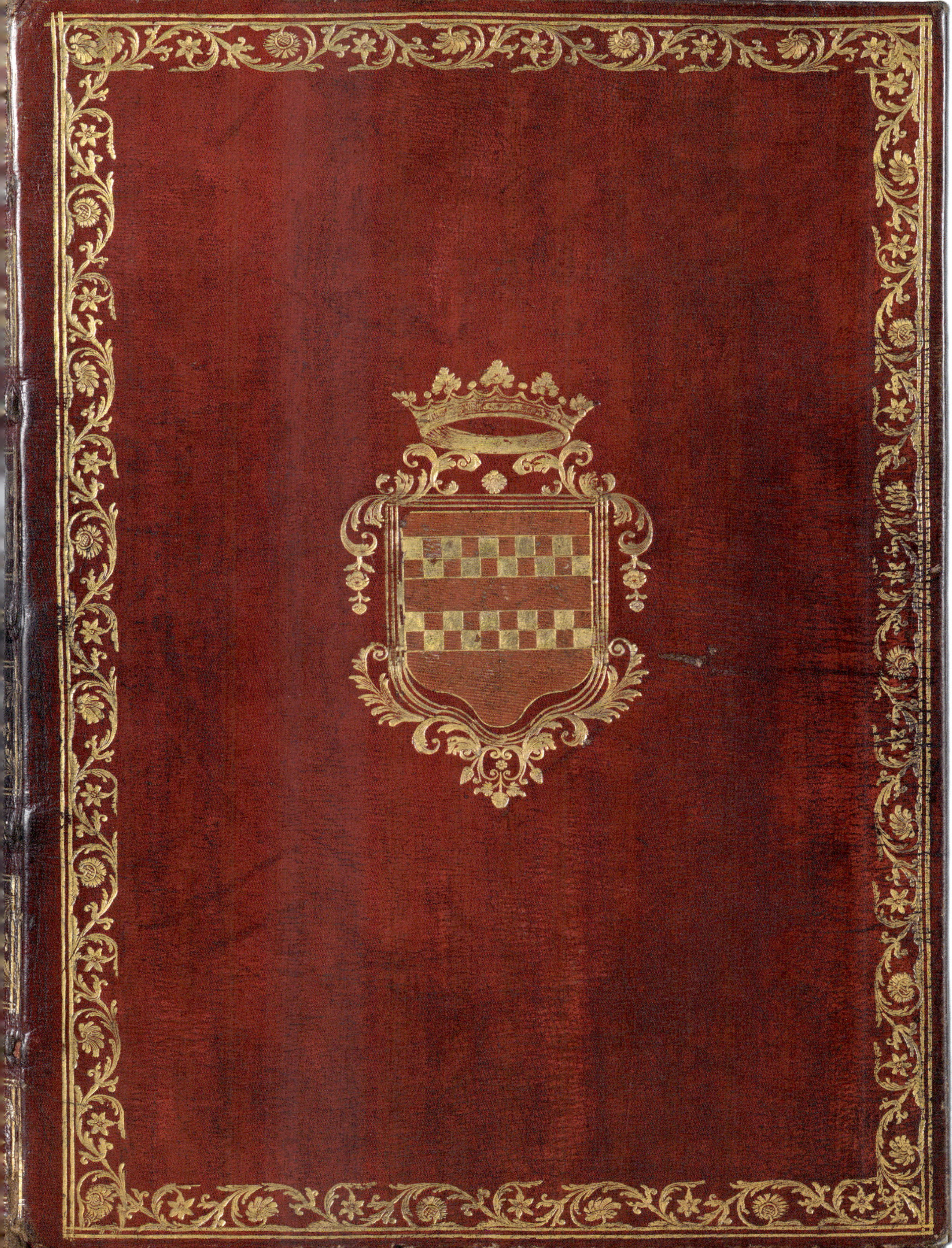

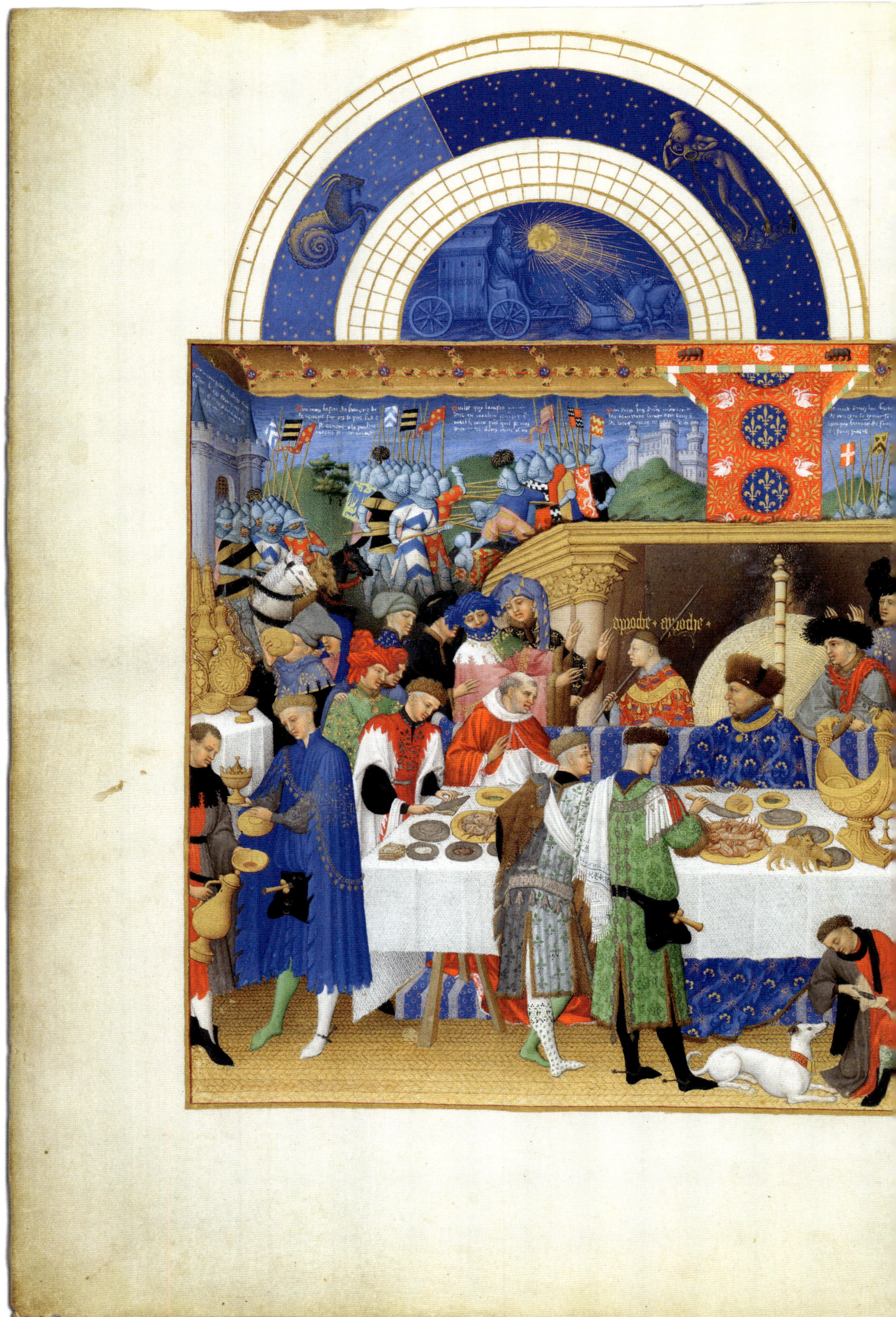
aproche aproche

| | | | | Janvier a. xxxi. iour<br>Et la lune. xxx. | La quantite<br>Des iours<br>heurez. ap[re]s | | Nombre<br>du<br>nouel. |
|---|---|---|---|---|---|---|---|
| iii. | A | | | | viii | xxvii | xix. |
| | b | iiii | N. | Octaves saint estienne. | viii | xxix. | |
| xi. | c | iii. | N. | Oct. s. iehan. segneueue. | viii | xxxi. | viii |
| | d | ii. | N. | Octaves des innocens. | viii | xxxiii | xvi. |
| xix. | e | Nonas | | saint symeon. | viii | xxxv. | v. |
| viii | f | viii | id. | | viii | xxxvii | |
| | g | vii | id. | saint fiambout. | viii | xxxix. | xiii. |
| xvi | A | vi. | id. | saint lucien. | viii | xli. | |
| v. | b | v. | id. | saint pol. premier hermite. | viii | xliii | ii |
| | c | iiii | id. | saint guillaume. | viii | xlv. | x. |
| xiii. | d | iii. | id. | saint sauveur. | viii | xlvii. | |
| ii. | e | ii. | id. | saint satur. | viii | xlix. | xviii |
| | f | Idus. | | saint hylaire. | viii | lii. | |
| x. | g | xix. | kl. | saint felix. | viii | lv. | vii. |
| | A | xviii | kl. | saint mor. | viii | lviii | xv. |
| xviii | b | xvii | kl. | saint marcel. | .ix. | o | |
| vii | c | xvi. | kl. | saint anthoine. | ix. | ii. | iiii. |
| | d | xv. | kl. | saint prisce. | .ix. | v. | xii. |
| xv. | e | xiiii | kl. | saint lomer. | ix. | viii. | .i. |
| iiii | f | xiii | kl. | saint sebastien. | .ix. | .x. | |
| | g | xii. | kl. | sainte agnes. | .ix. | xiii. | ix. |
| xii. | A | xi. | kl. | | ix. | xvi. | xvii. |
| i. | b | .x. | kl. | sainte emerancene. | .ix. | xix. | |
| | c | .ix. | kl. | saint babile. | .ix. | xxiii | vi. |
| ix | d | viii | kl. | | .ix. | xxvii | |
| | e | vii. | kl. | saint policarpe. | .ix. | xxx. | xiiii |
| xvii | f | vi. | kl. | saint iulien. | ix. | xxxiii. | |
| vi. | g | v. | kl. | sainte agnes. | ix. | xxxvi | iii. |
| | A | iiii | kl. | sainte paule | ix. | xxxix. | xi. |
| xiiii | b | iii | kl. | sainte baudour. | ix. | xlii | |
| iii. | c | ii. | kl. | Saint metran. | .ix. | xlv. | xix |

2

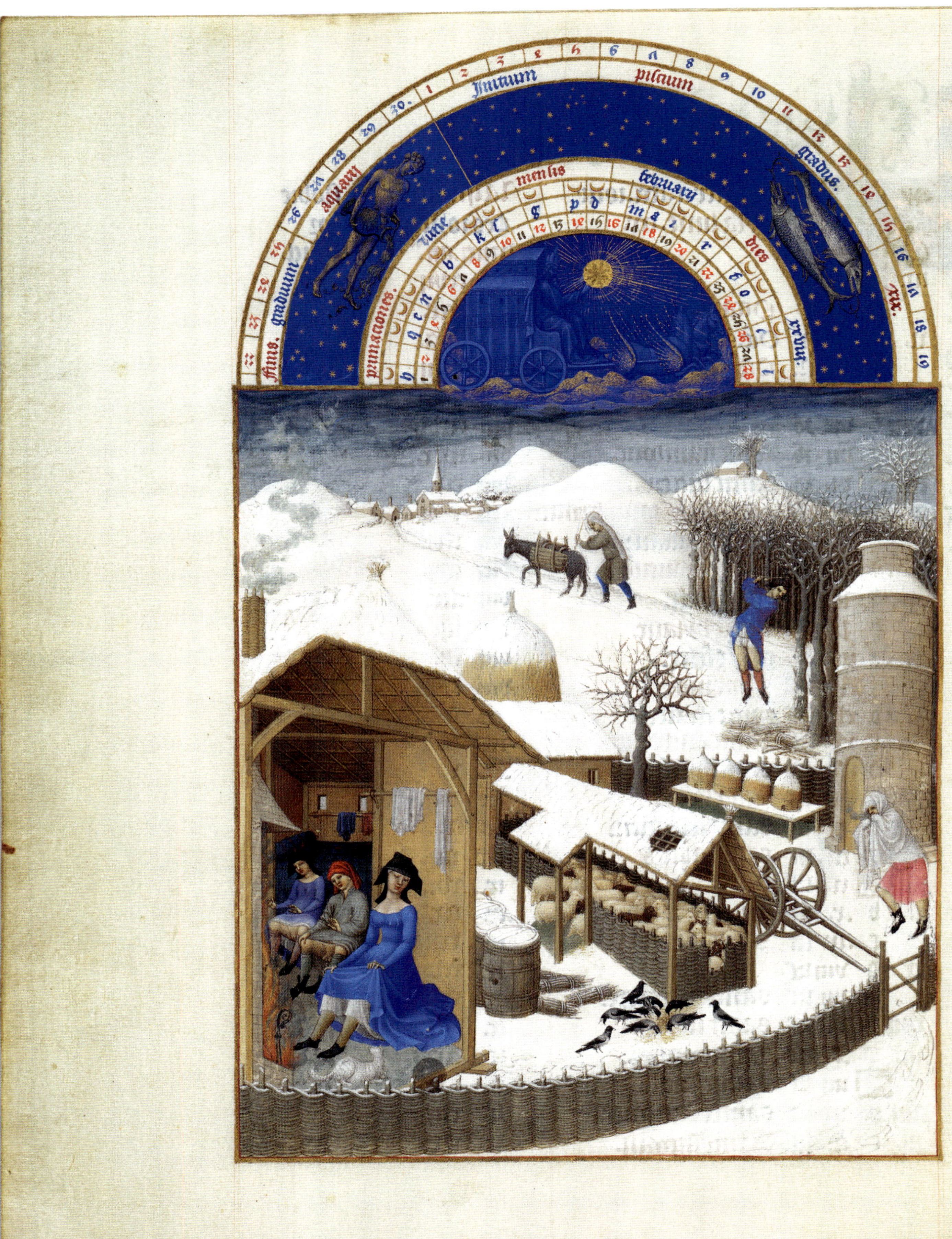

| | | | | Feurier a xxviij. iours<br>Et la lune. xxix. | La quantite des iours | | le nob. dor. nouel |
|---|---|---|---|---|---|---|---|
| | | | | | heure. | minu. | |
| | d | | | saincte bride. | ix. | xlv. | viij. |
| xi. | e | iiij. | no. | La purification. | ix. | xlviij | |
| xix | f | iij | no. | saint blaise. | ix. | li. | xvi. |
| viij | g | ij. | no. | saint auentin. | ix. | liiij | v. |
| | A | nonas. | | saincte agathe. | ix. | lvij. | xiij |
| xvi. | b | viij. | id. | saint amant. | x. | i. | |
| v. | c | vij. | id. | saincte helaine. | x. | v. | ij. |
| | d | vi. | id. | saint salomon. | x. | ix. | |
| xiij | e | v. | id. | saincte appoline. | x. | xv. | x. |
| ij. | f | iiij | id. | saincte scolastique. | x. | xviij | xviij |
| | g | iij. | id. | saint desier. | x. | xxi. | |
| x. | A | ij. | id. | saincte eulalie. | x. | xxvj. | vij. |
| | b | Idus. | | saint lucien. | x. | xxx. | |
| xviij | c | xvj | kl. | Saint ualentin. | x. | xxxiiij | xv. |
| vij | d | xv. | kl. | saint marcel. | x. | xxxvi | iiij |
| | e | xiiij | kl. | saincte iulienne. | x. | xxxix. | |
| xv. | f | xiij. | kl. | saint donace | x. | xliij. | [illegible] |
| iiij | g | xii. | kl. | saint symeon. | x. | xlv. | i. |
| | A | xi. | kl. | saincte susanne | x. | xlix. | ix. |
| xij | b | .x. | kl. | saint eleuthere. | x. | liij. | |
| i. | c | ix. | kl. | saint uictor. | x. | lvj. | xvij |
| | d | viij | kl. | saint pierre. | xi. | o. | |
| ix. | e | vij | kl. | saint policarpe. | xi. | iiij. | vi. |
| | f | vi. | kl. | saint mathias. | xi. | vj. | xiiij |
| xvij | g | v. | kl. | saint uictorin. | xi. | ix. | |
| vi. | A | iiij | kl. | saint uenice. | xi. | xij. | iij. |
| | b | iij. | kl. | saincte honorine. | xi. | xv. | |
| xiiij | c | ij. | kl. | saint iust. | .xi. | xix. | xi. |

3

Fols. 2v-3: February

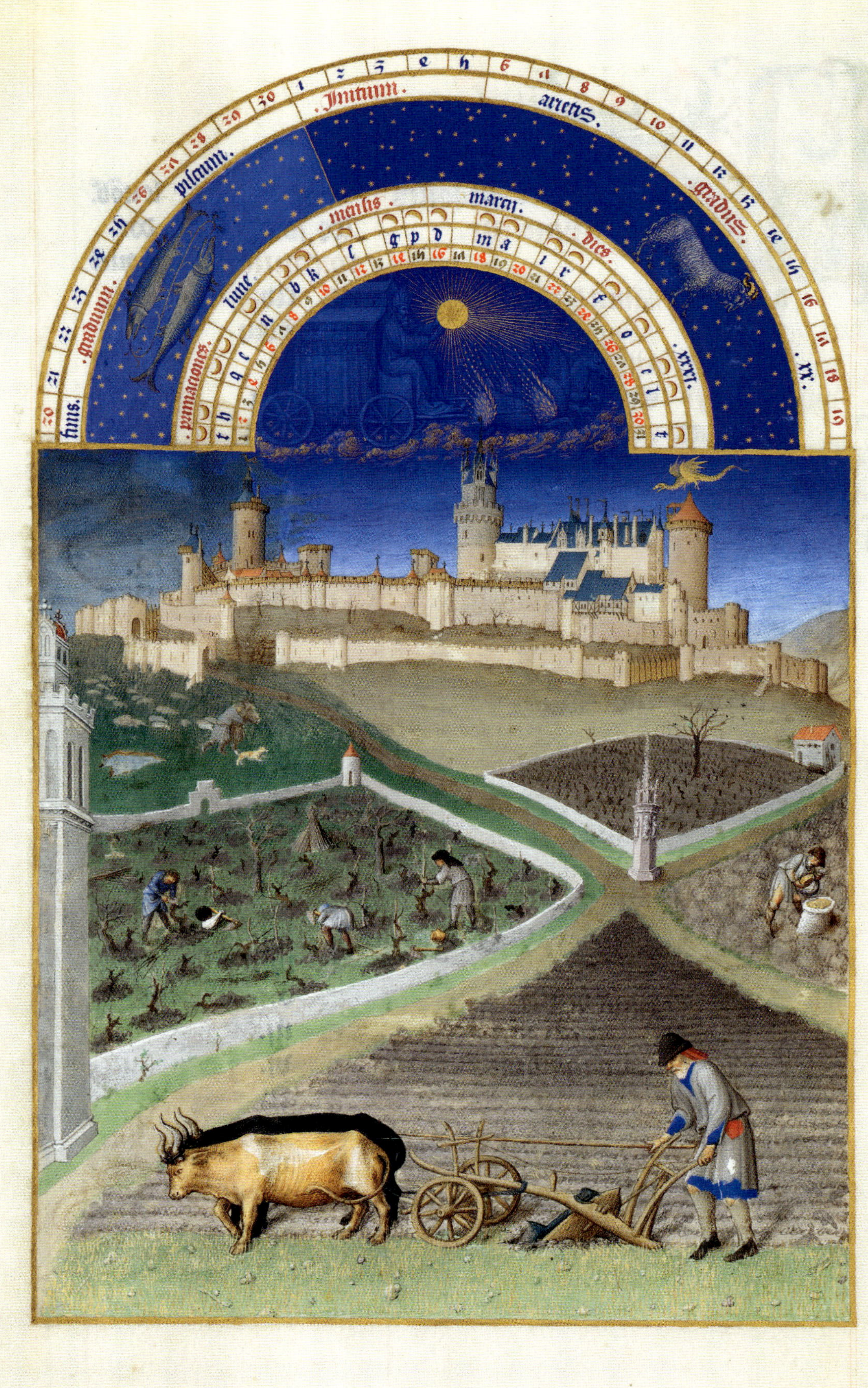

| | | | | Marcius habet dies xxxi. Luna habet dies xxx. | | Quantitas dierum. hore | minuta | Numerus aureus novus |
|---|---|---|---|---|---|---|---|---|
| iii. | d | Marcij | | saint aubin. | D | xi. | xxij. | xix. |
| | e | vi. | n. | saint pinne. | | xi | xxvj. | viij. |
| xi. | f | v. | n. | saint mauiin. | | xi. | xxx. | |
| | g | iiij | n. | Saint anduen. | | xi. | xxxiij. | xvi. |
| xix | | iij. | n. | saint saturnin. | | xi. | xxxvj. | v. |
| viij | b | ij. | n. | saint felice. | | xi. | xxxix. | |
| | c | pdie. | | saint thomas daquin. | | xi. | xliij. | xiij. |
| xvi | d | viij | id | saint potemaane. | | xi. | xlvj. | |
| v. | e | vij. | id | saint boutoul. | | xi. | l. | ij. |
| | f | vi. | id | saint alixandre. | | xi. | liij. | x. |
| xiij | g | v. | id | saint blanchart. | | xi. | lvij | |
| ij. | | iiij. | id | saint girgoire. | | xij. | o | xviij |
| | b | iij. | id | saint lubin. | | xij. | iiij. | |
| x. | c | ij. | id | saint innocent. | | xij. | viij | vij |
| | d | pdie | | saint longin. | | xij. | xij. | xv. |
| xviij | e | xvij. | kl | saint quiriace. | | xij. | xvj. | iiij. |
| vij | f | xvi. | kl | saint gertrud. | | xij | xx. | |
| | g | xv. | kl | saint offirn. | | xij | xxiiij. | xij. |
| xv. | | xiiij. | kl | saint astradose. | | xij | xxviij | i. |
| iiij | b | xiij. | kl | saint agapit. | | xij | xxxij | |
| | c | xij. | kl | saint benoit. | | xij | xxxvj | ix. |
| xii | d | xi. | kl | saint emerancaane. | | xij | xl. | xvij |
| i. | e | .x. | kl | saint theodoire. | | xij | xliiij | |
| | f | ix. | kl | | | xij | xlviij | vi. |
| ix. | g | viij | kl | | | xij | lij. | |
| | | vij. | kl | saint mondin. | | xij. | lvj. | xiiij |
| xvij | b | vi. | kl | saint ligier. | | xiij | i. | |
| vi. | c | v. | kl | saint ernoul. | D. | xiij | v. | iij. |
| | d | iiij | kl | saint eustace. | | xiij | ix. | xi. |
| xiiij | e | iii. | kl | saint nulle. | | xiij. | xiij. | |
| iij. | f. | ij. | kl. | saint albaur | | xiij. | xvij. | xix. |



Fols. 3v-4: March

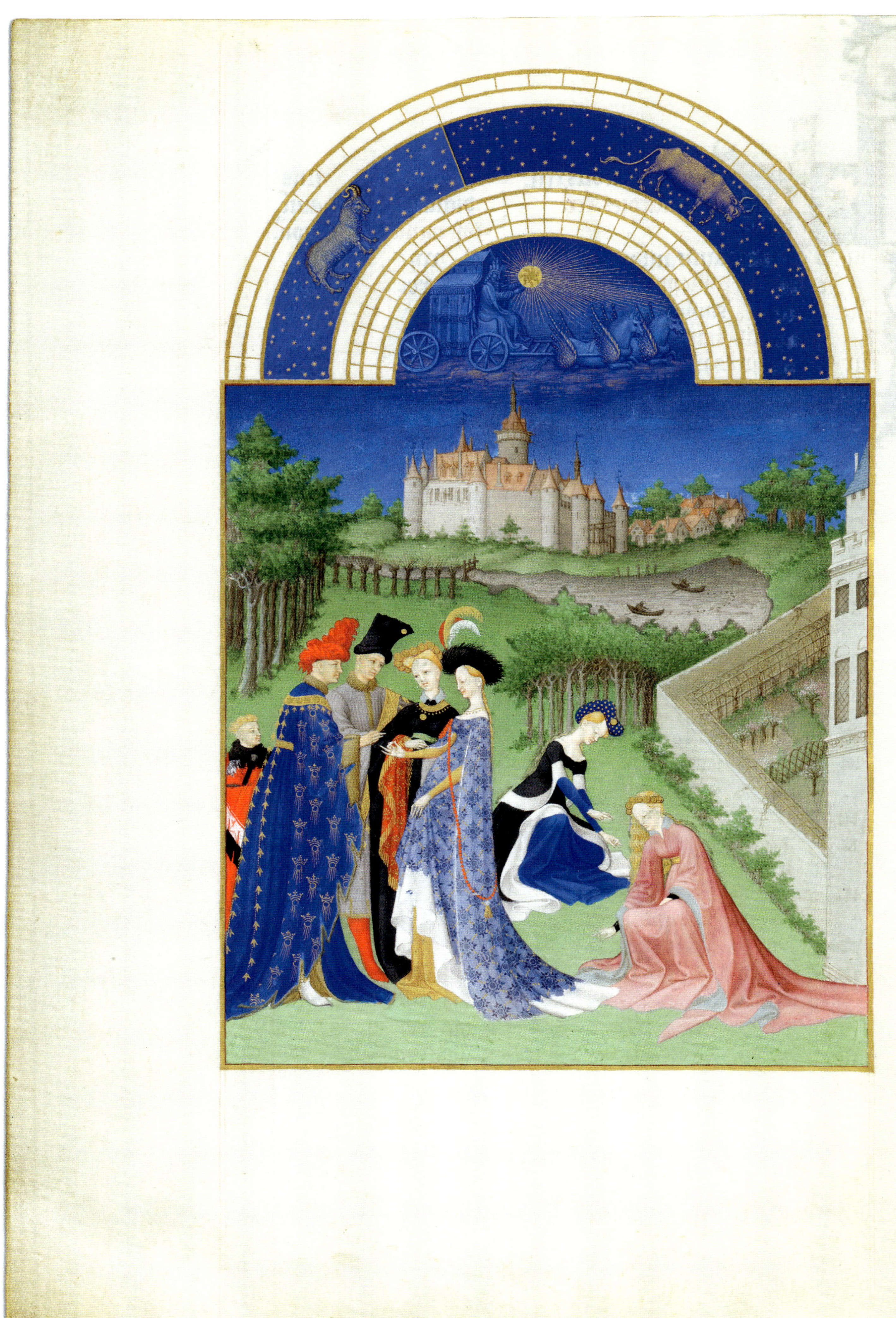

| | | Aprilis habet dies xxx. luna habet dies xxix. | | | Quantitas dierum. hore | minuta. | Nūs aur' novi |
|---|---|---|---|---|---|---|---|
| | g | Aprilis | saint valeri. | | xiij | xx. | vij. |
| xi. | | iiij n' | saint egipcienne. | | xiij | xxiiij | xvj |
| | b | iij. n' | saint pancrace. | | xiij. | xxvij | |
| xix | c | ij. n' | saint ambroise. | | xiij | xxx. | v. |
| viij | d | pridie | saint yrainne. | | xiij | xxxiij | xiij. |
| xvi. | e | viij id' | saint timothe. | | xiij | xxxvj | |
| v. | f | vij. id' | saint machaire. | | xiij | xlij. | ij. |
| | g | vi. id' | saint apolinaire. | | xiij | xlv. | |
| xiij | | v. id' | saint procor. | | xiij. | xlviij | x. |
| ij. | b | iiij id' | saint gobert. | D. | xiij | l. | xviij |
| | c | iij id' | saint lyon. | | xiij | liij. | |
| .x. | d | ij. id' | saint marcel. | | xiij | lv. | vij. |
| | e | pridie. | saint eufamie. | | xiij | lviij | |
| xviij | f | xviij kl' | saint valerien. | | xiiij | i. | xv. |
| vij | g | xvij. kl' | saint presime. | | xiiij | iiij. | iiij. |
| | | xvi. kl' | saint anaclet. | | xiiij | vij. | xij. |
| xv. | b | xv. kl' | saint leonide. | | xiiij | x. | |
| iiij. | c | xiiij kl' | saint mapolite. | | xiiij | xiij. | i. |
| | d | xiij. kl' | saint profeit. | D. | xiiij | xvj. | ix. |
| xij. | e | xij. kl' | saint victor. | | xiiij | xix. | |
| i. | f | xi. kl' | saint symeon. | | xiiij | xxij | xvij |
| | g | x. kl' | saint oportune. | | xiiij | xxvj. | |
| ix. | | ix kl' | | | xiiij | xxix. | vi. |
| | b | viij kl' | Vigile. | | xiiij | xxxij | xiij. |
| xvij | c | vij kl' | | | xiiij | xxxvj | |
| vi. | d | vi. kl' | saint clet. | | xiiij | xxxix | iij. |
| | e | v kl' | saint germain. | | xiiij | liij. | |
| xiiij | f | iiij. kl' | saint vital. | | xiiij | lv. | xi. |
| iij. | g | iij. kl' | saint pierre. | | xiiij | lviij | xix. |
| | | ij. kl' | saint eutrope. | | xiiij | lij. | viij |

Fols. 4v–5: April

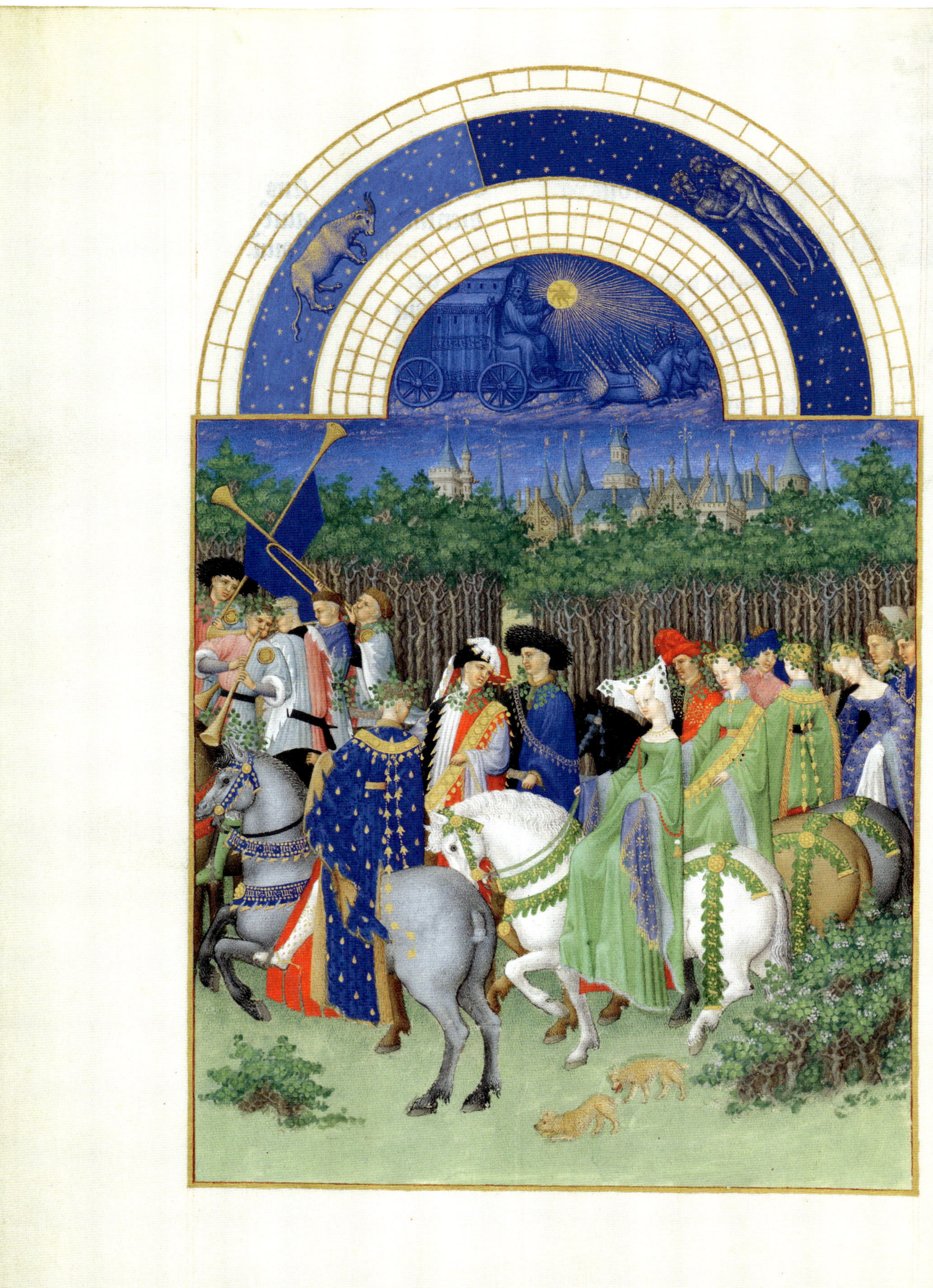

| | | | | May a. xxxi. iour. Et la lune. xxx. | La quantite des iours heures. min. | | Nombre dor nouvel |
|---|---|---|---|---|---|---|---|
| xi. | b | | | saint iaques s. phe. | xiiij | liiij | |
| | c | vi. | N. | sainct anastaise. | xiiij | lvij. | xvj |
| xix | d | v. | N. | saincte croys. | xiiij | lix. | v. |
| viij | e | iiij | N. | saint quiriace. | xv. | ij. | |
| | f | iij | N. | saint fortunat | xv. | .v. | xiij. |
| xvj | g | ij. | N. | saint iehan. | xv. | vij. | |
| v. | A | Nonas | | saint siluain. | xv. | x. | ij. |
| | b | viij | id. | saint beach. | xv. | xij. | x. |
| xiij | c | vij | id. | Saint nicolas. | xv. | xij. | |
| ij. | d | vi. | id. | saint gordian. | xv. | xvij | xviij. |
| | e | v. | id. | saint memert. | xv. | xix. | |
| x. | f | iiij | id. | saint ponciace. | xv. | xxi. | vij. |
| | g | iij. | id. | saint marcelin. | xv. | xxiiij | xv. |
| xviij | A | ij. | id. | saint boniface. | xv. | xxvj | iiij. |
| vij | b | Idus | | saint ysidoire | xv | xxviij | |
| | c | xvij | kl. | saint honore. | xv. | xxx. | xij. |
| xv. | d | xvi. | kl. | saint ambrose. | xv. | xxxij | i. |
| iiij | e | xv. | kl. | saint felix. | xv. | xxxv. | |
| | f | xiiij | kl. | saint yues. | xv. | xxxvij | ix. |
| xij. | g | xiij | kl. | saint vandrille. | xv. | xxxix. | |
| .i. | A | xij | kl. | saint audebert | xv. | xli. | xvij |
| | b | xi. | kl. | saint emille. | xv. | xliij | vi. |
| ix. | c | x. | kl. | saint disier. | xv | xliiij | |
| | d | ix. | kl. | saint donacien. | xv | xlv. | xiiij. |
| xvij | e | viij | kl. | saint urbain. | xv. | xlvj | |
| vi. | f | vij | kl. | saint augustin. | xv. | xlvij | iii. |
| | g | vi. | kl. | saint geron. | xv. | xlviij | xi. |
| xiiij | A | v. | kl. | saint germain. | xv. | xlix. | |
| iij. | b | iiij | kl. | saint maxime. | xv. | l. | xix. |
| | c | iij | kl. | saint felix. | xv. | li. | viij. |
| xi. | d | ij. | kl. | saint petronille. | xv. | lij. | xvj. |

Fols. 5v-6: May

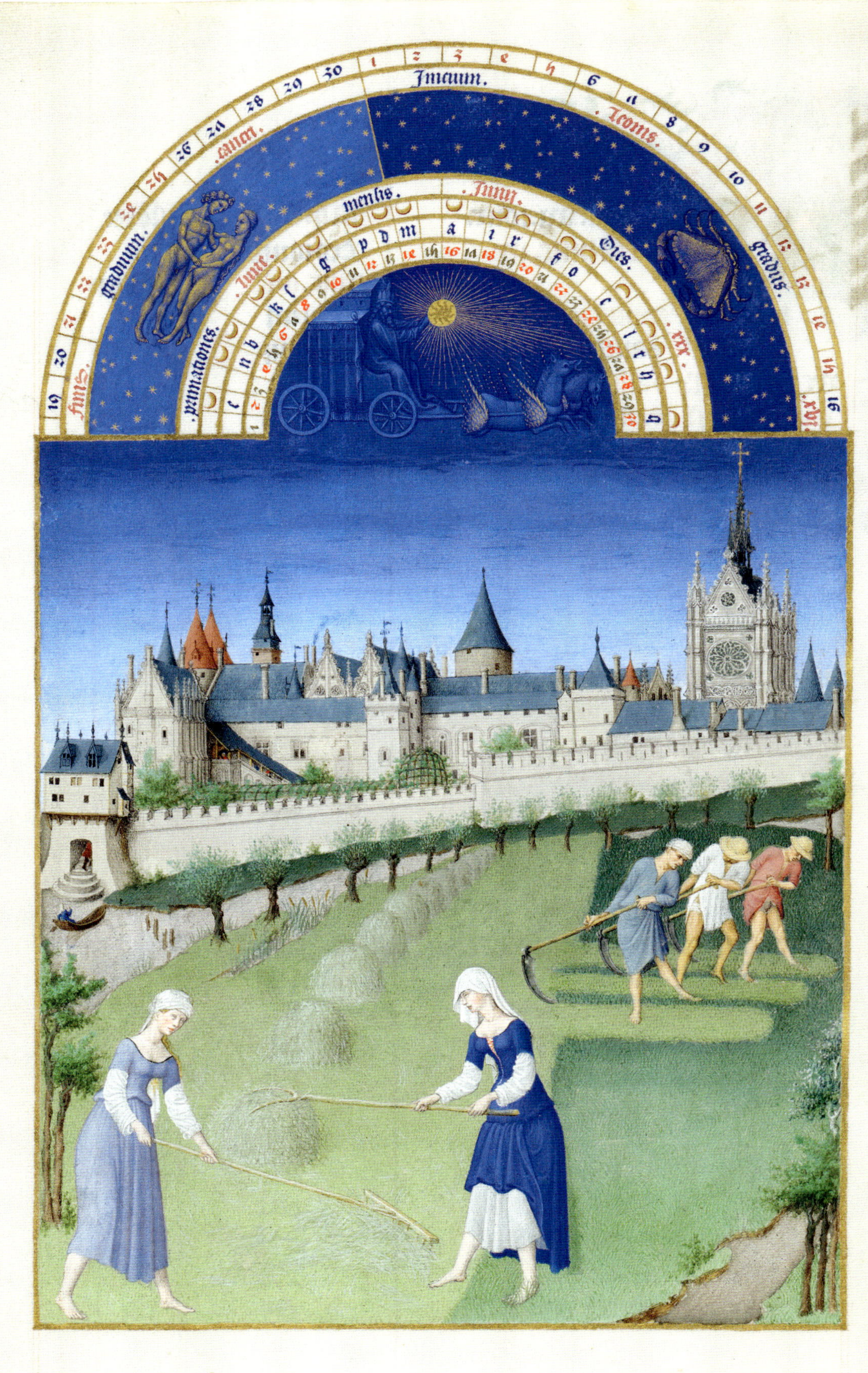

| KL | | | | Junius a .xxx. iours. Et la lune .xxix. | La q̃ntite des jours heurez.an. | | nombre dor nouel |
|---|---|---|---|---|---|---|---|
| | c | | | saint nicomede. | xv. | liii. | |
| xix. | f | iiii | no. | saint marcellin. | xv. | liiii. | v. |
| viii | g | iii. | no. | saint liffart. | xv. | lv. | |
| xvi. | A | ii. | no. | saint pontalin. | xv. | lv. | xiii |
| v. | b | nonas. | | saint boniface. | xv. | lvi. | ii. |
| | c | viii | id. | saint ponce. | xv. | lvi. | |
| xiii | d | vii | id. | saint proiet | xv. | lvii. | x. |
| ii. | e | vi. | id. | saint medart. | xv | lvii | xviii |
| | f | v. | id. | saint feliacn. | xv. | lviii | |
| x. | g | iiii | id. | saint landri. | xv. | lviii. | vii. |
| | A | iii. | id. | | xv | lix. | |
| xviii | b | ii. | id. | sainte basilide. | xv. | lix. | xv. |
| vii | c | Idus | | sainte fenieule. | xvi | o | iiii. |
| | d | xviii | kl. | saint rufin. | xvi | o | xii. |
| xv. | e | xvii | kl. | saint modest. | xvi | o | |
| iiii | f | xvi. | kl. | saint cir. | xvi. | o. | i. |
| | g | xv. | kl. | saint auit. | xv. | lix | |
| xii | A | xiiii | kl. | sainte marine. | xv. | lix. | ix. |
| i. | b | xiii. | kl. | saint geruais. | xv. | lix | xvii |
| | c | xii | kl. | sainte florence. | xv. | lviii | |
| ix. | d | xi. | kl. | saint leuffroy. | xv | lvii | vi. |
| | e | x. | kl. | saint paulin. | xv | lvi. | xiiii. |
| xvii | f | ix | kl. | Vigile. | xv. | lvi. | |
| vi. | g | viii | kl. | | xv. | lv. | iii. |
| | A | vii | kl. | | xv. | lv. | |
| xiiii | b | vi. | kl. | saint iehan.s.pol. | xv. | liiii | xi. |
| iii. | c | v. | kl. | saint lion. | xv. | liii | xix. |
| | d | iiii | kl. | Vigile. | xv. | lii | viii. |
| xi. | e | iii. | kl. | | xv. | li | |
| | f | ii. | kl. | saint marcial. | xv. | l. | xvi. |

Fols. 6v-7: June

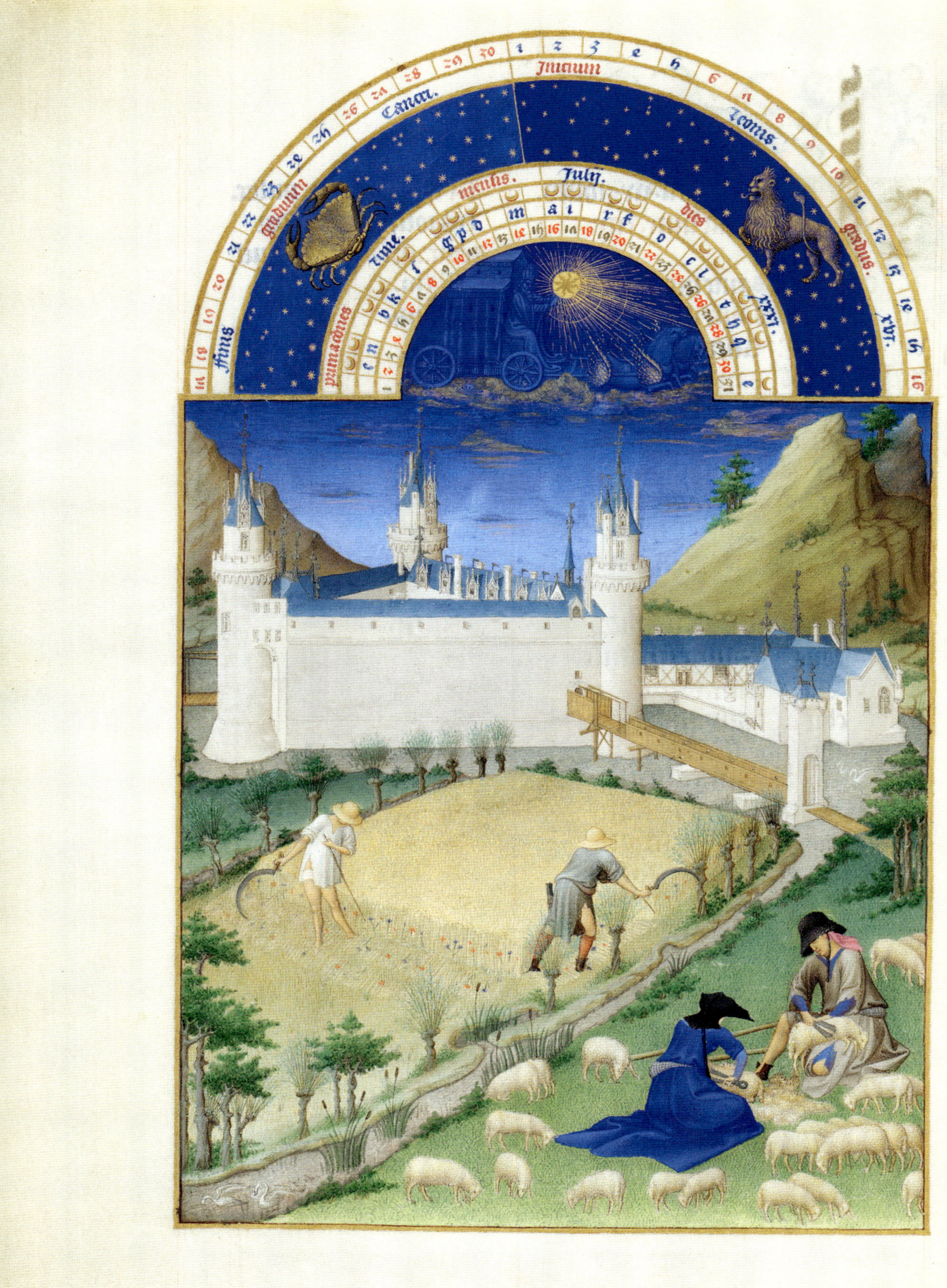

| | | | | Julius habet dies. xxxj. Luna habet dies xxix. | | Quantitas Dierum. | | Nus. aure. nou. |
|---|---|---|---|---|---|---|---|---|
| | | | | | | hore. | minuta. | |
| xix. | g | July | | Saint leonorin. | | xv. | .I. | |
| viij | A | vi. | N' | Saint procés. | | xv. | xlviij | .v. |
| | b | v. | N' | Saint apolin. | | xv. | xlv. | xiij. |
| xvj. | c | iiij. | N' | Saint martin. | | xv. | xliiij | |
| v. | d | iij. | N' | Saint dominique. | | xv. | xliij | ii. |
| | e | pdie | N' | Octaues saint pierre. | | xv. | xlij. | x. |
| xiij | f | Nonas. | | Saint thomas. | | xv. | xli. | |
| ij. | g | viij | id' | Saint claude. | | xv. | xxxviij | xviij. |
| | A | vij | id' | Saint tibault. | | xv. | xxxvi | |
| x. | b | vi. | id' | Les. vij. freres. | | xv. | xxxv. | vij. |
| | c | v. | id' | Saint benoit. | | xv. | xxxij | xv. |
| xviij | d | iiij | id' | Saint lisé. | | xv. | xxx. | iiij. |
| vij. | e | iij. | id' | Saint turien. | D. | xv. | xxviij | |
| | f | pdie | id' | Saint uaast. | | xv. | xxvi. | xij. |
| xv. | g | Idus. | | Saint florentin. | | xv. | xviii | |
| iiij. | A | xvij. | kl' | Saint alexis. | | xv. | xvij | .i. |
| | b | xvi. | kl' | Saint piat. | | xv. | xiiij | ix. |
| xij. | c | xv. | kl' | Saint arnoul. | | xv. | xij. | |
| i. | d | xiiij | kl' | Saint uist. | | xv | x. | xvij. |
| | e | xiij. | kl' | Sainte margarete. | | xv. | vij. | vi. |
| ix. | f | xij. | kl' | Saint uictor. | | xv | v. | |
| | g | xi. | kl' | | D. | xv. | ij. | xiiij. |
| xvij | A | x. | kl' | Saint appolinaire. | | xv. | o | |
| vi. | b | ix. | kl' | Sainte cristine. | | xv. | lvij | iij. |
| | c | viij | kl' | | | xv. | liiij | xi. |
| xiiij | d | vij | kl' | Saint marcel. | | xiiij | lij. | |
| iii | e | vi. | kl' | Les. vij. dormans. | | xiiij | xlviij | xix. |
| | f | v. | kl' | Sainte anne. | | xiiij | xlv | viij. |
| xi. | g | iiij. | kl' | Sainte marthe. | | xiiij | xliij. | xvi. |
| xix. | A | iij. | kl' | Saint abdon. | | xiiij | xlij. | |
| | b | pdie | kl' | Saint germain. | | xiiij | xli. | v. |

Fols. 7v-8: July

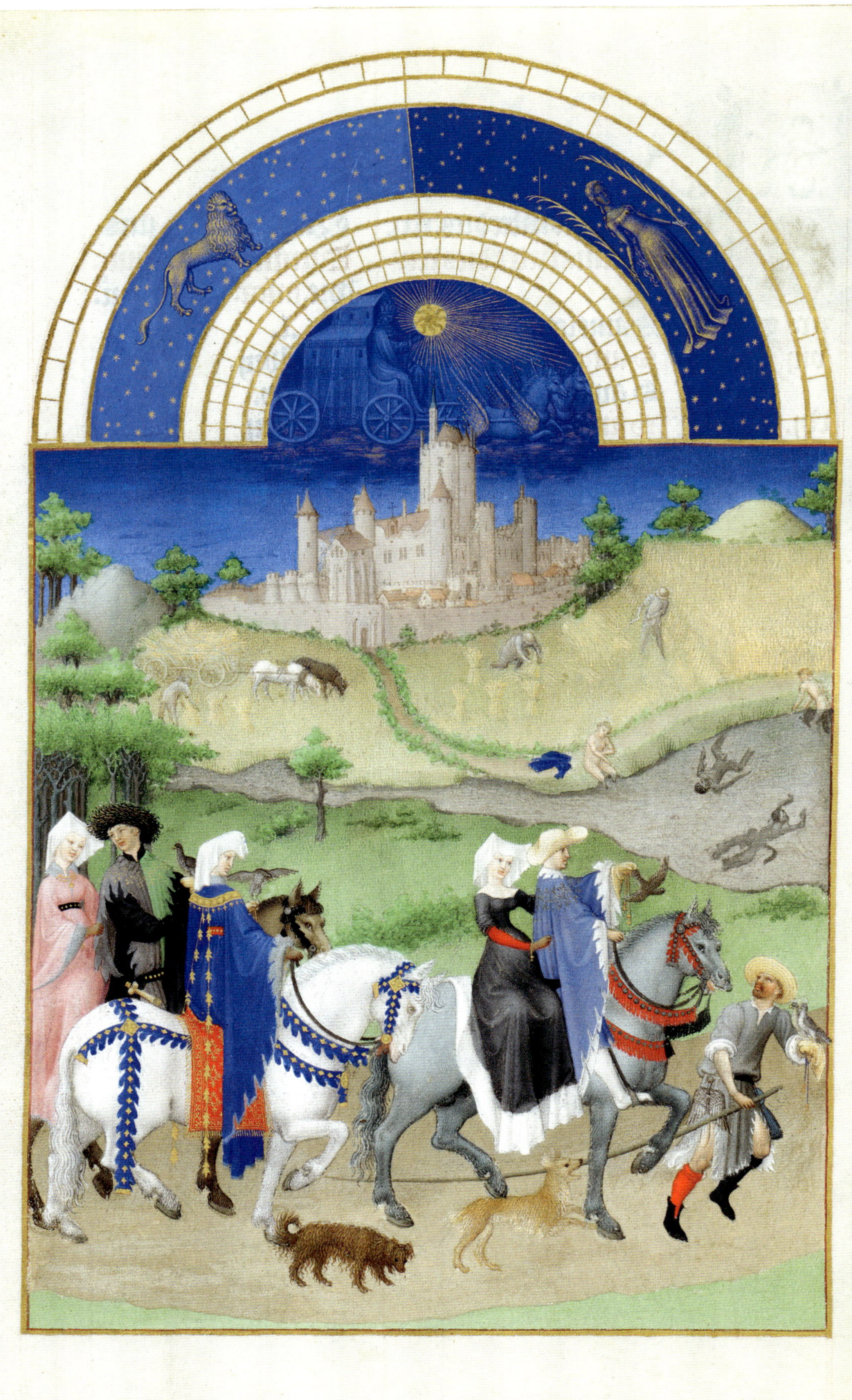

| | | | | Aoust a xxxi iours. Et la lune xxx. | La quantite des iours | | le nõbre dor |
|---|---|---|---|---|---|---|---|
| | | | | | hore | minut. | nouuel. |
| viij | c | | | saint pieur. | xiiij | xxxix | |
| xvi. | d | iiij | N' | saint esthienne | xiiij | xxxvi | xiij. |
| v. | e | iij | N' | saint esthienne. | xiiij | xxxij | ij. |
| | f | ii. | N' | saint osanne. | xiiij | xxix. | |
| xiij | g | Nonas. | | saint yon. | xiiij | xxvi | x. |
| ij | A | viij | id' | saint est. | xiiij | xxiij | xviij. |
| | b | vij | id' | saint donne. | xiiij | xix | |
| x | c | vi. | id' | saint iustin. | xiiij | xvi | vij |
| | d | v. | id' | saint naast. | xiiij | xiij | |
| xviij | e | iiij | id' | saint lorens. | xiiij | x. | xv. |
| vij | f | iij | id' | saint morice. | xiiij | iiij. | iiij. |
| | g | ij. | id' | saint epule. | xiij | lviij | xij. |
| xv. | A | Idus | | saint ypolite. | xiij | lv. | |
| iiij | b | xix. | kl' | E vigille. | xiij | lij. | i. |
| | c | xviij | kl' | La sompcion nr̃e dame. | xiij | l. | |
| xij | d | xvij | kl' | saint emanue. | xiij | xlviij | ix |
| i. | e | xvi | kl' | saint candre | xiij | xlv. | xvij |
| | f | xv. | kl' | saint agapit. | xiij | xlij | |
| ix. | g | xiiij | kl' | saint gruant. | xiij | xxxviij | vi. |
| | A | xiij | kl' | saint bernart | xiij | xxxiiij | xiiij |
| xvij | b | xij. | kl' | saint prime. | xiij | xxxi. | |
| vi. | c | xi. | kl' | saint syphorien. | xiij | xxvij | iij. |
| | d | x. | kl' | saint tymotee | xiij | xxv. | xi. |
| xiiij | e | ix | kl' | saint bertelemy. | xiij | xxij | |
| iij | f | viij | kl' | saint loys. | xiij | xxi. | xix. |
| | g | vij | kl' | saint abondin. | xiij | xvij | viij |
| xi | A | vi | kl' | saint ruffin. | xiij | xiij | xvi |
| | b | v. | kl' | saint iulien. | xiij | ix. | |
| xix. | c | iiij | kl' | saint iehan. | xiij | v. | v. |
| viij. | d | iij | kl' | saint fiacre. | xiij | i. | |
| | e. | ij | kl'. | saint paulin. | xiij | lvj. | xiij |



Fols. 8v-9: August

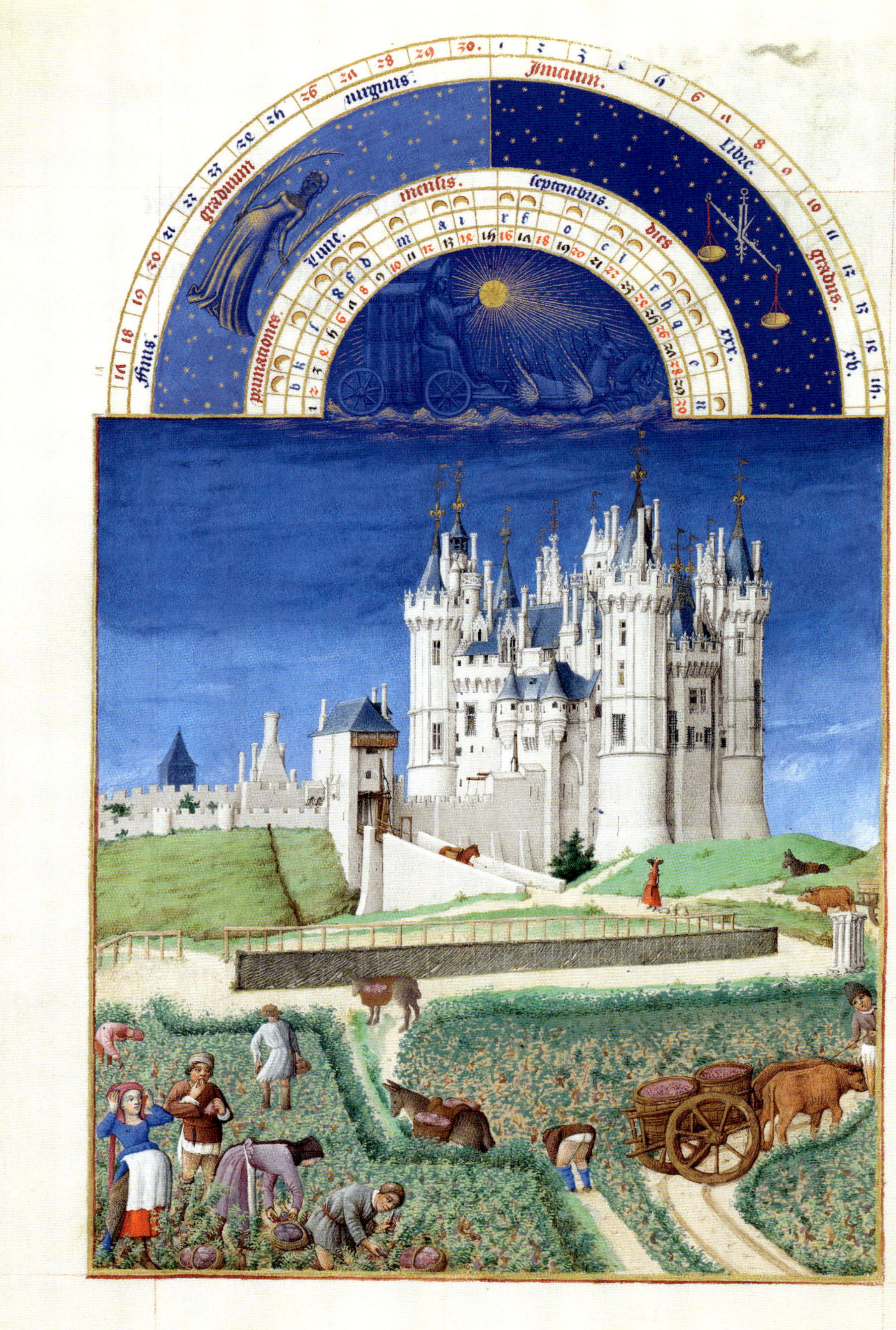

| | | | | Septembre a .xxx. iours. Et la lune .xxx. | la quãtite des iours | | le nõbre dor nouuel. |
|---|---|---|---|---|---|---|---|
| | | | | | hore | minut. | |
| xvi | f | | | saint leu. saint Gille. | xij. | xlij. | |
| v. | g | iiij | N | saint antoyne. | xij | xlix | ij |
| | A | iij | N | saint godegran. | xij | xlvj | x. |
| xiij. | b | ij. | N | saint marcel. | xij | xliij | |
| ij. | c | Nonas | | saint victorin. | xij | xl. | xviij |
| | d | viij | id | saint donacien. | xij | xxxvi | |
| x. | e | vij | id | saint clouit. | xij | xxxij | vij |
| | f | vi. | id | Nostre dame. | xij | xxvij | xv. |
| xviij | g | v. | id | saint omer. | xij | xxiiij | iiij |
| vij | A | iiij | id | saint gobert. | xij | xx. | |
| | b | iij | id | saint prothin. | xij | xvi. | xij |
| xv. | c | ij | id | saint sare. | xij | xij | |
| iiij. | d | Idus. | | saint regnalt. | xij | viij | i. |
| | e | xviij | kl | sainte croys. | xij | iiij | ix |
| xij | f | xvij | kl | saint nicomede. | xij | o | |
| i. | g | xvi. | kl | sainte eufemme. | xi. | lvij | xvij |
| | A | xv. | kl | saint lambert. | xi. | liij | vi. |
| ix. | b | xiiij | kl | saint ferrol | xi. | l. | |
| | c | xiij | kl | saint signe. | xi. | xlvj | xiiij |
| xvij | d | xij | kl | vigille. | xi. | xliij | |
| vi. | e | xi. | kl | sainte mathieu. | xi. | xxxix | iij. |
| | f | x. | kl | saint mourice. | xi | xxxvj | xi. |
| xiiij | g | ix. | kl | saint egle | xi. | xxxiij | |
| iij. | A | viij | kl | saint lier. | xi. | xxix | xix |
| | b | vij | kl | saint firmin. | xi | xxvi. | viij |
| xi. | c | vi. | kl | saint aprien. | xi | xxij. | xvi |
| xix | d | v. | kl | saint cosme. | xi. | xxix | |
| | e | iiij | kl | saint presme. | xi. | xv. | v. |
| viij | f | iij | kl | saint michiel. | xi | xij | |
| | g | ij. | kl | Saint geroume. | xi. | ix. | xiij. |

10

Fols. 9v-10: September

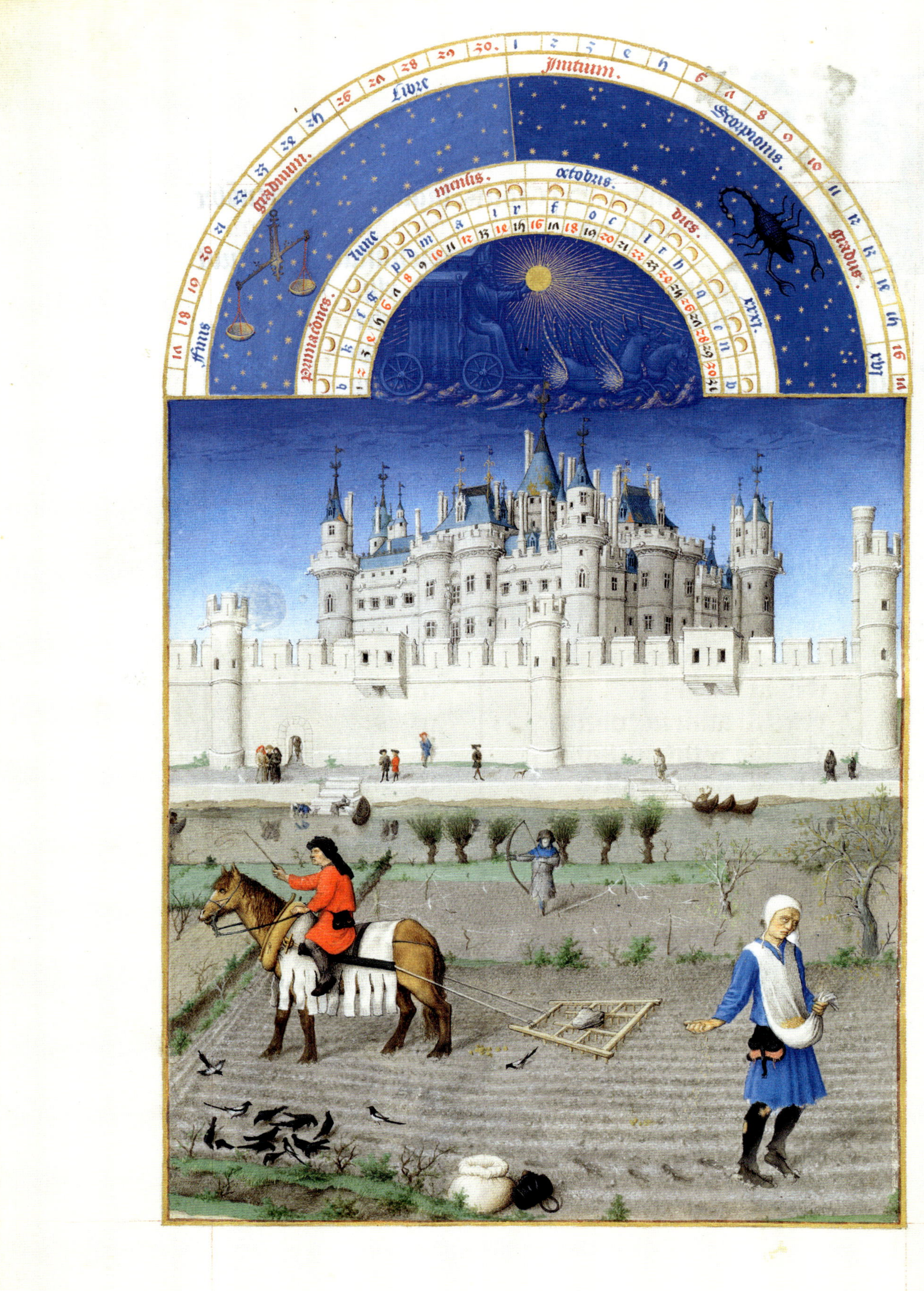
Libre
Initium
Scorpionis
mensis
octobris
dies

| | | | | Octobre a xxxi. iour. Et la lune. xxx. | La quãtite des iours | | le nõbre dor. |
|---|---|---|---|---|---|---|---|
| | | | | | Hore | minut. | nouuel. |
| xvi | A | | | saint Remy. | xi. | vi. | ii |
| v. | b | vi. | n' | saint ligier. | xi. | iii. | |
| xiii | c | v. | n' | saint victor. | xi. | o | x. |
| ii | d | iiii | n' | saint francoys | x. | lvi. | |
| | e | iii | n' | saincte aistine. | x. | liii | xviii |
| x. | f | ii. | n' | saincte foy. | x. | xlix | vii. |
| | g | Nonas. | | saint marc | x | xlv. | |
| xviii | A | viii | id' | saint demettre. | x | xlii | xv. |
| vii | b | vii | id' | saint denis. | x | xxxix | iiii |
| | c | vi | id' | saint gerion. | x | xxxvi | xii. |
| xv | d | v. | id' | saint macaire | x | xxxii | |
| iiii | e | iiii | id' | saint venant | x | xxx. | i. |
| | f | iii | id' | saint aurien. | x | xxvi. | |
| xii | g | ii. | id' | saint calixte. | x | xxi. | ix |
| i. | A | Idus. | | saint offrant. | x | xviii | xvii |
| | b | xvii | kl' | saint gabriel. | x | xv | |
| ix | c | xvi | kl' | saint cerbon. | x | xii | vi. |
| | d | xv | kl' | saint lucas. | x | ix | |
| xvii | e | xiiii | kl' | saint ptolome | x | v. | xiiii |
| vi. | f | xiii | kl' | saint capraise. | x | i. | iii. |
| | g | xii | kl' | Les. xi. mille vierges. | ix. | lvii | |
| xiiii | A | xi. | kl' | saint malon. | ix | liiii | xi. |
| iii | b | x | kl' | saint gracien. | ix | li | xix |
| | c | ix | kl' | saint maglour. | ix | xlviii | viii |
| xi. | d | viii | kl' | saint crespin. | ix | xlv. | |
| | e | vii | kl' | saint amant. | ix | xlii | xvi. |
| xix. | f | vi | kl' | Vigille. | ix | xxxix | |
| viii | g | v. | kl' | saint symon. s. iude. | ix | xxxvi | v |
| | A | iiii. | kl' | saint narcis. | ix | xxxiii | xiii |
| xvi | b | iii | kl' | saint lucain. | ix | xxx. | |
| v. | c | ii. | kl' | Vigille. | ix. | xxvi. | ii. |

Fols. 10v-11: October

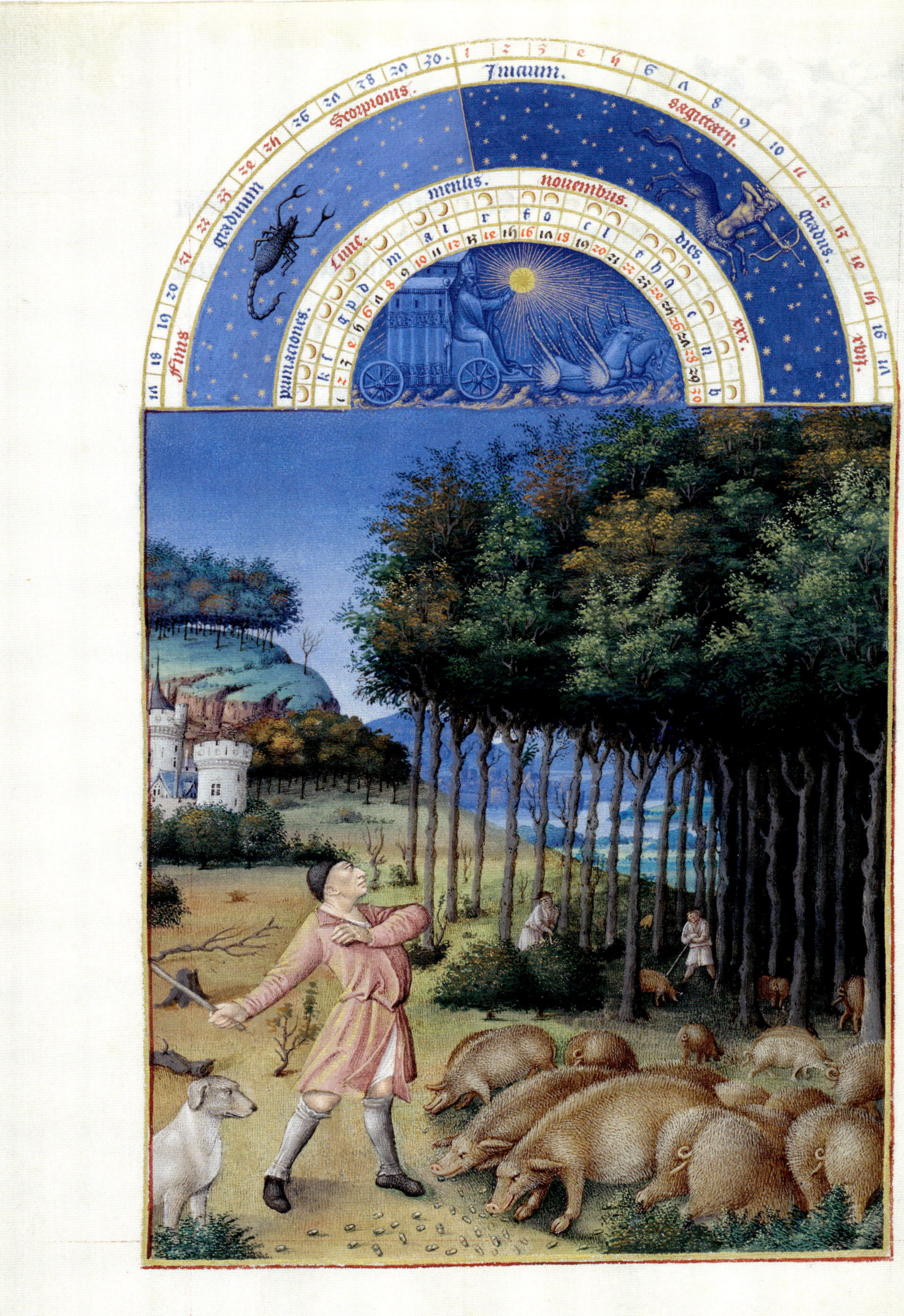

| | | | | Nouembre a xxx. iours. Et la lune xxx. | La quantite des iours hore | minut. | Le nõbre d'or nouuel |
|---|---|---|---|---|---|---|---|
| | d | | | La tous sains. | ix. | xxiii | |
| xiii | e | iiii | N | Le iour des mors. | ix. | xix. | x |
| ii. | f | iii. | N | saint marcel. | ix | xvi. | xviii |
| | g | ii. | N | saint clere. | ix | xiii | |
| x. | A | Nonas. | | saint lye | ix | .x. | vii |
| | b | viii | id | saint lienart. | ix | viii. | xv. |
| xviii | c | vii | id | saint lemulain. | ix | .v. | iiii |
| vii | d | vi. | id | les.iiii.coronnes. | ix | ii. | |
| | e | v. | id | saint mathelin. | ix | o | xii |
| xv. | f | iiii | id | saint ueram. | viii | lviii | |
| iiii | g | iii | id | saint martin. | viii | lv. | i. |
| | A | ii. | id | saint lyon. | viii | lii. | ix. |
| xii | b | Idus. | | saint brice. | viii | xlix. | |
| i. | c | xviii | kl | saint maclou. | viii | xlvi. | xvii |
| | d | xvii. | kl | saint eugene. | viii | xliii | |
| ix | e | xvi. | kl | saint fauste. | viii | xli. | vi. |
| | f | xv. | kl | saint aignen. | viii | xxxix | xiiii |
| xvii | g | xiiii | kl | saint mandin. | viii | xxxvii | |
| vi. | A | xiii. | kl | saint romain. | viii | xxxv | iii |
| | b | xii | kl | saint edmon | viii | xxxiii | xi. |
| xiiii | c | xi. | kl | saint coulumbain. | viii | xxx. | |
| iii. | d | x. | kl | sainte cecile. | viii | xxviii | xix |
| | e | ix | kl | saint climent. | viii | xxvi | viii |
| xi. | f | viii | kl | saint grisogone. | viii | xxiiii | xvi |
| | g | vii | kl | sainte katerine. | viii | xxii | |
| xix | A | vi. | kl | sainte geneuieue | viii | xx. | v. |
| viii | b | v. | kl | saint uital. | viii | xix | |
| | c | iiii | kl | saint rufin. | viii | xvii | xiii |
| xvi. | d | iii | kl | vigille. | viii | xv. | |
| v. | e | ii. | kl | saint andrieu. | viii | xiii | ii. |

12

Fols. 11v-12: November

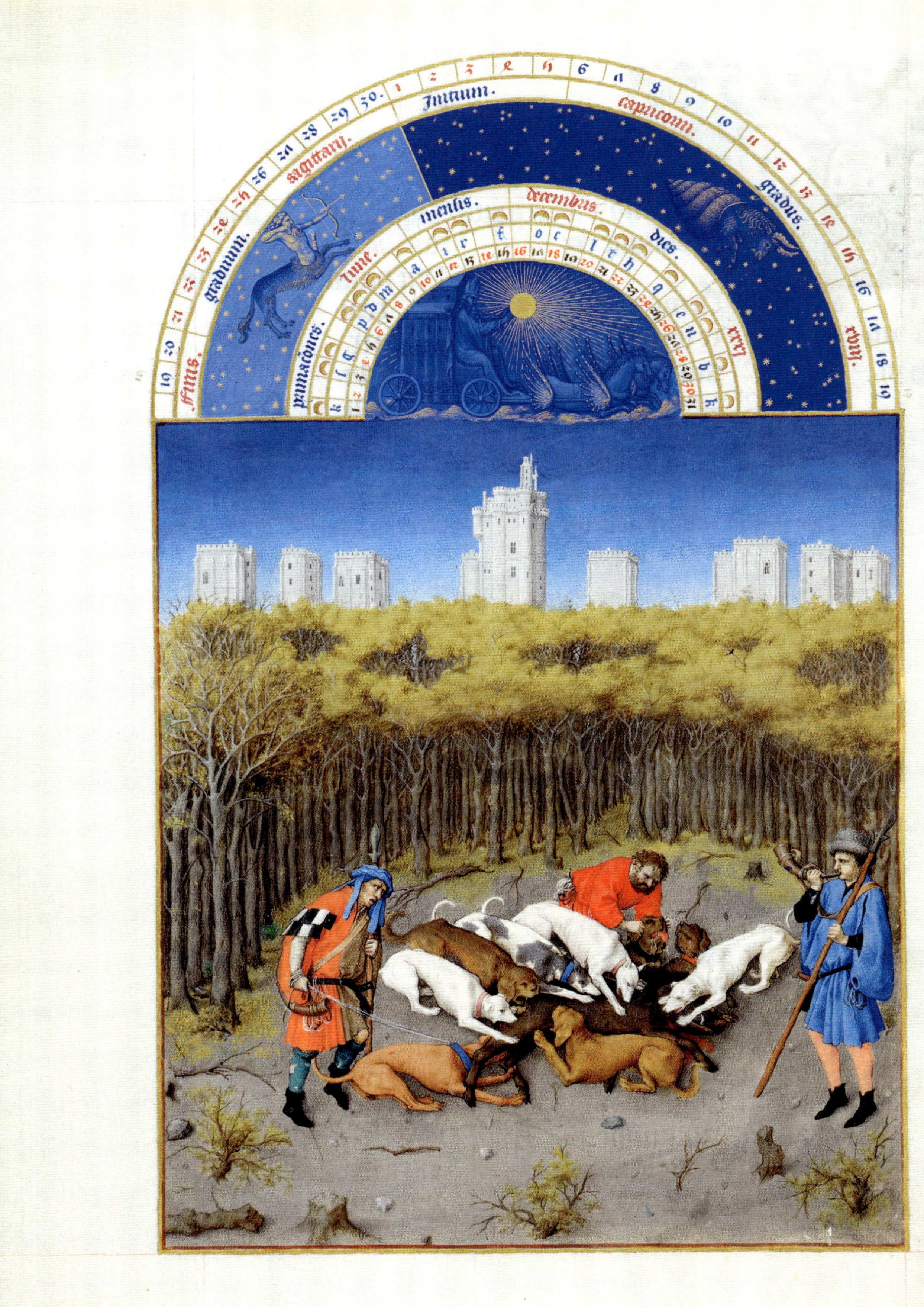

| | | | | Decembre a xxxi iour. Et la lune xxx. | La quantite des iours. | | le nõbre d'or. |
|---|---|---|---|---|---|---|---|
| | | | | | hore | minut. | nouuel. |
| | f | | | saint eloy. | viij | xij. | x |
| xiiij | g | iiij | n° | saint flaui. | viij | x. | |
| | A | iij | n° | saint claudien. | viij | viij | xviij |
| x. | b | ij. | n° | saint ambroise | viij | vij | vij. |
| | c | Nonas. | | saint barbe. | viij | vi. | |
| xviij | d | viij | id' | saint nicholas | viij | v. | xv. |
| vij | e | vij | id' | sainte faur. | viij | iiij. | iiij. |
| | f | vi | id' | Nostre dame. | viij | iij | xij. |
| xv. | g | v. | id' | saint apien. | viij | ij. | |
| iiij | A | iiij | id' | saint eulalie. | viij | .i. | i. |
| | b | iij | id' | saint fuscien. | viij | o | |
| xij | c | ij. | id' | saint ualeri. | viij | o | ix. |
| i. | d | Idus. | | saint aunen. | viij | o | xvij |
| | e | xix. | kl' | saint nicaise. | viij | o | |
| ix. | f | xviij | kl' | saint maxime | viij | o | vj. |
| | g | xvij | kl' | saint sapience. | viij | i. | |
| xvij | A | xvi | kl' | saint ladre. | viij | ij | xiiij. |
| vi | b | xv. | kl' | saint gracien. | viij | iij | iij. |
| | c | xiiij | kl' | saint satir. | viij | iiij | |
| xiiij | d | xiij | kl' | saint emille. | viij | v. | xi. |
| iij. | e | xij | kl' | saint thomas | viij | vi. | xix |
| | f | xi | kl' | saint uictor. | viij | vij | viij |
| xi. | g | x. | kl' | saint bertin. | viij | viij | |
| xix | A | ix. | kl' | Vigille. | viij | x. | xvi |
| | b | viij | kl' | Le iour de noel. | viij | xij | |
| viij | c | vij | kl' | saint estienne. | viij | xiiij | v. |
| | d | vi | kl' | saint iehan euuangeliste. | viij | xvi | xiij |
| xvi. | e | v. | kl' | Les innocens. | viij | xviij | |
| v | f | iiij | kl' | saint thomas. | viij | xx. | ij. |
| | g | iij | kl' | saint columban. | viij | xxij | |
| xiij | A | ij. | kl' | saint seluestre. | viij | xxiiij | x. |

13

Fols. 12v-13: December

Note to the reader:

# Maelwael – Van Lymborch The Standardized Form of Their Name

Pieter Roelofs

The Regional Archives in Nijmegen, the birthplace of Herman, Paul, and Johan van Lymborch in the Dutch province of Guelders, hold a series of 600-year-old aldermen's protocols. At first glance, these booklets may not seem very appealing, but they offer a wealth of historical information, not least about the world-famous book illuminators and their family.[1] From the last years of the fourteenth century onward, we come across their names quite regularly in these northern sources. Most of these entries were recorded in formal Latin with a pen and brown ink and refer to the "de Lymborch" family. However, a few sparse notes in the vernacular bring us even closer to the brothers and the way in which they were personally designated by their contemporaries. In the years around 1400, Herman, Paul, and Johan were known as the "Van Lymborch gebrueder" (Van Lymborch brothers), as recorded in the Nijmegen protocols.[2]

Ever since their rediscovery in the second half of the nineteenth century, the Van Lymborch brothers have been the subject of countless scholarly and popular books, catalogues, and articles. In recent decades, visitors have been offered the opportunity to see their innovative miniatures with their own eyes at exceptional exhibitions in Chantilly (2004, 2025), Nijmegen (2005), Los Angeles (2008–09), New York (2010), Paris (2004, 2012), and Amsterdam (2017).[3] While there is a broad consensus in the international art-historical literature on the importance and significance of the brothers' book illumination, until recently there was no unanimity regarding the spelling of their name.

The conventional English spelling of the name "Limbourg brothers," traditionally written without the preposition, in fact straddles two languages. More than a century ago, the name was based on the French appropriation "frères de Limbourg" and as a result it is still pronounced the French way—[Lemburg]—and not Limburg [Lɪmberg]. The Dutch name "Van Limburg" [Lɪmborg], which was still commonplace in the Netherlands and Belgium until a few years ago, was introduced into scholarly literature in 1919 by historian Johan Huizinga in his famous book *Herfsttij der Middeleeuwen* (*The Waning of the Middle Ages*), but does not refer back to any historical source.[4] The same observation holds for the German variant "die Brüder Limburg" [Lɪmburg], without the preposition, which became widespread in the German literature after the Cleves city archivist Friederich Gorissen used the spelling in two articles in 1954 and 1957.[5] Both spellings have led to confusion among experts to this day. For example, it has been noted in recent literature that the brothers' name derives from the Dutch province of Limburg, because their hometown of Nijmegen is said to have been located in this area.[6] This claim is incorrect: after all, the region as a whole is not related to the brothers' name. In the Late Middle Ages, Nijmegen belonged to the Duchy of Guelders and the geographical name Limburg did not come into use for the southern province until the nineteenth century.

The traditional multiple forms that are used to refer to the brothers require uniformity in an international context. That is why, in this book, we use the internationally standardized spelling "Van Lymborch brothers" [van Lɪmborg], based on the historical sources. The actual origin of the name of the three illuminators can be traced back to the city of Lymborch—now called Limbourg—the most important city in the duchy of the same name, located on the Vesdre river between Aachen and Liège in present-day Belgium.[7] Herman, Paul, and Johan were the three eldest children (of six) of Mechteld Maelwael and Arnold van Lymborch; the latter was referred to in Middle Dutch sources as "Arnt den beeltsnijder" (Arnt the sculptor) and in Latin sources as "Arnt de Aquis" (Arnt of Aachen) on account of his craft and origin. From 1389 onward, his name appears fifteen times in the Nijmegen aldermen's protocols and the archives of the Duke of Guelders.[8] Johannes van Lymborgh, who came from the Duchy of Lymborch, as it was called in the late fourteenth century, and was registered as a citizen of Nijmegen in 1366, is believed to have been the brothers' grandfather.[9]

For centuries, the use of a toponym as part of a name was useful for people to identify themselves outside their region of origin. Until well into the fifteenth century, the descendants of Arnold van Lymborch used the toponym "Lymborch," combined with the preposition "van" as a reference to the origin of their ancestry. As sons of Nijmegen, it is remarkable that Herman, Paul, and Johan did not opt for the addition "de Nimègue" in France. In Paris, the Duchy of Berry, and the Duchy of Guelders, on the other hand, they regularly used the surname of their mother Mechteld, also known as Metta Maelwael, daughter of the productive and successful local painter Willem Maelwael. For example, in 1400, Herman and Johan are mentioned in ducal sources in Burgundy as "Hermant Maleuel" and "Jacquemin Malauel, brothers, young children and cousins of Jehan Maleuel, painter and varlet de chambre" of Philip the Bold, Duke of Burgundy.[10] The good reputation of their uncle Johan Maelwael seems to have opened doors for the teenagers. Accordingly, Johan, the youngest of the three brothers, was mentioned in Nijmegen in 1413 as "Johannes dictus Jenneken Maelwael," the name under which his death was also recorded three years later.[11]

The majority of the Latin sources in Nijmegen—fifteen in total—refer to the three brothers, their father, and their younger brother Arnold as "de Lymborch." In the French archives of the Duke of Berry, the variants "de Limbourc" (thrice), "de Lumbourc" (once), and "de Limbourg" (once) were used between 1408 and 1415. The guidelines of the United Nations Conferences on the Standardization of Geographical Names (UNCSGN) serve as a starting point for the standardization of their names, including toponyms. The UN bases geographical names as much as possible on the original, local spelling, whereby it is important that the name can also be recognized and understood internationally.

Both their birthplace Nijmegen and the Duchy of Lymborch, as it was called around 1400, were part of the Middle Dutch-speaking area in the Late Middle Ages. Although there were different dialects and vernaculars, their name was written and pronounced more or less the same in both areas. "De Lymborch," the most common spelling in the northern documents, is, as mentioned, Latin. The preposition "de" indicates a person's origin and therefore has the same meaning as the Dutch "van" related to a toponym, as in such Dutch names as Van Eyck, Van Gogh, and Van Gaal.[12] In the period in which the brothers were active, the spelling "Van Lymborch" was common in everyday Middle Dutch, as illustrated by the fourteenth-century romance of Heinric and Margariete van Lymborch.[13] In the "Wapenboek Gelre" (Gelre Armorial) by herald Claes Heynenzoon, between around 1393 and 1402, a scribe added these words above the coat of arms of the Duke of Lymborch: "die hé[rtoge] vā[n] Lymborch" (meaning, the duke of Lymborch). Completed in 1405 by the same herald, the "Wapenboek Beyeren" (Beyeren Armorial) contains the same phrase, this time in full: "die hertoge van Lymborch." We also come across the form "Van Lymborch" in combination with a first name. For example, in 1419 the name "Derich van Lymborch" was recorded in a charter of the Duke of Guelders and, as mentioned above, the Nijmegen aldermen's protocols also refer to Herman, Paul, and Johan as the "Van Lymborch gebrueder."

Based on these historical arguments and the original sources, in 2018 the Maelwael van Lymborch Foundation and the Maelwael van Lymborch Studies Foundation proposed the use of the international, uniform variant, "Van Lymborch," instead of the multiple national forms. This naming has since become commonplace in several international publications, setting the standard for the future. In English, the full name is "Van Lymborch brothers;" in German, "Brüder Van Lymborch." This spelling restores the loss of the preposition "van" in both languages. In recent years, the actual historical name of Johan Maelwael has been embraced in the international scientific literature; now, Herman, Paul, and Johan van Lymborch have also been given back their original names.[14]

1 This text is a revised and greatly abbreviated version of Roelofs 2018. For the aldermen's protocols, see Gorissen 1954; Gorissen 1957; Niessen, Roelofs, and van Veen-Liefrink 2005; Roelofs 2005; Roelofs 2017a.

2 See, for example, a record in the Nijmegen aldermen's protocols of June 20, 1419. Gorissen 1954, no. 156.

3 See Chantilly 2004; Paris 2004b; Nijmegen 2005; Husband 2008; Paris 2012; Amsterdam 2017–18; Chantilly 2025.

4 Huizinga 1919, 445, 448, 496.

5 Gorissen 1954; Gorissen 1957.

6 König 2003, 39–40; Stumpel 2016, 12–13.

7 On this origin, see Meiss 1974, I, 67; Niessen, Roelofs, and van Veen-Liefrink 2005, 14.

8 Niessen, Roelofs, and van Veen-Liefrink 2005, 14–15.

9 Ibid., 14.

10 Deshaisnes 1886, II, 790–91 ("Hermant Maleuel et Jacquemin Malauel frères, jonnes enfans et nepveus de Jehan Maleuel paintre et varlet de chambre de mondit seigneur," Archives Départementales de la Côte d'Or, Dijon (ADCO), inv.no. B 1519, fols 158v-159r); Roelofs 2017a, 15. In the early fifteenth century, French sources also refer to the brothers as "Manuel" and "Maluel" on several occasions.

11 Niessen, Roelofs, and van Veen-Liefrink 2005, 24. A similar identification was also used for their father, who was referred to as "Arnoldi de Lymborch dicti Maelwael" in two Latin documents in 1415. See Ibid., 15.

12 With special thanks to Jef Janssens, Prof. emer. of medieval literature, Brussels, who has published extensively on the *Roman van Lymborch*, among other subjects.

13 Schellart 1952.

14 Johan Maelwael, long known in international scholarly literature by his Frenchified name "Jean Malouel," had his original name restored in Nijmegen 2005, followed by an exhibition at the Rijksmuseum in 2017. See Amsterdam 2017–18.

# JEAN, DUKE OF BERRY

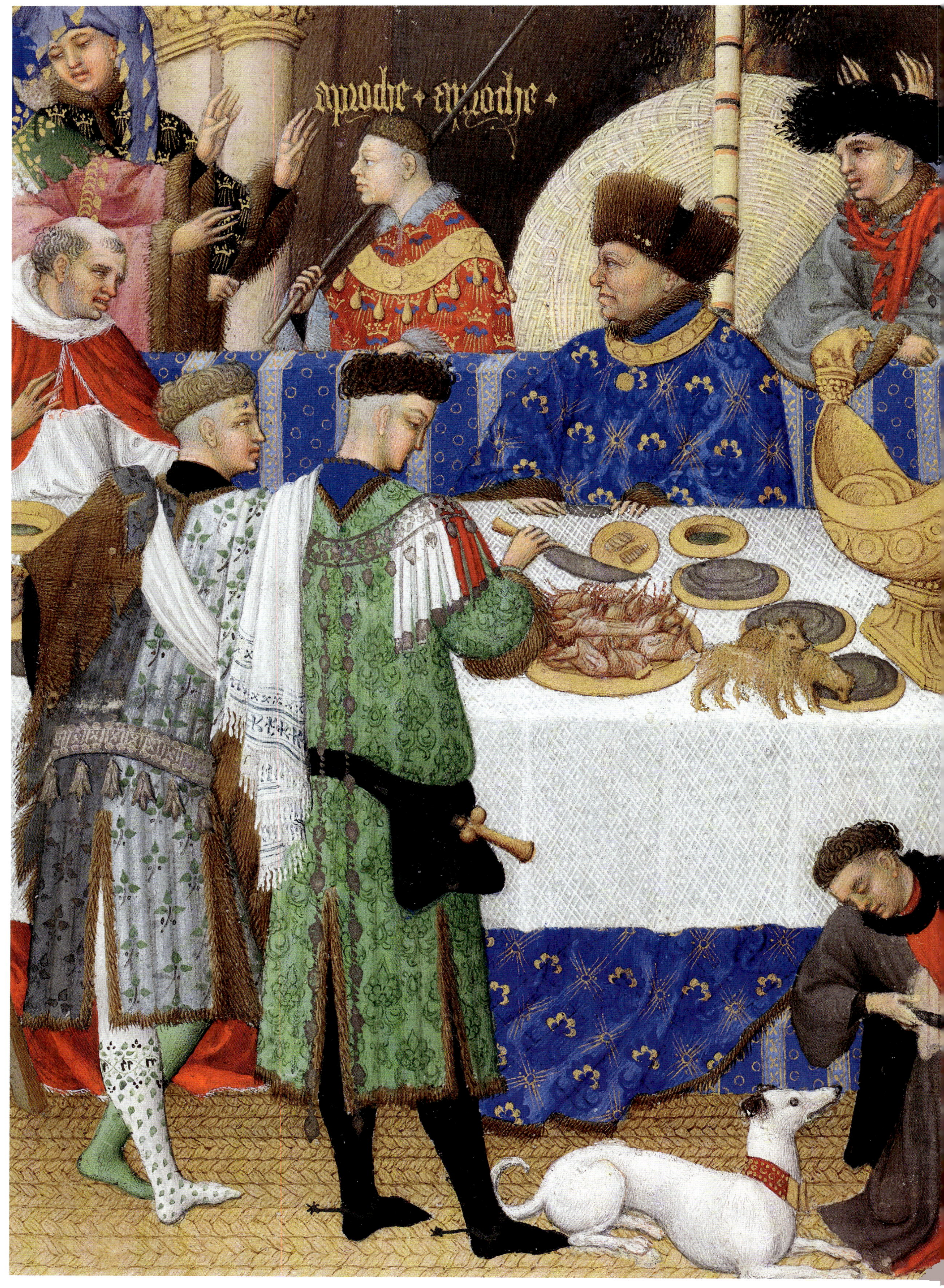
aproche aproche

# 1.

# The Duke of Berry in the Mirror of His *Très Riches Heures*

Mathieu Deldicque

Would Jean of Berry be remembered today if it were not for his fabulous book of hours? Didn't the precious manuscript, in a sense, make the duke? Rarely have a book and its patron been so closely associated in the collective unconscious.

Son, brother, and uncle of a king, as he himself liked to proclaim, Jean of Berry, "filz de roy de France, duc de Berry et d'Auvergne, comte de Poictou, d'Estampes, de Boullongne et d'Auvergne,"[1] was one of the most brilliant "princes des fleurs de lis."[2] Gifted with a strong personality, a shrewd diplomat rather than a man of war, he lived a particularly long life—dying at the age of seventy-six—and left his mark on his time and his peers. Above all, the duke was a wise patron of the arts. His two sons predeceased him, and he used his extensive artistic patronage to consolidate his political activity and ultimately memorialize a life that, although unsettled by trials of all kinds, was rich in achievements. He undertook the *Très Riches Heures* against a backdrop of political and military upheaval. The work's pages include many depictions of the duke's possessions and places that were dear to him, and also evocations of certain family events. At times, the famous manuscript is an unconscious mirror of the duke's life (figs. 1 and 2) and especially of ambitions that remained unfulfilled, just as the book itself was left unfinished.

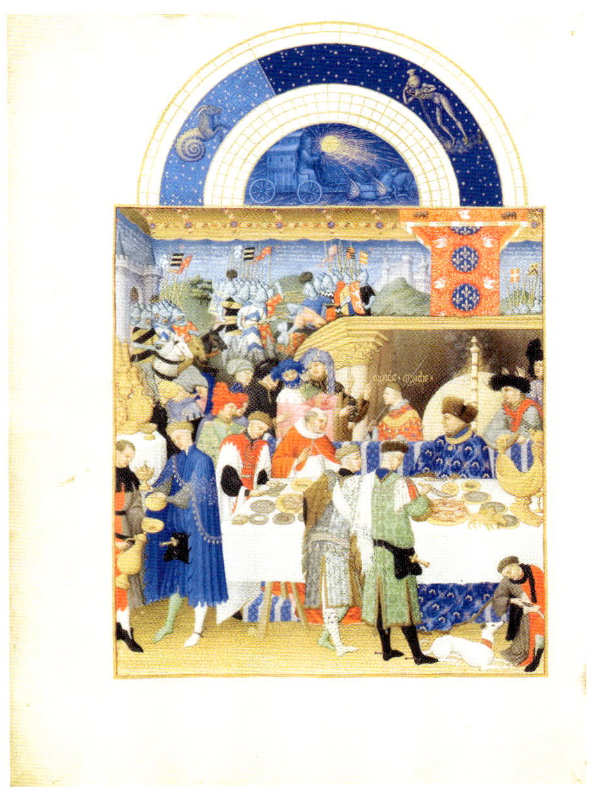

**Fig. 2** Van Lymborch brothers, *Très Riches Heures*, fol. 1v: January

**Fig. 1** Van Lymborch brothers, *Très Riches Heures*, fol. 1v: January, detail

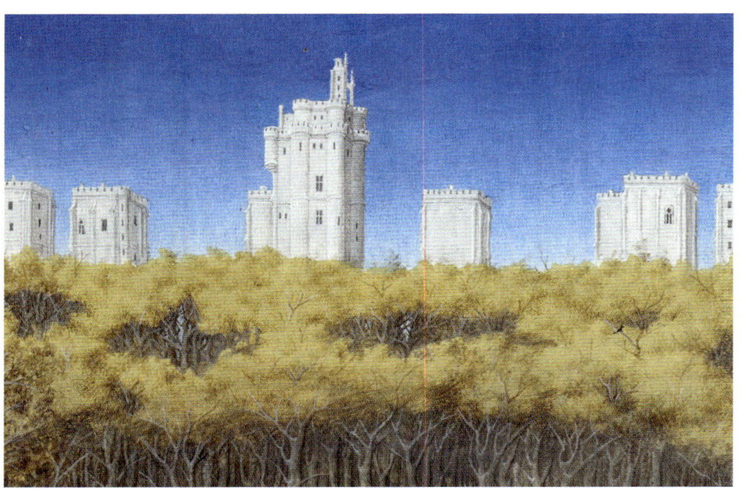

**Fig. 3** Van Lymborch brothers, *Très Riches Heures*, fol. 12v: December, detail

Jean of France, the future Duke of Berry, was born at the château of the Bois de Vincennes (fol. 12v; fig. 3) on November 30, 1340, the feast day of St. Andrew, a patron saint to whom the duke maintained a special devotion throughout his life.[3] He was the third son of John, Duke of Normandy, who became king of France under the name of John II the Good, and Bonne (or Guta) of Luxembourg, daughter of the king of Bohemia. His mother died nine years later, at an early age, from the Black Death, a scourge that spared no one in the kingdom, least of all the royal family, and which is, of course, represented in the *Très Riches Heures* (fol. 71v). Jean's birth was welcomed as a blessing for the young Valois dynasty, which was strengthened by it: Jean's grandfather, Philip VI of Valois, had ascended the throne in 1328 when the male heirs of the eldest branch of the Capetians had become extinct.

The future of the Valois rested on the descendants of the future Jean II, particularly as they faced claims to the throne of France from Edward II of England, who was also descended from the Capetians, on the female side. The Duke of Berry was born on the eve of a war that would last more than a hundred years and mark his entire life.

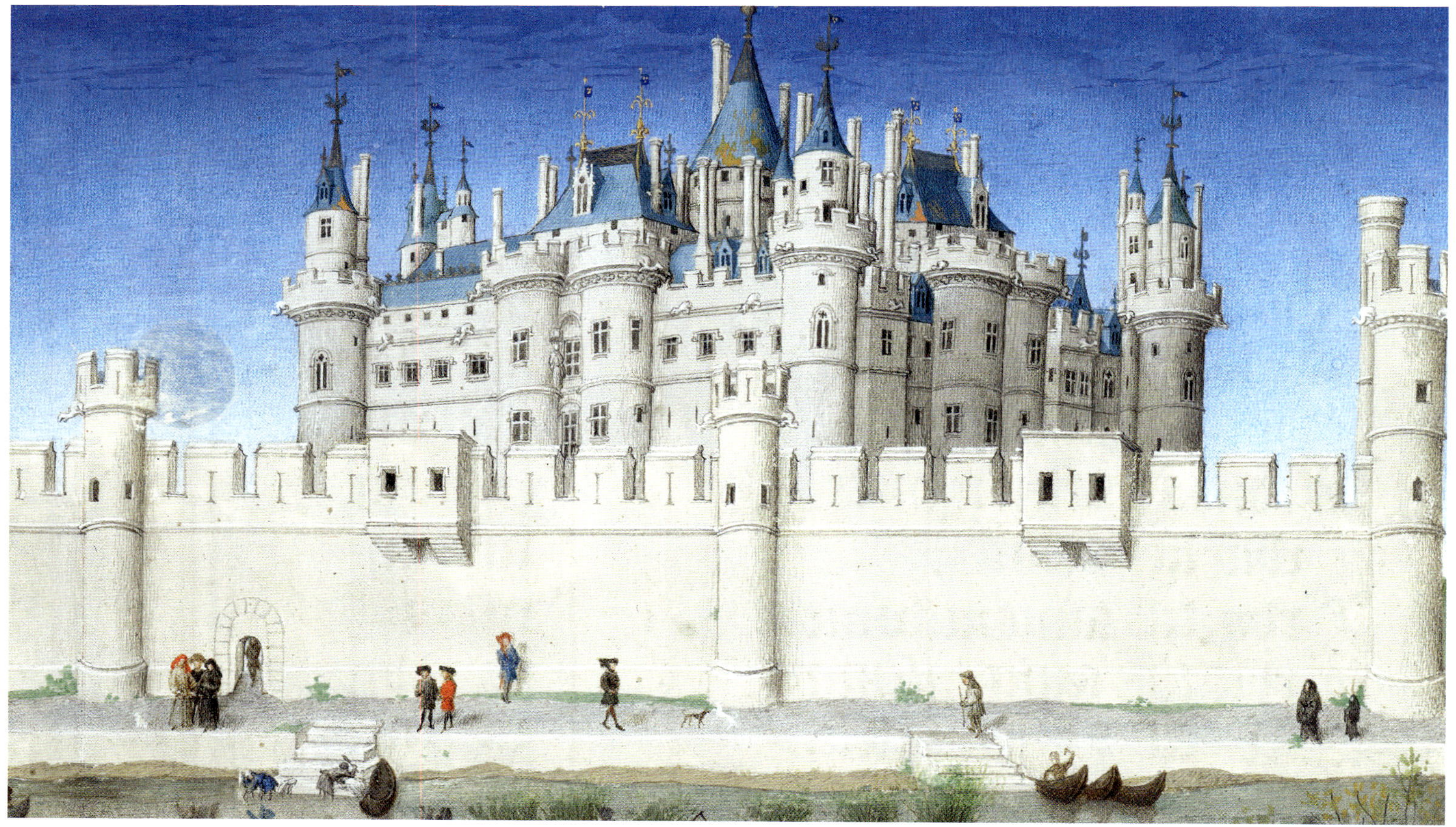

**Fig. 4** Van Lymborch brothers and Barthélemy d'Eyck, *Très Riches Heures*, fol. 10v: October, detail

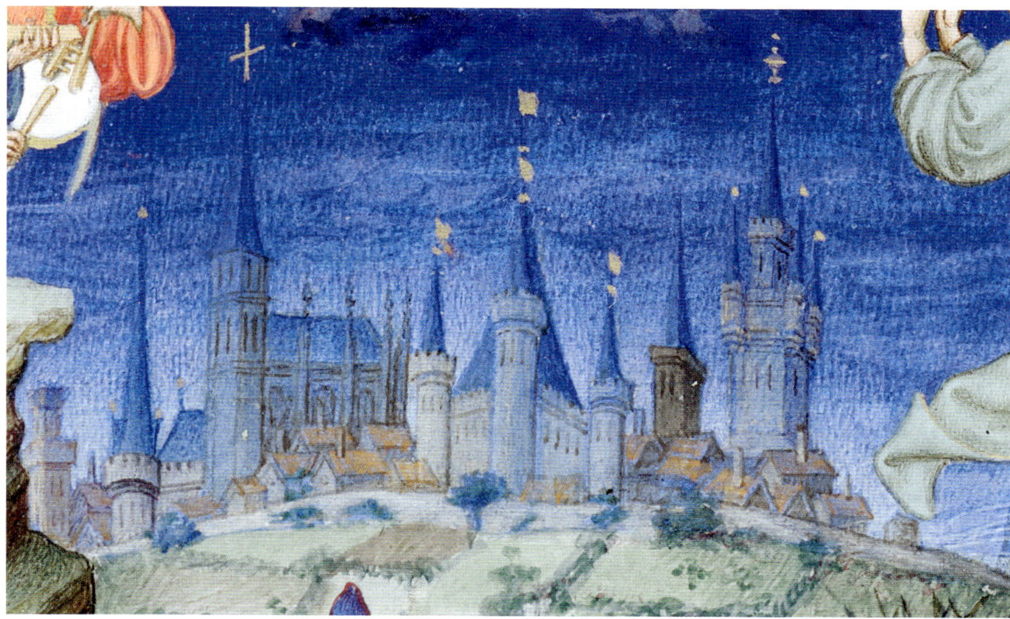

**Fig. 5** Van Lymborch brothers, *Très Riches Heures*, fol. 48: The Annunciation to the Shepherds, detail

## POITOU AND BERRY

The Crown relied on the system of appanages: territories entrusted to princes of the royal family that were designed to divide the kingdom and ensure closer governance. The king possessed "ressort et souveraineté" (competency and sovereignty), while the prince benefiting from the particular appanage was responsible for justice and administration. Unlike his older brother, Louis, who was given the duchy of Anjou, and his younger brother, Philip, who received the duchy of Burgundy, Jean had to create a new appanage for himself, a principality he strove to expand and consolidate his whole life. In 1356, while still in his teens, he was made Count of Poitiers and sent as the king's lieutenant general to Languedoc, a position he held from then on, representing the Crown, pacifying the region in the face of "routiers" (mercenaries), and facilitating the collection of taxes—not without controversy. This greed earned him a bad reputation, which historians, rarely kind toward him, have often held against him.[4] That same year, the catastrophic defeat suffered by his father King John II at Poitiers at the hands of the Black Prince's English troops hit him hard. The king was captured and held for ransom by the English for four years. Jean's older brother Charles (the future Charles V), who was regent while their father was in captivity, gave Jean the county of Mâcon in 1359. Jean's secret marriage in Rodez on October 17, 1359 to Jeanne d'Armagnac, the daughter of his mentor, Count Jean d'Armagnac, also anchored him in the regions beyond the Loire, where he settled permanently. After obtaining a papal dispensation, the marriage was made official in Carcassonne on June 24, 1360.

The Treaty of Brétigny on October 17, 1360 turned Jean's young life upside down. John II negotiated his own release in exchange for the freedom of three of his sons: Louis, Jean, and Philip. Under the terms of the treaty, Poitou was to be ceded to the English; before giving himself up as a hostage, Jean received the duchies of Berry and Auvergne in appanage by way of compensation. He was held captive in England for four years (from November 1360 to December 1364), a comfortable but idle confinement, mitigated by several months' leave in France. His stay in England gave him the opportunity to reflect on emblems, a field in which the English court was well advanced. The duke gradually built up an entire heraldic and emblematic system made up of arms, mottos and devices, emblems, and colors, which were ultimately brought together in the precious manuscript of the *Très Riches Heures*.[5]

The new Duke of Berry shared his father's second captivity; the king had returned to London to replace his other son, Louis of Anjou, who had escaped. The king died in London in 1364 and Jean of Berry, seemingly unmoved by the memory of his father, drew up an inventory of his possessions before returning to France. In the meantime, the Dauphin Charles had become Charles V, known as Charles the Wise.

The new king's political activity and intellectual interests served as a model for his brother.[6] The October miniature in the *Très Riches Heures* (fol. 10v; fig. 4) is adorned with the Louvre of Charles V—the fortress that the sovereign rebuilt and where he set up his famous library, one of the sources of inspiration for Jean. Alongside his brothers, and the king and queen, the duke took his place in the sculpted procession to be found on the Grand Staircase of the Louvre, finding himself on the "second step of the throne."[7]

## EMERGING FROM CRISES

The conflicts with the English soon resumed. In November 1369, Charles V restored to Jean of Berry his former appanage of Poitou. However, he first had to win it back. Assisted by Constable Bertrand du Guesclin, the duke led a victorious campaign and despite some difficulties entered Poitiers on August 7, 1372. Poitou appears several times in the *Très Riches Heures* in the form of detailed depictions: of the château in the background of July (fol. 7v); and of the town's main monuments behind the Annunciation to the Shepherds (fol. 48; fig. 5). The manuscript thus provides subtle proof of one of the duke's great military and symbolic achievements.

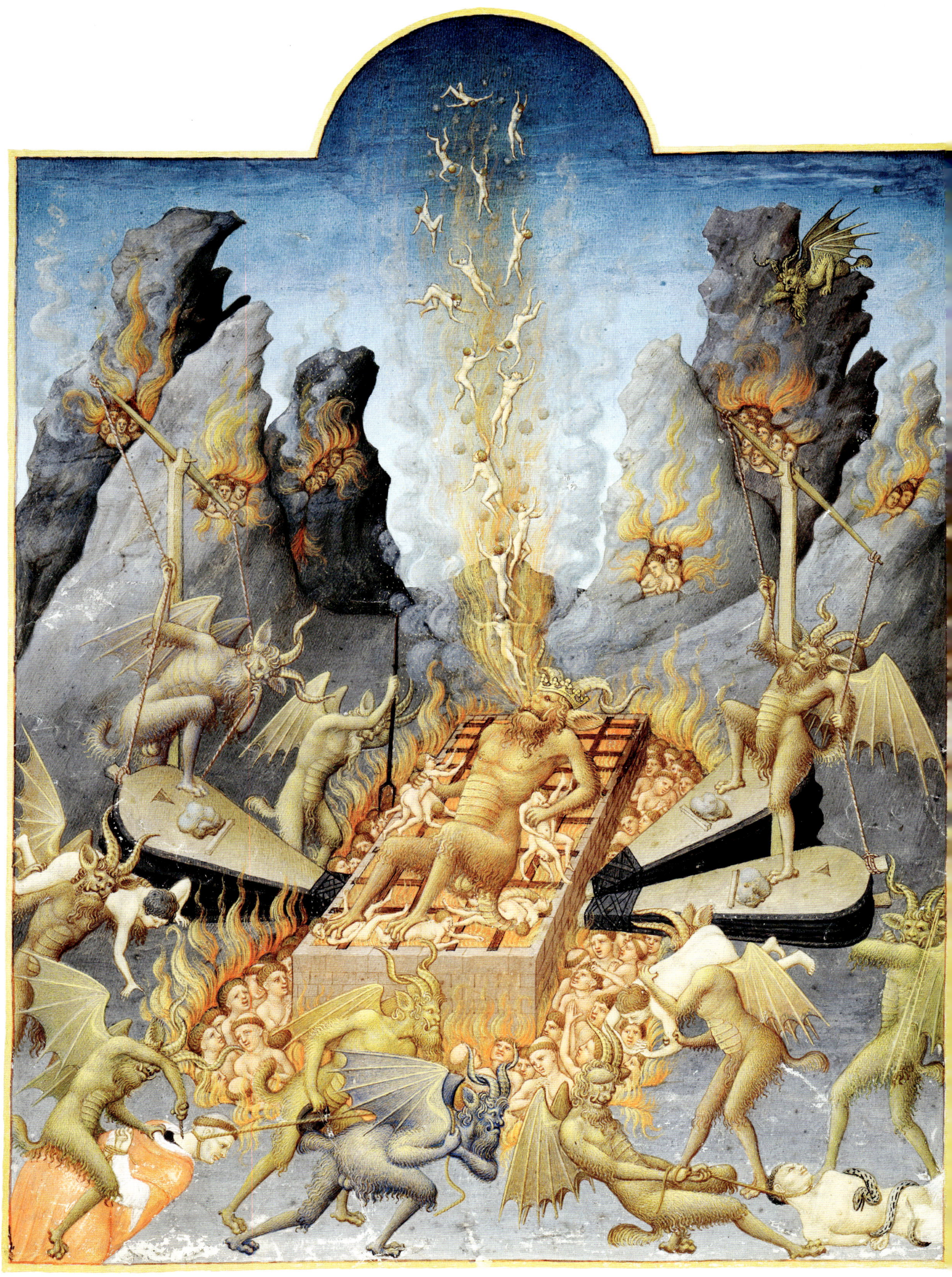

The reconquest of Poitou culminated in a long-term undertaking, again celebrated in his favorite manuscript: March shows the château of Lusignan and its multiple walls (fol. 3v). After an interminable siege lasting almost a year and a half, this powerful fortress surrendered to the duke on October 1, 1374. According to legend (recounted by Jean of Berry to Jean d'Arras in the *Roman de Mélusine*, written twenty years later), the fairy Mélusine, a former chatelaine, would appear in the form of a snake to whichever of the two opponents she had decided to make victorious. This prophetic vision is depicted in the miniature of March. The Duke of Berry was now at the head of a coherent principality that had been patiently put together.

The ravages of the Hundred Years' War were soon exceeded by the consequences of the Great Schism. In 1378, on the death of Pope Gregory XI, the cardinals in Rome appointed Urban VI as his successor. The French cardinals, gathering for a conclave in the city of Fondi, refused to accept this choice and instead appointed "Antipope" Clement VII, in Avignon (where the papacy had been based until 1376). It took almost forty years, a litany of popes and antipopes, and the Council of Constance of 1414–18 before the robe of the Catholic Church, torn by the conflict between two "obediences," was finally mended. Initially a supporter of Pope Clement, the Duke of Berry became, thanks to the election of Benedict XIII in 1394, a firm defender of the union of the Church. A shrewd diplomat, he led the long and difficult negotiations on behalf of the French side. It is probably not a coincidence that many clerics, recognizable by their tonsures (fol. 108; fig. 6), can be seen roasting in Satan's inferno in the *Très Riches Heures*.

The calendar, whose scope was unprecedented at the time, also illustrates for the first time a plan to reform the ecclesiastical reckoning of the dates of movable feasts in the religious calendar. The plan, championed by Pierre d'Ailly, first at the Council of Rome (1412–13), then at the Council of Constance (1414–18),[8] was a project defended by the unionist pope, the Duke of Berry's candidate. Since the calculation was based on the movements of the Sun and the Moon, the traditional reckoning had ended up producing discrepancies between the official calendar and the course of the stars. The duke addresses a prelate in the miniature of January: Is this Alamanno Adimari, cardinal of Pisa, legate of Pope John XXII in France,[9] or Simon de Cramaud, a unionist cardinal familiar to the duke?[10] In any event, the miniature bears witness to the importance that the Duke of Berry attached to resolving the schism.

The spiritual crisis was exacerbated by the political turmoil that marked the second half of the duke's life. The death of Charles V in September 1380 left his brothers in charge, on behalf of the young Charles VI, who was still a minor. Jean of Berry took possession of his new residence in Paris, the Hôtel de Nesle on the left bank of the Seine, together with the "séjour de Nesle," the gardens, stables, and fields beyond the ramparts. It is this "séjour de Nesle" that is to be admired in the miniatures of June, depicting the Île de la Cité (fol. 6v), and October, illustrating the Louvre palace (fol. 10v). From November 1388, after Charles VI had expressed his desire to govern the kingdom himself, the duke devoted more time to his estates and his own descendants. He had lost his first wife, Jeanne d'Armagnac, in January of the same year, and now set his sights on the very young Jeanne de Boulogne, the coveted heiress to the county of Auvergne. Froissart reports that the age difference between the couple surprised the king, who joked about it: "Bel oncle, que ferez-vous d'une telle fillette? Elle n'a que douze ans, et vous en avez soixante. Par ma foi, c'est grand'folie pour vous de penser de celle chose" (Fair uncle, what are you planning on doing with such a little girl? She is only twelve and you, sixty. By my faith, it is madness of you to think of such a thing). Nevertheless, the king gave his blessing to the union. The marriage contract was fiercely negotiated by Jeanne's cousin, Gaston Phoebus, himself a rival of Jean of Berry in Languedoc. The union remained childless, which may explain why the duchess is not portrayed in the *Très Riches Heures*, an eminently personal manuscript. The Duke of Berry lost his two sons by his first wife very early on—first Charles in 1383, then Jean in 1397. However, two daughters survived him: Bonne, who married first Amadeus VII of Savoy and then Count Bernard d'Armagnac; and Marie, who wed three times: Louis de Blois; Constable Philippe d'Artois, Count of Eu; and Jean de Bourbon, Count of Clermont, the future Duke of Bourbon. The calendar in the *Très Riches Heures* refers to the matrimonial alliances of the duke's descendants: April (fol. 4v) could portray the engagement of Bonne d'Armagnac, the duke's granddaughter, to Charles d'Orléans (1410),[11] or that of Marie of Berry to Jean de Bourbon (1400),[12] which could also be found in May (fol. 5v) or even August (fol. 8v).[13] Although the portraits are not necessarily characterized (unlike that of the duke in January), the para-heraldic decoration adorning the figures' outfits undoubtedly enabled the duke to identify them. As his daughters were unable to inherit the lands he had received in appanage, the duke knew he was doomed to see the new principality that he had patiently put together disappear after him, and which the manuscript, with its architectural portraits, both commemorated and recognized. No doubt he found some consolation in the prestigious marriages his descendants had contracted. Eventually, he would also have to give up his favorite residence, the château of Mehun-sur-Yèvre—"l'une des plus belles maisons de France" (one of France's most beautiful houses), according to Froissart—and the jewel of a domain that had come to him from his paternal grandfather, Jean de Luxembourg, king of Bohemia, an ideal prince and the founder of an imperial dynasty.[14] In the manuscript, this residence forms the setting for the Temptation of Christ (fig. 2, p. 73); the duke gave it to the Dauphin, Louis of Guyenne, in October 1414, but reclaimed it on the latter's death in December 1415.

**Fig. 6** Van Lymborch brothers, *Très Riches Heures*, fol. 108: Hell

**Fig. 7** Following pages: Van Lymborch brothers, *Très Riches Heures*, fol. 108: Hell, detail

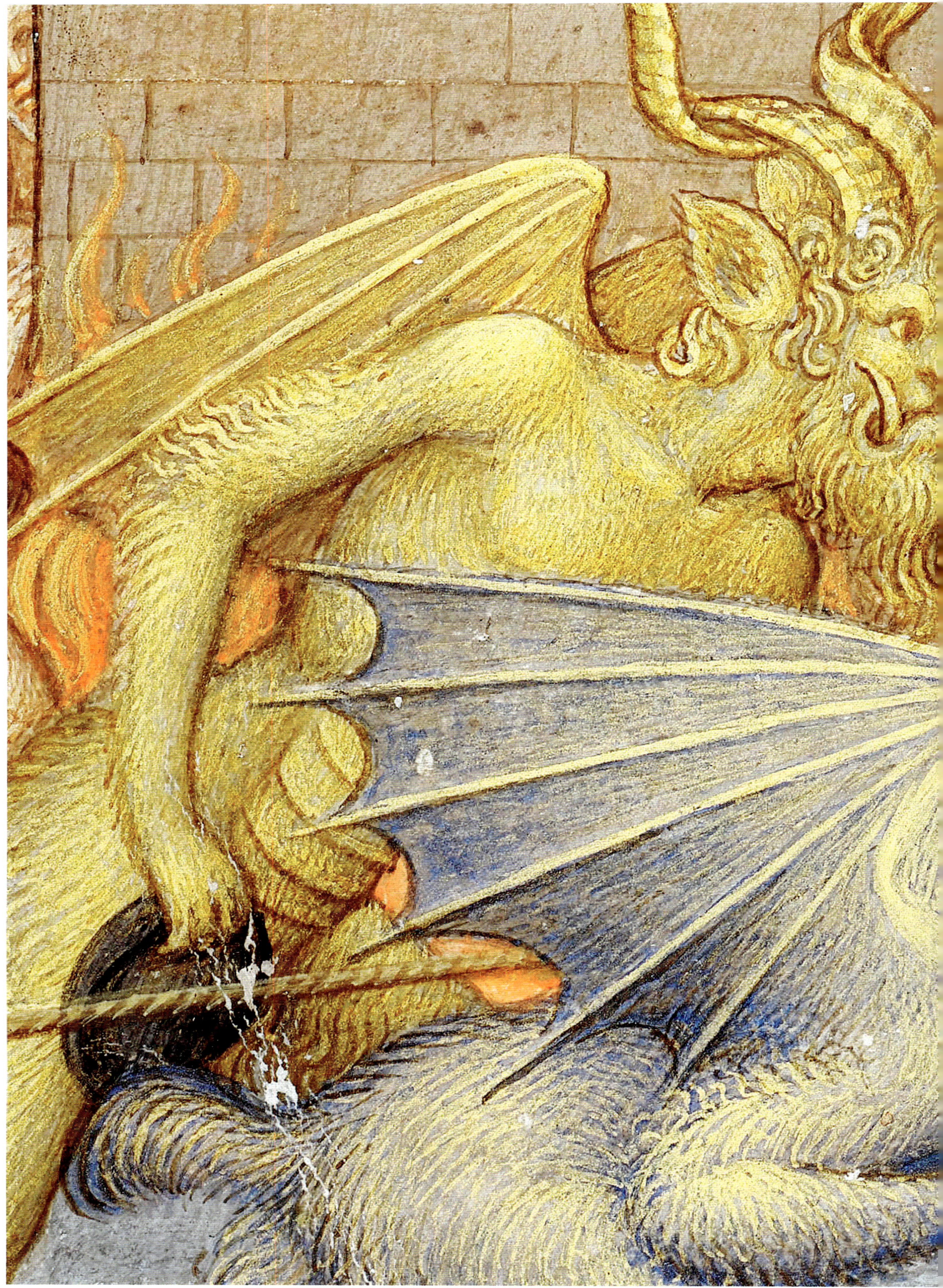

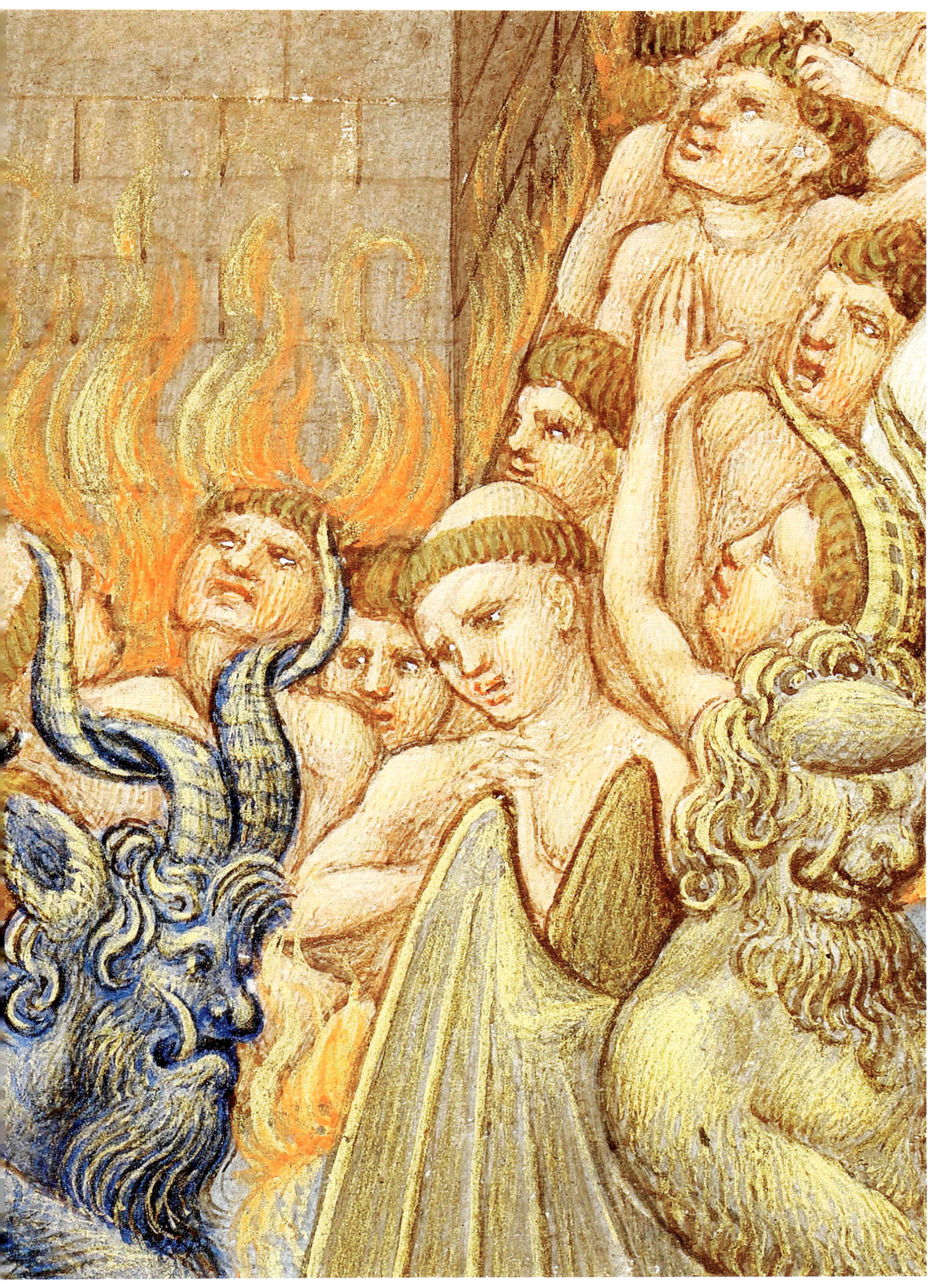

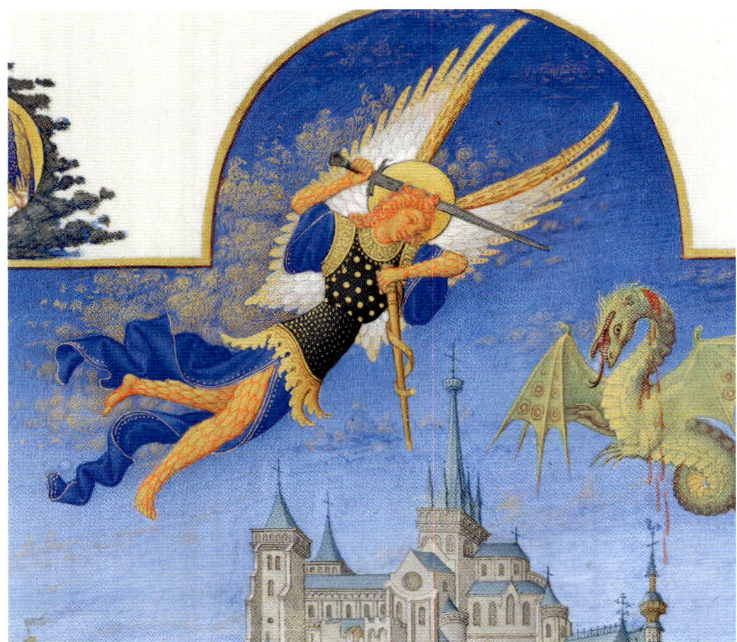

**Fig. 8** Van Lymborch brothers, *Très Riches Heures*, fol. 195: St. Michael Slaying the Dragon, detail

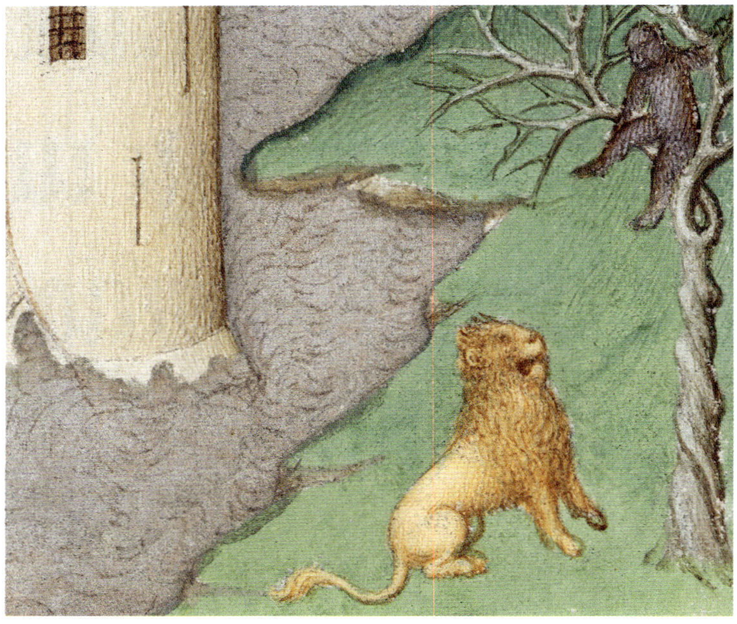

**Fig. 9** Van Lymborch brothers, *Très Riches Heures*, fol. 161v: The Temptation of Christ, detail

## THE BEAR VS THE LION

In the bottom right-hand corner of the Temptation of Christ, a lion (of Flanders?) sits watching a bear (of Berry?) up in a tree (fig. 9). The creation of the *Très Riches Heures* took place against the backdrop of the tumultuous struggle between the Armagnacs and the Burgundians, during which Jean of Berry repeatedly strove to maintain a balance between the two sides.[15]

The attack of madness suffered by King Charles VI in the forest of Le Mans on August 5, 1392 triggered a profound political crisis. The sometimes lengthy absences of the indispensable but now useless sovereign[16] placed his brother (the Duke of Orléans), his uncles (the Dukes of Berry and Burgundy), and his cousin (the Duke of Anjou) at the center of power. Opposing views of government sometimes had to coexist and the Duke of Berry, who held a central position in the king's council, now spent more time in Paris, a capital that is well represented in the *Très Riches Heures* (fol. 6v). The scene showing the Healing of the Possessed (fig. 10) could be a reminder of the terrible illness that deprived the kingdom of its head and whose cure remained unlikely. The hopes raised by a short-lived improvement in the condition of Charles VI—who made a vow to the archangel during a pilgrimage to Mont Saint-Michel in February 1394 (depicted on fol. 195; see fig. 8), a pilgrimage that the pious Duke of Berry took part in—were soon dashed.

The death of the Duke of Burgundy, Philip the Bold, in 1404 placed his son John the Fearless at the head of this powerful family. John soon set himself against his cousin, Louis, the Duke of Orléans, in almost every area. The Duke of Berry, who was tasked with creating a counterweight with Queen Isabeau of Bavaria and the Duke of Bourbon (who were looking after the Dauphin, Louis of Guyenne), was compelled to mobilize the king's army to avoid a fratricidal conflict. He was driven to join the Orléans side, soon to be known as the Armagnac side, after the assassination of the Duke of Orléans in Paris by John's agents on November 23, 1407.[17]

Jean of Berry tried his best to avoid a civil war, orchestrating a reconciliation ceremony between the Duke of Burgundy and the son of the Duke of Orléans in Chartres in 1409, but his efforts were in vain. A few months later, Jean de Montaigu, a loyal follower of both Orléans and Berry, was executed on the orders of John the Fearless. In 1410, the Count of Armagnac, the head of the party that took his name (and whose members were recognizable by the white band or scarf they wore, as in the January miniature), joined with other princes to form the League of Gien. In opposition to this alliance, John the Fearless, followed by the population of Paris, gained the support of Charles VI, who had temporarily regained his health.

The Peace of Bicêtre in 1410 was followed by more conflicts in 1411, which led to the burning of Jean of Berry's castle in… Bicêtre. The Englishmen of King Henry IV, jumping at the chance, were called in by both sides. The towns of Étampes and Dourdan, which feature prominently in the *Très Riches Heures* (fols. 8v and 4v), were seized in November and December 1411.

The royal army, led de facto by the Duke of Burgundy, laid siege to Bourges from June 11 to July 14, 1412; most of the treasures of the Sainte-Chapelle were melted down to mint

**Fig. 10** Van Lymborch brothers, *Très Riches Heures*, fol. 166: The Healing of the Possessed

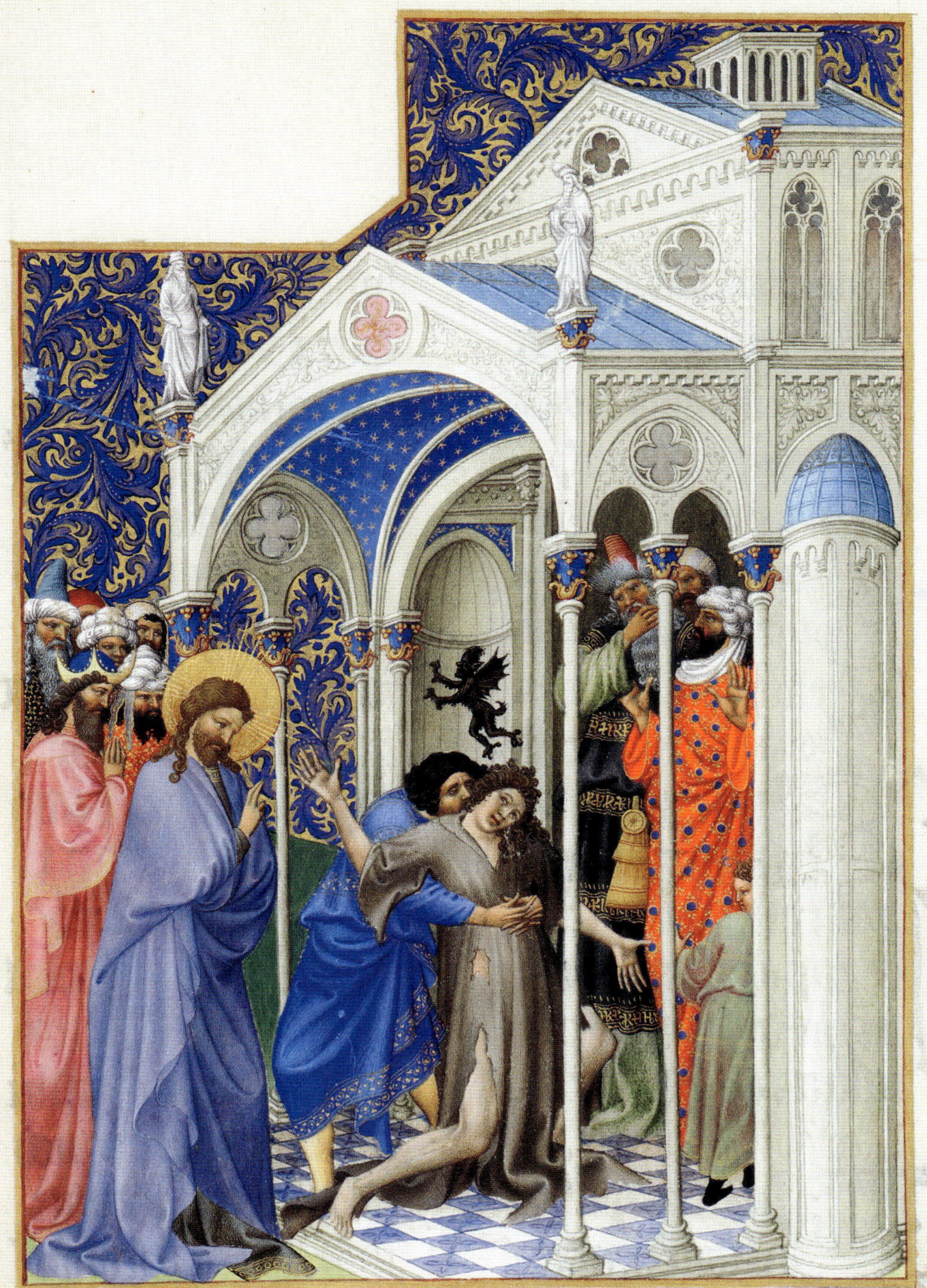

Dominica tercia in xl^a.

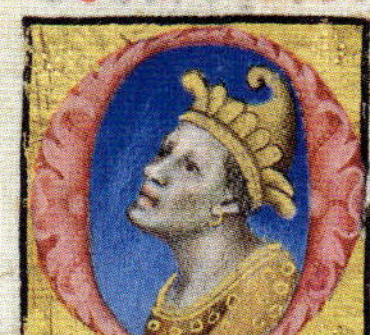

culi mei semper
ad dominum quia
ipse evellet de laqueo
pedes meos respice in me et
miserere mei quoniam u-
nicus et pauper sum ego. Ps.
Ad te domine levavi ani-

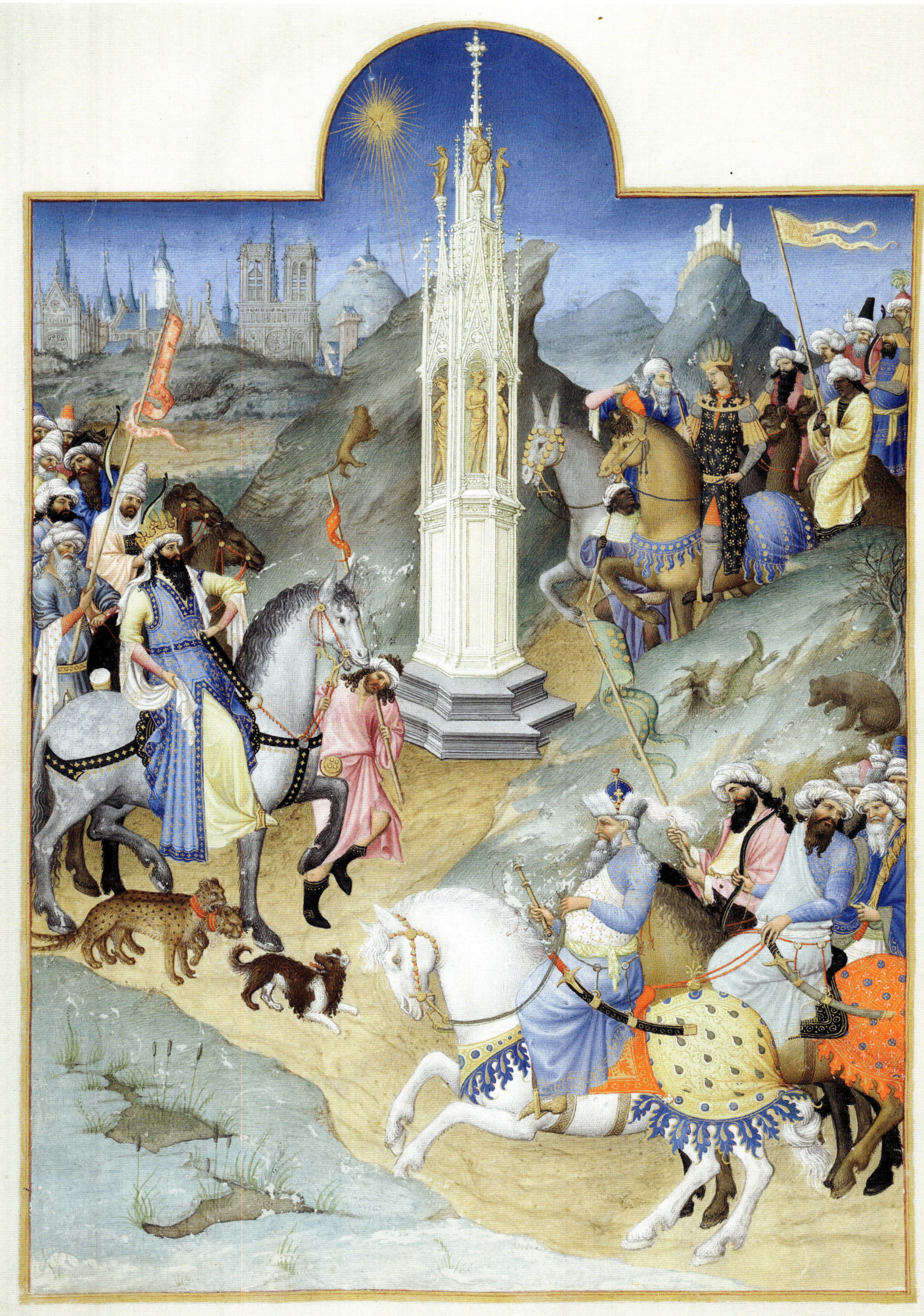

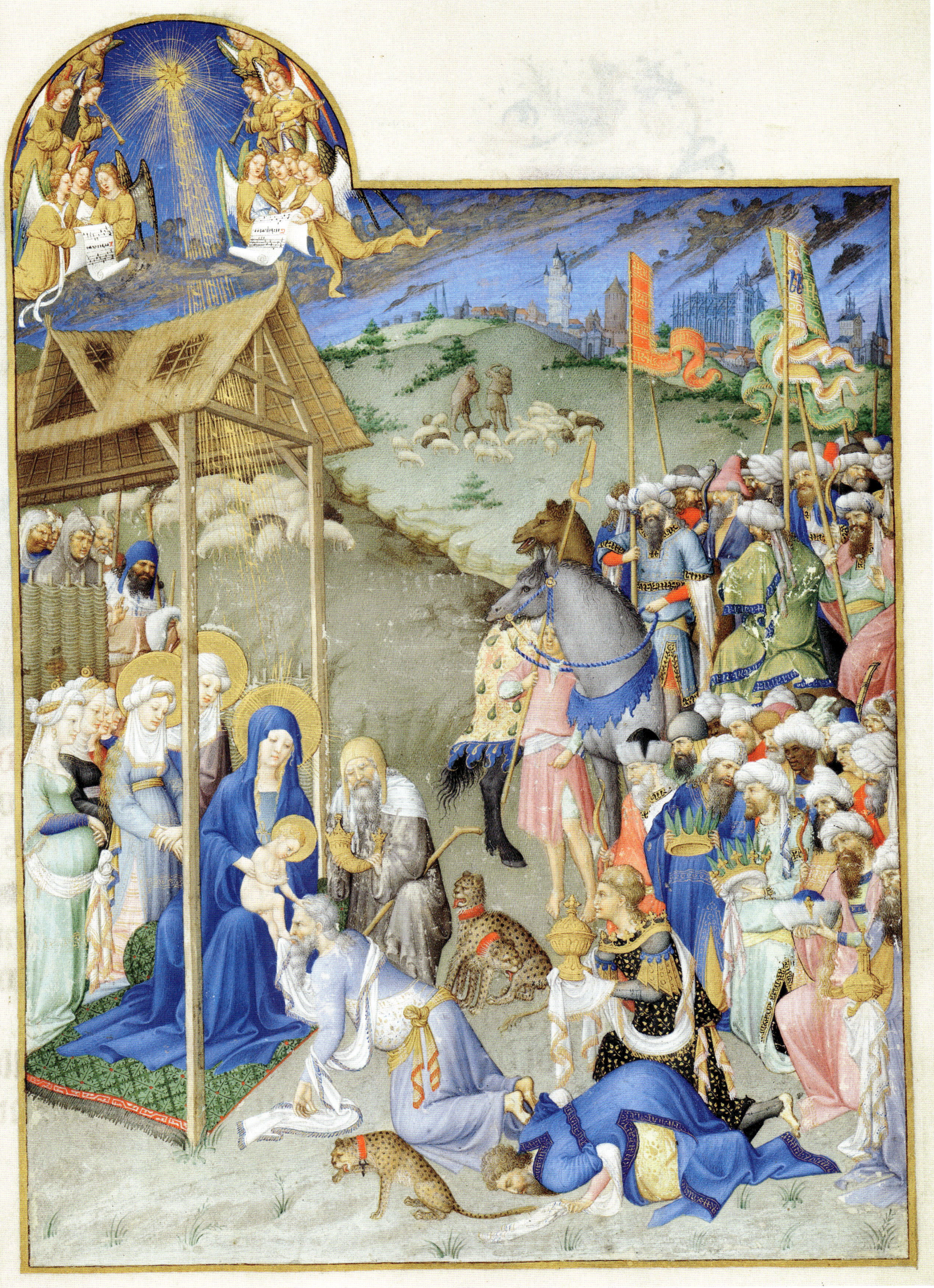

coins to pay the troops. A peace treaty was finally signed on August 22, under the aegis of the Dauphin. From then on, the Duke of Berry rarely left Paris. Contemplating the miniatures in his *Très Riches Heures* (then in the process of being created) no doubt enabled him, not without bitterness and perhaps with a sense of nostalgia, to journey through his residences and estates.[18] These trials were not his last, however. He still had to face the revolt of the "skinners," supporters of John the Fearless, led by the butcher Simon Caboche; the duke was even forced to take refuge in the house of his physician, Simon Aligret. The negotiations in September 1414 and again in February 1415 that would lead up to the "Peace of Arras" were a new attempt at reconciliation, as can be seen in the *Très Riches Heures*, whose serene miniatures can be read as a fervent manifesto for peace.[19] The January miniature has often been interpreted as a depiction of the sumptuous feast offered by Jean of Berry in January 1415 after the Peace of Arras.[20] The funerary ceremonies held in memory of Louis d'Orléans on January 5 and 7 brought the deceased's sons, Charles d'Orléans and Philippe, Count of Vertus, to Paris; they may appear among the young men in white bands,[21] although these could be the grandsons of Jean of Berry (the young man in the red, white, and black garment is probably Charles, since these are Orléans colors). Likewise, the diptych on folios 51v and 52[22] (figs. 11 and 12) could evoke these successive peace treaties; the three magi of different ages could refer to Jean of Berry (accompanied by a bear), the Duke of Burgundy in his maturity (with two leopards), and the young Dauphin (wearing a crown).[23] These exotic escorts more likely evoke the many wild animals that populated the ducal menageries and refer to the welcome Jean of Berry gave to the Byzantine emperor Manuel II Palaiologos in Paris in June 1400. The kneeling magus, dressed in a black tunic strewn with mayflowers and holding the golden chalice of myrrh on a shroud, which he offers to the Christ Child, one of the emblems of Charles VI, may be a portrait of the sovereign (fig. 13). This method was later used by Jean Fouquet, in a more realistic manner, to depict Charles VII on one of the leaves of the *Heures d'Étienne Chevalier.*[24]

This fragile peace soon shattered. Henry V of England landed near Harfleur and headed north. The king and the princes, including the Duke of Berry, settled in Rouen. The elderly duke advised Charles VI and the Dauphin against taking part directly in any fighting, as "mieux valait perdre bataille seule que roi et bataille" (better to lose the battle alone than the king and the battle)[25]:—the wise Berry could remember the defeat at Poitiers almost sixty years earlier. Events proved him right: in October 1415, at Azincourt, France suffered one of its most devastating military disasters and saw its knights decimated. One of Jean of Berry's sons-in-law, Jean de Bourbon, and the duke's grandsons, Charles d'Orléans and Charles d'Artois, Count of Eu, were among the prisoners of war. A few months later, on June 15, 1416, Jean of Berry died in Paris, at his Hôtel de Nesle, in the presence of his daughter, Marie of Berry, and two of his grandsons, Charles de Bourbon and Bernard d'Armagnac the younger.[26] In accordance with his wishes, the duke was buried in the Sainte-Chapelle in Bourges, which he had founded in 1392 and which, once completed and endowed, had been consecrated at Easter 1405. Starting in Paris, the prince's funeral cortege crossed Étampes and then Mehun-sur-Yèvre before reaching Bourges, a final journey that allowed the deceased to visit, one by one and for the last time, the landscapes depicted in the famous pages of his *Très Riches Heures*.

1 Barry et al. 2019.
2 First used in an official capacity in the Treaty of Valognes of 1355, this expression refers to the brothers and sons of Charles V.
3 On the Duke of Berry, see Autrand 2000 and above all the very scholarly work of Lehoux 1966–68.
4 Autrand 2000, 11–26.
5 See essay by Laurent Hablot, pp. 63–69.
6 Autrand 2000, 143–46.
7 Ibid., 182–92.
8 Lebigue 2014.
9 Ibid.
10 Châtelet 1999 and Autrand 2002.
11 Longnon and Cazelles 1969b; Meiss 1974a, I, 191–92. For a summary of the proposals, see Perkinson 2009.
12 Chantilly 2004, 40–43.
13 August (fol. 8v) shows Marie of Berry dressed like her husband in the two previous miniatures. Chantilly 2004, 40–43.
14 Autrand 2000, 44–63.
15 Slanicka 2002, 267–80.
16 Guenée 2004.
17 Guenée 1992.
18 Meiss 1974a, I, 201.
19 Autrand 2000, 455–59.
20 Autrand 2002 and Lebigue 2014.
21 Lebigue 2014.
22 Hablot 2018, 121.
23 Ibid.
24 Chantilly, Bibl. du musée Condé, Ms 71.
25 Quoted by Autrand 2000, 486, after Courteault et al. 1979, 67.
26 Lehoux 1956a.

**Figs. 11–12** Previous pages: Van Lymborch brothers, *Très Riches Heures*, fols. 51v and 52: The Meeting of the Three Magi and The Adoration of the Magi

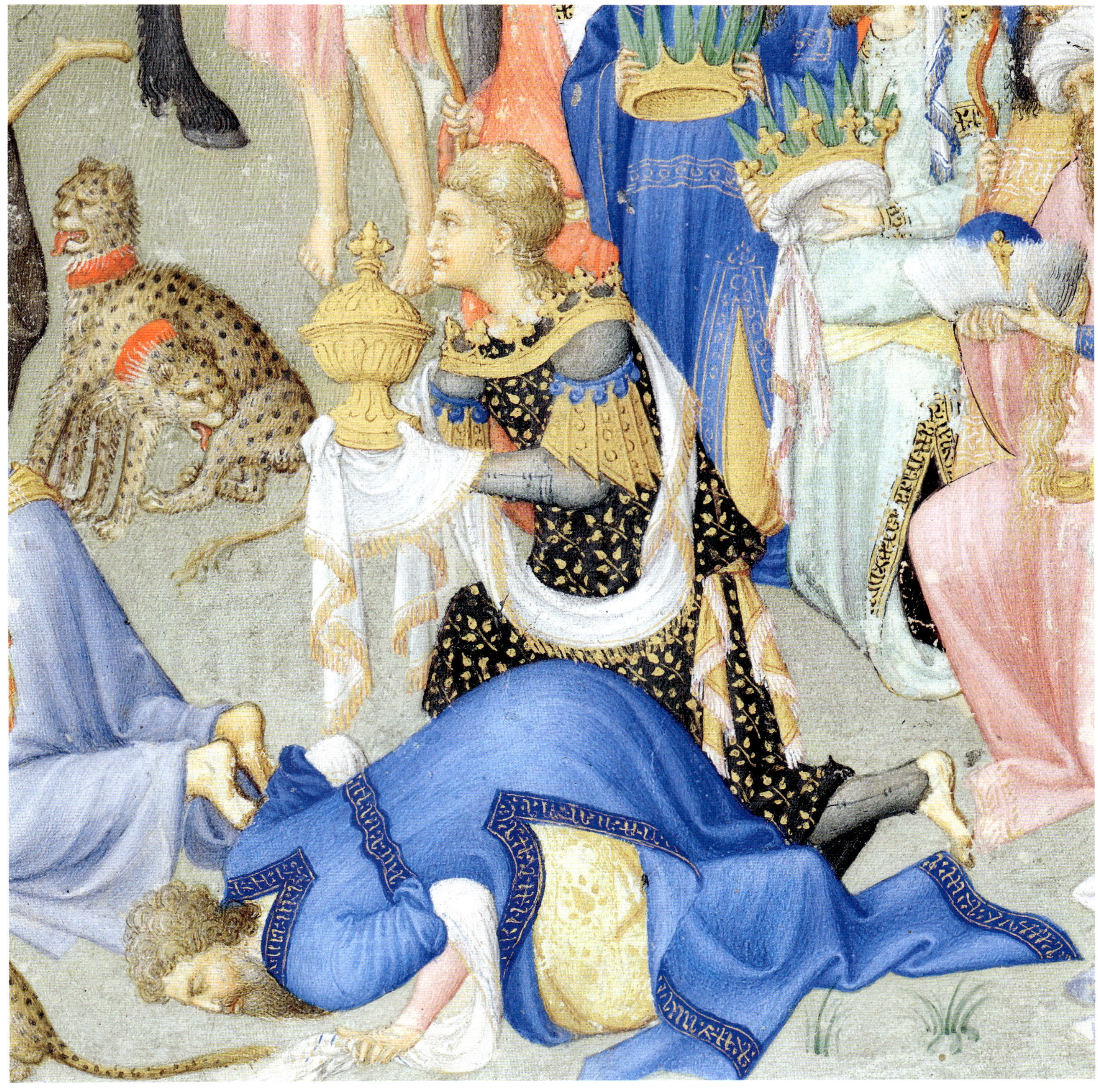

**Fig. 13** Van Lymborch brothers, *Très Riches Heures*, fol. 52: The Adoration of the Magi, detail

**Figs. 14–15** Following pages: Van Lymborch brothers, *Très Riches Heures*, fols. 12v and 52: December and The Adoration of the Magi, details

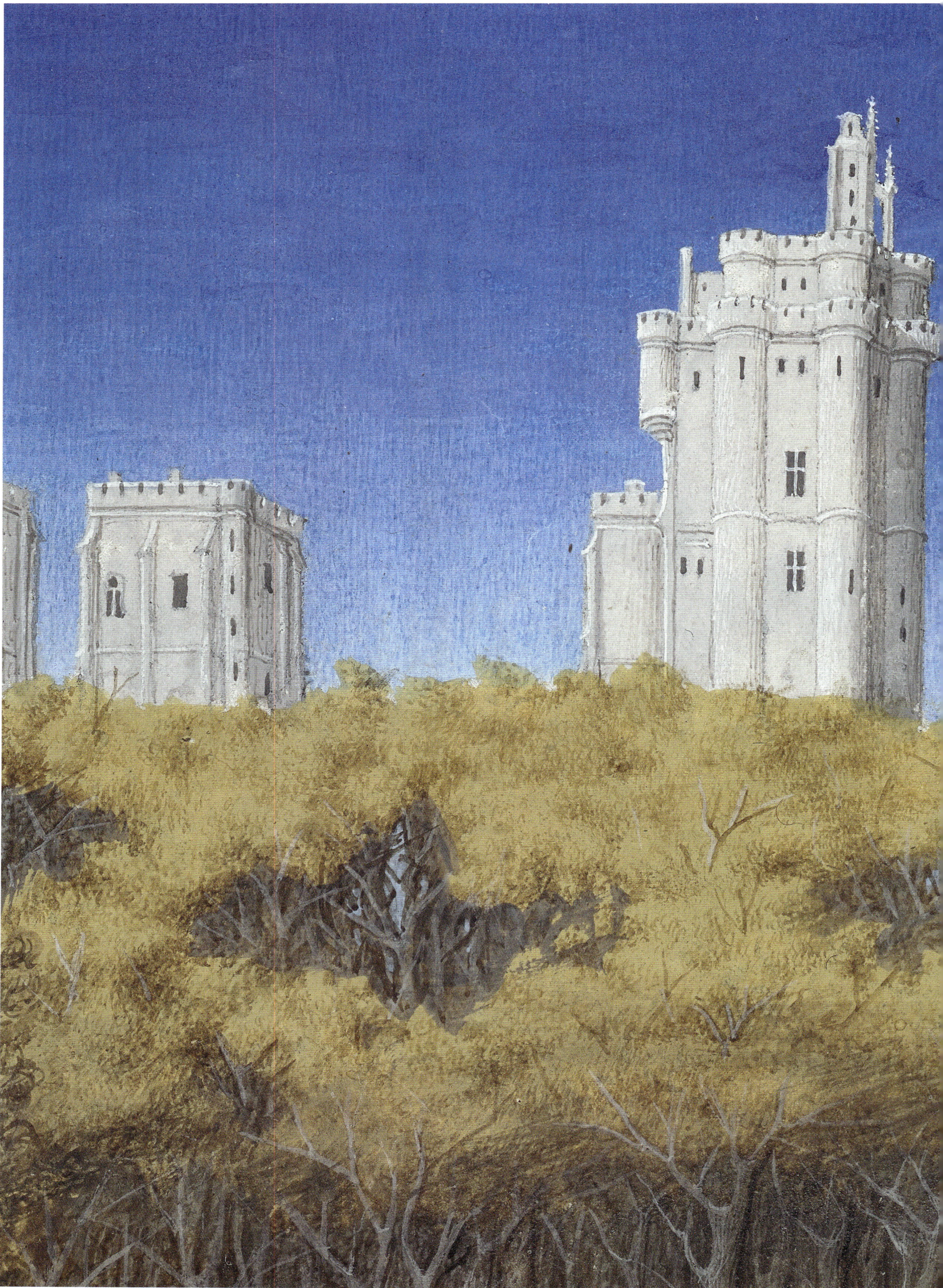

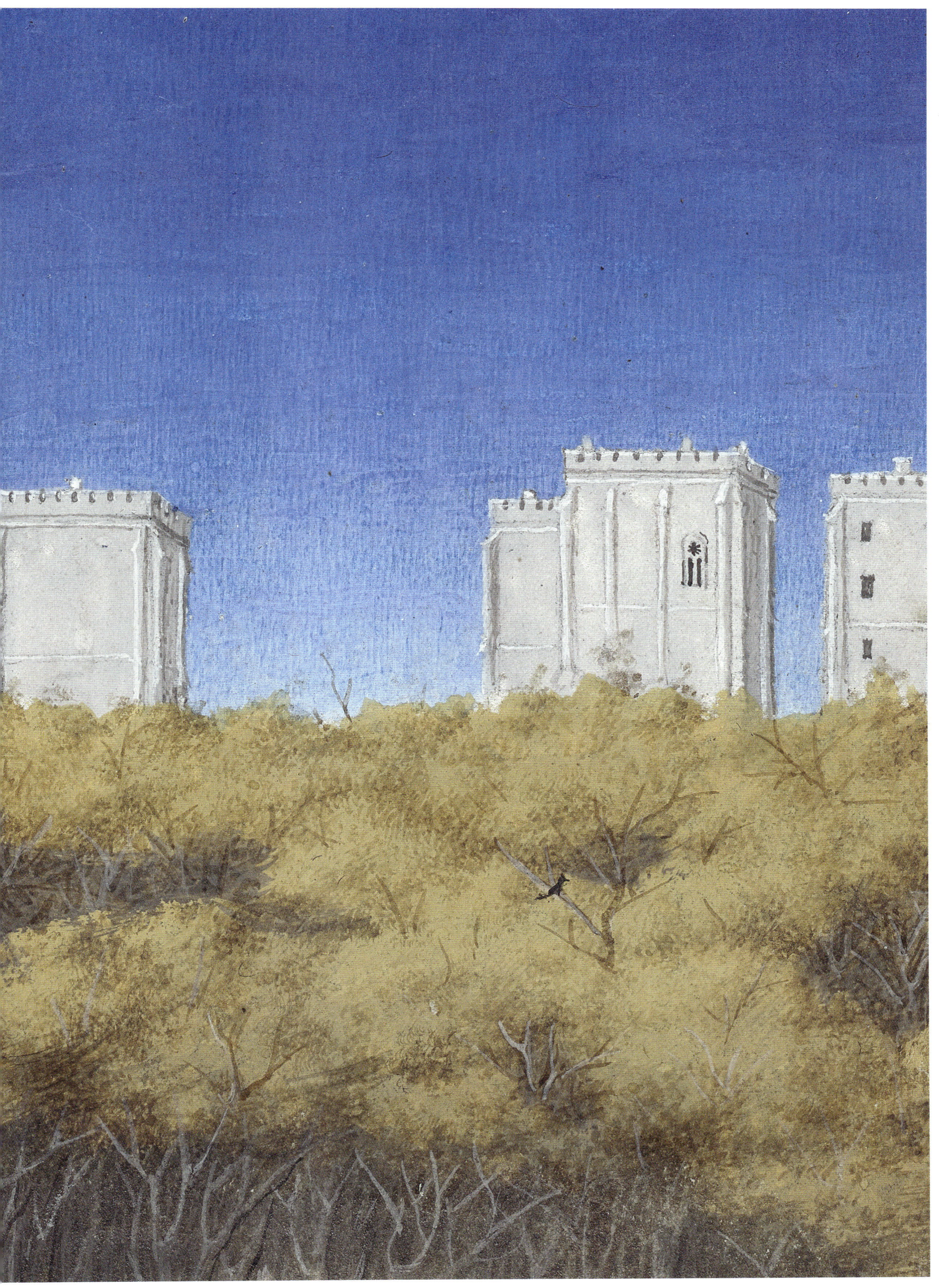

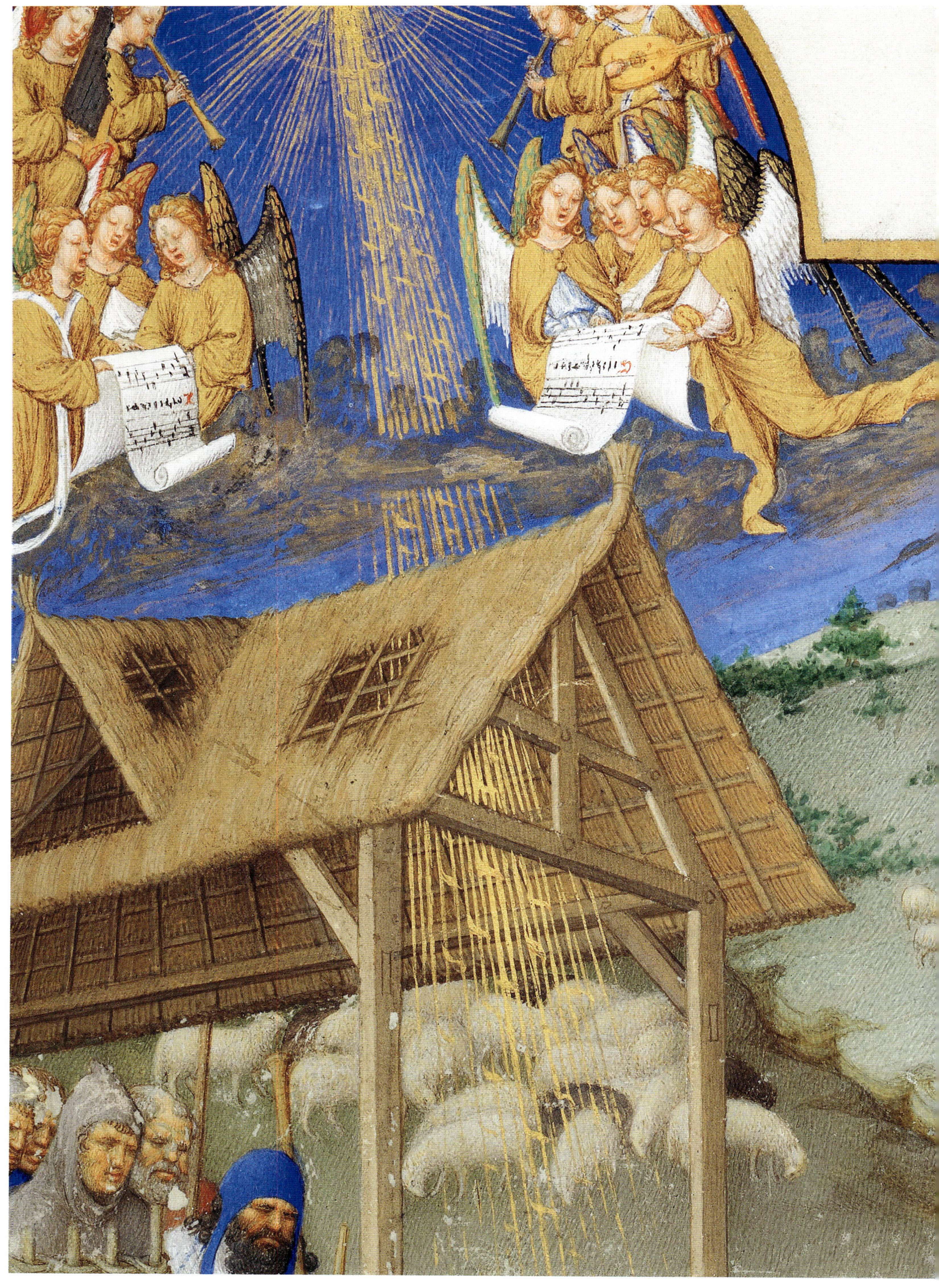

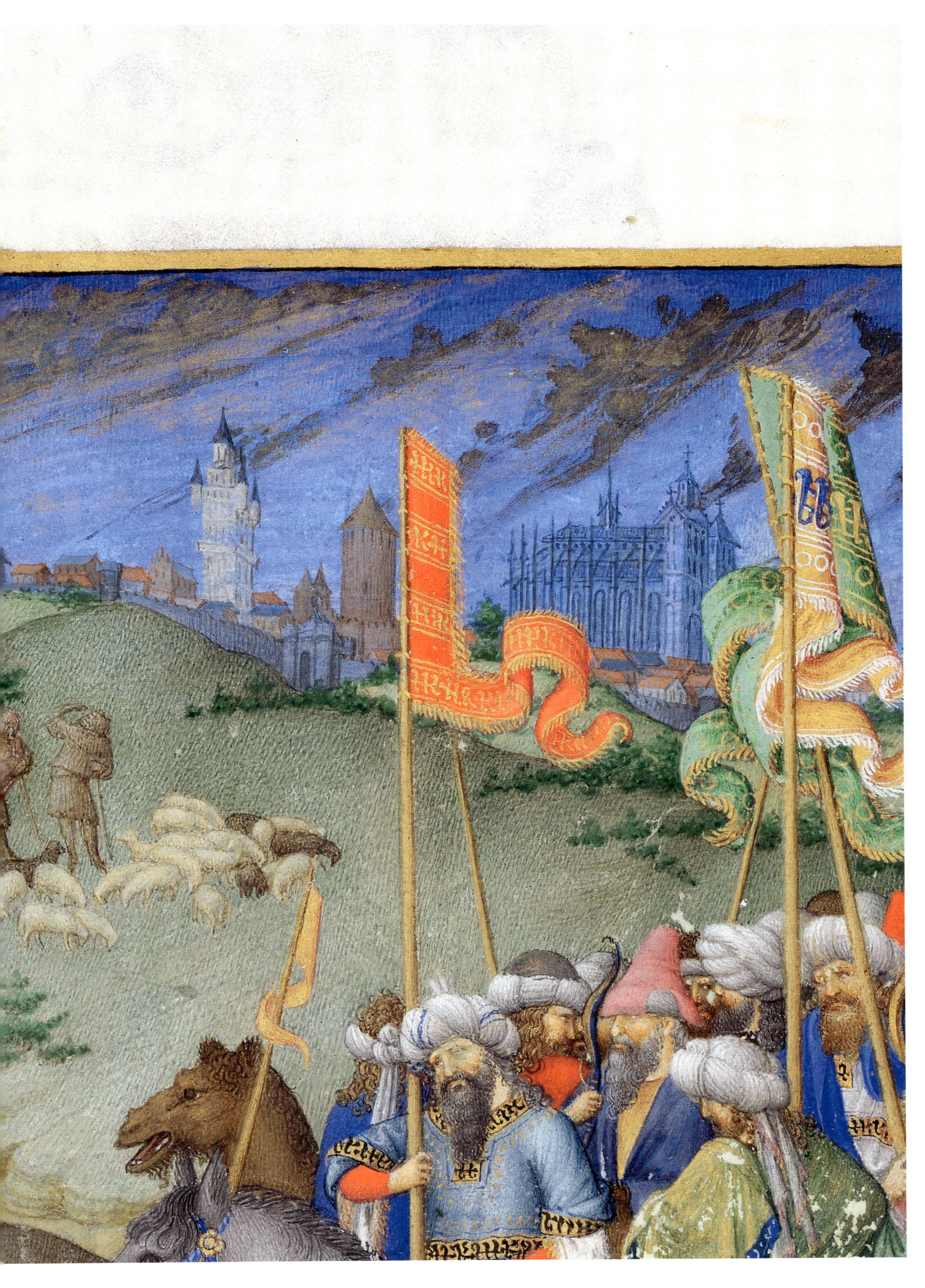

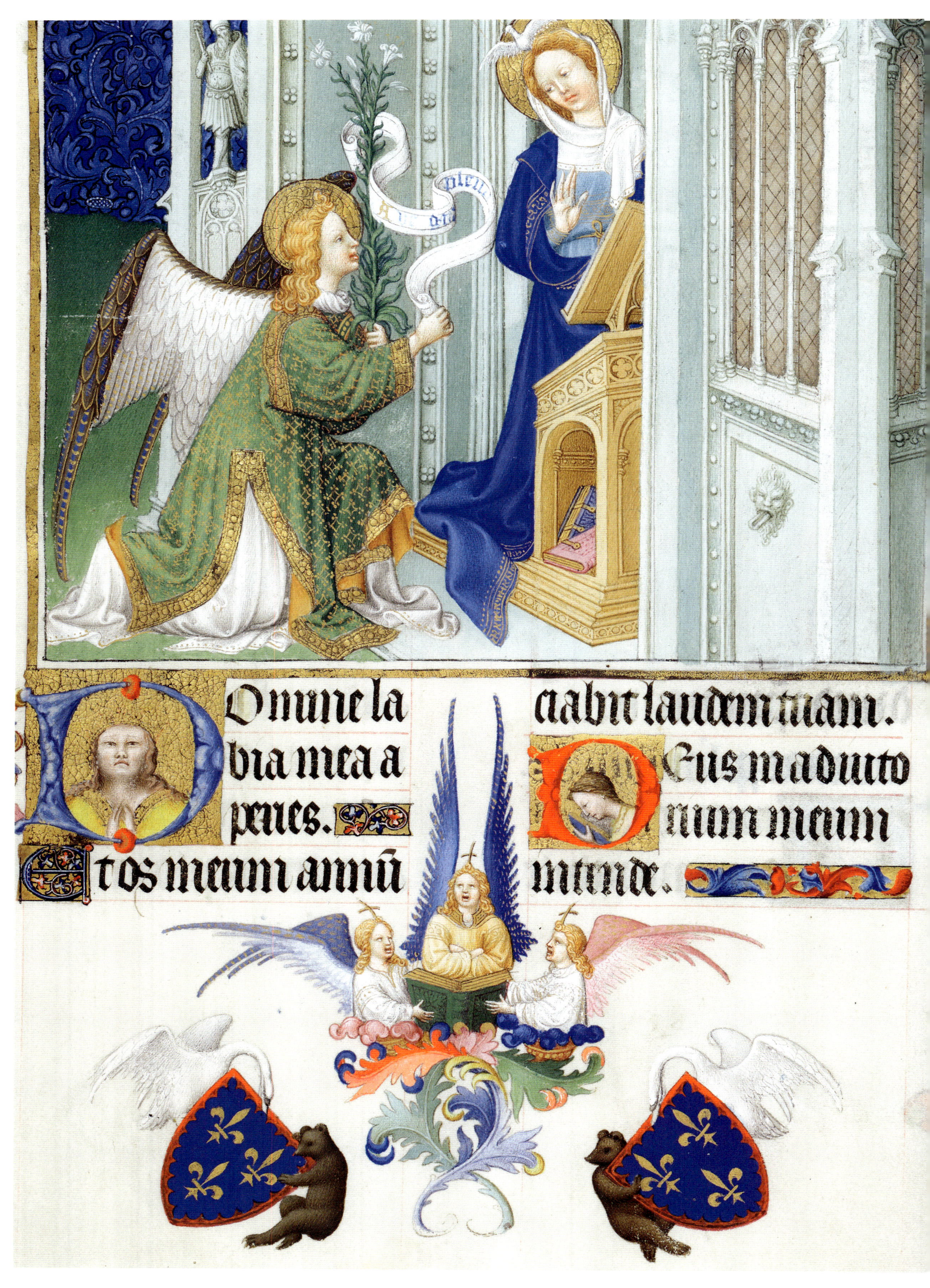

Domine la
bia mea a
peries.
Et os meum annū
ciabit laudem tuam.
Deus in adiuto
rium meum
intende.

# 2.

# The *Très Riches Heures*, an Emblematic Reflection of Jean of Berry

Laurent Hablot

I am Jean, Duke of Berry, this I truly know
Who while prisoner as hostage for my father
. . . Was so ardently smitten by Love's fire
For an Englishwoman, a servant of the god of Love
. . . For her I adopted a motto and placed on my shield
The wounded white swan: no other word was placed
there . . . [1]

It is with these verses, drawn from the mouth of his hero Cuer, that René of Anjou interpreted the emblems adopted a century earlier by his great-uncle, the Duke of Berry. These two men shared the same taste for power and beauty, and the connection between Jean of Berry and the Van Lymborch brothers is clearly reflected in the close collaboration between René of Anjou and the great Barthélemy d'Eyck, with a common denominator: a true passion for emblems and their staging in book decoration.

The *Très Riches Heures*, which these different painters all worked on, is a perfect illustration of this. The arms of Jean of Berry naturally occupy pride of place, but other elements also help to identify the prince: the bear, the swan, the orange branch, the cypher "EV" (which can also be read as "UE"), the portrait of the prince, his livery, and the ensigns of his party. All these pieces add up to turn this devotional book into a veritable political manifesto.

## HERALDIC HERITAGE

The Duke of Berry's prestigious arms—"d'azur semé de fleurs de lis d'or à la bordure engrelée de gueules" (a semé of gold fleurs-de-lis on a blue ground with engrailed red bordure)—repeatedly identify the patron of this precious work. Unlike those of his brother the king, his arms are not "full," but, with the addition of this red engrailed bordure, include a brisure (cadency mark) that makes it possible to recognize at first glance Jean of Berry as one of the younger fleur-de-lis princes, "son," "brother," and "uncle" of the king of France, as he liked to indicate in his titles. It was through this symbol of power that he expressed his feudal authority over his appanage by displaying it on his jurisdictional seals, the initial letters of his deeds, and the decorations of his hotels, palaces, fortresses, and chapels, as the frequent references to these arms in the folios of the Chantilly manuscript remind us.[2] As legend has it, lilies have, since Clovis, been the visible sign of the divine election of the Capetians and their ancestors. To demonstrate this "singulière affection de la benoicte trinité pour le royaume de France" (singular affection of the Blessed Trinity for the kingdom of France), Charles V reduced the number of lilies on his shield to three and made angels the usual bearers of this sign. Jean of Berry, in turn, continued this sacralization of the royal arms, as folios 26 (fig. 2) and 195 (fig. 3) of the *Très Riches Heures* remind us. Although the prince's arms and emblems no

**Fig. 1** Van Lymborch brothers, *Très Riches Heures*, fol. 26: The Annunciation, detail

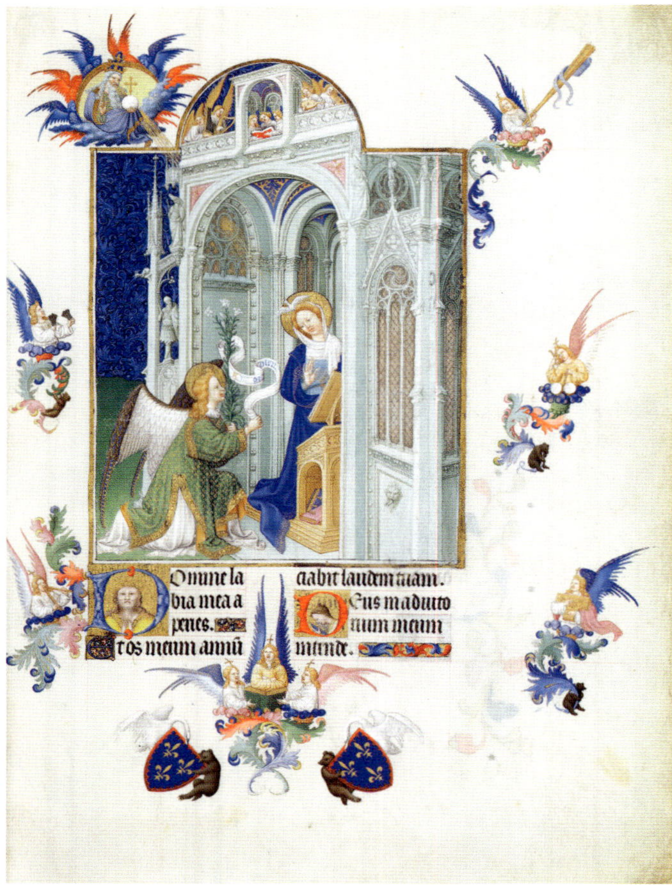

**Fig. 2** Van Lymborch brothers, *Très Riches Heures*, fol. 26: The Annunciation

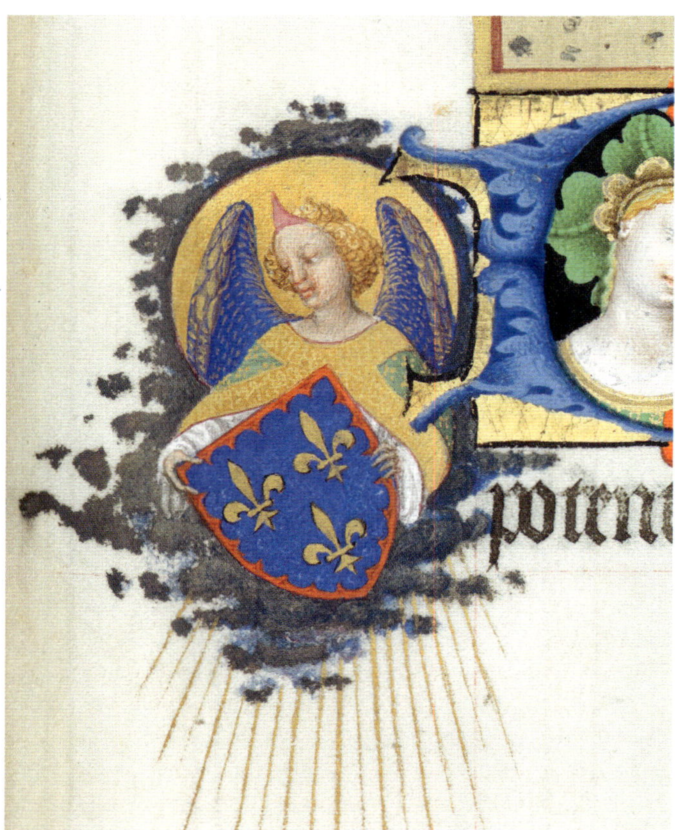

**Fig. 3** Van Lymborch brothers, *Très Riches Heures*, fol. 195: St. Michael Slaying the Dragon, detail

longer saturate the marginal decoration to the same extent as in the *Très Belles Heures* (before 1402) or in the *Grandes Heures* (1409),[3] their skillful integration into the decoration of the *Très Riches Heures* help to inscribe these sacred or secular images in space and time, creating a sense of reality that connects heaven and earth.

## BETWEEN COURTESY, SPIRITUALITY, AND POLITICS: THE BEAR AND THE SWAN

Two other emblematic figures stand out in the decoration: the bear and the swan. These two animals, used in some cases as heraldic "tenants" (supporters), belong in fact to a new register of emblems that appeared in the second half of the fourteenth century, the "devises" (devices). Sometimes supplemented by a phrase, a "mot" (motto), a monogram or letters, and a set of colors or "livrée" (livery), the device remains inseparable from the cultural and political changes of the mid-fourteenth century and from the widespread revival of the chivalric ideal, underpinned by the holding of tournaments, Arthurian literature, the consolidation of princely authority, and the promotion of courtesy and *devotio moderna*. The captivity of the French princes following the defeat at Poitiers (1356) clearly contributed to the spread of devices on the French side of the Channel. For the patron of the *Très Riches Heures*, as well as for his relatives, this event marked a significant turning point and the emergence of a unique emblematic expression. According to René of Anjou, it was during this enforced stay that the duke adopted his two devices—the bear ("ours") and the swan ("cygne")—as a symbolic reference to a lady named Ursine. While this reading may seem apocryphal, the bear that the Duke of Berry chose as his device was used frequently from 1364.[4] After this date, the bear appears everywhere on the artistic artefacts made for the duke, including seals, manuscripts, monuments, tiled floors, jewelry, and clothing. Depicted in a variety of guises and positions, the bear was shown muzzled or unmuzzled, alongside the swan or on its own, holding a banner or shield, or wearing the crested helmet topped with the great fleur-de-lis of the Capetians.

Symbolically, the former king of the animals is still admired and feared for its strength. This is even more celebrated when it is tamed, subdued, and muzzled. Its power was diminished, and the act of riding the bear was seen as overcoming fear. However, it was rather the significance of the emblem that seems to have motivated the duke's choice, perhaps by evoking the Berry apostle, the legendary Ursinus of Bourges or St. Ursin, or the homophony between the name of the duchy "Berry" and the word "bear." Whatever the reason, the animal became the veritable totem of the Duke of Berry, who maintained an almost-mimetic relationship with the animal, wearing bear-fur hats, modelling his features on those of the bear —as revealed, among other images, by the scene showing the exchange of gifts on New Year's Day in the *Très Riches Heures* (January)—and populating his menageries with bears, which sometimes even accompanied him on his travels.

The second device chosen by Jean of Berry was that of the swan. This appeared around 1377 and therefore well before his marriage in 1389 to Jeanne de Boulogne, whose mythical kinship with the Knight of the Swan is unrelated to this choice.

Perhaps the duke inherited this device, shared for a time by his brother Philip the Bold, from his mother-in-law Jeanne d'Auvergne? The swan—a "cygne" in essence and by homophony—was undoubtedly one of the most potent emblems of this age, nourished by the legend of the knight to whom it gave its name. In relation to Jean of Berry, however, the swan is depicted as "navré," that is, wounded on the breast rather than chained, as was usual; this brings it closer to the swan represented in the medieval bestiary, which, singing its last song, reveals its courage in the face of death and its longing to meet Christ. The duke's passion for this figure is apparent on all his movable and immovable artefacts, his jewels, his chapels, even the moats of his châteaux at Mehun-sur-Yèvre and Poitiers, which are depicted as populated with swans on the folios of the *Très Riches Heures* (July, fol. 7v; and 161v, fig. 2, p. 73).

## ORANGE TREE AND LAPDOG

On the canopy behind the duke in the illumination of January, orange-branch scrolls have been added to the emblematic decoration (fig. 4). This vegetal emblem was adopted on New Year's Day 1415, when, for this court feast, Jean of Berry commissioned "858 feuilles d'orenges pour faire la livrée de mondit seigneur le duc ledit jour" (858 orange leaves to make the livery of my lord the duke on the said day), minor goldsmithery artefacts intended to be sewn onto the livery dresses distributed to his courtiers.[5] Bearing both flowers and fruit, the orange tree was a symbol of fertility and prosperity, but also an exotic tree, rare and precious, evocative of the golden apple in the Judgment of Paris and of the Tree of Knowledge and thus, by extension, of the *lignum vitae* of the Wood of the Cross, revered by the duke. René of Anjou also added the orange tree to his emblems in the mid-fifteenth century.

Another relatively emblematic figure that appears frequently in the representations of Jean of Berry and is found in particular in the *Très Riches Heures*, in January, May, and August as well as at the Meeting of the Magi, is that of the lapdog. This emblem has been studied by the great scholar Paul Durrieu.[6]

## MOTTO AND CIPHER: A TASTE FOR LETTERS AND ENIGMAS

The duke's motto, "Le temps venra" (The time will come), appears as early as 1365 on his seal, together with the bear. It was used until his death, although it is curiously absent from the decoration of the *Très Riches Heures*. It may have been contracted in the cipher adopted by the duke—the intertwined letters "EV"—an enigma which to this day remains unsolved and which is found from 1407 engraved on a diamond or decorating manuscripts, as in the lower margins of Zodiacal Man (fol. 14v; fig. 5).

The cipher could refer to the first two letters of "Eveniet" in the Latin version of the motto, "Eveniet tempus," or, if read as "UE" and not "EV," to the first and last letters of "UrsinE." More simply, these intertwined letters could be read as meaning "En Vous" (In you) and thus as evoking the Virgin Mary.

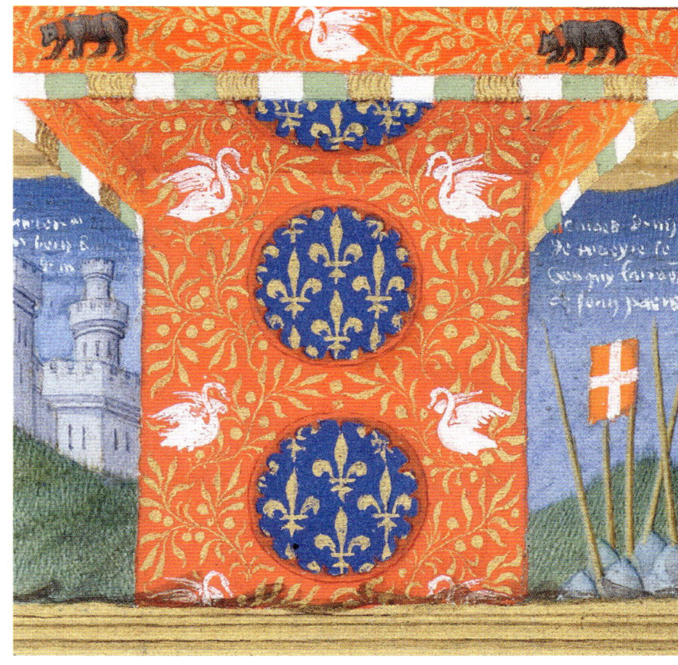

**Fig. 4** Van Lymborch brothers, *Très Riches Heures*, fol. 1v: January, detail

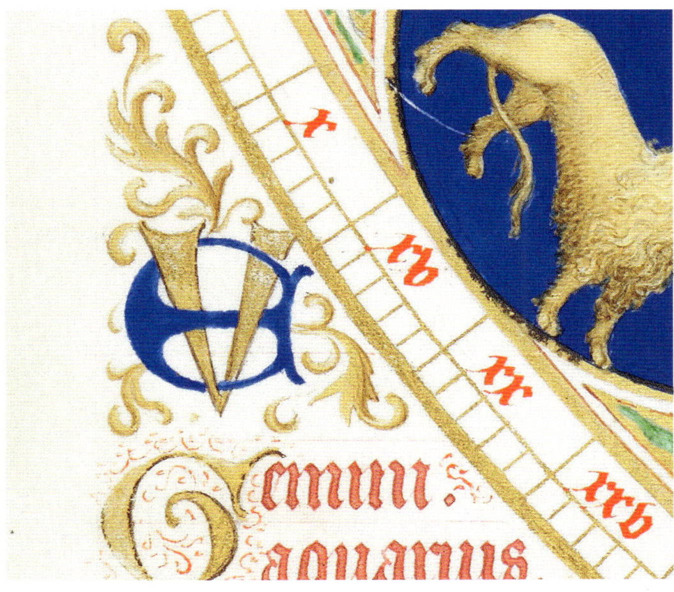

**Fig. 5** Van Lymborch brothers, *Très Riches Heures*, fol. 14v: Zodiacal Man, detail

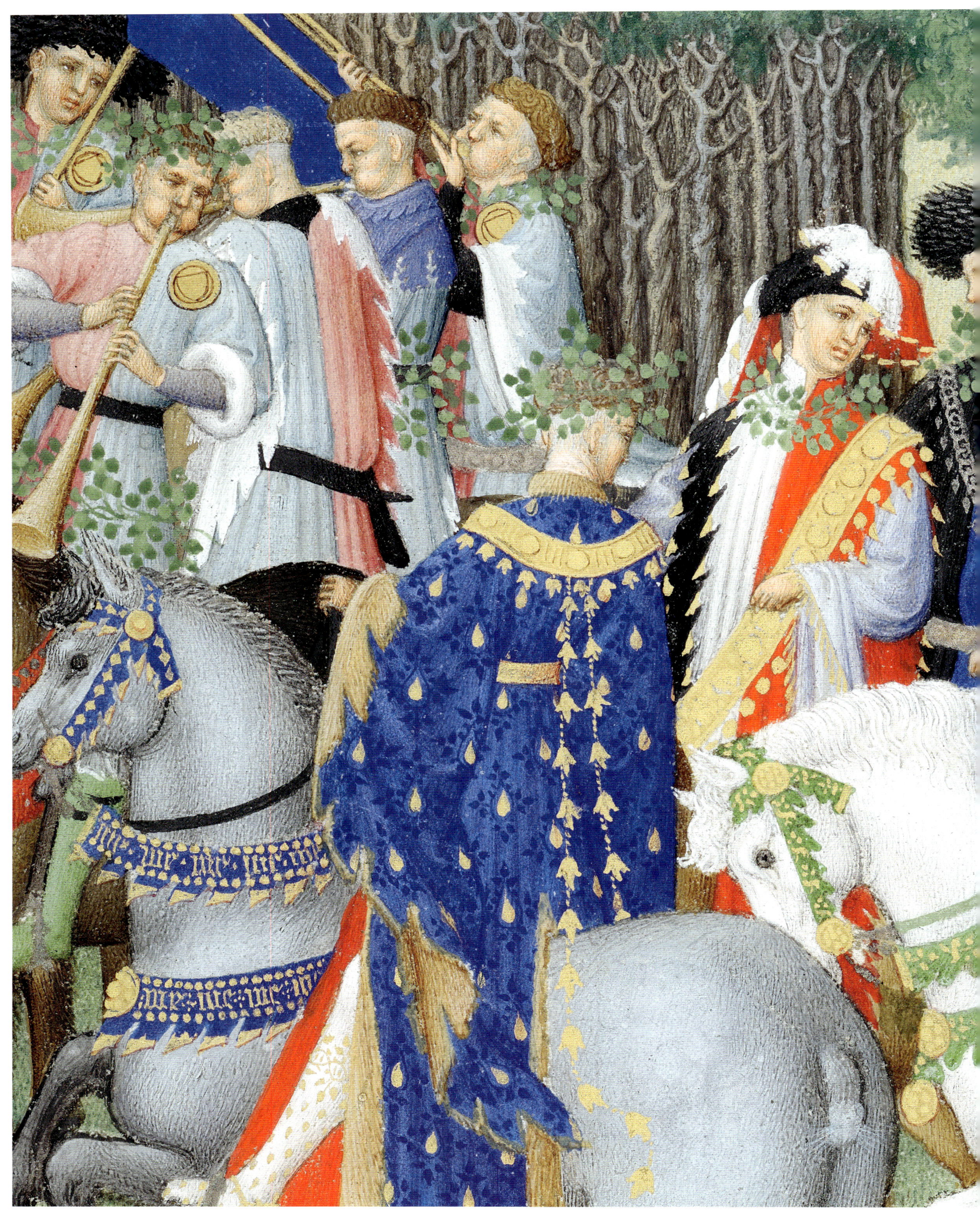

**Fig. 6** Van Lymborch brothers, *Très Riches Heures*, fol. 5v: May, detail

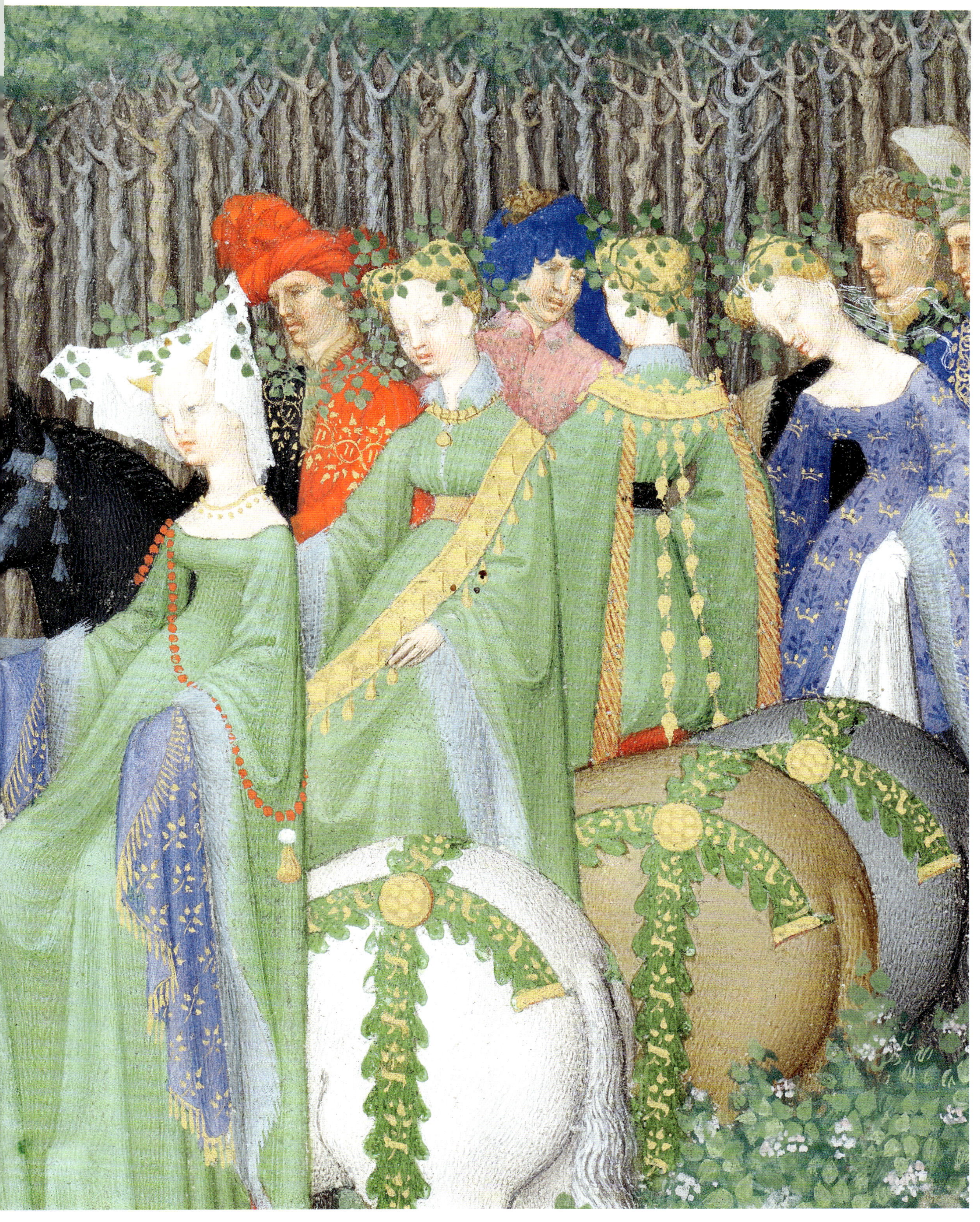

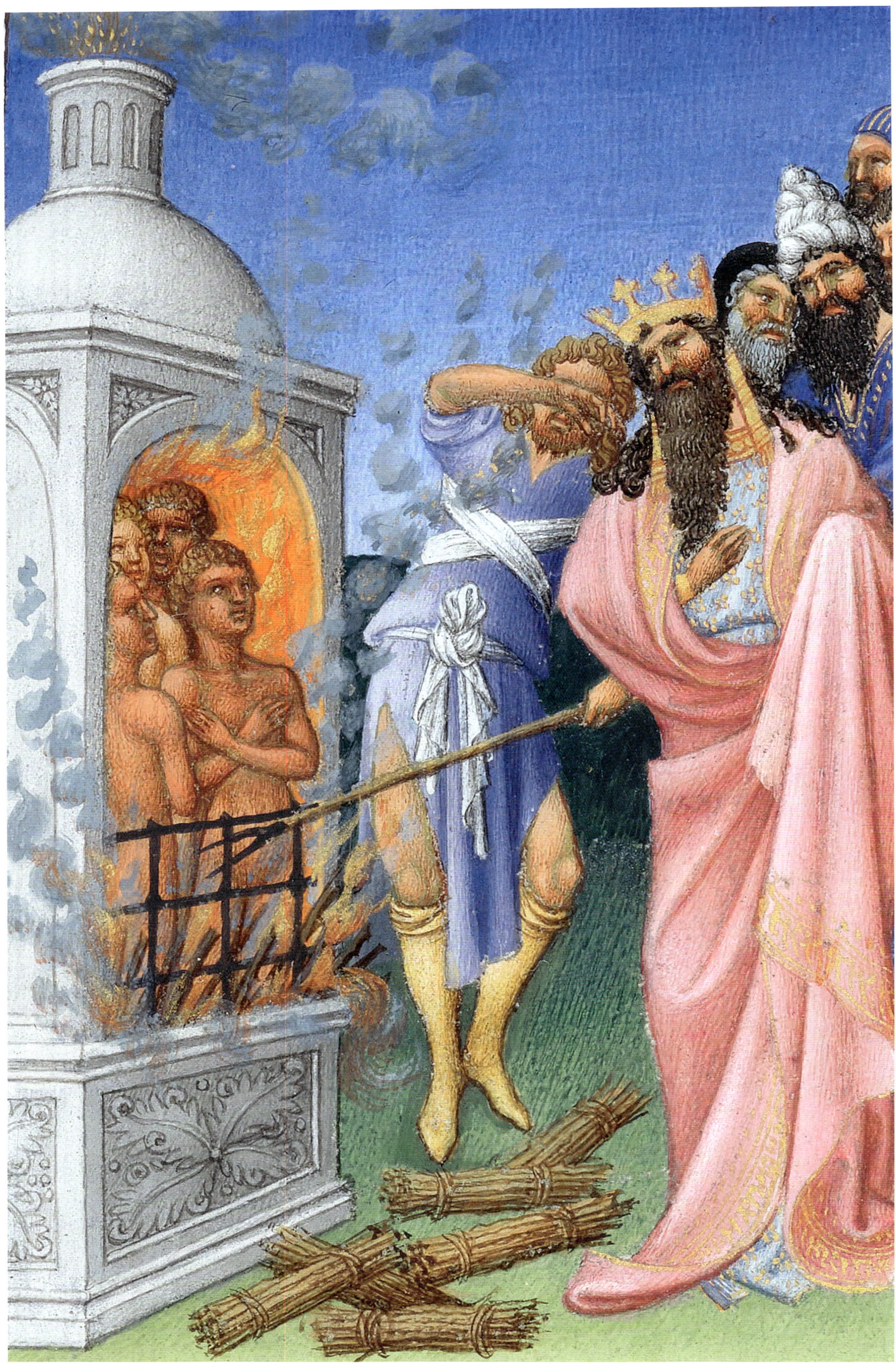

## POLITICAL EMBLEMS

In 1415, Jean of Berry was also the head of a political party, that of the "faux bandés armagnacs" (Armagnac rebels), as revealed in the *Très Riches Heures*. The manuscript not only shows the grey, red, and black livery of the ducal court for kitchen valets (January), falconers (August), and swineherds (November), it also shows several princely liveries that help us to identify the figures and give a political reading to the images, such as the engagement of Bonne d'Armagnac, Jean of Berry's granddaughter, to Charles of Orléans (May; fig. 6). Beside them stand two princes identified by their colors: Louis of Guyenne in red, black, and white, positioned at the center of the scene in accordance with his rank, and John of Bourbon, who wears the blue and black colors of his house.

With the exception of one of the meat-cutting servants at the January banquet and St. John (the duke's patron saint) at the foot of the Cross (fol. 156v; fig. 19, p. 157), both of whom may be wearing the famous white band of the Armagnacs, there is no trace of any other sign. By contrast, the sign of their Burgundian adversaries, the cross of St. Andrew,[7] is displayed on several occasions by the tormenters of the faithful and of Christ (fols. 40v (fig 7), 143, 146v) and those threatening the Virgin (fol. 147). As he perishes in the flames with his rebellious angels, Lucifer himself wears a stole covered with small crosses (fol. 64v; fig. 8).

But in 1415, the Duke of Berry, dean of the fleur-de-lis princes, wanted peace and harmony, as is likely symbolized by the gathering of the Magi, where three kings come together around the common ideal of venerating Christ. Three kings for three ages of life, three kings for three princes controlling the kingdom: the old Jean of Berry, the mature John the Fearless, and the young Louis of Guyenne. Three princes who, in February 1415, were engaged in peace negotiations that would lead up to the "Peace of Arras" (1435). The time had come ...

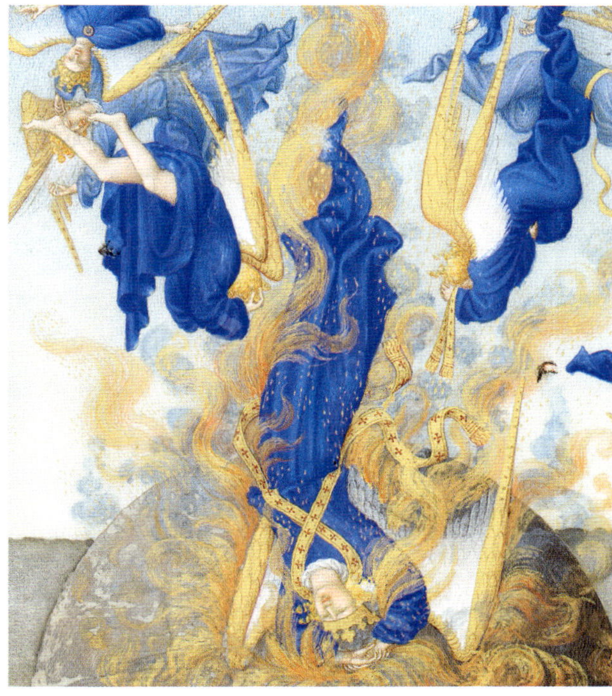

**Fig. 8** Van Lymborch brothers, *Très Riches Heures*, fol. 64v: The Fall of the Rebel Angels, detail

1 "Jehan, duc de Berry, suis-je de vérité saige / Qui en tenant prison et pour mon père ostaige ...Je fis si ardemment d'estre amoureux espris / D'une dame englaische, servante au Dieu d'amours /...Pour elle prins ung mot, et mis soubz mon escu / Le cygne blanc navré, autre mot puis ny fu..." Translation from Gibbs and Karczewska 2001, 163.

2 The weather vanes at Mehun-sur-Yèvre (fol. 161v) and Poitiers (fol. 7v) and the ceilings at Bourges (fol. 1v). On this subject, see Salamagne 2010.

3 The duke's emblematic decoration appears neither in the *Petites Heures*, illustrated by Jean Le Noir around 1380–90, nor in the psalter from the same period, illustrated by André Beauneveu. Still absent from the *Très Belles Heures* (painted in 1400), it was introduced after 1400 in the *Belles Heures*, unfinished by Jean d'Orléans, also Jean Le Noir. This emblematic decoration was reused in 1408 by Jacquemart de Hesdin in the *Grandes Heures*.

4 Blanc-Riehl and Nielen 2019.

5 Favière 1996.

6 Durrieu 1909.

7 Schnerb 2008.

**Fig. 7** Van Lymborch brothers, *Très Riches Heures*, fol. 40v: Three Hebrews in the Furnace, detail

**Fig. 9** Following pages: Van Lymborch brothers, *Très Riches Heures*, fol. 64v: The Fall of the Rebel Angels, detail

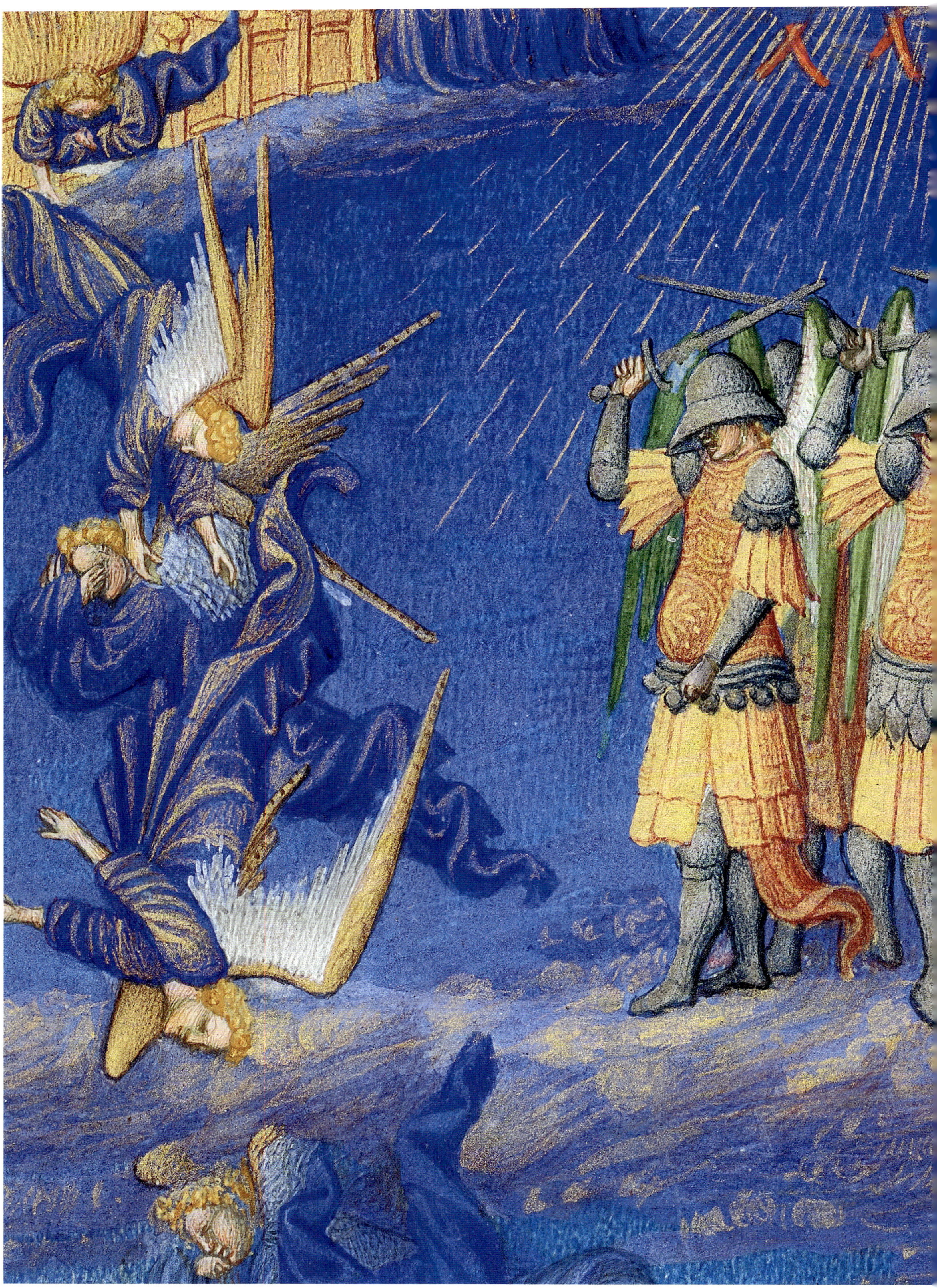

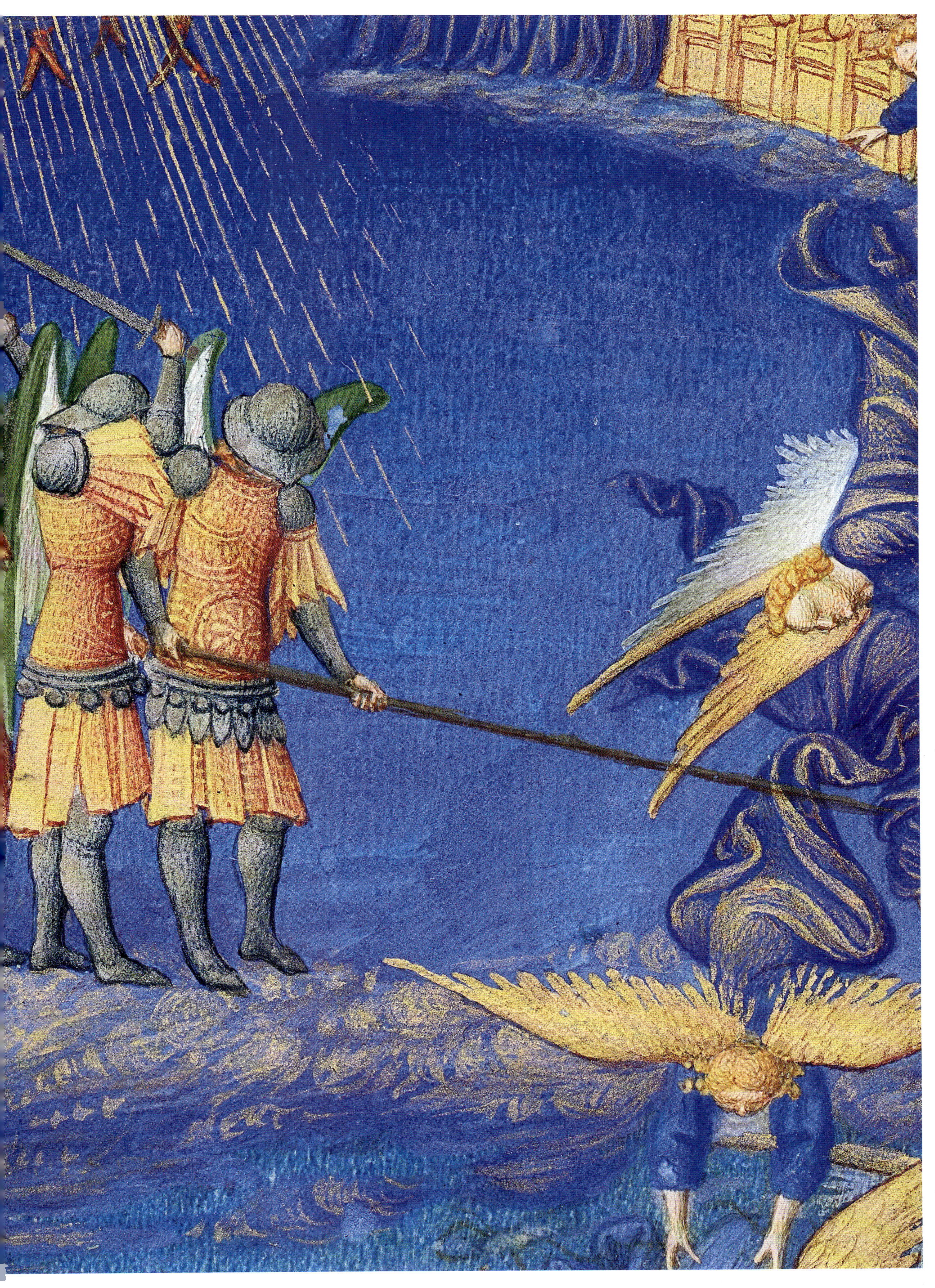

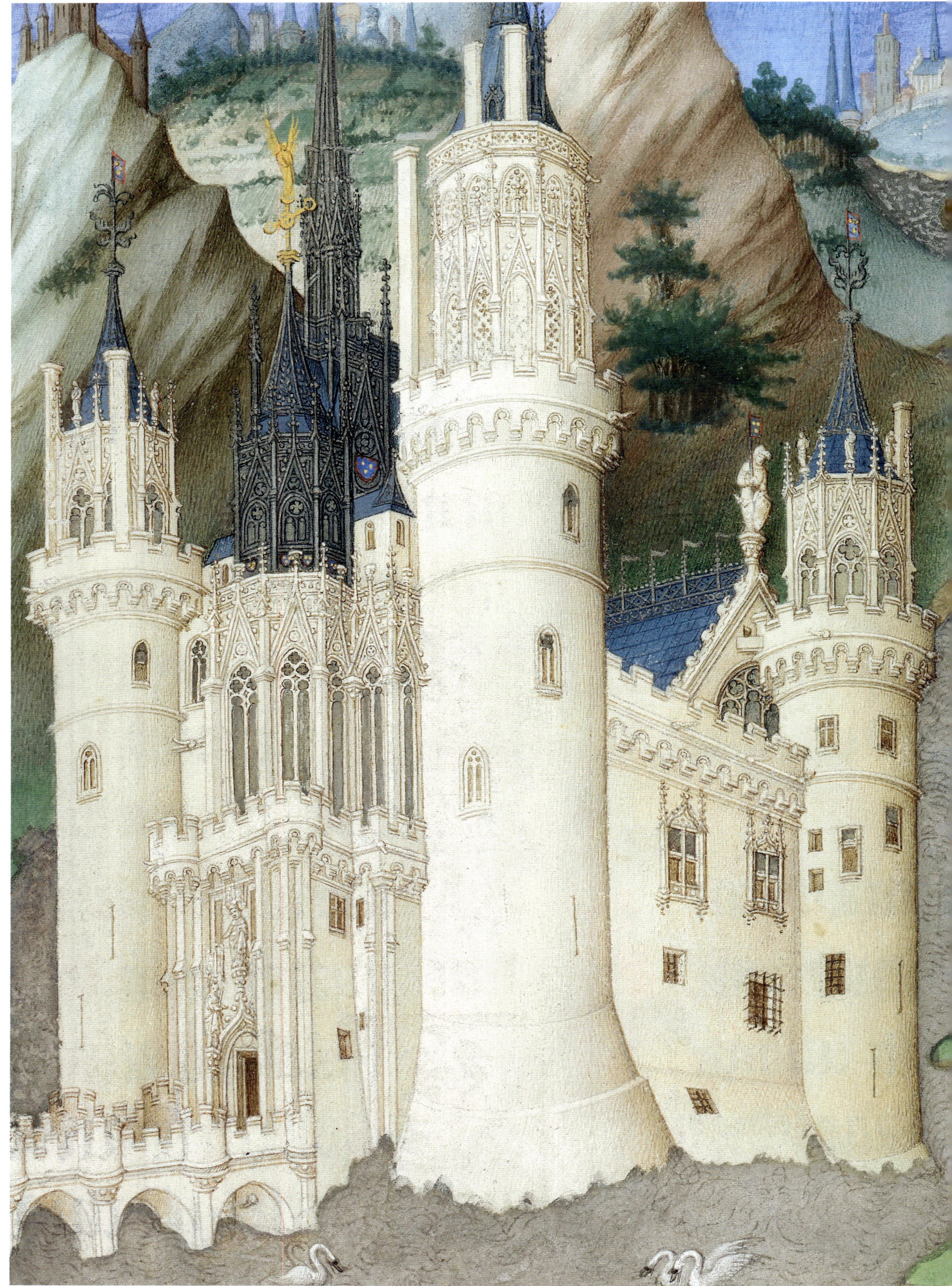

# 3.

# The *Très Riches* Collections of the Duke of Berry

Mathieu Deldicque

The miniature of the month of January in the *Très Riches Heures* immortalizes the pomp and splendor of one of the greatest art patrons of all time. It highlights most of the artistic resources available at the time: precious works in gold and silver, shimmering tapestries with figurative scenes, men wearing sumptuous fabrics, expertly sculpted capitals, a skillfully designed ceiling, and a throng of busy servants and other valets whose comings and goings reveal the duke's consummate mastery of the art of celebration. This abundance says a lot about Jean of Berry's feverish passion for works of art, beautiful objects, and admirable constructions, a passion without which his commissioning of the *Très Riches Heures* would be difficult to understand.

Jean of Berry belonged to a generation of princes who were traumatized by the upheavals of the Hundred Years' War, the defeat at Poitiers in 1356, the subsequent captivity of John II (also known as John the Good), the Parisian revolts, the Great Schism, and the companies of mercenaries roaming the countryside. The long period of relative calm in the conflict between the French and the English, from the Truce of Bruges (1375) to the defeat at Azincourt (1415), was an opportunity to put art at the service of the fleurs-de-lis princes and restore the legitimacy of the Valois. The architectural landscape was transformed as a result, the decorative arts were promoted, and illuminated manuscripts enjoyed a veritable golden age. The Duke of Berry was in the vanguard of all these fields.

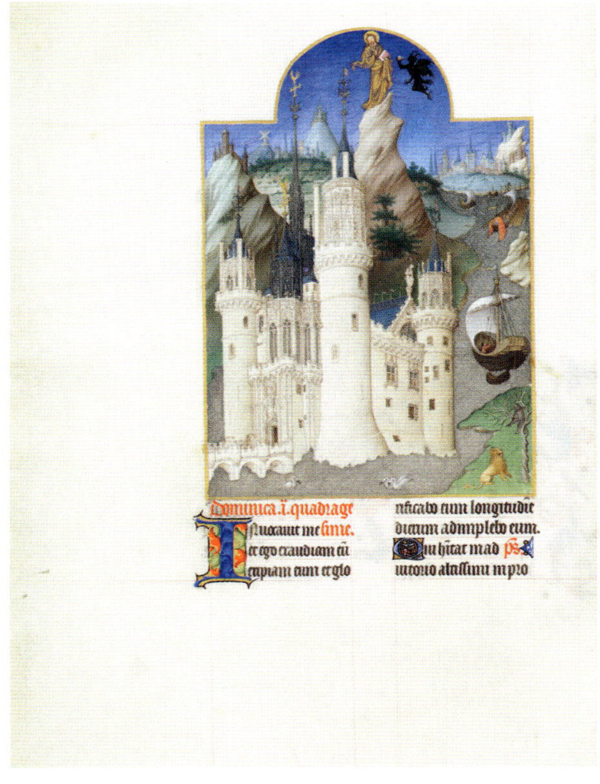

**Fig. 2** Van Lymborch brothers, *Très Riches Heures*, fol. 161v: The Temptation of Christ

**Fig. 1** Van Lymborch brothers, *Très Riches Heures*, fol. 161v: The Temptation of Christ, detail

The duke's celebrated collections have already been the subject of in-depth research, from Alfred de Champeaux, Paul Gauchery,[1] and Jules Guiffrey[2] to Millard Meiss.[3] The duke's biographers have also written extensively about his collections,[4] while the various aspects of his artistic patronage have been highlighted in turn, although a comprehensive study of his patronage has yet to be carried out.[5] The reputation of the first true collector of the modern era is due, above all, to his illuminated books, most of which escaped being melted down or destroyed. But these works of great financial value cannot be understood outside the broader context of a protean and resolutely avant-garde patronage of the arts.

Although his collections are no longer intact, the inventories give us an idea of their incredible wealth. The oldest surviving inventory, compiled between 1401 and 1403, describes 1317 objects. These registers were regularly updated to take account of acquisitions and transfers of ownership. The successive inventories collated by Robinet d'Étampes in 1412 list 1251 items, while the last account carried out by Jean Lebourne to liquidate the duke's estate lists 1335 items.[6] Inventories by object type—jewels[7] and tapestries[8]—round off our knowledge. This wealth of documentation conceals the fact that at least 95 percent of the documents from the Court of Accounts of Bourges relating to the duke's accounts have disappeared.[9]

In addition to patiently delving into the sources and among the works preserved, it is worth turning to the accounts of contemporaries, who were not mistaken in recognizing in Jean of Berry as the paragon of the collector and builder, one who "se délecte et aime gens subtils, soient clercs ou autres, beaux livres des sciences morales et histoires notables de polices romaines ou d'autres louables enseignements, moult aima et volontiers on vit tous ouvrages subtilement faits et par maîtrise beaux et polis, ornements riches, beaux édifices dont a fait faire maint en son pays, à Paris et ailleurs" (takes pleasure in and enjoys subtle minds, whether clerics or not, as well as beautiful books dealing with moral sciences and notable histories of Roman governments or other commendable teachings; he much enjoyed and was often seen appreciating the works produced with delicacy, beauty, and mastery, as well as the refined ornaments and wonderful buildings, several of which he had erected in his country, in Paris and elsewhere).[10]

## A PATRON AND HIS MODELS

Since the time of Louis IX (known as St. Louis), the kingdom of France had been engaged in a process of artistic centralization, one which intensified even further in the fourteenth century. The seat of both a powerful monarchy and a renowned university, the capital of books and beautiful objects that drew the best craftsmen, Paris was home to a refined court, where certain artists were given the role of court artist. Jean of Berry was born in 1340, in the splendor of the Valois period, of which he ultimately proved to be the most brilliant heir. It is often forgotten that he spent a lot of time with several eminent figures from the century of the so-called Accursed Kings that would soon come to an end. Queen Jeanne d'Évreux (d. 1370), wife of the late Charles IV, known as Charles the Fair (d. 1328), and Queen Blanche of Navarre (d. 1398), second wife of his grandfather Philip VI, were undoubtedly role models for him as art lovers. Queen Blanche, for example, left him her "plus belles heures," inherited from her own mother.[11] From the library of Charles V and then Charles VI, he acquired the famous *Book of Hours of Jeanne d'Évreux* illuminated by Jean Pucelle[12] as well as, no doubt, her *Bréviaire*.

Jean of Berry's education was initially entrusted to the care of his mother, Bonne of Luxembourg, who died early but who, like the great French queens of the fourteenth century, was a great lover of illuminated devotional books, as evidenced by her famous psalter illuminated by Jean Le Noir, a student of Jean Pucelle.[13] The duke's relations with his father, John the Good, were never excellent, but the king was able to instill in his sons, particularly Jean, a taste for books and objects. His court was attended by scholars such as Guillaume de Machaut, Philippe de Vitry, and even Petrarch, who visited in 1361.[14] He also amassed an interesting collection of manuscripts and launched several major literary ventures, including a French translation by Pierre Bersuire of three decades of Livy's *History of Rome* (part of Jean of Berry's library) and a monumental glossed translation of the Bible by the Dominican Jean de Sy, a work left unfinished following the defeat at Poitiers. While captive in England, John the Good also asked his chaplain, Gace de La Bigne, to write a treatise on hunting that would paint a portrait of the perfect huntsman but that would serve, in reality, as a treatise on good government for his son, Philip the Bold. The Duke of Berry also owned a copy, although not a very luxurious one.[15] John the Good also commissioned an important *Bible moralisée* (Moralized bible), with almost 5212 images by some fifteen artists, which incidentally served as a model for the Van Lymborch brothers.[16]

In his youth, Jean of Berry had been in contact with several artists, in particular the king's painter and valet Girard d'Orléans, who in 1352 decorated chairs for the young princes,[17] before accompanying John the Good during his English exile.[18] Jean of Berry came into possession of a book of hours at a very young age, which was restored in 1355–56.[19] His brothers—Charles, the future Charles V; Louis, the future Duke of Anjou; and Philip, the future Duke of Burgundy—enjoyed the same education in beauty provided by living in a courtly milieu. It was a fertile breeding ground for a generation of brilliant art patrons.

## THE TEMPTATION TO BUILD

Jean of Berry was not just a passionate collector of manuscripts and jewels. Eager to consolidate his hard-won territorial holdings and lay the foundations of his new dynasty, he launched an ambitious construction and renovation program (fig. 3).[20] He initiated almost twenty building projects (Thomas Rapin ascribes seventeen residences to him), most of which have, unfortunately, vanished. Only part of the palaces at Poitiers and Bourges survive, along with the ruins of the château of Mehun-sur-Yèvre. The duke's building activity—which, in line with many other facets of his patronage, proved to be excessive—intensified during the minority of Charles VI, when he came to power with his brothers (and gained some financial leeway). This is evident in the duchy of Berry (Bourges, Mehun-sur-Yèvre), in Auvergne (palace of Riom, château of Nonette), and in the palace of Poitou (Maubergeon

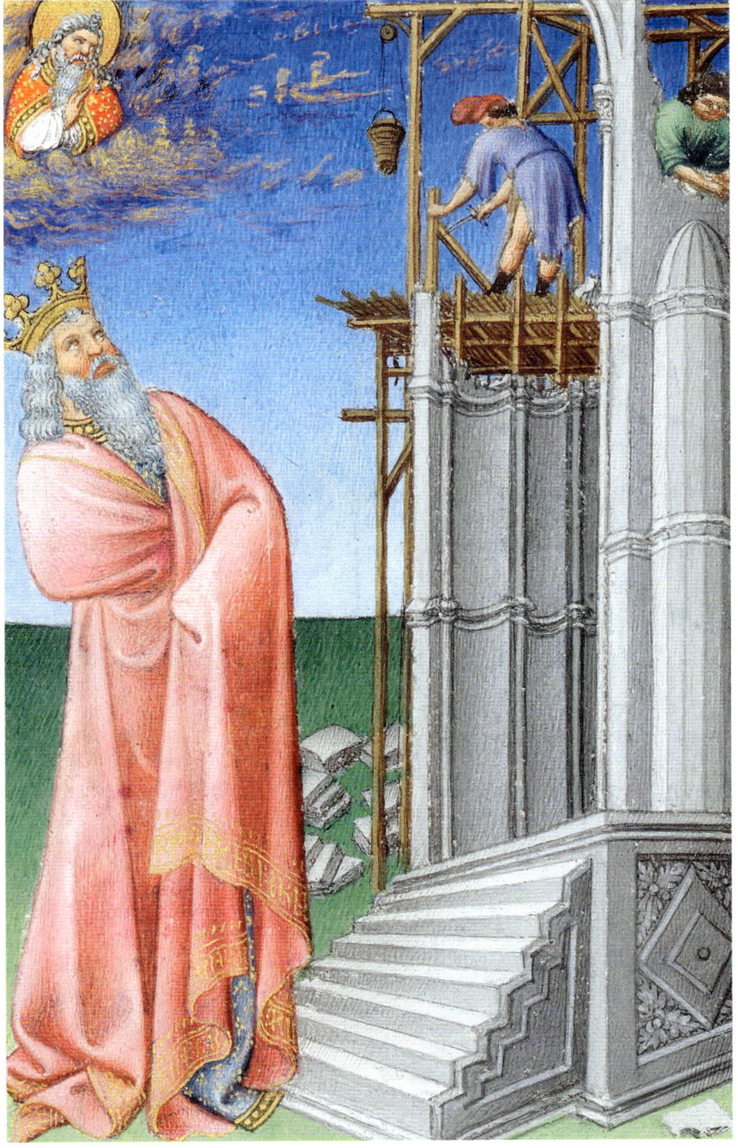

**Fig. 3** Van Lymborch brothers, *Très Riches Heures*, fol. 35v: The Judge of the Earth (Psalm 98)

Tower, and the fireplace in the great hall). These ambitious projects should not obscure the more modest ones, such as lightly fortified villas and hunting lodges, which were also part of his *art de vivre*. Paris and the surrounding region were not forgotten: the château of Bicêtre, described as a "hostel" by contemporaries, was the duke's main summer residence south of the capital, in addition to the Hôtel de Nesle, located opposite the Louvre. Rebuilt by the duke from 1381, it was one of his first large-scale projects, with a large central area given over to gardens, overlooked by galleries.[21] Jean of Berry was a pioneer in this regard. It was at the château of Bicêtre that he breathed his last, and where the Van Lymborch brothers drew images of the Parisian landscape for their *Très Riches Heures*. The duke was no doubt closely involved in its construction, as he was for the château of Mehun-sur-Yèvre. The latter benefited from a lengthy renovation starting in 1367, followed by a second one around 1384–85, which incited court historian Jean Froissart to enthuse about "l'une des plus belles maisons du monde" (one of the most beautiful houses in the world).[22] Mehun-sur-Yèvre was chosen to represent "tous les royaumes du monde avec leur gloire" (all the kingdoms of the world with their glory) in the miniature of the Temptation of Christ in the *Très Riches Heures* (fol. 161v; fig. 2). The château symbolizes the real artistic crucible sought by the duke. Taking a certain "plaisir en choses estranges" (pleasure in things from abroad), as he liked to say,[23] in the spring of 1382 Jean of Berry brought three Moorish tile makers from the Valence region to work under the supervision of Jean de Valence on the Mehun-sur-Yèvre sites as well as the palaces of Bourges and Poitiers.[24] The innovative program involved decorating ceremonial rooms and apartments with armorial tiles that were manufactured locally, thanks to the temporary importation of this type of knowledge, which was unknown in France at the time. Some of these tiles[25] were recovered during excavations at the château of Mehun-sur-Yèvre (fig 4).

Although personally involved in his ambitious commissions, the duke also relied on a highly centralized system that he had set up expressly for this purpose. He entrusted a single man with the task of directing all the work: first Guy de Dampmartin (1369 to 1397), then his brother Drouet (1397–98

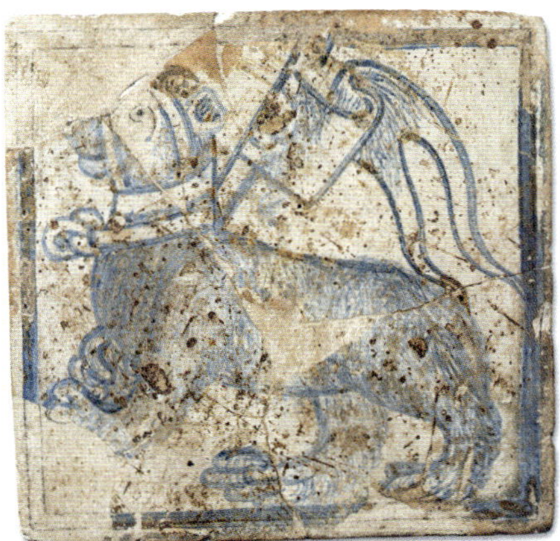

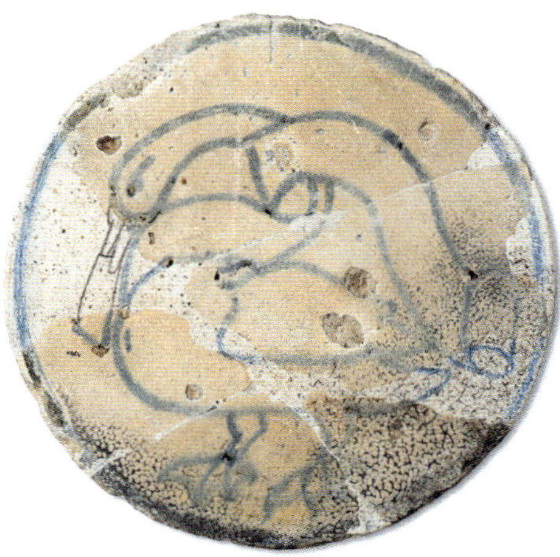

**Fig. 4** Tiles found in situ at the château of Mehun-sur-Yèvre: bear and phylactery, wounded swan, blue decoration on white background (Mehun-sur-Yèvre, château-musée Charles VII, inv. 981.1.1 [left], inv. 994.2.1 [right])

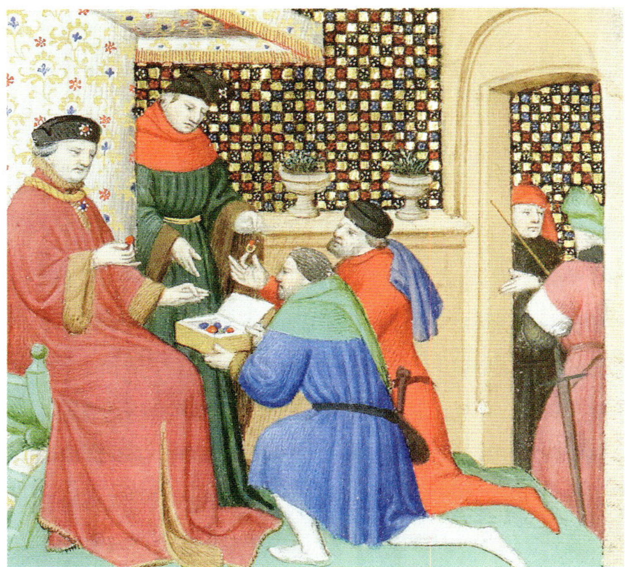

**Fig. 5** Bartholomew the Englishman, *Livre des propriétés des choses*, translated by Jean Corbechon, fol. 235v (Boucicaut Master): Jean of Berry receiving precious stones (Paris, Bibliothèque nationale de France, Ms. Français 9141)

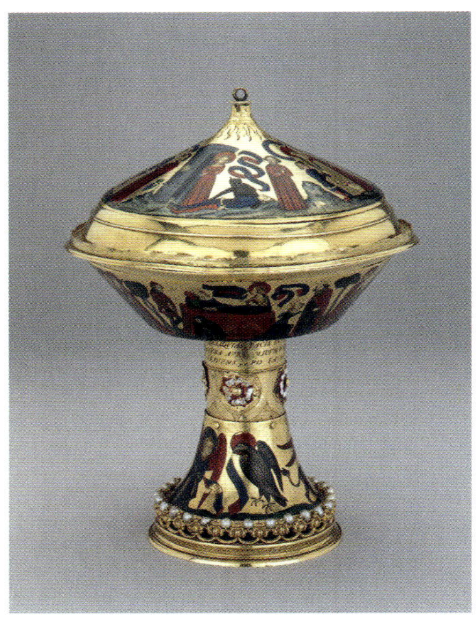

**Fig. 6** *St. Agnes Cup* (or *Royal Gold Cup*). Paris, third quarter of fourteenth century (London, British Museum, inv. 1892,0501.1)

to 1415).[26] The brothers, who were probably of Parisian origin, worked from 1365 on the royal Grande Vis du Louvre staircase, before entering the service of the Duke of Berry. Guy lived in Bourges from 1380, before settling in Poitiers in 1388, towns from where he supervised work on the ducal appanage. After serving as master of works to the Duke of Burgundy, Philip the Bold, Drouet replaced his late brother when he began working for the Duke of Berry: once again, as in the case of the painters and illuminators, this confirms the porousness of the artistic entourages of the dukes of Berry and Burgundy.

One building in particular testifies to Jean of Berry's direct involvement and architectural ambitions. In 1392, the duke wanted to build his own version of Sainte-Chapelle next to his palace in Bourges, with the intention of being buried there. The reference to the royal Sainte-Chapelle in Paris, built by his ancestor St. Louis and which also featured in his *Très Riches Heures* (the exterior in the month of June, the interior on folio 158), was clear. The Sainte-Chapelle in Bourges was the recipient of the duke's largesse, the reflection of his tastes and of his own collection. Although its treasure has disappeared, we do have the list, drawn up in May 1404—just before the canonic chapter was established—of the manuscripts, liturgical ornaments, and jewels he intended for it. These included the Last Judgment and the Annunciation to the Shepherds, a large cross, a monstrance, a chalice and paten, pax tablets, cruets, pontifical rings, forty liturgical and other books, a processional cross, reliquary pictures, and several shrines. This was not the duke's first attempt at erecting a Sainte-Chapelle, as he had already founded another at his palace in Riom in 1382.

Although it would be rather contrived to outline a "Duke of Berry style" on the basis of the civil or religious buildings he created, his princely commissions did lay the groundwork for the birth of flamboyant architecture, as can be seen in the windows of the "Belle Cheminée" (beautiful chimney) in the ducal palace at Poitiers (around 1390).

## PRECIOUS STONES, GOLD, AND SILVER

Even more than buildings, the fleurs-de-lis princes took great pleasure in precious works in gold and silver, a craft that they placed, along with precious textiles, at the top of the arts hierarchy. The inventories of Charles V, Louis of Anjou, Philip the Bold, and, of course, Jean of Berry are full of these "jewels." The Duke of Berry is rightly regarded as the first of these collectors of *objets d'art* and precious stones (fig. 5),[27] a reputation that Filarete, Dante, and Christine de Pizan were keen to propagate,[28] but which his detractors used against him—such as the anonymous author of the political pamphlet *Songe véritable*, who accused him of embezzling the king's money and spending it:

It's a very bad deal
To have rubies and sapphires,
Diamonds and so many other stones.
Don't believe it, don't even imagine it:
Your stones will not save your life,
For, it is certain, you will die soon,
And nothing in the world can prevent it[29]

All the merchants knew of the duke's passion for beautiful objects and sought him out, even when he was busy with particularly grave matters. Thomas de Saluces, for instance, reports that Jean of Berry interrupted important negotiations to receive merchants from Venice who had come to show him some precious stones.[30]

A reading of the inventories[31] reveals that the duke had a gargantuan appetite in this area: Works in gold, intaglios, cameos, gemstones, medals, and jewels (including rings bearing his effigy or emblems) compete with precious stones bearing evocative names ("le roy des rubins," "le Cuer de France," "le ruby de Berry"). A number of remarkable pieces have survived, providing eloquent testimony to one of the most extraordinary collections of jewels ever assembled. In addition to the gemstones, cameos, intaglios,[32] and medals, some rare masterpieces have miraculously escaped being melted down or being plundered.

The duke most likely commissioned the *St. Agnes Cup* (or *Royal Gold Cup*) in the British Museum (fig. 6)[33] in the third quarter of the fourteenth century, probably as a gift for his brother Charles V, who was born on the saint's feast day, although the cup was not delivered to Charles VI until 1391.[34] This covered hanap, decorated with scenes from the saint's life executed in *basse-taille* enamel on a gold background, bears witness to the magnificence of Jean of Berry's gifts. He was quick to place special orders with Parisian goldsmiths, who were enjoying a veritable golden age at the time.

The Toledo *Madonna*, an enameled statuette in the round on gold (currently owned by Toledo Cathedral's Capilla de los Reyes Nuevos), was originally part of the treasure of Mehun-sur-Yèvre, where it was listed in the first inventory of 1401–02 (fig. 7).[35] It appears to have been a gift from Jean of Berry to Eleanor of Castile, wife of the duke's nephew Charles III, king of Navarre, with whom he exchanged gifts on several occasions between 1404 and 1408. These enameled jewels were among the most sought-after objects of the period. With its iconographic theme close to *devotio moderna*, its structure close to that of an illuminated page, and its style reminiscent of André Beauneveu,[36] the piece demonstrates the extent to which the arts influenced one another at the time, under the watchful eye of a patron who neglected none.

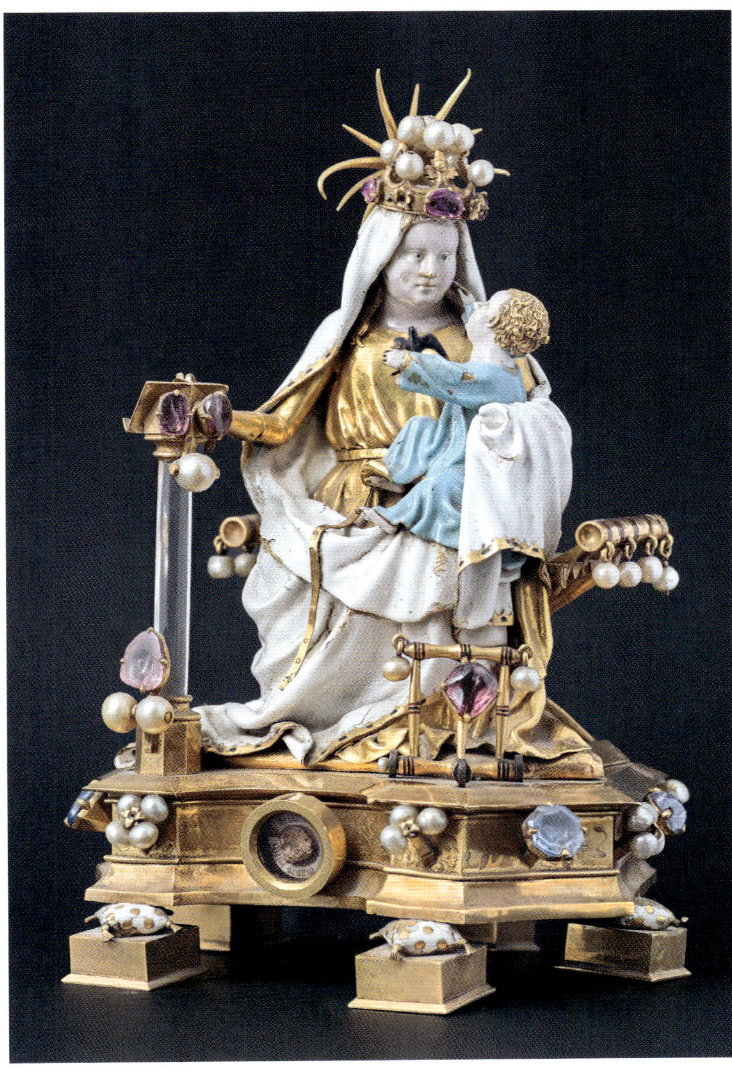

**Fig. 7** *Virgin and Child*, donated by Jean of Berry to the Queen of Navarre. Paris, before 1403 (Toledo, Treasure of the Cathedral)

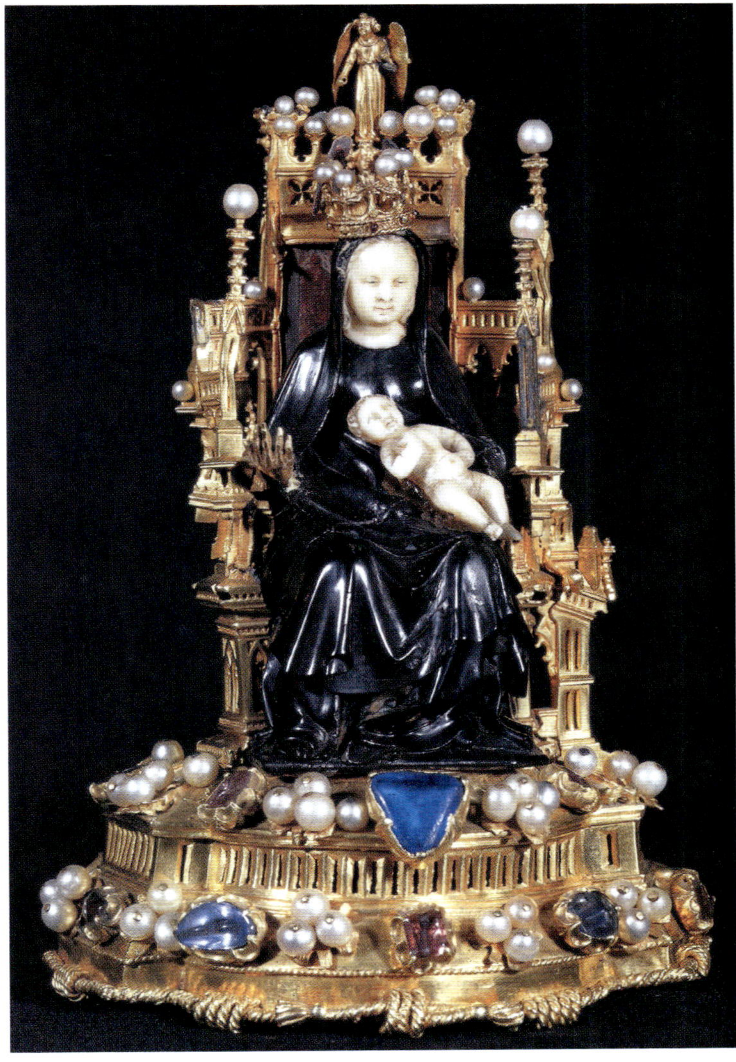

**Fig. 8** *Virgin and Child*, donated by Jean of Berry to the Queen of Castile. Paris, before 1403 (Burgos, Treasure of the Cathedral)

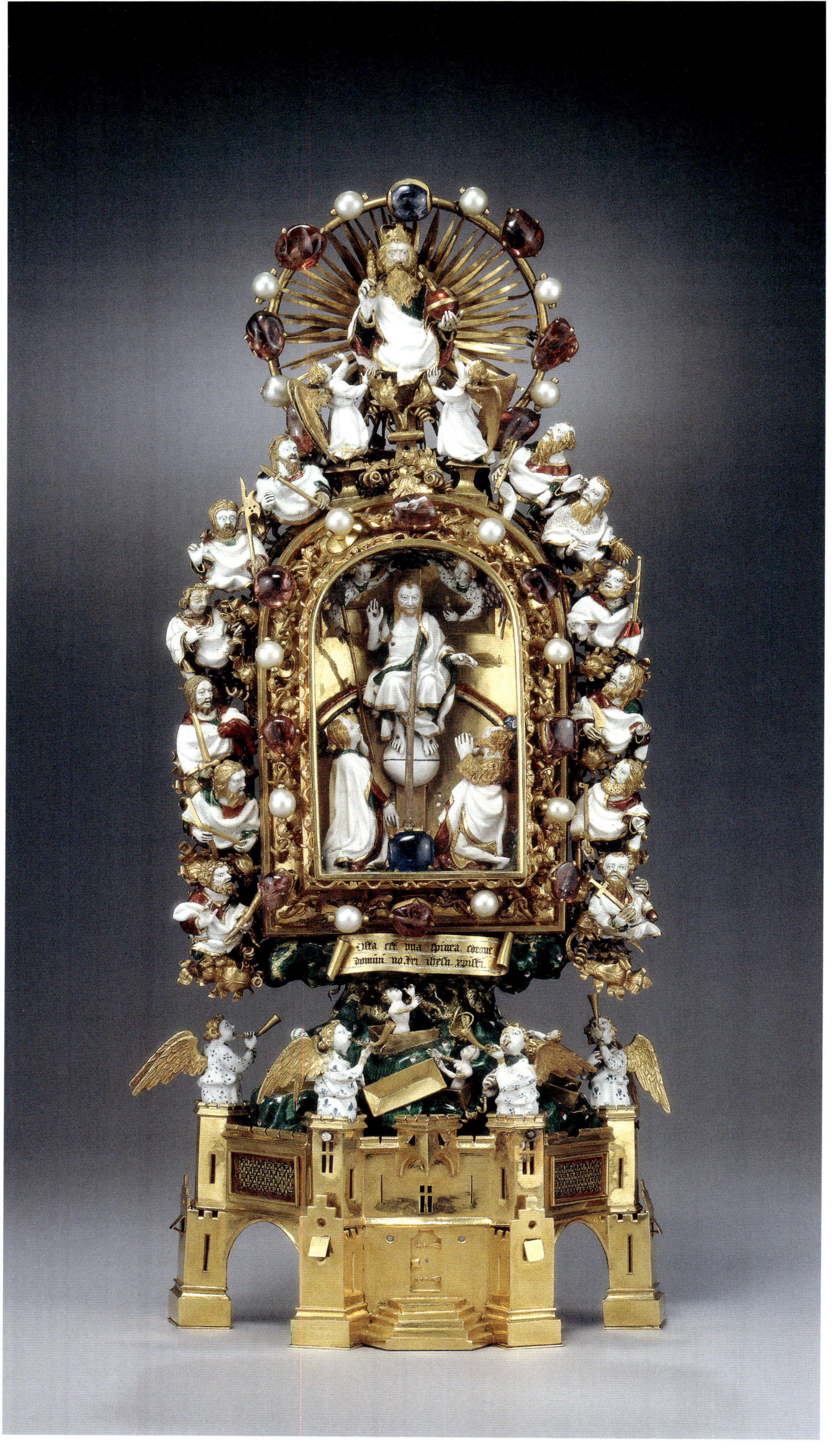

**Fig. 9** *Reliquary of the Holy Thorn*. Paris, 1403 and 1413 (London, British Museum, Waddesdon Bequest, WB.67)

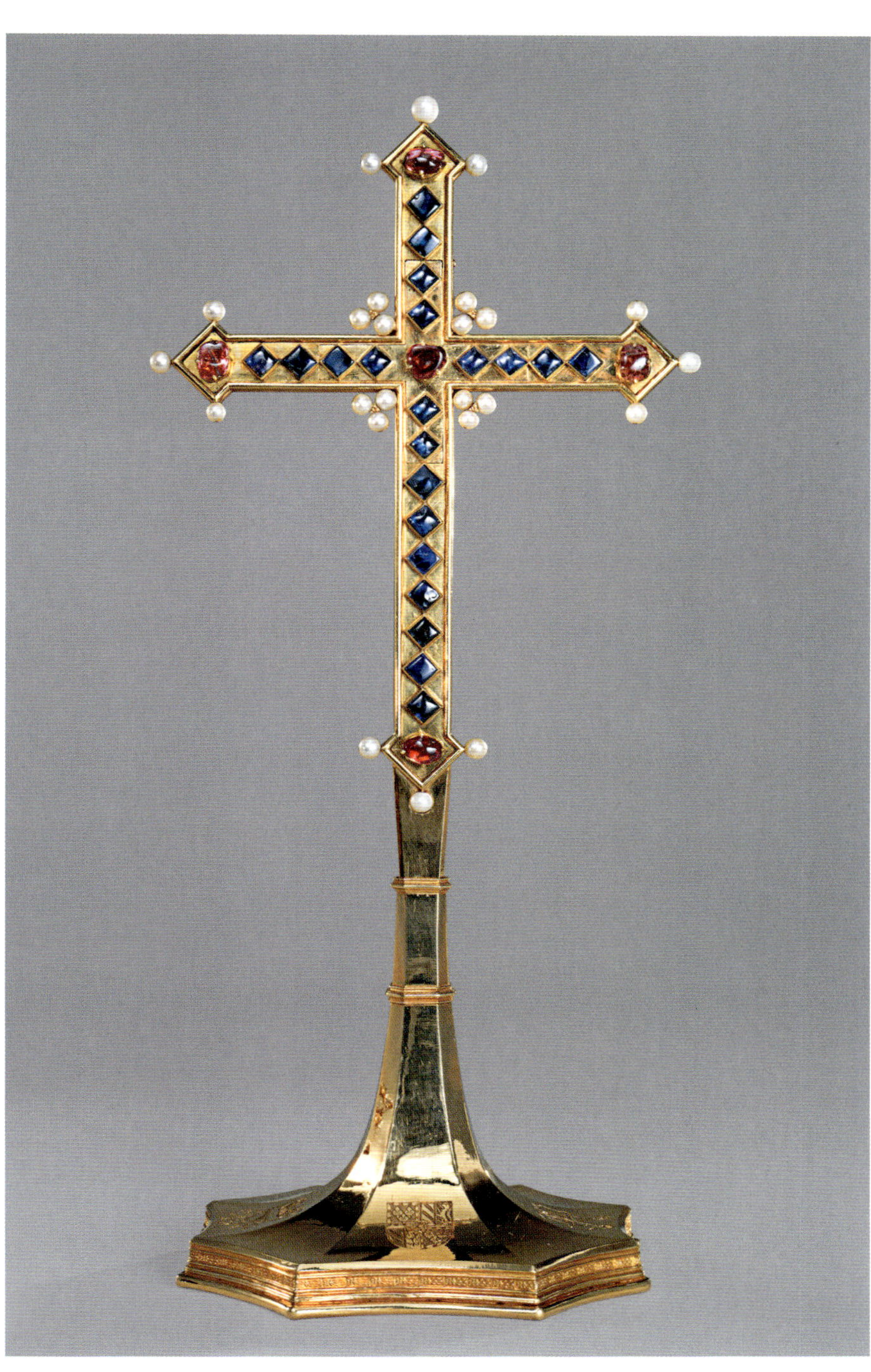

**Fig. 10** *Oath Cross of the Order of the Golden Fleece*. Paris, c. 1400 (Vienna, Kunsthistorisches Museum, Weltliche Schatzkammer, Inv. Dep. Prot. 1)

The Toledo *Madonna* recalls another in Burgos Cathedral (Capilla del Condestable; fig. 8), a Virgin sculpted in black jet with an ivory head and seated on a throne, holding an infant also in ivory, which corresponds to the description in one of the duke's inventories.[37] The duke offered his Madonna to another Iberian queen, Catherine, daughter of the Duke of Lancaster and wife of Henry III, king of Castile, whom he had at one time considered making his second wife.

Jean of Berry most likely gave either his brother Philip the Bold or his nephew John the Fearless a prime piece, the *Reliquary of the Holy Thorn* in the British Museum (fig. 9),[38] which features his arms.[39] Thanks to the 1401–03 inventory drawn up by Robinet d'Étampes, we know that the duke had four thorns (supposedly from Christ's crown of thorns) set in a gold crown cast at his request. He donated three of them to the Sainte-Chapelle in Bourges; the fourth was integrated into a new reliquary that he kept for his own use. This reliquary, which is missing from the 1413 inventory, was probably given to Philip the Bold or John the Fearless between 1403 and 1413, as it was found in the collection of their descendant, Charles V, in the seventeenth century.

Another of Jean's objects went to the dukes of Burgundy: his "petite croix appellé la croix à lozanges" (small cross called the cross with the lozenges),[40] which can be identified with the Oath Cross of the Order of the Golden Fleece (fig. 10).[41] Decorated with pearls and precious stones,

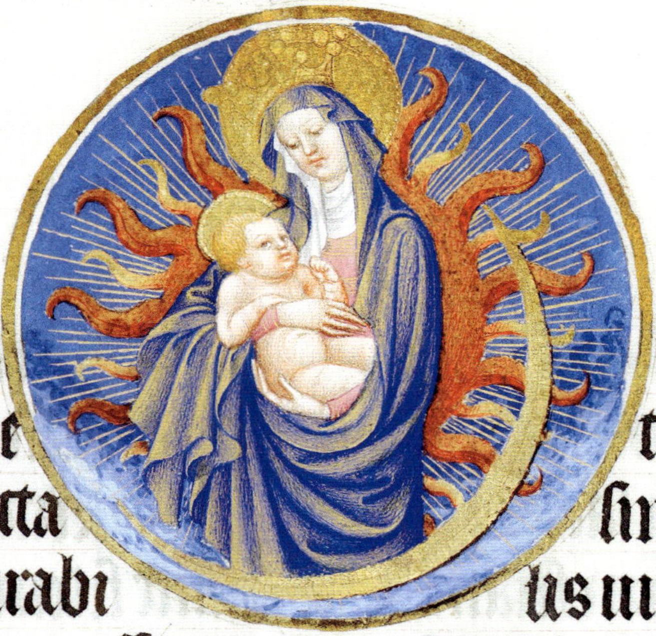

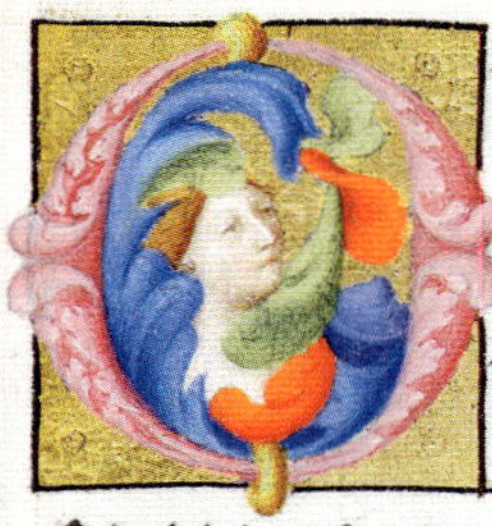

O in temerata et
in e ternum bene
dicta singularis at
que incomparabi lis virgo dei geni
trix maria gratissimum dei templum spiritus sancti
sacrarium ianua regni celorum. per quam post
deum totus vivit orbis terrarum de te dei genitrix
filius dei verus et omnipotens deus suam sacratis
simam fecit matrem assumens de illa sacratissimam
carnem per quem mundus qui perditus erat salua
tus est. Cuius preciosissimo sanguine suo mundus

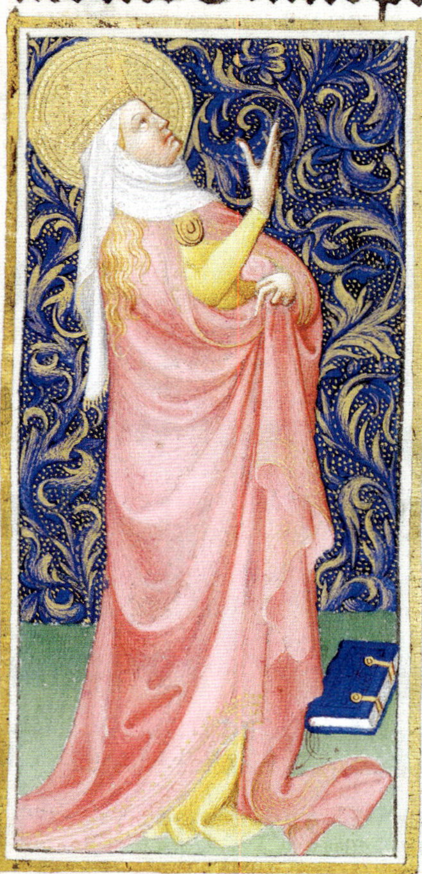

redemptus est. et
omnia peccata
ei remissa sunt
formans eam in
preciosissimo san
guine suo inves
eam eterne et in
commutabili
divinitatis sue
a quo bona cunc
ta procedunt per

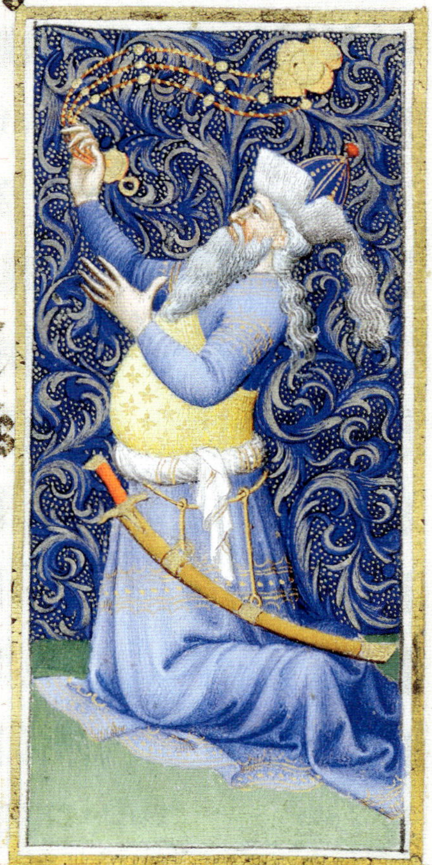

it features twenty-one sapphire lozenges and five ruby cabochons, and still has its original case bearing the arms of Jean of Berry. The stand was transformed under Philip the Good: Jean of Berry undoubtedly intended to present this exceptional gift to his father, John the Good, or his nephew, John the Fearless. The Van Lymborch brothers seem to have been aware of its existence, since a miniature of it appears in the *Belles Heures* (fol. 157). It also appears in the *Très Riches Heures* in the miniature for the Mass of the Exaltation of the Cross (fol. 193; fig. 2, p. 93), in which the reliquary containing pieces of the Cross is venerated by King Solomon and the Queen of Sheba. For its part, the stand of this illuminated cross recalls that of the cross with an enameled serpent at its foot mentioned in the duke's inventories.[42]

Close to the world of goldsmiths, and one of them indeed a goldsmith himself, the Van Lymborch brothers were ultimately merely the interpreters of one of their patron's devouring passions. The *Très Riches Heures* bear witness to their in-depth knowledge of the art of goldmithing, whether in the form of reliquaries (fol. 29; fig. 12), or fols. 71v–72), vases (fol. 52), incense burners (fol. 22; fig. 11), and necklaces or sashes (fols. 4v and 5v). The table set for the banquet in January is the perfect example.[43] At the end of the table is a nef (used to store and display cutlery) shaped like a ship, with a bear and a swan perched fore and aft. Naturally, it echoes the table nefs owned by Jean of Berry, such as the great golden ship whose base featured statuettes of the Twelve Peers of France while the stern featured a portrait of St. Louis,[44] or the salt cellar in the shape of a boat, known as the "pavilion."[45] The *Très Riches Heures* suggests other links with items in the duke's collections. For example, the Visitation on folio 38v, dedicated to a new feast (introduced into the liturgical calendar in 1389), can be compared with the most beautiful of the presents the duke's wife gave him during the exchange of New Year's Day gifts in 1415: "ung petit tabernacle d'or où il a ung ymaige de Nostre Dame grosse, dont le ventre est de nacle de perle, ceint d'une ceinture, tenant en sa main un livre et ung autre ymage de sainte Hélizabet qui embrasse ledit mage de Nostre Dame" (a small golden tabernacle containing an image of Our Lady, expecting, whose belly is made of mother-of-pearl, girded with a belt, holding a book in her hand and another image of St. Elizabeth, who embraces this image of Our Lady).[46]

Such comparisons bear witness to the connections between painting and goldsmithing around 1400 and which Jean of Berry seems to have relished. The Van Lymborch brothers were in close contact with the greatest Parisian goldsmiths and may not only have drawn inspiration from them for their illuminated manuscripts, but may also in turn have provided them with models or influenced their work. Only one surviving piece has been attributed to them, based on iconographic rather than strictly stylistic criteria. Augustus's vision of the Virgin and Child from the *Ara Coeli* appears in both the *Belles Heures* (fol. 26v) and the *Très Riches Heures* (fol. 22; fig. 11). It is repeated on a small painted enamel medallion,[47] sometimes attributed rather hastily to the youngest of the three Van Lymborch brothers, Arnold, who began his apprenticeship as a silversmith in Nijmegen in 1417 (fig. 13).

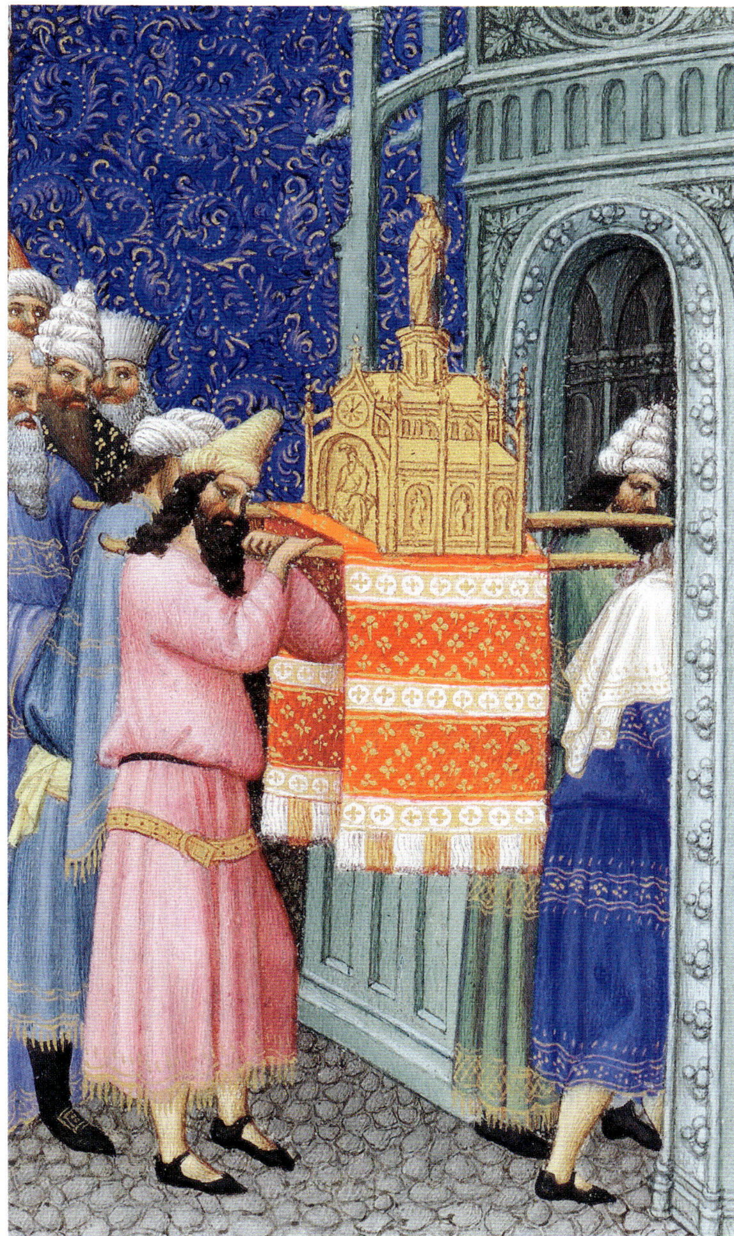

**Fig. 12** Van Lymborch brothers, *Très Riches Heures*, fol. 29: Liturgy of the Entry to the Sanctuary (Psalm 24)

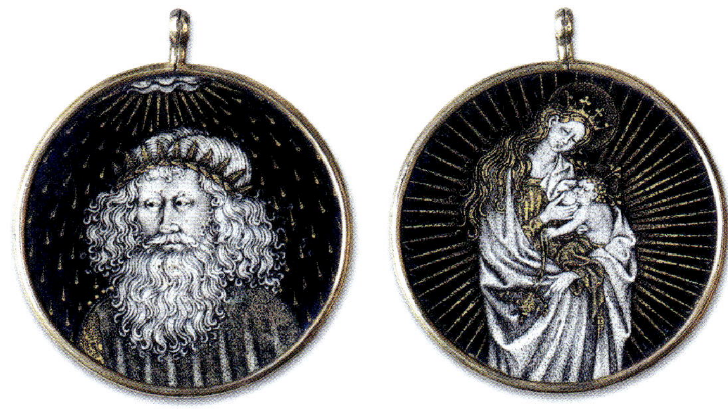

**Fig. 13** *Medallion with the Emperor Augustus's Vision of the Virgin and Child.* Paris, c. 1420 (?) (Baltimore, The Walters Art Museum, inv. 44.462)

**Fig. 11** Van Lymborch brothers, *Très Riches Heures*, fol. 22: Emperor Augustus

**Fig. 14** Following pages: Van Lymborch brothers, *Très Riches Heures*, fol. 52: The Adoration of the Magi, detail

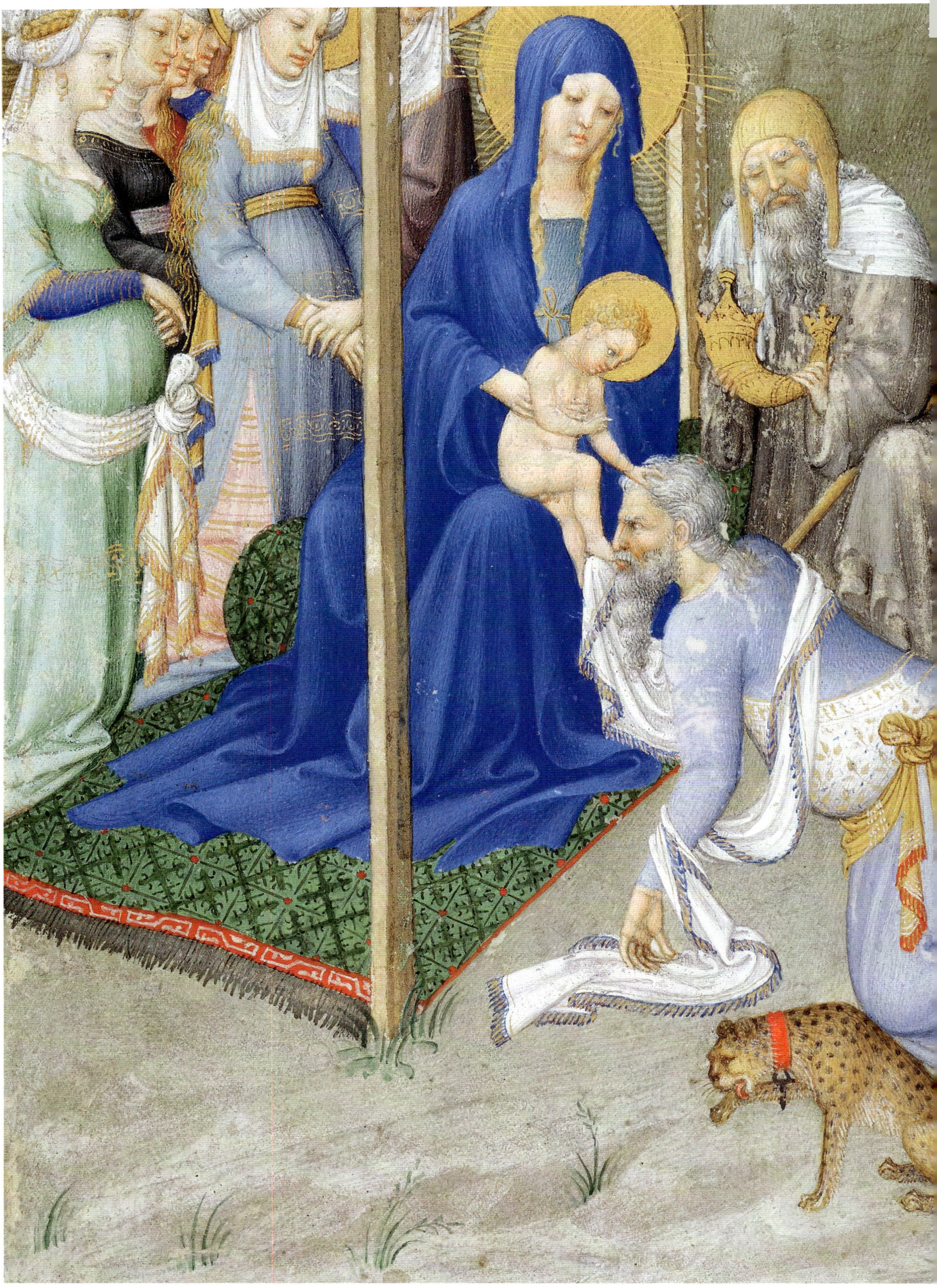

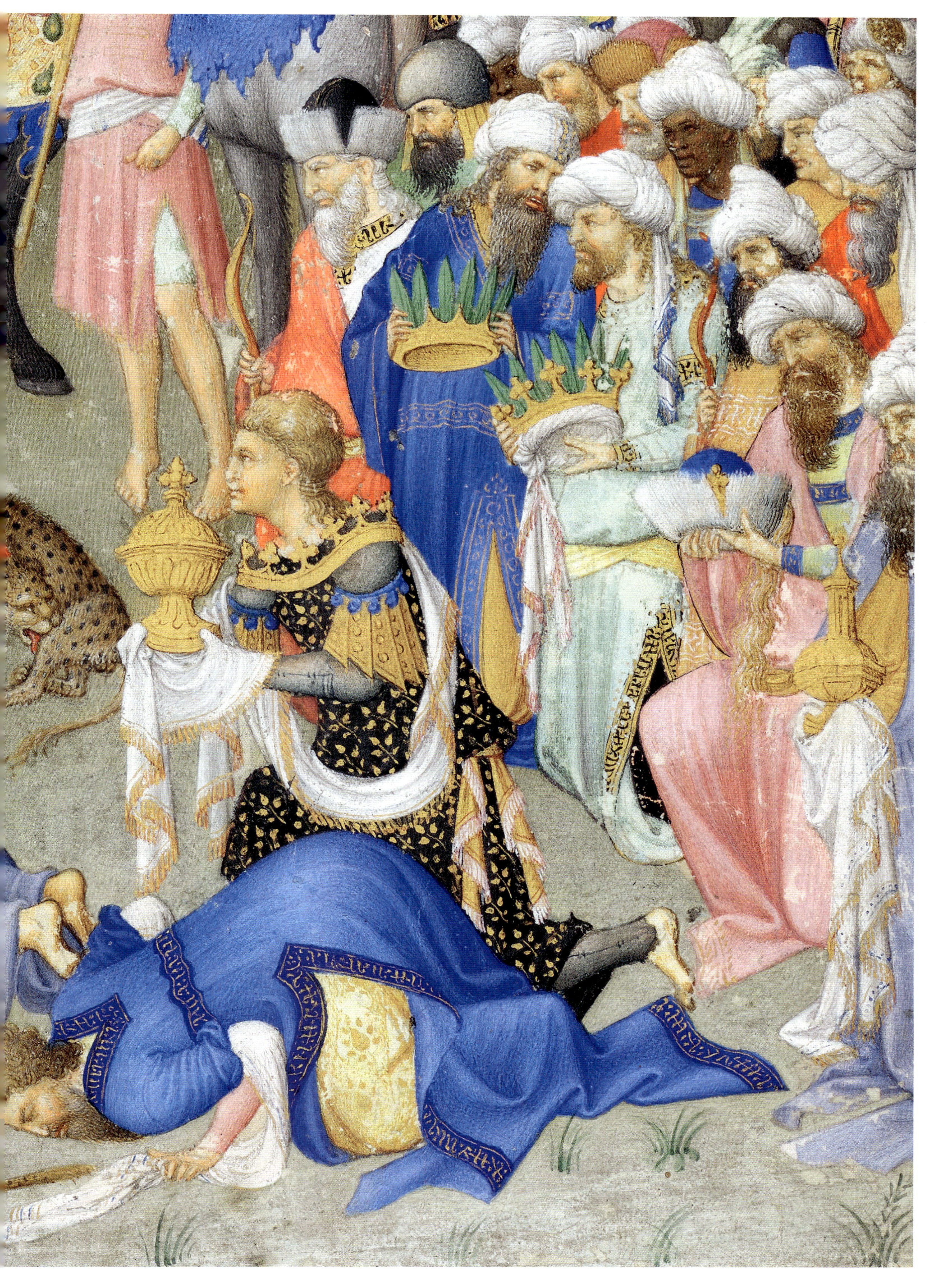

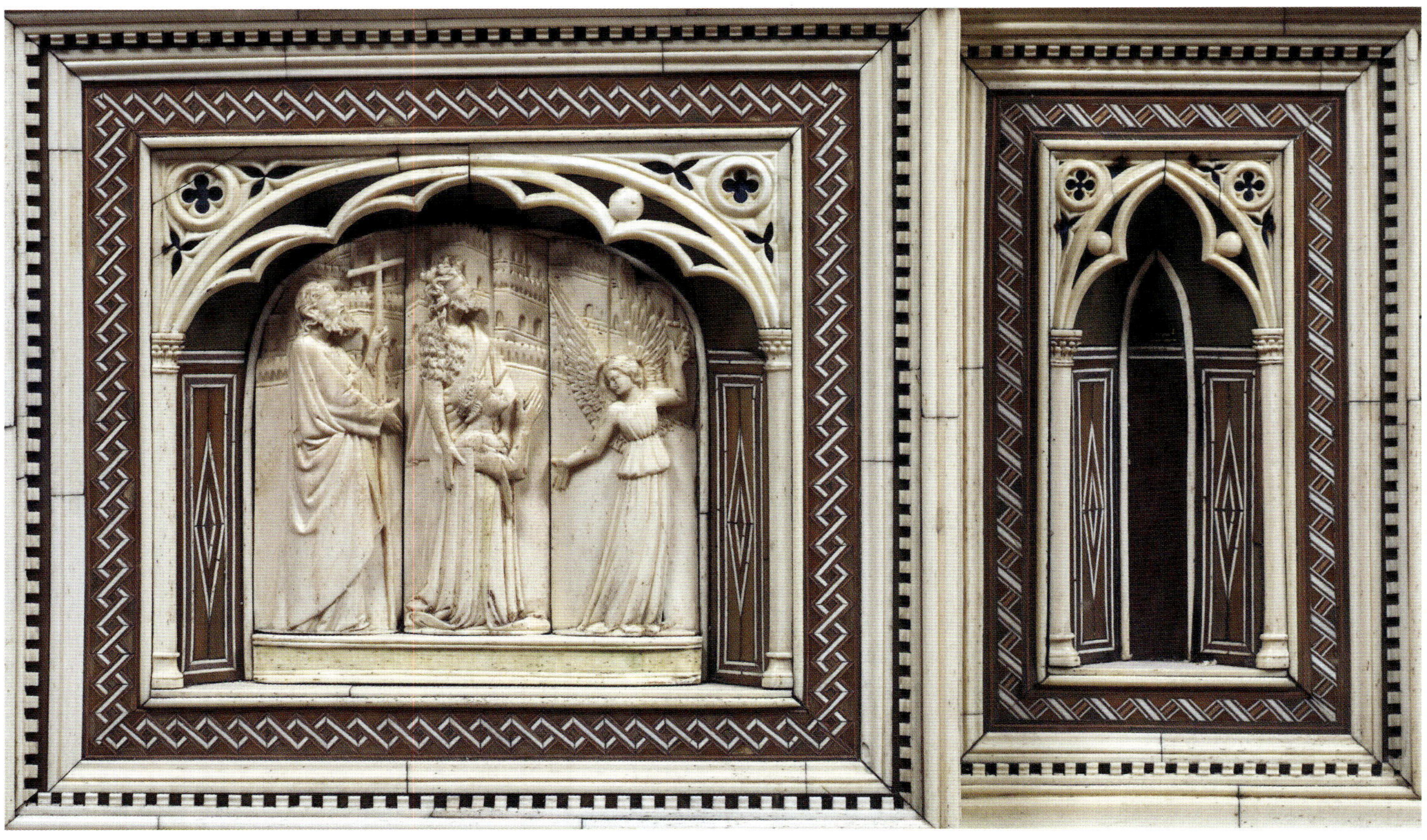

**Fig. 15** Florentine workshop of the Embriachi, *Poissy Altarpiece*, Jean of Berry accompanied by St. Andrew, St. John the Baptist, and an angel. Florence, c. 1400 (Paris, musée du Louvre, MR 379)

## GIFTS AND *ÉTRENNES*

During the *étrennes*—the exchange of gifts on New Year's Day—the duke was at liberty to draw on his collections and convert the selected items into gifts. Around 1400, with the monarchy weakened by the madness of Charles VI, the exchange of gifts between the princes during these celebrations reached an unprecedented peak and served as a veritable political instrument. These exchanges and gifts have been studied extensively[48]; they seem to have been the main means by which Jean of Berry's collections were enriched. For example, between the first and last of his inventories, between 1401 and 1416, the duke commissioned 119 objects, but received 358 as gifts from 136 different people, more than half of them as New Year's gifts. Conversely, he distributed 231 gifts.[49] When short of money, he did not hesitate to dip into the treasure of the Sainte-Chapelle in Bourges to select jewels that he could offer. He did this on June 4, 1415, when he gave his nephew, the Dauphin, Louis of Guyenne, two "tableaux d'or" (gold paintings) richly adorned with jewels; one had been bought from a certain Cendre Billot on the occasion of the 1409 New Year's Day gifts, the other had been given to him by Queen Isabeau in 1401.[50]

Jean of Berry also received gifts from his artists. In 1408, for example, the painter Jean d'Orléans presented him with "une belle pomme de musc" (a beautiful scented apple), the inside of which was decorated with one of his paintings.[51] After the fake book presented in 1410 as a New Year's gift,[52] Paul van Lymborch presented the duke with an agate salt cellar for the 1414 New Year's gift.[53] For the 1407 *étrennes*, Jean of Berry received a gold ring with a small emerald mounted in a bear, which he later passed on to Paul van Lymborch.[54]

Often portrayed as a predator of lands and artworks, Jean of Berry nonetheless displayed a level of piety that was long denigrated. His devoutness manifested itself in generous donations to churches and convents. In 1408, for instance, to mark the profession of faith of his niece, Marie de France, daughter of Charles VI, who had entered the Dominican convent of Poissy to pray for a cure for her father's madness, Jean of Berry presented this prestigious institution with an impressive bone altarpiece by the Florentine workshop of the Embriachi.[55] Although Baldassare degli Embriachi, who ran the workshop, arrived in Paris in 1401–02, this carefully crafted altarpiece, similar to a triptych illustrated with scenes from the lives of Christ and St. John the Baptist and St. John

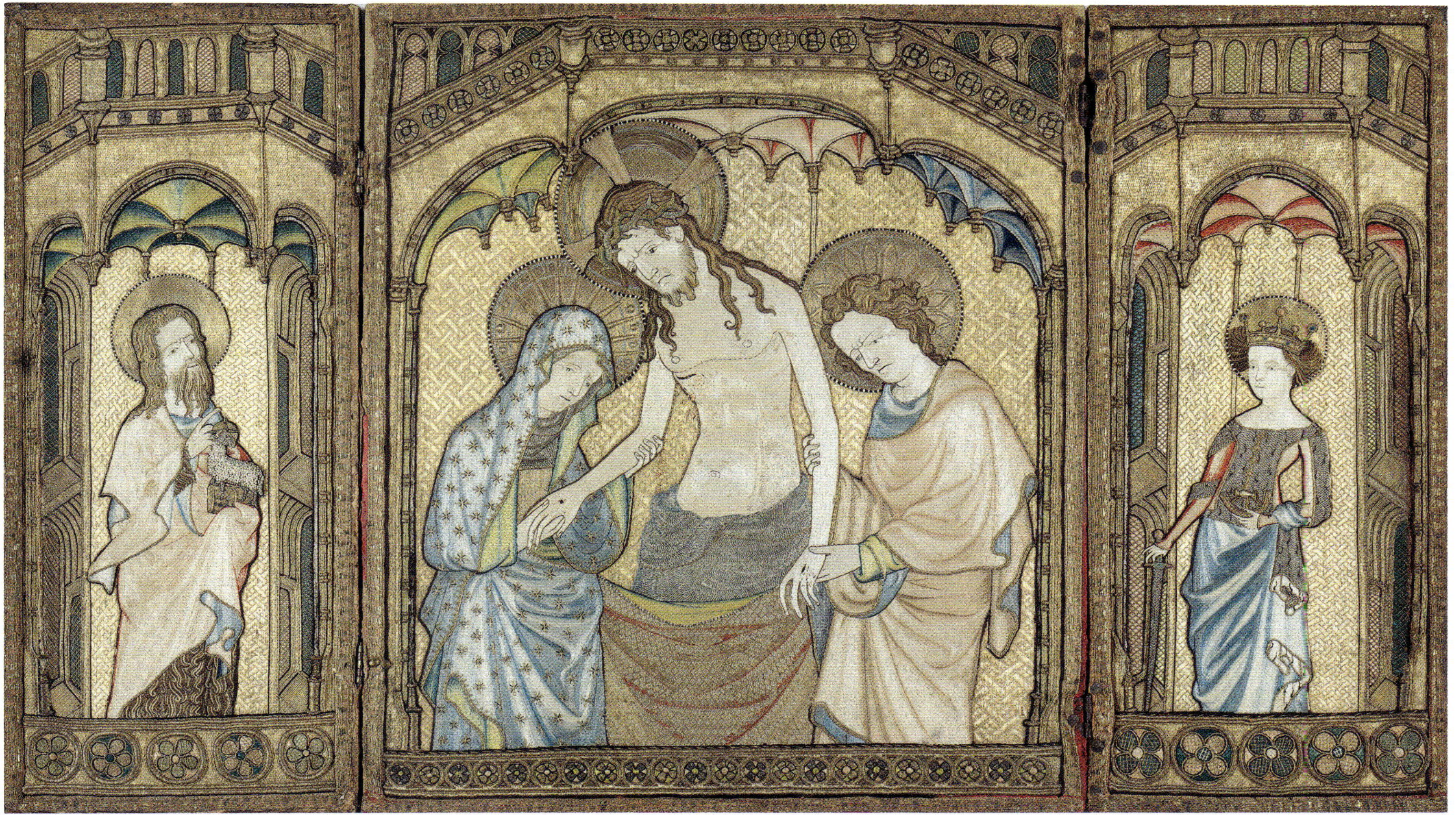

**Fig. 16** Embroidered triptych donated by the Duke of Berry. Paris, last quarter of the fourteenth century (Chartres, Treasure of the Cathedral)

the Evangelist, was more likely executed in Italy and then assembled in Poissy. The donors can be seen at either end of the base. The depiction of Jean of Berry, on the left, kneeling, flanked by an angel and St. Andrew and St. John the Baptist, is unlike any known portrait of him (fig. 15). On the right is his second wife, Jeanne de Boulogne, preceded by an angel and followed by St. John and St. Catherine. It is not easy to measure the role of the duchess in her husband's artistic patronage, as she lived far from the court and her effigy appeared very rarely, or only in commemorative contexts (such as on the praying figures in the Sainte-Chapelle in Bourges). The duke gave Marie de France another superb gift: the *Belleville Breviary*,[56] illuminated by Jean Pucelle among others, which had belonged to Charles V, and which his son Charles VI had given to Richard II of England, but which Henry IV of England had somehow ceded back to our duke.[57]

Many of the prelates in the entourage of Jean of Berry were recipients of his acts of kindness, such as the archbishop of Bourges, Guillaume de Boisratier, and the bishop of Chartres, Martin Gouges. Chartres Cathedral was particularly favored by the Duke, who presented it with an enameled gold Virgin in 1404; a reliquary of a hair of the Virgin that Pope Clement VII had given him in 1384; a gilded oval reliquary in 1406; and, that same year, a "grand tableau de broderie" (large embroidered painting) for the high altar, depicting the Assumption of the Virgin adored by the royal family.[58] A fabulous triptych of silk, gold, and silver on linen, executed in Paris in the last third of the fourteenth century, was also donated by Jean of Berry (fig. 16).[59] It depicts Christ supported by the Virgin Mary and St. John, an *Imago Pietatis* in line with the compassionate trend of the suffering Christ to which Jean of Berry was very attentive, as shown by the works the Van Lymborch brothers created for him.

Naturally, the Duke of Berry's loyal followers and protégés benefited from his generosity. Not only did he draw on his own collections for this purpose, but he also called on his own artists for special commissions. For example, he sponsored the covent of Célestins de Marcoussis, founded in 1404 by Jean de Montaigu, Grand Master of France (the foundation stone was laid in 1405 and the convent church consecrated in 1408). He presented the convent with an impressive Virgin and Child, executed by his sculptor Jean de Cambrai, and a large missal on which Jean de Montaigu had the duke's arms painted.[60]

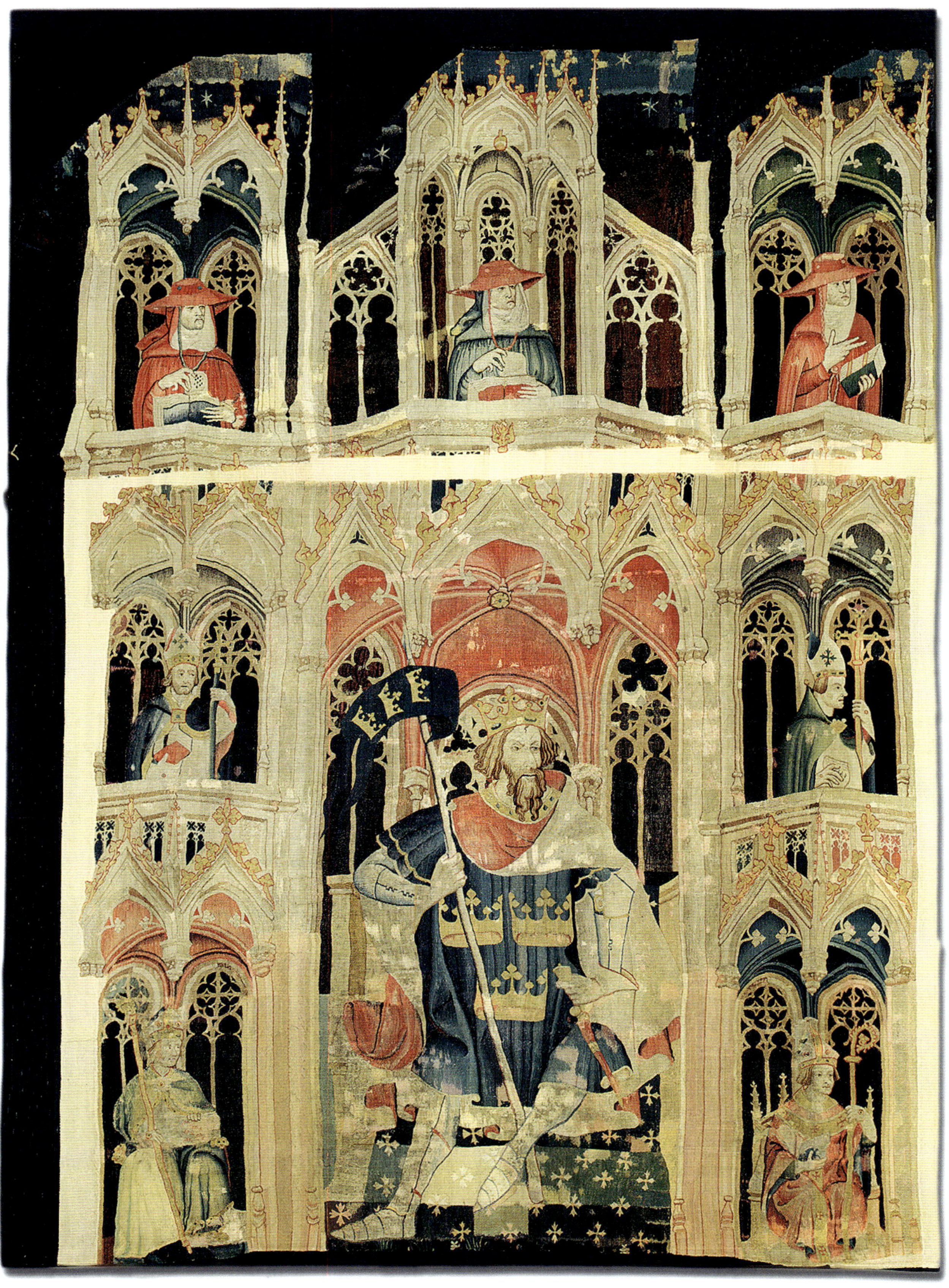

**Fig. 17** *Heroes Tapestries*: King Arthur. Paris or Southern Netherlands, c. 1400–10 (New York, The Metropolitan Museum of Art, The Cloisters Collection, Ms. Acc. 32.130.3a; 47.101.4)

## A COLLECTION IN PERPETUAL MOTION

A source of prestige, study, pleasure, and power, the duke's collections were not inalienable for all that, and on several occasions they were sacrificed to finance military campaigns, pay troops, or pay back debts of all kinds. During the Hundred Years' War, when gold and silver replaced currency reserves, works in silver and gold remained a convenient means of hoarding money. For example, the duke regularly tapped into the treasury of the Sainte-Chapelle in Bourges, since he considered it his personal bank. It was at his request that the gold and silver works were melted down during the terrible siege of Bourges in 1412, a depletion that he later compensated for by donating a large cross adorned with stones and cameos.[61] He also undertook in writing to return the gilded silver head of St. James, inlaid with precious stones and decorated with enamelwork bearing his arms, which he had taken from the treasury, or the equivalent sum.[62] His collections were also used to borrow money; the lender then kept the precious objects as a security. When the duke died, a number of items were still with his creditors, often the very merchants who had given them to him. Sometimes these gifts were resold by the recipients to merchants and then bought back by the Duke of Berry, as was the case with a gold cross set with stones given to his chapel, which was sold and later repurchased by the duke.[63]

Jean of Berry's collections were therefore a living thing, spread across his various homes. Items undoubtedly travelled from one to another, depending on events and visits that were planned. For example, the tapestries could have formed the backdrop for receptions. It has been suggested that the *Heroes Tapestries* in the Metropolitan Museum of Art, New York (fig. 17),[64] dating from 1400–10 and bearing the arms of Jean of Berry (ten times), Charles VI, and Burgundy may have belonged to him. We know from his inventories that the duke owned a more luxurious version, with gold and silver threads.[65]

Tapestries, jewels, and books were carefully recorded in the inventories. The first inventory in 1401–02 encompassed the holdings of the Hôtel de Nesle, the châteaus of Dourdan and Mehun-sur-Yèvre, and the Grosse Tour in Bourges. This was a way for the duke to keep track of his reserves of precious metal, plan donations, and consider future commissions.

## THE DUKE AND HIS ARTISTS

Et, quoy que il [Jean de Berry] deist encore, se tenoit il à Meun sur Ieurre et si tint plus de trois sepmaines, et devisoit au maistre de ses ouvriers de taille et de ponture, car en telles choses avoit il grandement sa fantasie, et regardoit maistre Andrieu Beau Nepveu à faire nouvelles images et pointures. (And whatever he may still say, he stayed in Mehun-sur-Yèvre and was there for more than three weeks. He spoke with the master about his stonecutters and carpenters working in sculpture and painting, for he had a great passion for these arts. He watched master André Beauneveu make new sculptures and paintings.)

This famous passage from Froissart's *Chronicles* is explicit regarding the Duke of Berry's close relationship with his artists, in this case the sculptor (and illuminator) André Beauneveu. He employed the greatest artists of his time, including the sculptor André Beauneveu, the architect Guy de Dampmartin, and the Van Lymborch brothers, setting them up in his appanages. The duke's artists were paid a regular salary, belonged to his household, and held the title of valet to the duke, who sometimes acted as godfather to their children. He also had a goldsmith in his employ, who worked mainly in Bourges, first Jean de Morcelles, originally from Flanders like many of the artists close to the duke, and then a certain Jehan Chenu.[66] Only one sculptor bore the title of valet. This was Jean de Cambrai, first mentioned as the duke's "imagier" (image-maker) in 1386–87, then as valet in the 1401–02 inventory.[67] Although André Beauneveu was also described as the duke's image-maker, he appears nowhere with the title of valet and it is likely that he never held such an office. On the other hand, the duke's residence was home to a number of painters and goldsmiths: Jean d'Orléans, François d'Orléans, Étienne Lannelier, and Michelet Saumon.[68]

Jean of Berry also got a great deal of his jewelry in Paris from independent artists, illuminators, and goldsmiths, such as Hermann Ruissel, Charles VI's principal goldsmith, who, toward the end of the duke's life, delivered some of his greatest jewels. Like the Van Lymborch brothers, he joined the court of the Duke of Berry on the death of Philip the Bold: The prince was a veritable predator. The leading Parisian merchants—Simon de Dammartin, Jean Tarenne, and Dino Rapondi—were the duke's friends and sold him many works of art; several of them were involved in the settlement of his estate.

**Fig. 18** Following pages: Van Lymborch brothers, *Très Riches Heures*, fol. 22: Emperor Augustus, detail

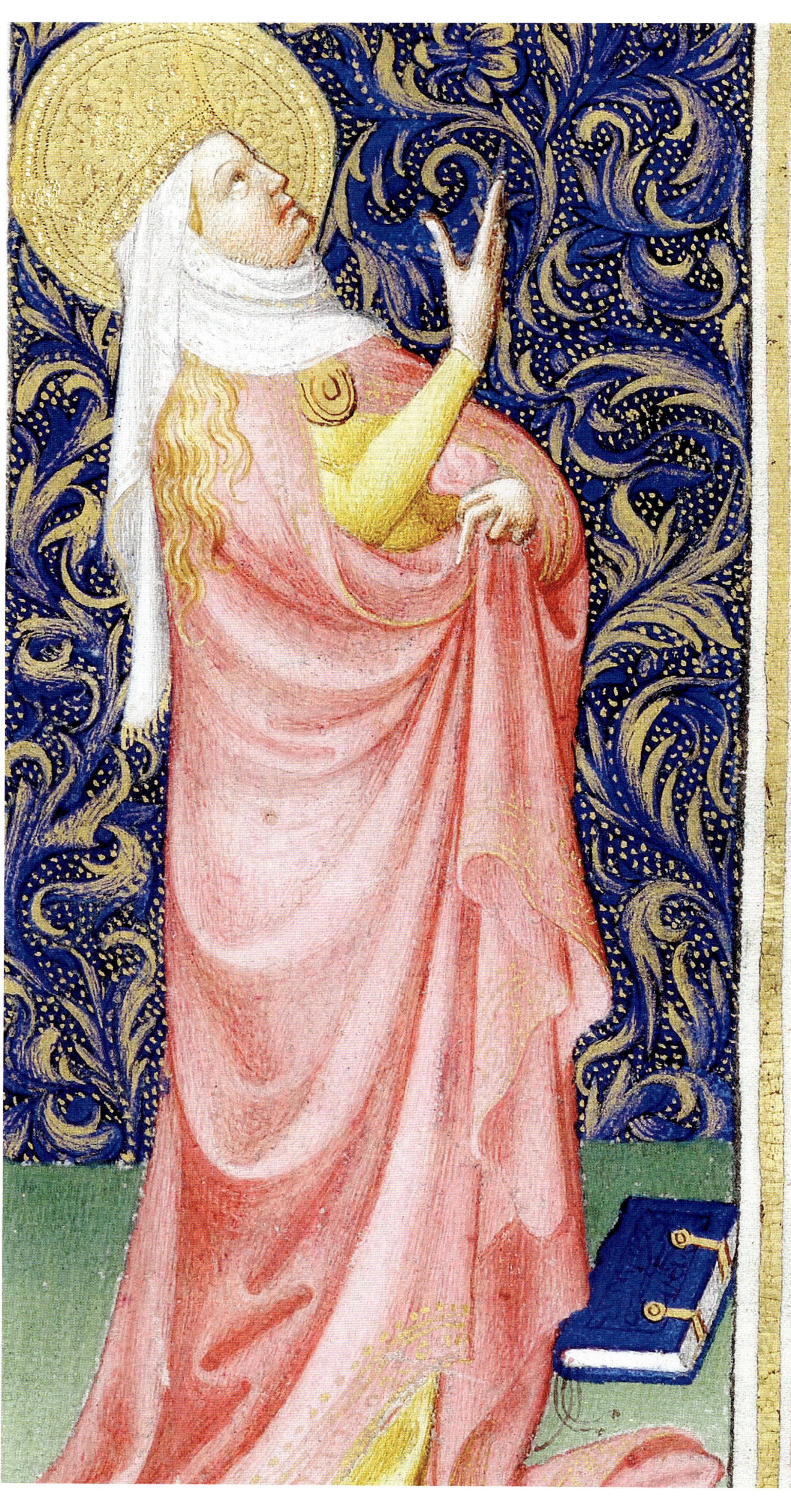

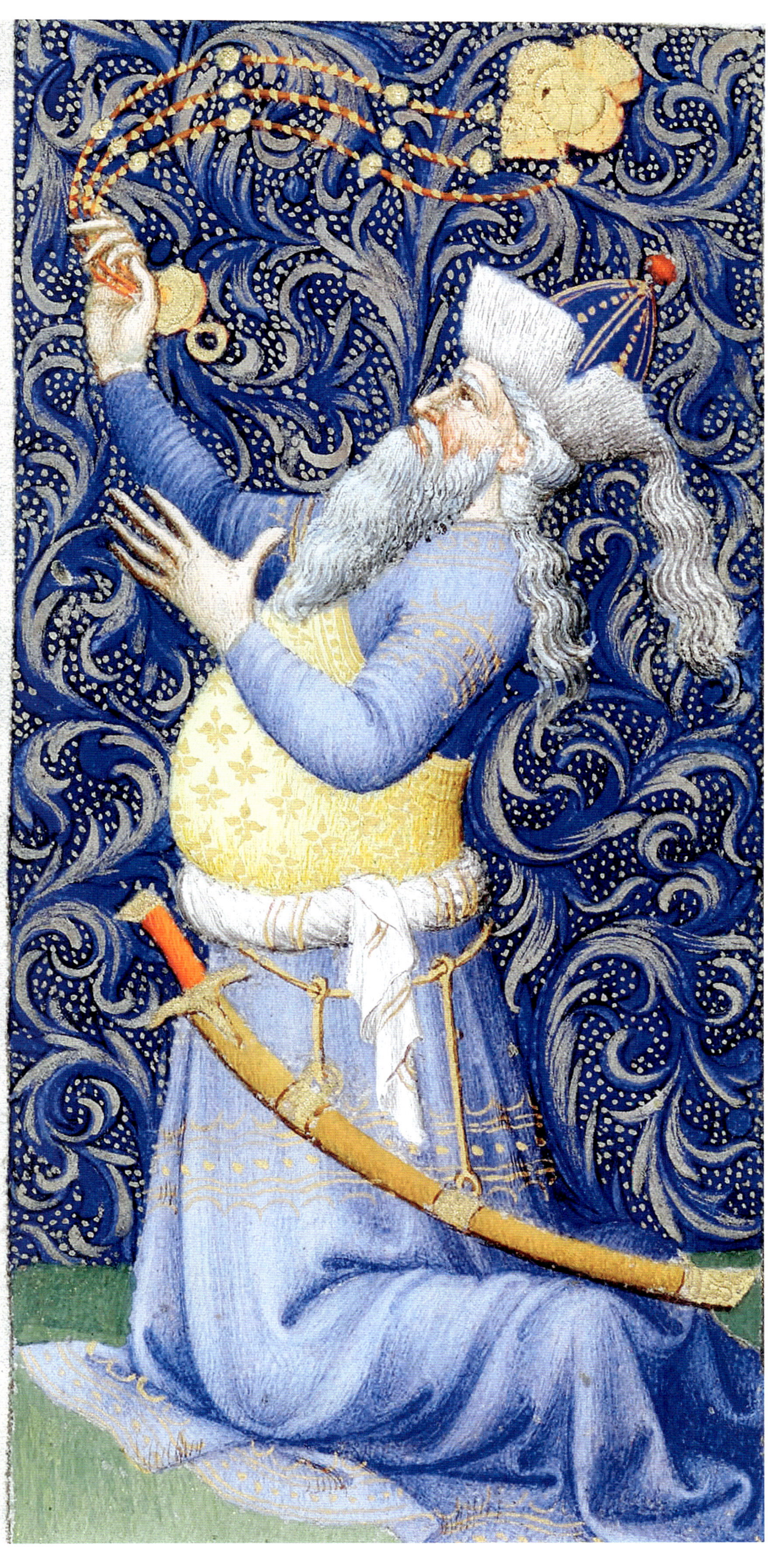

## ENDLESS EXPERIMENTATION

The artists at the court of Jean of Berry and the network of those he called on elsewhere reflected his tastes and concerns (fig. 19). While he shared his elder brother Charles V's interests in the 1370s, he gradually developed his own preferences from the following decade onward. He became a veritable talent scout and a connoisseur who was as innovative as he was demanding. For example, he long appreciated the great style of Jean Pucelle, in the tradition of the fourteenth century, employing his disciple Jean Le Noir, but he was also open to other generations, other periods, and other cultures, such as Italy (owning several manuscripts, paintings, and objects), the East, and antiquity. His patronage, which was particularly sensitive to iconographic innovations, led to the creation of new types of artworks.

His tastes can easily be perceived in his library, which was less intellectual than that of Charles V, but much more lavish. The many commissioned books of hours that it contained seem to have been his preferred field of experimentation. The *Très Belles Heures de Notre-Dame* showcase almost thirty years of artistic development encouraged by the duke, from the formulas of Jean Pucelle to those of the Van Lymborch brothers.[69] His *Petites Heures*, also of Pucellian inspiration (this was Jean Le Noir's last work), were completed by a second team led by Jacquemart de Hesdin, a singular figure from the north who was open to Italy. For his psalter, the duke even asked a sculptor, André Beauneveu, to become a painter. With the Van Lymborch brothers, he wanted to push to the limit the innovations proposed by some of the most distinctive artists of his time. An avid and passionate collector of artworks and precious books, Jean of Berry was ultimately also a collector of artists, whom he enjoyed pitting against one another, encouraging emulation among them but also between the arts. Through his demanding tastes, he played a resolutely central role in the flowering of the arts around 1400.

A collector and bibliophile who was as compulsive as he was generous, open to all forms of artistic expression, Jean of Berry did not hesitate to push his desires ever further. The incompleteness of the *Très Riches Heures*, which represents the culmination of all the duke's ambitions in terms of architecture, *objets d'art*, sculpture, and painting, clearly shows that his aspirations were so high that they were bound to remain unfulfilled.

1 Champeaux and Gauchery 1894.
2 Guiffrey 1894–96.
3 Meiss 1969 and 1974a.
4 Lehoux 1966–68; Autrand 2000.
5 Meiss devoted some insightful pages to this subject: Meiss 1967, I, 36–67. A brief summary was provided by Avril and Taburet-Delahaye 2004.
6 Guiffrey 1894–96.
7 For example, Paris, AN, J 947.
8 Paris, BnF, Ms. Français 20686, fols. 60–63v.
9 Rapin 2019, 101. See Paris, AN, KK 250–258.
10 Christine de Pizan, *Le Livre des fais et bonnes meurs du sage roy Charles V*, 1404.
11 Delisle 1885, 29. Is this the *Heures de Jeanne de Navarre*, mother of Blanche of Navarre (Paris, BnF, Ms. NAL 3145).
12 New York, Met, The Cloisters, Ms. Acc. 54.1.2.
13 New York, Met, The Cloisters, inv. 69.86.
14 Lehoux 1966–68, I, 35.
15 Chantilly, Bibl. du musée Condé, Ms. 487.
16 Paris, BnF, Ms. Français 167.
17 Paris, AN, KK 8, fol. 6.
18 Avril 1978, 22–23.
19 Paris, AN, KK 8, fol. 203: "Pour XVI esterlins d'argent XIII s. VI d. dont l'en fist I crochet à unes petites Heures pour Monseigneur Jehan de France, pour l'or [sic] et façon XXX s. pour tout XLIII s. VI d" (For 16 silver esterlin, 13 sous and 6 deniers, which he used to have a clasp made for a small book of hours intended for Monseigneur Jean de France; for the gold and the work, 30 sous; in all, 43 sous and 6 deniers).
20 See Raynaud 2006a and 2006b; Salamagne 2010; Rapin 2006, 2010, 2019.
21 Meunier 2006; Rapin 2012.
22 See the extensive study by Bon 2011.
23 In a letter addressed to the advisor Pierre Salmon, copied by the latter in his *Réponses à Charles VI et Lamentation au roi sur son état* (Paris, BnF, Ms. Français 23279, fol. 79). Salmon took it upon himself to act as intermediary with the Duke of Berry, recommending the services of a Sienese inlayer and mosaicist.
24 Rapin 2018.
25 Mehun-sur-Yèvre, musée Charles VII, invs. 981.1.1 and 994.2.1.
26 Raynaud 2006a and 2006b; Rapin 2006, 2010, 2019.
27 Kovács 2004, 165.
28 Meiss 1967, I, 35, 39, 50, 70, 307–08.
29 "En tresmalvaise marchandise,/ C'est en balays et en rubys,/ En dyamans et en saphirs,/ Et de plusieurs autres pierres,/ Ne le croy pas, ne pense mie/ Que tes pierres te vaillent vie,/ Car pour certain briefment mourras,/ Pour nulle riens ne demourras." Moranvillé 1891, 77–79.
30 In his *Livre du Chevalier Errant*: Tommaso III di Saluzzo ed. 2008, 453.
31 Guiffrey 1894–96.
32 See essay by Philippe Malgouyres, pp. 93–101.
33 London, BM, inv. 1892, 0501.1.
34 Kovács 2004, 169–70; Stratford 2022. The donation is documented: Paris, BnF, Ms. Français 21445, fol. 16.
35 Guiffrey 1894–96, II, no. 362. Kovács 2004, 129–37.
36 Kovács 2004, 133.
37 Guiffrey 1894–96, II, no. 364. See Gaborit-Chopin 1978, 15–16, 164; Kovács 2004b, 167; Paris 2004, no. 46.
38 London, BM, Waddesdon Bequest, inv. WB.67.
39 Lasko 1962, Tait 1986 and Cherry 2010.
40 Guiffrey 1894–96, II, no. 1161. Inventory of 1401–03.
41 Kovács 2004, 83–91; Berne, Bruges, and Vienna 2008–10, no. 10.
42 Guiffrey 1894–96, I, no. 7.
43 Van Rijen 2005.
44 Guiffrey 1894–96, II, no. 784; Kovács 2004, 293.
45 Guiffrey 1894–96, I, no. 649.
46 Ibid., I, 292 (no. 1109); Autrand 2002.
47 Baltimore, The Walters Art Museum, inv. 44.462. Dijon and Cleveland 2004–05, 49 (no. 14).
48 Buettner 2001; Hirschbiegel 2003.
49 Buettner 2001, 604.
50 Bourges, Arch. Dép. du Cher, 8 G 1452 [TSC 817].
51 Laborde 1872, 402.
52 See essay by M. Deldicque, pp. 145–71.
53 Guiffrey 1894–96, I, no. 1211.
54 Ibid., I, no. 415.
55 Paris, Louvre, inv. MR 379. Gaborit-Chopin, Alcouffe, and Bardoz 2003; Tomasi 2005.
56 Paris, BnF, Ms. Latin 10483-10484.
57 Paris 1981–82, no. 240.
58 Merlet and Mély 1886.
59 Paris 2004b, no. 148; Audebrand and Jourd'heuil 2025.
60 Chamarande, Arch. dép. de l'Essonne, 13J40, register of the foundation of the convent, fol. 8: "Item pour un grant escuçon des armes monseigneur de Berry fait par l'ordonnance dudit monseigneur le grant maistre en I grant messel donné par led. monseigneur de Berry pour ce.... V s" (Likewise, for a large shield of the arms of Lord Berry, made according to the order of the said Lord the grand master in a large messel given by the said Lord Berry for this . . . 5 sous).
61 Bourges 2004, 144–45.
62 Bourges, Arch. dép. du Cher, 8 G 1452, May 17, 1412.
63 Ibid., January 12, 1415.
64 New York, Met, The Cloisters, inv. 32.130.3a; 47.101.4.
65 Paris 2004, no. 134; Los Angeles and New York 2008–10, 17.
66 Kovács 2004, 311–12.
67 Paris, BnF, Ms. 7855, fol. 620; cited in Champeaux and Gauchery 1894, 28, 38.
68 Champeaux and Gauchery 1894, 103, 108–10, 164–66.
69 König 2006.

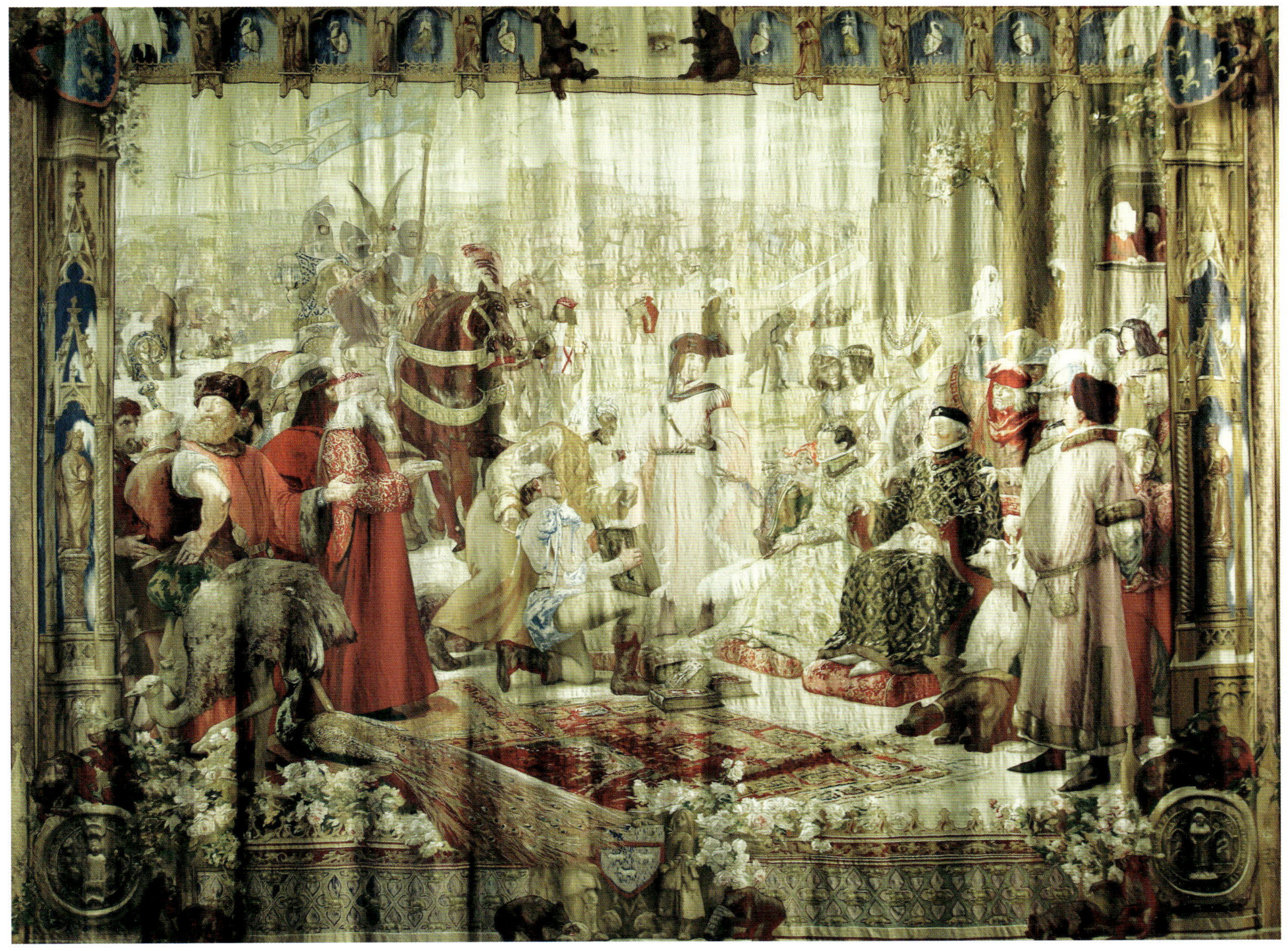

**Fig. 19** *The Duke of Berry Buying Objets d'Art*, tapestry woven by the Manufacture des Gobelins in 1911 after a design by Fernand Cormon for the Duke of Berry's palace in Bourges

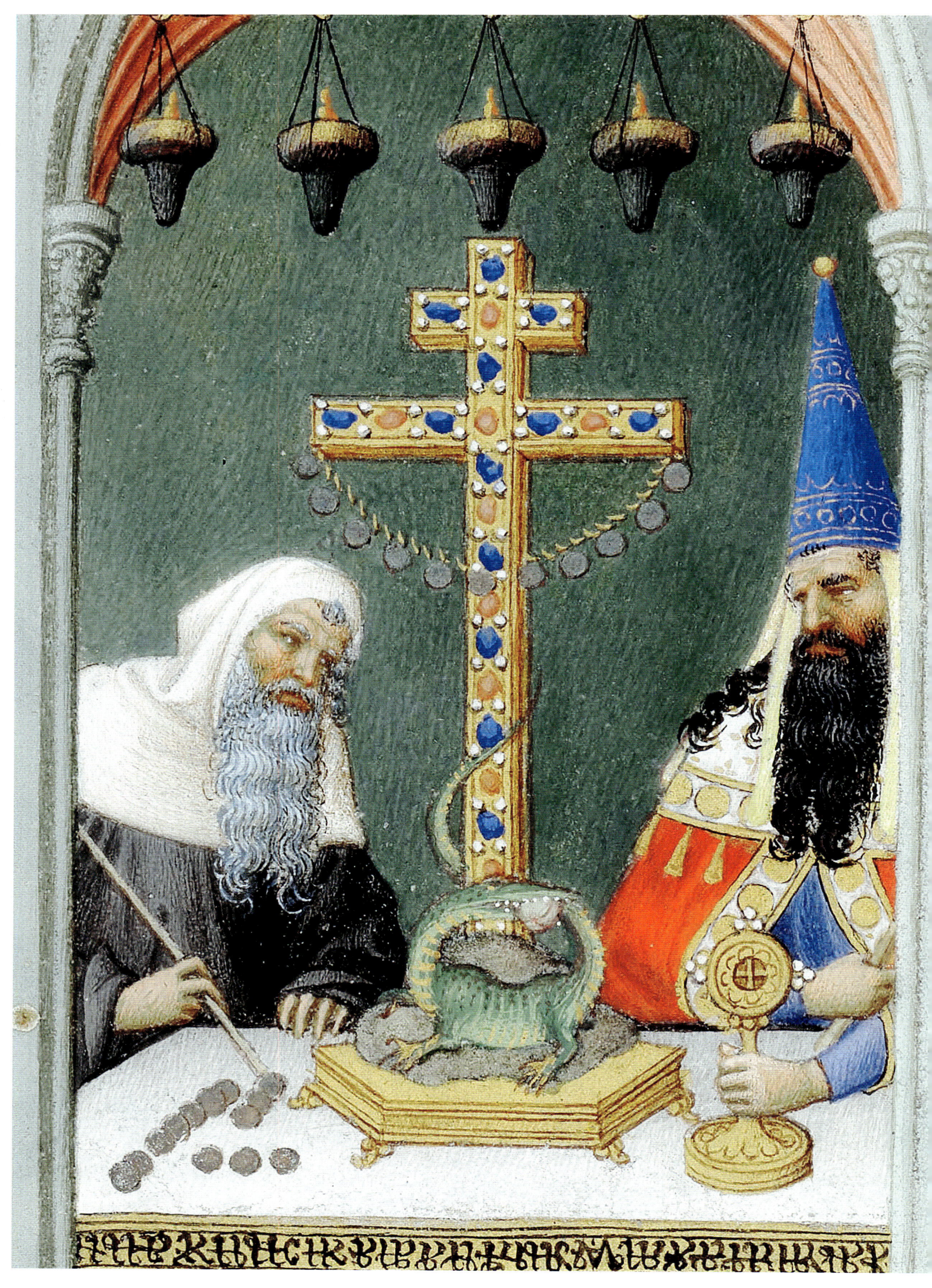

# 4.

# *Splendor principis*: Jean, Duke of Berry and Gemstones

Philippe Malgouyres

Reading the various surviving inventories of the Duke of Berry's treasures is enough to boggle the mind, leaving one at a loss for words to even begin describing his collections. It is also difficult because there are many of these documents and they largely overlap because the list of the duke's belongings was constantly being updated, in time with the purchases he made, the gifts he received or granted, and the major donations he made to shrines, first and foremost to the Sainte-Chapelle in Bourges. Simply describing his passion for gemstone objects and glyptics is an arduous task. Let us try to give some figures—to be treated with caution, given the gaps in these inventories and the repetitions. Leaving aside reliquaries and crosses, there are more than two hundred entries for hardstone objects, twice the number owned by the duke's brother, Charles V.[1] Most of these are secular, if we are to rely on the terminology used, and were intended to embellish the duke's dining table: some twenty ewers, as many goblets and hanaps, around forty salt cellars, some twenty pieces of cutlery (forks and spoons), to which we must add around twenty-five "pots" and vases. Liturgical objects were far fewer in number: five holy-water buckets and ten pairs of cruets (cruets of this type belonging to the royal collections were reassembled around 1528 by Pierre Mangot) (fig. 3).[2] In the inventory, the materials are differentiated with precision: rock crystal, agate, chalcedony, jasper, serpentine, porphyry, amethyst, garnet, and in the few cases where the compiler

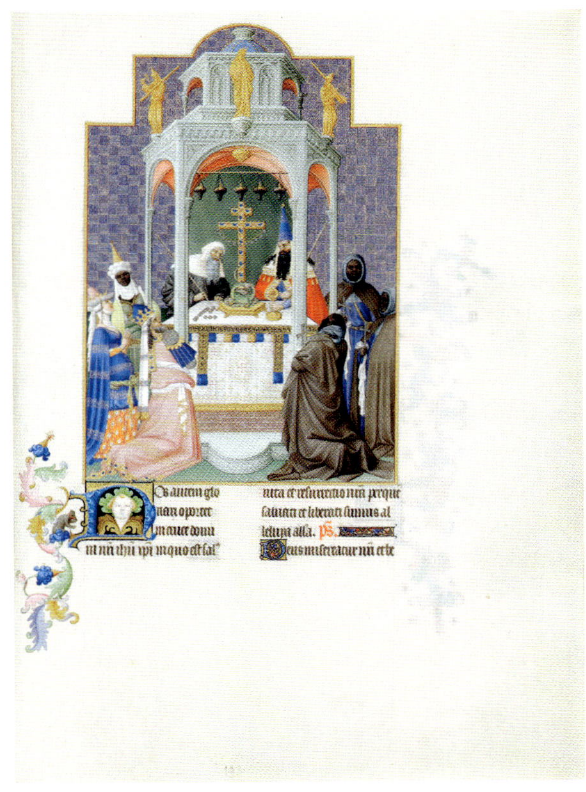

**Fig. 2** Van Lymborch brothers, *Très Riches Heures*, fol. 193: Mass of the Exaltation of the Cross

**Fig. 1** Van Lymborch brothers, *Très Riches Heures*, fol. 193: Mass of the Exaltation of the Cross, detail

was stumped, "pierre estrange" (strange stone). Rock crystal takes the lion's share, given for more than half of the objects listed, which obviously corresponds to preserved works; the vast majority of known Gothic stone vases are made of rock crystal, but this prevalence is not universal. Vases used for drinking—ewers, goblets, cruets, "pots"—are mostly made of rock crystal, and it is easy to imagine how wine could glorify the marvelous transparency of the quartz. Other stones were used for other shapes: Hanaps and bowls were usually made of jasper, salt cellars of agate or chalcedony (which also corresponds to the works that have been preserved).

Let us be clear: These hundreds of objects have not been specifically identified today. At best, the items listed in the inventories can be compared to similar objects that survive in large numbers. The list of medieval vases in hardstone compiled forty years ago[3] includes nearly six hundred references, but needs to be supplemented, in particular to include recut or transformed medieval vases. This is the case with the rock-crystal holy-water buckets, four of which appear in the inventories of Jean of Berry, and which survive in the form of situlas that were redecorated in the seventeenth century.[4] The large vase on display here (fig. 4) is a large crystal "pot" of the kind given in the inventory, with its faceting and double strapping typical of Gothic vases. In the seventeenth century it was recut, enriched with ovals and gadrooning, and fitted with handles. Such "modernization" of antique vases seems to have been one of the specialties of Gian Battista Metellino's workshop in Milan.[5] Louis XIV purchased many vases made in this workshop, but the circumstances surrounding the entry of this particular item into the royal collections are not known.[6] In most cases, it is easy to visualize these ewers, "goubelez à plusieurs quarres" (faceted goblets) or "hanap de jasper" (jasper hanaps). Just as in the Louvre's collections, there are also many examples in Lorenzo de' Medici's collection. The latter contains a large number of medieval vases.[7] All these vases have been attributed to workshops in Paris, Venice, or Prague. They are usually monolithic, with facets ("à quarres"). Sometimes, the handle is cut into the mass of the vase. Their sole ornamentation is a molding in the upper part that looks like strapping on a cask. The Duke of Berry owned a great many of these products issued from the luxury industry of his time. Are there rarer objects in this inventory? This is probably the case of the two large porphyry vases "de Romme" (from Rome), a "bien grant cruche" (a very large jug), and a "grant

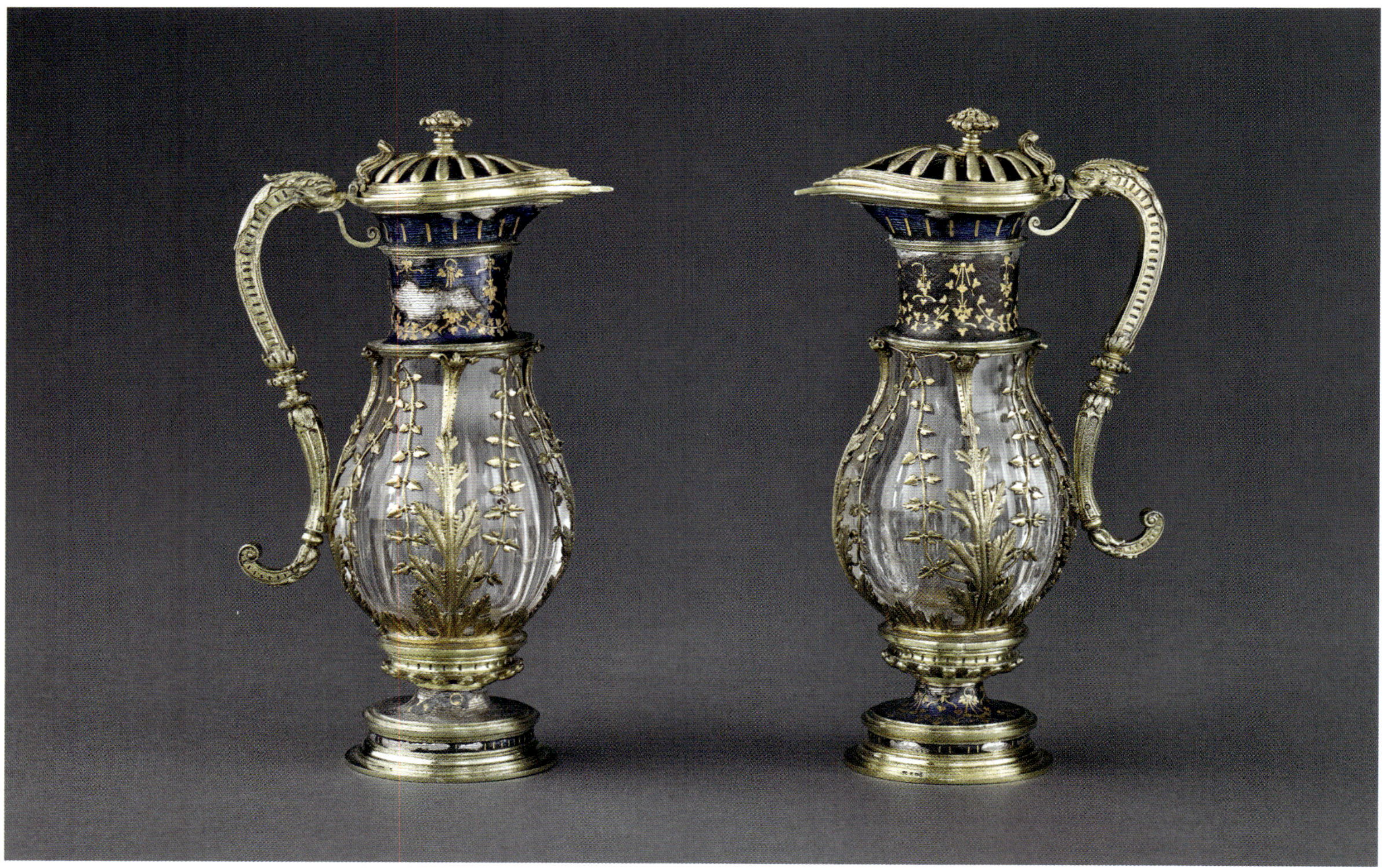

**Fig. 3** Pair of cruets, rock crystal, gilded and enameled silver, gold. France, fourteenth century. Mount attributed to Pierre Mangot (active between 1528 and 1551) (Paris, musée du Louvre, département des Objets d'art, inv. MR 548 et MR 549)

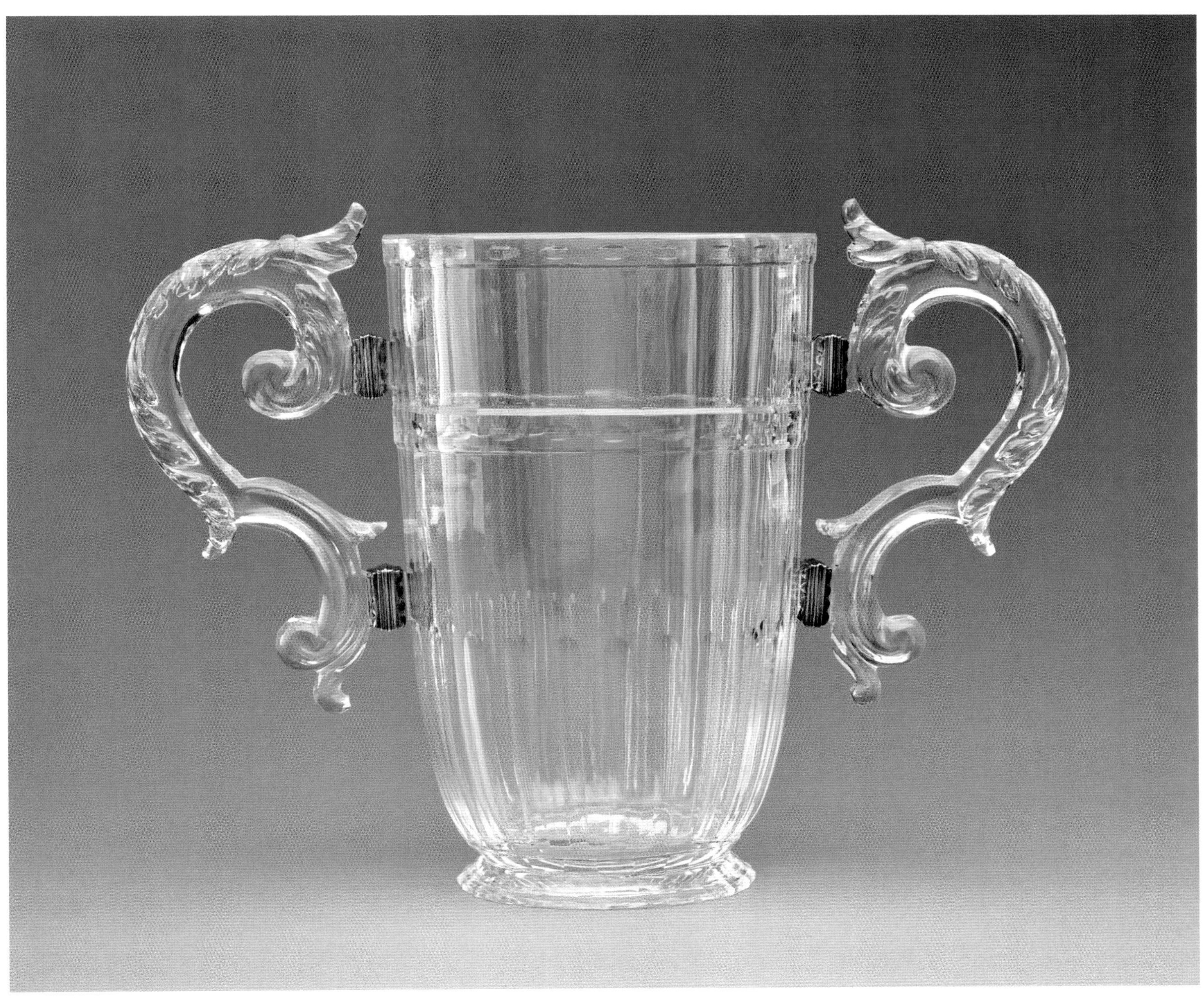

**Fig. 4** Vase. France, fourteenth century (recrafted and adorned with handles in Milan at the end of the seventeenth century) (Paris, musée du Louvre, département des Objets d'art, inv. MR 284)

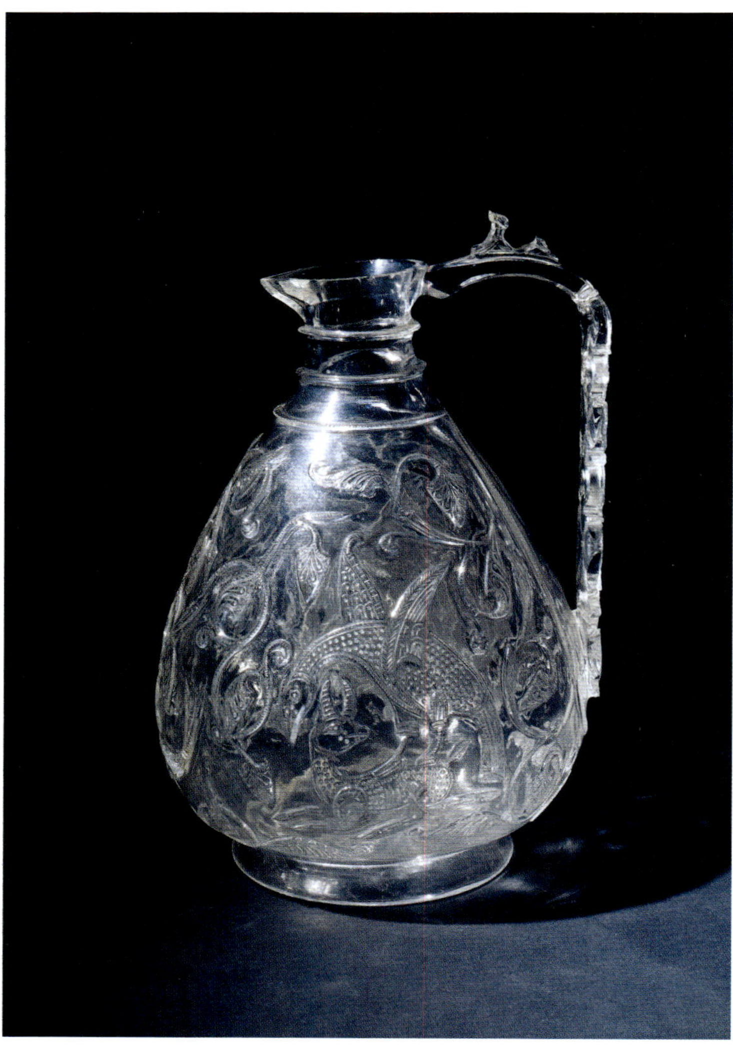

**Fig. 5** Ewer, rock crystal. Iraq or Egypt, eighth to tenth century (London, Victoria and Albert Museum, inv. 7904-1862)

bassin" (large basin),[8] which bring to mind ancient vases rather than Gothic artefacts. A "cassidoine" (chalcedony) pot is said to be "ouvré" (worked),[9] that is, with a sculpted decoration: Could this be one of the small sardonyx cameo vases inherited from antiquity? A reference to the decoration on two rock-crystal ewers—with "bestes" (animals)[10] or "fueillages et oiseaulx" (foliage and birds)[11]—recalls the splendid Islamic rock crystal ewers (fig. 5).[12] These two ewers were a gift to Jean of Berry, as were many other objects in his collection. The "petit pot de jaspre sur le vert, martelé" (small jasper pot on green, hammered),[13] a gift from Queen Isabeau in 1408, is reminiscent of a vase kept at the Prado.[14] The pot has been attributed to a Sassanid workshop because of its honeycomb decoration, which makes it look like a hammered metal vase.

These inventories could be analyzed in terms of the relationships they highlight: the gifts received from members of the Duke of Berry's family, and the vases given by the duke to his entourage. For example, in June 1408, Queen Isabeau gave him seven stone vases[15] including three rock-crystal "pots" with "pluseurs quarres" (multiple facets). Salt cellars, small precious objects, were the most numerous items in these exchanges of gifts, particularly on New Year's Day. The range of donors was vast, from European sovereigns (Martin I, King of Sicily; Charles III, King of Navarre)[16] to prelates and court nobles (Gérard de Montaigu, Bishop of Poitiers; Charles I d'Albret, Constable of France; Bernard VII, Count of Armagnac)[17] and even the duke's employees, such as Guillaume de Ruilly, "Garde des Joyaux" (keeper of the jewels), and Paul van Lymborch, who gave the duke "une petite sallière de gathe garnie d'or" (a small agate salt cellar trimmed with gold) as a New Year's gift in 1414.[18] On several occasions, the duke gave the painter rings inlaid with stones, two of which he himself had received as gifts.[19]

Gothic lapidaries were not only in thrall to the extraordinary clarity of crystal, but also appreciated opaque and brightly colored stones, particularly red jasper and all its more or less mottled shades. Half of the twenty-two hanaps inventoried in the duke's collection are made of jasper, including the cup of St. John the Baptist discussed below.

Amethyst, a macrocrystalline quartz like rock crystal, was rarer and considered a precious stone. Vases cut from its crystals are exceptional, but the duke owned eight of them (including two cruets donated to the Sainte-Chapelle in Bourges, of which we have an image).[20] Did amethyst's alleged property—to prevent intoxication (Greek "amethustos" meaning "not drunken")—motivate the making of such a goblet (fig. 6)? In any case, its lip allows one to drink from it and verify for oneself. With its inclusions, the stone's appearance recalls vases carved in Bohemia in the fourteenth century rather than any Italian or Parisian product.

In addition to these vases, almost all of which were intended to enhance the splendor of the duke's dining table, a number of other items were reserved for the Sainte-Chapelle in Bourges, in particular, pairs of cruets and crystal candelabras (noteworthy among these liturgical objects are the holy-water buckets and the "fouets," that is, holy-water sprinklers). An exceptional item is the gadroon cup (fig. 7), to which a head of St. John the Baptist was added to turn it into an object worthy of the treasure of the Sainte-Chapelle; this extraordinary artefact appears in the 1402 inventory of the Grosse Tour in Bourges.[21] The gold head of the Precursor,[22]

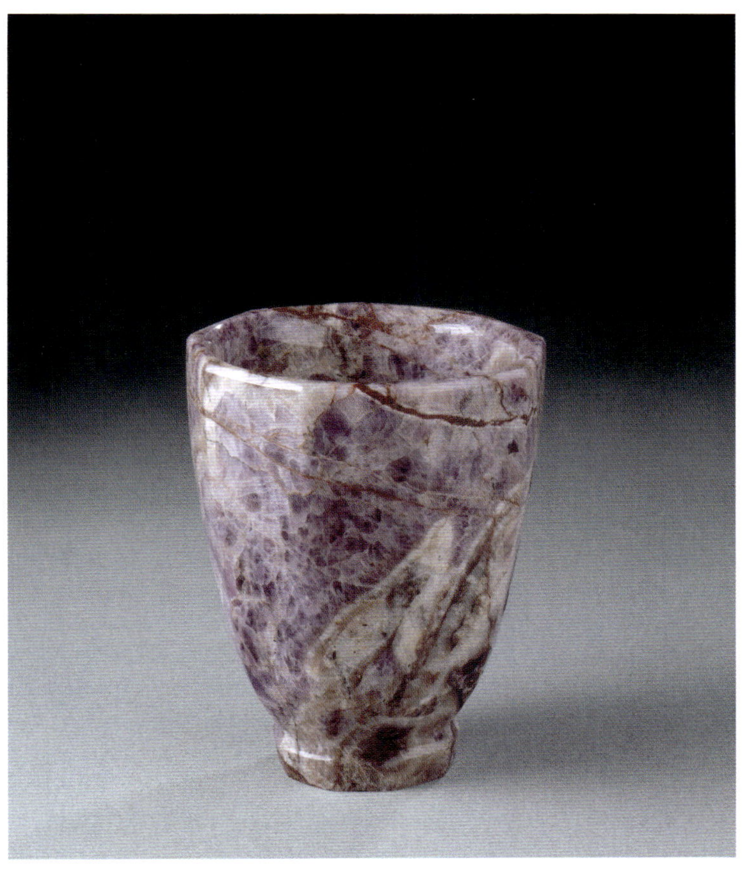

**Fig. 6** Goblet. Prague, fourteenth century (Paris, musée du Louvre, département des Objets d'art, inv. OA 2042)

placed in the cup that Herodias might have lifted from the banqueting table, was displayed on a gilded silver base weighing more than 50 kg. The Duke of Berry was forced to melt it down while under siege in Bourges in 1412, and only the cup has survived. Like the faceted decoration, the gadrooning animates the design of the vase by getting round the difficulty of creating smooth, regular sides. This type of decoration is mentioned in the inventories, but there are few examples; perhaps it is this less specifically medieval form that prevents us from identifying them today.

Jean of Berry also shared his brother Charles V's love of ancient glyptics. His reputation as an astute collector spread beyond the Alps. Antonio Averlino, known as Filarete (active 1433–65), who knew the great Italian collectors of his time (Niccolò Niccoli, Ludovico, patriarch of Aquileia, and Paolo Barbo), remembered him: "Come quando si loda ancora il duca di Berri della sua tanta dilectatione di queste cose; che dove avessi sentito, che fusse stata una cosa degnia, non guardava in danari; chè bisogniava che l'avesse, se possibile era" (We also praise the Duke of Berry for the great pleasure he took in these things [ancient cameos]; if it was something important, money was not an issue because it had to be had if possible).[23] Here again, it is difficult to convey an idea of the wealth of his collection, as any reading of the inventories poses problems of interpretation. First, the term "camahieu" refers not only to cameos ("camées"), but also to a type of stone,[24] namely

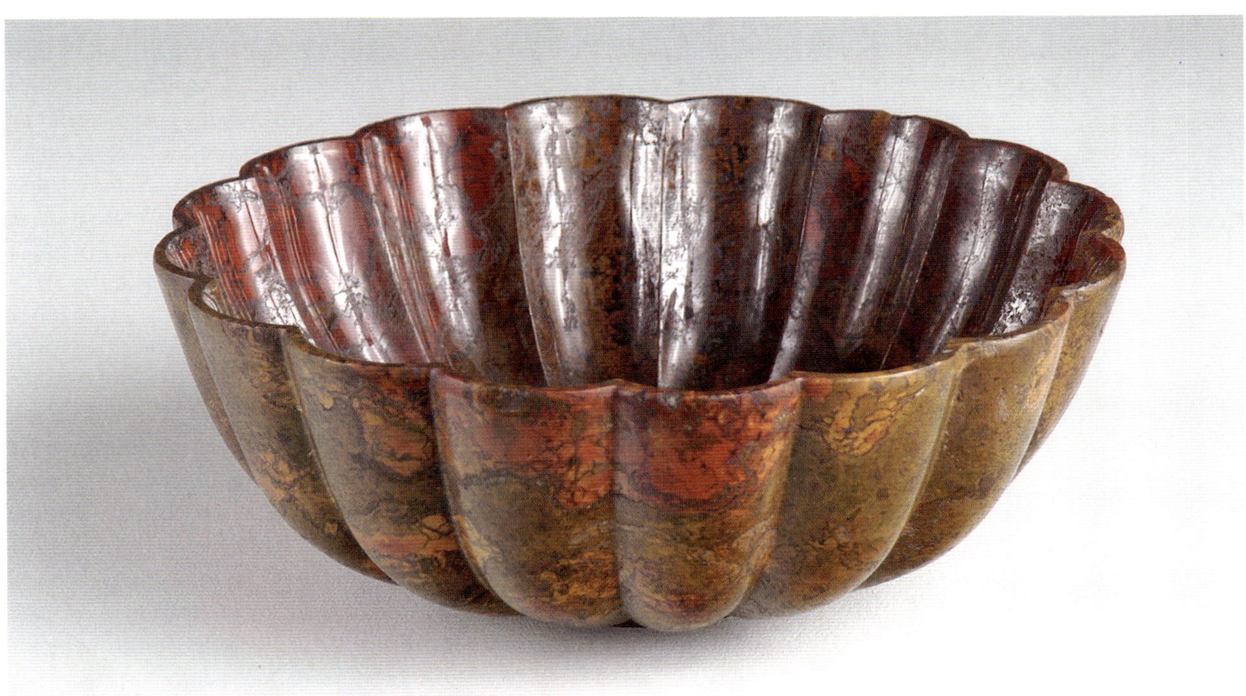

**Fig. 7** Gadroon cup given to the Sainte-Chapelle in Bourges by the Duke of Berry (Bourges, musée du Berry, inv. 1836.5.1)

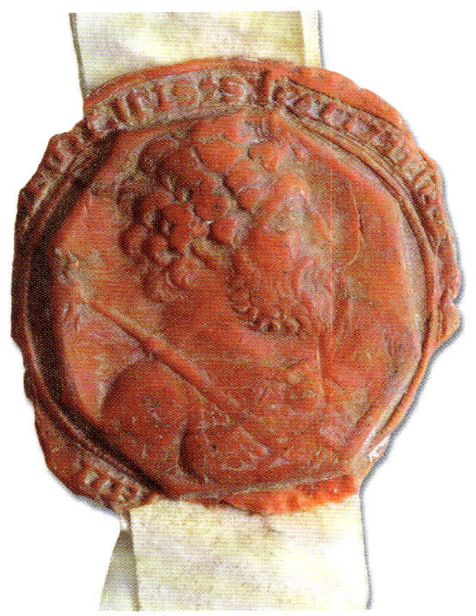

**Fig. 8** Seal of the Sainte-Chapelle in Bourges, impression of an intaglio (?) representing Marcus Aurelius (Bourges, Archives départementales du Cher)

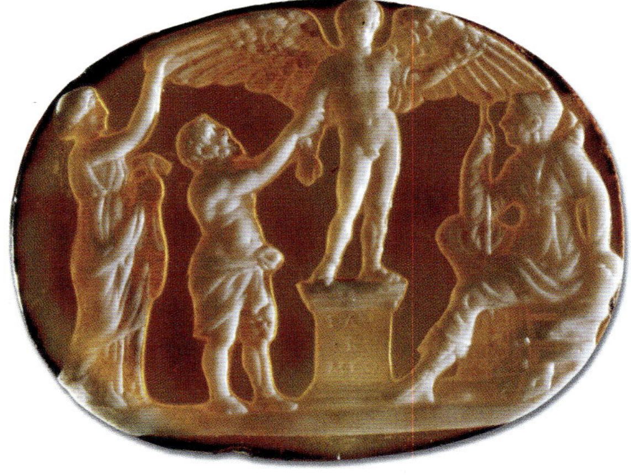

**Fig. 9** *Icarus, Daedalus, Pasiphae, and Artemis*, sardonyx cameo (Naples, Museo Archeologico Nazionale, no. 2, inv. 25838)

sardonyx. A distinction must be made between "camahieux" in which there is an image ("un grant camahieu ouquel sont deux beaux visaiges" [a large 'camahieu' with two fine faces])[25] and various subjects "en camahieu." The latter are not cameos, but often works in stone commesso, contemporaneous to the duke ("un petit tableau d'or... ouquel a un petit ymaige de Nostre Dame qui a le visaige et mains de camahieu, le corps jusqu'à la ceinture d'un saphir, tenant son enffant nu fait de camahieu" [a small golden painting . . . with a small picture of Our Lady whose face and hands are 'de camahieu,' whose body to the waist is a sapphire, and who holds her bare Child made 'de camahieu']).[26] In many cases, it is impossible to tell: What is to be understood by "a teste de camahieu"?[27] Furthermore, it may also be an intaglio, despite the mention of "camahieu": We have a clear example of this in the case of the "camayeu assis sur un cassidoyne, et oudit camayeu a une teste d'omme gravée à une main qui tient une espée, sur le bout de laquelle a un oisseaul volant" ('camahieu' placed on a chalcedony, and the said 'camahieu' shows the head of a man engraved, with a hand holding a sword with a bird in flight at its tip).[28] It is specified that this "camahieu" was mounted to form the seal of the chapter of the Sainte-Chapelle in Bourges.[29] The impression of this seal has been preserved[30] and shows that it was not a cameo but an intaglio, which is logical for a seal but contradicts the inventory. It depicts a bearded man in profile holding a scepter topped by an eagle (fig. 8).[31] We suggest this might be Marcus Aurelius; this lost stone can be tied to various bronze medallions of the same size in which the emperor holds a scepter.[32] On the other hand, it is very difficult to find anything approaching this large octagonal intaglio (about 4 cm per side) in the ancient stones that have survived.

What is immediately striking is the large number of medieval pieces, less biblical subjects than rings bearing the duke's emblems: bear, fleur-de-lis, even his effigy. Among the stones that could be considered antique given their description, we suggested recognizing in the "camahieu plat, longuet sur le roont, en façon de fons de cuve, où il a un petit ymaige nu sur un pillier en maniere d'une ydole et trois autres ymaiges" (flat 'camahieu,' somewhat elongated in a round way, like the bottom of a vat, where there is a small naked image on a pillar after the manner of an idol and three other images),[33] a well-known cameo from the collection of Lorenzo de' Medici with the story of Icarus (fig. 9).[34] Although a reading of the inventory is less rewarding here than its for the stone vases, we can grasp the importance of the duke's glyptic collection from the works preserved. The duke had two works of goldsmithery enriched with cameos, the stones of which still exist: the reliquary bust of St. Benedict donated to the Basilica of Saint-Denis, and the cameo cross intended for the Sainte-Chapelle in Bourges (figs. 10 and 12). The cameos stemming from these two works, which were destroyed during the Revolution, are all in the Musée du Louvre.[35] Some are antique,[36] others medieval. Of the latter, leaving aside the few Byzantine stones, it is clear that these cameos are highly skillful imitations, genuine fake antiquities.[37] We will give just one example, the most masterly (fig. 11). This laurelled profile is one of the nine cameos that adorned the Bourges cross. Commissioned from the goldsmith Hermann Rince and unfinished on the duke's death, it replaced a staurotheke reliquary that the duke was forced to surrender during the siege of Bourges in 1412.[38] It is known to us from various

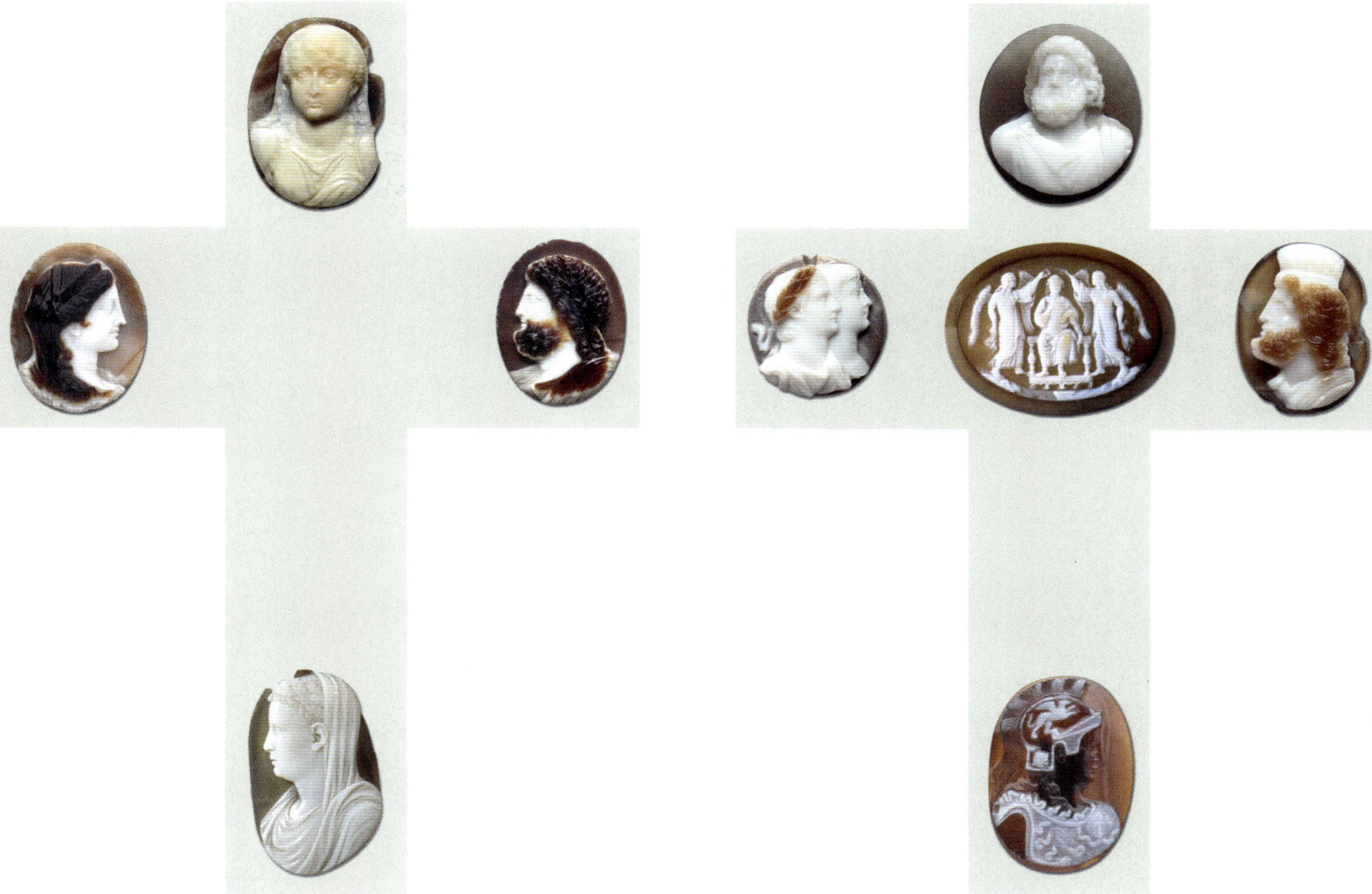

**Fig. 10** Reconstruction of the cameo cross at Bourges (front) (Paris, musée du Louvre, département des Objets d'art. Top: Agrippina the Elder (?), inv. MR 56. Left: Juno [Livilla (?)], inv. MR 49. Right: Jupiter [Drusus the Elder (?)], inv. MR 48. Bottom: Laurelled profile, inv. MR 54)

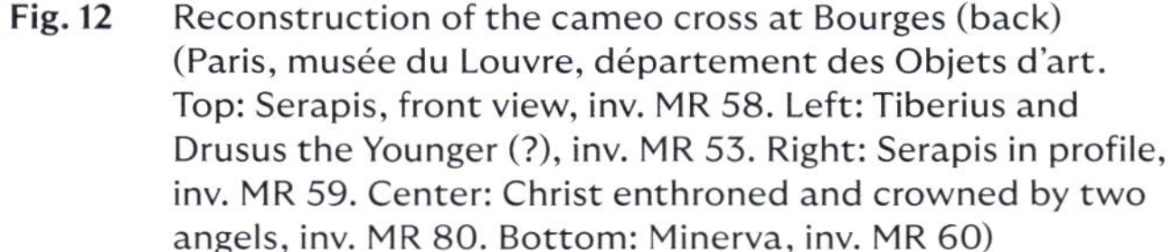

**Fig. 12** Reconstruction of the cameo cross at Bourges (back) (Paris, musée du Louvre, département des Objets d'art. Top: Serapis, front view, inv. MR 58. Left: Tiberius and Drusus the Younger (?), inv. MR 53. Right: Serapis in profile, inv. MR 59. Center: Christ enthroned and crowned by two angels, inv. MR 80. Bottom: Minerva, inv. MR 60)

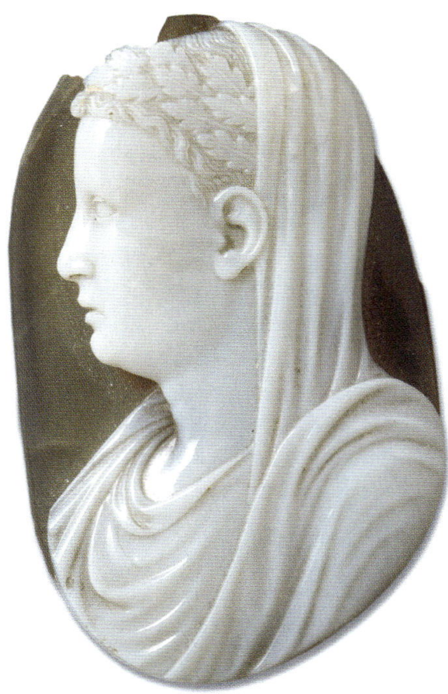

**Fig. 11** Laurelled profile, one of the nine cameos of the cross at Bourges (Paris, musée du Louvre, département des Objets d'art, inv. MR 54)

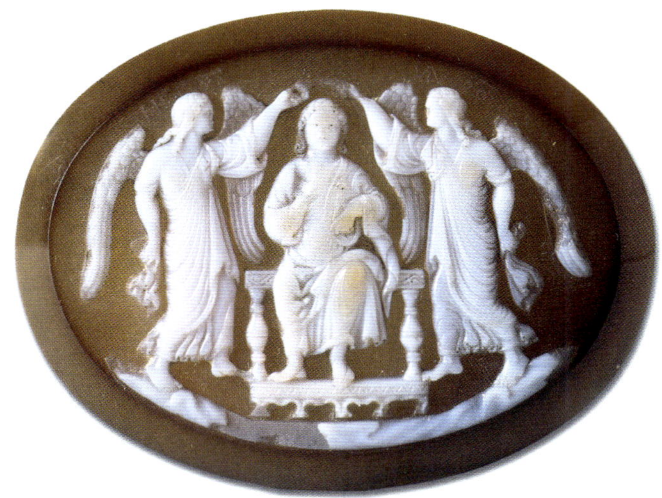

**Fig. 13** *Christ Enthroned and Crowned by Two Angels*, sardonyx cameo (Paris, musée du Louvre, département des Objets d'art, inv. MR 80)

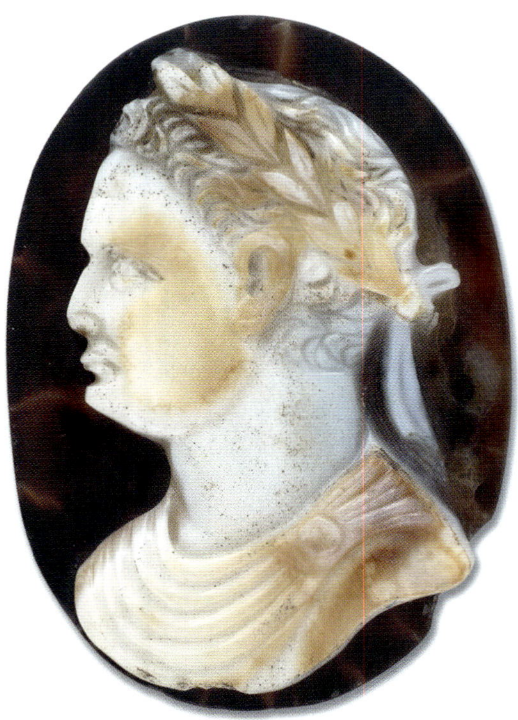

**Fig. 14** *Tiberius* (?), sardonyx cameo (Paris, musée du Louvre, département des Objets d'art, inv. MR 55)

inventories until it was taken apart in November 1793, and from a sketch by John Bargrave, a canon from Canterbury who travelled across Europe in the mid-seventeenth century.[39] The front featured, at the top, a portrait of Agrippina, two pendant portraits showing Livilla and Drusus the Elder as Juno and Jupiter,[40] and the cameo on display here. Initially listed as an antique in the Louvre ("the young Caligula"), it was later recognized as a medieval creation and can justifiably be called the masterpiece of Gothic glyptics. The fineness of the work and its Atticism surpass those of the Frederician cameos,[41] currently the only glyptic work from the medieval period that is reasonably well known. Wentzel's suggestion that it is a fake antique appears convincing[42]: Is it likely that Jean of Berry would have chosen anything other than the best and most precious piece in his collection to decorate his staurotheke reliquary? The subtle shifts in the outlines of the face, the perfect control of the cutting, and the graceful fluidity of the drapery stand in stark contrast to other, much cruder imitations made in the Middle Ages.[43] It can be compared with another large cameo that adorned the clasp of the cope on the reliquary bust of St. Benedict mentioned above (fig. 14).[44] This imperial profile, long considered to be antique, is also a medieval imitation,[45] whose Gothic sculptor seems to have been less taken by the fineness of the antique glyptic than by its vigor. It is possible that he wanted to represent Tiberius, who reigned when Christ died; in fact, the duke owned a piece of jewelry bearing the effigy of this emperor.[46]

A second Gothic cameo adorned the center of the Bourges cross, on the back. It shows Christ enthroned and crowned by two angels (fig. 13). At least, this is what the names of the archangels lightly engraved in Greek above the figures indicate. This Christ in Glory was a fitting counterpart to the suffering Christ on the Cross on the front. The choice of stone and the treatment of the surfaces make it possible to link it to the previous cameo and to remove it from the corpus of Frederician cameos in which it sometimes still appears. This is made all the easier by the fact that there is a genuine Frederician cameo depicting the same subject, a prototype of ours, which makes it possible to measure the insurmountable stylistic distance between the two.[47] Did the fourteenth-century lapidary behind the elegant copy of this rougher, more plastic cameo believe he was copying a work of his own time or a precious antique? It is difficult to tell. More broadly, this raises the question of replicas and copies of cameos made in the Gothic period, regardless of whether the models were medieval or antique.

Textual sources and the few surviving works give us an idea of the nature, if not exactly the wealth, of Jean of Berry's glyptic collections. We must bear in mind that, despite their importance, these objects are almost marginal in relation to the dizzying mass of goldsmithery and jewelry accumulated by the duke. In addition to conveying the discernment of this exceptional patron of the arts, they reflect the fascination of the time with stones and their properties, described in detail in the works of medieval lapidaries from Marbode to Albert the Great, and also a less well-documented interest in ancient glyptics, an interest powerful enough to have led to the creation of pastiches and copies so skillful that some continue to deceive specialists.

1 Alcouffe 2023, 57–58.
2 Paris, Louvre, dép. Objets d'art, invs. MR 548 and MR 549. Bimbenet-Privat 2022, I, 71–72 (no. 8).
3 Hahnloser and Brugger-Koch 1985.
4 Among others, Paris, Louvre, dép. Objets d'art, inv. MR 308 and MR 291 (Malgouyres 2023a, 256–57 [no. 143]).
5 The case of this vase, which is exceptionally well preserved, confirms this origin (Arbeteta Mira 2001, 280), as does the clumsy setting of the handles.
6 We thank Yves Carlier for pointing out to us the "très beau vase de cristal de roche portant 9 poulces de haut" (very nice rock-crystal vase, nine inches high) inventoried at Versailles in June 1774, on the death of Louis XV, in the cupboards of the King's cabinet (AN, $O^1$820, piece 215, no. 0 54). This vase appears in successive Versailles inventories with indications of its diameter and handles, enabling its identification. However, it does not appear in the inventories of Louis XIV's collections (we acknowledge Christine Chabot, Bertrand Rondot, and Emmanuel Sarméo for their help).
7 Dacos, Giuliano, and Pannuti 1980.
8 Guiffrey 1894–96, I, 205 (no. 787), 213 (no. 819).
9 Ibid., I, 193 (no. 771).
10 Ibid., I, 209 (no. 806).
11 Ibid., I, 214 (no. 826).
12 London, V&A, inv. 7904–1862.
13 Guiffrey 1894–96, I, 210–11 (no. 810).
14 Arbeteta Mira 2001, 112–13 (no. 8).
15 Guiffrey 1894–96, I, 210–11 (nos. 809–13), 214 (no. 823).
16 Ibid., I, 181 (nos. 685, 686).
17 Ibid., I, 176–81 (nos. 667, 668, 687).
18 Ibid., I, 180 (no. 681), 323–24 (no. 1211).
19 Ibid., I, 125 (no. 415), 128 (no. 421), 135–36 (no. 457).
20 Sketch by John Bargrave reproduced in Bourges 2004, 150.
21 Guiffrey 1894–96, II, 80 (no. 652).
22 The piece as a whole weighed around 7.5 kg. Unfortunately, we were unable to obtain the weight of the cup, which would have given us a better idea of the nature and dimensions of this golden head.
23 Filarete 1896, 659 (book XXIV).
24 Among others, "un camayeu tout plain, garni d'argent et de mauvaise perrerie" (a full 'camayeu,' set with silver and poor stones). Guiffrey 1894–96, II, 139 (no. 1096).
25 Ibid., I, 70 (no. 196).
26 Ibid., I, 37–38 (no. 72).
27 Ibid., I, 64 (no. 174).
28 Ibid., II, 37 (no. 228).
29 Ibid., II, 306–307.
30 Gandilhon 1933, 1133 (no. 552) and pl. IV.
31 Bourges, Arch. dép. du Cher.
32 Gnecchi 1912, with the scepter: 27 (no. 2, fig. 5, pl. 59 [AD 173]); the portrait is closer to 31 (no. 35, fig. 9, pl. 61).
33 Guiffrey 1894–96, I, 143 (no. 481).
34 Naples, Museo Archeologico Nazionale, no. 2, inv. 25834. Dacos, Giuliano and Pannuti 1980, 40 (no. 2). See Malgouyres 2023b.
35 On the cameos from Bourges, see Blanchet 1900. On those in the reliquary, see Montesquiou-Fezensac and Gaborit 1973–77, 34–39, pl. 18–20, and Paris 1981–82, 212–13.
36 On ancient cameos, see Malgouyres 2023b.
37 Malgouyres [forthcoming].
38 Philippe Bardelot in Bourges 2004, 144–45.
39 Bourges 2004, 150.
40 Malgouyres 2023b. They are reproduced in Paris 2021–22, 22, 23 (fig. 9).
41 It has long been excluded from this group, but is still considered as such by Giuliano 2003, 67–68, 104 (fig. 19).
42 Wentzel 1954, 70 (fig. 49), 72.
43 Malgouyres [forthcoming].
44 Paris, Louvre, dép. Objets d'art, inv. MR 55.
45 Montesquiou-Fezensac and Gaborit 1973–77, III, 36 (pl. 18A); Paris 1981–82, 212–13 (no. 171, A); Paris 2021–22, 22–23 (no. 13), 25 (Paris?, 14th c.) (notice by Philippe Malgouyres).
46 Guiffrey 1894–96, I, 70–71 (no. 197).
47 Munich, Staatliche Münzkabinett, inv. 1207. They are reproduced side by side in Magdebourg 2006, 283, and in Malgouyres 2022, 44–45 (figs. 5, 7). Helmut Trenk (in Magdebourg 2006, 284) considers these essential differences to be of little significance and suggests justifying them by a slight dating discrepancy in the Sicilian production.

**Fig. 15** Following pages: Van Lymborch brothers, *Très Riches Heures*, fol. 193: Mass of the Exaltation of the Cross, detail

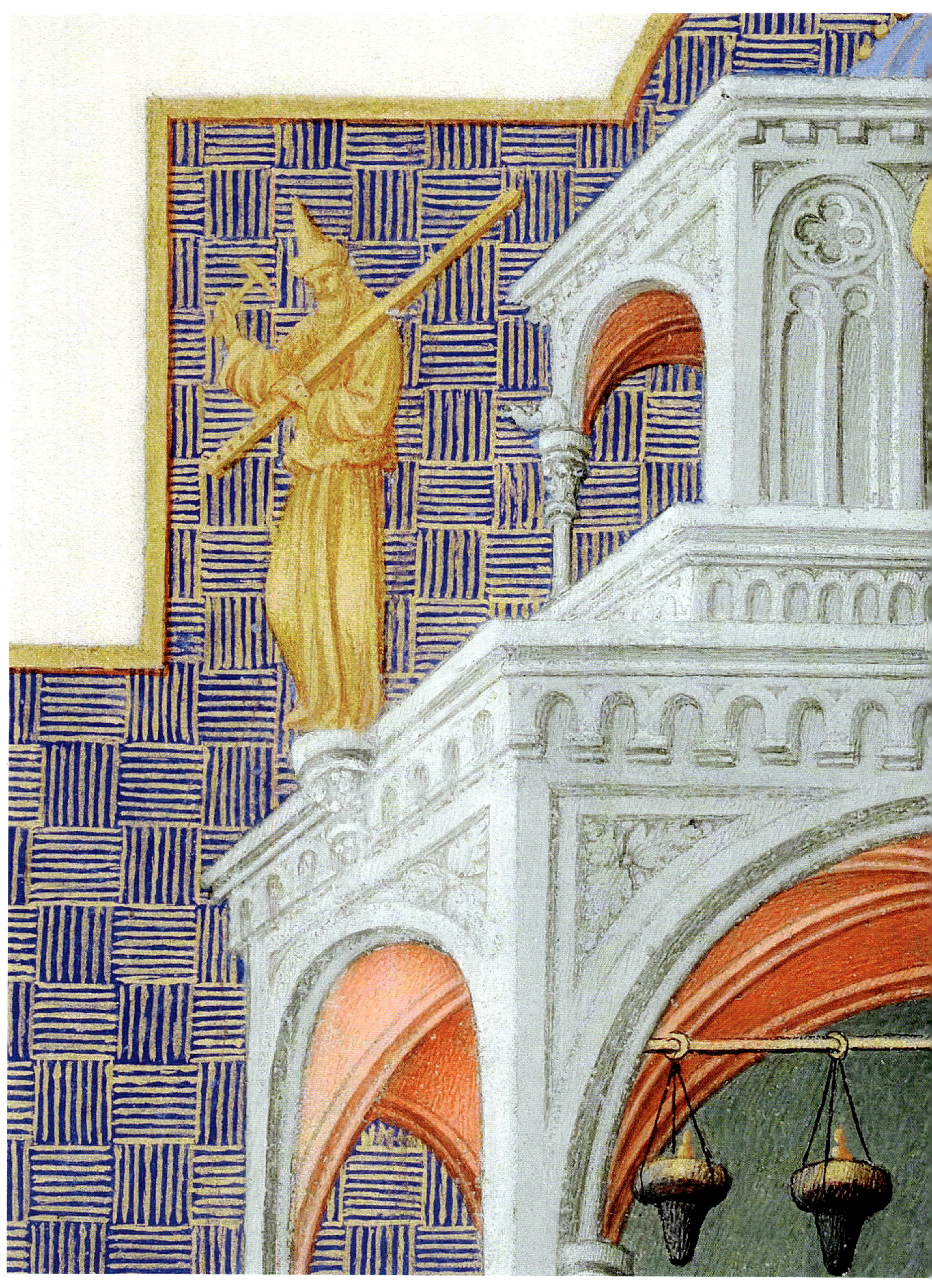

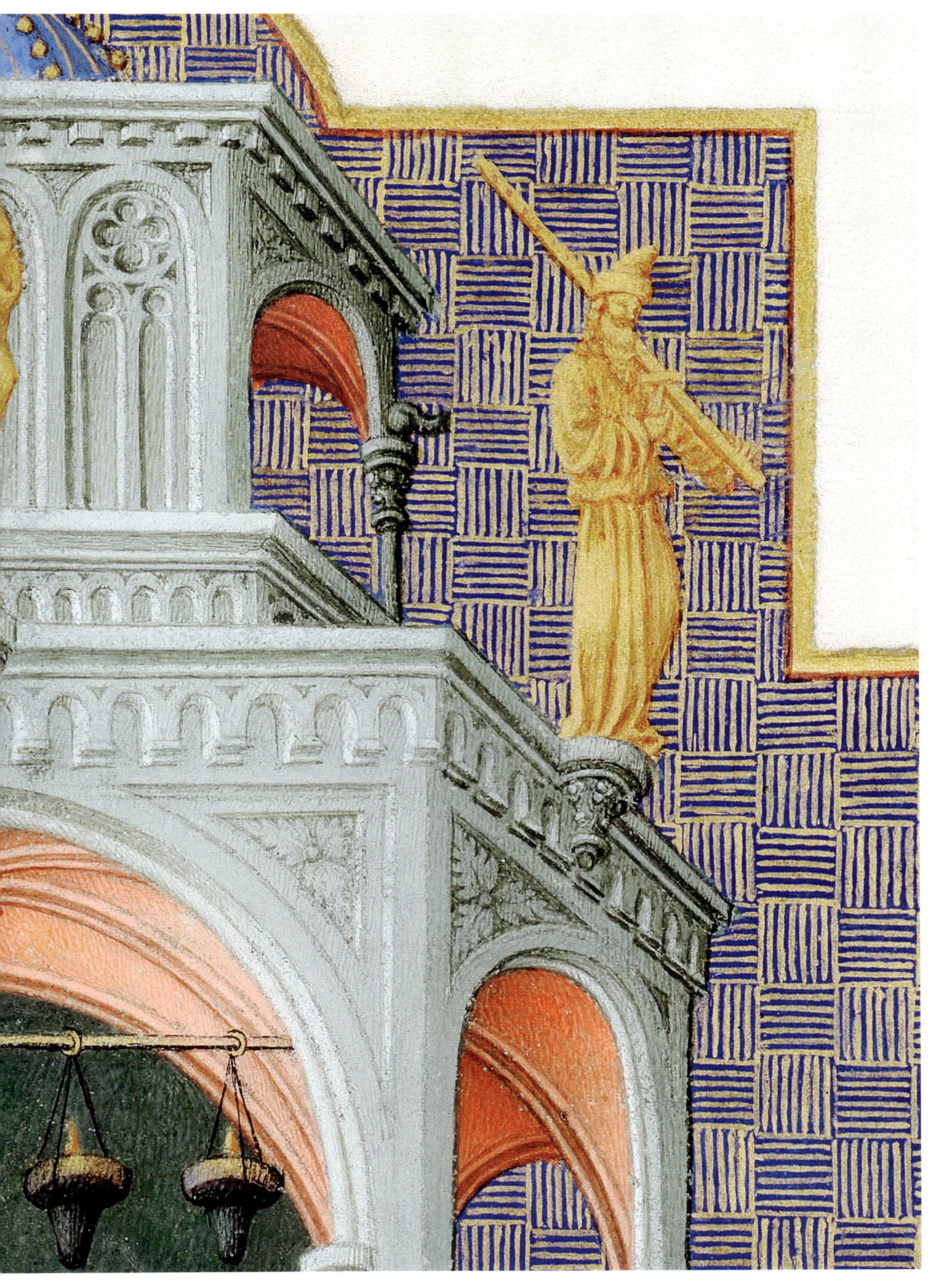

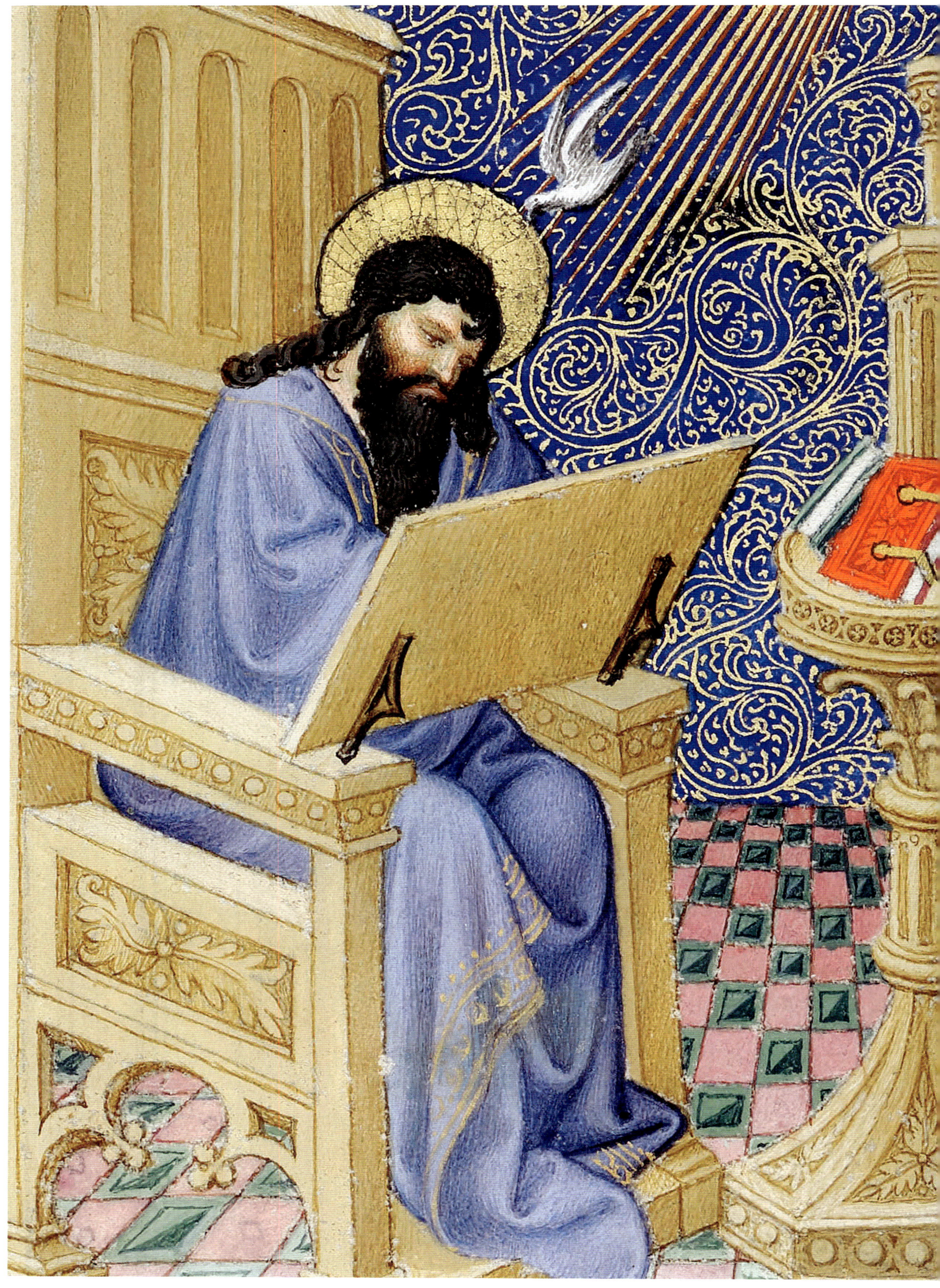

5.

# Where Learning Meets Luxury: The Library of Jean of Berry

Véronique de Becdelièvre

While his role in political, military, and diplomatic spheres is often little known, Jean of Berry is certainly remembered as a great bibliophile with a passion for art. As early as 1830, the magnificence of the manuscripts in his library fascinated researchers.[1] Perhaps it is because of the quality of their execution that so many volumes have, happily, been preserved: 127 manuscripts have been identified,[2] representing more than one-third of the original library, and they are now the showpieces of libraries in France and abroad.

However, a study of the inventories of the collection drawn up between December 1401 and autumn 1416, and of the books that have come down to us, shows that, beyond the image of the luxury-loving bibliophile so often conveyed, the Duke of Berry's library was the product of reasoned choices by a literate prince who cared as much about the texts as he did about the richness of his works. Alongside sumptuous books of hours, we discover a highly diversified collection that encompasses encyclopedias, early humanism and contemporary authors.[3]

## SOURCES: INVENTORIES AND MARKS OF OWNERSHIP

The approximately three hundred works that make up the library, kept mainly in the duke's Mehun-sur-Yèvre residence, are known thanks to three inventories that still exist today. To these works we must add thirty-four manuscripts,

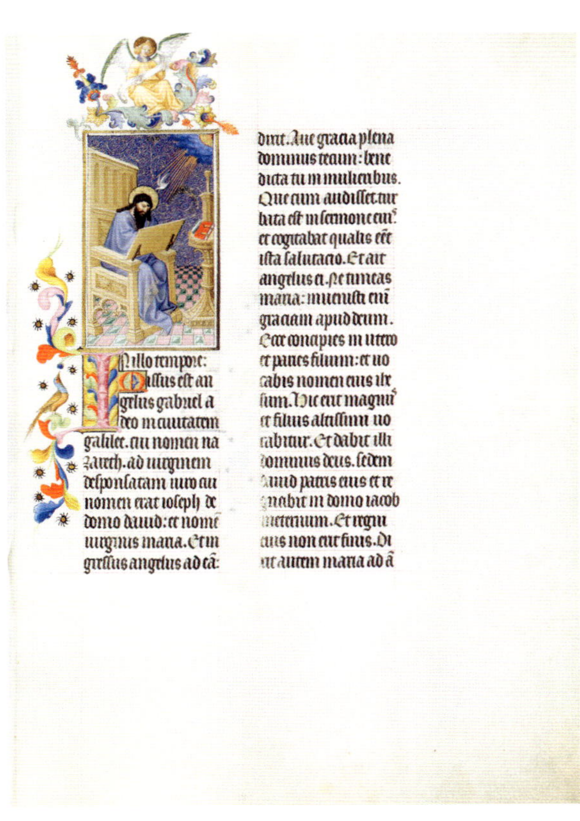

**Fig. 2** Van Lymborgh brothers, *Très Riches Heures*, fol. 18: The Evangelist Luke Writing

**Fig. 1** Van Lymborgh brothers, *Très Riches Heures*, fol. 18: The Evangelist Luke Writing, detail

which were not inventoried, but have now been identified thanks to their marks of ownership.

The first document, kept at the Bibliothèque nationale de France,[4] lists all the jewels and manuscripts recorded in the duke's residences between December 2, 1401, and February 23, 1403. Compiled by the "Garde des Joyaux," the keeper of the duke's jewels, Guillaume de Ruilly, who was succeeded in 1402 by Robinet d'Étampes, it lists 129 manuscripts.[5]

The second inventory is in the Archives nationales.[6] The first part contains the jewels listed by Robinet d'Étampes before January 31, 1413, while the second contains those acquired from then until June 15, 1416, the date of Jean of Berry's death. It lists 181 manuscripts, 59 of which appear in the previous inventory. More detailed than the first inventory, it mentions the incipits of the second or third leaf and the provenance of the works.[7]

Finally, manuscript 841 in the Bibliothèque Sainte-Geneviève is the record compiled by Jean Lebourne, secretary and controller of expenses of the duke's estate upon his death. It lists the objects found in Bourges, Mehun-sur-Yèvre, and Paris.[8]

These sources must be supplemented by the documents issued on the occasion of the founding of the Sainte-Chapelle in Bourges, consecrated on April 18, 1405, and intended to endow it with a treasure. Marginal annotations on an inventory of books drawn up between 1404 and 1406 mention if the books were removed and sometimes the incipits of the second and last leaves.[9] In total, sixty-seven manuscripts were removed from the ducal library between 1405 and 1416 and given to the clergy of the Saint-Chapelle.

These sources are invaluable in terms of intellectual heritage and the execution of the works, since they mention

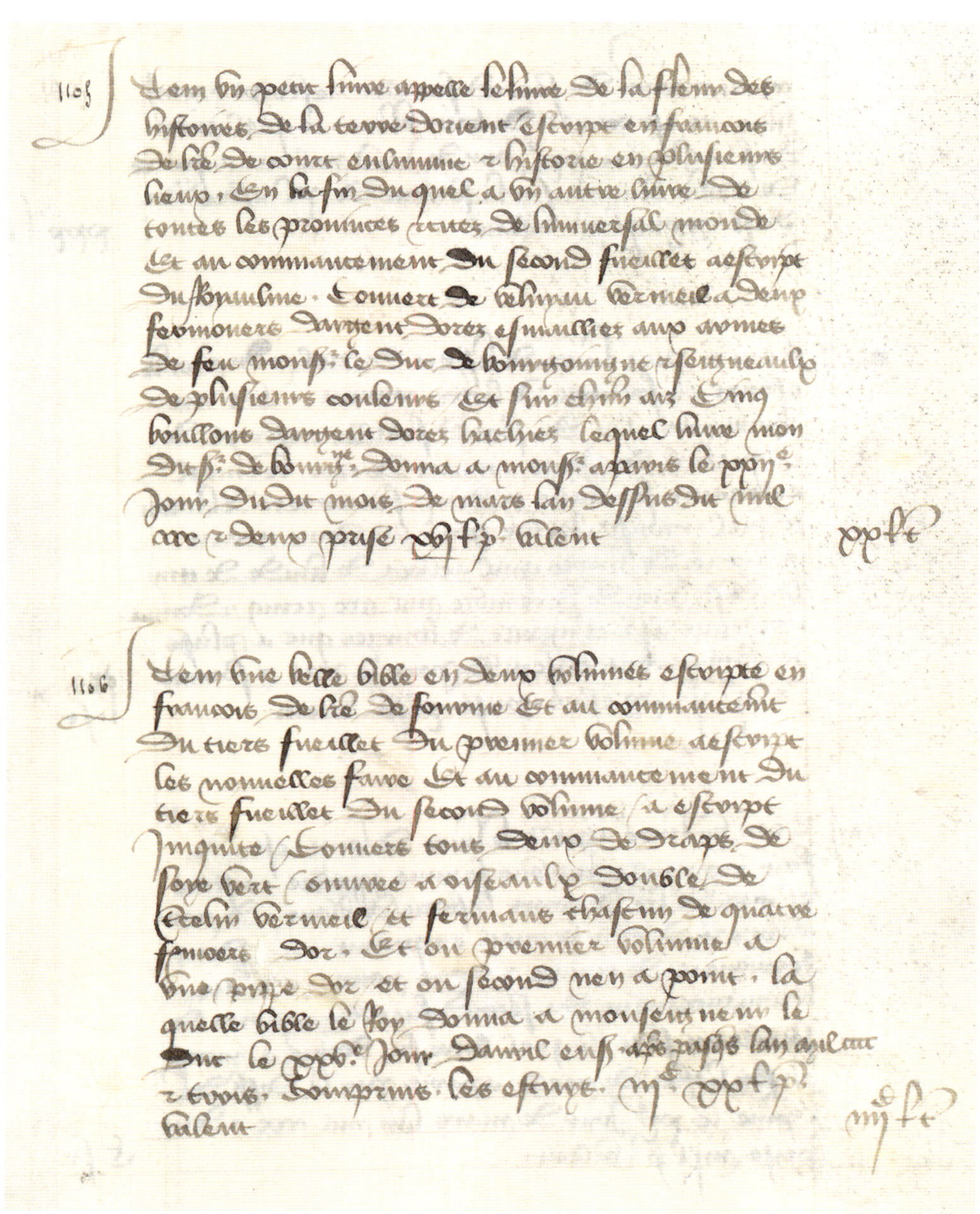

**Fig. 3** Correspondence of article 1106 of the 1416 inventory (left) (Paris, Bibliothèque Sainte-Geneviève, ms. 841, fol. 159v) with the incipit of the third leaf of the *Grande Bible historiale complétée* (right) (Paris, Bibliothèque nationale de France, Bibliothèque de l'Arsenal, ms. 5212, fol. 3r, line 1)

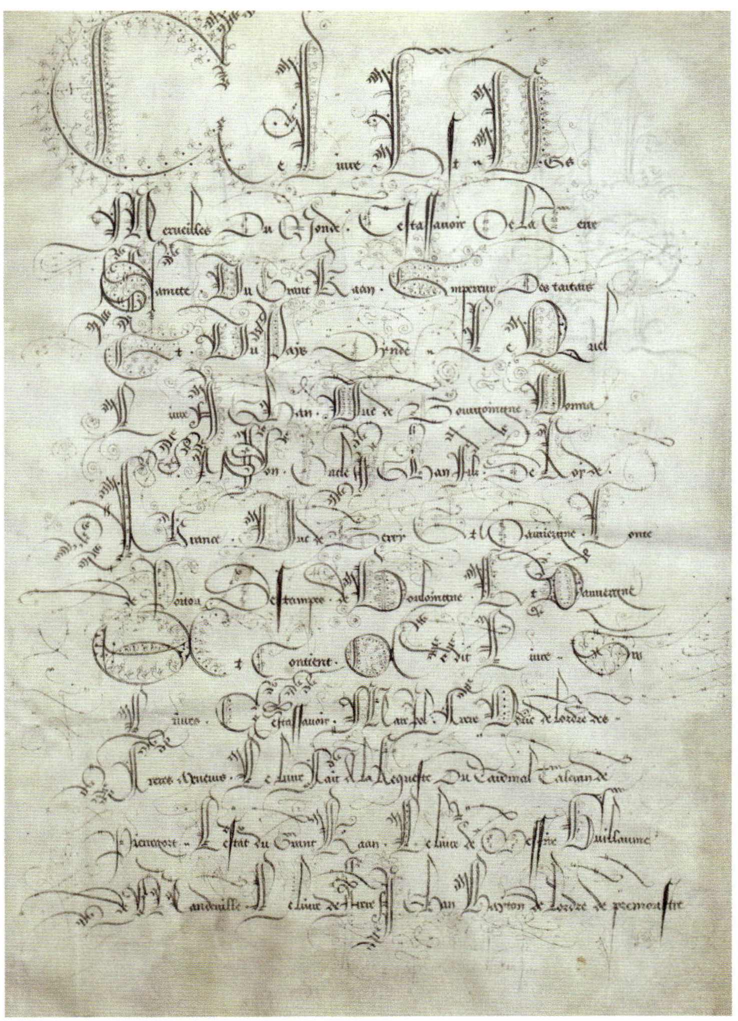

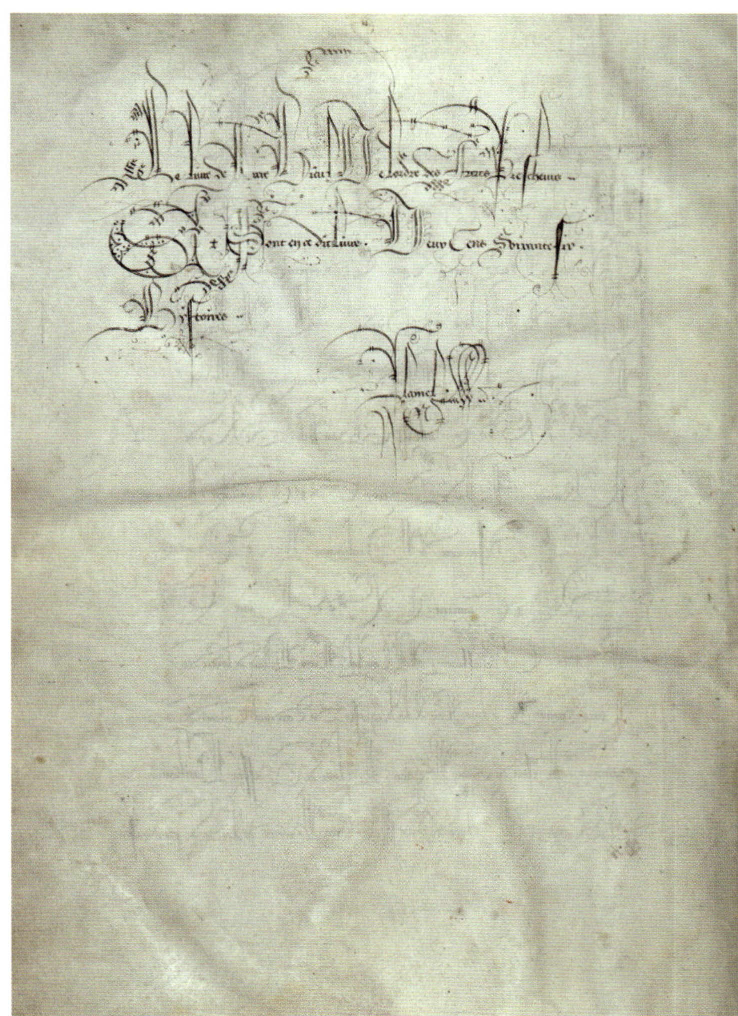

**Fig. 4** Bookplate calligraphed by Jean Flamel in Marco Polo, *Devisement du monde* and other texts on overseas lands (fol. 42v), Paris, Ahun, 1410–12, c. 1470 (Paris, Bibliothèque nationale de France, département des Manuscrits, Français 2810, fol. Ar-v)

authors and titles, but also "histoires" or illuminations and bindings. They also trace the changes within the library between 1401 and 1416 and shed light on the duke's policy of increasing his collections through purchases, commissions, and donations.[10] The description of the painting on the frontispiece and the mention of the incipit have been as useful as the actual title in identifying many manuscripts. Take, for example, the *Grande Bible historiale complétée*, which was divided into two volumes in the early fifteenth century. As indicated in article 1106 of the inventory of 1416, the "tiers fueillet du premier volume" (third leaf of the first volume) begins with the words "les nouvelles fere," which recur in the first line of the third leaf (fig. 3).[11] Article 1106 also mentions the provenance of the *Grand Bible*: It was a gift from King Charles VI dated April 25, 1403, listed in the inventories of the jewels at Vincennes in 1391.

Another means of identification is to be found in the duke's bookplates, calligraphed on the flyleaves by his secretary Jean Flamel, and his autograph signature (sometimes scratched), which is inscribed on many of the last leaves. Manuscript Français 2810 (Paris, Bibliothèque nationale de France) collects Marco Polo's *Devisement du monde* (Description of the World, known as Book of the Marvels of the World) and other texts on overseas history, and bears a bookplate in Cadel letters at the beginning of the volume, attesting that the book, given to his uncle by the Duke of Burgundy, John the Fearless, in 1413, belonged to "Jehan, filz de roy de France, duc de Berry et d'Auvergne, conte de Poitou, d'Estampes, de Bouloingne et d'Auvergne" (fig. 4).

The duke's coat of arms—"d'azur semé de fleurs de lis d'or à la bordure engrelée d'azur" (a semé of gold fleurs-de-lis on a blue ground with engrailed red bordure)—adorn the illuminations, initials, and marginal borders. It is thanks to the coat of arms that the manuscript of St. Augustine's *The City of God*, kept in Cambridge but missing from the inventories, was identified. In the *Grandes Heures*,[12] the borders of folio 96r contain sixteen quatrefoil medallions alternating the duke's

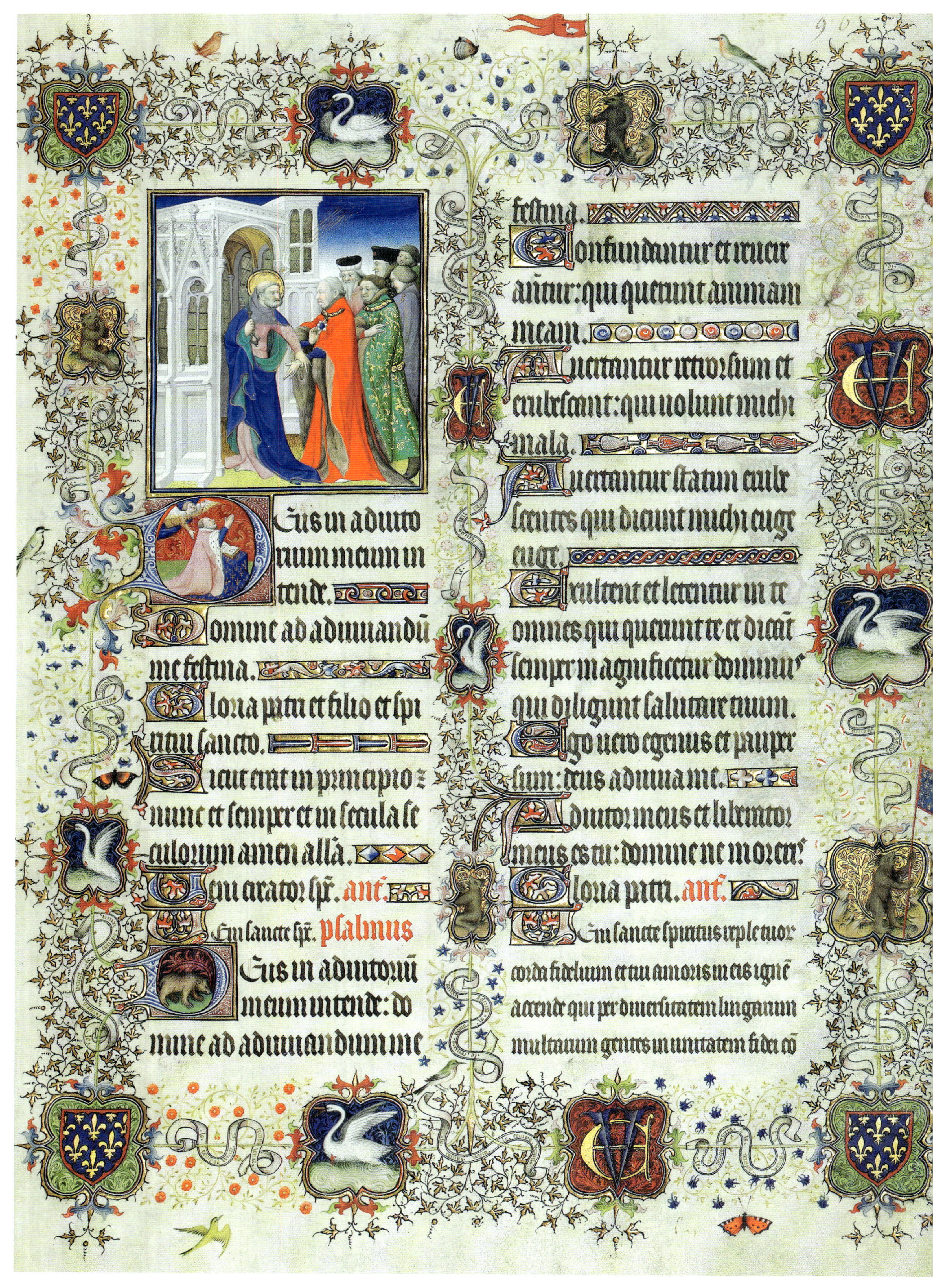

96

Deus in adiutorium meum intende.
Domine ad adiuuandū me festina.
Gloria patri et filio et spiritui sancto.
Sicut erat in principio et nunc et semper et in secula seculorum amen alla.
Veni creator sp̄s. ant.
Veni sancte sp̄s. psalmus
Deus in adiutoriū meum intende: domine ad adiuuandum me festina.
Confundantur et reuereantur: qui querunt animam meam.
Auertantur retrorsum et erubescant: qui volunt michi mala.
Auertantur statim erubescentes qui dicunt michi euge euge.
Exultent et letentur in te omnes qui querunt te et dicāt semper magnificetur dominus qui diligunt salutare tuum.
Ego vero egenus et pauper sum: deus adiuua me.
Adiutor meus et liberator meus es tu: domine ne moreris.
Gloria patri. ant.
Veni sancte spiritus reple tuorum corda fidelium et tui amoris in eis ignē accende qui per diuersitatem linguarum cunctarum gentes in unitatem fidei cō

arms, emblems (wounded swan and bear), and cipher (interlaced "VE" or "EV"), linked by scrolls bearing the motto "Le temps venra" (The time will come) (fig. 5). To these various elements, the illuminator of the evangeliary in the Sainte-Chapelle in Bourges added the helmet with its fleur-de-lis crest in the center of the upper border of the painting that opens the manuscript.

Dedication scenes and liturgical works are sometimes adorned with a portrait of the Duke of Berry, as in the manuscript of the *Très Belles Heures* in which Jacquemart de Hesdin depicted the duke praying before the Virgin and Child (fig. 6).[13] These images tell us about the duke's private devotion and his worship of Our Lady, but also of St. Andrew, whose feast day coincided with his birthday; the Pseudo-Jacquemart and the Mazarine Master painted him kneeling before St. Andrew in both the evangeliary (fig. 7) and lectionary (fig. 8) of the Sainte-Chapelle in Bourges.[14]

## THE CLASSIC COLLECTION OF THE LIBRARY, WITNESS TO TEXTUAL AND ARTISTIC EVOLUTIONS

Like every medieval princely library, Jean of Berry's library included a large section devoted to the *Biblica* and to liturgical and devotional books.

Fifteen bibles have survived, bearing witness to the evolution of the text during the Middle Ages. Among the Latin bibles, the *Biblia sacra* stands alongside the *Vulgate parisienne*, which brings together the text of St. Jerome and the glossary of Hebrew names by Étienne Langton. The Biblioteca Apostolica Vaticana holds a two-volume *Bible glosée* (Glossed bible) that the duke gave to Pope Clement VI before 1394.[15] The library contained eleven French bibles, including eight *Grandes Bibles historiales complétées*, a text composed in the first quarter of the fourteenth century by combining the *Bible historiale* by Guiart des Moulins and the thirteenth-century

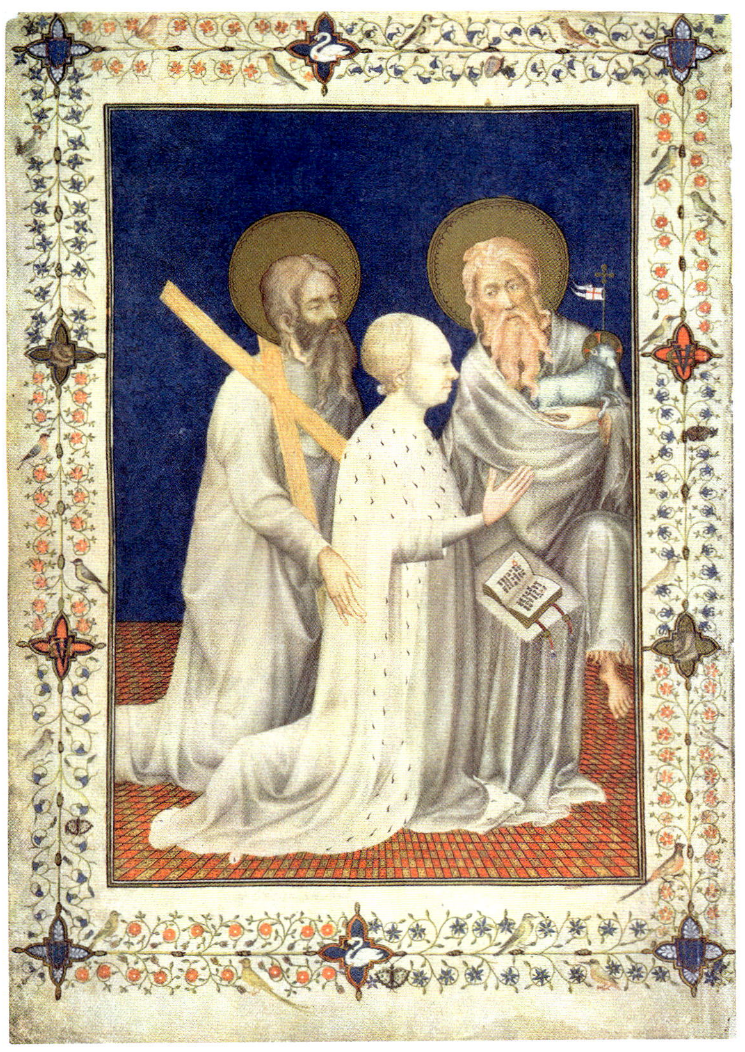

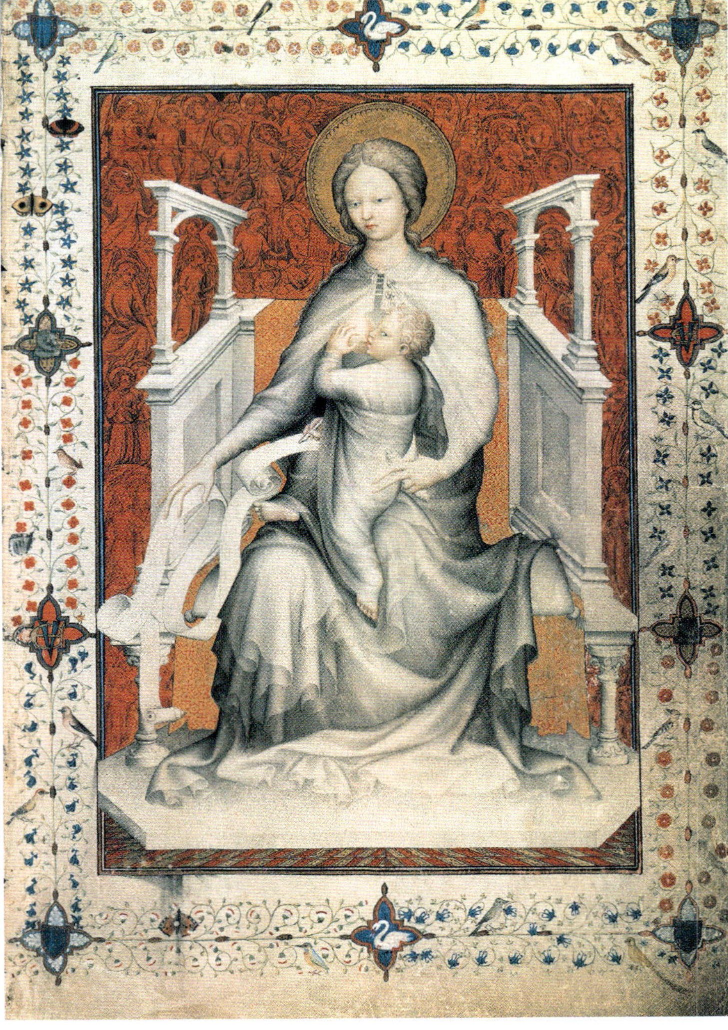

**Fig. 6** The Duke of Berry kneeling in prayer flanked by his patron saints on the left page, and the enthroned Virgin nursing the infant Jesus on the facing page, in Jacquemart de Hesdin, *Brussels Hours*, Paris, before 1402–03 (Brussels, Bibliothèque royale de Belgique, ms. 11060-61, pp. 10–11)

**Fig. 5** Borders containing the arms, emblems, cipher, and motto of Jean of Berry, in the *Grandes Heures du duc de Berry*. Paris (?), before 1409 (Paris, Bibliothèque nationale de France, département des Manuscrits, Latin 919, fol. 96)

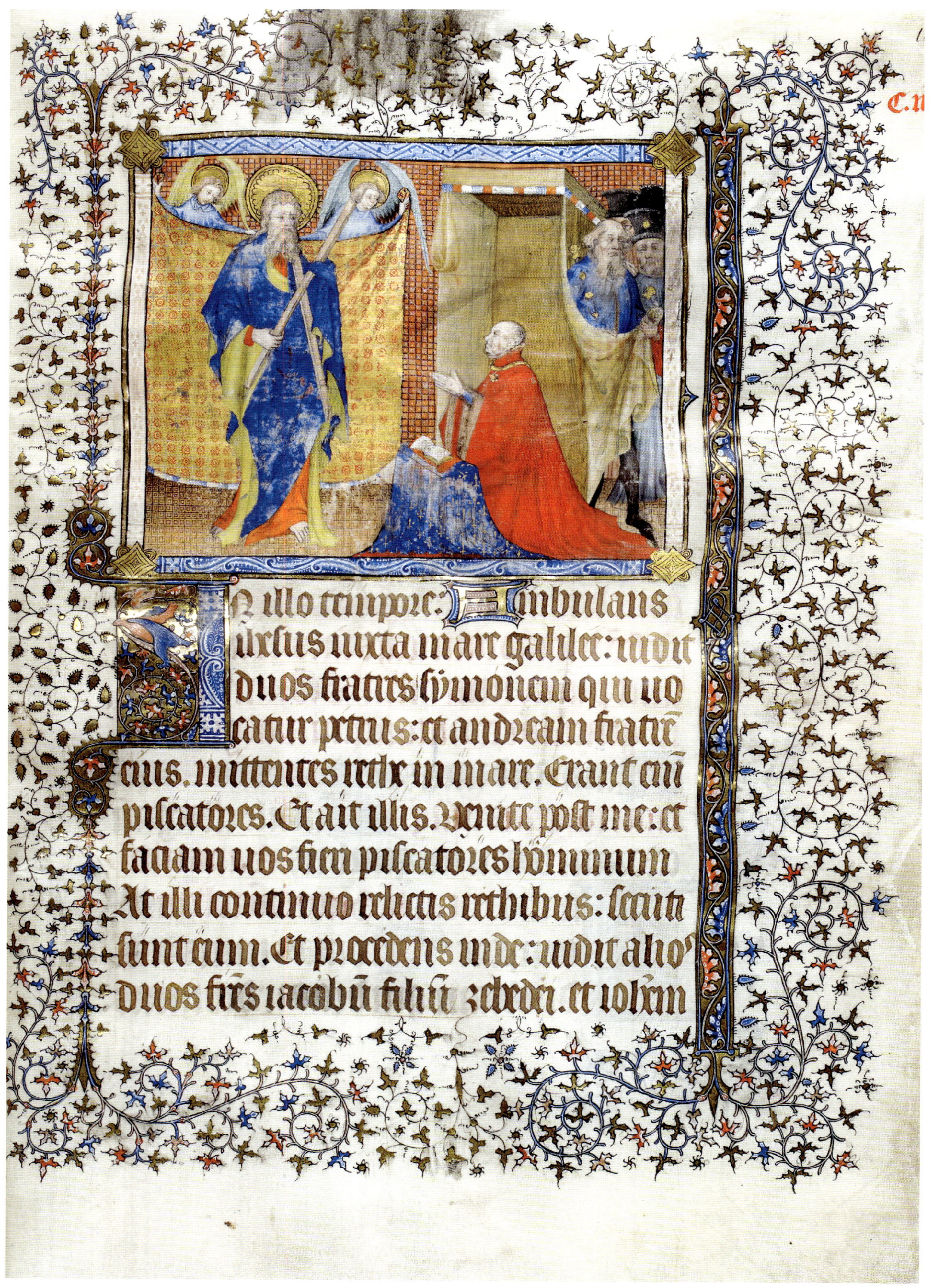

**Fig. 7** Pseudo-Jacquemart and the Mazarine Master, *Evangeliary of the Sainte-Chapelle in Bourges*, fol. 181, Paris, c. 1410, detail (Bourges, Bibliothèque municipale, ms. 48)

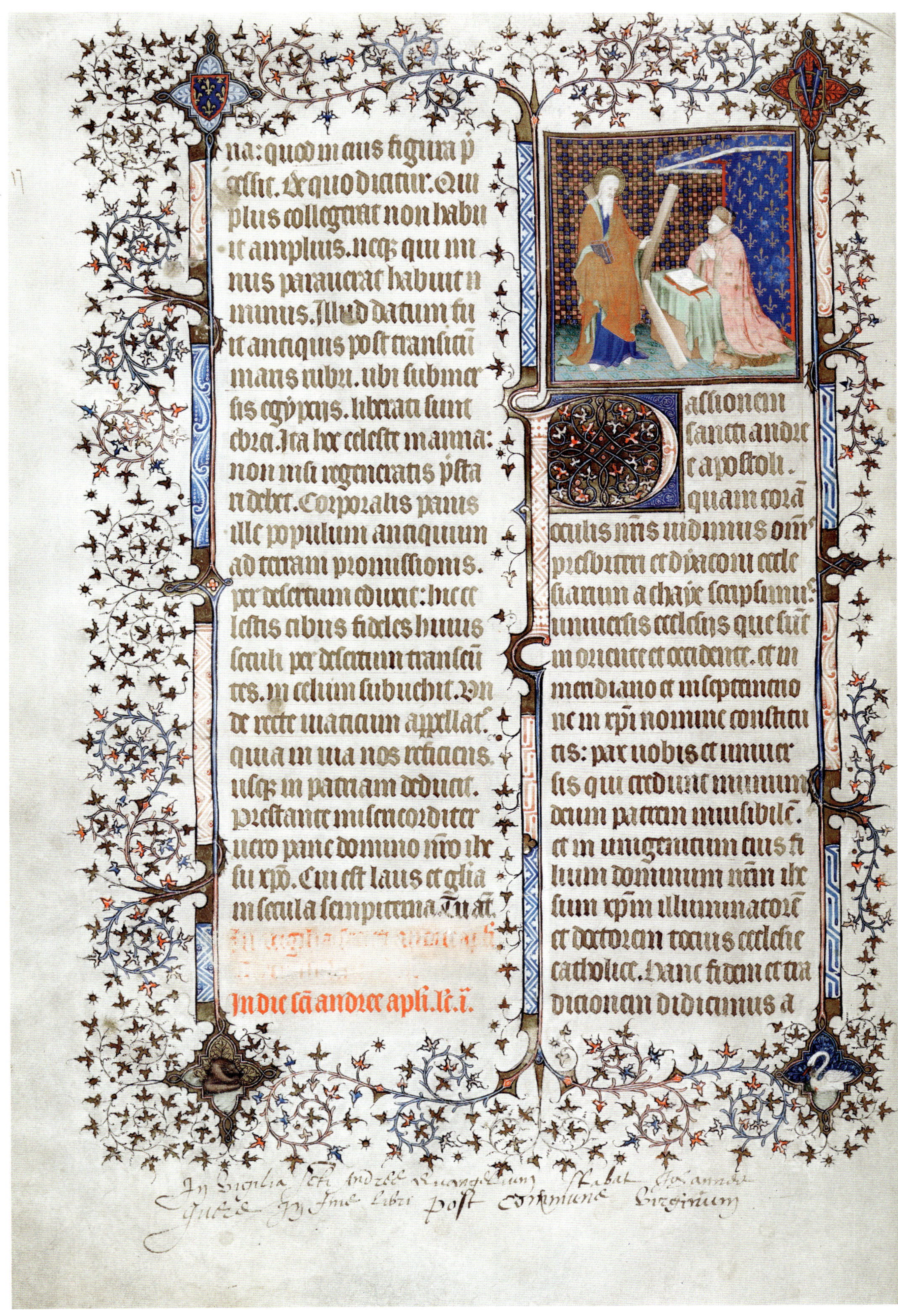

**Fig. 8** Pseudo-Jacquemart and the Mazarine Master, *Lectionary of the Sainte-Chapelle in Bourges*, fol. 17v, Paris, c. 1410, detail (Bourges, Bibliothèque municipale, ms. 35)

*Bible française* (French bible). One of the finest copies is undoubtedly the bible commissioned by the duke's chamberlain, Jean de Vaudetar, for King Charles V, borrowed by Louis I of Anjou, who gave it to the duke.[16] To complete his versions of the *Bible française*, Jean of Berry was given two royal bibles containing the latest translations commissioned by King Charles V from Raoul de Presles and the Dominican Jean de Sy.[17]

Among the liturgical books, twenty breviaries, twelve missals, and eighteen books of hours have been recorded in the libraries and inventories. The latter sometimes provide information on the richness of their illustrations: The *Petites Heures*[18] includes a "kalendrier très richement décoré" (very richly decorated calendar) and the *Heures* are "trés richement historiées en plusieurs lieux" (very richly historiated—that is, decorated with pictures—in several places). The manuscript of the *Très Riches Heures*, unfinished at the time of the Duke of Berry's death, was still in "cayers que faisoient Pol et ses frères, très richement historiez et enluminez" (gatherings that Paul and his brothers were making, very richly historiated and illuminated).[19]

According to Christine de Pizan, Jean of Berry liked fine books on moral and political science, Roman history, and didactic writings. The inventories list several "mirrors of princes" in French. The translation of Gilles de Rome's *De regimine principum* for Guillaume de Belesvoies stood alongside that by Jean Golein. Durand de Champagne's *Miroir des dames* (Mirror of Ladies) existed in two copies, now in the British Library and the Royal Library of Belgium.[20]

The books on history cover three main themes. Ancient history, a source of memorable examples, is represented by, among others, the *Histoire ancienne jusqu'à César* (Ancient History until Caesar) and the *Faits des Romains* (Exploits of the Romans). There was also Orosius's *History Against the Pagans* and Livy's *History of Rome* in Pierre Bersuire's translation. Jean of Berry had borrowed a manuscript of the *First Decade* from King Charles VI: a working copy by the translator, "escript de mauvaise lettre, mal enluminé et point historié" (badly written, poorly illuminated, and hardly historiated), according to the inventory of the library of the Louvre in 1380. Despite its lack of artistic refinement, it was undoubtedly chosen for its textual interest as the first state of the translation.[21] Similarly, as in the Louvre library, the collection also included the recent translation of Valerius Maximus's *Factorum et dictorum mirabilium libri novem*. This translation was begun for Charles V by Simon de Hesdin and, after the latter's death, continued by Nicolas de Gonesse for the duke.

The history of France is certainly illustrated by Froissart's *Chronicles*, but above all by the *Grandes Chroniques de France*, a vast historical compilation begun by Primat, a monk of Saint-Denis, later revised and expanded in the fourteenth century to include the deeds of the reigns of John the Good (Jean le Bon) and Charles V.[22] Jean of Berry owned six copies of this official history of the kingdom, which was intended to demonstrate the legitimacy of the French dynasty and assert royal power in the midst of the Hundred Years' War. Five of these copies have been identified; they make up a veritable anthology of the various writings, which, depending on the manuscript, conclude in 1350, 1379, or 1380.

The prince's interest in the government of the French kingdom during this period of turmoil was undoubtedly aroused by the manuscript of *La Prinse et mort du Roy Richart d'Angleterre*, which Jean de Montaigu had given him as a gift between September 1405 and January 1406.[23] Ownership of a universal chronicle entitled the *Chroniques de Burgos*, translated by the Carmelite Jean Golein, was linked to the political desire to enhance the glory of the kingdom through the history of the nations. Two copies were published in 1403 and 1407.[24]

Similarly, while Poitou was still being claimed by England, the duke commissioned Jean d'Arras to write the *Roman de Mélusine*, which, completed in 1394, allowed him to reassert his legitimacy over the county in his capacity as heir to the Lusignan family; although the inventories fail to mention the text by Jean d'Arras, they do cite two copies of the Latin chronicle that undoubtedly served as his source.[25]

Finally, the appeal of the East and plans for crusades and overseas travels are attested to by literature on the Holy Land and other Asian countries, as evidenced by two copies of Marco Polo's *Devisement du monde*.[26]

Unusually for a princely library, however, Arthurian novels and *chansons de gestes* (a type of epic poem) are rare: a single manuscript of the *Cycle du Graal* (The Grail Cycle), Wace's *Roman de Brut*, and a single *chanson de geste*, *Les quatre fils Aymon* (The Four Sons of Aymon). Courtly literature is mainly illustrated by the *Roman de la Rose*, mentioned four times; three volumes have been found. Manuscripts of the *Ovide moralisé* (Moralized Ovid) and poems by Guillaume de Machaut can be counted among the lyrical or allegorical works.

## A MODERN COLLECTION: CONTEMPORARY TRANSLATORS AND AUTHORS AND HUMANISM

Translations and treatises highlight the emergence of new models of rationality, among others through the works of Aristotle, present in the library in the French version by Nicole Oresme. Among the translations commissioned by King Charles V are three copies of the *Livre des Proprietés des choses* (On the Properties of Things) by Bartholomew the Englishman, translated by Jean Corbechon. Two of them are illustrated by the Virgil Master, the third by the Boucicaut Master. The duke owned seven copies of St. Augustine's *The City of God*, in the translation by Raoul de Presles.

The collection contains few purely scientific works, with the exception of four copies of Nicole Oresme's *Traité de la Sphère* (Treatise of the Sphere), Gossuin de Metz's *L'Image du monde* (The Image of the World), and two volumes of Galen's works donated to the Sainte-Chapelle in Bourges. There are no works on mathematics, so highly prized by King Charles V, but the duke had a keen interest in astronomy, astrology, and magic. The Morgan Library holds a manuscript of Abū Ma'shar's *Introduction to Astrology*.[27] Several books on divination and magic are mentioned in the inventories.

Among the Parisian humanists close to Jean of Berry we find Gontier Col, diplomatic adviser to King Charles VI, Laurent de Premierfait, the author of many translations, and Jean Lebègue, the clerk of the "Chambre des Comptes" (Court of Accounts). Their commitment to the production of illuminated manuscripts of ancient authors and contemporary Italian literature is particularly evident in the duke's library.[28] The most famous example is probably *Térence des ducs*, a

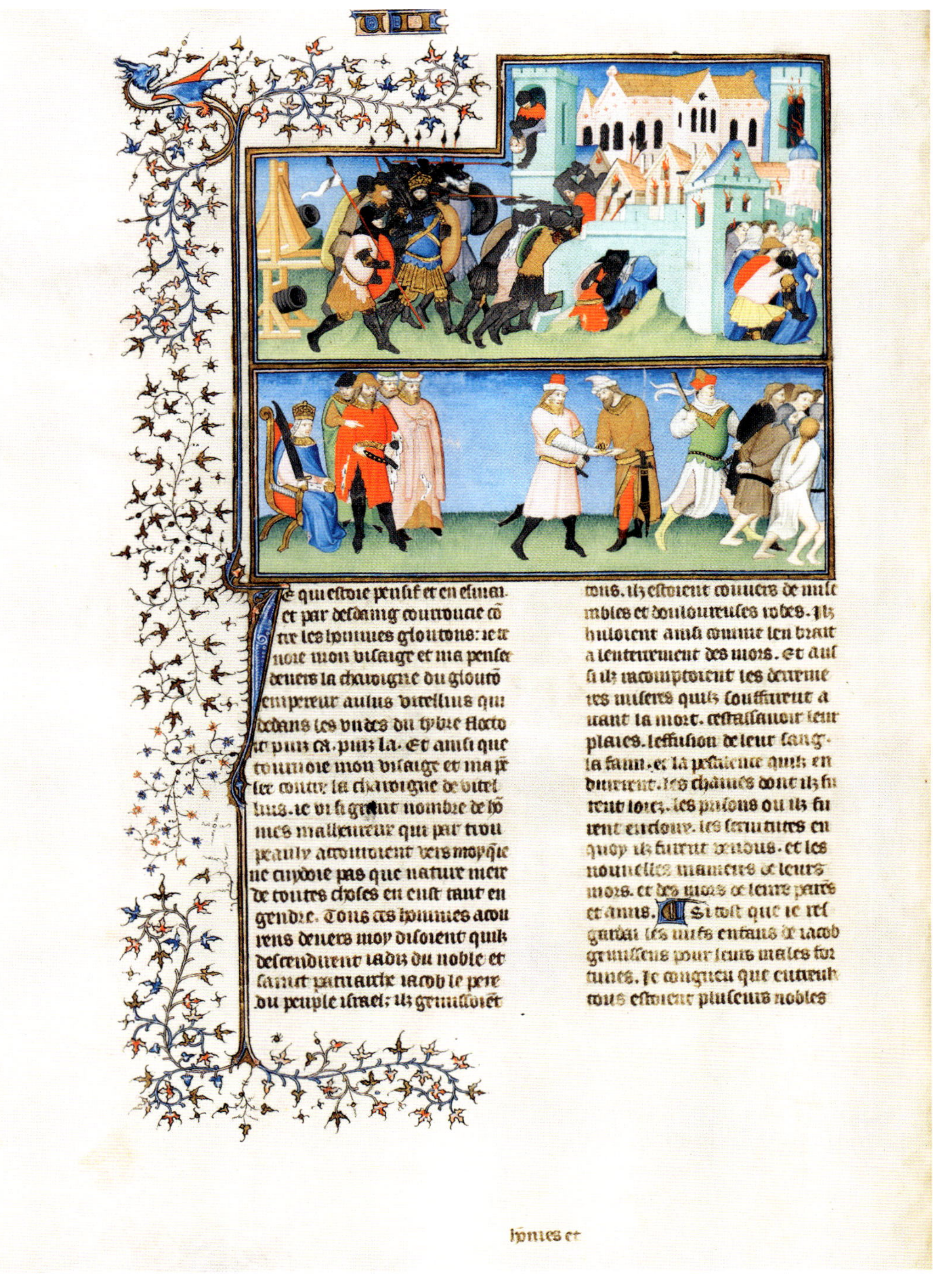

**Fig. 9** Luçon Master, *The Destruction of Jerusalem*, in Boccaccio, *Cas des nobles hommes et femmes*. Paris, April 15, 1409 and January 1411 (Genève, Bibliothèque de Genève, ms. 190/2, fol. 96v)

collection of comedies by Terence, produced around 1411 and superbly decorated with 132 illuminations executed by four hands.[29] The translation of *De amicitia* begun by Laurent de Premierfait for Louis de Bourbon around 1405–06 was dedicated to Jean of Berry; the original manuscript has not survived.

The Duke of Berry owned Petrarch's *Remedies for Fortune Fair and Foul*, probably in the translation by Jean Daudin produced for Charles V before April 1378. A new translation of Boccaccio's *De casibus virorum illustrium* was undertaken by Laurent de Premierfait in 1409–10 and dedicated to the duke. A luxurious copy, illustrated by the Luçon Master with the assistance of the Master of the Térence des ducs, was presented to him as a New Year's Day gift in January 1411 (fig. 9).[30]

Between 1403 and 1414, ten copies of Christine de Pizan's poetic, moral, and didactic works were added to the library. The movements of the books recorded in the inventory of 1413 seem to indicate that the author offered them almost immediately to her patron. The presentation at the Hôtel de Nesle on March 20, 1403, of the *Chemin de long estude* (The Book of the Path of the Long Study), begun in October 1402, indicates that the work was finished on that date. The *Mutacion de Fortune* (Book of the Mutability of Fortune), completed in November 1403, was presented to the prince in March 1404. The *Livre des fais et bonnes meurs du sage roy Charles V* (Book of the Deeds and Good Practices of King Charles V the Wise), composed at the request of Philip the Bold between January 1 and November 30, 1404, was presented to him as a New Year's Day gift on January 1, 1405. On January 1, 1410, he received the *Sept psaumes allégorisés* (Seven Psalms, Allegorized), begun on June 26, 1409. The library held four copies of the *Roman de la Rose*, and Jean of Berry was not left unmoved by the dispute that opposed Christine de Pizan and Jean Gerson to the humanists Jean de Montreuil and the Col brothers, Gontier and Pierre, since a copy of the *Débat sur le Roman de la Rose* (Debate on the Roman de la Rose) has been identified in the Bancroft Library in Berkeley.[31]

## A WELL-INFORMED BIBLIOPHILE

A reading of the inventories reveals the care with which the library was built up. Although Jean of Berry entrusted his books to the care of Guillaume de Ruilly and then Robinet d'Étampes, he monitored the expansion of his collections closely. In addition to his calling on the services of prestigious artists, three points are worth highlighting: the connection with Italy, the search for specific texts, and the acquisition of royal manuscripts by means of donations or loans.

Italian manuscripts were acquired early on: the so-called *Girona Bible*, produced in Bologna between 1281 and 1289, was "borrowed" from King Charles V on March 6, 1384.[32] Twelve works in the 1401–03 inventory are said to be written in "lettre boulonnoise" (Bolognese script) or "lombarde" (Lombard script) and some are decorated with "ouvrages roumains" (Romanesque ornamentation). This enthusiasm for manuscripts from Naples or Northern Italy can be explained by the political climate of the time and Jean of Berry's family ties with the dukes of Milan, as evidenced by the presence in the library of a copy of the works of Seneca, known as the *Sénèque des ducs*. Produced in Northern Italy, the manuscript was a diplomatic gift made in March 1402 to Jean of Berry by his brother-in-law, Jean Galéas Visconti, who was anxious to obtain the support of the duke and the neutrality of France in his campaign against Rupert of the Palatinate. It is now divided into two parts, the first containing Seneca's philosophical works,[33] the second his tragedies.[34] The decoration has been attributed to two artists, one of whom illuminated a book by Petrarch that belonged to the duke of Milan's chancellor. In the historiated letter introducing the first tragedy, *Hercules furens*, the second (anonymous) artist depicted the philosopher in a half-body pose, teaching with a book in his hand. The framing vignettes, ornamented with birds and drolleries, bear witness to the Parisian influence on the secondary decoration (fig. 10). Among the Neapolitan works is the so-called *Anjou Bible*, illuminated by the painter Cristophoro Orimina (active 1335–60) and his workshop,[35] and the copy of *Histoire ancienne jusqu'à* César, now in the British Library.[36]

The humanist duke was interested in contemporary authors and artists, but he did not hesitate to seek out older versions to add to his collections. The oldest manuscript in the library identified to date is a bilingual psalter[37] composed in England in the second quarter of the eleventh century and donated to the Sainte-Chapelle in Bourges in 1405; the Latin text and the Anglo-Saxon translation stand side by side, illustrated with thirteen pen and ink drawings. A psalter by Thomas of Canterbury is also mentioned, described as "bien ancient" (very old). In July 1403, a copy of the *Sentences*, dating from the third quarter of the twelfth century, was added to Jean Lombard's *Commentaires sur les Psaumes* (Commentaries on the Psalms). The *Épîtres glosées de saint Paul*[38] (Glossed Epistles of St. Paul) is typical of academic output in the thirteenth century. A book of hours entitled *Heures à l'usage d'Angleterre* (Hours for Use in England) was decorated by Master Honoré before 1293. The library did not include a chronicle by Guillaume de Nangis, so, wishing to show the manuscript to Emperor Sigismund of Luxembourg in 1416 and also to have it copied, the duke borrowed it from the abbey of Saint-Denis.[39] Decorated with superb zoomorphic hybrid initials, the *Livre des profits ruraux* (Book of Rural Profit) by Pierre de Crescens is one of the earliest copies of the text, composed between 1305 and 1309 for Charles II of Anjou.[40] Many unilluminated volumes bear witness to the duke's interest in texts. The *Dialogues* of Gregory the Great, now in the Royal Library of Belgium,[41] only contains a historiated initial at the beginning of the volume. A single scene in a lower border adorns the copy of Galen's *Oeuvres*, copied between 1320 and 1340 in southern France.[42]

The search for exceptional pieces is evident in the choice of royal manuscripts, most of which were illuminated by renowned artists. Among the twenty works from the library of Charles V and Charles VI, the *Book of Hours of Jeanne d'Évreux*[43] and her *Bréviaire*[44] stand out, decorated with grisaille paintings attributed to Jean Pucelle. The Parisian artist was highly regarded by the duke, whose collection included three other manuscripts decorated by the painter from the royal library: the *Belleville Breviary*, the *Miracles of Notre-Dame* by Gautier de Coinci, and the *Savoy Hours*. In *the Grande Bible historiale complétée* from the Arsenal and Hamburg, we can perceive the hand of artists close to the court: Jean Le Noir, a disciple of Pucelle, the Master of the *Bible of Jean de Sy, and* the Master of the *Coronation of Charles VI*. It is to these artists, and the Master of the Coronation Book of Charles V, that we owe the decoration of the very fine copy of The City of God, one volume of which is kept in Angers and the other at Harvard College.[45]

## CALLING ON PRESTIGIOUS ARTISTS

As a patron, Jean of Berry surrounded himself with prestigious illuminators, who sometimes took their names from the illustration of ducal manuscripts. It is to the Master of the Berry Apocalypse that we owe the iconographic cycle of the *Expositio super septem visiones Libri Apocalypsis*, and to the Master of Berry's Cleres Femmes that we owe the decoration of manuscript Français 598 held in the Bibliothèque nationale de France. The painter of manuscript Français 12595 in the Bibliothèque nationale is known as the Master of Berry's second *Roman de la Rose*. The Master of Flavius Josephus and the Orosius Master worked on the Bibliothèque nationale manuscripts Français 247 and Français 301, respectively.

The inventories specify that the psalter, "escript en latin et françoys, tres richement enluminé" (written in Latin and French, very richly illuminated), was by André Beauneveu, who was appointed "surintendant de toute peinture et de sculpture" (superintendent of all painting and sculpture) to the Duke of Berry from 1386. He is also credited with the grisaille diptych of the *Très Belles Heures* in the Royal Library of Belgium

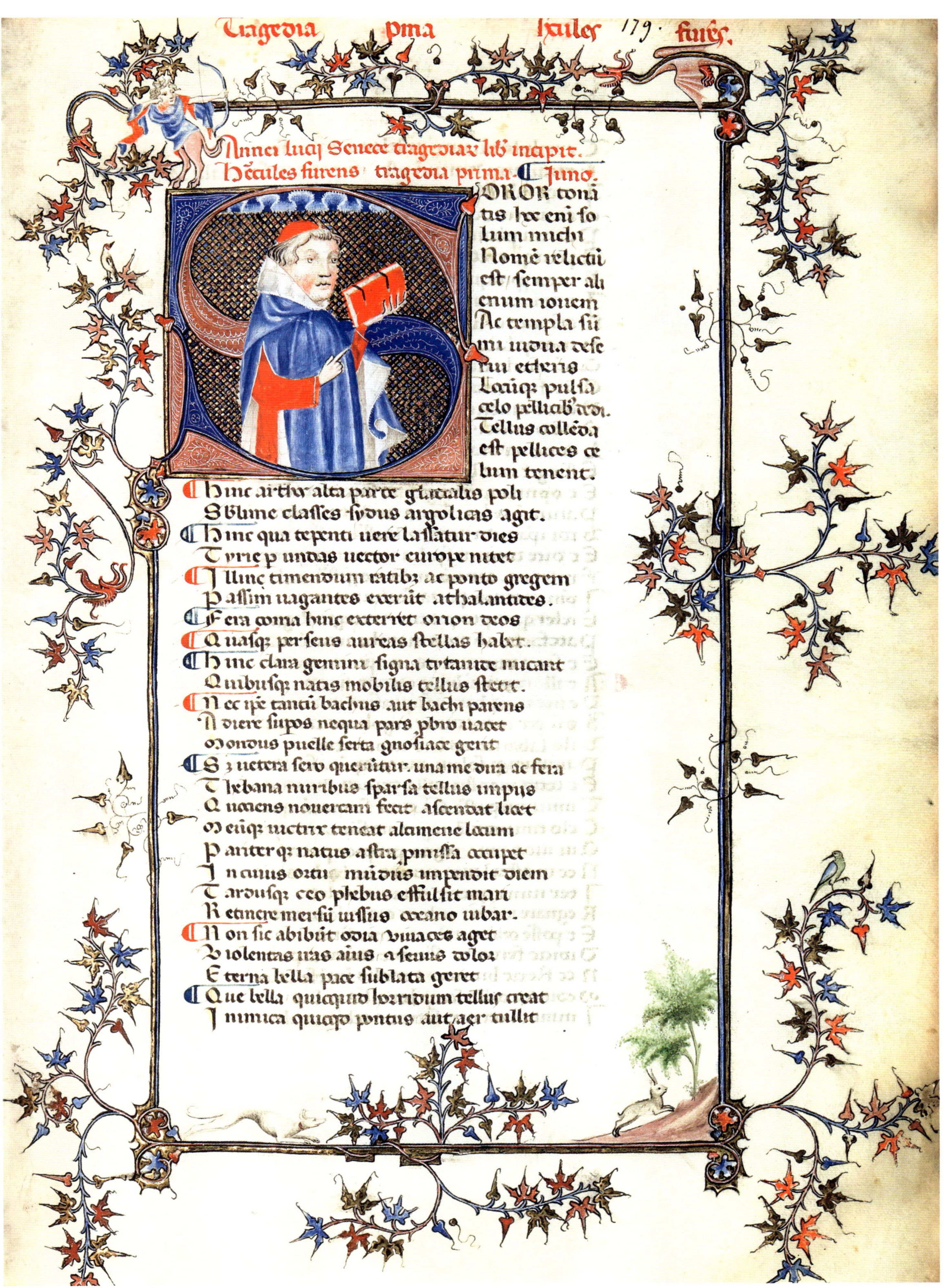

**Fig. 10** Anonymous Italian artist, painting of Seneca introducing the tragedy *Hercules furens*, in Seneca, *Tragedies*, fol. 179. Northern Italy (Pavia?), c. 1390 (Paris, Bibliothèque nationale de France, département des Manuscrits, Latin 8055)

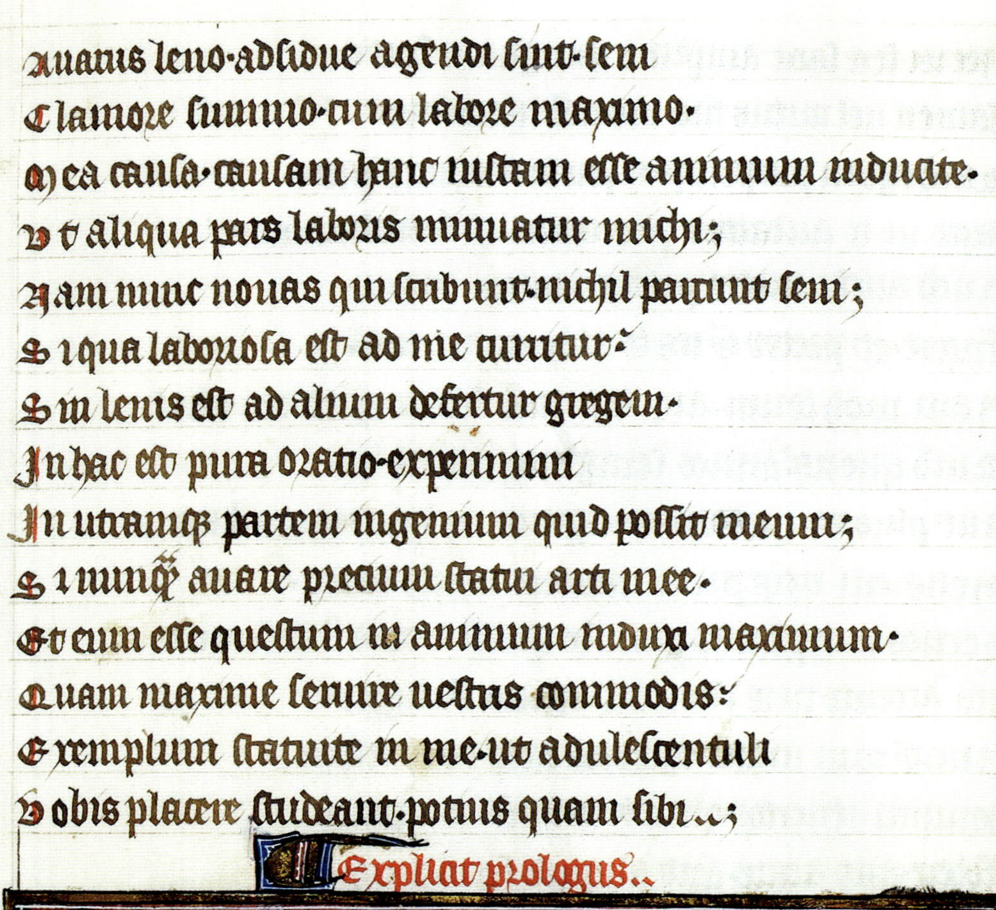

Auarus leno · adsidue agendi sunt · seni
Clamore summo · cum labore maximo ·
Mea causa · causam hanc iustam esse animum inducite ·
Vt aliqua pars laboris minuatur michi;
Nam nunc nouas qui scribunt · nichil parcunt seni;
Si qua laboriosa est ad me curritur ·
Si lenis est ad alium defertur gregem ·
In hac est pura oratio · experimini
In utramque partem ingenium quid possit meum;
Si numquam auare precium statui arti mee ·
Et eum esse questum in animum induxi maximum ·
Quam maxime seruire uestris commodis:
Exemplum statuite in me · ut adulescentuli
Vobis placere studeant · potius quam sibi ..;

Expliat prologus ..

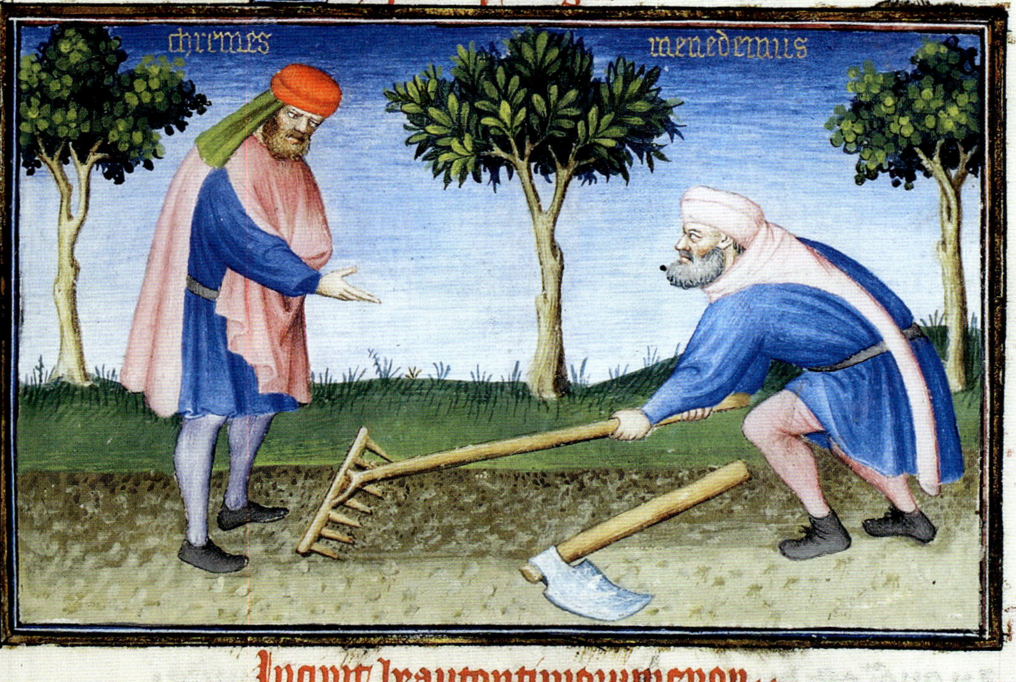


Incipit heautontimorumenon ..

Chre. Quamquam hec inter nos nuper notitia admodum est:
Inde adeo quod agrum in proximo hic mercatus es ·

**Fig. 11** The Orosius Master, painting introducing the comedy *Heautontimoroumenos*, in Terence, *Comedies*, fol. 52. Paris, c. 1407 (Paris, Bibliothèque nationale de France, département des Manuscrits, Latin 7907A)

in Brussels. The style of the Virgil Master, who was employed by the duke between 1390 and 1410, is recognizable in at least eight manuscripts in the collection.

The names of the Mazarine Master, the Egerton Master, and the Orosius Master, who worked on four other books in the library, including a second copy of the comedies of Terence (fig. 11),[46] recur for manuscripts composed in the first decade of the fifteenth century. Another artist commissioned by illustrious patrons was the Bedford Master, who worked on the decoration of Marco Polo's *Livre des merveilles*[47] (Book of the Marvels of the World) and the *Grandes Heures du duc de Berry*.[48]

Was it the Abbot of Bruges, Lubert Hautschild, with whom Jean of Berry exchanged manuscripts, or Philip of Burgundy who introduced the duke to the Flemish artistic movement? The movement is evident mainly in the books of hours. The last years of the fourteenth century and the first decade of the fifteenth were marked by the presence of Jacquemart de Hesdin, who worked in Bourges from 1384 to 1413: He succeeded Jean Le Noir in decorating the *Petites Heures*, before they were completed by Johan van Lymborch after 1410, and executed the full-page paintings of the *Très Belles Heures* preserved in Brussels. He was often assisted by the Pseudo-Jacquemart. The latter was involved in the second part of the *Très Belles Heures de Notre-Dame*, known as the *Turin-Milan Hours*, now partly lost. Six miniatures from the *Psautier à l'usage de Bourges* (Psalter for Use in Bourges)[49] are attributed to him. Such works were covered with precious bindings; the inventories describe silk covers, silver or gold clasps embellished with enamels and gems, and precious metal pipes trimmed with tassels, pearls, and gems.

It was in 1404, when their patron the Duke of Burgundy died, that the brothers Herman, Paul, and Johan van Lymborch, nephews of the painter Johan Maelwael, entered the service of Jean of Berry. A year later, they were already entrusted with the illustration of the *Belles Heures* manuscript, decorated with 172 illuminations and now in The Metropolitan Museum. After 1410, Johan completed the decoration of the *Petites Heures*. Between 1412 and 1416, Paul and Johan contributed to the illustration of the *Très Belles Heures de Notre-Dame*.[50] Their emblematic work remains the *Très Riches Heures du duc de Berry*.

Gifted with a unique talent for finding rare artefacts, the Duke of Berry built up a prestigious, eclectic, and learned collection. In addition to his patronage of the greatest artists and authors of his time, his knowledge of texts, his taste for *belles-lettres*, his interest in Italian artists and the early humanists, and his pursuit of choice items in royal or princely collections all made the library into a place of excellence, a harmonious marriage of luxury and learning.

1 Barrois 1830.
2 Sometimes divided up and spread over different institutions.
3 For a general presentation of the Duke of Berry's library, see Guiffrey 1894–96, I, CXL–CLXXXIV; Robin 2008.
4 Paris, BnF, Ms. Français 11496.
5 Guiffrey 1894–96, II, 1–166. Guiffrey assigned class mark B to the items in this inventory. See also the general catalogue drawn up on the basis of all the inventories by Delisle 1868–81, III, 170–194, and Delisle 1907, II, 219–326: 297 titles are listed.
6 Paris, AN, KK 258.
7 Guiffrey 1894–96, I, 1–336 (class mark A). On this inventory, see Meiss and Off 1971.
8 Ibid., II, 205–91 (class mark SG), and Hiver de Beauvoir 1860.
9 Paris, BnF, Ms. NAF 1363, fol. 14–18v (inventory of jewels and books delivered to the Sainte-Chapelle in Bourges) and BnF, Ms. Latin 17173, fol. 228–229v (receipt for books delivered to Arnoul Belin on July 5, 1406). Guiffrey 1894–96, II, 167–186; Rabel 2004, 154–171: list of "livres de la Sainte-Chapelle de Bourges provenant de Jean de Berry" (books from the Sainte-Chapelle in Bourges coming from Jean of Berry), 168–71.
10 For a chronology of the library's growth, see Meiss and Off 1971.
11 Paris, BnF, Biblio. de l'Arsenal, Ms. 5212.
12 Paris, BnF, Ms. Latin 919.
13 Brussels, KBR, Ms. 11060-61, page 14.
14 Evangeliary: Bourges, BM, Ms. 48, fol. 181. Lectionary: Bourges, BM, Ms. 35, fol. 17v. See also the portrait of the duke between St. Andrew and St. John the Baptist in the *Très Belles Heures* or *Heures de Bruxelles*, Brussels, KBR, Ms. 11060-61, page 10.
15 Vatican City, BAV, Ms. Vat. Lat. 50–51.
16 The Hague, Museum Meermanno-Westreenianum, Ms. 10 B. 23.
17 London, BL, Ms. Lansdowne 1175; Paris, BnF, Ms. Français 15397. On the *Bible française*, see Berger 1884 and *DLF* 1994, 179–96.
18 Paris, BnF, Ms. Latin 18014.
19 Paris, BSG, Ms. 841 (inv. 1416), art. 1164. The manuscript, not yet bound, was valued at 500 livres tournois.
20 London, BL, Ms. Add. 29986; Brussels, KBR, Ms. 9555-58.
21 Oxford, Bodl. Library, Ms. Rawlinson C 477. See Tesnière 2000.
22 On the *Grandes chroniques de France*, see Hedeman 1991; Brix 2024.
23 On the manuscript, see Hedeman 2011.
24 Inventory of 1413: A 913 and A 955. The latter item has been identified with the London manuscript, BL, Ms. Royal 19 E VI. See Aubert 2014 and 2015.
25 Inventory of 1413: A 980 and A 981.
26 Paris, BnF, Ms. Français 2810 and Ms. Français 5631.
27 New York, Morgan Library, Ms. 785.
28 See Hedeman 2022.
29 Paris, BnF, Bibl. de l'Arsenal, Ms. 664.
30 Geneva, BGE, Ms. Fr. 190/2.
31 Berkeley, Bancroft Library, Ms. UCB 109.
32 Girona, Arxiu Capitular de la Catedral, Ms. 6.
33 Paris, BnF, Ms. Latin 8717.
34 Paris, BnF, Ms. Latin 8055, pages 179–456.
35 Leuven, KU, Maurits Sabbe Library, Ms. 1. On this manuscript, see Watteeuw and Van der Stock 2010.
36 London, BL, Ms. Royal 20 D I.
37 Paris, BnF, Ms. Latin 8824.
38 Bourges, BM, Ms. 124.
39 London, BL, Ms. Royal 13 E IV.
40 Paris, BnF, Ms. Latin 9328.
41 Brussels, KBR, Ms. 9553.
42 Bourges, BM, Ms. 299, fol. 50v.
43 New York, Met, The Cloisters, Ms. Acc. 54.1.2.
44 Chantilly, Bibl. du musée Condé, Ms. 51.
45 Angers, BM, Ms. fr. 162; Cambridge, Harvard College Library, Hofer Collection, Ms. Typ. 201.
46 Paris, BnF, Ms. Latin 7907 A.
47 Paris, BnF, Ms. Français 2810.
48 Paris, BnF, Ms. Latin 919.
49 Paris, BnF, Ms. Français 13091.
50 Paris, BnF, Ms. NAL 3093.

**Fig. 12** Following pages: Van Lymborgh brothers, *Très Riches Heures*, fol. 38v: The Visitation, detail

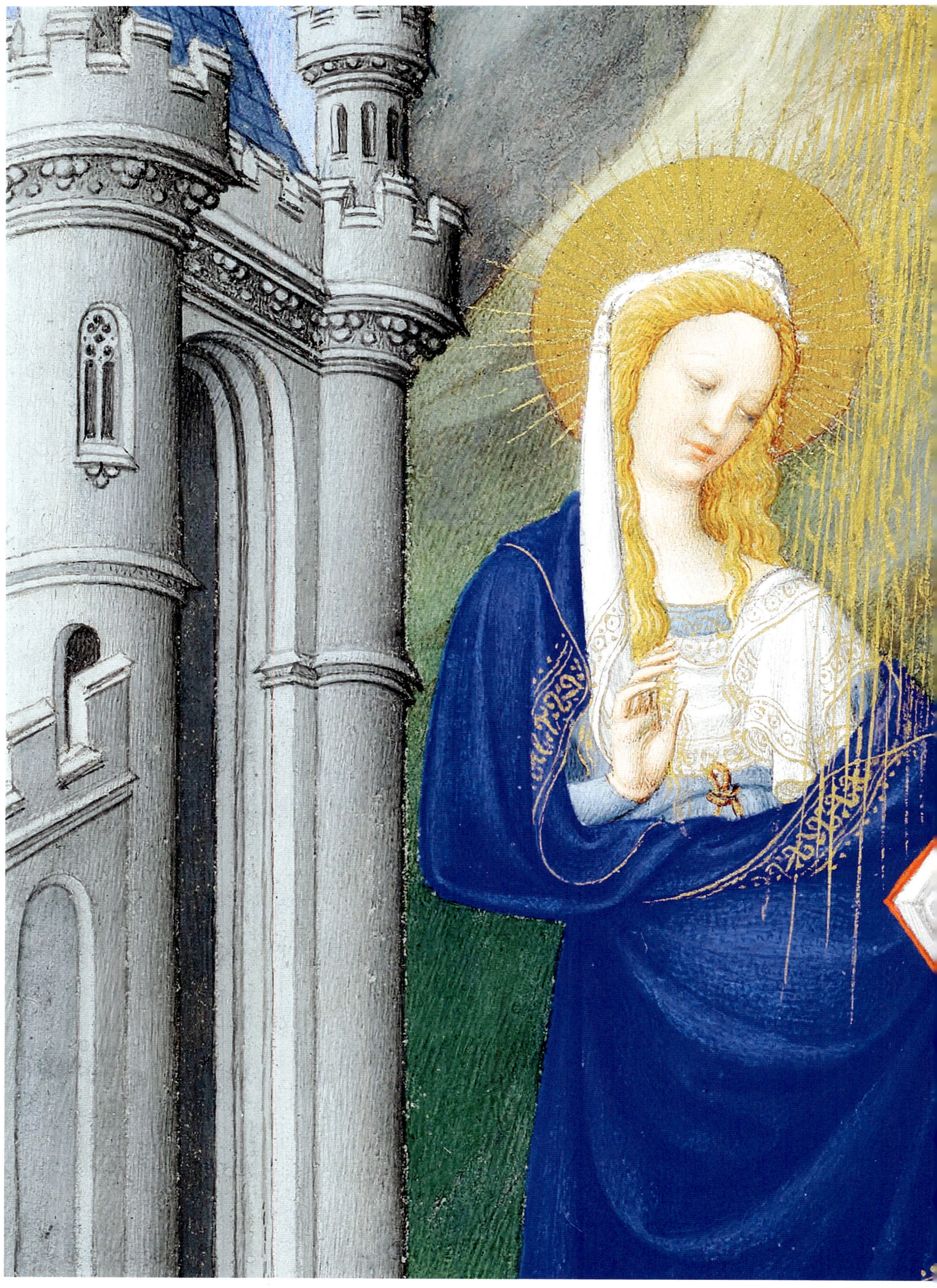

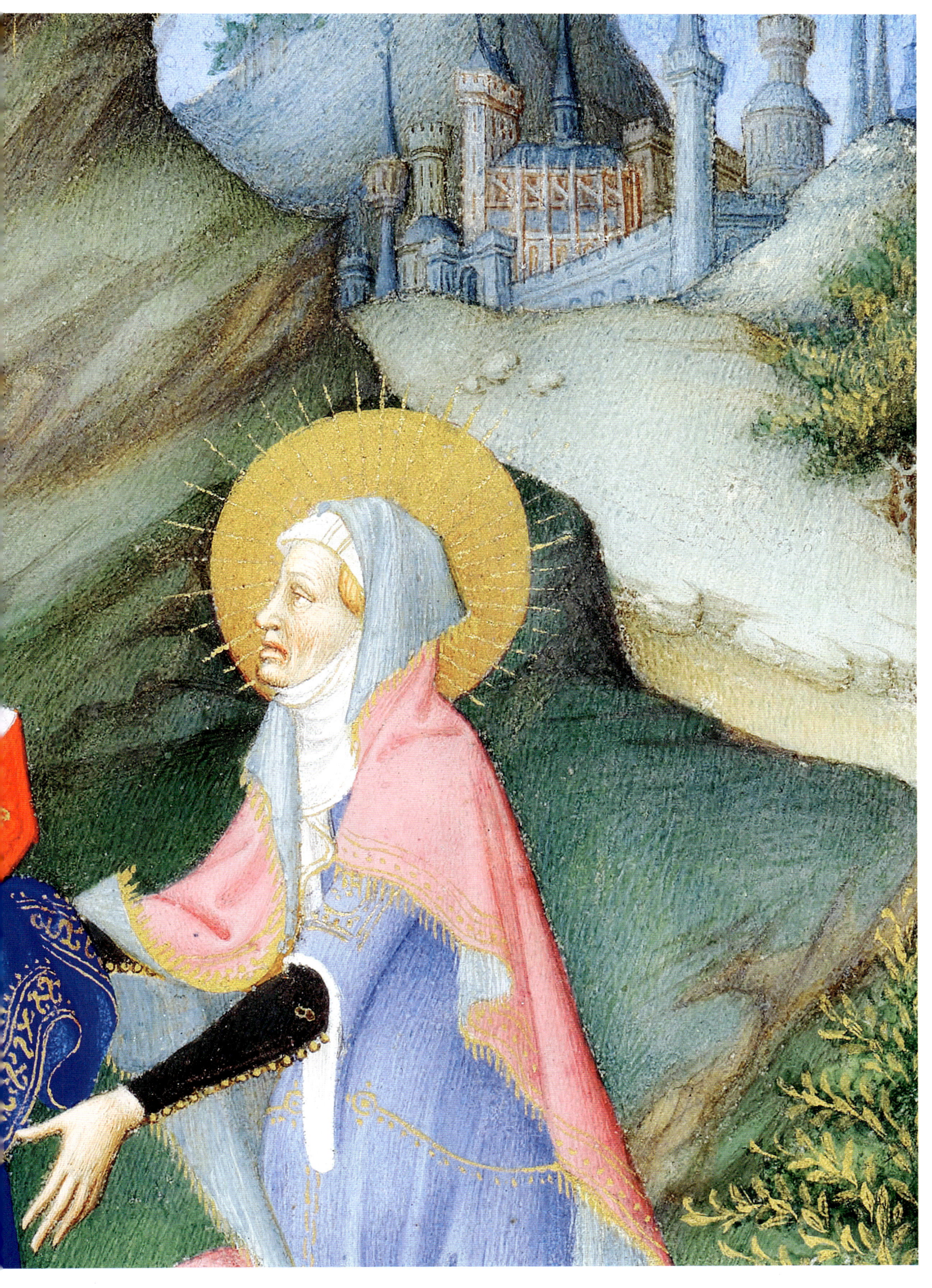

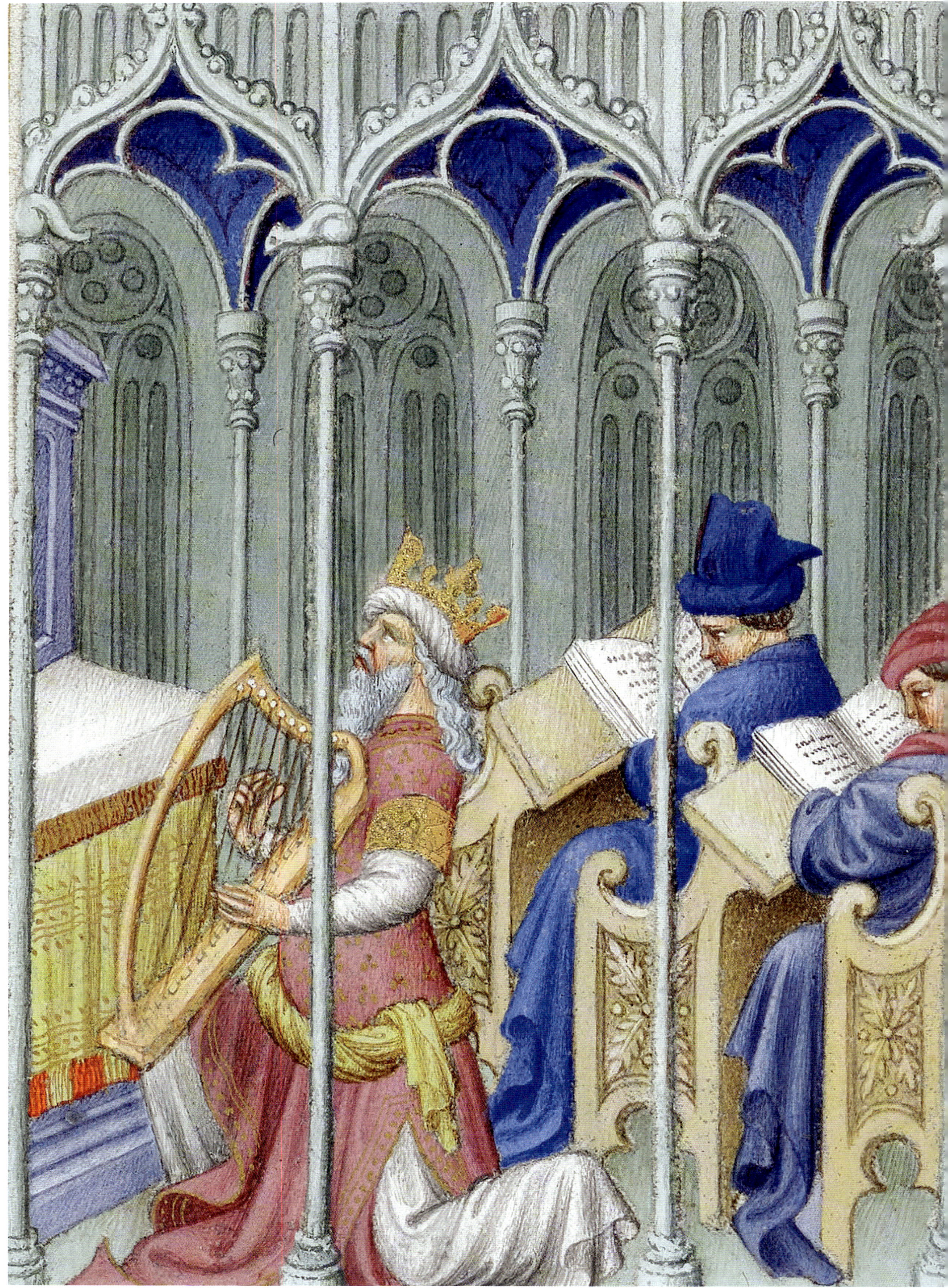

6.

# Devotion and Pleasure: The Duke of Berry's Books of Hours

Marie-Pierre Dion

The books of hours are the "monuments that give the most accurate idea of Jean of Berry's tastes and sense of luxury," wrote Léopold Delisle. Eighteen books of hours, to which we must add six psalters and thirteen breviaries, represent an extraordinary scale. Although these books have lost their ornate bindings, they have stood the test of time better than other treasures, and today they make up the most celebrated part of the Duke of Berry's collections. Among them, six books of hours commissioned by the duke himself stand out more for their quality than for their quantity. These are works of art that the most talented illuminators took turns working on for many years under the prince's direction. They have been the subject of extensive monographs and facsimiles, and have been placed all the more easily in the wider context of the Duke of Berry's artistic patronage because they are described in the same inventories as the other treasures and their illuminations sometimes mirror them.[1] Another approach to the books of hours in the context of the princely library or of the subset made up by the spiritual books was outlined first by Léopold Delisle, and then by Millard Meiss.[2] It shows the attention paid by the prince to texts and the breadth of the fields of knowledge put to use for the prayer books.

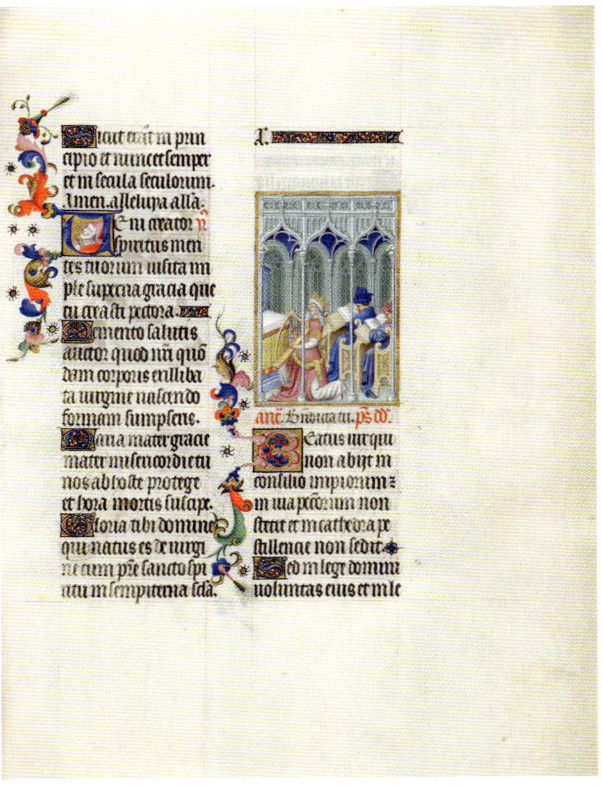

**Fig. 2** Van Lymborch brothers, *Très Riches Heures*, fol. 45: The Two Ways (Psalm 1): David kneels with his harp and sings a psalm while the faithful read their psalter

**Fig. 1** Van Lymborch brothers, *Très Riches Heures*, fol. 45: The Two Ways (Psalm 1), detail

## THE PRINCE'S PIETY

The *Très Riches Heures* opens with a feast presided over by the Duke of Berry. This may have raised doubts about the latter's devotion, which, however, was very real if we measure it by the number of representations of the duke at prayer across his books of hours. Christian ideals, the hope of an afterlife, and the anticipation of Christ's return as the Redeemer permeated everyday life, society, and knowledge in the medieval West. Members of the royal family played an important role in religious practices (fig. 2). They built chapels, founded chapters, donated relics and liturgical ornaments, promoted certain forms of devotion, and commissioned perpetual masses. The Duke of Berry, who distinguished himself by his Saintes-Chapelles and his passion for relics, spent a lot of time at prayer every day, surrounded by chaplains and confessors, most of them Dominicans, who advised him.[3] He had to show that the power he held by God's will placed him in line with the kings of France and St. Louis. "Always animated by an ardent devotion to the service of God, he kept in his house a large number of chaplains, who sang aloud, day and night, the praises of the Lord and celebrated mass, and he was sure to compliment them whenever the service had lasted longer and been held with more pomp than usual."[4] (fig. 3)

In such a context, it was traditional in royal and princely circles to own psalters, breviaries, and, from the late thirteenth century, books of hours, sumptuously illuminated *objets d'art* "historiated" with miniatures, bound in brocade or embroidered silk, and decorated with precious stones and armorial clasps. As devotion to the Virgin Mary grew, the books of hours were articulated around the Little Office of the Virgin to give the laity access to the standard texts of the liturgy of the canonical hours (fig. 4). Beyond reading such works, the making of a book of hours was itself an act of piety aimed at securing the benevolence of heaven.[5] For high-ranking figures, the large number of books of hours is the rule. Valentina Visconti, the Duke of Berry's sister-in-law, brought six of them from Italy. This is just one example of the luxury that surrounded the princes in the last years of the Middle Ages.

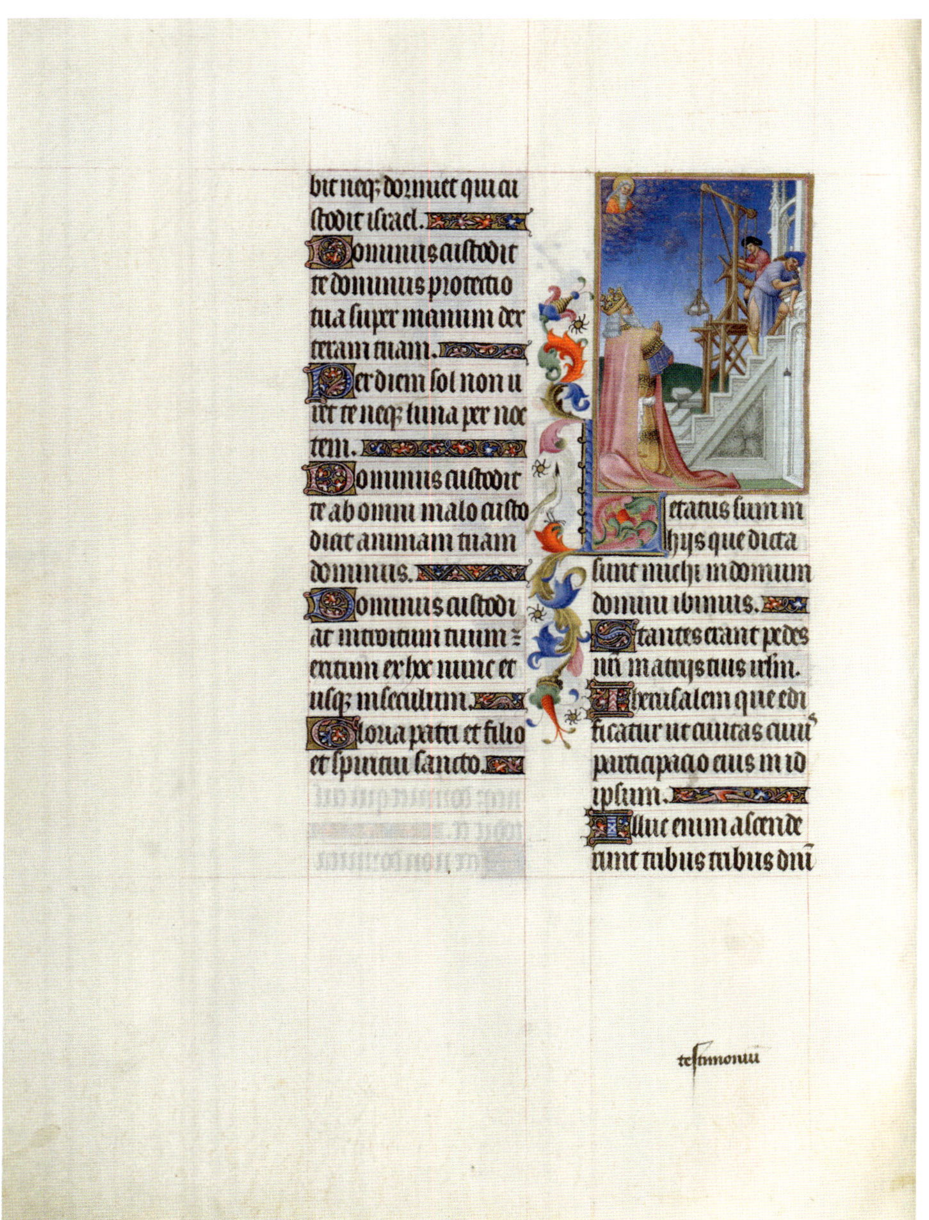

**Fig. 3** Van Lymborch brothers, *Très Riches Heures*, fol. 49v: Salutation to Jerusalem (Psalm 122)

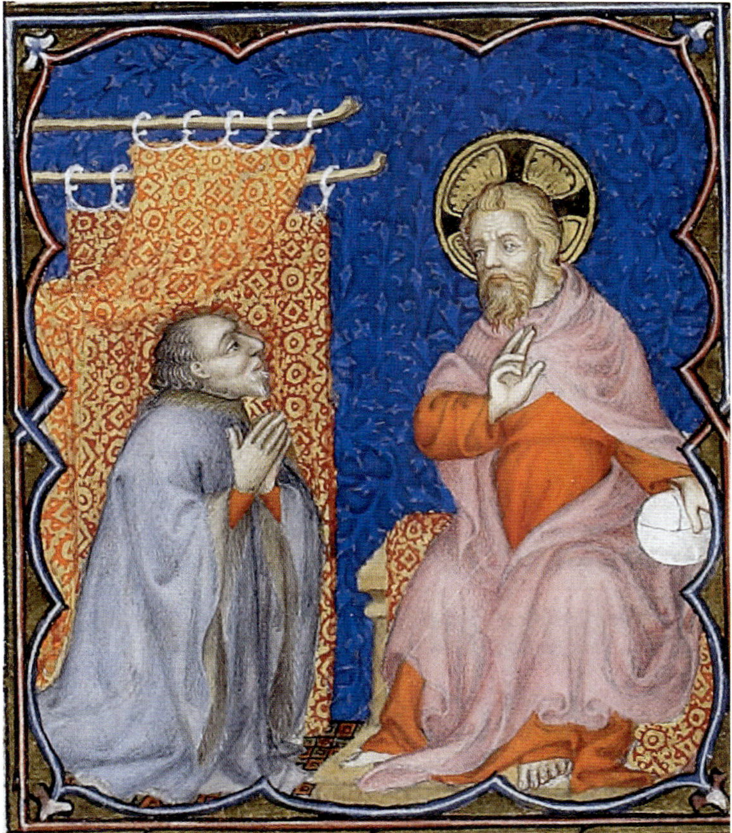

**Fig. 4** Pseudo-Jacquemart, The Duke at prayer before Christ, fol. 115v, in *Petites Heures*, Paris or Bourges, c. 1375–80 and c. 1385–90 (Paris, Bibliothèque nationale de France, département des Manuscrits, Latin 18014)

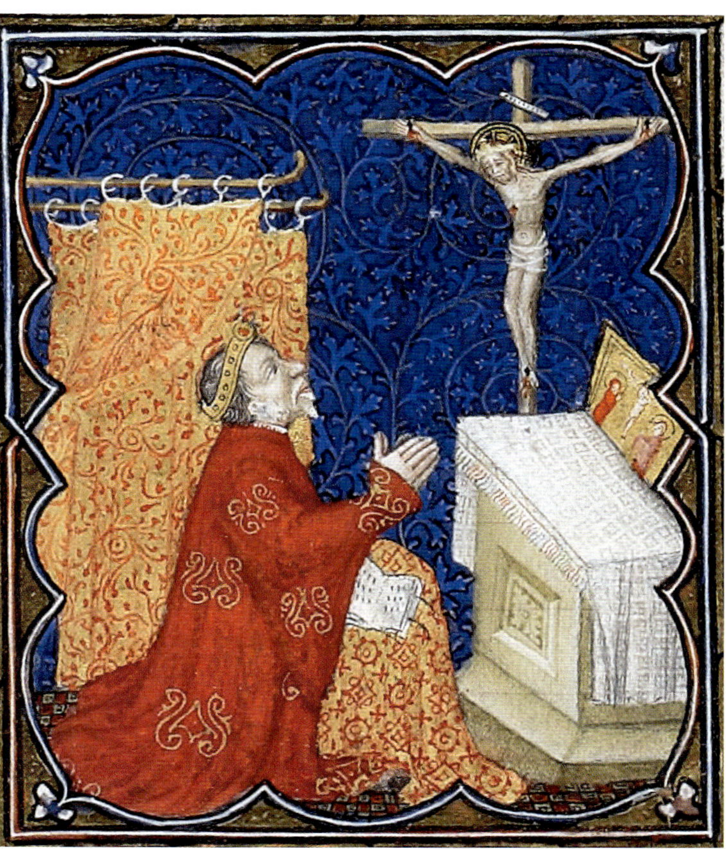

**Fig. 5** Pseudo-Jacquemart, The Duke at prayer before a crucifix, fol. 176v, in *Petites Heures*, Paris or Bourges, c. 1375–80 and c. 1385–90 (Paris, Bibliothèque nationale de France, département des Manuscrits, Latin 18014)

Books of hours could freely contain a great number of images: They punctuated reading, stimulated devotion, and supported meditation.[6] The Duke of Berry was particularly fond of such customizable works, in which arms, emblems, and other signs of belonging abound. The six books of hours he commissioned make up an exceptional series of books, named after the terms used to describe them in the inventories of the fifteenth century. The first book is the *Petites Heures*,[7] illuminated under the direction of Jean Le Noir from 1375 and then Jacquemart de Hesdin from 1385. Jean of Berry added a traveler's prayer illustrated by the Van Lymborch brothers, a sign that he was still using the book around 1410. Work on the *Très Belles Heures de Notre-Dame*[8] began around 1380–90 under the direction of the Master of the Parement of Narbonne; after an interruption, it continued until 1409 with other illuminators, and even until 1412 with the Van Lymborch brothers. The ambitious plan, which initially included hours, prayers, and a missal, was revised by Jean of Berry, who had the hours separated from the volume around 1405.[9] Meanwhile, in 1402, the prince received the *Très Belles Heures*, known as the *Brussels Hours*,[10] which he had commissioned from Jacquemart de Hesdin. With the Pseudo-Jacquemart and promising painters such as the Boucicaut Master and the Bedford Master, Hesdin completed the exceptionally large *Grandes Heures*[11] in 1409, shortly after the Van Lymborch brothers had put the finishing touches to their *Belles Heures*.[12] In 1411 or 1412, the Duke of Berry commissioned the Van Lymborch brothers to work on the *Très Riches Heures*,[13] but died before they were finished.

Through his books of hours, the Duke of Berry manifested his rank and portrayed both himself and his models of "wisdom"—King David, the Magi, Emperor Constantine—his devotion to the Trinity, the Cross and the Virgin (figs. 5, 9, and 12). The Duke of Berry's patron saints—St. John the Evangelist, St. John the Baptist, and St. Andrew—were honoured in all his prayer books, notably in the *Très Belles Heures*, or *Brussels Hours* (fig. 5, p. 108). The Duke of Berry owned only devotional books following Parisian liturgical use, which was also that of Notre-Dame Cathedral and the Sainte-Chapelle, two key sites of royal devotion. Only the litanies of the psalter illuminated by André Beauneveu and the calendar of the *Très Belles Heures* mention—alongside saints specifically from Paris (St. Genevieve) or linked to the royal court (St. Louis)—saints of Bourges (Ursinus and William of Bourges).

## INHERITED BOOKS OF HOURS

Only the calendar of the *Très Belles Heures de Notre-Dame* commemorates Jean of Berry's close relatives: Jeanne d'Armagnac (his first wife), his parents, and his brothers. However, he maintained spiritual links with his father, John II (John the Good, d. 1364), through the books of hours. On October 23, 1408, the duke received from his nephew Louis II of Anjou "unes Heures esquelles le roi Jehan père de Monseigneur, apprist à lire; et tout au commancement est le kalendrier; et après, plusieurs enseignemens en françoys de bien vivre selon Dieu" (a book of hours in which King John, the father of Monseigneur, learned to read; at the very beginning is the calendar; then come several lessons in French on how to live well according to God).[14] The Duke of Berry embellished his father's book by adding enameled clasps bearing his arms, a *pipe* (bookmark) set with a ten-carat ruby and a purple damask case lined with black taffeta. As early as 1375,

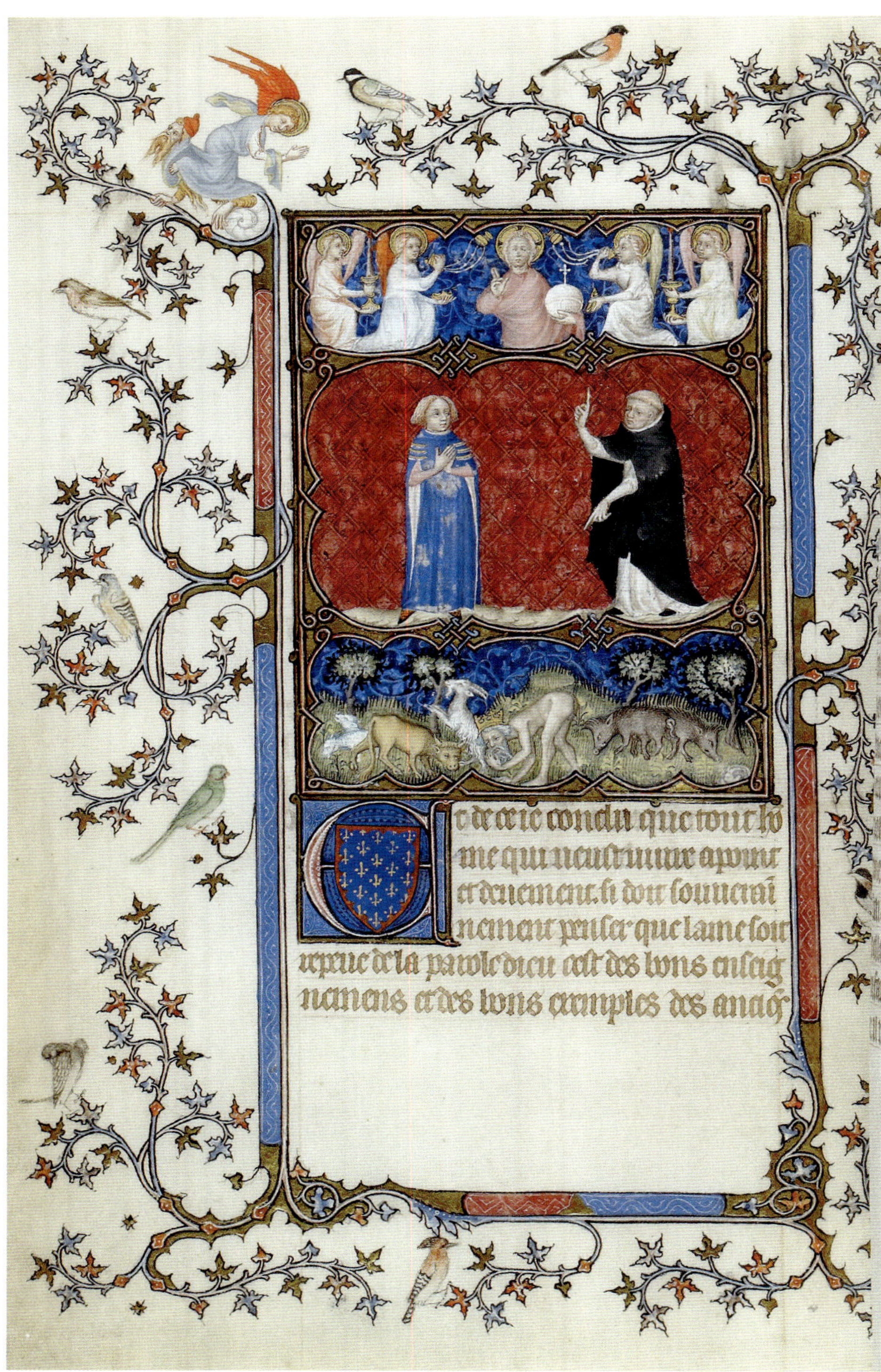

**Fig. 6** Jean Le Noir and Pseudo-Jacquemart, *The Appraiser of the World* (A Dominican Shows the Prince God among the Angels and Nebuchadnezzar among the Animals), fol. 9v, in *Petites Heures*, Paris or Bourges, c. 1375–80 and c. 1385–90 (Paris, Bibliothèque nationale de France, département des Manuscrits, Latin 18014)

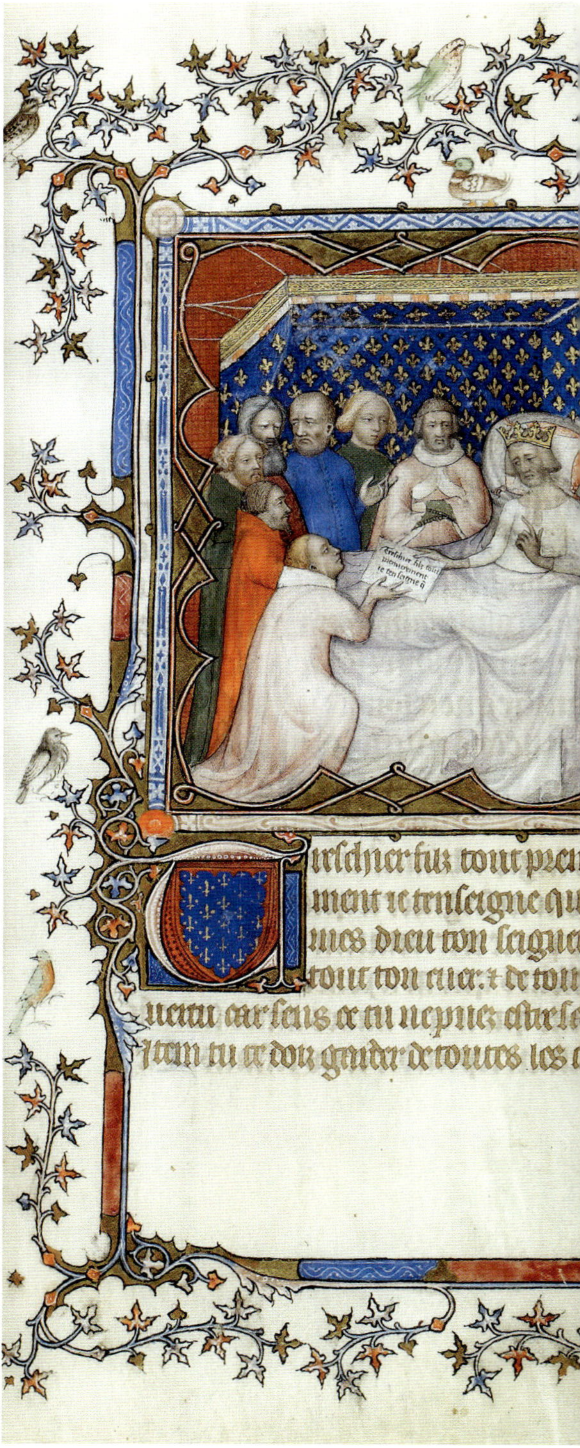

**Fig. 7** Jean Le Noir and Pseudo-Jacquemart, *The Teachings of St. Louis*, fol. 17, in *Petites Heures, Paris or Bourges*, c. 1375–80 and c. 1385–90 (Paris, Bibliothèque nation[ale] de France, département des Manuscrits, Latin 18014)

the duke had didactic texts of his father's book copied into his *Petites Heures*, after the calendar. The first, *L'Estimeur du monde* (The Appraiser of the World), contains general precepts of Christianity, addressed to princes and nobles (fig. 6). The book emphasizes the importance of regular morning and evening prayer and of daily mass, and provides advice on how to conduct oneself at church services and religious ceremonies.[15] It was followed by a brief version of the famous *Enseignements de saint Louis* (Teachings of St. Louis) (fig. 7).

Jean of Berry also kept "unes heures de la Trinité et de Nostre Dame, où il a pluseurs commemoracions de Sains, lesquelles furent de madame la duchesse de Normandie" (a book of hours of the Trinity and Our Lady, with several commemorations of saints, which belonged to the Duchess of Normandy), his mother, who introduced him early on to reading and religious practice. The refinement, culture, and devotion of Bonne of Luxembourg (d. 1349) are evident in her prayer book illuminated by Jean Le Noir, a pupil of Jean Pucelle (fig. 8).[16] Jean

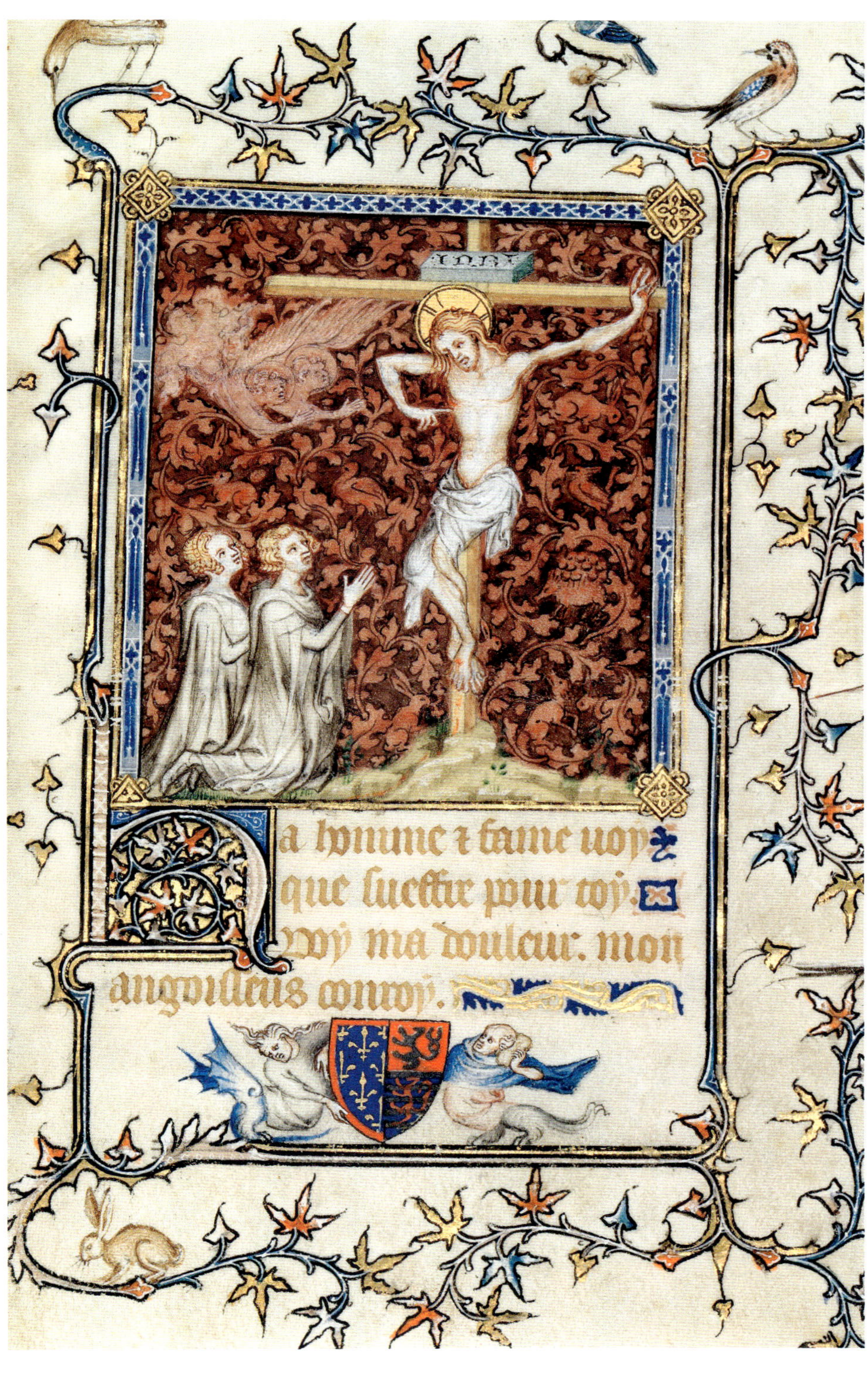

**Fig. 8** Jean Le Noir, Bonne de Luxembourg at Prayer, fol. 327, in *The Prayer Book of Bonne of Luxembourg*, Paris, c. 1348–49 (New York, The Metropolitan Museum of Art, The Cloisters Collection, Ms. Acc. 69.86)

of Berry entrusted the execution of the first book of hours he commissioned (*Petites Heures de Jean de Berry*) to the same artist. He had the *Traité sur les six degrés de charité* (Treatise on the Six Degrees of Charity) (fols. 278v–281) (fig. 10) copied from Bonne's prayer book, a sign of the prince's demanding piety (fig. 9).[17] The birds painted in a realistic manner in his mother's prayer book also adorn the margins of the same *Petites Heures* from the 1370s, the *Très Belles Heures de Notre-Dame* around 1390, and the *Très Riches Heures*.

Queen Jeanne d'Évreux (d. 1371), wife of Charles IV (known as Charles the Fair, d. 1328), was another model of devotion, admired by all at the French court for her extensive religious patronage. Through the intermediary of Charles VI, Jean of Berry recovered the queen's famous *Hours*,[18] illuminated by Jean Pucelle and her *Bréviaire*. The importance of personal devotional books for members of the royal family can be seen in a miniature from the *Hours of Jeanne d'Évreux*, in which a dove brings to St. Louis, held captive by the Saracens, the prayer book he had lost in battle (fig. 11). Equally admired as Jeanne d'Évreux, Blanche of Navarre (1331–98), widow of Philip VI (d. 1350), carefully divided her books among her heirs: Anticipating Jean of Berry's wishes, she left him her "plus belles heures" (most beautiful hours) inherited from her mother, a sign that Jean of Berry must have been a connoisseur of precious manuscripts.[19]

## THE MAJOR COMMISSIONS

It was not until the 1370s that the Duke of Berry, aged thirty, personally commissioned a book of hours. The *Petites Heures* was particularly rich in terms of textual and artistic content. As it integrated texts drawn from the books of hours of John II (John the Good) and Bonne of Luxembourg, it can be seen as a son's modest memorial to his parents. Roger S. Wieck pointed out that, at the same time, Charles V acquired a sumptuous book, the *Savoy Hours*, executed in the workshop of Jean Le Noir between 1335 and 1340 for Blanche of Burgundy (1288–1348), wife of the Count of Savoy and granddaughter of St. Louis.[20] Charles V lengthened the book with sixty illuminated leaves by the Master of the Bible of Jean de Sy. Impressed by the work, the Duke of Berry immediately

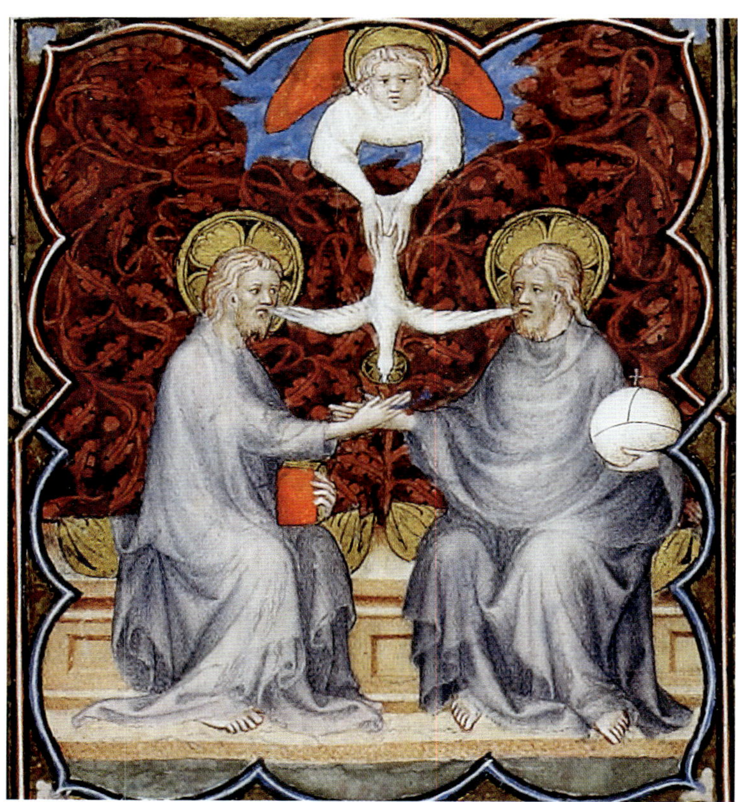

**Fig. 9** Master of the Trinity and Pseudo-Jacquemart, The Throne of Grace (Pentecost), fol. 137, in *Petites Heures*, Paris or Bourges, c. 1375–80 and c. 1385–90 (Paris, Bibliothèque nationale de France, département des Manuscrits, Latin 18014)

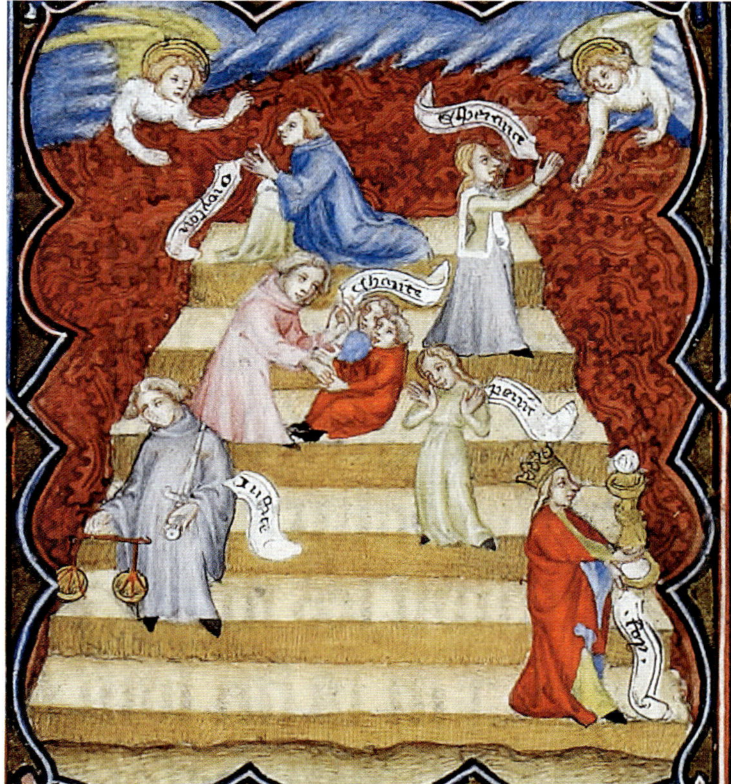

**Fig. 10** Master of the Trinity and Pseudo-Jacquemart, Six Degrees of Charity, fol. 278v in *Petites Heures*, Paris or Bourges, c. 1375–80 and c. 1385–90 (Paris, Bibliothèque nationale de France, département des Manuscrits, Latin 18014)

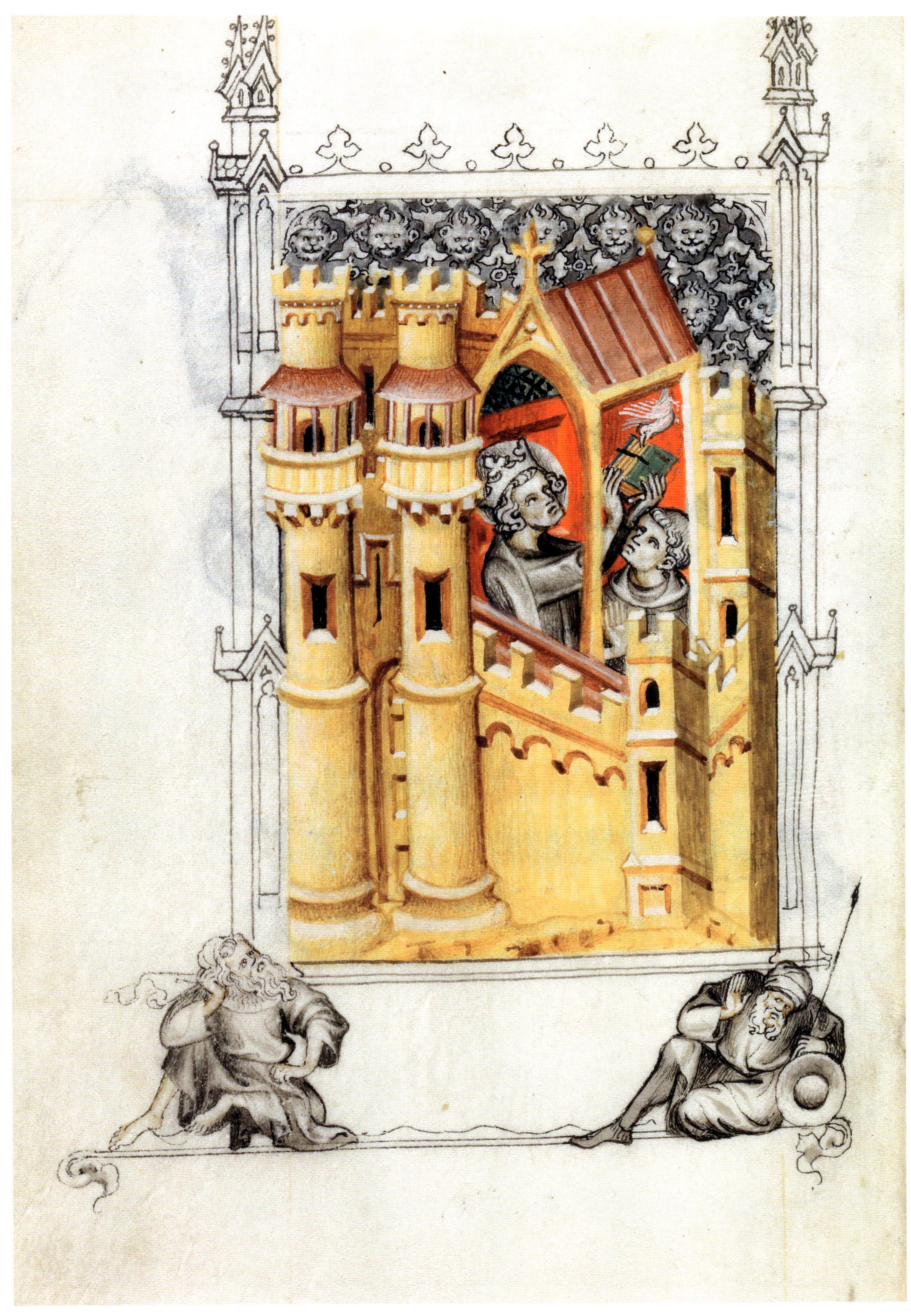

**Fig. 11** Jean Pucelle, The Miracle of the Breviary, fol. 154v, in *Heures of Jeanne d'Évreux*, Paris, c. 1324–28 (New York, The Metropolitan Museum of Art, The Cloisters Collection, Ms. Acc. 54.1.2)

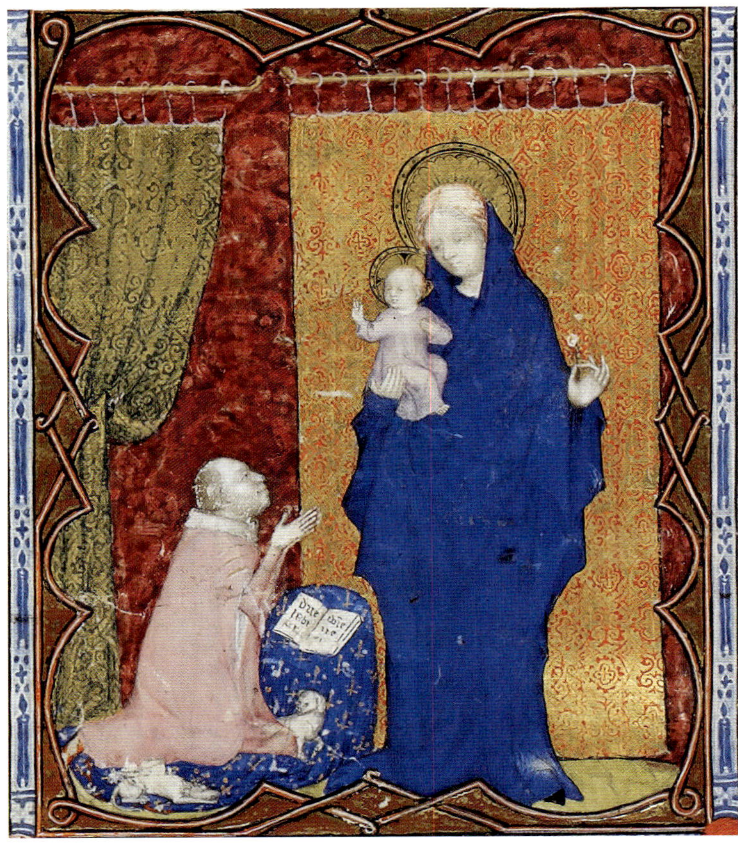

**Fig. 12** Pseudo-Jacquemart, The Duke of Berry at prayer before the Virgin and Christ, fol. 97v, in *Petites Heures*, Paris or Bourges, c. 1375–80 and c. 1385–90 (Paris, Bibliothèque nationale de France, département des Manuscrits, Latin 18014)

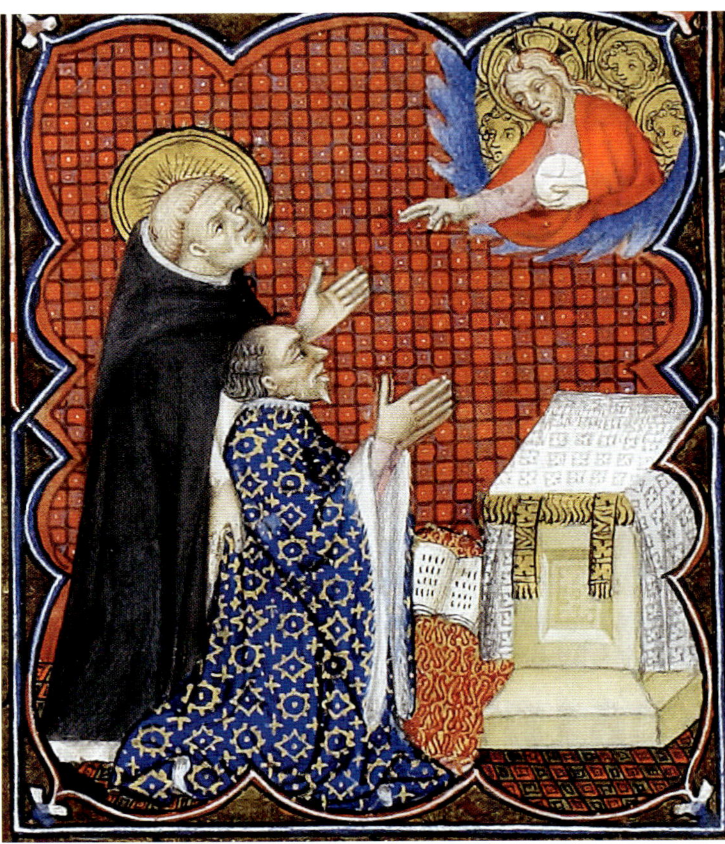

**Fig. 13** Pseudo-Jacquemart, The Duke of Berry at prayer with St. Thomas Aquinas, fol. 117v, in *Petites Heures*, Paris or Bourges, c. 1375–80 and c. 1385–90 (Paris, Bibliothèque nationale de France, département des Manuscrits, Latin 18014)

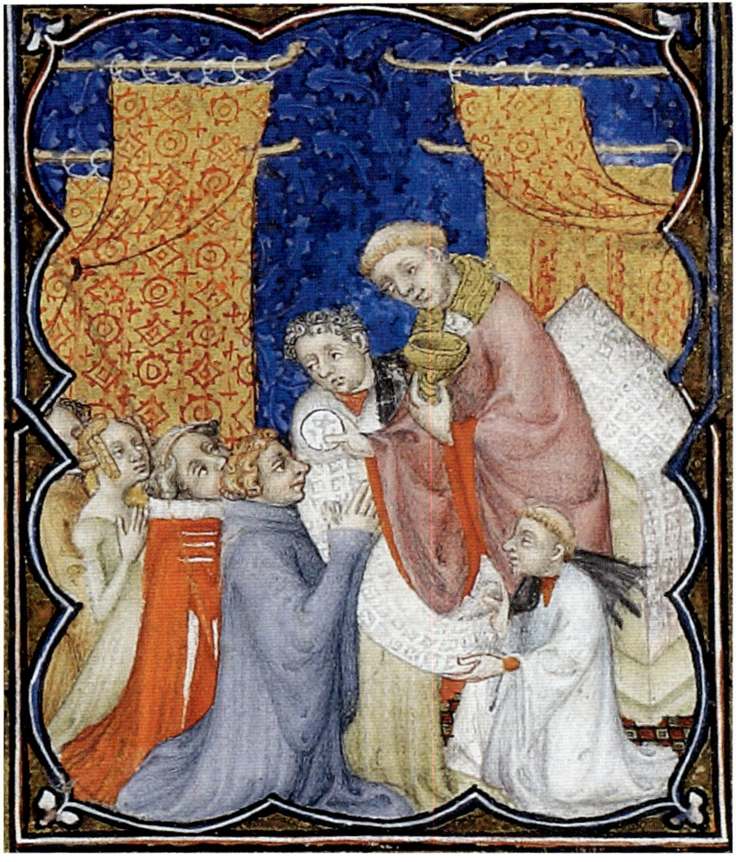

**Fig. 14** Pseudo-Jacquemart, The Duke of Berry Receiving Communion, fol. 173v, in *Petites Heures*, Paris or Bourges, c. 1375–80 and c. 1385–90 (Paris, Bibliothèque nationale de France, département des Manuscrits, Latin 18014)

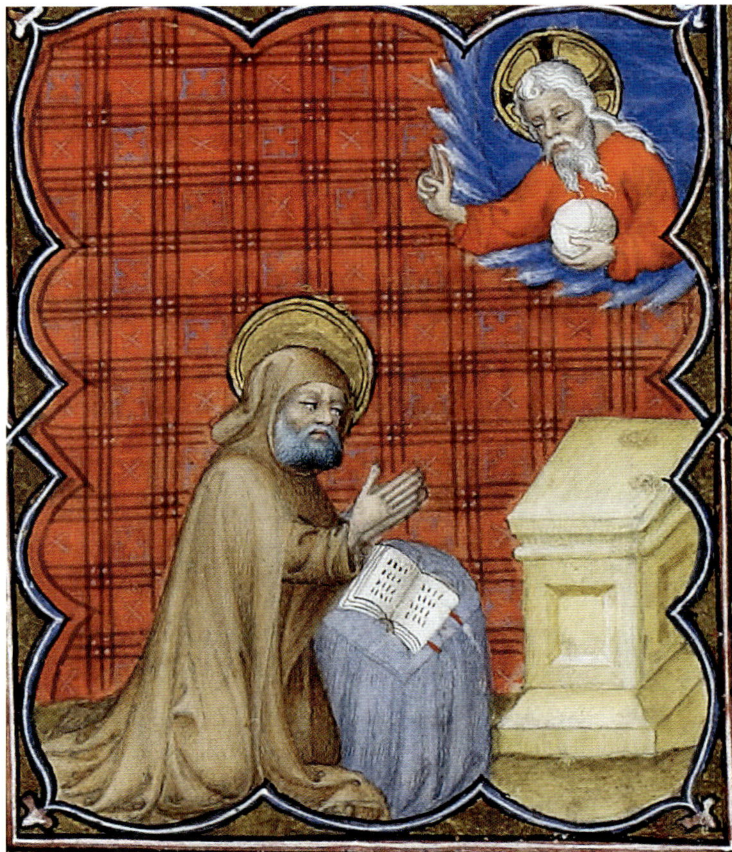

**Fig. 15** Pseudo-Jacquemart, St. Jerome at prayer, fol. 123v, in *Petites Heures*, Paris or Bourges, c. 1375–80 and c. 1385–90 (Paris, Bibliothèque nationale de France, département des Manuscrits, Latin 18014)

imitated the king, adding to his *Petites Heures* the Office of the Holy Spirit and Prayers to recite during Mass, illustrated with images of himself performing acts of devotion, just as Charles V and Blanche of Burgundy had done before him (figs. 13–15). A similar act of emulation between Jean of Berry and Philip of Burgundy can be seen in the parallel commissions for the *Très Belles Heures de Notre-Dame* and the *Grandes Heures*[21] of Philip the Bold.[22]

As the book of hours gradually took shape over the course of the fourteenth century, it comprised parts that were relatively constant. First, after the calendar, comes the Canonical Office of the Hours of the Virgin, followed by the Seven Penitential Psalms, the Litany of the Saints, and the Office of the Dead. All these elements appear in the six books commissioned by the Duke of Berry, but the remainder of the content varies. The Hours of the Cross and the Hours of the Holy Spirit appear in either full or abridged form, with the *Grandes Heures* containing both versions of the Hours of the Holy Spirit. The first four books of hours, commissioned before 1400, do not contain extracts from the Gospels, or the two Prayers to the Virgin ("Obsecro te" and "O intemerata"), which only became widespread in the early fifteenth century.

Three of the Duke of Berry's manuscripts were completed by a category of liturgical texts that are rare in books of hours. The propers of the various liturgical feasts are, of course, present in the missal of the *Très Belles Heures de Notre-Dame*, ultimately separated from the Hours, but also appear in the *Belles Heures*, for the main feasts, and in the *Très Riches Heures*. In 1412, the Duke of Berry exchanged the *Très Belles Heures de Notre-Dame* given to his keeper of the jewels, Robinet d'Étampes, for a missal, a sign of his desire to concentrate on the texts during Mass. Finally, a unique feature of the *Très Riches Heures* is that they allow you to follow the Hours for each day of the week, a practice that originated in the Southern Netherlands.[23]

On the other hand, the *Très Riches Heures* are devoid of simple devotional texts, prayers, and appeals to the saints. They contain only canonical texts, composed in two columns like those in breviaries, with rubrics in Latin, lending them a severe appearance reinforced by the book's incompleteness. Paul Durrieu hypothesized that on two occasions the Duke of Berry put together a "set" of books of hours, comprising, on the one hand, a large ceremonial volume for the chapel, and on the other, a portable, personal volume to be kept on one's person.[24] The *Belles Heures* would then be the counterpart to the *Très Riches Heures*, just as the *Petites Heures*—with its varied content, entreaties to saints, and numerous devotional prayers, often in French—would be the counterpart to the solemn *Grandes Heures* covered in precious stones.

In the *Grandes Heures* (fol. 96), St. Peter welcomes the Duke of Berry and his family at the entrance to Heaven, symbolized by a chapel. Jean of Berry is portrayed as an old man so as to situate the "vision" in the distant future and contrast it with the historiated initial in which the duke appears younger. In the *Très Riches Heures*, the last book of hours commissioned by the Duke of Berry, death is more present in the prince's prayers; now aged over seventy, he was preparing to "bien mourir" (die well) (fig. 16). The Office of the Dead is illustrated with a complete cycle instead of the usual single image.

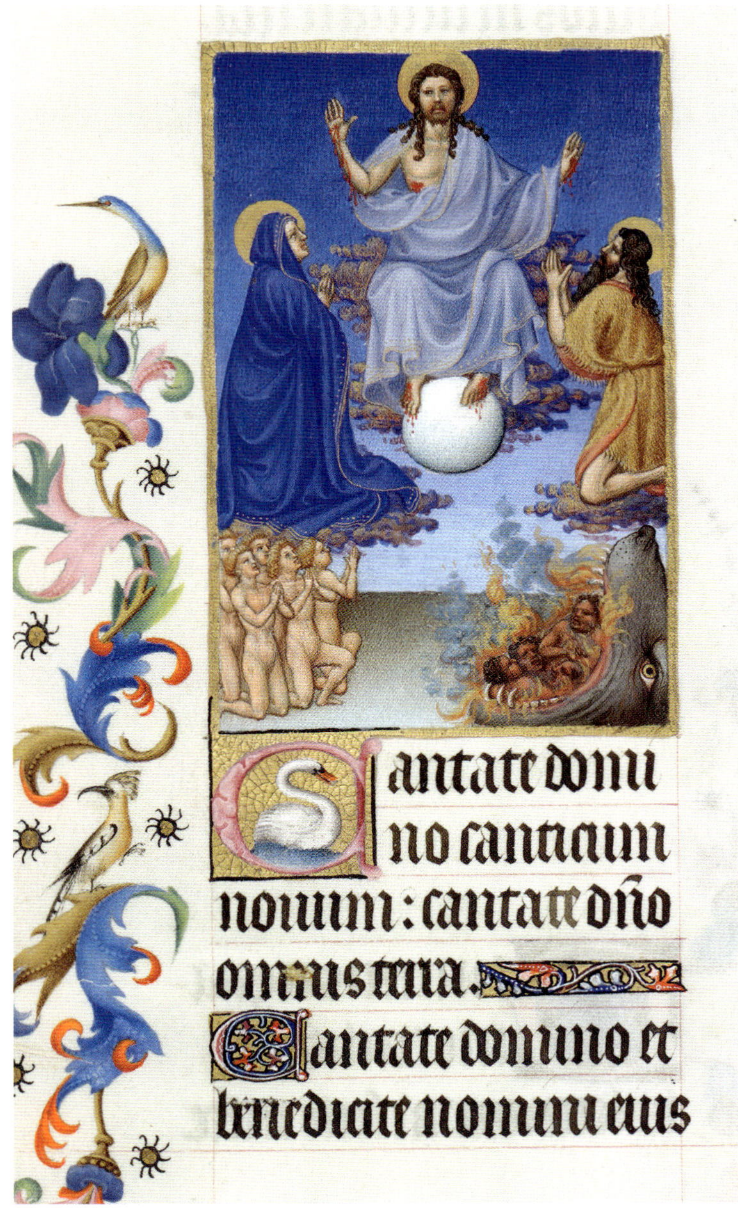

**Fig. 16** Van Lymborch brothers, *Très Riches Heures*, fol. 34: The Last Judgment (Psalm 96), detail

**Fig. 17** Following pages: Van Lymborch brothers, *Très Riches Heures*, fol. 34: The Last Judgment, detail

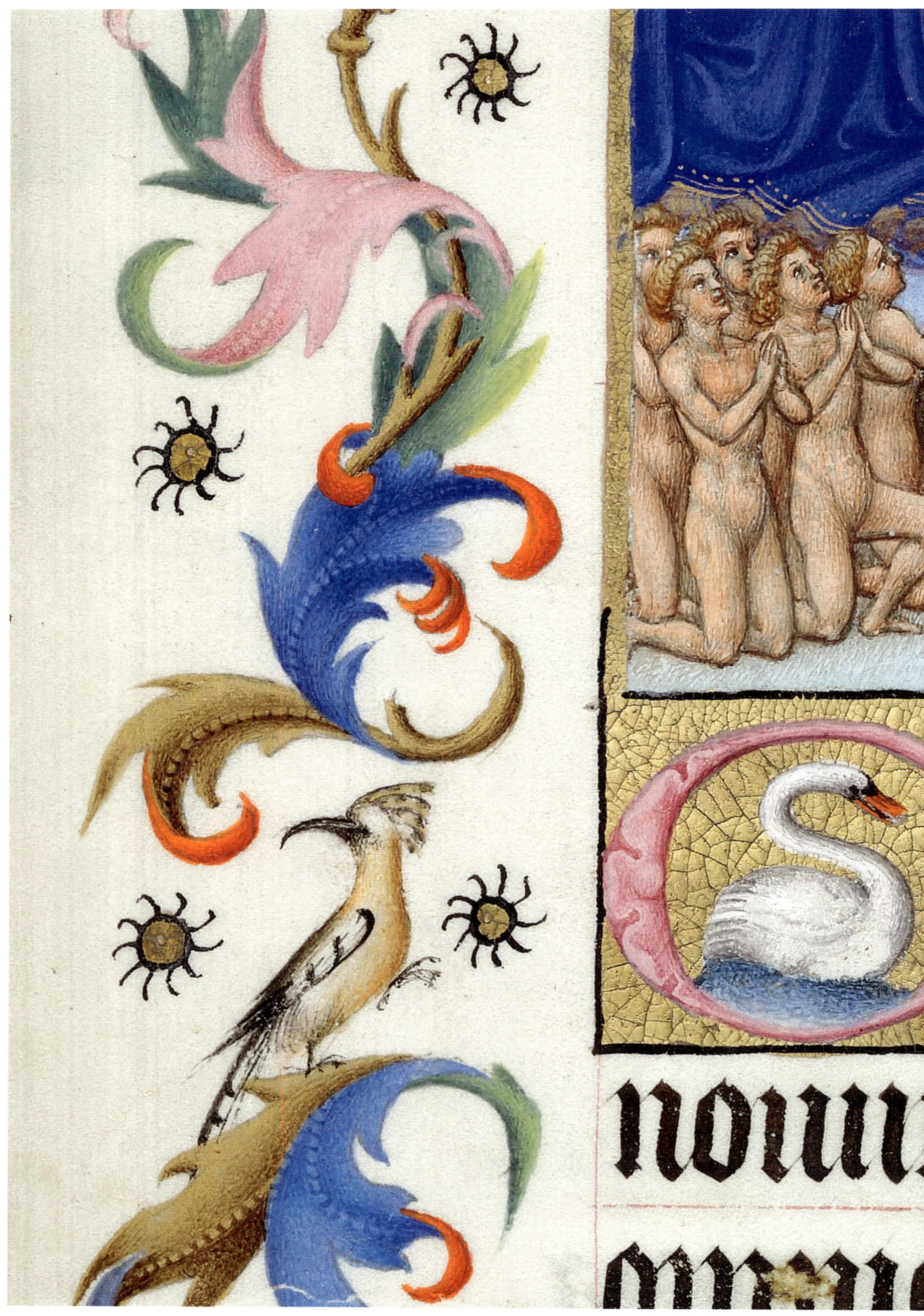

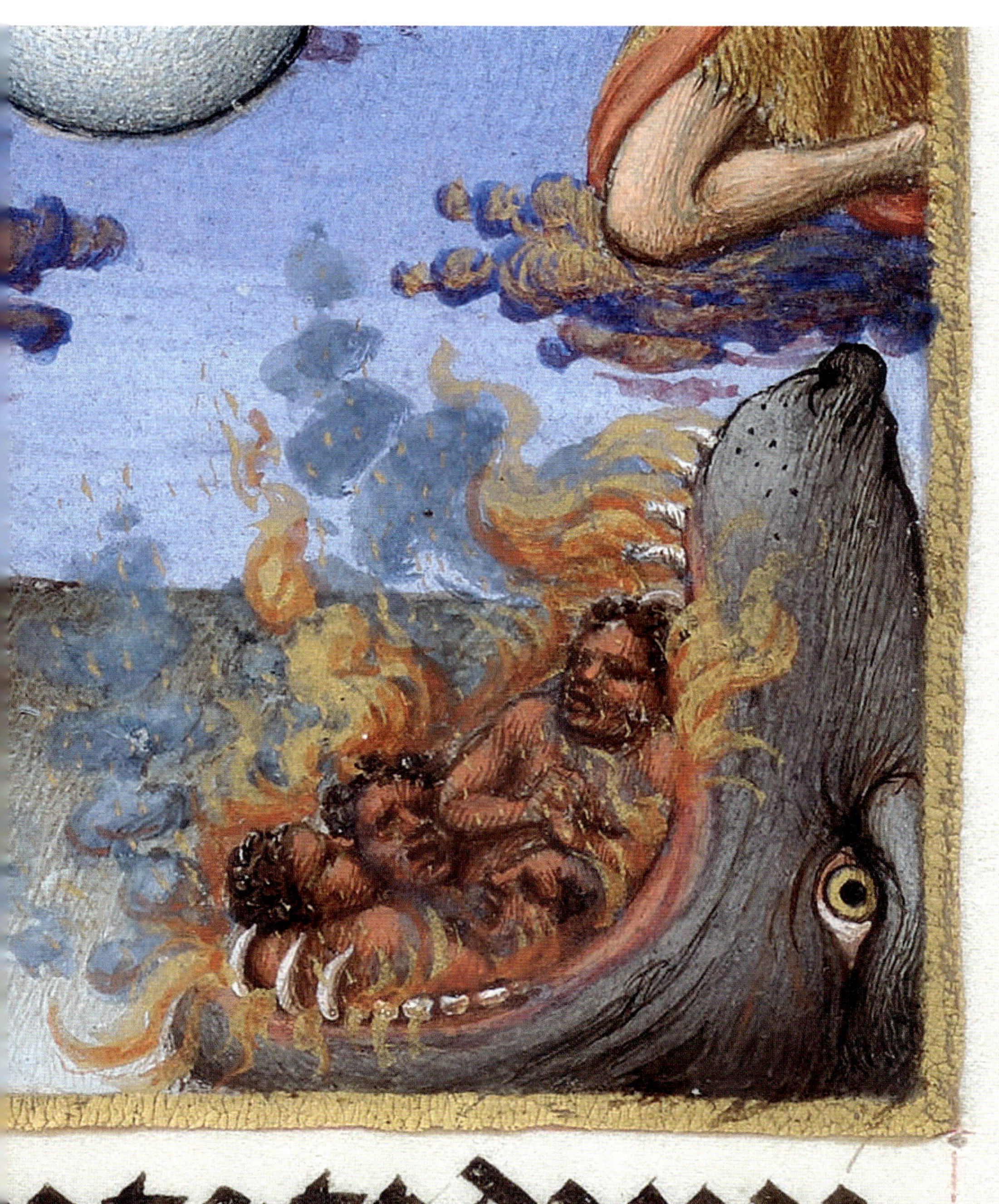

ntate domi

o canticum

cantate dño

ra

Auferens bella usq;
ad finem terre arcum
conteret et confringet
arma et scuta cōburet igñ.
Vacate et videte qm̄
ego sum deus exaltabor
in gentib; et exaltabor
in terra.
Dominus virtutū
nobiscum susceptor
noster deus iacob.
Pfetizăt filij chore mi
litantē et triumphātē
ecclīam in monte syon.

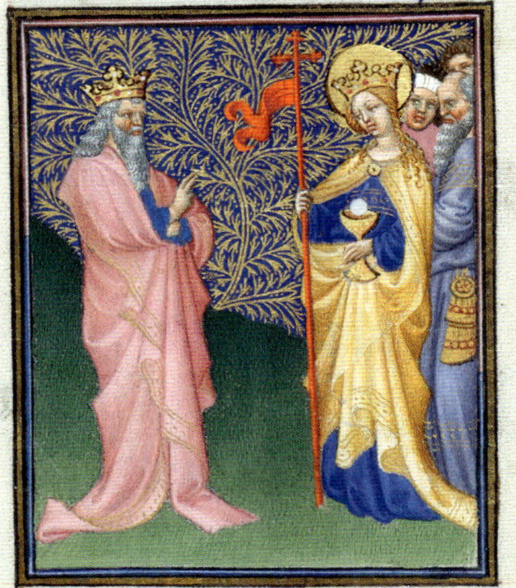

Fundamenta
eius in monti
bus sanctis diligit do
minus portas syon sup
omnia tabernacula
iacob.
Gloriosa dicta sunt
de te civitas dei.
Memor ero raab: et ba
bilonis scientium me.
Ecce alienigene et ty
rus et populus ethyopū
hij fuerunt illic.
Numquid syon di
cet homo et homo natus
est in ea: et ipse fundavit
eam altissimus.
Dominus narra
bit in scripturis popu
lorum: et principum
horum qui fuerunt in
ea.

## RENEWED HOURS

The sumptuous patron of the arts, who had books of hours made for his "devocion et plaisance" (devotion and pleasure),[25] owned enough of them to be able to offer some as gifts—for example, to the King of Spain, the Duke of Burgundy (*Très Belles Heures*), and the Queen of England, who received Bonne of Luxembourg's *Heures de la Trinité et de Nostre Dame*. Among those offered to him, we note a volume "d'ouvrage romain" (from Italia) and Hours containing the "Psalms compiled by Petrarch".[26]

The creation of the commissioned books of hours reveals that the prince was closely involved in the work, intervening with his illuminators to perfect the books. The books of hours, breviaries, and devotional treatises served as models or sources of inspiration[27]; the hours were equipped with *pipes* (bookmarks) to facilitate the presentation, comparisons, and copying.[28] The *Grandes Heures*, for example, contains miniatures reproduced from the *Très Belles Heures de Notre-Dame*, and the Resurrection (fol. 8) was inspired by the *Breviary of Charles V*, which the Duke of Berry acquired in December 1408.[29] Up to the Van Lymborch brothers, marginal drolleries were copied from the *Belleville Breviary*.[30] Other correspondences connect the books: The flower-strewn scene of Christ's entry into Jerusalem, painted in the *Très Riches Heures*, echoes the *Meditations* attributed to St. Bonaventure, which the Duke of Berry had translated and adapted.[31]

The complexity of the images required close collaboration between illuminators and clerics. The *Très Belles Heures de Notre-Dame* combines four cycles of images per page, with large miniatures, historiated initials, an illustrated band at the bottom of the page, and decorated margins. The more sober *Très Riches Heures* adds a second, smaller cycle of images for the Psalms to the large paintings. *Tituli* in blue and gold letters formed carefully worded captions to remind the reader of the essential principles of the Christian faith, and provide keys for moving from the Old to the New Testament: Psalm 87, attributed to the sons of Korah who celebrate Jerusalem, is illustrated by David and the Church Triumphant, for, as the title reminds us, Zion prefigures the Church (fig. 18).[32]

In addition to the desire to perfect the images or clarify the layout of the leaves, there were many other reasons for commissioning new books of hours. Certain texts might suddenly seem essential: "Obsecro te," a prayer to the Virgin and a request to accompany death, was included in the last two books of hours.[33] The litanies were updated in the *Très Riches Heures* with the appearance of Albert of Sicily, celebrated by the Carmelites from 1411. The images also echoed newly acquired relics, such as the hand of St. Elizabeth, ostensibly extending toward the Virgin of the Visitation in the *Très Riches Heures* (fol. 38v; fig. 19).[34]

One of the most important driving forces behind the making of the *Très Riches Heures*, at least during the last execution campaign in the prince's lifetime, may well have been the reform of the Church calendar, which had long been a subject of discussion and whose outcome seemed imminent in the 1410s.[35] In Rome (1412–13), Constance (1414–18), and soon Basel, the calendar's imperfection was on the agenda of councils, along with the various ills of the Church and the Great Schism.[36] Under the supervision of the prince's advisers,

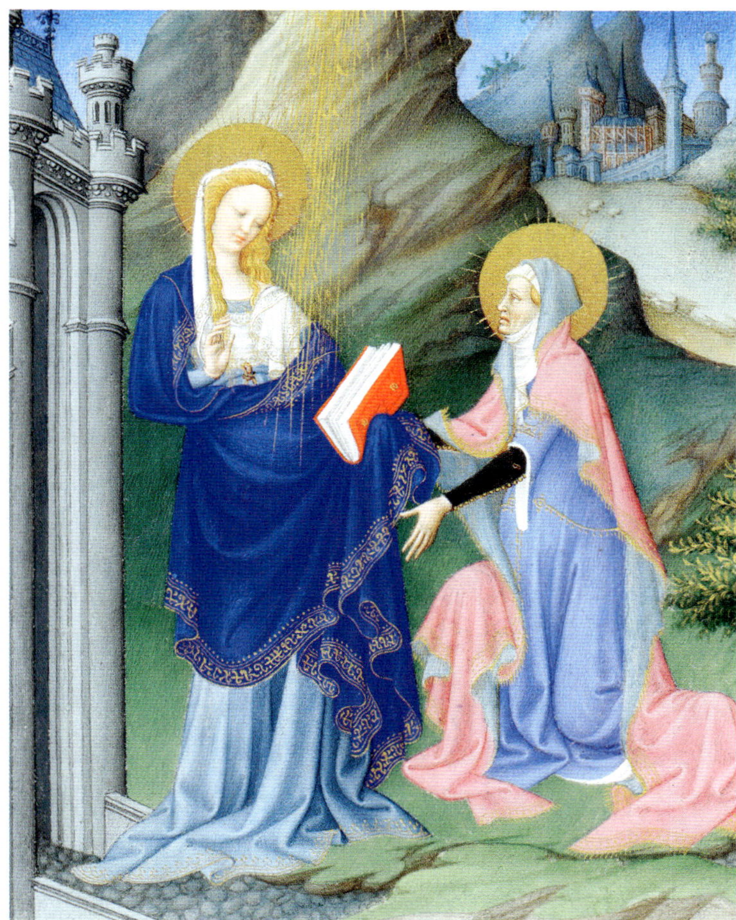

**Fig. 19** Van Lymborch brothers, *Très Riches Heures*, fol. 38v: The Visitation, detail

**Fig. 18** Van Lymborch brothers, *Très Riches Heures*, fol. 32: Zion, Mother of All Humanity (Psalm 87)

benedicite filij hominũ
domino.
Benedicat israel do
minum: laudet et super
exaltet eum in secula.
Benedicite sacerdotes
domini domino: bene
dicite servi domini do
mino.
Benedicite spiritus
et anime iustorum
domino: benedicite sancti
et humiles corde dño.
Benedicite anania
azaria misael domino
laudate et superexaltate
eum in secula.
Benedicamus pa
trem et filium cum scõ
spiritu laudemus et su
perexaltemus eum in se
cula.

Benedictus es dñe
in firmamento celi et
laudabilis et gloriosus
et superexaltatus eum
in secula. Amen.

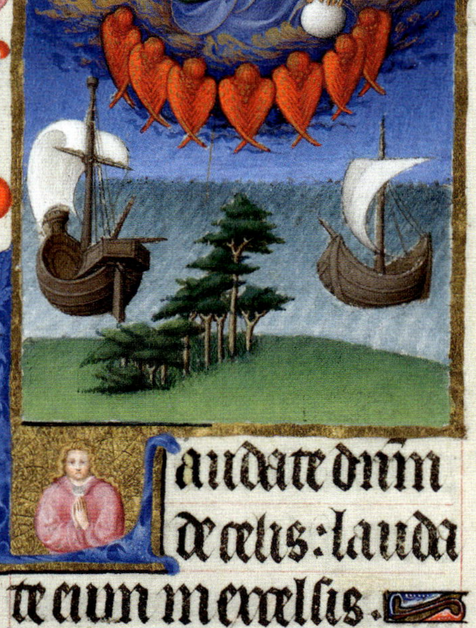

Laudate dñm
de celis: lauda
te eum in excelsis.
Laudate eum om
nes angeli eius: lauda

such as the physician Simon Aligret (d. 1415) and the renowned astronomer Lubert Hautschild from Bruges, the "nombre d'or novel" (new golden number), in French in the calendar of the *Très Riches Heures*, corrected the lunar calculation according to a table drawn up in 1345 by Jean de Murs and Firmin de Beauval. Cardinal Alamanno Adimari, archbishop of Pisa, legate of John XXIII in France and advocate of the Union of the Church, occupies the place of honour in the opening scene of the *Très Riches Heures*, to the right of the Duke of Berry, who for many years fought to put an end to the Great Schism, and who was a keen astrologer (fig. 20).

As well as looking back on a life gone by, the calendar could offer a peaceful vision of a unified Christian world, living in harmony with the rhythm of the celestial spheres.

1 Villela-Petit 2013a; König 2006.
2 Delisle 1884; Meiss 1969 and 1974a.
3 Pons 2005; Villela-Petit 2007, 393.
4 Bellaguet 1839–52, VI, 33.
5 Henryot 2022, 44.
6 Corresponding to each part of the text is a traditional cycle of images. Excerpts from the Gospels are accompanied by effigies of the Four Evangelists, while the prayers to the Virgin are accompanied by a depiction of the mother of Christ. Each liturgical division of the *Hours of the Virgin* corresponds to a fixed subject: the Annunciation for Matins, the Visitation for Lauds, the Nativity for Prime, the Annunciation to the shepherds of the birth of Christ for Terce, the Magi for Sext, the Presentation of the Child Jesus in the Temple for Nones, the Flight into Egypt or the Massacre of the Innocents for Vespers, and the Coronation of the Virgin for Compline. The hours of the Passion naturally provide material for one or more compositions depicting the death of Christ.
7 Paris, BnF, Ms. Latin 18014.
8 Paris, BnF, Ms. NAL 3093.
9 The book contains a prayer for the king and could have been commissioned as a gift for Constantine, his devotion to the Trinity, the Cross. Paris 1968 (175, note by F. Avril).
10 Brussels, KRB, Ms. 11060-61.
11 Paris, BnF, Ms. Latin 919.
12 New York, Met, The Cloisters, Ms. 54.1.1. a, b.
13 Chantilly, Musée Condé, Ms. 65.
14 Guiffrey 1894–96, I, 257 (968).
15 Manion [1991] 2020, 178–79.
16 New York, Met, The Cloisters, Ms. 69.86.
17 This is a paraphrase of St. Bonaventure's treatise *De triplice via*. Heck 1995.
18 New York, Met, The Cloisters, Ms. 54.1.2.
19 Buettner 2004.
20 Wieck 1991 and 2005. Charles VI offered the *Savoy Hours* to the Duke of Berry on July 7, 1409, as indicated by the bookplate calligraphed by Jean Flamel and reported by Paul Durrieu before the fire that ravaged Turin Library in 1904. Fragments are currently held in the Beinecke Library at Yale University.
21 The *Grandes Heures* is in two volumes: Cambridge, Fitzwilliam Museum, Ms. 3-1954 and Brussels, KBR, Ms. 11035-37.
22 Wieck 2005, 133.
23 Korteweg 2005, 139. Sunday mass is dedicated to the Trinity, that of Monday to the commemoration of the dead, Tuesday to the Holy Spirit, Wednesday to all the saints, Thursday to the Blessed Sacrament, Friday to the Holy Cross, and Saturday to the Virgin Mary.
24 Durrieu 1904, 13–15.
25 See the suggestive articles by Jean-Yves Ribault (1999) and Michael Camille (2001).
26 Delisle 1884, XXI, XXII, XXIX, XXXV, XXXVI.
27 Meiss 1967, I, 296.
28 Villela-Petit 2013a, 53.
29 Paris, BnF, Ms. Latin 1052. Meiss 1967, I, 296; Paris 1981–82, 344–346 (298, note by F. Avril).
30 Paris, BnF, Ms. Latin 10483-10484. König 2006, 25, 28.
31 The Duke of Berry had the *Meditationes Vitae Christi* (Meditations on the Life of Christ) translated and adapted. See Meiss and Beatson 1977 and Villela-Petit 2013a, 53–54.
32 Manion 1995.
33 This prayer was intended to protect those who recited it from violent death. Henryot 2022, 41.
34 Villela-Petit 2013a, 55.
35 Meiss 1967, I, 49 and chap. XL; Lebigue 2014; Solan Bethmale 2016, 25–31.
36 Based on an insufficiently precise calculation of the length of the solar year and of the lunar months, the Julian calendar used in the Middle Ages no longer corresponded to astronomical facts. Over the centuries, the spring equinox, supposed to occur every March 21, kept arriving earlier and earlier in the year, March 11 or 12 in the years 1415–16.

**Fig. 20** Van Lymborch brothers, *Très Riches Heures*, fol. 41v: Cosmic Praise (Psalm 148)

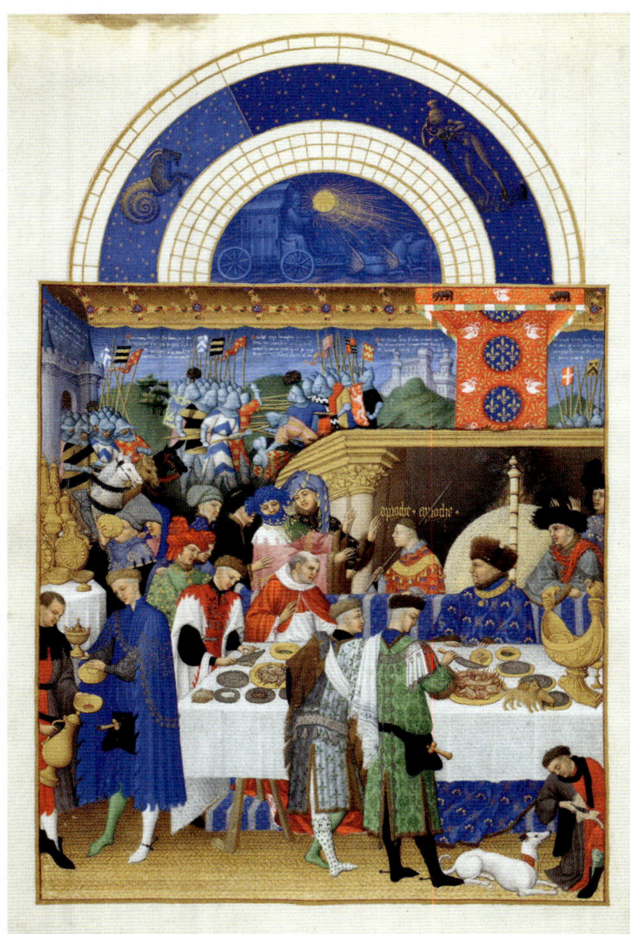

Van Lymborch brothers, *Très Riches Heures*, fol. 1v: January

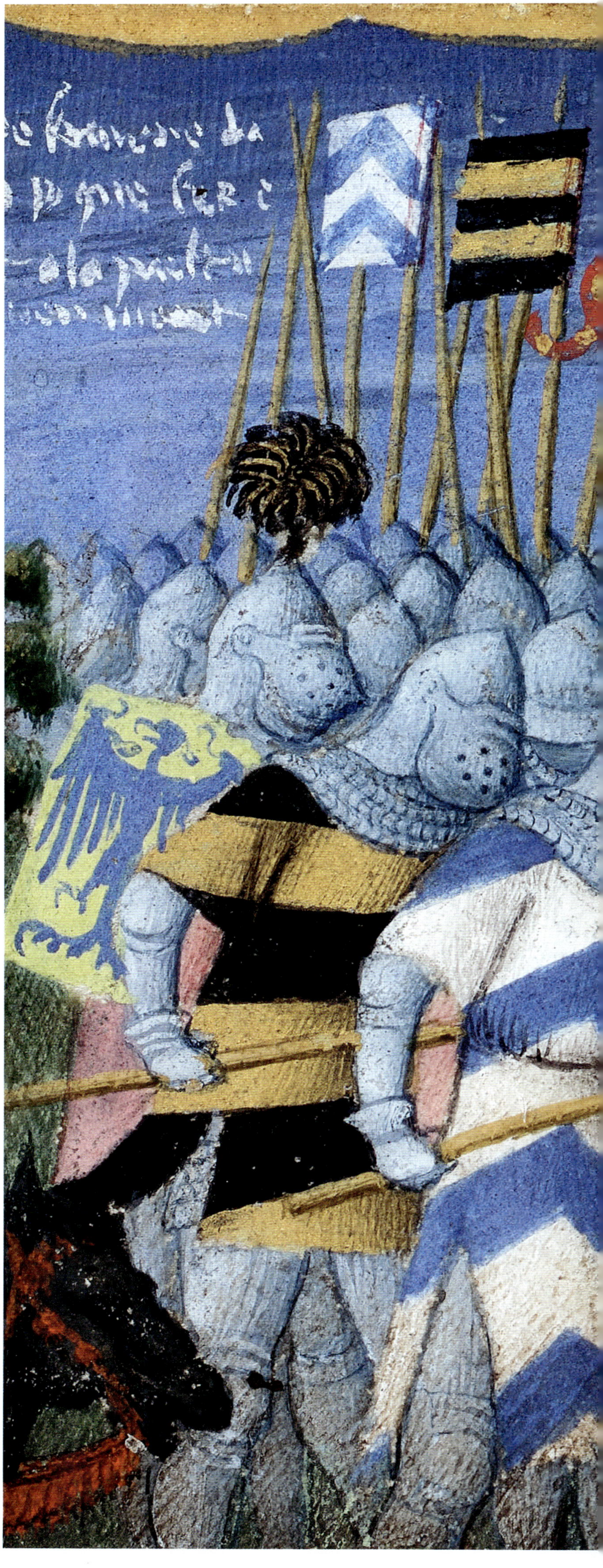

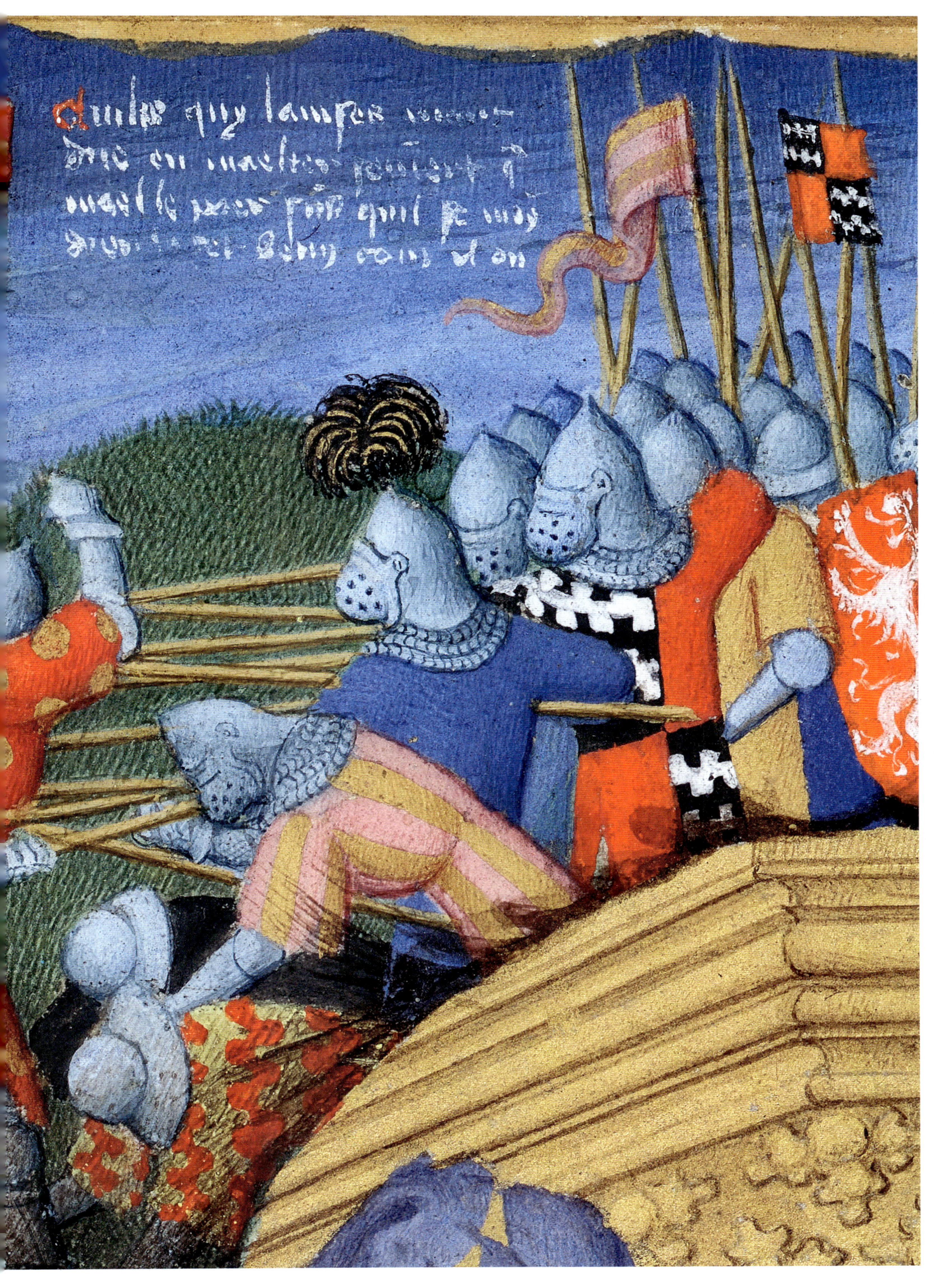

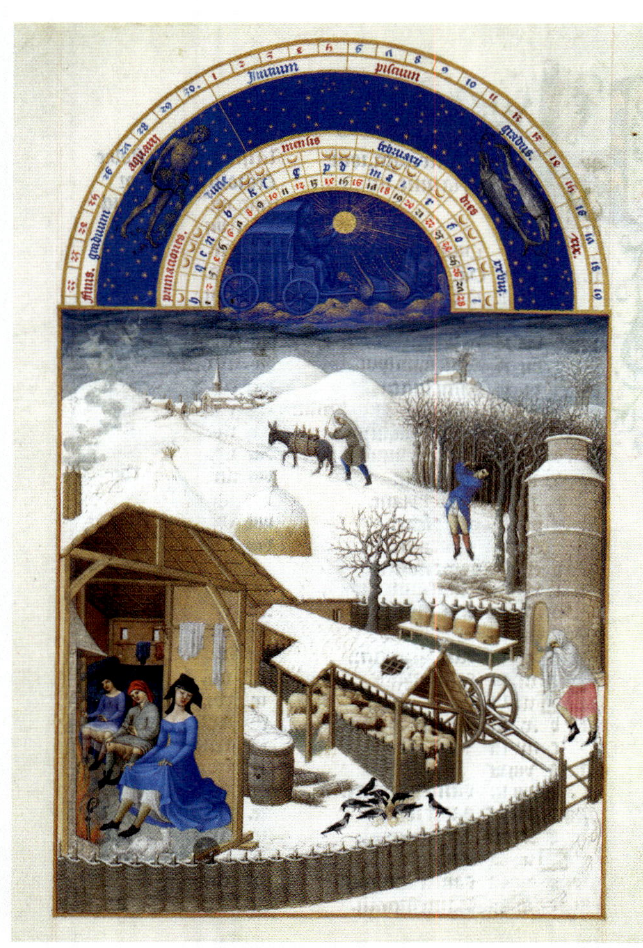

Van Lymborch brothers, *Très Riches Heures*, fol. 2v: February

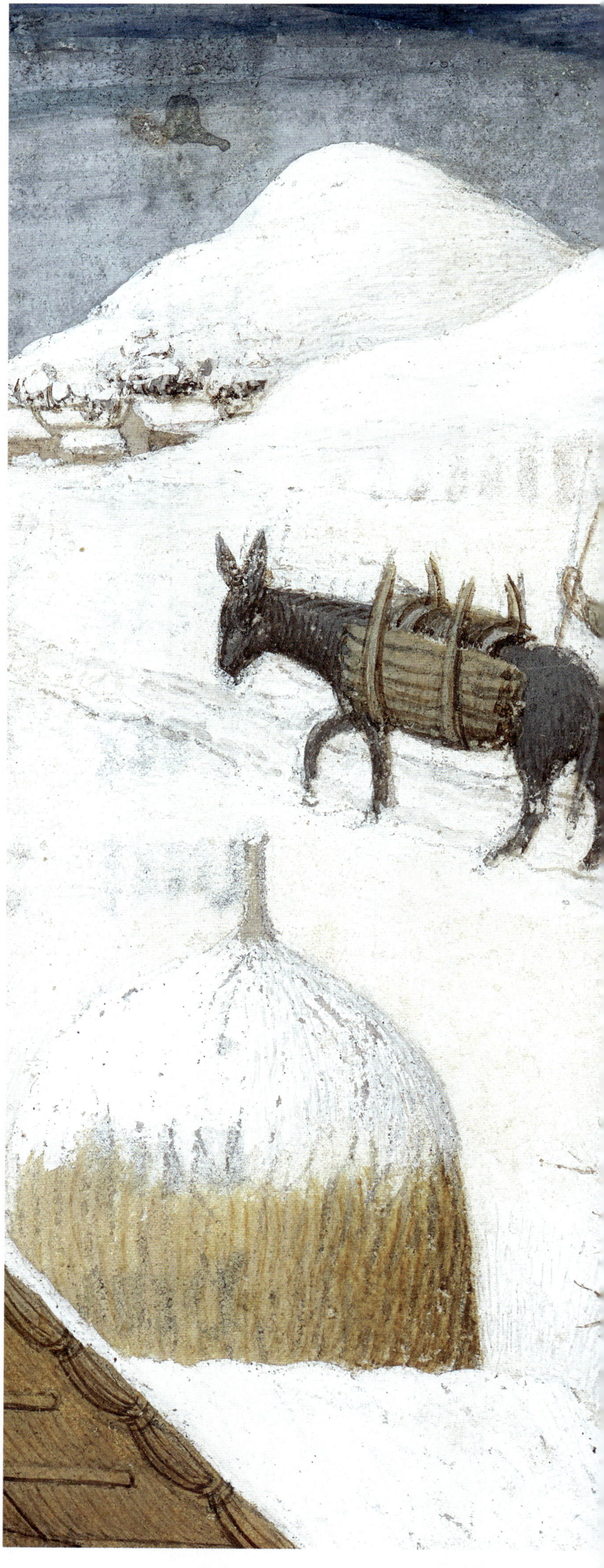

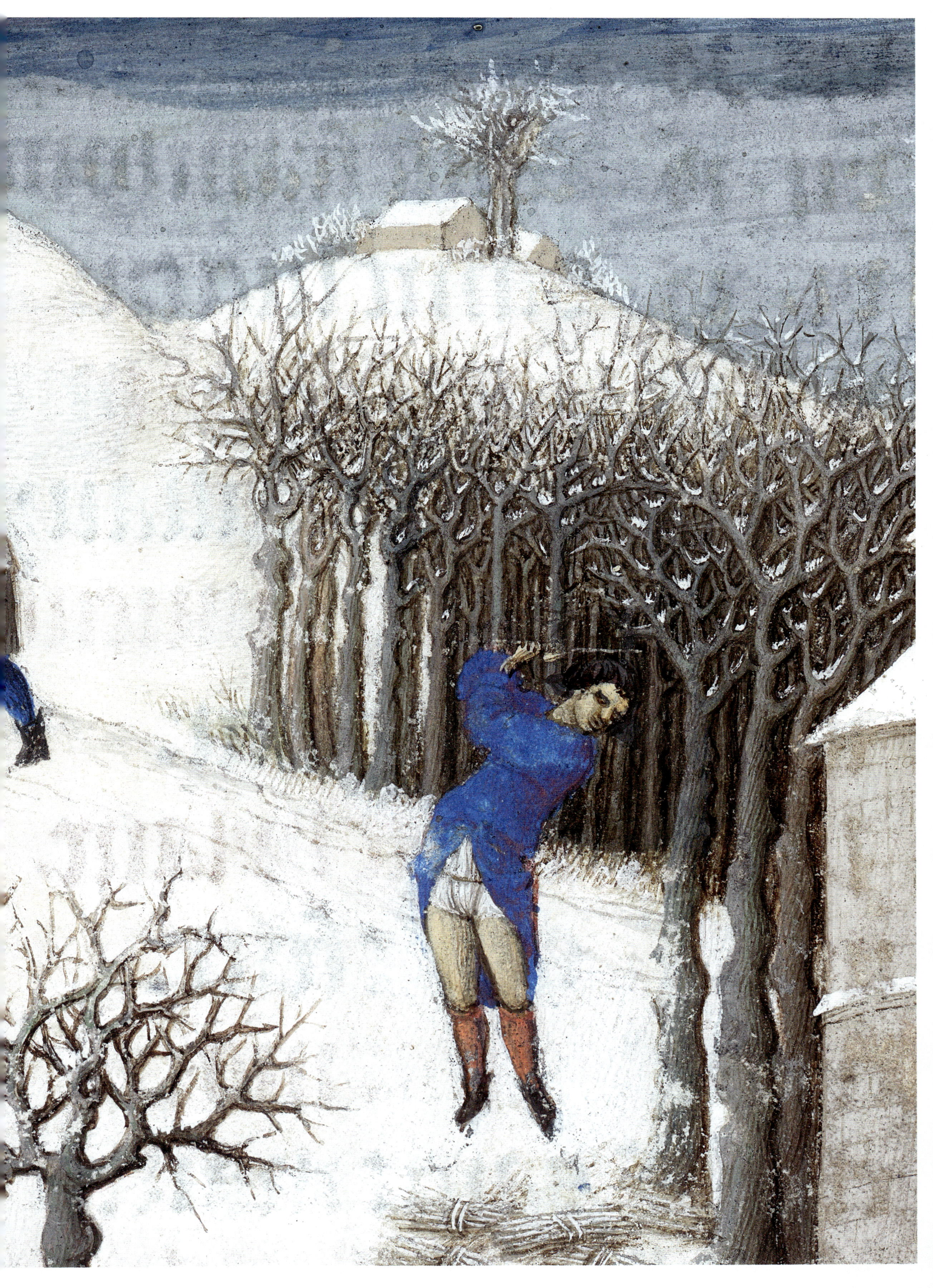

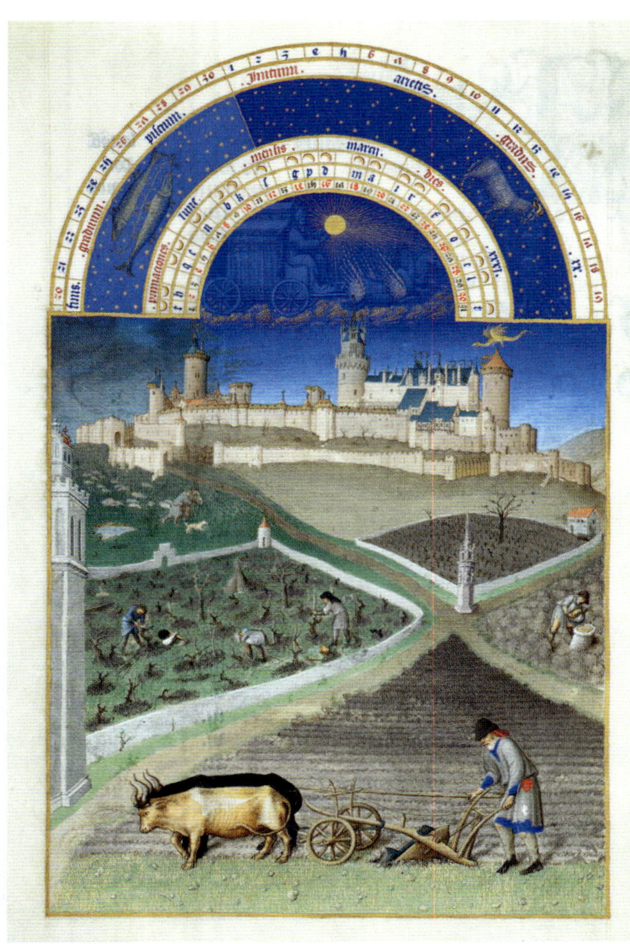

Van Lymborch brothers, *Très Riches Heures*, fol. 3v: March

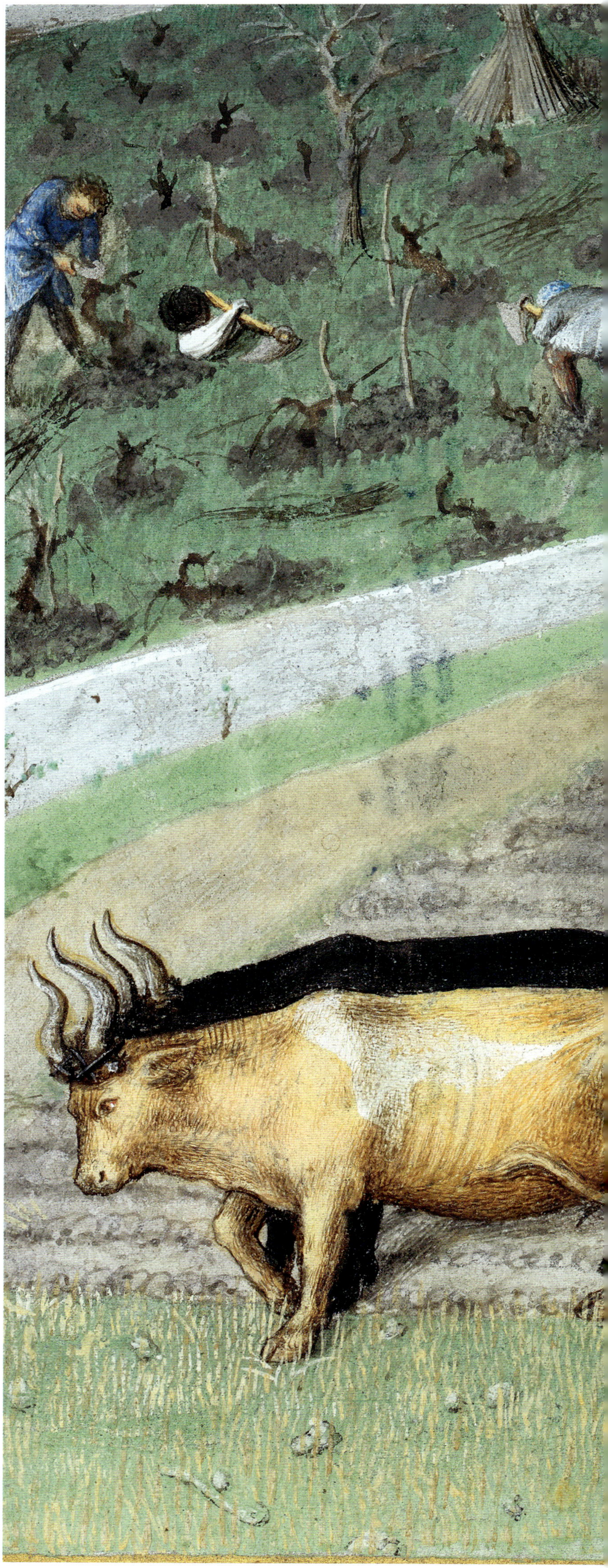

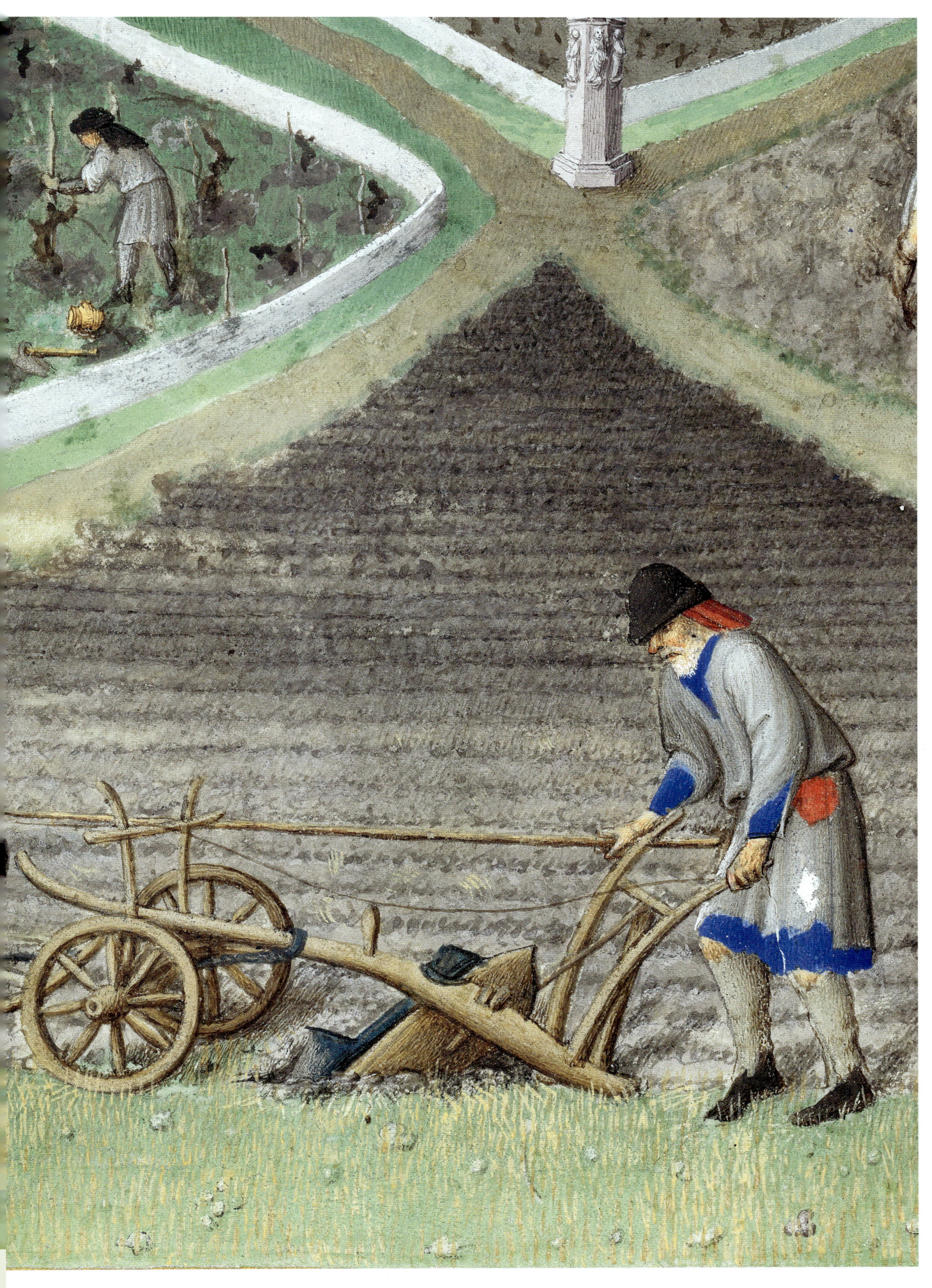

# THE VAN LYMBORCH BROTHERS

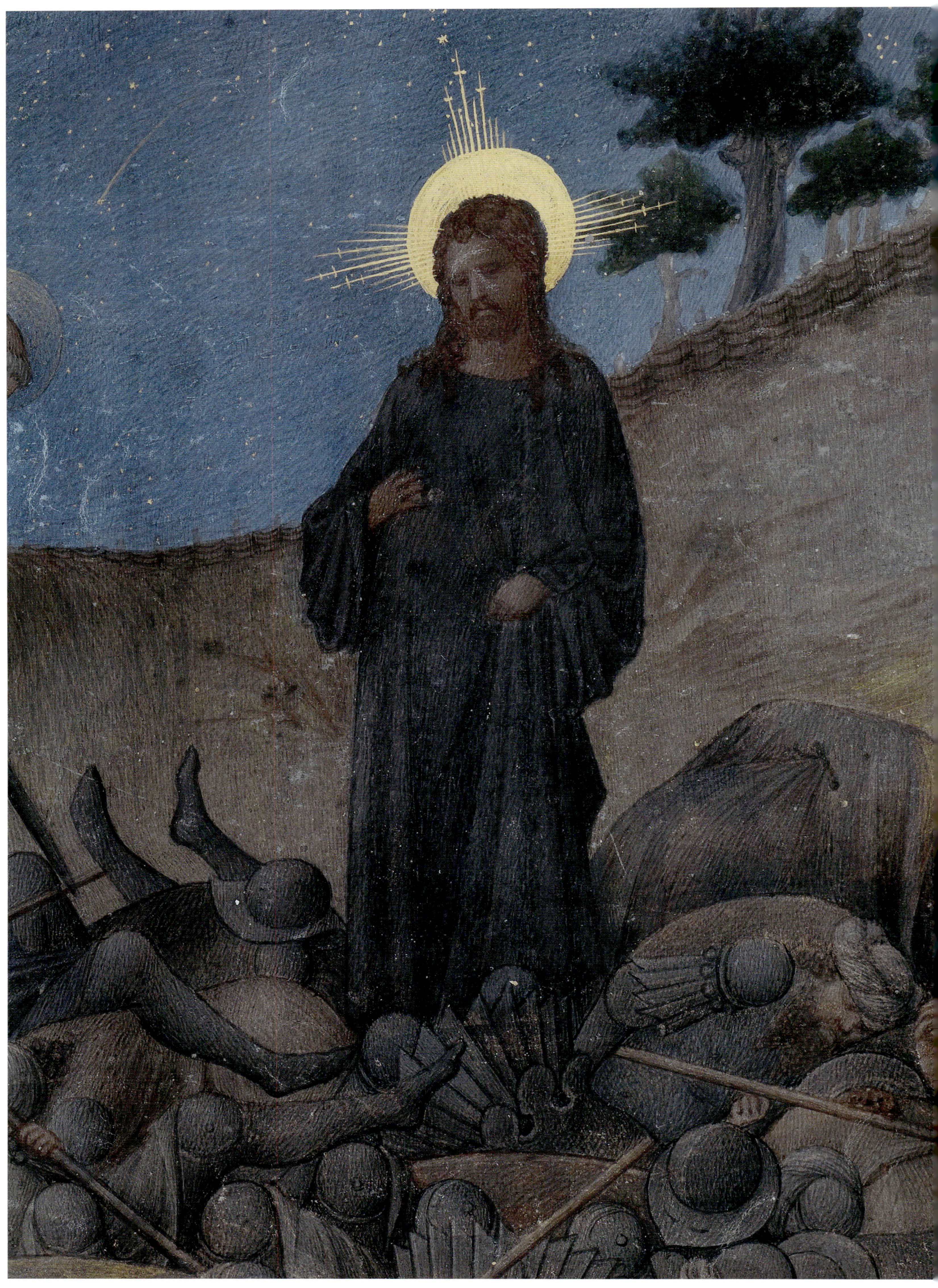

7.

# The Ultimate Masterpiece of the Van Lymborch Brothers

Mathieu Deldicque

The acquisition of the *Très Riches Heures du duc de Berry* by the Duke of Aumale in 1856 played a fundamental role in the rediscovery of the Van Lymborch brothers, a role that is often overlooked. In fact, it was only in 1881, when Léopold Delisle linked their final and most extraordinary masterpiece to the record of "unes très riches heures" (a very rich book of hours) in the inventory drawn up after the Duke of Berry's death that "Pol and his brothers" (also mentioned in the inventory) began to recover their artistic identity.In 1904, following the first archival study devoted to them a few years earlier,[1] another expert in the Musée Condé collections, Paul Durrieu, a graduate of the École Nationale des Chartes and a member of L'Institut de France, published the first monograph on the three brothers.[2] However, it was not until Millard Meiss's magnum opus, seventy years later, that the three painters were properly contextualized, their body of work enriched, and, above all, the pictorial revolution they set in motion understood.[3] The exhibitions devoted over the last twenty years to the *Très Riches Heures*[4] and the *Belles Heures*[5] in addition to the *Maelwael Van Lymborch Studies*[6] have helped to deepen our knowledge of the brothers, so much so that they are now among the most-studied artists of the French Middle Ages. No doubt the most recent analyses of their final masterpiece presented in this book will shed even more light on these prodigies of illumination.

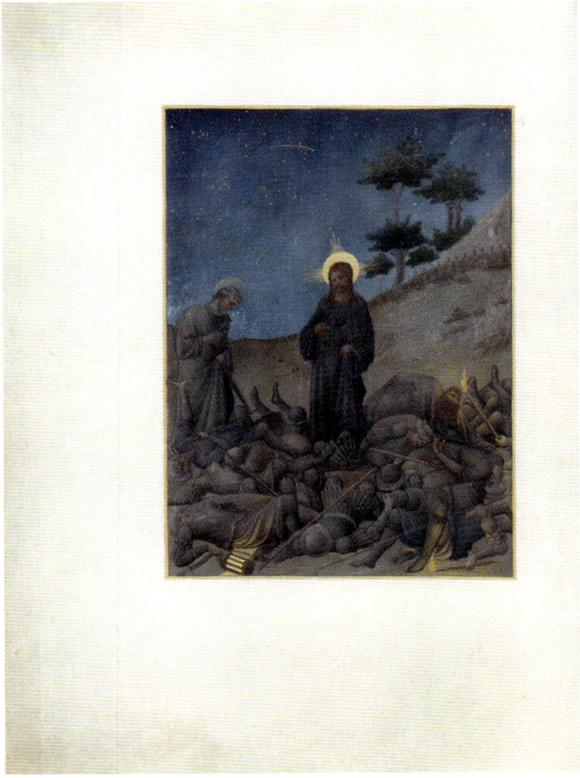

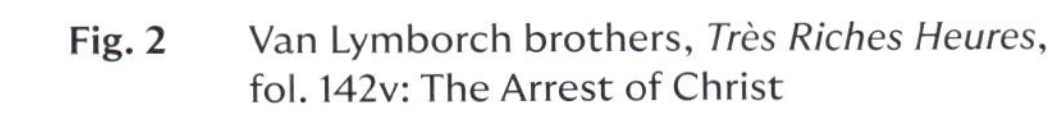

**Fig. 2** Van Lymborch brothers, *Très Riches Heures*, fol. 142v: The Arrest of Christ

**Fig. 1** Van Lymborch brothers, *Très Riches Heures*, fol. 142v: The Arrest of Christ, detail

**Fig. 3** Following pages: Van Lymborch brothers and Jean Colombe, *Très Riches Heures*, fols. 71v–72: The Procession of St. Gregory or The Institution of the Great Litany

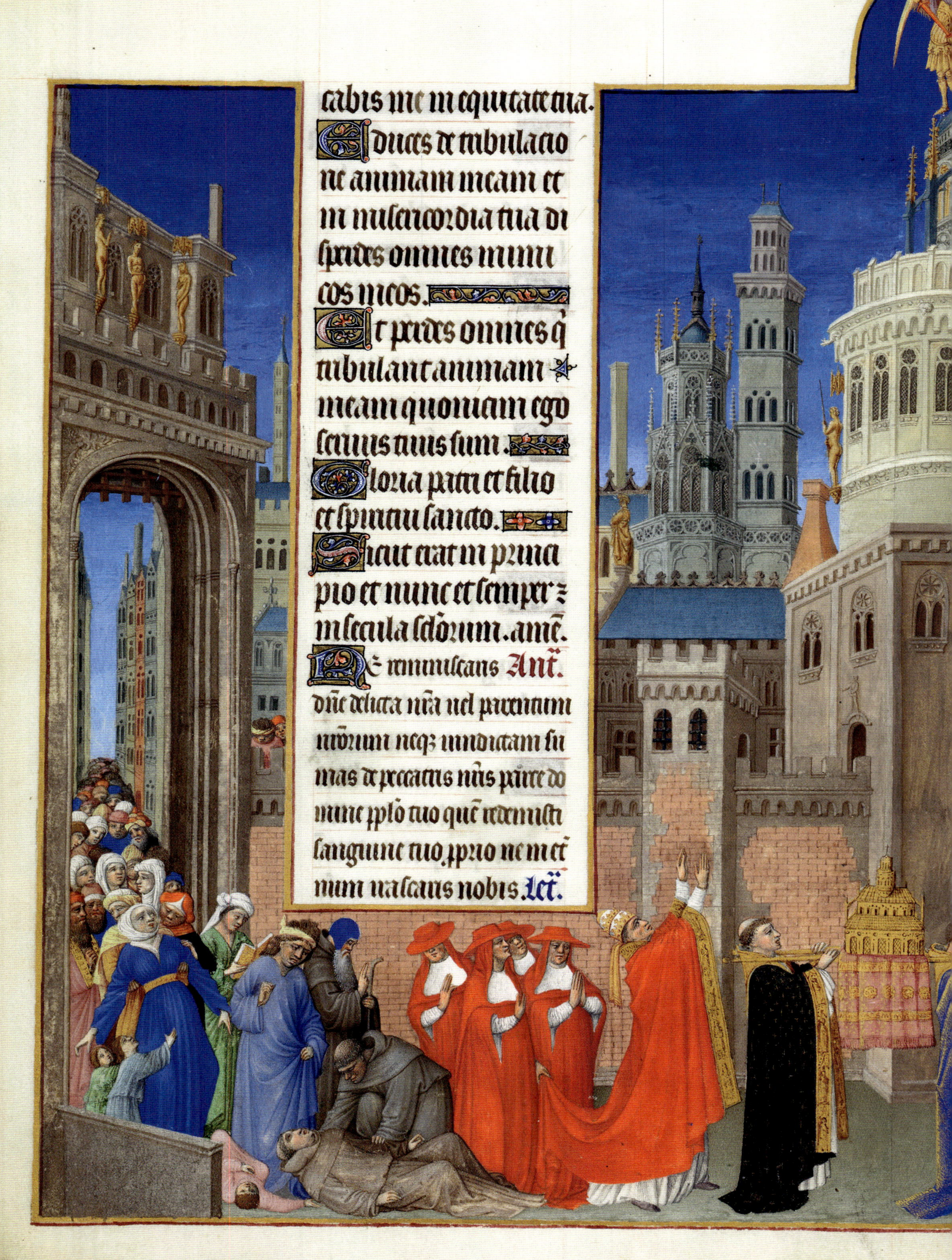

cabis me in equitate tua.
Educes de tribulatio
ne animam meam et
in misericordia tua di
sperdes omnes inimi
cos meos.
Et perdes omnes q̄
tribulant animam
meam quoniam ego
seruus tuus sum.
Gloria patri et filio
et spiritui sancto.
Sicut erat in princi
pio et nunc et semper &
in secula seculorum. amen.
Ne reminiscaris Ant.
dñe delicta nr̄a uel parentum
nr̄orum neq̄ uindictam su
mas de peccatis nr̄is parce do
mine p̄plo tuo quē redemisti
sanguine tuo, ꝑpro ne in et
num irascaris nobis. Let.

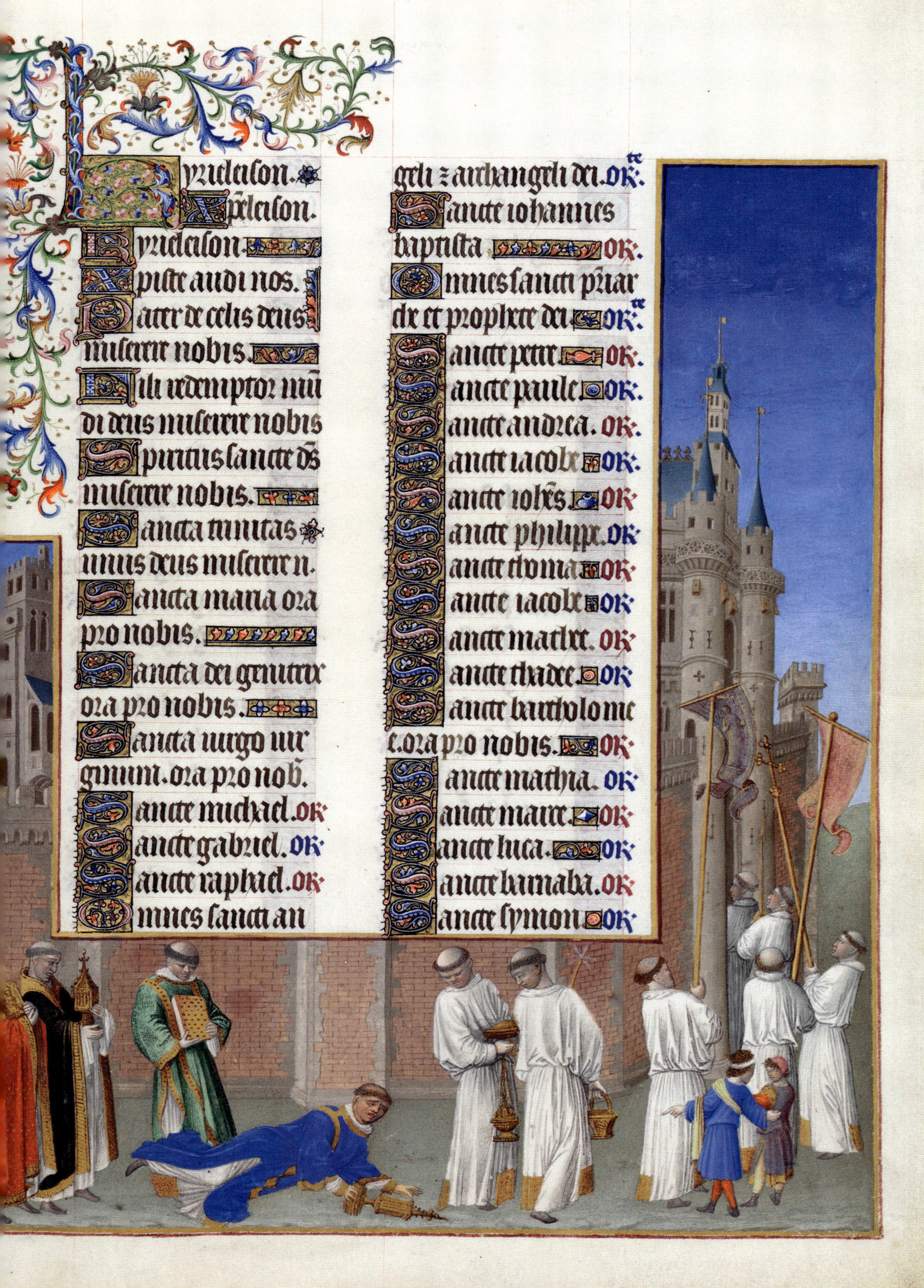
Kyrieleison.
Xpeleison.
Kyrieleison.
Xpiste audi nos.
Pater de celis deus
miserere nobis.
Fili redemptor mun-
di deus miserere nobis
Spiritus sancte deus
miserere nobis.
Sancta trinitas
unus deus miserere n.
Sancta maria ora
pro nobis.
Sancta dei genitrix
ora pro nobis.
Sancta virgo vir-
ginum. ora pro nob.
Sancte michael. or.
Sancte gabriel. or.
Sancte raphael. or.
Omnes sancti an-
geli et archangeli dei. or.
Sancte iohannes
baptista. or.
Omnes sancti patriar-
che et prophete dei. or.
Sancte petre. or.
Sancte paule. or.
Sancte andrea. or.
Sancte iacobe. or.
Sancte iohannes. or.
Sancte philippe. or.
Sancte thoma. or.
Sancte iacobe. or.
Sancte mathee. or.
Sancte thadee. or.
Sancte bartholome-
e. ora pro nobis. or.
Sancte mathia. or.
Sancte marce. or.
Sancte luca. or.
Sancte barnaba. or.
Sancte symon. or.

## THE CHILDREN OF NIJMEGEN AND THE DUKE OF BURGUNDY

Appearing like comets in the star-filled sky of International Gothic (fig. 2), the Van Lymborch brothers nevertheless came from a universe whose contours were already well charted. Ever since Friedrich Gorissen's excavation of the archives in the 1950s, we are well familiar with their environment.[7] Their family came from a village in Limburg, between Aachen and Liège, where their grandfather Johannes lived before they moved further north to Nijmegen, capital of the wealthy duchy of Guelders. Johannes's son, Arnold de Lymborgh, a woodcarver, worked for the Duke of Guelders. He married Mechteld (or Metta) Maelwael, sister of the great painter Johan Maelwael,[8] who themselves came from a line of painters attached to the Duke of Guelders, specializing in heraldic paintings. Arnold and Metta had at least six children, the three eldest of whom are the illuminators we are interested in, Herman (b. c. 1385), Paul (b. c. 1386–87), and Johan (b. c. 1388).

The Van Lymborch-Maelwael family lived quite comfortably in Nijmegen. The three brothers probably began their training in the family workshop—their painted figures, whose corporal presence is worthy of sculpture, retain traces of this background. It was probably Arnold's death (after 1395) that altered the destiny of Herman, Paul, and Johan.

The boys, still children, were taken in by their uncle, who was making his debut in Paris, working for Queen Isabeau of Bavaria, great-niece of the Duchess of Guelders. He received his first documented commission in the autumn of 1396, before becoming painter to Philip the Bold, Duke of Burgundy, in August 1397. It was at this time, 1396–97, that Herman and Johan, aged twelve and nine, respectively, were sent at their uncle's instigation to work for the Parisian goldsmith Alebret de Bonne, who supplied the Duke of Burgundy, among others. An epidemic of the plague, heralding the one they would depict much later in the *Très Riches Heures* (fols. 71v-72r; fig. 3), sent them back to Nijmegen in 1399. This proved to be an ill-fated journey, however, as they were captured on their way through Brabant, which was in conflict with Guelders, and held hostage in Brussels for six months, from November 1399 to May 1400. These "jonnes enfants" (young children), then aged fifteen and twelve, were freed thanks to the reputation of their uncle Johan Maelwael among the painters and goldsmiths of Brussels and to his intervention with Philip the Bold, who paid their

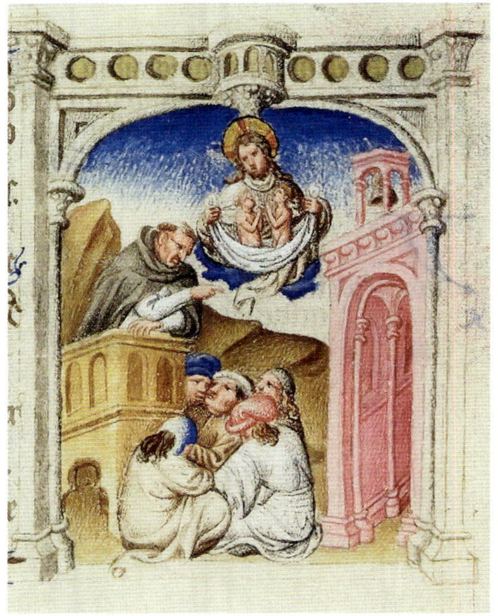

**Fig. 4** Van Lymborch brothers, *Bible moralisée*, fol. 8: Abraham and the Church (Paris, Bibliothèque nationale de France, département des Manuscrits, Français 166)

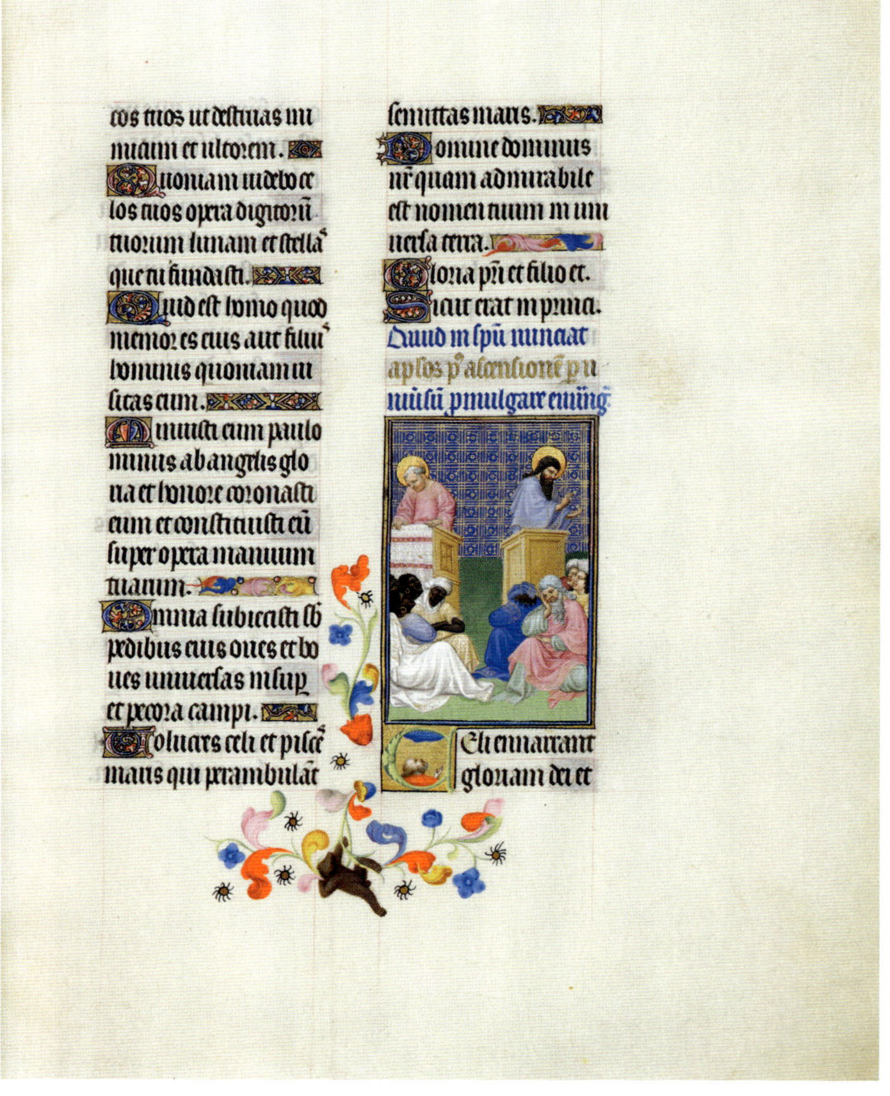

**Fig. 5** Van Lymborch brothers, *Très Riches Heures*, fol. 28: Yahweh, Sun of Righteousness (Psalm 19): Scene of the Apostles Preaching the Gospel to All the Peoples of the Earth

ransom. We do not know whether the two brothers continued on to Nijmegen or returned to France, but it is in Dijon that we pick up their track, along with that of their uncle, in the service of Philip the Bold, no doubt in gratitude for for their release. A clue that they may have seen the sculptures in the Chartreuse de Champmol, on the outskirts of Dijon, and in particular to the *Well of Moses* sculpted by Claus Sluter and painted by Van Lymborch in 1402, may be perceived in the *Très Riches Heures*: depicted from behind, Mary Magdalene embracing the foot of the sculpted Cross recurs in the Descent from the Cross (fol. 156v).[9] Paul, the only one of the three brothers not to have been held captive, was no doubt able to continue his training as a painter with his uncle, before he too entered the service of Philip the Bold.

On February 9, 1402, the Duke of Burgundy hired Paul and Johan for a period of four years in Paris, "pour faire les ystoires d'une très belle et très notable Bible" (to make the histories of a very beautiful and notable bible), a task to which the adolescents were to devote themselves exclusively, in return for accommodation and a substantial salary of ten sous per person per day. They were housed in the residence of Jean Durant, the duke's "physician," located in the cloister of Notre-Dame. This doctor, who was well versed in astrology—a field that fascinated the Van Lymborch brothers as much as the Duke of Berry—not only provided them with accommodation, but also saw to it, while overseeing the publishing venture, that they were provided with the precious materials they needed for their work, and all the while receiving now Philip the Bold, now a certain Jean of Berry . . .

The death of the Duke of Burgundy in April 1404 left unfinished the very first known work by the Van Lymborch brothers, the *Bible moralisée* (Moralized bible),[10] which is often identified with the one commissioned in 1402 and which was eventually to include almost 5000 miniatures. The three quires they painted were based on patterns from the *Bible moralisée* of John the Good,[11] probably on loan from the Duke of Burgundy. They served as a matrix for many of the iconographies later picked up in the *Belles Heures*[12] and the *Très Riches Heures*, particularly for the small vignettes illustrating the psalms, such as God Blessing Creation (fol. 2v, and *Très Riches Heures*, fol. 41v), Preaching from the Pulpit (fols. 8 and 28r, respectively), the Figure of the Church (fols. 8 and 28; figs. 4 and 5), or Longing for God with David Asleep (fols. 8v and 39v; figs. 6 and 7), among many other examples.[13]

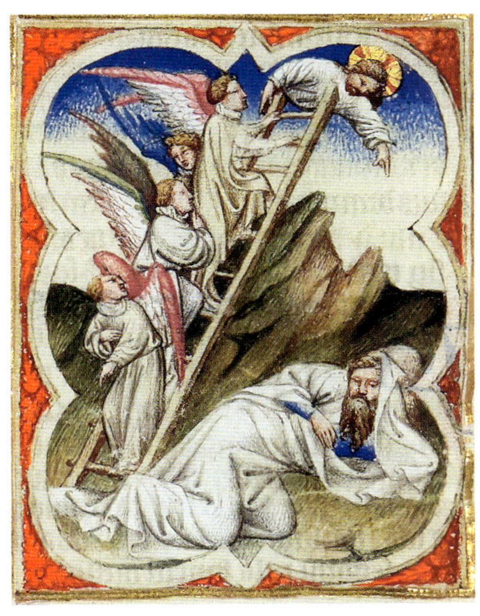

**Fig. 6** Van Lymborch brothers, *Bible moralisée*, fol. 8v: Jacob's Ladder (Paris, Bibliothèque nationale de France, département des Manuscrits, Français 166)

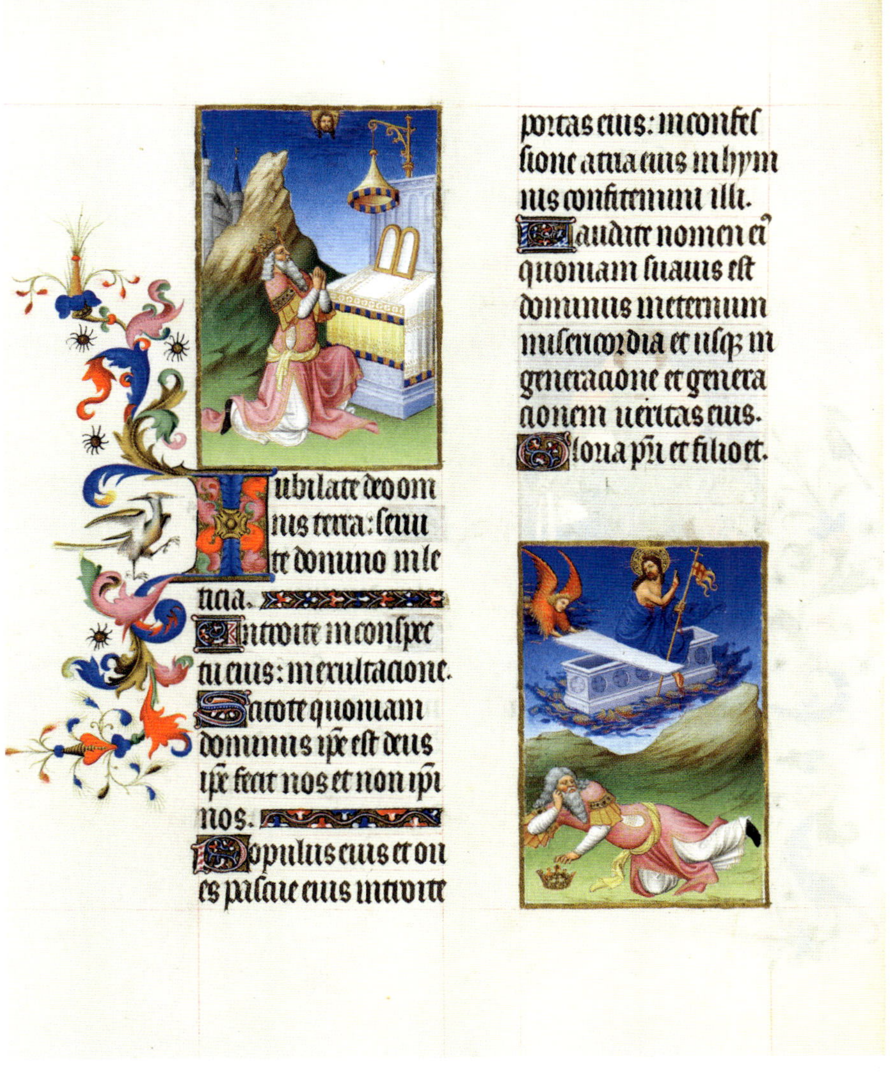

**Fig. 7** Van Lymborch brothers, *Très Riches Heures*, fol. 39v: Call to Praise (Psalm 100) and The Desire for God (Psalm 63): Asleep, David Sees Christ Coming Out of His Tomb and Blessing Him

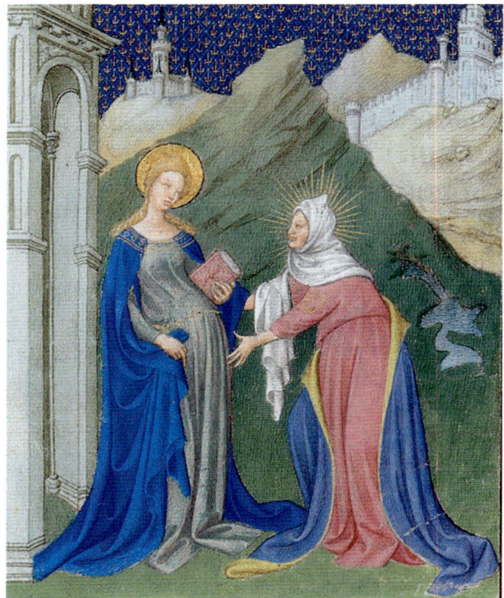

**Fig. 8** Van Lymborch brothers, *Belles Heures*, fol. 42v: The Visitation, detail (New York, The Metropolitan Museum of Art, The Cloisters Collection, Ms. Acc. 54.1. a, b)

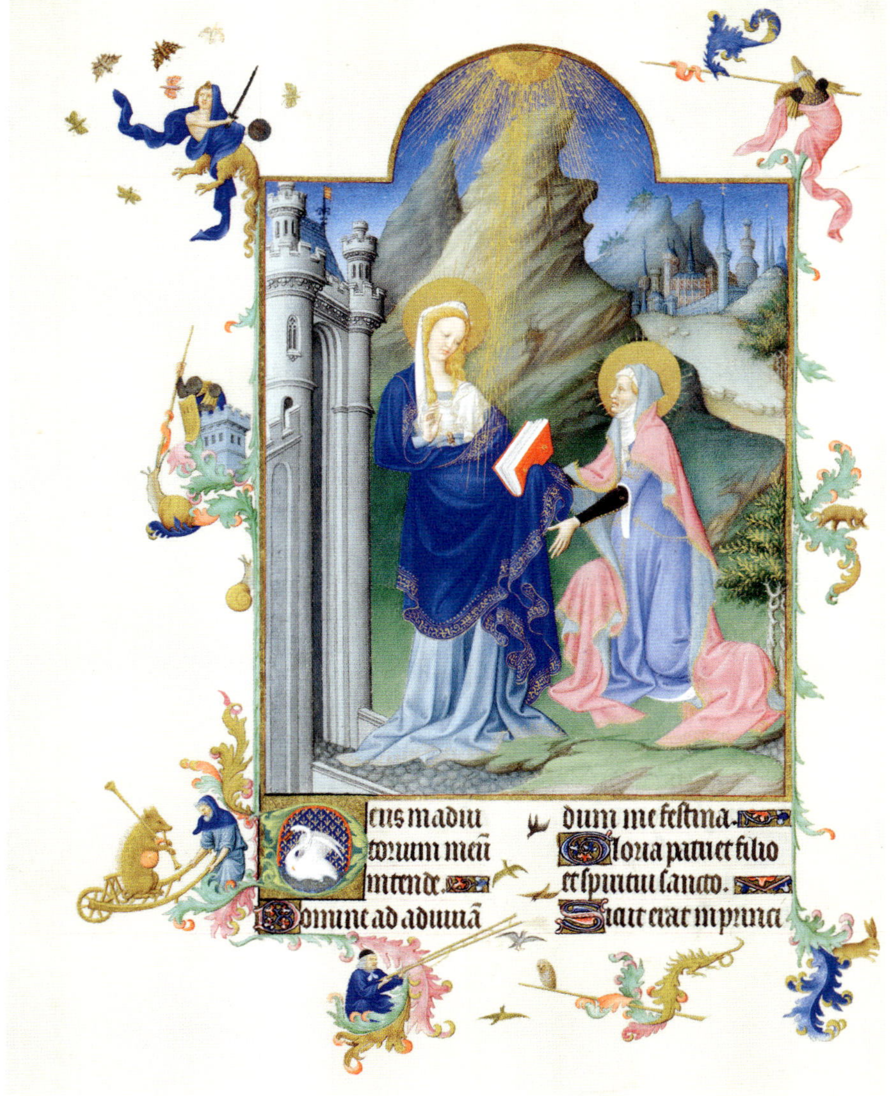

**Fig. 9** Van Lymborch brothers, *Très Riches Heures*, fol. 38v: The Visitation

What about the third brother, Herman, who did not take part in this undertaking? It is possible that upon his release he returned to his apprenticeship as a goldsmith. Éva Kovács has suggested identifying him with the goldsmith nicknamed "little Herman," from whom Jean of Berry purchased several objects on August 25, 1403.[14] The advanced training in goldsmithing of at least one of the brothers would explain the great richness of materials and the refined craftsmanship that can be seen in their great masterpiece at Chantilly.[15]

## THE DUKE OF BERRY'S CRAFTSMEN AT WORK

There was no shortage of opportunities to meet the man who was to become their greatest patron, and it was quite natural that after the death of Philip the Bold in April 1404 the brothers entered the service of his brother Jean of Berry. This was the beginning of one of the most fruitful alliances between artists and patron in the history of art, and one that would only end with the death of all those involved.

The Van Lymborch brothers first illustrated a charter drawn up in favor of the Sainte-Chapelle in Bourges and dated April 18, 1405, now lost. Around this date, "Paul et ses deux frères, enlumineurs" (Paul and his two brothers, illuminators),[16] received nine gold coins and then twelve more, in all likelihood not just in payment for this miniature, but perhaps also for other works that have not survived or, better still, for creations to come.[17] The duke was very fond of splendorous books of hours and was keen to use these works as a means to stimulate emulation among his favorite illuminators.

Toward the end of 1405, he commissioned the brothers to complete an ambitious book of hours (*Trés Belles Heures de Notre Dame*),[18] long in the making and which he was anxious to see finished.[19] They painted two pages that fitted into a pre-existing frame: the Adoration of the Trinity and Creation, on the one hand, and the Invocation of the Spirits and St. Anthony and the Satyr, on the other. A third miniature showing the Duke of Berry—which is only known today through a nineteenth-century reproduction—had been added at the end of the work by the artists, as they had done for the *Petites Heures*. We suggest

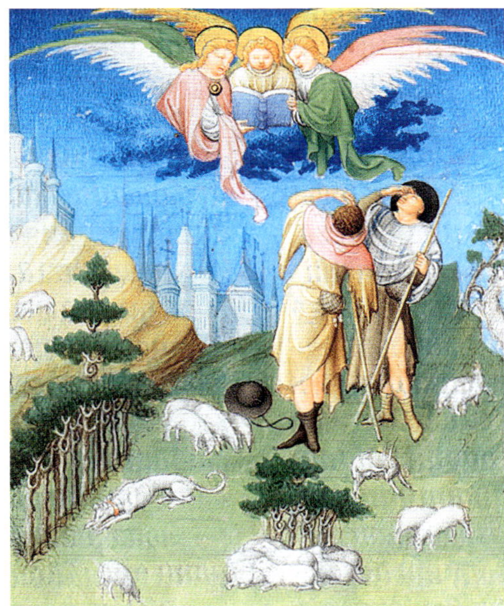

**Fig. 10** Van Lymborch brothers, *Belles Heures*, fol. 52: The Annunciation to the Shepherds, detail (New York, The Metropolitan Museum of Art, The Cloisters Collection, Ms. Acc. 54.1. a, b)

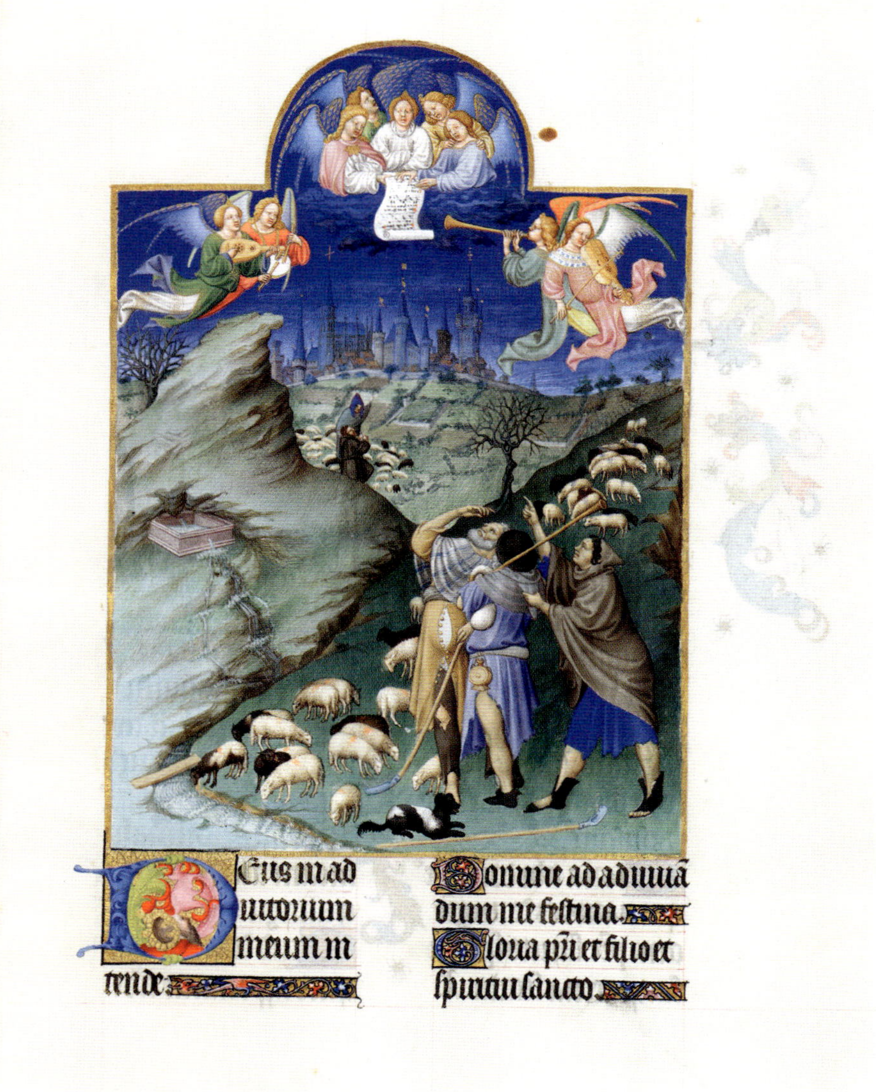

**Fig. 11** Van Lymborch brothers, *Très Riches Heures*, fol. 48: The Annunciation to the Shepherds

situating this work around 1405, based on the comparisons suggested by Timothy Husband between the Van Lymborch miniatures and the compositions of the same period, painted in the same *Très Belles Heures* by the Master of St. John the Baptist and the Master of the Holy Spirit, before the three brothers produced their first great masterpiece soon afterwards.[20]

Clearly satisfied with this conclusive test, Jean of Berry entrusted his young and talented protégés, also in 1405, with the decoration of a new book of hours, the *Belles Heures*, "lesquelles Heures Monseigneurs a fait faire par ses ouvriers" (which Hours Monseigneur had made by his craftsmen), as noted in the fourth inventory of his possessions drawn up by Robinet d'Étampes.[21] The term "ouvrier" (craftsman), far from being pejorative, rather shows how close the three brothers were to their patron. By late 1408 or early 1409, after almost three years of work, the illuminators had completed the revolutionary decoration of this manuscript.

The originality of the format of the illuminations in the *Belles Heures* struck the authors of the *Très Riches Heures*, as did their iconographic creativity, so that the former served as a prototype for the latter. Many of the compositions in the *Très Riches Heures* derive directly from them: The Visitation (fol. 38v; fig. 9) seems to be a culmination, with its heightened, courtly grace, of that in the *Belles Heures* (fol. 42v; fig. 8); the same holds for the Annunciation to the Shepherds (fol. 48; fig. 11 / fol. 52; fig. 10) and the Adoration of the Magi (fol. 54v; fig. 15 / fol. 52; fig. 12, p. 55). While the Institution of the Great Litany to combat the plague is broken down into four images in the *Belles Heures* (fols. 73–74v), it is the subject of a single composition spread over a double page in the *Très Riches Heures* (fols. 71v–72; fig. 3). As they moved from one book to the other, the miniatures took up more space on the page, and we get see the extent to which the atmospheric horizons deepened considerably, along with the wealth of detail and the embodiment of the scenes.[22] This close relationship between the works further bolsters the idea that the *Belles Heures* was highly regarded by Jean of Berry and played a key role in his growing fondness for the Van Lymborch brothers.

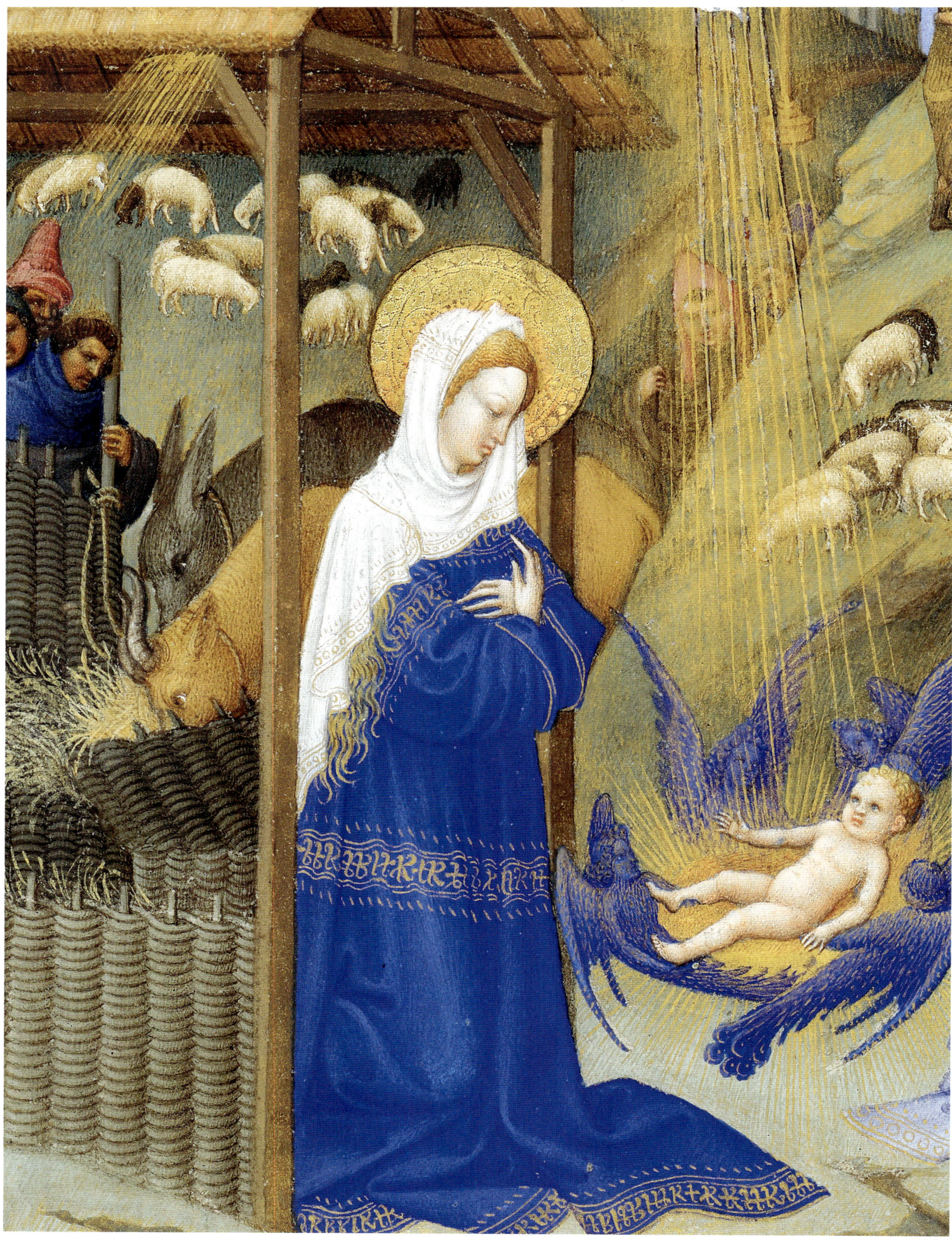

**Fig. 12** Van Lymborch brothers, *Très Riches Heures*, fol. 44v : The Nativity, detail

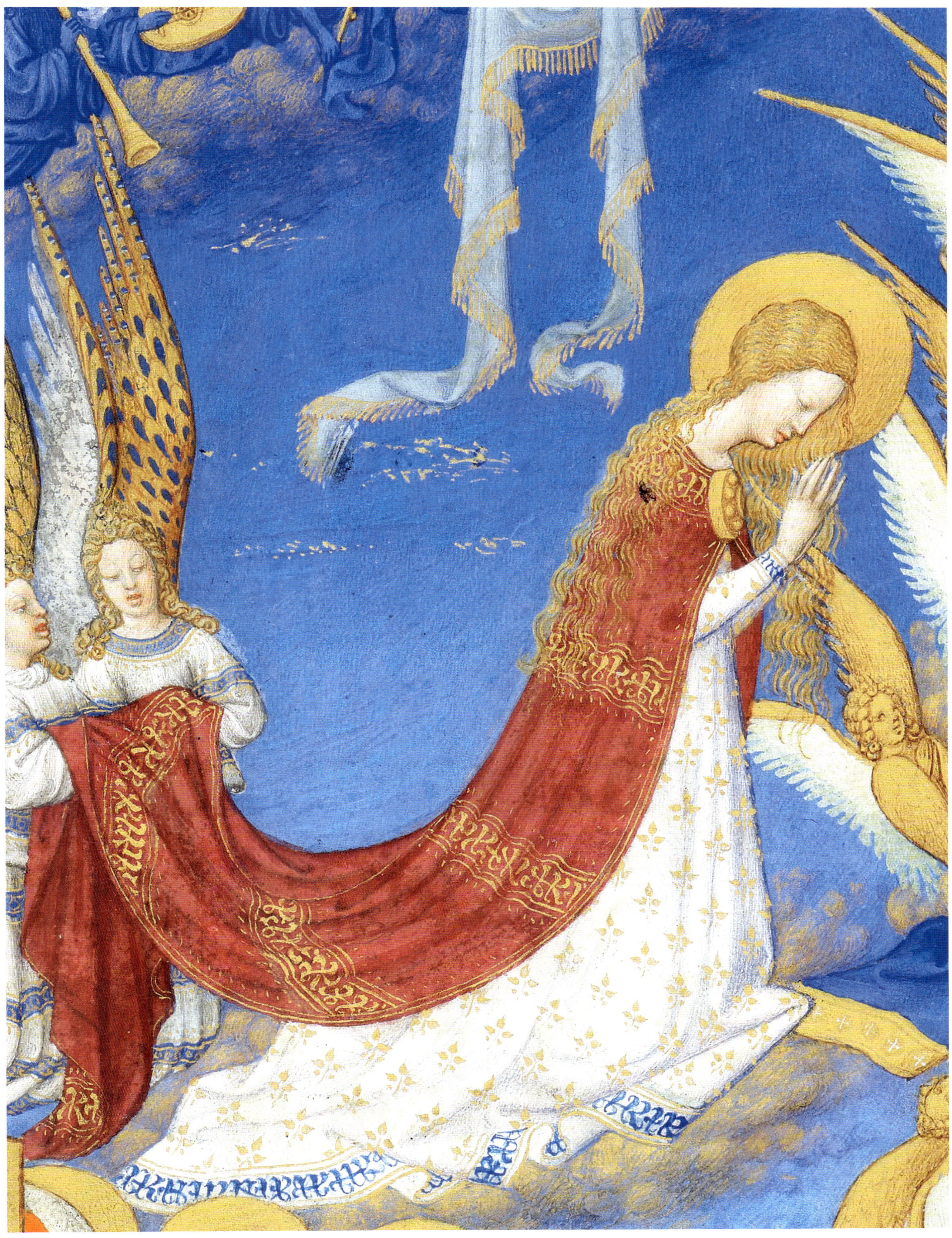

**Fig. 13** Van Lymborch brothers, *Très Riches Heures*, fol. 60v: The Coronation of the Virgin, detail

**Fig. 14** Following pages: Van Lymborch brothers, *Très Riches Heures*, fol. 48: The Annunciation to the Shepherds, detail

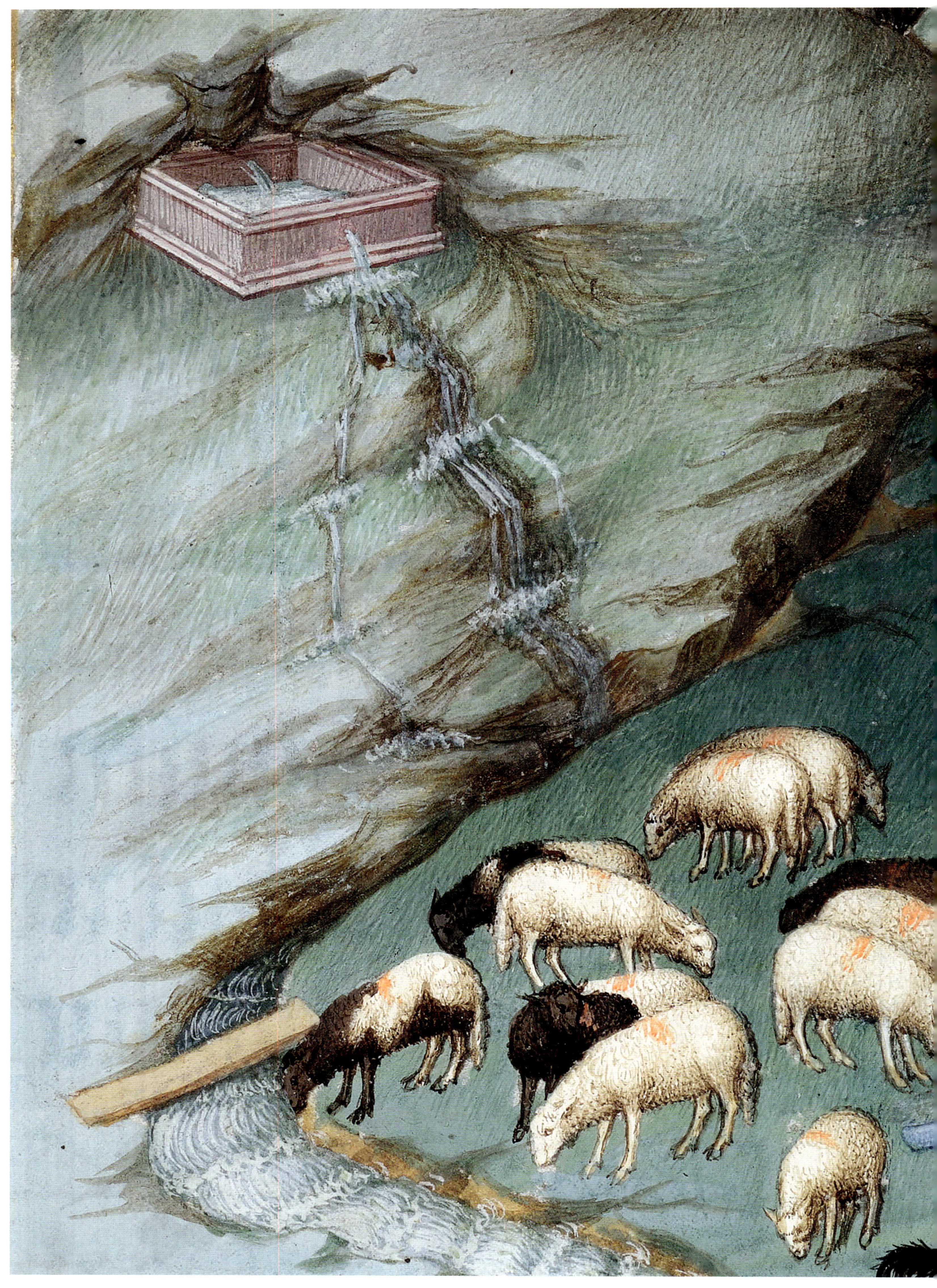

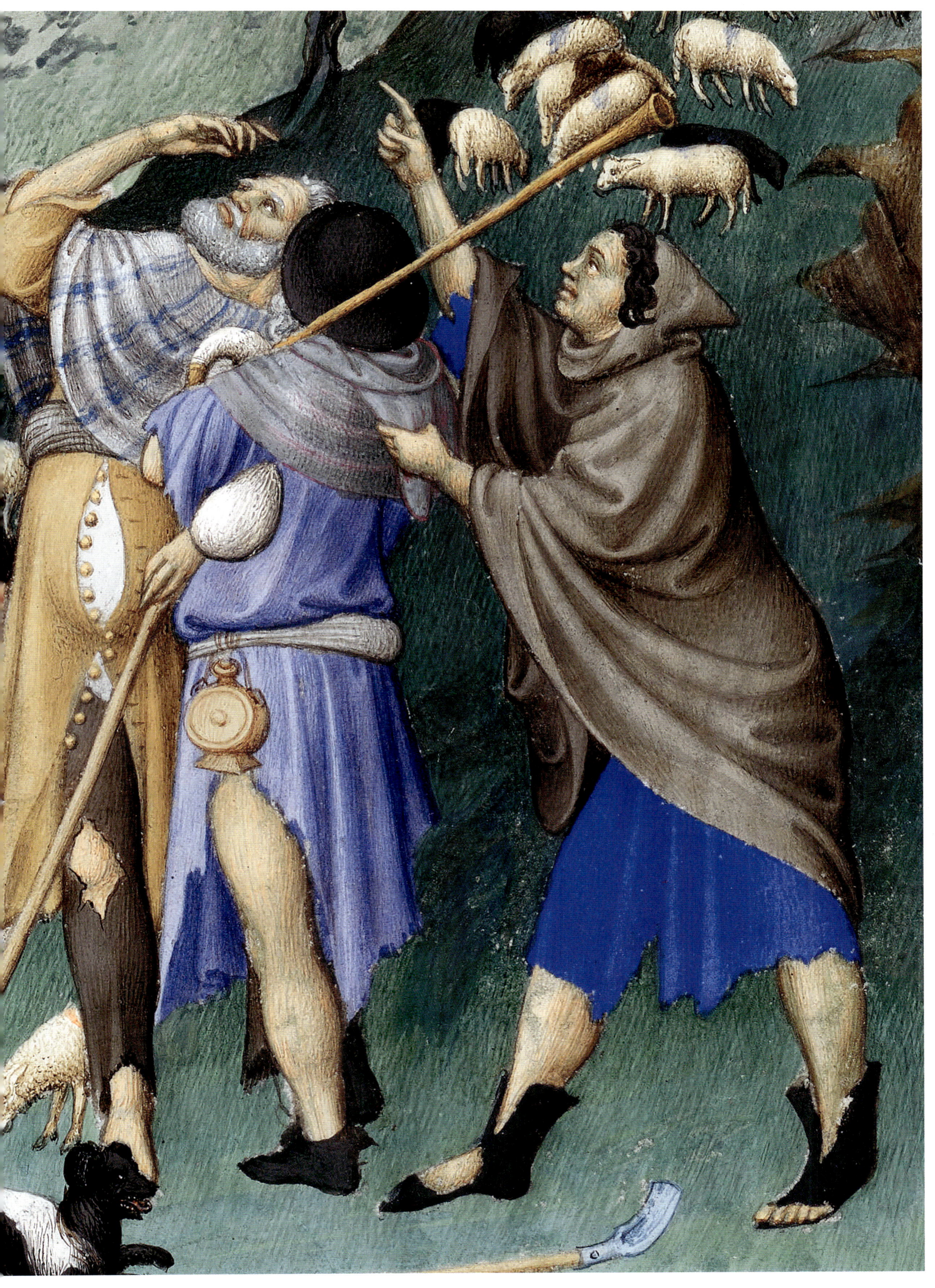

The other contributions of the three brothers were more sporadic: Consider the isolated miniature of St. Christopher Carrying the Christ Child, from an unknown book of hours (fig. 16),[23] which is similar to the *Belles Heures* (c. 1408–10), or the page added around 1412 to the *Petites Heures* showing Jean of Berry setting off on a pilgrimage (fol. 288). In addition to the illuminated charter mentioned above and the page from the lost *Belles Heures de Notre-Dame*, the latter miniature shows that the Van Lymborch brothers also specialized in portraying their duke, including in group scenes where the other figures are not singled out, as in the month of January in the *Très Riches Heures*.[24] Following the example of Jean de Cambrai, whose portraits, given their realism, are the sculpted equivalents of those of the Van Lymborch brothers, the brothers went along with Jean of Berry's fascination with his own image and the abundant use he made of it. This pronounced interest in portraiture did not stop there: in November 1408, Paul van Lymborch, who we know was an easel painter,[25] was working at the duke's château in Bicêtre, no doubt on the series of portraits of French kings and Roman emperors that could be admired there. For his part, Johan Maelwael painted a likeness of John the Fearless in 1413 for King John I of Portugal.

The oeuvre of the Van Lymborch brothers has recently been enriched by several drawings formerly attributed to the Master of St. Jerome, an artist once considered a member of the Van Lymborch entourage or one of their followers, but who today is readily identified with one of the three brothers.[26] In addition to the frontispiece of the *Bible moralisée* (Moralized bible) (fol. A; fig. 17), which is more accomplished than the illuminations of the quires of the same work executed by Paul and Johan between 1402 and 1404, and probably dating from around 1410, we can now add four marginal drawings from the *Heures Douces* (fols. 105, 108v–109, 110), completed in 1409, and preparatory drawings for miniatures painted afterwards for the *Psalter of Henry VI*, begun before 1415).[27] As for the frontispiece of the Valerius Maximus manuscript,[28] perhaps intended

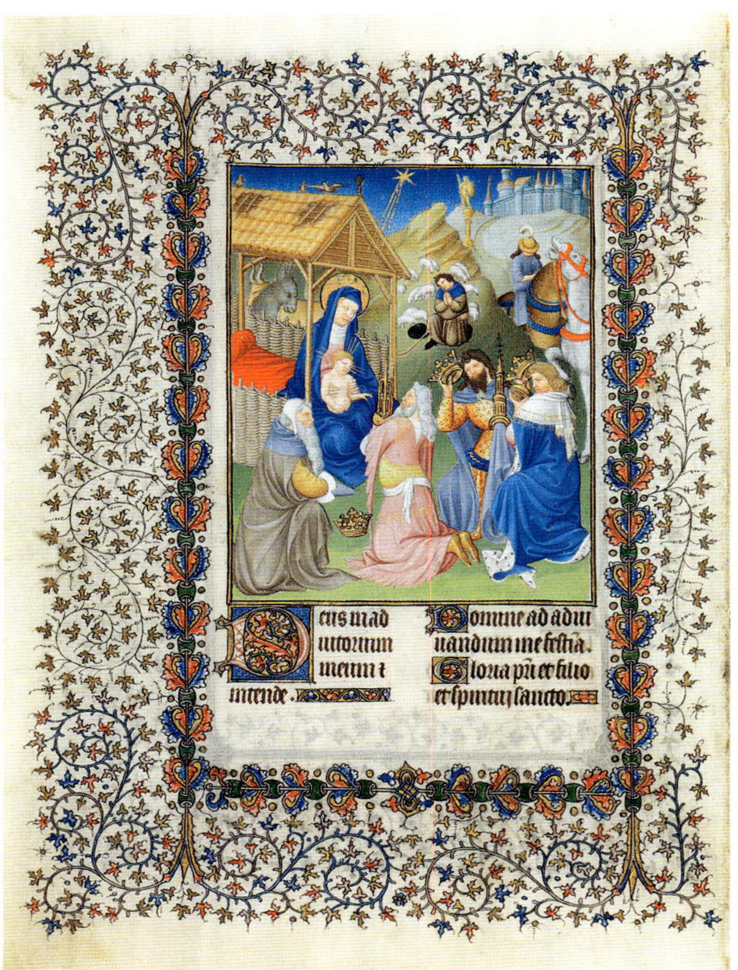

**Fig. 15** Van Lymborch brothers, *Belles Heures*, fol. 54v: The Adoration of the Magi

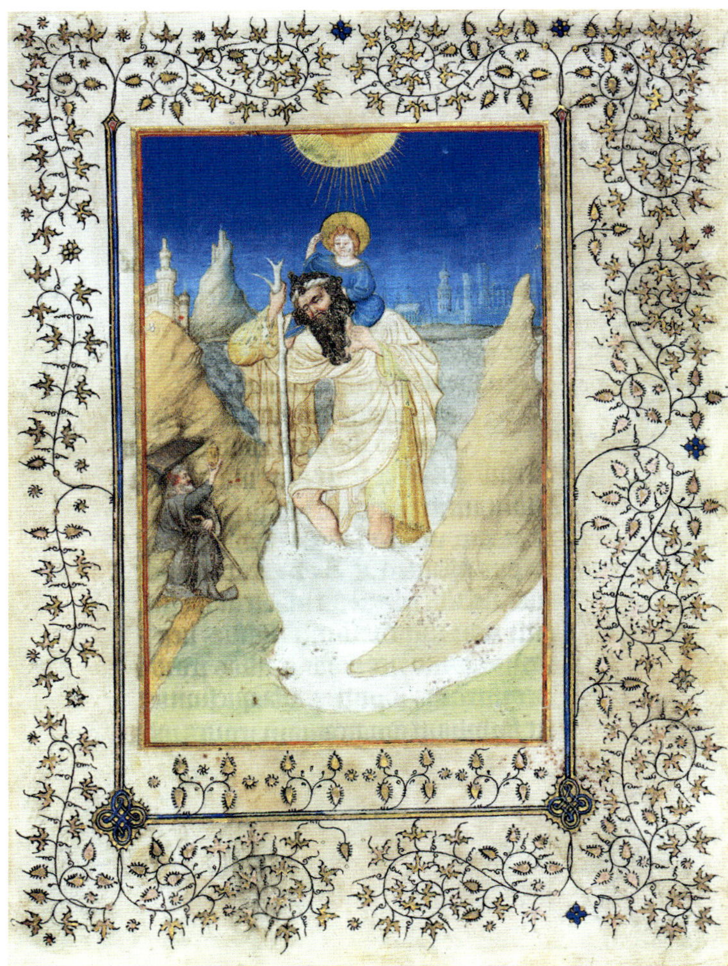

**Fig. 16** Van Lymborch brothers, *St. Christopher Carrying the Christ Child, leaf from a book of hours* (Washington, National Gallery of Art, Acc. No. B-13, 520)

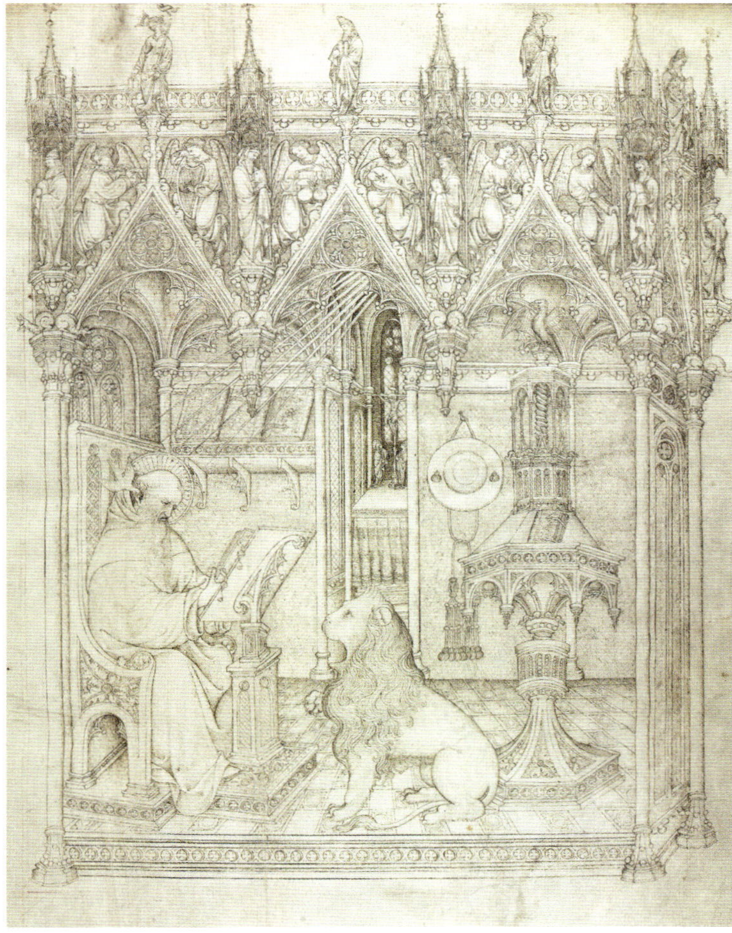

**Fig. 17** Van Lymborch brothers, *Bible moralisée*, fol. A: St. Jerome in His Study (Paris, Bibliothèque nationale de France, département des Manuscrits, Français 166)

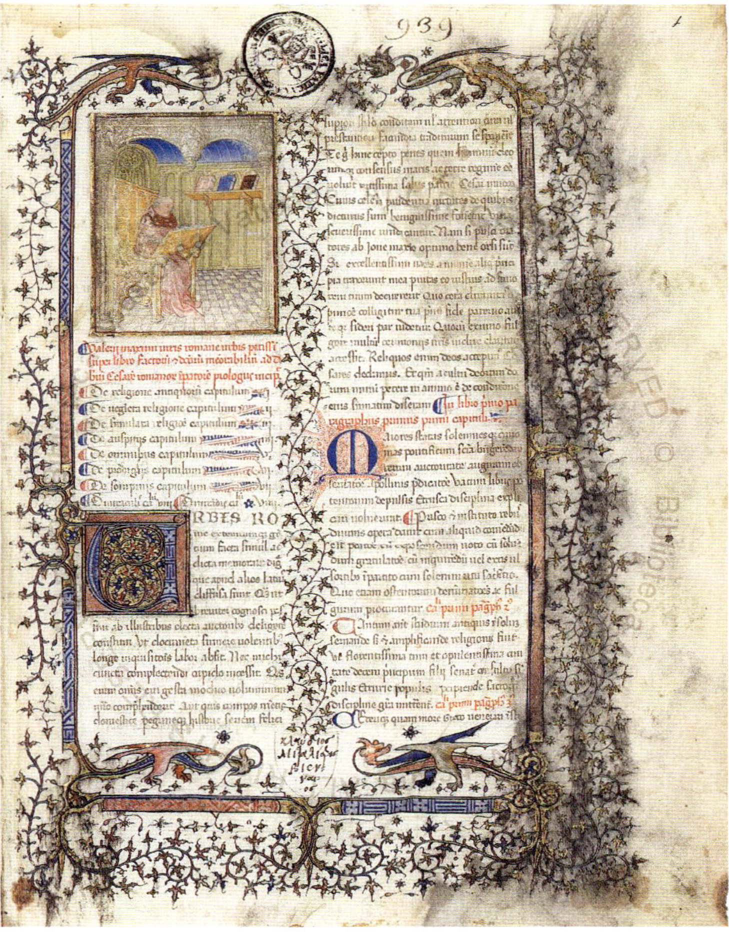

**Fig. 18** Entourage or follower of the Van Lymborch brothers (?), Valerius Maximus, *Facta et dicta memorabilia*, fol. 1 (Rome, Vatican Library, Cod. Reg. Lat. 939)

for Jean of Berry or at any rate for a member of the royal family (fig. 18), it has been attributed both to the Van Lymborch studio and to the Van Lymborch brothers themselves. This miniature seems to us to be a little earlier than the generally accepted date of around 1410[29] and should rather be compared with those of the *Bible moralisée* of 1402–04 (excluding the frontispiece, which is later, as we have seen). The interior of the study, with its paneled barrel vault, can be seen, for example, on folio 7v. Rather than an echo of the miniature in the *Belles Heures* depicting St. Jerome translating the bible (fol. 187v), the illumination of the Valerius Maximus is either the result of an earlier inspiration, featuring a shortish figure—a motif destined for a brilliant development, culminating in the frontispiece of the *Bible moralisée*—or the work of a collaborator or follower not far removed from the Spitz Master.

## MONSEIGNEUR WANTS HIS PEOPLE TO BECOME RICH

However, this list obscures one fact: The *Belles Heures* is the only manuscript whose decoration was completed by the Van Lymborch brothers. The relative slowness in completing a rather small undertaking can be explained by the fact that these illuminators, some of whom were also painters or goldsmiths, had other tasks. They regularly returned to Nijmegen on business or for family reasons. As court artists, and as such exempt from the constraints of the market and the constant pursuit of clients, they were among Jean of Berry's regular entourage, taking part in the duke's life and sometimes accompanying him on his travels.

In fact, the duke wanted "his people to become rich," as his treasurer Jean de Bétizac told the king's council, which reproached him for enriching himself at the expense of the inhabitants of Béziers.[30] Like the treasurer, the Van Lymborch brothers were greatly favored by their patron, Paul, in particular, who enjoyed a special place in the ducal entourage. The Duke of Berry, who liked to marry his entourage off to eligible parties, took it upon himself to provide Paul with a rich heiress. The duke considered giving him the very young Gillette, daughter of the late Gilles Le Mercier, a wealthy merchant from Bourges.[31] The duke had housed the young girl in his château at Étampes (the same one depicted in the month of August); she had been subjected to a particularly gruesome abduction, probably committed as early as August 1406 by the duke's henchmen at the Parisian house where the Bishop of Puy was staying: they "avoient rompu l'uiz et avoient prinz une bible, breviaire, ceincture et autres chosettes, et une fillette" (had broken into the room and taken a bible, breviary, belt and other things, and a little girl).[32] Besides the young heiress, the duke's men also took advantage of the opportunity to take anthing that pleased their master, including precious manuscripts and *objets d'art*. This being said, by no stretch of the imagination could one put all these predatory acts on the same footing and equate Jean of Berry's delight in parchment with his delight in carnal pleasures . . . [33]

Aged only eight in 1408, Gillette was about to marry "un peintre alemant qui besoignoit pour lui en son hotel de Wincestre lez Paris" (a German painter who worked for him in his residence in Wincestre near Paris)—that is, Paul van Lymborch, who was then working on the Bicêtre site—against the wishes of her mother and her family, who filed a complaint with the Paris parliament in November. The king intervened on January 7, 1409, and on February 11 an arrangement was reached between the parties. The marriage still took place, probably in 1412, when Gillette had reached marriageable age—the same age at which Jeanne de Boulogne had married the elderly Jean of Berry. We do not believe that Gillette can be recognized, in January of the *Très Riches Heures*, in the man (!) in the blue hood near the dresser on the left of the picture; nor that the man in the grey hat drinking in front of him is one of the Van Lymborch brothers, as has sometimes been suggested. On the other hand, this brilliant miniature bears witness to the brothers' intimate knowledge of aristocratic life. This is what enabled them to paint with such acuity the many court scenes that punctuate the calendar in the Chantilly manuscript.

Jean of Berry was, as Christine de Pizan wrote, "debonaire a ses serviteurs" (generous with his servants), so much so that the Van Lymborch brothers were showered with gifts, jewels, and precious stones, particularly on the occasion of the *étrennes*, the exchange of gifts on New Year's Day. In 1408, for example, Paul received a ring with a small emerald mounted in a bear, which was the duke's emblem and a sign of his favor.[34] In 1411, he was given one of the most beautiful houses in Bourges, where he could live nobly, no doubt in the company of his brothers. Paul and Johan were appointed valets to Jean of Berry no later than 1411. Their rise to prominence is reflected in the sumptuousness of the gifts they gave their patron: On January 1, 1415, Paul presented him with a small agate salt cellar adorned with gold and gems. But, above all, it is an oft-reported anecdote that reveals how close our protagonists were. For the *étrennes* of 1411, the brothers offered the Duke a fake book, executed in a trompe l'oeil style: "un livre contrefait d'une pièce de bois paincte en semblance d'un livre, ou il n'a nuls fueillets ne riens escript, couvert de veluiau blanc à deux fermouers d'argent dorez esmaillez aux armes de monseigneur" (a fake book made from a piece of wood painted to resemble a book, with no leaves and nothing written in it, covered in white velum, with two silver clasps gilded and embellished with monseigneur's arms).[35] This witty gesture, a further demonstration of the skill of the artists, was no doubt also an allusion to their work rhythm, which was anything but moderate. And indeed, around 1411, they received an exceptional commission from the duke: This fake book presaged the failed delivery of an impossible masterpiece.

## THE CREATION OF THE *TRÈS RICHES HEURES*

Usually, 1411 is the year given as marking the beginning of the creation of the most ambitious, if not the most beautiful, manuscript of the Duke of Berry, a book that the inventory after the duke's death named, for posterity, the *Très Riches Heures*. Among the confessors featured on folio 73r is St. Albert: Albert of Sicily, a Carmelite venerated for his miracles (d. 1306), whose feast day was not established until 1411, as Patricia Stirnemann has shown.[36] After the copying, almost three illumination campaigns were carried out over the five years of creation, bringing together twenty-four craftsmen: four copyists, nine illuminators, eight painters of initials, and the three Van Lymborch brothers.[37] Inspired by the example of the *Grandes Heures* of Jacquemart de Hesdin, whose ambition paved the way for the *Très Riches Heures*, this was a colossal bookmaking venture, as all the elements of the decoration had to be painted, including the line ends, a practice that was completely unheard of at the time. Nevertheless, the masterpiece took shape as the paintbrushes were applied, without being subject to a predetermined plan. Three successive campaigns have been identified, thanks to the changes noted in the craftsmen and artists: The full illuminated pages were only introduced during the second campaign, while the last (probably 1415–16) concerned the calendar. The five years of work, interrupted by various journeys or parallel tasks, were not enough, with the result that none of the quires that make up the work was completed during the lifetime of the Van Lymborch brothers.

The brothers were rewarded with several payments for progress on the manuscript. Between October 1, 1413, and March 31, 1414, "Paoul, Jehannequin, and Harmant, frères" were remunerated together, although it was usually Paul who, acting as the overseer, was paid. Was he responsible for coordinating the publication of this work and distributing the decoration, not only among his brothers, but also among all the craftsmen involved? On October 24, 1413, he received six ecus, on November 7 ten ecus, and on November 9 the substantial sum of 100 ecus, "pour consideracion des bons et agreables services quil luy a faiz, fait chascun jour et espere que fasce ou temps a venir" (in consideration of the good and appreciable services he has rendered, rendered each day and hopes to render in the future).[38]

Where the work on the manuscript was done has never been precisely determined. There may well have been several locations, as the three brothers, although they lived in Bourges, also accompanied their master on his travels. After 1404, however, the Duke of Berry mainly lived in Paris; we know, for example, that he was there between March and August 1415. It was also in Paris that some of the illuminators who contributed to the decoration were active, foremost among them Haincelin de Haguenau (the Bedford Master), who, during the third illumination campaign (1414–15), drew the miniature of the Christmas Mass (fol. 158; fig. 3, p. 258), which mirrors a drawing of an unfinished missal intended for the Dauphin,[39] and four borders (fols. 86v, 152, 158, 182).[40] Did the Van Lymborch brothers take some of the leaves with them? Or, more likely, did the squires remain in Paris, awaiting their return, which would explain the three campaigns of decoration and the changes in the craftsmen? We know that in 1416 the manuscript was not mentioned among the possessions found in Bourges or at the château of

**Fig. 19** Van Lymborch brothers, *Très Riches Heures*, fol. 156v: Descent from the Cross

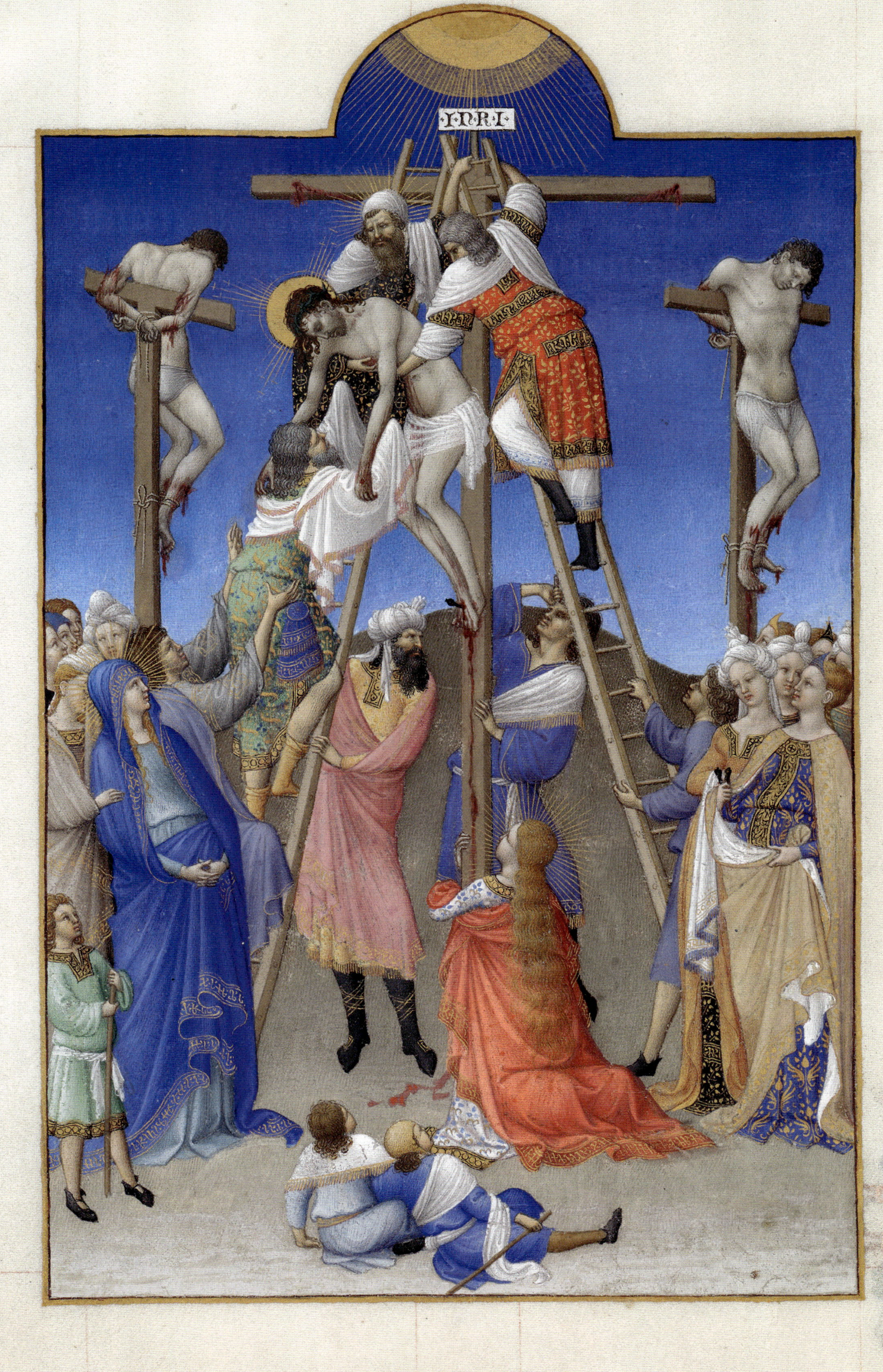
INRI

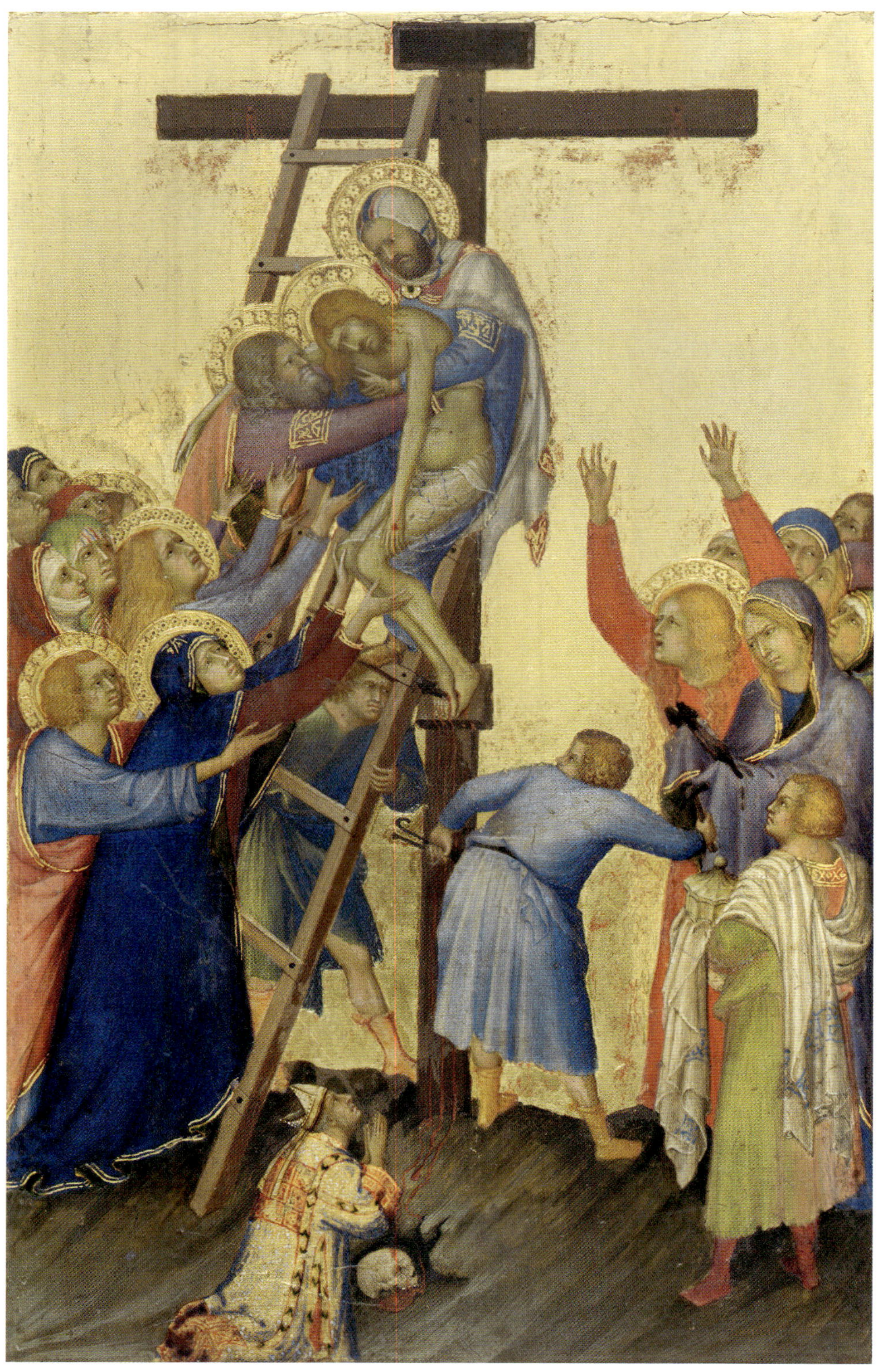

**Fig. 20** Simone Martini, Descent from the Cross, *Orsini Polyptych* (Antwerp, Koninklijk Museum voor Schone Kunsten, inv. 260)

Mehun-sur-Yèvre and brought to Paris for inventory. It was obviously already there.

Of the three brothers, who was responsible for what? Unravelling the tangle of hands in the Van Lymborch oeuvre, with its seemingly homogeneous style, is a delicate exercise. Millard Meiss went furthest in his attempt to divide the corpus into three groups corresponding to Paul, Johan, and Herman, sometimes questionably.[41] In Meiss's view, according to a rather anachronistic conception of a teleological progression of art history, Paul was the most avant-garde of the three. Some scholars have taken the analysis even further, at times distinguishing two different methods in a single miniature.[42] Of course, it is possible that each of the three brothers had his own specialty: Johan, the goldsmith (active in Paris in 1413), was perhaps the most experienced in architectural drawings, sometimes similar to the graceful, gold-plated structures of his time (in which case he could be identified with the Master of St. Jerome), or in ornate backgrounds; while Paul, the painter, may have focused on the duke's portraits or on coloring the miniatures. The subtle differences in palette noted here and there could also reflect different sensibilities.[43]

One should bear in mind, however, that depending on circumstances, travel opportunities or various obligations, the brothers may have worked jointly or separately, executing a miniature from start to finish, or assuming only one stage or part of another, alternating with the other brothers. While the underdrawings of the *Belles Heures* revealed by infrared reflectography seem to corroborate the existence of three distinct authors,[44] it is difficult, if not impossible, to draw the same conclusions for the *Très Riches Heures*, given the seemingly perfect harmony between the hands.

## THE TRANSEPT CROSSING OF A CATHEDRAL-LIKE BOOK

Three men, three brothers, for one book. A book that is a world unto itself, reflecting a multitude of sources and inspirations, ancient and modern, from the north and east and Italy—sources and inspirations that fit effortlessly into the great tradition of precious book illumination of the fourteenth century, and which ushered in a revolution in the making of pictures for books that perfectly echoed the political horizons of the time.[45]

The aim here is not to offer an exhaustive counterpoint to the study presented in this book on the links between the *Très Riches Heures* and the art of the north,[46] but to return to the Italian coloring of the manuscript. Let us not forget that Paul van Lymborch's hypothetical journey (or journeys) to the Italian peninsula[47] are highly unlikely; we now know the extent to which sources and patterns circulated in France.[48]

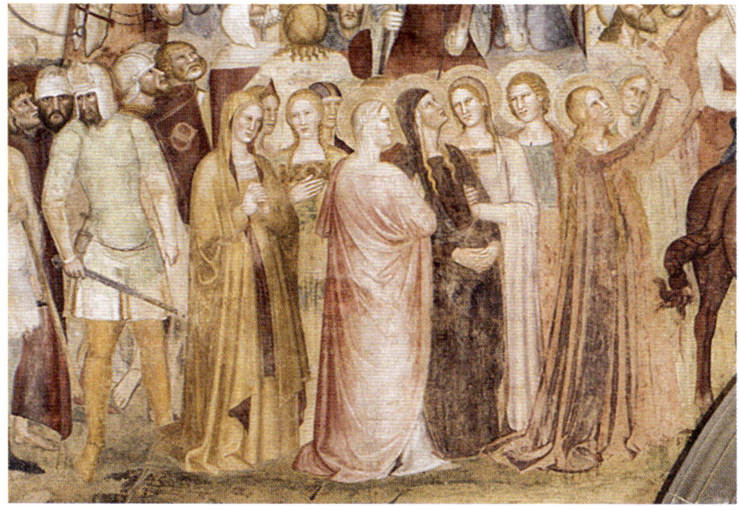

**Fig. 21** Andrea da Firenze, *Crucifixion:* Virgin, detail. c. 1365–67 (Florence, Church of Santa Maria Novella, Spanish Chapel)

The Van Lymborch brothers had access to several Italian paintings found on this side of the Alps. They took the time to admire and assimilate them, as in the case of the painting of *The Fall of the Rebel Angels* (fig. 1, p. 174), the source of folio 64v on the same theme. The Carrying of the Cross on folio 147r stems from Simone Martini's *Orsini Polyptych*, then in the Chartreuse de Champmol, which inspired Jacquemart de Hesdin, as well as the Descent from the Cross of the Van Lymborch brothers (fol. 156v; fig. 19).[49] The latter is also a perfect illustration of their perfect syncretism: The pyramidal composition, resting on the dead Christ with his limp arms, derives from Simone Martini's painting (fig. 20),[50] while Mary Magdalene was drawn from the *Crucifixion* in the same polyptych, with the exception of the motif of her arms embracing the Cross. This was taken from the Great Cross in the Chartreuse de Champmol, polychromed by Johan Maelwael in 1402, as mentioned above. The same miniature features the dignified figure of the Virgin standing with her hands clasped in sorrow, which can be seen on Florentine crucifixions of the fourteenth century, such as the paintings by Jacopo del Casentino (c. 1340–45, Oberlin, Ohio, Allen Memorial Art Museum) or Andrea da Firenze (1370–77, Vatican City, Vatican Museums),[51] or frescoed on the walls of the Spanish chapel in the Santa Maria Novella church, Florence (fig. 21).[52] There was no need to travel to admire these decorations, as drawings and books of models circulated widely on both sides of the Alps. For example, the Presentation of Jesus in the Temple, also called the Purification of the Virgin (fol. 54v; fig. 25) is

**Fig. 22** Following pages: Van Lymborch brothers, *Très Riches Heures*, fol. 156v: Descent from the Cross, detail

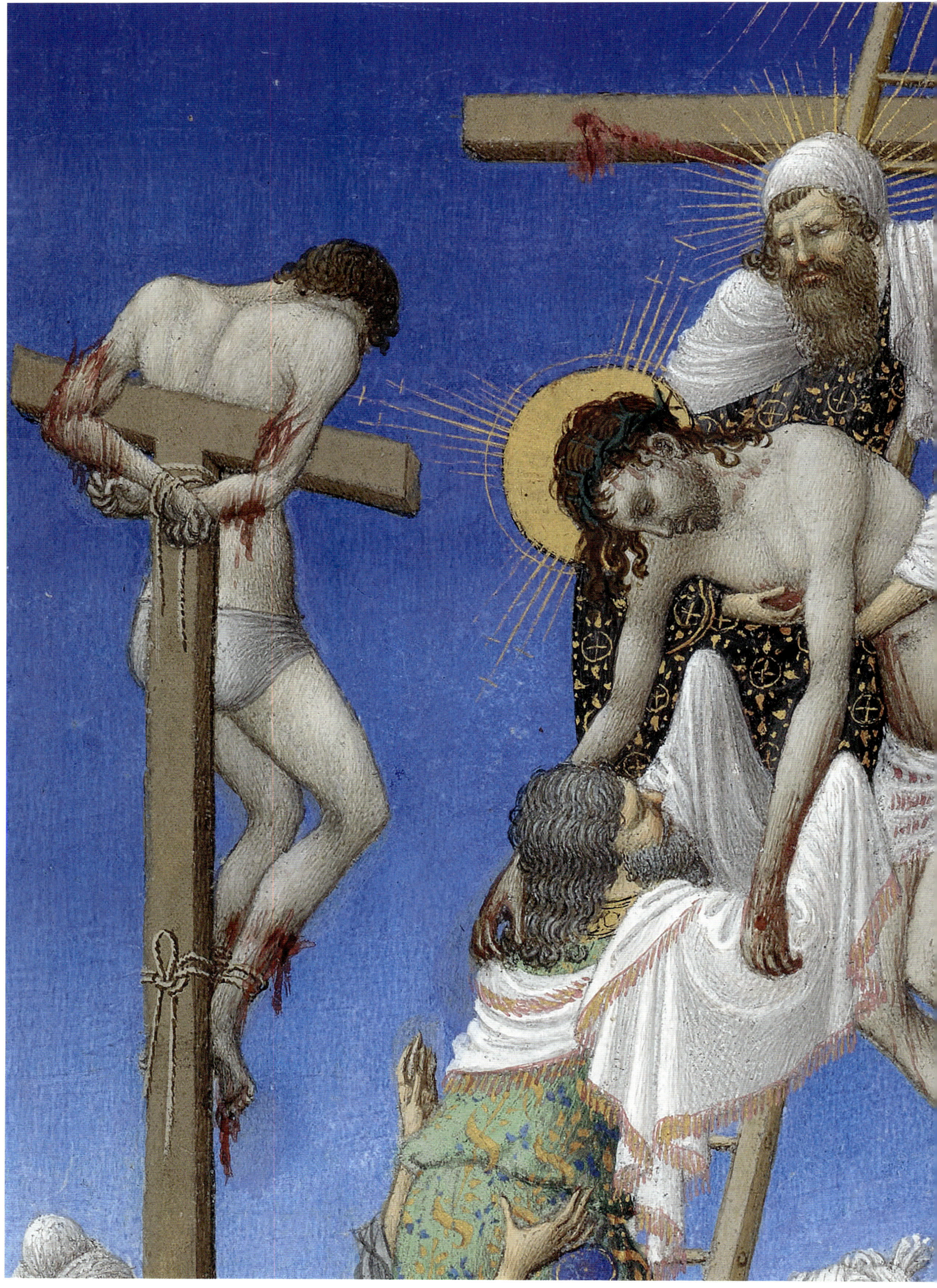

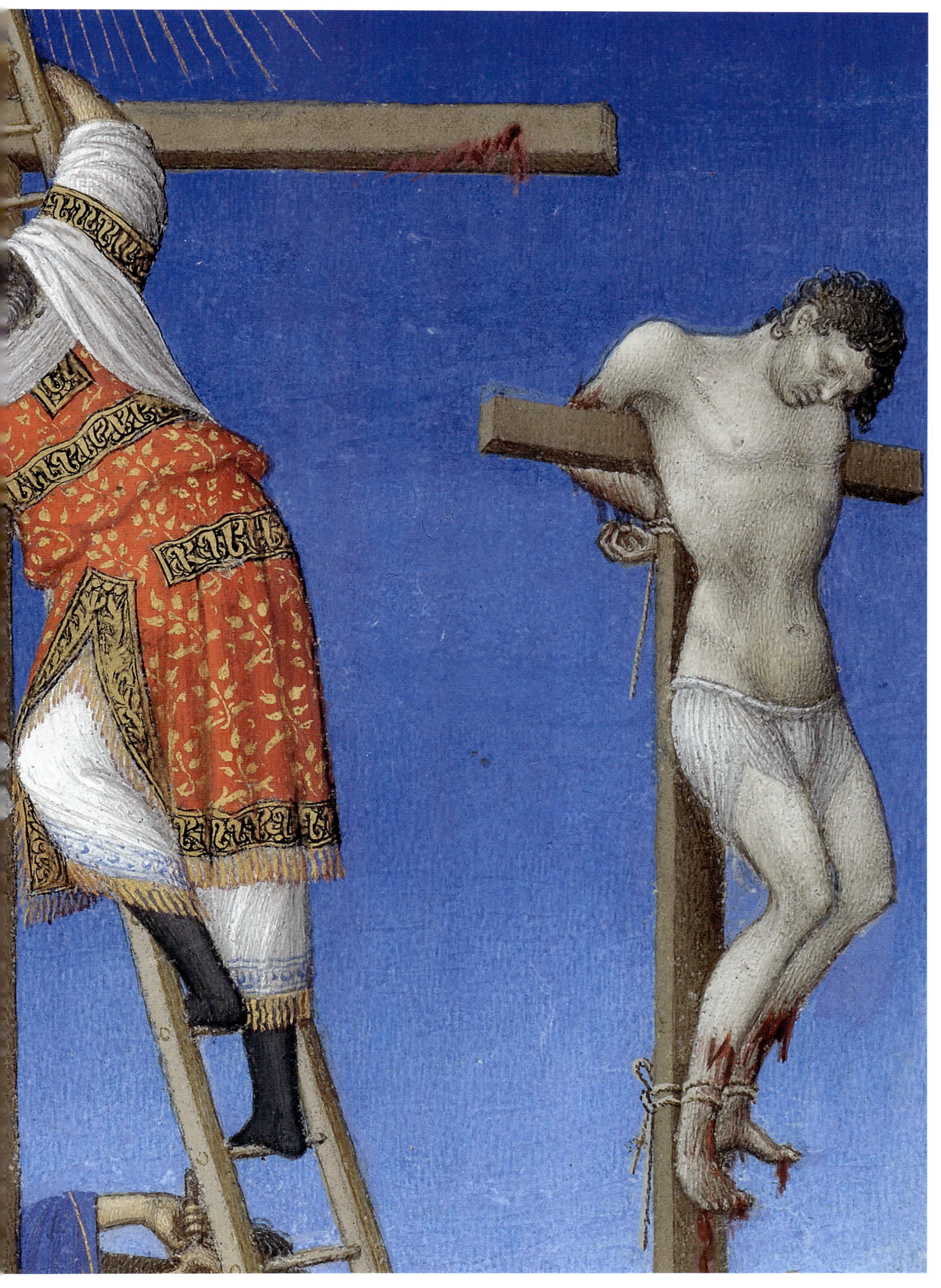

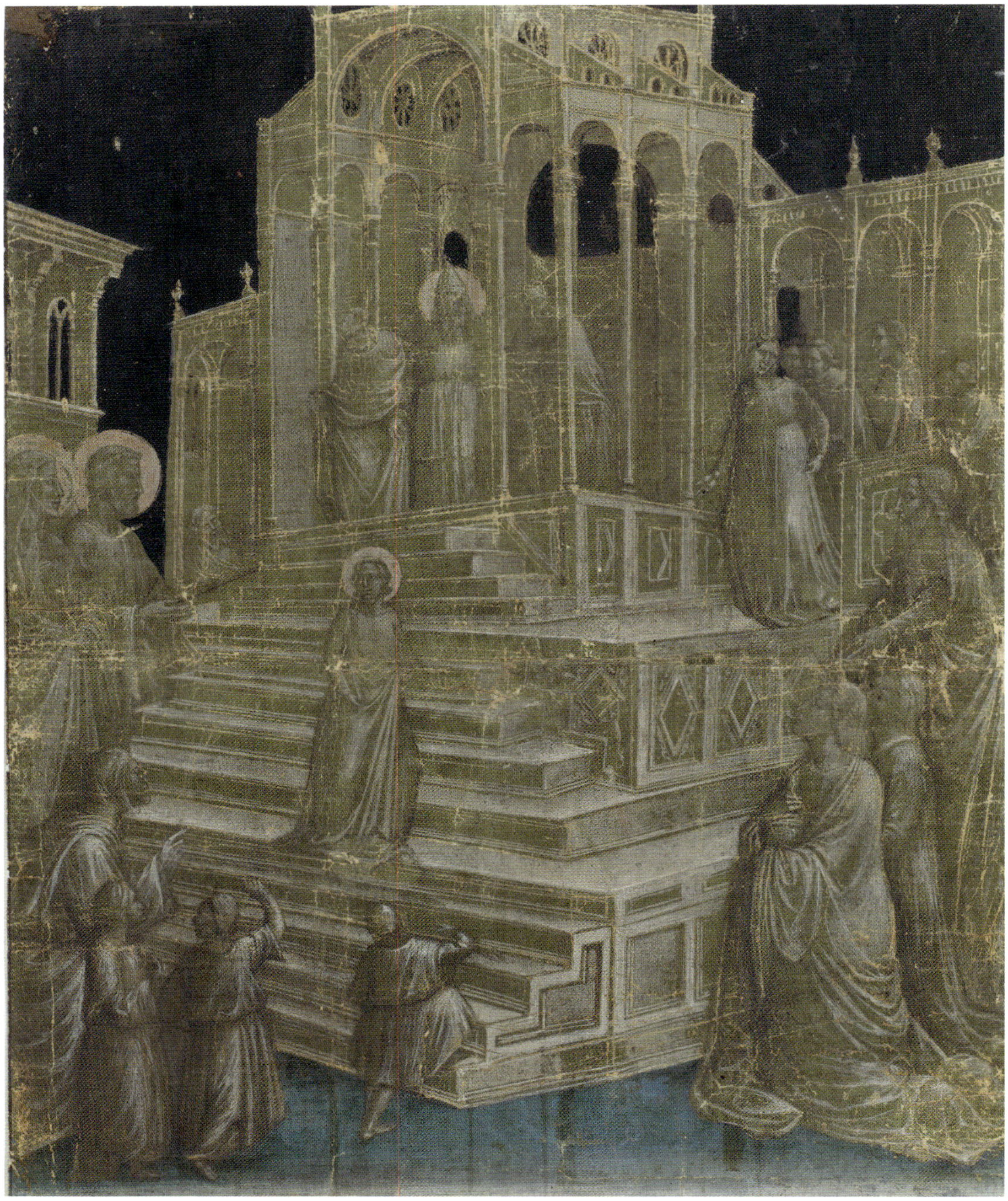

**Fig. 23** Taddeo Gaddi, *The Presentation of the Virgin in the Temple*. c. 1330 (Paris, musée du Louvre, département des Arts graphiques, inv. 1222)

similar to the *Presentation of the Virgin in the Temple* frescoed by Taddeo Gaddi in the Baroncelli chapel in Santa Croce church, Florence (1328–38; fig. 24), which was known from certain graphic documents, such as the presentation drawing in the Louvre (fig. 23).[53] Other motifs may have circulated thanks to sketchbooks, such as the dogs mauling their prey (fol. 12v), a motif disseminated by means of manuscripts (*Livre d'Heures et Missel à l'usage des Frères Mineurs*)[54] and drawings (fig. 11, p. 252).[55]

One of the most remarkable images in the *Très Riches Heures* shows a bird's-eye view of Rome reduced to its ancient and Christian monuments, as described in the twelfth-century guide to the *Mirabilia urbis romae*: the tomb of Romulus and Remus, the columns of Trajan and Antoninus Pius, the Dioscuri, the equestrian statue of Marcus Aurelius, and more (fol. 141v;

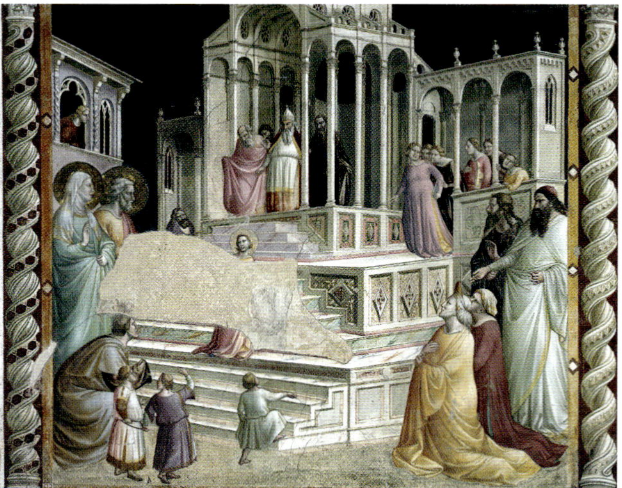

**Fig. 24** Taddeo Gaddi, *The Presentation of the Virgin in the Temple*. 1328–38 (Florence, Church of Santa Croce, Baroncelli Chapel)

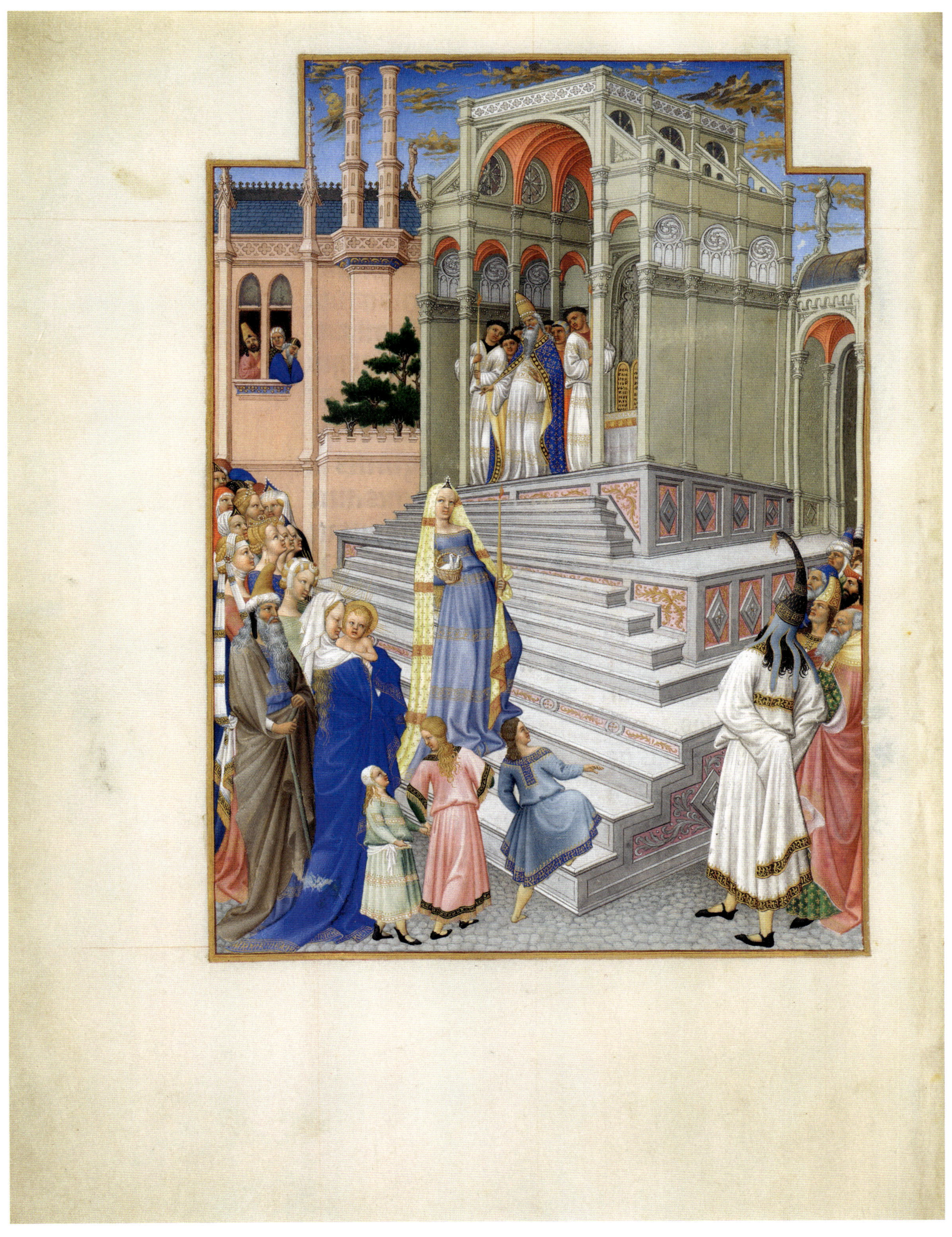

**Fig. 25** Van Lymborch brothers, *Très Riches Heures*, fol. 54v: Purification of the Virgin
**Fig. 26** Following pages: Van Lymborch brothers, *Très Riches Heures*, fol. 54v: Purification of the Virgin, detail

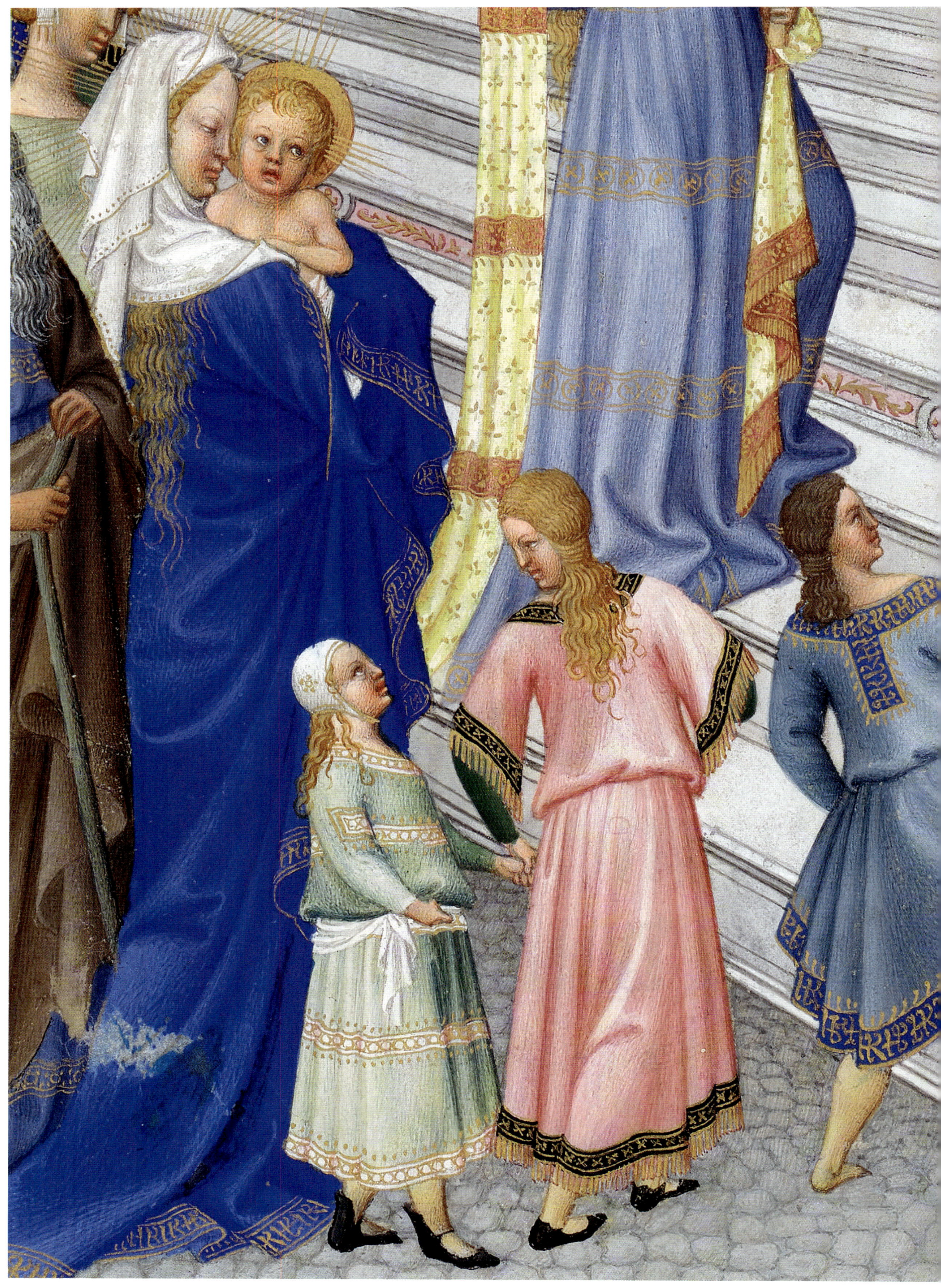

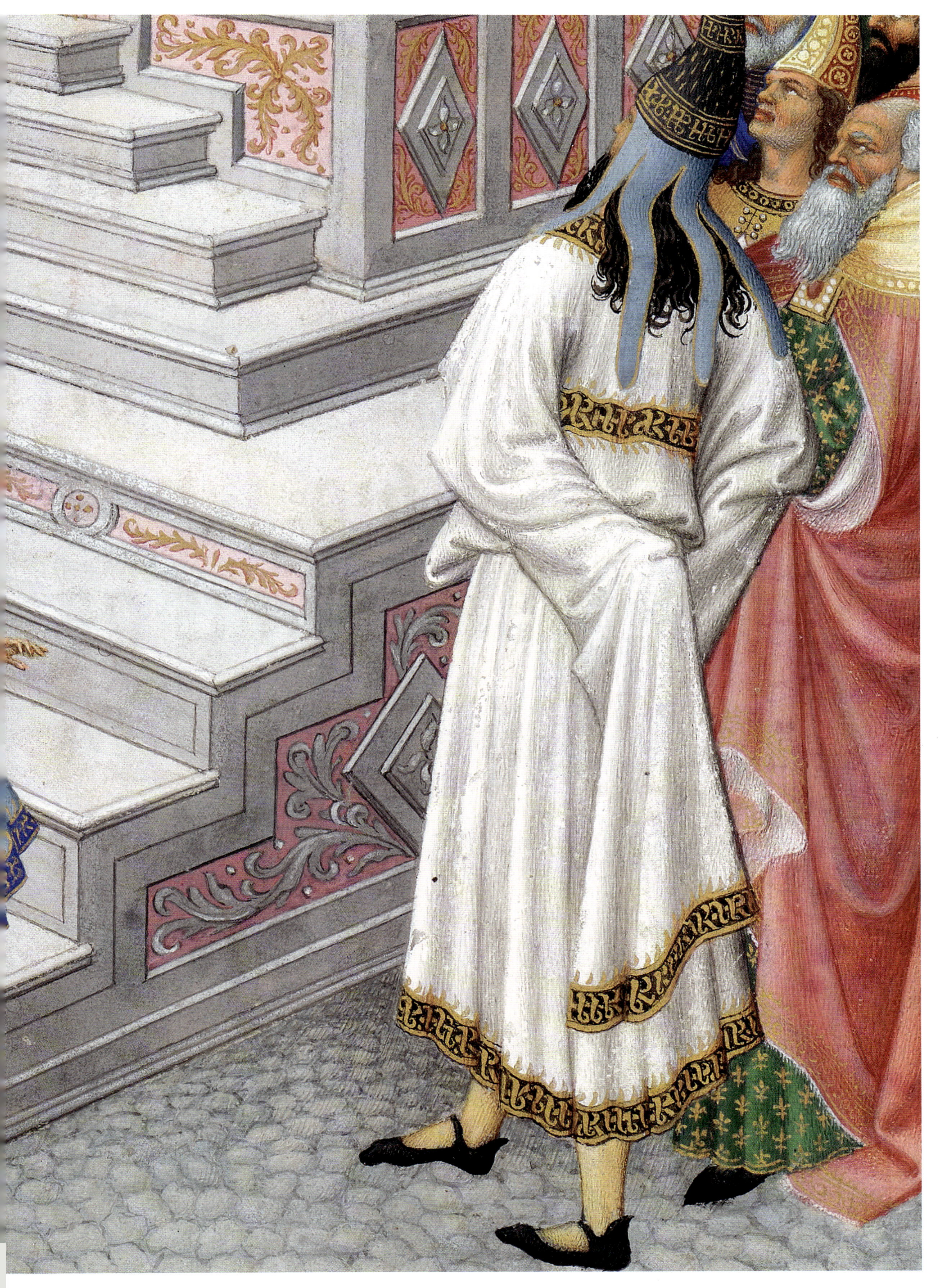

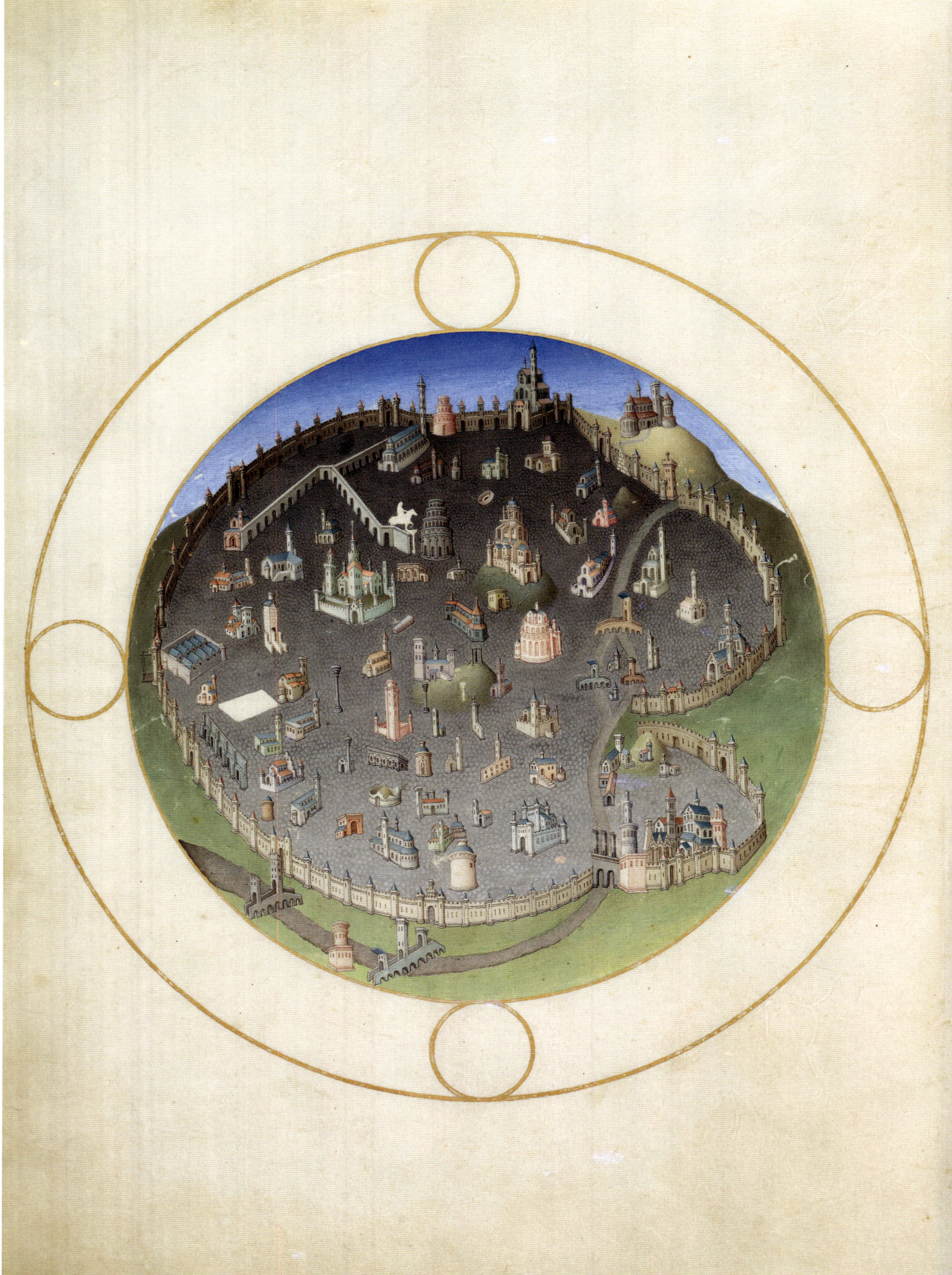

fig. 27). The Van Lymborch brothers used an Italian graphic source known to Parisian illuminators of the time and dating from before 1379, the year in which the statue of St. Michael was destroyed at the top of the Castel Sant'Angelo.[56] The guide also mentions a statue of a defeated barbarian, a kneeling Persian, a Roman copy of a Greek marble (fig. 28),[57] which was also known to the Van Lymborch brothers, probably from the same source, as they used its contorted position for Adam in their Terrestrial Paradise (fol. 25v; fig. 29).

In addition to using these learned sources, the Van Lymborch brothers were attentive to their environment, featuring in their works meteorological events that were unknown in France. For example, the eclipse that occurs during the Death of Christ (fol. 153; fig. 30) is even more intense than the one in the *Belles Heures* (fol. 145v), and echoes that of 1406, described in the *Chronique du religieux de saint Denis*, which they must have witnessed. Wasn't this act of looking with a curious gaze at everyday life, at humans and nature, the true springtime of the Renaissance, ushered in by the Van Lymborch brothers?

The three Van Lymborch brothers were cut down in their youth, between the ages of around twenty-eight and thirty-one. Were they victims of an accident, epidemic, or illness? We know that Johan breathed his last before March 1416, while Herman and Paul died in October of the same year, just a few months after their great patron, Jean of Berry, who had died in June. United even in death, the illuminators of the prince and the prince of illuminators left behind their great and "rich" common work, brilliantly unfinished.

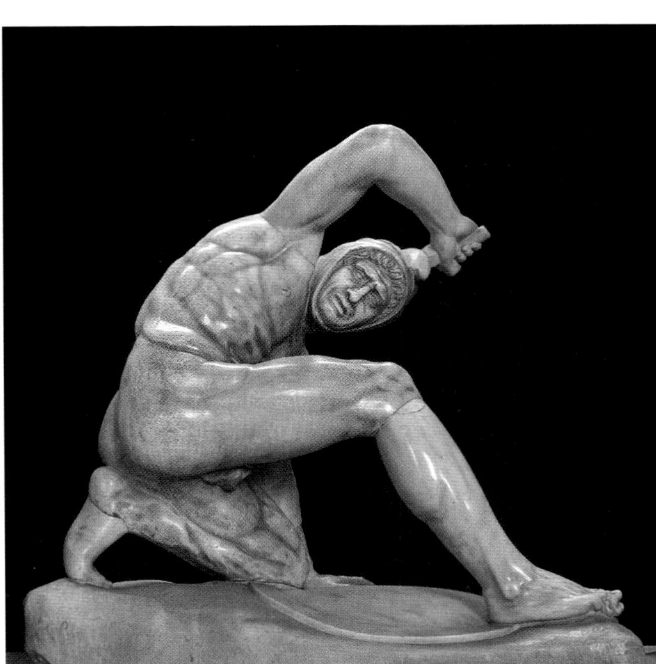

**Fig. 28** Roman copy after a Greek statue, *Kneeling Persian* (Vatican, Vatican Museums, inv. 2794)

**Fig. 27** Van Lymborch brothers, *Très Riches Heures*, fol. 141v: Map of Rome

1 Champeaux and Gauchery 1894.
2 Durrieu 1904.
3 Meiss 1974a.
4 Chantilly 2004. See also Stirnemann and Villela-Petit 2013.
5 Nijmegen 2005; Los Angeles and New York 2008–10; Paris 2012.
6 *Maelwael Van Lymborch Studies*, I, 2018 and II, 2022.
7 Gorissen 1954, 1957. Since then, see Niessen, Roelofs, and van Veen-Liefrink 2005; Roelofs 2005; Camps 2018; Stufkens and Verhoeven 2023. What follows draw on these studies.
8 On Maelwael, see Amsterdam 2017–18.
9 Nash 2008, 728–29.
10 Paris, BnF, Ms. Français 166.
11 Paris, BnF, Ms. Français 167.
12 New York, Met, The Cloisters, Ms. 54.1.1. a, b
13 Stirnemann and Villela-Petit 2013, 94–95.
14 Kovács 2004, 285 note 11.
15 See essays by D. Thiébaut, pp. 175–76, and É. Ravaud, pp. 337–38.
16 Guiffrey 1894–96, II, 26 (no. 122).
17 Niessen, Roelofs, and van Veen-Liefrink 2005, 20.
18 Paris, BnF, Ms. NAL 3093.
19 Husband 2012a, 26–31.
20 Husband 2012b, 44–47. For another opinion, with a dating around 1412–13, see Paris 2012, no. 1.
21 Guiffrey 1894–96, I, 253 (no. 960).
22 On the development between the *Belles Heures* and the *Très Riches Heures*, see Stirnemann 2018, who suggests that Johan Maelwael might have been involved in the latter (fol. 19v or 26), based on the *Man of Sorrows* painting. We disagree, especially as the *Man of Sorrows* has now been attributed to Paul van Lymborch.
23 Washington, NGA, Ms. Acc. No. B-13, 520.
24 Perkinson 2009.
25 See essay by D. Thiébaut, pp. 174–93.
26 Stirnemann and Villela-Petit 2013, 73–117; König 2018; Villela-Petit 2018c; essay by I. Villela-Petit, pp. 232–33.
27 London, BL, Ms. Cotton Domitian A.XVII. Villela-Petit 2018a, 65.
28 Vatican City, BVA, Ms. Cod. Reg. Lat. 939.
29 See, for example, Nijmegen 2005, no. 103, following Meiss 1974a, I, 16, 245, and Husband 2012a, 32–34.
30 Ainsworth and Varvaro 2004, IV, chap. 7, 400–410.
31 Ribault 1990a.
32 Meiss 1974a, I, 74.
33 This is what Camille 2001 suggested in a grotesque and rather extreme article.
34 Guiffrey 1894–96, I, no. 415.
35 Ibid., I, 323 (no. 994).
36 In Chantilly 2004, 48.
37 See Stirnemann's 2006 insightful study.
38 Meiss 1974a, I, 77.
39 Paris, Bibl. Mazarine, Ms. 406.
40 Stirnemann and Rabel 2005; Stirnemann 2009.
41 Meiss 1974a, I, 89–96, 110–112. Hulin de Loo (1903) had already proposed a division.
42 Eberhard König, for example, saw two artists at work in the Fall of the Rebel Angels (fol. 64v). König 1976, 104 note 12.
43 On the palette of the Van Lymborch brothers, see Villela-Petit 2004d; essay by É. Ravaud, pp. 331–41.
44 Lawson 2005 and 2008.
45 Nash 2022 and De Bruijn Kops 2022.
46 See essay by P. Roelofs, pp. 196–205.
47 Winckler 1930.
48 Schmidt 2005 and Husband 2012b.
49 Nash 2024a.
50 Antwerp, KMSKA, inv. 260.
51 Villela-Petit 2010c, 51.
52 Meiss 1974a, I, 172 and 240.
53 Paris, Louvre, dép. des Arts graphiques, inv. 1222. Meiss 1974a, I, 157–58 and note 345.
54 Paris, BnF, Ms. Latin 757.
55 See essay by M. Deldicque on Barthélemy d'Eyck, p. 253.
56 Meiss 1974a, I, 209–14.
57 Vatican City, Vatican Museums, inv. 2794.

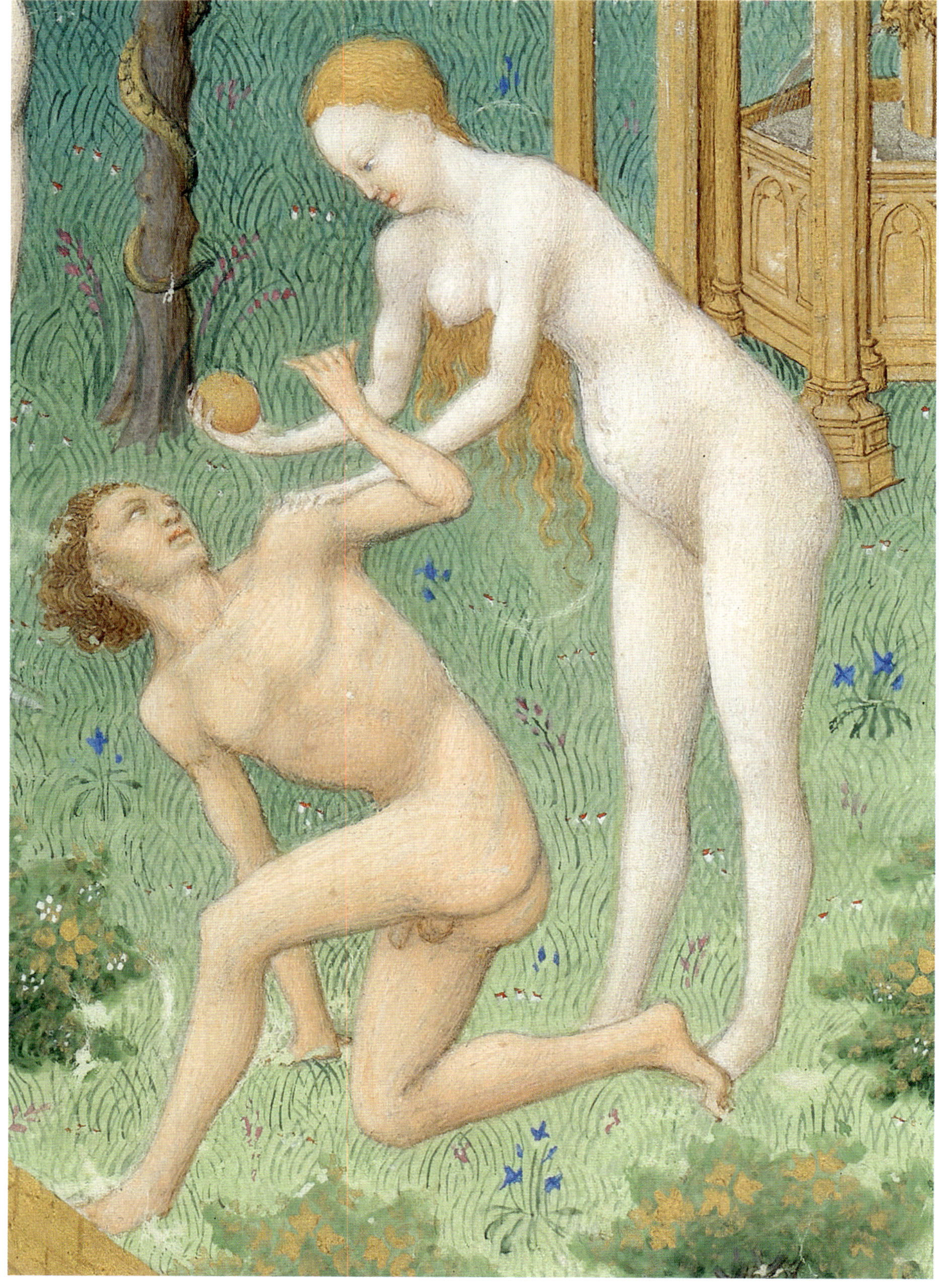

**Fig. 29** Van Lymborch brothers, *Très Riches Heures*, fol. 25v: Adam and Eve Expelled from Paradise, detail

**Fig. 30** Van Lymborch brothers, *Très Riches Heures*, fol. 153: The Death of Christ

**Fig. 31** Following pages: Van Lymborch brothers, *Très Riches Heures*, fol. 153: The Death of Christ, detail

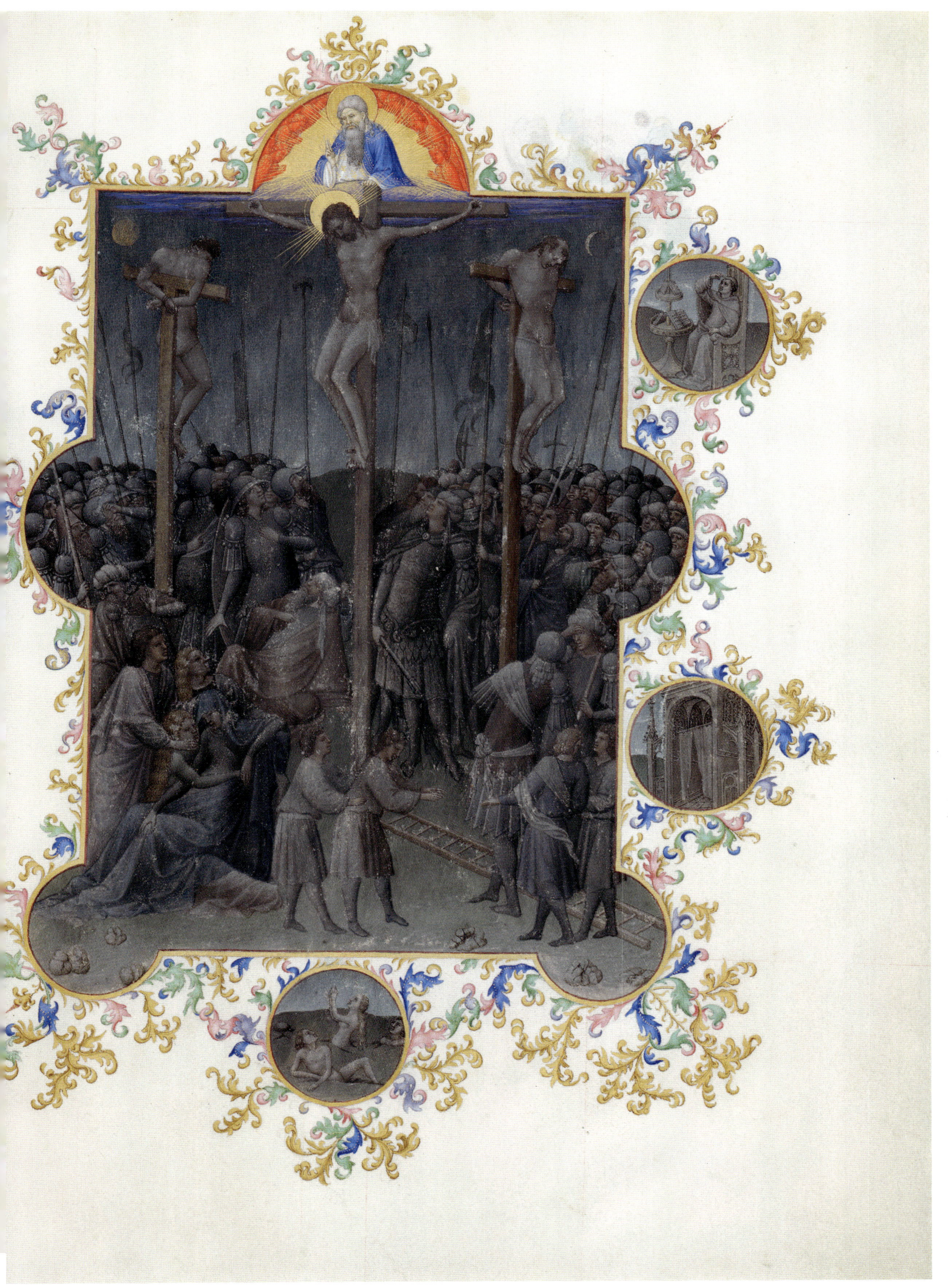

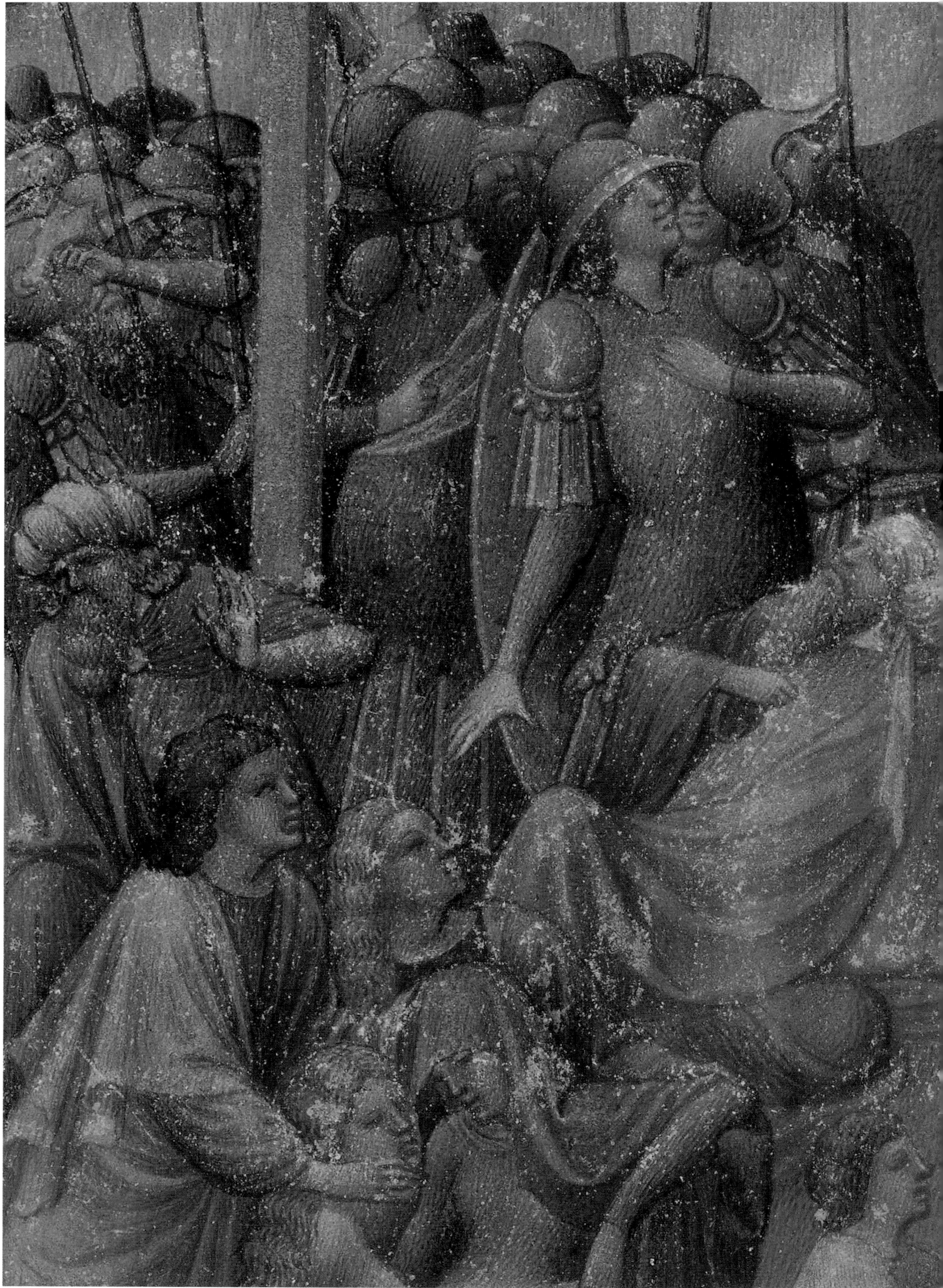

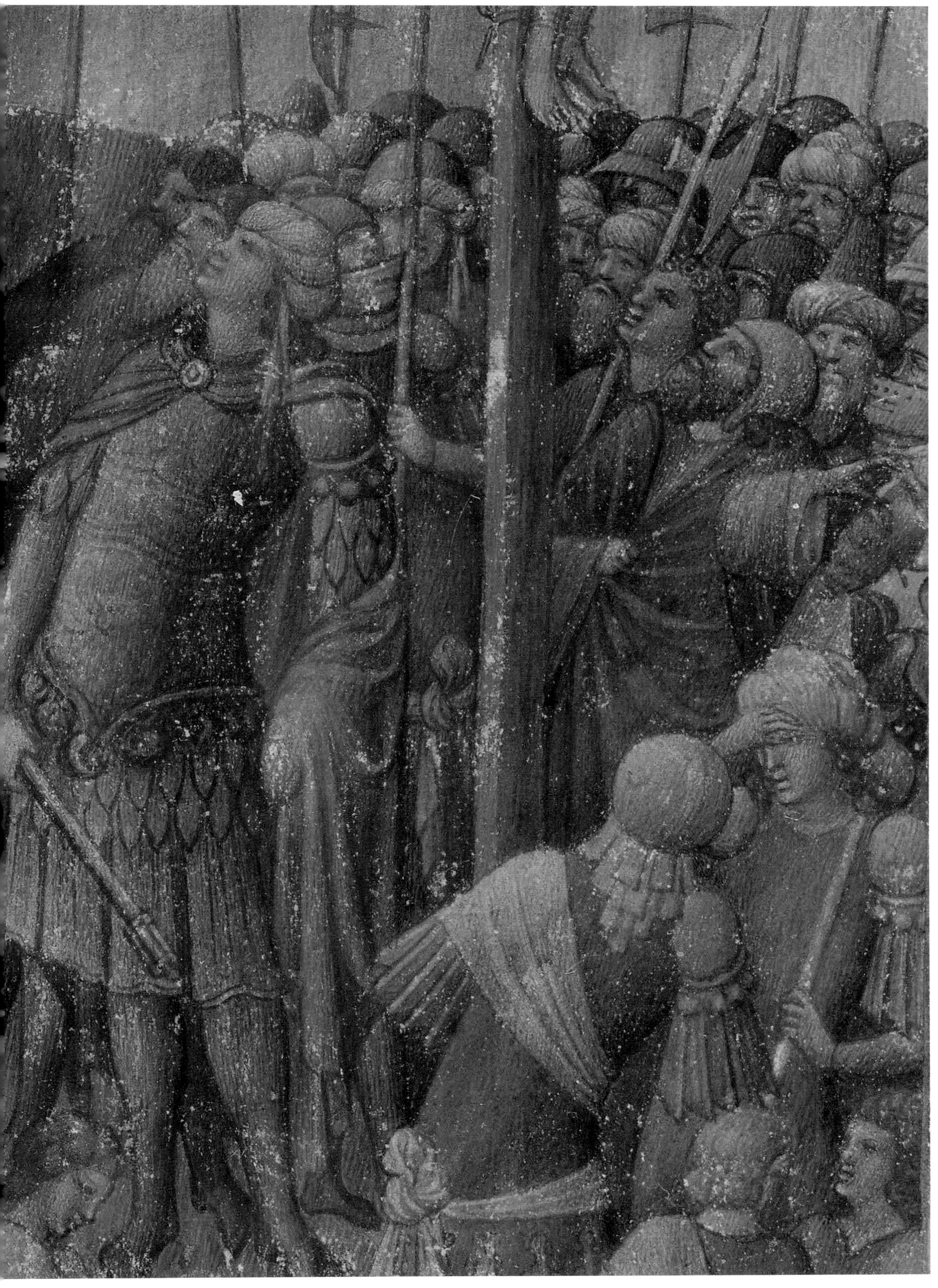

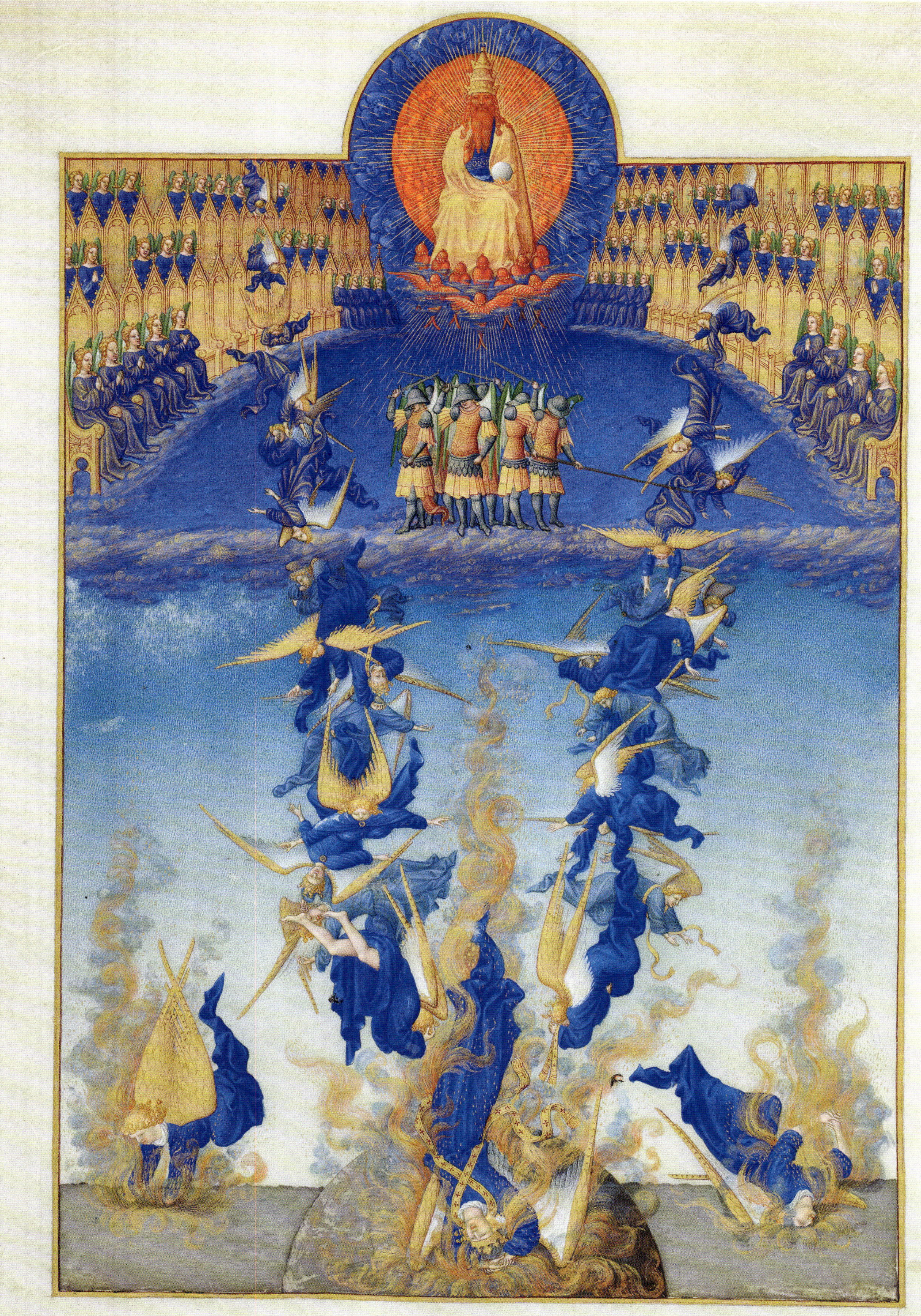

# 8.

# The Van Lymborch Brothers, Painters on Panel?

Dominique Thiébaut

The notion that the three Van Lymborch brothers—still celebrated for their talents as illuminators by Guillebert de Metz in 1434,[1] nearly twenty years after their deaths—also practiced, in parallel, painting in a broad sense, including panel painting, would not, a priori, be surprising given the customs of their time. As Nicole Reynaud wrote in 2006, "in Northern Europe in the fifteenth century [but this also holds for the previous century], the painter's craft encompassed the painting of miniatures, an art in which painters were also trained, whereas an illuminator by trade, put in the same category as artisans of the book, had to limit his work to parchment."[2] Let us recall the exemplary case of Jean Fouquet, the greatest French painter of the fifteenth century, who produced both a coherent group of painted panels and some admirable miniatures, including those in the *Hours of Étienne Chevalier*, almost all of which are held at the Musée Condé.

## WERE HERMAN, PAUL, AND JOHAN "PAINTERS"?

What do we know about the training of the three brothers, and how are they described in the documentary sources that have come down to us?[3] Born in Nijmegen between 1385 and 1390 into a family that included artists on both their mother's and father's sides,[4] the three brothers left their native city most likely after the death of their father, the woodcarver Arnold van Lymborch, probably at too young an age to have received a very advanced artistic instruction. In 1399, Herman, the eldest of the three brothers, and Johan, the youngest,[5] were apprenticed in Paris to the goldsmith Alebret de Bolure,[6] probably on the recommendation of their uncle and guardian, Johan Maelwael,[7] who in 1397 became official painter to the Duke of Burgundy, Philip the Bold. Under the statutes of the Paris guild, their training was meant to last six to eight years, but it was abruptly interrupted in the autumn of 1399 by a plague epidemic that forced the goldsmith to send them back to the Duchy of Guelders. Imprisoned for more than six months in Brussels, did the youths return to Nijmegen upon their release in May 1400,[8] or did they turn around and return to Paris? This remains an open question. In any case, Johan is mentioned on February 9, 1402, with his brother Paul as the Duke of Burgundy's "enlumineur" (illuminator) for a bible, which has often been identified with the *Bible moralisée* (Moralized bible) in the Bibliothèque nationale de France.[9] Nothing is known of Paul before this date, but we cannot reject the hypothesis that he arrived in France with his brothers.[10] This time, he and Johan were referred to as "paintres" (painters) in a document dated January 12, 1403 relating to a gift granted by the duke,[11] and then as "paintres et historieurs"[12] (painters and miniaturists) in a payment dated January 17, 1404 relating to the said bible, which suggests that both of them had been specifically trained as painters. On the other hand, the imprecise term "ouvriers"

**Fig. 1** Van Lymborch brothers, *Très Riches Heures*, fol. 64v: The Fall of the Rebel Angels

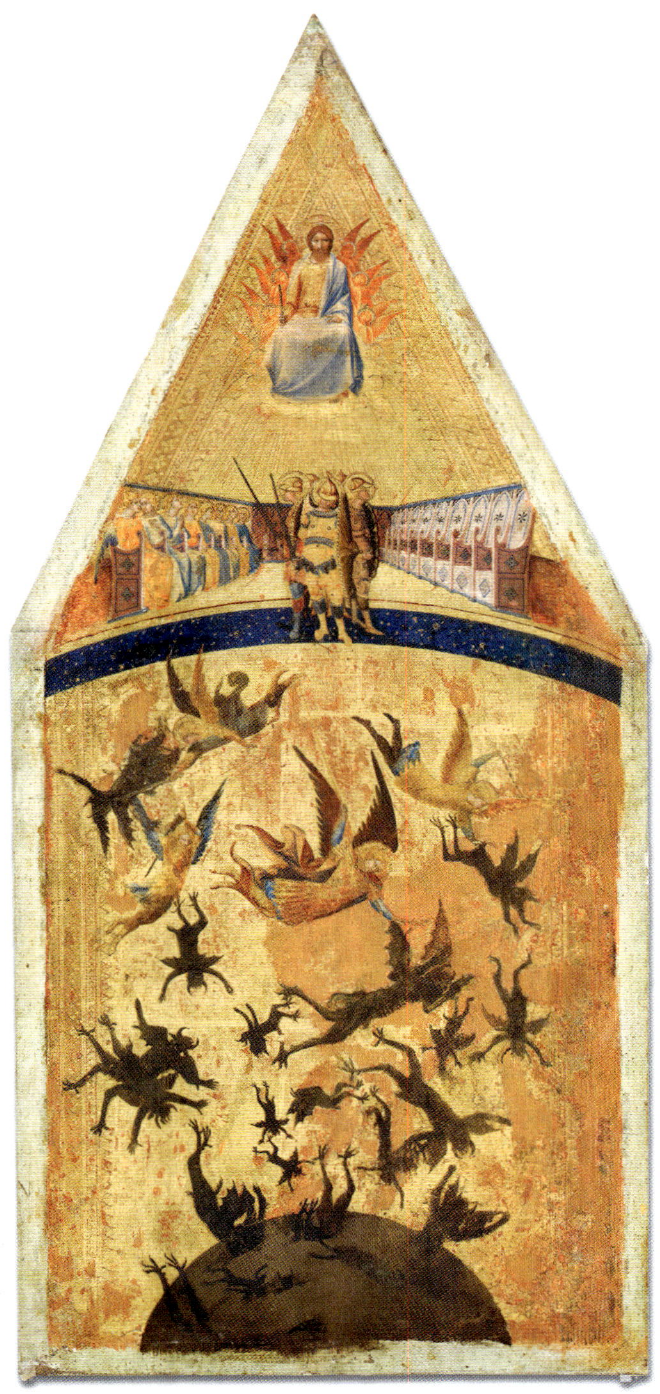

**Fig. 2** Painter of the Memmi family, *The Fall of the Rebel Angels*, interior of a painted panel divided in two and transferred from wood to canvas (Paris, musée du Louvre, département des Peintures, DL 1967-1 A [on deposit from musée du Berry, Bourges])

(craftsmen) of Monseigneur [Jean, Duke of Berry] used around 1408–09 by Robinet d'Étampes to refer to the authors of the New York *Belles Heures*[13] does not tell us anything about their professional status or the identity of the brothers involved in the execution of the manuscript. As for the documents relating to the three brothers collectively, they identify them as "illuminators"[14] and then as the duke's "valets de chambre."[15] In my view, there is therefore nothing to suggest that Herman, the eldest, practiced painting; conversely, nothing allows us to rule out the possibility that Johan learned this trade. In addition to his trade as an illuminator, Herman most likely also worked as a goldsmith: Éva Kovács has suggested identifying him with "petit Herman," the goldsmith from whom Jean of Berry bought several objects on August 25, 1403, including an amethyst salt cellar.[16] She has further suggested that his brother Johan was a certain "Hansse Melluel" registered with the guild of Parisian goldsmiths in 1413.[17] Was the latter the same "Jean de Nimègue" who in September 1403 sold to the duke "un annel d'or" (a gold ring) and supplied him, on an unspecified date, with a chess set and board?[18] This is the opinion of Inès Villela-Petit.[19] If these hypotheses are correct, Johan would therefore have been active as a painter, illuminator, and goldsmith, his contribution in the last field not being limited to providing designs for jewels, as some painters were called upon to do, but extending to the making of these precious objects. Nevertheless, in view of the events described above, his training as a painter could only have been short-lived. If he did practice this trade, it was probably limited to the period when he worked for Philip the Bold, perhaps even to heraldic designs, in line with a family trade that has been well demonstrated on his mother's side.[20] The same cannot be said of Paul, assuredly the "paintre alemant" (German painter) mentioned in 1408[21] and 1434[22] in the service of Jean of Berry, and who continued to be called a painter after the death of his Burgundian patron (1404). That Jean of Berry saw him as the most gifted of the siblings,[23] and therefore entrusted him with a wide range of prestigious painting projects, is suggested by the eminent position reserved for him in relation to his brothers in the texts and gifts from the Duke of Berry. It is also tempting to imagine that Johan Maelwael, convinced of his young nephew's remarkable talents, took the decision, as soon as the latter arrived in France, to initiate him himself into all aspects of the painter's trade.[24]

## A SOURCE OF INSPIRATION: PRECIOUS PANEL PAINTINGS IN FRANCE AROUND 1400

On French soil, the curiosity of the three youths was no doubt aroused when they discovered, among other treasures, paintings on panel—but also on canvas—visible in churches and public places or hidden away in sumptuous princely residences to which, however, their uncle, as court painter, had access. Critics have rightly pointed out several references in both the *Belles Heures* and the *Très Riches Heures* to Sienese paintings of remarkable quality that seem to have been on view in France as early as the fourteenth century,[25] and which the Van Lymborch brothers may have seen directly. These include, in particular, Simone Martini's small quadriptych of the Passion (now shared between the Louvre, the Royal Museum of Fine Arts in Antwerp, and the Gemäldegalerie in Berlin), which likely arrived in the Chartreuse de Champmol in the late fourteenth century,[26] and a double-sided panel attributed to a member of the Memmi family (showing, on the front, *The Fall of the Rebel Angels*; figs. 1 and 2),[27] which may have been among Jean of Berry's possessions at the time.[28] The "Italianism" of the Van Lymborch brothers, highlighted by critics since Waagen,[29] is not limited to borrowings of motifs and compositions. It is also evident in the spatial arrangement of scenes and their emotional content, in many iconographic and decorative decisions, and in the use of delicate modeling and a varied palette dominated by light hues; there can be no talk of plagiarism, however, since, on the contrary, this Italian influence drove the brothers to produce works of remarkable creativity and intelligence. The hypothesis that Paul and his brothers made one or more journeys to Italy, refuted by some critics because of the diversity of their sources of inspiration, ranging from Florence and Siena to northern Italy,[30] has recently been reintroduced.[31] In Dijon, the Van Lymborch brothers undoubtedly studied closely the ambitious and innovative works then in progress at Champmol, whether the famous sculpted group known as the *Well of Moses*, commissioned from Claus Sluter in 1395 and colored by their uncle in 1402–03, a piece whose monumental power could hardly leave them indifferent,[32] or the altarpieces sculpted by Jacques de Baerze and polychromed by Melchior Broederlam between 1390 and 1399.[33] Moreover, Paul may have been directly involved in the execution of the five altarpieces intended for the chapels in the church of Champmol, which Johan Maelwael began painting in 1398.[34] In any case, the artistic relationship between the uncle and his nephews has been demonstrated by the almost literal reuse of one of Maelwael's formal ideas in an illumination in the *Belles Heures*, the Lamentation over the Body of Christ (fol. 149v; fig. 3): As Philippe Lorentz has judiciously pointed out,[35] the Christ figure, with compressed waist and dangling arms, and with its particular cropping below the knees, derives in fact from the *Large Round Pietà* (fig. 4).[36] This precious *tondo*, produced for Philip the Bold—whose arms appear on the reverse, an indication that it could not have been executed after 1404—is almost unanimously attributed by specialists to Philip the Bold's official painter and considered a masterpiece of painting in France around 1400.

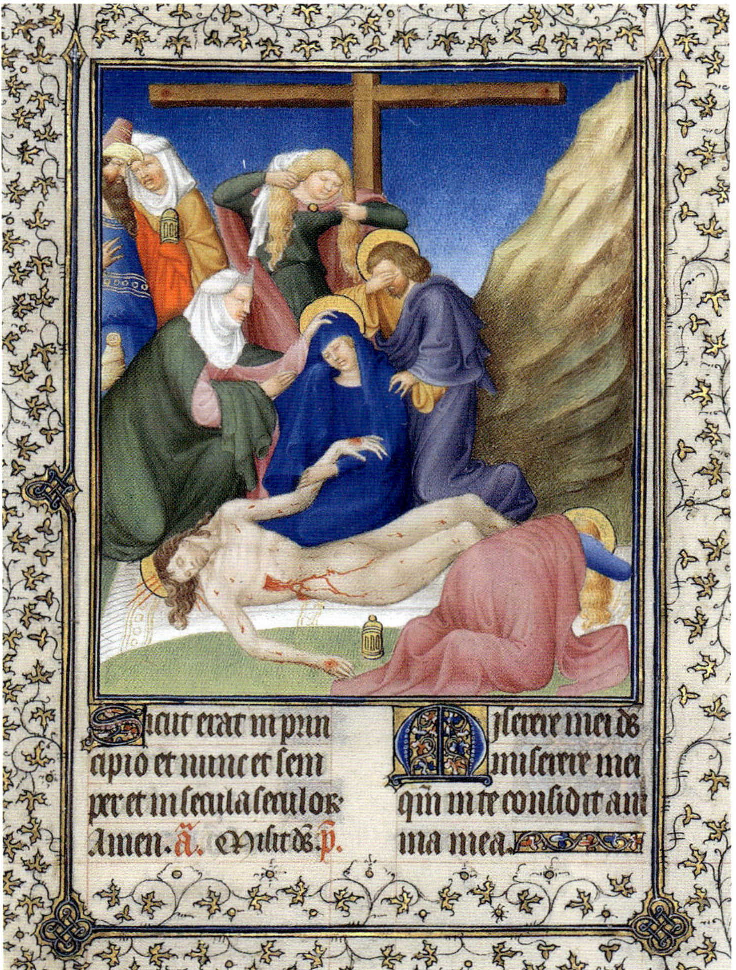

**Fig. 3** Van Lymborch brothers, *Belles Heures*, fol. 149v: Lamentation over the Body of Christ (New York, The Metropolitan Museum of Art, The Cloisters Collection, 1954 [Ms. Acc. 54. 1. 1])

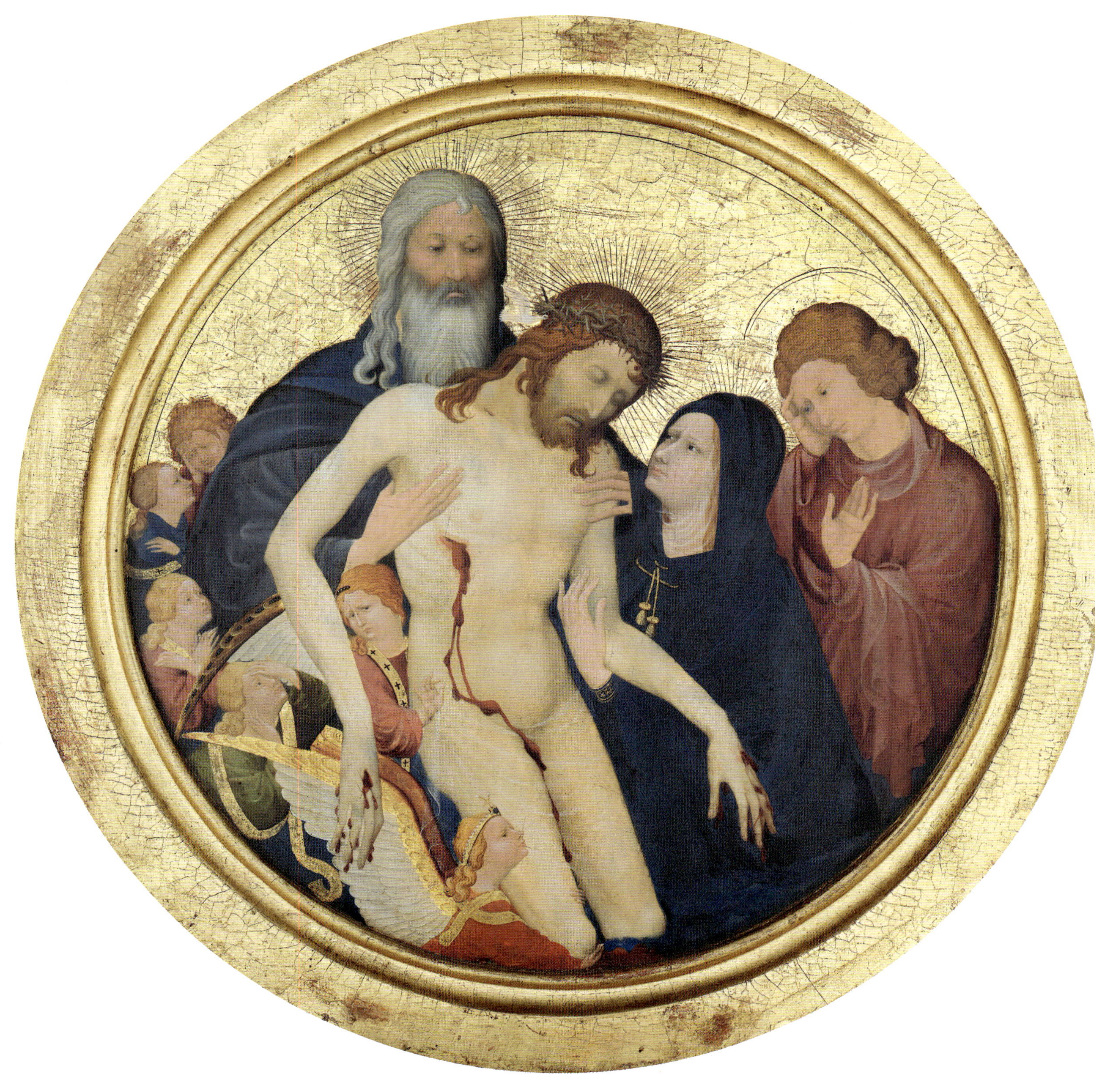

**Fig. 4** Attributed to Johan Maelwael, *Large Round Pietà* (Paris, musée du Louvre, département des Peintures, M.I. 692)

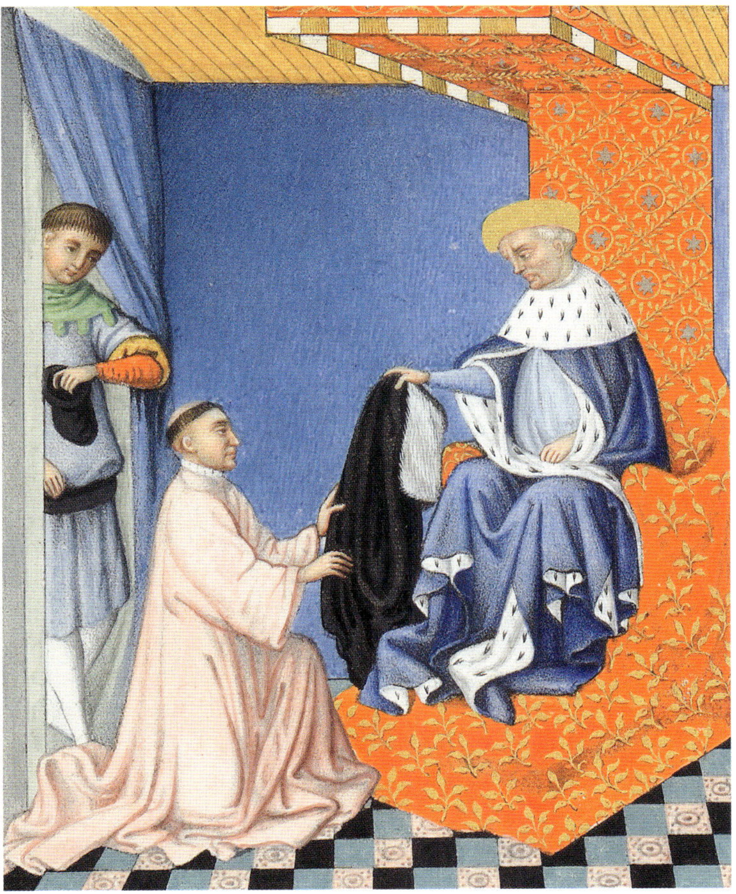

**Fig. 5** Foundation charter of the Sainte-Chapelle in Bourges after the facsimile by Auguste de Bastard: detail of the initial showing the portrait of the Duke of Berry (Bourges, Archives départementales du Cher, J 771)

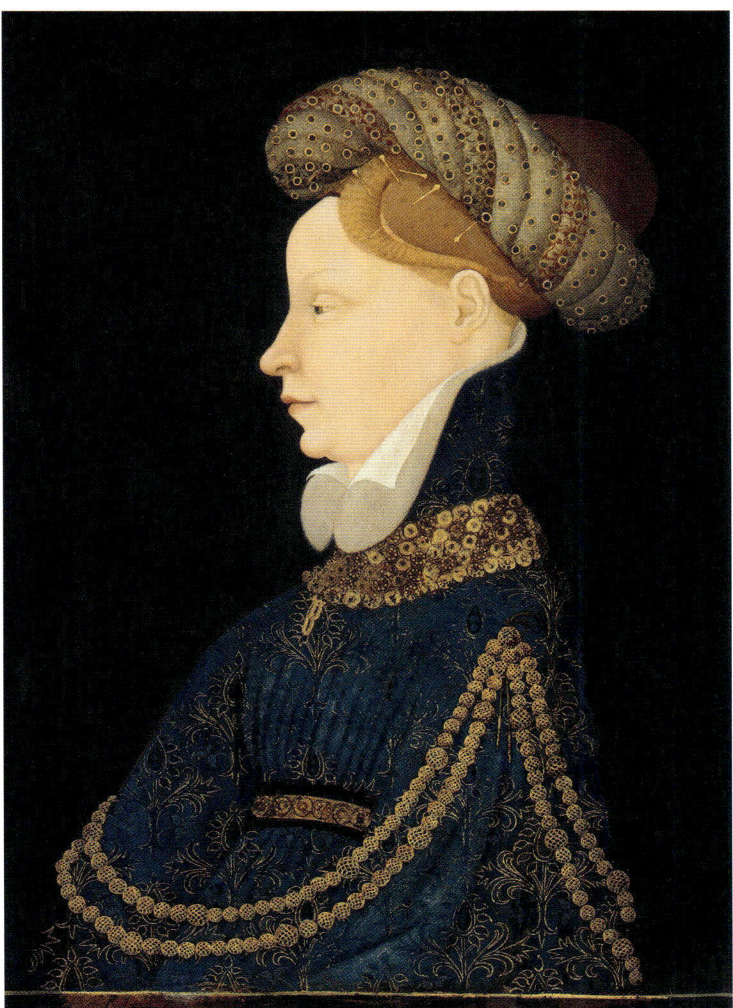

**Fig. 6** Anonymous Franco-Flemish painter, *Profile Portrait of a Lady.* c. 1410–20 (Washington, National Gallery of Art, Andrew W. Mellon Collection, 1937.1.23)

## PANEL PAINTINGS BY THE VAN LYMBORCH BROTHERS?

It remains that no painting on panel made with certainty by the Van Lymborch brothers has survived, starting with the "hoax gift"[37] given by the three brothers to their prince for the exchange of gifts on New Year's Day in 1411, a "livre contrefait d'une pièce de bois paincte en semblance d'un livre, où il n'a nuls fueillets ne rien escript" (a fake book made from a piece of wood painted to resemble a book, containing neither pages nor any text),[38] a book that may have been created by Paul alone. While the nature of the work that Paul carried out in 1408 for the Duke of Berry in his château of Bicêtre[39] remains, in our opinion,[40] a mystery, the great American specialist Millard Meiss, followed by Inès Villela-Petit,[41] did not rule out the possibility that the painter was then busy completing the famous gallery of historical portraits in the great hall (destroyed when the ducal residence was sacked in 1411). As court artists, the Van Lymborch brothers were certainly called upon by their patron to work as portraitists, in one form or another. According to Meiss (who hardly convinced critics on this point), it was they who invented a self-standing, half-length portrait of Jean of Berry in profile, a trace of which has come down to us in a drawing by Roger de Gaignières.[42] The rather unflattering likenesses of the old duke in the *Petites Heures* (fol. 288v) and the *Très Riches Heures* (fol. 1v; January), preceded by the one that adorned the initial of the foundation charter of the Sainte-Chapelle in Bourges around 1405, known from Auguste de Bastard's facsimile (fig. 5),[43] reveal in any case an undeniable talent for observation.

The half-length *Profile Portrait of a Lady* on a dark background (fig. 6) has been attributed to the Van Lymborch brothers, or to their circle, some even going so far as to interpret it as the portrait of a lady of Jean of Berry's court.[44] Admittedly, the slim chest, the ostentatious luxury of the coiffure and clothing, and the supple contours of the face and collar recall the elegant ladies of April and May of the *Très Riches Heures* (figs. 7 and 8),[45] but given the extensive damage and repainting, particularly in the gilded areas, one must be prudent. As for the rather rudimentary underdrawing visible in the infrared reflectography, unfortunately, it does little to help clarify what remains of the original.[46]

**Fig. 7** Following page: Van Lymborch brothers, *Très Riches Heures*, fol. 4v: April
**Fig. 8** Following page: Van Lymborch brothers, *Très Riches Heures*, fol. 5v: May

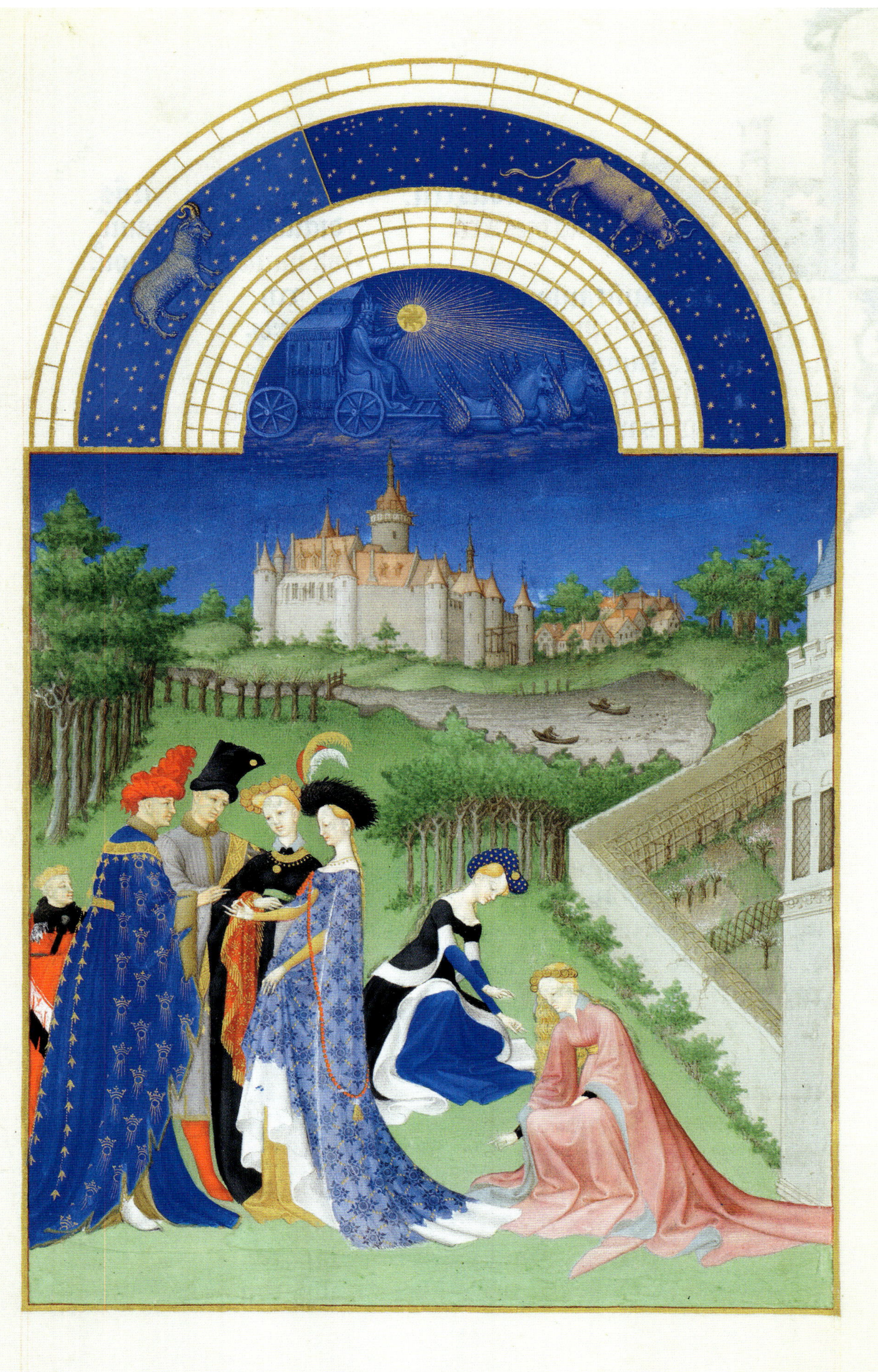

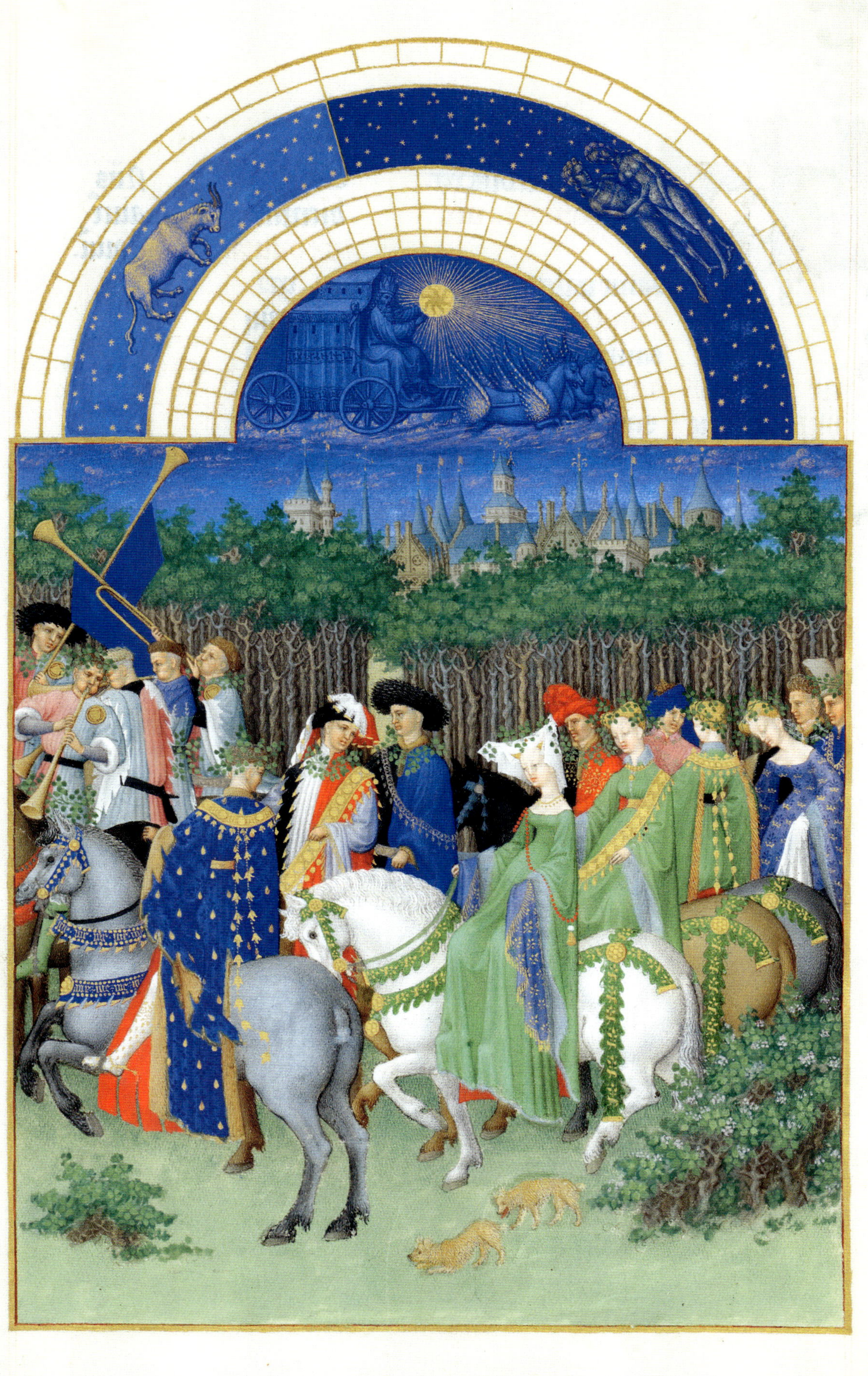

## THE *MAN OF SORROWS* OF VIC-LE-COMTE

Nevertheless, we tend to believe that one painting of prime importance could be attributed to one of the Van Lymborch brothers, Paul, in all likelihood.[47] This is a *Man of Sorrows*, discovered by a second-hand dealer in an outbuilding of the presbytery of Vic-le-Comte in Auvergne in 1985, but in fact mentioned as being "à la cure" (in the presbytery) since 1952,[48] and which the Musée du Louvre was able to acquire in 2012 (fig. 10).[49] (For the sake of convenience, we will refer to it here as the *Christ* of Vic.) This painted panel—which, unfortunately, has been stripped of the lower part of its frame, but apart from a centimeter or two is, we believe, complete in terms of the painted surface—bears a striking resemblance to the *Large Round Pietà* (fig. 4). It has the same central figure, but inverted, of the dead Christ, cut off in the same way at the level of the calves, with his head softly leaning over his right shoulder, his arms hanging down and with his elbows bent,[50] supported here not by God the Father, but by St. John the Evangelist, and the same idea of the raised hand, with open palm, which is now that of the Virgin . . . In 2012, faced with this work of exceptional beauty, we advanced therefore the name of Maelwael,[51] all the while noting differences with the *tondo* in the Louvre which have become increasingly obvious to us over the years: first, a monumentality and more elongated proportions that, we believe, the vertical format of the painting and its larger dimensions alone cannot explain; more fluid lines, less sharp, as well as a marked concern for depth,

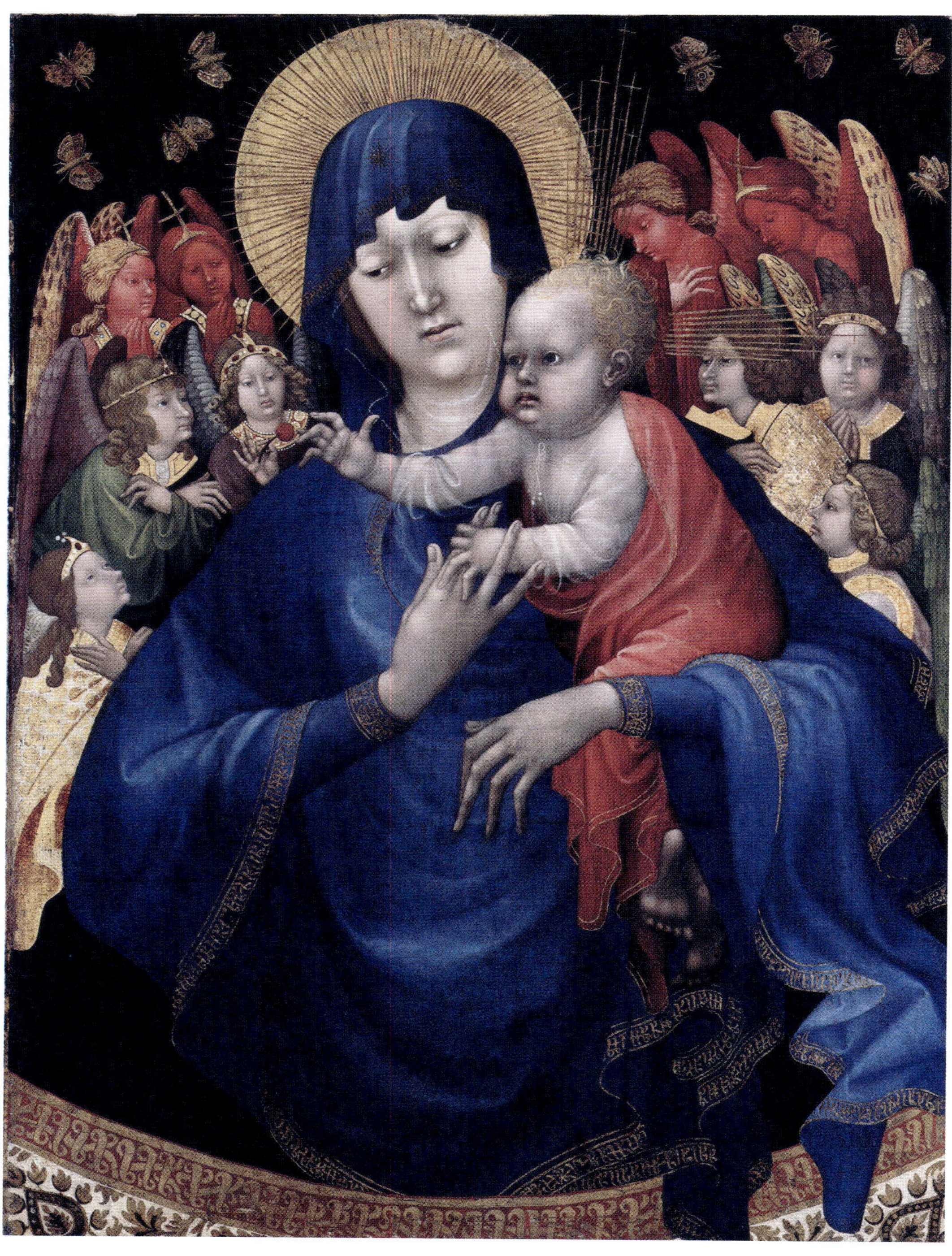

**Fig. 9** Johan Maelwael, *Virgin and Child with Butterflies*, c. 1410–15 (Berlin, Gemäldegalerie, Kat. Nr. 87.1)

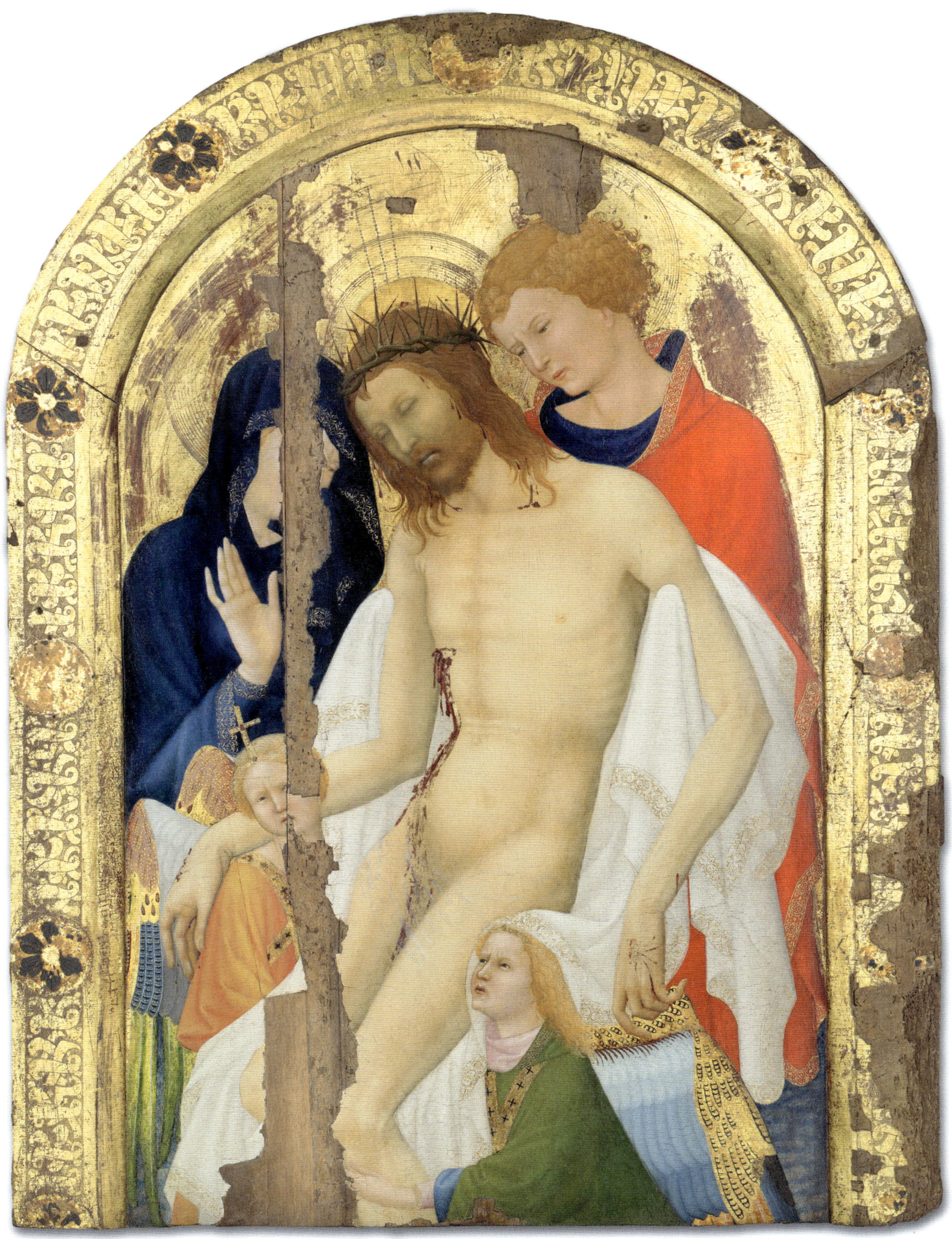

**Fig. 10** Attributed to the Van Lymborch brothers (Paul?), *Man of Sorrows* (Paris, musée du Louvre, département des Peintures, R.F. 2012-1)

**Fig. 11** Following pages: Van Lymborch brothers, *Très Riches Heures*, fol. 5v: May, detail

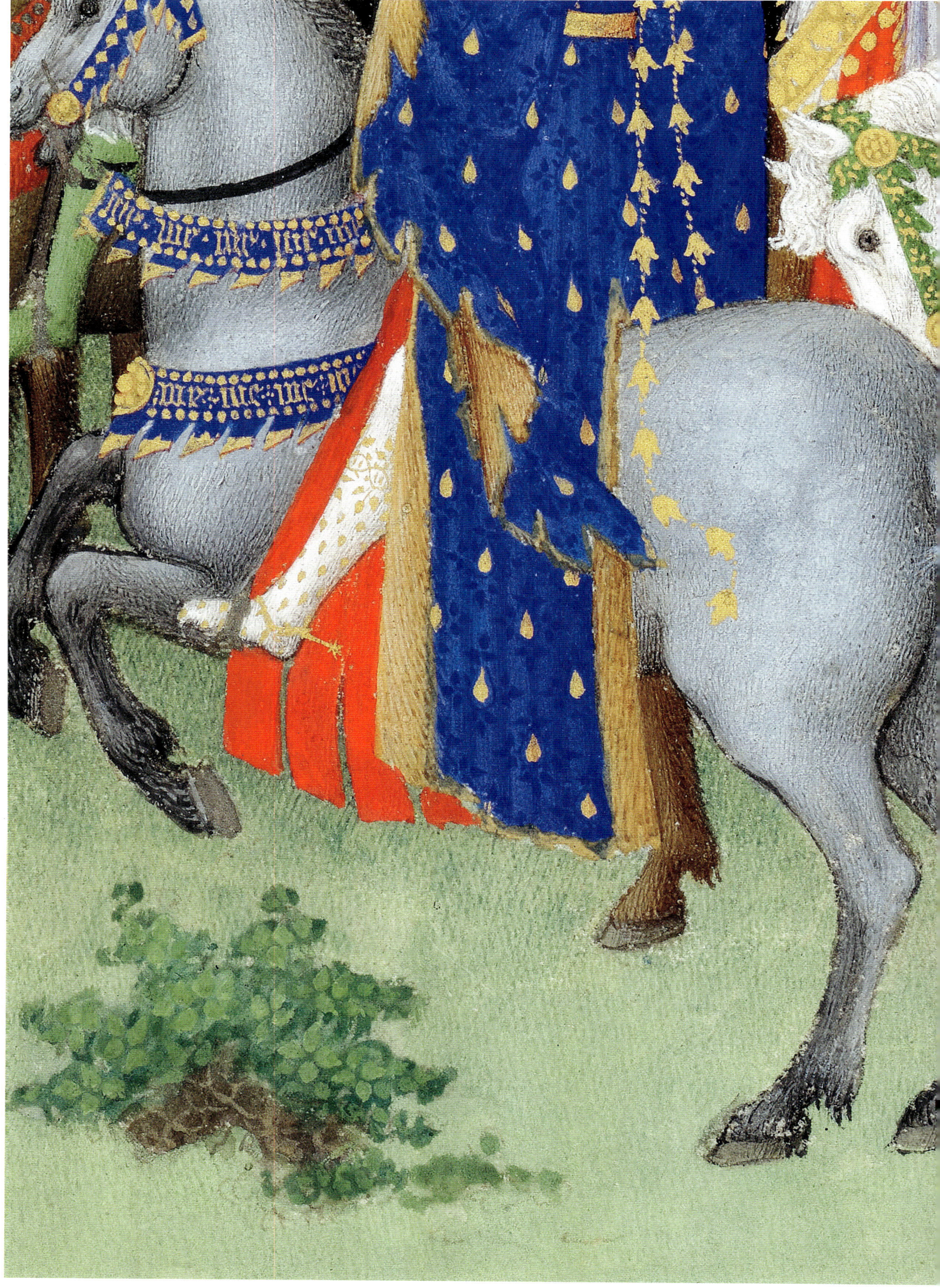

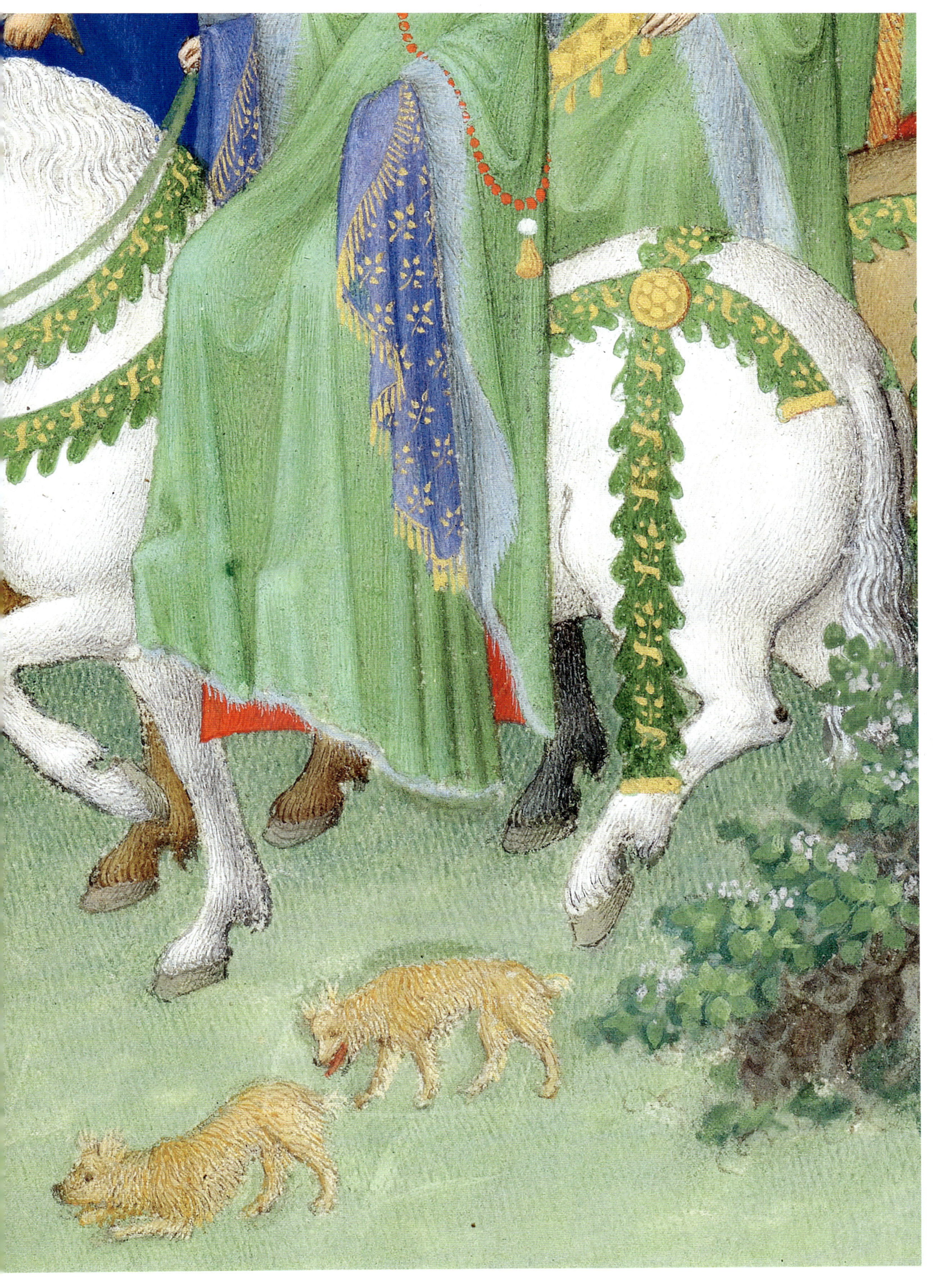

evident, among other things, in the bold foreshortening of the apostle's neckline. If we compare the *Christ* of Vic with the works now attributed to Maelwael by most specialists—the *Large Round Pietà* and the *Virgin and Child with Butterflies* in Berlin (fig. 9)—the range of colors appears softer, more luminous, and more contrasted: alongside salmon-orange, a rare hue at the time, and pale pink, characteristically combined with green, we have, as a counterpoint, as in the *Belles Heures* (fol. 149; fig. 12), bright colors, the vermilion red of the apostle's cloak, and, in various places, a skillfully modulated ultramarine blue. A striking element here, from both a visual and symbolic point of view, is the place given to the superb white shroud, whose fabric, as if swollen from within, has a vaporous texture. Despite successive cleanings, the body of Christ has also retained this smooth, "fused" texture, as have the flesh tints, in particular the Virgin's beautiful hand, elements that indicate a mastery of oil painting, but also, despite the difference in binding medium, call for comparison with the later nudes in the *Très Riches Heures* of Zodiacal Man (fol. 14v; fig. 13) and of Adam and Eve Expelled from Paradise (fol. 25v; fig. 15). Several poetic

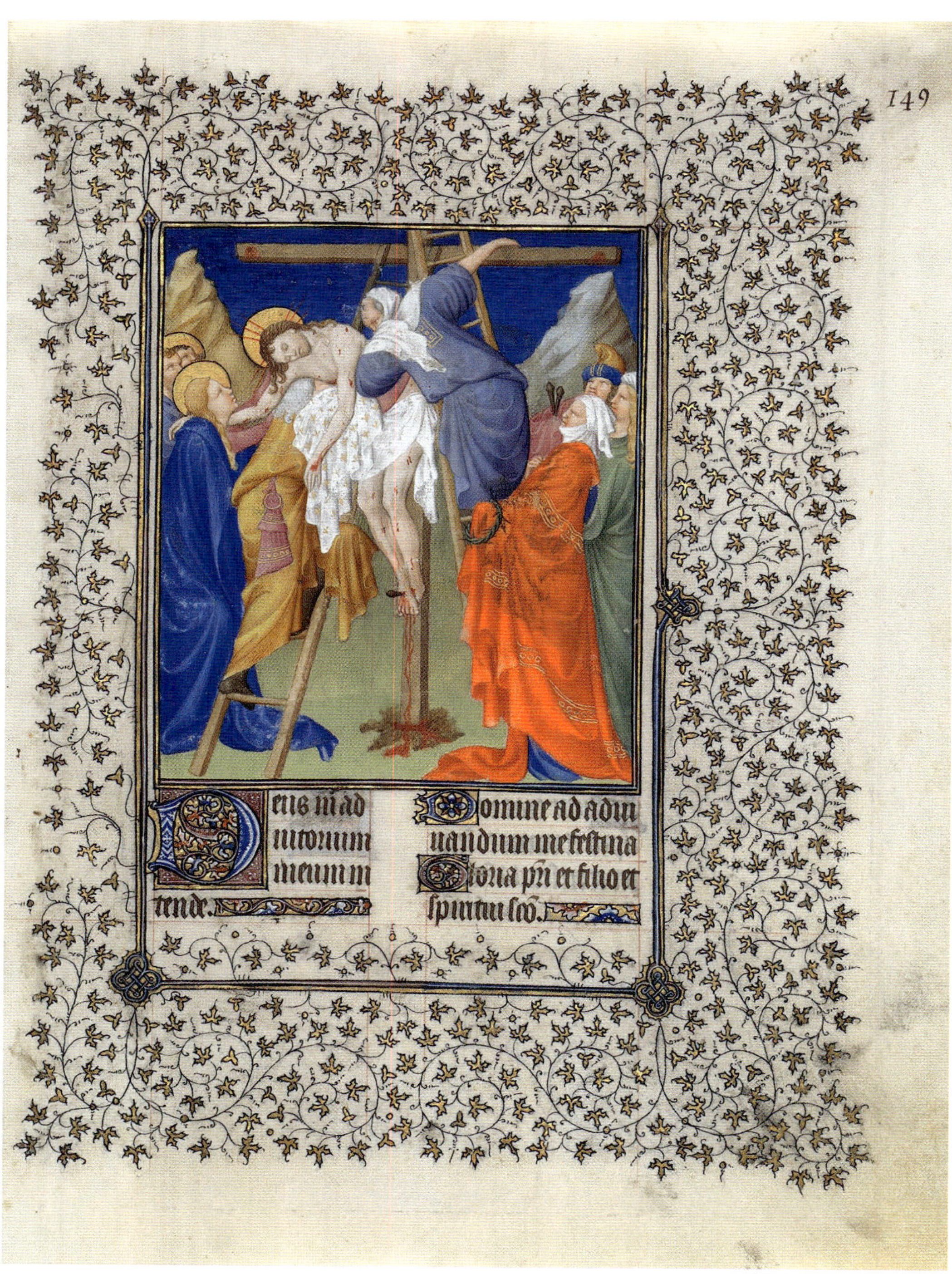

**Fig. 12** Van Lymborch brothers, *Belles Heures*, fol. 149: Descent from the Cross (New York, The Metropolitan Museum of Art, The Cloisters Collection, 1954 [Ms. Acc. 54. 1. 1])

**Fig. 13** Van Lymborch brothers, *Très Riches Heures*, fol. 14v: Zodiacal Man
**Fig. 14** Following pages: Van Lymborch brothers, *Très Riches Heures*, fol. 14v: Zodiacal Man, detail

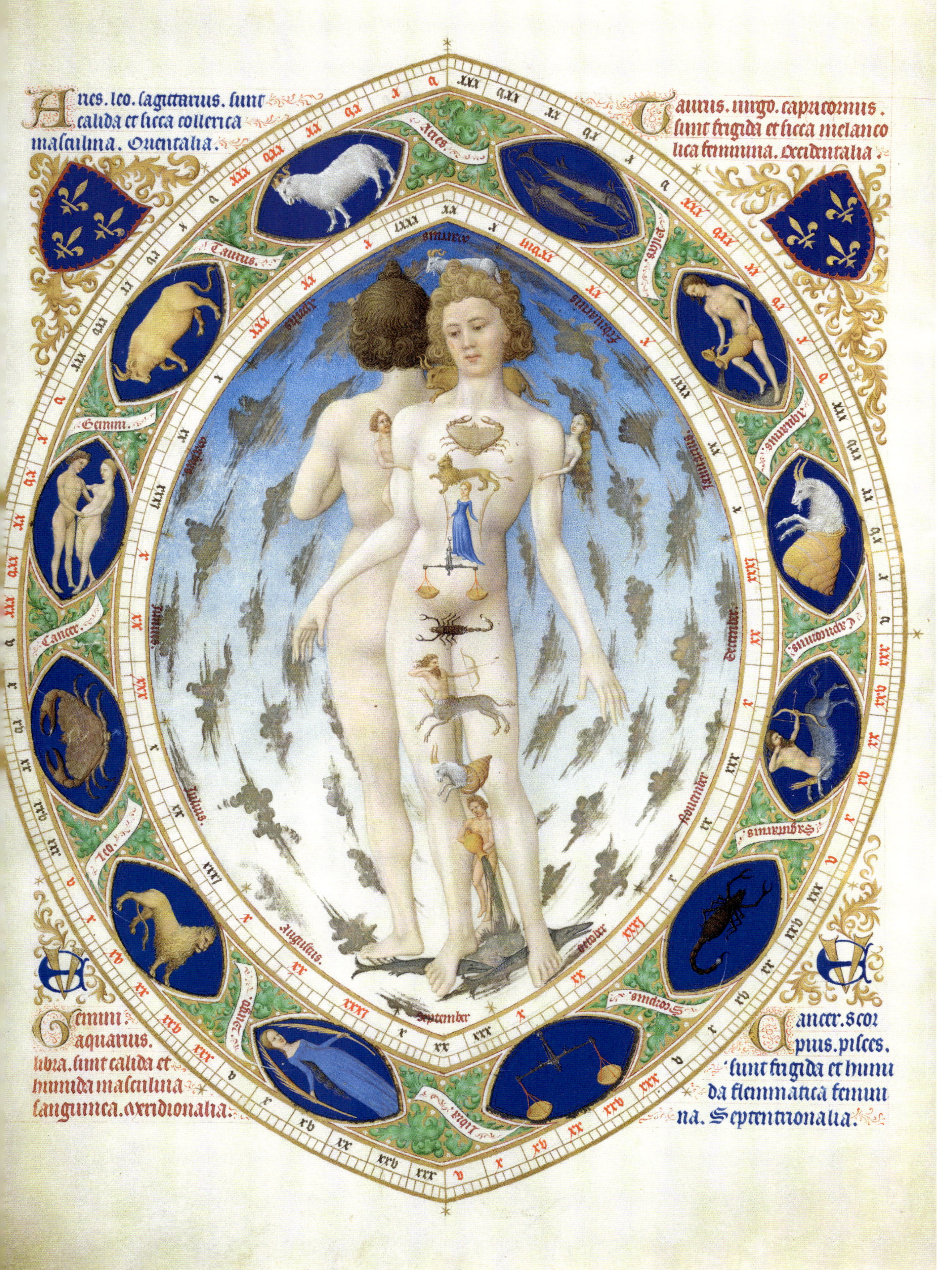
Aries. leo. sagittarius. sunt
calida et sicca collerica
masculina. Orientalia.
Taurus. virgo. capricornus.
sunt frigida et sicca melanco
lica feminina. Occidentalia.
Gemini.
aquarius.
libra. sunt calida et
humida masculina
sanguinea. meridionalia.
Cancer. scor
pius. pisces.
sunt frigida et humi
da flegmatica femini
na. Septentrionalia.

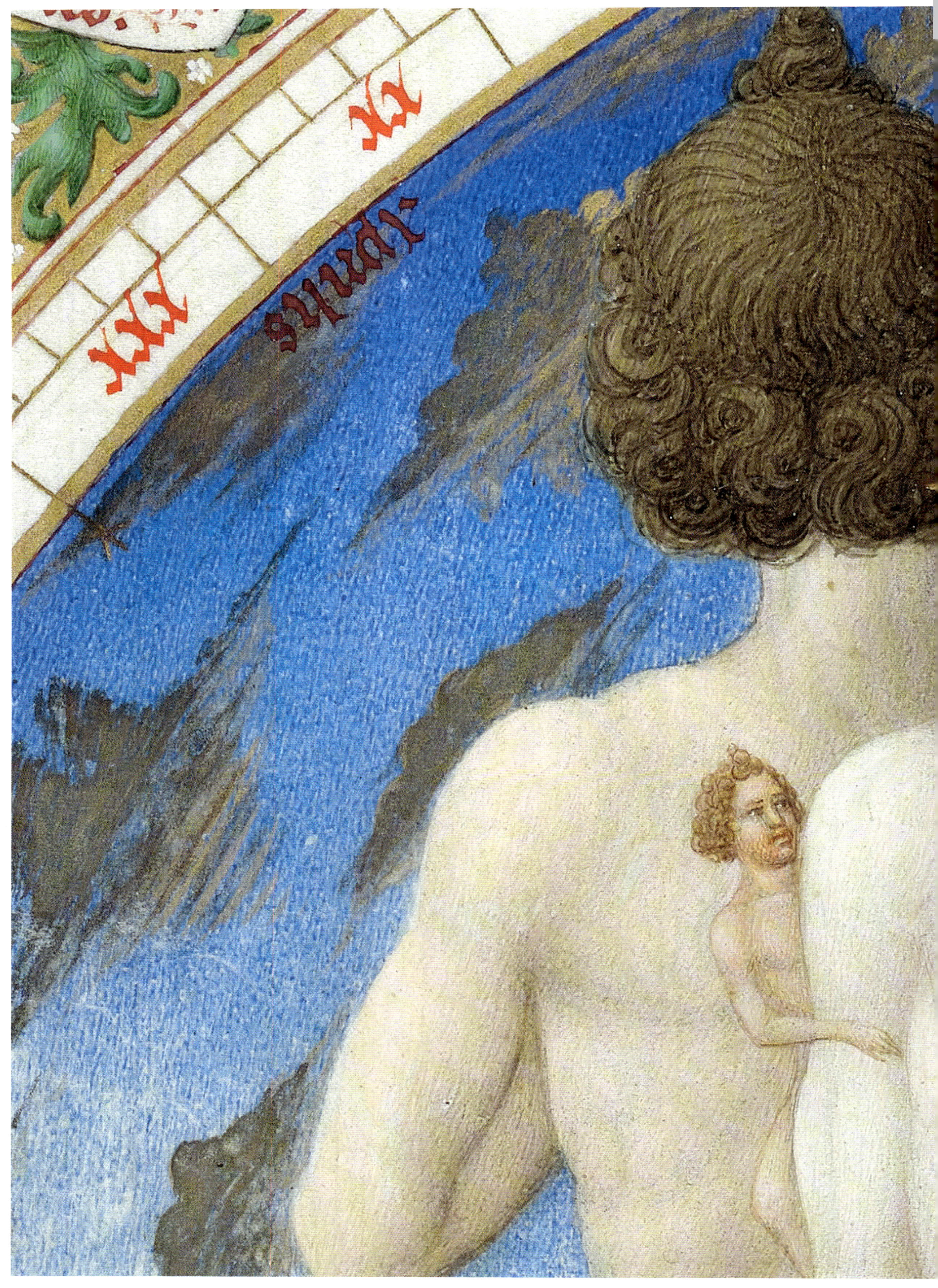

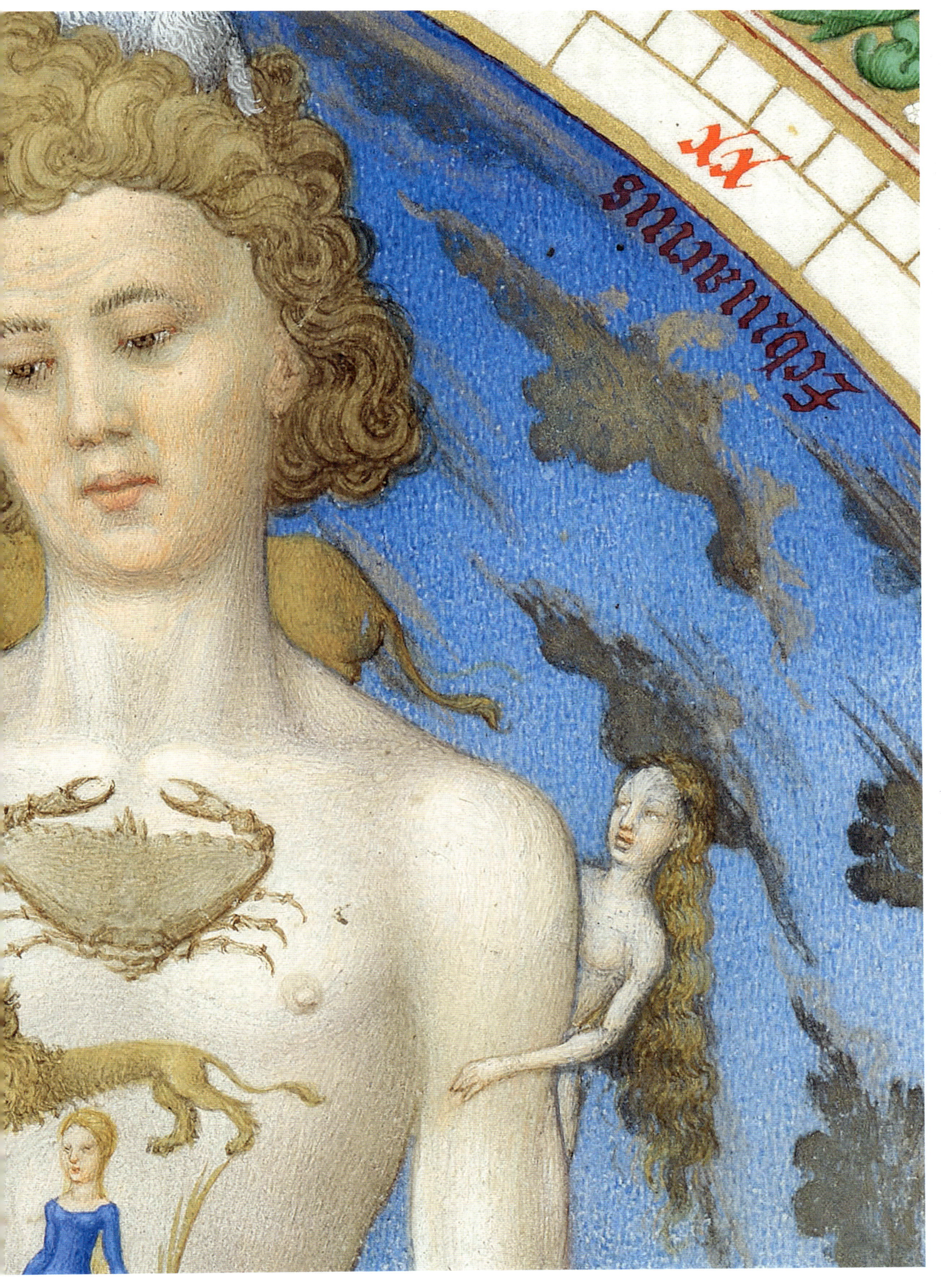
xx
Februarius

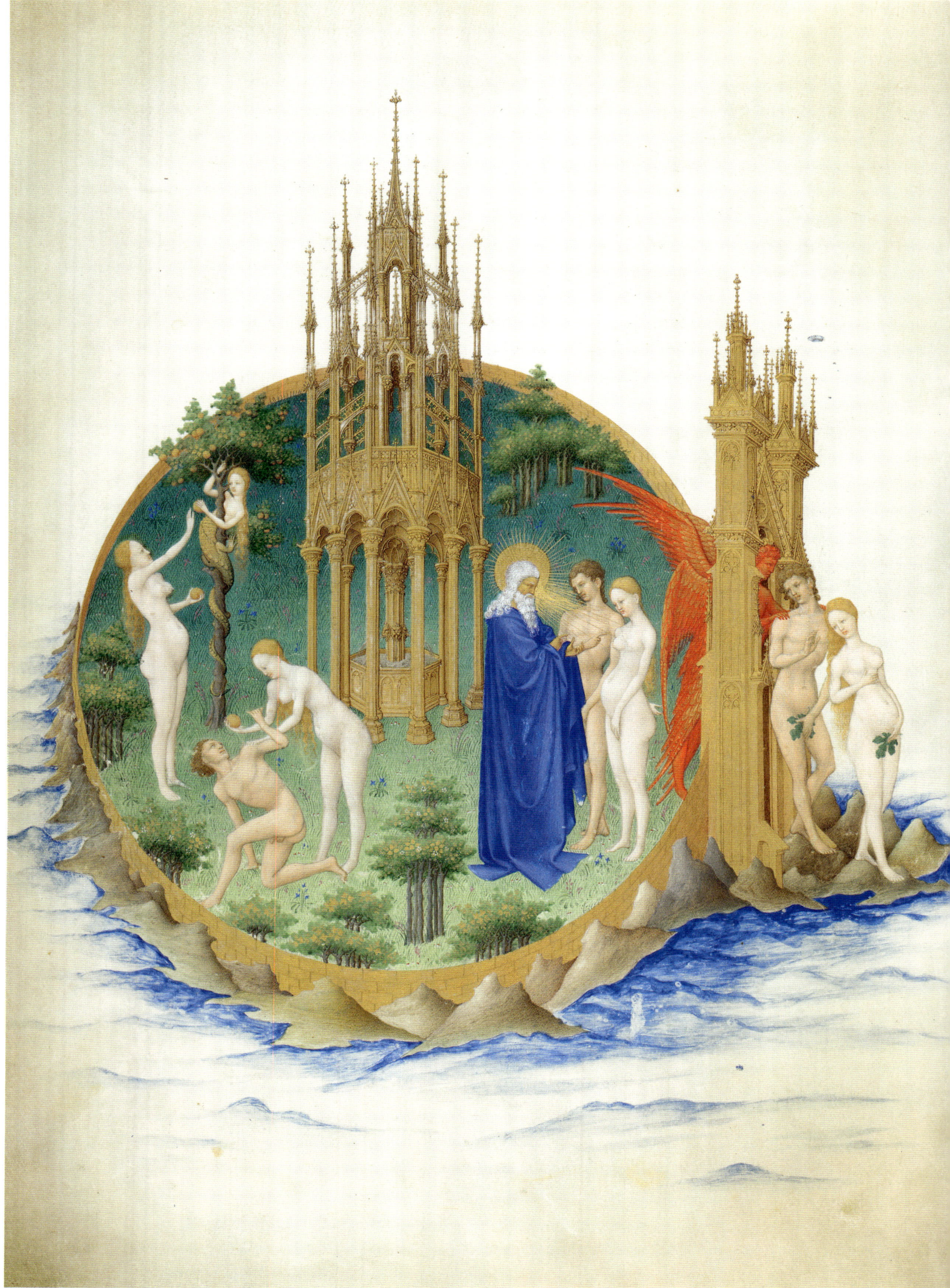

or significant details—such as the angel's crown hidden under a piece of the shroud, and St. John's hands veiled as a sign of concern and respect—reveal the imagination of the painter of Vic. There are no pathetic gestures here—consider the apostle and the angels of the *Large Round Pietà*—but rather a subtle and hypersensitive emotion, tending toward greater gentleness and serenity: Christ's already sallow face expresses not suffering, but inner peace (figs. 4 and 10).

From a technical perspective, the analysis of the scientific documents has proven disappointing,[52] both in terms of refuting the identity of the maker of this work with that of the *tondo* and supporting the attribution of the painting to one of the Van Lymborchs. On the basis of infrared photographs and infrared reflectography (figs. 16–18), the underdrawing hardly differs from one painting to another: Linear in each case, though it appears more supple in the *Christ* of Vic and has a specific line around the eyebrows, which curiously end in a comma, an element that we would tend to regard as a signature of the "Vic Master" (fig. 18). However, there is no visible trace of this unusual detail on the infrared photographs of the *Belles Heures*,[53] nor on those of the *Très Riches Heures* recently taken by the C2RMF (Centre de Recherche et de Restauration des Musées de France), perhaps because of the reduced size of the images. The underdrawing of the Chantilly miniatures shows pronounced cross-hatching and particularly abundant decorative patterns at this stage, which contrast with the more simplified outline of the two painted panels.[54] Conversely, the *Christ* of Vic and several pages from the *Belles Heures*[55] and the *Très Riches Heures*[56] exhibit the same masterful and varied use of silver and, especially, gold. Whether matt or burnished—these two decorative techniques are sometimes combined, as seen in Christ's halo (fig. 17),[57]—gold

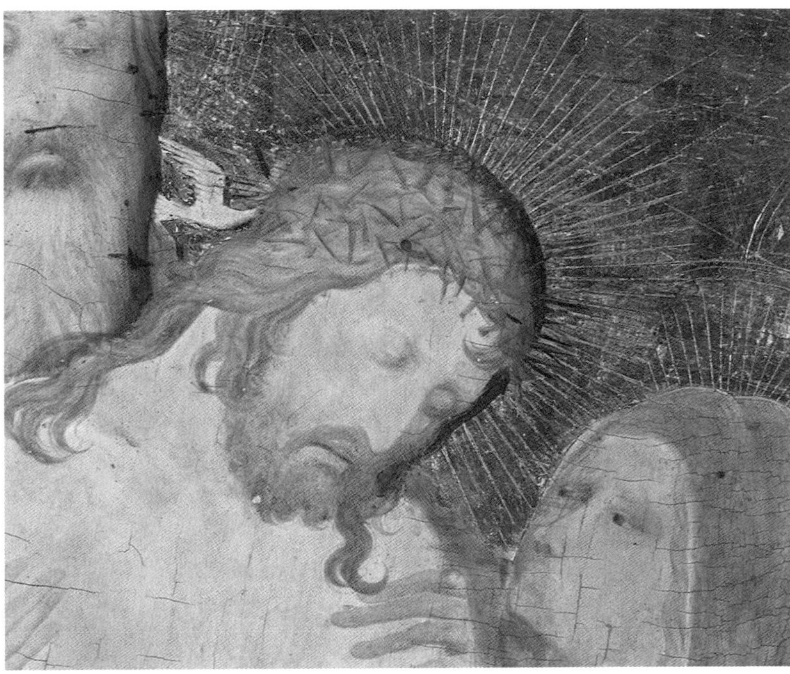

**Fig. 16** Attributed to Johan Maelwael, *Large Round Pietà*: detail of the face of Christ, infrared reflectography. Photo E. Lambert, J.-L. Bellec – C2RMF

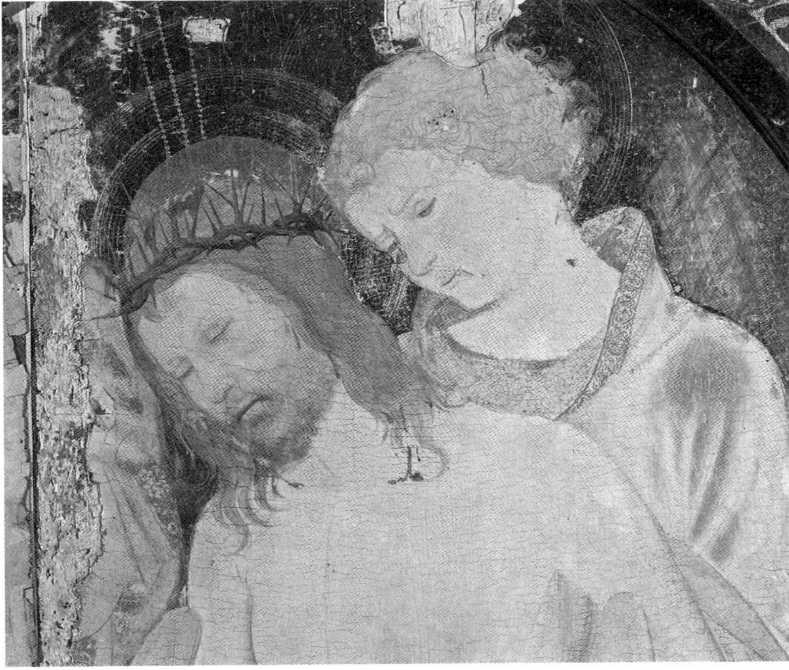

**Fig. 17** Attributed to the Van Lymborch brothers (Paul?), *Man of Sorrows*: detail of the face of Christ, infrared reflectography. Photo E. Lambert, J.-L. Bellec – C2RMF

**Fig. 15** Van Lymborch brothers, *Très Riches Heures*, fol. 25v: Adam and Eve Expelled from Paradise

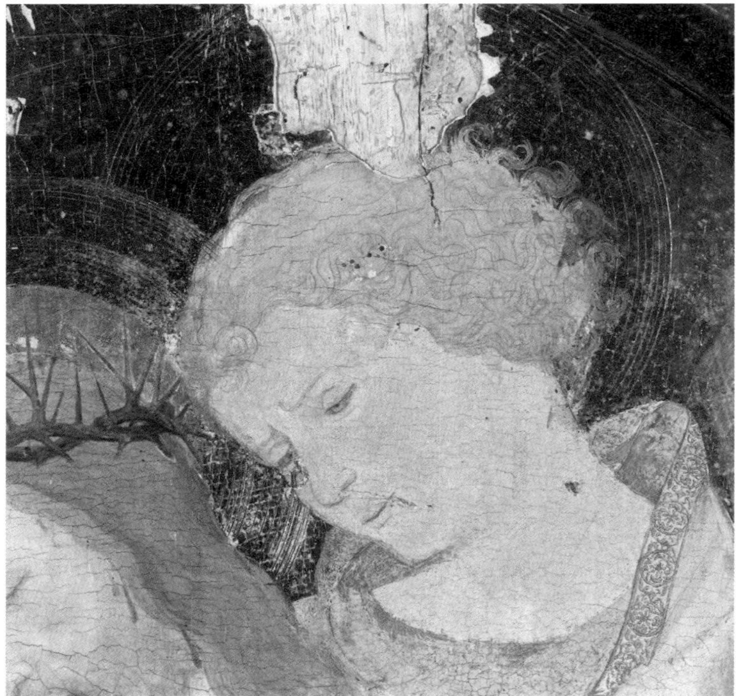

**Fig. 18** Attributed to the Van Lymborch brothers (Paul?), *Man of Sorrows*: detail of the face of St. John the Evangelist, infrared reflectography. Photo E. Lambert, J.-L. Bellec – C2RMF

leaf can be incised, punched, and occasionally overlaid with a glaze. Regardless of the specific technical methods employed, the intricate patterns adorning the frame, the angels' wings, and the fabrics in the painting—along with those lavishly laid on backgrounds, textiles, and jewels in the miniatures—are, for most, unmatched in originality, elegance, and sumptuousness. As for the pigments used in both paintings, they are to be found to a greater or lesser extent in the illuminations, but in these the palette is considerably more varied.[58]

Two other material elements are of interest in determining the paternity of the *Christ* of Vic. First, the use of walnut for its support,[59] a species rarely imported and rather used locally, in Burgundy and south of the Loire, which seems to rule out a priori that it was executed in Paris: Most of the surviving paintings that can be linked to this source[60] are, in fact, painted on oak imported from the Baltic regions.[61] However, as the accounts of the Burgundian Court and surviving painted panels show,[62] both walnut and local oak were used in Dijon. Nevertheless, the experienced carpenters who worked on the Champmol site would not have used planks so defective and knotty that inserts had to be added before painting could begin, as was the case for the *Christ* of Vic, nor would they have failed to cover the entire panel with cloth, or at least to line the joint between the two planks. This negligence, which is responsible for the loss of the paint on the faces of the Virgin and the angel on the left, suggests that the support was made in a provincial center with little experience of producing painted panels. What a contrast between, on the one hand, the mediocrity of the support and, on the other, the sumptuousness of the decoration on the finely grained frame, alternating pseudo-Kufic characters and superb floral medallions in relief, the generous use of metallic leaves and precious pigments, and the extraordinary quality of the pictorial execution, so apt to satisfy the taste of the most refined prince of the time, Jean of Berry.

The provenance of the painting, namely Vic-le-Comte, a place where his presence can hardly be considered fortuitous, does not contradict the hypothesis that the work was commissioned by the duke. On the contrary. Let us recall that in 1389 Jean was given the County of Auvergne—whose capital was Vic—as a dowry from his second wife, Jeanne, daughter of John II, Count of Auvergne. Perhaps the princely couple wanted to decorate the former chapel of the count's palace with a painted altarpiece, for example in the wake of the death of John II (1404), or a few years later? What could have been more natural than for Berry to ask his favorite painter, Paul van Lymborch, to work in Bourges, a town not very far from Vic after all, where the artist may already have been living intermittently. But we are well aware, of course, that this involves a lot of suppositions.

1 We wish to acknowledge the following for the help they gave us in various ways during the writing of this essay: Anne-Isabelle Berchon, Philippe Bon, Sophie Caron, Anne Chapoutot, Aurélia Cohendy, Sara Colson, Mathieu Deldicque, Marie-Pierre Dion, Joanna Dunn, Nathalie Gallier, Lore Gauterie, Catherine Granger, Armelle Parent, Claudia Rabel, Marina Rouyer, André Stufkens, Élisabeth Taburet-Delahaye, Bénédicte Verny, and, especially, Béatrice de Chancel-Bardelot, Élisabeth Ravaud, and Inès Villela-Petit, with whom we had very fruitful discussions. In his *Description de la ville de Paris au xv^e siècle* ([1434] ed. 1855, 84), Guillebert de Metz mentions the three illuminators among the "artificieux ouvriers" (ingenious craftsmen) who ensured the city's excellence.

2 Reynaud 2006b, 242. See the rich and stimulating contribution by Inès Villela-Petit (2021b, in particular 129–31) on the specific case of the Van Lymborch brothers.

3 See the corpus of documents compiled by Millard Meiss (1974a, I, 71–81).

4 Niessen, Roelofs, and van Veen-Liefrink 2005, 14–15; Roelofs 2005, 36–40.

5 On the place of the three brothers in this group of six siblings, see Niessen, Roelofs, and van Veen-Liefrink 2005, 15.

6 Registered in the guild of Parisian goldsmiths in 1388, Alebret de Bolure (or Bolme?) is mentioned in 1393–94 as a supplier to the Duke of Burgundy. Inès Villela-Petit (2013b, 15–16) does not rule out the possibility that the three brothers arrived in Paris as early as 1396 with their uncle, Johan Maelwael, who was mentioned as being in the capital in the service of Queen Isabeau of Bavaria in September 1396.

7 Johan Maelwael, born c. 1370–75, present in Paris in 1396, died in Dijon in 1415. Following Patrick M. De Winter, Anne van Buren (Van Buren, Marrow, and Pettenati 1996, 487 note 15) is in favor of identifying him with the painter known as "Malohé" and then "Malouhé," who in 1395 owed the City of Dijon a tax from which he would eventually be exempted.

8 Meiss 1974a, I, 72.

9 Paris, BnF, Ms. Français 166. Meiss 1974a, I, 72–73, 81–101.

10 See note 6 above.

11 Meiss 1974a, I, 73.

12 Meiss 1974a, I, 73–74.

13 New York, Met, The Cloisters, 1954 (Ms. Acc. 54.1.1). See Meiss 1974a, I, 75–76.

14 Around 1405, see Meiss 1974a, I, 74.

15 Paul, the first to receive this distinction, was awarded it on November 9, 1413, and the three brothers on August 22, 1415; see Meiss 1974a, I, 77, 79.

16 Guiffrey 1894–96, I, 171–72 (no. 650); Henwood 1982, 154; Kovács 2004, 285 note 11.

17 Henwood 1982, 160; Kovács 1984, quoted by Inès Villela-Petit (2013b, 78, and 2023b, 19 note 28).

18 Guiffrey 1894–96, I, 123 (no. 401), 90 (no. 296).

19 Villela-Petit 2023b, 18–19.

20 Roelofs 2005, 40–41, 43; Hablot 2018, 118–21.

21 November 21, 1408, see Meiss 1974a, I, 75.

22 February 1, 1434, see Ibid., I, 80–81.

23 Should the "Paoul" mentioned in 1521 by Jean Pèlerin, known as the Viator, on the frontispiece of his treatise *De artificiali perspectiva* (Toul, P. Jacques, 1521, fol. 1) among some twenty painters, be identified with Paul van Lymborch, as suggested by Paul Durrieu (1904, 80), followed, among others, by François Avril (1971, 1024) and by Willy Niessen, Pieter Roelofs, and Mieke van Veen-Liefrink (2005, 13, 27 note 3)? This is open to question.

24 Patricia Stirnemann (2018) envisages Maelwael as being active in the field of illumination, in particular as a participant in the *Très Riches Heures*. On this subject, see the reflections of Rob Dückers (2017).

25 See the articles by Victor M. Schmidt on the subject, in particular Schmidt 2005, 179; Husband 2012b, 65–69; Nash 2024a.

26 On the echoes of Simone Martini's quadriptych in their illuminations, see the very detailed analysis by Susie Nash (2024a, 241–49).

27 Paris, Musée du Louvre, on loan from Bourges, Musée de Berry, inv. R.F. 1967-1 A.

28 The provenance of this painted panel—whose two sides were separated and transposed onto canvas in the 1950s—is indeed linked to the region of Berry. As Béatrice de Chancel-Bardelot kindly pointed out to us, it came from the collection of Louise de Bourbon-Chalus (1861–1959), whose château was located in Ville-Perdue, 7km from Mehun-sur-Yèvre. According to Élisabeth Mognetti (2018), who investigated the legacy of this panel in the Parisian milieu, the personality of Jean of Berry is precisely "the crux of her investigation." It cannot be ruled out that the altarpiece to which this double-sided painting most likely belonged, whether fixed or portable, was still complete in the early fifteenth century.

29 In relation to the Martyrdom of St. Mark (fol. 19v of the *Très Riches Heures*), Gustav Friedrich Waagen evokes a "strong Italian influence" (Waagen 1857, 255, cited by Durrieu 1904, 45 note 2).

30 In particular François Avril (1979).

31 Nash 2024a, 249–52.

32 On the echoes of the lost Mary Magdalene from the *Well of Moses*—Mary Magdalene who, according to Susie Nash's demonstration (2008, 724, 727–33; 2024b, 997, 999 [fig. 3], 1006, 1015), knelt alone, from behind, with her hair flowing, embracing the base of the Cross—in the *Bible moralisée* (fol. 24), the *Très Belles Heures de Notre-Dame* (Paris, BnF, Ms. NAL 3093, fols. 119, 126v), and the *Très Riches Heures* (fol. 156v; fig. 19, p. 158), see Nash 2008, 728; Villela-Petit 2013b, 83.

33 Dijon, Musée des Beaux-Arts.

34 In the opinion of Susie Nash (2022, 15, 17, 20), of the five altarpieces in question delivered to Maelwael, two have survived: the *Martyrdom of St. Denis*, *"parfait"* (completed) in 1416 by Henri Bellechose (Paris, Louvre), and the later *Martyrdom of St. George* (Dijon, Musée des Beaux-Arts, on loan from the Louvre), which was painted later.

35 Lorentz 2004a, 293; Paris 2004b, 294 (no. 183).

36 Paris, Louvre, inv. MI 692.

37 Warnke [1985] 1989, 52, 185.

38 Meiss 1974a, I, 76.

39 Given the facts related in the document of November 21, 1408, the "painter alemant qui besoignoit pour lui [le duc Jean] en son hôtel de Wincestre lez Paris" (a German painter who worked for him [Jean, Duke of Berry] in his residence in Wincestre near Paris) can only be Paul; see Meiss 1974a, I, 75.

40 Philippe Lorentz (2004a, 293) is of the same opinion.

41 Meiss 1974a, I, 225; Villela-Petit 2022, 154–56.

42 Paris, BnF, Estampes, Oa 13, Rés, fol. 15. Meiss 1963, 51–53; Meiss 1974a, I, 225.

43 Bourges, Arch. dép. du Cher, Ms. J 771.

44 Washington, NGA, Andrew W. Mellon Collection, inv. 1937.1.23. For an extensive bibliography and a physical description of the painting, we refer you to the gallery's excellent online catalogue.

45 Meiss (1974a, I, 228, 471 note 640)—who dated the portrait to c. 1420—noted that, despite certain elements reminiscent of Maelwael and the Van Lymborch brothers, "volume is now compressed and sacrificed for fluctuating outline."

46 See incidentally Bernard Berenson's 1932 assessment of the painting's condition, quoted by Patricia Rubin (2011, 21, 380 note 69). For a physical description of the work, see the "Technical Summary" in the online catalogue cited above in note 44. We wish to thank Joanna Dunn, painting conservator at the NGA in Washington, for kindly showing us the infrared reflectography of the painting.

47 Thiébaut 2015.

48 Salmon 2012, 28–29.

49 Paris, Louvre, inv. RF 2012 1. Thiébaut 2012, 7–25.

50 See Rob Dückers' highly evocative montages of the figure of Christ (2017, 62).

51 Thiébaut 2012.

52 There are several reasons why it is difficult to compare panel paintings and illuminations, among others, of course, the difference in scale between them, but also the diversity of media used for the underdrawing and the binding medium in the final stage. We wish to thank Élisabeth Ravaud, who kindly discussed these issues with us and refer you to her essay, pp. 331–45.

53 See Lawson 2012, 352–53 figs. 91a, 92, 93, 94.

54 See essay by É. Ravaud, p. 334.

55 Lawson 2012, 354–55 fig. 95.

56 See essay by É. Ravaud, pp. 337–38

57 Thiébaut 2012, 8.

58 On the pigments used by painters and illuminators, see Villela-Petit 2022, 134–37, and essay by É. Ravaud, pp. 335–38.

59 On the reverse, however, are two original dovetailed crossbeams that, as dendrochronological analysis has shown, are made of Baltic oak; see Gonzalez et al., 2017, 35.

60 These are mainly pictures painted in the fifteenth century; see Marette 1961; Sterling 1987–90.

61 The *Large Round Pietà* was very probably painted on oak, but the presence of the painted reverse prevents a dendrochronological analysis from being carried out to determine whether it is of Baltic or local origin. According to Élisabeth Ravaud, however, the density of the wood rings visible on the X-ray suggests a Nordic provenance.

62 See Prochno 2002a; Nash 2010.

**Fig. 19** Following pages: Van Lymborch brothers, *Très Riches Heures*, fol. 25v: Adam and Eve Expelled from Paradise, detail

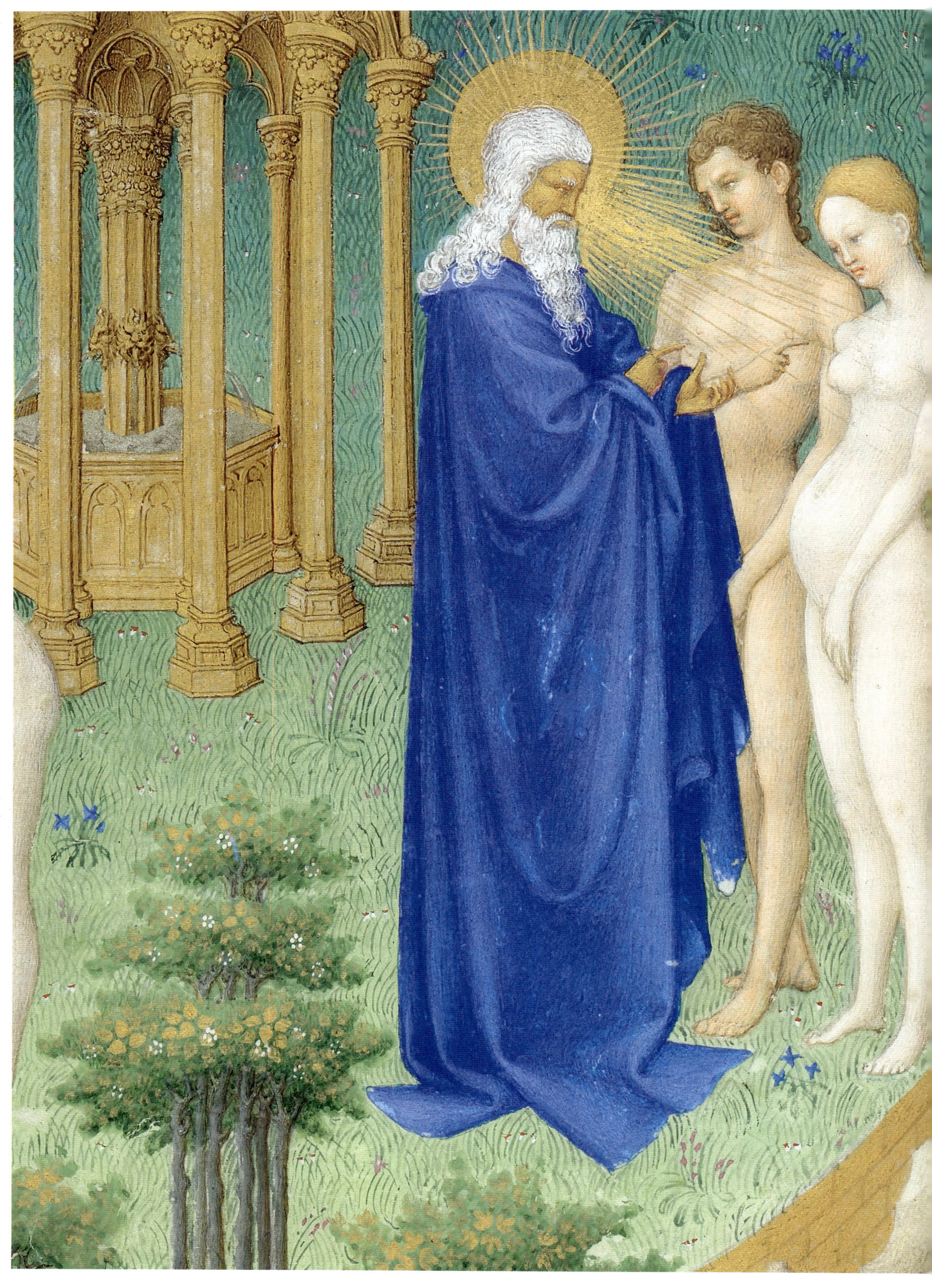

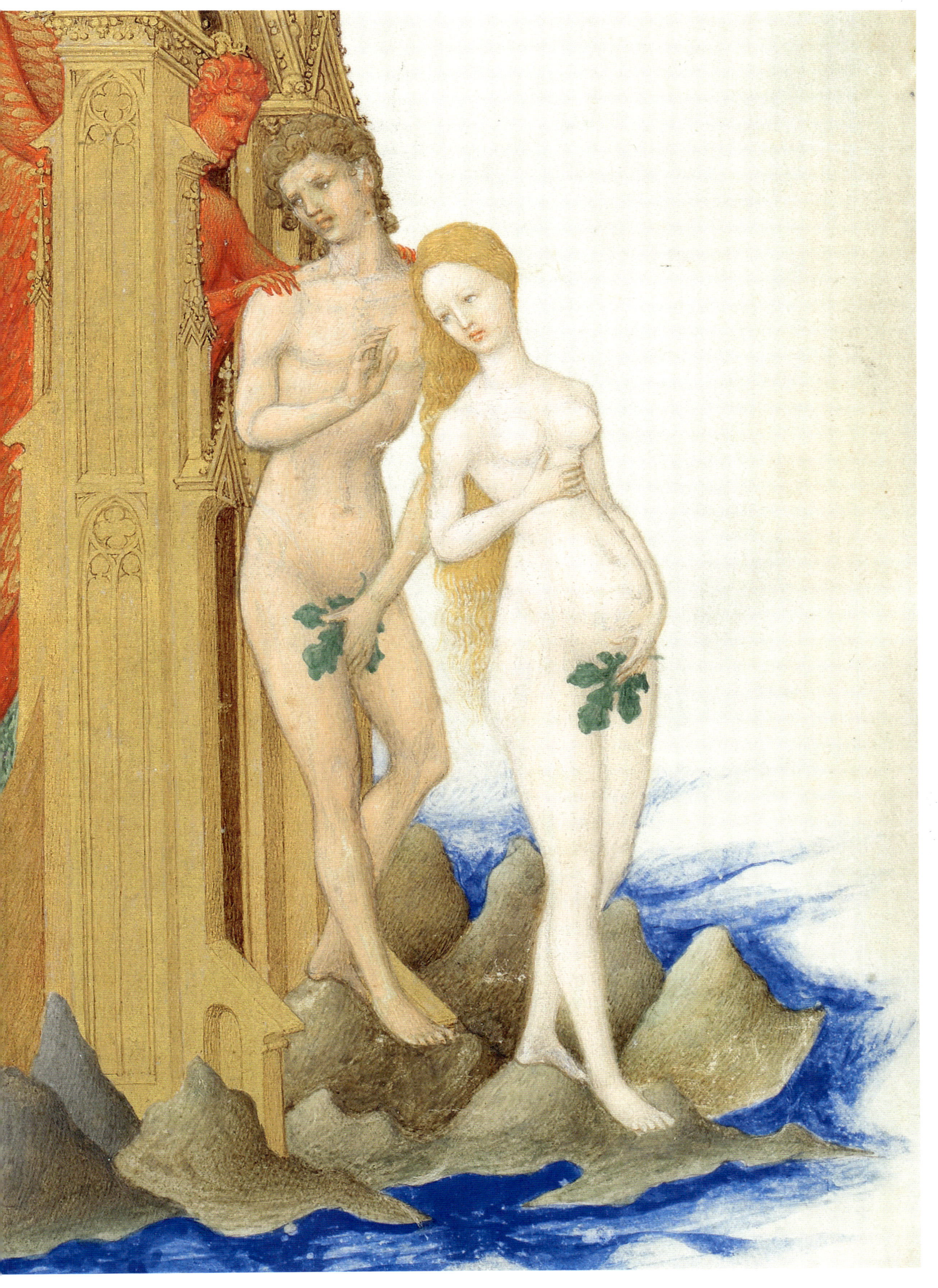

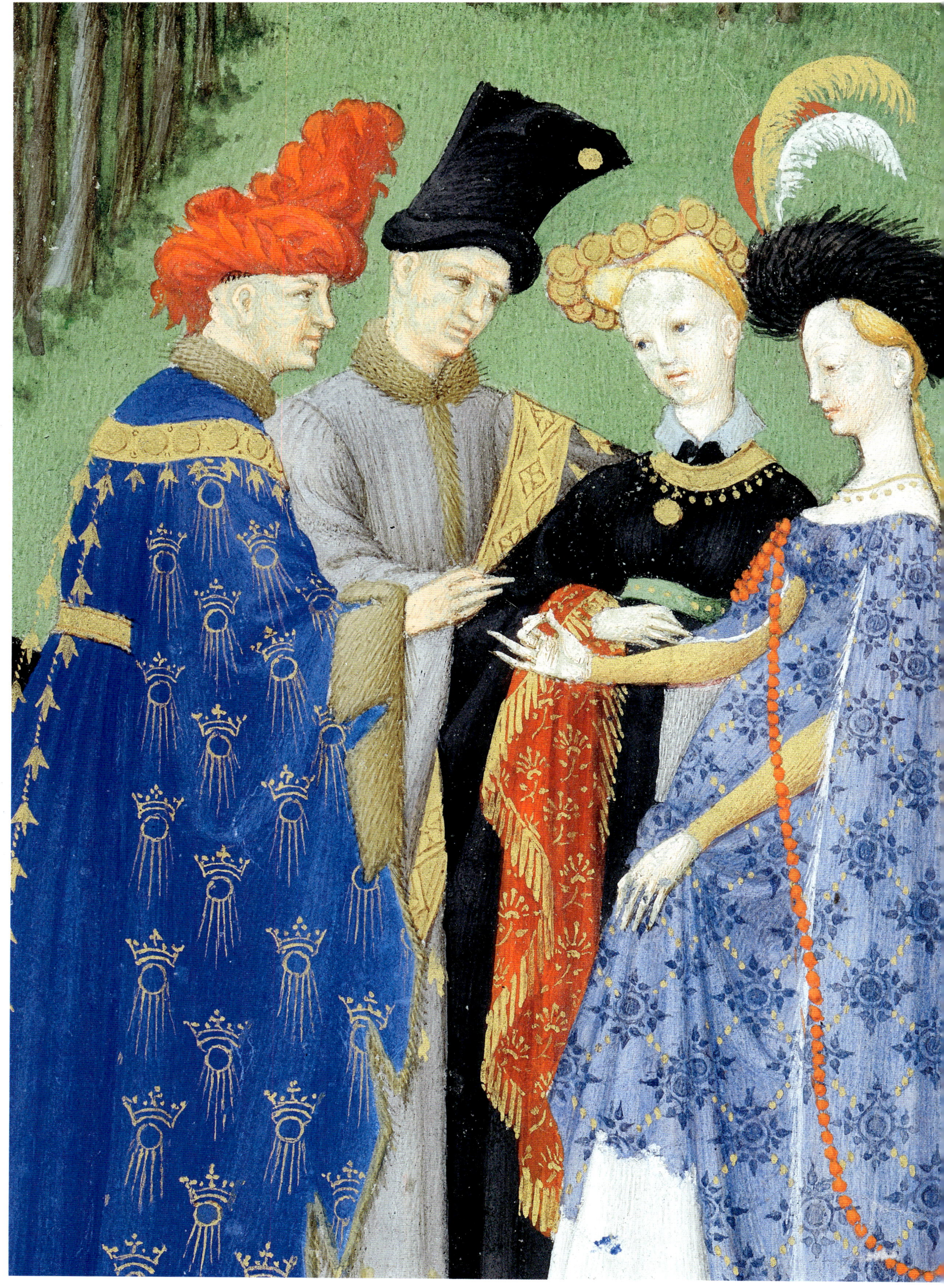

# 9.

*In memory of Clemens Verhoeven (1949–2023), founder of the Maelwael Van Lymborch Foundation*

# The Van Lymborch Brothers and the North: Crosscurrents between Nijmegen, Bourges, and Paris

Pieter Roelofs

Barely a few quires—a set of vellum leaves preserved in a box at the Hôtel de Nesle in Paris—is all that was left in 1416 of one of the most impressive private devotional commissions in Western Europe in the late Middle Ages. Its creators were dead, as was its patron. Only a pile of unbound leaves of what should have been a particularly rich book of hours—"d'unes très riches Heures"—remained as evidence of their shared ambition to create a luxurious, technically unrivalled, and visually spectacular manuscript.

Neither the patron, Jean of France, Duke of Berry, nor "Pol et ses frères"—as the brothers Herman, Paul, and Johan van Lymborch were named in the duke's estate inventory—would ever see the anticipated conclusion of their partnership.[1] But although the international collaboration that had begun some ten years earlier between the powerfully rich French duke driven by a lively passion for collecting, and these three exceptionally talented young artists from the distant Duchy of Guelders, was brutally interrupted by death, it amazed the nobleman, made the painters' fortunes, and, above all, produced several impressive works of art and devotion. The few completed leaves of their last, unfinished project—"très richement historiez et enluminez" (very richly historiated and illuminated)—were enough for the Van Lymborch brothers to lay a milestone in history and, since the manuscript was rediscovered in the 1850s, to rank among the most admired artists of their time.

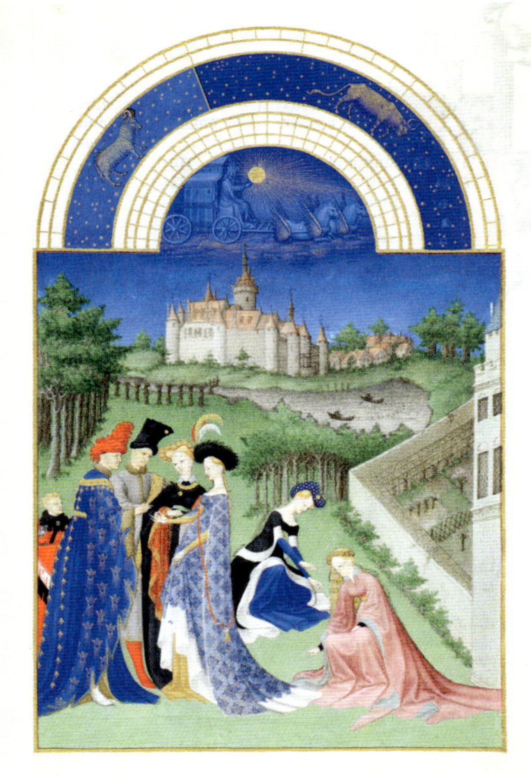

**Fig. 2** Van Lymborch brothers, *Très Riches Heures*, fol. 4v: April

**Fig. 1** Van Lymborch brothers, *Très Riches Heures*, fol. 4v: April, detail

It was above all the synergy between Jean of Berry and the Van Lymborch brothers in the flourishing cultural centers of Bourges and Paris that led to this masterly undertaking. However, it is undeniable that the innovative character, technical perfection, and cultural significance of their creations are in part due to the talent, training, and practice of the brothers. The foundations were laid not in the Île-de-France, where their mastery was given concrete expression, but in their hometown of Nijmegen, more than 600 kilometers to the north.

A key question, then, is how the work of the Van Lymborch brothers relates to their training in the Duchy of Guelders, the land of their youth. What role did the close political, dynastic, and cultural ties between their region and the French court play in their development? What was the relationship of Marie d'Harcourt, Duchess of Guelders, with France and the Duke of Berry, in particular? And what can we say about the interaction between the work of Herman, Paul, and Johan van Lymborch and the art of around 1400 in the Northern Netherlands and the Lower Rhine?

## NETHERLANDISH ORIGINS

Even though Nijmegen city archivist Herman van Schevichaven demonstrated as early as 1914 that the Maelwael-Van Lymborch family (traditionally in French, Malouel-de Limbourg) originated from Nijmegen, and Cleves city archivist Friedrich Gorissen published numerous sources from the Guelders archives from 1954, the Van Lymborch brothers have been described by several authors as Flemish, Belgian, French, or German, even recently.[2] For a long time, their Netherlandish origins were considered irrelevant to their art. In 1953, French art historian Jean Porcher wrote, half-jokingly: "As far as their country of origin is concerned, it does not seem that they got much out of it, other than themselves, which was essential."[3]

It is true that it is not easy to make the connection between the work of the Van Lymborch brothers and the art of the northern regions. This near absence of visual connections even led the Dutch art historian Herman Colenbrander to question, as recently as 2006, whether the authors of the Musée Condé's *Très Riches Heures* had been correctly identified.[4] It was Rob Dückers—co-curator of the acclaimed 2005 exhibition about the Van Lymborch brothers at the Museum Het Valkhof in Nijmegen[5]—who was the first to draw a broader parallel between the work of the Van Lymborch brothers and their uncle Johan Maelwael (traditionally in French, Jean Malouel) and the painting and book illumination in the Duchy of Guelders and surrounding regions between around 1380 and 1420.[6]

Clearly, the concept of a national or regional character of art in the late Middle Ages does not reflect the practice of the time. Indeed, given the abundant and continuous circulation of artists, works, materials, and ideas, fluid exchanges took place between the different regions of Europe. As André Stufkens, president of the Maelwael Van Lymborch Studies Foundation, wrote recently, it is striking to note the extent to which the brothers drew on almost the entire world known at the time, particularly for their miniatures in the *Très Riches Heures*—not only the near world, in France, the Netherlands, and Italy, but also the far world, from China to Byzantium and from the Levant to North Africa.[7]

## MULTITALENTED CITIZENS OF GUELDERS IN FRENCH SERVICE

It is generally accepted that Herman, Paul, and Johan van Lymborch worked on the illumination of the *Très Riches Heures* during the last three to five years of their short lives, between around 1411–13 and 1416. Even though they were only in their late twenties at the time, they could already boast a skyrocketing carreer. In the space of a decade and a half, these talented teenagers from the Duchy of Guelders had developed into "valets de chambre" operating at the heart of power in Bourges and Paris. In the preceding period, after the death in 1404 of their former patron, Philip the Bold, Duke of Burgundy, they had already completed their first masterpiece for Jean of Berry, namely the *Belles Heures*, and, as Mathieu Deldicque describes elsewhere in this book, had managed to secure a solid position in his inner circle at the ducal court.[8]

While Paul was primarily active as a painter and illuminator, Herman and Johan worked from an early age as goldsmiths, a trade that their younger brother Arnold would later also practice. In their illuminations, punchwork as a decorative technique and the exceptional application of gold leaf in places where other illuminators applied shell gold with a brush are striking examples of the overlap between the two professions. It is precisely in this mastery of multiple disciplines that the knowledge of various materials and the versatile technical skills, secured through their training, are embedded and culminate in their contribution to the *Très Riches Heures*.[9]

The trio were raised in Nijmegen in a rather affluent family of craftsmen. Three successive generations of the Maelwael-Van Lymborch family had excelled in diverse artistic techniques and media, from goldsmithing to painting, sculpture to embroidery. The ducal accounts show that William and Herman Maelwael, the brothers' grandfather and great-uncle, were the main suppliers of heraldic paintings, gilding, and embroidery to the dukes of Guelders at the end of the fourteenth century, and that they were sometimes assisted in their tasks by the young Johan Maelwael. The archives also reveal that their father, Arnt van Lymborch, as a woodcarver, repeatedly executed "carved works" for various rooms in the ducal court.[10]

The mix of disciplines within a single workshop shows that the boundaries between different trades were not clearly defined in the late Middle Ages—hence the wide-ranging practice of the Van Lymborch brothers as illuminators, goldsmiths, decorative painters, and perhaps also panel painters.

## BETWEEN FRANCE AND GUELDERS

During their years in the service of the Duke of Berry, the Van Lymborch brothers undertook several long journeys to their hometown of Nijmegen, often to attend to their financial affairs. In the summer of 1410, for example, Herman and Johan traveled to Nijmegen to sell everything they owned in the city and county to their mother Metta Maelwael and her heirs. The trips continued while they worked on the *Très Riches Heures*. Local aldermen's protocols indicate that Johan visited Nijmegen in December 1413 and July 1414, shortly after his mother's death.[11] In March 1415, the year before their untimely deaths, Paul and Johan traveled over 600 kilometers one way for the last time.

Although the Duchy of Guelders lagged behind the neighboring County of Holland and Duchy of Brabant in terms of population and urbanization, by 1400 it was the dominant principality in the Lower Rhine region. Guelders formed the flow-through area for the great trade waterways of the Lower Rhine, Waal, IJssel, and Meuse, making it a meeting point of multiple regions. In Nijmegen, the largest city between Cologne and Utrecht, stood the Valkhof Castle on the moraine. It was built in 1155 by Emperor Frederick Barbarossa on the historical site where Emperor Charlemagne had founded a palatinate in the eighth century and where Empress Theophanu died in 991. In the Van Lymborch brothers' time, the Duke and Duchess of Guelders—Willem I van Gulik (William of Guelders) and Katherine of Bavaria, followed shortly after 1400 by Reinoud IV van Gulik (Reinald of Guelders) and Marie d'Harcourt[12]—repeatedly stayed in the castle with their itinerant court.

The houses and workshop of the Maelwael-Van Lymborch family were located in Burchtstraat, the main thoroughfare between the castle and the Church of St. Stephen. Noble families and civil servants in the service of the duke usually lived in spacious "town castles" built in stone. That both Johan Maelwael and the Van Lymborch brothers had managed to find their way south from Nijmegen was due in no small part to the good reputation of their family workshop at the court of Guelders, and to the close dynastic and political ties that the dukes and duchesses of Guelders maintained with both France and Burgundy. Indeed, within this international context, art also played a role in broad diplomacy between sovereigns. Via the beaten path between north and south, Rutger van Lymborch, a younger brother of the three painters, would also have found his way to the Île-de-France, following in their wake. From 1414 until his death in 1435, he was canon of the chapter of the Sainte-Chapelle in Bourges, founded shortly before by Jean of Berry. This honorable position was undoubtedly due to his religious devotion, but also to personal relationships and patronage.[13]

## MARIE D'HARCOURT, DUCHESS OF GUELDERS

In the late Middle Ages, it was not uncommon for influential women to play a role in cultural and political relations, including in the patronage of artists. In late summer 1396, Johan Maelwael received his first documented commission in France from Queen Isabeau of Bavaria, for more than thirty fabric designs, to be executed in gold thread on velvet of various colors, accompanied by mottos.[14] It is assumed that it was a recommendation from Katherine of Bavaria, Duchess of Guelders, that opened the door to her second cousin.[15] Thanks to the double marriage of her brother William and her sister Margaret, celebrated in 1385, Katherine, whose father was the Duke of Bavaria and Count of Holland, was also the sister-in-law of Margaret of Burgundy and John the Fearless, children of Philip the Bold, Duke of Burgundy—the same man for whom both Maelwael and the Van Lymborch brothers worked.

The ducal court of Guelders may have been involved in the transition of the Van Lymborch brothers to Jean of Berry, which took place almost immediately after the death of Philip the Bold. The direct link between the Duchess of Guelders and the Duke of Berry has been virtually ignored in art historical literature—until now. In spring 1405, Reinald IV, Duke of Guelders, younger brother and successor to William I, married Marie d'Harcourt, daughter of Jean VI, Count of Harcourt and Aumale, and Catherine de Bourbon, at Crécy. Marie was also the beloved niece of King Charles VI, and it was the king himself who set the date and venue for the wedding and financed it. According to the customs of the time, this union was mainly a political and state alliance between the king of France and the duke of Guelders. The marriage contract bears witness to this; drawn up in formal Latin, it emphasizes that the union strengthened the long-standing ties between the two regions.[16] To represent Reinald IV and the new court to which Marie came to belong, the coat of arms of the Duke of Guelders was frequently displayed in and around Crécy on objects commissioned by the ducal court as early as the 1380s, gilded or painted by various members of the Maelwael-Van Lymborch family.

As a result of Marie d'Harcourt's arrival in Guelders, numerous French citizens visited the Guelders court from 1405 onward. In 1407, for example, the duchess received both "des Conincx ende Comenstavels vriende van Franckrijk" (the king's and the constable's friends of France) and "heren Gankourt" (gentlemen of Gancourt) and their entourage. Two years later, her guests included "twe Fransoysse riddere" (two French knights).[17] A personal letter written by the Duchess of Guelders in December 1415 to her "dear and much-loved niece" Mary of Burgundy, Countess of Cleves and La Marck, daughter of John the Fearless—nephew of Jean of Berry—and Margaret of Bavaria, shows that France remained dear to the hearts of both noblewomen, even in the north, and that they closely followed events in their native country. Barely six weeks after the bloody battle of Azincourt, in which Anthony of Burgundy, uncle of the Countess of Cleves, was killed alongside many others, and Marie's elder brother, Jean VII d'Harcourt, was captured by the English, the Duchess of Guelders wrote to her niece about the "calamity that has struck our family and our friends in France" and asked her to write at any time if she had good news from France.[18]

Marie d'Harcourt had probably already met Jean of Berry, brother of her uncle Charles V, in her early years. She shared with him a love of richly illuminated manuscripts. The fact that the Duchess of Guelders, along with the Queen of England, the Queen of Cyprus and others, belonged to the select circle of those who maintained cordial relations with the duke outside France has not, until now, been highlighted in the literature devoted to the Van Lymborch brothers.[19] On August 23, 1413, she sent two diamonds set in a gold ring to the Duke of Berry as a gift.[20] Two months later, she received from him a small ruby mounted on a gold ring, purchased the previous year from a Venetian merchant in Paris.[21] These gifts are comparable to the gold rings set with diamonds or an emerald that Paul van Lymborch received from the duke as a token of esteem between 1408 and 1413.[22] In the absence of sources, we can only speculate whether Paul, or one of his brothers, played a role in the exchange of these gifts between Berry and Guelders.

From a French point of view, the Duchy of Guelders may have been considered a peripheral region in the late fourteenth to early fifteenth century, but within the Low Countries, the Duchy could count itself among the liveliest centers of art at the time, according to leading German-American art historian Erwin Panofsky.[23] Thanks in part to court patronage, the duchy had become a cultural melting pot, where the towns and various ducal castles saw the comings and goings of artists and artworks from surrounding regions including the Rhineland, Westphalia, the Maasland, Utrecht, and Brabant.[24] Within this dynamic cultural climate, where influences from all directions converged, the two previous generations of the Maelwael-Van Lymborch family had done good business, and Herman, Paul, and Johan van Lymborch found a perfect breeding ground from which they could develop their international artistic careers at the crosscurrents between the Guelders and French courts.

## PAINTING IN THE DUCHY OF GUELDERS AND SURROUNDINGS, C. 1400

It is not easy to reconstruct the artistic environment in the Duchy of Guelders in which Herman, Paul, and Johan van Lymborch were trained from an early age and on which they, in turn, exerted their influence in their late twenties. We do not know of any certain works produced by the Maelwael-Van Lymborch family in Guelders. In the northern Netherlands and the Lower Rhine, only a small number of paintings, drawings, and manuscripts from the late fourteenth and early fifteenth centuries have survived the ravages of time, escaping fire, wars, religious conflicts, natural disasters, destruction, or neglect. Representative examples are equally rare in the fields of goldsmithing, stained glass, embroidery, and sculpture.[25]

There are no monumental paintings from the period of the Van Lymborch brothers in the Duchy of Guelders. The few painted panels directly linked to the principality date from after their time. For example, the Mary Magdalene altar in Zutphen, located in the northeastern part of the Duchy of Guelders, was painted in Upper Guelders or adjacent East Brabant around 1415–20, and the so-called *Roermond Passion* from around 1435 can be traced to Munster Abbey in Roermond.[26] The *Crucifixion with St. Anthony, Mary, John the Evangelist, and St. Catherine* from the parish church of Sts. Peter and Paul in Kranenburg (Germany) was once attributed to the Maelwael workshop in Nijmegen, but in fact it seems to have been executed in the Duchy of Cleves around around 1420–30.[27]

The earliest known panel paintings from the area include two works from the diocese of Utrecht: the *Calvary of Hendrik van Rijn*, commissioned by the canon, provost, and archdeacon of St. John's church in Utrecht around 1363, and the *Lords of Montfoort*, made around 1385, which once adorned the Virgin altar in St. John's church in Linschoten, a village southwest of Utrecht (fig. 3).[28] While the gilded escutcheons visible in the background of the first work underline the versatility and diversity of the materials and techniques used in early painting workshops—in line with the workshop practice of the Maelwael-Van Lymborch family—the second panel demonstrates above all how quickly the motifs of French art of the period spread northward. The "Virgin seated on a throne" motif was developed at the French court around 1380 by artists such as André Beauneveu and Jacquemart de Hesdin. We find it again a few decades later in the *Belles Heures* of the Van Lymborch brothers.[29]

In the Duchy of Guelders, several castles and secular buildings were adorned with decorative wall paintings, such as those Paul van Lymborch likely created in 1408 at the behest of Jean of Berry in the Château de Bicêtre near Paris.[30] Ducal accounts for the years from 1395 to 1405 mention a "gemaelde camer" (painted room) at the château of Rozendaal, near Arnhem, and a certain "Claesken die maelre" (Nicholas the painter) who worked there in 1415 and 1416 repainting part of the fire-damaged interior.[31] A few years earlier, in 1408 and

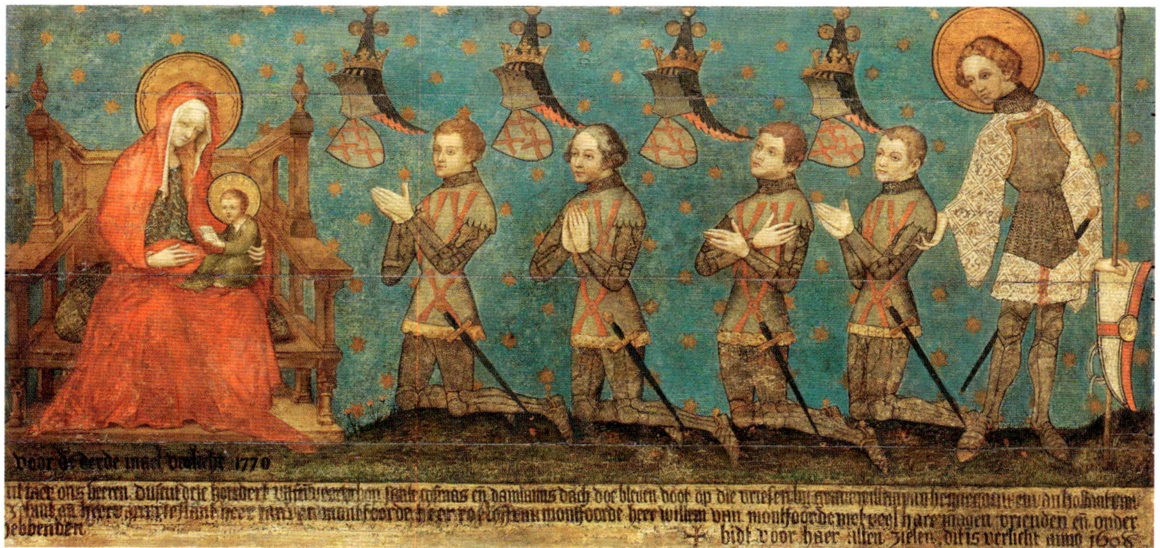

**Fig. 3** Anonymous, *The Lords of Montfoort*. Utrecht (?), c. 1385 (substantial restorations in 1608, 1770, and 1886) (Amsterdam, Rijksmuseum, SK-A-831, bequest of H. van der Lee, Woerden)

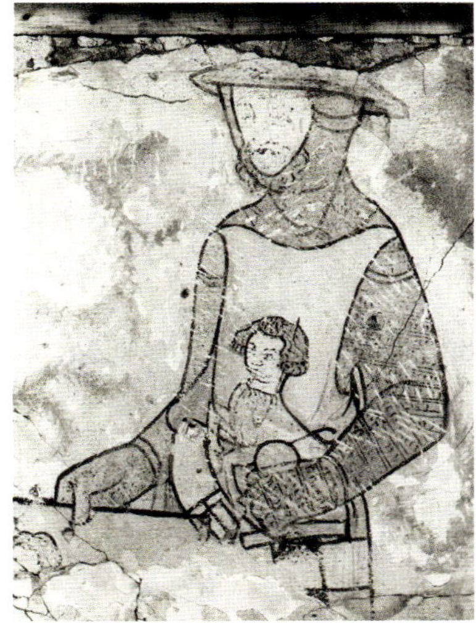

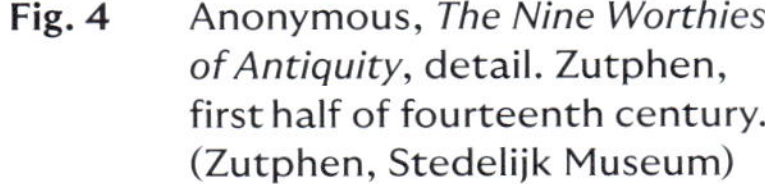

**Fig. 4** Anonymous, *The Nine Worthies of Antiquity*, detail. Zutphen, first half of fourteenth century. (Zutphen, Stedelijk Museum)

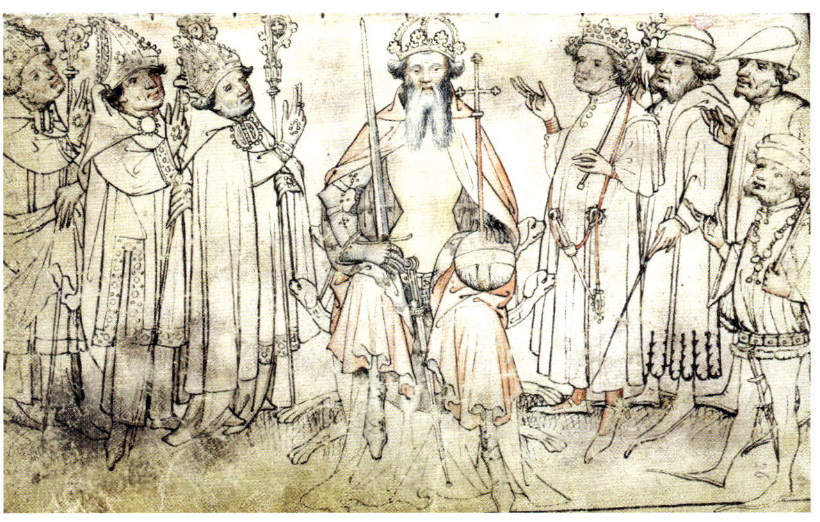

**Fig. 5** Herman or William Maelwael (?), *The Emperor with the Seven Prince Electors*, in *Wapenboek Gelre*. Northern Netherlands. c. 1393–1402 (Brussels, Bibliothèque royale de Belgique, ms. 15652-56)

1409, "meister Johan die maelre" (master Johan the painter) was entrusted with painting work at Hattem castle, in the far north of the duchy.[32] The documents mention not only the payment made to the servant who built the scaffolding, but also the cost of the oil and color that the painter used on the wall. To our knowledge, this is the first mention in the Northern Netherlands of the use of oil paint in murals, which is consistent with Cennino Cennini's observations in *Il libro dell'arte*, his treatise on painting techniques, published around 1400, that this material was widely used in this way by northern artists.[33]

It is likely that the decorations of Bicêtre, Rozendaal, and Hattem present technical or aesthetic affinities with examples by Jean de Beaumetz and his workshop in the Duke of Burgundy's château in Germolles, Mellecey, around 1390, or by the Master of La Manta in the Sala Baronale (baronial hall) of Castello della Manta, Piedmont, around 1416–20; several authors have recognized similarities with the figures of the Van Lymborch brothers in the latter.[34] The theme of the La Manta paintings, the Nine Worthies of Antiquity—from Hector of Troy and Julius Caesar to Charlemagne and Godfrey of Bouillon—matches that of the oldest secular mural in the Northern Netherlands. This depiction, which includes six nearly life-size knightly figures in secular attire, complete with chain mail, surcoat, and storm hat, and armed with shield, sword, and lance, was unexpectedly discovered years ago during construction work in a building in the historic center of the aforementioned Guelders town of Zutphen, about fifty kilometers northeast of Nijmegen. It dates from the first half of the fourteenth century (fig. 4).[35] The Van Lymborch brothers are likely to have seen similar murals in several places in their native region during their younger years.

A drawing in the *Wapenboek Gelre* (Guelders armorial) of the emperor with the seven prince electors (fig. 5)[36] suggests—given its horizontal format, linear character, and monumentality reminiscent of the wall decorations in the style of that of Zutphen—that this depiction also shows a mural found in one of the castles of the court of Guelders around 1400. The drawing is traditionally attributed to William Maelwael, grandfather of the Van Lymborch brothers, or to his brother Herman. Given their prominent role as suppliers to the Guelders court of banners, pennants, messenger boxes and other items bearing the duke's arms, it is reasonable to assume that one of these brothers worked on the armorial between 1393 and 1402.[37] The *Wapenboek Gelre*, compiled by Claes Heynenzoon, herald and king of arms to Duke William I, contains more than 1700 coats of arms of princes, clerics, and nobles from all over Europe—including about one-tenth from France, starting with the King of France, the Duke of Burgundy, the Duke of Berry, and the Duke of Anjou—and is the oldest and most comprehensive work of its kind from the Netherlands.[38] In their youth, the Van Lymborch brothers had a front-row seat to many similar heraldic commissions in the family workshop. Although no explicitly heraldic work by them has come down to us, we do find Jean of Berry's arms in the *Belles Heures* and *Très Riches Heures*.[39]

## REFINED RELATIONS

Twenty years ago, Rob Dückers showed that the Van Lymborch brothers used, among other things, a repertoire of figures with which they had become familiar in their native region, especially in the *Belles Heures*. For this, he presented examples from both book illumination around 1400 in Utrecht

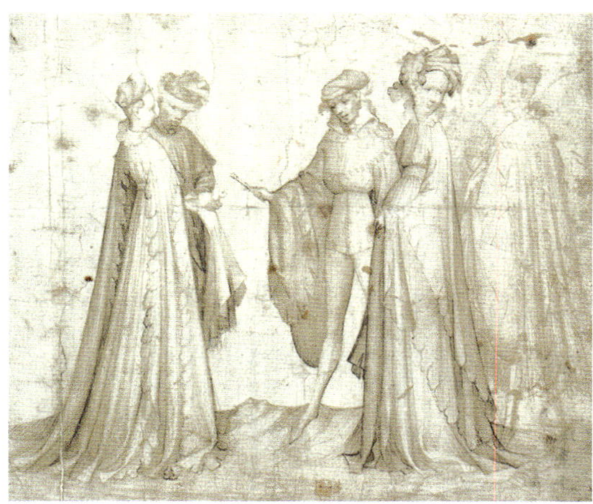

**Fig. 6** *Young People in Courtly Dress*. Guelders (?), 1410–15 (Uppsala, Universitetsbibliotek)

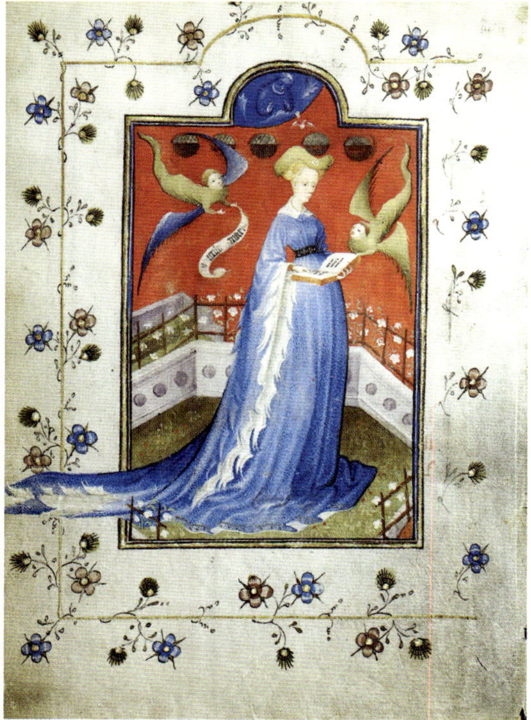

**Fig. 7** Master of Mary of Guelders, *Mary of Guelders*, in the *Book of Hours of Mary of Guelders*. Arnhem, Guelders, or Utrecht, c. 1415 (Berlin, Staatsbibliothek zu Berlin, Preussischer Kulturbesitz, Ms. Germ. Qu 42)

and The Hague, as well as from panel painting in Brabant and Westphalia.[40] The most direct visual link between the *Très Riches Heures* and the art of the Northern Netherlands of the same period can be seen in a drawing, kept in the University Library in Uppsala, Sweden, that has been associated with the Guelders court around 1415 since it was first published (fig. 6).[41]

The scene in silverpoint, enhanced with pen and ink, presents an allegorical depiction of courtly love, with an elegant company dressed in court attire. On the left, a man carries a dog that is being petted by a lady in profile at his side. On the right, another man holds out a flute to the animal, while the lady beside him turns with a smile toward the female figures sketched delicately behind her. The slender silhouettes, with their elegant long dresses and courteous gestures, lend the scene a distinguished atmosphere that evokes a world similar to the engagement scene depicted by the Van Lymborch brothers for the month of April in the *Très Riches Heures* (fol. 4; figs. 1, 2, and 8).[42]

The question arises as to how the drawing in Uppsala and the miniature in the Duke of Berry's book of hours relate to each other. It is generally believed that the Van Lymborch brothers' work on the *Très Riches Heures* preceded the drawing, but it is equally possible that the latter was produced earlier and came to their attention as a model. Indeed, the group of figures in the April miniature resembles, in posture and gesture as much as interaction, a more compact variant of the quartet of figures in the drawing.

## IN DIALOGUE WITH THE BROTHERS

The woman on the left in the Uppsala drawing bears a striking resemblance, in both posture and costume, to the figure of Marie d'Harcourt in her personal book of hours, executed by Northern Netherlandish illuminators at the Guelders court around 1415 (fig. 7) and now preserved in two volumes in Berlin[43] and Vienna.[44] The duchess stands in a small enclosed garden, the *hortus conclusus*, next to a banner reading "O milde Maria" (O mild, Mary), in reference to the Virgin Mary, her namesake. The long train of her elegant blue *houppelande*, or gown, crosses the frame and stretches into the margin. Viewed in mirror image, this figure also recalls in elegance and design the lady standing on the right on the April miniature of the *Très Riches Heures*; similarly, the shape of the frame, uncommon in the north in the early fifteenth century, recalls the frames of the Van Lymborch brothers.[45]

Drawing on a series of remarkable similarities between the work of the so-called Master of Mary of Guelders in her book of hours, and the *Belles Heures*, Erwin Panofsky suggested in 1953 that the Duchess of Guelders must have owned a manuscript illuminated by the Van Lymborch brothers, now lost.[46] Panofsky was unaware, however, that the brothers had maintained close ties with their native Nijmegen until shortly before their death, and that the illuminator of the duchess's book of hours could have had direct knowledge of their work. As Rob Dückers has also demonstrated in several publications over the past twenty years, it is striking how widely and extensively compositions or motifs by the Van Lymborch brothers were adopted, used, or adapted by book illuminators in the Northern Netherlands in the first half of the fifteenth century.[47] The creations of Herman, Paul, and Johan van Lymborch were passed on to subsequent generations through these book illuminators. Remarkably, these similarities all concern the *Belles Heures* and, with the exception of the Uppsala drawing and the miniature in Marie d'Harcourt's private book of hours, no link with the *Très Riches Heures* has yet been identified in the north. It is plausible that during their trips to Nijmegen in 1410, 1413, 1414, and 1415, the brothers brought with them drawings, models, or even miniatures that captured the imagination of book illuminators in the north and served as examples for them. For a long time, however, the finished quires of their most ambitious book of hours were seen only by the Duke of Berry and his confidants.

Both the sparse surviving paintings from the decades around 1400 and the written sources on the cultural climate in the Duchy of Guelders reveal a picture of the environment in which the Van Lymborch brothers were artistically formed. The close ties between the courts of Guelders and France gave them a springboard that took them from the periphery to the beating heart of artistic production in France. Marie d'Harcourt, Duchess of Guelders, maintained, just like her neighboring princess Mary of Burgundy, Countess of Cleves and La Marck, direct and warm contact with her family in France during those days, including Jean, Duke of Berry, the patron of the Van Lymborch brothers. The direct survival of their inventions, especially from the *Belles Heures*, in northern manuscripts from the period between about 1415 and 1450 shows that illuminators in these regions had direct access to models by the brothers. The brothers' frequent journeys to their hometown Nijmegen also gave rise to a clearly identifiable dialogue between their work in Île-de-France and the artistic production of the Northern Netherlands and the Lower Rhineland. Although only a modest number of quires of their most ambitious book of hours for Jean of Berry had been completed at the time of their early deaths in 1416, the impact of this art—preserved in a small box at the Hôtel de Nesle in Paris—has generously outlived Herman, Paul, and Johan van Lymborch and is still evident more than 600 years later.

1 Inventory of Jean of France, Duke of Berry, Paris 1416, Paris, BSG, inventory Berry B, no. 1164: "Item, en une layette plusieurs cayers d'unes très riches Heures, que faisoient Pol et ses frères, très richement historiez et enluminez, prisez vc liv. t." (Item, in a box several quires of a very rich book of hours, made by Paul and his brothers, very richly historiated and illuminated, valued at 500 livres tournois.) Guiffrey 1894–96, I, CLXV, and II, 280 (no. 1164); see also Nijmegen 2005, 378–79 (no. 105) (note by P. Roelofs).

2 Van Schevichaven 1914; Gorissen 1954; Gorissen 1957. For a brief historiography of the Maelwael-Van Lymborch family, see Stufkens and Verhoeven 2018. For the use of the internationally accepted appellation "Van Lymborch," following, for example, the names of Van Eyck, Van Spaendonck, Van Gogh, and Van Dongen, see Roelofs 2018.

3 Porcher 1953a, 53: "Pour ce qui est de leur pays d'origine, il n'apparait pas qu'ils en aient tiré grandchose, sinon eux-mêmes, ce qui est bien essentiel."

4 Colenbrander 2006, 14–16, 29–35.

5 *De gebroeders Van Limburg. Nijmeegse meesters aan het Franse hof 1400–1416* (The Limbourg brothers: Masters of Nijmegen at the French court, 1400–1416), Museum Het Valkhof, Nijmegen, August 28–November 20, 2005.

6 Dückers 2005.

7 Stufkens 2020, 4.

8 See essay by M. Deldicque, pp. 145–69.

9 On this subject, see Van Rijen 2005, 175; Lawson 2005, 154.

10 On this point, see Niessen, Roelofs, and van Veen-Liefrink 2005, 14–15; Roelofs 2017a, 13–15; Ubl 2017, 49–53.

11 Gorissen 1954, 210 (no. 118), 211 (nos 126-28), 130–32; Niessen, Roelofs and van Veen-Liefrink 2005, 24.

12 On Nijmegen around 1400 and the history of the Valkhof, see Lemmens 2005a.

13 Champeaux and Gauchery 1894, 142; Gorissen 1954, 215 (no. 148), 220 (no. 177); Meiss 1974a, I, 70; Niessen, Roelofs, and van Veen-Liefrink 2005, 15.

14 Guiffrey 1878, 167; Gorissen 1954, 197 (no. 40); Roelofs 2005, 41; Roelofs 2017b.

15 Rickert 1957, 74; Ph. Lorentz in Dijon and Cleveland 2004–05, 96.

16 Duisburg, Staatsarchiv Nordrhein-Westfalen; J. Oosterman in Nijmegen 2018–19, 47; J. Kuys in Nijmegen 2018–19, 48–49.

17 On Messrs. Gankourt, see Nijsten 1992, 319 note 96, with source reference; for the other two mentions, see J. Oosterman in Nijmegen 2018–19, 184. Arnhem, Gelders Archief, 0001, Archief van de graven en hertogen van Gelre, inv. 2956 [old 246], fol. 60v. With special thanks to Johan Oosterman, Radboud Universiteit, Nijmegen.

18 Duisburg, Staatarchiv Nordrhein-Westfalen; Van Spaen 1808, 70–71; Nijmegen 2018–19, 181–83.

19 Guiffrey 1894–96, I, XLVI. Some authors claim, without citing sources, that she also corresponded with the duke. See e.g. Baumeister 1984, 236; J. Oosterman in Nijmegen 2018–19, 19, 80.

20 Guiffrey 1894–96, I, LXVI, and II, 316 (no. 1181): "Item, deux petis diamens poinctus, assis en ung annel d'or, que la duchesse de Guesles [sic] envoya en don à Monseigneur, le XXIIIe jour d'aoust l'an mil quatre cens et Treize" (Item, two small pointy diamonds, set in a gold ring, which the Duchess of Guelders sent as a gift to Monseigneur on August 23, 1413).

21 Guiffrey 1894–96, II, 304–05 (no. 1142). The duke had bought two rings from the merchant Loys Gradenigo for the sum of 638 gold ecus. From the same Gradenigo, Jean of Berry bought in 1412 a small ruby called "grain d'orge" worth some 3,000 gold ecus, which he pledged to the Van Lymborch brothers in August 1415 against a loan of 1,000 gold ecus. See Guiffrey 1894–96, II, 102–03 (no. 349).

22 Gorissen 1954, 215 (no. 145), 208 (no. 102), 214 (no. 144); Niessen, Roelofs, and van Veen-Liefrink 2005, 21.

23 Panofsky 1953, 100–06.

24 Nijsten 1992, 188–222; Nijmegen 2005, *passim*; Roelofs 2017a, 13.

25 For examples, see e.g. Cleves and Düsseldorf 1984–85; Kevelaer et al. 2001–02; Nijmegen 2005; Lemmens 2005b, 216–25; Amsterdam 2017–18; Nijmegen 2018–19.

26 Nijmegen 2005, nos. 40–41, 280–83 (notes by P. Roelofs); Roelofs 2017a, p. 15.

27 Nijmegen 2005, no. 51, 300–01 (note by P. Roelofs).

28 Amsterdam, Rijksmuseum, inv. SK-A-831, bequest of H. van der Lee, Woerden. On *The Calvary of Hendrik van Rijn*, see Amsterdam 2017–18, 82–83 (no. 1) (note by M. Ubl).

29 Nijmegen 2005, 282–83 (no. 41) (note by P. Roelofs).

30 Champeaux and Gauchery 1894, 140; Gorissen 1954, 170: "peintre alemant qui besoignoit pour lui en son hotel de Wincestre lez Paris" (a German painter who worked for him in his residence in Wincestre near Paris). These decorations were lost in the fire of 1411.

31 Arnhem, Gelders Archief, 0001, Archief van de graven en hertogen van Gelre, inv. 2902 [old 225], fol. 241r (1395); inv. 2922 [old 226], fol. 267r (1396); Brussels, Archives générales du Royaume, Chambre des comptes 27000 p. 4 (1404–05); p. 7 (1405–06), "die gemaelde camer op der cappellen" (the painted room in the chapel); Nijsten 1992, 194.

32 Arnhem, Gelders Archief, 0001, Archief van de graven en hertogen van Gelre, inv. 3304 [old 462], fols. 2r, 3r (1408); inv. 3305 [old 463], fols. 4v, 5r; Nijsten 1992, 194. With special thanks to Lobke Roenhorst, Gelders Archief, Arnhem.

33 Frezzato 1994, 129, chap. lxxxix, 168, chap. cxlv: "ti voglio insegnare a lavorare di olio in muro o in tavola, che l'usano molto i tedeschi" (I want to teach you how to work with oil on a wall or table, which the Germans use a lot). The word "tedeschi" (or "Germans") was also used around 1400 to designate artists north of the Alps in general, including on several occasions for Paul van Lymborch. On Paul van Lymborch as a painter, see also Villela-Petit 2021, 134.

34 Roques 1963, 148 note 19; Van den Bergen-Pantens 1983, 229; Ubl 2017, 49.

35 Zutphen, Stedelijk Museum. Padberg Evenboer 2023a, 2023b and 2024.

36 Brussels, KBR, Ms. 15652-56.

37 Roelofs 2017a, 15. The same manuscript also contains a portrait of the Guelders herald.

38 Flokstra and Jahn 2003; Amsterdam 2017–18, 90–91 (no. 5) (note by P. Roelofs). Regarding the French arms in the armorial, see fols. 46r–52r.

39 On the Van Lymborch brothers and heraldic painting, see Hablot 2018.

40 Dückers 2005, 68–72.

41 Nijmegen 2005, 254–55 (no. 24) (note by P. Roelofs).

42 This connection was first made by Dodgson 1935, LLX.

43 Berlin, SBB, Ms. Germ. Qu 42.

44 Stange 1938, 116, was the first to note this similarity.

45 Nijmegen 2005, 250–53 (nos. 22–23) (notes by R. Dückers).

46 Panofsky 1953, 101 (fols. 19v, 39v, 50v, 284v).

47 Dückers 2005; Dückers 2009, 152; Dückers 2017.

**Fig. 8** Following pages: Van Lymborch brothers, *Très Riches Heures*, fol. 4v: April, detail

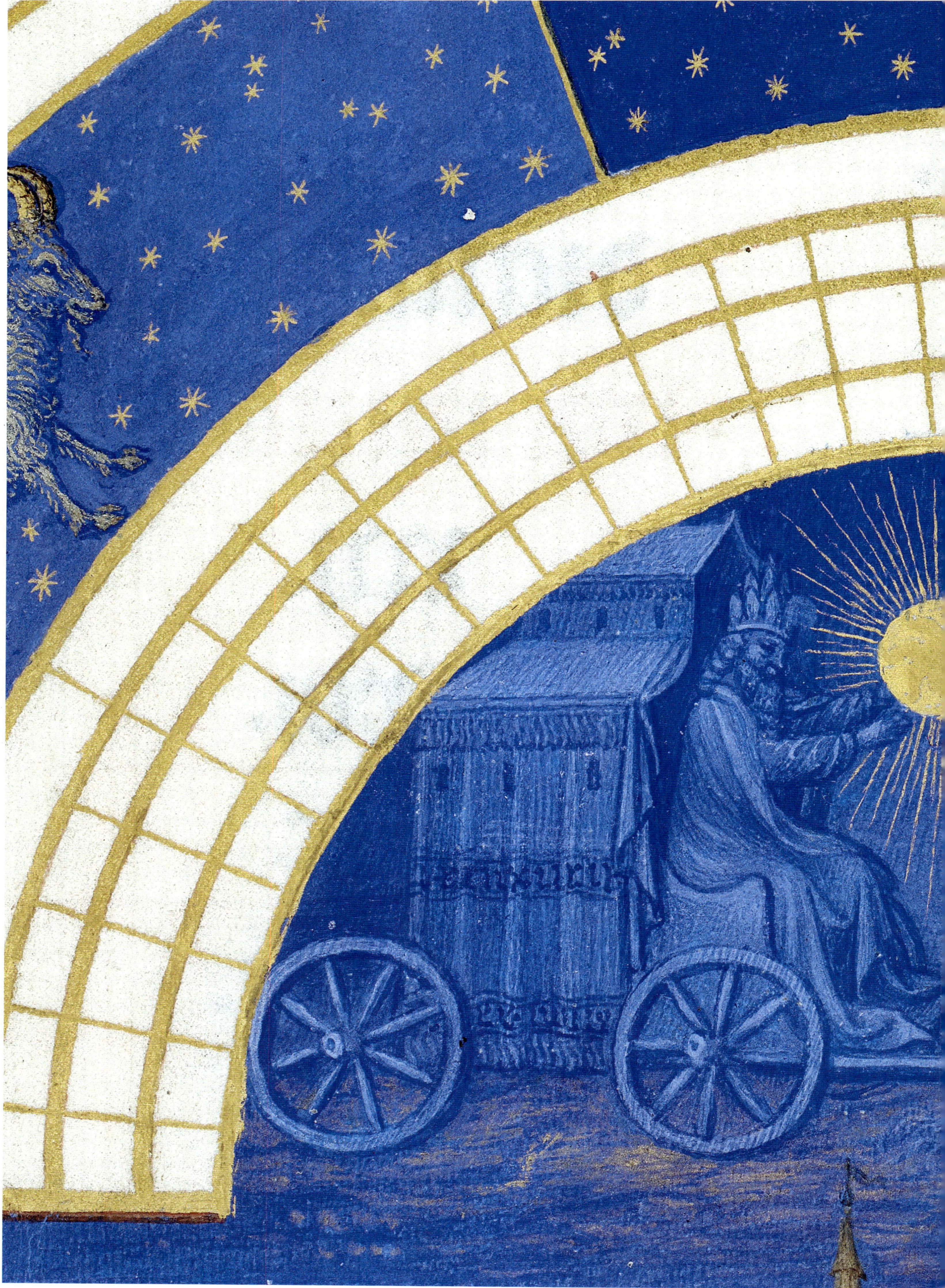

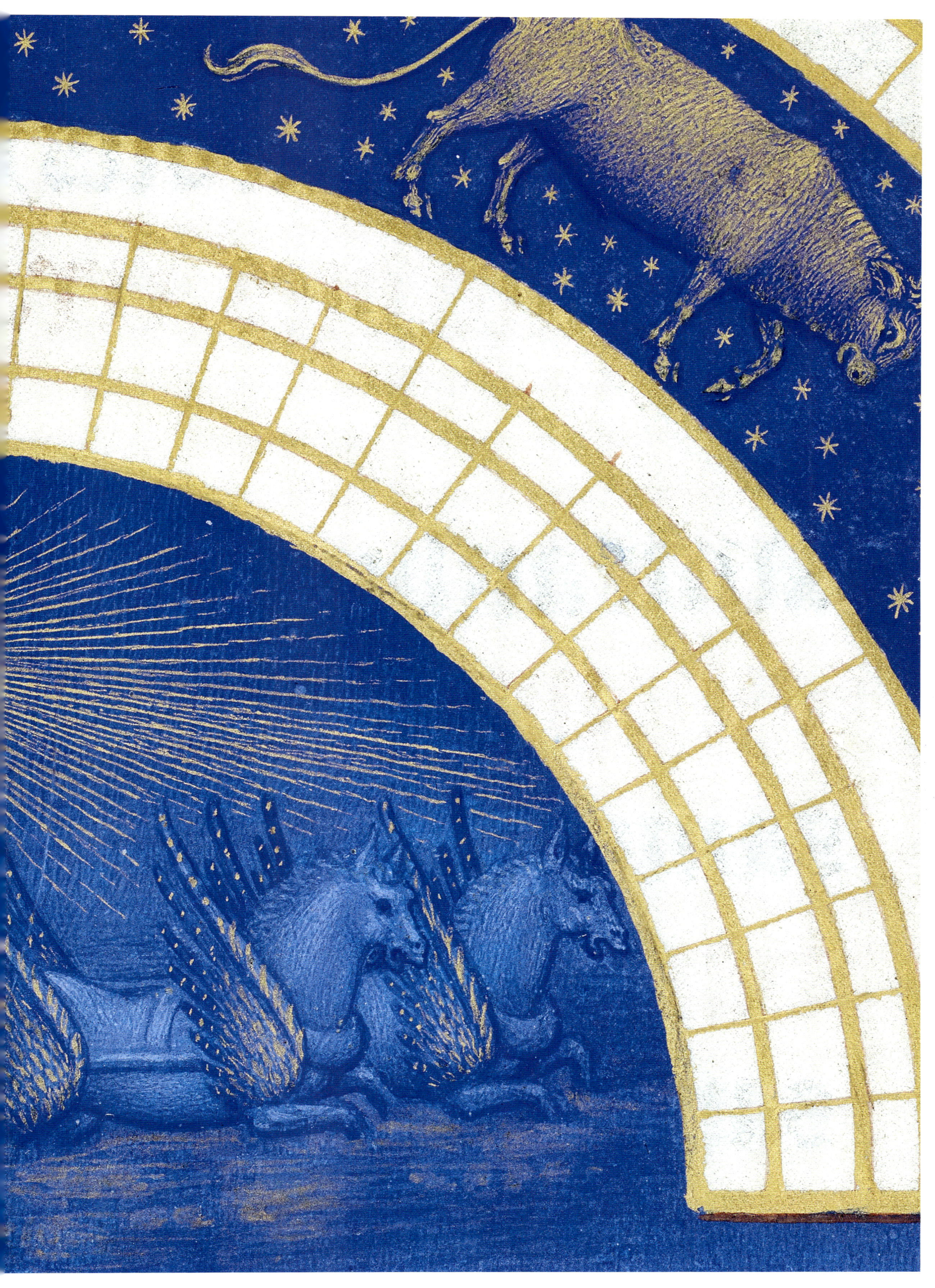

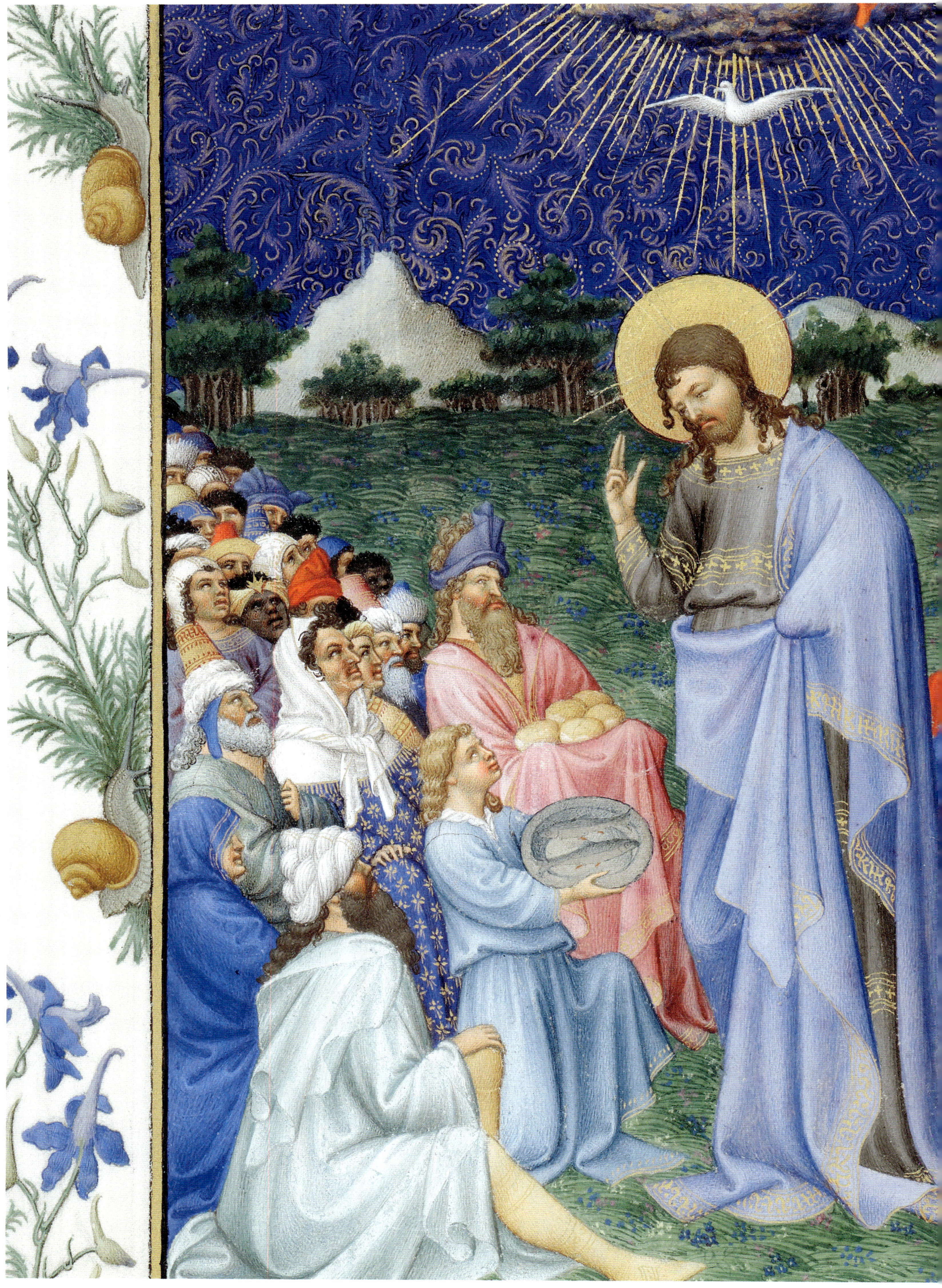

10.

# The Decoration of the *Très Riches Heures* and the Triumph of the Acanthus in Paris

Inès Villela-Petit

The illumination of Jean of Berry's *Très Riches Heures* was a collective undertaking like many elaborate manuscripts, but it differed from the usual practices in Paris, where decoration was the responsibility of specialist ornamentalists, on account of its original distribution of roles.[1] The *Très Riches Heures* is, in fact, the only princely manuscript of the period where the "vignette makers," namely, Pierre Gilbert and his workshop,[2] limited themselves to filling in the small ornate initials and line ends in the text without adding the traditional vine scrolls in the margins. The decoration of the large initials and their extensions into the margins was reserved for the proponents of a new ornamental style based on the antiquizing motif of acanthus leaves.[3] The taste for brightly colored, thick acanthus borders populated by playful putti and a variety of fauna had spread while Giovanni di fra Silvestro was in Paris between 1397 and 1407.[4] Originally from Bologna, where the profession was less specialized and did not make a distinction between the ornamentalist and the miniature painter, the Italian illuminator was entrusted with the historiated initials of the Duke of Berry's *Très Belles Heures* around 1400. The sumptuous books of hours he subsequently produced, notably around 1405–07 for the Dauphin, Louis of Guyenne,[5] were closely scrutinized by the Parisian masters, prompting them to reclaim the domain of ornamentation and go beyond the frame of narrative "histories."

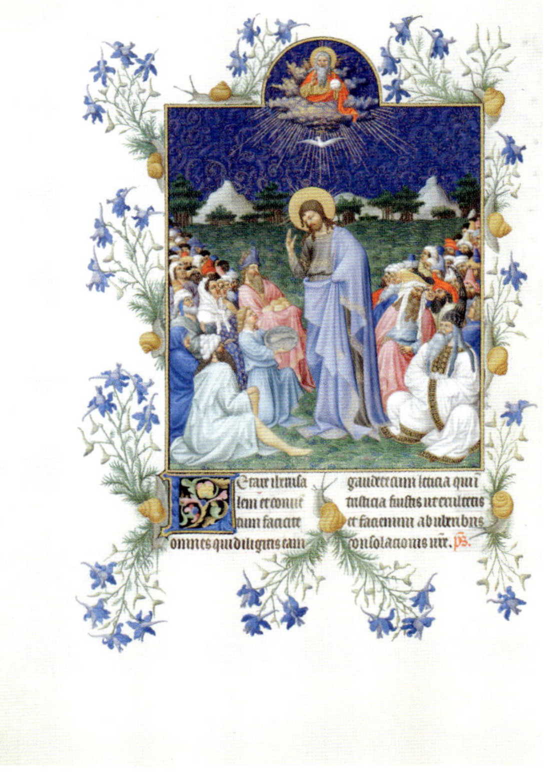

**Fig. 2** Van Lymborch brothers (miniature and border) and Master of the Breviary (initial), *Très Riches Heures*, fol. 168v: The Multiplication of the Loaves. 1412–16

**Fig. 1** Van Lymborch brothers, *Très Riches Heures*, fol. 168v: The Multiplication of the Loaves, detail

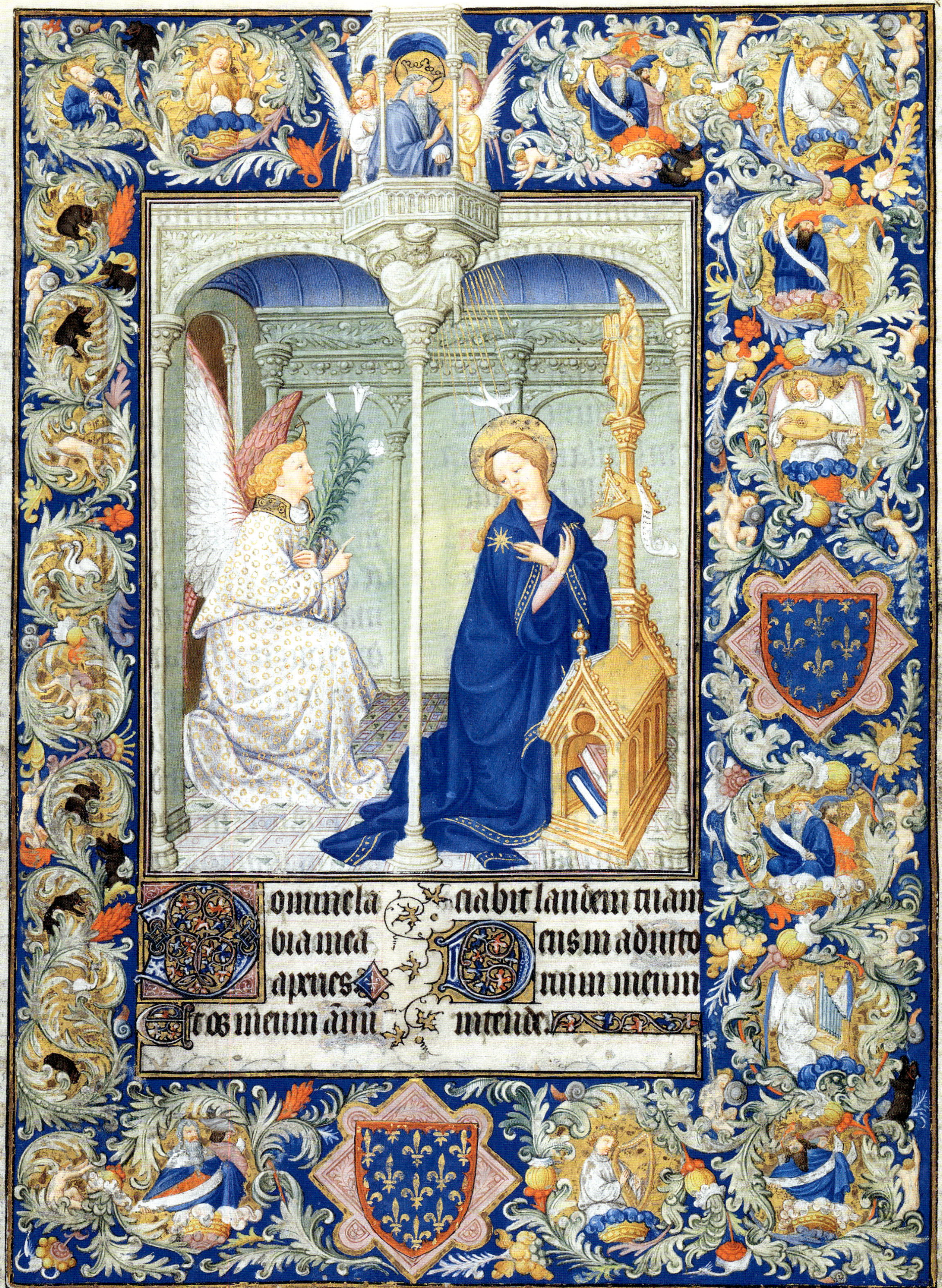
Domine la
bia mea
aperies
Et os meum anu
ciabit laudem tuam
Deus in adiuto
rium meum
intende

**Fig. 4** Michelino da Besozzo, *Visconti Prayer Book*, fol. 6v: The Adoration of the Magi. c. 1400 (New York, The Morgan Library & Museum, MS M.944)

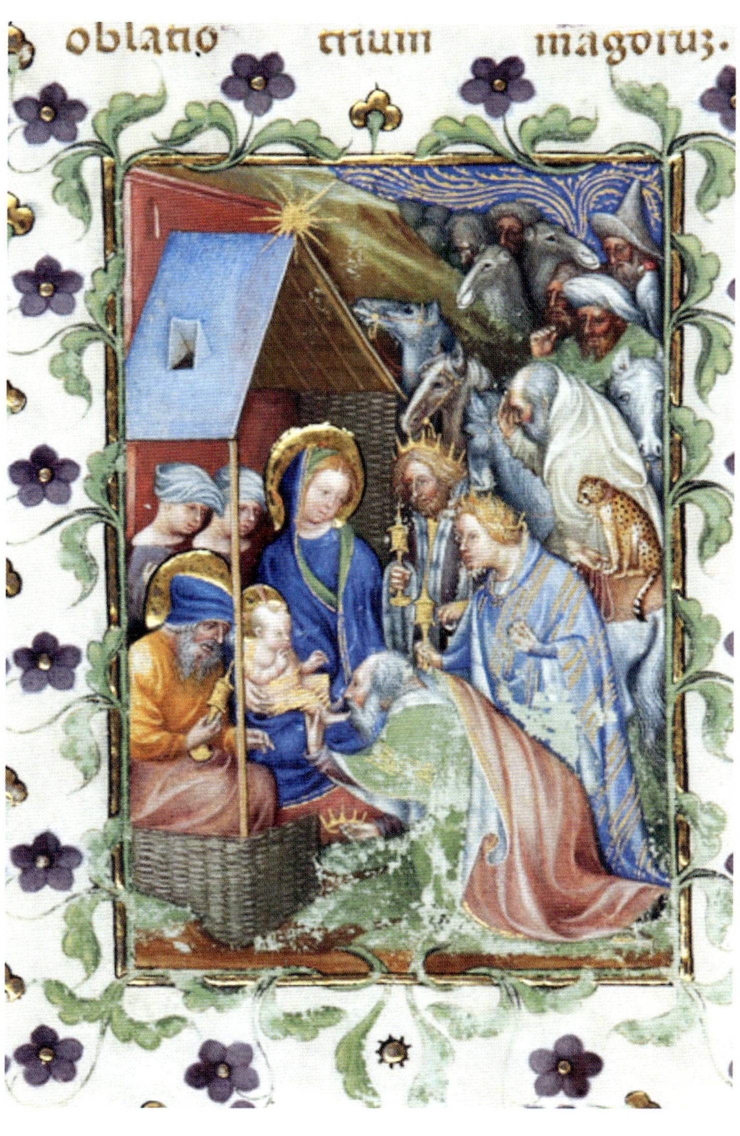


**FROM VINE SCROLLS TO NATURALISTIC FLOWERS**

The Van Lymborch brothers created their own ornamental style as early as 1405 to decorate the founding charter of the Sainte-Chapelle in Bourges.[6] The rich border that highlights the Annunciation in their *Belles Heures* features all the elements of this style, with its small acanthus leaves, the Lilliputian bears that cling to them, and the half-bodied figures perched on floral corollas (fol. 30; fig. 3). This overloaded effect was replaced in the *Très Riches Heures* by refined selectivity. The corners of the Zodiacal Man (fol. 14v; fig. 14, p. 186) and the borders of the Death of Christ (fol. 153; fig. 31, p. 171) are enlivened by small sprigs of bronze or polychrome acanthus, sometimes populated by bears (the Duke of Berry's emblem), and angel musicians emerging from a crown of petals (fol. 26; fig. 5). Around the Visitation, the acanthus gives way to drolleries (fol. 38v; figs. 5 and 6) in the Parisian tradition perpetuated by the Pseudo-Jacquemart in the duke's *Grandes Heures*[7]: hybrid creatures fighting imaginary enemies, a cleric catching larks, a bagpipe-playing pig in a wheelbarrow— all motifs that Barthélemy d'Eyck would later recall in a Provençal book of hours.[8] As for the clumps of field larkspur (*Delphinium consolida*) threatening the Multiplication of the Loaves (fol. 168v; fig. 1), saved by an invasion of large Burgundy snails (*Helix pomatia*), they recall the naturalistic flowers painted by Michelino da Besozzo in the borders of a Milanese prayer book intended for the Visconti (fig. 4).[9]

**Fig. 3** Van Lymborch brothers, *Les Belles Heures du duc de Berry*, fol. 30: The Annunciation (New York, The Metropolitan Museum of Art, the Cloisters Collection, 54.1.1. a, b)

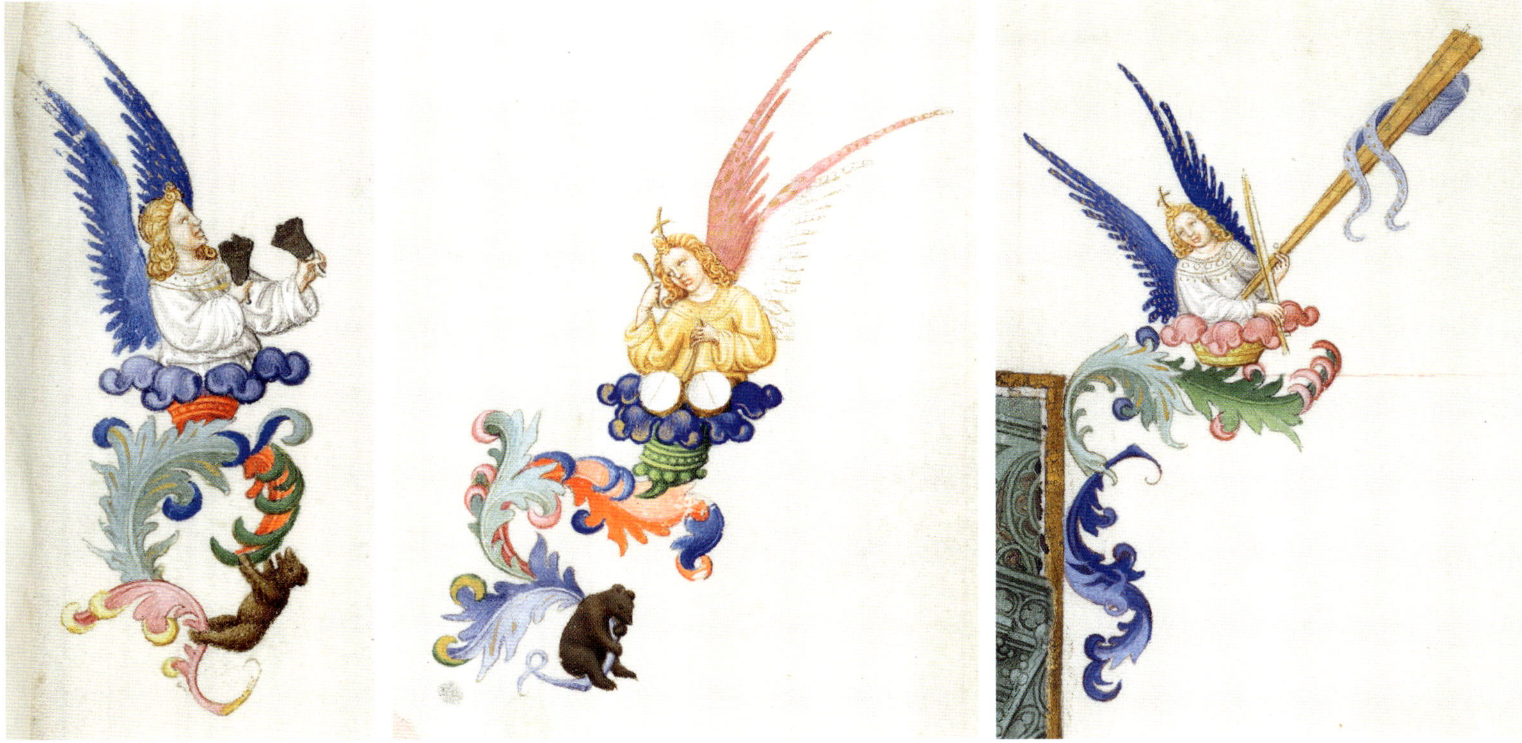

**Fig. 5** Van Lymborch brothers, *Très Riches Heures*, fol. 26, detail: angel musicians emerging from a crown of petals. 1412–16

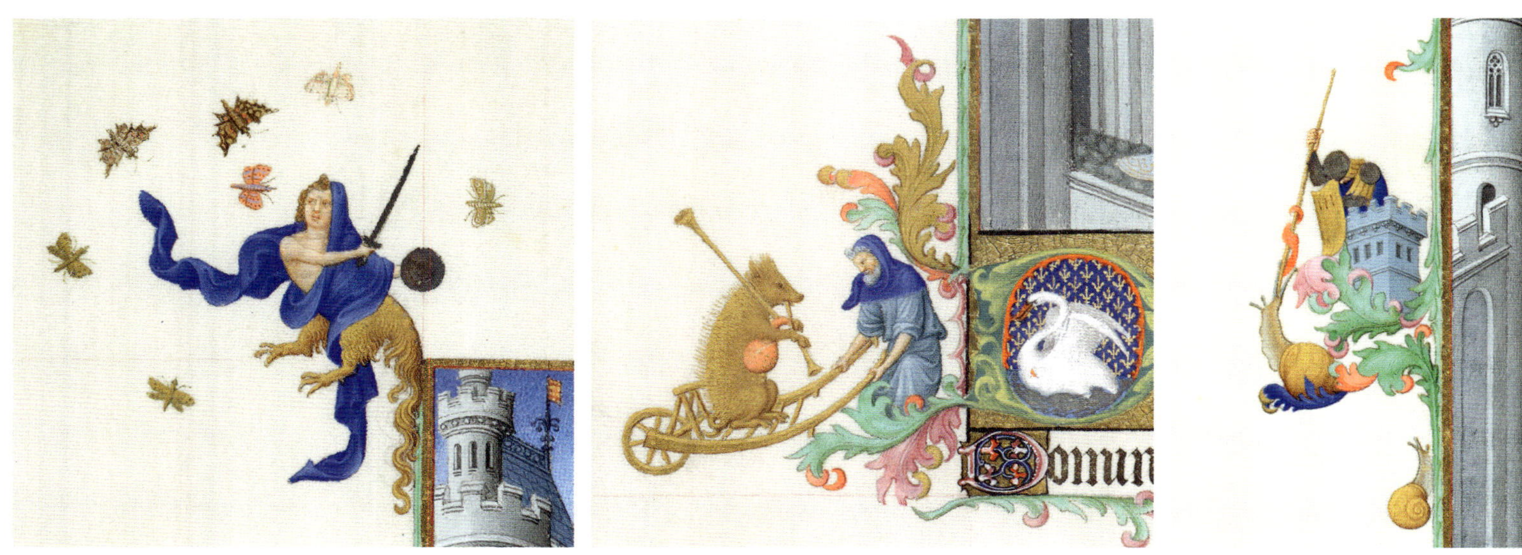


**Fig. 6** Van Lymborch brothers, *Très Riches Heures*, fol. 38v, detail: drolleries. 1412–16

This manuscript may have been in France—perhaps through Valentina Visconti (d. 1408), Duchess of Orléans, or Isabelle de Valois (d. 1409), courted in 1403 by Giovanni Maria Visconti, the new Duke of Milan—since its Adoration of the Magi (fol. 6v) also seems to have inspired several details in that of the *Très Riches Heures* (fol. 52).[10] Lastly, the wisps of smoke rising from the furnace (fol. 40v; fig. 7) and the dark clouds casting golden rays around Mont Saint-Michel (fol. 195; fig. 2, p. 231) are a highly original form of marginal decoration that plays on the materiality of the image's frame.

## VARIATIONS ON THE ACANTHUS

The involvement of the Van Lymborch brothers as ornamentalists remained limited, however, and the ornamented or historiated initials in the *Très Riches Heures* were entrusted to several other hands.[11] The first was the Master of the Breviary of John the Fearless, who invented acanthus leaves with composite florets, inspired by Prague manuscripts from the time of Kings Wenceslas and Sigismund of Luxembourg, perhaps via the initials of the Orosius Master[12] and the florets of another Bohemian master who, around

**Fig. 7** Van Lymborch brothers (miniature) and Master of the Breviary (initials), *Très Riches Heures*, fol. 40v: Three Hebrews in the Furnace. 1412–16

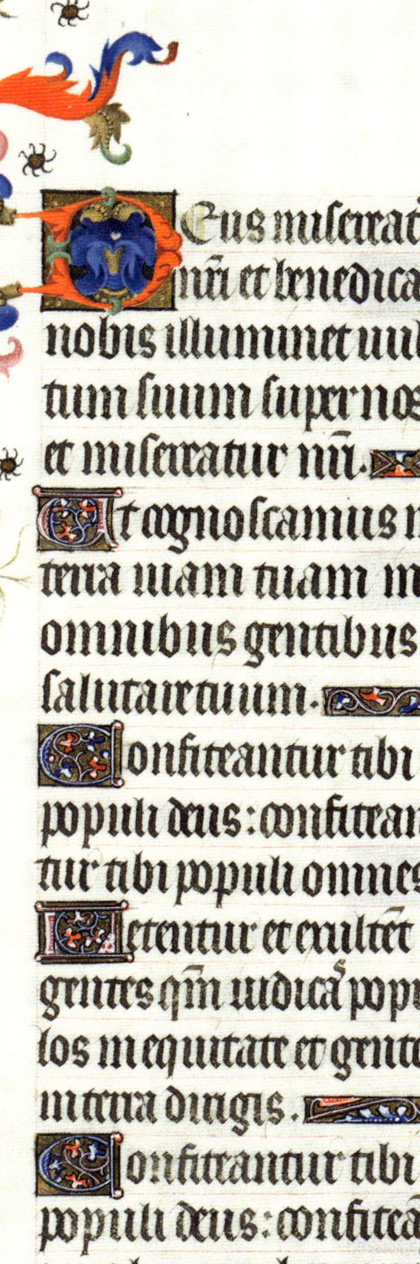

Deus misereatur nostri et benedicat nobis illuminet vultum suum super nos et misereatur nostri.

Ut cognoscamus in terra viam tuam in omnibus gentibus salutare tuum.

Confiteantur tibi populi deus: confiteantur tibi populi omnes.

Letentur et exultent gentes quoniam iudicas populos in equitate et gentes in terra dirigis.

Confiteantur tibi populi deus: confiteantur tibi populi omnes terra dedit fructum suum.

Benedicat nos deus deus noster benedicat nos deus et metuant eum omnes fines terre.

Gloria patri et filio.

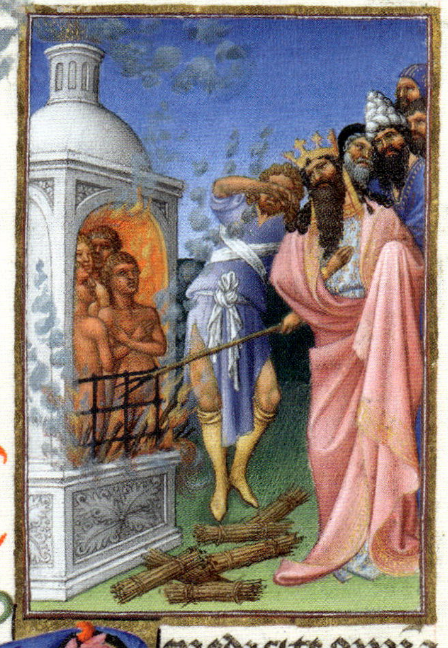

Benedicite omnia opera domini domino: laudate et superexaltate eum in secula.

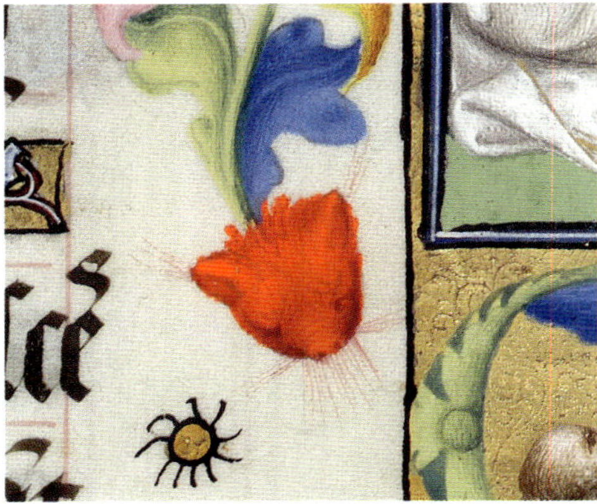

**Fig. 8** Master of the Breviary, *Très Riches Heures*, fol. 28v, detail: glowing cat's head. 1412–16

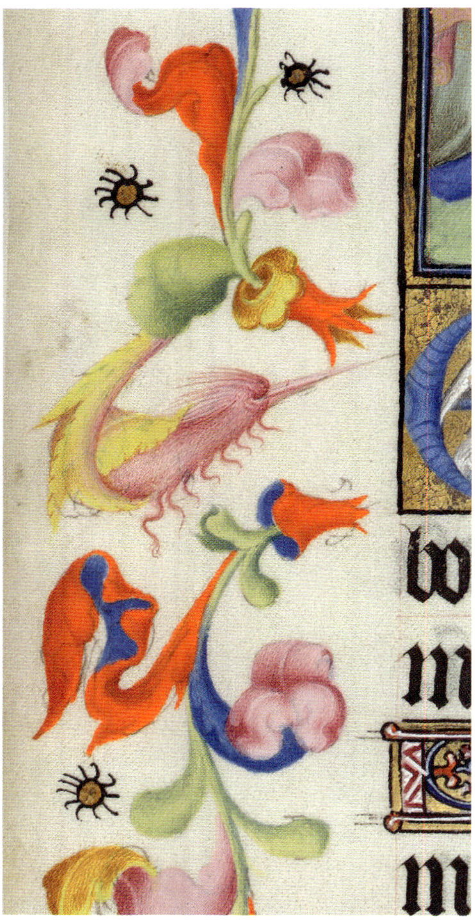

**Fig. 9** Master of the Breviary, *Très Riches Heures*, fol. 31, detail: pink hoopoe. 1412–16

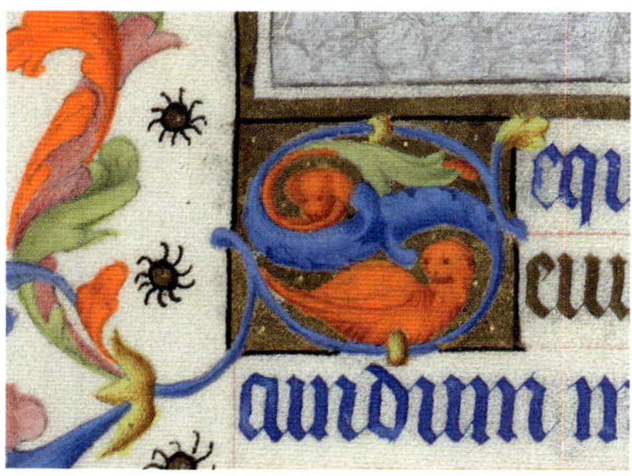

**Fig. 10** Master of the Breviary, *Très Riches Heures*, fol. 19v, detail: bright orange puppy and weasel. 1412–16

1400, illuminated a copy of the *Grandes Chroniques de France* for King Charles VI.[13] The Van Lymborch brothers also tried their hand at fantastical florets (fols. 18–18v, 193). The acanthus of the Master of the Breviary are complemented by flowers in their natural state and small perching birds. Giovanni di fra Silvestro and the Prague illuminators were equally fond of pareidolia, which transform acanthus leaves into animal creatures, such as the dragon-like scrolls in Konrad de Vechta's Bible.[14] The Master of the Breviary delighted in concealing in his vegetal designs a glowing cat's head (fol. 28v; fig. 8), a pink hoopoe (fol. 31; fig. 9), and a bright orange puppy and weasel (fol. 19v; fig. 10), while the Van Lymborch brothers transformed a sprig of acanthus into a twirling blue dragon or a golden lizard at the moment it catches a worm (fol. 38v).

The enrichment of the program for the *Très Riches Heures* led to a second ornamental campaign and the appointment of the Pseudo-Jacquemart (Jeannin Petit?). The latter reduced the acanthus motif to lobed leaf florets projecting a gold roundel in the form of a pistil, reserving his imaginative powers for the decoration of the initials, which displayed arms, emblems, figures, and drolleries. The Pseudo-Jacquemart was joined or replaced by the Egerton Master, recognizable by the scowling figures populating his initials (fols. 144v, 147v; fig. 11).[15] He adopted the same regular structure for the acanthus, but tended to extend and curl them, a tendency that would be confirmed in the *Hours of René of Anjou*, his eponymous manuscript.[16] Lastly, in 1415–16, a third campaign led by Haincelin de Haguenau (also known as the Bedford Master) focused on the calendar and some full pages (fol. 86v).[17] The rather uncluttered decorative style of the Van Lymborch brothers then underwent a radical change: The borders grew, filled with scrolls of floreted acanthus bearing natural violets, which delineated medallions housing angels, small scenes or the shepherds of the Christmas Mass. The pages ornamented in this way would have brought the *Très Riches Heures* in line with the richest manuscripts of Louis of Guyenne: the book of hours of 1408,[18] the so-called *Bedford Hours*,[19] and the unfinished missal. Haincelin was assisted by two collaborators, named after the initials of the calends of the calendar: the exquisite Master of the KL of January with his filiform acanthus; and the Master of the KL of August, principal ornamentalist of the *Hours of Charles VI* in 1415,[20] author of the border of the Chantilly *Bible historiale* (fol. 1) and close to the Master of the Breviary. However, their work came to a halt in mid-June 1416 with the death of Jean of Berry.

Jean Colombe completed the decoration of the *Très Riches Heures* in 1485, in part based on the inspirational drawings of his predecessors. He adopted their vocabulary and compositional methods, such as Haincelin's acanthus medallions (fol. 158), reproduced in his own style (fol. 152v), while favoring trompe l'oeil frames, two-tone blue and gold acanthus, red rose stems, and ornate initials in monochrome or painted white in the manner of Florentine *bianchi girari* or white vine-stem. The illuminator added his own creative outbursts to the masterpiece, such as a phoenix in flame-like acanthus (fols. 96, 110v), a dragon and a carnation (fol. 138v; fig. 12), a snail (fol. 159), and a large green grasshopper (*Tettigonia viridissima*) (fol. 164v; fig. 13).

## ACANTHUS MAKERS[21]

**Van Lymborch brothers**: fols. 14v, 18–18v, 26, 38v, 153, 168v, 193. And backgrounds covered with acanthus in monochrome blue, fols. 18v, 29, 39, 45v, 166, 168v, 171.
**Master of the Breviary** (Master of the Iris): fols. 17–18v, 19v–20, 22, 26–28, 29, 30–31, 32–34v, 35v–36v, 37v, 39–40v, 41v–45v, 46v–49v, 161–162v, 166–166v, 168–168v, 171–171v, 173–173v, 192–192v, 193v–195v, 198v.
**Pseudo-Jacquemart** (Dry Master): fols. 59–63v, 65–65v, 66v, 67v, 112–113, 116–116v, 119v, 122.
**Egerton Master** (Master of Widener 6): fols. 144v, 147v, 149v–150, 152, 153v, 155v–156, 157v.
**Haincelin de Haguenau** (Bedford Master): fols. 4, 5, 86v, 158, 182.
**Master of the KL of January** (Spindly Master): fols. 2, 3, 6, 7, 8, 72, 86, 89–89v, 158v, 165–165v, 182v, 189v.
**Master of the KL of August** (Plush Master): fols. 9, 10, 11, 12, 13.
**Jean Colombe**: fols. 50–50v, 52v–54, 55–58v, 68v, 70–70v, 74v–78v, 79v–81v, 82v–85v, 87v–88, 90, 91v, 92v, 93v–94v, 96, 97v, 98v–99v, 100v, 101v, 102v–103v, 104v–105v, 106v–107, 110–111v, 114–115v, 117–118v, 120, 121–121v, 123–129, 130–133, 134–136v, 137v–140v, 145v, 152v, 159, 160–160v, 163–164v, 167, 169–169v, 170v, 172, 174–174v, 181v, 183–188v, 189v–191v, 196–197v, 199–204v.

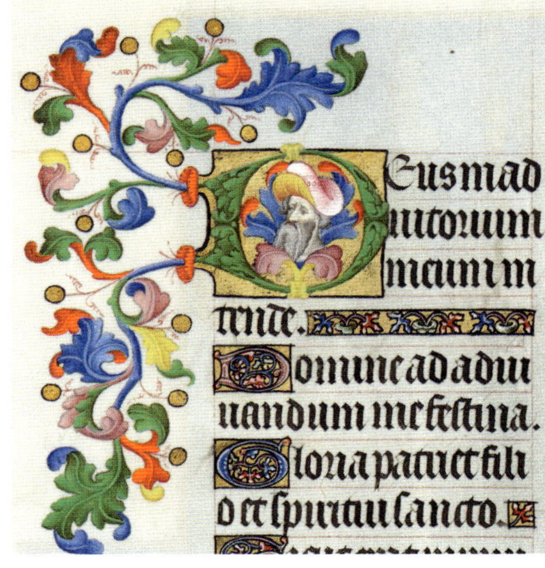

**Fig. 11** Egerton Master, *Très Riches Heures*, fol. 147v, detail: figure in an initial. 1412–16

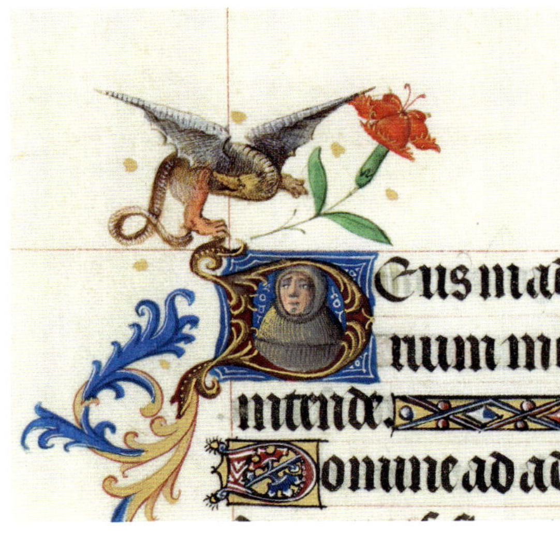

**Fig. 12** Jean Colombe, *Très Riches Heures*, fol. 138v, detail: dragon and carnation. 1485

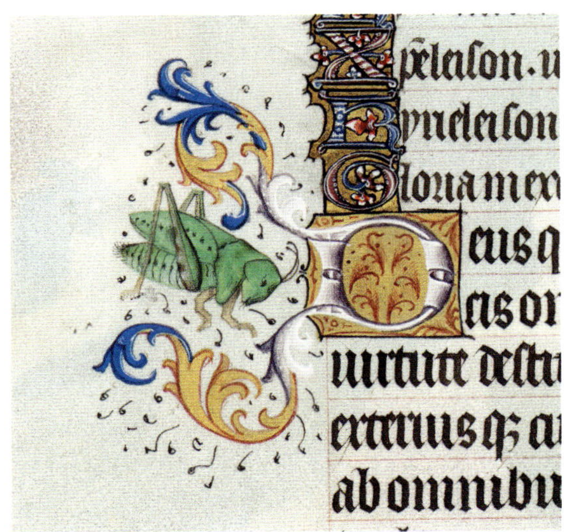

**Fig. 13** Jean Colombe, *Très Riches Heures*, fol. 164v, detail: large green grasshopper. 1485

1 Villela-Petit 2008; Villela-Petit 2012c; Hofmann 2014.
2 Dogaer 1967; Farber 1993; Villela-Petit 2019.
3 Hofmann 2007; König 2007, 26–30; Villela-Petit 2023.
4 Meiss 1969, I, 229–46; Calkins 1981; Medica 2010–11; Medica 2012.
5 London, BL, Ms. Add. 29433.
6 Villela-Petit 2022.
7 Paris, BnF, Ms. Latin 919.
8 Villela-Petit 2013c.
9 New York, Morgan Library, Ms. M. 944. Eisler 1995; Mulas, Visioli, and Zaggia 2015.
10 See also the columbine flowers painted by Jean Fouquet in the *Hours of Simon de Varie*. Marrow 1985.
11 Meiss 1974a, I, 178–84, 308–24; Stirnemann 2006.
12 Villela-Petit 2003, 59–61; Villela-Petit [forthcoming].
13 Paris, BnF, Ms. Français 2608. Paris 2004b, 272–73 (no. 168) (note by F. Avril); Schmidt and Ramirez-Weaver 2005; Studničková 2006.
14 Antwerp, Museum Plantin-Moretus, Ms. M 15.2. Watteeuw and Reynolds 2013, 104–21 (nos. 28-29).
15 Also known as the "Master of Widener 6" after the *Heures de Philadelphie* (Philadelphia, Free Library, Ms. Widener 6). Meiss 1956.
16 London, BL, Ms. Egerton 1070.
17 Stirnemann 2009; Villela-Petit 2013b.
18 Oxford, Bodl. Library, Ms. Douce 144
19 London, BL, Ms. Add. 18850.
20 Paris, Bibl. Mazarine, Ms. 469.
21 The following distribution, which differs slightly from those of Millard Meiss and Patricia Stirnemann (see note 11) and my previous study (see note 3), where I identified the Master of the Iris with Haincelin de Haguenau and the Master of the KL of August with the Master of the Breviary, is based solely on the acanthus in the borders. The outline of the initials and the decoration were not always carried out by the same artist.

**Fig. 14** Following pages: Van Lymborch brothers, *Très Riches Heures*, fol. 168v: The Multiplication of the Loaves, detail

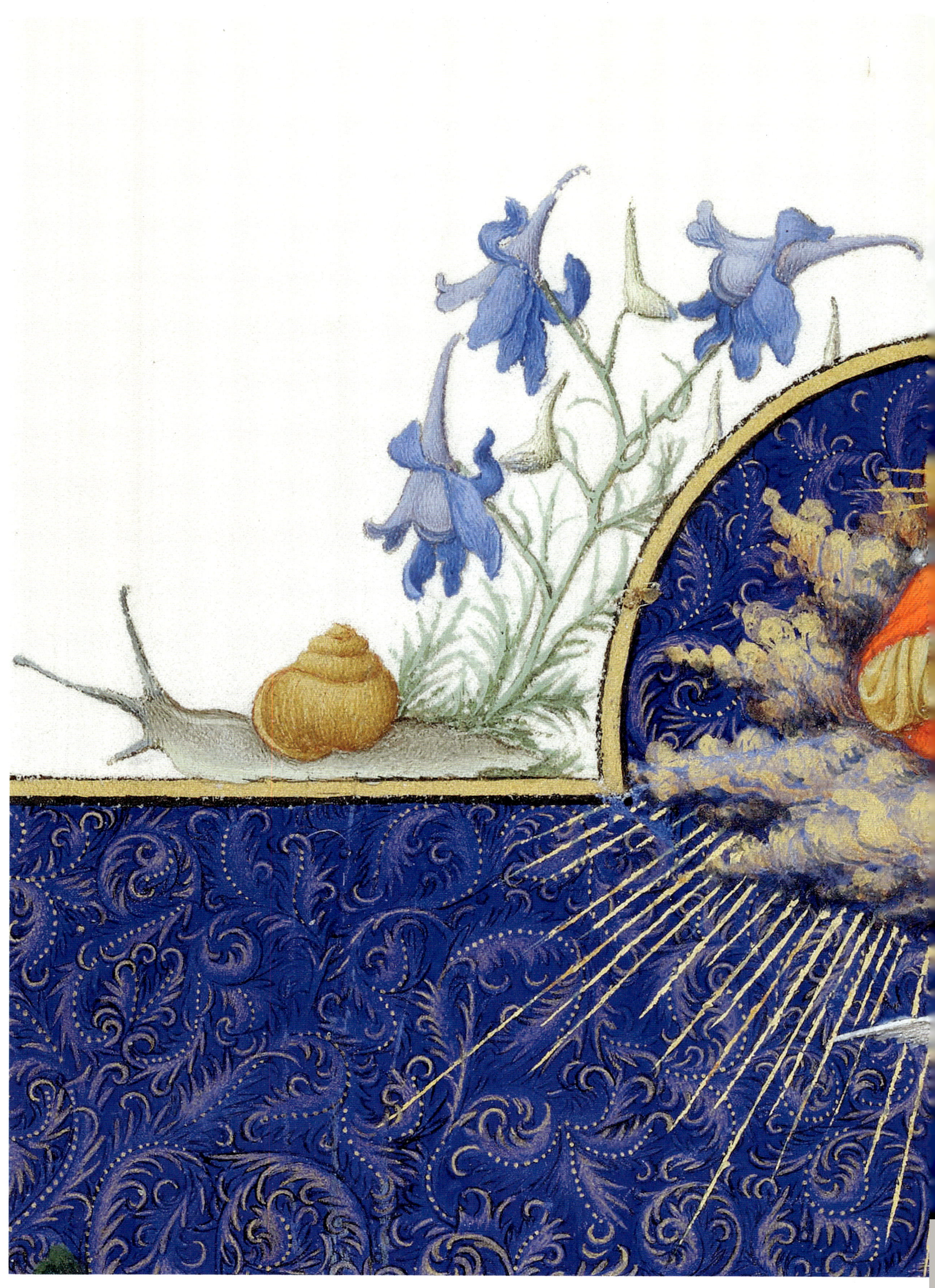

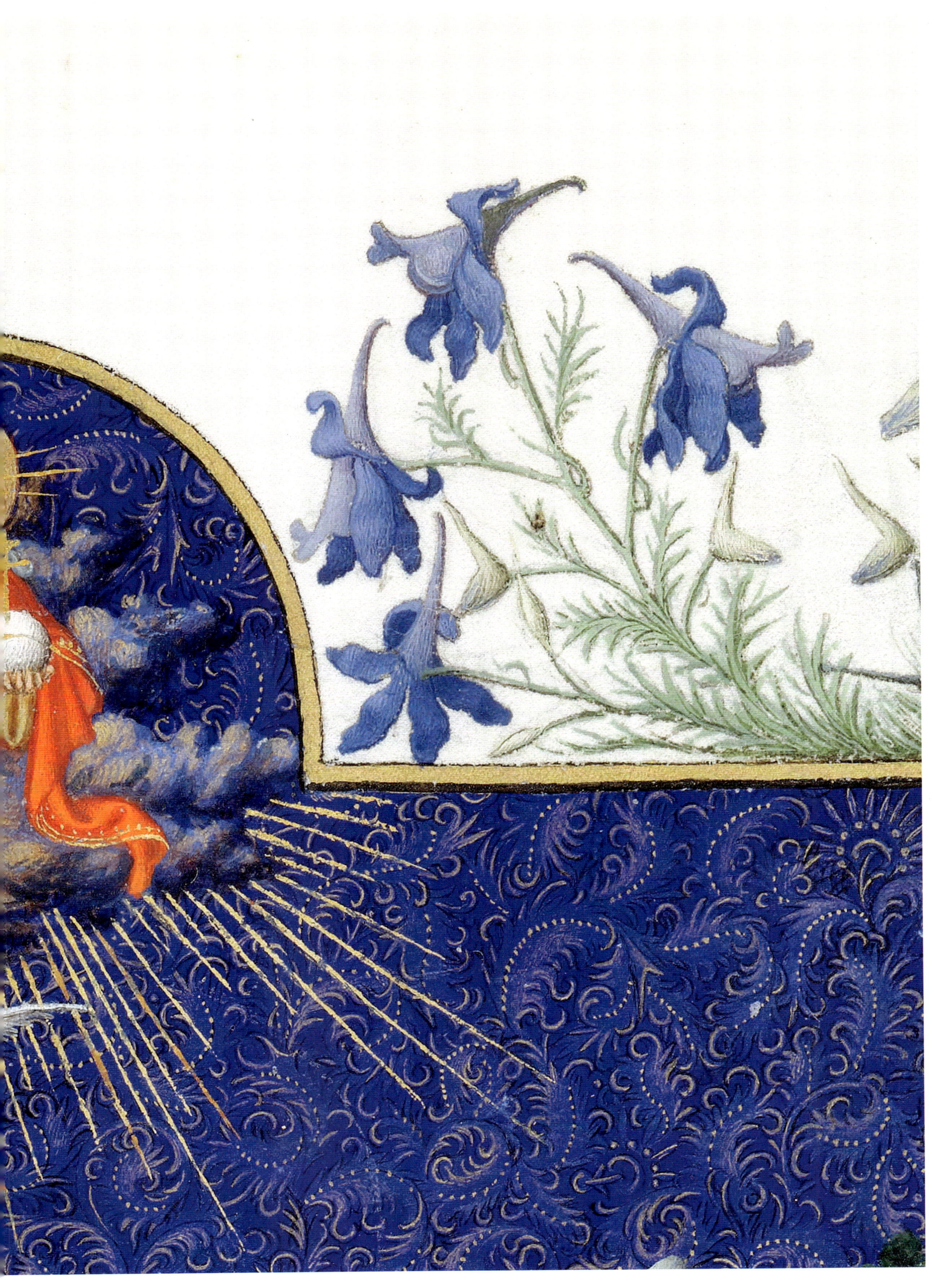

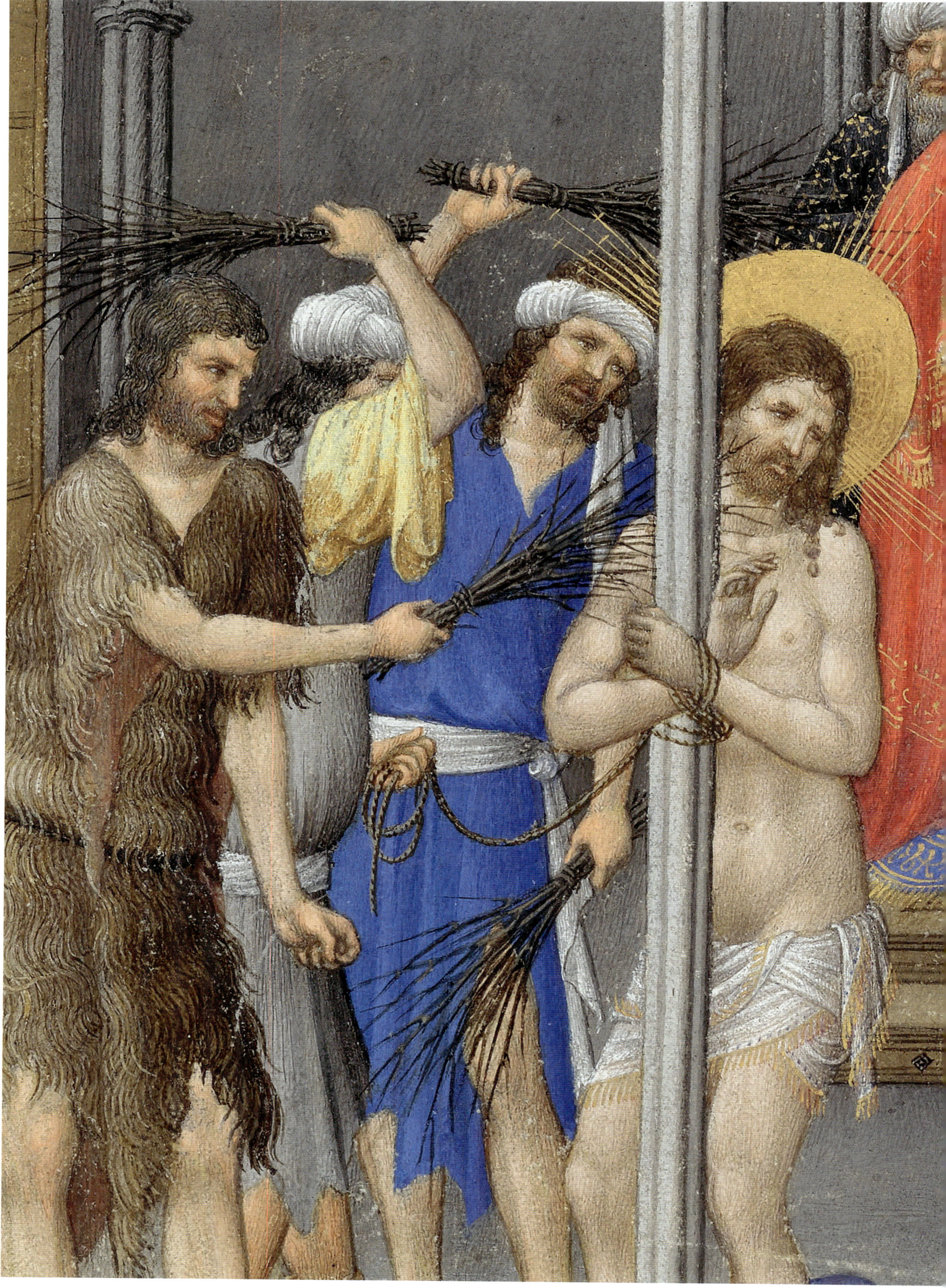

# 11.

# The Van Lymborch Brothers and Their Contemporaries

Inès Villela-Petit

Paul van Lymborch was not the only official painter to Jean of Berry.[1] Jacquemart de Hesdin had held the title since 1384, as had Michelet Saumon in 1413–15,[2] and the king's painters were also held in esteem by the duke.

## RIVALRY AND COLLABORATIONS

The compositions of Jean d'Orléans (d. c. 1408) in the *Très Belles Heures de Notre-Dame* were put to good use by the Van Lymborch brothers, who were tasked with completing the first volume[3]; the brothers also remembered the dreamlike landscapes of the Master of the Holy Spirit, which anticipated their visions of châteaux. The completion of the Duke of Berry's *Belles Heures*, illuminated by Paul and his brothers, preceded by several months the *Grandes Heures*, dated July 1409, whose illustration was overseen by Jacquemart.[4] The concurrence of the two undertakings was not accidental. Under the prince's kindly gaze, a positive spirit of competition was kindled, one which resulted in an abundance of ideas for pictures. Outdoing the full-page images of the *Grandes Heures* seems to have been the ambition of the second campaign for the *Très Riches Heures*. For example, the now detached Carrying of the Cross in the former (fig. 5)[5] was answered in the latter with a spectacular double-page spread capturing two moments on the road to Calvary: Christ Leaving the Praetorium and Christ Carrying the Cross (fig. 3).[6]

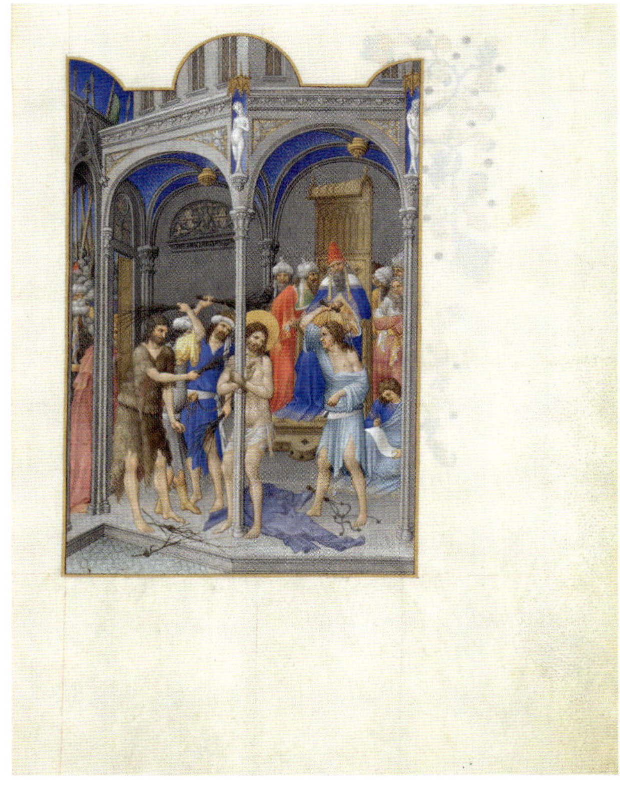

**Fig. 2** Van Lymborch brothers, *Très Riches Heures*, fol. 144: The Flagellation of Christ

**Fig. 1** Van Lymborch brothers, *Très Riches Heures*, fol. 144: The Flagellation of Christ, detail

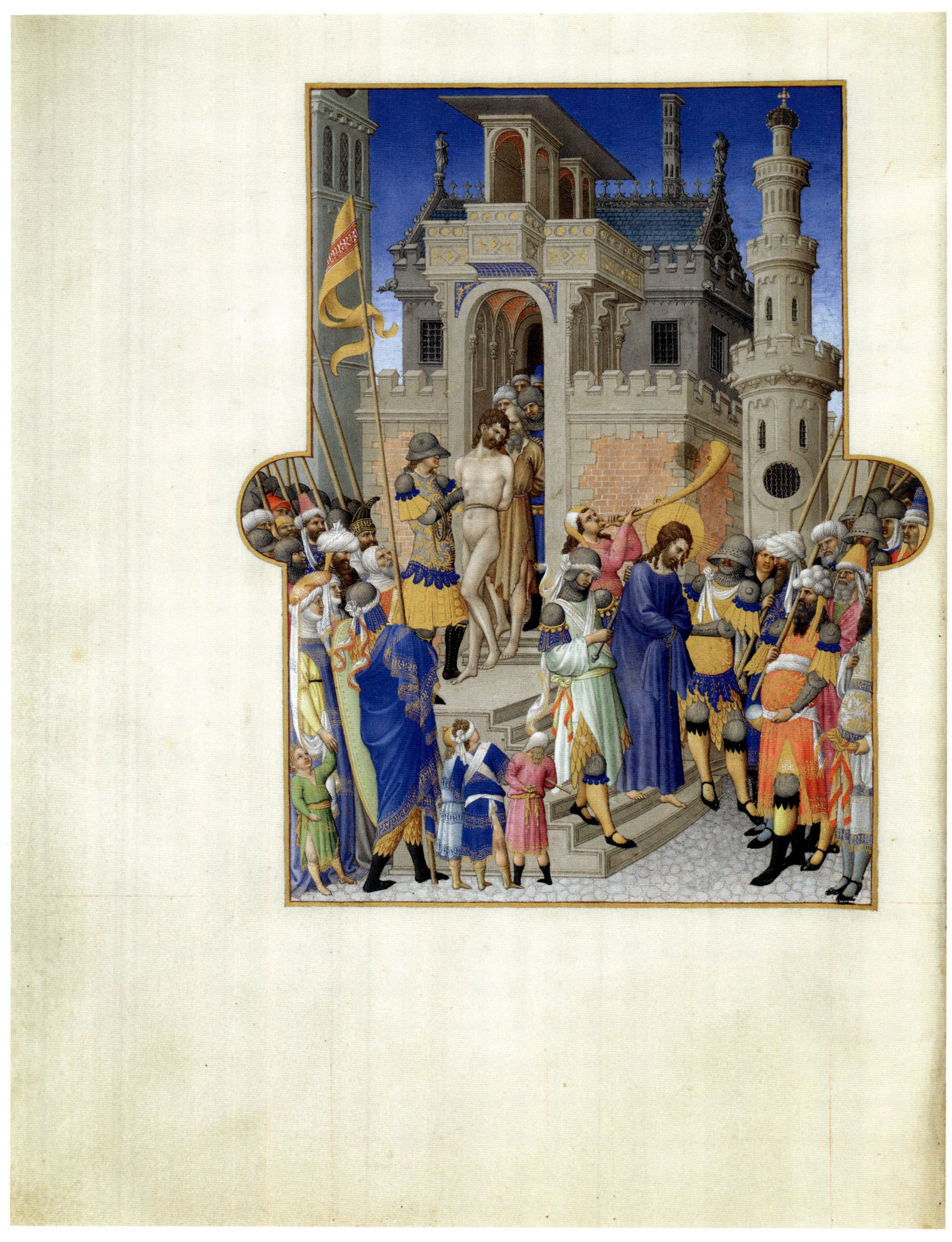

**Fig. 3** Van Lymborch brothers, *Très Riches Heures*, fols. 146v–147: Christ Leaving the Praetorium and Christ Carrying the Cross

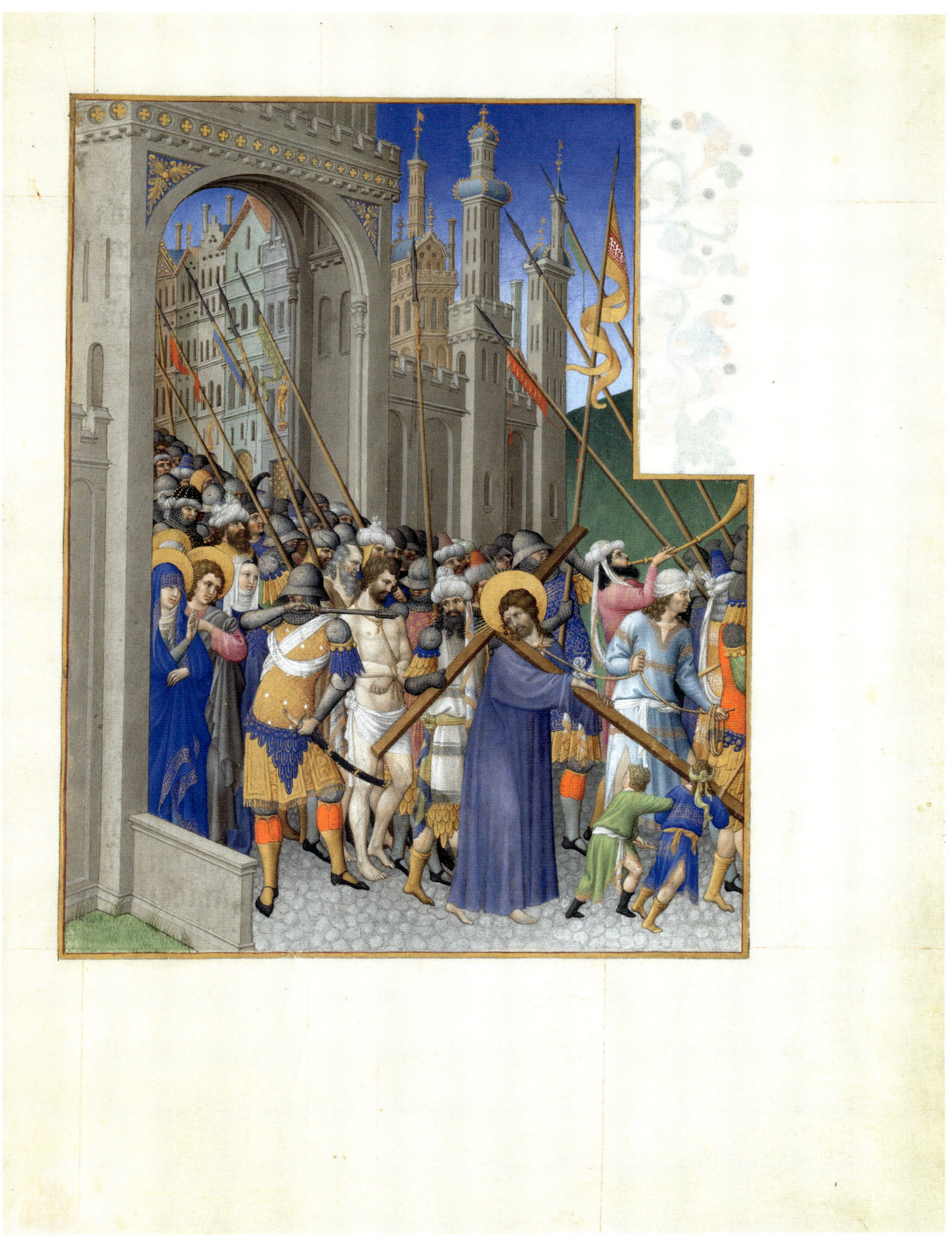

**Fig. 4** Following pages: Van Lymborch brothers, *Très Riches Heures*, fol. 146v: Christ Leaving the Praetorium, detail

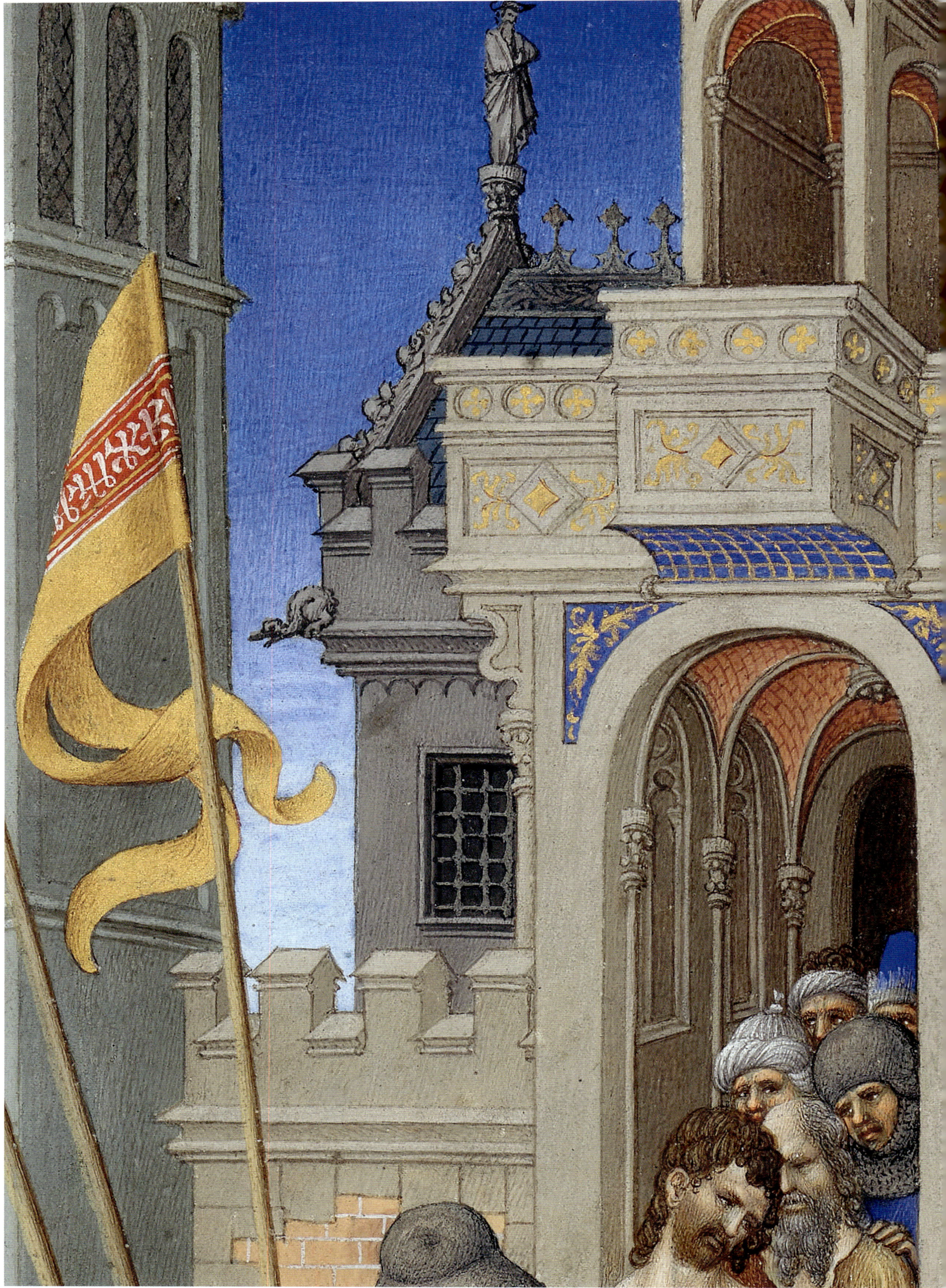

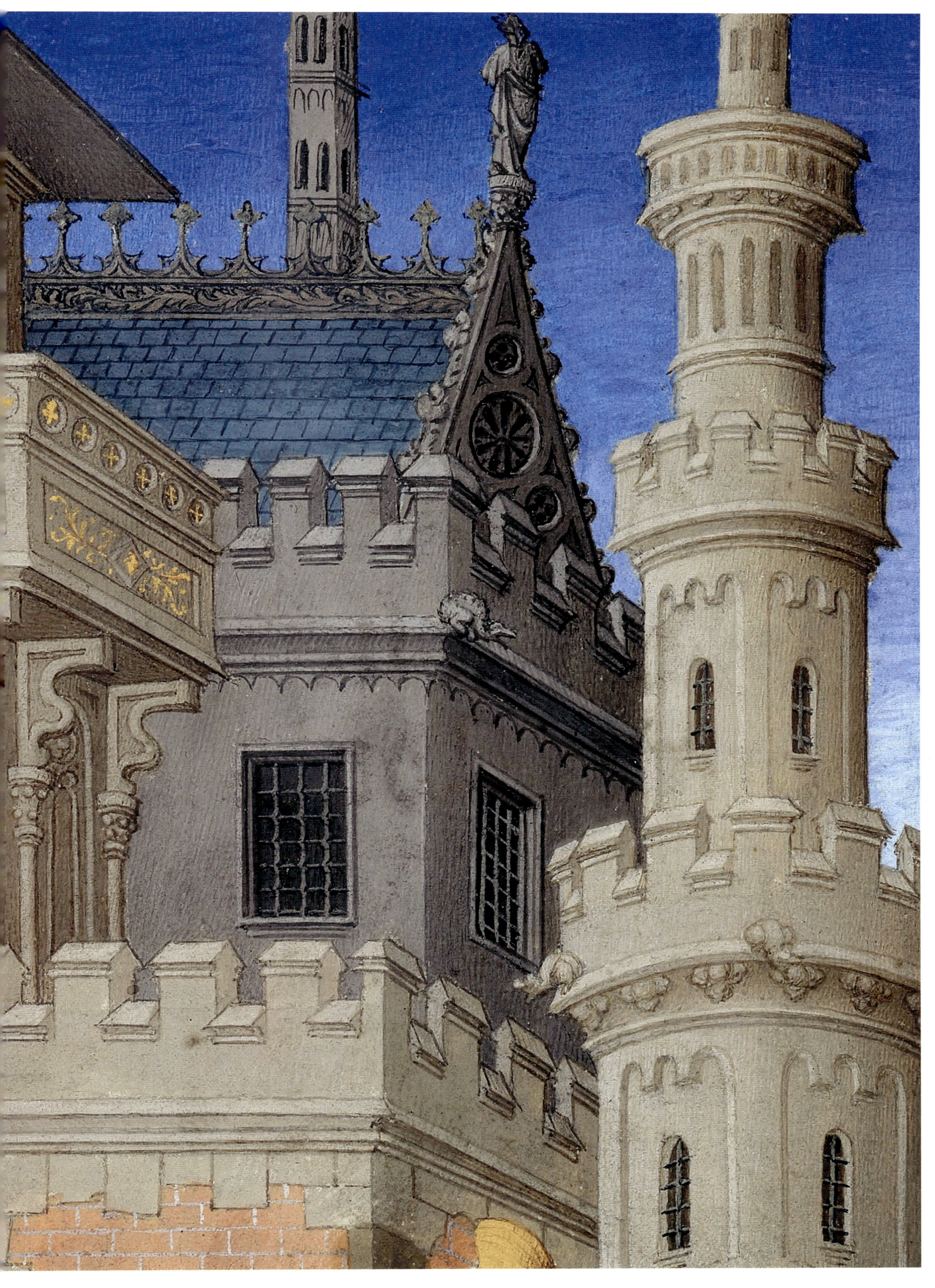

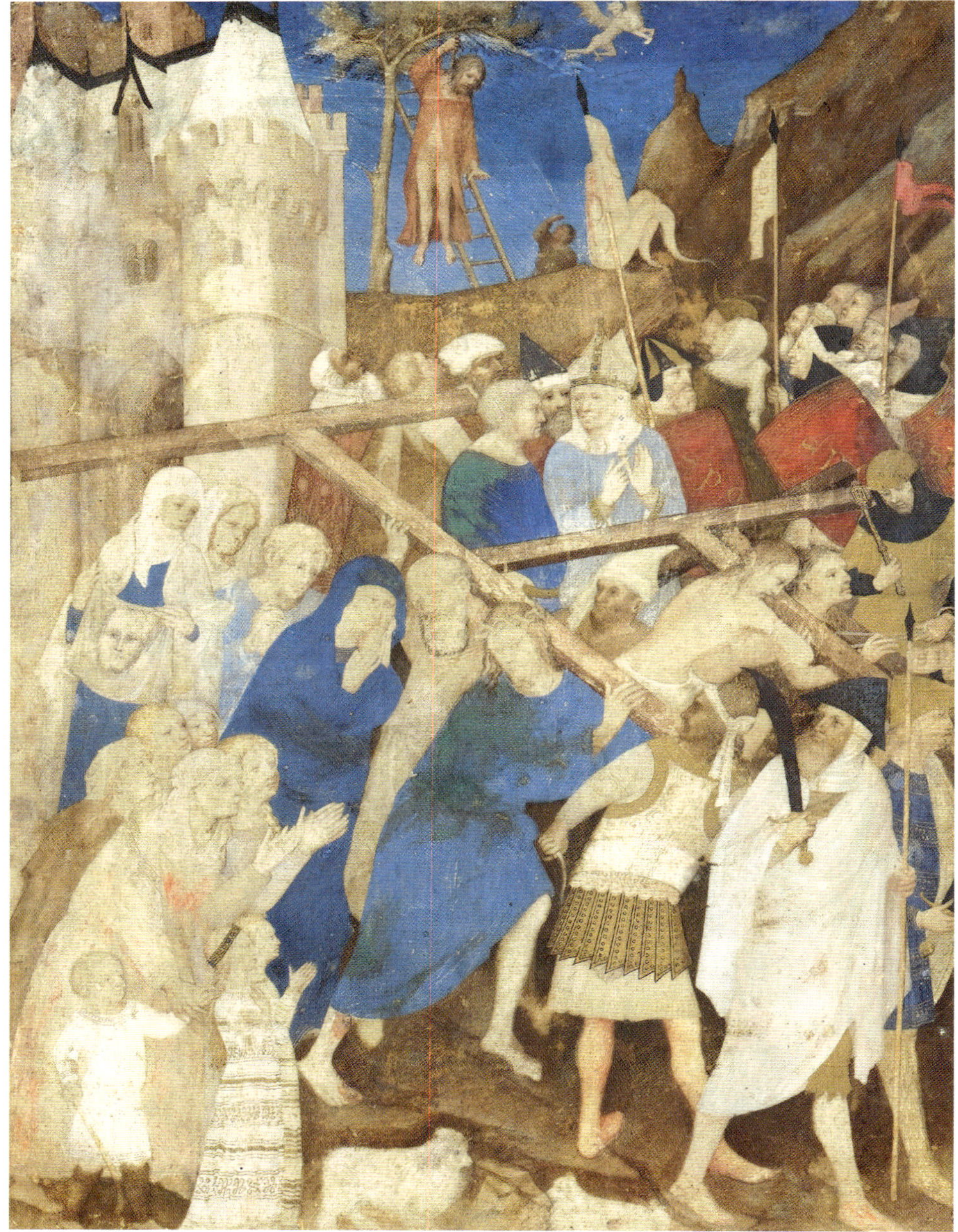

**Fig. 5** Jacquemart de Hesdin, *Grandes Heures*: Carrying of the Cross. Bourges, 1409 (Paris, musée du Louvre, département des Peintures, RF 2835)

Beyond the rivalries illustrated in 1398 by a dispute between the painter "Jehan de Houllande" (Jean of Holland) and Jacquemart de Hesdin along with his brother-in-law Jeannin Petit—both of whom were accused of stealing pigments and patterns from the palace in Poitiers[7]—the scale of the princely commissions often meant that work had to be carried out with others. In March 1404, to ensure progress was made on the *Bible moralisée* (Moralized bible) of Philip the Bold, the Van Lymborch brothers were joined by three other masters, Alemannic- or Middle Dutch-speakers like themselves: Ymbert Stanier, Jacques Cœne, and Haincelin de Haguenau.[8] Haincelin (also known as the Bedford Master) would also lend them a hand in the *Très Riches Heures*.[9] He even took advantage of this opportunity to memorize scenes and expressive details, such as the Meeting of the Three Magi (fol. 52), which he reproduced in the book of hours known as the *Bedford Hours*,[10] illuminated for the Dauphin, Louis of Guyenne, and in two other "Bedfordian" books of hours executed around the same time, which were perhaps presented to the Dauphin's sisters, Jeanne, Duchess of Brittany,[11] and Michelle, Countess of Charolais.[12] In terms of lavish artistic commissions, the young Dauphin followed in the footsteps of his great-uncle, Jean of Berry. He seems to have borrowed his illuminators from time to time, for example to enrich his psalter (fig. 6),[13] while in return Haincelin painted a portrait of the Duke of Berry and his family being welcomed by St. Peter into paradise in the *Grandes Heures* (fol. 96).

This closeness is revealed by a first book of hours for the Dauphin,[14] "very richly illuminated" under the direction of Haincelin,[15] and completed before April 15, 1408. As a result, Haincelin became the official illuminator for the Dauphin in 1409. And yet the manuscript, decorated in the workshop of Pierre Gilbert (the principal ornamentalist of the *Belles Heures*) is associated with the name of the Van Lymborchs for the three processions or litanies drawn in its margins[16]: St. Gregory (fol. 105), the relics (fols. 108v–109), and the flagellants (fol. 110). However, their intervention was actually far more extensive. The architecture of the Annunciation (fol. 28; fig. 7), which depicts both the interior and the roofs, the statuette on a console (misinterpreted during the coloring process), the ball capitals, the pilaster strips, and the small columns, the acanthus in the corners, but also the masonry vault (like that of the Annunciation in the *Petites Heures by Charles d'Orléans*[17]) and the lectern (which has an equivalent in the *Belles Heures*: fol. 183), and the angel Gabriel with his coiled hair and his tuft of hair surmounted by a small cross, reveal an underdrawing by the Van Lymborch brothers. The type of building with a corner statuette topped by a dome, which has analogues in the *Belles Heures* (fols. 184v and 187v), comes from the Crucifixion altarpiece painted by Melchior Broederlam for the Chartreuse de Champmol,[18] where Paul had undoubtedly trained. A drawing by the Van Lymborch brothers is also perceptible on other pages, such as the detail of the large shield with a human mask in the Crucifixion (fol. 111v), of which the *Belles Heures* offers many examples (fols. 142, 145, 152v, 156, 198); and the Last Judgment (fol. 128v), which prefigures those in the *Très Riches Heures* (fols. 34–34v) and the *Seilern Hours*. Some of the marginal drolleries also bear their mark, such as the spectacular nude man surprised from behind (fol. 3v, fig. 8), who evokes

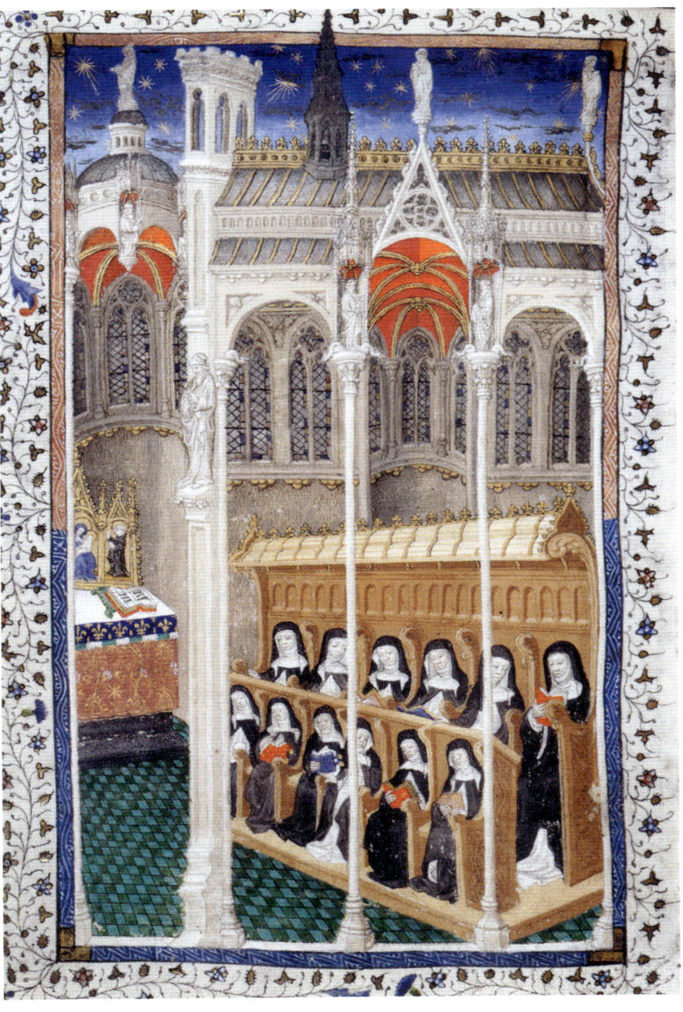

**Fig. 6** Van Lymborch brothers, *Psalter of Louis of Guyenne*, fol. 177v: Dominican Sisters in Church. c. 1413–15 (colored c. 1425) (London, British Library, MS Cotton Domitian A.XVII)

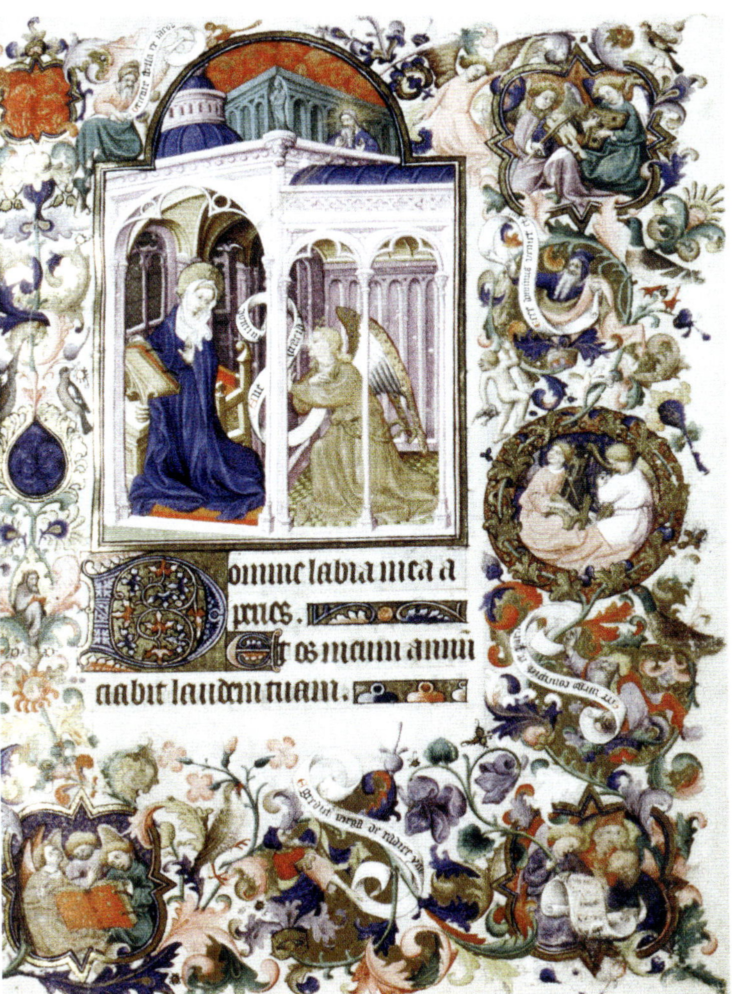

**Fig. 7** Van Lymborch brothers and Haincelin de Haguenau (Bedford Master), *Hours of Louis of Guyenne*, fol. 28: The Annunciation. 1408 (Oxford, Bodleian Library, MS. Douce 144)

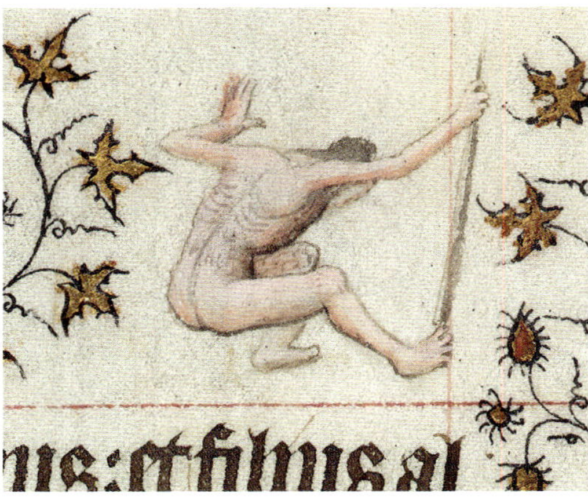

**Fig. 8** Van Lymborch brothers, *Hours of Louis of Guyenne*, fol. 3v: nude seen from behind. 1408 (Oxford, Bodleian Library, MS. Douce 144)

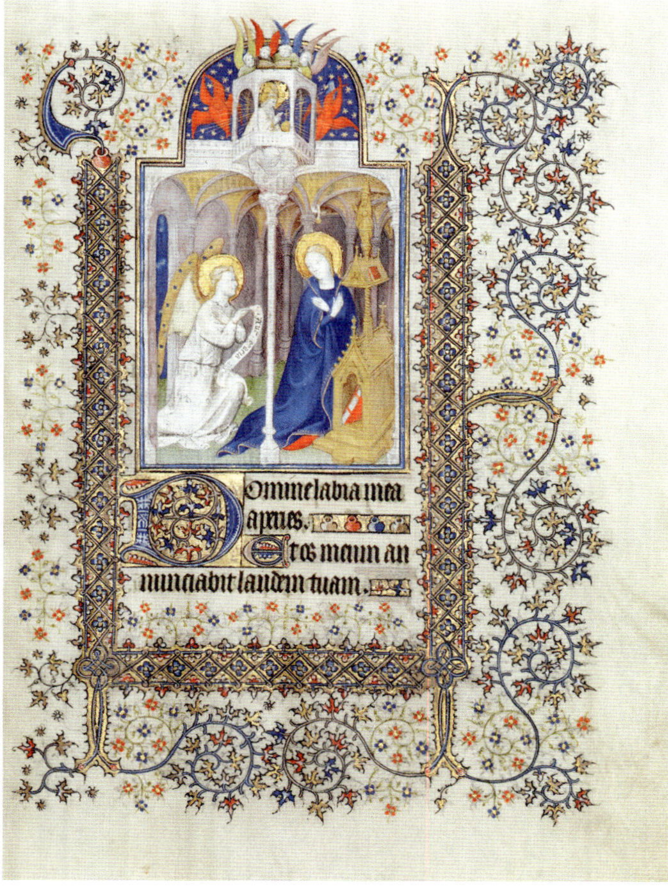

**Fig. 9** Mazarine Master, *Hours of Jean de Sainte-Maur*, fol. 45: The Annunciation. c. 1412 (Paris, Bibliothèque nationale de France, département des Manuscrits, NAL 3107)

the wounded Gauls of ancient sculpture and may have been inspired by the risen figures portrayed in the portal of Bourges Cathedral.[19] The illustration of the *Heures Douce* may have been undertaken for Jean of Berry, and may have been interrupted in November 1408 when the duke left Paris following the announcement that John the Fearless was returning, before being resumed for the benefit of the Dauphin.

## THE BENEFITS OF COPYING

Although the *Belles Heures* is uniquely homogeneous, with the three brothers already forming a team, their compositions were prematurely distributed among the circle of illuminators in the service of the Duke of Berry. The Egerton Master reproduced scenes from the calendar, first in the *Grandes Heures* and then in a book of hours for the duchess, Jeanne de Boulogne.[20] Even more significant are the reproductions by independent workshops, for example the Annunciation from the *Belles Heures* in the book of hours of the Touraine lord Jean de Sainte-Maur, entrusted to the Mazarine Master (fig. 9),[21] or the cemetery in the Office of the Dead (fol. 99) reinterpreted by the Orosius Master in the Dauphin's breviary[22] and later by the Giac Master in the *Hours of René of Anjou*.[23] Other details in the *Hours of Jean de Sainte-Maur* reveal a familiarity with the work of the Van Lymborch brothers, in particular the celestial apparitions of seraphim in orbs, and the pulpits of the evangelists topped by the statuette of a prophet.

If it is true that many of their own compositions were reproduced deliberately, it is no less true that the Van Lymborch brothers themselves reproduced the work of others. For example, at the end of the *Belles Heures*, to illustrate the Mass of All Saints (fol. 218), they integrated a twin version of the Virgin and Child in a medallion at the center of the celestial court that was painted by the Virgil Master on the frontispiece of a copy of the *Golden Legend* completed on September 8, 1404.[24] Such meaningful details as the symbols of the Four Evangelists, the Keys of St. Peter, and Mary Magdalene's ointment jar, which are absent from the work of the Van Lymborch brothers, suggest that they proceeded independently, drawing from a shared source—perhaps an altarpiece by Johan Maelwael intended for the chapel of the Virgin at the Chartreuse de Champmol. In 1399, Philip the Bold's painter had acquired "II compas de fer pour compasser l'ouvraige" (two iron compasses to measure the work), tools that fit with this circular construction.[25] The version in the *Belles Heures*, which became famous in its own right, was later reproduced by the Spitz Master[26] and in the *Grandes Heures de Rohan*.[27] It remains that the *Golden Legend*—or a similar manuscript[28]—seems to have served as a source of inspiration for the illustrations of the masses for the dead and the services of the *Belles Heures*, such as the centaur (fols. 46 and 192, respectively), the Beheading of John the Baptist (fols. 280v and 212), and St. Catherine and the doctors (fols. 386 and 16), but also as a prototype for the Resurrection of the Dead in the *Très Riches Heures* (fols. 4 and 34v). Similarly, the plowman in the month of March in the *Très Riches Heures* (fol. 3v) was probably inspired by "un homme touchant ses bœufs en l'arée" (a man touching his oxen in the ploughed soil) in the frontispiece of a Latin treatise on agronomy or *Coultivement de la terre* (Cultivating the earth) inventoried in the duke's library in 1402,[29] of which the Virgil Master gave his own version as early as 1403 in a manuscript of the *Georgics* also intended for Jean of Berry.[30]

Although the Virgil Master was not indebted to the Van Lymborch brothers in his early manuscripts,[31] he later drew inspiration from the court of Pilate—or Nero—in the *Belles Heures* (fols. 135v and 215v), of which he proposed an enlargement for the frontispiece of a collection of the science writings of Alchandreus and Boethius.[32] The panoptic architecture he erected seems to want to rival some of the spectacular drawings in the *Très Riches Heures* (fols. 86v, 157v–158) or their equivalents by Haincelin de Haguenau.[33] The figure of Pontius Pilate has also been dressed as the emperor Domitian in the scene of the martyrdom of St. John at the head of the Chantilly Apocalypse (fol. 36),[34] while the Death of Alexander the Great, Poisoned (fol. 24v; fig. 10) is reminiscent of the banquet in January in the *Très Riches Heures*. A spirit of emulation seems to have played a role in the creation of this masterpiece

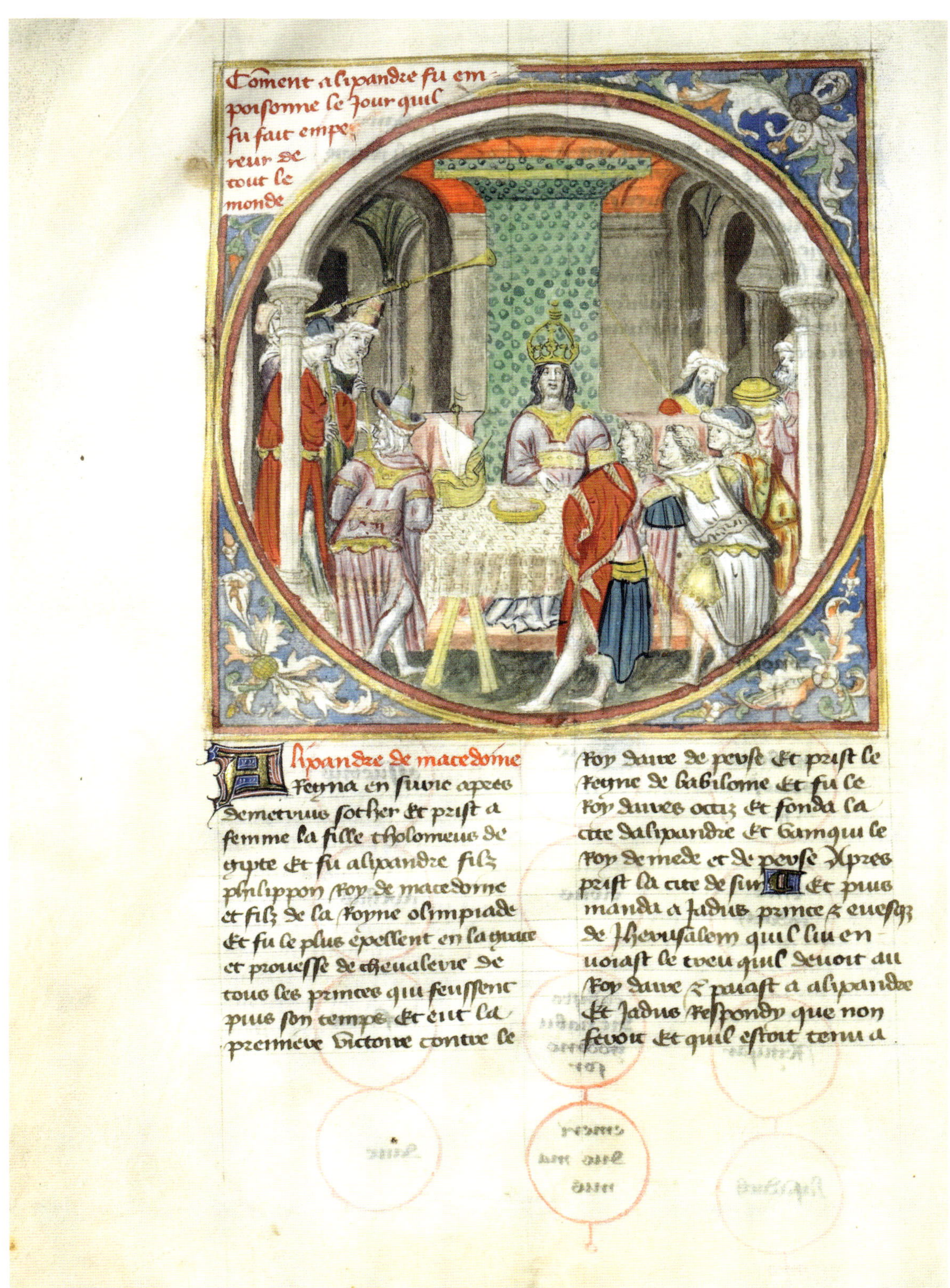

**Fig. 10** Master of Virgil, *Bible historiale* of Guiart des Moulins, followed by *Apocalypse*, fol. 24v: The Death of Alexander. c. 1416 (Chantilly, Bibliothèque du musée Condé, ms. 28)

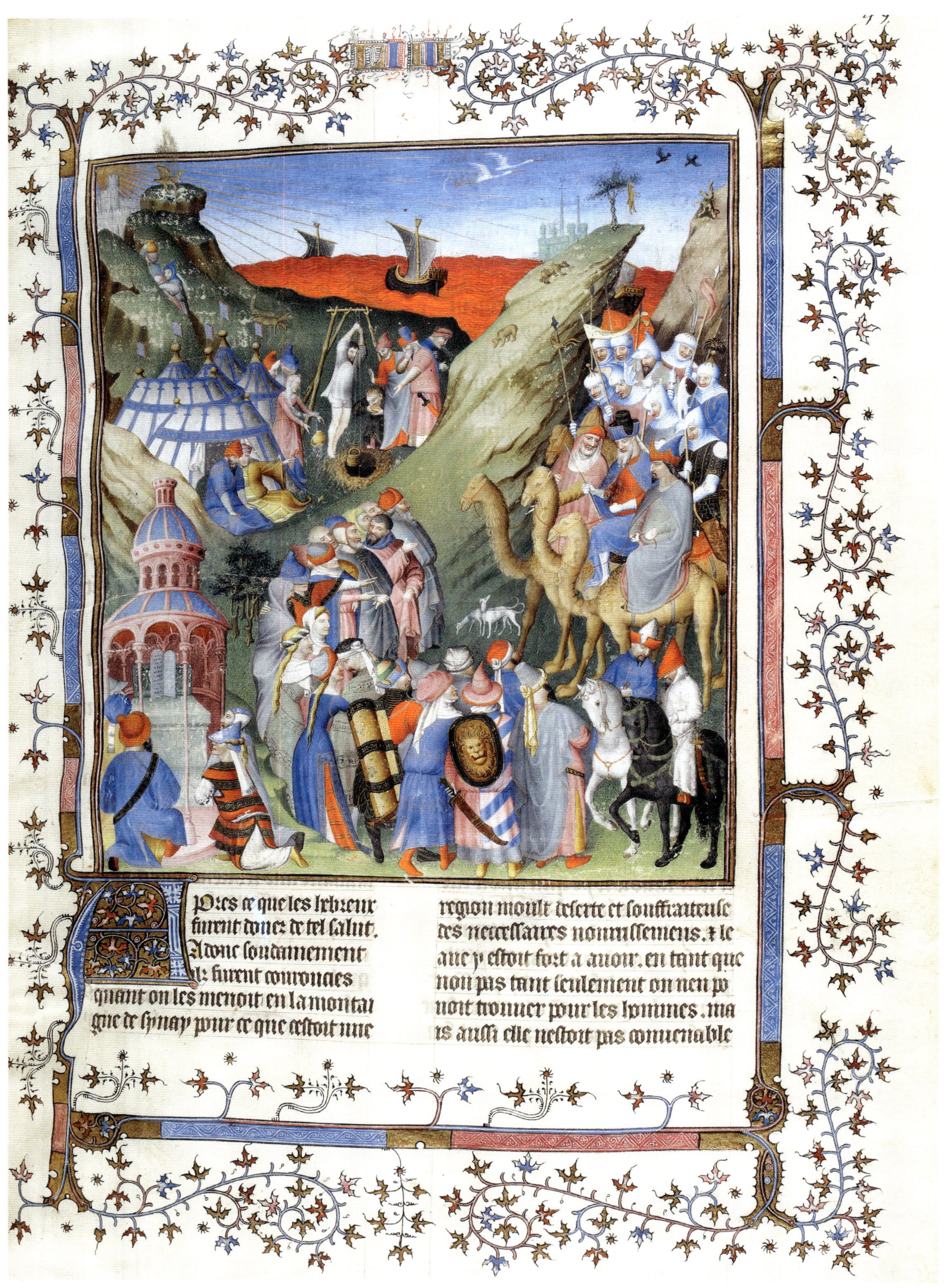

**Fig. 11** Michelet Saumon (?) (Master of the Roman Texts), *Les Antiquités judaïques* by Flavius Josephus, fol. 49: Israelites in the Wilderness. 1416 (Paris, Bibliothèque nationale de France, département des Manuscrits, Français 247)

by an illuminator trained in the workshop of Perrin Remiet at the end of the fourteenth century. Subverting the tradition of the "ink portrait,"[35] he achieved an exceptional level of freedom in terms of tone and color, with his slender buildings and his suggestion of subtle elements, such as the smoke from the censer hurled at the earth by the angel in Revelation 8:5 (fol. 54v), which is close to the smoking chimney in the coldness of February in the *Très Riches Heures* (fol. 2v). The ties between the three Van Lymborch brothers and the Parisian illuminators must have been all the closer as Jean of Berry and his court did not leave Paris after September 1413.

Their status as courtiers must also have facilitated the brothers' access to the princely collections.[36] The *Très Riches Heures* echoes the landscapes illuminated by golden rays and the architecture lit up by silver windows found in the book of hours of Marshal Boucicaut and his wife Antoinette de Turenne, first cousin of the Duchesse of Berry.[37] The Van Lymborch brothers also seem to have been familiar with the volume of Terence's *Comedies* presented to the duke by his treasurer Martin Gouges in January 1408,[38] and its human figures with their faces hidden by their hats. This motif, compatible with the brothers' quest for expressiveness, was immediately adopted for the flagellants in the *Belles Heures* (fol. 74v), the peasants in their calendar (fols. 7 and 8), and then those in the *Très Riches Heures* (fol. 7v). In return, the Master of the Roman Texts (Michelet Saumon?) had the opportunity to contemplate both the *Belles Heures* (the very red Red Sea on fols. 196 and 198) and the *Très Riches Heures* in the making—the small building of the Adoration of the Cross (fol. 193), and the Procession of the Magi (fols. 51v–52)—which he borrowed freely in the pages of a large volume of *Antiquités judaïques* (Antiquities of the Jews) begun for Jean of Berry (fig. 11).[39] The Master of the Roman Texts, early designated as "l'enlumineur du duc Jehan de Berry" (the illuminator of the Duke of Berry),[40] left the manuscript unfinished in 1416. His perceptive portraits, lively poses, and taste for exoticism and craggy landscapes make him the great rival of the Van Lymborch brothers in terms of the duke's favors—which is precisely what Michelet Saumon was.

To claim that the borrowings among these artists were reciprocal and stimulating is certainly not to insult the genius of the Van Lymborch brothers. These borrowings circulated in the form of drawings, even if copying from memory cannot be ruled out. In practice, the method varied: a tracing of the motif using *carta lustra*, for which Jean Lebègue's *Liber colorum* provides a recipe,[41] or from a model-book.[42] Their range was even more diverse, from a detail to an overall composition, from faithful replication to reinterpretation. Re-uses of this kind occurred naturally within the oeuvre of the Van Lymborch brothers; for instance, the figure of Pilate who becomes Nero, or the structure of the Holy Sepulchre in the *Belles Heures* (fol. 185v), transformed into a convent of Dominican nuns in the psalter of Louis of Guyenne (fol. 177v), or into a cathedral for the funeral of Canon Raymond Diocrès in the *Très Riches Heures* (fol. 86v). Learning to copy was an essential part of an artist's training, but copying cannot be limited to the years of learning. It is, in turn, a ferment for *inventio*, nourishing creation[43]; a homage to great works, a copy was a rich addition to the model-books and imaginaries of those who could recognize these masterpieces.

1 Villela-Petit 2013a.
2 Villela-Petit 2021.
3 Boespflug and König 1998; Villela-Petit 2011a; Husband 2012b.
4 Meiss 1969, I, 256–85; Meiss and Off 1971; Paris 2004b, 104–09 (no. 43) (note by I. Villela-Petit).
5 Villela-Petit 2011b.
6 Chantilly, Bibl. du musée Condé, Ms. 65, fols. 146v–147.
7 Remission granted by King Charles VI in May 1398 for the murder of Perrot Garnier; see Guérin 1893, 299–301 (no. 841).
8 The manuscript (Paris, BnF, Ms. Français 166) is missing one half. Most recently: Amsterdam 2017–18, 116–17 (no. 18) (note by I. Villela-Petit).
9 Reynolds 2005; Stirnemann and Rabel 2005; Stirnemann 2009.
10 London, BL, Ms. Add. 18850, fol. 75. König 2007, 73–74, 87.
11 Lisbon, Fundação Gulbenkian, Ms. LA 237, fol. 71v.
12 Vienna, ÖNB, Ms. cod. 1855, fol. 70v.
13 London, BL, Ms. Cotton Domitian A.XVII.
14 Oxford, Bodl. Library, Ms. Douce 144.
15 Lebailly 2005.
16 Letort 2022.
17 König 2016.
18 Dijon, Musée des Beaux-Arts.
19 We wish to thank Pierre-Yves Le Pogam and François Queyrel for their richly suggestive parallels.
20 London, BL, Ms. Add. 32454. Meiss 1974a, I, 103; Villela-Petit 2023, 18–19.
21 Paris, BnF, Ms. NAL 3107, fol. 45. Bartz 1999; Paris 2004b, 284 (no. 176), 286 (note by I. Villela-Petit).
22 Châteauroux, BM, Ms. 2, fol. 395v. Villela-Petit 2003, 92–93.
23 Paris, BnF, Ms. Latin 1156A, fol. 114.
24 Paris, BnF, Ms. Français 414, fol. 1. Paris 2004, 299–300 (no. 187) (note by F. Avril).
25 Prochno 2002b; Prochno 2002a, 334.
26 Los Angeles, Getty Museum, Ms. 57, fol. 176v.
27 Paris, BnF, Ms. Latin 9471, fol. 29v.
28 The only copy mentioned in the duke's library—"un très bel livre de la Légende dorée, historié au commancement et en pluseurs autres lieux très richement" (a very beautiful copy of the Golden Legend, very richly historiated at the beginning and in several other places)—entered the library before 1402. This could be the common model; see Guiffrey 1894–96, I, 230 (no. 876).
29 Rabel 2004, 162, 167 note 64, 171 (no. 83).
30 Florence, Bibl. Laurenziana, Ms. Med. Pal. 69, fol. 18.
31 Villela-Petit 2006a.
32 Los Angeles, Getty Museum, Ms. 72, fol. 2.
33 Paris, Bibl. Mazarine, Ms. 406, fol. 7.
34 Chantilly, Bibl. du musée Condé, Ms. 28. Meiss 1974a, I, 252–56, 296–303.
35 Villela-Petit 2012a.
36 Villela-Petit 2012b.
37 Paris, Musée Jacquemart-André, Ms. 2. Meiss 1969; Châtelet 2000; Guineau and Villela-Petit 2002; Guineau and Villela-Petit 2003.
38 Paris, BnF, Ms. Latin 7907A.
39 Paris, BnF, Ms. Français 247, fol. 25, 49, partly 194.
40 According to a note added to the volume after 1470 in the Bourbon library (fol. 311v). Paris 2003, 310–27 (no. 34) (note by F. Avril); Villela-Petit 2021, 55–57.
41 Merrifield 1999, 292–95 (no. 305); Villela-Petit 2006b.
42 Scheller 1995; Lorentz 2004b.
43 Villela-Petit 2004b; Villela-Petit 2010a, 408–411 ("L'invention et la copie").

**Fig. 12** Following pages: Van Lymborch brothers, *Très Riches Heures*, fol. 144: The Flagellation of Christ, detail

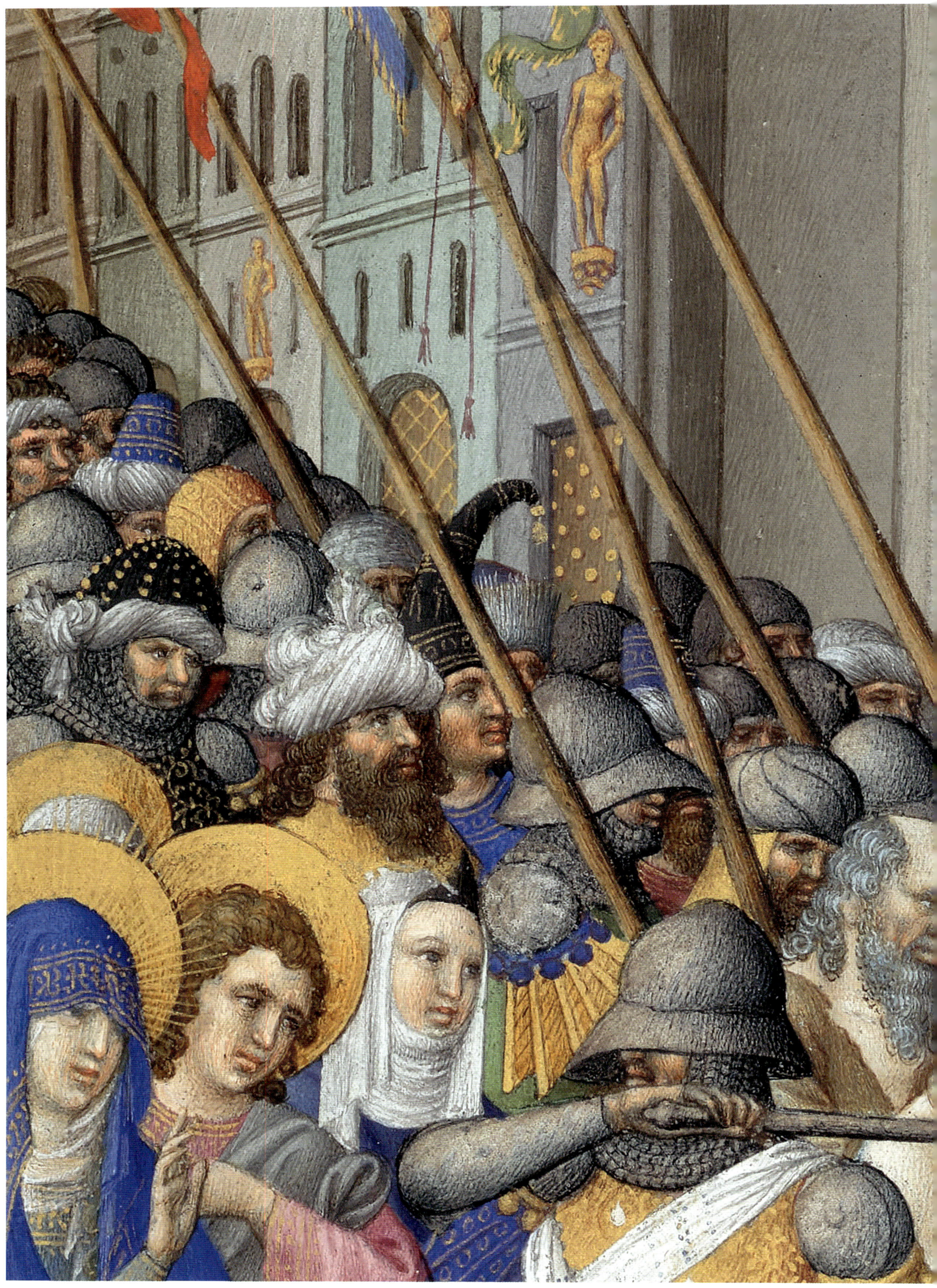

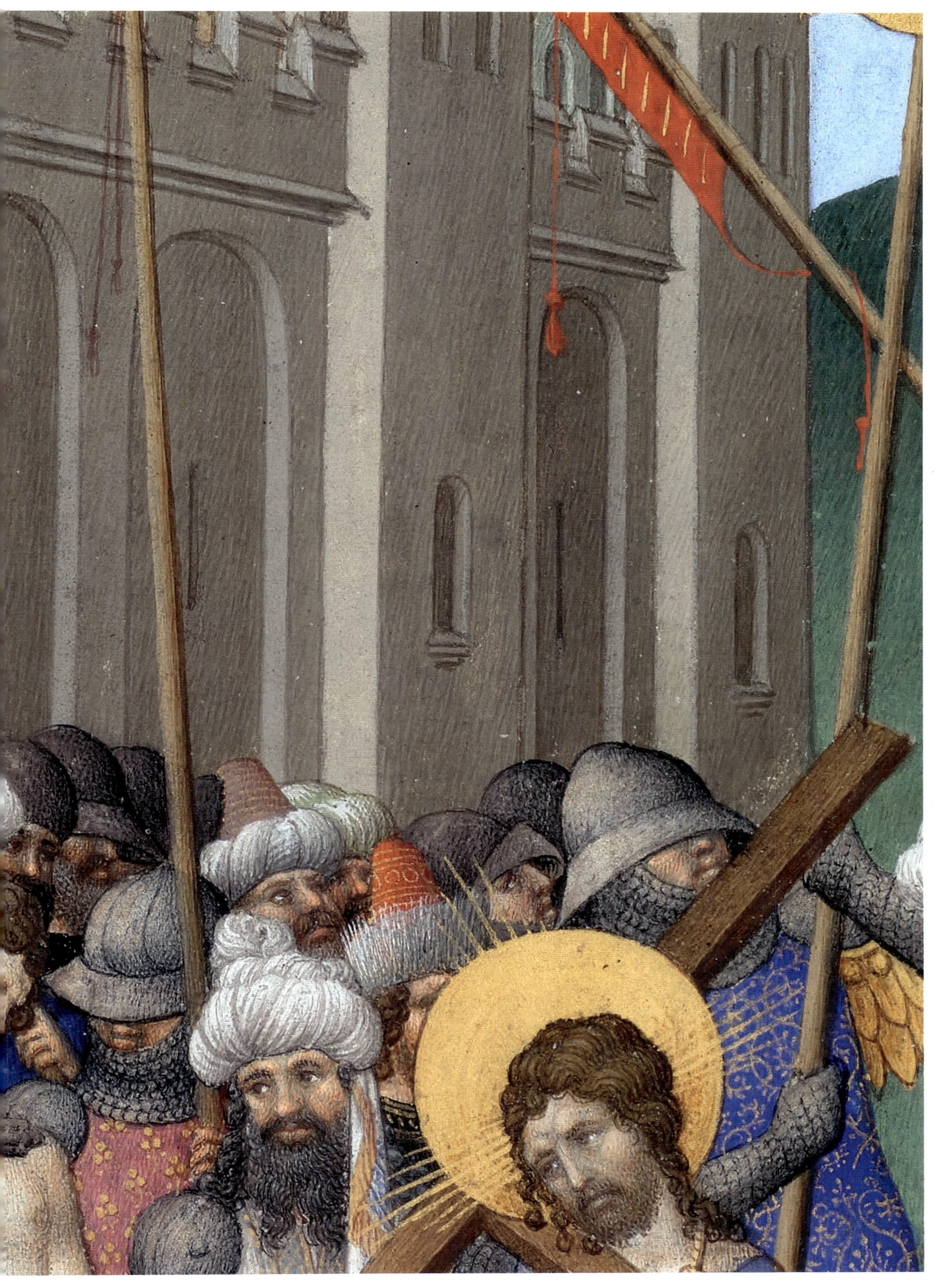

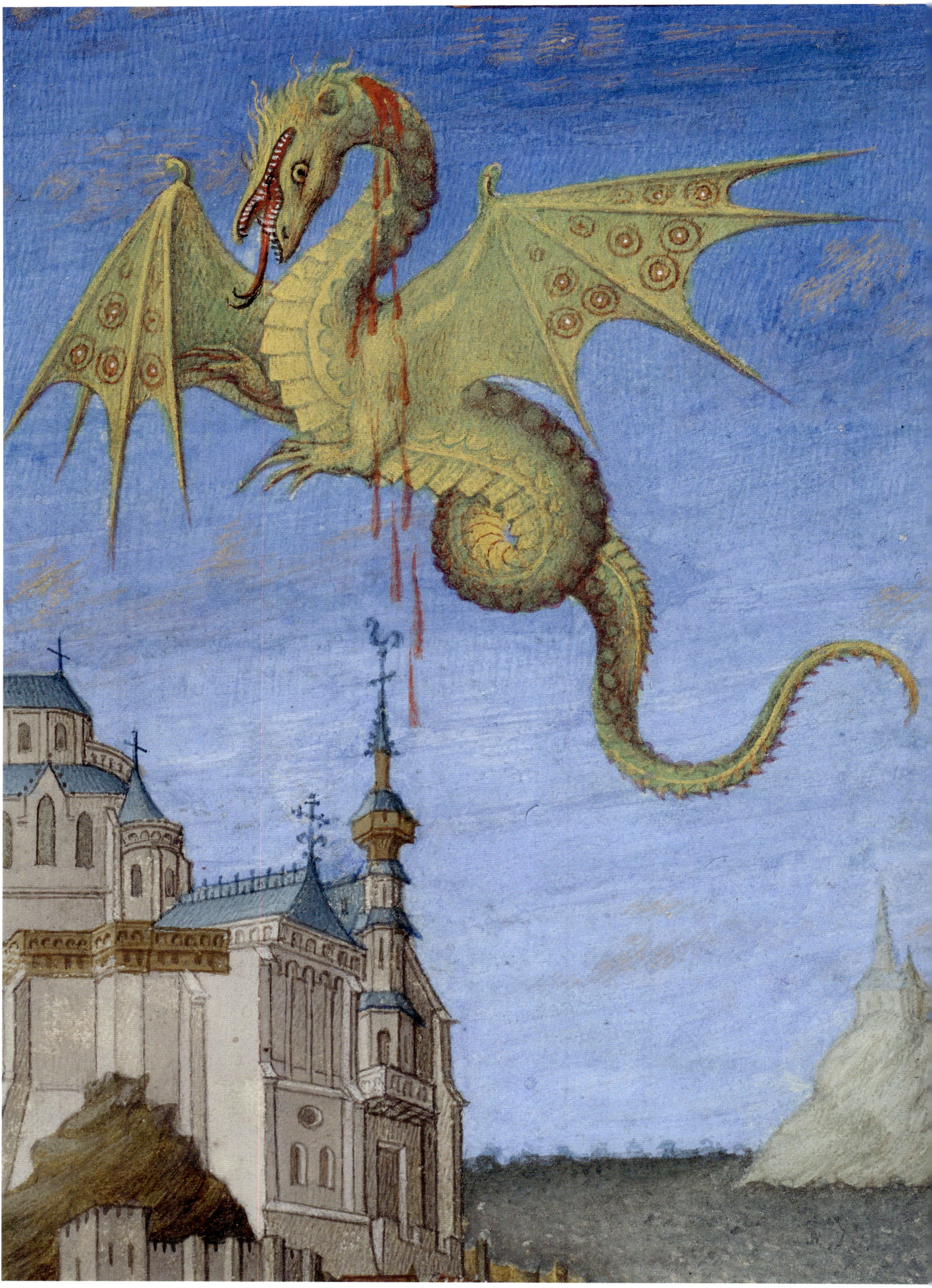

12.

# The Legacy of the Van Lymborch Brothers in French Illumination of the First-half of the Fifteenth Century

Inès Villela-Petit

The long-lasting fame of the Van Lymborch brothers' masterpiece was already underway in their lifetime. One of the most enlightening adaptations is the scene of the martyrdom of St. Mark—until then devoid of any iconographic tradition—which illustrates the extracts from the Gospels to be found in the *Très Riches Heures* (fol. 19v); the *Breviary of John the Fearless* gives an abridged version in its sanctorale (fol. 282v).[1]

## THE BREVIARY MASTER, A CONTEMPORARY

The illumination of this manuscript began some time after May 22, 1412, when the Duke of Burgundy gave 300 francs to his wife, Margaret of Bavaria, "pour la façon d'un Bréviaire et autres livres qu'elle fait faire" (for the making of a breviary and other books that she was having made).[2] The Breviary Master was the ornamentalist of the two initials on folio 19v of the *Très Riches Heures*, which, if we follow the usual order of execution, enabled him to examine the underlying design of the Van Lymborch brothers. The distribution of the leaves among the ornamentalists determined the stock of compositions that each could plunder at will. To this we can add patterns from the Van Lymborch workshop that were already circulating, but also those from the *Très Belles Heures* painted by Jacquemart de Hesdin, patterns that the Breviary Master combined in a precious book of hours illuminated between

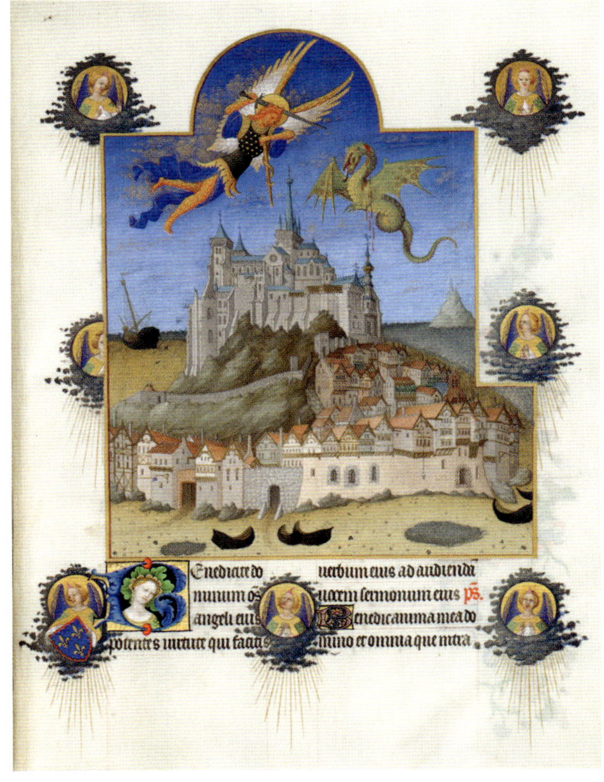

**Fig. 2** Van Lymborch brothers, *Très Riches Heures*, fol. 195: St. Michael Slaying the Dragon. 1412–16

**Fig. 1** Van Lymborch brothers, *Très Riches Heures*, fol. 195: St. Michael Slaying the Dragon, detail

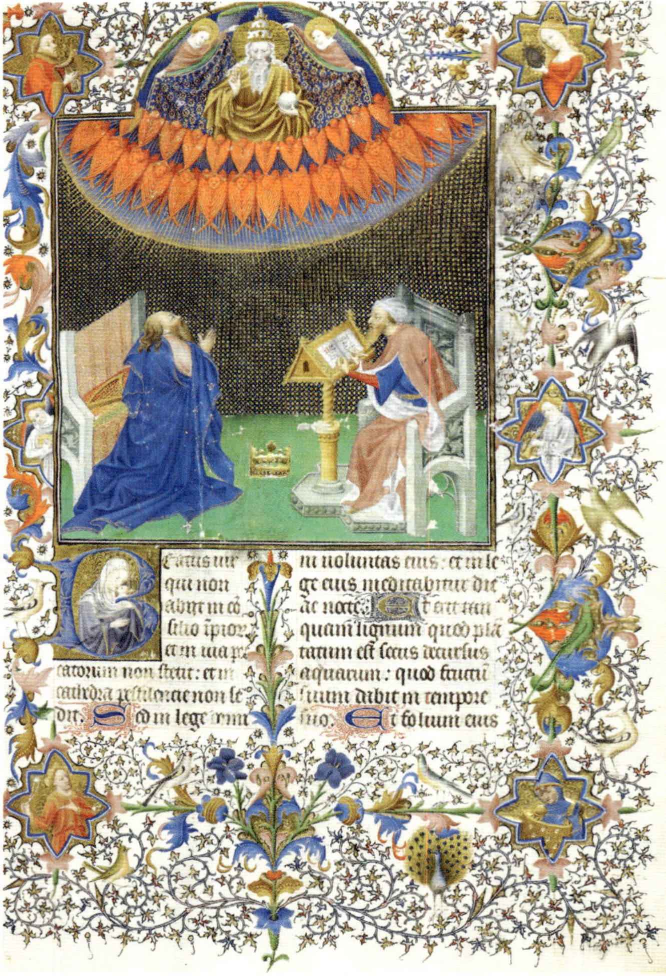

**Fig. 3** Breviary Master, *Breviary of Margaret of Bavaria*, fol. 8: David at Prayer and His Scribe. 1412–19 (London, British Library, Add. MS 35311)

1408 and 1412, perhaps for Jean of Berry, but left incomplete.[3] Indeed, it was in the service of the Berry court that this painter first surfaced, in a collection presented to the duke's daughter Marie at Pentecost 1406.[4] He was then associated with the Van Lymborch brothers in this "ducal workshop," which enabled him to gather drawings, even if his Burgundian sympathies undoubtedly kept him away from it.[5] He then completed Philip the Bold's old prayer book[6] with a refined version of the half-length Madonnas of the *Belles Heures* (fols. 26v, 209). He was also familiar with the Van Lymborch compositions added to the *Très Belles Heures de Notre-Dame*,[7] adapting the Pilgrimage scene of Jean of Berry into that of the Ascension in the breviary to which he owes his name,[8] or into the Flight into Egypt.[9] Drawing on the Emperor Augustus adoring the Lord, he recomposed a David at prayer for the second volume of the eponymous breviary (fig. 3). A detail in the border of the latter leaf—a quatrefoil that is home to an angel partly hidden by the miniature, as if the angel were passing behind the image—bears witness to his careful observation of the *Très Riches Heures*, where this process was used during the first illustration campaign (fol. 195; fig. 2). However, the Breviary Master's shimmering pointillist style contrasts with the Van Lymborch brothers' clean, precise work.

## THE VAN LYMBORCH BROTHERS AND THEIR DISCIPLE: THE SPITZ MASTER

The question of the Van Lymborch brothers' followers needs to be partly revised to take account of the drawings attributed to a supposed emulator, the "Master of St. Jerome."[10] Named after the St. Jerome in his study serving as the frontispiece to Philip the Bold's *Bible moralisée* (Moralized bible) (fol. A), he is distinguished by the sumptuousness of his architectural constructions, comparable to the architectural elevations of the Musée de l'Œuvre de Notre-Dame in Strasbourg,[11] and by refined details, perhaps a legacy of his training as a goldsmith, like that received by Herman and Johan van Lymborch, so that these drawings were appreciated in and of themselves.[12] Yet these Gothic superstructures have equivalents in the Fountain of Life and the Gate of Paradise from the *Très Riches Heures* (fol. 25v; fig. 15, p. 190), and in the view of the duke's château at Mehun-sur-Yèvre (fol. 161v; fig. 2, p. 73). In fact, the other drawings in the corpus are not subsequent to but contemporary with the Van Lymborch brothers, whether the litanies in the margin of the *Heures du Dauphin* of 1408,[13] or the architectures added to a psalter also illuminated for Louis of Guyenne, which was adapted and colored around 1425 for Henry VI of England.[14] There is therefore no chronological obstacle to reintegrating the "St. Jerome" style into the brothers' oeuvre, a style that is in keeping with the variability to be expected of a three-handed creation. These extraordinarily inventive drawings are inseparable from it and draw on the same sources.

The case of the *Book of Hours for the Use of Rome* known as the *Seilern Hours* (formerly in London in the collection of Count Antoine Edward Seilern und Aspang) seems partly of the same kind. Described as "by far the best manuscript painted by a follower of the Van Lymborchs," it is the only known work by the "Seilern Master," although the latter was initially identified with one of the three brothers ; Meiss himself recognized in his art the refinement and elegance of the one he identified as "Jean de Limbourg."[15] Here again, the question is obscured by the presence of several hands, all the more difficult to analyze as these *Seilern Hours* are known to us only through black and white photographs.[16] In addition to the Van Lymborch hand—which gives the workshop's compositions some more spatial breathing space, as in the Annunciation, the Last Judgment, and the Entombment—other illuminations are already characteristic of the style of the Spitz Master. The delicate floral or acanthus borders on one side, and the large acanthus leaves extending from the frame on the other, correspond closely to this distribution. Both left the book of hours unfinished. It was completed around Ghent in the 1440s, undoubtedly in part on the basis of drawings by the Van Lymborch brothers, which are still recognizable in the architecture of the Presentation in the Temple and the details of the Coronation of the Virgin.

If the "Seilern Master" is, like the "Master of St. Jerome," identifiable to the Van Lymborchs, then there remains this Spitz Master, who trained under them and was their main epigone. He inherited their designs, or appropriated them as soon as they died, and made use of them for his own benefit. His books of hours contain some thirty patterns, drawn from the *Belles Heures* and the *Très Riches Heures*, but also from the *Seilern Hours* (fig. 4) and a leaf showing St. Christopher from a lost book of hours.[17] Among his sources was at least one of the full pages that typify the second campaign of the *Très Riches Heures*: the Flagellation of Christ (fol. 144; fig. 2, p. 217), which he reproduced in the *Spitz Hours* (fig. 6).[18] One of the border medallions reproduces the Crown of Thorns from the *Seilern Hours*, while the small acanthus leaves and miniaturized fauna pay homage to the ornamentalist style of the Van Lymborch brothers. However, he substituted their naturalism with a picturesque, decorative style that saturates the surfaces: backgrounds with gold scrolls, brocaded textiles, and skies strewn with flowers (fol. 33v). A comparison of the Carrying of the Cross in the *Spitz Hours* (fol. 31; fig. 5) with that in the *Belles Heures* (fol. 138v) shows a definite relationship, with the same figures quoted identically. But the more coherent composition of the Spitz Master and the weaknesses of the leaf of the *Belles Heures*—Christ's atrophied foot, the absence of Simon of Cyrene replaced by St. John and a contorted soldier, and the crossbeam of the Cross ending in the sleeve of the Virgin—attest to a common source, and not an act of copying. Even within the Van Lymborch workshop, the drawings were sometimes misinterpreted, no doubt because the lead pencil left a line with little contrast unless it was repeated in ink.[19]

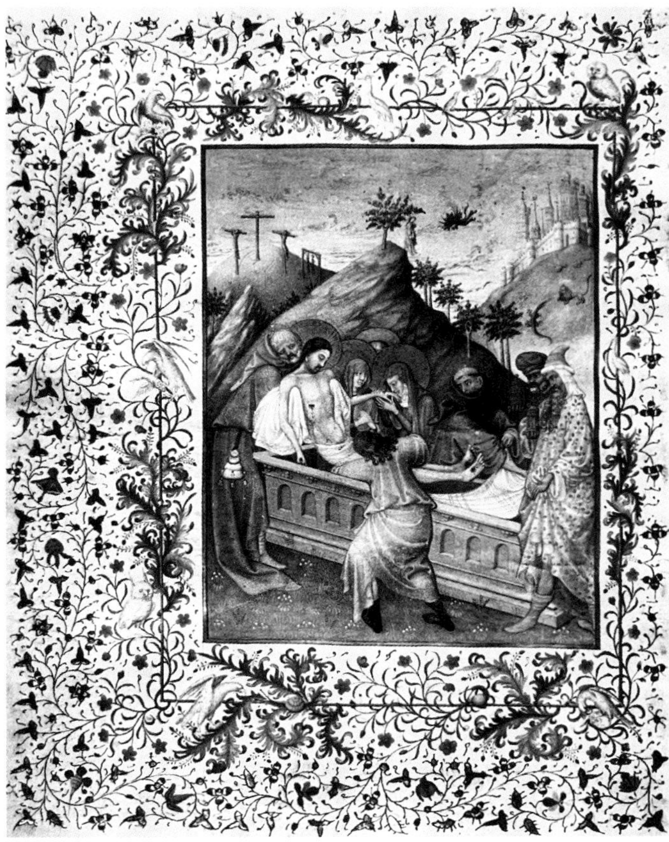

**Fig. 4** Van Lymborch brothers, *Seilern Hours*: The Entombment of Christ. 1415–16, outer border by a Ghent illuminator, around 1440 (London, private collection)

## DRAWINGS AND REAPPEARANCES

Two drawings, inserted on tabs in books of hours dating from 1425–30, may have been Van Lymborch originals.[20] The full-page Marriage of the Virgin, colored by the Master of Morgan 453,[21] stands out in this illuminator's work for its complex architecture, modelled on the Annunciation in the *Très Riches Heures* (fol. 26), but also for its figures, such as the man in a greatcoat who reproduces the lost portrait of the Duke of Berry from the *Très Belles Heures de Notre-Dame*. A different

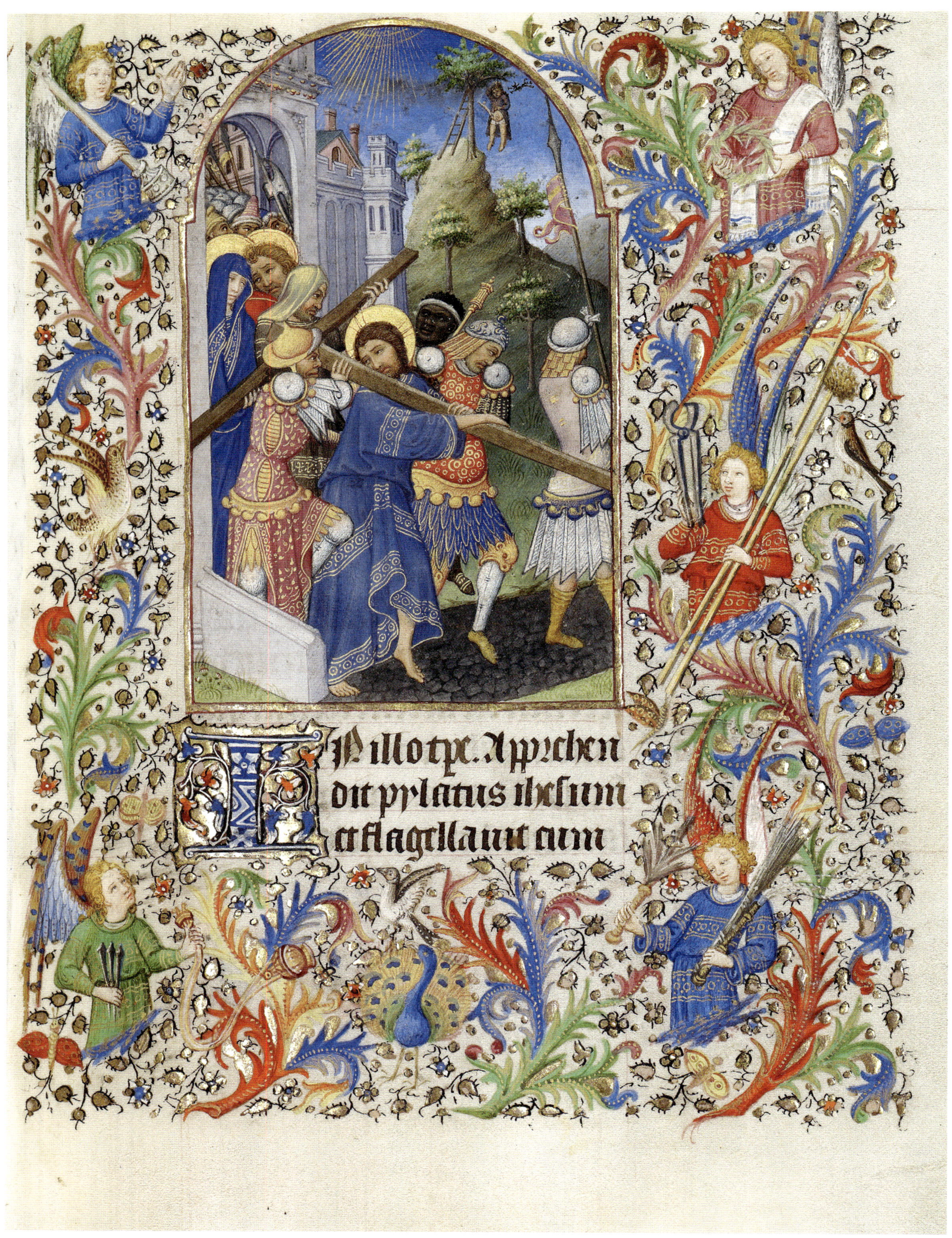

**Fig. 5** Spitz Master, *Spitz Hours*, fol. 31: Christ Carrying the Cross. 1420–24 (Los Angeles, The J. Paul Getty Museum, MS 57)

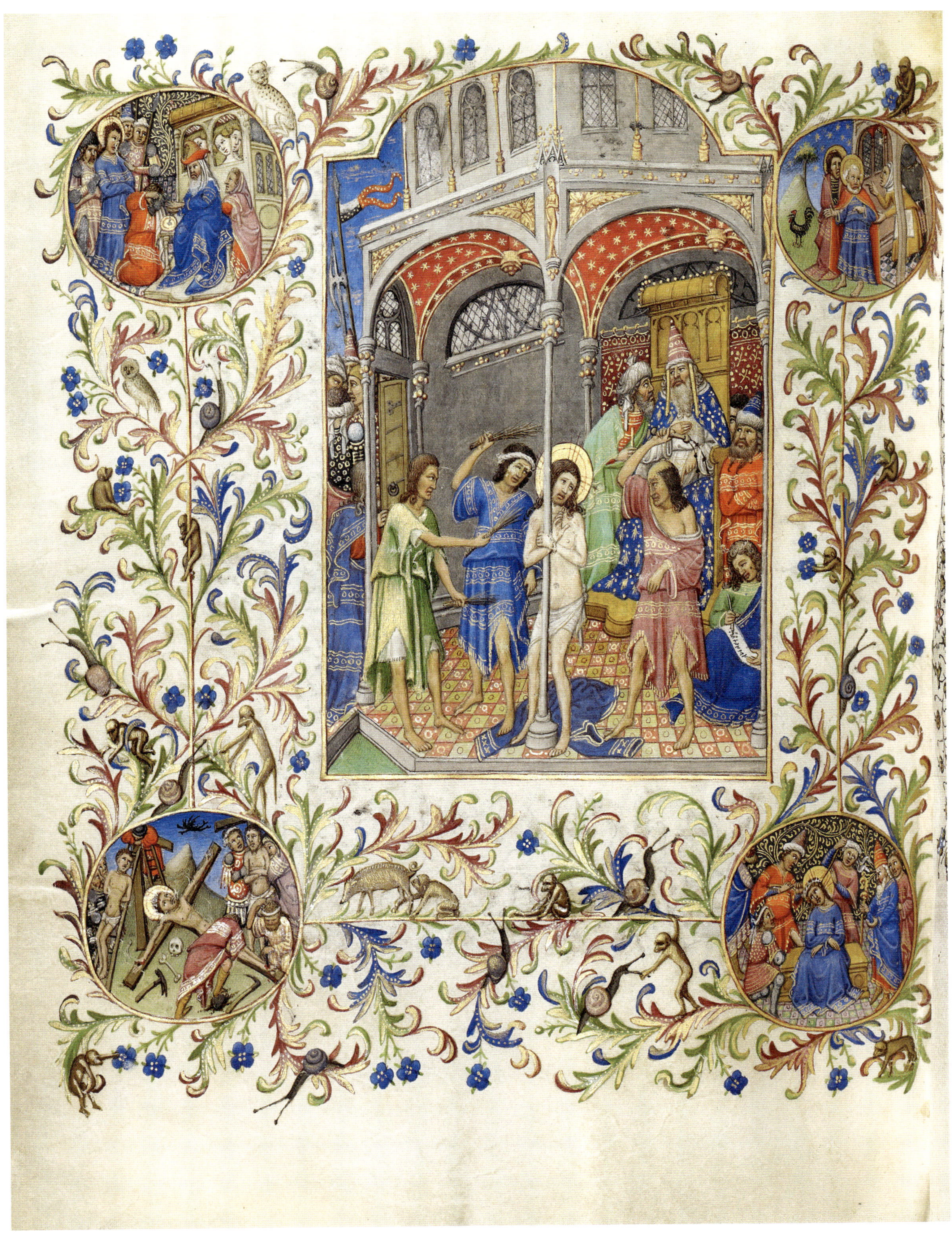

**Fig. 6** Spitz Master, *Spitz Hours*, fol. 172v: The Flagellation of Christ. 1420–24 (Los Angeles, The J. Paul Getty Museum, MS 57)

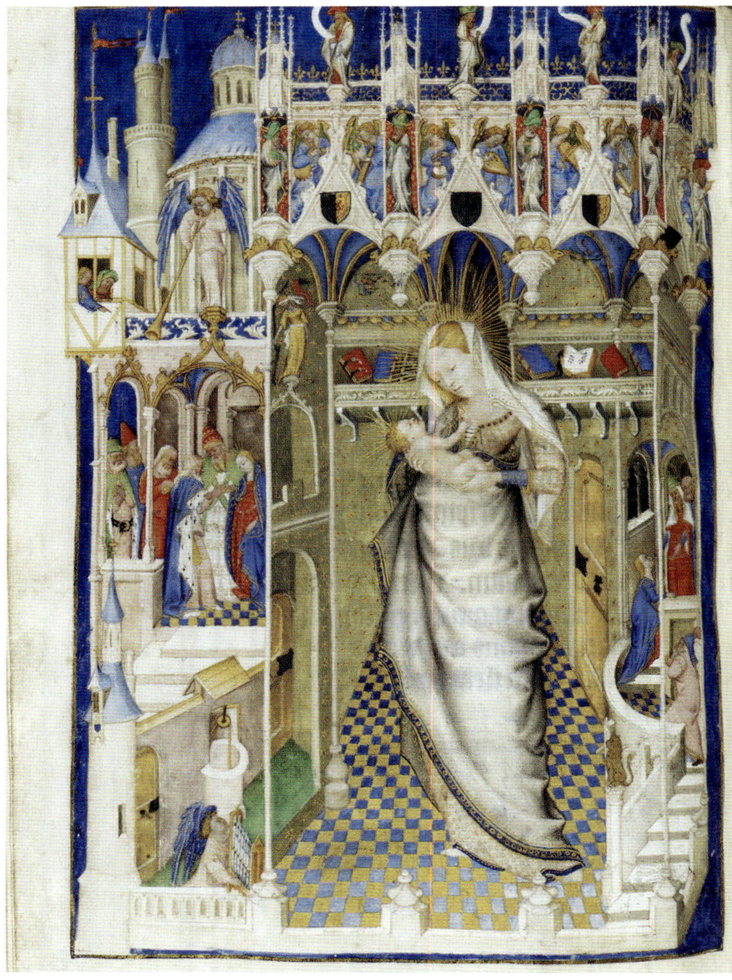

**Fig. 7** Rohan Master and Giac Master (figurines), *Hours of Yolande of Anjou*, fol. 141v: Virgin and Child. c. 1431 (Cambridge, Fitzwilliam Museum, MS 62)

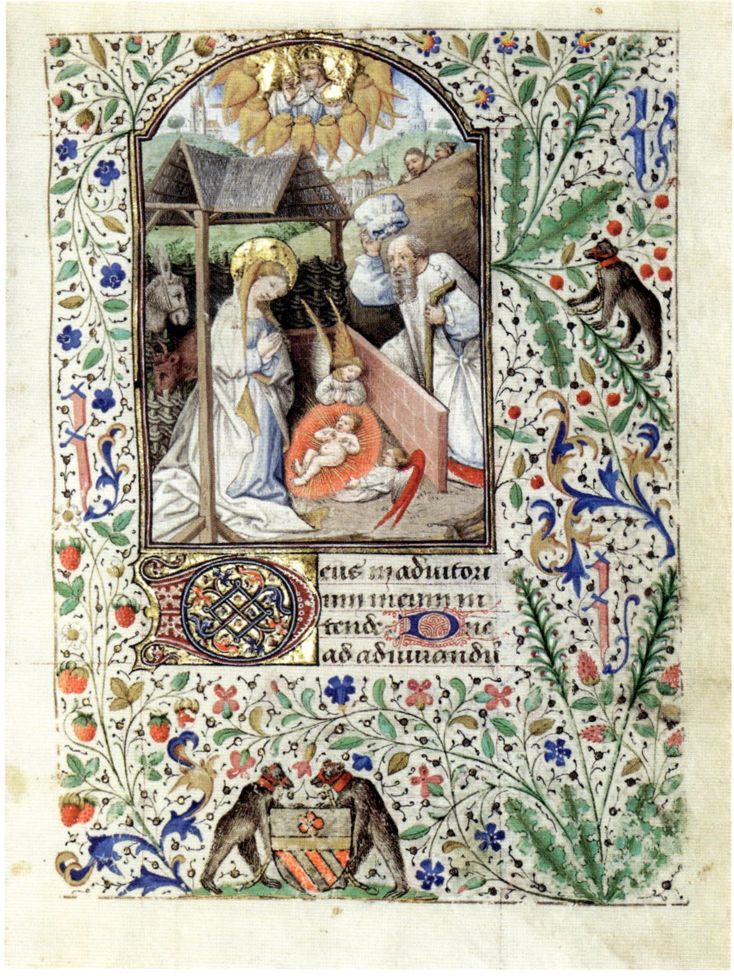

**Fig. 8** Jean Haincelin (Dunois Master), fol. 13: The Nativity of Jesus. 1445–50 (Paris, Bibliothèque nationale de France, département des Manuscrits, NAL 3226)

version of the Marriage of the Virgin appears in the *Hours of Thomas Malet*, Receiver of the castellany of Lille, and Jeanne de Lannoy, whom he married in 1444,[22] alongside a number of compositions that date back to the Van Lymborch brothers, such as the Virgin giving Communion to St. Avoye (fol. 241) or the funeral service bearing the arms of a first owner, "d'azur à cinq cotices d'or" (azure with five gold cotices) (fol. 167). As for the Master of the Harvard Hannibal, the brilliant Parisian heir to the Boucicaut-Mazarine workshop and occasional collaborator of the Spitz Master, he was already using Van Lymborch patterns for the Annunciation and Last Judgment[23] around 1417, and he adopted the architectural design that served as a model for both the Christmas Mass of the *Très Riches Heures* (fol. 158; fig. 3, p. 258) and the missal of Louis of Guyenne (fol. 7). Three books of hours by the Master of the Harvard Hannibal retain the original theme, which must have been a Requiem Mass.[24]

The architectural designs of the Van Lymborch brothers also fascinated the Giac Master from his time in Troyes, where the court of Charles VI and Isabeau of Bavaria, fleeing the troubles in Paris, settled in January 1418. The Annunciation in the *Book of Hours for the Use of Troyes* of Demoiselle Jacquette[25] is based on that in the *Hours of 1408* (fol. 28) or an equivalent. The illuminator also seems to have been familiar with several compositions from the *Belles Heures*, such as the half-length Trinity.[26] However, it was undoubtedly in Angers, at the court of Yolande of Anjou, that this precursor of the Rohan Master studied the two Van Lymborch manuscripts acquired by the Duchess of Anjou after the death of Jean of Berry: the *Belles Heures*, in April 1417 at the latest, and the *Bible moralisée*, which the Duke of Berry had received from John the Fearless in 1407. The latter was fitted with a red and gold textile binding, "couverte à bendes de veloux cramoisi et de drap d'or" (covered with strips of crimson velvet and gold cloth), which corresponds to the Aragonese arms[27] ("d'or à quatre pals de gueules," or four pallets gules). The hours known as the *Heures d'Antoine de Buz*[28] took over from the *Belles Heures* several unusual themes, always reworked with the expressionism that characterizes the Giac Master, such as the book wheel (*Belles Heures*, fol. 15), whose statuette of Moses at the top became a Virgin and Child; the shepherd turning his back (fol. 52); the Virgin seen from behind from the Flight into Egypt (fol. 63); the Throne of Grace with seraphim (fol. 204); the half-length Trinity (fol. 155); and the Virgin and Child asleep (fol. 209). In the *Hours of Yolande of Anjou*,[29] who became Duchess of Brittany in 1431,[30] the Giac Master combined the iconographic types of the

Trinity and the Last Judgment, while the Master of the Rohan Madonnas superimposed the half-length Trinity and the Virgin with crescent moon (fol. 136v). He built a case for his full-length Madonna and the surrounding scenes (fol. 141v; fig. 7), combining the architecture of the St. Jerome in the *Bible moralisée* with the architectural frames of the Mazarine Master.[31] The Van Lymborch patterns were reinterpreted after 1434 in the *Hours of René of Anjou*, notably the Madonna of the Crescent Moon,[32] and reminiscences of the Raymond Diocrès cycle from the *Belles Heures* (fols. 94–94v) can still be discerned after 1436 in the *Hours of Viscount Alain IX de Rohan* or *Grandes Heures de Rohan*,[33] where a horseman from the Meeting of the Magi in the *Très Riches Heures* (fol. 51) makes an appearance in the Flight into Egypt (fol. 99). Similarly, the Master of Marguerite d'Orléans, an adept of the ornate style, adapted several compositions from the *Belles Heures* in the *Hours of Marguerite d'Orléans* illuminated for this young princess, Dame de Clisson since her marriage in 1423 to Richard d'Étampes.[34] Adoration of the Magi, Arrest of Christ, Martyrdom of St. Catherine,[35] but also, between 1426 and 1430, in the *Hours of Marie de Rieux*, wife of Louis d'Amboise. The *Belles Heures* and the frontispiece of the *Bible moralisée* went through unexpected reinterpretations by the Breton illuminators, as in the hours of Anne de Kerenrais and Jean de Montauban.[36] The Master of Marguerite d'Orléans was still faithful to his patterns in a book of hours illuminated for Charles VII after the king's return to Paris on November 12, 1437.[37]

It was then that the eclipse of the *Très Riches Heures* came to an end. The death of Jean of Berry in mid-June 1416 had left the quires not only unfinished, but also unavailable due to the duke's succession and their sequestration.[38] The sketchbooks and copies made earlier continued to serve as before, but most of the calendar's superb full pages, the last to be added to the work during the time of the Van Lymborch brothers, remained without immediate successors. The manuscript only reappeared with the recapture of Paris by Jean d'Orléans on April 13, 1436. The book of hours of Jean d'Orléans, who became Count of Dunois in 1439, included several compositions from it, including the January banquet, the Coronation of the Virgin, and the Adoration of the Cross (fols. 1v, 60v, 193), alongside landscapes of Eyckian inspiration.[39] The Dunois Master, identifiable with Jean Haincelin, the heir to Haincelin de Haguenau, made use of it in manuscripts dating from 1445–50, such as the hours of the Chancellor Guillaume Jouvenel des Ursins,[40] whose Nativity (fig. 8)[41] is an adaptation of the one in the *Très Riches Heures* (fol. 44v). Finally, it fell to Barthélemy d'Eyck to reconnect with the spirit of the Van Lymborch brothers. He probably only got hold of the *Très Riches Heures* between late June and early August 1446, on the occasion of the Joyeuse Garde tournament, which gathered in Saumur his patron King René of Anjou, King Charles VII, and Dunois.[42] His later work was then imbued with it.[43]

1 London, BL, Ms. Harley 2897. Meiss 1974a, II, 232–237, fig. 619.
2 Jeannot 2012.
3 [De Hamel] 1999.
4 Paris, BnF, Ms. Français 926, fol. 52.
5 [De Hamel] 1999, 16. The litanies include the patron saints of Poitou, of which Jean of Berry was the count, but the wolf mauling a sheep in the Annunciation to the Shepherds (fol. 80v) was part of the "war of signs" that followed the assassination of Louis d'Orléans (November 23, 1407) and shows his wolf emblem in an unfavorable light. See Hablot 2000.
6 Brussels, KBR, Ms. 11035-37, fol. 6v.
7 Meiss 1963; Avril, Reynaud, and Cordellier 2011, 140–156 (nos. 77–80) (notes by I. Villela-Petit).
8 London, BL, Ms. Harley 2897, fol. 188v.
9 Madrid, Museo Lazaro Galdiano, reg. 15701-21. Paris 2004b, 270–272 (nos, 166–67) (notes by F. Avril).
10 Meiss 1974a, I, 405; Villela-Petit 2013b.
11 Bengel and Dupeux 2019, in particular drawing no. 5.
12 Villela-Petit 2013b.
13 Villela-Petit 2018b.
14 London, BL, Ms. Cotton Domitian A.XVII. Backhouse 2004.
15 Paris 1955–56, no. 91, 93 (note by J. Porcher); Meiss 1974a, I, 237–39, 330; Avril 1975; König 2003b, 50–53; Clark 2005; Van Bergen 2016.
16 In particular Meiss 1974a, II, figs. 424–25, 469, 625–33; König 2003b, figs. 15–16, 18–19, 25.
17 Washington, NGA, Ms. 1946.21.10. Nijmegen 2005, 380–81 (no. 106) (note by G.T. Clark).
18 Los Angeles, Getty Museum, Ms. 57. Clark 2003; Clark 2004.
19 Seidel 2018.
20 Cleveland 1967–68, 288; New York 1982–83, 8 (no. 11); Clark 2016, 119–27, 140–48.
21 New York, Morgan Library, Ms. M.453, fol. 30v.
22 Baltimore, Walters Art Museum, Ms. W.281, fol. 30v.
23 New York, Morgan Library, Ms. M.455, fols. 23, 166v.
24 Oxford, Bodl. Library, Ms. Liturg. 100, fol. 115; Baltimore, Walters Art Museum, W.287, fol. 149; Los Angeles, Getty Museum, Ms. 19, fol. 113. Paris 2004b, 144–45 (no. 70) (note by I. Villela-Petit); König 2007, 71–76.
25 Paris, BSG, Ms. 1278, fol. 77. Meiss 1974b; Châlons-en-Champagne, Troyes, and Reims 2007–08, 92 (no. 7) (note by F. Avril); Villela-Petit 2010b.
26 Paris, BSG, Ms. 1278, fol. 21v.
27 Amsterdam 2017–18, 116–17 (no. 18) (note by I. Villela-Petit).
28 Cambridge (MA), Houghton Library, Ms. Richardson 42.
29 Panayotova 2014.
30 Cambridge, Fitzwilliam Museum, Ms. 62, fol. 99.
31 Paris, BnF, Ms. Latin 10538, fol. 31 and 116.
32 Paris, BnF, Ms. Latin 1156A, fol. 18v.
33 Paris, BnF, Ms. Latin 9741, fol. 21 and 167.
34 König 1991; Paris 1993–94, 28–29 (no. 5) (note by F. Avril); Paris 2024, 162–63 (no. 88) (note by M. Hermant).
35 Paris, BnF, Ms. Latin 1156B, fols. 89, 133, 175.
36 Paris, BnF, Ms. Latin 18026, fols. 18, 64, 112, 121, 126, 136, 155. Paris 2024, 166–67 (no. 91) (note by M. Deldicque).
37 Paris, BnF, Ms. Rothschild 2534, fol. 124.
38 Reynolds 2005; Villela-Petit 2018b.
39 London, BL, Ms. Yates Thompson 3, fols. 1, 114, 184. Châtelet 2008.
40 Paris 2024, 82 (no. 45) (note by M. Hermant).
41 Paris, BnF, Ms. NAL 3226, fol. 13, fig. 9.
42 Based on elements pointed out by Patricia Stirnemann in the illustration for September in the *Très Riches Heures* (fol. 9v), which shows the tilt barrier in front of the château. See Angers 2009–10, 244–47 (no. 12) (note by R.M. Ferré).
43 Villela-Petit 2013c.

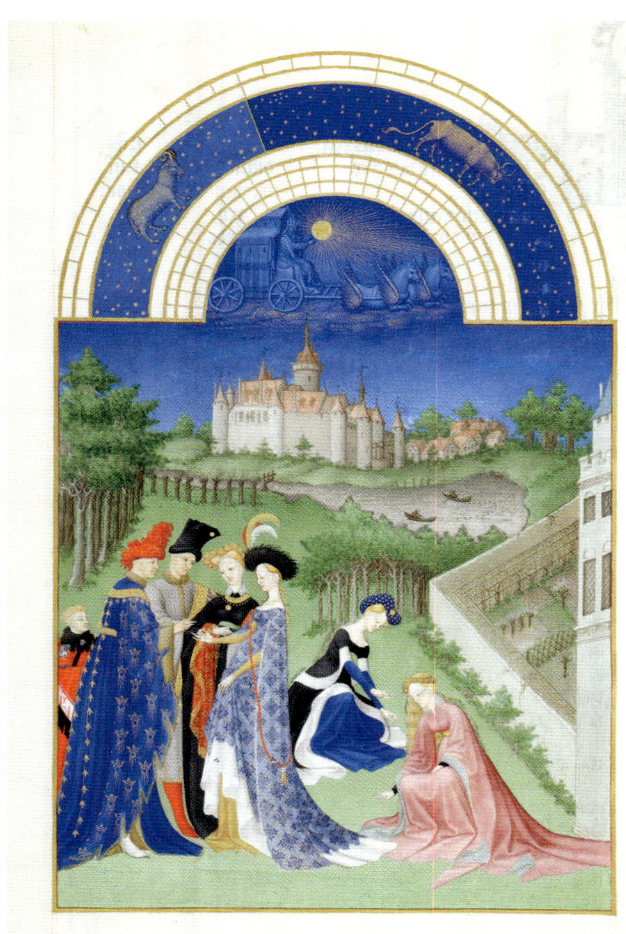

Van Lymborch brothers, *Très Riches Heures*, fol. 4v: April

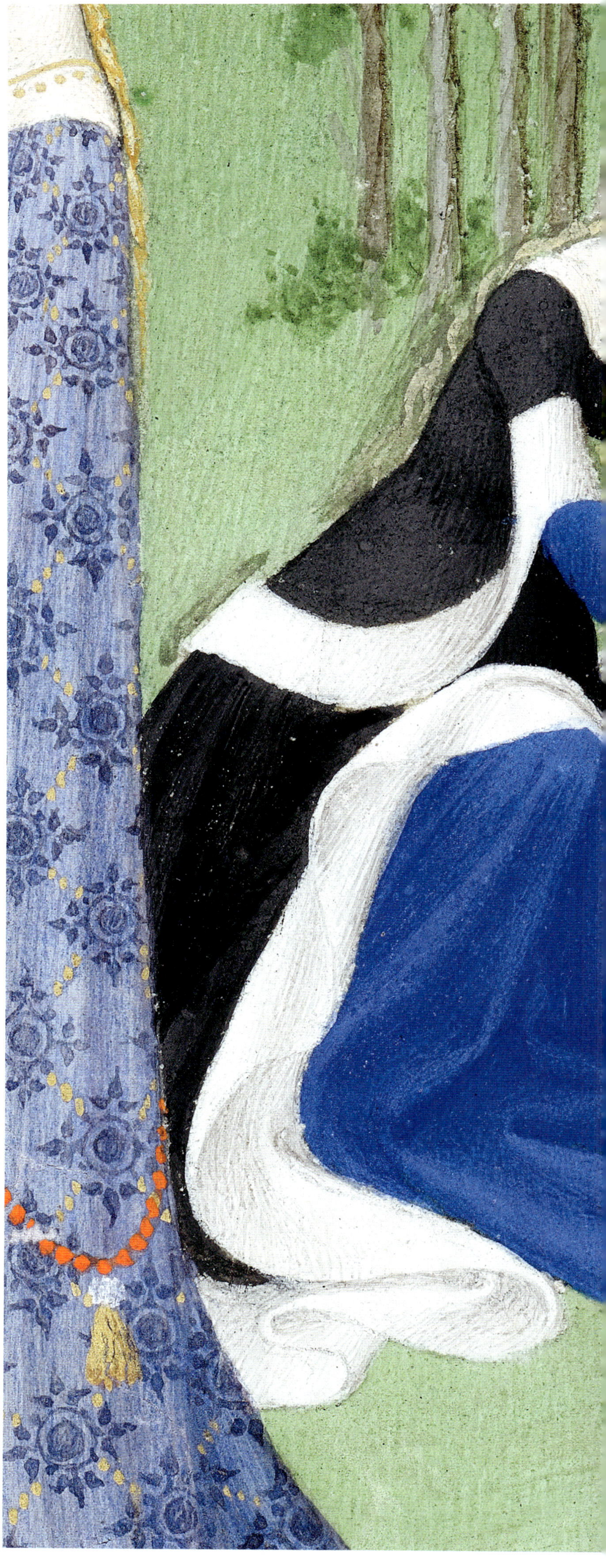

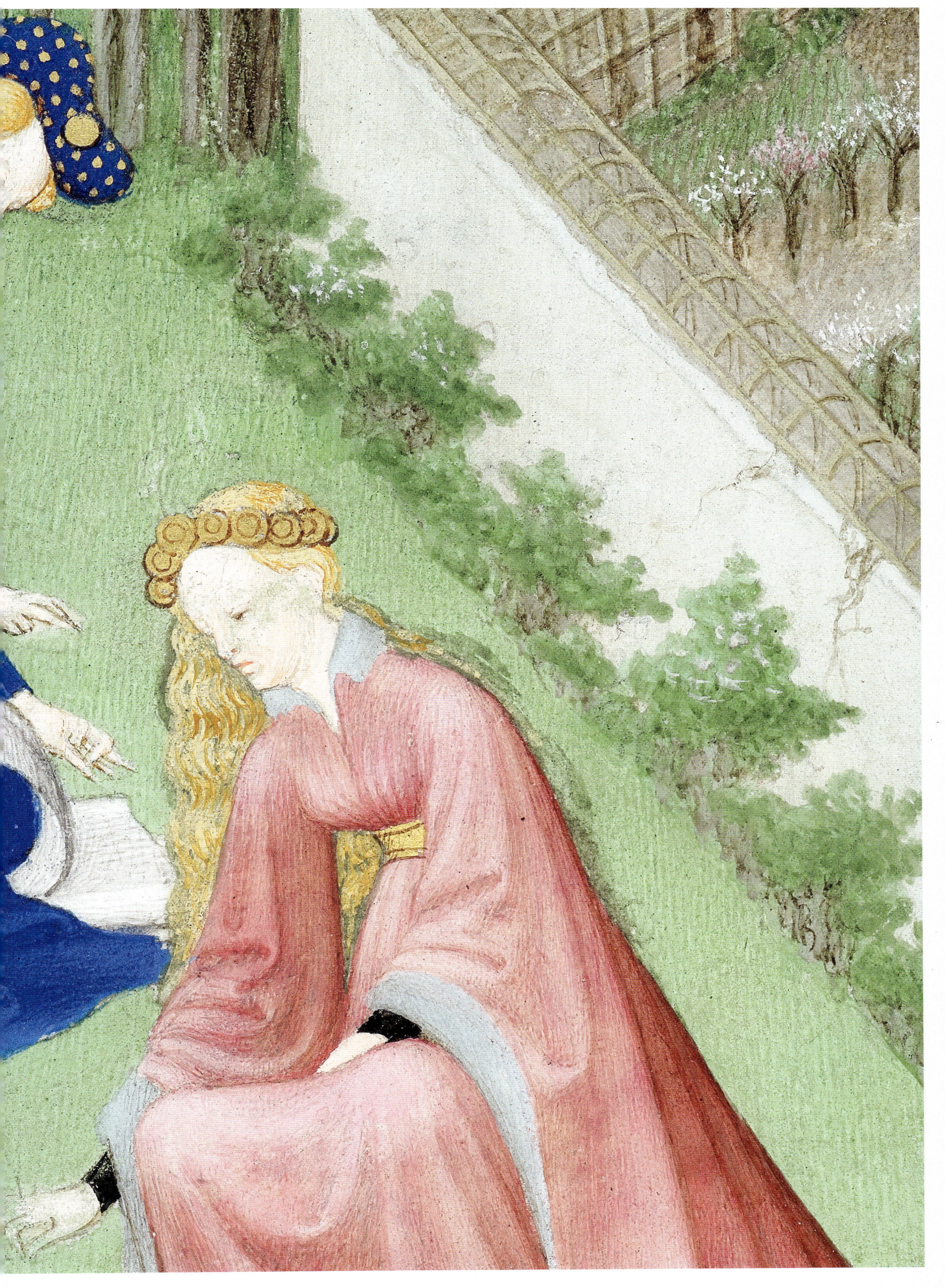

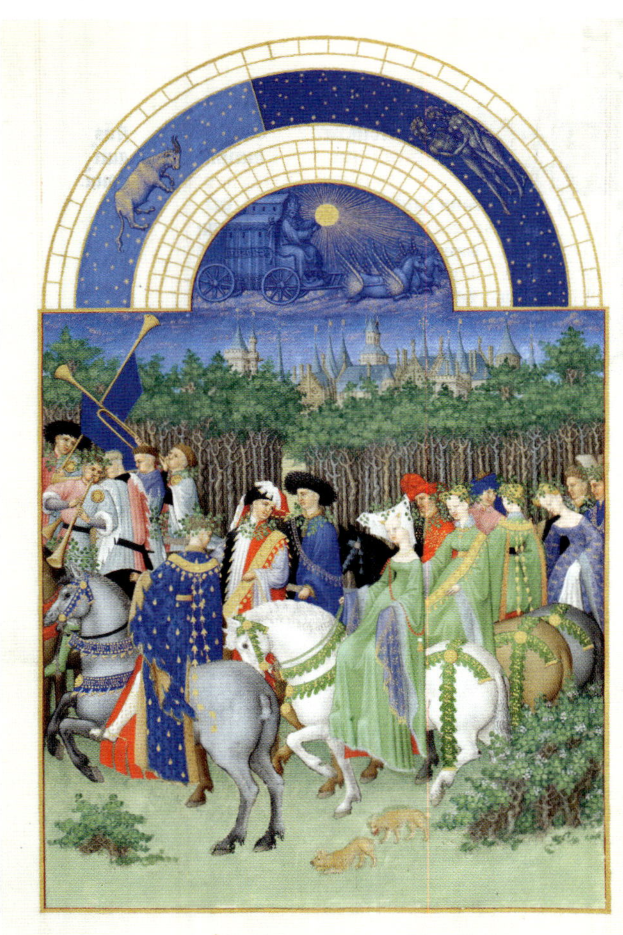

Van Lymborch brothers, *Très Riches Heures*, fol. 5v: May

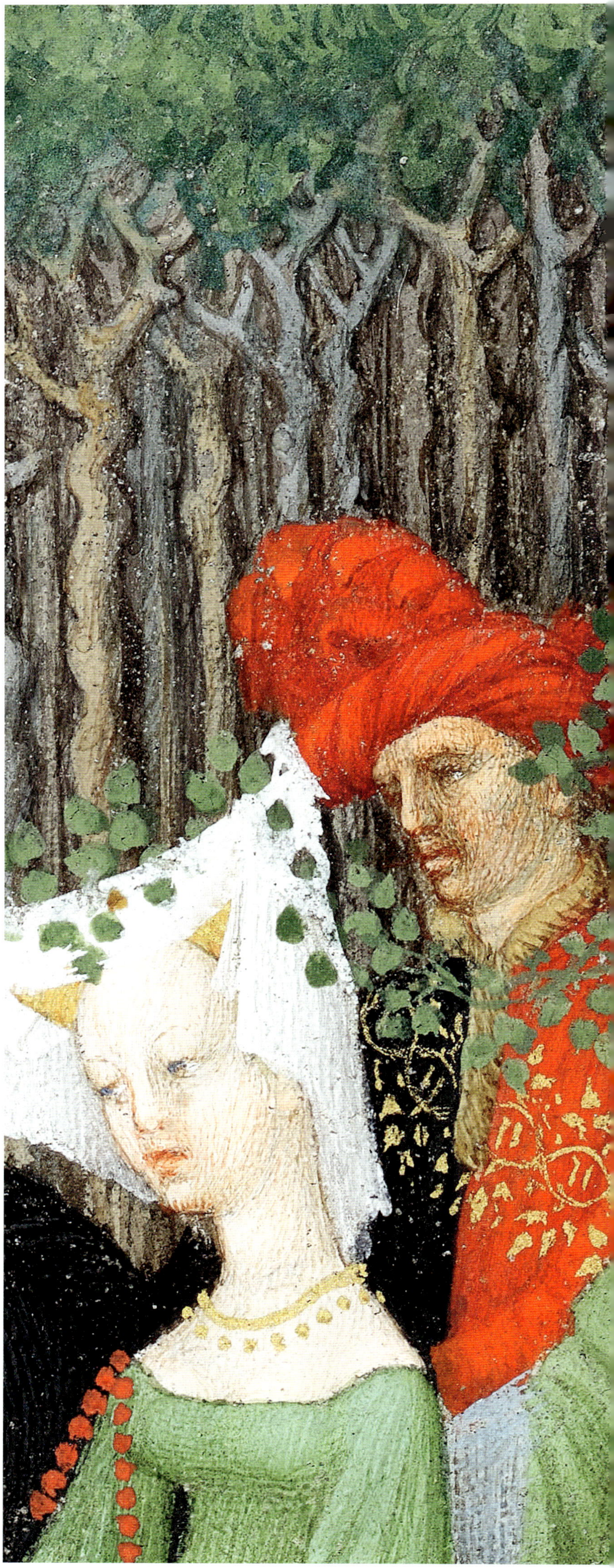

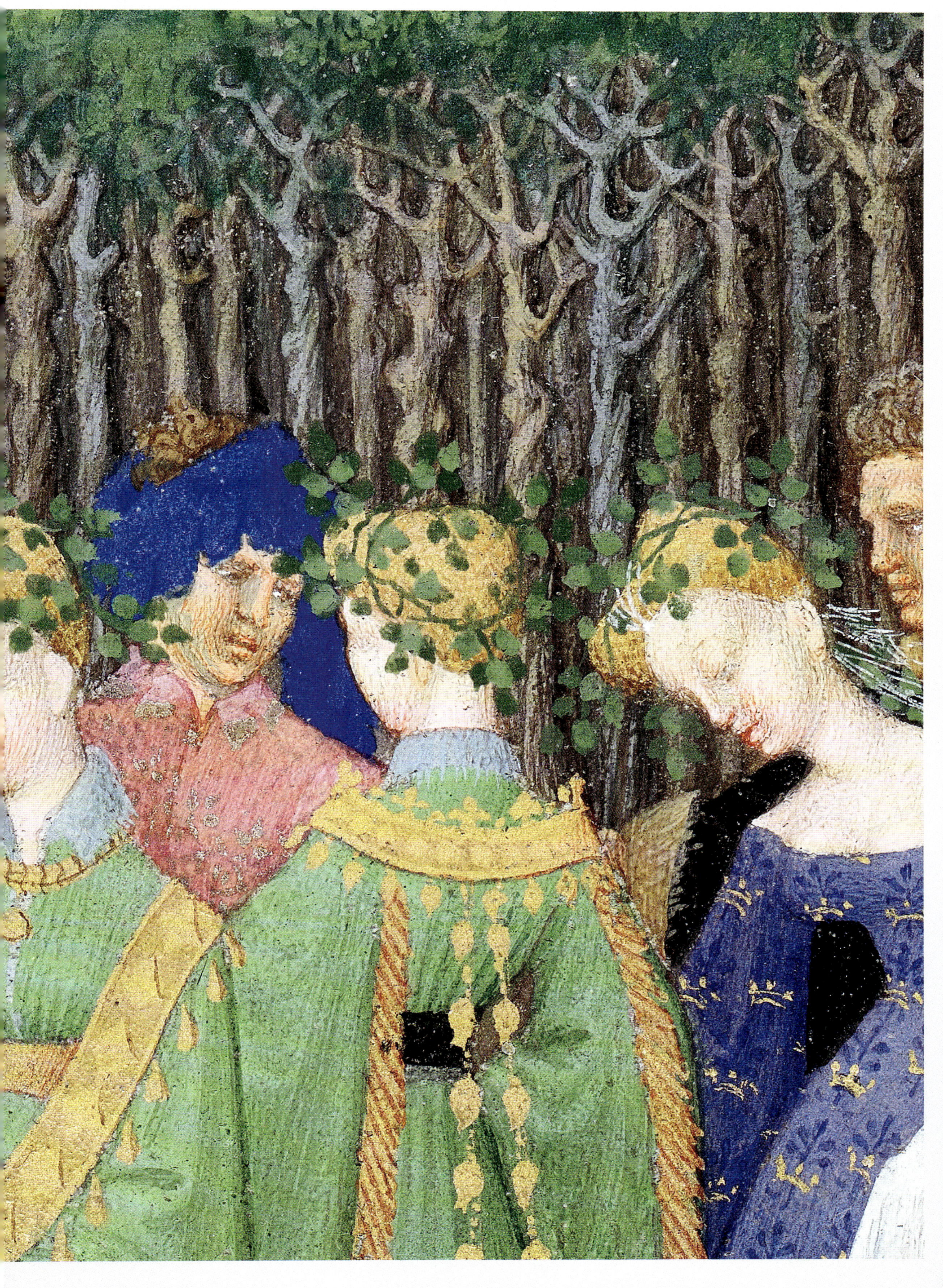

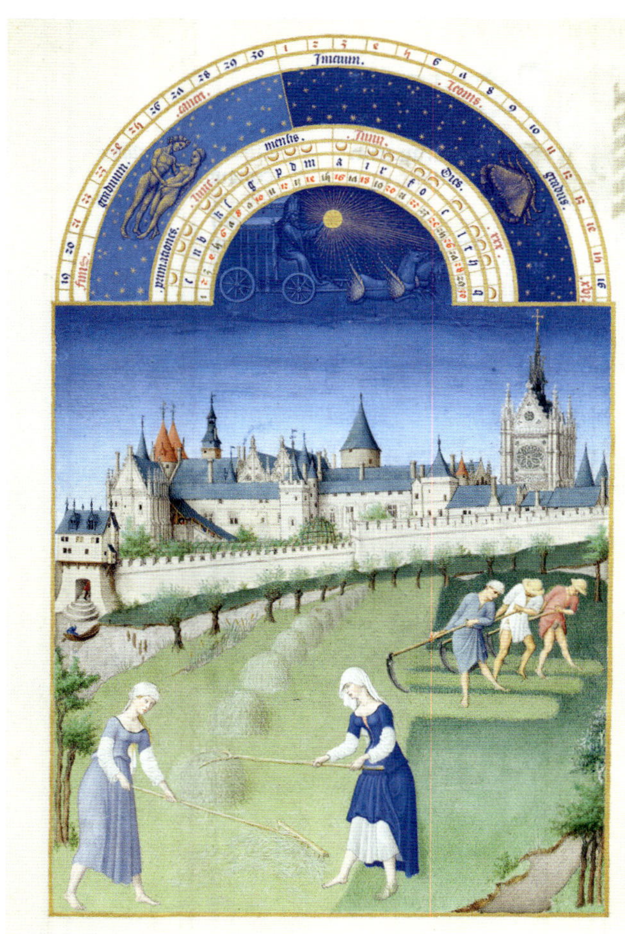

Van Lymborch brothers, *Très Riches Heures*, fol. 6v: June

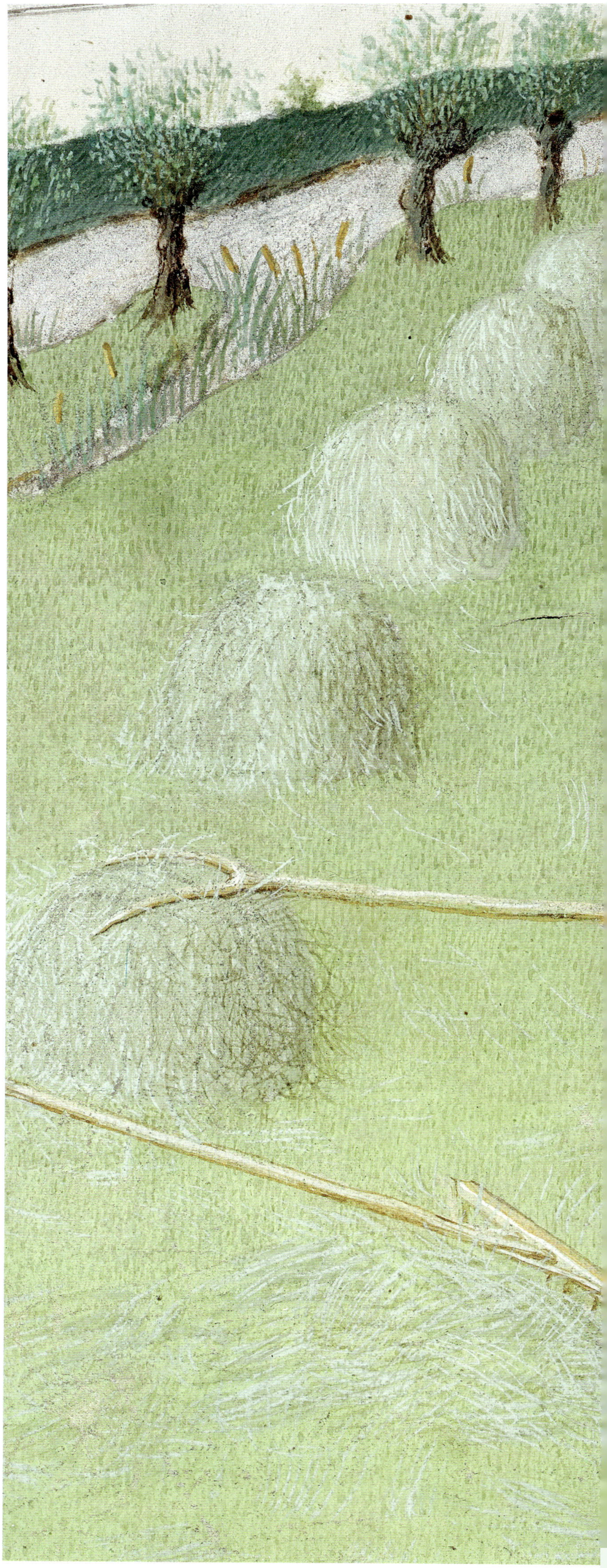

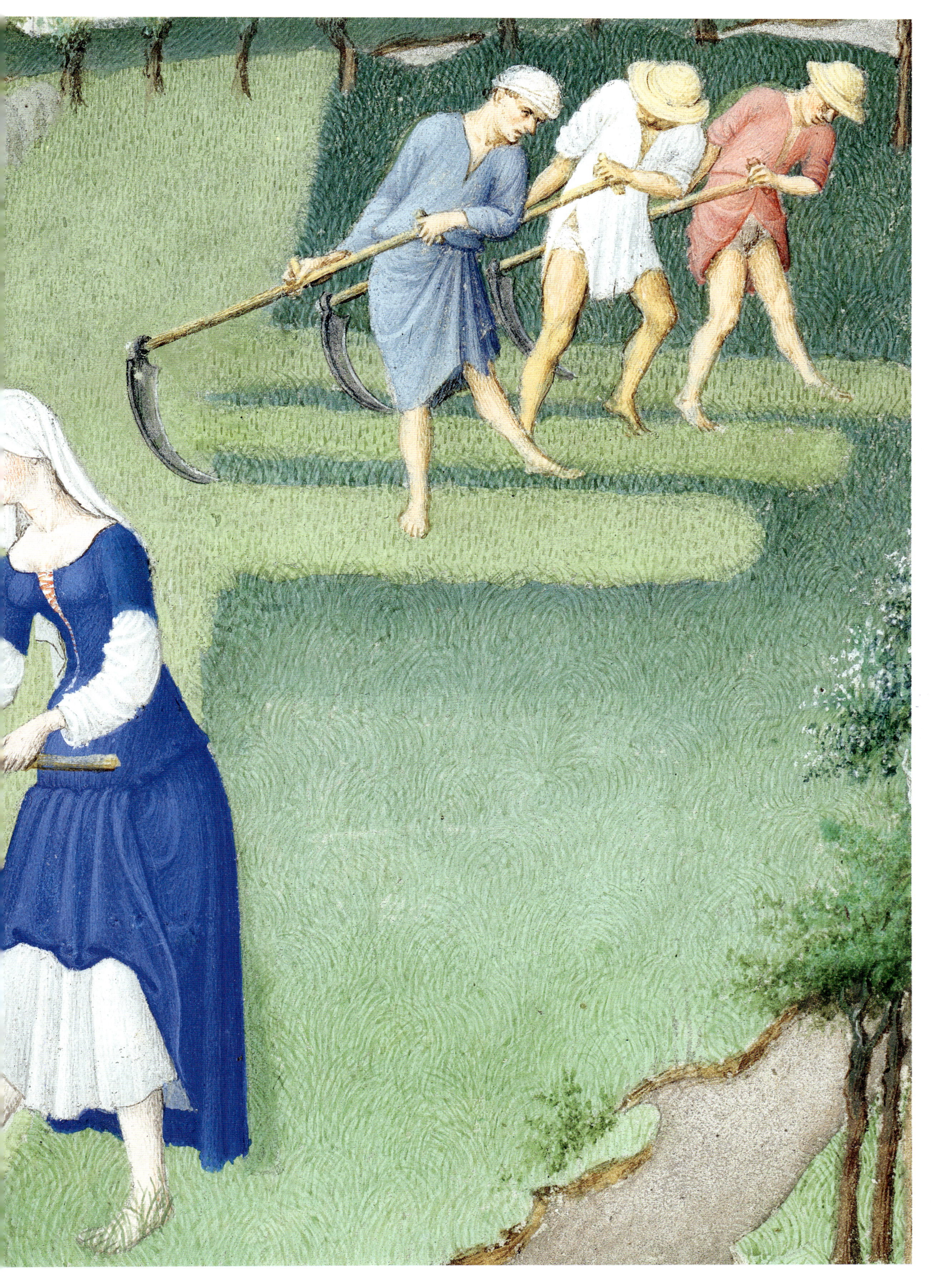

# THE OTHER DECORATION CAMPAIGNS

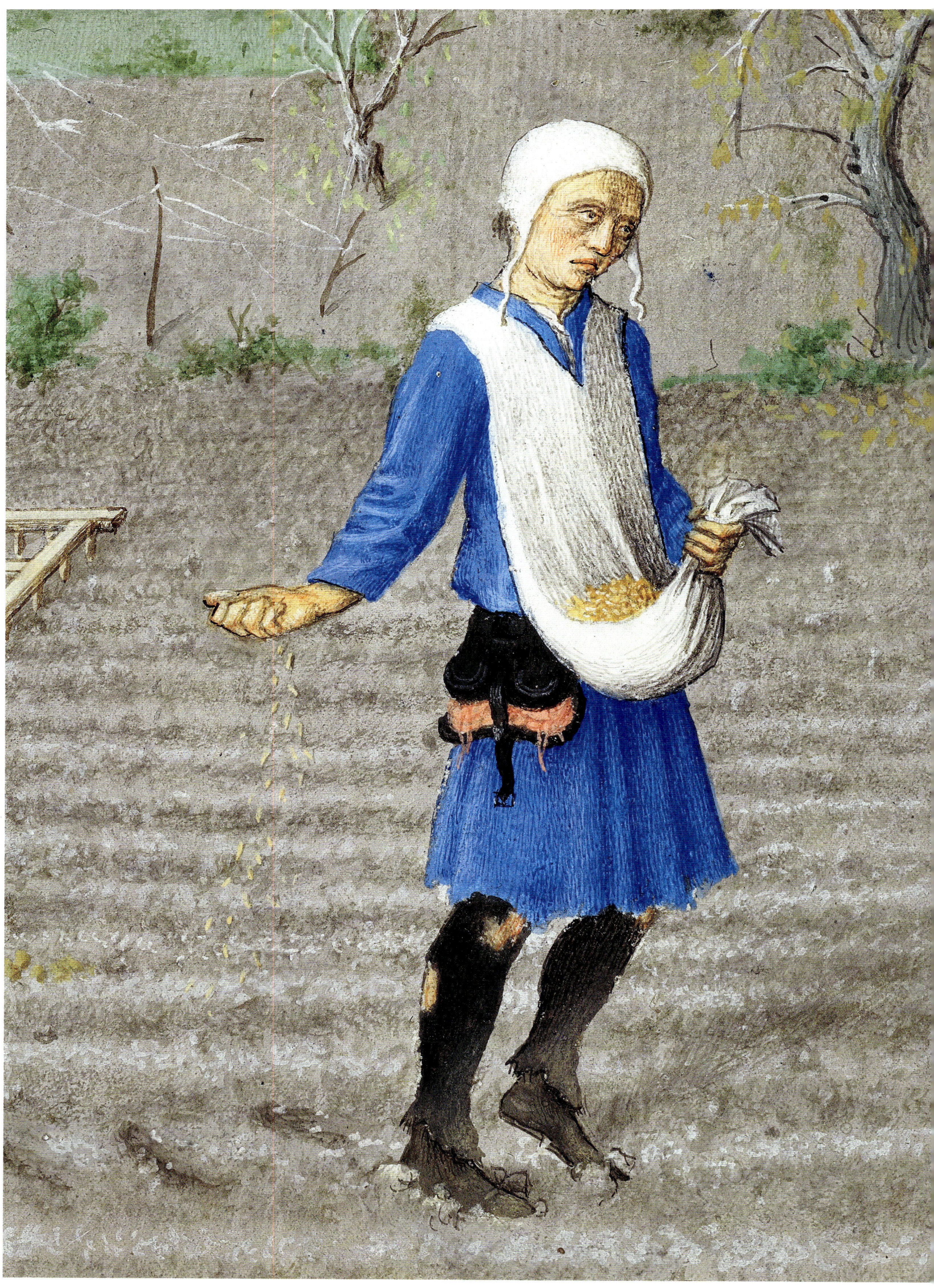

13.

# The Contribution of Barthélemy d'Eyck, Master of the Uncompleted

Mathieu Deldicque

While the Van Lymborch brothers and Jean Colombe are mentioned in fifteenth-century archives as having participated in the decoration of the *Très Riches Heures du duc de Berry*, no trace is found of other decoration campaigns or other intermediary hands. Over time, however, specialists have identified another figure who made substantial innovations in the calendar and helped to turn the famous manuscript into the meeting point of many generations of artists in the last century of the Middle Ages, all of whom contributed to making it a testament of Gothic art and the cradle of a nascent Renaissance in embryonic form.

Some of the pages that Millard Meiss attributed to a Paul van Lymborch ahead of his time[1] were first removed by Luciano Bellosi. He suggested instead that another painter, active in the mid-fifteenth century, was responsible for some of the miniatures for the months of March, June, September, October, and December,[2] namely three bifolia left uncompleted by the Van Lymborch brothers in the second quire. In addition to these five illuminations, the Procession of St. Gregory or the Institution of the Great Litany (fols. 71v–72; fig. 3, pp. 146–47) were also attributed to him.[3] Initially, it was the cut of the costumes worn by the characters in the scenes in question that drew attention: In the month of October, for example (fig. 2), the figures strolling along the banks of the Seine are dressed in short tunics in dark colors, beige or black, and hats typical of the 1440s that Philip the Good would not

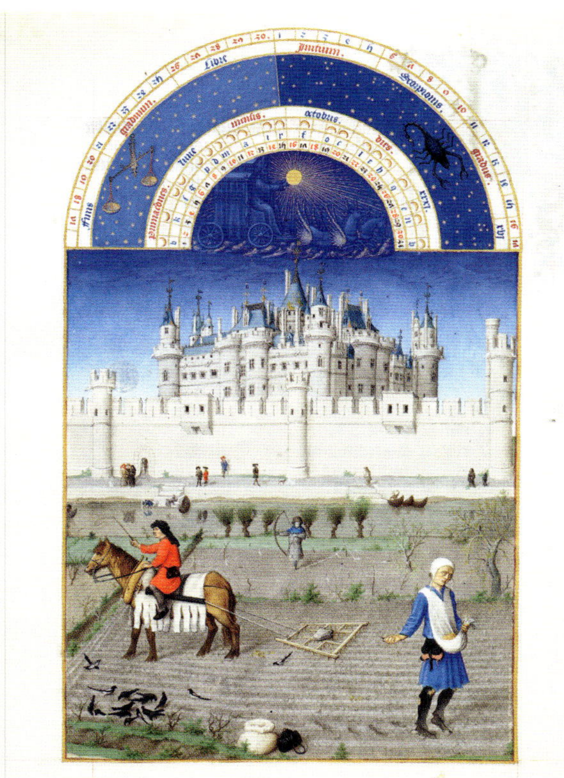

**Fig. 2** Barthélemy d'Eyck, *Très Riches Heures*, fol. 10v: October

**Fig. 1** Barthélemy d'Eyck, *Très Riches Heures*, fol. 10v: October, detail

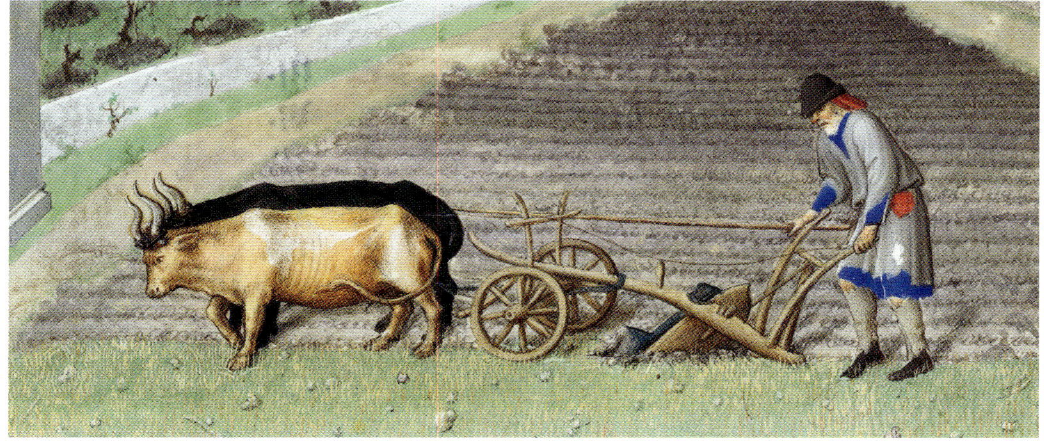

**Fig. 3** Barthélemy d'Eyck (over an underdrawing by the Van Lymborch brothers), *Très Riches Heures*, fol. 3v: March, detail

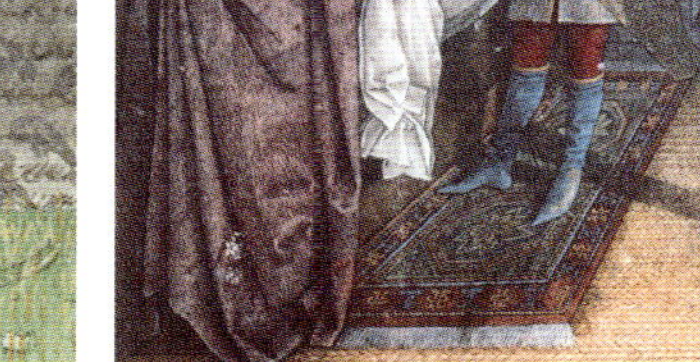

**Fig. 4** Barthélemy d'Eyck, The Dream of King René: Cuer's Heart Is Given over to Desire, in René of Anjou, *Book of the Love-Smitten Heart*, fol. 2 (Vienna, Österreichische Nationalbibliothek, Codex Vindobonensis 2597)

have disowned in the frontispiece of the *Chronicles of Hainaut* painted by Rogier van der Weyden in 1446–47.[4]

However, beyond a style of dress whose precise dating, in particular that of its dissemination to certain regions, gives rise to much debate, it was a stylistic analysis that made it possible to recognize the intermediary master in question, whose identification is now barely disputed.[5] According to Bellosi, the illuminator in question, whom he called the "Master of the Second Quire," was well acquainted with Flemish innovations and betrayed a pronounced Eyckian character. Paying close attention to reality, he employed pictorial principles unknown to the Van Lymborch brothers thirty years earlier, such as reflections of buildings or plants in the transparent waters, and above all the phenomenon of shadows, such as that cast by the plowman, plow, and oxen in March (fig. 3), a pictorial innovation that only broke through in the 1420s, in both northern and southern Europe, in the wake of the great masters Jan van Eyck and Masaccio.

According to Bellosi, this artist moved in the entourage of Charles VII and René of Anjou and had painted miniatures in which the châteaux in the background had no obvious connection with the possessions of the Duke of Berry (Saumur, Vincennes, Louvre, Palais de la Cité). However, this was to ignore the fact that, in addition to their actual links with the Duke of Berry,[6] these buildings had indeed been either painted or drawn by the Van Lymborch brothers, and that they were in fact pages left unfinished by the latter. Bellosi recognized the hand as that of the Master of King René, also known as the Master of the Love-Smitten Heart, after the famous manuscript in the Austrian National Library (fig. 4), whose author was King René himself. The discovery of the joint participation of this still-anonymous illuminator and Enguerrand Quarton in the decoration of a book of hours[7] with links to the *Annunciation* painting in Aix-en-Provence—executed around 1443–44 for Pierre Corpici, King René's supplier, for his chapel within the cathedral—and that of a document linking Quarton and an illuminator[8] subsequently made it possible to identify the Master of the Love-Smitten Heart and the Master of the Aix Annunciation with one and the same artist: Barthélemy d'Eyck.[9]

## KING RENÉ'S PAINTER

Barthélemy d'Eyck was the son of a certain Ydria Exters, originally from the region of Maaseik in the diocese of Liège, and probably related on his father's side to the Van Eyck brothers, whom he may have been in contact with in the 1430s, perhaps during his formative years (perhaps in Bruges, where Jan Van Eyck went regularly on his multiple missions and travels for the Duke of Burgundy). He is first documented in Aix-en-Provence in 1444 (alongside Enguerrand Quarton). We then find him in the service of King René of Anjou, from 1446 to the early 1470s, as valet, carving valet (in charge of cutting the meats), and then equerry to this great patron of the arts. Perhaps it was during King René's trip to Flanders in 1433 that the artist caught his eye. He probably entered his service around 1435 and remained there for more than thirty years, enjoying (like the Van Lymborch brothers and the Duke of Berry) a relationship whose closeness is revealed by the layout of the sovereign's apartments; for example, the artist had the use of recessed cabinets adjoining the king's apartments in his various residences between Provence and Anjou.[10] He was a versatile artist, a panel painter, banner painter, illuminator, and designer of embroidery models for the king and his entourage. A court painter who lived nobly, having spent much of his career in Provence, he ended his days in Anjou, where we lose track of him after 1471–72.

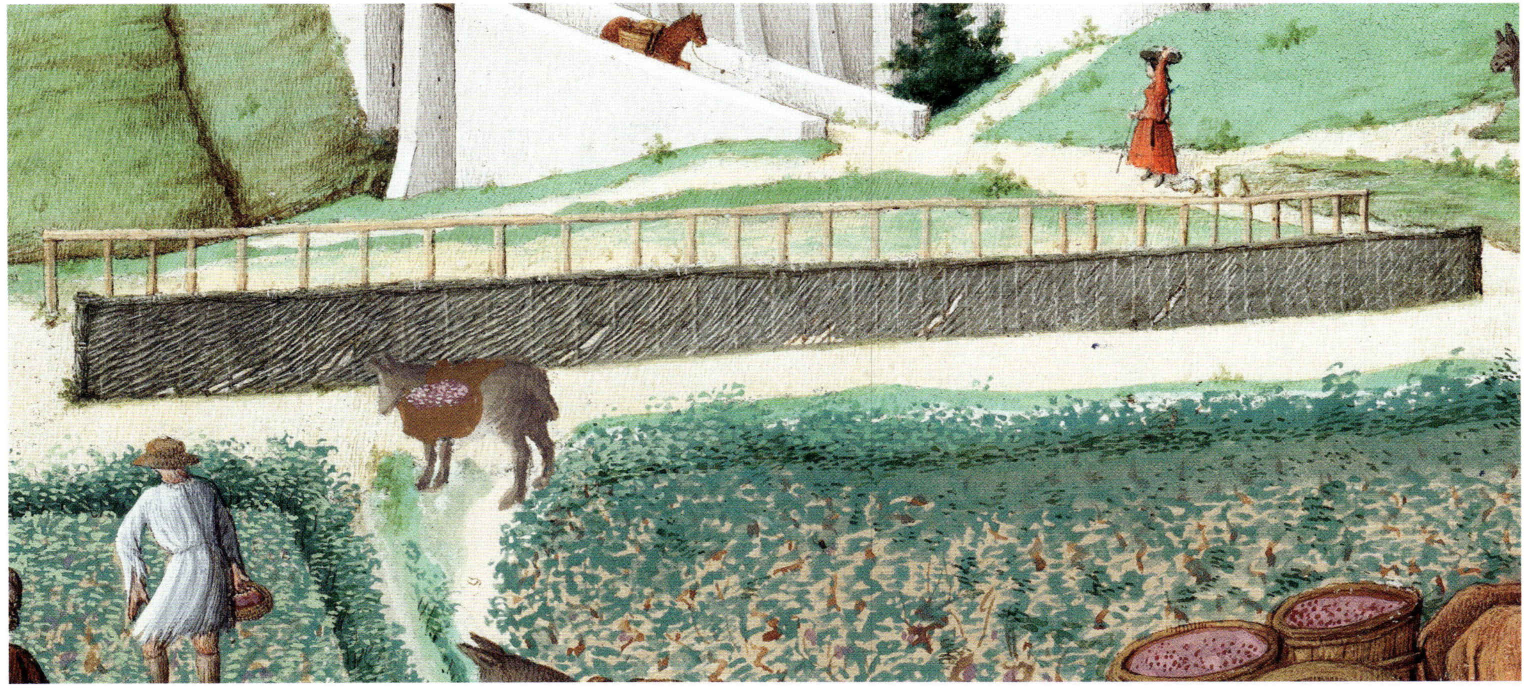

**Fig. 5** Barthélemy d'Eyck, *Très Riches Heures*, fol. 9v: September, detail

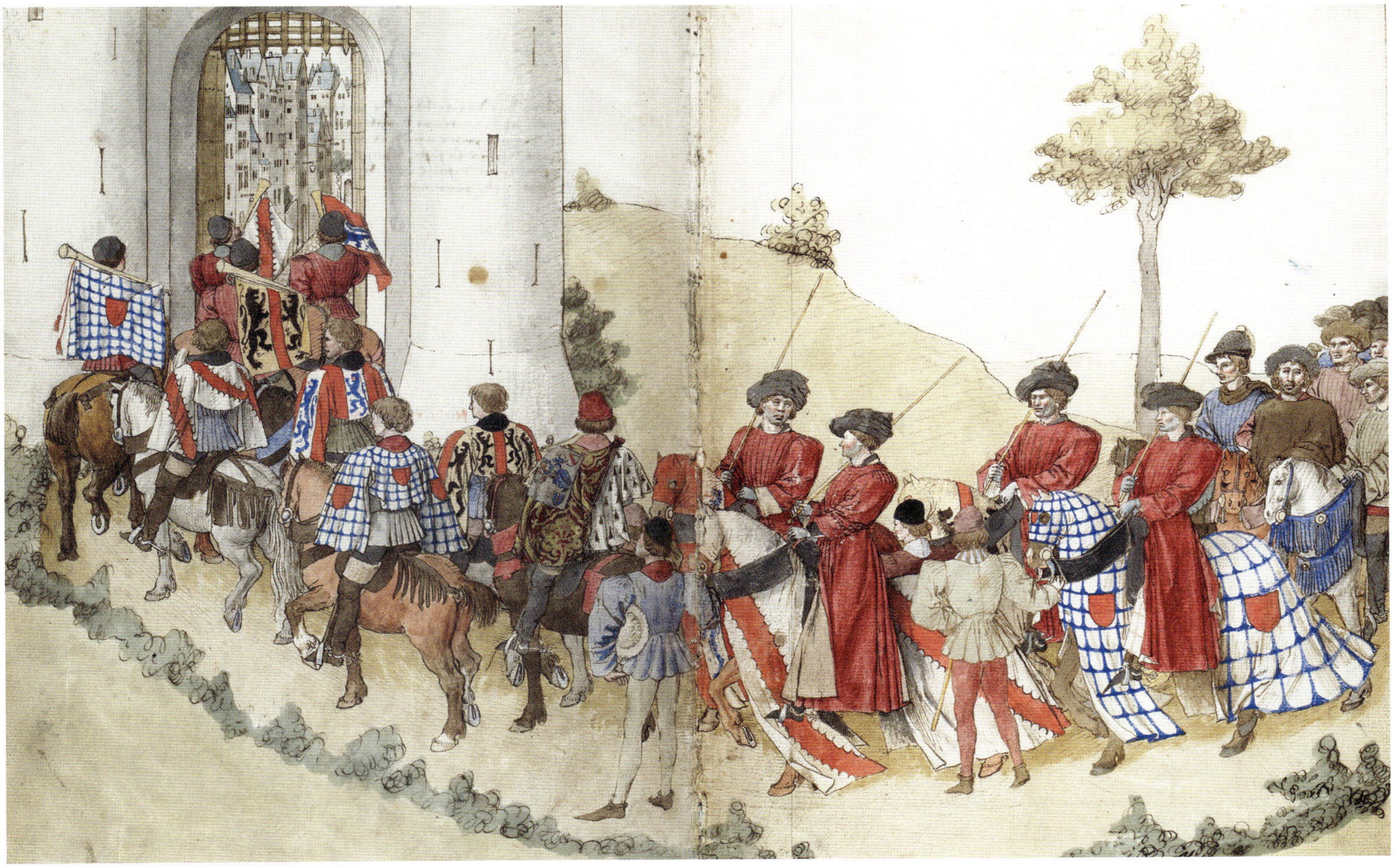

**Fig. 6** Barthélemy d'Eyck, The Heraldic Judges Make Their Entrance, in René of Anjou, *Tournament Book*, fols. 57v–58 (Paris, Bibliothèque nationale de France, département des Manuscrits, Français 2695)

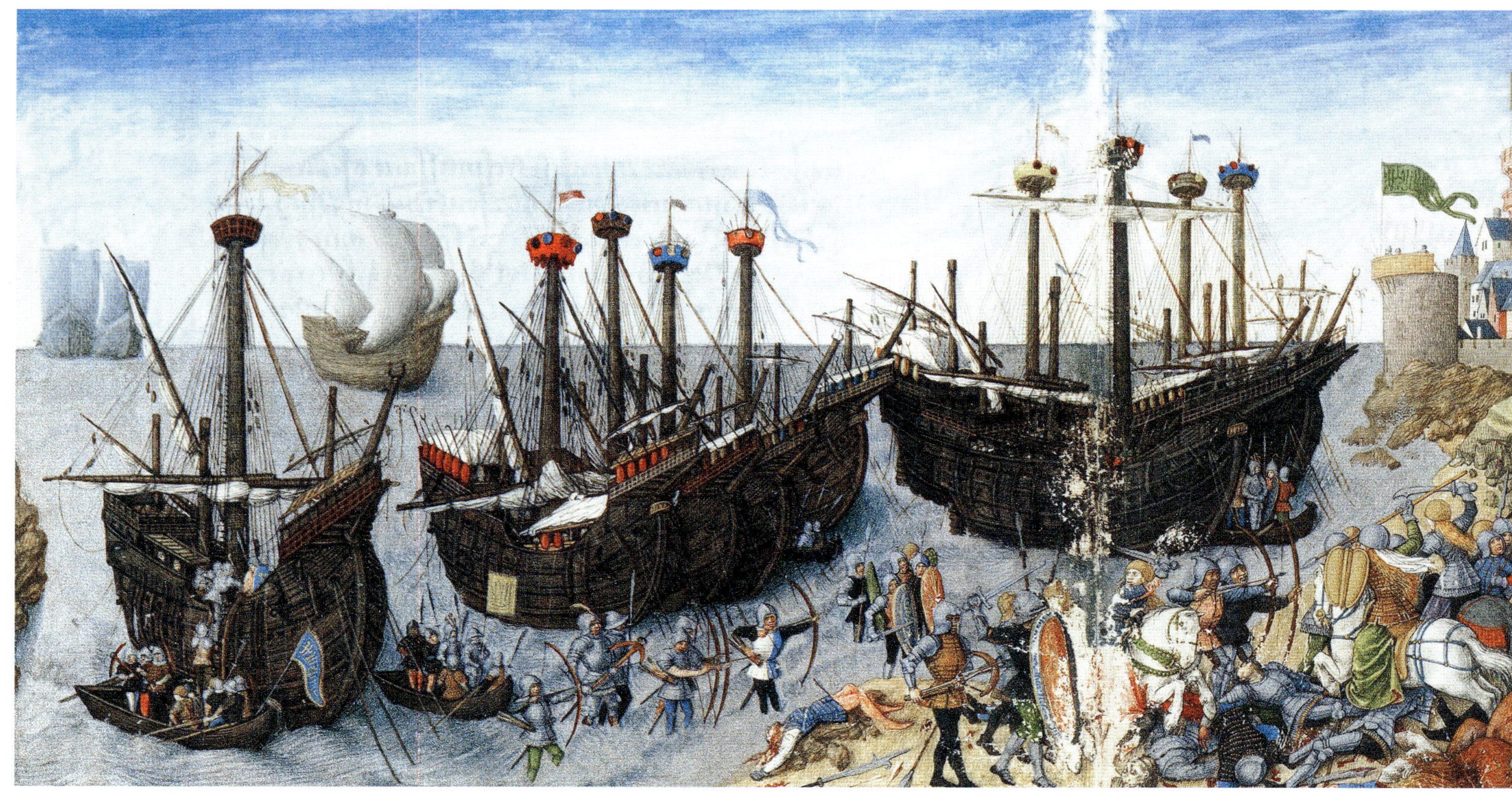

**Fig. 7** Barthélemy d'Eyck, Theseus's Victory over the Amazons, in Boccaccio, *Teseida*, fols. 18v–19 (Vienna, Österreichische Nationalbibliothek, Codex Vindobonensis 2617)

Barthélemy d'Eyck's greatest masterpieces were executed in the 1460s, foremost among which are the *Heures du René d'Anjou* (between 1459 and 1463),[11] Boccaccio's *Teseida* (c. 1460; fig. 7),[12] the *Tournament Book* (*Livre des tournois*, c. 1464–65; fig. 6),[13] and, of course, the *Book of the Love-Smitten Heart* (*Livre du Cœur d'amour épris*, c. 1465; fig. 9),[14] the latter two both written by René of Anjou.

### THE "PAS DE SAUMUR" OF 1446

While no document links Barthélemy d'Eyck to the *Très Riches Heures*, chronological markers can be established through observation and comparison. For instance, Patricia Stirnemann has suggested that the miniature of September contains, at the foot of the Château de Saumur, a reminder of the "Pas de Saumur," a famous tournament organized there in the summer of 1446 by the chivalry-loving King René in honor of Charles VII and attended by more than a hundred participants (fig. 5). A tilt barrier is indeed visible in front of the vines, separated by a wicker parapet, and, to the right, is a cluster of white columns—the remains of marble steps originally guarded by lions and a dwarf—to which was attached the shield that the joust participants had to strike with their spears.[15] This element is a *terminus post quem* for the miniature's execution. Were the pages completed by King René's illuminator in Saumur itself, in a relatively short period of time during the actual tournament (June 26 to August 7, 1446)? This would explain why this second campaign itself remained unfinished. In any case, the presence of so many potential owners of the manuscript at this event—Jean de Dunois, Charles VII, King René, but also the ladies of their entourage and their retinue—opens up the field of possibilities.[16]

### IN THE FOOTSTEPS OF THE VAN LYMBORCH BROTHERS

The *Très Riches Heures* inspired Barthélemy d'Eyck throughout his career, so much so that the works that most demonstrate the artist's admiration for the decoration of this work are further markers that help to date his own work. The book of hours in the Morgan Library, to which Barthélemy contributed around 1445–50, takes up certain formulas from the *Très Riches Heures*, including the famous banquet of the Van Lymborch brothers from February (fol. 2) and the iconic figure of the sower (November, fol. 11) taken from October, imagined by the Van Lymborch brothers and completed by Eyck.[17]

His later works also seem to have assimilated the lesson of the brothers from Nijmegen. The wonderful chiaroscuro of their night scenes (142v; fig. 2, p. 145, and fol. 153) appears to have left a lasting impression on him. Such chiaroscuro is also evident in the twilights and nocturnal light of the scenes in the *Book of the Love-Smitten Heart* (fig. 4). The layout of several pages also owes a debt to the Van Lymborch brothers: In the *Tournament Book* (fols. 57v–58), when the heraldic judges make their entrance (fig. 6),[18] the open gates of the town reveal the houses clustered along the main street, as can be seen in the Procession of St. Gregory in the *Très Riches Heures*.

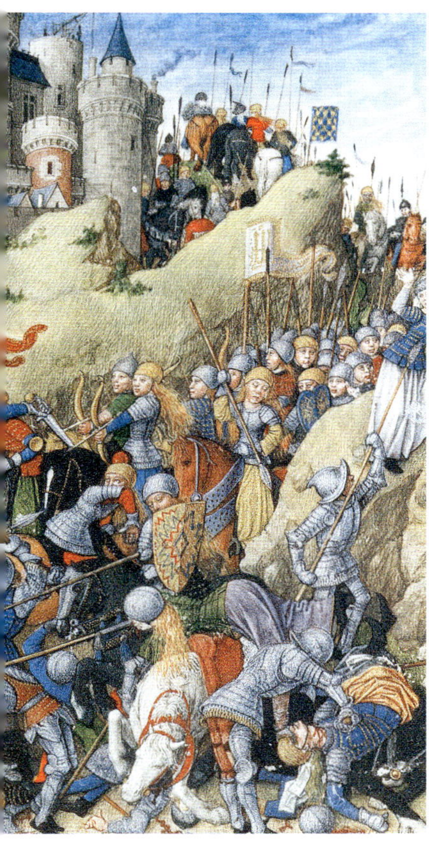

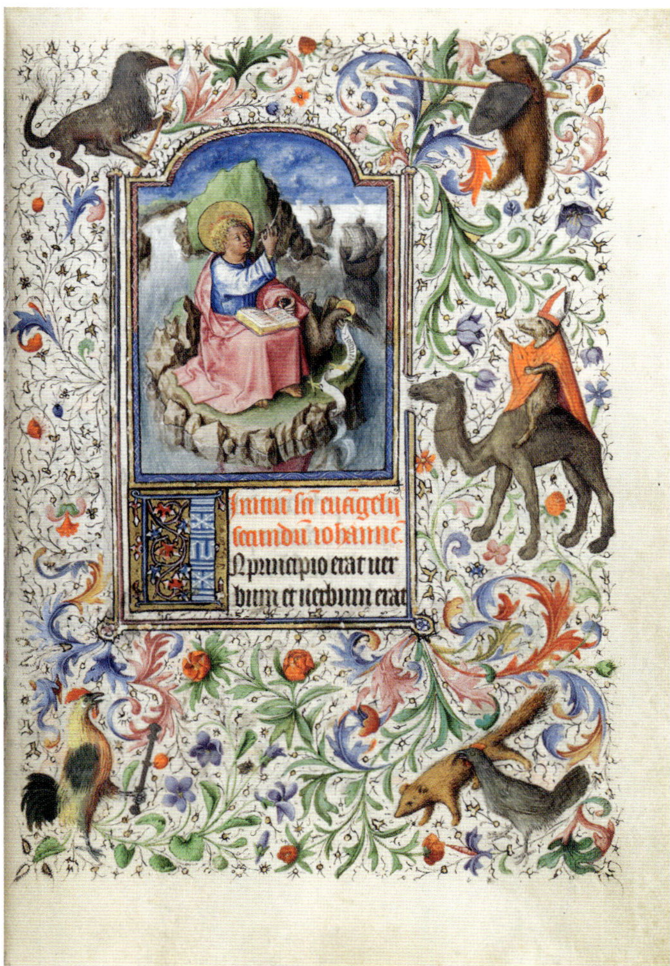

**Fig. 8** Barthélemy d'Eyck and Enguerrand Quarton, fol. 13: St. John on the island of Patmos, in *Hours for the Use of Rome*, Provence, c. 1447 (New York, The Morgan Library & Museum, MS M.358)

The presence of a château displaying sumptuous architecture in the background of the scene of the Liberation of Arcita in the *Teseida* (fol. 64) or of Theseus's Victory over the Amazons (fols. 18v–19; fig. 7) demonstrates his adherence to the Van Lymborch topos. The latter example shows that, following in their footsteps, Barthélemy d'Eyck set out to conquer the illuminated double-page spread.

His contribution to the *Très Riches Heures* was respectful and ultimately relatively modest. He was content to complete the scenes sketched by the Van Lymborch brothers and almost never set to work on a blank leaf (except for September). In fact, he never even completed his own work: The month of September was completed by Jean Colombe. This new element definitively invalidates the hypothesis that Barthélemy d'Eyck added a château linked to the Anjou family and his patron King René. In fact, the artist merely continued a pre-existing image.

However, these miniatures clearly reveal his language and style[19]: the impassive, almost sullen faces, the slightly bulging eyes with black pupils raised to the heavens, the white complexions contrasting with the rosy complexions of the Van Lymborch brothers' figures. The famous shadows, of course, found much later, in his *Tournament Book* and his *Book of the Love-Smitten Heart* (fig. 9), the bold reflections on water in the months of June and especially October, transposed to the surface of the seas surrounding St. John on the island of Patmos (fig. 8), in the book of hours partly illuminated by Barthélemy d'Eyck are all personal traits of the artist. Like the Van Lymborch brothers, he paid attention to the trivial details of everyday life. The dung left by the horse on

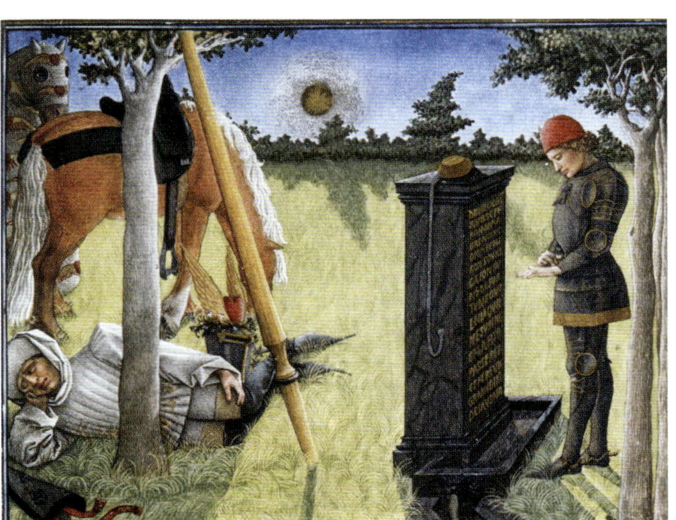

**Fig. 9** Barthélemy d'Eyck, Cuer Reads the Inscription Engraved on Fortune's Fountain at Dawn, in René of Anjou, *Book of the Love-Smitten Heart*, fol. 15 (Vienna, Österreichische Nationalbibliothek, Codex Vindobonensis 2597)

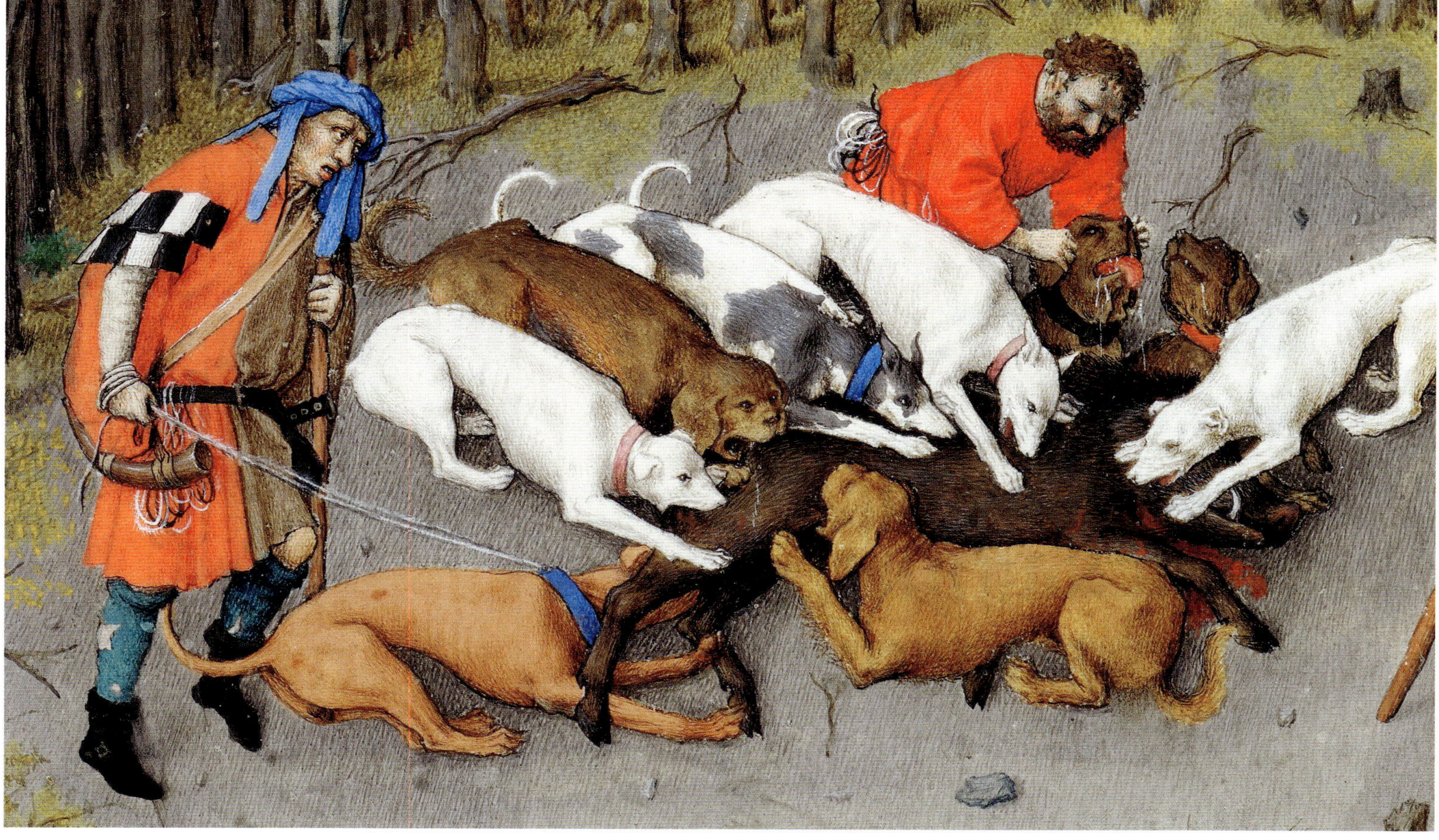

**Fig. 10** Barthélemy d'Eyck (over an underdrawing by the Van Lymborch brothers), *Très Riches Heures*, fol. 12v: December, detail

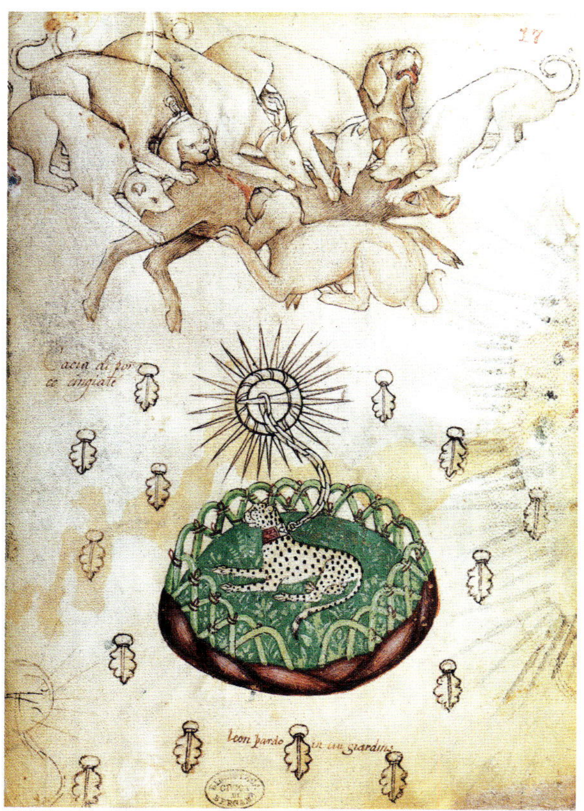


**Fig. 11** Workshop of Giovannino de' Grassi, Wild Boar Hunt, in *Sketchbook*. Milan or Pavia, last decade of 14th c., fol. 17 (Bergamo, Palazzo Nuovo, Biblioteca Civica Angelo Mai, Cassaf. 1.21)

the ploughed field (and which the magpie almost seems to covet), the inhabitants of Paris washing their clothes in the Seine in October, the dogs foaming at the mouth over the wild boar in December: Aren't these the worthy successors of the swimmer in August, who floats freely in the Van Lymborch brothers' distant pond, or the peasants warming their private parts by the warmth of the fire in February? A key player in the dissemination of Flemish *Ars nova*,[20] Barthélemy d'Eyck defended a more direct approach to the world and gave free rein to that Nordic sensibility to detailed verisimilitude whose seeds were already present in his predecessors.

## TO ITALY AND BACK?

Much has been written about Barthélemy d'Eyck's probable trip to the Italian peninsula and the traces that such a journey would have left on the pages of the *Très Riches Heures*.[21] According to the will of Jeanne II, the last Angevin queen on the throne of Naples, who died in 1435 without issue, René had inherited the title of King of Sicily and Jerusalem, as well as the County of Provence. He occupied Naples from May 1438 to June 1442 before relinquishing the throne to his opponent, Alfonso of Aragon. This period coincided with the introduction of *Ars nova* in Naples, notably through the painters Colantonio and Antonello da Messina. Did Barthélemy d'Eyck follow King René to Naples, where his father-in-law, the embroiderer Pierre du Billant, is recorded in January 1440?[22]

This would explain the openness of the Neapolitan milieu to *Ars nova*. Indeed, this is the hypothesis put forward by Nicole Reynaud, who attributes to Barthélemy d'Eyck the leaves from the so-called *Cockerell Chronicle*, a copy of the *Universal Chronicle* illuminated by a Lombard painter present in Naples, Leonardo da Besozzo.[23] Was it absolutely necessary to make the journey to Italy to gain access to this manuscript? Chased out of Naples, René and his retinue returned to France via Florence, then the capital of the Quattrocento, the Florence of Fra Angelico, Domenico Veneziano, and Donatello,[24] then via the north of the peninsula. In reality, the Italianisms of Barthélemy d'Eyck attributed to these potential artistic encounters are not so obvious. Ultimately, there is only one clearly Italian-inspired element in the pages of the *Très Riches Heures du duc de Berry*. In December (fig. 10), the ferocious hallali or bugle call sounding the death of a wild boar stems from a Lombard model, which has come down to us via a sketchbook from the workshop of Giovannino de' Grassi, an illuminator in the service of the Viscontis (fig. 11). Critics are divided: Is this a motif sketched by the Van Lymborch brothers and painted by Barthélemy d'Eyck,[25] or a scene due entirely to the latter?[26] Proponents of the latter hypothesis have speculated that the painter accompanied King René to see the collections of illuminated manuscripts of the Viscontis in Pavia (where Giovannino de' Grassi's composition was available), perhaps during another stay in Italy by the sovereign in 1453. Here again, analyses carried out for the present catalog shed a definitive light on the question. The preparatory drawing for the hallali is indeed by the Van Lymborch brothers, who thus had access to the Lombard model, as some had conjectured. Barthélemy d'Eyck colored in and completed the composition, particularly with regard to the whip; this explains the awkward cohabitation of the dogs, almost levitating above the ground of the clearing, and the whips, whose dimensions are somewhat disproportionate to their animals. The artist allowed himself a certain amount of freedom, relinquishing a number of typical Van Lymborch details at the painting stage.

## BARTHÉLEMY D'EYCK'S FERTILE *NON FINITO*

Barthélemy d'Eyck's intervention in the famous manuscript happened therefore rather discreetly, in small touches: certain parts of the months of March, June, September, October, and December. He almost never tackled an entirely blank leaf, except, most likely, in the month of September (whereas the boar hunt scene was drawn by the Van Lymborch brothers). Contrary to what has been suggested,[27] we should not look for his hand in the Procession of St. Gregory, drawn by the Van Lymborch brothers and completed by Jean Colombe[28] (fol. 71v–72). His work was sporadic, and the artist even abandoned a miniature in progress, that of September (fol. 9v), which he left to Colombe. This *non finito* was in fact almost a habit with Barthélemy d'Eyck, as many of his masterpieces were left in a state of incompletion.

There is no certainty that the *Très Riches Heures* ever belonged to King René, even though the memory of the Pas de Saumur and the involvement of his favorite illuminator may support this hypothesis. It should nevertheless be noted that the great bibliophile entrusted at least one other unfinished manuscript to his painter, the Egerton Hours,[29] also in the early 1440s. Finally, when Jean Colombe took over from Barthélemy d'Eyck in the decoration of the *Très Riches Heures*, it was not the first time that the illuminator from Bourges was completing what his predecessor had left behind. Already around 1470–75, he had illuminated his sketches in a copy of *Mortifiement de vaine plaisance* (The mortification of vain pleasure), composed by René of Anjou.[30] In the mid-fifteenth century, through the *Très Riches Heures* and other masterpieces, the true personality of Barthélemy d'Eyck came into view, that of a conduit.

1 Meiss 1974a, I, 195–201. Châtelet 2010 still attributes these pages to the Van Lymborch brothers and rejects the intermediary master.
2 Bellosi 1975. König 1976 evoked the "October painter."
3 König 1976, 100 note 2.
4 Brussels, KBR, Ms. 9242.
5 See Châtelet 1998 or Reynolds 2005 for another viewpoint.
6 See essay by M. Deldicque, pp. 45–57.
7 Avril 1977.
8 Sterling 1983, 11–15, 127–37, 173–83.
9 On the rediscovery of Barthélemy d'Eyck by historians, see Thiébaut 2004.
10 On Barthélemy d'Eyck, see Reynaud 1989; F. Avril in Paris 1993–94, 224–25; Thiébaut 2004; Ferré 2009.
11 Paris, BnF, Ms. Latin 17332.
12 Vienna, ÖNB, Ms. Cod. Vind. 2617.
13 Paris, BnF, Ms. Français 2695.
14 Vienna, ÖNB, Ms. Cod. Vind. 2597.
15 Stirnemann 2021. On the relation between the Pas de Saumur held in 1446 and the later manuscript representing it (Saint-Petersburg, National Library of Russia, Ms. fr. F. p. XIV, 4), see Angers 2009–10, no. 12.
16 See by M. Deldicque, pp. 286–89.
17 See essay by É. Ravaud, pp. 342–44.
18 Gautier and Hermant 2024, 13.
19 For other examples, see the insightful analyses of Villela-Petit 2013c.
20 Deldicque 2024b.
21 Beyer 2002; Thiébaut 2006, 40–47; Toscano 2024.
22 Robin 1985, 81.
23 Reynaud 1989; Paris 1993–94, no. 121.
24 Angelini 2018.
25 Meiss 1974a, I, 214–16; Scheller 1995, 276–91; Schmidt 2005, 181–82.
26 Bellosi 1975; Sricchia Santoro 2017, 30, 52 note 44; Toscano 2024, 250–51.
27 König 1996, 77; Villela-Petit 2013c, 137.
28 See essay by É. Ravaud, pp. 344–45.
29 London, BL, Ms. Egerton 1070. Angers 2009–10, no. 2.
30 Metz, BM, Ms. 1486.

**Fig. 12** Following pages: Barthélemy d'Eyck (over an underdrawing by the Van Lymborch brothers), *Très Riches Heures*, fol. 12v: December, detail

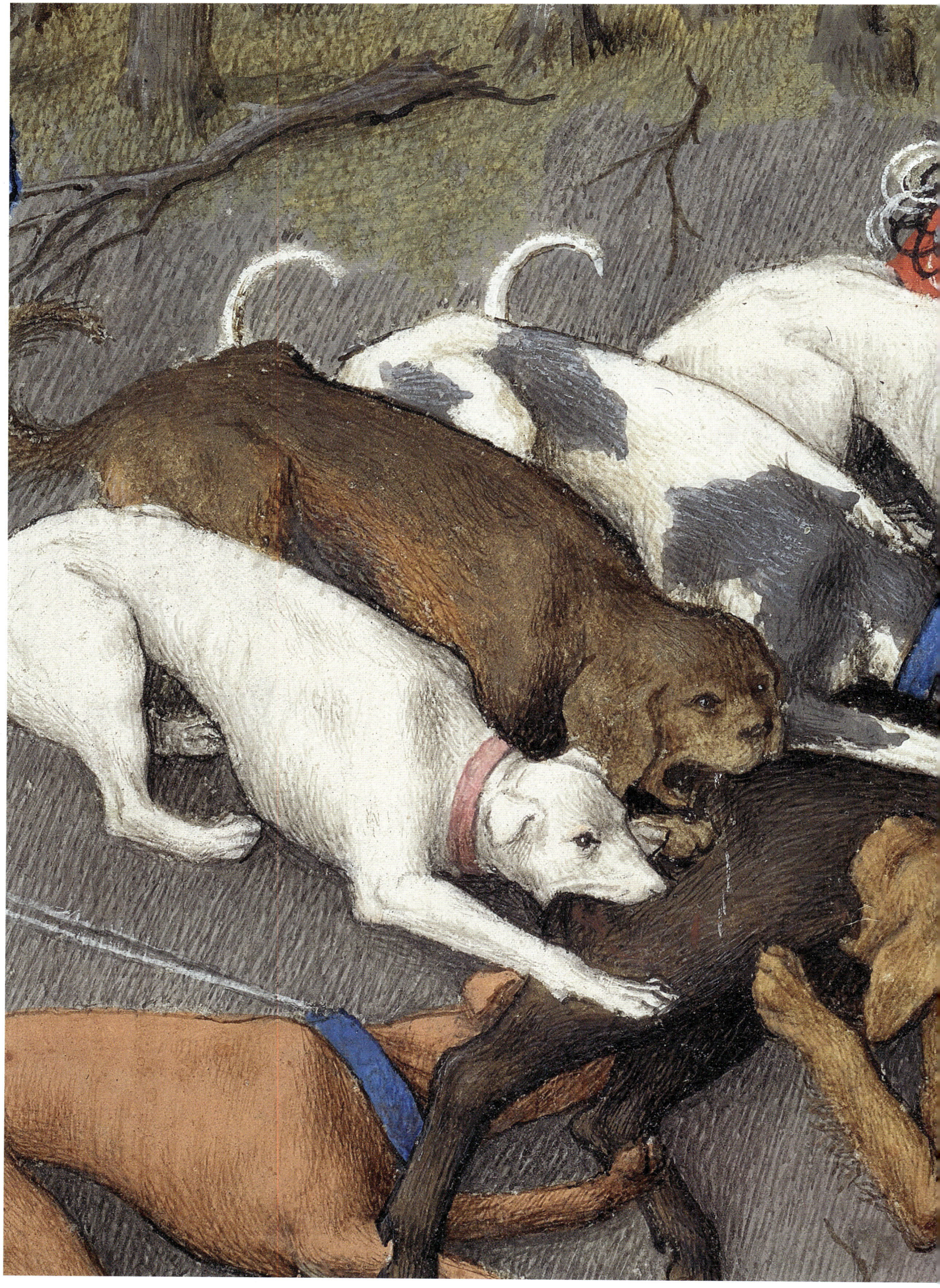

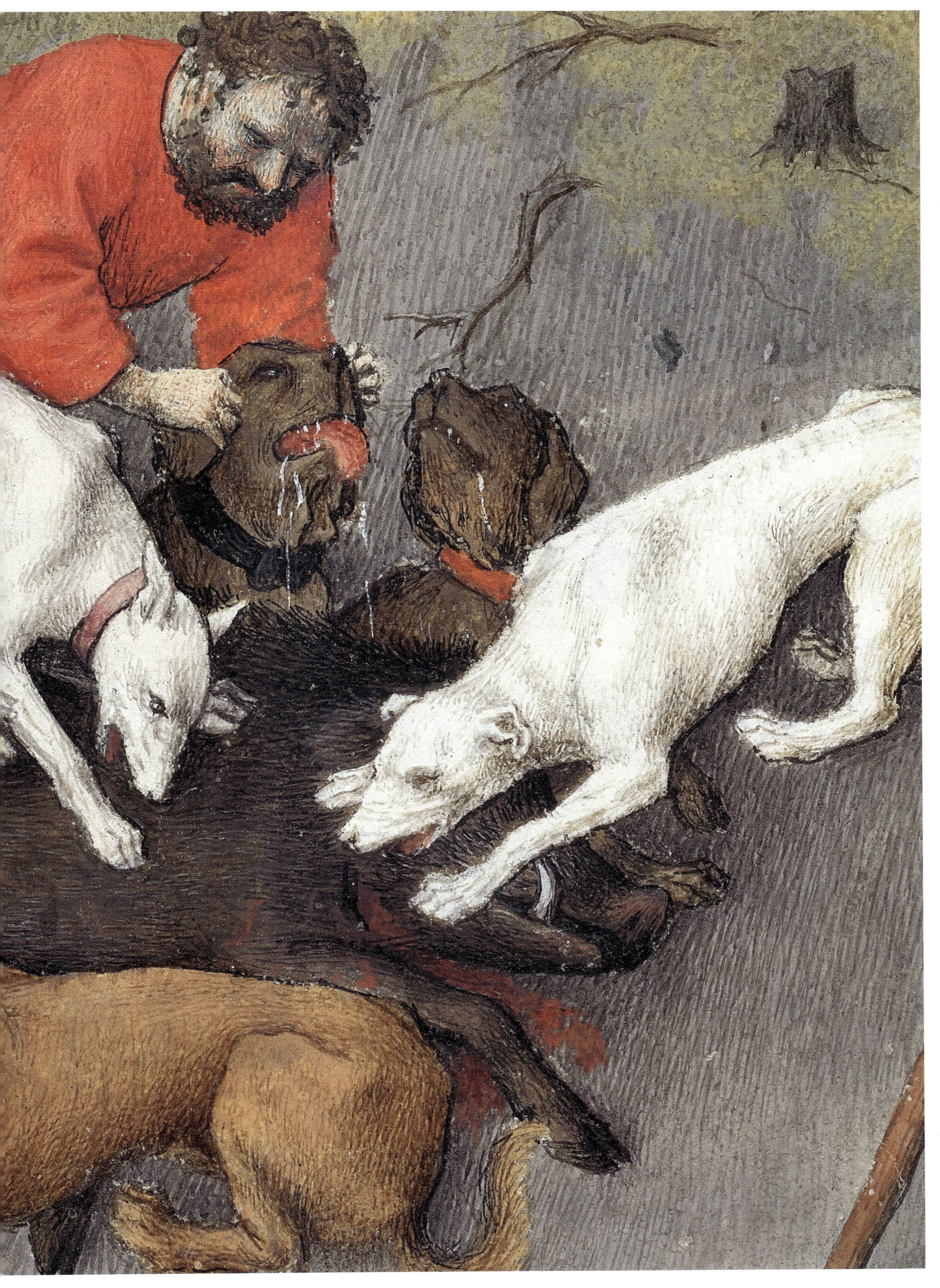

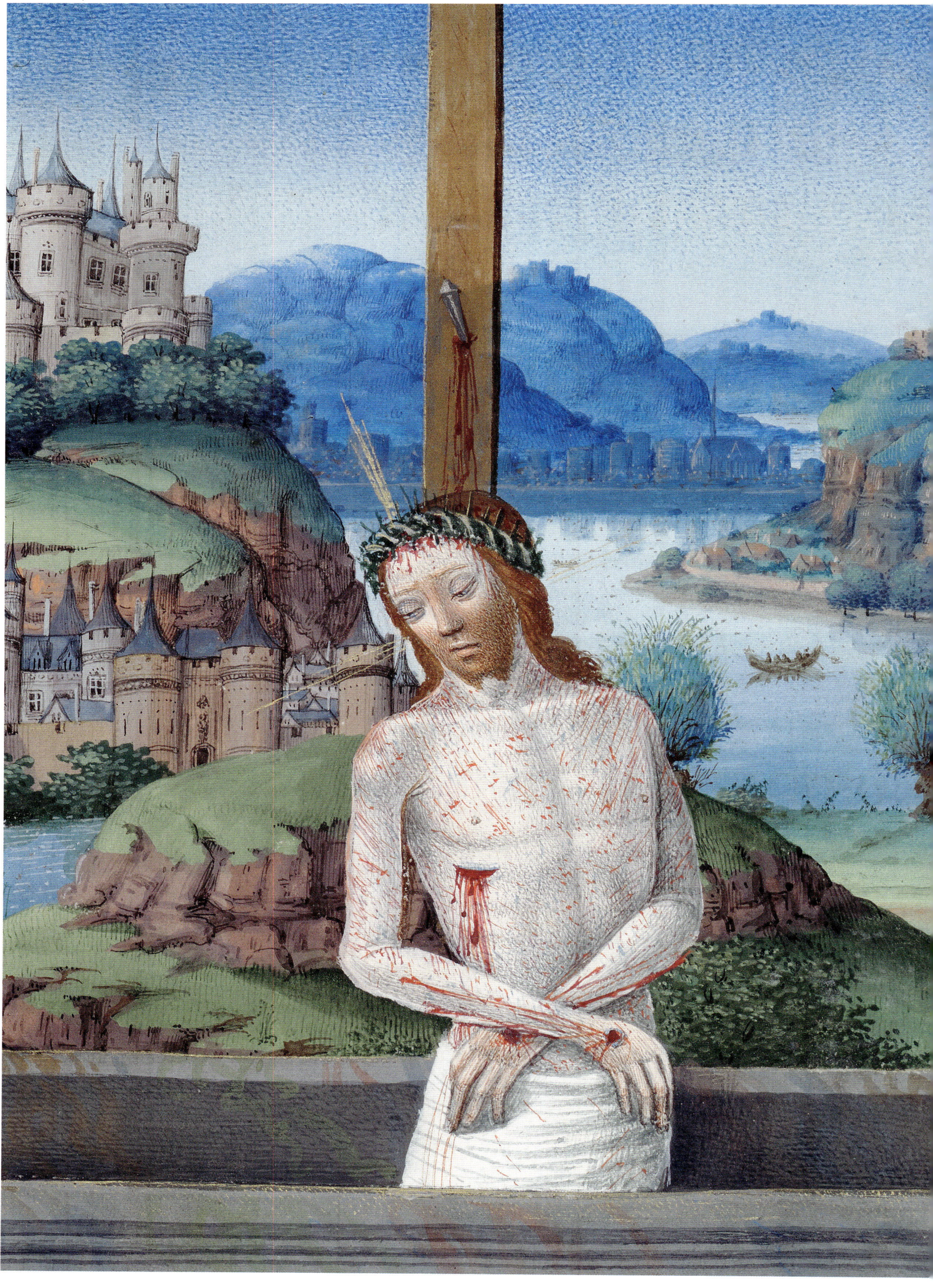

14.

# The Contribution of Jean Colombe and the Influence of the *Très Riches Heures* on Berry Illumination

Marie Jacob-Yapi

When the young Duke of Savoy Charles I (fig. 1) hired the Bourges illuminator Jean Colombe in 1485 to complete the decoration of the book of hours he had possibly inherited from his late aunt, the Queen of France, Charlotte of Savoy (d. 1483), some sixty miniatures, including twenty-four full-page ones, and more than 300 initials containing figures had still to be painted or finished.[1] Some were already well underway. Among the big "hystoires" (narrative scenes), the Funeral of Raymond Diocrès (fol. 86v) and the Christmas Mass (fol. 158v; fig. 3) had already been drawn by the Van Lymborch brothers.[2] The latter had also probably sketched some elements of the Resurrection (fol. 182), as the motif of the huge oblong tomb running diagonally across the miniature and the soldier flat on his back in the foreground is to be found in another of their works for Jean of Berry, the *Belles Heures*, dated between around 1405 and around 1408–09 (fols. 73v and 152v). The painting of the month of September in the calendar (fol. 9v) had already been started in the 1440s by Barthélemy d'Eyck, who had had time to complete the château of Saumur in the background, including the tilt barrier and the cluster of columns.

When this work was commissioned, Jean Colombe (c. 1440–93) was at the height of his career. Since 1470, he had been called upon by the highest officials in the kingdom of France, including Jean Robertet (secretary to Louis XI), Louis de Laval-Châtillon (Grand Master of the Waters and Forests), Louis, Bâtard de Bourbon (Admiral of France), and many others.

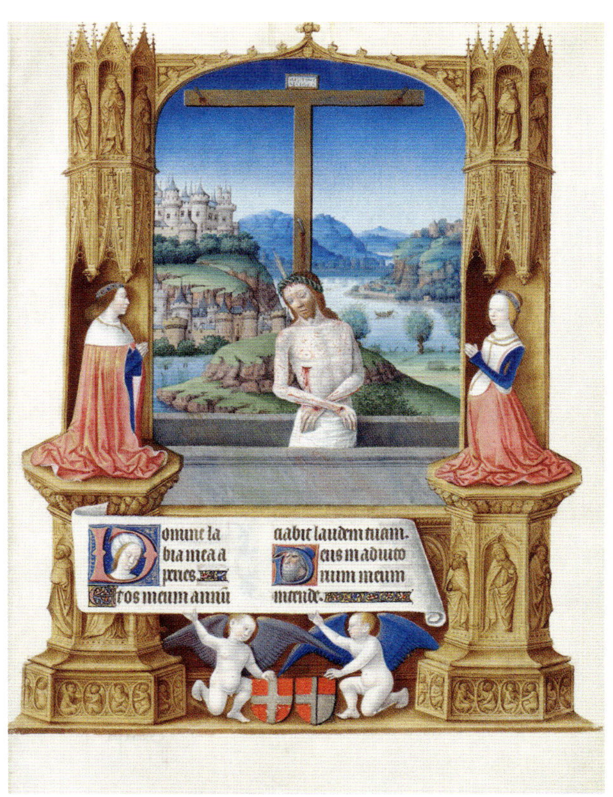

**Fig. 2** Jean Colombe, *Très Riches Heures*, fol. 75: Man of Sorrows with Charles of Savoy and Blanche of Montferrat

**Fig. 1** Jean Colombe, *Très Riches Heures*, fol. 75: Man of Sorrows with Charles of Savoy and Blanche of Montferrat, detail

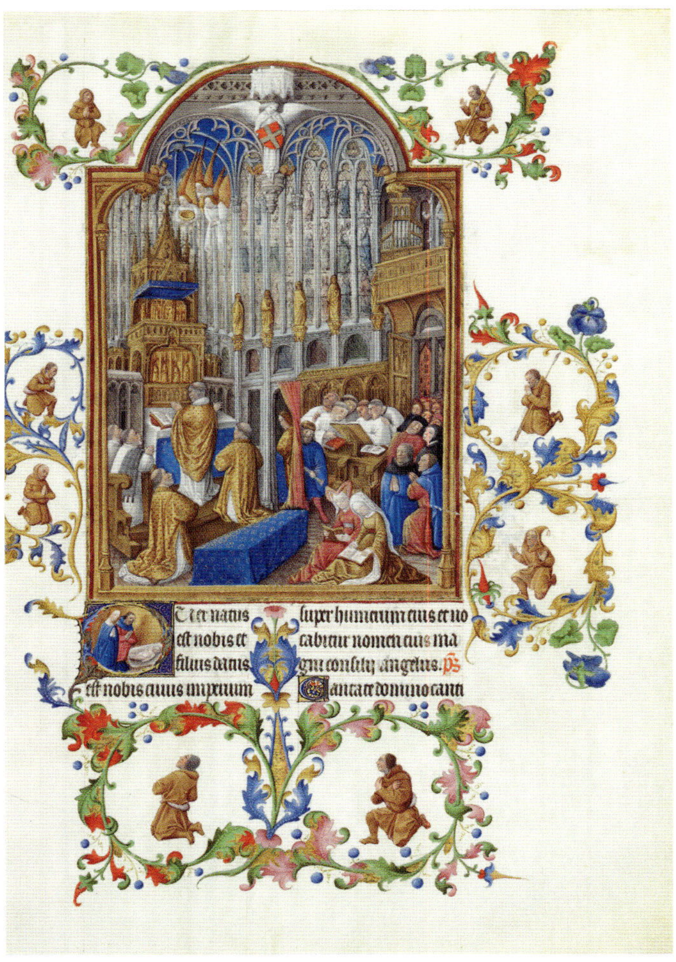

**Fig. 3** Miniature left unfinished and completed by Jean Colombe, *Très Riches Heures*, fol. 158: Christmas Mass

He had worked for Queen Charlotte of Savoy, who had taken him under her protection when Charles, still a child, had come to live in Touraine with his sisters and younger brother following the death of their mother Yolande of France, Louis XI's sister, in August 1478 (he stayed there until 1483).[3]

As the head of a flourishing workshop, Jean Colombe almost systematically called on other illuminators to help him fulfill his contracts, and the *Très Riches Heures* is no exception. At least one assistant was involved in their illustration. The latter was tasked in particular with painting the frames of seven large miniatures (fols. 82, 95, 100v, 122v, 126, 133v, 201), frames that stand out from those of his master by their colored marble columns enhanced with gilded scrolls, which he sometimes topped with an entablature in the form of a scalloped branch. The clusters of small figures standing in his Gothic structures have wide, black-rimmed faces, with drooping mouths. It was this same assistant decorator who, several years later, shortly after 1490, painted some of the frames for the book of hours known as the *Hours of Louis d'Orléans*,[4] a manuscript begun in Toulouse by the second master of the *Missal of Jean de Foix*[5] and completed in Bourges in the joint workshops of the painter Jean de Montluçon and Jean Colombe. Marie Mazzone, who believes she has identified the hand of this assistant in some fifteen manuscripts, recently suggested identifying him with Jean Colombe's eldest son, Philibert Colombe.[6]

## THE ART OF JEAN COLOMBE

In terms of style, it made sense to entrust Jean Colombe with the task of finishing this manuscript. Indeed, unlike that of other French artists of the 1480s, his style was still very much influenced by the Gothic aesthetic of the early century.[7] Neither his vertical arrangement of space, nor his female models with their striking hips, long blonde hair, and almond-shaped eyes clashed with the Van Lymborch style, nor indeed did his gilded pinnacled frames. Compare, for instance, the female nudes and the framing of the Purgatory scene (fol. 113v; fig. 4) with the expulsion from Paradise of the Van Lymborch brothers (fol. 25v; fig. 15, p. 190). But that is as far as it goes. While we can observe, here and there, the direct influence of the Van Lymborch brothers' work on certain inflections of his color palette—such as the guard of honor formed by angels on either side of Christ during the Ascension (fol. 184), treated in perspective with subtle transparency effects in the manner of the clouds beneath the twenty-four elders of the Apocalypse at the beginning of the Gospel of St. John (fol. 19)—and while the iconographic decision to turn the western facade of Bourges Cathedral into a protagonist in its own right in the Presentation of the Virgin in the Temple (fol. 137; fig. 6) is directly related to the architectural portraits painted by the Van Lymborch brothers in the calendar pages, the comparisons end there. Above all, Jean Colombe displayed in this manuscript the art for which he was renowned. In other words, Colombe did what Colombe did best, and this was undoubtedly what his young client wanted of him.

Indeed, Jean Colombe took up many of the formulas that had made him so successful, starting with layout. Following the approach he had adopted shortly before 1470

**Fig. 4** Jean Colombe, *Très Riches Heures*, fol. 113v: Purgatory
**Fig. 5** Following pages: Jean Colombe, *Très Riches Heures*, fol. 113v: Purgatory, detail

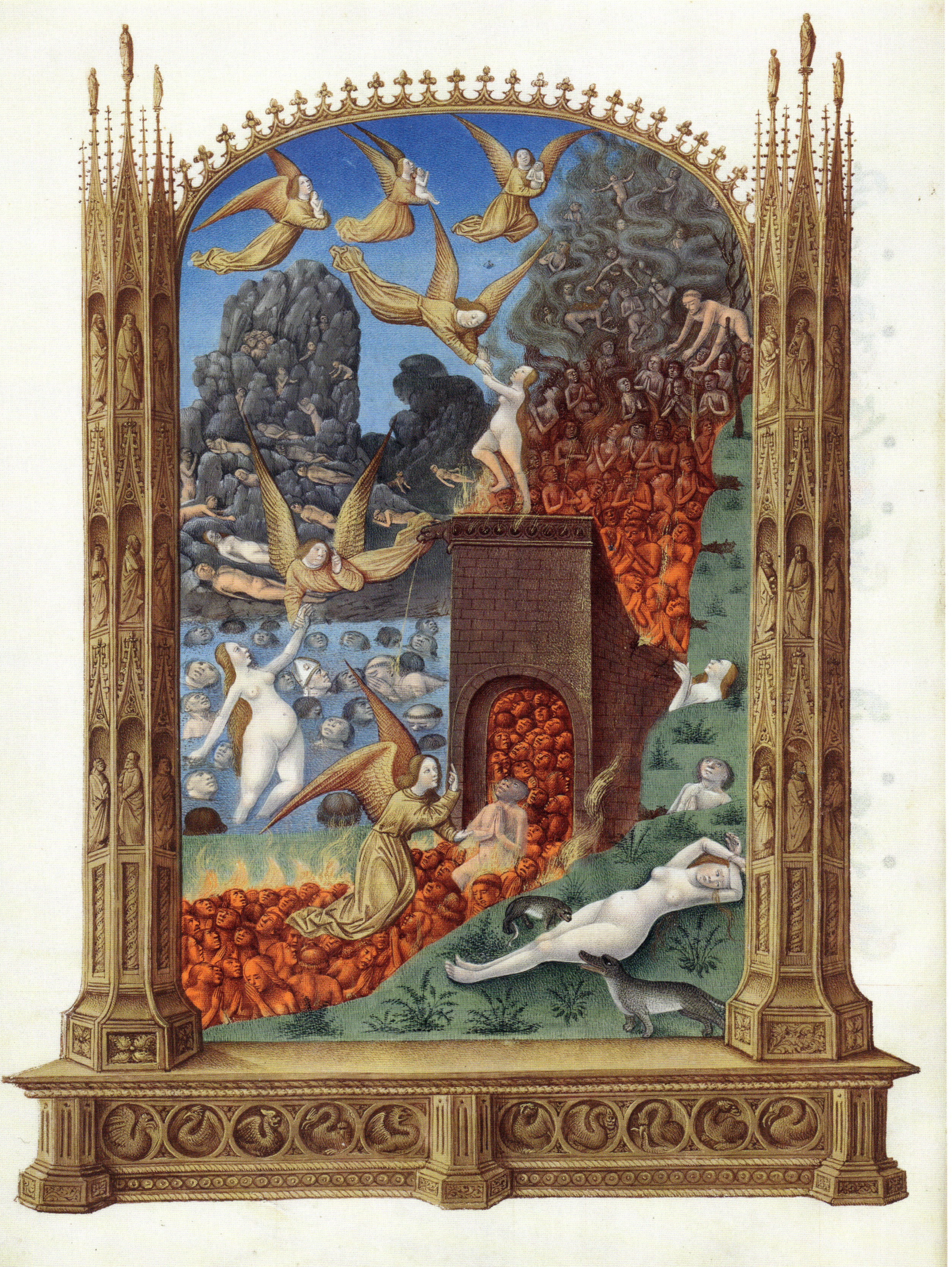

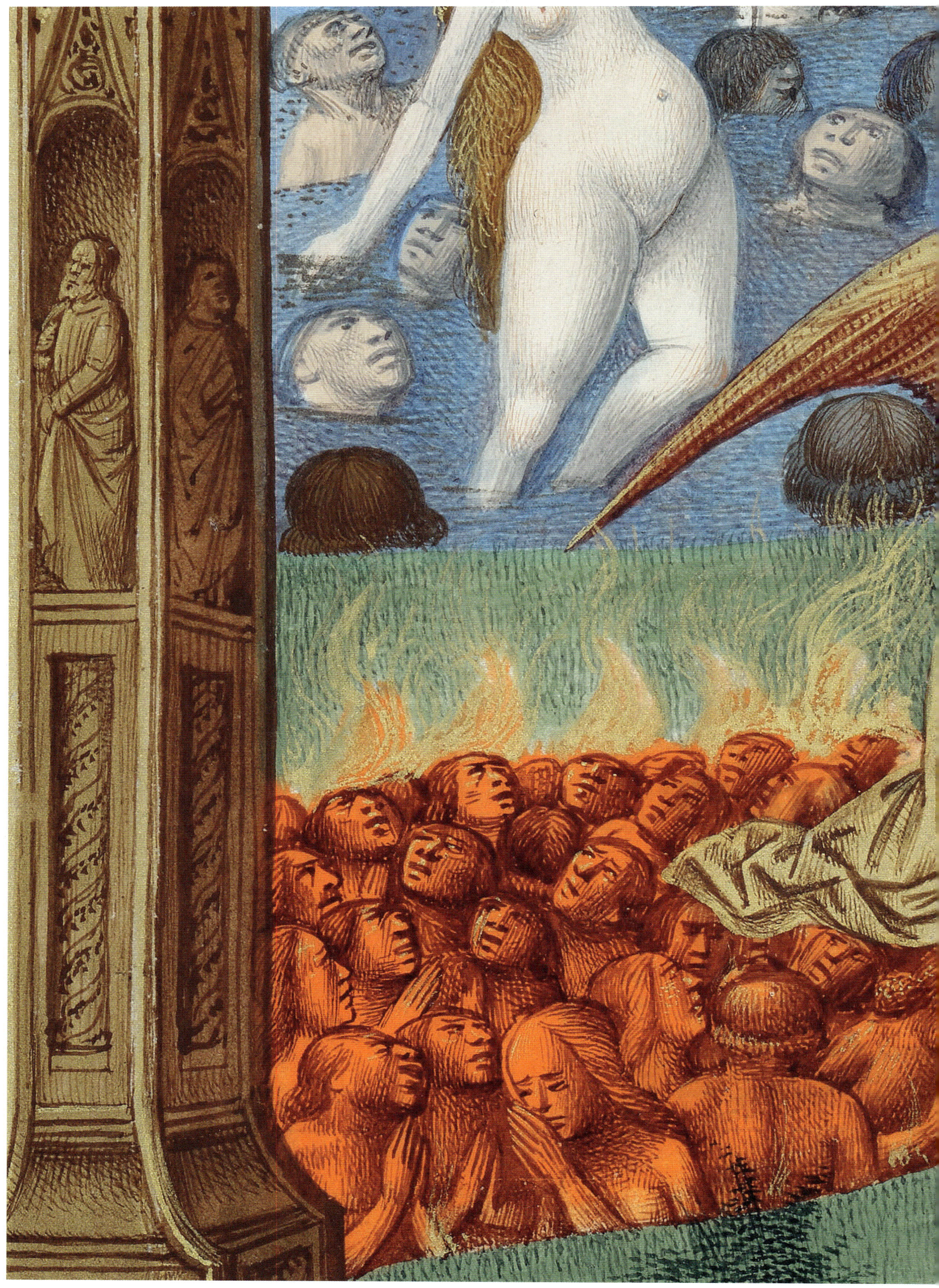

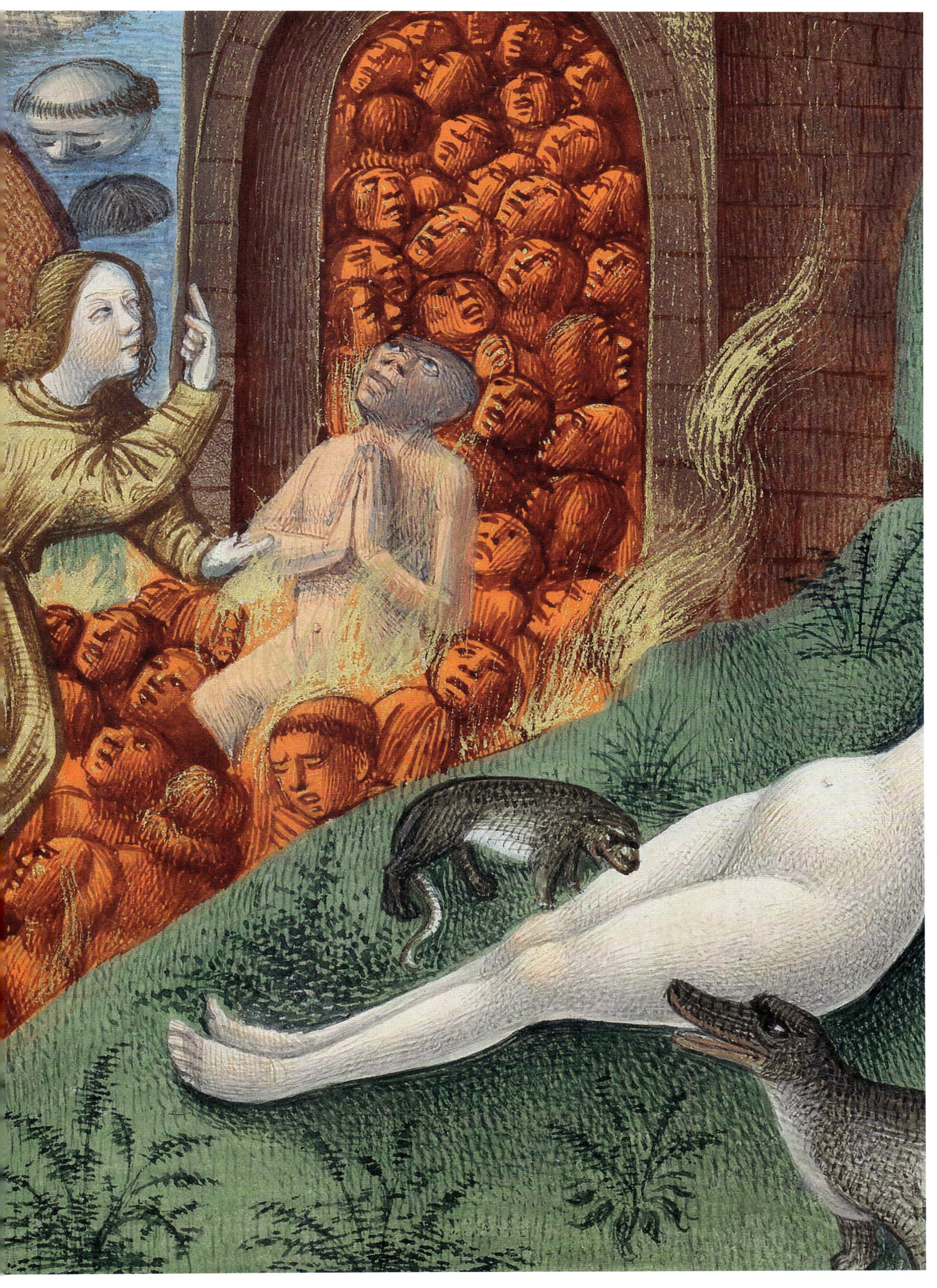

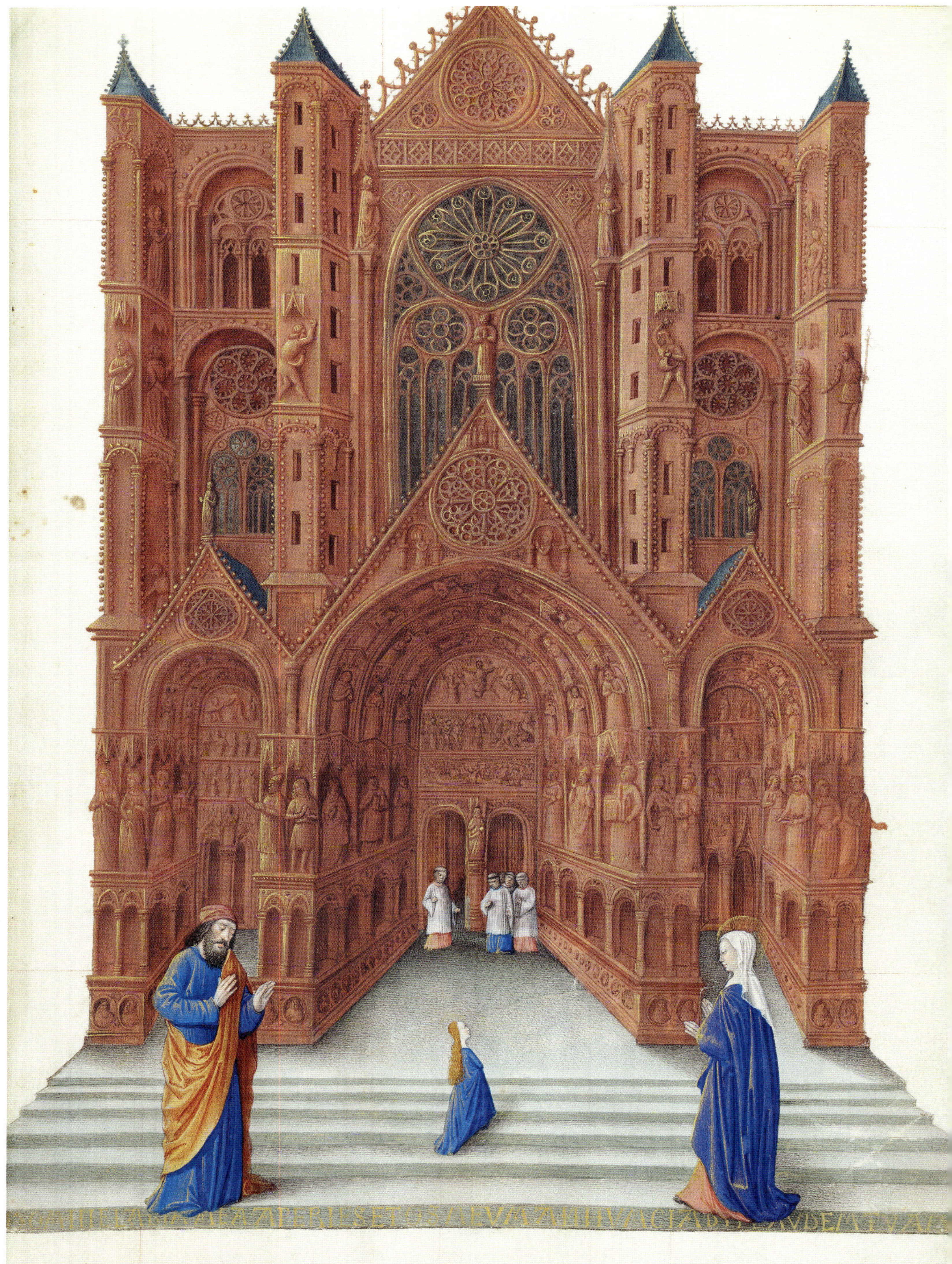

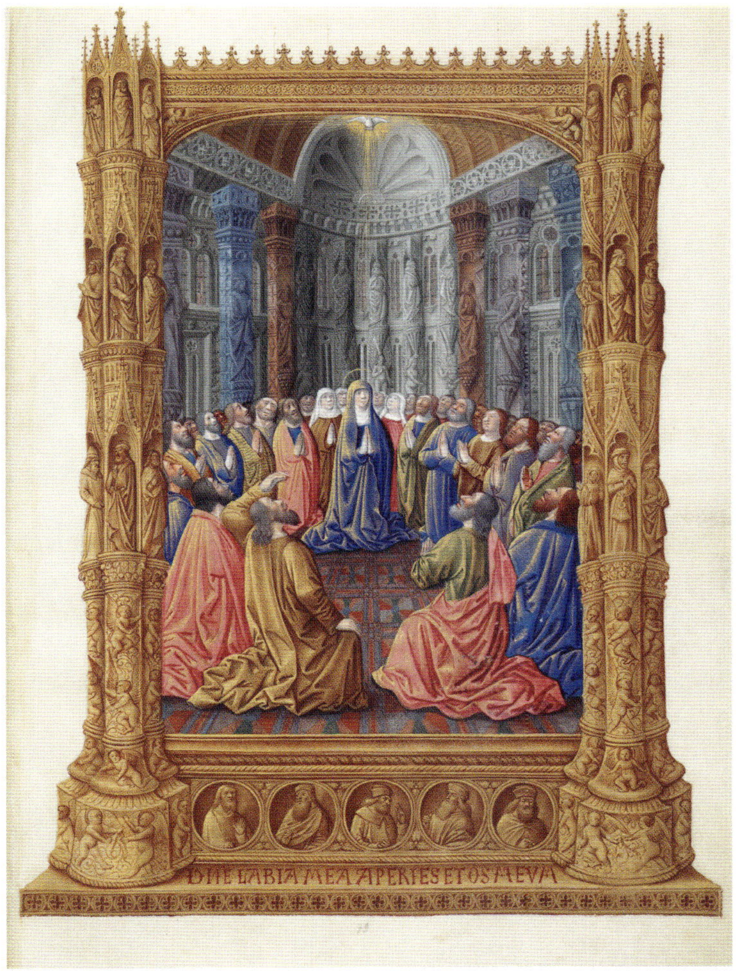

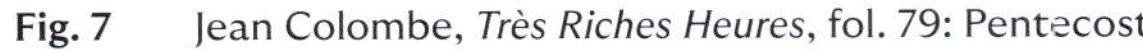

**Fig. 7** Jean Colombe, *Très Riches Heures*, fol. 79: Pentecost

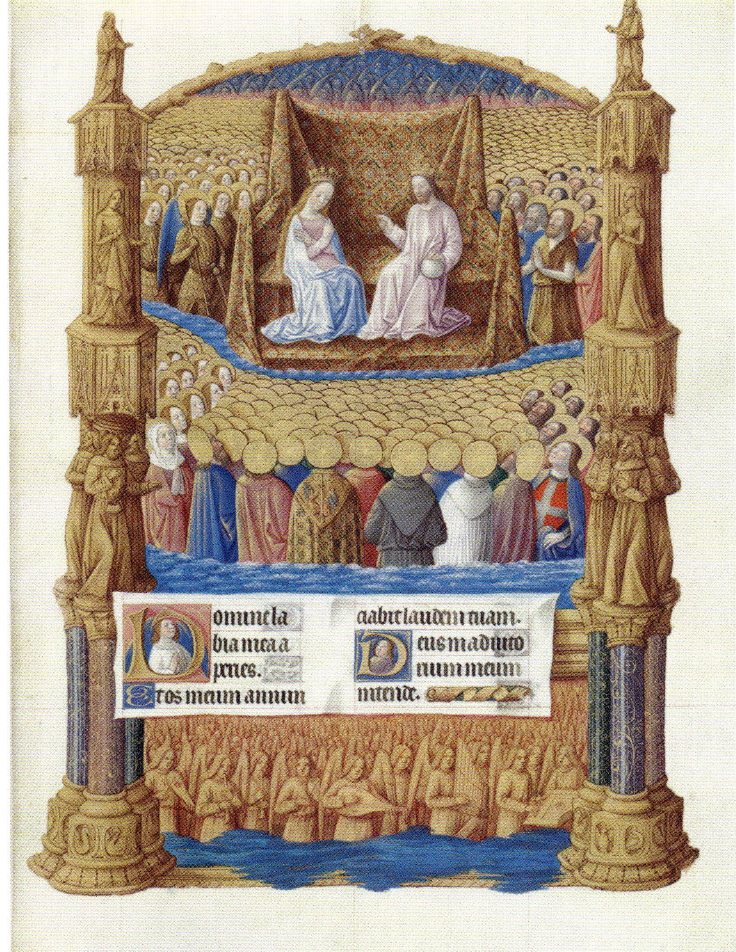

**Fig. 8** Jean Colombe, with the collaboration of the Montluçon workshop, *Très Riches Heures*, fol. 126: The Celestial Court

in the *Bureau Hours*[8] and then developed in the *Hours of Louis de Laval*, most of his large paintings are set in impressive, gilded, Gothic architectural frames surmounted by ogee arches that give them the appearance of tabernacles. He had borrowed the idea from an Angevin illuminator, the Master of Smith-Lesouëf 30, who had introduced the motif in the early 1460s in the hours known as the *Hours of Mary Stuart*[9] and in the book of hours in the Bibliothèque nationale de France that earned him his nickname.[10] But Jean Colombe gave his frames a singular monumentality by adorning them with a lot of bas-reliefs and statues nestling beneath tapering pinnacles. This sensitivity to sculpture, which he had inherited from his father Philippe and his brother Michel Colombe, was given majestic expression in the double portrait of Charles I of Savoy and his wife Blanche of Montferrat kneeling in prayer beneath historiated high canopies on either side of the *Man of Sorrows* (fig. 2). To leave as much room as possible for his large paintings, the illuminator from Bourges rewrote the first lines of the text, now with capitals engraved on the base of his frames, now on a fictitious parchment scroll, two methods he had learned in the late 1460s from Jean Fouquet when he completed Fouquet's *Robertet Hours*. He then used them in several of his books of hours, but in the *Très Riches Heures*, unlike the other manuscripts, he indulged more freely in trompe-l'oeil effects. The fragment of parchment hanging casually from the border of the frame depicting Christ and the Canaanite Woman (fol. 164), with its initial "R" in relief imitating an ancient inscription, is particularly successful in this respect.

His leaves feature several compositions that are typical of his repertoire. The Pentecost scene (fol. 79; fig. 7)—with the dove of the Holy Spirit descending upon the Virgin kneeling in the center among the Holy Women, the apostles, and other disciples, in a sumptuous architectural setting adorned with a sculpted colonnade and a semi-dome—follows a pattern that he returned to throughout his career. Further on, the depiction of the Celestial Court, for the week's Wednesday Office (fol. 126; fig. 8), blends the two visions of Paradise he had developed in the *Hours of Louis de Laval* on folios 177v and 320,

**Fig. 6** Jean Colombe, *Très Riches Heures*, fol. 137: The Presentation of the Virgin in the Temple

**Fig. 9** Following pages: Jean Colombe, with the collaboration of the Montluçon workshop, *Très Riches Heures*, fol. 126: The Celestial Court, detail

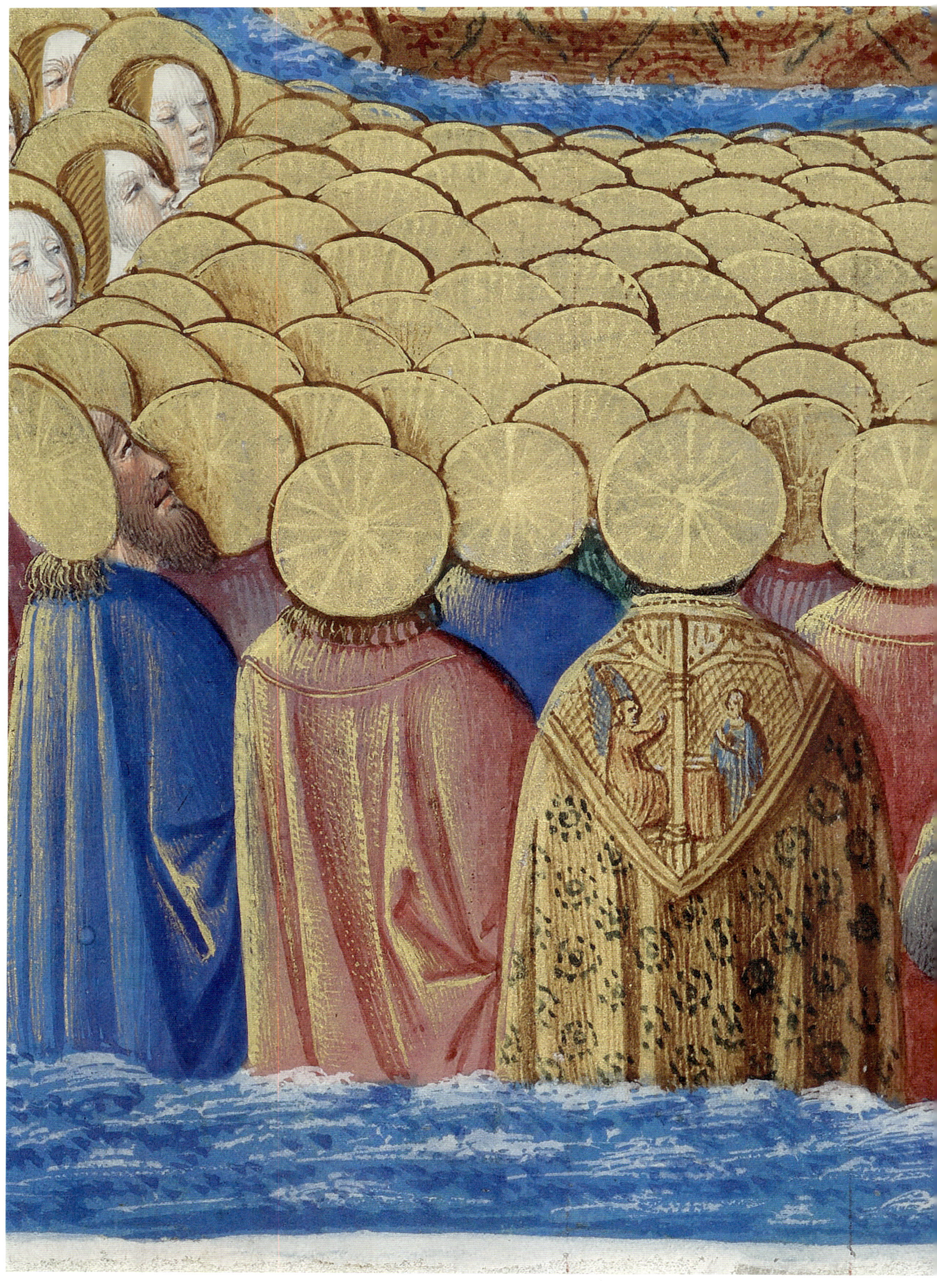

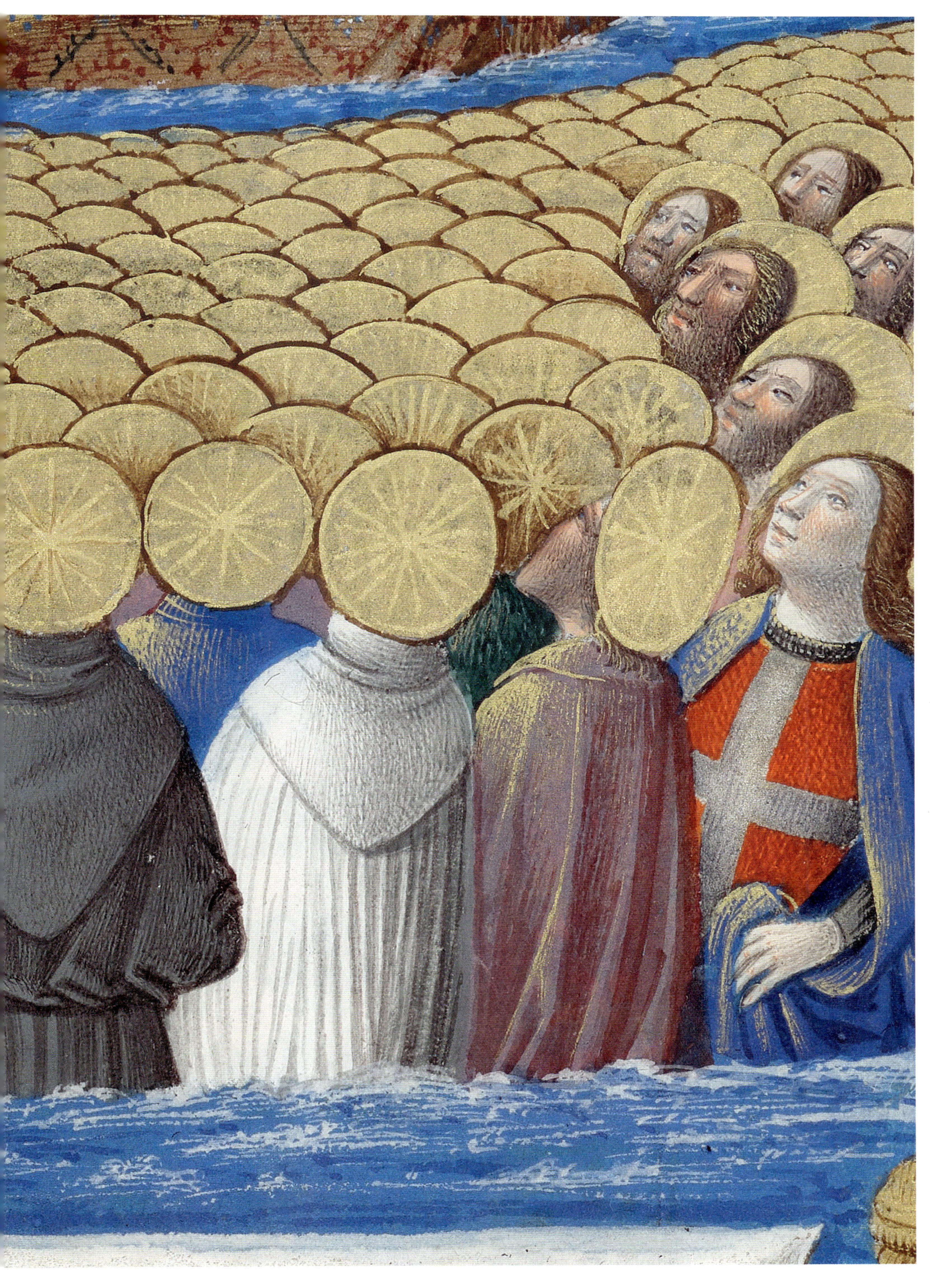

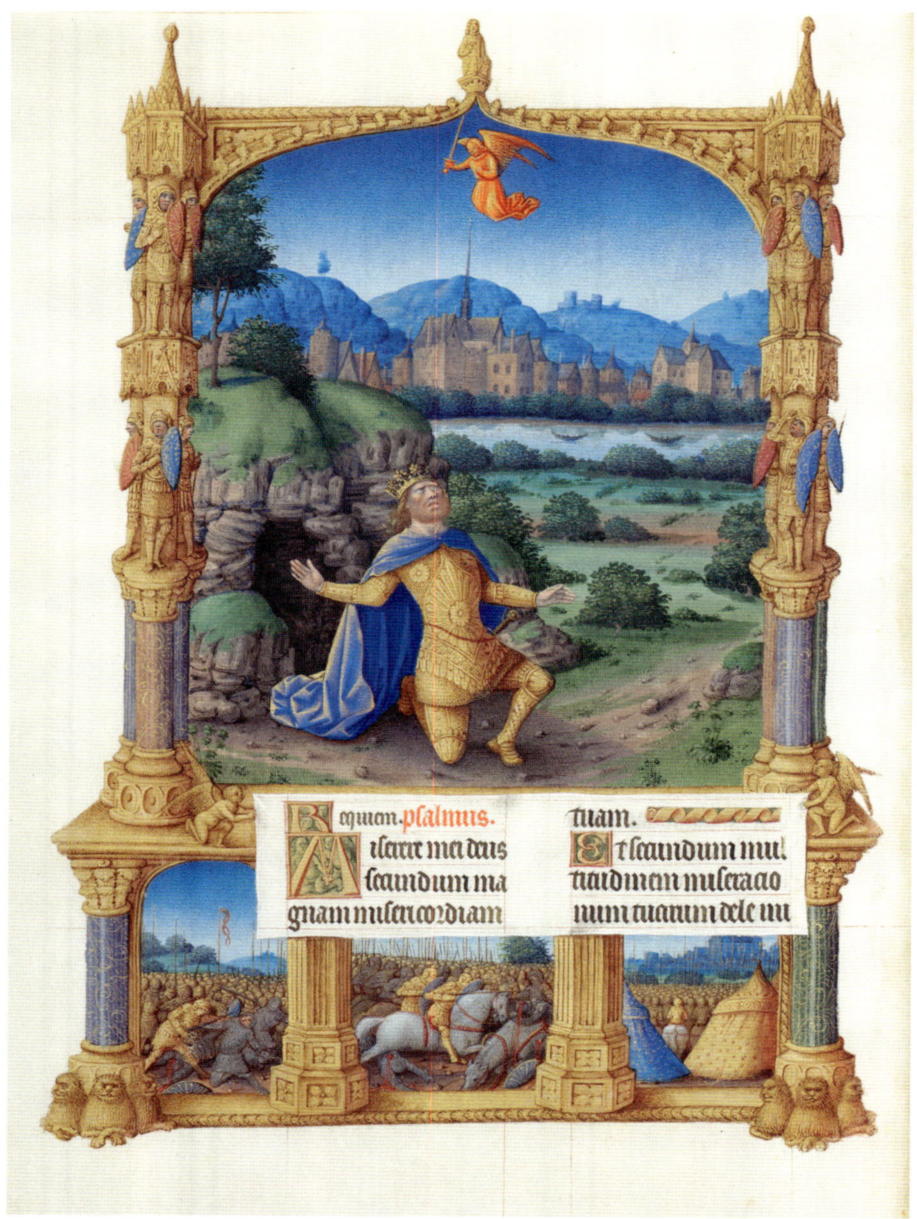

**Fig. 10** Jean Colombe, *Très Riches Heures*, fol. 100v: David at Prayer

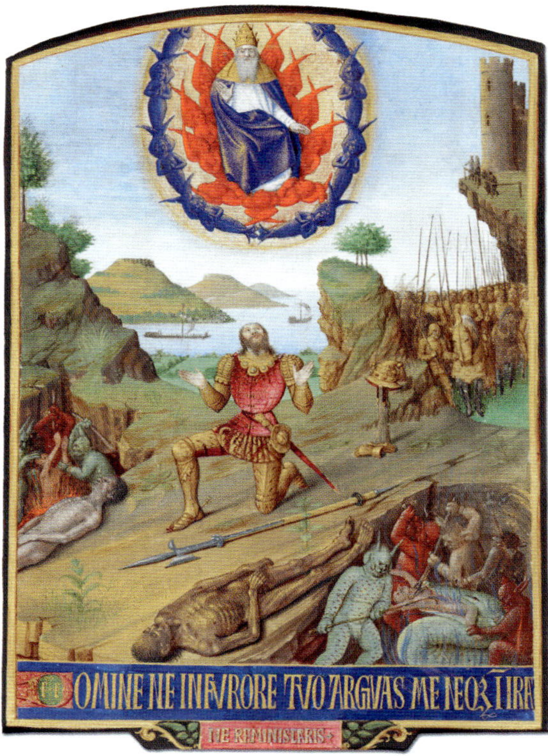

**Fig. 11** Jean Fouquet, *Hours of Étienne Chevalier*: David at Prayer (London, British Library, Add. MS 37421)

relegating the group of musician angels to the base, beneath the inset text. The image of Christ and Mary seated on a large throne covered with embroidered cloth—with Christ wearing a loose white garment with fine light-purple hatching, holding a globe in his left hand, and blessing his Mother, whose eyes are lowered and whose arms are crossed on her chest—was inspired rather by the model he used, around 1480, in the small book of hours acquired in 1979 by the Bibliothèque nationale de France.[11]

As is often the case in Jean Colombe's manuscripts, traces of Jean Fouquet's paintings abound. Jean Robertet, the king's secretary, had entrusted the young Berry illuminator with the task of completing a book of hours that the master from Tours had left unfinished. In the 1470s, he had regularly collaborated with several illuminators of Tours from Fouquet's sphere of influence, including the Master of the Yale Missal—whom Samuel Gras recently suggested identifying with Guillaume Piqueau—with whom he worked, among others, on the eponymous missal[12] and two manuscripts for Louis de Laval, his *Hours* and *Histoire des neuf preux et des neuf preuses* (History of the nine worthies and nine lady worthies).[13] These repeated contacts with the art of Fouquet left a deep impression on him, and this can be clearly felt in the *Très Riches Heures*.[14] The image of David at Prayer (fol. 100v; fig. 10)—in the prime of life, dressed in armor, kneeling on the ground, arms outstretched, imploring God—stems from a model developed around 1450 by the Touraine painter in the *Hours of Étienne Chevalier* (fig. 11).[15] Other elements in the small miniatures inserted in the columns of text also bear the mark of the Touraine painter, for example the Virgin and Child at the head of the Mass for the Nativity of Mary (fol. 191v; fig. 12). This type of monumental Madonna, cut at knee level, with her cloak loosely draped around the infant, is a variant of a lost painting by Jean Fouquet that was very popular with Jean Colombe and the illuminators of Touraine between 1470 and 1490, as François Avril has clearly shown.[16]

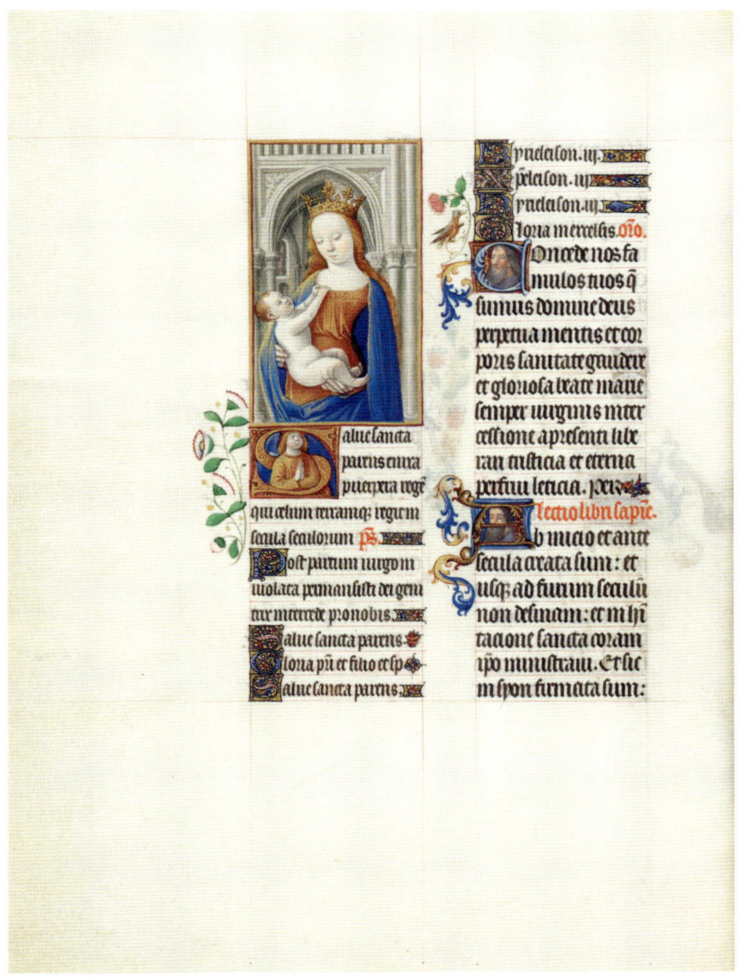

**Fig. 12** Jean Colombe, *Très Riches Heures*, fol. 191v: Virgin and Child

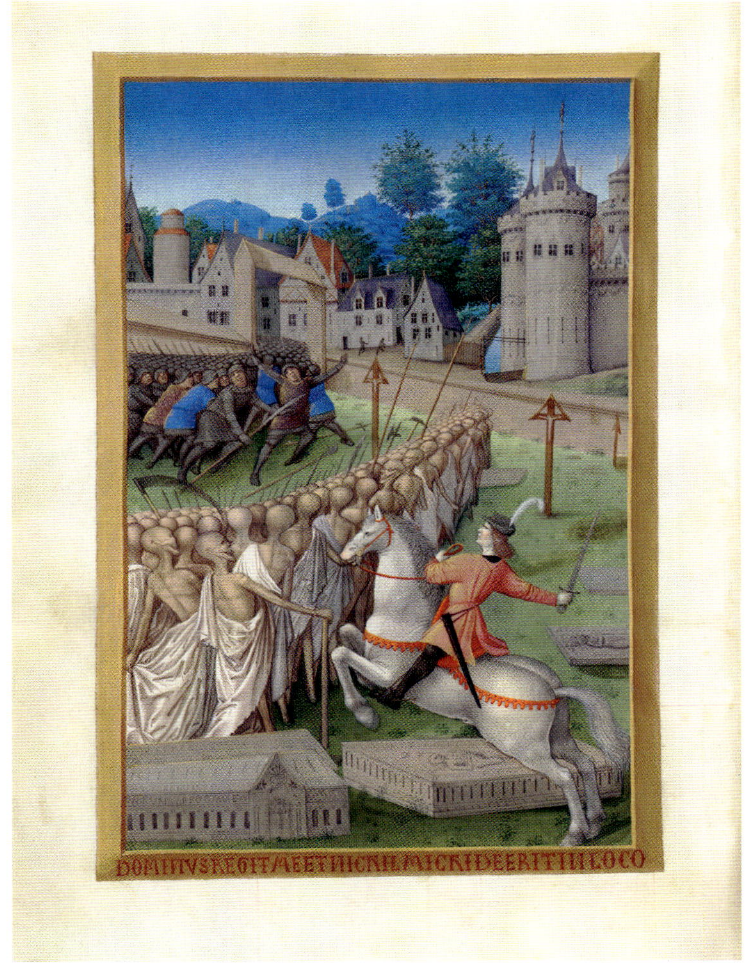

**Fig. 13** Jean Colombe, *Très Riches Heures*, fol. 90v: The Legend of the Grateful Dead

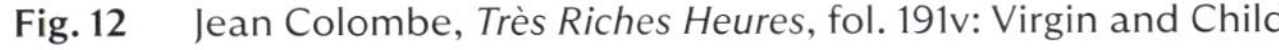

## REGARDING CERTAIN SINGULARITIES

Although Jean Colombe reused many of his habitual compositions, his illustrations in the *Très Riches Heures* stand out from the countless books of hours to come out of his workshop thanks to several singular images. This is the case, for instance, of the strange miniature that introduces the second nocturne of the Office of the Dead (fol. 90v; fig. 13). In a cemetery, a column of the dead, armed with spears, scythes, axes, and sticks, stands between a young rider and a group of fleeing soldiers. Colombe had never painted such a scene before. Long interpreted as representing the fourth horseman of the Apocalypse described in the Book of Revelation (6:8), the true subject of this miniature was identified a few years ago by Klara H. Broeckhuijsen as an illustration of the legend of the Grateful Dead,[17] which appeared in the early thirteenth century and was popularized by Jacques de Voragine in his *Legenda aurea*. The depiction of this legend in the *Très Riches Heures* is quite remarkable since, despite the theme's popularity in literature, few artists had previously attempted to portray it, and of the five examples from the fifteenth century that have been recorded, this is the only one of French origin.

Two other miniatures catch the eye—the Man of Sorrows at the beginning of the Hours of the Cross (fol. 75; fig. 1) and the Vision of Purgatory for the Monday Office (fol. 113v). This representation of the Man of Sorrows—depicted half-length and in three-quarter view, wearing a crown of thorns and with his head bowed, with one hand over the other, the stigmata clearly visible—is quite traditional and dates back to Byzantine archetypes, but the treatment of the bloody body is more unusual. Christ's skin has been covered with laceration marks painted using fine gray hatching. Jean Colombe probably found inspiration for this image of the martyred body when he saw the striking vision of the Man of Sorrows painted by the Master of the Parement of Narbonne (Jean d'Orléans) around 1400 in the *Très Belles Heures de Notre-Dame* (fol. 126,

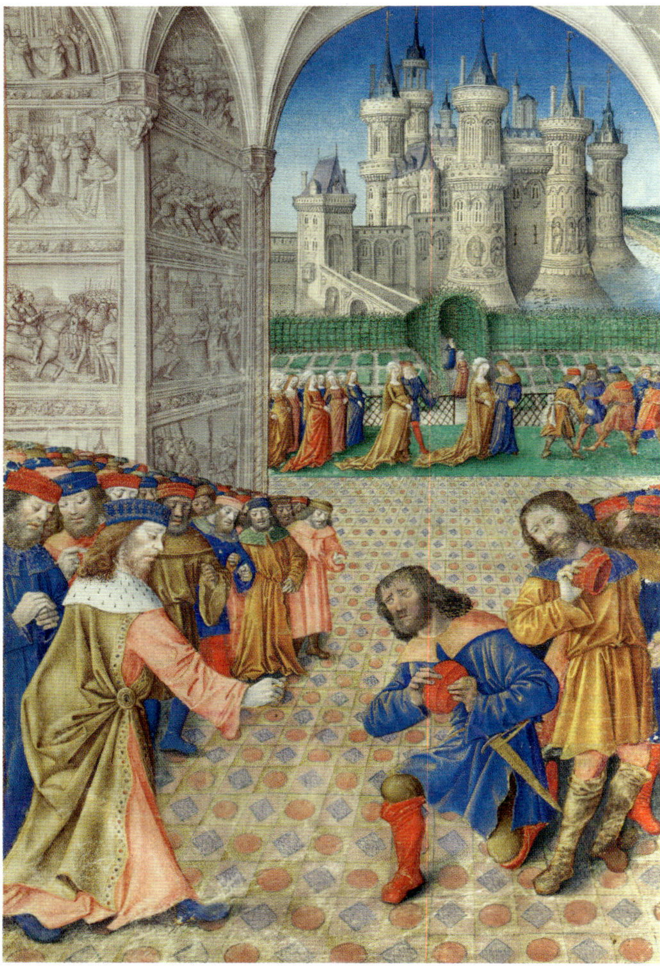

**Fig. 14** François Colombe, *Histoire de la destruction de Troye la Grant*, fol. 15v: Priam and the Greek envoys (Paris, Bibliothèque nationale de France, département des Manuscrits, NAF 24920)

fig. 14), under which Marguerite de Beauvilliers had asked the Bourges illuminator in the 1460s to add her portrait and arms, as Christine Seidel recently observed.[18] As for the large painting of Purgatory, with its juxtaposition of torture scenes and of angels carrying souls away from the burning gate of Hell, it is not strictly speaking a creation of Jean Colombe. The illuminator found his inspiration in a miniature painted by the Coëtivy Master in the manuscript of Dante's *Divine Comedy* (fol. 30)[19] commissioned around 1460–65 by Louis XI's younger brother, Charles de France, at the time Duke of Berry.[20] Coincidentally or not, among the mass of manuscripts attributable to the Colombe workshop that have come down to us, the only other book of hours to feature a Man of Sorrows, Purgatory, and Coronation of the Virgin with illustrations similar to those in the *Très Riches Heures* is the one executed shortly before, around 1480, for Anne of France, the cousin of Charles I.[21]

## THE *TRÈS RICHES HEURES* AFTER THE *TRÈS RICHES HEURES*

The experience of putting the finishing touches to the *Très Riches Heures du duc de Berry* left a lasting impression on Jean Colombe. Most of the manuscripts he subsequently illuminated contain quotations from the miniatures of his illustrious predecessors. The footers of the calendar in the Franciscan missal kept in Lyon contain several borrowings from the compositions of Barthélemy d'Eyck, from the three reapers in the month of June (fol. 3v) and the horse pulling a harrow in the month of October (fol. 4v) to the terrible hallali or bugle call sounding the death of the wild boar in the month of December (here for the month of November, fol. 6).[22] More than the pages of Barthélemy d'Eyck, however, it was above all those of the Van Lymborch brothers that fired his imagination. The copy of Benvenuto da Imola's *Romuleon*, which Colombe illuminated for the French admiral Louis Malet de Graville, is a veritable compendium of quotations from their paintings. For example, he reproduced the view of the Palais de la Cité in the month of June of the calendar to represent the palace of the Numidian king Syphax (fol. 197). Below that, to illustrate the meal with Scipio and Hasdrubal, he used motifs from the January banquet: The cupbearer, on the right, filling a cup behind a dresser, and the curious boat-shaped vessel on the table, which is none other than the famous "salliere du pavillon" (pavilion salt cellar) mentioned in Jean of Berry's inventory.[23]

Colombe conveyed his admiration for the *Très Riches Heures* not only to his sons, Philibert and François, who succeeded him at the head of the workshop around 1493, but also to his other colleagues in Bourges. The success of the new illustration layout for the calendar among illuminators in Bourges from the 1490s onward cannot otherwise be explained. Full-page miniatures for the months of the year can be found in the *Boisrouvray Hours*, the *Spencer Hours*, and in the *Hours of Jean Lallemant l'Aîné*,[24] as well as in a book of hours with the ciphers "G" and "H" auctioned recently.[25] But when it comes to the motifs themselves, instead of the Van Lymborch pages, which in their view had undoubtedly become too "Gothic," it was the later contributions, his own and those of Barthélemy d'Eyck, that aroused the interest of this new generation. The David at prayer from the *Hours of Louis d'Orléans* (fol. 67),[26] executed shortly after 1490 in the Montluçon workshop, as well as the St. John the Baptist and the two angels of the Baptism (fol. 88v), are almost identical to the figures painted by Jean Colombe in the *Très Riches Heures* on folios 100v and 109v, respectively. Only the Nativity scene (fol. 25), with its snowy landscape for a backdrop, could have been inspired by the month of February of the Van Lymborch brothers.[27] In *Histoire de la destruction de Troye la Grant* (History of the destruction of Troy),[28] a book dated around 1500, the Colombe sons based Priam's palace on the château of Saumur depicted by Barthélemy d'Eyck in the calendar (fol. 15v; fig. 14). The month of September in the *Boisrouvray Hours*, painted by a follower of the Montluçon workshop, then run by Jean's son Jacquelin, features Colombe's aproned woman putting her headdress back on; the month of October (fol. 10v) combines Barthélemy d'Eyck's motif of the plowman with that of the sower from the month of October; and the representation of the acorn harvest in the month of November (fol. 11v) is an inverted copy of that by Jean Colombe.[29] Another illuminator from Bourges, known as the Master of Spencer 6, also borrowed the iconography of the month of October from the book of hours that gave him his nickname (fol. 11v)[30] from manuscript 651 in the Bibliothèque de l'Arsenal[31] and from a manuscript bearing the arms of the Bouer family from Berry, held by the University of Leeds.[32]

1 The engagement of Jean Colombe to finish the *Très Riches Heures* is documented by an initial payment in the accounts of the receivers and treasurers general of the dukes of Savoy dated August 31, 1485: "Expediri mandavit viginti quinque scutos auri cugni regis ad rationem triginta quatuor gros. pro singulo scuto per ipsum Johanem accedentem Franciam in villa de Burges tunc expediendos Johanni de la Columbe pro illuminatura et historiatione certarum orarum canonicarum ipsius illustrissimi domini nostri ducis eidem Johanni Columbe in maiore quantitate debitos, ut per ipsius domini nostri licteram. datam Rippolis die ultima augusti mile iiii[e] lxxxv[o]—xxv scut auri regis" (He ordered the payment of 25 gold crowns from the king's treasury, at a rate of 34 gros per crown, to Johan, who was coming to France in the village of Bourges. These funds were to be given to Jean Colombe for the illumination and decoration of certain canonical hours for his most illustrious lord, our duke. This payment was to be made in a larger quantity, as authorized by the letter from our lord, issued at Rippolis on the last day of August 1385–25 gold crowns from the king). Turin, Archivio di Stato, inv. 16, reg. 138, fol. 143v; ed. in Dufour and Rabut 1870, 110–11). On this record, see Jacob 2013. On how the manuscript arrived in the hands of Charles I of Savoy, see most recently Reynaud 2007, 275.

2 On the attribution of these two drawings and their links with models of the Bedford Master, see Stirnemann and Rabel 2005, and Villela-Petit 2013b.

3 For an overview of Jean Colombe's career before the *Très Riches Heures* contract, see Paris 1993–94, 326–38; Ribault 2001; Jacob 2012, 23–48 (with bibliography); Seidel 2017.

4 Saint-Petersburg, National Library of Russia, Lat. Q. V. I. 126.

5 Paris, BnF, Ms. Latin 16827.

6 Mazzone 2018. For Katja Airaksinen-Monier, it is rather Jacquelin de Montluçon (Airaksinen-Monier 2014, 166–68).

7 On the links between Jean Colombe's art and Berry painting of the 1400s, see Seidel 2017.

8 Private collection.

9 Private collection.

10 On the Angevin origin of these frames, see Paris 2003, 256, 407, and Seidel 2017, 37–38.

11 On this manuscript, see Paris 1993–94, no. 183, 334–35.

12 New Haven, Yale, Beinecke Library, Ms. 425.

13 Vienna, ÖNB, Ms. cod. 2577-2578. Gras 2016, I, 228–339.

14 On the influence of Jean Fouquet's art on Colombe, see Paris 2003, 253–56.

15 London, BL, Ms. Add. 37421.

16 See Paris, BnF, Ms. Latin 13305, fol. 239; Épinal, BMI, Ms. 100, fol. 98v. On the Fouquettian origin of this type of Virgin and Child, see Avril 2023.

17 Broeckhuijsen 2002.

18 Seidel 2017, 18.

19 Paris, BnF, Ms. Italian 72.

20 Paris 1993–94, 62.

21 John Plummer had suggested that this book of hours was commissioned by Charlotte of Savoy around 1473–74 for the marriage of her daughter Anne to Pierre de Beaujeu (New York 1982–83, 53–54 [no. 70]). Christine Seidel, followed by François Avril, considers, on the basis of stylistic elements, that this dating should be pushed forward to around 1480 (Seidel 2017, 285; Avril 2023, 43 note 3).

22 According to François Avril, Jean Colombe may have entrusted the execution of some of the miniatures in this manuscript to Jean de Montluçon (Paris 1993–94, 339).

23 A fuller list of Jean Colombe's borrowings from the *Très Riches Heures* can be found in Jacob 2012, 174–77.

24 Private collection.

25 Paris, Hôtel Drouot, June 5, 2020, lot 23.

26 Saint-Petersburg, National Library of Russia, Ms. Lat. Q. V. I. 126.

27 On borrowings from the *Très Riches Heures* in the *Hours of Louis d'Orléans*, see Sterligov 1980, II, 70–74.

28 Paris, BnF, Ms. NAF 24920.

29 Paris 1993–94, 340; Reynaud 2007, 276–77 note 19.

30 New York 2005–06, 280–81.

31 Châlons-en-Champagne, Troyes and Reims 2007–08, 186 (no. 43) (note by F. Avril).

32 Leeds, Brotherton Coll. Ms. 8, 10; Ker 1983, 41.

**Fig. 15** Following pages: Jean Colombe, *Très Riches Heures*, fol. 90v: The Legend of the Grateful Dead, detail

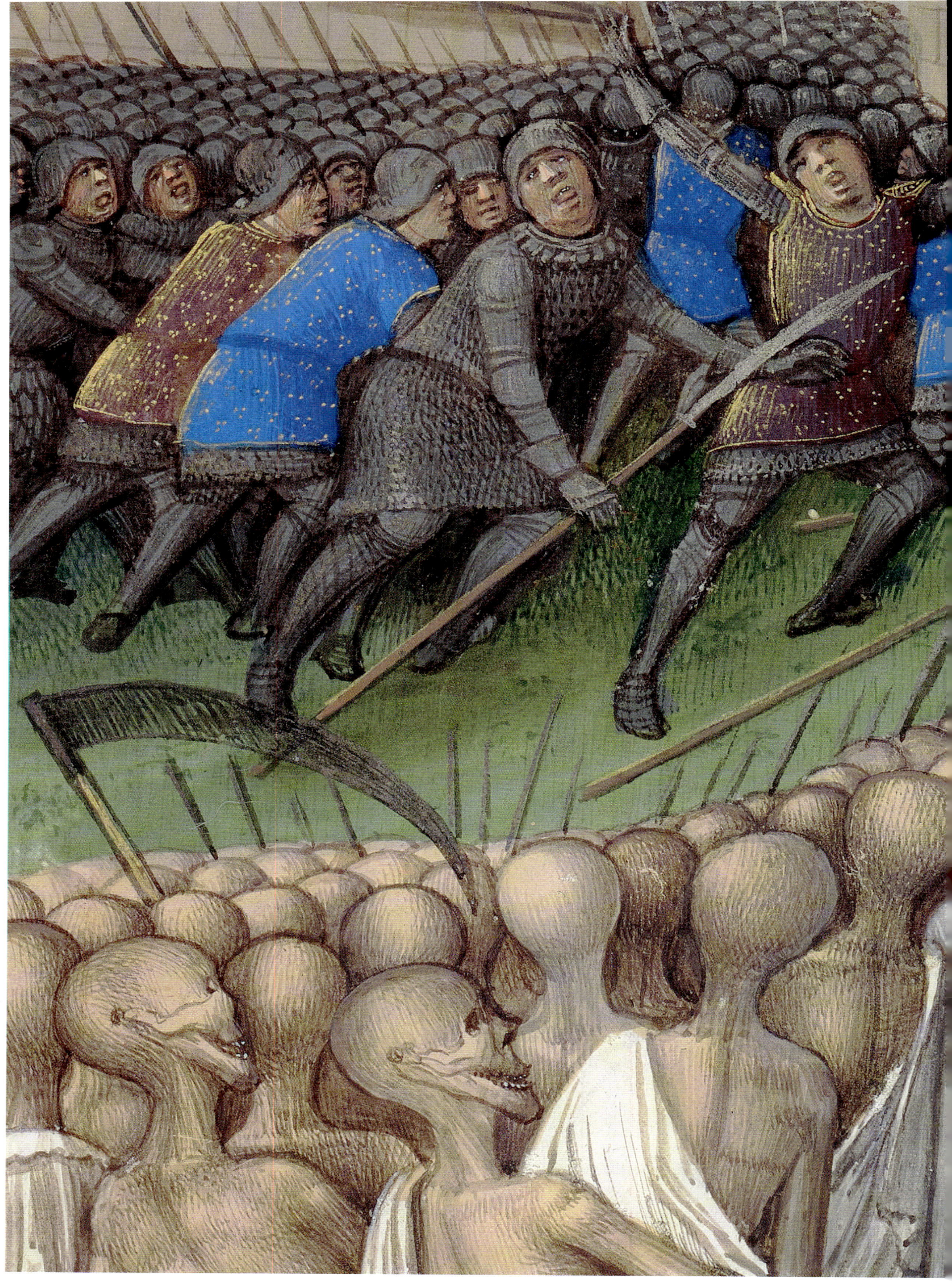

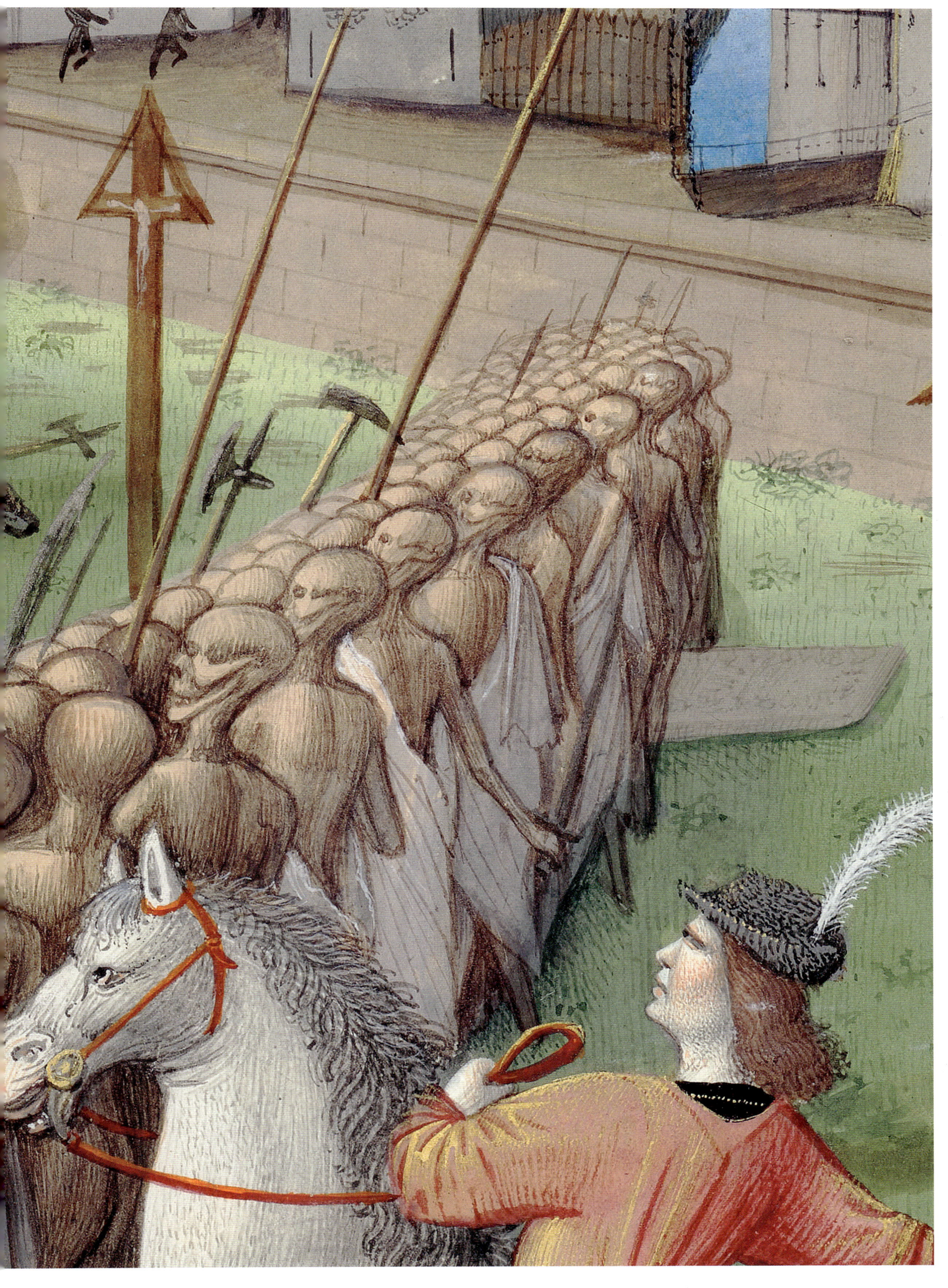

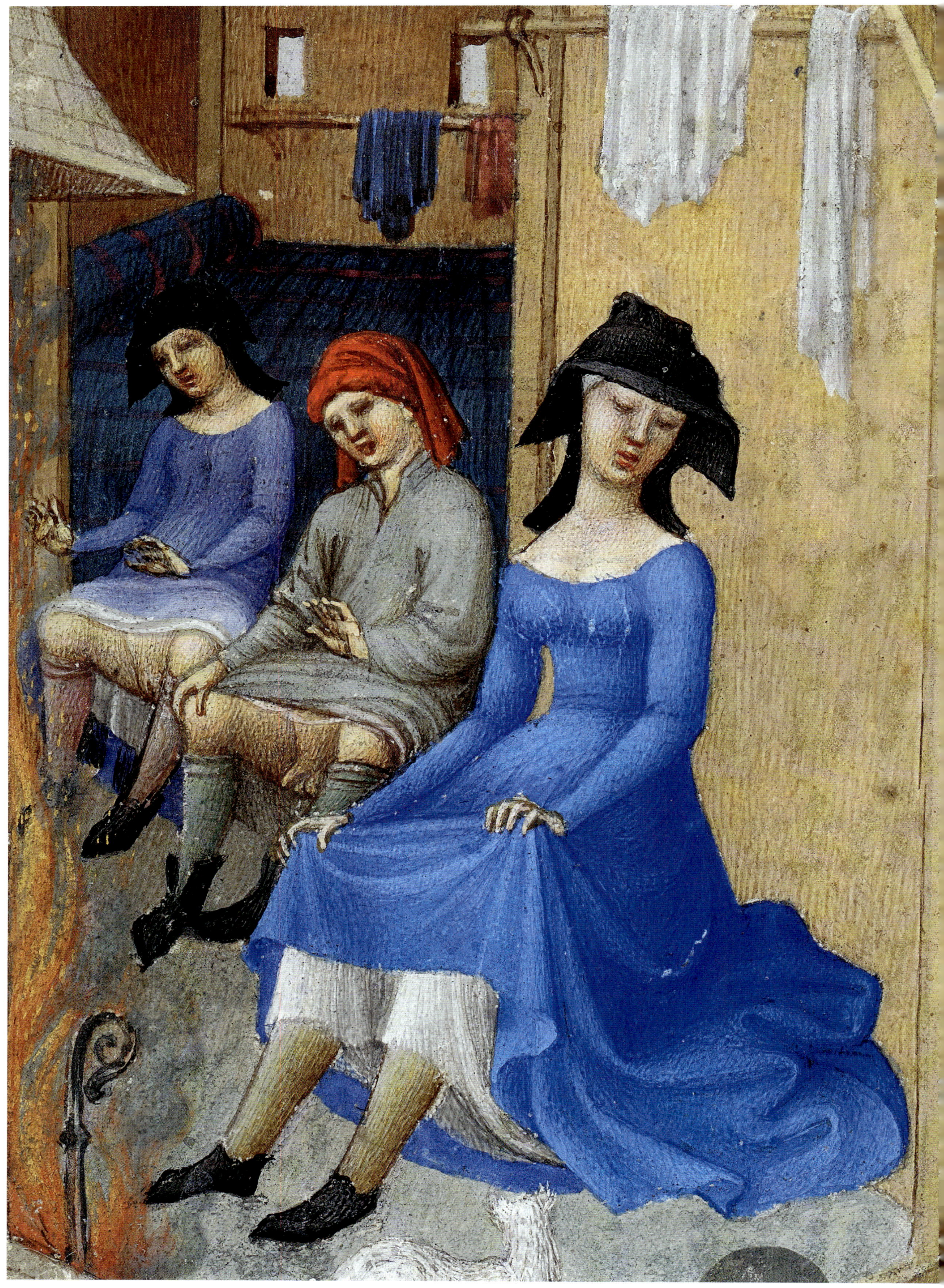

15.

# The *Très Riches Heures* and Calendars in Flemish Manuscripts from the 1520s

Till-Holger Borchert

In the early decades of the sixteenth century, Gerard Horenbout, one of the most accomplished Flemish artists of the time, had the opportunity to study the famous calendar and other miniatures executed by the Van Lymborch brothers and later illuminators including Barthélemy d'Eyck and Jean Colombe in the *Très Riches Heures* of Jean of France, Duke of Berry. Although these miniatures had been painted more than a century earlier, their innovative character and unusual format—they were the first full-page calendar illustrations—prompted the artist to reconsider his own work. They were a source of inspiration for the miniatures that Horenbout contributed to the calendar of the famous *Grimani Breviary*, unquestionably the most ambitious manuscript in early sixteenth-century illumination in Flanders (figs. 6–9).[1]

Horenbout gives his own version of what he saw.[2] His miniature for the month of January, for example, depicts a gentleman's supper, echoing the Van Lymborch image of the Duke of Berry's supper. However, Horenbout reorganizes the interior while taking care to retain several details, such as the dresser on the left, on which the precious tableware is displayed. Although he replaces the tournament tapestry in the duke's manuscript with a "millefleurs" tapestry, he retains the tournament motif, which he turns into a stone bas-relief on the lintel of the fireplace. Horenbout also took liberties with the representation of the figures. He altered their arrangement, but without changing the overall character of the image.

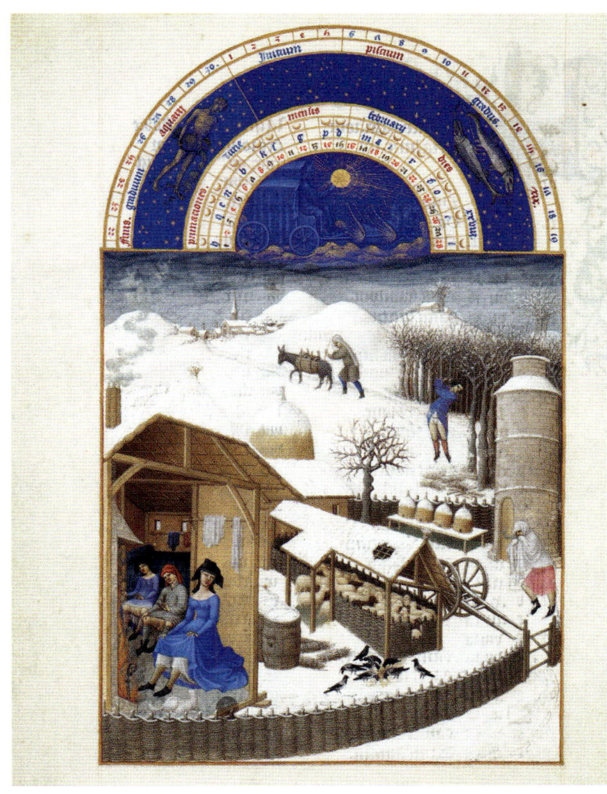

**Fig. 2** Van Lymborch brothers, *Très Riches Heures*, fol. 2v: February

**Fig. 1** Van Lymborch brothers, *Très Riches Heures*, fol. 2v: February, detail

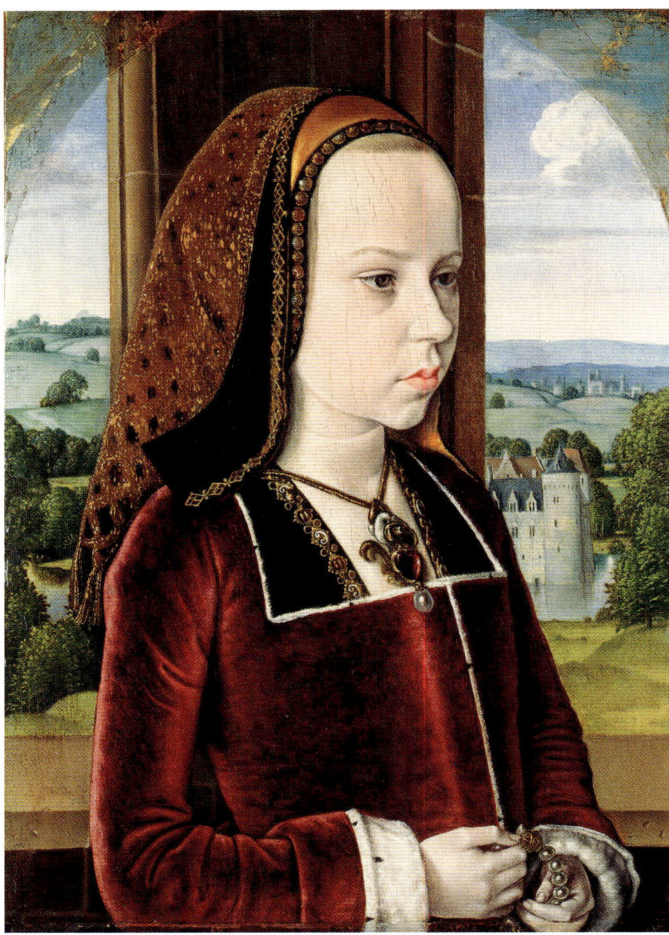

**Fig. 3** Jean Hey, *Margaret of Austria* (New York, The Metropolitan Museum of Art, Acc. No. 1975.1.130)

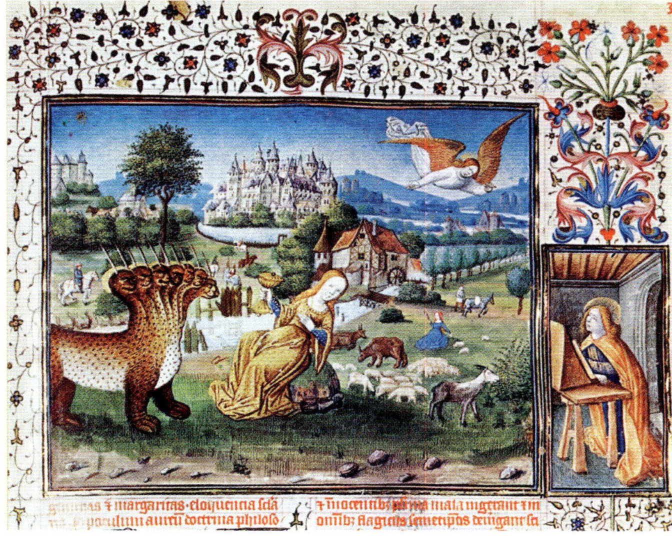

**Fig. 4** Jean Bapteur, Péronet Lamy, and Jean Colombe, *Figured Apocalypse of the Dukes of Savoy*, fol. 37 (San Lorenzo de Escorial, Real Biblioteca de Escorial, Ms Escorial E. Vit. V)

However, he added the figure of a falconer on the left; the man, who wears the collar of the Order of St. Anthony around his neck, is not part of Jean of Berry's entourage as seen in the *Très Riches Heures*. Horenbout may have got the idea from the miniature for the month of August by the Van Lymborch brothers, in which a group of gentlemen and ladies are depicted on horseback.

The winter scene chosen by the Van Lymborch brothers for February was reworked by Horenbout to improve the illusion of space. The Van Lymborch miniature showed a simple dwelling in a snow-covered, rather revolutionary landscape. Horenbout modified the building, adding white "graffiti" representing the symbols of the Burgundian Order of the Golden Fleece on one wall. In the Duke of Berry's manuscript, a woman and a young couple are warming themselves by an open brazier in the house; the young man and woman have lifted their clothing and are exposing their genitals, a detail that Horenbout moves (and also justifies): He depicts a young boy urinating in the fresh snow, which turns yellow—a detail much admired by a commentator who was almost contemporary with the artist.[3]

The pictorial inventions of the Van Lymborch brothers and others who contributed to the *Très Riches Heures* calendar were still considered appropriate for illustrating a luxurious manuscript in the sixteenth century. The miniatures we owe to Horenbout, themselves a reinterpretation of these "prototypes" that had no antecedents, became a model for several calendars found in precious manuscripts—prayer books, breviaries, and other religious codices—intended for an elite clientele made up of cultivated patrons in the Burgundian Netherlands and elsewhere in Europe.[4]

Illuminators, more so than painters on panels, were generally in touch with the great artistic achievements of previous generations since illustrated manuscripts were sometimes not completed until several decades after the work had begun. The task of finishing this kind of project was usually entrusted to craftsmen in a different time and place from the miniature-painters who had started the work. This is why a number of manuscripts served as catalogues of models, enabling younger artists to find pictorial solutions in the work of their predecessors, or to use the miniatures of the past as prototypes for their own creations.[5]

Nonetheless, the reaction in Flanders to the *Très Riches Heures* possesses a characteristic of its own, over and above what can reasonably be considered a common practice among illuminators, namely the appropriation of older artistic compositions. Horenbout was not involved in the completion of the *Très Riches Heures*; the manuscript was not finished when the Van Lymborchs died, and was completed around 1485, by which time it had come into the possession of the House of Savoy.[6]

On the other hand, Horenbout took a spontaneous interest in the work once it was concluded; he consulted the precious prayer book, either because he was stimulated to study its calendar, or out of professional curiosity—a curiosity that was sufficiently compelling to make him view the work. Horenbout made the miniatures in the *Très Riches Heures* calendar his own by adapting them for the *Grimani Breviary*, and other artists followed his example. His reinterpretation of the work of the different months of the year—even if these themes were already commonplace in Flemish art of the time—shaped the iconography of Flemish calendars for the next fifty years, if not longer, and his influence extended far beyond book illumination.[7]

Simon Bening used repeated motifs modeled on Horenbout's calendar miniatures, which he had copied, in several of the manuscripts he illuminated after settling in Bruges in 1520.[8] Bening trained and worked in Ghent under his father Alexander (himself a famous and prolific illuminator known as the Master of the First Prayer Book of Maximilian)[9] and collaborated regularly with Horenbout's workshop. Bening moved to Bruges after his father's death in 1519, and from 1530 onward was undoubtedly the most prominent illuminator in the Netherlands.

## THE *TRÈS RICHES HEURES* IN MARGARET OF AUSTRIA'S LIBRARY

The *Très Riches Heures* was most likely in the possession of Margaret of Austria (1480–1530) (fig. 3) when Horenbout viewed it. The Austro-Burgundian princess, who had a considerable interest in the arts, was a fervent collector as well as a leading patron of Netherlandish artists. Her artistic patronage and her collections embody the importance, both political and cultural, of the Valois-Burgundy ancestry to the House of Habsburg. As a direct descendant of the Valois dukes of Burgundy—she was the daughter of Mary of Burgundy—Margaret asserted her lineage brilliantly through the arts and culture.[10]

Margaret of Austria was one of the greatest bibliophiles of her time. Two inventories drawn up during her regency of the Netherlands, in about 1520 and 1523–24, provide ample proof of this.[11] Although it is not possible to identify the *Très Riches Heures* with any certainty in these documents, they do bear witness to the extraordinary breadth and wealth of Margaret's library. They list 340 manuscripts, plus forty-six printed volumes, covering a remarkable variety of subjects and including devotional books, religious and educational works, philosophical texts, genealogies, and chronicles, as well as volumes of chivalric and courtly literature, and music manuscripts. Margaret owned one of the most important princely libraries in Europe in the first half of the sixteenth century, keeping most of her books in a dedicated space in the west wing of the Hof van Savoye, her palace in Mechelen.[12]

Margaret's love of books must have begun in childhood and seems to have fully matured in her early adult years. Following her mother's death, the three-year-old was betrothed in 1483 to the French king, Charles VIII, and raised at the French court in Amboise until 1491. Books from the rich library of the late Queen of France, Charlotte, were used to further the education of Margaret and other princesses.[13] After Charles VIII annulled the marriage in 1491, so that he could marry Anne of Brittany, Margaret was sent back to the Burgundian Netherlands. By this time, in 1493, the thirteen-year-old princess was already in possession of a lavishly illustrated Neapolitan *Bible moralisée* (Moralized bible) and two missals.[14]

In the Netherlands, the princess settled in Mechelen, where Margaret of York was tasked with her education. The latter, the widow of Charles the Bold and godmother to the young Margaret, owned several richly illuminated religious manuscripts, which reflected her great piety. When Margaret of York died in 1503, her goddaughter inherited her books.[15]

Before Margaret of Austria returned permanently to the Burgundian Netherlands and took up residence in Mechelen in 1506, she had already been married twice, on both occasions being widowed early. Her first husband, John, Prince of Asturias, heir presumptive to the Spanish throne, died in Salamanca in 1497, two years after their marriage. Margaret's second marriage, to Philibert II of Savoy, lasted from 1501 until his untimely death three years later.

When Margaret left Spain in 1499, she owned several manuscripts and incunabula, mainly books of hours and magnificently illustrated devotional works, but also copies of secular texts such as Christine de Pizan's *Livre des trois vertus* (The book of the three virtues) and Jean de Mandeville's *Livre des merveilles* (Mandeville's travels).[16]

In Savoy, although very busy with political matters, Margaret was able to take advantage of the ducal library in Chambéry. The library had been built up by great bibliophiles, including Amadeus VIII and Charles I, the latter having secured the services of Jean Colombe, the French illuminator from Bourges.[17] Margaret was probably familiar with Colombe's work through the books in the Amboise library, as the artist had previously worked for King Louis IX of France and his wife, Charlotte of Savoy.

In their marriage contract, Philibert had guaranteed Margaret that, in addition to an annual dowry, she would receive "tapisseries, bagues, bijoux et autres biens meubles qui appartiendraient en propre à la princesse ou bien à sa cour" (tapestries, rings, jewels, and other movable property that would be the sole property of the princess or her court).[18] This contract enabled Margaret to claim ownership of a selection of works from the dukes' library collections, including an *Apocalypse* (fig. 4) produced for Amadeus VIII and lavishly illustrated by Jean Bapteur and Péronet Lamy. Like the *Très Riches Heures*, this unfinished manuscript was completed by Jean Colombe around 1486, or later.[19] On her journey north, Margaret also took novels of chivalry such as *L'Histoire du Saint Graal* and *Le Roman de Merlin*, two volumes that had also been illuminated by Colombe.[20]

The hypothesis that the *Très Riches Heures* was among the treasures Margaret brought back to the Burgundian Netherlands is based on strong indirect evidence.[21] The precious manuscript belonged to the Dukes of Savoy; the fact that the famous calendar miniatures by the Van Lymborch brothers were the main source of inspiration for the *Grimani Breviary* corroborates the suggestion that the *Très Riches Heures* was in the Burgundian Netherlands from 1506 onward; lastly, the fact that Gerard Horenbout was officially in the service of Margaret of Austria as a court painter from April 1515 provides another argument that she was in possession of the manuscript.

And yet, it is not possible to identify with certainty the *Très Riches Heures* in Margaret's library. It may be that it corresponds to the volume described as "une grande heure," which was kept—along with two missals and three prayer books—in the palace chapel, which was used for the official ceremonies of her court.[22] It has also been suggested that the *Très Riches Heures* was the volume described as "une riche heure en parchemin, bien historiee et enlumynee, couverte de satin noir" (a rich book of hours in parchment, nicely historiated and

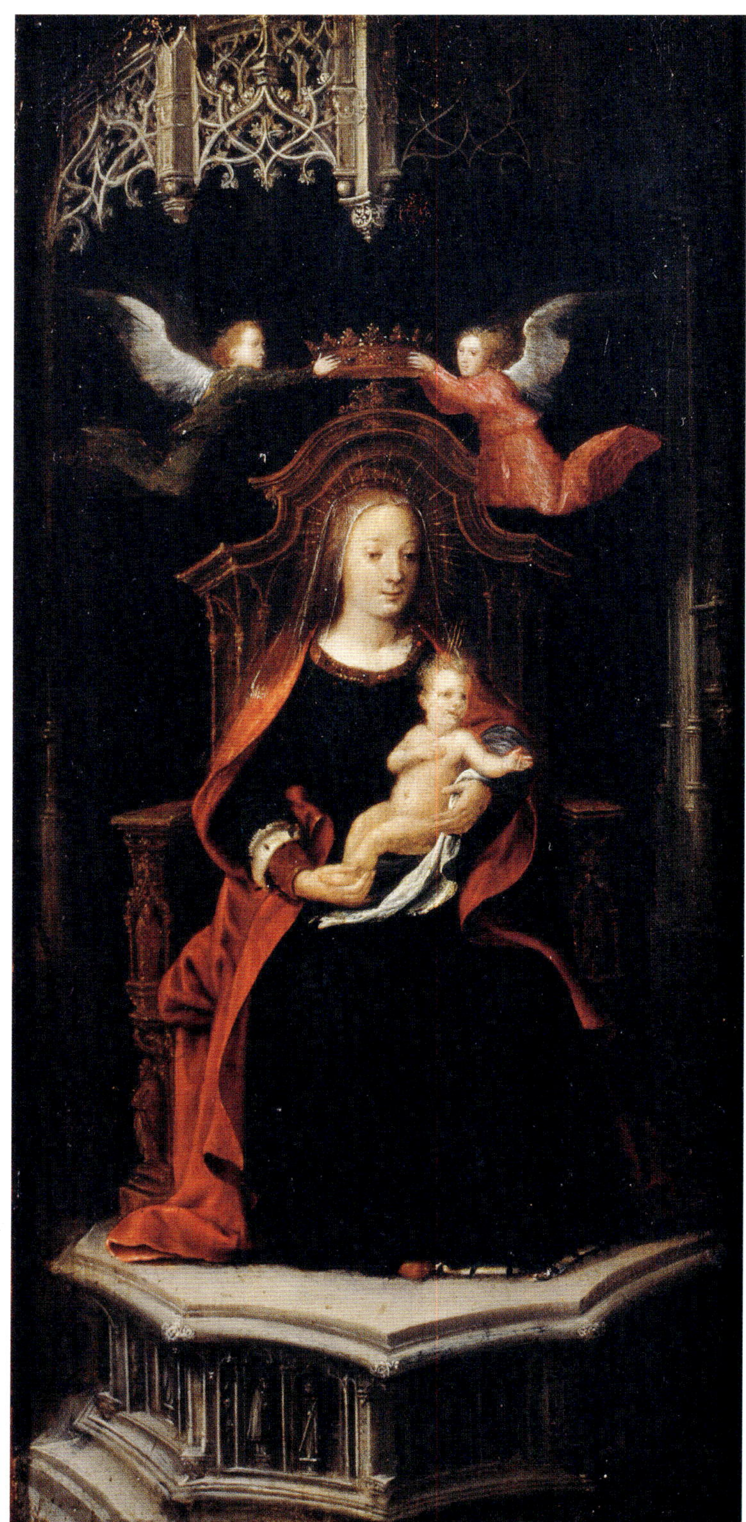

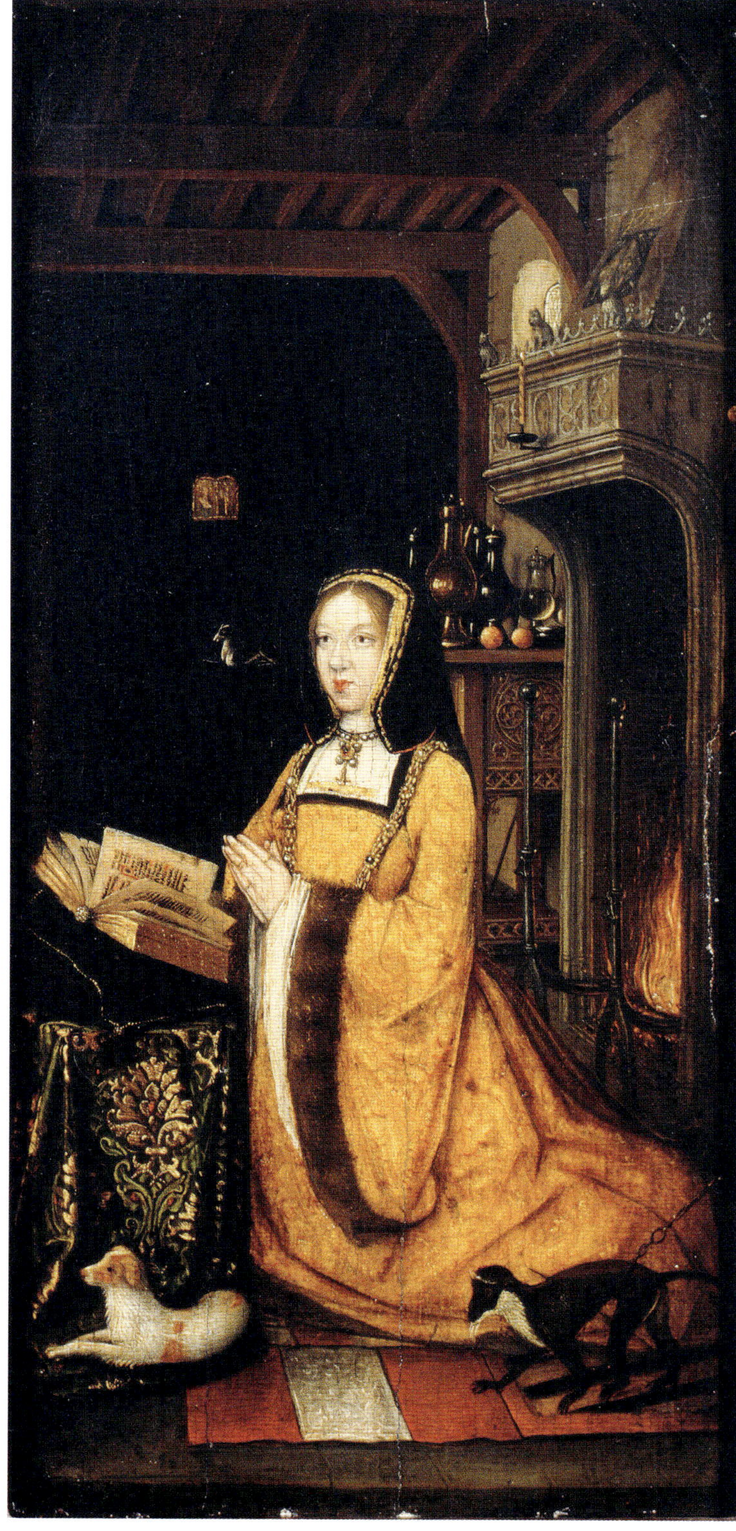

**Fig. 5** Master of 1499, *Margaret of Austria Adoring the Virgin* (Ghent, Museum voor Schone Kunsten, Acc. No. 1973-A)

illuminated, covered in black satin) that Margaret, according to the 1523–24 inventory, kept in her small cabinet (fig. 5).[23]

This room, located next to her bedroom, served as her *studiolo*; in it she displayed *objets d'art* and curiosities, including small paintings, sculptures, model books, drawings, manuscripts, medals, jewelry, and *naturalia*.[24] It was an intimate place devoted to knowledge, one that the regent of the Netherlands also used for her devotional practice. When Albrecht Dürer visited Mechelen in June 1521, Margaret of Austria personally showed him the paintings in her palace; together they visited the library, a room decorated with the most representative works, but she also introduced him to the smaller, more artistically original creations she kept in her bedroom and small cabinet.[25]

Dürer was not the only one to have the opportunity to observe the palace and the works it housed; other visitors included Erasmus and Antonio de Beatis, who admired Margaret's richly decorated library and her collection. Given the princess's interest in the arts, it is safe to assume that certain artists were occasionally allowed to visit and observe the collections. It is therefore not surprising that Gerard Horenbout had the opportunity to study the *Très Riches Heures*, probably around 1515, when he replaced Jacopo de' Barbari as Margaret's court painter and valet.

## THE CALENDAR, A SOURCE OF INSPIRATION

At the time, Gerard Horenbout was an established master with a successful career spanning almost thirty years. He became a master in Ghent in 1487 and worked in the city until he and his family moved to England in the mid-1520s. He oversaw a busy workshop where he trained his children. He was both a painter and an illuminator, and also created tapestries and stained-glass windows. However, the only documented works by Horenbout are the miniatures for the *Sforza Hours*, for which he was paid by Margaret of Austria in 1520.[26] But these miniatures are of little use in giving an overview of Horenbout's work: Their Italianate style has no equivalent in Flemish illumination, and shows that the workshop attempted to reproduce the older illuminations found in the then unfinished work.[27]

The attribution of the calendar in the *Grimani Breviary* to Horenbout is based on circumstantial evidence: Not only did the artist have access to the *Très Riches Heures* in Mechelen, but his name—Gerardo da Guant (Gerard of Ghent)—was associated by Marcantonio Michiel with the illuminators of the manuscript he saw in Cardinal Grimani's palace in Venice in 1521.[28] Although these miniatures were influenced by the prototypes created by the Van Lymborch brothers, the mastery of the pictorial space, colors, and physiognomies of the figures confirm the hypothesis that Gerard Horenbout should be identified with the Master of James IV of Scotland.[29]

One of Ghent's most important illuminators, this master owes his name to a prayer book made for the King of Scotland around 1500.[30] From around the 1490s until the 1520s, Horenbout collaborated with illuminators from Ghent and Bruges, creating miniatures for a number of precious manuscripts. Examples of his early work can be found in the *Isabella Breviary*, for which Horenbout worked with the Master of the Dresden Prayer Book and Bruges-based painter Gerard David.[31] On more than one occasion, he collaborated with Alexander Bening, notably on the breviary of Eleanor of Portugal,[32] the *Isabella Hours*,[33] and the magnificent breviary preserved in Antwerp's Museum Mayer van den Bergh,[34] which may have been commissioned by Margaret of Austria to celebrate the marriage of her sister-in-law, Maria of Aragon, to Manuel I of Portugal in 1500.[35]

More than ten years later, around 1510–15, both artists participated in the illumination of the *Grimani Breviary*. It was probably the Bening workshop in Ghent (where the aging Alexander worked with his son Simon) that coordinated this complex project. The *Grimani Breviary* has no fewer than 833 leaves. In addition to decorated margins on almost every page, the volume contains eighty-nine miniatures, often arranged in pairs on facing leaves; they either occupy the entire page, or are set in frames painted in trompe l'oeil, typical of Flemish precious manuscripts of this type.[36] Simon, his elderly father, and their assistants painted most of the breviary's miniatures, which clearly show links with the inventions of Hugo van der Goes (figs. 6–9).

In addition to the Bening and Horenbout workshops, the hand of another artist, known as the "Master of the David Scenes in the Grimani Breviary"—perhaps one of Horenbout's assistants—has been identified, who contributed a few miniatures.[37] Gerard David, who had already been involved in decorating the *Isabella Breviary* and that of Museum Mayer van den Bergh, was also involved in the illumination.[38]

As with most Flemish precious manuscripts of the early sixteenth century, the identity of the patron who commissioned the *Grimani Breviary* is not known to us. But the heraldic clues it contains—such as the emblem of the Order of the Golden Fleece (fol. 2v; fig. 4) and the arms of the Habsburgs of Austria (fol. 10v; fig. 5)—suggest it was a prominent member of the Burgundian Habsburg dynasty. It has been suggested that Margaret of Austria herself commissioned the work, as a gift for her father, Maximilian I, or for her nephew, the future emperor Charles V. No tangible evidence supports this conjecture, however.[39]

The breviary was purchased—and modified—by Antonio Siciliano, ambassador to the Duke of Milan, who visited the regent and admired her collections in Mechelen in 1514. This diplomat had a keen interest in the arts and took advantage of his stay to commission and/or purchase Flemish works, which soon found their way into the collections of Venetian nobles. Exactly when and for how much he acquired this superb breviary is not known. The Venetian humanist Marcantonio Michiel reports that he sold it to Cardinal Grimani of Venice in 1520 for 500 ducats, almost a hundred times the usual price of a printed book.[40]

Had it not been for the example of the *Très Riches Heures*, Horenbout's calendar would probably not have existed in this form; this appears self-evident if we compare the work with earlier calendars illuminated by the Ghent artist or his contemporaries. By the end of the fifteenth century at the latest, the depiction of the work and tasks related to each month of the year had become a regular theme in Flemish art. The Master of the Dresden Prayer Book, to name just one of the artists involved, played an important role in the development of this standard.[41]

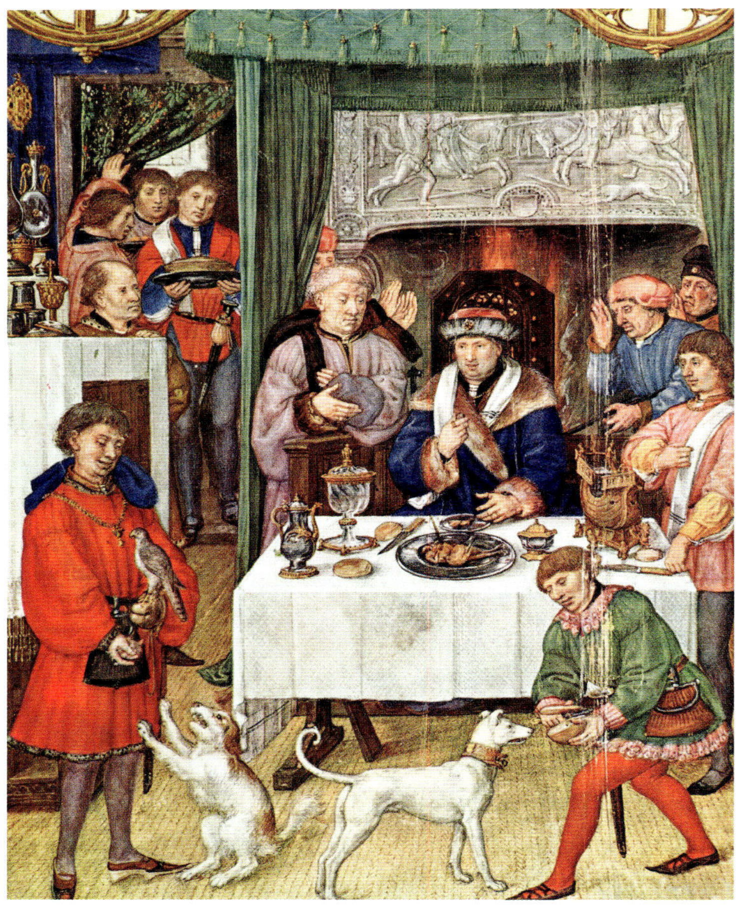

**Fig. 6** Alexandre Bening, Simon Bening, and Gerard Horenbout, *Grimani Breviary*, fol. 1v: January, c. 1510–20 (Venice, Biblioteca Nazionale Marciana, cod. Lat. I, 99)

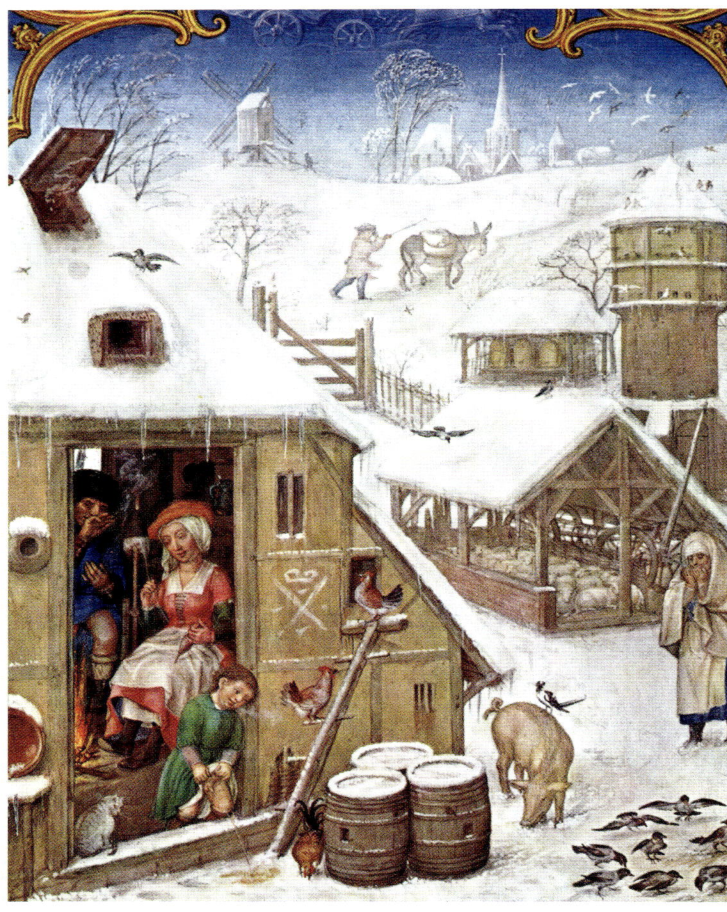

**Fig. 7** Alexandre Bening, Simon Bening, and Gerard Horenbout, *Grimani Breviary*, fol. 2v: February, c. 1510–20 (Venice, Biblioteca Nazionale Marciana, cod. Lat. I, 99)

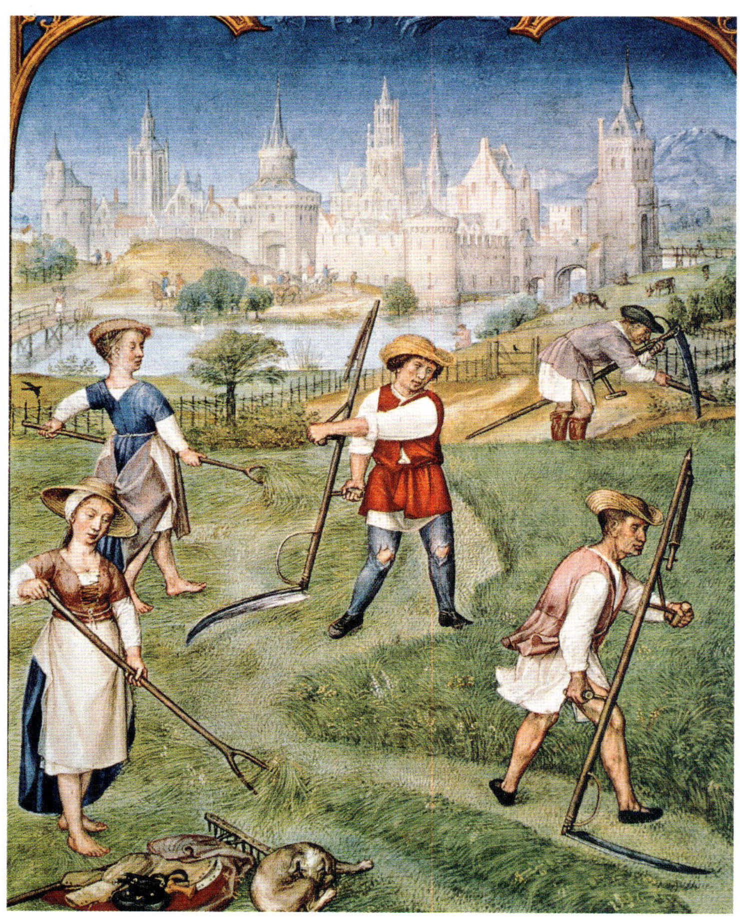

**Fig. 8** Alexandre Bening, Simon Bening, and Gerard Horenbout, *Grimani Breviary*, fol 6v: June, c. 1510–20 (Venice, Biblioteca Nazionale Marciana, cod. Lat. I, 99)

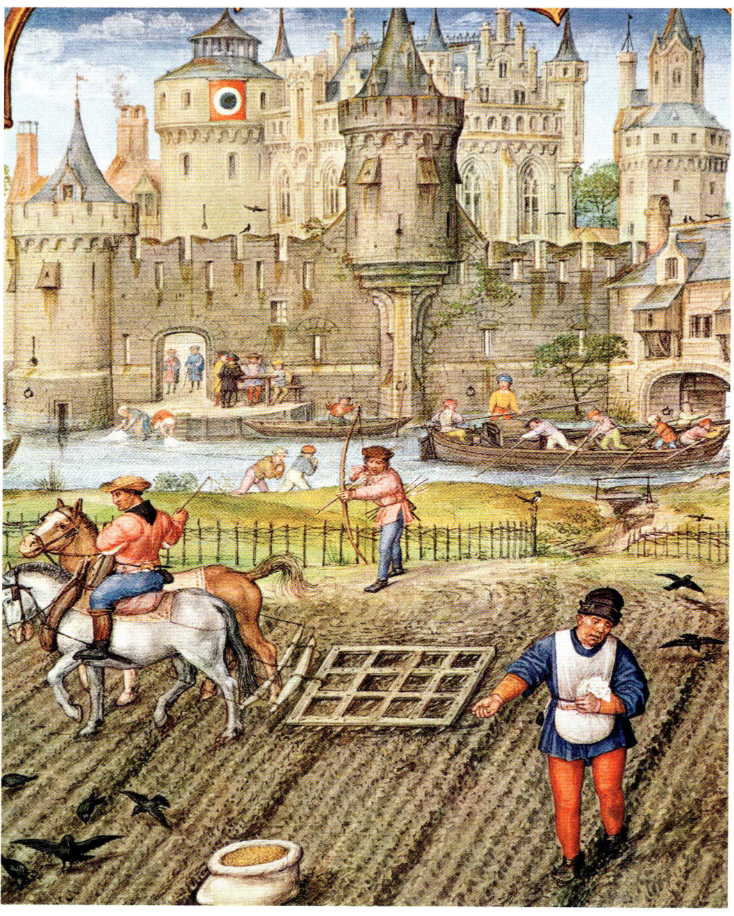

**Fig. 9** Alexandre Bening, Simon Bening, and Gerard Horenbout, *Grimani Breviary*, fol. 10v: October, c. 1510–20 (Venice, Biblioteca Nazionale Marciana, cod. Lat. I, 99)

By adapting certain miniatures from the calendar of the *Très Riches Heures* in his work, Horenbout unwittingly made an essential contribution to the homogenization of Flemish calendar iconography. The motifs and compositions by the Van Lymborch brothers that he revisited in the calendar of the *Grimani Breviary* present features that were to become increasingly common in the representation of the months and seasons found in Flemish art. Through the models used in various manuscripts executed by Simon Bening's workshop in Bruges, these elements were another source of influence for Pieter Bruegel in his *Four Seasons*.[42]

1 Venice, Bibl. Marciana, cod. Lat I, 99, fols. 1v–13r.
2 For a detailed comparison of the Horenbout miniatures with those of the Van Lymborch brothers, see König and Heyder 2016, 71–95.
3 Frimmel 1886 (1974), 104.
4 Los Angeles and London 2003–04, 313–487.
5 Borchert 2024, 22.
6 Villela-Petit 2018b.
7 Pearsall and Salter 1973, 152–60; Hansen 1984, 33–60; Kren and Rathofer 1988; Kren 1988, 350–61, 376–81.
8 See, e.g., the *Hennessy Hours* (Brussels, KBR, Ms. II 15), fol. 1v; the *Petites Heures* (London, BL, Ms. Egerton 1147), fol. 6v; and the calendar fragment held in Munich (BSB, Ms. Clm 236737), fol. 2v (see Wolf 2006, 95).
9 Los Angeles and London 2003–04, 190–91 (note by Th. Kren).
10 Eichberger 2002, *passim*, especially 145–63; Eichberger 2018.
11 Lille, Arch. dép. du Nord, Chambre d des Comptes de Lille no. 123925, 4 (fragment of an inventory of the library of c. 1520); Paris, BnF, Cinq cents de Colbert 128, fol. 5v (inventory of 1523–24). Checa Cremades 2010, III, 2412 (no. 1520) & 2429 (nos. 1523/4).
12 Debae 1995, *passim*; Eichberger 2002, 124–33, 167–75; Legaré 2005, 217–18.
13 Legaré 2005, 214–15; Rivière Ciavaldini 2018, 94–96.
14 Zimmermann 1883; Legaré 2005, 219.
15 Blockmans 1992, 33–44; Morgan 1992; Legaré 2005, 207–14.
16 Debae 1995, x–xi; Legaré 2005, 216–17.
17 On the library of Amadeus VIII, see Saroni 2004, *passim*; on Colombe's work for the House of Savoy, see Seidel 2011.
18 Lille, Arch. dép. du Nord, B 434 no. 17892, cited by Debae 1995, xi.
19 San Lorenzo, Real Bibl. de Escorial, Vitr. 1, see Bartz and Seidel 2011.
20 Brussels, KBR, Ms. 9246, see Debae 1995, 70–77 (no. 45); Paris, BnF, Arsenal, Ms. 3479, see Debae 1995, 30–35 (no. 30).
21 On the provenance of the *Très Riches Heures*, see Villela-Petit 2018b, and essay by M. Deldicque, pp. 283–89.
22 Debae 1995, 3–8 (Paris, BnF, Colbert 128, Chapelle, 3).
23 Ibid., 494 (no. 367); identification proposed by Eichberger 2002, 197–98.
24 Eichberger 2002, 195–205, 372–88.
25 Ibid., 373–74; Eichberger 2021, 145–46.
26 Campbell and Foister 1986, 719–21; Krieger 2012, 41–72.
27 London, BL, Ms. Add. 34294; see Evans and Brinkmann 1995, 566–86; Los Angeles and London 2003–04, 429–31; Krieger 2012, 67–72, 439–58.
28 The other two artists mentioned —erroneously—by Michiel are Zuan Memelin (Hans Memling) and Livieno da Anversa (Lieven van Lathem); see Frimmel 1886 (1974), 104; König and Heyder 2016, 14–15, 19–20; on the reliability or not of Marcantonio Michiel's *Notizie*, see Campbell 1981, 468.
29 Los Angeles and London 2003–04, 166–67; Krieger 2012, 438–39; König and Heyder 2016, 25–31.
30 Vienna, ÖNB, Ms. 1897; see Los Angeles and London 2003–04, 371–73; Krieger 2012, 48–60.
31 London, BL, Ms. Add. 18851; see Los Angeles and London 2003–04, 347–51.
32 New York, Morgan Library, Ms. M 52; see Los Angeles and London 2003–04, 321–24; Krieger 2012, 169–208.
33 Cleveland Museum of Art, inv. 1963.256; see Los Angeles and London 2003–04, 358–61.
34 Antwerp, Museum Mayer van den Bergh, inv. 946; see Los Angeles and London 2003–04, 324–28; Dekeyzer 2004, *passim*; Krieger 2012, 208–26.
35 Dekeyzer 2004, 157–80.
36 J.C. Heyder, in König and Heyder 2016, 48–59; As-Vijvers 2013, 303–18.
37 Los Angeles and London 2003–04, 383–85 (note by E. Morrison); Morrison 2006, 149–57.
38 Ibid., 344–45 (note by M.W. Ainsworth).
39 König and Heyder 2016, 16, 220.
40 Frimmel 1886 (1974), 104.
41 Hansen 1984, 193–203, 223–26, 229–46; Kren 1988, 357–58.
42 Borchert 2019, 96–108.

**Fig. 10** Following pages: Van Lymborch brothers, *Très Riches Heures*, fol. 2v: February, detail

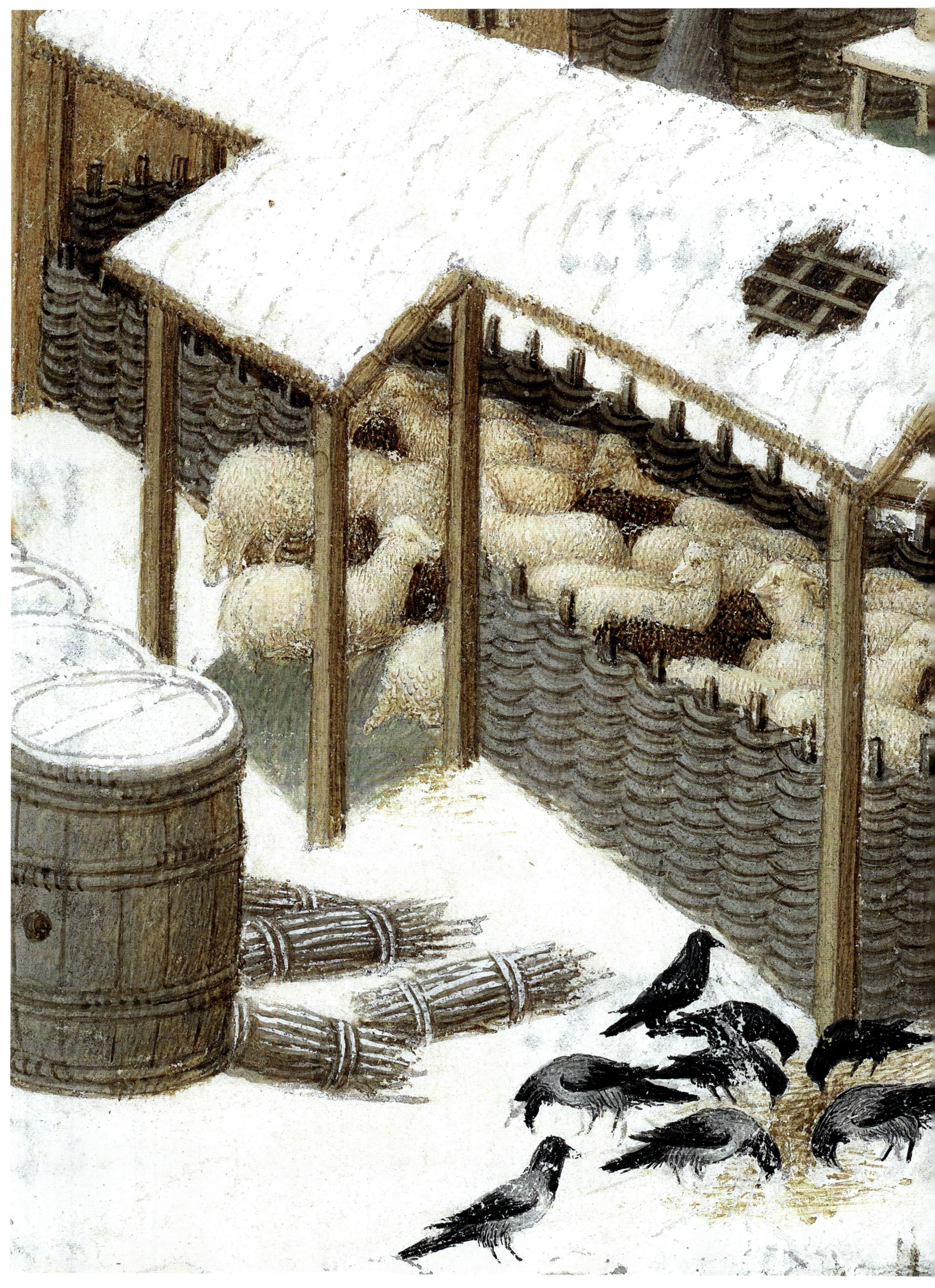

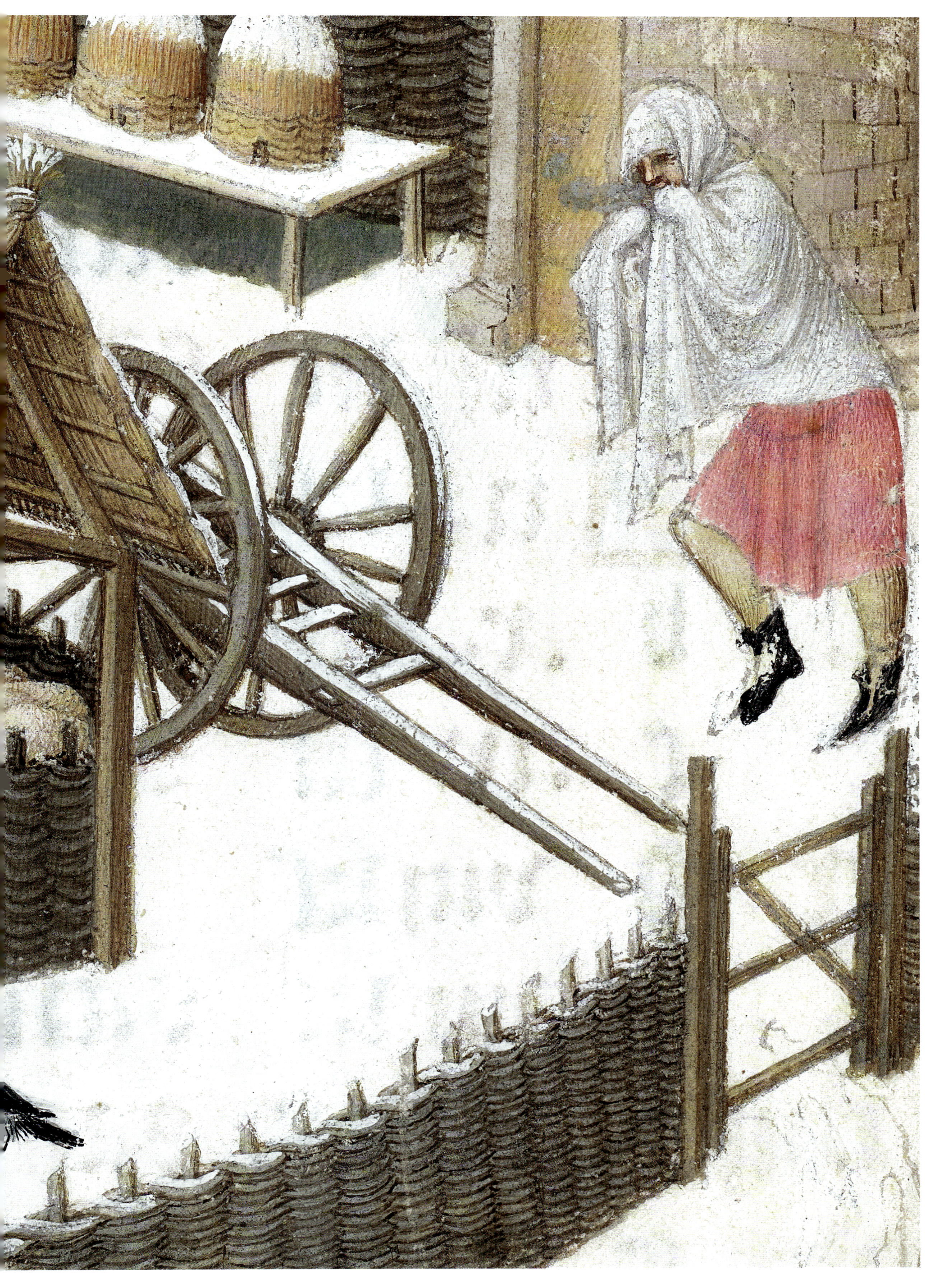

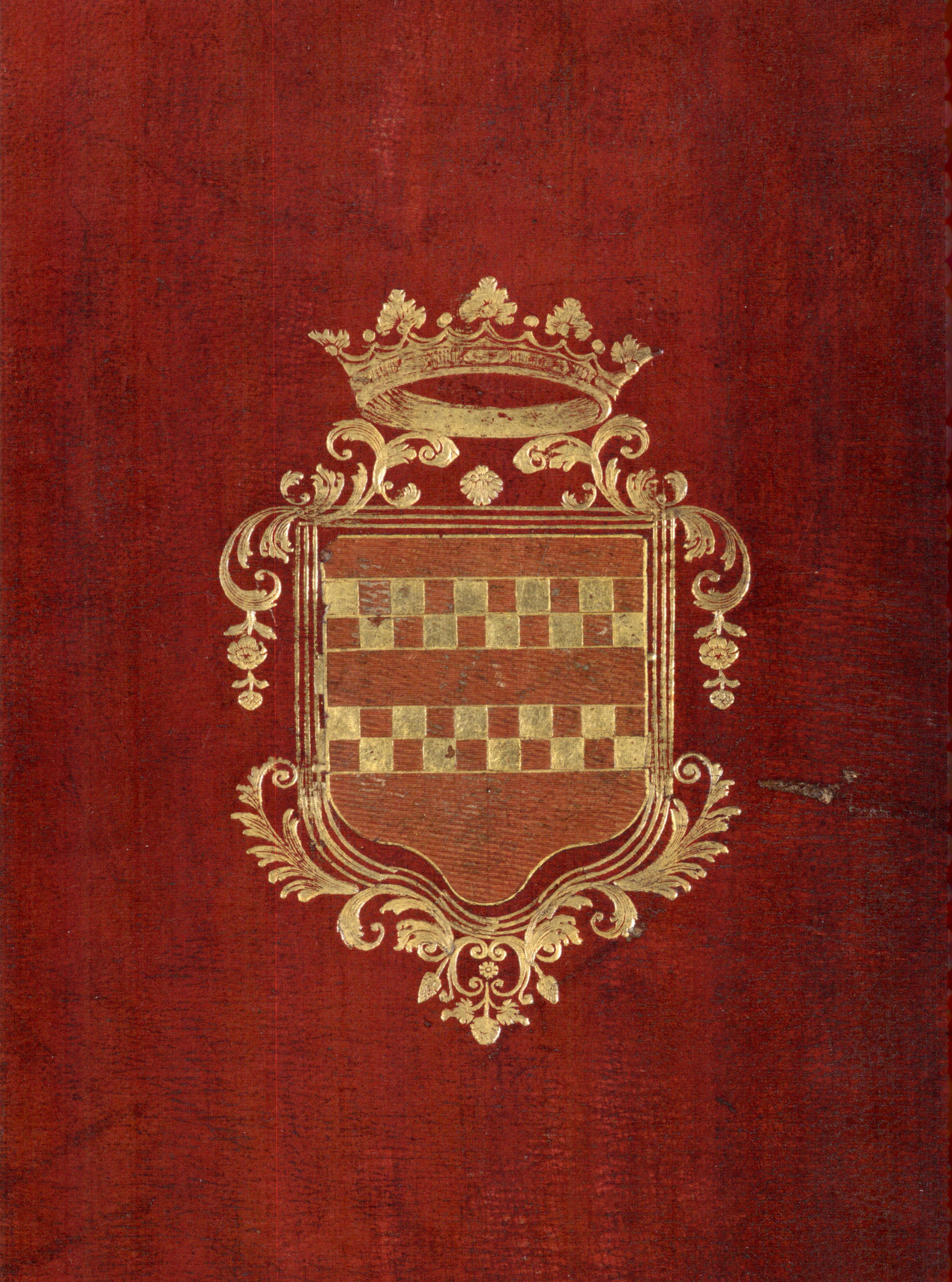

# 16.

# The *Très Riches Heures*: A Tentative History

Mathieu Deldicque

On June 15, 1416, the Duke of Berry breathed his last, just a few months after the death of Johan van Lymborch. The death of the patron prince put a brake on the creation of his *Très Riches Heures*, which became even more orphaned when Paul and Herman van Lymborch in turn departed this world in the autumn of the same year. The illuminators from Nijmegen had been part of the ducal court, and their unfinished manuscript was among the items Jean of Berry left behind. The Duke of Berry also left a large number of debts that had to be discharged. His will, drawn up on May 25, 1416, accompanied by codicils,[1] provided for the settlement of thirty-four creditors. The duke had appointed as executors his grandson, Charles d'Artois, Count of Eu, and his son-in-law, the Duke of Bourbon, both of whom had been held prisoner since the defeat at Azincourt in 1415. As his illness progressed, Jean of Berry made a number of changes on June 8. Fearing he would die before the executors he had designated returned, he appointed his youngest daughter, Marie of Berry, Duchess of Bourbon, in their place.

On August 8, royal letters ordered that the executors of his will should divide all his assets collected in Paris between his two daughters from his first marriage, the Countess of Armagnac and the Duchess of Bourbon, and his creditors. The ducal collections in Bourges, Mehun-sur-Yèvre, and Paris were brought together in the Parisian residence of Bernard d'Armagnac, the duke's son-in-law, so that all parties concerned could be paid. The collections were inventoried, so that they could either be divided among the heirs or sold—some debts, too large, would remain unpaid.

### THE LIQUIDATION OF THE DUKE OF BERRY'S ESTATE

It is in this inventory that we find the earliest surviving reference to the *Très Riches Heures*. The manuscript is described thus: "Item en une layette plusieurs cayers d'une tres riches heures que faisoient Pol et ses freres tres richement historiez et enluminez ; prisez V$^{c}$ liv. t" (Item, in a box several quires of a very rich book of hours, which Paul and his brothers were working on, very richly historiated and illuminated, valued at 500 livres tournois).[2] It is listed among the duke's "autres biens appartenant à l'exécution" (other goods part of the execution), which, according to the agreement between the executors and the creditors, were "baillez et delivrez" (given and delivered) by the executors to representatives of the creditors.[3] No mention is made of the geographical origin of the manuscript, which was not among the duke's belongings in Bourges and Mehun-sur-Yèvre, nor among the books kept in Mehun and brought to Paris, nor among those from Bourges. However, the calendar painted by the Van Lymborch brothers after their other contributions to the manuscript, around 1415, reveals it was probably Paris, which inspired the illuminators to

**Fig. 1** Front board of the binding of the *Très Riches Heures*

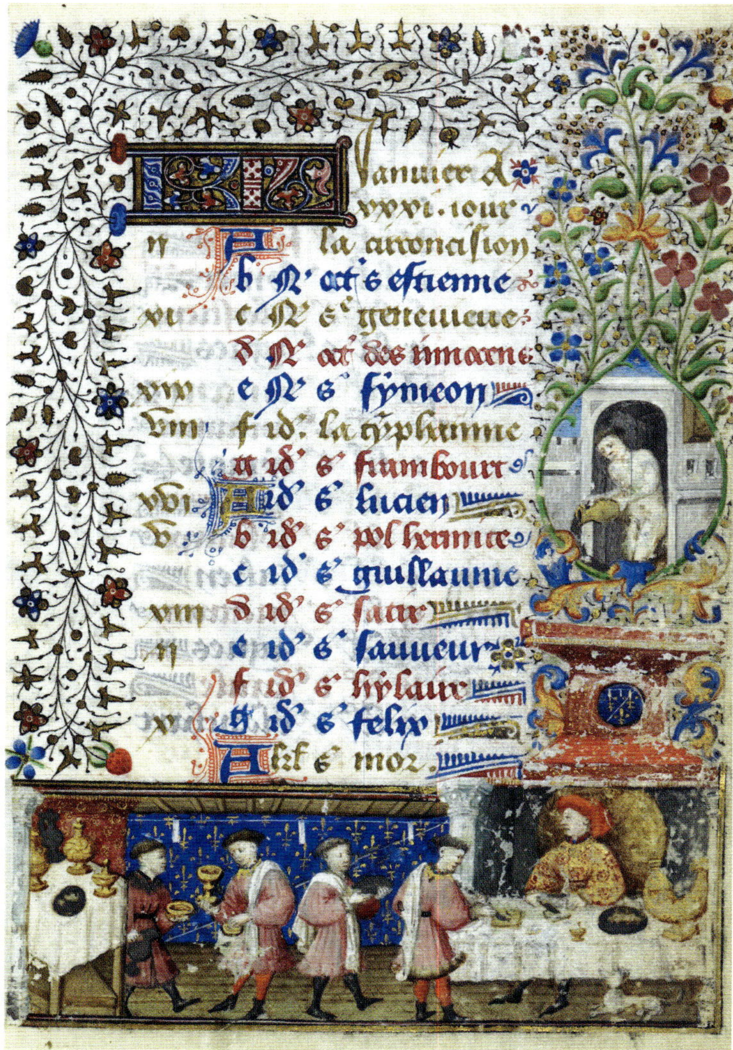

**Fig. 2** Jean Haincelin, *Dunois Hours*, fol. 1 (London, British Library, Ms Yates Thompson 3)

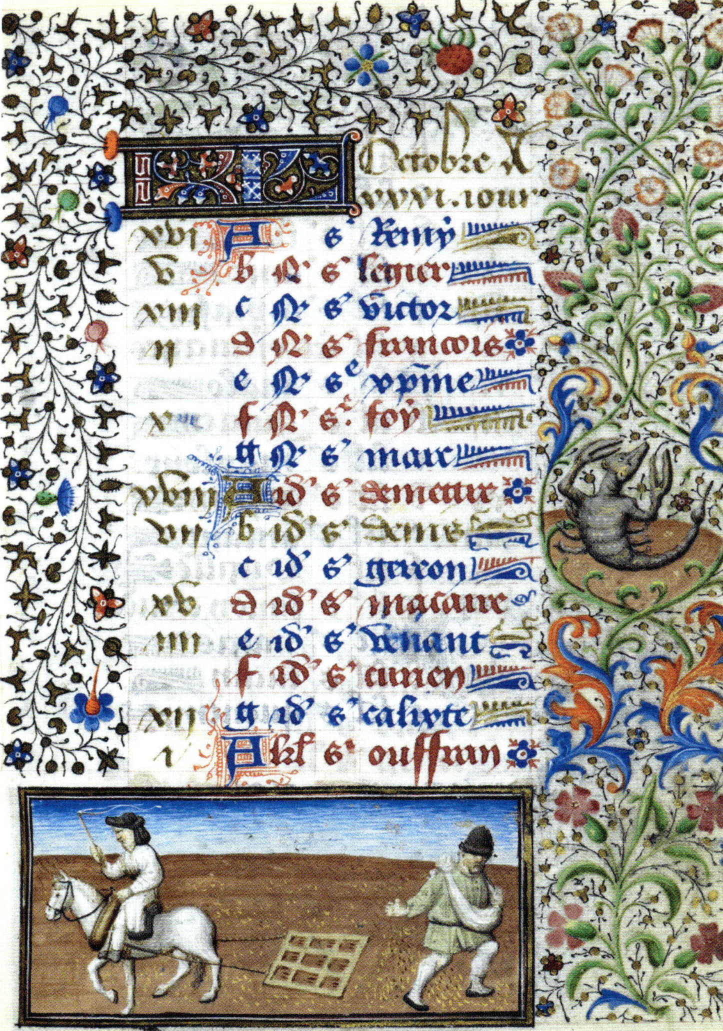

**Fig. 3** Jean Haincelin, *Dunois Hours*, fol. 4 (London, British Library, Ms Yates Thompson 3)

create several cityscapes. In any case, the *Très Riches Heures*, which was less valuable than other manuscripts due to its incompleteness, was among the assets withdrawn from the estate to pay the duke's debts.[4]

The other assets, in particular the books, were divided up after being appraised by four booksellers attached to the University of Paris, namely Regnault du Montet, Olivier de l'Empire, Jehan Marlais, and Denis Courtillier. Marie of Berry received forty-one manuscripts on the death of her father.[5] The reason she obtained so many, while her sister Bonne and husband Bernard d'Armagnac received only five, is because part of her dowry had not been paid. Furthermore, as executor, Marie of Berry requested that she be compensated in goods, jewels, and books worth 40,000 livres tournois (less than the remainder of her dowry, which amounted to 70,000 livres). Thus, neither of the duke's daughters came into possession of the *Très Riches Heures*.[6]

The Count of Eu, the duke's grandson, also needed 20,000 livres so that he could be released from his English jail. It was also necessary to remunerate nearly 500 loyal servants. Two sales were organized, unfortunately without any inventory of their contents, including one between October 18, 1417 and April 25, 1418 for the benefit of the impecunious Charles VI, "pour le fait de sa guerre" (for the purpose of his war). Was the *Très Riches Heures* part of this sale?

The rest went to the duke's creditors, which included a large number of important Parisian merchants. Pierre de l'Esclat and Jean Sac (both from Genoa), Audebert Catin (a moneychanger), and Étienne de Bonpuis (a furrier), representatives of all the creditors, were entrusted with holding part of the estate's assets until the executors had completed payment of the debts. Catin was one of the duke's official suppliers, as was Bonpuis, a fervent Armagnac and one of Jean of Berry's major financial backers.[7] The *Très Riches Heures* may also have been among the remaining goods delivered to these four. Having been removed from the Armagnac residence, the manuscript may have been kept in Bonpuis's residence. The long process of selling or allocating property was severely disrupted when the Burgundians entered Paris on May 28 and 29, 1418, imprisoning, murdering, or driving into exile many members of the Armagnac party involved in the administration of the Duke of Berry's property. Bonpuis fled Paris on June 10, 1418, and his

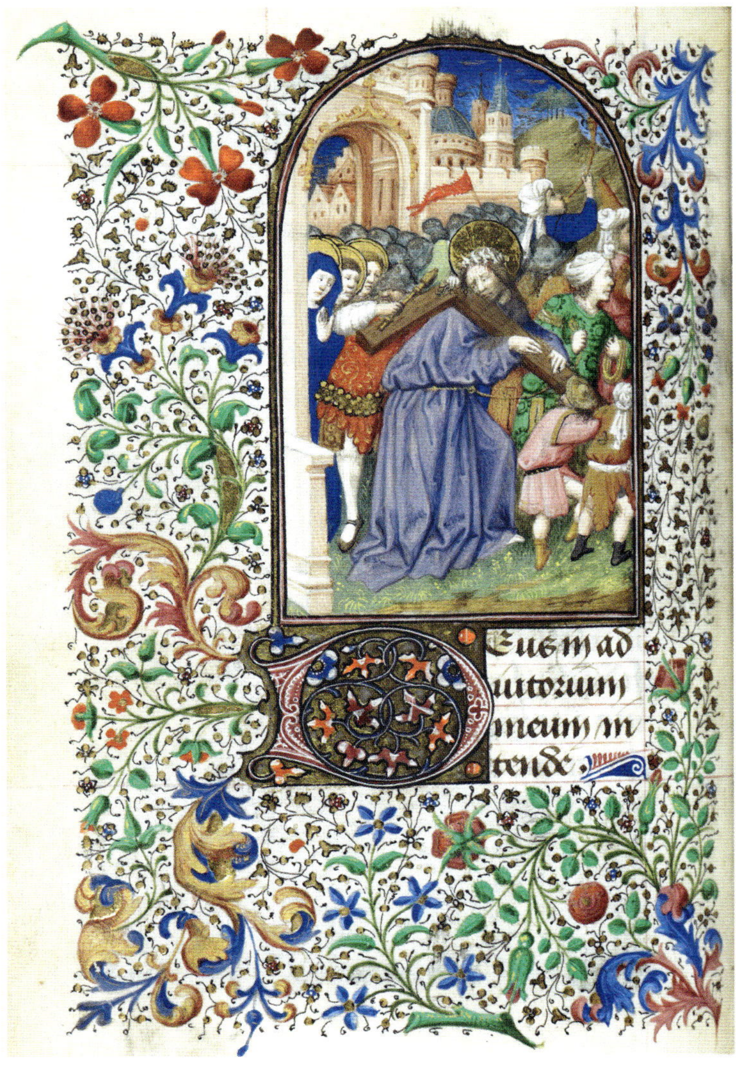

**Fig. 4** Jean Haincelin, *Dunois Hours*, fol. 136v (London, British Library, Ms Yates Thompson 3)

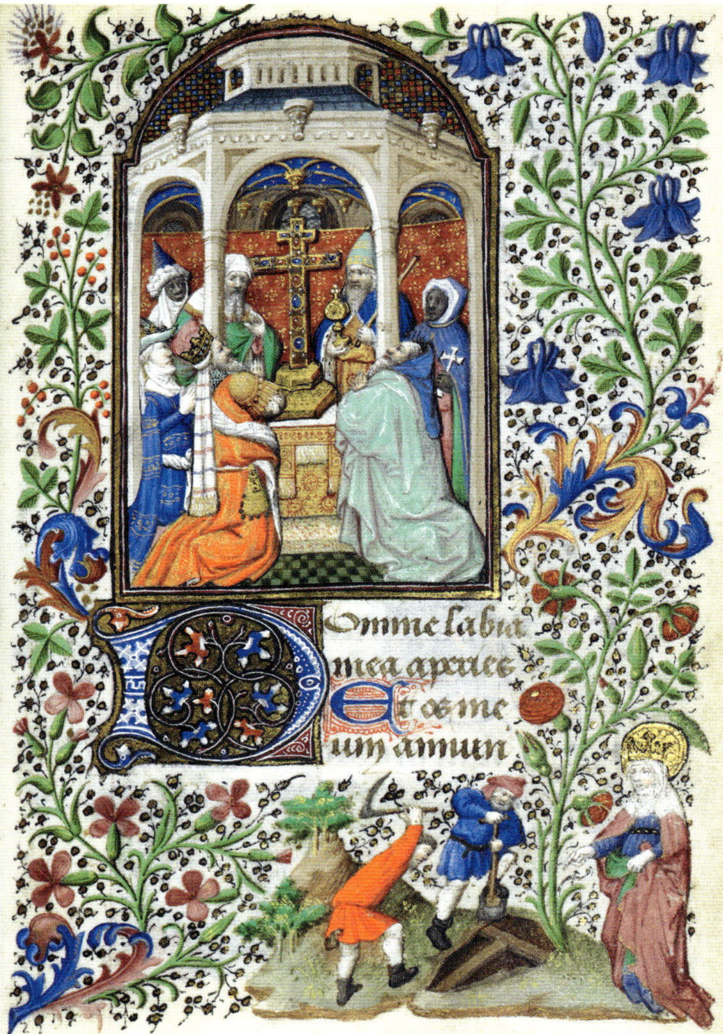

**Fig. 5** Jean Haincelin, *Dunois Hours*, fol. 184 (London, British Library, Ms Yates Thompson 3)

property was confiscated by the Anglo-Burgundian administration. Pierre de l'Esclat was executed on June 12. Catin and Sac pledged their allegiance to the John the Fearless, Duke of Burgundy. Who took possession of the *Très Riches Heures*? Catin, who was married to Marie de Breuil, mother of Gillette la Mercière, Paul van Lymborch's wife?[8] Or did Bonpuis flee Paris with the manuscript? Did he put it in a safe place or sell it before he escaped? Were his possessions looted during his exile?

## THE REAPPEARANCE OF A MODEL MANUSCRIPT

In the face of all these questions and grey areas, the history of the *Très Riches Heures* is one that, as is often the case, must be discovered indirectly. The manuscript inspired the artists who had the opportunity to examine it. It is by charting the sequence of repeated motifs that we can follow its trail, albeit intermittently and with a few exceptions. If we consider, for example, the influence the manuscript may have exerted on Haincelin de Haguenau (the Bedford Master), it is probably not because it was present in his workshop after the death of the Duke of Berry,[9] since the illuminator worked on the manuscript alongside the Van Lymborch brothers, in particular on four borders.[10]

After the death of the Van Lymborch brothers and the Duke of Berry, the *Très Riches Heures* unquestionably disappeared from sight and does not seem to have inspired any more artists. One must wait for the recapture of Paris in April 1436 by Charles VII (who had left the city as Dauphin) to pick up any trace of it. At the time, the royal troops were commanded by Arthur de Richemont and Jean d'Orléans, Count of Dunois, known as the Bastard of Orléans. The latter's book of hours, the *Dunois Hours*,[11] decorated around 1440 by Jean Haincelin (the Dunois Master), son of Haincelin de Haguenau, includes no fewer than eighteen quotations from the *Très Riches Heures* (figs. 2–5).[12] Such an abundance of motifs common to both works implies privileged and direct access to the Duke of Berry's hours, and not the use of a hypothetical pattern book passed on by Haguenau; after all, he had participated only modestly in the decoration of the *Très Riches Heures*, and had surely seen only a few leaves.[13] The portrait of the Count of Dunois in the month of January (fig. 2) is a clear transposition

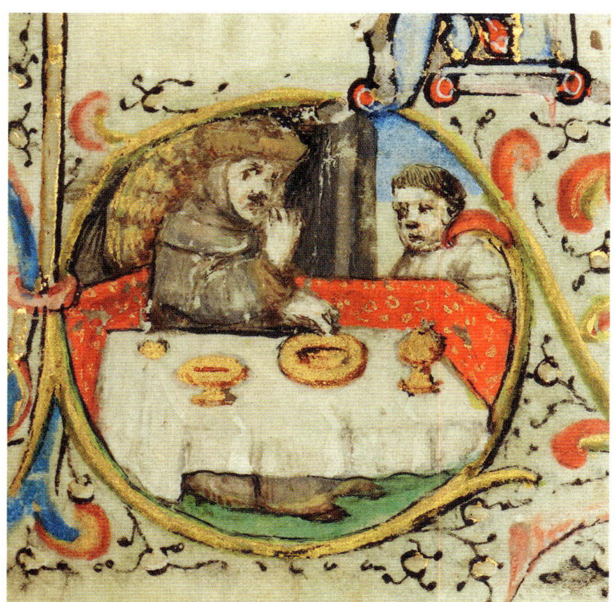

**Fig. 6** Jean Haincelin, *Coëtivy Hours*, fol. 1, detail (Dublin, Chester Beatty Library, WMs. 82)

of January from the *Très Riches Heures*: The Bastard of Orléans stands with his back to a fireplace, protected from the fire by a wicker screen, facing a banquet table featuring a nef of gold, served by a carving valet (in charge of cutting the meats) and cupbearers carrying gold and silver plates, cups, and ewers from a dresser. The month of October (fol. 10) also inspired the *Dunois Hours* (fig. 3) and, more faithfully still, another book of hours from the same workshop, the *Book of Hours for the Use of Paris*. Curiously, the rider's clothing in October in the *Dunois Hours* is white. As suggested by Inès Villela-Petit,[14] this detail indicates that the motif had indeed been drawn by the Van Lymborch brothers but left white, before being colored in by Barthélemy d'Eyck, a fact confirmed by the analyses carried out for the present catalog.

Was it the illuminator, Jean Haincelin, or the patron, Dunois, who came into possession of the *Très Riches Heures*? If we follow the second hypothesis, the work did not remain long in Dunois's library as it does not appear in his estate inventory.[15] Did it come briefly into his possession, thus enabling his chosen illuminator to draw inspiration from it? It is worth noting that the book was probably not yet bound, and therefore not a bibliophilic artefact. There is every reason to believe that it was acquired either by a bookseller or by Jean Haincelin himself, who used it as a repertoire of motifs. He used it again in 1445–50 for the *Coëtivy Hours* (fig. 6).[16] At the end of his career, the same Jean Haincelin also portrayed the Duke of Berry on the frontispiece of Laurent de Premierfait's 1466 translation of Boccaccio's *Cas des nobles hommes et femmes* (On the fates of famous men and women), intended for Jacques d'Armagnac (fig. 7).[17]

## THE ENIGMA OF BARTHÉLEMY D'EYCK'S INTERVENTION

Barthélemy d'Eyck's contribution to the calendar of the *Très Riches Heures* is another chronological marker. Without dwelling on the specifics,[18] we know that it must be dated 1446, since the illuminator added to the month of September a reminder of the marble steps of the "Pas d'armes" (passage of arms) at Saumur, the great 40-day tournament organized in June 1446 by King René in honor of Charles VII (September). This second decoration campaign was a rapid one, and d'Eyck probably only had the *Très Riches Heures* in his possession between late June and early August 1446, during the tournament. The event was attended by King Charles VII, Dunois, and d'Eyck's patron King René (the artist was attached to his court and worked almost exclusively for his master and the House of Anjou): all three are potential owners of the manuscript.

Let us take a closer look at these three possibilities. Did Dunois take the manuscript to the Pas de Saumur, where King René's illuminator may have briefly contributed to the work? Some have even speculated that the work was then passed on to his son, François de Longueville, who was entrusted with the education of the young Duke Charles of Savoy, a later owner of the *Très Riches Heures*.[19] No source corroborates this hypothesis, however.

Perhaps we should take a closer look at the House of Anjou. Barthélemy d'Eyck was official painter to King René, who was the brother-in-law of Charles VII. The Anjou family possessed several important manuscripts of the Duke of

**Fig. 7** Jean Haincelin, Boccaccio, *Cas des nobles hommes et femmes*, translation Laurent de Premierfait, fol. 1 (Chantilly, Bibliothèque du musée Condé, ms. 860)

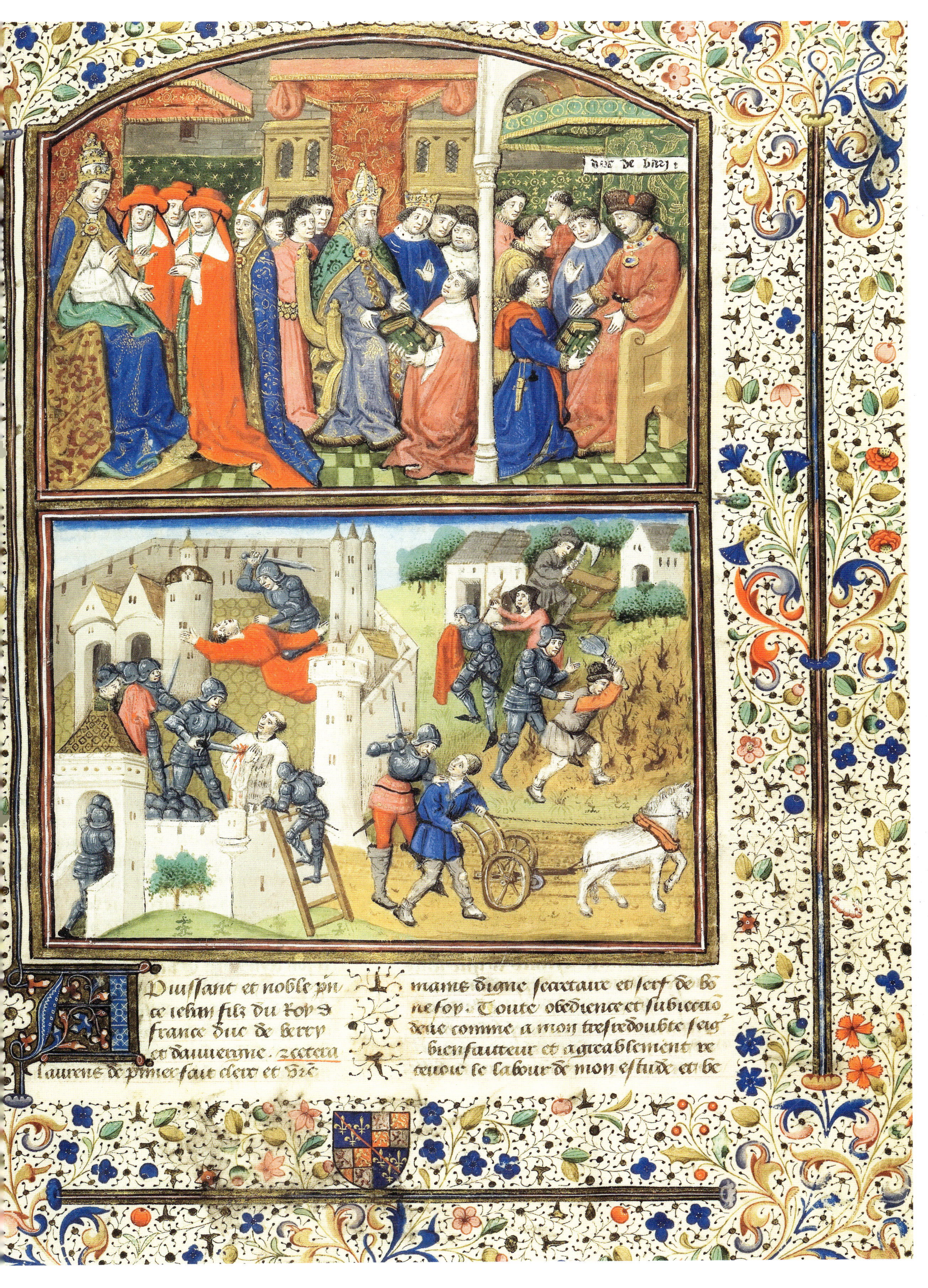
Puissant et noble prin
ce iehan filz du roy de
france duc de berry
et dauuergne. zcetera
laurens de primierfait clerc et
mains digne secretaire et serf de bo
ne foy. Toute obedience et subiectio
deue comme a mon tresredoubte seig
bienfaitteur et agreablement re
cevoir le labour de mon estude et be

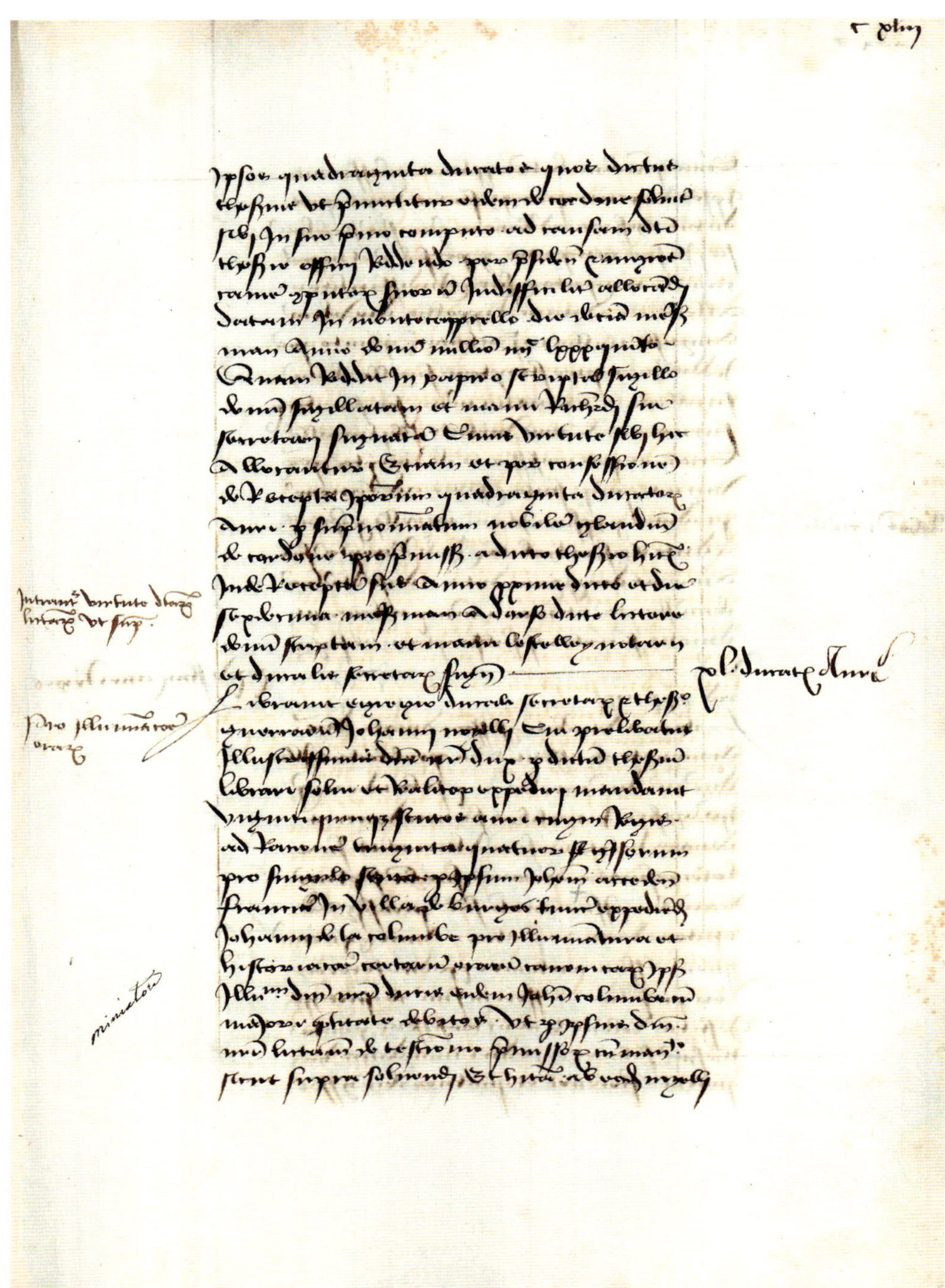

**Fig. 8** Accounts of the receivers and treasurers general of the Dukes of Savoy in 1485: payment to Jean Colombe to complete the *Très Riches Heures du duc de Berry* (Turin, Archivio di Stato, inv. 16, Reg. 138, fol. 143)

Berry and the Van Lymborch brothers. The *Belles Heures*, for example, belonged to Yolande of Aragon, niece by marriage to the Duke of Berry, mother of René and Marie of Anjou, and therefore mother-in-law of Charles VII. Yolande of Aragon had acquired the manuscript for 300 livres tournois (the manuscript was initially estimated at 875 livres tournois) from the executors of Jean of Berry's will in 1417.[20] She took it with her to Anjou, where its compositions exerted a certain influence on the Rohan Master,[21] whose masterpiece includes a timid echo of the *Très Riches Heures*,[22] possibly known thanks to the circulation of drawings. King René also came into possession of the *Bible moralisée* (Moralized bible), partly illuminated by the Van Lymborch brothers. Should the *Très Riches Heures* be added to this collection, as has been suggested without any real documentary evidence?[23] If so, why did René of Anjou not have his illuminator complete the manuscript, rather than contenting himself with such a partial and rapid contribution?

The third possibility centres on King Charles VII. Was the manuscript given to him by Dunois or someone else, or did he acquire it from a Parisian bookseller, in memory of the uncle to whom he was so attached (let's not forget that he completed Jean of Berry's tomb and also established his capital in Bourges, employing many of the late duke's loyal followers)? Several members of the king's entourage could have presented him with such a gift, and we know that Jean Haincelin acted as supplier for many of them.[24] Could d'Eyck have acted at the request of Charles VII, owner of the work, in the summer of 1446, during the king's stay with his brother-in-law in Saumur? In this case, the impecunious "little king of Bourges" would not have had the time to further complete the manuscript's decoration. Although we do not believe it is certain that the manuscript belonged to the king—the role of the illuminator Jean Haincelin being, in our view, the real reason for the manuscript's influence on the works in the royal milieu in the 1440s—it is nevertheless a serious possibility.

## THE *TRÈS RICHES HEURES* IN SAVOY

We have known that the *Très Riches Heures* became part of the estate of the House of Savoy since Paul Durrieu's work in 1904.[25] The illuminator Jean Colombe was recruited by Duke Charles I of Savoy and received a first payment, which was recorded in the accounts of the receivers and treasurers general of the Dukes of Savoy on August 31, 1485 (fig. 8).[26] According to Durrieu, the manuscript had been directly inherited by the House of Savoy, thanks to the marriage of Bonne, the Duke of Berry's eldest daughter, to Amadeus VII, ancestor of Charles I, who had Colombe portray himself and his wife on the manuscript (fol. 75; fig. 2, p. 257). For Millard Meiss, this hypothesis does not hold up: According to him, the manuscript could not have been taken to Savoy so early since some of its motifs had time to inspire several later workshops, notably in Paris.[27]

As Jean Colombe was the protégé of Queen Charlotte of Savoy, wife of Louis XI and aunt of Charles I of Savoy, it was long assumed that the *Très Riches Heures* may have left the French court to enter the Savoy collections after the queen's death, the engagement of Colombe being explained as having been suggested by the queen to her nephew. Nicole Reynaud has proposed that the Chantilly manuscript be recognized in the queen's estate inventory, drawn up in Tours between December 1483 and March 1484, in the mention (fol. 81v) of "ung autre livre en parchemin, appellé les Heures de monseigneur de Berry, bien hystorié" (another parchment book, called the Hours of Monseigneur of Berry, well historiated). But is this really the *Très Riches Heures*? In fact, there is every reason to believe that this reference concerns the *Grandes Heures de Jean de Berry*, which had remained in the royal collections. As Louis XI clearly did not inherit any books from his father Charles VII, with whom relations were notoriously poor, it is hard to imagine how his wife Charlotte could have come into possession of the work.[28]

If it is not necessary that the manuscript was in the possession of Charlotte of Savoy, we can turn to Charles I of Savoy's mother, Yolande of France, the daughter of Charles VII and Marie of Anjou. In fact, her husband, Amadeus IX, appears in the foreground of the Celestial Court miniature (fol. 126; fig. 8, p. 263). Unfortunately, no inventory is known to exist.

The book's history becomes clearer in the next generation. Charles I died in 1490 and was succeeded by his son, Charles John Amadeus, acting under his mother's regency, and then, very briefly, by his relative Philip II, who left the duchy to his own son, Philibert II. The latter married Margaret of Austria, aunt of Charles V, who, after the death of her husband in 1504, was forced to leave Savoy in 1506 to assume the regency of the Netherlands. She took with her to Mechelen several books from the rich library of the Dukes of Savoy, including the famous *Très Riches Heures*, still unbound! The manuscript was then inventoried in 1523–24 in her palatine chapel[29] and inspired the artists of her court.[30]

## GENOA, TWICKENHAM, THEN CHANTILLY

On the death of Margaret of Austria in 1530, the manuscript passed to her treasurer general of finances, Jean Raffault, lord of Neufville. It subsequently reached Genoa, probably in the luggage of Ambrogio Spinola, commander-in-chief of the Spanish forces, and remained in the Ligurian capital, where it was bound in the eighteenth century to honor one of his descendants, Vincenzo Spinola. Left without an heir, Vincenzo Spinola chose his cousin Gian Battista Serra as his executor. The latter probably had his arms placed over those of his ancestor on the front board of the binding (fig. 1).[31] After a four-century European journey through the libraries of some of the greatest bibliophiles of the modern era, it was in Genoa that the Duke of Aumale had the good fortune to be offered the chance to acquire the "king of manuscripts" in 1856. Thanks to him, the precious work would soon conclude its journey via Twickenham on the edge of London to the château he was to rebuild, a castle whose singular silhouette would recall in many ways the prodigious edifices of the calendar of the *Très Riches Heures*, now in Chantilly.

1 Guiffrey 1894–96, I, 1–3, and II, 191–204.
2 Paris, BSG, Ms. 841, fol. 168v. Guiffrey 1894–96, II, 280 (no. 1164).
3 Guiffrey 1894–96, II, 260.
4 This essay on the history of the *Très Riches Heures*, a subject that has never ceased to provoke conjecture, seeks to complement research carried out on the subject, including: Durrieu 1904; Lehoux 1956b; Meiss 1974a, I, 321–24; Chantilly 2004; Reynolds 2005; Reynaud 2007; Châtelet 2008; Châtelet 2010; Villela-Petit 2018b; Angelini 2018; Stirnemann 2021.
5 Mattéoni 2022, 109–30.
6 Meiss 1974a, I, 321–23.
7 Lehoux 1956b.
8 Rouse and Rouse 2000, II, 23–24, 99, 105–06, 123–25.
9 Reynolds 2005; Stirnemann and Rabel 2005.
10 Stirnemann and Rabel 2005.
11 London, BL, Ms. Yates Thompson 3.
12 Reynolds 2005.
13 Châtelet 2008, 20.
14 Villela-Petit 2013c.
15 Jarry 1890.
16 Dublin, Chester Beatty Library, Ms. W 082.
17 Chantilly, Bibl. du musée Condé, Ms. 860.
18 See essay by M. Deldicque, pp. 247–53.
19 Châtelet 2008, 22; Châtelet 2010, 9–10, 83.
20 Guiffrey 1894–96, II, 299–300.
21 Panayotova 2014.
22 Villela-Petit 2013c: in the *Grandes Heures de Rohan* (Paris, BnF, Ms. Latin 9471), the horseman from the Meeting of the Three Magi in the *Très Riches Heures* (fol. 51) appears in the Flight into Egypt (fol. 99).
23 Angelini 2018, 34 note 15.
24 Deldicque 2024a.
25 Durrieu 1904, 9.
26 For the record in the accounts, see essay by M. Jacob-Yapi, p. 269, note 1. On Jean Colombe's contribution, see the same essay.
27 Meiss 1974a, I, 321–23; see also Stirnemann and Rabel 2005; Reynolds 2005.
28 Paris 2024, 62.
29 "une grande heure escripte a la main, lesquelles n'ont point de couverte ne fermeilletz" (a large book of hours written by hand, with neither cover nor clasps). (Debae 1995, 3, 7).
30 See essay by T.-H. Borchert, pp. 273–79.
31 De Hamel 2016, 561. For a study of the manuscript's current binding, see essay by C. Barbe and F. Malo, pp. 349–61.

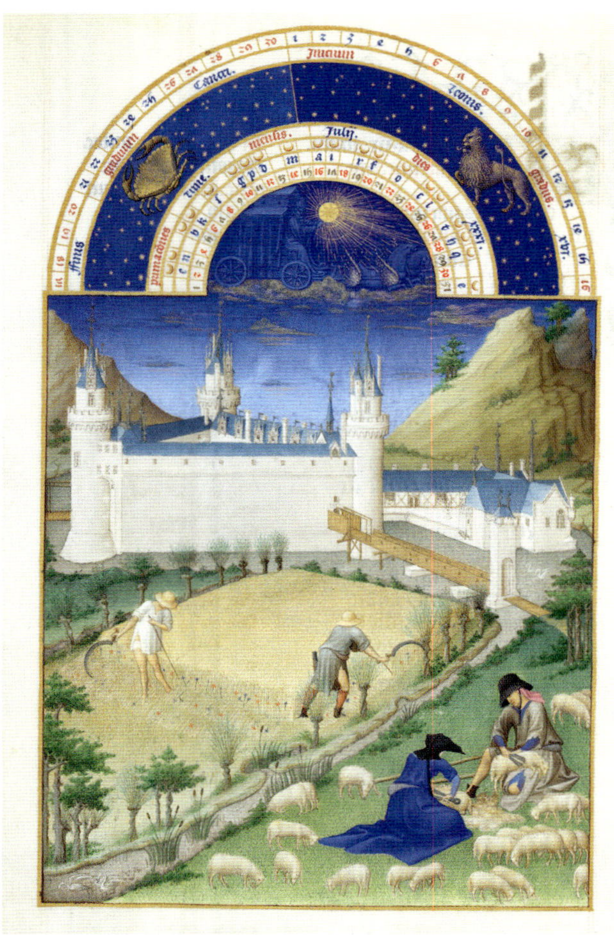

Van Lymborch brothers, *Très Riches Heures*, fol. 7v: July

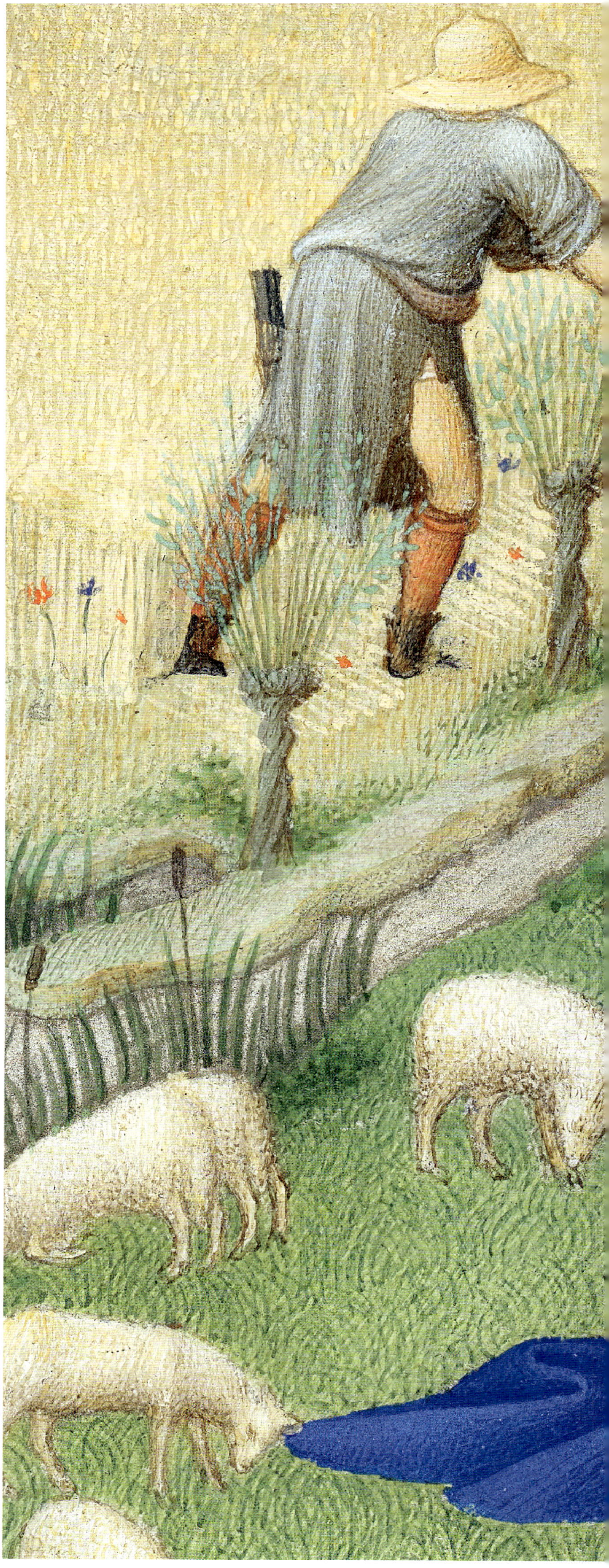

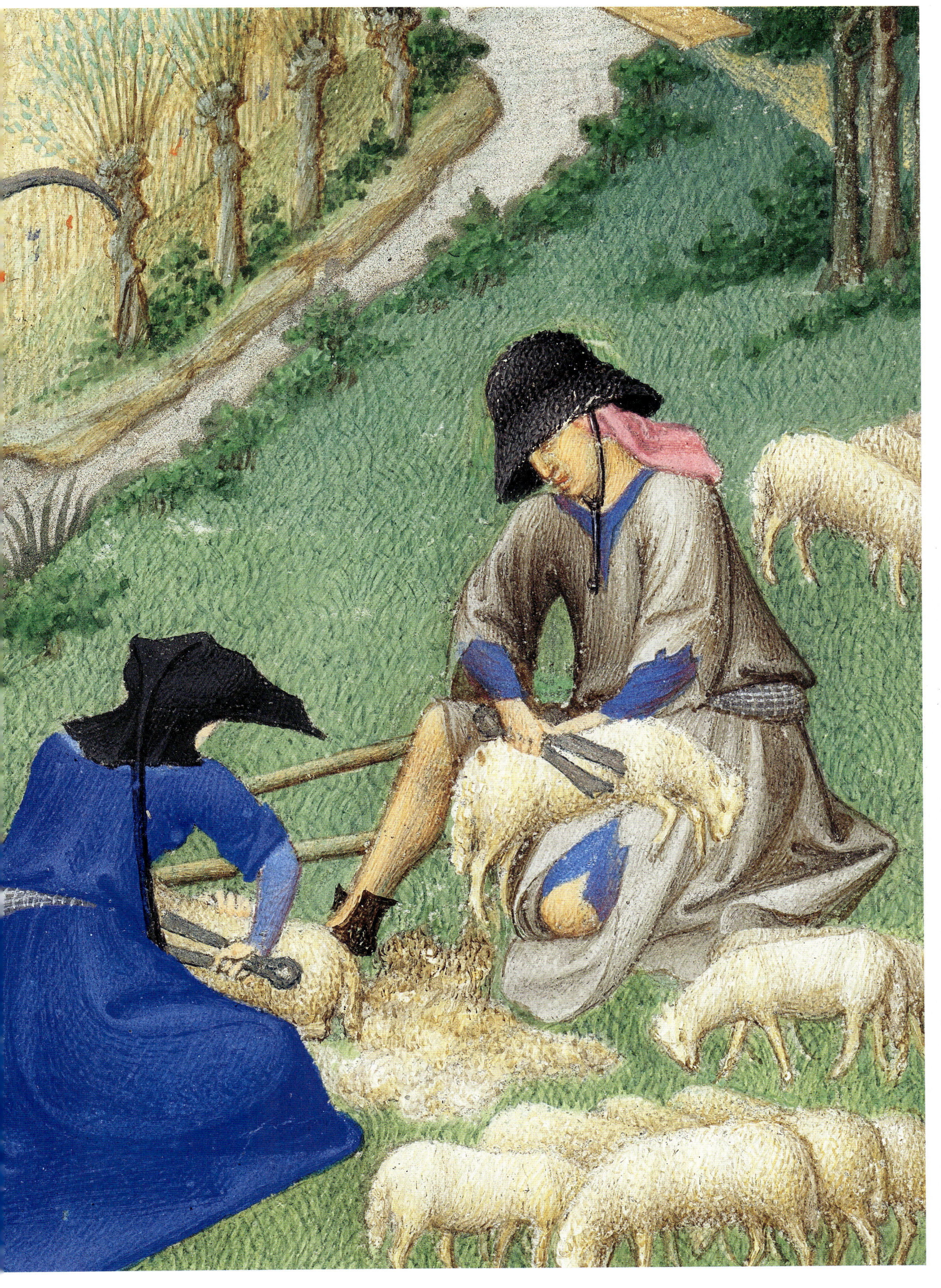

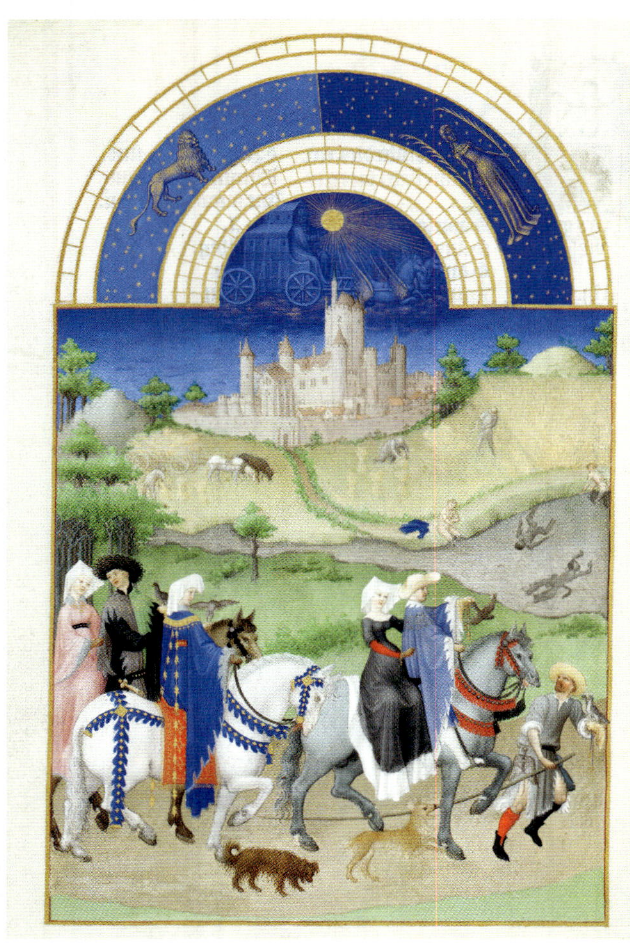

Van Lymborch brothers, *Très Riches Heures*, fol. 8v: August

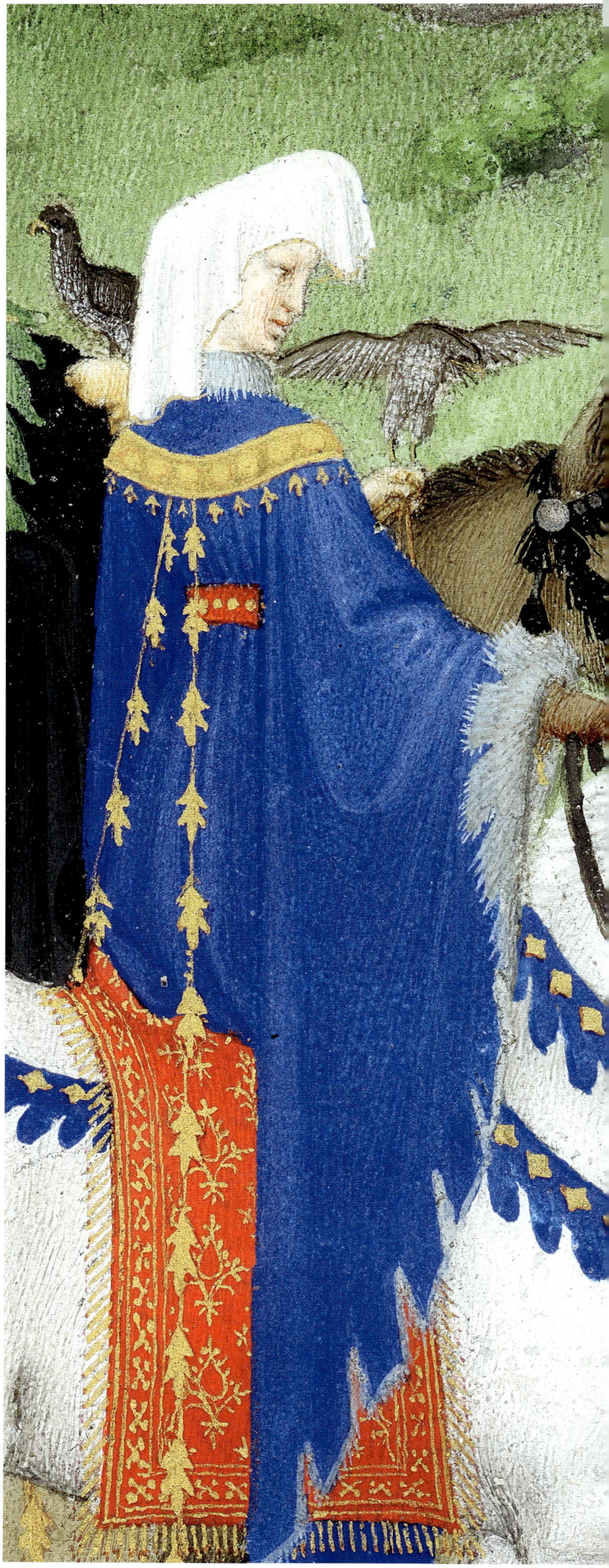

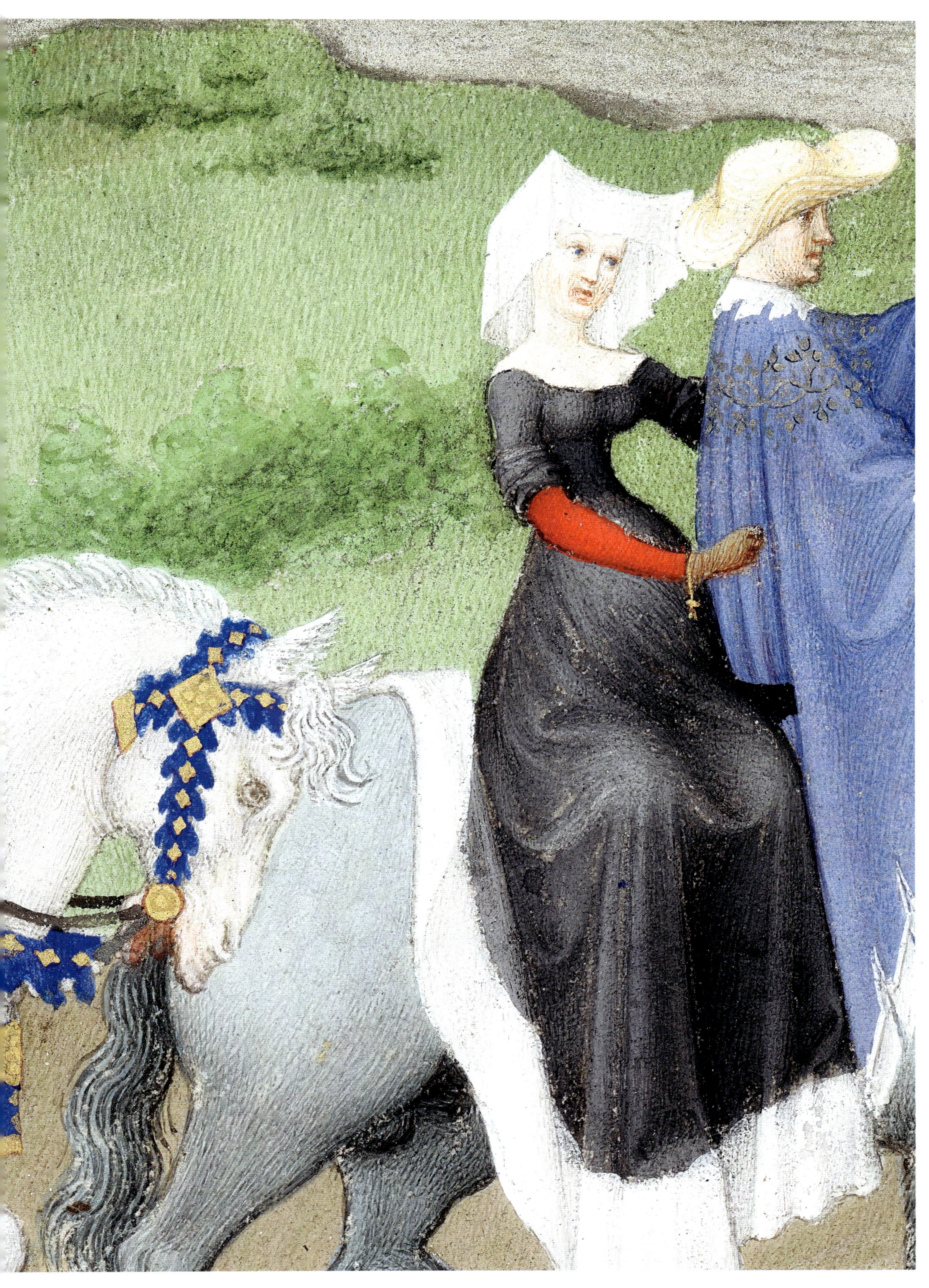

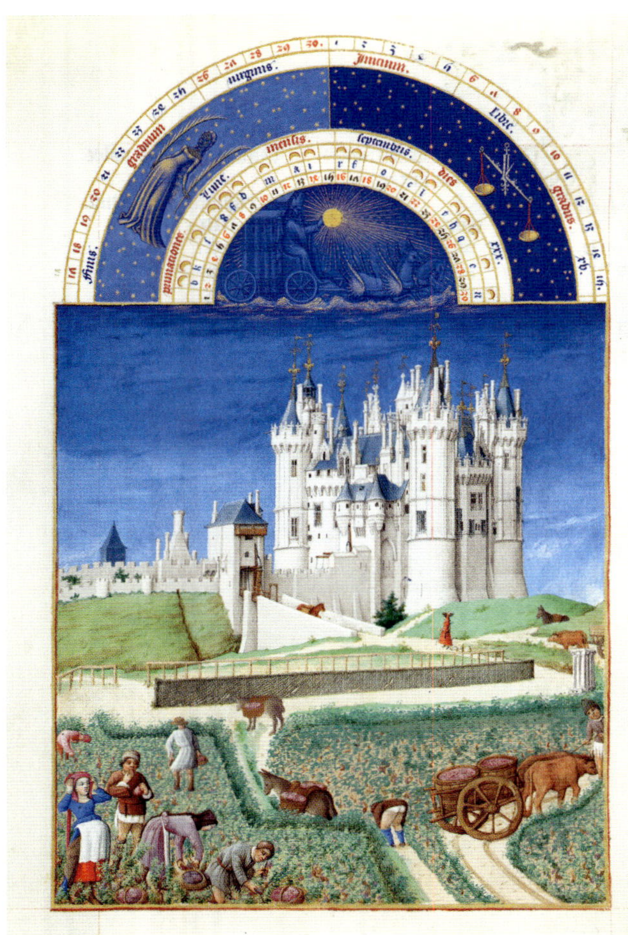

Van Lymborch brothers, *Très Riches Heures*, fol. 9v: September

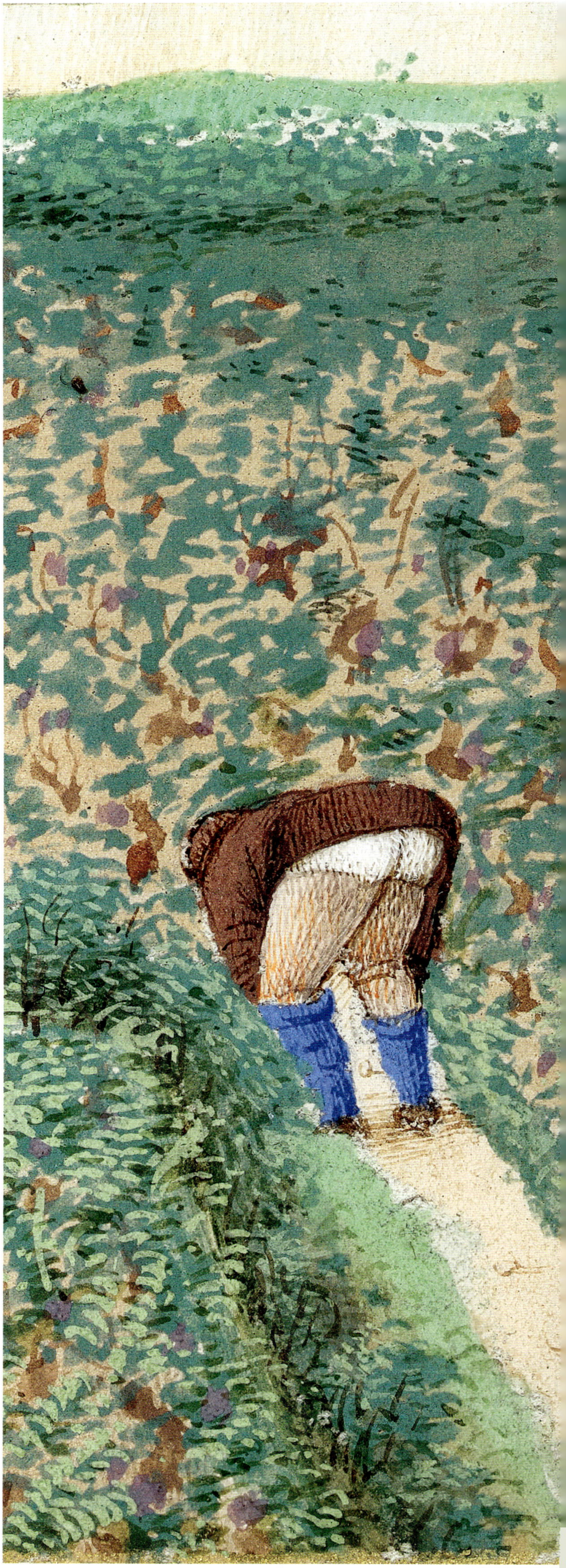

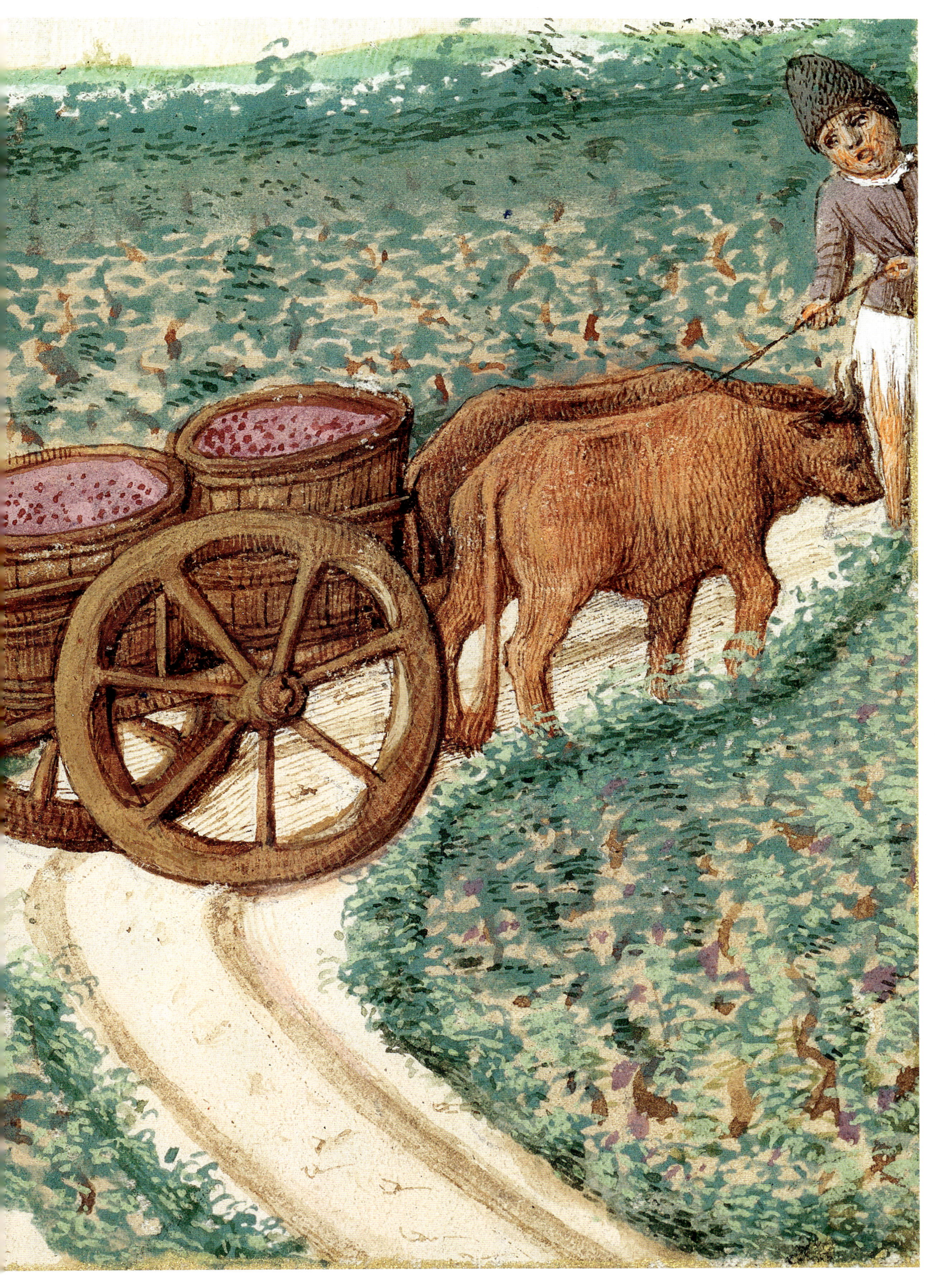

# REDISCOVERY & RECOGNITION

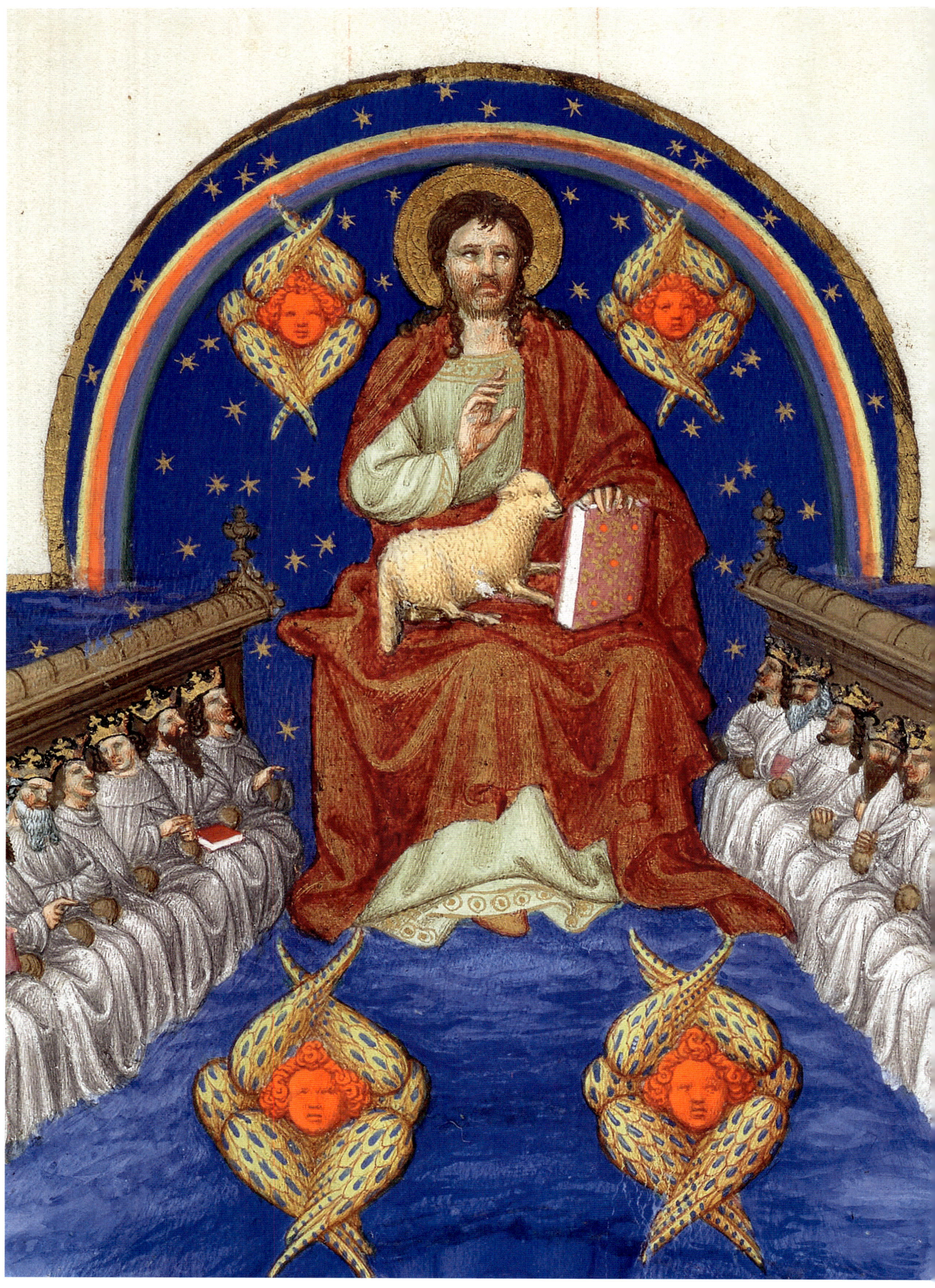

17.

# From Genoa to Chantilly: The Invention of the *Très Riches Heures* of the Duke of Berry

Marie-Pierre Dion

"Je suis en marché pour acheter à Gênes le plus beau manuscrit que j'aye vu, au point de vue de l'art, après le Julio Clovio du roi de Naples" (I am seeking to buy in Genoa the most beautiful manuscript I have seen, in terms of the art, after the Giulio Clovio of the King of Naples), wrote Henri d'Orléans, Duke of Aumale, on January 11, 1856, referring for the first time to the *Très Riches Heures.*[1] Forty years later, his preference for the *Farnese Hours* composed by Giulio Clovio, described as the "Michelangelo of Miniatures," had melted away. The Duke of Aumale devoted twelve pages to a note on the book of hours he still called the "Heures du duc de Berry." "Ce livre tient une grande place dans l'histoire de l'art: j'ose dire qu'il n'a pas de rival" (This book occupies a significant place in the history of art; I dare say it has no rival), he emphasized as he finished writing the note on the manuscript, a few months before his death in 1897. The prince was only thirty-three when he discovered the manuscript, but was already one of the most important private bibliophiles in England, where he was living in exile. The acquisition, which was no accident, endowed his collection with an unrivalled prestige, which the prince would strive to preserve at his estate in Chantilly, located about forty kilometers above Paris.

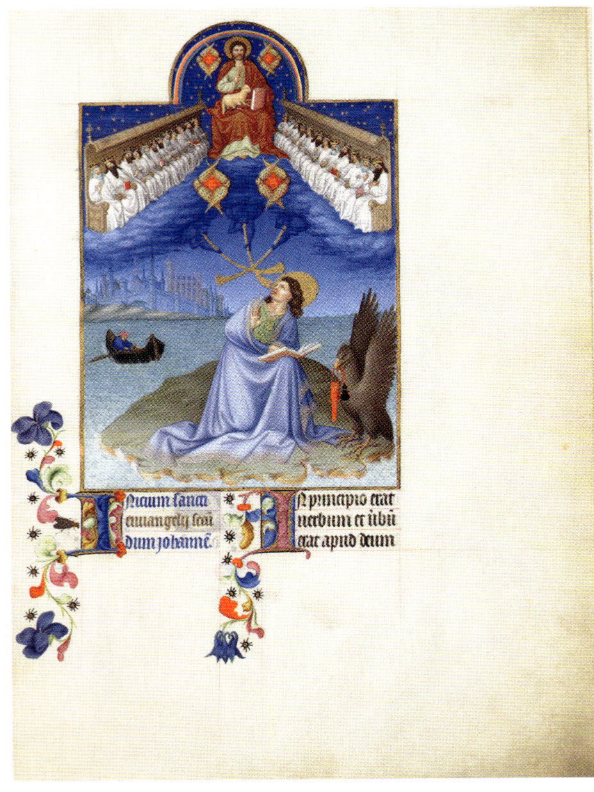

**Fig. 2** Van Lymborch brothers, *Très Riches Heures*, fol. 17: St. John at Patmos

**Fig. 1** Van Lymborch brothers, *Très Riches Heures*, fol. 17: St. John at Patmos, detail

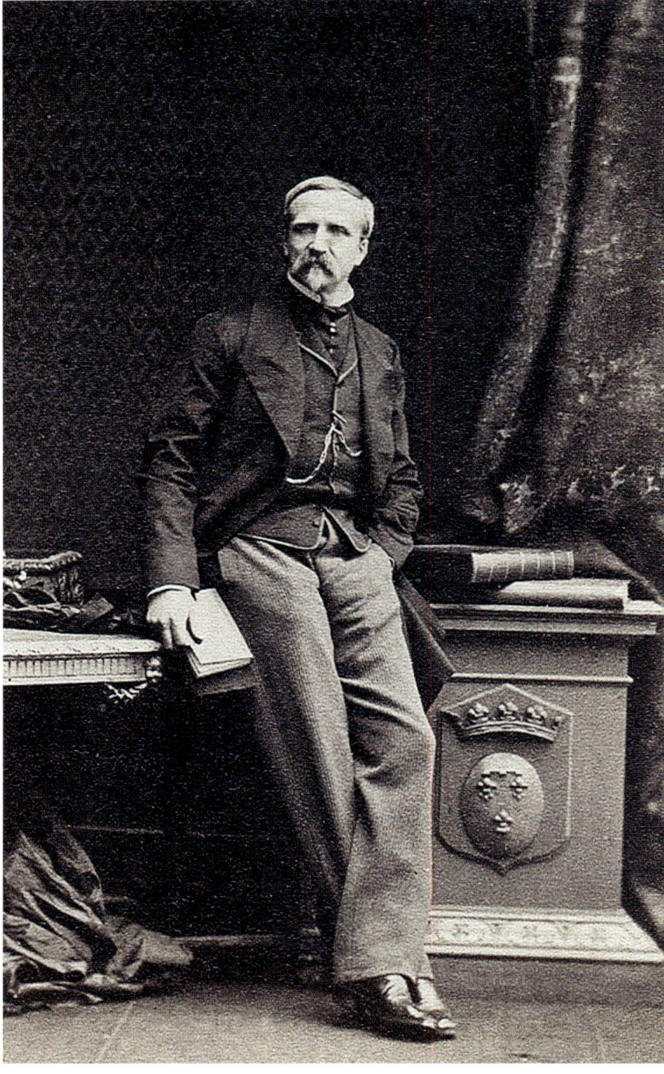

**Fig. 3** Camille Silvy, *Henri d'Orléans, Duke of Aumale (1822–1897), Full-length, Leaning on Books Placed on a Pedestal Bearing the Orléans Arms*. London, March 5, 1861 (Chantilly, musée Condé, inv. 2007-6-1-15)

## THE BIBLIOPHILE'S GRAND INTENTION

Born in 1822, Henri d'Orléans (fig. 3) was a member of the royal Bourbon family, the fifth son of Louis Philippe, future "King of the French." Henri was descended through his father from Philippe d'Orléans, the brother of Louis XIV. He was given the title Duke of Aumale, and his godfather was Louis VI Henri Joseph de Bourbon, Prince of Condé, who was his great-uncle and had no direct heirs. Louis Philippe's political strategy favored a coming together of the last remaining "princes of the blood," who had been kept at a distance by Louis XVIII. The Prince of Condé, son of the former leader of the Army of the Émigrés, named Henri d'Orléans, grandson of the regicide Philippe Égalité, as his universal heir. This made the Duke of Aumale one of France's richest men and the owner of, among other things, the vast Chantilly estate. Aumale was a younger son destined for a military career, famous for his military achievements in Algeria. A well-educated and cultured prince, he was enrolled, like his brothers, at the Collège Henri IV, a prestigious secondary school in Paris. Keen on history, he was fascinated at an early age by Louis II de Bourbon, known as "le Grand Condé," who brought glory to Chantilly. The château of Chantilly, which rivaled Versailles, had been largely destroyed during the French Revolution, but Aumale set about rebuilding it.[2]

Among the possessions of the Condé family that Aumale inherited were 900 manuscripts, the only items that remained out a collection of more than 30,000 works held at the Palais Bourbon in Paris before the Revolution. The manuscripts were returned to Louis V Joseph de Bourbon-Condé in 1815.[3] Between military campaigns, the Duke of Aumale admired the miniatures in the manuscripts with his young wife, Maria Carolina of Bourbon-Two Sicilies, and pondered the journey made by the books, undertaking to untangle the tangled inheritances to understand how they had been passed down to the Condés over the centuries.[4] After the French Revolution in 1848 and the fall of the July Monarchy, the prince went into exile in England, along with his collection: "le loisir que Dieu m'a donné sans que je le lui demande, m'a permis de faire avec eux une connaissance plus intime" (the leisure that God has given me without my asking him enabled me to become more intimately acquainted with them).[5] Meticulous examination of the surviving manuscripts, analysis of early inventories, reading the texts with the help of their first printed editions and of modern studies—what he called "appareiller" (equipping) his collections—provided the Duke of Aumale with a solid knowledge of aristocratic, medieval, and modern libraries. This enabled him to expand the various elements of the collection he had inherited[6] with both taste and coherence. Before he died in 1897, he had acquired 550 manuscripts, 13,000 rare printed books, and thousands of historical documents.

The young prince carefully noted the books' ancient and prestigious origins. He identified forty-three books once owned by Antoine de Chourses and his wife Catherine de Coëtivy, granddaughter of Agnès Sorel and Charles VII, books that had come down to the Condés through successive inheritances and which thus linked the library to the Valois family.[7] The prince also discovered fifty books from the third House of Bourbon, direct descendants of St. Louis, allied to the Valois on several occasions through marriages.[8] The memory of the Duke of

Berry hangs over these two great aristocratic libraries of the late Middle Ages. Jean of Berry's name appears in bookplates and in dedications to translations of Boccaccio by Laurent de Premierfait owned by the Chourses-Coëtivy and the Bourbons. "Les livres du Duc de Berry sont aujourd'hui les plus précieux joyaux des collections publiques et privées qui les possèdent" (The books of the Duke of Berry are today the most precious jewels in the public and private collections that own them), noted Aumale, echoing Count Auguste de Bastard's famous work, *La Librairie du Duc de Berry* (1830), which reproduced several illuminations in hand-colored lithographs.[9]

Beyond the collection he inherited, the Duke of Aumale exemplified the taste that characterized the Orléans family and its princely pageantry. In 1791, his grandfather Philippe Égalité broke up one of France's most important collections of paintings, the Galerie d'Orléans in the Palais-Royal in Paris, while his library was confiscated in 1793.[10] Aumale's father Louis Philippe reconstituted a private collection—scattered in 1851, 1852, and 1857—and instilled in his son a taste for rare books, which left Aumale with a vivid memory of the Penthièvre family's legacy.[11] In turn, Aumale felt it his duty to gather the scattered elements of the Orléans collection: "M. Louis Bonaparte a pris soin d'étouffer dans son essor ma passion de bibliophile et l'a réduite aux proportions d'un goût modeste que j'essaierai de satisfaire sans trop de folie" (Mr. Louis Bonaparte [the future Napoleon III] took care to stifle my budding passion as a bibliophile and reduced it to the proportions of a modest taste that I will try to satisfy without too much folly).[12] Louis Philippe gave his son as part of his inheritance the collection of the wealthy English Francophile Frank Hall Standish (1799–1840), which was valued at 133,000 francs. This collection of 3427 volumes is the second most important subset of the the duke's library (known as the Cabinet des livres; fig. 4) after the Bourbons-Condés inheritance. From 1851 onward, it inspired in Aumale the same passion for rare printed books that he already had for manuscripts. Among Louis Philippe's books most cherished by the prince, *Le Livre de chasse* (The Hunting Book) by Gaston Phébus entered the national collections in 1848,[13] while an edition of the *Livre de Mélusine*—a text commissioned by the Duke of Berry—inherited from the Penthièvre family, was purchased by Aumale in July 1856.

Following the Decree of 1852, which obliged him to mobilize his considerable landed wealth and reinvest his funds, Aumale gained a financial independence that soon made him the undisputed head of the family. While the Musée des Souverains (Museum of Sovereigns), which opened in the Louvre on February 13, 1853, reduced the Orléans dynasty to a mere shadow, the Duke of Aumale defended his family's rank and reputation by continuing to collect rare works. In terms of books, he followed in the footsteps of eighteenth-century connoisseurs, acquiring rare editions, often of illustrious provenance, in the most perfect condition possible. These books fall within the scope of high bibliophily and the most distinguished "collectionism" of the nineteenth century, that of classical scholarship and art. Aumale, who was also putting together a display of antiques and a gallery of paintings, established himself as an "expert collector surrounded by experts."[14] John Charles Robinson, a curator at the Kensington Museum in London (the precursor to the Victoria and Albert Museum) from whom the duke bought several manuscripts and a series of Italian cuttings, reinforced his idea of collecting pieces to create "a history of the art of the miniaturist and of decoration on vellum." Through his acquisitions, Aumale gradually established essential milestones in the history of the manuscript book "in its most dazzling form," including the *Très Riches Heures du duc de Berry* , the "apogee" in his eyes of manuscript illumination.[15]

The prince's exile in England—he lived in Orleans House in Twickenham, on the edge of London from 1852 to 1871—had a profound impact on the reconstruction of the collection, which now provided a reflection of his distant homeland. Books were not simply a remedy for forced military inaction, but a new battleground. The quality of Aumale's collections and his work as a historian enabled him to assert himself as the guardian of French history and national identity, through landmark studies or resounding writings against the Second Empire, such as *Lettre sur l'histoire de France* (Letter on the History of France) in 1861.[16] In 1856, his publications on the Chourses-Coëtivy library and Gace de La Buigne's hunting treatise belonging to the Duke of Berry were circulated discreetly, due to imperial censorship, by Alfred Auguste Cuvillier-Fleury. This historian, bibliophile, and the duke's secretary also spoke of the new acquisitions around him in France: "[cela] profite à votre renommée d'homme intelligent [et] ne nuit pas à votre destinée de prince, quelle qu'elle puisse être dans les décrets insondables de la Providence; et tout ce qui vous rappelle légitimement et sans fanfare à l'attention et à l'estime du public me paraît bon" ([this] benefits your reputation as an intelligent man [and] does not harm your destiny as a prince, whatever it may be in the unfathomable decrees of Providence; and anything that legitimately and without fanfare recalls you to the attention and esteem of the public seems a good thing to me).[17]

Aumale liked to buy books that were exiled, like himself, waiting patiently—according to his motto, "J'attendrai" (I will wait)—to be able to bring them back to France. In the meantime, books opened doors to the elite of British society. Excluded from European courts and official receptions, the Duke of Aumale joined the narrow and prestigious circles of the Philobiblon Society and the Fine Arts Club, playing an active part in their academic and social activities.[18] This is when he met Gustav Friedrich Waagen, the first curator of Berlin's Gemäldegalerie, who had travelled from Germany to talk about the importance of illuminated manuscripts to the history of art.[19] The duke cultivated his image as a French prince in exile. In 1856, he published accounts dating from the English captivity of King John the Good, found among the Condé archives. "The editor [Aumale] must more than once have regretted the times when England could be a prison for a French prince, but not a place of exile," wrote his friend Albert de Broglie, alluding to Jean of Berry, held hostage in England after the Treaty of Brétigny, from 1360 to 1366, a limited time, unlike endless exile.[20] From now on, the flattering comparisons between the two bibliophile princes would continue.

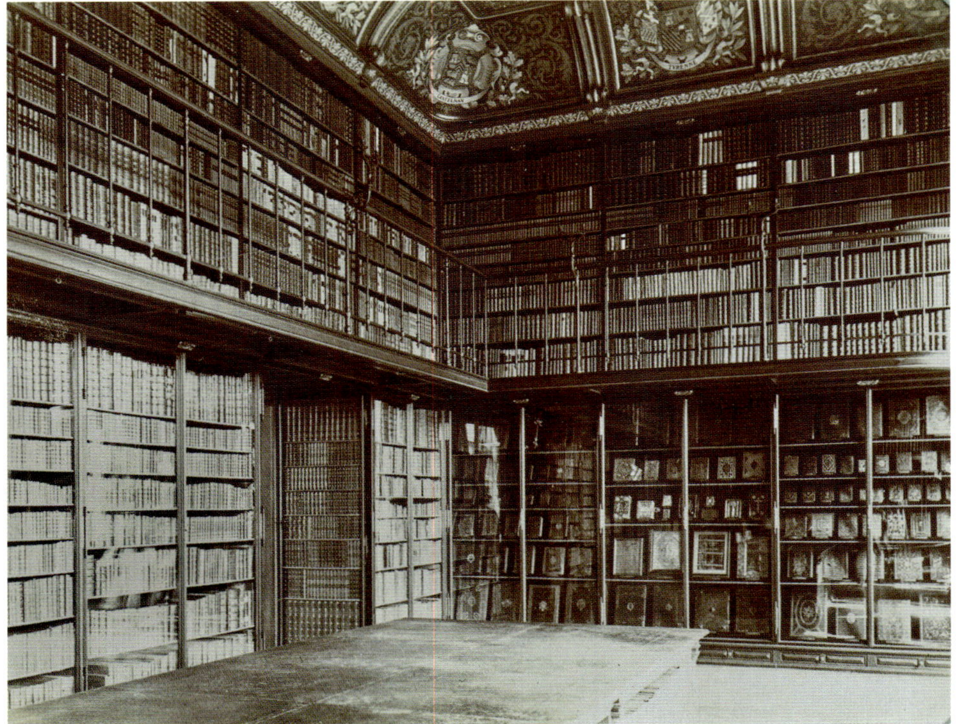

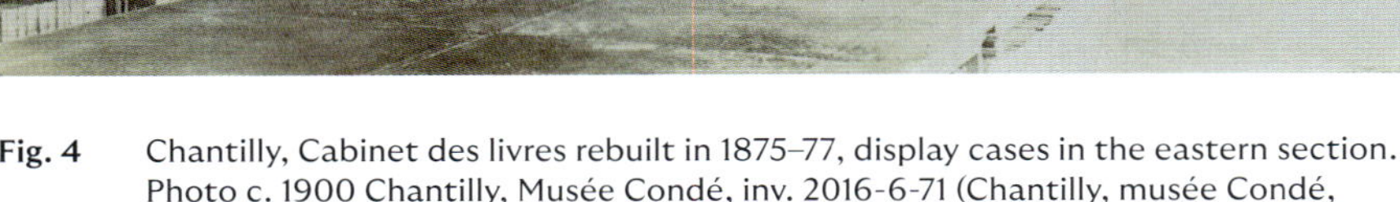

**Fig. 4** Chantilly, Cabinet des livres rebuilt in 1875–77, display cases in the eastern section. Photo c. 1900 Chantilly, Musée Condé, inv. 2016-6-71 (Chantilly, musée Condé, inv. 2016-6-71)

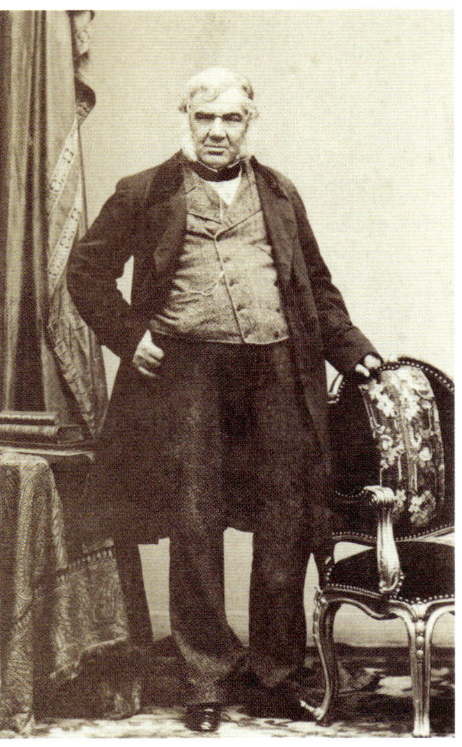

**Fig. 5** Hughes & Mullins, *Antonio Panizzi*. Ryde, UK, 1888, after an original dated c. 1860 (Florence, Alinari Foundation)

## THE ACQUISITION OF THE *TRÈS RICHES HEURES*

While he was seeking to buy the *Très Riches Heures* in January 1856, Aumale was also negotiating the purchase, in Brussels, of the *Livre des proprietés des choses* (On the properties of things) by Bartholomew the Englishman, which he suspected also came from the Duke of Berry. One might assume that he immediately recognized the Duke of Berry in the illumination of January in the *Très Riches Heures* and immediately decided to acquire a book that was princely in every respect. However, the ties he had forged since 1848 with Antonio (known as Anthony) Panizzi, an Italian patriot and political refugee in London who had been appointed chief librarian of the British Museum, were decisive (fig. 5).[21]

In a famous passage from his catalog, which contributed to the legend of the manuscript, the Duke of Aumale set the scene:

> In December 1855, I left Twickenham to go and visit my mother, who was ill at the time in Nervi, near Genoa. Panizzi had enabled me to view an interesting manuscript that had been brought to his attention by a friend of his in Turin. I was introduced to the 'Hours of the Duke of Berry,' kept at the time in a boarding school for young ladies at Villa Pallavicini, on the outskirts of Genoa. A quick inspection allowed me to appreciate the beauty, style, and originality of the miniatures and all the decoration. I recognized the portrait of the prince, his arms, the dungeon at Vincennes, etc. I was told, as was customary, that my competitors were serious; I did not respond to this warning, which seemed banal and which was, however, more legitimate than I thought. My mind was made up, and I put the matter in Panizzi's hands. Within a month, the 'book of hours with miniatures, bearing on the cover the Serra and Spinola arms of Genoa' (as described in the receipt), was in my possession, sold by Baron Felix de Margherita, of Turin, who himself had inherited it from Marquis Jean-Baptiste Serra, for the principal sum of 18,000 francs. Adding 1,280 francs, commission, appraisal, and shipping costs, we arrive at the total price of 19,280 francs, which I actually paid. (fig. 6)[22]

What did a French prince, linked to the Bourbons-Sicilies by his mother and wife, have in common with the ardent, pro-Risorgimento, Italian activist who had had to flee the Duchy of Modena in 1823? Aumale had been a regular visitor to the British Museum's library since 1849: John Holmes, a prominent bibliographer and curator of manuscripts, gave him J. Barrois's *Bibliothèque protypographique* (1830), a book that, wrote Aumale, "introduced us to the libraries of Charles V and his brothers."[23] Panizzi, who was in charge of the printed collections, was one of Aumale's close advisors from 1850, when the Standish collection was sold, and was a regular guest at Orleans House.[24] Nicolas Barber has shown how real bonds of friendship were forged between the two men, both exiles who loved their respective homelands and shared many links with Italy and a taste for books; the sympathy felt by the duke, a liberal faithful to the ideals of the Enlightenment, for the Italian patriot is clearly apparent in the collections at Chantilly.[25] On his return from Turin, Panizzi told Aumale about the sale of the manuscript, and supported the duke's dealings with Chevalier Angelo de Mengaldo, a former friend of Byron and a fervent nationalist, who acted as intermediary between buyer and seller.

Some twenty kilometers separated Nervi, where Aumale was visiting his mother, from Pegli, where a meeting was organized at Villa Pallavicini. The manuscript Aumale discovered was covered in a red morocco Italian binding and belonged to a number of prominent Francophile families. Vincenzo Spinola di San Luca, a minister plenipotentiary of the Republic of Genoa in Paris, divided the succession to his immense estate between his four cousins, sons of Giacomo Serra. One of them, Gian Battista Serra, known as Serra the Jacobin, senator of the short-lived Ligurian Republic (1799), inherited the manuscript. Baron Felice de Margherita, for his part, asserted that he owned the book, thanks to his father, Luigi de Margherita, former mayor of Turin and a magistrate. The latter had a personal connection to Serra's family, having legitimized his daughter before she married Felice.

Were there other factors in the Duke of Aumale's favor? His mother, Queen Maria Amalia, came to visit what the duke described as a "boarding school for young girls," a philanthropic foundation created in 1850 by Bianca De Simoni Rebizzo, another Risorgimento figure. In any case, the Duke of Aumale won out over Adolphe de Rothschild, who would later acquire the *Belles Heures*. This manuscript was also offered to the Duke of Aumale, who noted in his diary on April 14, 1880: "pas de vues" (no views), namely, nothing comparable to the images in the Van Lymborch calendar.[26]

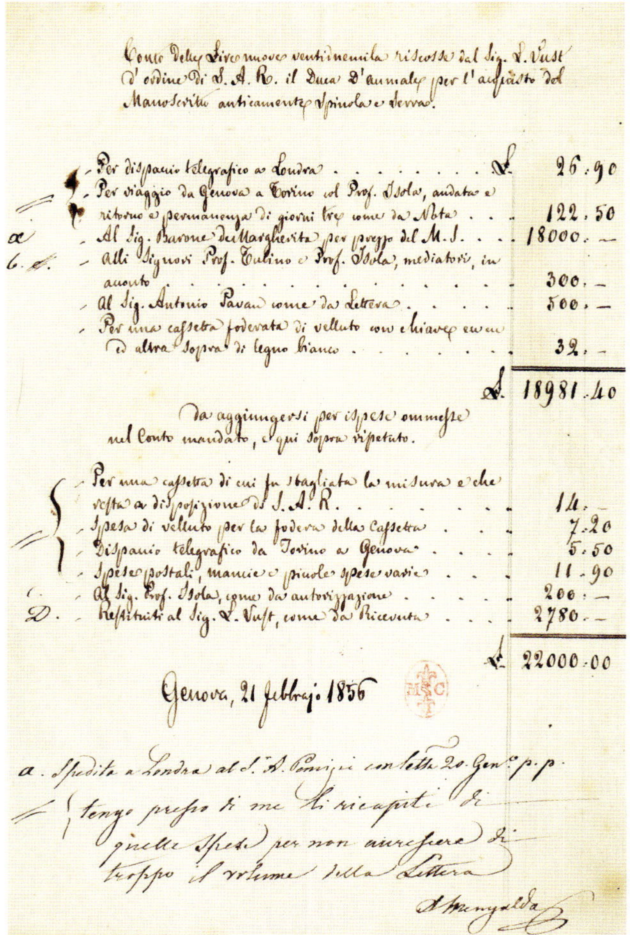

Conto delle Lire nuove ventiduemila riscosse dal Sig. L. Vust d'ordine di S. A. R. il Duca d'Aumale per l'acquisto del Manoscritto anticamente Spinola e Serra.

| | | |
|---|---|---|
| | Per dispaccio telegrafico a Londra | £ 26.90 |
| | Per viaggio da Genova a Torino col Prof. Isola, andata e ritorno e permanenza di giorni tre come da Nota | 122.50 |
| a | Al Sig. Barone de Margherita per prezzo del M. S. | 18000.– |
| b | Alli Signori Prof. Tulino e Prof. Isola, mediatori, in acconto | 300.– |
| | Al Sig. Antonio Pavan come da Lettera | 500.– |
| | Per una cassetta foderata di velluto con chiave ed un'altra sopra di legno bianco | 32.– |
| | | £ 18981.40 |

da aggiungersi per spese ommesse nel Conto mandato, e qui sopra ripetuto.

| | | |
|---|---|---|
| | Per una cassetta di cui fu sbagliata la misura e che resta a disposizione di S. A. R. | 14.– |
| | Spesa di velluto per la fodera della Cassetta | 7.20 |
| | Dispaccio telegrafico da Torino a Genova | 5.50 |
| | Spese postali, mancie e piccole spese varie | 11.90 |
| c | Al Sig. Prof. Isola, come da autorizzazione | 200.– |
| D | Restituiti al Sig. L. Vust, come da Ricevuta | 2780.– |
| | | £ 22000.00 |

Genova, 21 febbrajo 1856

a. Spedita a Londra al S. A. Panizzi con lett. 20 Gen. p.p.

tengo presso di me li ricapiti di quelle spese per non accrescere di troppo il volume della Lettera

A. Mengaldo

Fig. 6 Angelo de Mengaldo, *Account of the use of the 22,000 francs received from Louis Wüst by order of HRH the Duke of Aumale for the acquisition of the manuscript bearing the arms of the Spinola and Serra families.* Genoa, February 21, 1856 (Chantilly, Bibliothèque du musée Condé, Na 10-161)

## THE VALORIZATION OF THE MANUSCRIPT

Henri d'Orléans soon became aware that "the manuscript bought in Genoa"—the "wonderful book," as the curators of the British Museum called it—would be the jewel of his collection. Shipped on February 3, 1856 from Genoa to London, where it arrived at the British Museum, the manuscript was unpacked on February 15. It immediately raised a number of questions for the prince, as Aumale pointed out to Cuvillier-Fleury on February 18: "Je vais préparer une série de notes et questions que je vous enverrai en vous priant de les soumettre aux conservateurs de la Bibliothèque que je m'obstine à appeler nationale bien qu'elle soit l'œuvre des rois, parce que cela met tout le monde d'accord" (I shall prepare a series of notes and questions that I will send to you, asking you to submit them to the curators of the Library, which I insist on calling national, even though it is the work of kings, because that puts everyone in agreement).[27] On February 25, he said he has already been to the photographer's twice, despite the bad weather.[28] On February 26, the manuscript was presented to Queen Victoria at Buckingham Palace. Word spread: "Je suis écrasé de demandes de gens qui veulent voir mon manuscrit de Gênes" (I am overwhelmed with requests from people who want to see my manuscript from Genoa), Aumale wrote on March 16.[29] New forms of presentation emerged when the Aumale hosted the Fine Arts Club at Orleans House on May 21, 1862, perhaps the first exhibition organized by a bibliophile (fig. 7).[30]

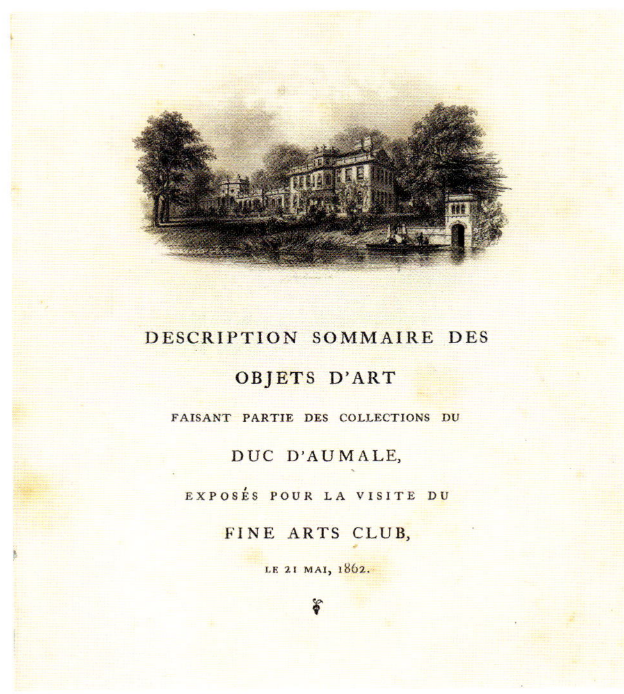

DESCRIPTION SOMMAIRE DES
OBJETS D'ART
FAISANT PARTIE DES COLLECTIONS DU
DUC D'AUMALE,
EXPOSÉS POUR LA VISITE DU
FINE ARTS CLUB,
LE 21 MAI, 1862.

Fig. 7 Henri d'Orléans, *Description sommaire des objets d'art faisant partie des collections du duc d'Aumale, exposés...* [at Orleans House, Twickenham, May 21, 1862: one of the first private presentations of the *Très Riches Heures du duc de Berry*]. (Chantilly, Bibliothèque du musée Condé, V-G-24)

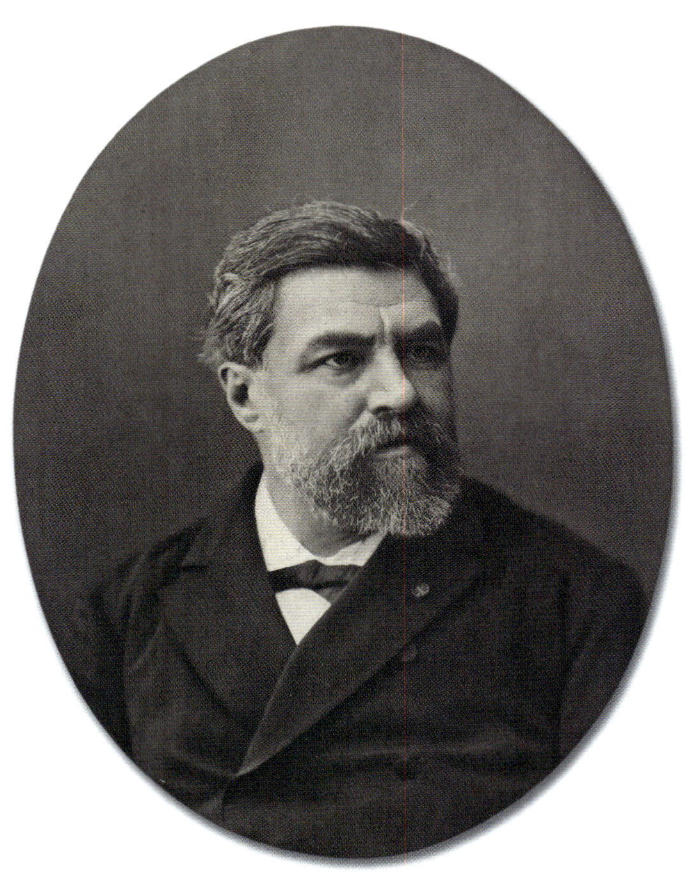

Fig. 8 Léopold Delisle, General Administrator of the National Library in Paris, from 1874 to 1905. Héliogravure by Paul Dujardin, c. 1880 (Chantilly, musée Condé, inv. PH1097)

The duke assigned a card to each miniature, to record the progress made in terms of research as he traveled, visiting libraries and consulting the leading experts of the day. Waagen was invited to see the manuscript, and devoted ten pages to it in his guide to the collections held in England, identifying it with the *Grandes Heures* of the Duke of Berry.[31] It wasn't until 1881, after Aumale had returned to France, that Léopold Delisle (fig. 8), head of the Bibliothèque nationale, and a colleague at the Institut de France, identified the Van Lymborch brothers by re-examining Waagen's hypothesis and the Duke of Berry's estate inventory of 1416: The only unfinished book of hours mentioned in it is "une très riche heures que fesoient Pol et ses frères" (a very rich book of hours that Paul and his brothers were making). From then on, the Duke of Aumale sometimes used the expression "très riches heures" in quotation marks. This authorized Count Paul Durrieu to consecrate this aesthetically refined name, after having used it as the title of the first major monograph on the manuscript in 1904.

Given the importance of the Duke of Aumale's bookplates and initials in the Cabinet des livres, it is surprising not to see any of his markings on the volume, which remained as the prince had discovered it in 1856. Only the class mark was traced in pencil on the first flyleaf. Since 1877, the Château de Chantilly, the Cabinet des livres, and a precious wooden case have jointly protected the book and served as its showcase (figs. 9 and 10).[32] Various accounts indicate that only the Duke

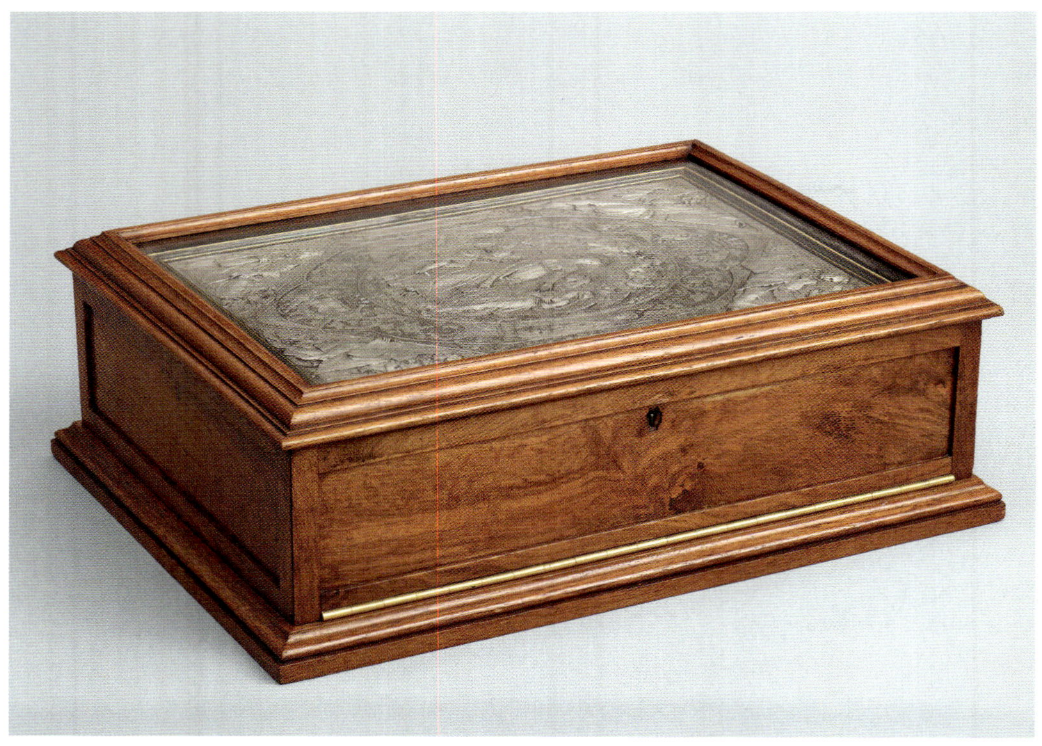

Fig. 9 Case of *Les Très Riches Heures du duc de Berry*. London, Hunt & Roskell, 1867 (Chantilly, Bibliothèque du musée Condé, ms. 65)

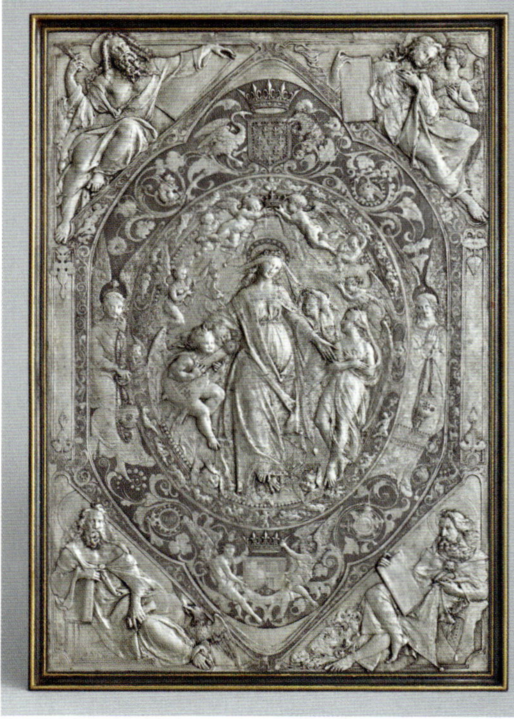

Fig. 10 Antoine Vechte, *The Coronation of the Virgin*, platinum plaque adorning the case of the *Très Riches Heures du duc de Berry*, London, Hunt & Roskell, 1867 (Chantilly, Bibliothèque du musée Condé, CMs65)

of Aumale was allowed to turn the pages; some reveal his concern when the book was handled by others. The number of "great scholars," "learned scientists," and "discerning critics" was limited: The careful and selective use of high-end reproductions in the catalog reflects a scholar who values the texts themselves and is confident about the manuscript's condition. Acquisitions of French masterpieces—the *Hours of Étienne Chevalier* (fifteenth century) by Fouquet, the *Breviary of Jeanne d'Évreux* (fourteenth century), and the *Ingeborg Psalter* (thirteenth century)—concentrated the bibliophile's attention. This focus, coupled with a sense of nationalism, made him a pioneer in the approach to the French Primitives of the late Middle Ages and early Renaissance.

The splendor of the restored château, its partial opening to the public from 1878, the attraction the Duke of Aumale exerted on many people, his election to the French Academy, then to the Academy of Fine Arts within the Institut de France, and his prestige within the army aroused the suspicion of republicans. A tactless action committed by the Count of Paris led to the duke being excluded from the army in July 1886 and to a second exile from 1886 to 1889.[33] Looking at the *Très Riches Heures* consoled him, according to Durrieu. The prince's innovative will of June 3, 1884, in which he bequeathed his great work at Chantilly to the Institut de France, was then made public. The bequest "à un corps illustre qui [lui] a fait l'honneur de [l']appeler dans ses rangs" (to an illustrious body which [had] done [him] the honor of calling [him] to its ranks) was transformed into an immediate donation with the right to use and enjoy. In doing so, Aumale made a political gesture full of flair for the benefit of the sovereign nation, in response to the government and to the detriment of a dynastic succession.

Thus the "Heures du duc de Berry," soon to be known as the *Très Riches Heures*, smoothly joined the public collections, in accordance with the bibliophile's wishes. A life's work, the Cabinet des livres that houses the collections was built as a private study library as much as a showpiece, while gradually becoming more museum-like to establish itself as a liberal model of a shared collection. Admired and then obscured for more than three centuries, the *Très Riches Heures* became the ultimate reference for books of hours and the art of illumination. Instead of hiding the library and its manuscript away from view, the prince ensured that they remain accessible and influential for the long term.[34]

1 Letter from Henri d'Orléans to his former private tutor, later his friend and secretary, Alfred-Auguste Cuvillier-Fleury (*ACF*, II, 276–77). The *Farnese Hours*, composed for Cardinal Alexander Farnese, have been in the collection of the Morgan Library & Museum in New York since 1903 under ref. M 69.
2 Cazelles 2013, 9–27.
3 Hermant 2022.
4 Aumale 1900–11, I, XXII.
5 Aumale 1854, 10.
6 Jacquemard 2021; Dion 2025.
7 Aumale 1854, 15.
8 Le Grand Condé came into possession of books left in Moulins when the Bourbonnais was awarded to him after the Treaty of the Pyrenees. Mattéoni 2022, 8, 35, 272.
9 Aumale 1854, 2–3. See Bouquillard 2021.
10 Schmid 2018; Paul-Marcetteau 1991.
11 Louis Philippe was the grandson of Louis Jean Marie de Bourbon, Duke of Penthièvre, Admiral of France, Grand Huntsman of France, and a great bibliophile. Delisle 1905, XXXIII–XXXV; Vial 2019.
12 *ACF*, II, 107 (letter of February 29, 1852).
13 Paris, BnF, Ms. Français 616.
14 Jacquemard 2021, 175.
15 Aumale 1900–11, I, XXIII; Urso and Mulas 2014, 23 ff.
16 Stammers 2023. On Aumale as historian, press patron, and pamphleteer, see Cazelles 2013, 171–91, 218–42, 249–54.
17 Chantilly, Arch. du musée Condé, PA 2 PA 22/11 (lists of addresses); *ACF*, II, 338 (letter of July 27, 1856).
18 McKitterick 2019, 44–99, 136–39.
19 Ibid., 111.
20 Arch. du musée Condé, 2 PA 22/11, 422. Letter of August 11, 1856.
21 Miller 1988, 235–241; Toulet 2013.
22 Aumale 1900–11, I, 60. This is a substantial sum compared to the 9,175 francs paid for Nicolas Poussin's *Le Massacre des Innocents* in 1854.
23 Chantilly, Bibl. du musée Condé, 38-C-9; Aumale 1854, 3.
24 Barber 2003, 140.
25 Garnier 2023. From 1857, Robert de Chartres, nephew of the Duke of Aumale, trained as an officer in Turin; he took part in the war of unification until the proclamation of the kingdom of Italy in March 1861.
26 Chantilly, Arch. du musée Condé, PA 18/82 1880. See De Hamel 2004, 11 ff.
27 *ACF*, II, 287, 288. Léopold Delisle, librarian at the "imperial library," mentions the manuscript as early as 1868. Delisle 1868–81, I, 67.
28 Letter to Panizzi, edited by Nicolas Barber 2002, 146.
29 *ACF*, II, 299 (letter of March 16, 1856).
30 *A Visit to the Fine Arts' Club...* [1862]; Toulet 2005, 18.
31 Waagen 1857, supplement, 247–49.
32 Chantilly, Arch. du musée Condé, Na 40/3.
33 Cazelles 2013, 409 ff.
34 Toulet 2010.

**Fig. 11** Following pages: Van Lymborch brothers, *Très Riches Heures*, fol. 17: St. John at Patmos, detail

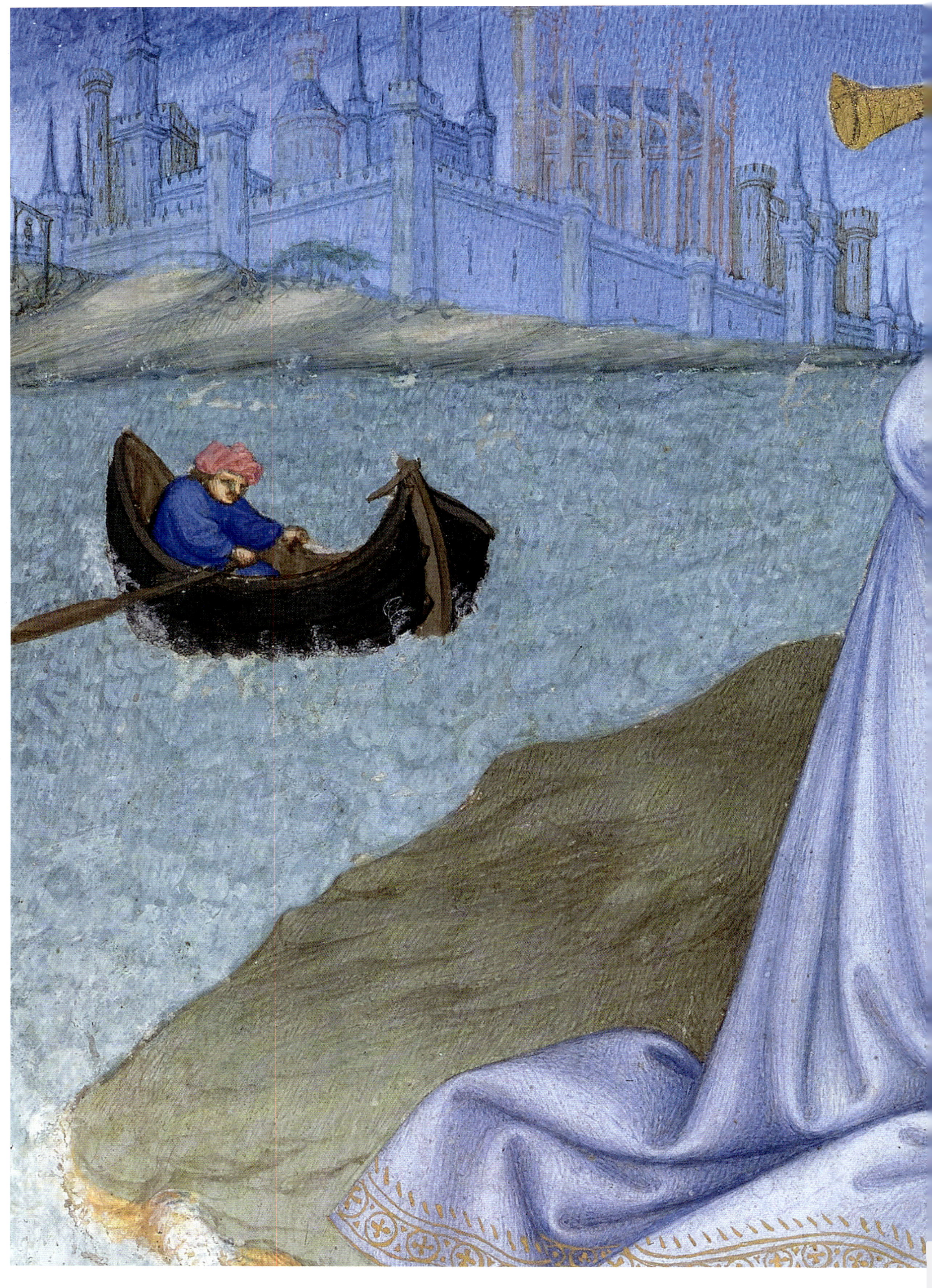

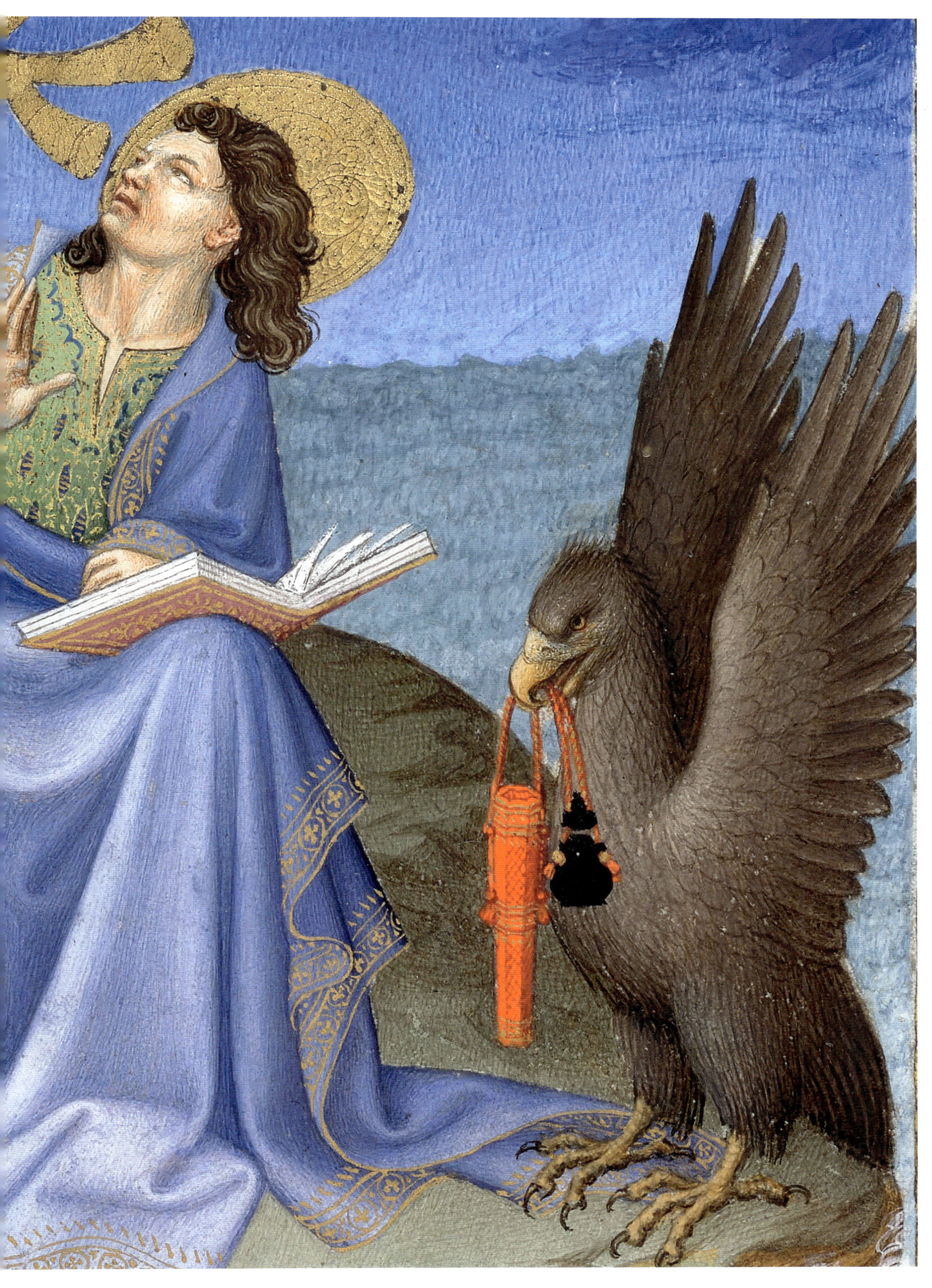

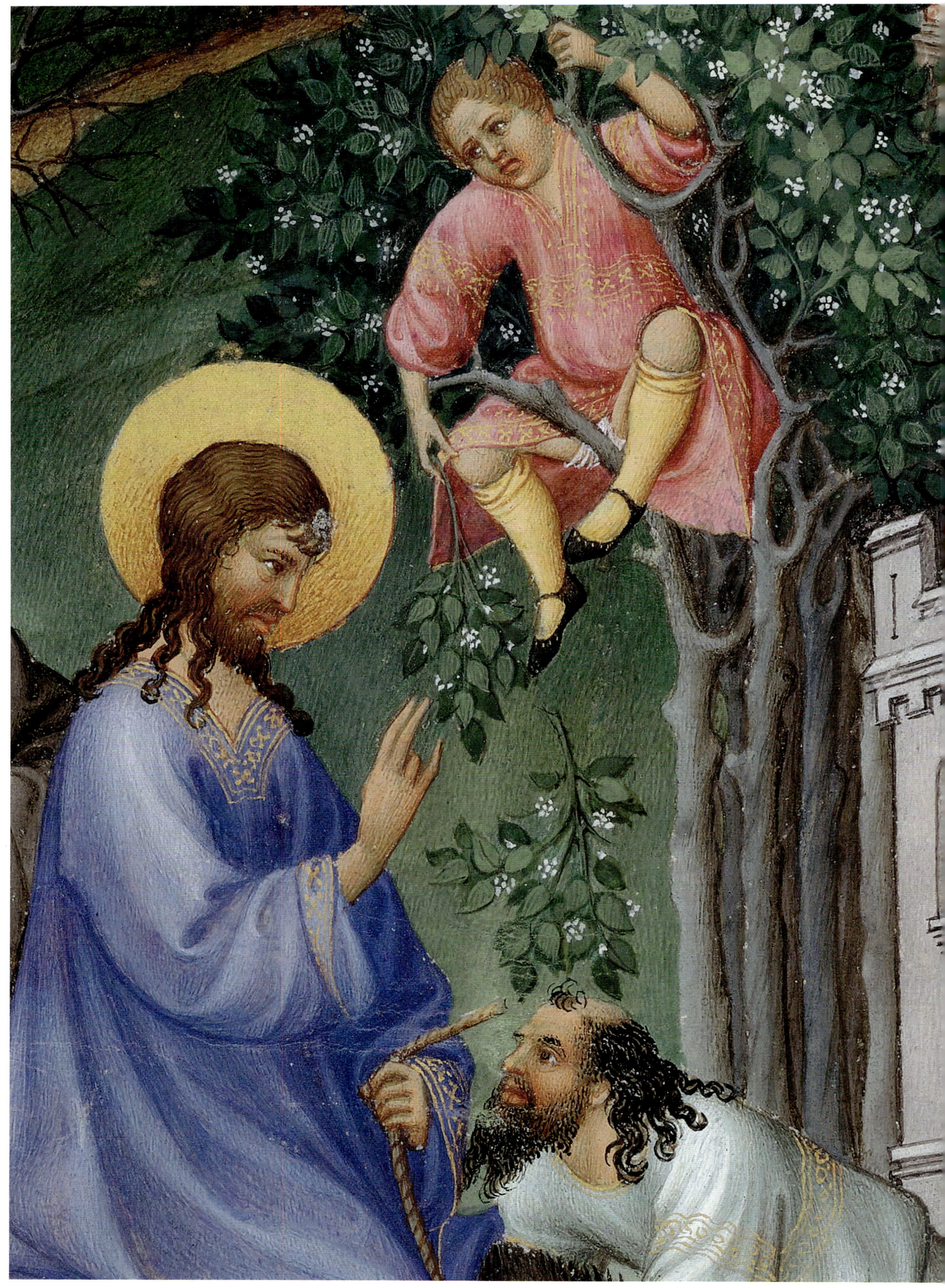

# 18.

# From "Wonderful Book" to Mythical Manuscript

Marie-Pierre Dion

The *Très Riches Heures du duc de Berry* changed hands several times before any trace of it was lost in the early sixteenth century. The prestigious red morocco binding decorated with the Spinola arms, in which the book resurfaced two and a half centuries later, is typical of the 1760s. It was from this period onward that books of hours, once disparaged by bibliophiles, became an object of admiration and particular distinction in the world of book collectors.

"The fact is that it is one of the most beautiful things to be seen,"[1] wrote the Duke of Aumale after familiarizing himself with his new manuscript. The arrival of the "wonderful book"—as the curators of the British Museum call it—at Twickenham, on the outskirts of London, marked the start of its ever-growing reputation. Thanks to several factors, the *Très Riches Heures* acquired an unprecedented reference value as a resource—as the quintessential manuscript of fifteenth-century France for historians, as a masterpiece to be admired by the public, and as an exceptional work accompanied by a multitude of reproductions and citations.

The reputation of the *Très Riches Heures* in the twentieth and twenty-first centuries is now an area of research in its own right. It was initiated in 1990 by Michael Camille, echoing Walter Benjamin's famous essay "The Work of Art in the Age of Mechanical Reproduction."[2] Pursued further by Emmanuelle Toulet, Laurent Ferri and Hélène Jacquemard, as well as Fabienne Henryot,[3] this field questions the uses to which heritage is put, yesterday and today.

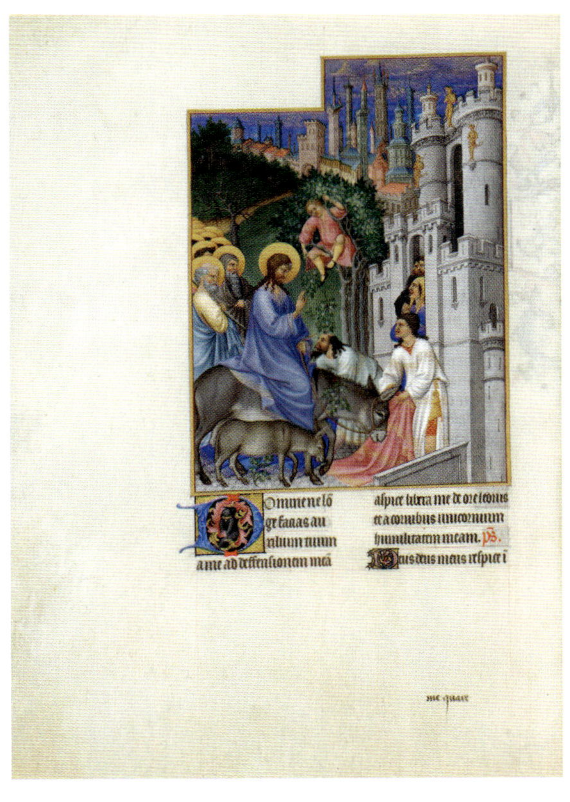

**Fig. 2** Van Lymborch brothers, *Les Très Riches Heures*, fol. 173v: The Entry of Jesus into Jerusalem (Mass for Palm Sunday)

**Fig. 1** Van Lymborch brothers, *Les Très Riches Heures*, fol. 173v: The Entry of Jesus into Jerusalem (Mass for Palm Sunday), detail

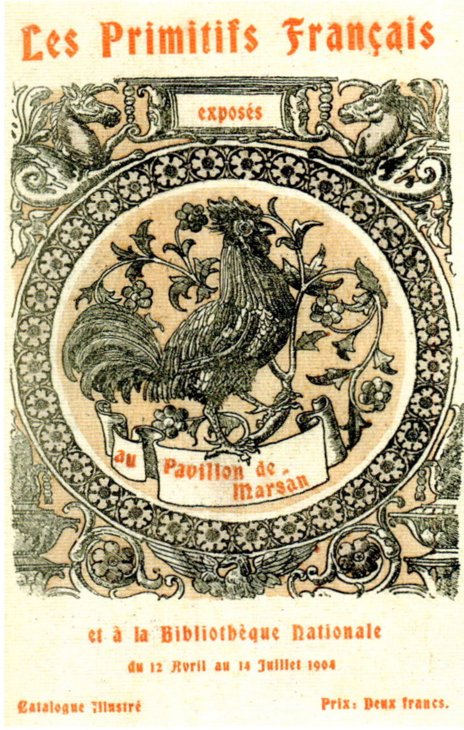


**Fig. 3** *Les Primitifs français*... Catalogue of the first public exhibition where the *Très Riches Heures* were presented through 12 photogravures. Paris, 1904 (Chantilly, Bibliothèque du musée Condé, 8 NF 3323)

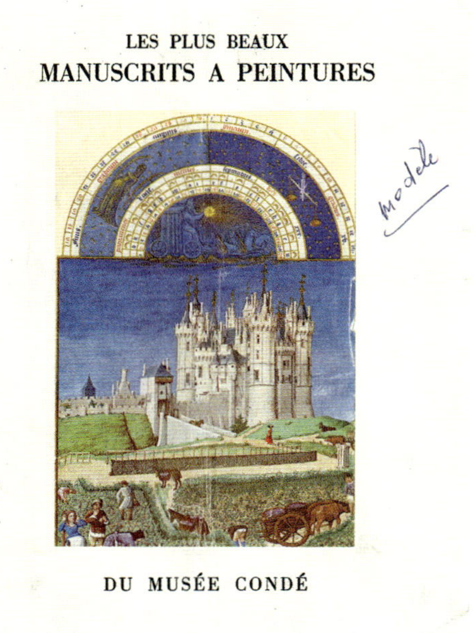


**Fig. 4** *Les Plus beaux manuscrits à peinture du musée Condé*, first exhibition catalogue (annotated model) featuring the *Très Riches Heures*, written by Jean Longnon, Chantilly, Library of the Condé Museum, 1956 (Chantilly, Arch. du musée Condé, Ms. 6 W 136)

## THE KEYS TO FAME

The rediscovery of books of hours in the nineteenth century, the enduring appeal of these intimate volumes with the public, and the popularity of the château of Chantilly, itself a place of myth and legend, laid the foundations on which the Duke of Aumale built the longlasting fame of the *Très Riches Heures*.

When the manuscript was put on display in the library of Orleans House, the duke's residence in Twickenham, in 1856, books of hours were no longer seen as liturgical and spiritual aids but were valued as aesthetic and symbolic objects from the Middle Ages. England was ahead of the competition in this respect, thanks to its flourishing market in rare books, societies of bibliophiles, and pioneering exhibitions.[4] By the end of the century, the most beautiful books of hours had become a luxury reserved for the wealthiest bibliophiles and an object of fetishization.

The Duke of Aumale benefited from favorable circumstances to expand the Bourbon-Condé collection, which numbered a single manuscript book of hours in 1851, but more than seventy pieces, if we include printed works, in 1897.[5] He also made the most of innovations in academic knowledge: A focus on archives and the analysis of forms highlighted the importance of France in the art and production of books of hours in the fifteenth and sixteenth centuries. Through his acquisitions and close ties with the scholarly world, the duke helped to draw attention to French medieval art, a valorization that served the nationalist cause and manifested itself brilliantly in the *Exposition des primitifs français* (French Primitives exhibition) of medieval and early Renaissance art, held at the Louvre and the Bibliothèque nationale in 1904 (fig. 3).

The duke did not share the simple enthusiasm for fifteenth-century books of hours that motivated collectors in France and around the world, favoring instead intellectual and artistic "monuments." His interest was in the long history of the book, acquiring from the bookseller Boone, in 1858 and 1860, two monastic psalters that were among the earliest to feature a calendar of saints and the Little Office of the Virgin.[6] In 1853, when he expressed interest in a book of hours from the seventeenth century, a "masterpiece by Jarry,"[7] he was also an exception. Since the manuscript of the *Très Riches Heures* cannot be exhibited anywhere other than Chantilly, according to the terms of its donation to the Institut de France, one of the keys to showcasing it is to link it to other remarkable pieces within the same collection. In 1891, the prince acquired forty leaves from the *Hours of Étienne Chevalier*, painted by Jean Fouquet between 1450 and 1460; These miniatures, which had been cut out and had become true small paintings, shed light on the *Très Riches Heures* and underlined the status of the collection as a major resource.

To the quality of his books, the Duke of Aumale added the appeal of his carreer as a bibliophile and the attractions of a princely residence. The presentation of the collections in their original home is key; the château is a setting that allows visitors to enter the world of the collector. The impression made on visitors is remarkable. Even if they do not see the original manuscript—meant to remain in its case—they feel a sense of ownership of it. For Emmanuelle Toulet, one might even suppose a form of latent assimilation between the châteaux of the Duke of Berry as depicted in the *Très Riches Heures* calendar and the château of Chantilly itself.[8] In any case, anything that draws attention to the one reinforces the celebrity of the other.

The rare occasions when the manuscript has gone on public display have always occurred alongside major events in Paris on a related theme. In 1937, it was shown, with other manuscripts, on the occasion of the International Exposition, "to give the highest, most complete, and most attractive idea of the château of Chantilly."[9] In 1956, it was displayed along with other treasures in the galleries of the castle during the Bibliothèque nationale's major exhibition on "painted manuscripts in France" (fig. 4).[10] This was when Italian novelist Umberto Eco discovered the manuscript; after his debut novel *The Name of the Rose*, a murder mystery set in 1327, he wrote a preface to a book on the *Très Riches Heures*, saying: "These miniatures were one of the paths that enabled me to approach the Middle Ages." In 2004, as part of a series of exhibitions on the arts in France around 1400—held at the Louvre, Dijon, Blois, and Bourges—the *Très Riches Heures* was exhibited along with eleven other illuminated manuscripts from the duke's collections in the chapel at Chantilly, in a special display case on loan from the Louvre (fig. 5).

In accepting the Duke of Aumale's donation, the Institut de France undertook to "take the necessary steps to ensure that the galleries and collections of Chantilly, under the name of Musée Condé, are open to the public twice a week for six months of the year, and that students, men of letters, and artists can at all times find there the work and research facilities they need." A codicil to the will allocated the sum of 50,000 francs for the completion and printing of catalogs. The manuscript catalog was published under the aegis of Léopold Delisle, one of the members of the newly formed Collège des conservateurs of Chantilly, and head of the Bibliothèque nationale until 1905. In 1898, a twelve-seat study room was opened, for use by students and researchers. Abbé Victor Leroquais, a specialist in liturgical books, prepared special lectures on the *Très Riches Heures* for his students at the École Pratique des Hautes Études. Thanks to its accessibility to academics, the *Très Riches Heures* became the most studied manuscript of the late Middle Ages. Scholars such as Léopold Delisle, Hulin de Loo, Paul Durrieu, Henry Martin, and Jean Porcher were succeeded by Millard Meiss, professor of art history at Princeton from 1958 to 1974. His innovative approach and monumental five-volume investigation of the *Très Riches Heures* brought the study of the manuscript into the scientific era and resulted in a series of lectures at the Collège de France.[11] The greatest names in art history cited and reproduced the book, including Louis Réau, Émile Mâle, André Malraux, Erwin Panofsky, Charles Sterling, and Carl Nordenfalk, to name but the first to do so.

To accompany the publications, courses, and conferences, new photographs of the manuscript were taken regularly, keeping pace with advances in technology. The curators of the Musée Condé used these reproductions as stand-ins for the original masterpiece. For example, visitors to the Château de Chantilly in the 1920s encountered the autochromes of Jules Gervais-Courtellemont (fig. 6).[12]

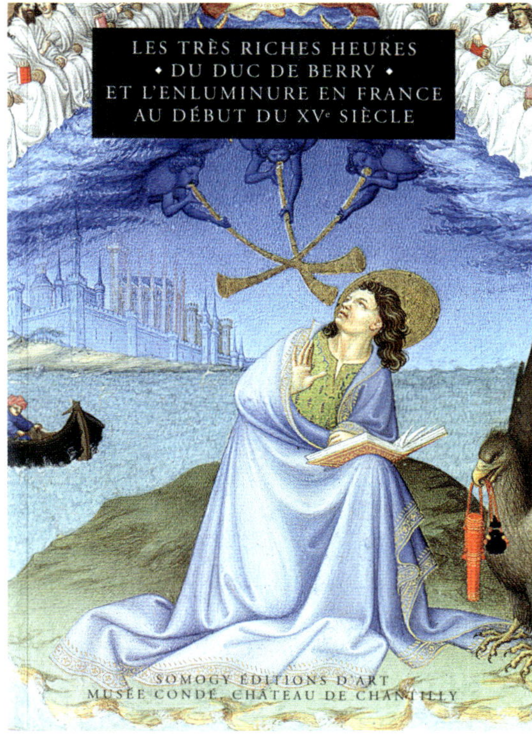


**Fig. 5** *Les Très Riches Heures du duc de Berry et l'enluminure en France au début du* XVe *siècle*, catalogue of the first exhibition dedicated to the *Très Riches Heures*, edited by Patricia Stirnemann and Emmanuelle Toulet, Paris, Somogy/Chantilly, Musée Condé, 2004 (Chantilly, Bibliothèque du musée Condé, 75 A-TRH 21)

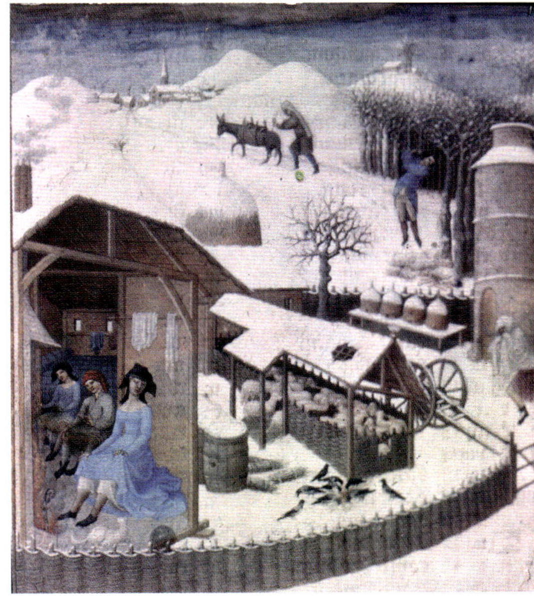

**Fig. 6** Jules Gervais-Courtellemont, *Les Très Riches Heures du duc de Berry, Février*, autochrome plate, Paris, c. 1910 (Paris, Cinematheque Robert-Lynen, AHA0039)

## CHALLENGES INVOLVED IN REPRODUCTION

The new images resonate strongly at key moments in French history. Following the first heliogravures produced in 1884 and 1900, sixty-four plates signed by Paul Dujardin, one in color, the others in velvety sepia, were printed on luxurious paper to accompany the first major monograph by the eminent scholar Paul Durrieu, commissioned by Léopold Delisle.[13] "One day Mr. Léopold Delisle, administrator of Chantilly, received a visit from a German who asked him for permission to publish a facsimile of the *Très Riches Heures* of the Duke of Berry. Not wanting this monument of French art to be published by a German, he refused the offer, claiming that the Comte de Durrieu had already undertaken that very task with the help of a Parisian publisher. Thus, Mr. Durrieu was unknowingly charged with this important historical work, and Plon-Nourrit et Cie—after other, perhaps more qualified, publishers had refused—had to reproduce the magnificent miniatures of this book of hours, purely out of patriotism."[14] Protected by an imposing neo-medieval case, this publication (1904) printed on loose leaves served as a reference for medievalists for sixty years (fig. 7).

The author established the name of the manuscript and ensured its presence at the ambitious and impressive French Primitives exhibition in 1904, which marked the first public presentation of the *Très Riches Heures* in France (fig. 3).[15] Ten leaves of miniatures attributed to the Van Lymborch brothers and two paintings by Jean Colombe were displayed under glass alongside other "facsimiles of first-rate manuscripts," including phototypes of the *Turin Hours* (most of which had been destroyed in a fire in Turin Library a few months earlier, on January 21)[16] and photogravures of the *Très Belles Heures* (also known as the *Brussels Hours*). In the catalog, the Duke of Berry's manuscripts, both originals and facsimiles, were listed in chronological order; the entry for the *Très Riches Heures* was referred to Durrieu's volume.

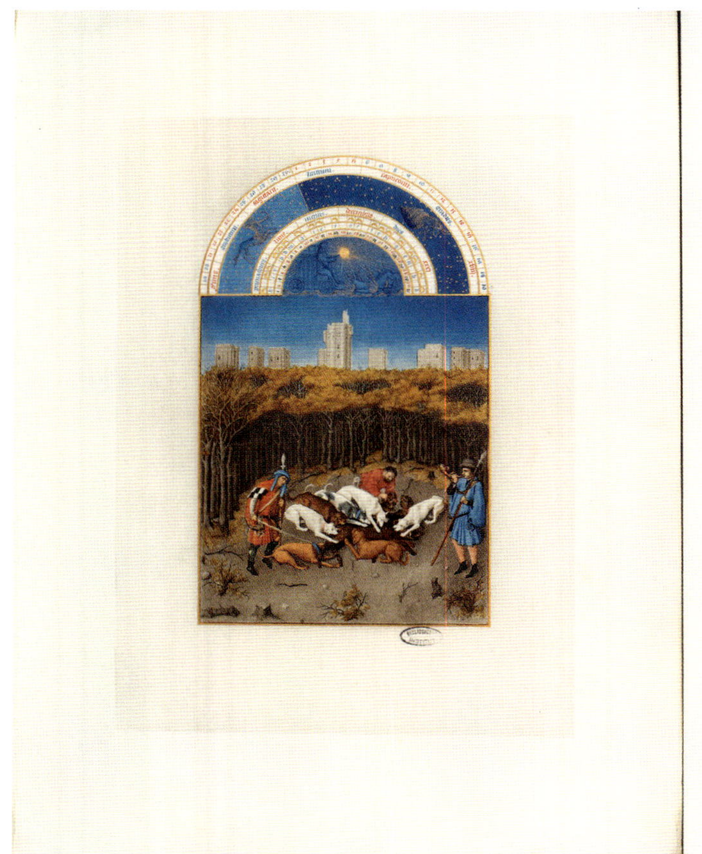

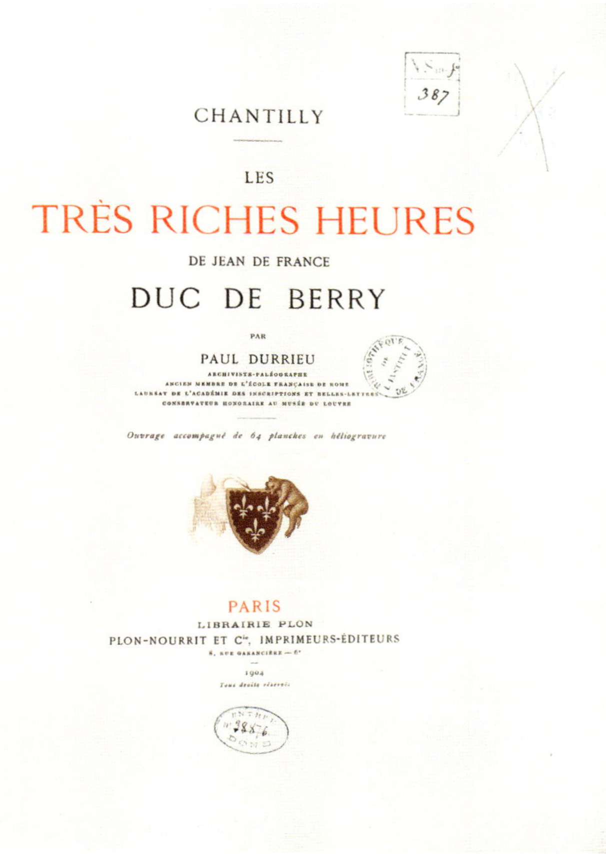

CHANTILLY

LES

TRÈS RICHES HEURES

DE JEAN DE FRANCE

DUC DE BERRY

PAR

PAUL DURRIEU

ARCHIVISTE-PALÉOGRAPHE

ANCIEN MEMBRE DE L'ÉCOLE FRANÇAISE DE ROME

LAURÉAT DE L'ACADÉMIE DES INSCRIPTIONS ET BELLES-LETTRES

CONSERVATEUR HONORAIRE AU MUSÉE DU LOUVRE

*Ouvrage accompagné de 64 planches en héliogravure*

PARIS

LIBRAIRIE PLON

PLON-NOURRIT ET Cie, IMPRIMEURS-ÉDITEURS

8, RUE GARANCIÈRE — 6e

1904

*Tous droits réservés*

**Fig. 7** Title page and heliogravure frontispiece in three colors (December), by A. Coret, printed by C. Wittmann, in Paul Durrieu, *Les Très Riches Heures de Jean de France, duc de Berry*, Paris, Plon-Nourrit et Cie, 1904 (Paris, Bibl. Mazarine, Ms. Fol. NS 315)

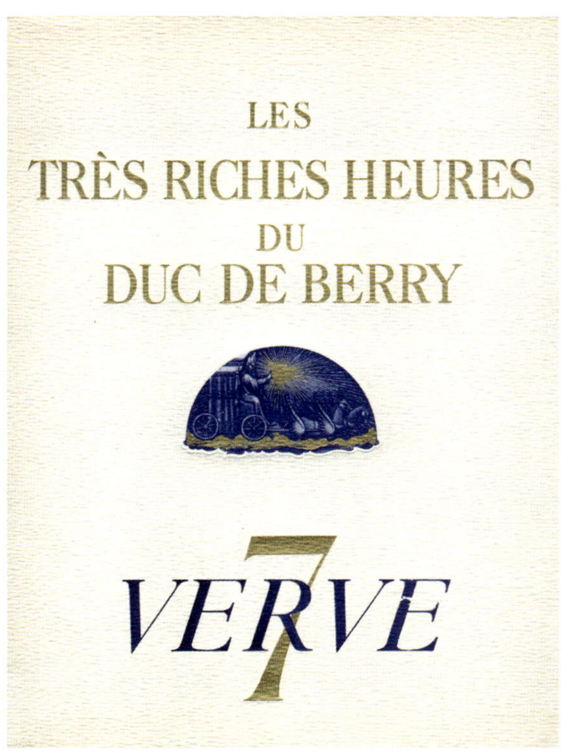


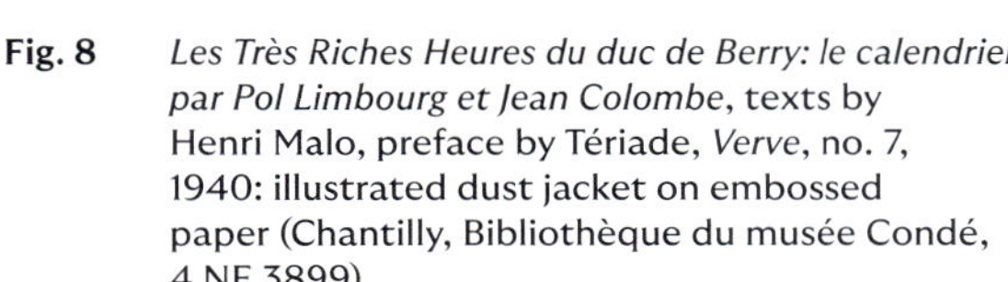

**Fig. 8** *Les Très Riches Heures du duc de Berry: le calendrier par Pol Limbourg et Jean Colombe*, texts by Henri Malo, preface by Tériade, *Verve*, no. 7, 1940: illustrated dust jacket on embossed paper (Chantilly, Bibliothèque du musée Condé, 4 NF 3899)

**Fig. 9** *Les Très Riches Heures du duc de Berry: le calendrier par Pol Limbourg et Jean Colombe*, texts by Henri Malo, preface by Tériade, *Verve*, no. 7, 1940: back cover (Chantilly, Bibliothèque du musée Condé, 4 NF 3899)

After the Turin fire, before the First World War, the safeguarding of cultural heritage became a major concern. The Société française de reproductions de manuscrits à peintures was founded on January 1, 1911 by Alexandre de Laborde (a friend of Durrieu's). Jacques Meurgey, member of the Society, published a lengthy note on the *Très Riches Heures* in his illustrated catalog of the painted manuscripts at Chantilly in 1930.[17] The safeguarding of manuscripts also aided projects by art critic and publisher Tériade, a pioneer of the modern artist's book, who previously had co-founded avant-garde magazine *Minotaure* (1933–39) and was interested in illuminated manuscripts. In 1937, Tériade launched *Verve*, a high-end art magazine in France and the US, with a print run of 15,000 copies. In 1940—after issue no. 7, devoted to the calendar of the *Très Riches Heures*—distribution ceased in the US and the print run dropped to 3,000.

Also in 1937, three exhibitions in Paris—*Masterpieces of French Art* (Palais de Tokyo), *The Masters of Independent Art, 1895–1937* (Petit Palais), and *The Most Beautiful French Manuscripts from the Eighth to the Sixteenth Century* (Bibliothèque nationale)—highlighted art with a French identity. Tériade included the exhibitions in *Verve*, acting as the first "imaginary museum." After contributing to various content before the war, Henri Malo, assistant curator at Chantilly, was involved in two issues in 1940 devoted to the *Très Riches Heures* (figs. 8–10) and also helped to keep the publication going during the Occupation. He granted image rights, provided texts and advice, and used his contacts within the Vichy government to facilitate the magazine's circulation.[18] He also persuaded

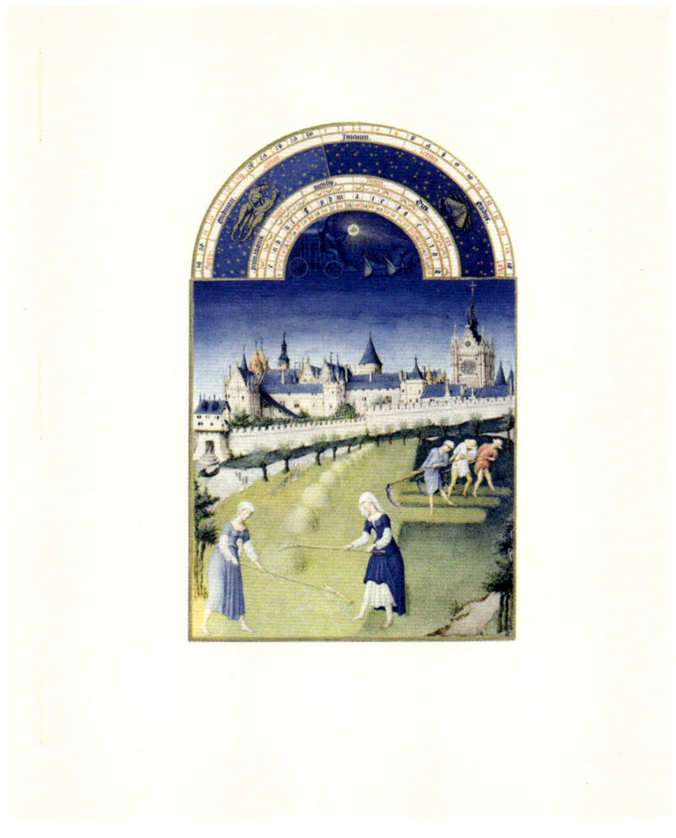

**Fig. 10** *Les Très Riches Heures du duc de Berry: le calendrier par Pol Limbourg et Jean Colombe*, texts by Henri Malo, preface by Tériade, *Verve*, no. 7, 1940: June, plate printed by Draeger (Chantilly, Bibliothèque du musée Condé, 4 NF 3899)

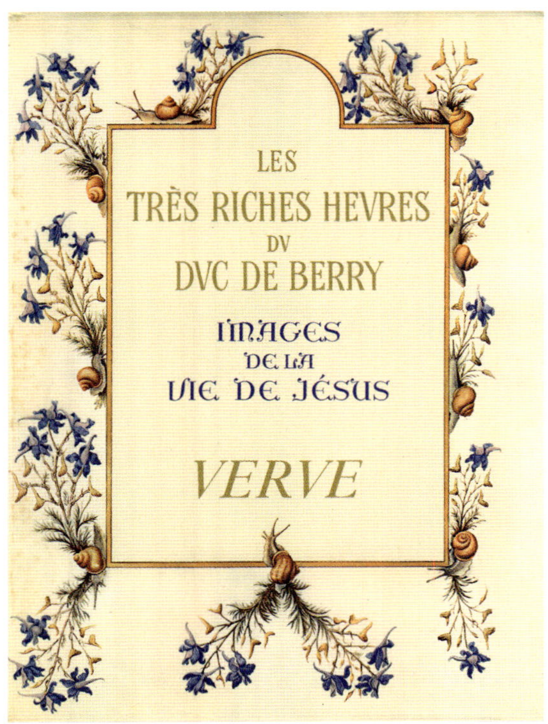


**Fig. 11** Illustrated dust jacket, *Les Très Riches Heures du duc de Berry: Images de la vie de Jésus*, texts by Henri Malo, preface by Tériade, *Verve*, no. 10, 1943 (Chantilly, Bibliothèque du musée Condé, 75 A-TRH 3)

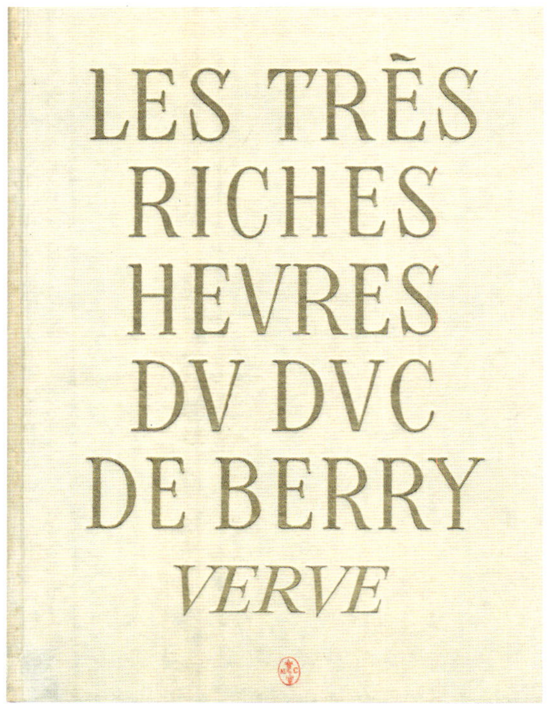


**Fig. 12** Ivory cover with gilded title, *Les Très Riches Heures du duc de Berry: le Calendrier* and *La Vie de Jésus par Pol Limbourg et Jean Colombe*, texts by Henri Malo, Paris, Éditions Verve, 1945 (reprint of issues 7 and 10) (Chantilly, Bibliothèque du musée Condé, 4 NF 1162)

Tériade of the artistic and commercial appeal of devoting another issue of *Verve* (no. 10) to the religious paintings in the manuscript (fig. 11).[19] Isolated in Berry, where he was in charge of the collections evacuated from Chantilly, he organized the photographic shoot by the Draeger company under difficult conditions. His letters provide an insight into the equipment and the meticulous color studies done in watercolor.[20]

The issue of *Verve* (no. 7, April 1940) devoted to the *Très Riches Heures* calendar caused a sensation among critics and art lovers. For the first time, the illuminations of the months were published in color, in the same dimensions as the originals, on white paper with wide margins, giving them a luxurious yet modern look, under a lightly embossed cover decorated with the Sun's chariot and the constellations, or under a gold lettered cardboard cover (figs. 8 and 12).

During this tumultuous period, the magazine left a profound mark by presenting, in the brightest and most luminous colors, "the elegance, refinement, and strength of old France," according to Tériade. This sentiment was echoed in an article by Adrienne Monnier in *Verve* no. 8, published on June 1, 1940, shortly after the German invasion and before the fall of France. She compared the manuscript to a "talisman," a "magic emerald" reflecting "the true nature of France, our country and its people dressed in bright colors, the gestures of work as pure as those of Mass, women in flowery dresses, fresh running water, branches, desires and loves; beautiful châteaux in the distance; a comforting sky; our animals close to us; our days colored with hope and finely woven."[21]

After the war, the miniatures were reproduced on small color postcards, treasured as souvenirs. A book on the *Très Riches Heures* by Jean Porcher, curator at the Bibliothèque nationale, went through several large print runs; with its vignette-framed title page, it was very reminiscent of a book of hours (fig. 13). It left a vivid impression on Umberto Eco,[22] and also on the renowned essayist and philosopher Pascal Quignard, who recalled "a very small, square volume, in large ivory cardboard, slightly embossed, light, fascinating, quite dry, the book of hours of the Duke of Berry; the vignettes were glued one by one from page to page."[23]

The end of the twentieth century was marked by two new types of publication. Between 1969 to 1974, four albums with commentary by curators from the Musée Condé were published in four different languages.[24] The books resembled facsimiles, but contained only the illustrated pages of the manuscript. On one side, the image; on the other, a commentary on paper of the same shade as the illuminated folios, to give the impression of parchment and lend unity to the work. Printed in offset by Draeger and distributed at affordable prices, they were a useful tool for students and researchers. The English, Dutch, and German versions had a foreword by the US art historian Millard Meiss, who contextualized the vision of the *Très Riches Heures* by placing it within the network of exchanges developing across the West, particularly from Tuscany to the Flemish lands (fig. 14).

The first limited-edition, luxury facsimile of the *Très Riches Heures* appeared in the 1980s.[25] The complete and meticulous reproduction of the book-object—text, illustration, binding—was part of a movement aimed at new bibliophiles, who were offered a Plexiglas showcase for the book. A volume of commentaries contains a presentation of the manuscript

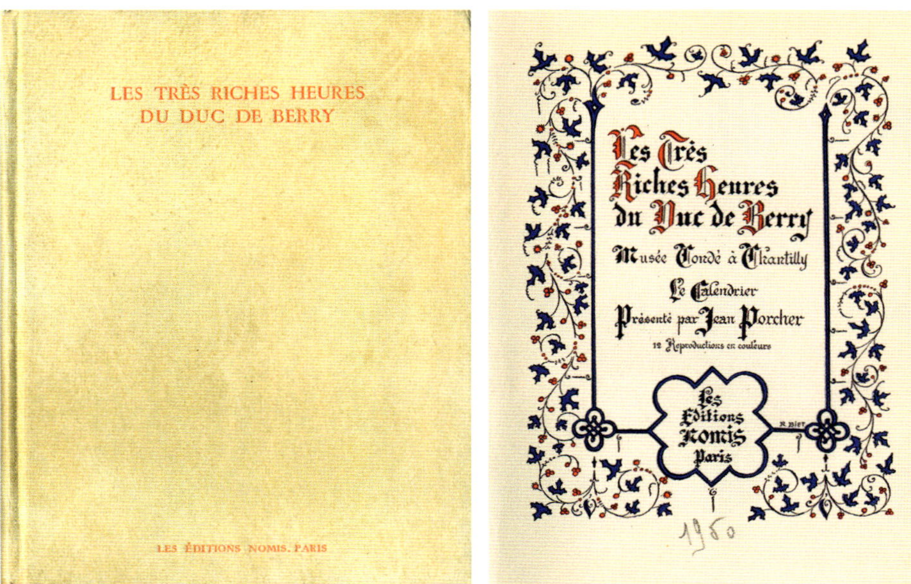


**Fig. 13** Cover and title page, Jean Porcher, *Les Très Riches Heures du duc de Berry*, Paris, Éditions Nomis, 1950 (Chantilly, Bibliothèque du musée Condé, 75 A-TRH 4)

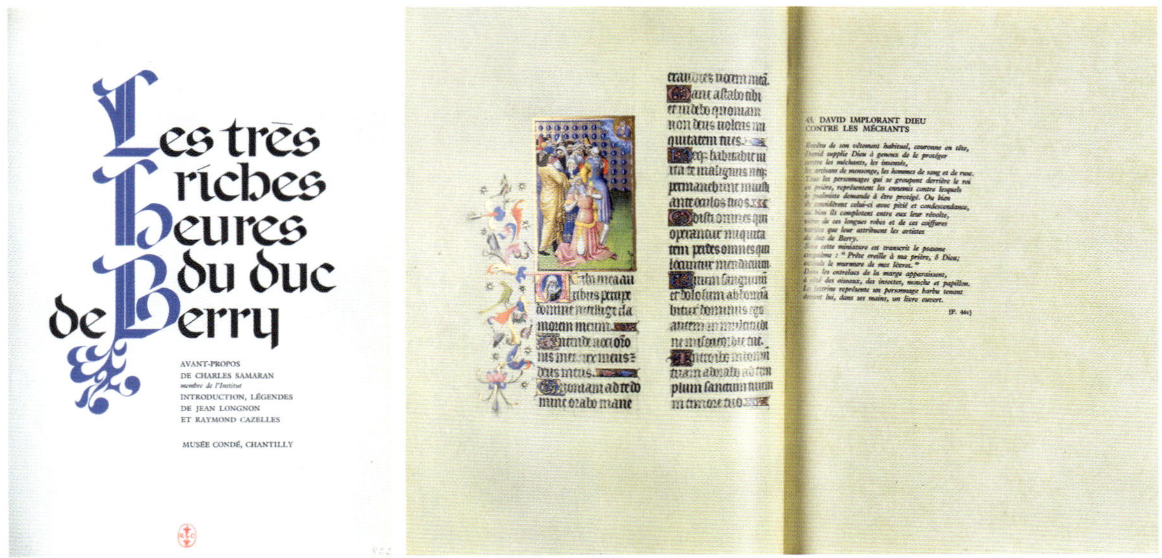


**Fig. 14** Cover and double-page spread, *Les Très Riches Heures du duc de Berry*, introduction and captions by Jean Longnon and Raymond Cazelles, Paris, Vilo, 1969 (Chantilly, Bibliothèque du musée Condé, 75-A-TRH10)

but also the transcription and translation of all the prayer texts. The price put the facsimile beyond the reach of most libraries and readers, while the publisher's advertisements warned that the *Très Riches Heures* would never be on public display again. The scandal was commensurate with the manuscript's reputation. *The New York Times* gave it a prominent headline, helping to entrench the idea that the world's most famous manuscript is also the most inaccessible.[26] And then, as if in a facetious echo of this story, in an episode of the British television comedy series *Mr. Bean*, the eponymous hero consults and clumsily destroys a manuscript that appears to be a facsimile of the *Très Riches Heures*.

### THE *TRÈS RICHES HEURES* ON SCREEN

The *Très Riches Heures* made some fine television appearances, notably in parts eight and nine of the documentary series *Le Temps des cathédrales* (The Time of the Cathedrals), in which medievalist Georges Duby commented on several pages of the manuscript.[27] The arrival of new technologies into the life of the book was more laborious, but the hopes raised made the headlines again, as did a CD project in 1990 that was ultimately abandoned ten years later.[28] Finally, in 2004, a CD-ROM was published, which "contains a very good facsimile of the manuscript of the illuminated hours created at the

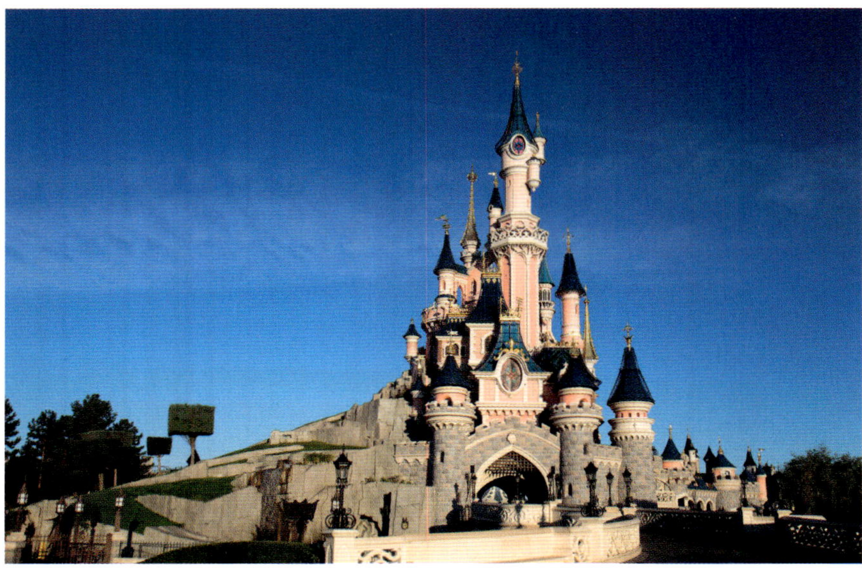

**Fig. 15** Sleeping Beauty's Castle, Disneyland Paris

instigation of the Duke of Berry. However, it is singularly lacking in commentary."[29] Producing high-quality images, adapting the format of the book to different screen sizes, restoring the vision of the book, turning the pages, giving free access to the document while respecting rights holders, facilitating research and comparison, offering sufficient commentaries without discouraging the general public—these were all the parts of the equation to be solved to do justice to the original. Today, the major scientific portal Biblissima, a constantly updated Wikipedia page, and a digital book that can be leafed through, published online with commentaries by the Museé Condé, all contribute to this goal.

## CASTLES FOR THE CINEMA

Reproductions of the Van Lymborch brothers' castles on film were instrumental in shaping an ideal image of the Middle Ages in the collective imagination. Jacques Prévert was inspired by the miniatures in *Verve* magazine when he was writing the screenplay for Marcel Carné's film *Les Visiteurs du Soir* (The Devil's Envoys), released in December 1942. The invitation to the preview, designed by René Péron, was taken directly from the illustrations of the manuscript, as was the castle recreated in the film (fig. 16).

Marcel Carné recalled this episode in his memoirs: "We had talked about it [with set designer Georges Wakhévitch] for a long time while contemplating the miniatures in the *Très Riches Heures*, and I had insisted that the walls should have the color of new stone, just as they existed when they were built. If I had asked for a set to be built, it was precisely so that it would look new. . ."[30] The château, "shining like a mirror," was designed by Alexandre Trauner.[31] At the beginning of the film, we see another castle perched on a hill in the distance, a field and, in the foreground, peasants at work. The image, inspired by the miniature of March in the *Très Riches Heures*, was recognized by several critics, who considered it faithful to what landscapes must have been like in the Middle Ages: "Certain images evoke pictures that have been in our eyes since childhood: the plowman from 500 years ago, throwing the grain into this black earth, while the castle that both protects and exploits him looms in the distance," said one. The beginning of the film was inspired by the month of March and can be recognized in the derivative images (fig. 17).[32]

British actor and director Laurence Olivier also drew on the *Très Riches Heures* for the setting of *Henry V*, his 1944 film version of Shakespeare's play. The castle of Charles VI, king of France, and the farmhouse scene where Gower, Pistol, and Fluellen exchange words immediately conjure up images from the manuscript.

The miniatures in the *Très Riches Heures* also inspired the set designers of Walt Disney, who himself visited the château of Chantilly on July 3, 1935.[33] The manuscript is directly mentioned in the "prop book" that opens the 1959 film *Sleeping Beauty*, designed by Eyvind Earle: The castle fills the center of the page of the neo-medieval illuminated book. The poetry of the Van Lymborch brothers' miniatures permeates not only the castle in *Sleeping Beauty*, but also the film's landscapes and the representation of nature. Along with Viollet-le-Duc's drawings and the architectural extravagances of King Ludwig II's castles in Bavaria, the Van Lymborch miniatures of September (the château of Saumur) and of October (the Louvre) also inspired the castle in the Disneyland Paris amusement park, which opened in 1992 (fig. 15).[34]

## FASCINATION WITH THE CALENDAR

On the threshold of the 2000s, Umberto Eco recommended reading the manuscript as a whole, rather than focussing, as many have, on just the calendar.[35] The miniatures have been widely used for documentary purposes, as a way of

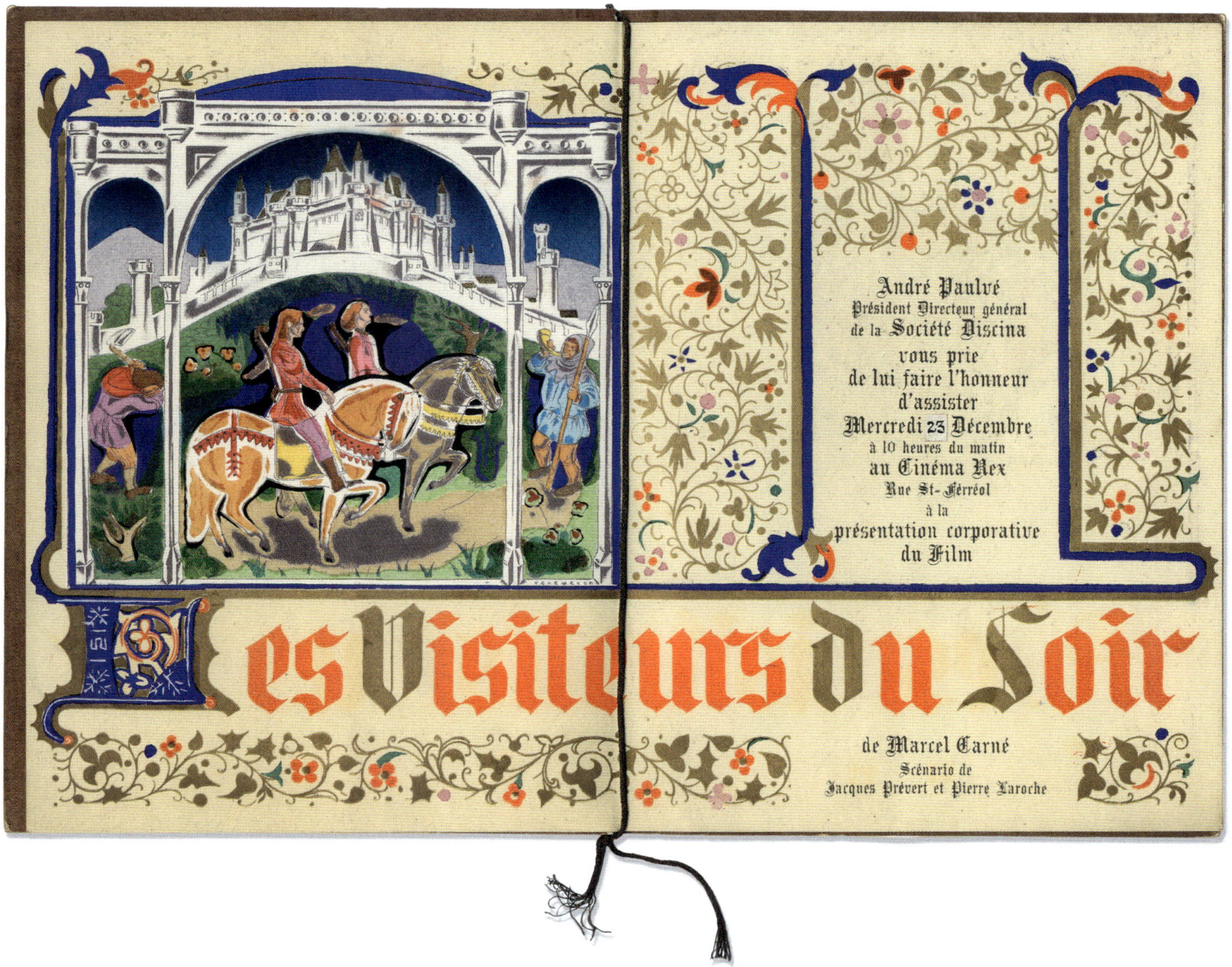

Les Visiteurs du Soir

André Paulvé
Président Directeur général
de la Société Discina
vous prie
de lui faire l'honneur
d'assister
Mercredi 23 Décembre
à 10 heures du matin
au Cinéma Rex
Rue St-Férréol
à la
présentation corporative
du Film

de Marcel Carné
Scénario de
Jacques Prévert et Pierre Laroche

**Fig. 16** Invitation card to a private screening of Marcel Carné's film *Les Visiteurs du soir* (*The Devil's Envoys*), at Cinéma Madeleine, December 5, 1942 (private collection)

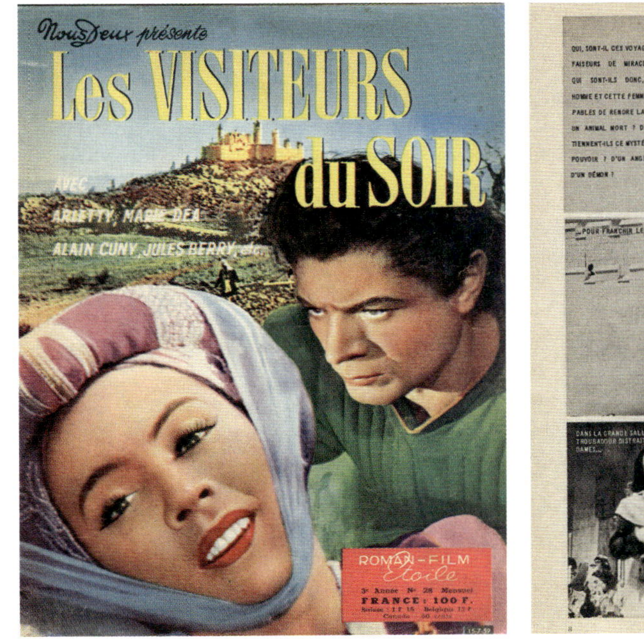


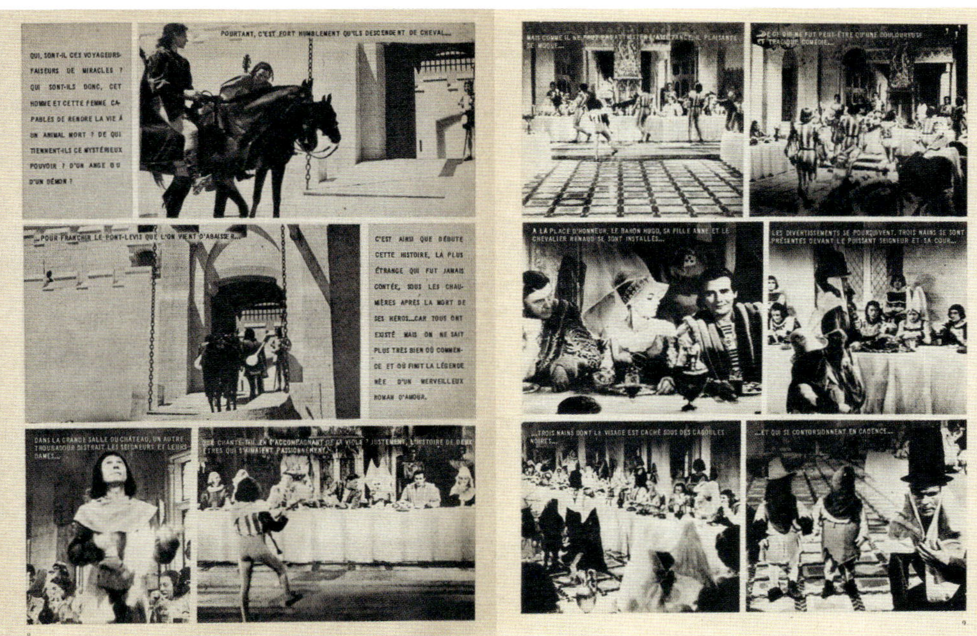


**Fig. 17** *Les Visiteurs du soir: roman-photo* (*The Devil's Envoys*: *photo romance*), in *Nous Deux*, 28 (July 15, 1959) (private collection)

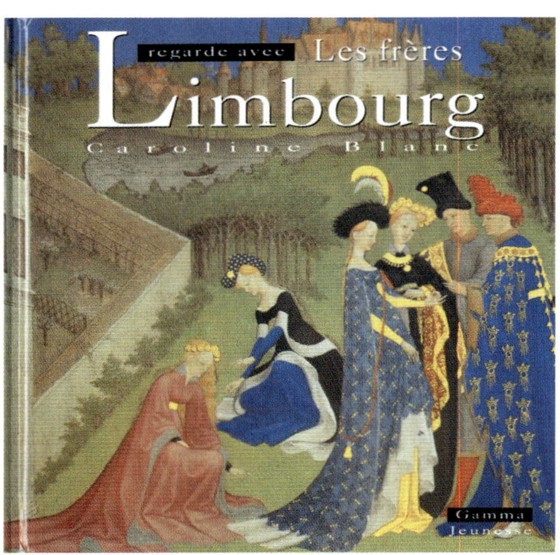


**Fig. 18** Cover image (reversed from the original), Caroline Blanc, *Les Frères Limbourg*, Paris, Gamma Jeunesse, 1993 (private collection)

exploring the lives of people in the Middle Ages and the history of medieval art. An object of cultural consumption and sharing on social media, the manuscript is now subjected to fragmentation, rapid visualization, and erratic browsing (fig. 18).

The images of the calendar months have frequently captured the attention of the media. On January 5, 1948, *Life* magazine printed several hundred thousand cheap copies of "the world's most famous calendar" in twelve full-page color photographs, slightly larger than the original illuminations, and censoring the genitals of the peasants in the month of February (fig. 19).[36]

The French government commissioned large posters of the magnificent view of the month of September to promote the châteaux of the Loire and tourism in France (fig. 20), while the French postal service issued two stamps in 1965 and 2013 with print runs of over seven and five million, respectively (fig. 21).

School textbooks have been another important vector. Fabienne Henryot notes that as early as 1908, images from the *Très Riches Heures* were featured on magic lantern slides for schools, as part of a series dedicated to to the history of miniature art. Textbooks and teaching materials have frequently used images from the *Très Riches Heures* calendar, especially after 1975 and 2000, when French teaching methods promoted the use of images (fig. 22). In the twentieth century, the two most frequently used illuminations were those depicting agricultural work in March and June. The very brief accompanying information made it difficult to contextualize them or to

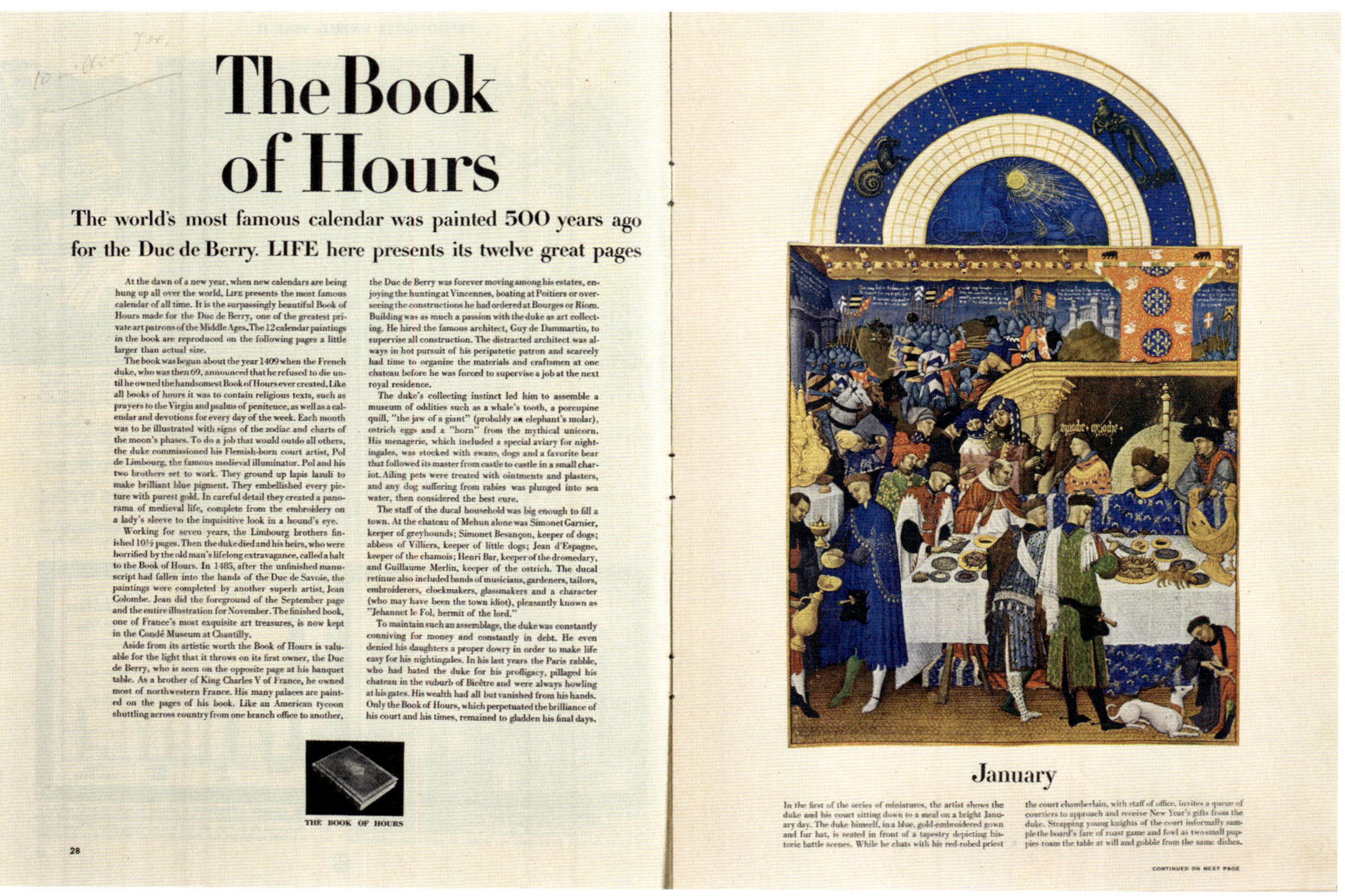

# The Book of Hours

**The world's most famous calendar was painted 500 years ago for the Duc de Berry. LIFE here presents its twelve great pages**

At the dawn of a new year, when new calendars are being hung up all over the world, LIFE presents the most famous calendar of all time. It is the surpassingly beautiful Book of Hours made for the Duc de Berry, one of the greatest private art patrons of the Middle Ages. The 12 calendar paintings in the book are reproduced on the following pages a little larger than actual size.

The book was begun about the year 1409 when the French duke, who was then 69, announced that he refused to die until he owned the handsomest Book of Hours ever created. Like all books of hours it was to contain religious texts, such as prayers to the Virgin and psalms of penitence, as well as a calendar and devotions for every day of the week. Each month was to be illustrated with signs of the zodiac and charts of the moon's phases. To do a job that would outdo all others, the duke commissioned his Flemish-born court artist, Pol de Limbourg, the famous medieval illuminator. Pol and his two brothers set to work. They ground up lapis lazuli to make brilliant blue pigment. They embellished every picture with purest gold. In careful detail they created a panorama of medieval life, complete from the embroidery on a lady's sleeve to the inquisitive look in a hound's eye.

Working for seven years, the Limbourg brothers finished 10½ pages. Then the duke died and his heirs, who were horrified by the old man's lifelong extravagance, called a halt to the Book of Hours. In 1485, after the unfinished manuscript had fallen into the hands of the Duc de Savoie, the paintings were completed by another superb artist, Jean Colombe. Jean did the foreground of the September page and the entire illustration for November. The finished book, one of France's most exquisite art treasures, is now kept in the Condé Museum at Chantilly.

Aside from its artistic worth the Book of Hours is valuable for the light that it throws on its first owner, the Duc de Berry, who is seen on the opposite page at his banquet table. As a brother of King Charles V of France, he owned most of northwestern France. His many palaces are painted on the pages of his book. Like an American tycoon shuttling across country from one branch office to another, the Duc de Berry was forever moving among his estates, enjoying the hunting at Vincennes, boating at Poitiers or overseeing the constructions he had ordered at Bourges or Riom. Building was as much a passion with the duke as art collecting. He hired the famous architect, Guy de Dammartin, to supervise all construction. The distracted architect was always in hot pursuit of his peripatetic patron and scarcely had time to organize the materials and craftsmen at one chateau before he was forced to supervise a job at the next royal residence.

The duke's collecting instinct led him to assemble a museum of oddities such as a whale's tooth, a porcupine quill, "the jaw of a giant" (probably an elephant's molar), ostrich eggs and a "horn" from the mythical unicorn. His menagerie, which included a special aviary for nightingales, was stocked with swans, dogs and a favorite bear that followed its master from castle to castle in a small chariot. Ailing pets were treated with ointments and plasters, and any dog suffering from rabies was plunged into sea water, then considered the best cure.

The staff of the ducal household was big enough to fill a town. At the chateau of Mehun alone was Simonet Garnier, keeper of greyhounds; Simonet Besançon, keeper of dogs; abbess of Villiers, keeper of little dogs; Jean d'Espagne, keeper of the chamois; Henri Bar, keeper of the dromedary, and Guillaume Merlin, keeper of the ostrich. The ducal retinue also included bands of musicians, gardeners, tailors, embroiderers, clockmakers, glassmakers and a character (who may have been the town idiot), pleasantly known as "Jehannet le Fol, hermit of the lord."

To maintain such an assemblage, the duke was constantly conniving for money and constantly in debt. He even denied his daughters a proper dowry in order to make life easy for his nightingales. In his last years the Paris rabble, who had hated the duke for his profligacy, pillaged his chateau in the suburb of Bicêtre and were always howling at his gates. His wealth had all but vanished from his hands. Only the Book of Hours, which perpetuated the brilliance of his court and his times, remained to gladden his final days.

THE BOOK OF HOURS

28

## January

In the first of the series of miniatures, the artist shows the duke and his court sitting down to a meal on a bright January day. The duke himself, in a blue, gold-embroidered gown and fur hat, is seated in front of a tapestry depicting historic battle scenes. While he chats with his red-robed priest the court chamberlain, with staff of office, invites a queue of courtiers to approach and receive New Year's gifts from the duke. Strapping young knights of the court informally sample the board's fare of roast game and fowl as two small puppies roam the table at will and gobble from the same dishes.

CONTINUED ON NEXT PAGE

**Fig. 19** The Book of Hours . . . , *Life*, January 5, 1948, 22 (Chantilly, Musée Condé, 2-NF-148)

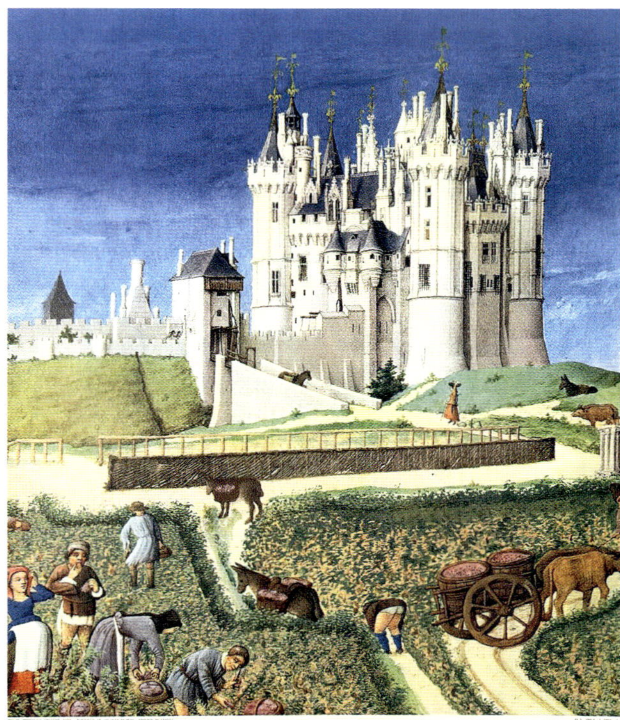

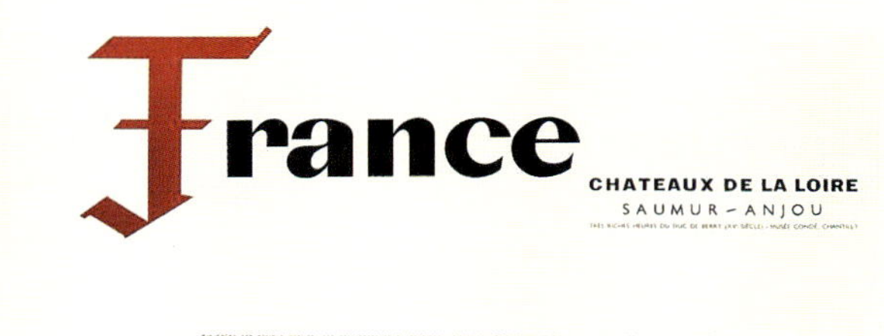


**Fig. 20** *France. Châteaux de la Loire*, poster designed by Jacques Dubois, printed by Draeger. Paris, Ministère des travaux publics, Direction du tourisme, 1956 (private collection)

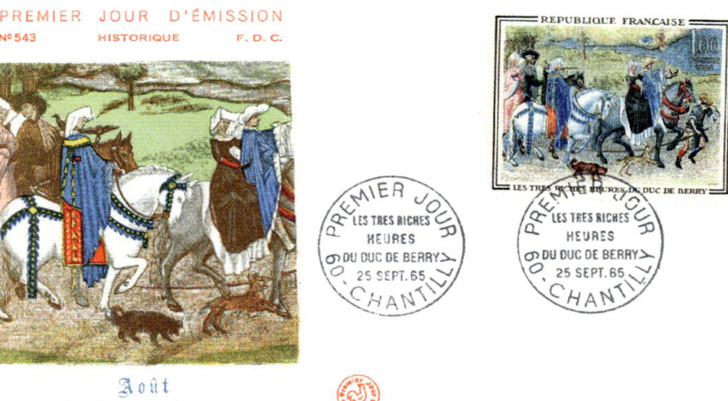


**Fig. 21** "First Day" envelope of the stamp designed and engraved by René Cottet, based on a detail from the illumination of August. Chantilly, 1965 (private collection)

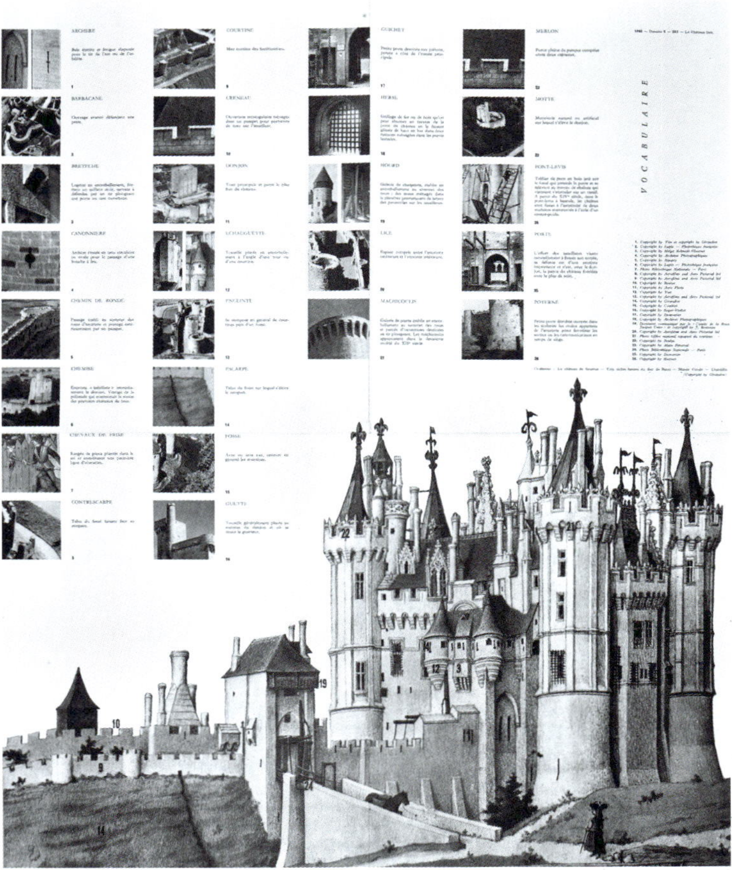


**Fig. 22** *Le Château fort*, educational file by Jean and Marie-Clotilde Hubert, illustrated fold-out board, Paris, *La Documentation photographique*, no. 5-253, March 1965 (private collection)

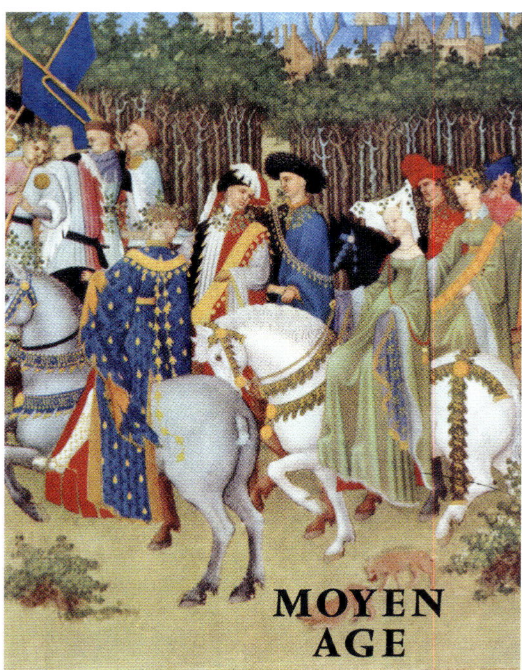


**Fig. 23** André Lagarde and Laurent Michard, *Moyen Âge*, Paris, Bordas, 1963 (private collection)

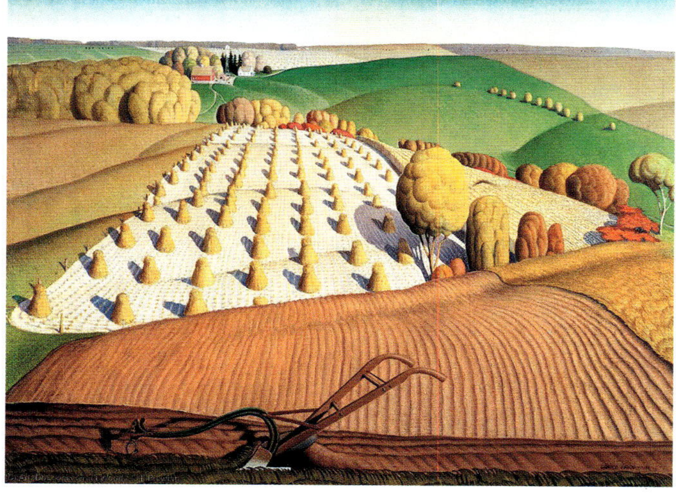

**Fig. 24** Grant Wood, *Fall Plowing*. 1931 (John Deere Collection [Moline, Illinois, USA])

appreciate the singularity of the manuscript, but it did help to establish the *Très Riches Heures* in the collective imagination of the Middle Ages. The famous "Lagarde & Michard" textbook, with several million copies in circulation, featured the month of May on its cover (at least between the 1960s and 1990s). The book also included February, retouched to illustrate the literature of fabliaux, April to sum up the spirit of courtly literature, and the miniature of Hell to evoke religious theater (fig. 23).

Few illuminations have inspired artists so intensely. American painter Grant Wood—creator of the instantly recognisable *American Gothic* (1930)—studied Flemish painting and drew inspiration from scenes of rural life in the *Très Riches Heures* (fig. 24).[37] French artist Bernard Buffet used the Duke of Berry's sulky expression in his painting *Académie Goncourt* (The Goncourt Academy).[38]

Some artists have focused their attention on the calendar. In 1975, Belgian conceptual artist and poet Marcel Broodthaers presented his version of the *Très Riches Heures du duc de Berry* in two panels (fig. 25). The right panel features Éditions Braun postcards showing the calendar miniatures without their emblematic tympanum, while the left panel features an alphabet book applied to the manuscript. Following in the footsteps of Magritte, Broodthaers was alluding to the fetishism of the manuscript and the imaginary it generates in the collective memory.

At the beginning of the twenty-first century, an active center for research and celebration of the Van Lymborchs emerged in Nijmegen: the Maewael Van Lymborch House, where the painters once lived. Still, Polish playwright Beniamin M. Bukowski was astonished by the Van Lymborch brothers' lack of fame. He turned them into the heroes of *The Amazing Limbourg Brothers* (2015), a play with a singular structure. Twelve scenes—one for each month, one for each year that the painters knew their patron—show the brothers at work, in moments devoted to creation or pondering existential interrogations on art, death, and vanity. The play interweaves medieval and contemporary cultural codes, highlighting the power of representations and the fragility of historians' hypotheses. "We live in times of reproducibility without remembering the original. Recall the banquet the Van Lymborch brothers painted for me," says the Duke of Berry character. "Even though it was only reproduced on paper, I remember it better than those I attended . . . "[39]

Does the manuscript's fame lie in the power of its images, their incomparable beauty, their evocative power, and the unique moment they represent in the history of art? Or does it lie in the humanity of a calendar evoking the universal theme of time, with the rotation of landscapes through the seasons? Or is it perhaps linked to the number of reproductions in circulation and the long periods when the book remained out of sight?

"The only rival in terms of renown, *The Book of Kells*, is regularly shown to the public in the library of Trinity College, Dublin, and it seems to me that there is no reason why the same should not be the case at the Musée Condé," wrote art historian Jonathan Alexander.[40] Between the vast stage of a university library and the intimate setting of the galleries at Chantilly, the battle is an unequal one, but it is far from lost, since the Cabinet des livres is currently being restored.

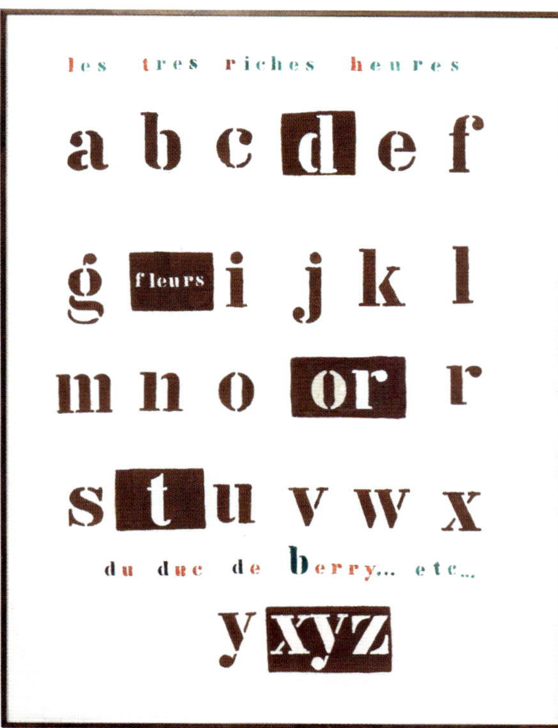


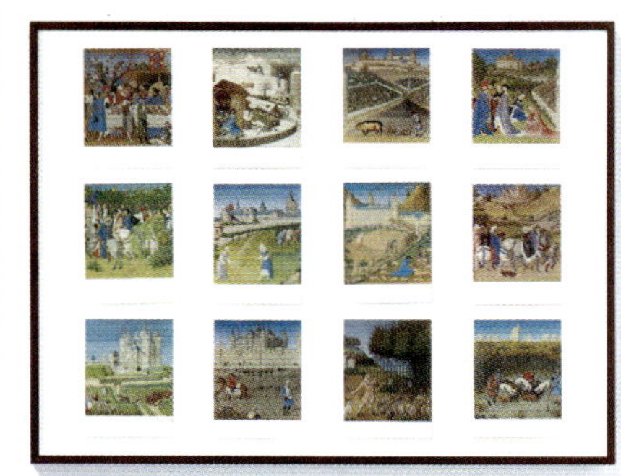

**Fig. 25** Marcel Broodthaers, *Très Riches Heures du duc de Berry*. 1975 (Courtesy Michael Werner Gallery)

1 *ACF*, II, 299 (letter of March 16, 1856).
2 Camille 1990, 72–74.
3 Toulet 2005; Ferri and Jacquemard 2018; Henryot 2022.
4 Munby 1972; Henryot 2022, 156 ff.
5 Chantilly, Bibl. du musée Condé, Ms. 74: *Hours of Marguerite de Coëtivy*, France, c. 1504. This book of hours was removed from the Condé collection in 1830 and returned to the Duke of Aumale in 1851. In the eyes of the latter, this was one of "the most interesting" volumes in the Condé collection; the originality of the illuminations, influenced by the art of Jean Bourdichon, played a key role in the prince's interest in French books of hours. Chantilly 2019–20. On the reconstruction of the Chantilly book collection, see Dion 2025.
6 Chantilly, Bibl. du musée Condé, Ms. 7 and Ms. 8.
7 Chantilly, Bibl. du musée Condé, Ms. 88: *Hours of François de Beauvilliers, Duc de Saint-Aignan*. Henryot 2022, 188.
8 Toulet 2005, 26.
9 Chantilly, Arch. du musée Condé, 6 W 108.
10 Chantilly 1956; Paris 1955–56.
11 Meiss 1968, 1969, 1974a.
12 Chantilly, Arch. du musée Condé, Na 98-32. Gustave Macon, *Le duc de Berry*, 1922 (handwritten lecture text and letters to Jules Gervais-Courtellemont).
13 Durrieu 1904 ; about Paul Durrieu, see Roman 2021.
14 Handwritten note at the top of the copy kept at the Getty Research Institute, 84-B2857 (conversation with Léopold Delisle, August 1907). Chantilly, Arch. du musée Condé, 4-W-19.
15 Paris 2004a.
16 Ninety-three leaves were lost in a fire in the library in Turin where they had been kept since 1720.
17 Meurgey 1930, 59–71 (no. 30).
18 The Catenacci Prize of the Academy of Fine Arts was awarded to Verve, thanks to Henri Malo, in 1940. On the relations between Tériade, Henri Malo, and Marshal Pétain, a member of the College of Curators of the Musée Condé, see Ferri 2020, 625, and Kolokytha 2014.
19 Henri Malo signed a presentation of the *Très Riches Heures du duc de Berry* in the "Memoranda (Collections publiques de France)" series published by Henri Laurens in 1933. It served as the basis for issue no. 10 of *Verve*.
20 Le Cateau-Cambrésis, Musée Matisse, Tériade collection, box 6, letters 1941–42.
21 Monnier [1940] 1976.
22 Cazelles 1988a, 7–9.
23 Cazelles 1988a; Quignard 2023, 19.
24 Starting with Longnon and Cazelles 1969a.
25 Cazelles and Rathofer 1984, 2 vols., 980 copies printed. The commentary was published in French and German.
26 Lewis 1987.
27 *Le Temps des cathédrales*. 8. *Le Bonheur et la mort*. 9. *Vers les temps nouveaux*, directed by Roland Darbois, based on the work of Georges Duby, Paris, Antenne 2, 1979.
28 "It will be possible to journey through *Les Très Riches Heures du duc de Berry* at lower cost. All you will need, besides a TV set, is a Kodak photo-CD player, connected to the small screen by a Péritel cable. After highlighting an image, using a remote control you can choose your program by selecting images from an index where each photo is numbered. Depending on which button you press, you can leaf through the images quickly, pause on a subject, explore it by enlarging it, make it move in all directions, frame it differently." "Les *Très Riches Heures du duc de Berry* sur disque compact: une première à cette échelle pour une oeuvre d'art," *Le Journal des Arts*, May 1, 1994.
29 *01.net*, May 6, 2004.
30 Georges Wakhévitch was a Franco-Russian set and costume designer who created several hundred sets for film, theater, opera, and ballet. Marcel Carné observed that "the sets were designed to be covered with staff, usually obtained by pouring plaster over a layer of horsehair" (Carné 1975, 125).
31 Arletty 1971, 148. Alexandre Trauner was the set designer on many of Marcel Carné's films.
32 Ducrocq 1942, quoted in Gasiglia-Laster 1995. On April 12, 1942, the newspaper *Comœdia* published a scale model assembling pieces of the miniatures from the months of March and October.
33 Paris and Montreal 2006–07, 232–36. To celebrate his tenth wedding anniversary, Walt Disney visited several French sites he had seen while on leave as an ambulance driver in 1918, including Chantilly. The filmmaker had a set of documents, including reproductions of the *Très Riches Heures*, which were used by Disney Studios for *Snow White and the Seven Dwarfs* (1937).
34 New York, London, and San Marino 2021–22, 82–91.
35 Cazelles and Rathofer 1988, 7–9.
36 "The Book of Hours: The World's Most Famous Calendar was Painted 500 Years ago for the Duc de Berry. LIFE here Presents its Twelve Great Pages," *Life*, January 5, 1948, 20–41; echoed by Jason Farago, "Searching for Lost Time in the World's Most Beautiful Calendar," *The New York Times, Art, Books, History*, April 17, 2023.
37 Chicago, Paris, and London 2016–17.
38 Fontevraud 2024.
39 Bukowski 2018, 10–71.
40 Quoted in Toulet 2005, 26.

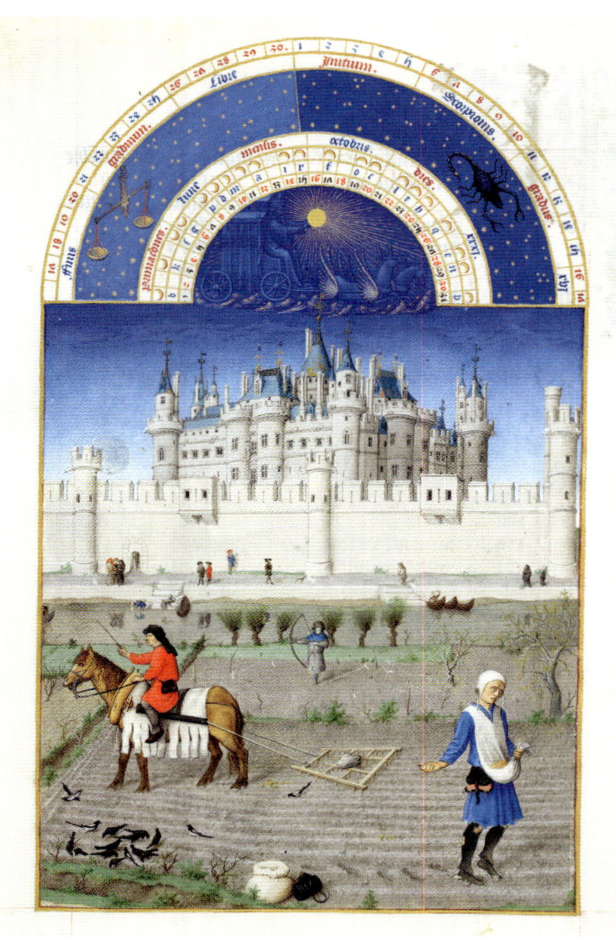

Van Lymborch brothers, *Très Riches Heures*, fol. 10v: October

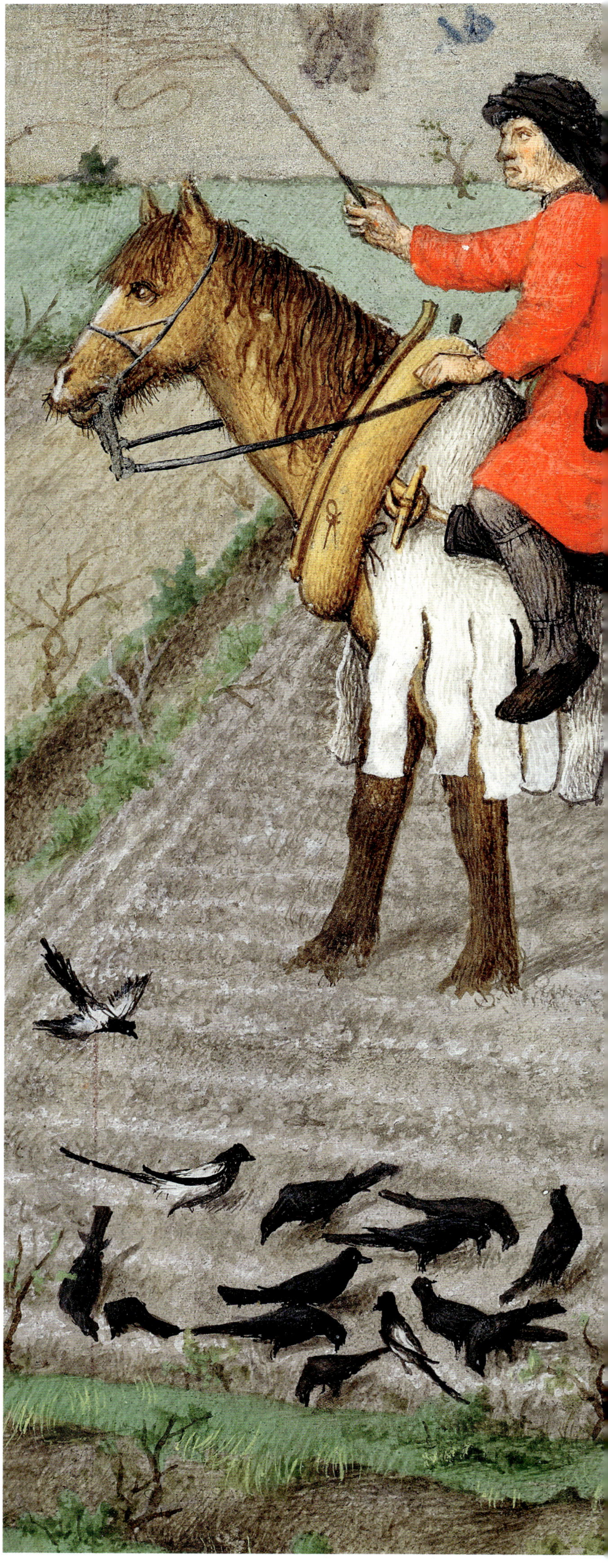

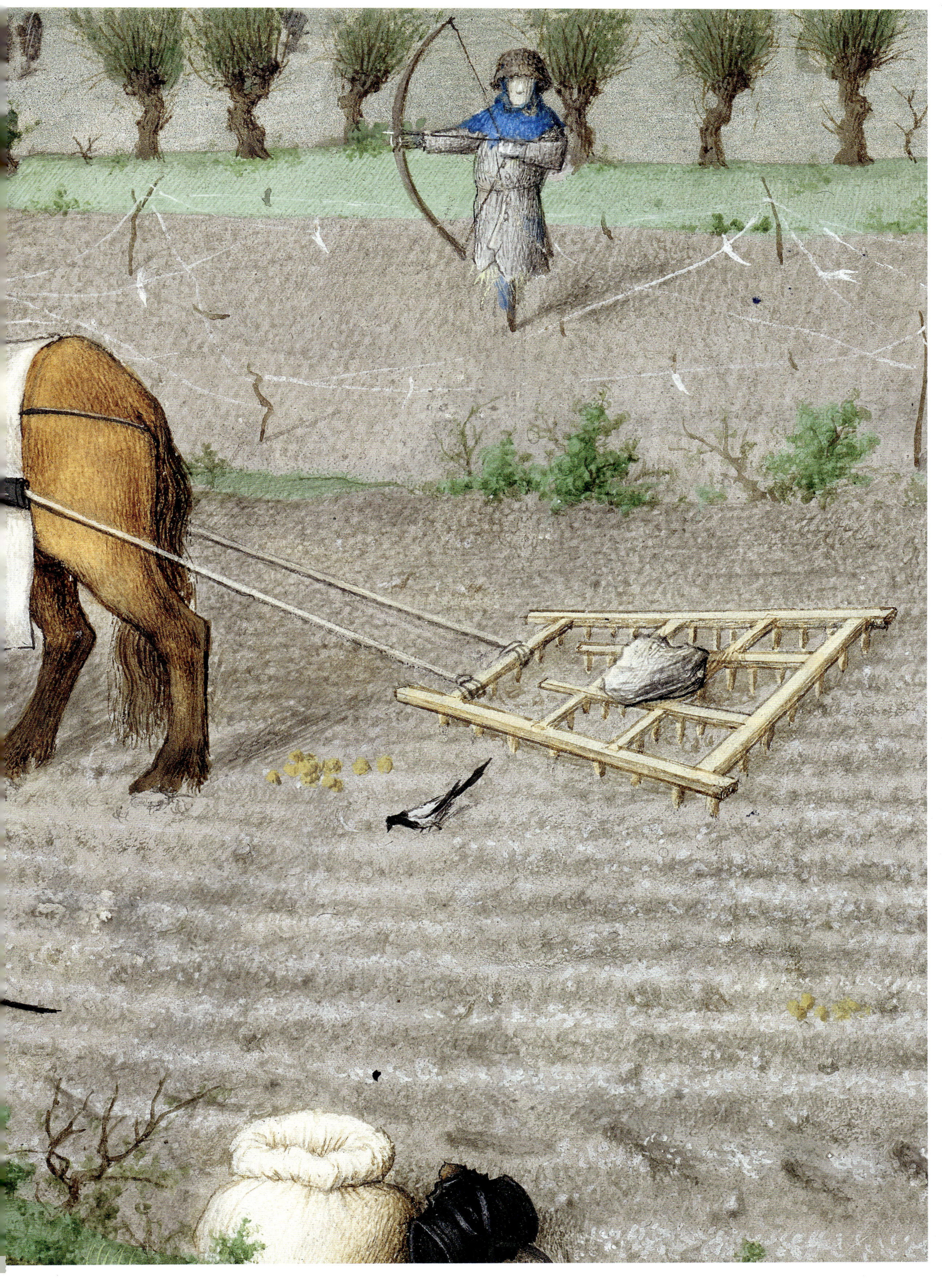

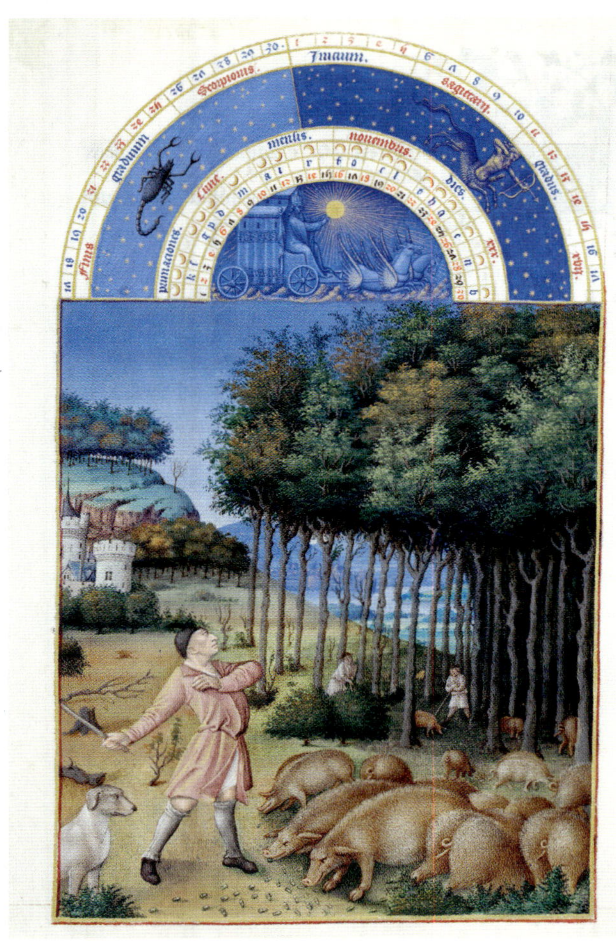

Van Lymborch brothers, *Très Riches Heures*, fol. 11v: November

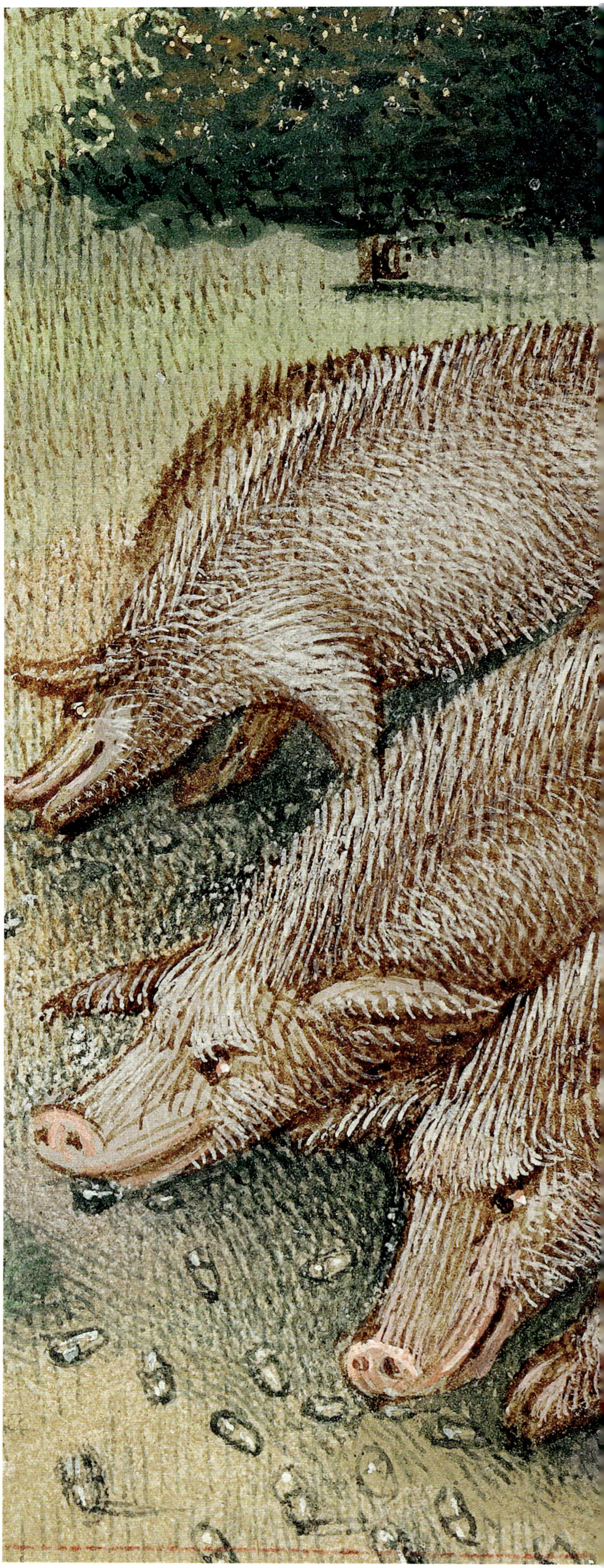

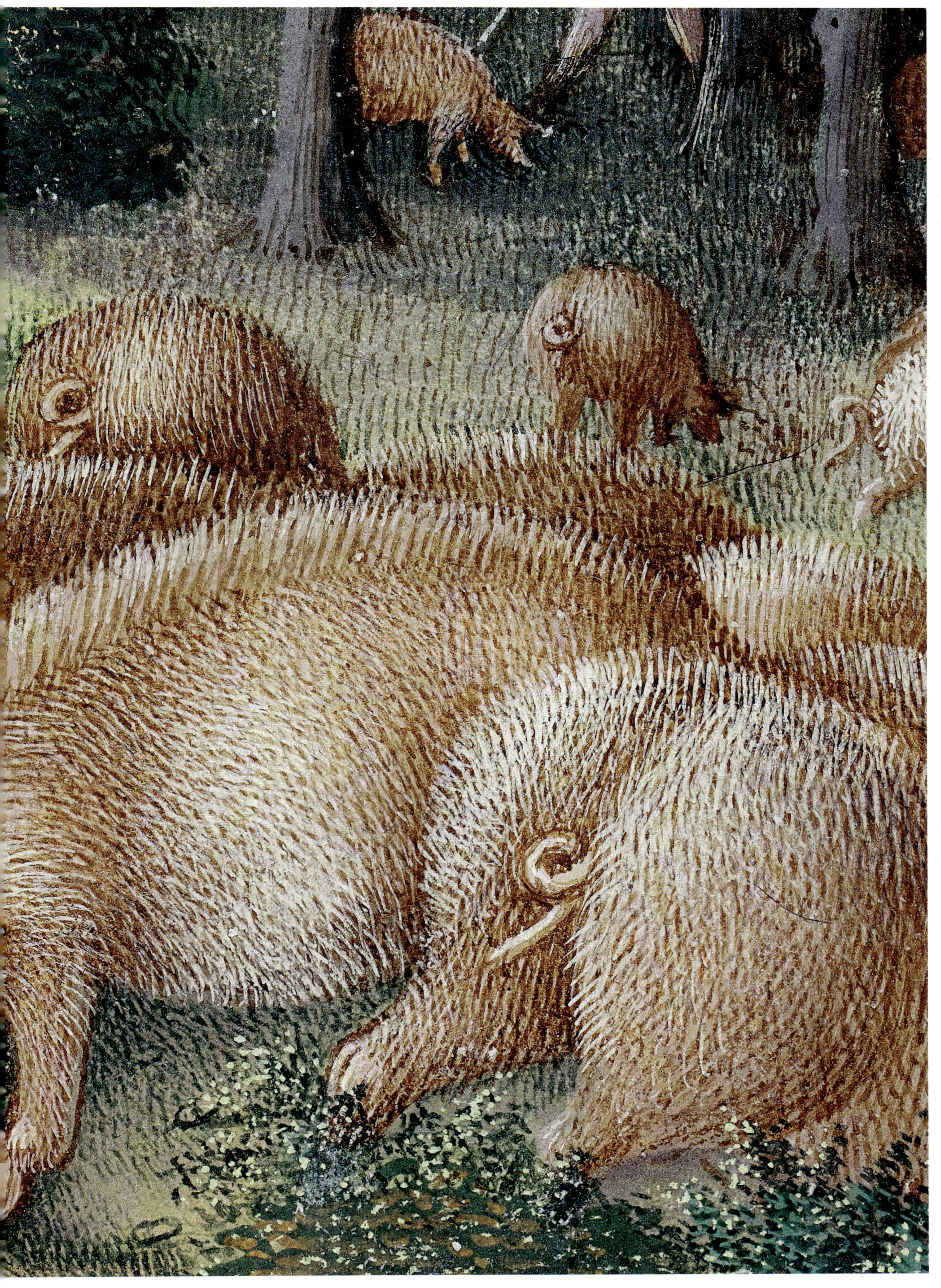

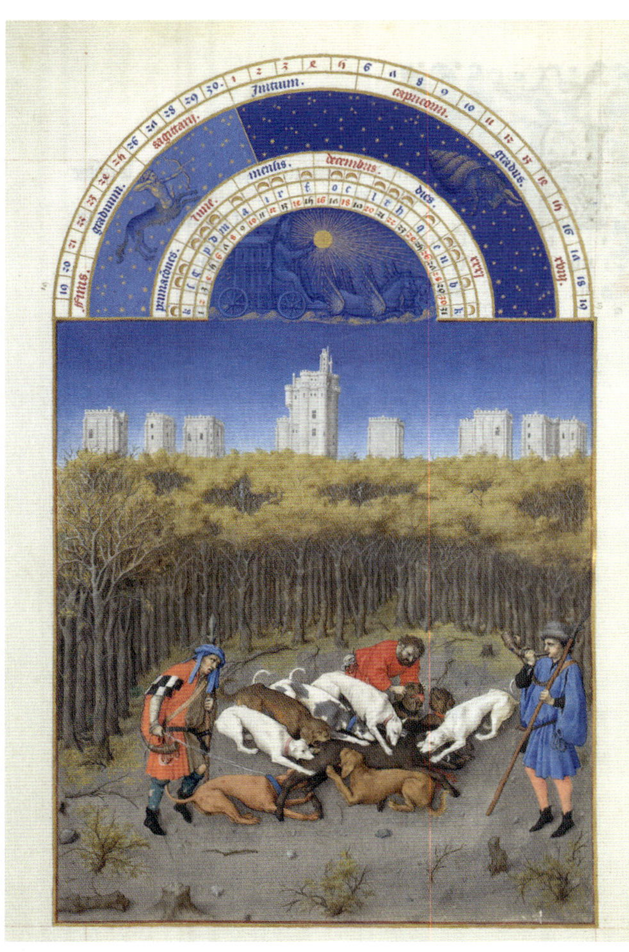

Van Lymborch brothers, *Très Riches Heures*, fol. 12v: December

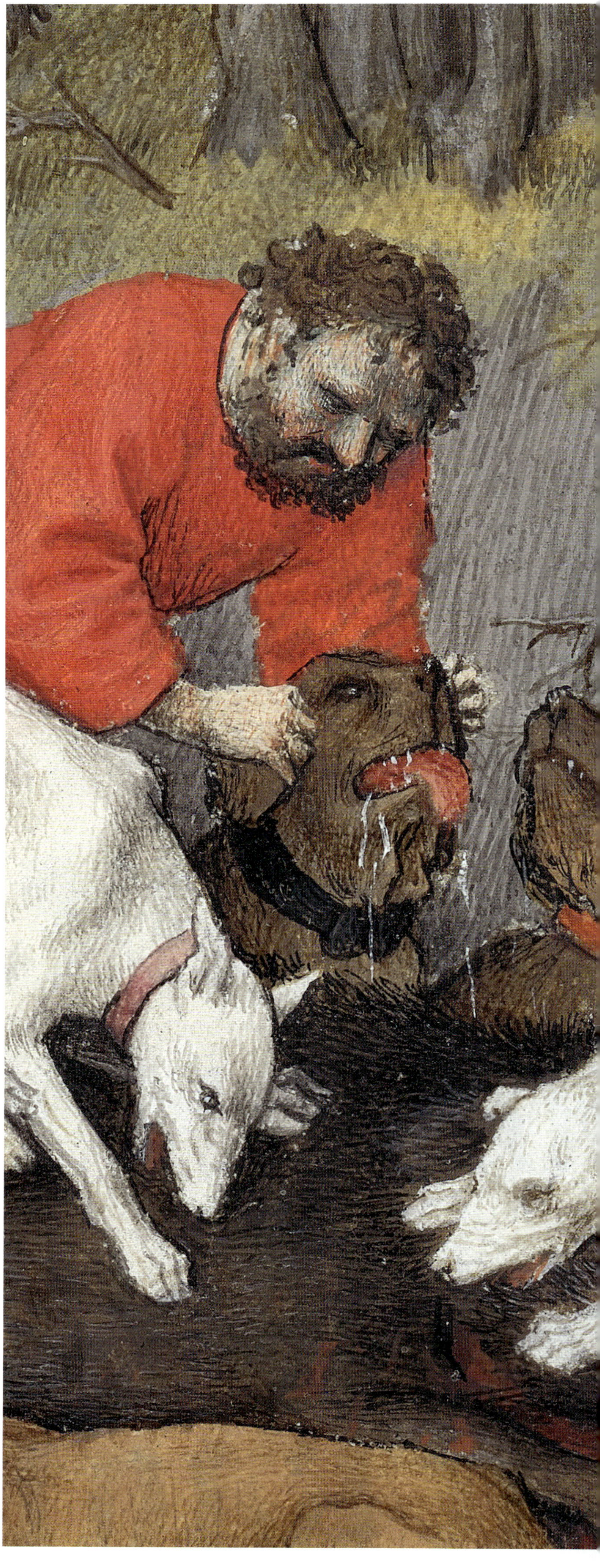

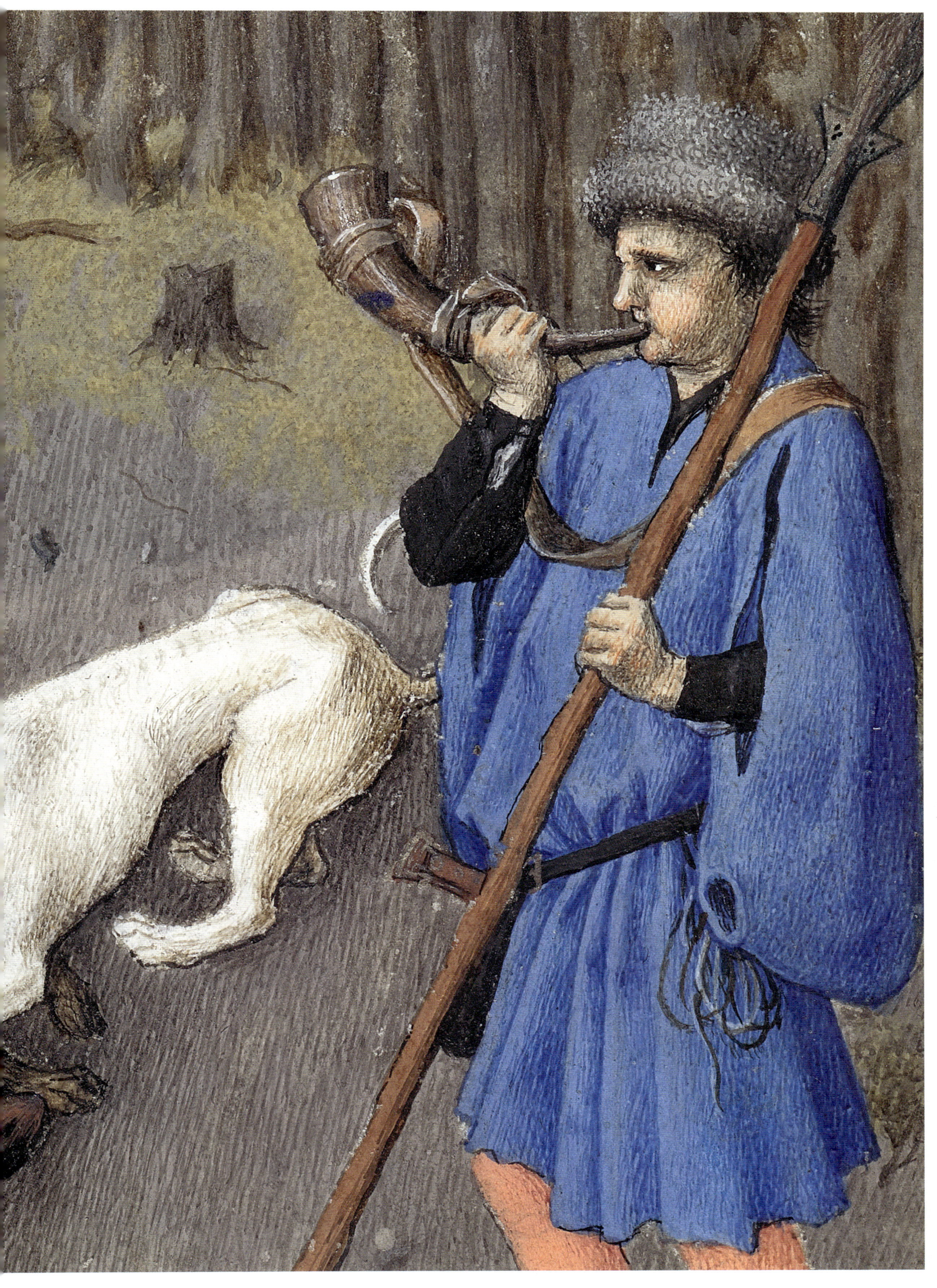

# ANALYSES & RESTORATION

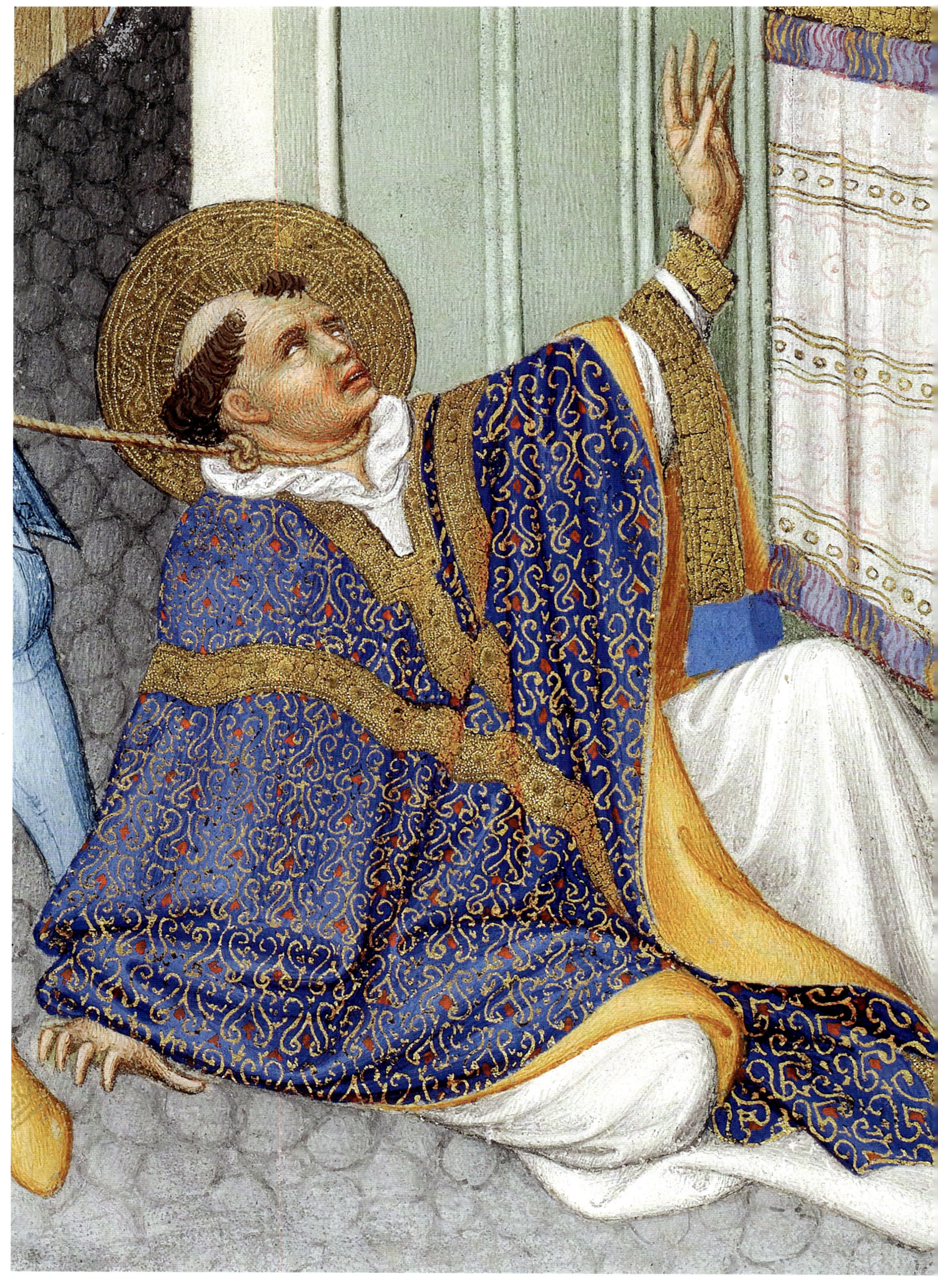

19.

# Materials and Techniques of the *Très Riches Heures du duc de Berry*

Élisabeth Ravaud, Anne Michelin, Kilian Laclavetine, Éric Laval, and Laurence Clivet[1]

The manuscript of the *Très Riches Heures du duc de Berry* contains 206 folios, illustrated with sixty-six large illuminations, sixty-five small ones, and many ornate margins. The production of the book spanned the fifteenth century. Stylistic analysis and a review of the literature reveal four main creative phases. The manuscript was commissioned by the Duke of Berry from the Van Lymborch brothers around 1411. The brothers died prematurely, leaving the manuscript unfinished in the form of unbound quires. The marginal medallions that are present on a number of folios have been attributed to the Bedford Master (Haincelin de Haguenau), whose intervention would dated from 1414–16 and preceded the death of the duke, in June 1416. Drawings by the artist that are similar to some of these illuminations raise the question of a more significant intervention.[2] A third hand, called the Intermediate Master, has been identified on some of the calendar leaves. Experts agree that this campaign was carried out by Barthélemy d'Eyck around 1446. The fourth contributor is easy to recognize on account of his style and the history of the manuscript. He was Jean Colombe, a painter engaged around 1485 to complete the manuscript inherited by Charles, Duke of Savoy.

In what condition was the manuscript left by the Van Lymborch brothers? Did the subsequent artists start from a blank page, or did they follow underlying indications? What characteristics define the production, and what palette was used at each stage of the process? Leaving aside the state of

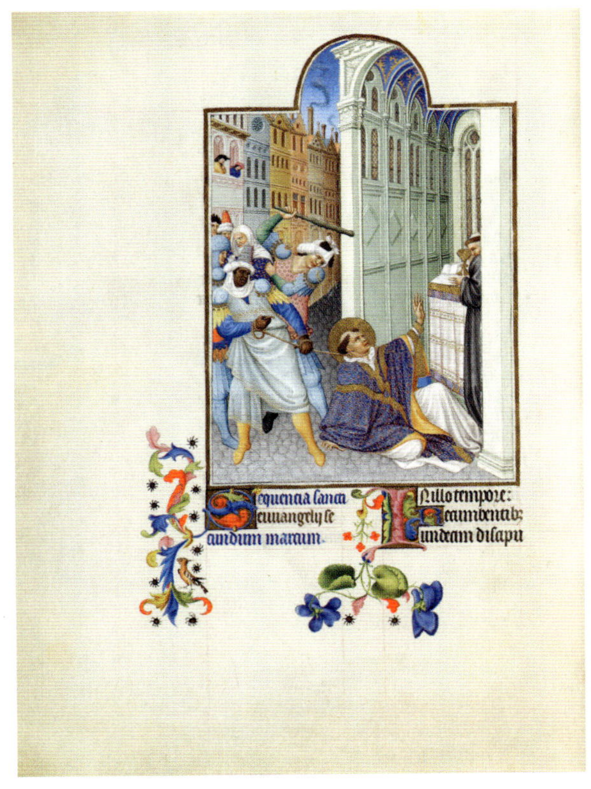

**Fig. 2** Van Lymborch brothers, *Très Riches Heures*, fol. 19v: The Martyrdom of St. Mark

**Fig. 1** Van Lymborch brothers, *Très Riches Heures*, fol. 19v: The Martyrdom of St. Mark, detail

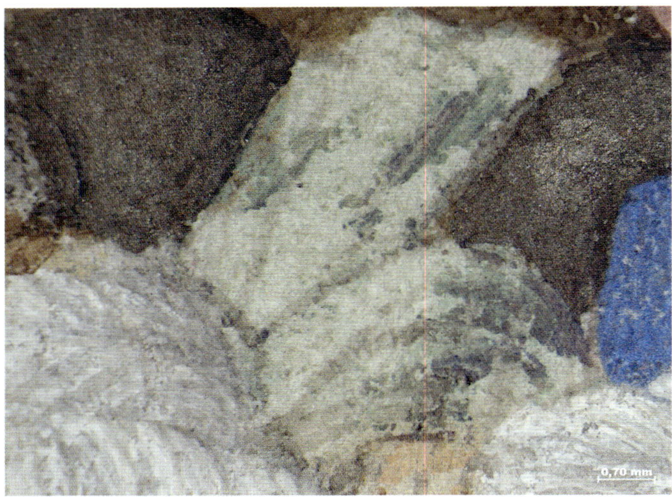

**Fig. 3** Detail under the microscope of an underdrawing in the paint loss of a turban (fol. 52). Photo É. Ravaud – C2RMF

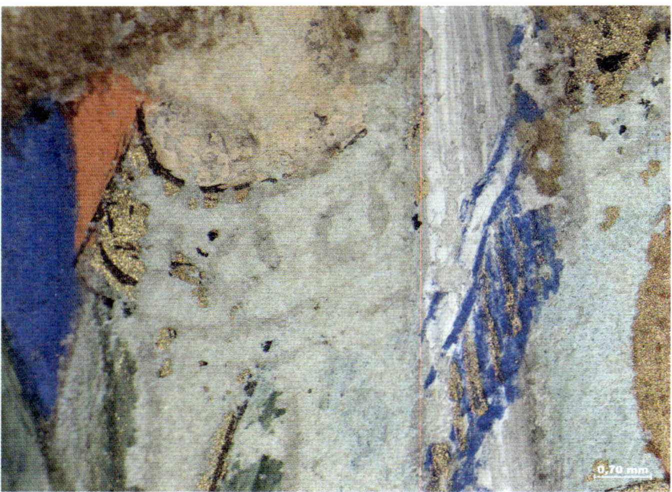

**Fig. 4** Detail under the microscope of the drawn decoration of a neckline in a paint loss in a figure (fol. 52). Photo É. Ravaud – C2RMF

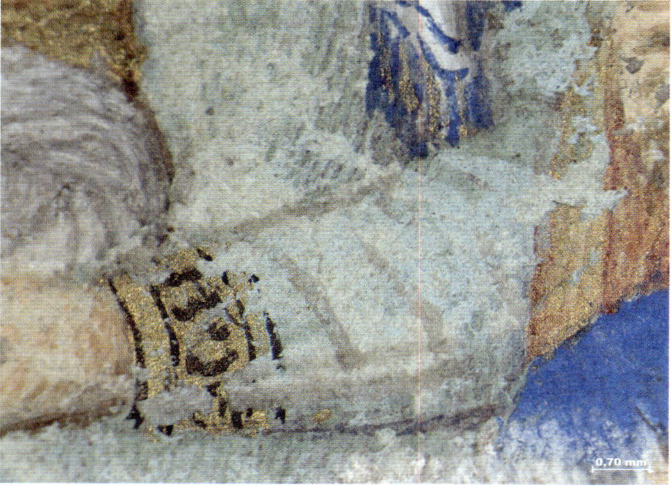

**Fig. 5** Detail under the microscope showing the shading of the arm at the stage of the underdrawing (fol. 52). Photo É. Ravaud – C2RMF

preservation (described by the restorers), these are the main questions that were raised during a major technical study carried out at the Centre de Recherche et de Restauration des Musées de France (C2RMF), in collaboration with the Centre de Recherche sur la Conservation (CRC), in 2023 and 2024.

Thirty-six large illuminations were examined, according to a sampling established with the curators of the Musée Condé. The examinations carried out consisted of an imaging file,[3] the systematic part of which included photographs in direct light, in infrared light,[4] under ultraviolet radiation (fluorescence and reflectance), and the making of false color composites: false color infrared (FCIR) and false color ultraviolet (FCUV). Microscopic examination[5] was carried out on all the selected sheets. Depending on conservation issues, photographs under raking light at different angles completed the documentation. Non-invasive analyses were carried out on a selection of this corpus: hyperspectral imaging[6] in the visible spectrum on sixteen leaves; X-ray fluorescence (XRF) spectrometry[7] on thirteen folios; X-ray diffraction (XRD) on three folios; fiber optic reflectance spectroscopy (FORS) on nine folios; and Fourier transform infrared spectroscopy (FTIR)[8] on five folios.

The support of the manuscript was studied by Coralie Barbe and Florence Malo, the restorers in charge of the manuscript. It consists of vellum skins, used transversely to form bifolia. The restorers counted twenty-eight quires, most often composed of four bifolia, sometimes two (quires 2, 3, 28), once three (quire 20), or with an odd number of folios due to the insertion of a folio (quires 5, 8, 9, 15, 19, 27). The skins were prepared with a calcium-based filler, as indicated by XRF spectrometry, but also a little chlorine, iron, lead, potassium, and silica. Traditionally, this would be lime.[9] Traces of substantial smoothing can be seen in the photograph of folio 51v under raking light.

Vertical lines were used to mark out two columns of text per folio. They were traced with a diluted red lake, from short incised marks at the edge of the folio. This lake strongly absorbs ultraviolet (UV) rays. Hyperspectral analysis helps rule out the use of carmine- or madder-based lakes. The use of brazilwood is possible but not definitive. The ruling is present on all the illuminations inserted in the text, but also in some illuminations without text, such as folios 153 and 156. For the calendar, the frame and the compartments of the lunette were traced with a similar red lake.

The different phases in the application of the paint layer will be described by grouping the folios by artist.

## THE LEAVES ATTRIBUTED TO ONLY THE VAN LYMBORCH BROTHERS

The first phase of execution is the preparatory drawing, essential for planning the work. It should be light and unobtrusive, so as not to be visible in the final phase.

The most abundant and visible drawing is made from a material with a liquid medium. In unpainted areas or when the line can be seen directly in paint losses, it is light gray in color, and suggests a highly diluted ink (figs. 3, 4, and 5). Microscopic examination shows that the ink contains a few scattered dark grains. Micro-paint losses frequently coincide with the path of this drawing, suggesting a lack of adhesion between the layers (fig. 6).

The material of the drawing has the particularity of being clearly visible under UV radiation and less visible under infrared radiation.[10] Under FCIR, it takes on a reddish hue (fig. 7). XRF spectrometry has identified the presence of iron, copper, and minute traces of zinc. These elements attest to the use of a drawing material made of vitriolic ferrogallic ink (also known as iron gall ink).[11] The relative visibility of the drawing under infrared and UV light varies within a single leaf. It depends on the absorption and reflection characteristics of the drawing material, its concentration and those of the surrounding or overlying painted layers, as well as their thickness. Generally speaking, the drawing is rather more visible under UV light, but in the colors that absorb it strongly the line remains relatively legible under infrared light. The somewhat blurred contours and noticeable width of ink lines in UV light reflect a slight diffusion of the ink in the parchment. Finally, the absorption of a few lines here and there by infrared light alone could suggest a drawing stage prior to the ink line.

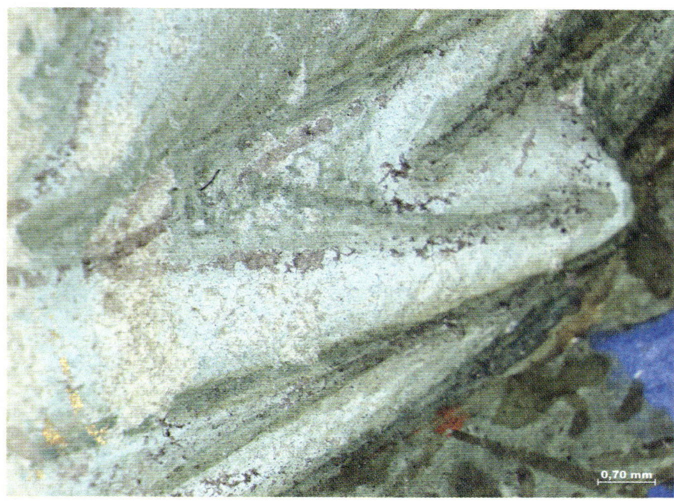


**Fig. 6** Detail under the microscope showing the wear of the painted layer on the line of the drawing (fol. 52). Photo É. Ravaud – C2RMF

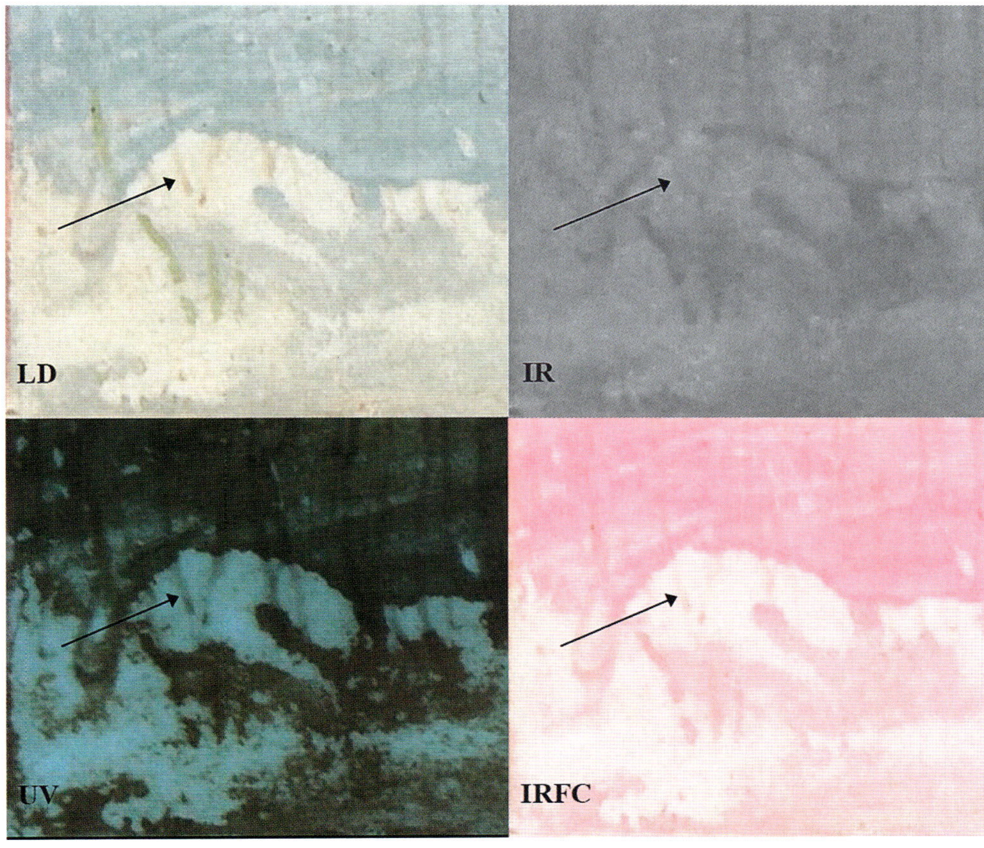


**Fig. 7** Behavior of the drawing by the Van Lymborch brothers in imaging: direct light (LD), infrared light (IR), ultraviolet light (UV), false color infrared composite (IRFC). Photo L. Clivet – C2RMF / Composition É. Ravaud – C2RMF

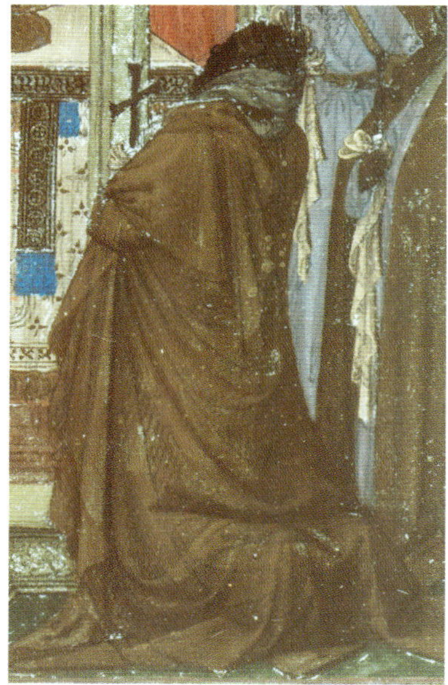

**Fig. 8** UV photograph showing the underdrawing of the drapery (fol. 193v), detail. Photo L. Clivet – C2RMF

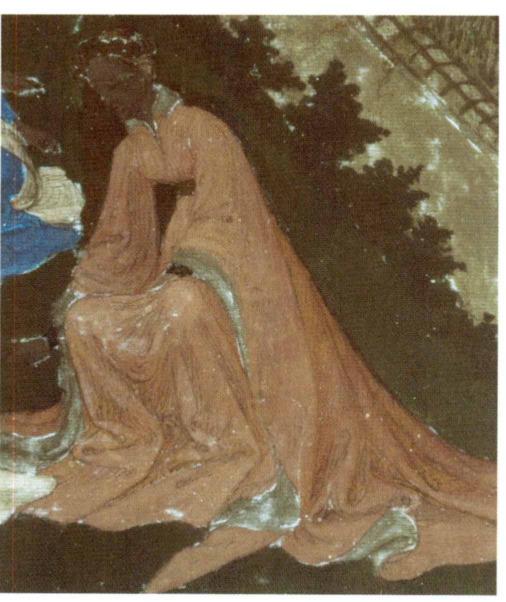

**Fig. 9** UV photograph showing the underdrawing of the drapery (fol. 5v), detail. Photo L. Clivet– C2RMF

XRF spectrometry analysis of the black ink of the text reveals the presence of iron, copper, zinc, and sulfur, indicating the use of a fairly concentrated vitriolic ferrogallic ink.

Ferrogallic ink has been known since antiquity. Many treatises give recipes for it, and its use is commonplace in many texts from this period and in later Renaissance drawings. The binding medium is made of fruit gum or gum arabic. The book *De Coloribus faciendis* recommends a binding medium of plum or apple gum to prevent the ink from running.[12] This type of ink tends to crack, and in paintings where it is used for the underdrawing, the micro-cracks impact on the overlying painted layer, leading to loss of material.[13]

In the *Belles Heures* manuscript of 1406, the drawing, traced in diluted black or brown ink,[14] was mainly studied by infrared light: The drawn and unpainted motifs are clearly visible in UV light, which suggests the use of a ferrogallic ink-based material.

Drawings are relatively abundant in illuminations in general. They mark the contours, folds, and areas of some important shadows by parallel hatching, either straight or, often in the folds, curved and short (figs. 8 and 9), or by wash-drawn areas (fig. 5).

Clothing ornaments are indicated in a rather extensive but synthetic way. Lines are supple and flexuous. In the drapery, hooks can be seen at the end of fold lines. The ink is probably more diluted for the drawing of flesh tones (faces, bodies, fingers) so that it is not visible after painting. Indeed, it is often difficult to detect by means of imaging, whereas it can be seen under the microscope. In the drapery, the concentration is probably higher, and the drawing can be seen under certain colors (fig. 10).

The preparatory drawings of the Van Lymborch brothers can be seen on all the leaves attributed to them. To the extent that scientific imaging allows us to read the underlying drawings beneath the paint layer, there seems to be no significant difference between the three types of illumination (those inserted in the text, those outside the text, and the calendar), though perhaps there is a greater flexibility of the drawing in the calendar.

Micro-paint losses are frequently observed along the line of the drawing, often at the limit of the form (fig. 6), suggesting interaction between the drawing material and the painted layer. The micro-cracking that develops in ferrogallic inks (fig. 11) is probably the source of fragmentation of the overlying paint layer and loss of adhesion. A paint's ability to resist ink shrinkage depends on the nature of the pigment, and it appears that lead white is one of the most sensitive due to its rigid, brittle character, linked to a very low binding content.

The painted layer was studied by specifying the palette before considering the painting technique. The palette was studied through interpretation of the scientific imaging file, XRF spectrometry, FORS, hyperspectral imaging, and observation under a microscope. The main pigments identified are presented below.

#### Blues

The abundance of lapis lazuli is certainly one of the particularities of the *Très Riches Heures*, and perhaps one of the origins of its name since this pigment was far more expensive than any other. The Duke of Burgundy's accounts reveal the exorbitant cost of this precious blue, brought back from Afghanistan in the form of a stone by merchants who were often Italian.[15] It was sold on in several qualities, depending on the complex and time-consuming refining processes that were essential to transform the ore into pigment. The quality of this blue is therefore a good indicator of the Duke of Berry's considerable means. Lapis is identified in false color composites, hyperspectral imaging, and under the microscope with its bright blue and luminous grains. X-ray diffraction shows the presence of lazurite. XRF spectra are remarkable for the intensity of aluminum and silicon, elements that are generally difficult to detect unless present in large quantities, and the low iron content, testifying to the quality of the pigment. The rather high potassium content reflects the refining process. This lapis is used alone or simply lightened with lead white. A lighter underlayer of lead white was often used to reflect light. It is sometimes mixed with red lake to obtain deep purple-blue shades (fig. 12). It is also used as a mixture for green colors.

Indigo is the second most common blue used in the illuminations. Under the microscope, its dull blue grains can be seen in clear matrices. It is identified by cross-referencing data from false color composites and hyperspectral imaging. It is used on its own or mixed with other colors.

Azurite does not appear to have been used in the folios studied and analyzed.

#### Reds

Vermilion is frequently found in illuminations and is easily characterized by XRF spectrometry due to the presence of mercury. It is often associated with minium or red lake.

Red lake is quite abundant in the leaves illuminated by the Van Lymborch brothers. Fragments of red thread are visible under the microscope in these leaves, indicating that the lake originated from the re-processing of garments dyed in red, a common procedure at the time.[16] Generally speaking, it exhibits a salmon fluorescence, distinct from the absorption of UV observed for the red lake used for ruling. These characteristics would suggest a madder and/or kermes lake.[17]

Minium was observed in several illuminations, generally in association with vermilion. The absence of elements other than lead in the XRF spectrometry confirms the diagnosis. FCUV and FCIR composites are also discriminative. In the hyperspectral imaging, minium is identified alone or mixed with vermilion.

#### Yellows

Yellow ochre is omnipresent, identified in hair, buildings, and landscapes. There is reason to believe that this is the beautiful ochre of Berry, from the deposit at Saint-Georges-de-la-Prée, not far from Tours,[18] in the duke's appanage. The fourteenth-century *Liber coloribus illuminatorum*[19] no doubt references it when it mentions that the "most desirable" ochre is taken from a deposit "near Tours," as later reiterated in the Montpellier manuscript.[20] Its very fine granulometry allows for extremely thin layers.

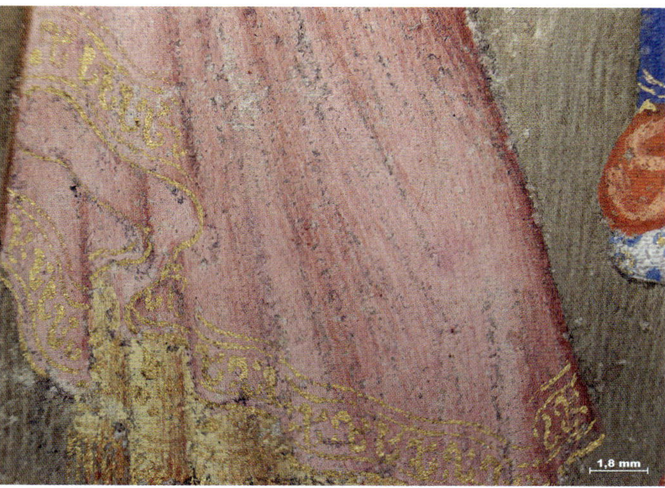


**Fig. 10** Detail under the microscope showing the underdrawing appearing beneath the painted layer (fol. 156v). Photo É. Ravaud– C2RMF

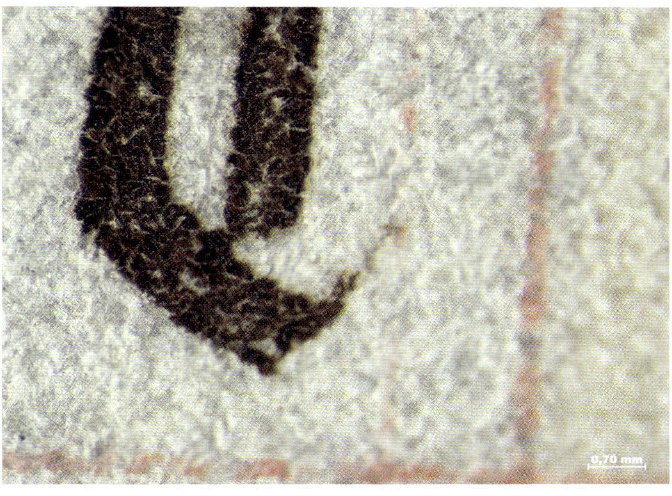


**Fig. 11** Detail under the microscope highlighting the fragmentation of the ink layer (fol. 2). Photo É. Ravaud – C2RMF

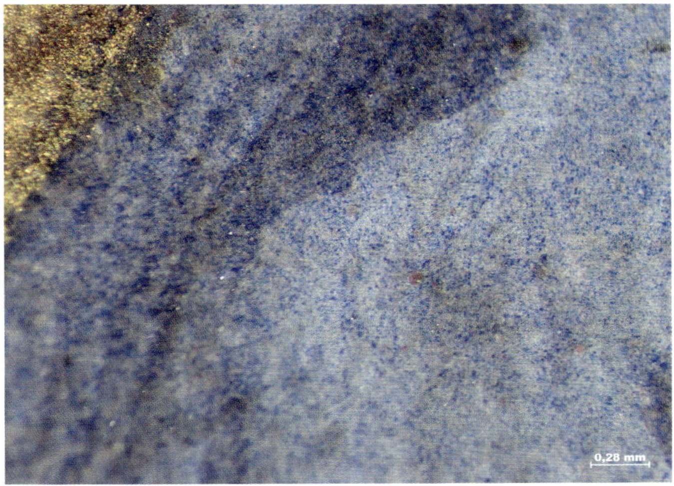


**Fig. 12** Detail under the microscope showing a grain of red lake in a layer of lapis (fol. 1v). Photo É. Ravaud – C2RMF

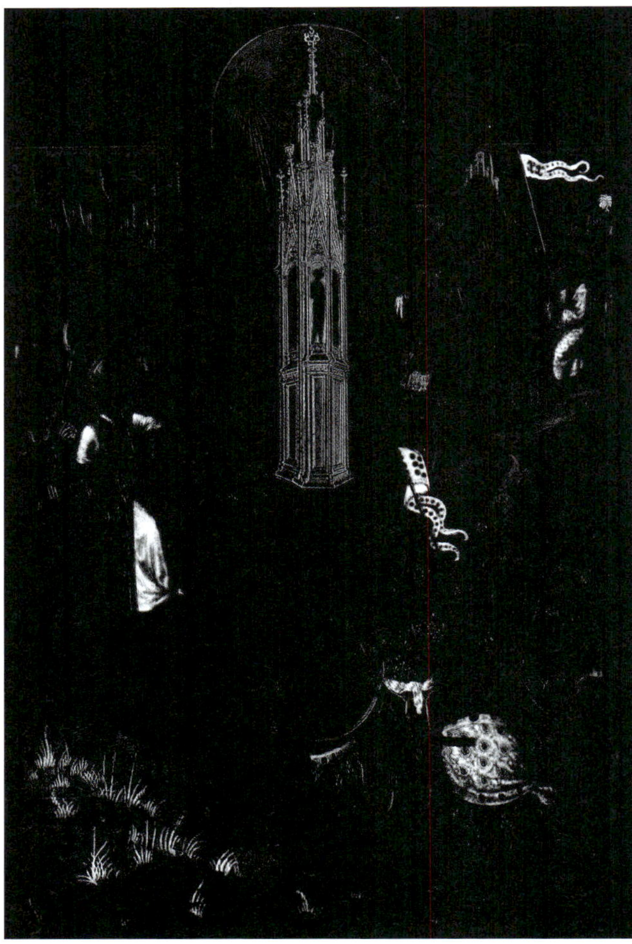

**Fig. 13** Mapping of lead-tin yellow using hyperspectral imaging (fol. 52). Photo A. Michelin – MNHM

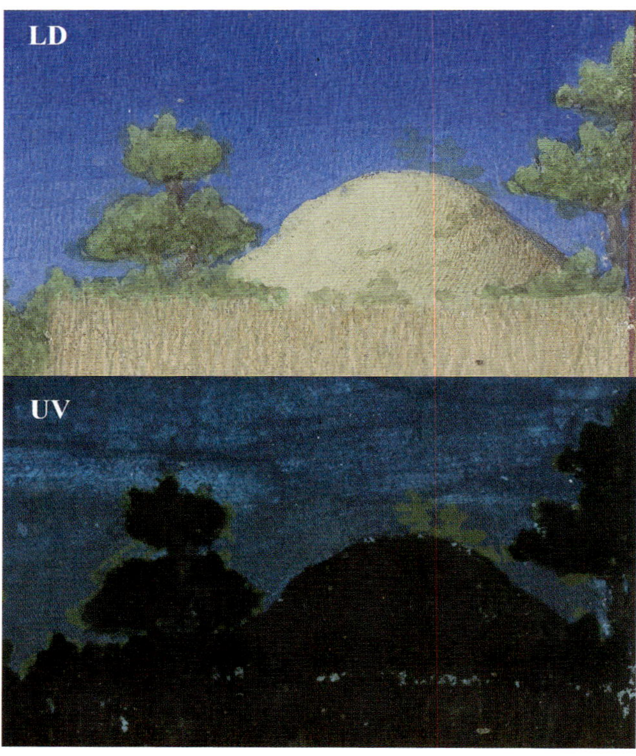


**Fig. 14** Direct light (LD) and ultraviolet (UV) photographs (fol. 8v), detail. Photo L. Clivet – C2RMF

A yellow has been identified on the basis of its lemon-yellow hue and the presence of lead and tin elements in XRF spectrometry. Its behavior on the false color UV composite points to lead-tin yellow (type I).[21] Lead-tin yellow is used relatively seldom for its own color (some tunics, belts, turbans), but it is used frequently mixed with lead white and especially in mixtures to create greens. The exceptions are two illuminations (fols. 51v and 52), where yellow is more abundant (fig. 13). It also appears there as an underlayer to a vermilion red in a tunic (fig. 24).

Lead-tin yellow (type I) is the variety identified in the *Belles Heures*, as in most of the paintings executed for the Chartreuse de Champmol.

Orpiment does not seem to have been used for colored areas as such. It has, however, been suspected in several of the gilded areas described below.

**Browns**

These consist of earthen tones or mixtures. XRF spectrometry suggests the presence of vermilion alongside earthen tones in several brown colors. Hyperspectral analysis occasionally identifies hematite, carbon black or a little vermilion in the mixture.

**Greens**

Greens are obtained in different ways, usually by mixing. Often, this is by mixing blue and yellow; indigo and lead-tin yellow, also known as "vergaut," is frequently identified. The use of copper green is attested by hyperspectral imaging, probably verdigris with XRF identification of the copper. It is frequently used in mixtures, most often with indigo. Two other transparent greens are seen in the illuminations, mainly in foliage and shrubs. One produces a yellow-green fluorescence under UV radiation (fig. 14). The other, a darker shade of olive, absorbs UVs. They are reminiscent of the many organic greens used at the time, notably bladder green obtained from buckthorn.[22]

**Blacks**

They are *a priori* carbon blacks.

**Whites**

These are essentially made of lead white, which is also present in all other colors. XRD analysis reveals a clear predominance of hydrocerussite (around 90%), with cerussite being absent or only present in tiny quantities. In FORS, the hydrocerussite signal is particularly strong in gray and pink hues. This composition differs from the lead whites most often encountered, obtained in acid pH,[23] and would be favored by a basic environment. This could be "blancum Apulicum," the synthesis of which in basic pH is described in the fourteenth-century *De Coloribus, Naturalia exscripta et collecta*.[24] An "Album de Apuleya" is quoted several times in the *Liber coloribus illuminatorum*.[25] In the *Third Book of Eraclius*,[26] a "blancum de pullia" appears. A similar name, "blanc de Puille," appears among the supplies of pigments delivered to the Duke of Burgundy's painters.[27] The use of another white, calcite-based, is identified by infrared spectrometry, in clear areas containing no lead-based material.

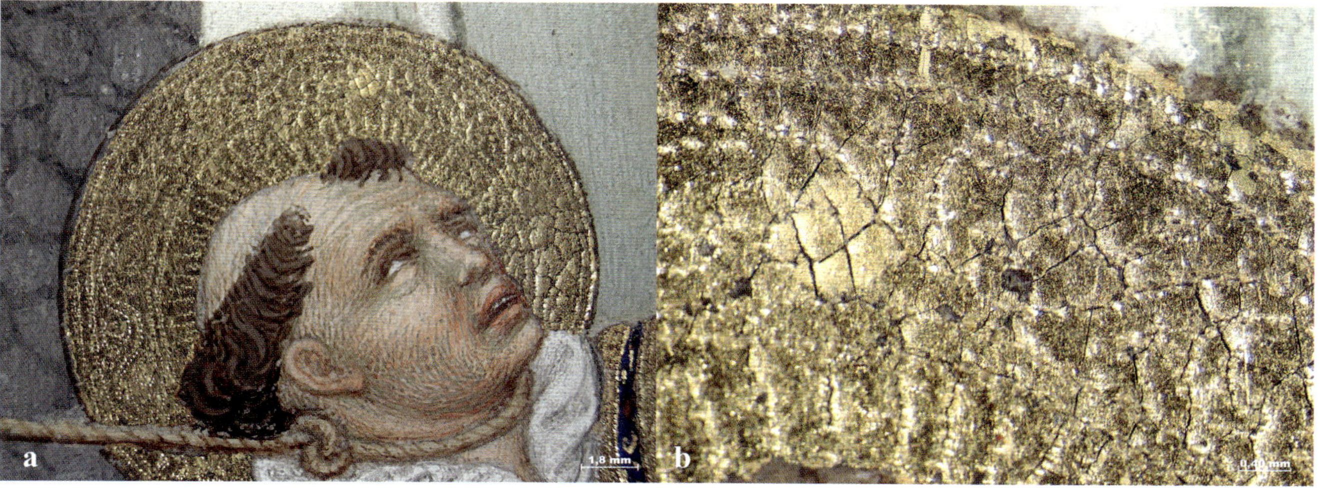


**Fig. 15** a) Detail under the microscope of St. Mark's burnished gilded halo (fol. 19v), b) at higher magnification on a paint loss showing a gray bole. Photo É. Ravaud – C2RMF

**Metallic Decors**

Gold and silver are used abundantly in the manuscript folios attributed to the Van Lymborch brothers.

The Van Lymborch brothers used gold in a wide variety of forms—sometimes difficult to distinguish from each other, to achieve multiple color and optical effects. Burnished gold leaf is used quite sparingly,[28] particularly on the representation of St. Mark's halo (fol. 19). The bole appears dark gray in a small loss in the halo, which also features delicate fine punching (fig. 15). The same color can be seen in the burnished gilding of the initials and the burnished gold dots in the margin.

Unburnished gold leaf is more frequently observed (fig. 16). It appears to be a specific feature of French illumination at the time.[29] Used for fairly simple geometric shapes, such as halos, tableware and architectural elements, its irregular surface gives it a matt appearance and a lighter tone in contrast with the burnished gold. The gilding is mostly applied directly over the parchment, sometimes on top of the paint layer.

The suns on the astrological lunettes[30] show two tones and two levels of roughness,[31] allowing a second star motif to be identified (fig. 17). It is possible that this difference is due in part to the color of the central motif's underlayer applied beneath the gold leaf. In folio 156v, Christ's halo, similar to the dark part of the suns, reveals a gray or pinkish-gray underlayer, which would explain the darker tone of the gold and the increased absorption of infrared radiation observed. Moreover, a higher degree of polishing of this underlayer may have favored a more even application and better reflection of the gold leaf. In several darker, unburnished gold areas, arsenic was detected by XRF. This could indicate the presence of orpiment in the underlayer. This pigment has already been identified in gilding mordants on fourteenth-century paintings.[32] Elsewhere, the color of the underlayer is difficult to distinguish, probably barely pigmented or not at all.

The gold leaf is quite pure, with minor copper impurities in XRF spectrometry.[33]

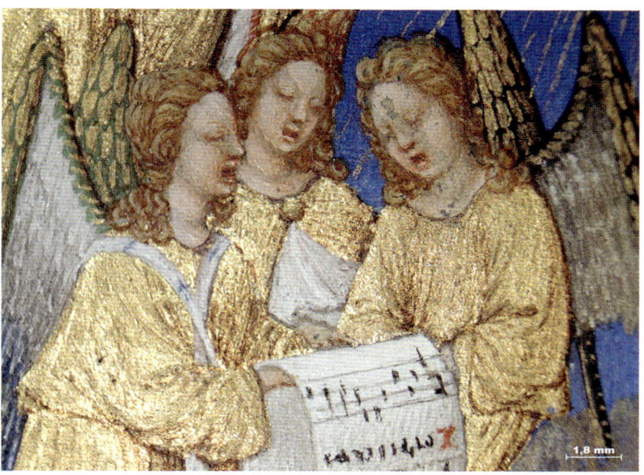


**Fig. 16** Detail under the microscope of the angels' albs gilded with unburnished gold leaf (fol. 52). Photo É. Ravaud – C2RMF

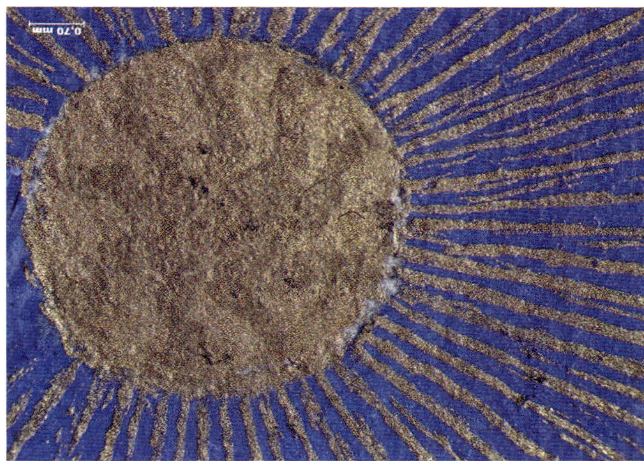


**Fig. 17** Detail under the microscope of a sun in two tonalities of gold (fol. 9v). Photo É. Ravaud – C2RMF

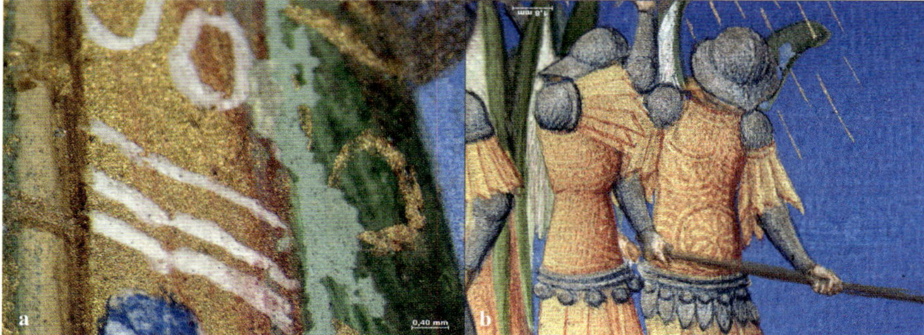

**Fig. 18** Detail under the microscope of red glazes on gilding: a) modeling the shadow (fol. 52), b) defining the motifs of a suit of armor (fol. 64v). Photo É. Ravaud – C2RMF

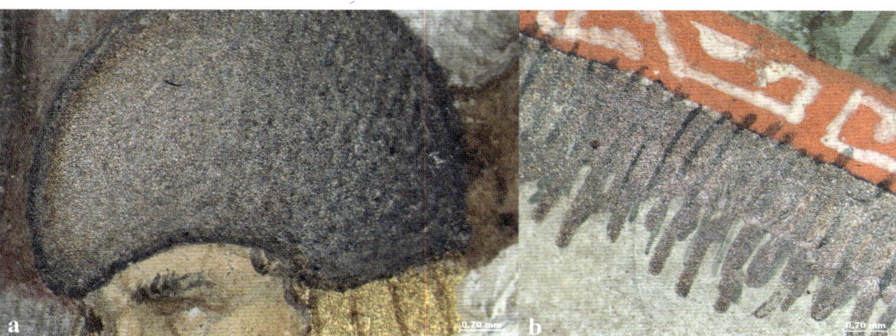

**Fig. 19** Detail under the microscope of silver decorations: a) with a non-burnished sheet modeled on the surface by colored glazes, b) with shell silver forming a thickened drop at the end of the stroke (folio 52r). Photo É. Ravaud – C2RMF

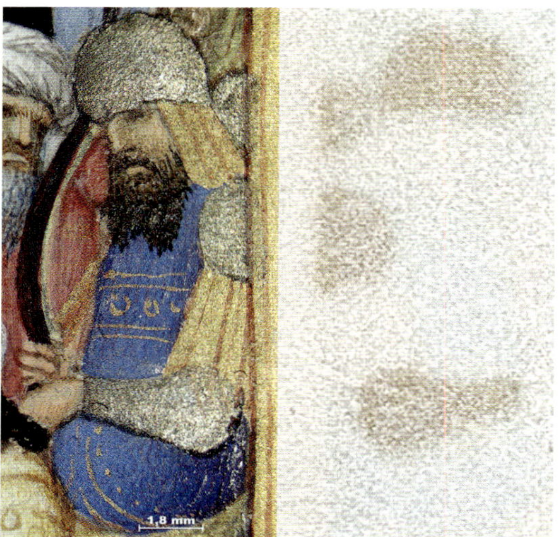

**Fig. 20** Details showing the browning of the parchment on the reverse of the silver leaf: on the left fol. 51v, on the right fol. 51. Photos É. Ravaud – C2RMF (left), Musée Condé, Chantilly (right)

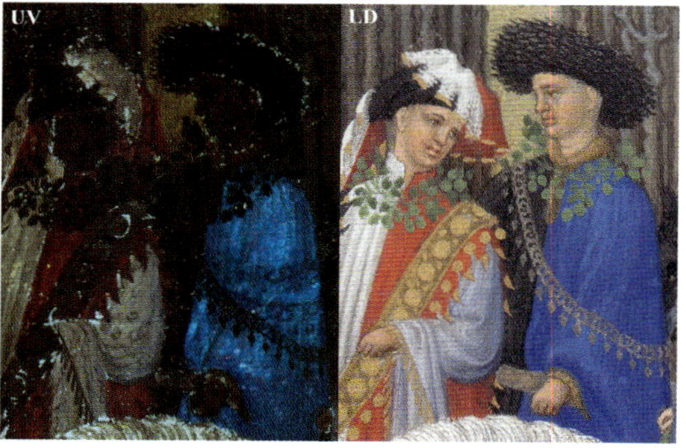


**Fig. 21** Detail of two figures in ultraviolet (UV) and direct light (LD). The blue clothing ornaments planned at the drawing stage (UV) were abandoned or shifted at the painting stage (LD). Photo L. Clivet – C2RMF

Shell gold is also used for gilded decorations. It allows for light, vaporous brushstrokes and complex shapes in illuminations. Microscopic observation under raking light reveals brushstrokes and variations in the thickness of the gilded paint. Different techniques are combined in the illuminations.

Colored glazes applied to the gilded decorations make it possible to modulate them, producing a *cangianti* effect or to clarify details (fig. 27).

Silver decorations are also frequent, mainly in the form of unburnished silver leaf and shell silver (fig. 19). Microscopic observation did not reveal a clear-cut layer of color under the silver leaf, which leads us to consider the hypothesis of a colorless or lightly pigmented organic fixative. The reverse side of the silver areas systematically showed browning, indicating interaction between the unstable and reactive underside of the silver leaf and the adhesive (fig. 20).

The changes made between the drawing phase and the painting phase are sometimes directly visible to the eye, while others are revealed through scientific imaging (fig. 21). The elaboration of decorative motifs on fabrics, for example, is regularly abandoned at the painted phase, testifying to a simplification of the garments in the course of the creative process. An important modification is the left foreground of folio 51v, initially dotted with many short shrubs that were drawn but never painted. The Van Lymborch brothers sometimes altered the size or build of certain figures at the painting stage, such as the sheep shearer in the month of July.

### Painting Technique

The chosen binding medium and its concentration (or dilution) influence the painting technique and the effects obtained. A high amount of binding medium is used for precise, fine brushstrokes with a viscosity that can even impart a certain relief and gloss (fig. 22). One diluted with water is used for very fluid washes covering large areas, such as skies or foregrounds, or to obtain a fusion of color while still wet, as can be seen in the foliage (fol. 25v). Microscopic examinations and photographs taken in raking light clearly highlight these variations in terms of texture, which are particularly visible in the flesh tones, where the highlights are much thicker than the thinner shadows.

Treatises on illumination prior to the production of the *Très Riches Heures* often recommended tempering colors with egg white, sometimes beaten and thinned with water and, in the case of greens, with wine. Other recipes recommend the use of vegetable gum, often from the plum tree or acacia (gum arabic).[34] These treatises explain the possible use of several binding media, depending on the pigments used. The non-destructive analyses carried out during this study did not enable us to identify with certainty the binding medium or binding media used, due to the weakness of the signals collected.

Depending on the size of the motif and the precision of the modeling, the artists used different brushes to produce strokes of varying width. In finely modeled areas, the brushstroke is one-fifth to one-quarter of a millimeter (190–230 microns). In large surfaces, such as the sky, the brushstrokes are wider (around 400 microns) in the underlayer, visible in UV light, with a second layer of fine strokes on the surface. Fragments of paintbrush hairs, in a variety of colors, were observed on numerous occasions, embedded in the painted material.

Several layers are usually applied one on top of the other.[35] When they involve a single pigment mixed with lead white, the lower layers are the lightest, with the most white (fig. 18a in the green area).

The colors may be similar in tone, such as a minium underlayer and a vermilion surface layer enhanced with red lake (fig. 23). Sometimes, however, the colors are completely different, raising the question of a pentimento, as in the sheet laid over one of the horses, where a red color can be seen overlaid with lead-tin yellow (fig. 24).

Gradations are obtained by working on the thickness of the color, as with the lapis lazuli blue cap (fig. 25). The layer is very thin on the side that is lit, revealing the support, and increases in thickness toward the shade. The highlights can be accentuated with fine, semi-transparent brushstrokes of lead white (fig. 26). For the light colors, pure lead white completes the highlights. Sometimes the shadows are of a different pigment, in monochrome (fig. 27a) or with *cangianti* effects, as in the woodcutter's blue garment with red lake shadows (fig. 27b).

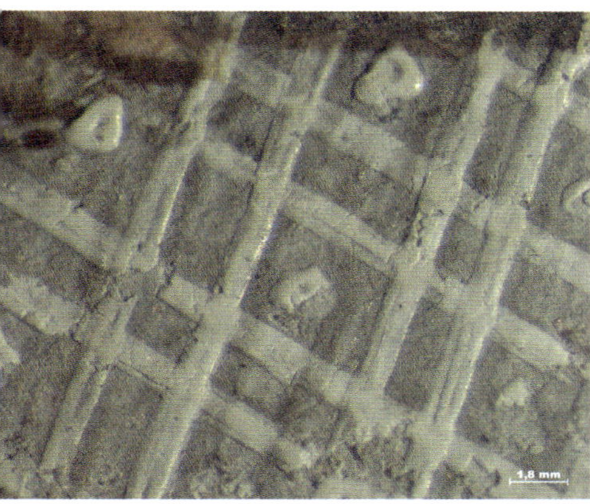


Detail under the microscope of the tablecloth showing the relief and gloss of the motifs (fol. 1v). Photo É. Ravaud – C2RMF

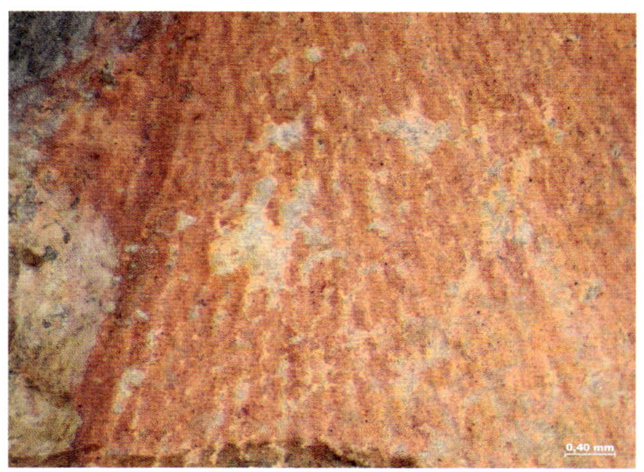


**Fig. 23** Detail under the microscope of worn drapery showing the two superimposed layers, orange then red (fol. 52). Photo É. Ravaud – C2RMF

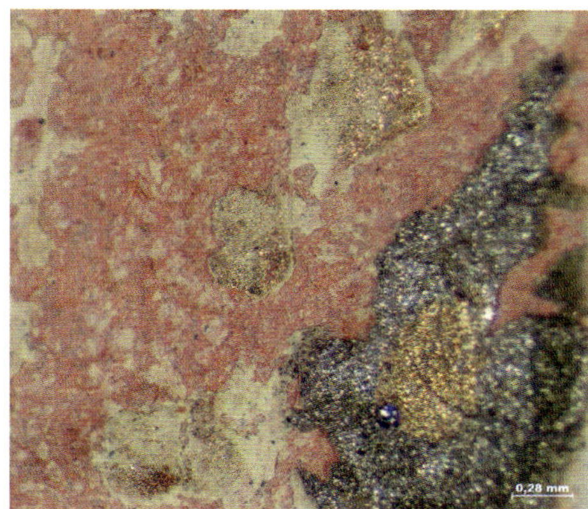


**Fig. 24** Detail under the microscope of worn drapery showing a yellow layer with gold and silver motifs covering a red layer (fol. 52). Photo É. Ravaud – C2RMF

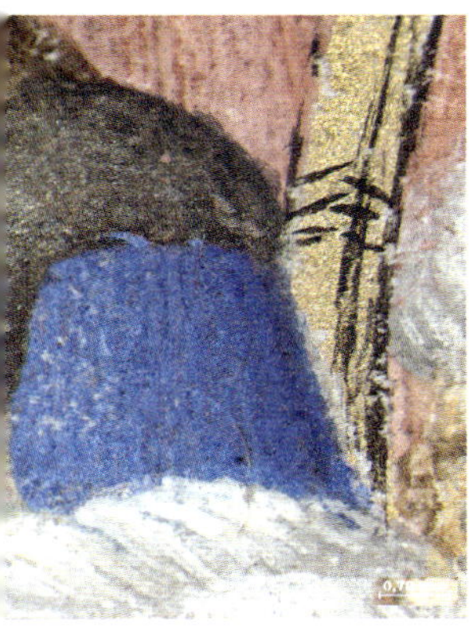

Detail under the microscope of a hat painted in shades of lapis lazuli (fol. 51v). Photo É. Ravaud – C2RMF

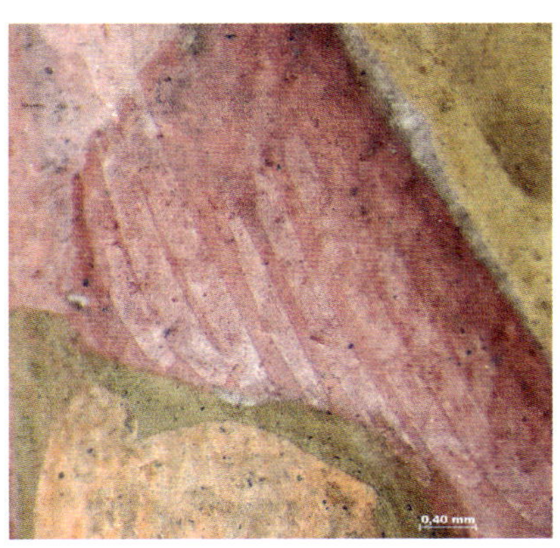


**Fig. 26** Detail under the microscope of a red lake gradation where the light is enhanced by white hatching (fol. 51v). Photo É. Ravaud – C2RMF

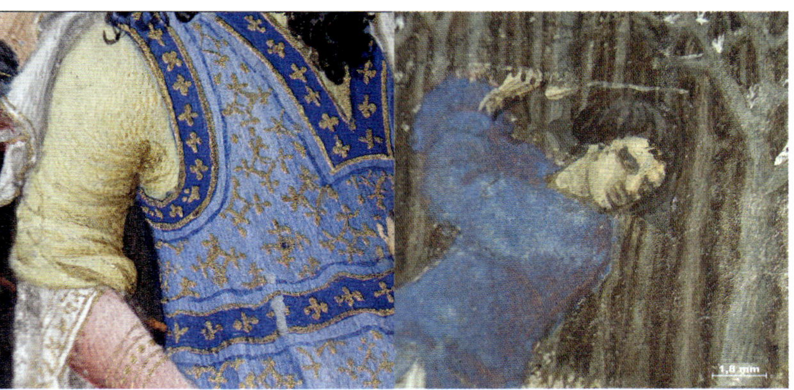


**Fig. 27** Detail under the microscope of examples of shading: a) by a brown color on the yellow arm of a Magus (fol. 51v), b) by a sharp *cangianti* of red lake shadows on the woodcutter's blue garment (fol. 2v). Photo É. Ravaud – C2RMF

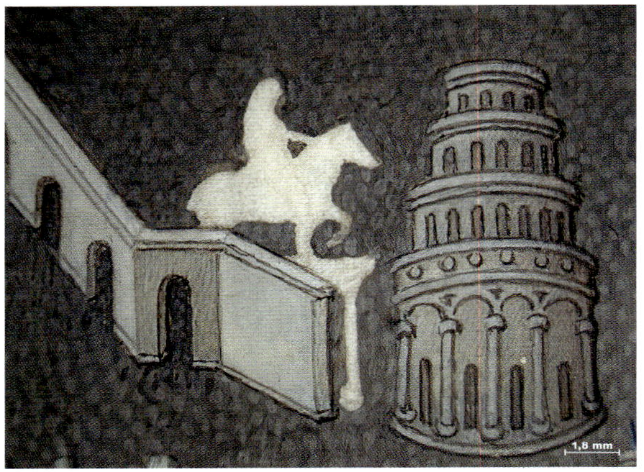


**Fig. 28** Detail under the microscope of the reserve of a motif on the painted background (fol. 141v). Photo É. Ravaud – C2RMF

Characters or motifs in the foreground are left in reserve and painted on the background last, as is clearly visible on folio 141v, where some small motifs were not painted (fig. 28), or in folio 25v, where the moving of the figures made it necessary to complete the background accordingly.

Light flesh tones are shaped by two main hues. The finer shadows are gray-brown in color, richer in earthen tones depending on the analysis, sometimes taking on a greenish hue. The highlights, standing out in relief under raking light, are made up of pink touches, richer in lead white and vermilion applied a second time, sometimes complemented by semi-transparent reddish transition hatches. The eyes come to life with touches of pure white in the conjunctiva.

There is a certain disparity in the execution of the faces: Some are soft and subtly modeled, with well-constructed volumes (figs. 30 and 32), while others show more contrasting modeling, with a certain coarseness and a less coherent volumetric rendering (fig. 29). When the face decreases in size, light and shadow areas are juxtaposed without transition (fig. 31). Do these variations betray the hands of the different brothers?

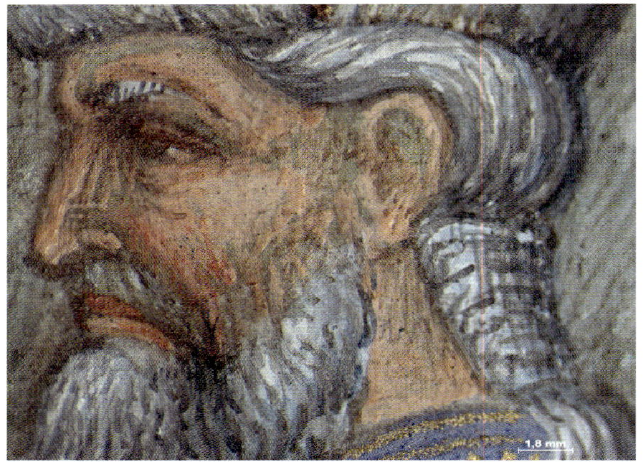


**Fig. 29** Detail under the microscope of a character's face (fol. 52). Photo É. Ravaud – C2RMF

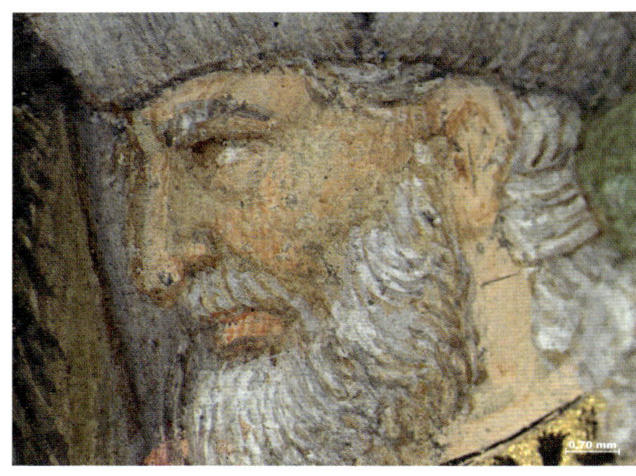


**Fig. 30** Detail under the microscope of a Magus's face (fol. 51v). Photo É. Ravaud – C2RMF

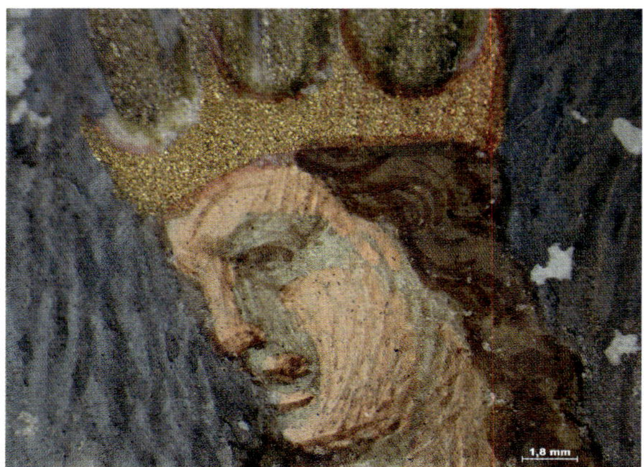


**Fig. 31** Detail under the microscope of a Magus's face in the distance (fol. 51v). Photo É. Ravaud – C2RMF

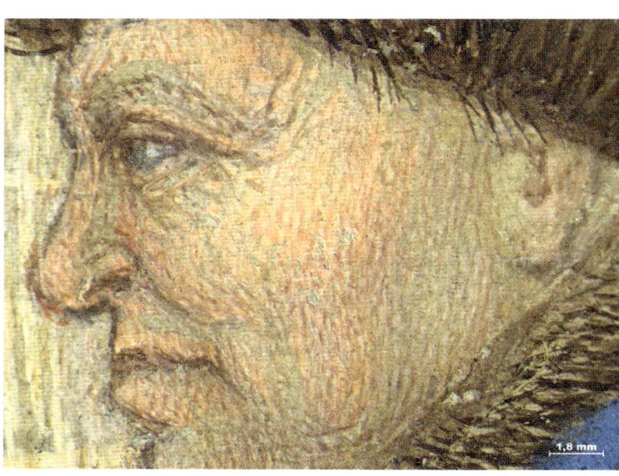


**Fig. 32** Detail under the microscope of the Duke of Berry's face (fol. 1v). Photo É. Ravaud – C2RMF

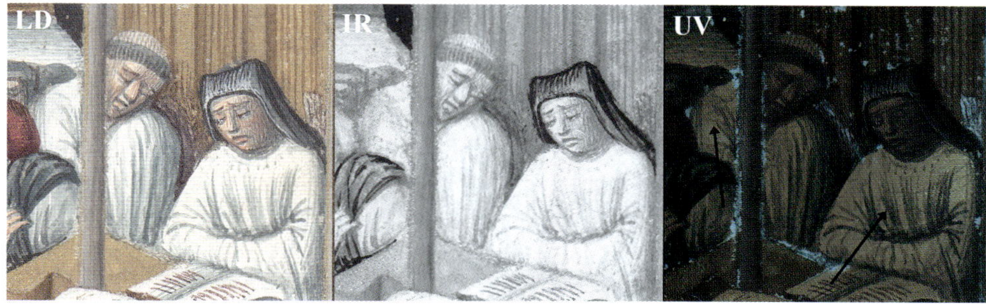


**Fig. 33** Fragments of the underdrawing in infrared (IR) and ultraviolet (UV) light, not visible in direct light (LD) (fol. 86v). Photo L. Clivet – C2RMF / Composition É. Ravaud – C2RMF

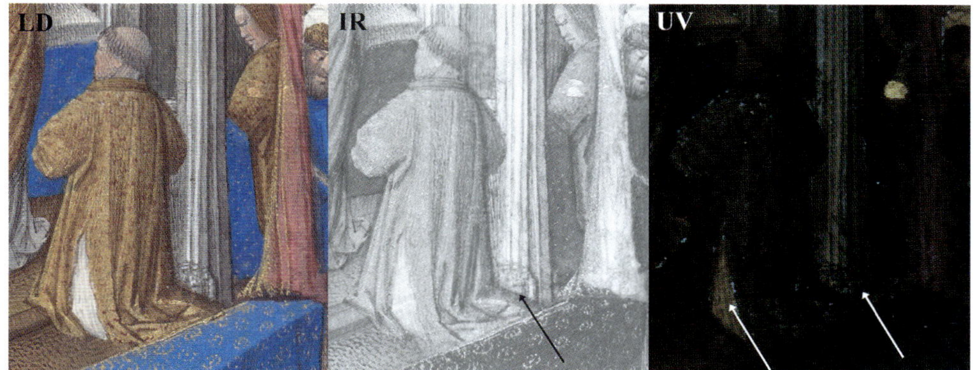


**Fig. 34** Fragments of the underdrawing in infrared (IR) and ultraviolet (UV) light, not visible in direct light (LD) (fol. 158). Photo L. Clivet – C2RMF / Composition É. Ravaud – C2RMF

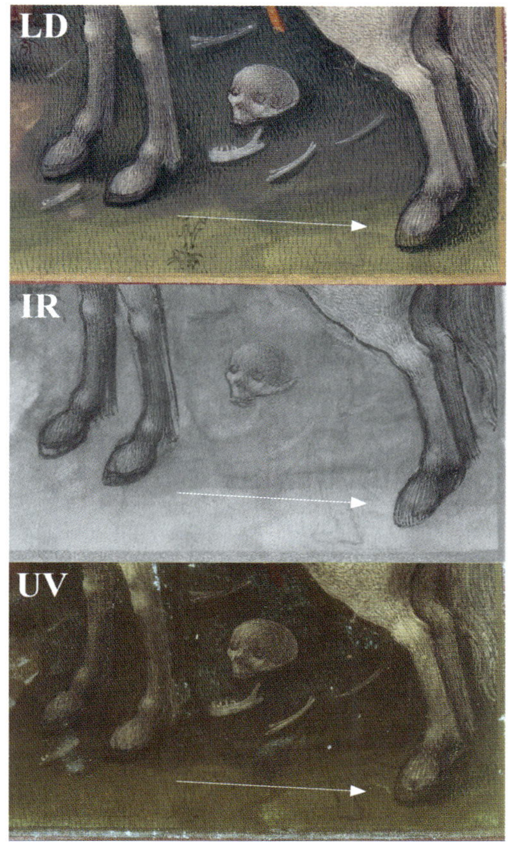


**Fig. 35** Details of direct light (LD), infrared (IR), and ultraviolet (UV) photographs showing the figure seated in the foreground (fol. 152v). Photo L. Clivet – C2RMF

### THE BEDFORD MASTER (HAINCELIN DE HAGUENAU)

This master produced several margins whose foliage scrolls form a succession of medallions. Four folios were analyzed: the Death of Raymond Diocrès (fol. 86v), the Crucifixion (fol. 152), the Christmas Mass (fol. 158), and the Resurrection (fol. 182). The existence of drawings similar to the two compositions of the Death of Raymond Diocrès and the Christmas Mass, painted later by Jean Colombe, raises the question of a broader intervention by the Bedford Master.[36]

The margins were drawn with an ink whose infrared and UV behavior shows clearer infrared absorption, while retaining some UV amplification. The FCIR composite is predominantly gray. The ink thus appears to have a slightly different composition than that observed on the folios attributed to the Van Lymborch brothers. It could be ferrogallic ink mixed with carbon black. In the illuminations themselves, the importance of detecting the drawing is directly linked to the density and opacity of the surface-painted motifs, but the same behavior as can be seen using in the margins scientific imaging.

In the Death of Raymond Diocrès, the foliage medallions in the margins, painted by the Bedford Master or his workshop, were completed in the center by Jean Colombe. However, an underdrawing can be detected by infrared and UV analysis, indicating several small modifications to the painted motifs. In the illumination, an underdrawing is detectable in abundance, but is only visible on small surfaces (clothing, drapery, architecture, altarpieces, etc.). These multiple indications suggest that a relatively complete drawing is present under the painted composition, which follows it quite closely (fig. 33).

In the Christmas Mass, the foliate margins include a drawing in the same ink as the preceding folio, but also a first tracing visible only in infrared, which would have preceded the ink tracing. No drawing other than that of Colombe has been identified with any certainty at the center of the medallions. In the illumination, the drawing is visible, in fragmented form, throughout the composition. The painting seems to follow its layout fairly closely (fig. 34).

The Crucifixion reveals margins where a double layer of drawing is identifiable. The less contrasted line is similar to those in earlier folios. It is covered by a second line, rich in carbon black, probably by Colombe, who also colored the margins. The illumination reveals that the composition was laid out via a drawing that can be detected in infrared and UV light. It includes a crouching figure in the right foreground, with other motifs that are difficult to read (fig. 35). Certain characteristics of the images in UV light suggest that some of the color areas may have been sketched out in paint.

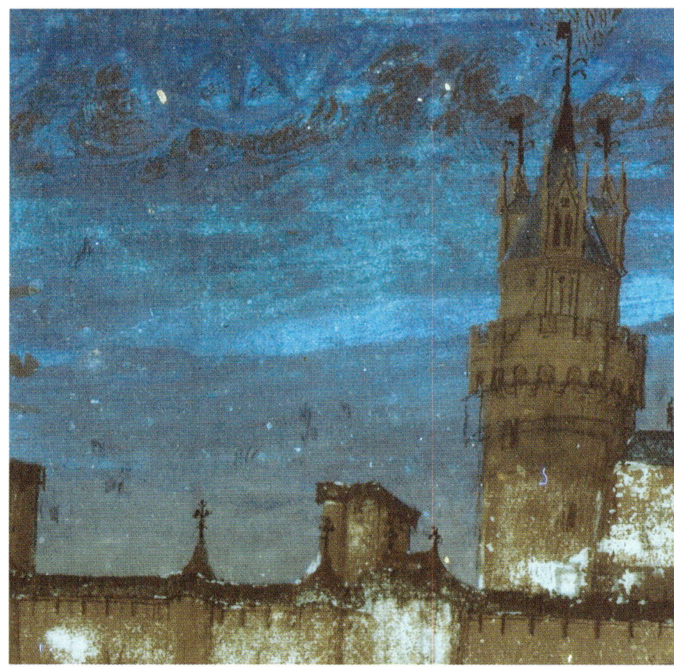

**Fig. 36** Detail of (lightened) UV photograph showing modifications to the castle (fol. 3v). Photo L. Clivet – C2RMF

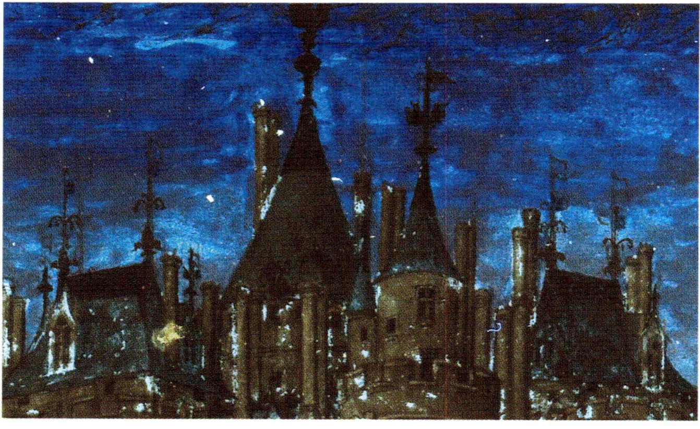

**Fig. 37** Detail of the UV photograph showing the underdrawing at the top of the castle (fol. 10v). Photo L. Clivet – C2RMF

On the other hand, no underdrawing has been detected in the Resurrection (fol. 182). The margins show a similar drawing to the folios 86 and 158. The center of the medallions did not reveal any underdrawing other than that of Colombe.

The similarity of the ink's behavior between the margins and the drawing detected beneath the illuminations on the Death of Raymond Diocrès (fol. 86v), the Crucifixion (fol. 152), and the Christmas Mass (fol. 158) suggests that the Bedford Master may indeed have been the author of these drawn compositions. Only folio 86v reveals a drawing in the medallions attributable to this artist.

The palette of margins painted by the Bedford Master is quite rich. Burnished gold on a dark gray bole with very fine punched decoration, unburnished gold leaf, sometimes modulated with colored glaze, unburnished silver leaf, vermilion, minium, UV-absorbing red lake (brazilwood?), lapis lazuli, indigo, copper green (probably verdigris) enriched with lead-tin yellow (type I), a transparent olive green modeling the green areas (organic green?), brown (earth with traces of manganese), carbon black, and lead white. Orpiment also may be present in a red mixture, judging by XRF spectrometry.

## BARTHÉLEMY D'EYCK

The artist intervened on leaves of the calendar previously worked on by the Van Lymborch brothers. These are the months of March (fol. 3v), June (fol. 6v), September (fol. 9v), October (fol. 10v), and December (fol. 12v).[37] A specific intervention is also suggested on folio 71, based on an initial work by the Van Lymborch brothers. On these folios, where several hands may have been involved, the interpretation of scientific imaging is particularly complex and must be treated with caution. While the underdrawing by the Van Lymborch brothers has already been described, that of Barthélemy d'Eyck remained to be defined due to the lack of a thoroughly studied illumination that could serve as a reference for imaging analysis. As art historians have shown, the artist was sensitive to the optical phenomena of cast shadows and water reflections, criteria used to identify him within the manuscript. Observation reveals that his painting technique is characterized by the use of fine, contrasting striations for modeling and for core and cast shadows. Examination of these leaves also highlights the presence of very dark brushstrokes, generally underlining the outline of a motif in shadow, made of a material that strongly absorbs infrared radiations but hinders detection of the underdrawing.

In the leaves on which Barthélemy d'Eyck seems to have worked, we used scientific imaging to discover if there was a preliminary sketch by the Van Lymborch brothers.

In the leaves for the months of March, October, and December, the castle painted by the Van Lymborch brothers features a preliminary drawing in ferrogallic ink. In March, for the first castle represented in the calendar, the imaging reveals numerous modifications both at the drawing stage and between this and the painted phase, as evidenced by the large tower partly painted on the sky (fig. 36). Examination of the leaf for October reveals a drawing in an ink that reveals the intervention of the Van Lymborch brothers, covering the entire castle down to its base (fig. 37). In December, the drawing beneath the castle in a UV-absorbing ink points to typical Van Lymborch gargoyles, though ultimately not painted. At the foot of the castle, these artists have indicated the tops of the foliage in very free curving lines, marking the beginning of the forest.

Examination of the foreground of these three illuminations in which the hand of Barthélemy d'Eyck is detectable shows the existence of an underdrawing attributable to the Van Lymborch brothers. For example, the peasant with his plow and ox team, and the other small figures in the background of March, feature a drawing in ferrogallic ink, as do the birds in the lower right, subsequently covered with a thin, light-gray layer (fig. 38). On the leaf for October, while the figures on the riverbank show no traces of a drawing by the Van Lymborch brothers, all the motifs in the foreground—figures, farming tool, scarecrow, trees along the riverbank—have underlying lines indicating the existence of a drawing by the brothers (fig. 39). A drawing only visible in infrared, probably made by Barthélemy d'Eyck, revisits the figure on horseback, tracing new folds in the clothes of the rider and, to a lesser degree, of the sower. The foreground scene of December, an Italian model of which has been identified in the work of Giovannino de' Grassi (Bergamo), was arranged by the Van Lymborch brothers. Particularly noteworthy are the collar of the dog on the left, decorated with small circles, and the drawing on the body of the white dog (fig. 40).

In the two folios for the months of June and September, imaging cannot confirm or exclude the existence of a Van Lymborch drawing. Essentially, we detect a drawing visible in infrared, without UV amplification, indicating the use of a carbon black-based material. In June, the underlying outline of the castle is particularly abundant in the roofs, with many straight lines, abandoned dormer windows, and vertical construction

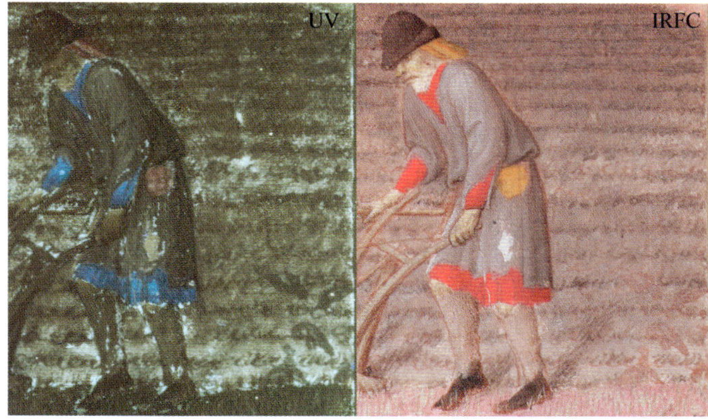


**Fig. 38** Details of ultraviolet (UV) and false color infrared (FCIR) photographs showing the underdrawing in ferrogallic ink in the plowman's blue garment and the birds, ultimately painted over (fol. 3v). Photo L. Clivet – C2RMF / Composition É. Ravaud

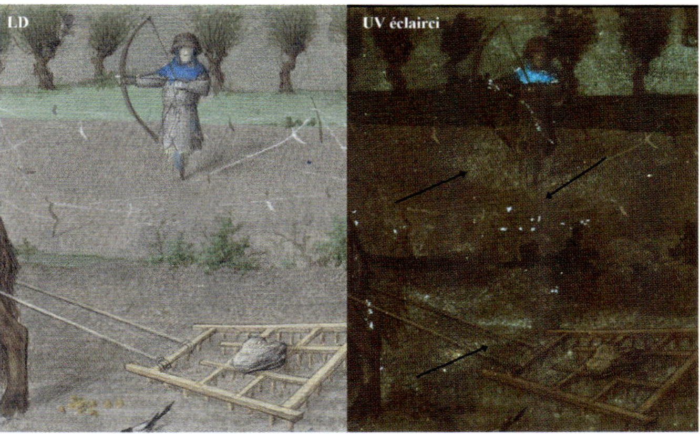


**Fig. 39** Details of direct light (LD) and ultraviolet (UV) photographs showing the underdrawing of the scarecrow, stretched wires, and plow (fol. 10v). Photo L. Clivet – C2RMF

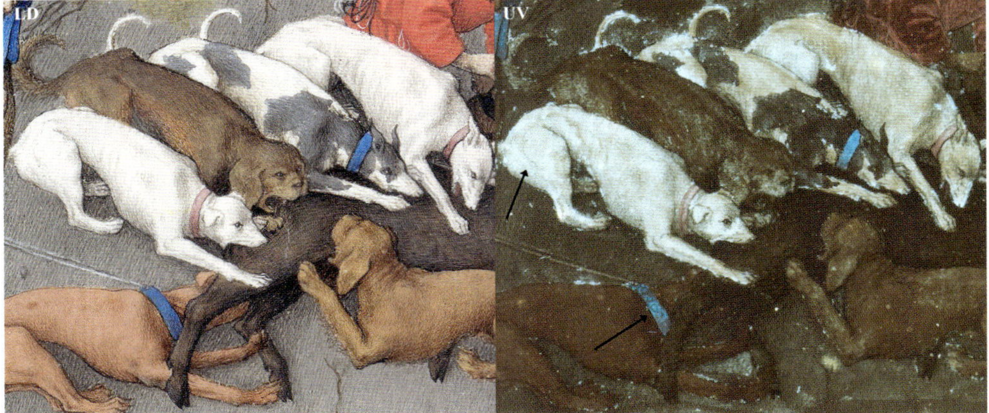


**Fig. 40** Details of direct light (LD) and ultraviolet (UV) photographs showing the underdrawing of the central group of animals with the collar decorated with small circles and the lines on the white dog (fol. 12v). Photo L. Clivet – C2RMF / Composition É. Ravaud

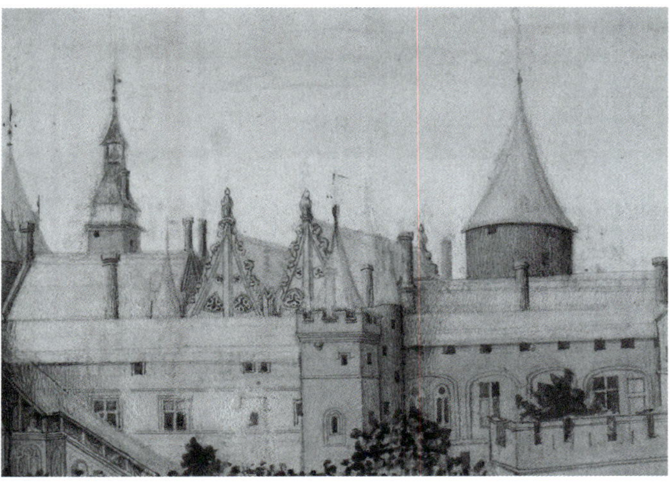

**Fig. 41** Detail of the infrared (IR) photograph showing the abundant underdrawing of the castle (fol. 6v). Photo L. Clivet – C2RMF

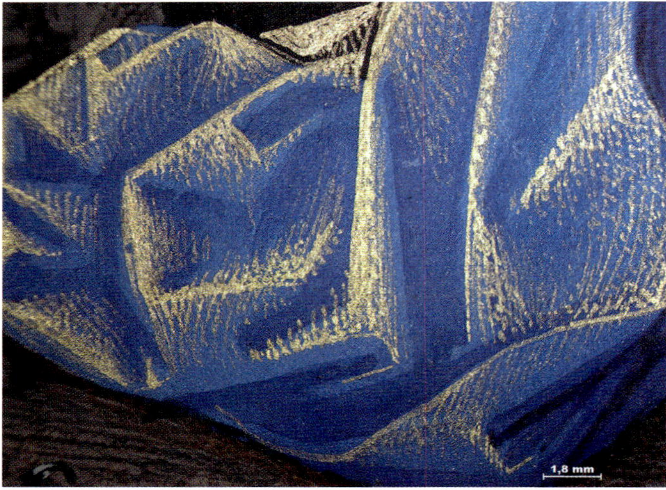

**Fig. 42** Detail under the microscope of drapery with gold shell highlights (fol. 100v). Photo É. Ravaud – C2RMF

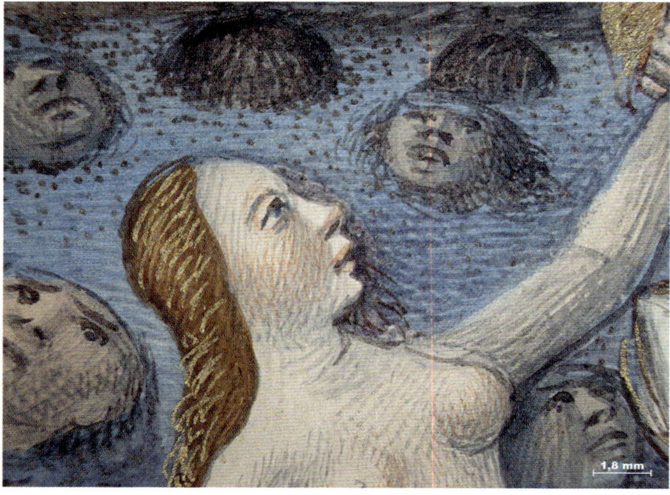

**Fig. 43** Detail under the microscope of a face (fol. 113v). Photo É. Ravaud – C2RMF

lines (fig. 41). At the painted stage, we note the core and cast shadows carried by contrasting tight vertical striations and the varied opening of the windows. In the foreground, the imaging does not reliably visualize a sketch beneath the figures, while in the landscape, the drawn lines of the women's tools and millstones are visible in infrared light. In September, rare modifications to the castle can be observed at the drawing stage. The grassy area at the foot of the castle was painted before the barrier and tilt.

Barthélemy d'Eyck thus used first and foremost a carbon-based material for drawing.

The color palette he employed is relatively limited, depending on the subjects depicted: buildings, landscapes, and peasants. The colors identified are vermilion red, a slightly fluorescent red lake, lapis lazuli blue, indigo, azurite, ochres, copper green (probably verdigris), and a fluorescent green.

## JEAN COLOMBE

Jean Colombe's style is easily recognizable in pictorial terms, and so the attribution of his leaves poses no particular issue.

The underdrawing is not very visible, as the contours are often surrounded by materials that absorb infrared and UV radiation themselves, at the painted stage. No significant pentimento has been observed. The material of the drawing observed on the leaves attributed to Jean Colombe differs from that used by the Van Lymborch brothers in that it is essentially visible under infrared radiation, indicating the use of a predominantly carbon-based material. He may also have used red lake, visible in certain paint losses.

The palette differs from that of the preceding artists. Azurite is the main blue, widely used on its own or as an underlayer for lapis lazuli, or in mixtures for dark purple hues. Indigo is also widely used, often in mixtures, particularly for greens and grays. It enhances the shading of foliage. Lapis is present, sometimes on its own but more often combined with azurite. Copper green is also widely used. Colombe favored yellow hues, notably lead-tin yellow (type I), as well as the orange color provided by minium. Yellow ochres and vermilion are regularly used. Red lake is identified pure or in combination with azurite for purple colors. This lake also models the gold Renaissance frames. He uses little silver and lots of shell gold.

The painting technique is characterized by a fairly dense covering material. The modeling makes extensive use of shell gold for clothing and hair highlights (fig. 42). For flesh tones, a recognizable painted reddish-brown hatching is used (fig. 43). Several folios show that Colombe did not hesitate to paint landscape backgrounds completely before adding motifs in the foreground.

On several folios painted by Jean Colombe, underlying elements can be identified.

In the Cathedral (fol. 137), blue areas are sometimes visible in small paint losses, aligned on two verticals, probably corresponding to an arrangement originally intended for a text. Blue, also seen in losses in the frame of folio 113v, could have the same significance.

The foreground of the month of September was painted by Colombe. Only the cart and oxen on the right have a detectable underdrawing, but its characteristics make attribution uncertain.

In November (fol. 11v), the entire lower scene under the astrological lunette, was painted by Colombe. In the main character's clothing, a few rare indications can be detected under UV light, but these could be modifications made during the painting phase by Colombe. The entire landscape in the distance was painted before the forest.

An abundant drawing in ferrogallic ink can also be seen under the Procession (fol. 71), painted by Colombe. Here, attribution to the Van Lymborch brothers appears almost certain, insofar as the architectural composition is evocative in itself, similar to Christ Carrying the Cross (fol. 147), and the buildings are adorned with gargoyles that were drawn but not painted.

## CONCLUSION

This first scientific study of the famous *Très Riches Heures* manuscript has shed new light on the materiality and production of numerous folios through strictly non-invasive approaches. It should be remembered that this study is not exhaustive and only considers a sampling of illuminations. Nevertheless, it has provided important insights into the genesis of many folios, by identifying the underdrawings, distinguishing their materials, and giving a first glimpse of the artists' palettes. It opens up new perspectives that can be complemented by future investigations.

The materials used in the folios studied and attributed to the Van Lymborch brothers are very similar to those identified in the *Belles Heures*. Their application, however, is different. The diversity in the use of metal leaf in the *Très Riches Heures* is quite remarkable. Burnished gold is rarely encountered, while unburnished gold leaf is more frequently used, sometimes with the subtlety of an underlayer modifying the shade of the gold, as well as shell gold. Silver is also used more frequently, either as unburnished leaf or as shell silver. Within restricted limits, guaranteeing the stylistic unity of all the leaves executed by the Van Lymborch brothers, variations in the painting technique raise the question of the hands of the different brothers. Folios in which an underdrawing attributable to the Van Lymborch brothers has been detected have made it possible to clarify the state of progress of the manuscript at the time of their death.

The intervention by the Bedford Master appears to be confirmed in several illuminations whose margins he also designed. The scope of the intervention by Barthélemy d'Eyck has been clarified, most often on the basis of a drawing by the Van Lymborch brothers, notably in the month of December. Jean Colombe's palette follows the general evolution of painting practices in the fifteenth century, with the virtual disappearance of silver, the decline of lapis lazuli in favor of azurite, the generous use of lead-tin yellow, and with a painting technique that is quite characteristic.

1 Our sincere thanks to Ms. Marie-Pierre Dion, general curator of libraries at the Musée Condé, who is responsible for the manuscript, for her kindness and help in handling the work and for ongoing discussions throughout the study; Mr. Mathieu Deldicque, director of the Musée Condé, for the trust he placed in us; Coralie Barbe and Florence Malo, restorers, for our very fruitful discussions on the manuscript; Stéphane Penaud for making a lectern specifically designed for the analyses; and Martina Lange Brejon de Lavergnée and Evelyne Sohonow, of the C2RMF's art handling department, who were called on often.
2 Stirnemann and Rabel 2005.
3 Laurence Clivet, photographer at C2RMF, was responsible for the entire photographic campaign.
4 The choice of infrared photography rather than infrared reflectography was based on the much finer resolution of the images, essential in the search for any underdrawing. The same protocol was used for the study of the *Belles Heures*.
5 Élisabeth Ravaud from C2RMF carried out the microscopic examinations.
6 Anne Michelin from CRC carried out the hyperspectral analyses.
7 Éric Laval from C2RMF carried out the XRF examinations.
8 Kilian Laclavetine from C2RMF carried out the FORS, XRD, and FTIR analyses.
9 Chahine 2013, 215.
10 The infrared photograph was taken at a wavelength of 900 nanometers. In the folio, where infrared reflectography (900–1,700 nm) was also carried out, this line fades even more clearly.
11 Recent literature distinguishes between ferrogallic inks according to the origin of the iron. In the case of metallic iron, the ink is called non-vitriolic; if the iron comes from vitriol, the ink is called vitriolic. See Cohen et al. 2023.
12 Manuscript by Jean Le Bègue, "De Coloribus faciendis," in Merrifield 1849, II, 158–59.
13 London 2002–03, 30–32.
14 Lawson 2012.
15 Prochno 2002a; Nash 2010.
16 This practice generally concerns fabrics dyed with kermes or madder, not brazilwood, which is used directly, grated and ground.
17 Fluorescence is, however, an inconsistent physical characteristic in these lakes, depending on the manufacturing process. Further investigations are needed to clarify this point.
18 Ribault 1990.
19 Thompson 1926.
20 Clarke 2011.
21 X-ray diffraction analysis yielded no specific results.
22 Purging buckthorn or *Rhamnus catharticus*: bark or fruit.
23 Gonzalez 2016; Gonzalez et al. 2017.
24 Thompson 1935.
25 Thompson 1926.
26 Merrifield 1849, II, chap. XLII, "How to gilt on parchment," 238.
27 Nash 2010.
28 There is no burnished gilded background.
29 Thompson 1926.
30 There are other motifs in the manuscript, such as the divine light on fol. 156v.
31 The lighter part is rougher, while the darker part is smoother, without reaching the level of burnished gold.
32 Howard and Najorka 2017.
33 Generally less than 1% in illuminations.
34 *Liber de coloribus Illuminatorum Siue Pictorum*.
35 Distinguishing two or three layers of different tones under the microscope may possibly underestimate the actual number of layers.
36 Stirnemann and Rabel 2005.
37 Villela-Petit 2013b.

**Fig. 44** Following pages: Van Lymborch brothers, *Très Riches Heures*, fol. 19v: The Martyrdom of St. Mark, detail

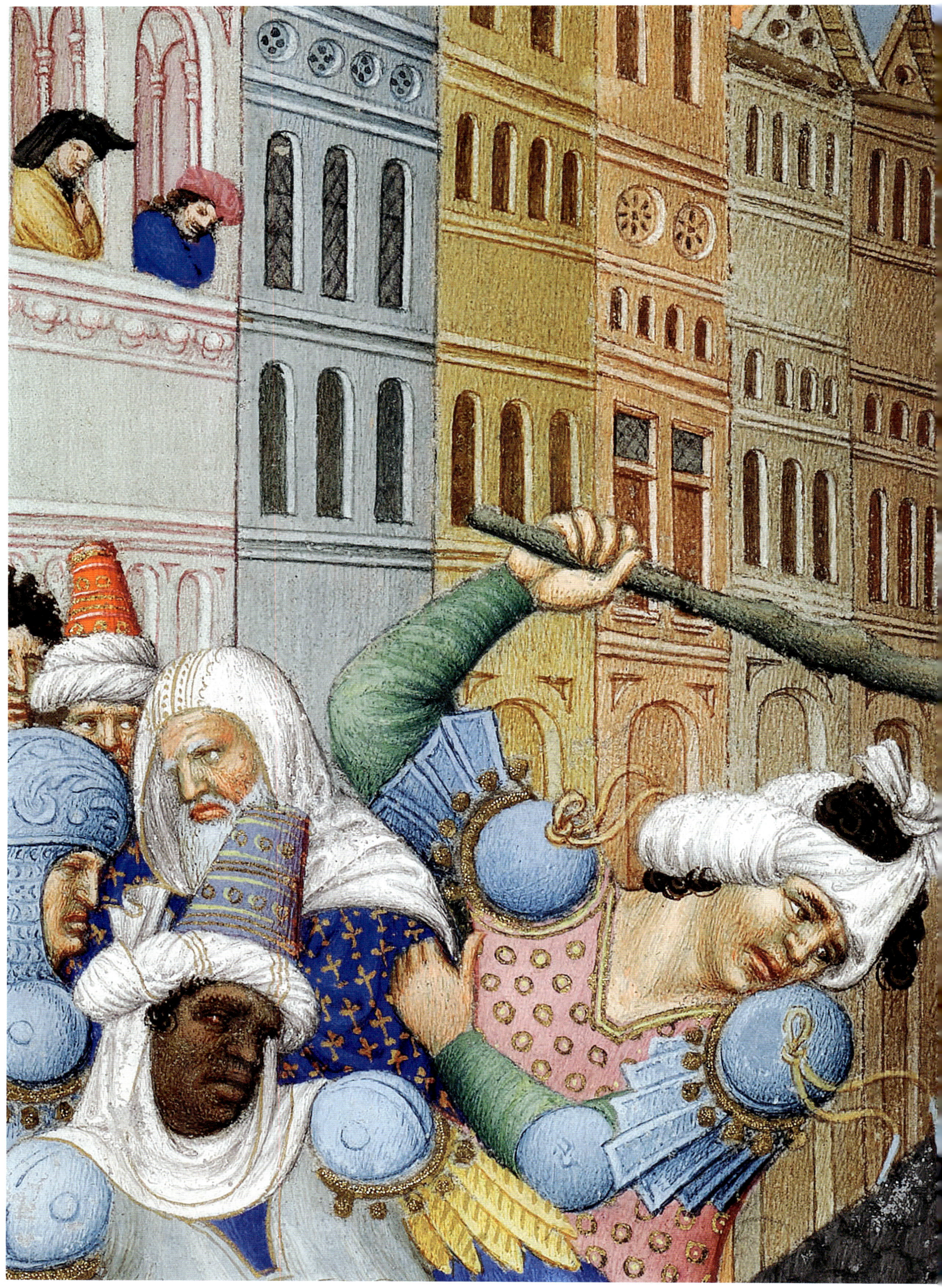

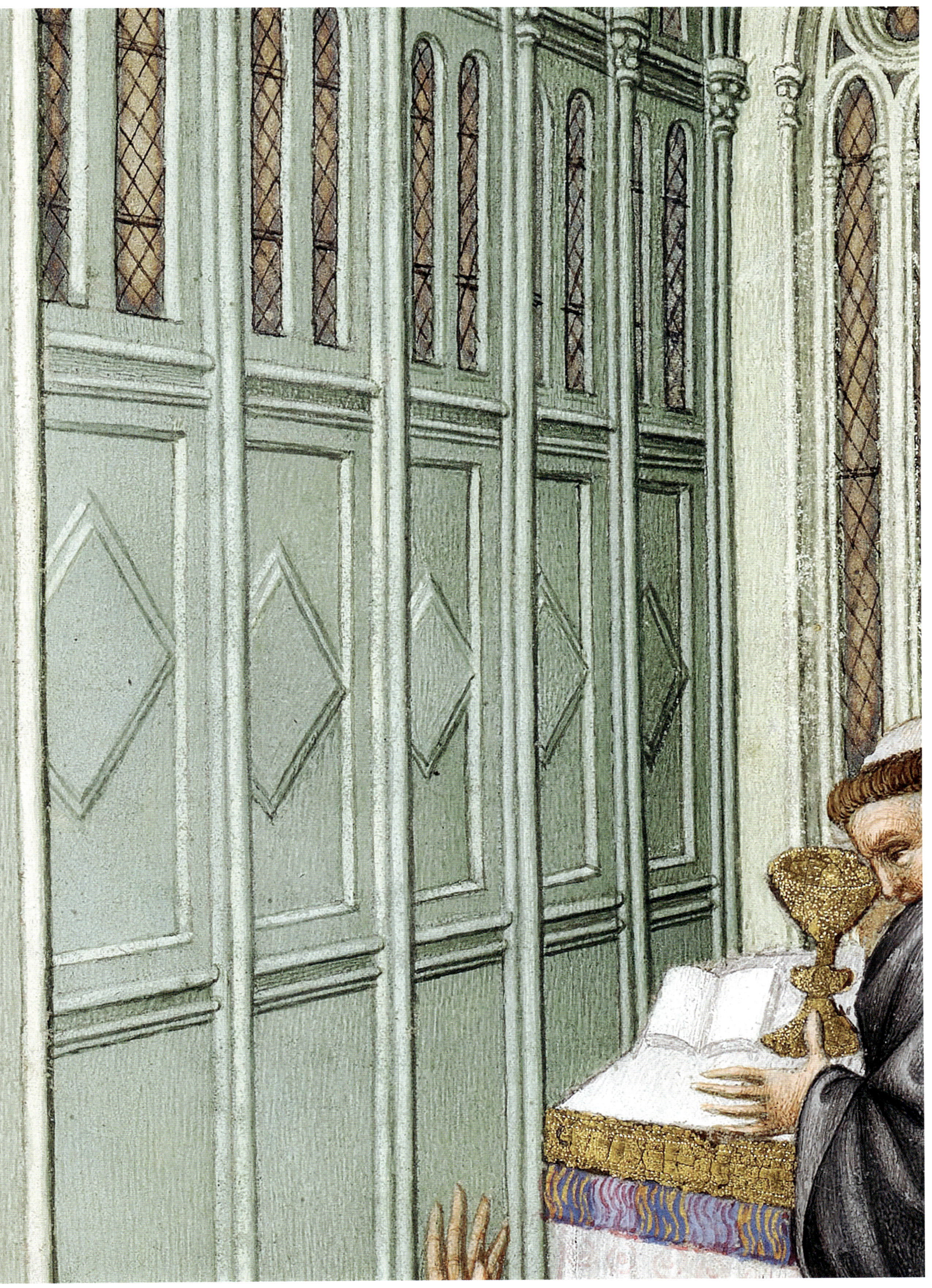

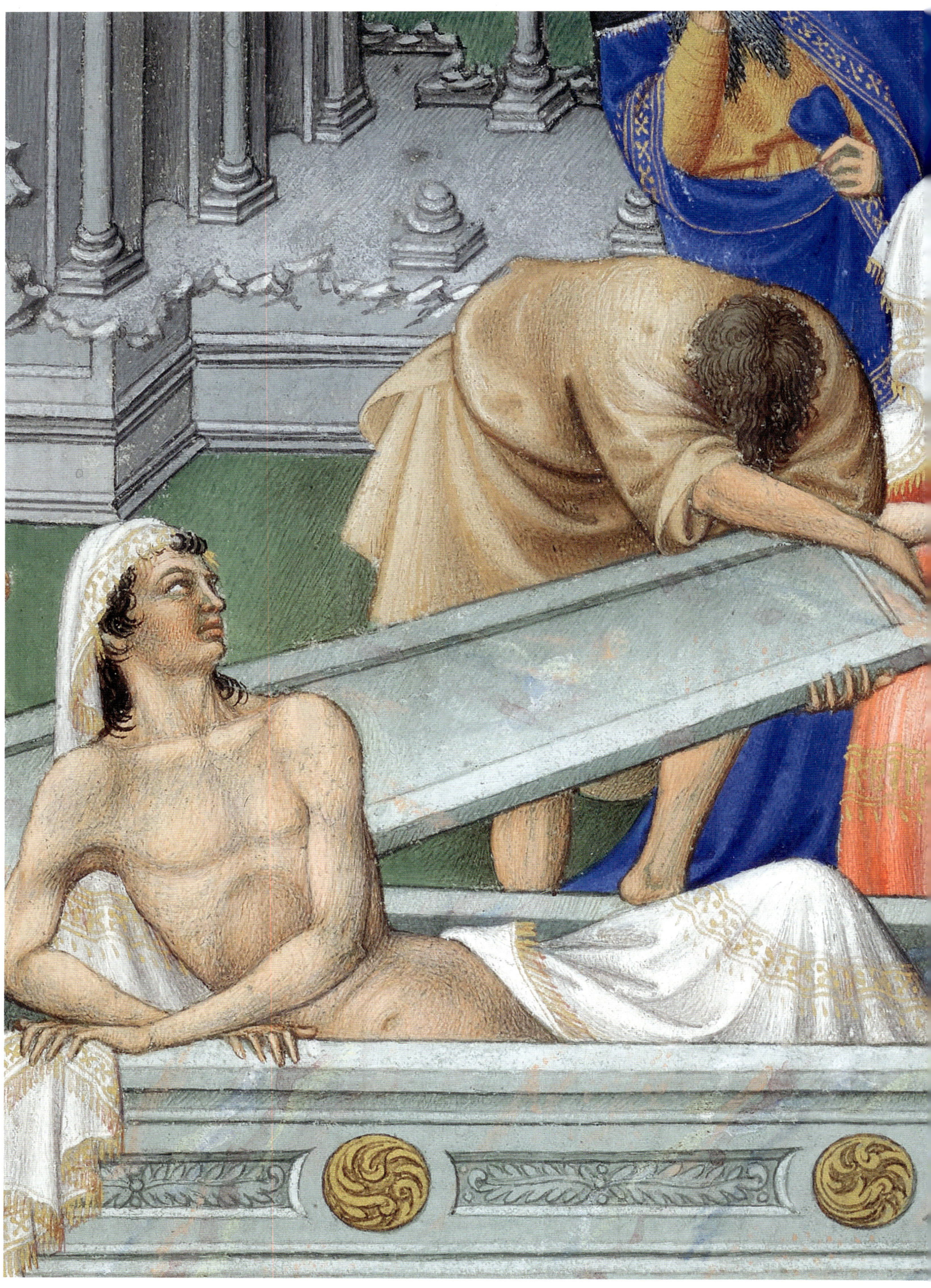

# 20.

# Defining the Preservation-restoration and Exhibition of the *Très Riches Heures*

Coralie Barbe and Florence Malo

"Révélez ; je ne suis nullement disposé au mystère en ce qui concerne mes raretés et d'ailleurs, le livre ne peut qu'y gagner" (Reveal; I am not at all inclined to mystery when it comes to my rarities, and besides, the book can only gain from it), wrote the Duke of Aumale to his former tutor, Alfred-Auguste Cuvillier-Fleury, who became his Parisian representative in 1856, the year he acquired the *Très Riches Heures*.[1]

What did the Duke of Aumale mean by the injunction "reveal"? If we put aside the religious meaning of the notion of revelation, we are left with two explanations: on the one hand, it can mean bringing to light what is unknown, and on the other, making someone or something suddenly known.

It was in the midst of this reflection that we were contacted in 2022 by the curators of the Musée Condé at Chantilly, who were concerned about the state of deterioration of the *Très Riches Heures* and were contemplating a research and development project for the manuscript. Several tears and dark stains visible on the first bifolia of the book were a cause for concern. In addition, several of the miniatures showed lifting of the pictorial layer, visible to the naked eye. Finally, the Bibliothèque nationale de France had already expressed concern about the preservation of the illuminations in this bound form, given the considerable undulations of the parchment leading to the embrittlement of the pictorial layers. How could the material preservation of the manuscript be improved over the long term? What was the actual condition

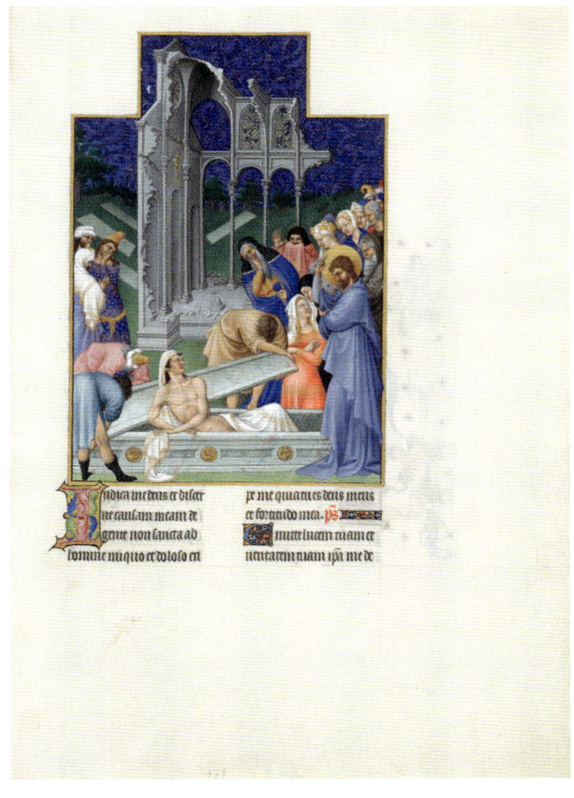

**Fig. 2** Van Lymborch brothers, *Très Riches Heures*, fol. 171: The Resurrection of Lazarus

**Fig. 1** Van Lymborch brothers, *Très Riches Heures*, fol. 171: The Resurrection of Lazarus, detail

of the miniatures? And as for the binding, which was evidently carried out at a later date, was it detrimental to their preservation, as is often the case with manuscripts bound later? Finally, was it possible to optimize the display of this precious manuscript without denaturing it?

As this catalog goes to press, the restoration of the manuscript is not yet complete and will not be finished until after the exhibition. However, in order to satisfy the requirements of the Duke of Aumale, we shall "reveal" the necessary elements of historical, stylistic, and technical reflection that have gone into developing the preservation-restoration project for the masterpiece of the Van Lymborch brothers.

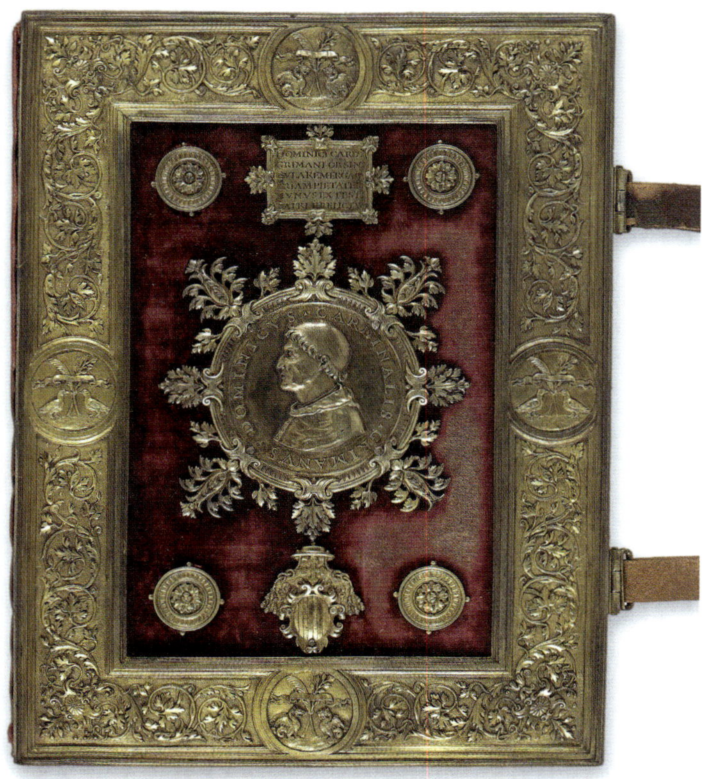

**Fig. 3** *Grimani Breviary*, front cover (Venice, Biblioteca Nazionale Marciana, cod. Lat. I, 99)

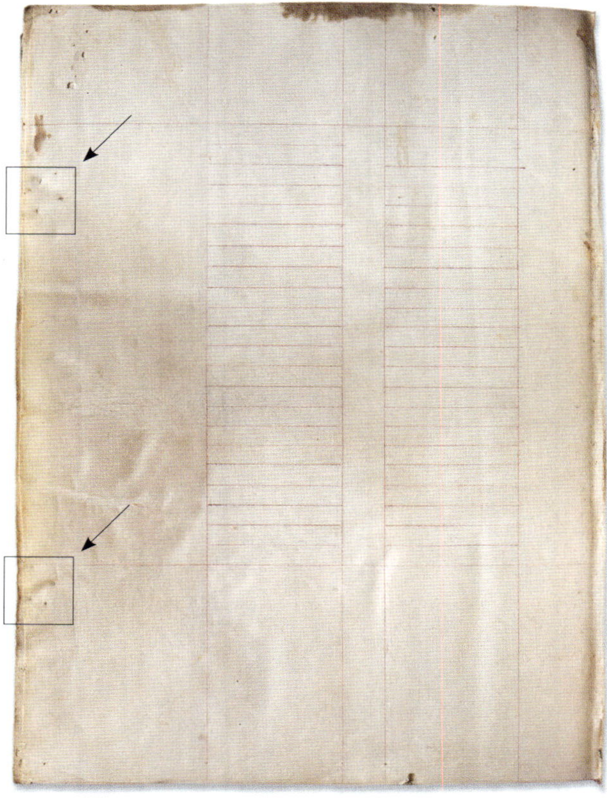

**Fig. 4** Traces left by the clasps of the *Très Riches Heures*

## A BRIEF MATERIAL HISTORY OF THE *TRÈS RICHES HEURES*

The Duke of Berry's estate inventory of 1416 established that the manuscript was still in progress and consisted of a set of loose quires, simply enclosed in a wooden case.[2] Paul Durrieu concluded from the mention of the manuscript in the 1523 inventory that it was then present in the Chapel of the Dukes at Margaret of Austria's palace in Mechelen. This inventory mentions, among other things, a "grand heure escripte à la main lesquelles n'ont pas de couvert ne fermeilletz" (a large book of hours written by hand with neither cover nor clasps), "depuis couvert de velours et y mis ung fermilet d'argent" (since then, covered in velvet and fitted with a silver clasp).[3] According to Christopher de Hamel, it was Martin des Ableaux, one of the jewelers at the court of Margaret of Austria, who first bound this precious manuscript.[4] The presence of the manuscript at the Mechelen court can also be deduced from the similarities between the *Très Riches Heures* and the *Grimani Breviary*, now kept in Venice.[5] As the inventory indicates, this initial binding may have resembled that of the *Grimani Breviary*, namely a binding covered in red velvet, decorated with various metal clasps (fig. 3). Indeed, the manuscripts of the princes of the time were frequently adorned with precious oriental and Italian silks. Jean of Berry's library contained 309 manuscripts, nearly half of which were decorated with fabric.[6] To prevent the parchment leaves from becoming distorted, metal clasps were attached to the boards. The metallic traces (probably silver) observed on the last leaf of the manuscript would have been left by the clasps of the binding, which has now disappeared (fig. 4).

On the death of Margaret of Austria in 1530, the manuscript was held by Jean Raffault, Lord of Neufville, her treasurer general of finances. It is likely that it was then brought from the Netherlands by Ambrogio Spinola, commander-in-chief of the Spanish forces in the Netherlands; indeed, it bears the Spinola arms on its back cover. In the 1830s, the manuscript passed to the Serras, a Genoese family allied to the Spinolas, whose arms were placed over those of the Spinolas on the front cover.[7] The Duke of Aumale, who acquired the manuscript in 1856, was probably careful to preserve it intact, keeping it in its full red morocco binding adorned with armorial bearings. To protect and enhance the book, he commissioned renowned jeweler Antoine Vechte to make a case in burr walnut covered with a chased and repoussé silver plate (fig. 5).[8]

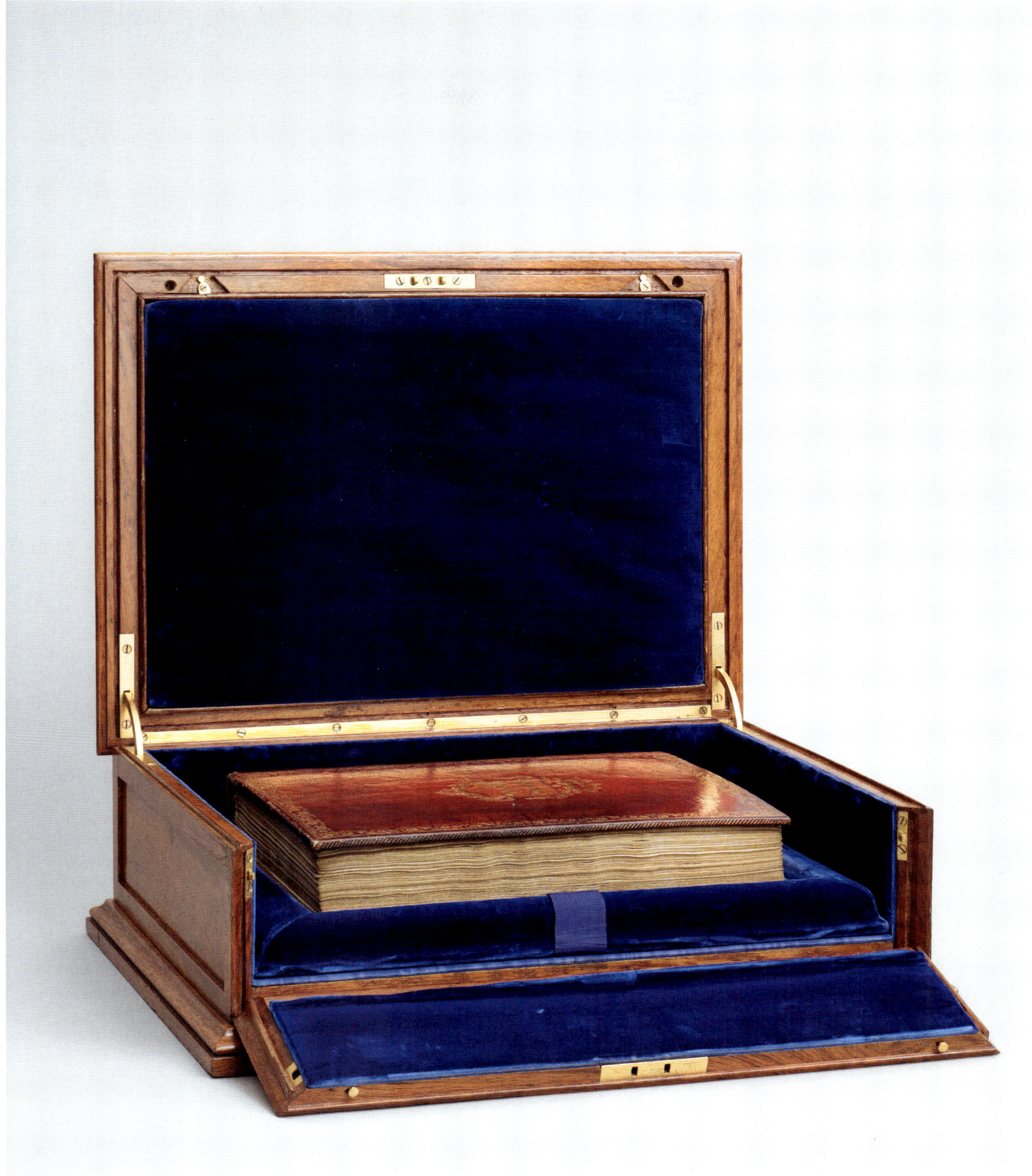

**Fig. 5** The manuscript in a case decorated with a goldsmith's plaque crafted by Antoine Vechte

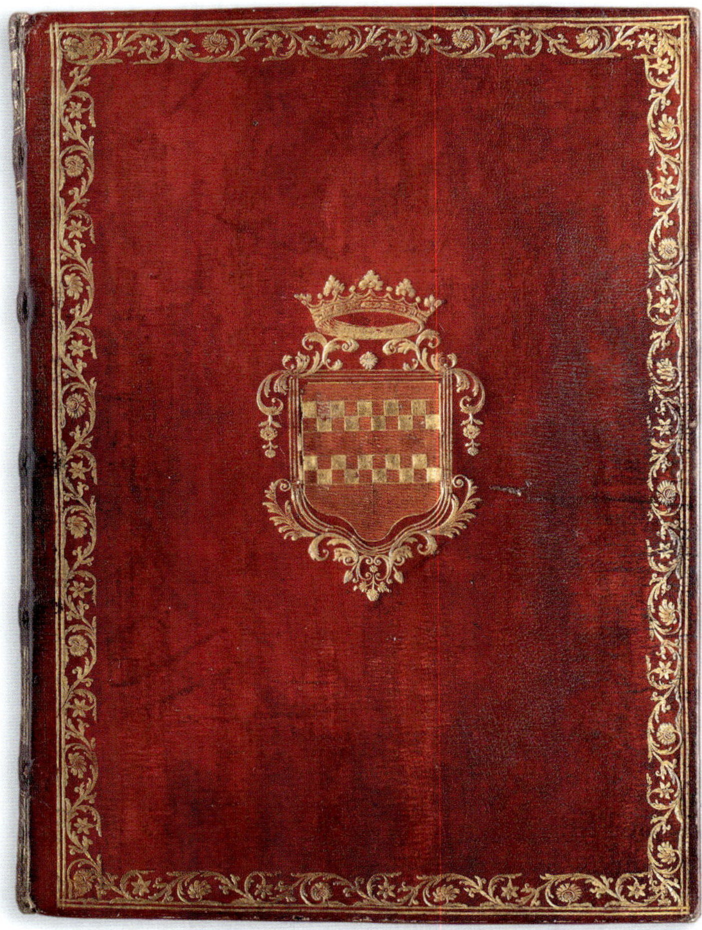

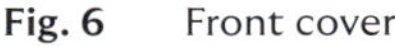

**Fig. 6** Front cover

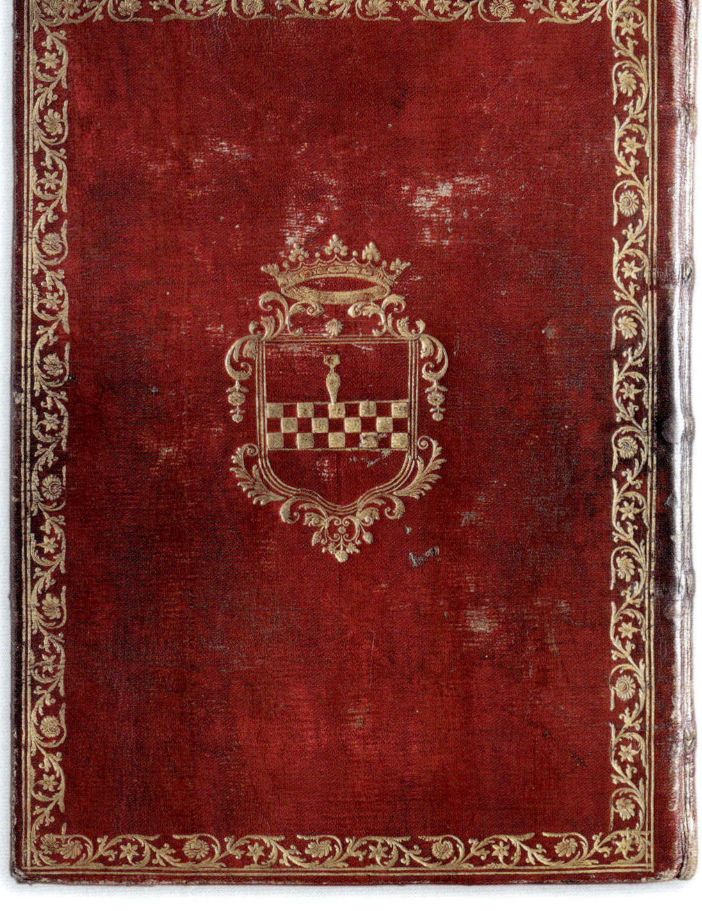

**Fig. 7** Back cover

## CODICOLOGICAL STUDY OF THE *TRÈS RICHES HEURES*: THE "SPINOLA" BINDING

The binding (figs. 6–8) would have been carried out between 1629, when Ambrogio Spinola brought the manuscript to Genoa, and its bequest to the Serra family in the 1830s. The Spinola arms in the center, "d'or à une fasce échiquetée de trois traits d'argent et de gueules, surmonté d'un robinet de gueules en pal fiché dans la fasce" (gold, a chequered band of three silver and red stripes, surmounted by a red faucet placed vertically on the band), are topped by a patrician crown typical of Genoese nobility.[9] As a result of comparing the *Très Riches Heures* with another remarkable manuscript, the *Spinola Hours* (now in Los Angeles),[10] Christopher de Hamel suggested that it was Vincenzo Spinola, son of Domenico Spinola and Benedetta Serra, who commissioned these bindings. Vincenzo had no heir, and his executor was his nephew Gian Battista Serra, who probably had his arms placed over those of his ancestor on the front cover.[11] The *Spinola Hours*, painted in Bruges in 1510 by Gerard Horenbout, probably at the request of Margaret of Austria, was sold in the same year as the *Très Riches Heures*, 1856.[12] De Hamel considers the two bindings to be identical in every respect.[13]

Although they cannot be directly compared, the two leathers used to bind the manuscripts appear to be very similar. Made from high-quality goat leather, the morocco was tanned with stable vegetable tannins, probably extracted from oak bark, a common tannin in the eighteenth century. It was then dyed, on the surface only, with various natural colorants (a few abrasions reveal the pale skin), and primed with various substances (oils, waxes, egg, gums) to improve its appearance, color, gloss, and feel. A special feature of the surface is that it has been stamped with hatching, creating slight reliefs. This technique appeared in the early nineteenth century and produced long-grain leathers particularly appreciated during the First French Empire.[14] In this instance, it seems to have been obtained by manual pressure with a copper plate engraved with grooves of varying fineness.

Minute differences on the edges and spines are also observable. The edges of the *Spinola Hours* are embossed with lozenges containing small flowers, while those of the *Très Riches Heures* are "simply" gilded. From a structural point of view, the spine of the *Très Riches Heures* features five relatively flat bands, characteristic of Italy in the second half of the eighteenth century, which also saw the spread of the fashion for long spines.[15] From a decorative point of view, the spine is typical of the eighteenth century: It features five bands and six compartments ornamented using small metal stamps, including a central stamp with a daisy motif, rather than the tulip adorning the *Spinola Hours*.[16] Far less typical is the fact that none of the

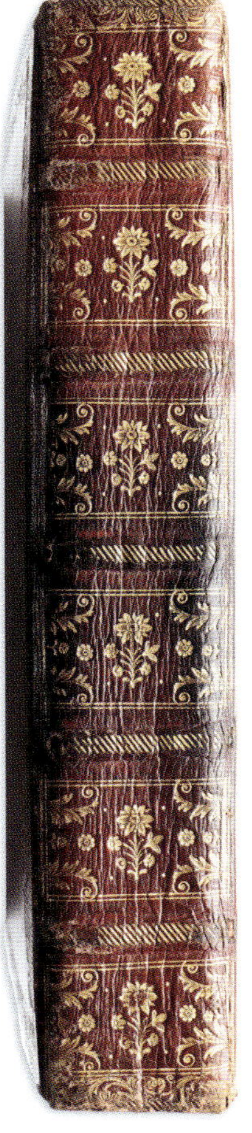

**Fig. 8** Spine

**Fig. 9** Green moiré silk front lining

compartments was reserved for the title of the work. This peculiarity tells us something about the precious nature and use of these manuscripts, which were not intended to be kept on library shelves.

Finally, it was necessary to compare the endpapers, added by the bookbinder to protect the leaves of the manuscript from prolonged contact with the acidic materials used for the binding (wood, leather, cardboard, etc.), as their appearance and assembly, unusual for the period, could have been the result of a later intervention.

Indeed, on each side of the *Très Riches Heures* we find a bifolium of endpapers made of rather thick parchment of mediocre quality, folded over a few centimeters to be sewn, and a counterguard—also known as the "lining"—in green moiré silk (fig. 9).

While the finest eighteen-century Italian bindings sometimes feature silk linings,[17] most of these are found on books whose leaves are made of paper, not parchment. Here, the binder chose to sew a bifolium of mediocre parchment and glue a loose silk lining to the inside of the cover. However, the appearance of the lining is intriguing on two counts. First, its assembly, which was rare in the eighteenth century (we have found no equivalent example in heritage collections) and more commonly referenced in the twentieth century[18]: The four edges of a piece of green moiré silk were folded and glued under tension onto a board, the latter being glued in full to the inside cover. At the time, the usual practice was to line the silk with paper and then glue the lined paper to the inside of the cover. The edges of the silk gradually fray, a phenomenon sometimes limited by the use of an ornate roulette straddling the two materials, leather and silk. Second, this lining, initially loose, was applied at a slight angle, so that it awkwardly covers the border on the edges of the binding. A comparison with the binding of the *Spinola Hours* left no room for doubt: The green silk and parchment endpapers of these two bindings, separated in 1856, therefore predated this year, and were probably contemporary with their bindings.[19]

## "I LACKED THE AUDACITY": THE INTERVENTION OF GUSTAVE MACON

To complete the material study of the binding of the *Très Riches Heures*, we still had to explore the restoration work it may have experienced. Although no restoration campaign was commissioned by the Duke of Aumale, who died in 1897, Gustave Macon, first assistant curator of the Musée Condé, appointed by the prince himself, decided at the start of the twentieth century to dismantle and reassemble the manuscript: ". . . I will not hesitate to let myself be called a vandal

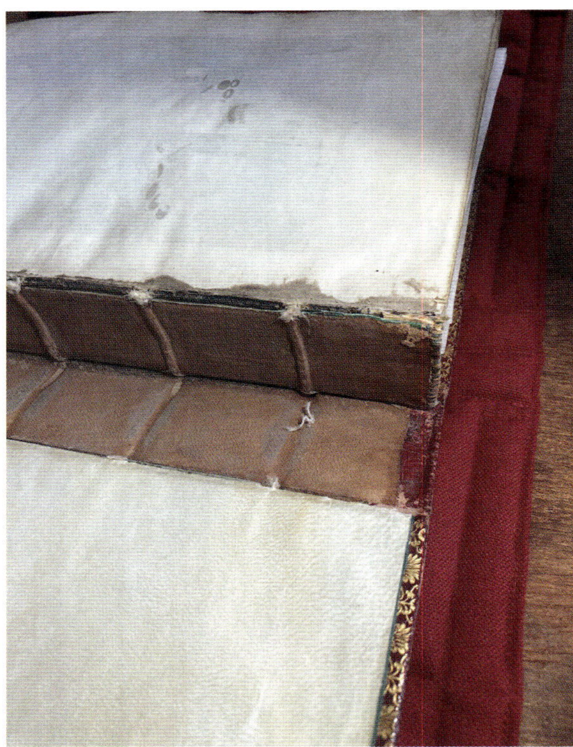

**Fig. 10** Rear of the parchment leaves consolidated with a piece of sheepskin leather and lining of the original spine with the same leather in the early twentieth century

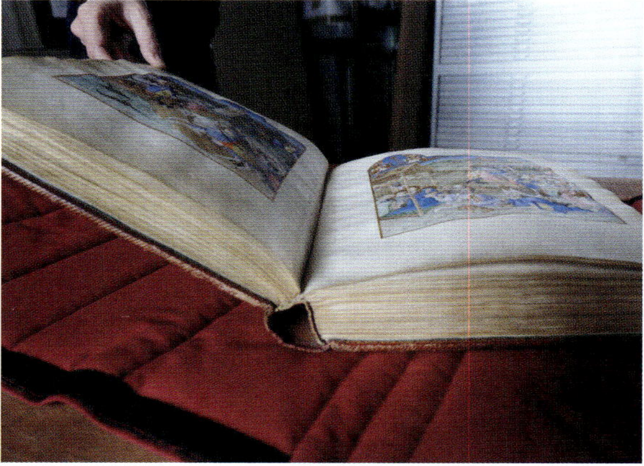

**Fig. 11** Behavior of the "broken spine" and leaves when the volume is opened

as I express the wish that some twenty of them [the leaves] be extracted from the book and framed like the miniatures by Jean Fouquet cut out from the *Hours of Étienne Chevalier*, now lost; this is the only way to save them from certain deterioration. I regret not doing this when, twenty years ago, I dismantled the volume to make it easier to photograph the book, studied the composition of the book, noted the shortcomings and the rearrangements made at the end of the fifteenth century: I would have been the subject of abuse at the time, but they would thank me today; all scholars and art enthusiasts would be pleased . . . I lacked the audacity. May Monseigneur the Duke of Berry forgive me!"[20]

Carried out in anticipation of the publication of the first facsimile of the manuscript by Paul Durrieu in 1904, is this intervention visible today?

Dismantling the leaves to take photographs meant reassembling them afterward. Although Macon did not dare to "sawbind" the parchment leaves—namely, to cut grooves to accommodate the sewing supports, as was customary in the twentieth century—he used hemp threads of a fairly fine diameter to resew the seams. However, these threads do not follow the relief left by the original bands on the spine leather, giving the latter a relatively smooth appearance. The boards are held together quite precariously with these threads, and the front board is in danger of coming loose. The back of the leaves was then consolidated in the traditional way, with several layers of green paper and brown basane leather. Far more surprisingly for the early twentieth century, this same leather was used to line the inside of the red morocco spine (fig. 10). This made it possible to avoid gluing the spine in full again, as had originally been the case, and the structure now functions as a broken spine, giving the leaves greater mobility (fig. 11). Finally, to replace the endbands of the Spinola binding, of which residues of pink and cream thread are visible between leaves 71 and 72, two industrially produced yellow and green endbands were put in place.

## 206 LEAVES AND 63 FULL-PAGE MINIATURES

### 28 Quires—Collation

Drawing on the collation carried out by Macon, Raymond Cazelles, curator of the Musée Condé between 1971 and 1983, counted a total of thirty-one quires, considering three unbound leaves as quires in their own right.[21] Our survey limits the total number of quires (mostly quaternions) to twenty-eight, the three leaves in question—25, 108, and 141—actually belonging to the corresponding quires. A total of twelve unbound leaves were counted among the most beautiful miniature pages (Earthly Paradise, Adoration of the Magi, etc.), a sign that these were designed separately.[22] They were all painted on the hair side of the parchment, the smoothest and most suitable for a delicate paint layer.[23] After being painted, these single leaves were assembled with the rest of the work, either by sewing or gluing. Quire eight, which contains no fewer than five single leaves, including three of the most beautiful miniatures in the manuscript (namely, the Purification of the Virgin, the Adoration of the Magi, and the Meeting of the Three Magi), shows that it was assembled by collage and is subject to the most significant deformations.

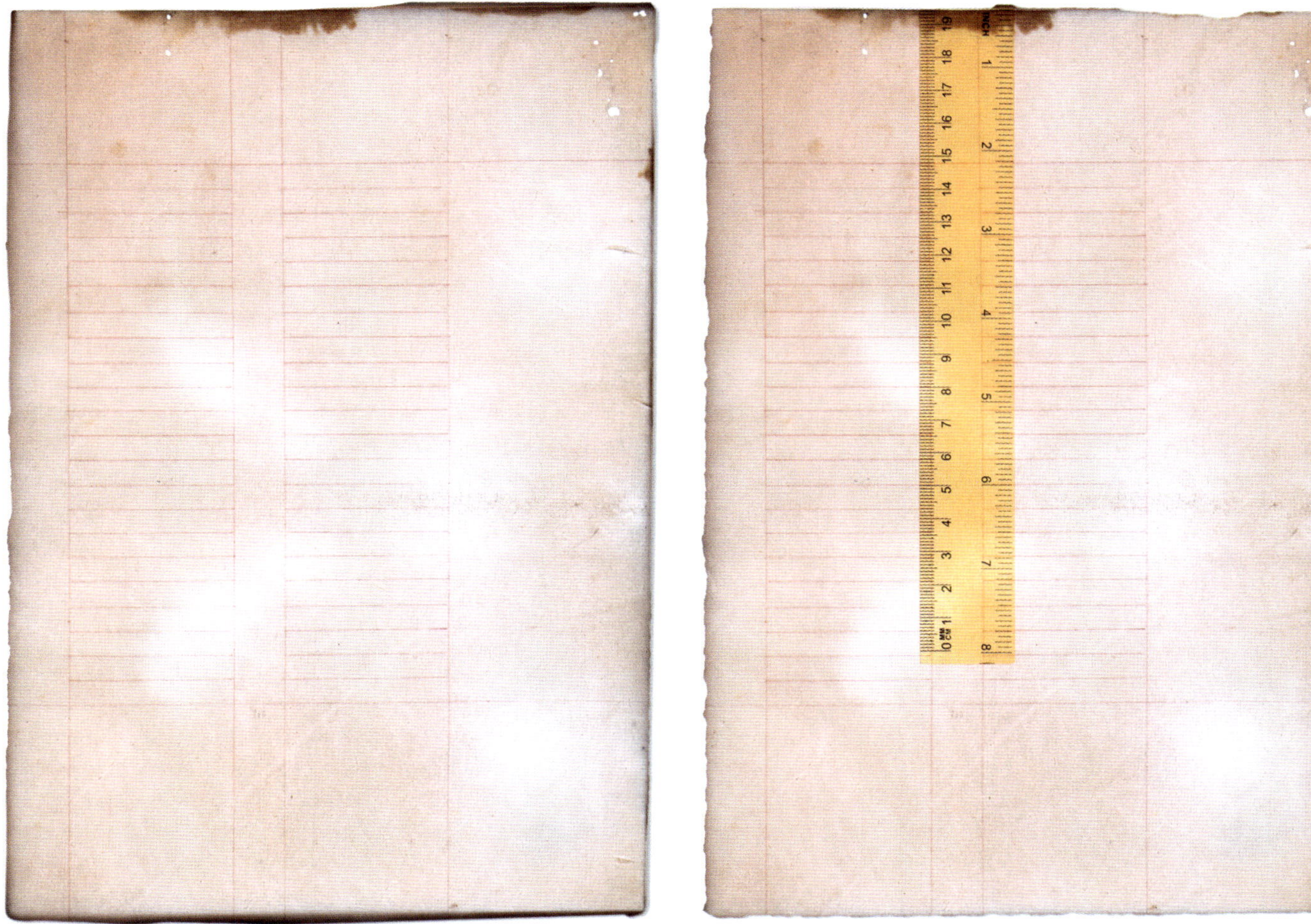

**Fig. 12** Leaves in transmitted light and estimation of space between the prominent pelvic bones

**206 Parchment Leaves**

The parchment support was examined leaf by leaf with the naked eye, using an LED lamp in direct and transmitted light. The vellum is of excellent quality, with a homogeneous structure and identical preparation on both sides (hair and flesh). Identification of the animal species is made difficult by the meticulous preparation of the parchment, which has been harmoniously sanded and primed, limiting observation of any hair follicles.[24] The thickness of the leaves varies from 0.1 mm to 0.2 mm. This is a low figure, which testifies to the importance of the work on the skin and the youth of the animals used to produce the leaves. This assertion is corroborated by the traces of skeletons visible on many leaves. In her article on the *Belles Heures*,[25] Margaret Lawson expressed surprise at the width of the animals' pelvises: between 5.7 cm and 10 cm. She assumed that, if it is a calf, it was a very small animal, even a fetus.[26] In the *Très Riches Heures*, several leaves feature the mark of the pelvis of the animals used, visible in transmitted light, particularly in the gutter. The distance between the two most prominent points of the animal's pelvis is estimated at around 10 cm, which is in line with the measurement taken by our colleague on the *Belles Heures* (fig. 12). Furthermore, unlike the *Belles Heures*, the parchment leaves of the *Très Riches Heures* were folded with the backbone perpendicular to the spine of the volume, resulting in greater deformations in the gutter.

**Some Interleaves . . .**

The use of *serpentes*, pieces of cloth or paper interleaved between the pages of a book to protect painted or printed images, is attested in medieval manuscripts intended for private devotion.[27] Although today's loose *serpentes* in Japanese paper were added in 2003,[28] traces of earlier *serpentes*, made of lightweight laid paper, can be found in the folds of quires, similar to the paper used for the *serpentes* traditionally found from the eighteenth century onward in books illustrated with drawings or prints. These *serpentes* may have been added by the author of the Spinola binding to protect the miniatures or to replace earlier textile *serpentes*, of which no trace remains, however.

**. . . and Sixty-Three Full-Page Miniatures**

The work consists of 206 handwritten leaves with a very regular script, copied in pen and ink, probably of a metallogallic nature, obtained from metallic salts (iron and copper sulfates) and tannins of vegetable origin, to which a binding medium was added, generally gum arabic. The text is copied on two columns with twenty-two ruled lines, visible thanks to marginal perforations and fine horizontal and vertical lines drawn with pen and red ink.

The body of the book is richly illustrated with miniatures painted by various artists: there are sixty-three large miniatures, four intermediate miniatures, and seventy-two small miniatures in the text columns.

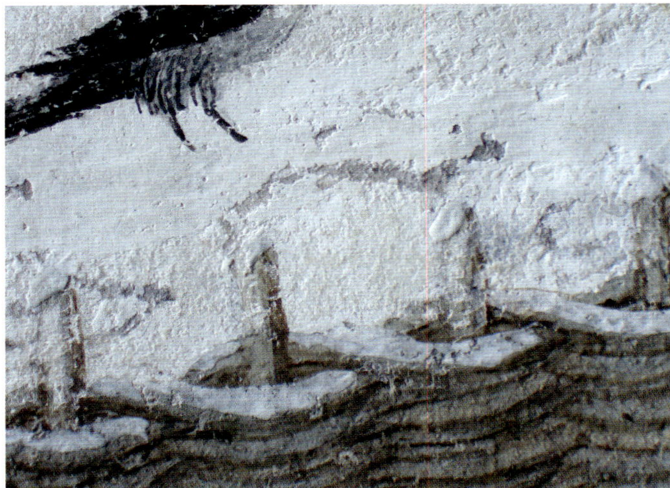

**Fig. 13** Observation under binocular loupe of the degradation of lead whites in the miniature of February

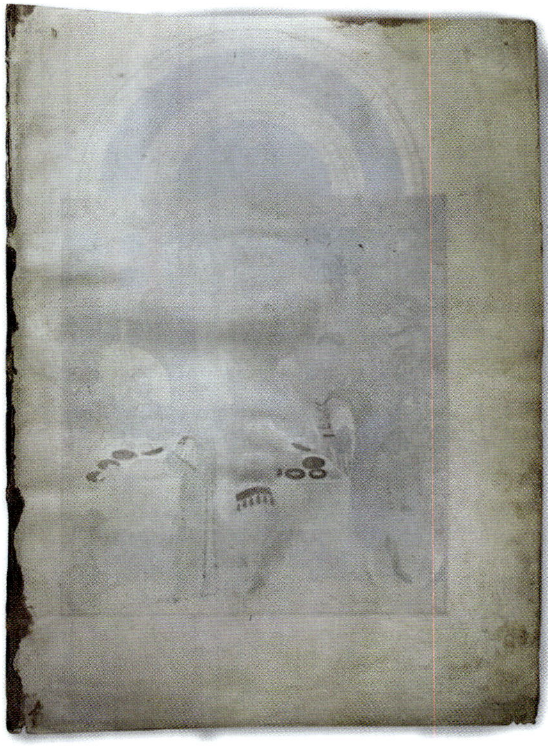

**Fig. 14** Degradation of the silver on the back of January, The Duke's Banquet

The paint layers were applied with brushes of varying widths, with thin, fluid strokes, as well as washes or glazes of varying transparency, depending on the area. In the fifteenth century, many pigments were available from apothecaries and merchants, and the palette used by the Van Lymborch brothers speaks for itself in this regard. Here, we briefly address the question of lead whites, widely used in a pure state to paint the clothes of figures or for the snow in the month of February (fol. 2v), or mixed with various colors to desaturate certain tones and obtain pinks, greens, yellows, light blues, etc. Lead white is a pigment frequently found in medieval manuscripts. Appreciated for its opacity and covering power, it is usually mixed with glair (egg white) or gum arabic. Its presence is usually easily identifiable, as it often forms a fragile layer that tends to crumble, crack, and flake, producing gaps in the paint layer. Unfortunately, the *Très Riches Heures* is no exception to this rule. Similarly, in the *Belles Heures*, there is a lack of cohesion between the pigment and the binding medium, and/or a lack of adhesion between the paint layer in which the lead white is present and the support.[29] This physico-chemical degradation (fig. 13) has yet to be fully explained. Binder dehydration could be one of the causes of the loss of cohesion. Another would be the thickness of the paint layer: A thick paint layer will not adapt well to bound parchment leaves, which are subject to variations in terms of dimensions as well as deformation and handling.[30]

The silver used to represent bodies of water and the glass found in buildings such as churches seem to be of the "shell" type, namely, obtained by grinding a sheet of silver mixed with a binding medium. Unfortunately, these layers are easily visible in direct light, due to the tarnishing resulting from their oxidation, but also in transparency on the reverse side of the leaves, in the form of dark spots that detract from the aesthetic appreciation of the miniatures. This deterioration is particularly noticeable on the verso of the manuscript's opening miniature, the month of January (fol. 1; fig. 14), depicting the banquet organized by the Duke of Berry, notably in the area of the silver tableware.

## THE PRESERVATION-RESTORATION PROJECT FOR THE *TRÈS RICHES HEURES*

The manuscript is in a precarious state of preservation, requiring a preservation-restoration treatment. Parchment, pictorial layers, silver, sewing: How do the constituent elements of this manuscript interact with each other? Do the Spinola binding or the restoration work carried out at the start of the twentieth century harm the preservation of the precious miniatures? How can we ensure their preservation, while allowing them to be put on temporary display?

## GENERAL DIAGNOSIS

The manuscript shows signs of use: The covers and spine are slightly abraded. All the leaves are very dusty and there are numerous fingerprints. Its dismantling at the start of the twentieth century also weakened it (fig. 15). The front cover, which risks coming loose, was not perfectly put back in place when

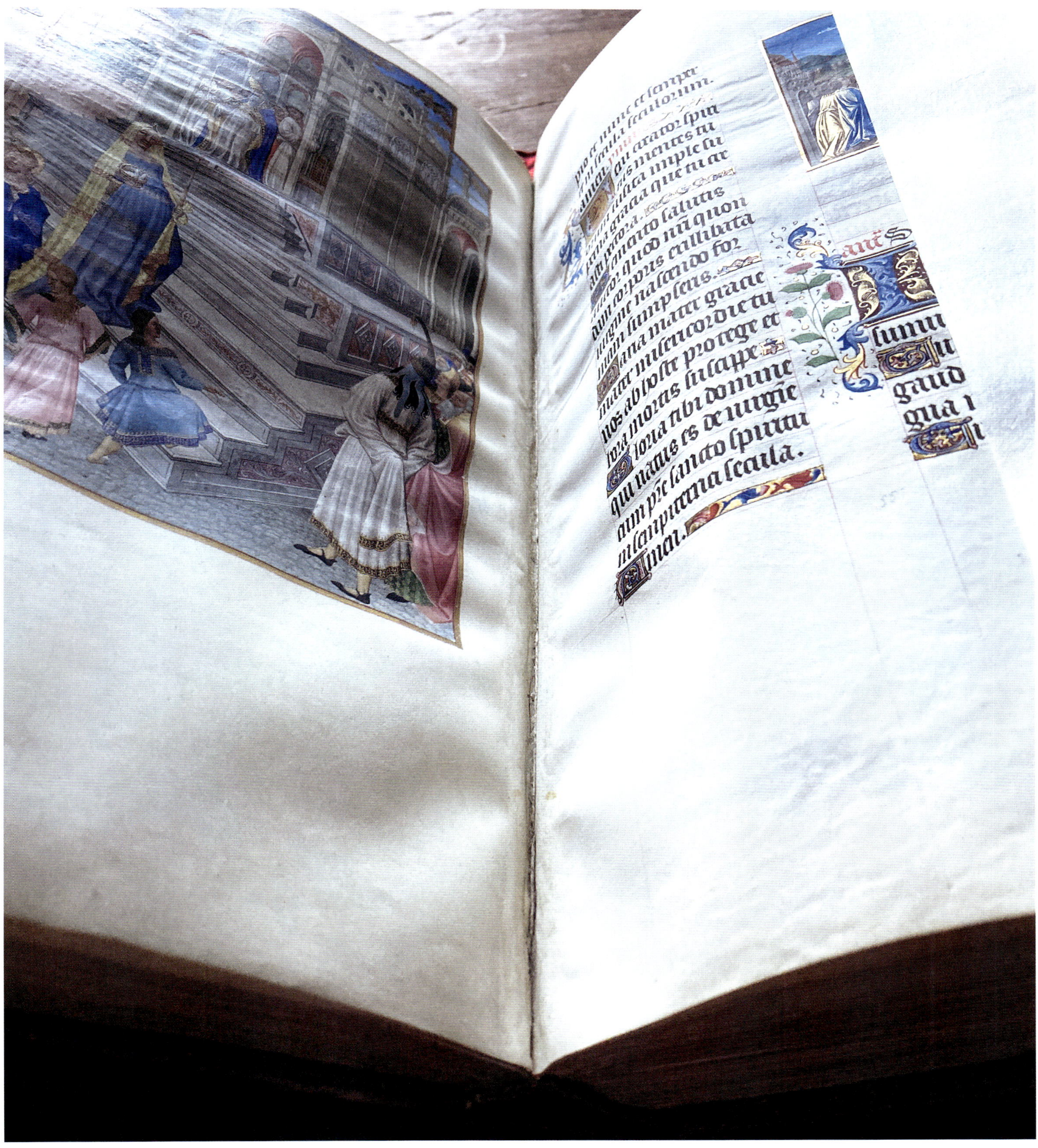

**Fig. 15** Deformation of fols. 54v and 55, The Purification of the Virgin

the body of the book was reinserted into the covers, and an extra thickness, due to the cardboard of the cover, is perceptible at the upper clasp. The spine of the binding is blackened in the center, probably as a result of the humidity made necessary by its temporary detachment. The sewing, redone using hemp threads, is quite tight, and the layer of adhesive that was applied to the spines of the quires to facilitate their cohesion has caused the inner margins of the parchment leaves to crinkle. Conversely, the disassembling of the morocco spine from the quires makes it easier to open the volume (figs. 10 and 11). The new sewing is still strong and holds all the sections together properly, with the exception of the first, which is in danger of coming loose. This loosening is accentuated by the fact that the bottoms of the first two bifolia show breaks, tears, and gaps linked to brown stains (fig. 16) whose nature, yet to be identified, could be tannic, coming from the wood or leather of an earlier binding.

The 206 leaves are made of parchment, a hygroscopic material whose dimensions vary with thermo-hygrometric (temperature and humidity) fluctuations. To limit this deformation, medieval bookbinders placed clasps on the covers; these exerted pressure and kept the leaves relatively flat. In fact, most illuminated manuscripts still in their original binding feature miniatures that are in a very good state of preservation. When paper replaced parchment, this habit was lost, and bookbinders simplified materials and techniques. Thus, the bookbinder responsible for making the new binding of the *Très Riches Heures* did not feel it necessary to add these protective elements. As a result, this medieval manuscript includes several relatively deformed leaves, the causes of which, in addition to the above, are manifold. The first is inherent to the material itself, a parchment made of more or less homogeneous collagen fibers (the fibers on the animal's spine being thicker and denser than those on the sides). In the case of the *Très Riches Heures*,

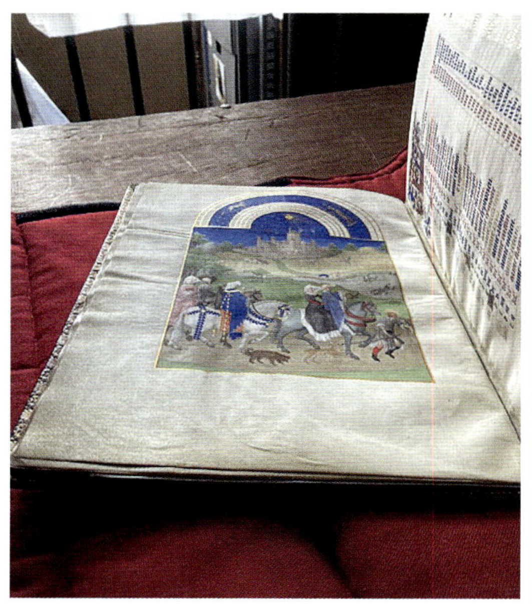
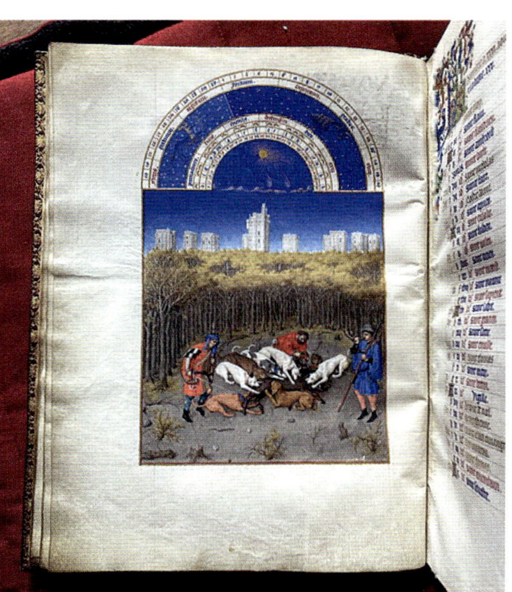
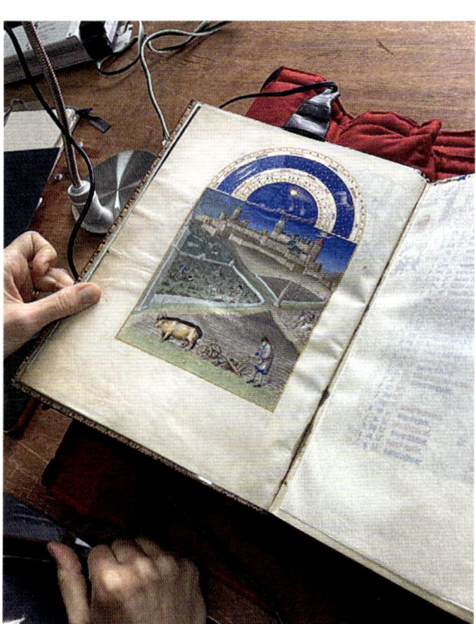
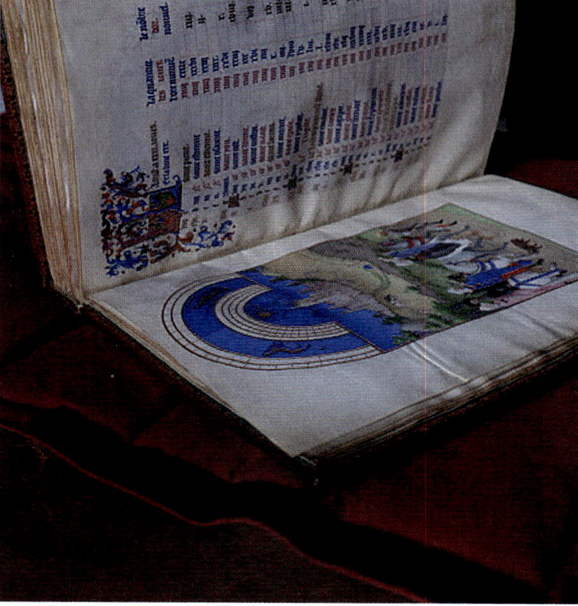
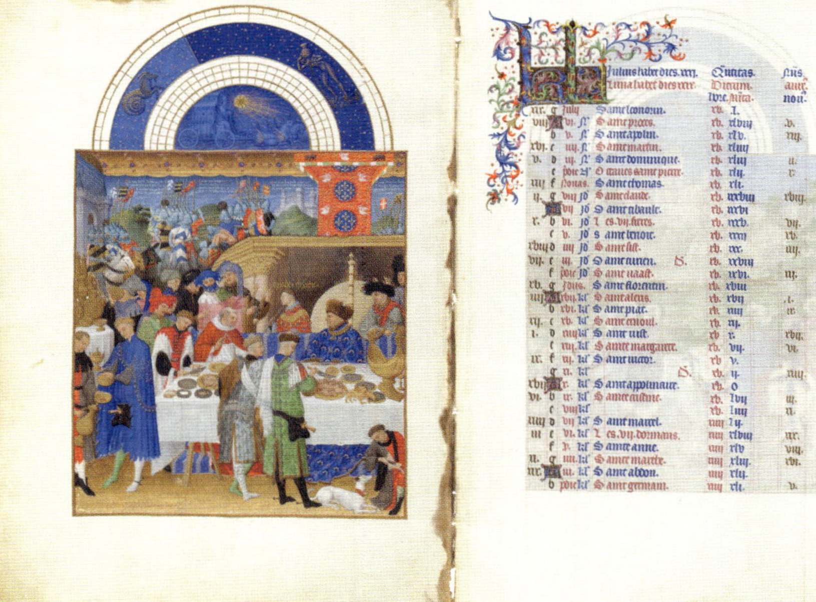

**Fig. 16** First quire of the manuscript, loose and showing large brown stains (Photo RMN)

the leaves are crossed perpendicularly by the spine. The most heterogeneous areas, namely the neck and lower edges, are located on the manuscript's outer margins, which show pronounced undulations. Conversely, the gutter should, in theory, be more homogeneous and therefore mechanically more stable. The history of this manuscript decided otherwise, and the deformation of this margin, often observed in medieval manuscripts, can here be attributed to the following operations:

- The three successive "bindings" or assemblies undergone by these leaves, in the form of seams and important moisture deposits due to the application of layers of adhesive.
- The assembly by gluing of independent leaves, carried out during the binding in the sixteenth century, and potentially performed again by the bookbinder in the eighteenth century, then by Gustave Macon.
- Successive additions and removals of tissue papers by gluing.

Once this diagnosis had been made, it was necessary to assess the impact of the parchment's undulations on the pictorial layers of the large miniatures. Indeed, a paint layer will be better preserved and will therefore adhere more to its support if the latter is flat and moderately deformed during consultation.

To do this, we estimated the amplitude ("thickness") and penetration ("length") of these undulations empirically, namely by using a ruler placed on the surface of the manuscript's gutters. The amplitudes of the undulations vary approximately between 1 mm and 4 mm, while their penetration varies between 3 cm and 6 cm, subsiding along the length. Since the margins of the miniatures range from 3 cm to 4.5 cm, we estimated that a range of 1 cm to 3 cm from the left or right edges of the miniatures is likely to be affected by these deformations. Moreover, these undulations, relatively pronounced at the beginning of the volume, diminish from folio 96 onward (that is, halfway through the work). In all, there are eight large miniatures for which the impact of these marginal undulations on the adhesion of the paint layer to the support has been deemed serious. These are the months of September and December and the Meeting of the Three Magi (fol. 51), as well as miniatures with little or no margins, namely Zodiacal Man (fol. 14), Terrestrial Paradise (fol. 25), the Procession of St. Gregory (fols. 71 and 72), Job on the Dung Hill (fol. 82), and the Funeral of Raymond Diocrès (fol. 86). No impact was deemed alarming. Similarly, the undulations visible on the outer margin, which are relatively pronounced on some leaves, have little impact on the pictorial layer at the left or right edges of the miniatures (fig. 17).

To complete this assessment, we carried out a rigorous examination of the pictorial layers of the miniatures, exposed for this purpose under a binocular loupe (fig. 18).[31] To do this, all the leaves, whether loose or bound, had to be properly fixed. A stainless steel plate, sheathed in new parchment, was used, along with a set of magnets whose interface was protected by alum-tanned skin. Weakened areas (chipped or flaked) were assessed for strength using a paper point,[32] following the method described by conservators Debora D. Mayer and Alan Puglia,[33] and a complete mapping of the state of conservation of each miniature tested was carried out.

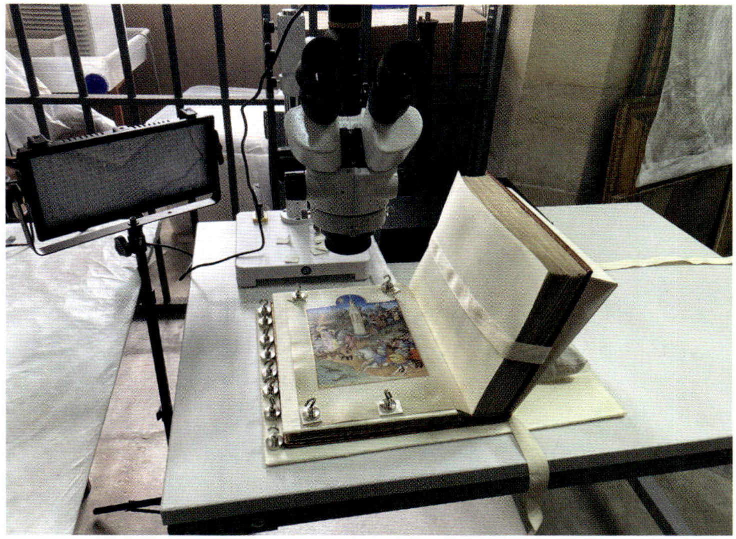

**Fig. 17** Diagram showing the amplitude and penetration of the undulations on the leaves

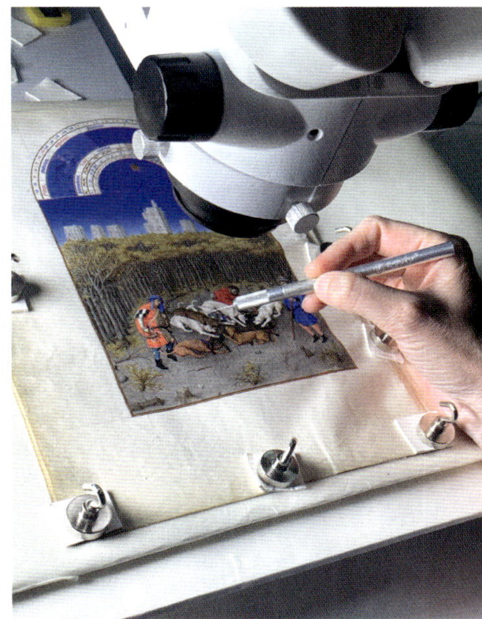

**Fig. 18** Setting up the manuscript for examination under binocular loupe

The paint layers tested show two main types of degradation: loss of internal cohesion (due to degradation of the binding medium) and loss of adhesion to the substrate.

While most layers generally adhere well to the parchment base, white presents cohesion and adhesion problems, both when used alone and when mixed. This is the case with the lighter shades of certain garments, such as green, pink, and yellow. This loss of cohesion and adhesion results in gaps, the edges of which are more or less stable: Some are stable, while others feature emerging flakes. Other gaps are caused by friction or abrasion.

In all, eleven of the fourteen miniatures observed to date have been judged to be in "very good" to "fairly good" condition. Only three miniatures are in "mediocre" or "poor" condition. These are, unsurprisingly, the month of February, due to the abundance of white, and the two miniatures facing each other, the Meeting of the Three Magi and Adoration of the Magi (fols. 51v–52), due to their use or handling and their being reassembled on parchment tabs.

While it cannot reasonably be asserted that the paint layers are free from brittleness caused by the undulations of their support or by their very nature, the total number of miniatures actually affected does not seem to warrant dismantling for treatment.

Do these miniatures merit separate treatment, or could we envisage treatment in situ, without dismantling the binding? How could the special status of the *Très Riches Heures* influence their preservation and presentation?

If, as Christopher de Hamel asserts, the book of hours is itself an "art museum," for which the museum would be a more appropriate location than the library,[34] it may be tempting to present it to the public as exhaustively as possible, as was done with the *Anjou Bible*, exhibited in Leuven in 2010,[35] or with the manuscript of the *Belles Heures* of the Duke of Berry, forty-seven double pages of which were exhibited between 2008 and 2010 in Los Angeles and New York, then in Paris in 2012.[36] Added to this temptation is the fact that, for obvious preservation reasons, but also for reasons tied to the duke's will (the manuscript cannot be loaned out), the *Très Riches Heures* has very rarely been exhibited.[37] However, it should be remembered that in the term "book of hours," there is of course "hours," but also "book," a word that designates both the container and the contents, as well as the different parts of the latter. In this respect, the approach of the Duke of Aumale, a well-informed bibliophile, deserves to be mentioned. Works whose bindings he considered uninteresting were given new bindings. Such a scrupulous bibliophile was always attentive to the provenance of his works, and the Spinola and Serra families added to the prestige of the manuscript. It is also worth pointing out that the forty miniatures cut from the *Book of Hours of Étienne Chevalier*, painted by Jean Fouquet, acquired by the duke in 1891 and now on permanent display at the Château de Chantilly, are pretty much an exception in his collection.

It is no doubt for all these reasons that he chose to present the *Très Riches Heures* in a case of burr walnut covered with a chased and embossed platin plate, made by Antoine Vechte, a renowned jeweler, which both protects and enhances the magnificence of this book of hours.

## CONCLUSION

From its first binding in the time of Margaret of Austria through its second binding with the Spinola arms to its dismantling in order to be photographed at the start of the twentieth century, the *Très Riches Heures* and its magnificent illuminated leaves have been subjected to a number of vicissitudes. The first leaves, detached and weakened by handling and showing significant brown stains, warranted urgent restoration work. In addition, the last sewing is tight and the layers of adhesive applied subsequently are quite generous. However, in view of the careful examination of the large miniatures, and the trauma that a third dismantling would represent, it has been considered more prudent, on a collegial basis, to carry out a restoration of the manuscript without dismantling it. Added to this is the fact that the binding, of prestigious provenance, would probably not have been reusable after the leaves had been treated and reassembled. Indeed, the leaves would certainly have increased in volume following the treatment in question, and the binding, already tight, would have struggled to accommodate such an increase in thickness.

In the case of the *Belles Heures* and the *Anjou Bible*, the question of the provenance of the bindings, both dating from the 1970s and of poor workmanship, enabled our colleagues in Leuven and New York to intervene in greater depth on the leaves, and allowed for an exhaustive display of the leaves. In the case of the *Très Riches Heures*, the historical and technical constraints mentioned here justified an intermediate intervention.

So, with the first quire already detached— and the second, which also requires consolidation—the whole calendar will be detached, consolidated, and displayed. The stabilization protocol, which will be carried out on an ad hoc basis in areas identified as unstable, is currently being drawn up. The protocol for the assembly of the calendar leaves within the display cases is also being studied. The structure of the bound work will be stabilized for the duration of the exhibition. At the end of the exhibition, the calendar leaves thus "revealed" will be returned to their original position inside the precious morocco binding bearing the Spinola-Serra arms.

1 Toulet 2001.
2 Durrieu 1904, 6.
3 Durrieu 1903, 328.
4 De Hamel 2016, 553.
5 Venice, Bibl. Marciana, cod. Lat I, 99. Durrieu 1903, 328.
6 Coilly 2001, 8.
7 Ferri and Jacquemard 2018, 72.
8 Ibid, 72. It should be noted that this case was replaced in 2022 by a preservation box and that it is now kept separately.
9 This central ornament was not struck from a single plate, as would soon be the case with mass-produced bindings, but was made with a series of small metal stamps. These include ornamental garlands in the Rococo style. Each cover features a fine gilded vegetal frame with a repeated motif of winding leaves and daisy-like flowers, framed by a double gold rim.
10 *Spinola Hours*, Los Angeles, Getty Museum, Ms. Ludwig IX 18 (83.ML.114).
11 De Hamel 2016, 561.
12 Ibid., 561.
13 The dimensions of the *Très Riches Heures* are 29 × 21 × 4.5 cm, while those of the *Spinola Hours* are 23.5 × 16.5 × 6.4 cm.
14 Chahine 2013, 235.
15 Petrucci Nardelli 1989, 50.
16 It is a spine with five raised bands, marked with thin golden hatchings; compartmentalized into six panels by a double gilt fillet, each marked at the center with a fleur-de-lis in the shape of a daisy, adorned with corner fleurons featuring scrolls of foliage and pinecones; golden dots and small daisies in the field. At the head, an ornate (floral) gilded palette, repeated upside down at the tail. The headbands are marked with golden hatchings. The hatching pattern found on the raised bands and headbands is also present on the edges of the binding, applied with gold using a roulette. The covers are adorned with a gold roulette, with a frieze featuring an alternating pattern of flowers and palmettes.
17 Petrucci Nardelli 1989, 47.
18 Zigzag endpapers with silk and leather (20th c.), American Institute for Conservation (AIC). "BPG Endpapers," https://www.conservation-wiki.com/wiki/BPG_Endpapers (accessed November 2, 2024).
19 We warmly thank Elizabeth Morrison and her collaborators for providing the necessary photographs and for discussing these manuscripts with them. We also thank Fabienne Le Bars, assistant director of the Réserve des livres rares, Bibliothèque nationale de France, for our discussions on this subject.
20 Macon 1926.
21 Cazelles 1988, 230.
22 These are leaves 25, 51, 52, 54, 55, 57, 64, 108, 141, 142, 143 and 198.
23 It should be noted that folios 25, 51, 64, 108, 141, 142, and 143 were painted on parchment with a slightly different appearance from the other leaves: although it is of similar thickness, it is stiffer, likely from older animals, and its surface has a more pearlescent finish.
24 We are leaning toward goat or lamb. A DNA analysis is underway.
25 *Belles Heures du Duc de Berry*, New York, MET, Ms 54.1.1.
26 Lawson 2012, 349.
27 Laffitte 2007.
28 Eve Menei's 2003 report on her intervention mentions the elimination of old tissue papers and the addition of new ones. We kindly thank Eve Menei for the information she provided.
29 Lawson 2012, 356.
30 Van Dyke 2015.
31 Euromex StereoBlue Zoom 7-45X trinocular loupe with remote stand.
32 VIDU paper point, diameter 0.25 mm.
33 Mayer and Puglia 2016.
34 De Hamel 2016, 513.
35 "The Anjou Bible – Naples 1340 – A Royal Manuscript Revealed" (Leuven 2010).
36 See Los Angeles and New York 2008–10, and Paris 2012.
37 The Duke of Aumale's bequest of his collections to the Institut de France, dated 1886, prohibits the manuscript from being exhibited anywhere other than the château of Chantilly. It was exhibited there in 1956 and then in 2004, in the château's chapel, as part of a series of exhibitions on the arts in France around 1400 (Ferri and Jacquemard 2018, 75).

**Fig. 21** Following pages: Van Lymborch brothers, *Très Riches Heures*, fol. 171: The Resurrection of Lazarus, detail

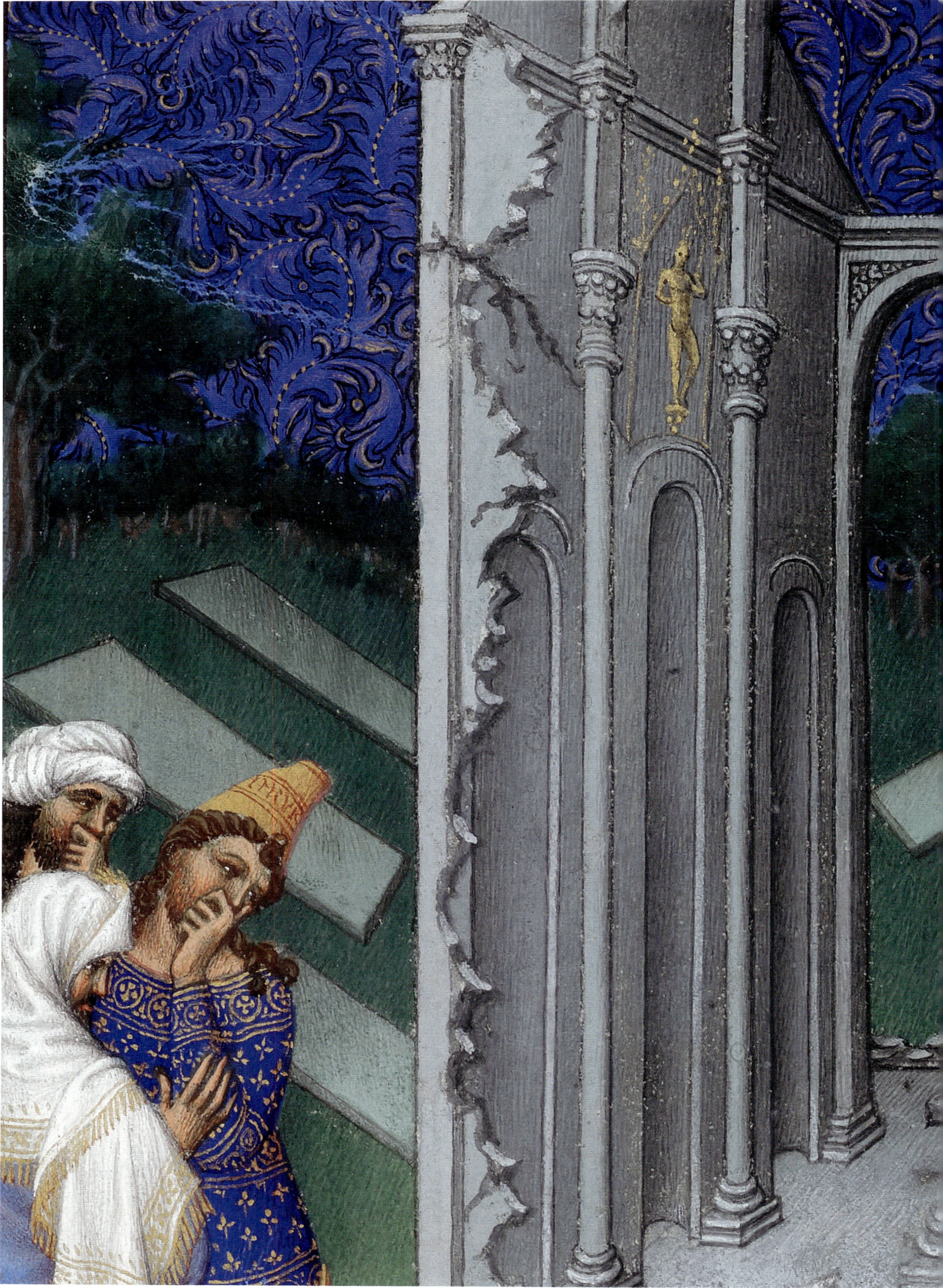

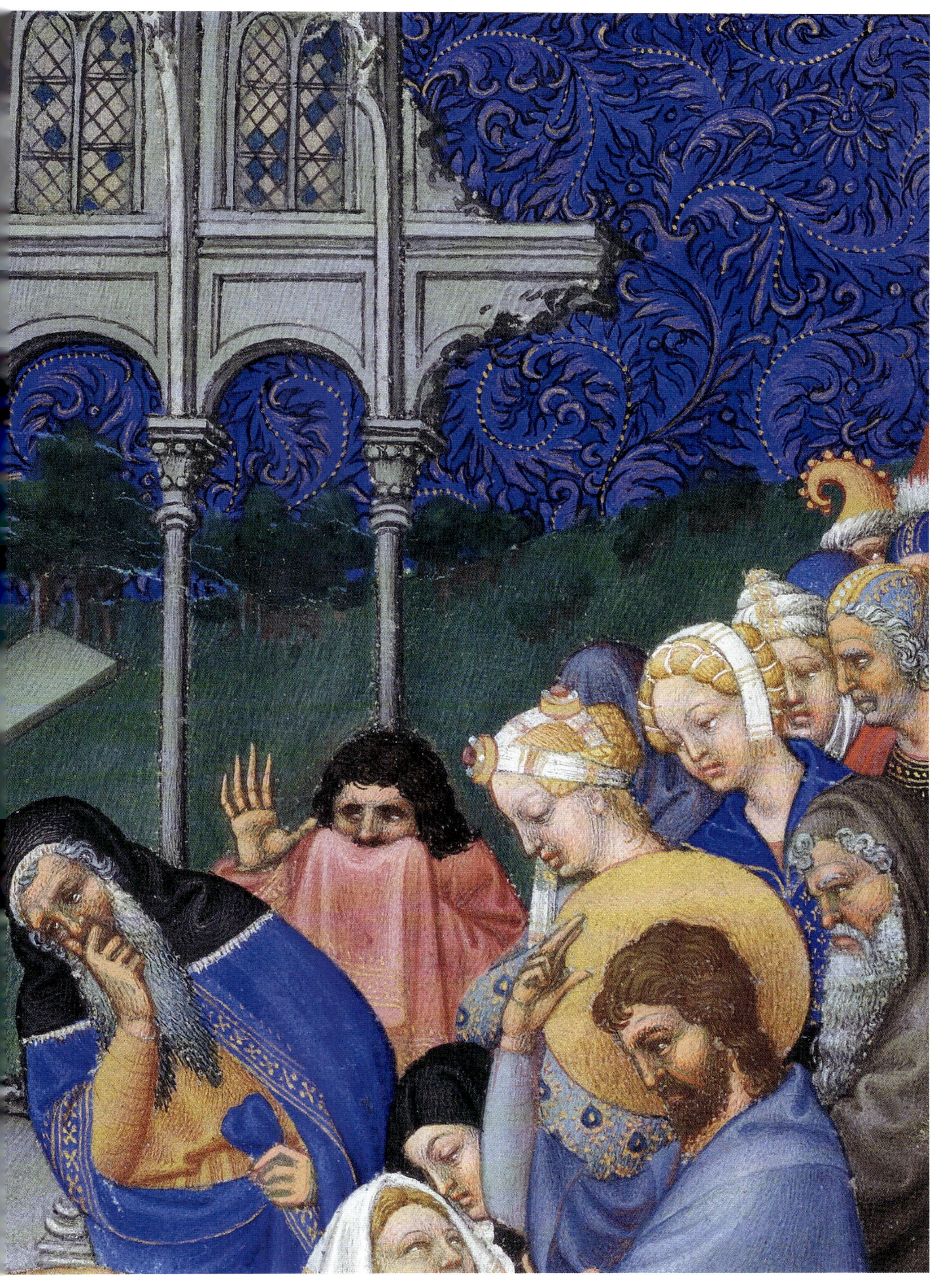

## BIBLIOGRAPHY


**ACF**
*Correspondance du duc d'Aumale et de Cuvillier-Fleury*, Paris, Plon-Nourrit, 1910–14, 4 vols.

**Ainsworth and Varvaro 2004**
Peter F. Ainsworth and Alberto Varvaro (eds.), *Jean Froissart. Chroniques, 2: livre III (du voyage en Béarn à la campagne de Gascogne) et livre IV (années 1389–1400)*, Paris, Le livre de poche, 2004.

**Airaksinen-Monier 2014**
Katja Airaksinen-Monier, *Vision and Devotion in Bourges Around 1500: An Illuminator and His World*, PhD diss., University of Edinburgh, 2014 [unpublished].

**Alcouffe 2023**
Daniel Alcouffe, "Le cristal de roche dans les collections royales françaises," in Paris 2023–24, 56–63.

**Angelini 2018**
Alessandro Angelini, "Sulla presenza di Barthélemy d'Eyck a Firenze. Continuazione di una conversazione con Dominique," in Michel Laclotte (ed.), *Regards sur les primitifs. Mélanges en l'honneur de Dominique Thiébaut*, Paris, Hazan and Louvre éditions, 2018, 30–35.

**Arbeteta Mira 2001**
Letizia Arbeteta Mira, *El tesoro del Delfín: alhajas de Felipe V recibidas por herencia de su padre Luis, Gran Delfín de Francia*, Madrid, Museo Nacional del Prado, 2001.

**Arletty 1971**
Arletty, *La Défense*, Paris, La Table Ronde, 1971.

**As-Vijvers 2013**
Anne Margreet As-Vijvers, *Re-Making the Margin: The Master of the David Scenes and Flemish Manuscript Painting around 1500*, Turnhout, Brepols, 2013.

**Aubert 2014**
Stéphanie Aubert, "Jean Golein et les Chroniques de Burgos," in *Histoire littéraire de la France*, 43/2, Paris, Boccard, 2014, 339–91.

**Aubert 2015**
Stéphanie Aubert, "Les Chroniques de Burgos, genèse d'une traduction à la cour de Charles V," in Joëlle Ducos and Michèle Goyens (eds.), *Traduire au XIVe siècle. Evrart de Conty et la vie intellectuelle à la cour de Charles V*, Paris, Champion, 2015, 313–26.

**Audebrand and Jourd'heuil 2025**
Fabienne Audebrand and Irène Jourd'heuil, "Un triptyque brodé offert par Jean de Berry au trésor de la cathédrale de Chartres," forthcoming, 2025.

**Aumale 1854**
Henri d'Orléans, Duke of Aumale, "Notes sur deux petites bibliothèques françaises du XVe siècle," in *Bibliographical and Historical Miscellanies [of the] Philobiblon Society*, 1, 1854, 1–64.

**Aumale 1900–11**
Henri d'Orléans, Duke of Aumale, *Chantilly. Institut de France. Musée Condé, Cabinet des livres. Manuscrits*, Paris, Plon, 1900–11, 3 vols.

**Autrand 2000**
Françoise Autrand, *Jean de Berry, L'art et le pouvoir*, Paris, Fayard, 2000.

**Autrand 2002**
Françoise Autrand, "Le Jour de l'an 1415 à la cour du duc de Berry," *Bulletin de la Société nationale des Antiquaires de France*, [1999] 2002, 275–88.

**Avril 1971**
François Avril, "Les Limbourg," in *Encyclopaedia Universalis. IX. Interférences – Liszt*, Paris, Encyclopaedia Universalis France, 1971, 1024–25.

**Avril 1975**
François Avril, "La peinture française au temps de Jean de Berry," *Revue de l'art*, 28, 1975, 40–52.

**Avril 1977**
François Avril, "Pour l'enluminure provençale. Enguerrand Quarton, peintre de manuscrits," *Revue de l'art*, 35, 1988, 9–40.

**Avril 1978**
François Avril, *L'Enluminure à la cour de France au XIVe siècle*, Paris, Chêne, 1978.

**Avril 1979**
François Avril, "Les Limbourg," in Michel Laclotte (ed.), *Petit Larousse de la Peinture*, Paris, Librairie Larousse, 1979, I, 1031.

**Avril 2023**
François Avril, "Un tableau perdu de Fouquet et ses répliques enluminées," *Art de l'enluminure*, 87, 2023, 8–45.

**Avril and Taburet-Delahaye 2004**
François Avril and Élisabeth Taburet-Delahaye, "Jean de Berry, bibliophile et amateur d'art," in Paris 2004b, 98–99.

**Avril, Reynaud, and Cordellier 2011**
François Avril, Nicole Reynaud, and Dominique Cordellier (eds.), *Les Enluminures du Louvre: Moyen Âge et Renaissance. Catalogue raisonné*, Paris, Hazan, 2011.

**Backhouse 2004**
Janet M. Backhouse, "The Psalter of Henri VI (London, BL, ms Cotton Dom. A. XVII)," in Frank Olaf Büttner (ed.), *The Illuminated Psalter: Studies in the Content, Purpose and Placement of its Images*, Turnhout, Brepols, 2004, 329–36.

**Barber 2003**
Nicolas Barber, "Henri d'Orléans, Duc d'Aumale: A French Bibliophile in England," in Antoine Caron (ed.), *Actes du XVIIe congrès de l'Association internationale de bibliophilie* (Paris, September 21–27, 1991), Paris, AIB, 2003, 127–48.

**Barrois 1830**
Joseph Barrois (ed.), *Bibliothèque protypographique, ou Librairies des fils du roi Jean, Charles V, Jean de Berri, Philippe de Bourgogne et les siens*, Paris, Crapelet, 1830.

**Barry et al. 2019**
Mélissa Barry et al., "Imitatio regis?," in Guyotjeannin and Mattéoni 2019, 21–35.

**Bartz 1999**
Gabriele Bartz, *Der Boucicaut-Meister, Ein unbekanntes Stundenbuch*, Ramsen, Heribert Tenschert, 1999 (Illuminationen. Studien und Monographien, 1; Katalog XLII).

**Bartz and Seidel 2011**
Gabriele Bartz and Christine Seidel, *Die Apokalypse der Herzöge von Savoyen*, Simbach am Inn, Anton Pfeiler, 2011.

**Baumeister 1984**
Annette Baumeister, "Illuminierte Handschriften im Besitz der Grafen und Herzöge von Jülich, Kleve und Berg," in Cleves and Düsseldorf 1984–85, 235–44.

**Bellaguet 1839–52**
[Michel Pintoin], *Chronique du religieux de Saint-Denys, contenant le règne de Charles VI de 1380 à 1422*, published in Latin for the first time and translated by M.L. Bellaguet, Paris, Impr. de Crapelet, 1839–52, 6 vols.

**Bellosi 1975**
Luciano Bellosi, "I Limbourg precursori di Van Eyck? Nuove osservazioni sui 'Mesi' di Chantilly," *Prospettiva*, 1, 1975, 23–34.

**Bengel and Dupeux 2019**
Sabine Bengel and Cécile Dupeux, *Dessins. Cathédrale de Strasbourg*, Strasbourg, Musées de Strasbourg, 2019.

**Berger 1884**
Samuel Berger, *La Bible française au moyen-âge. Étude sur les plus anciennes versions de la Bible écrites en langue d'oïl*, Paris, Imprimerie nationale, 1884.

**Beyer 2002**
Andrea Beyer, "Éclectisme des princes et des commanditaires: Naples et le Nord," in *Le Siècle de Van Eyck, 1430–1530. Le monde méditerranéen et les Primitifs flamands* (Bruges, Groeningemuseum, March 15–June 30, 2002), Ghent and Amsterdam, Ludion, 2002, 118–27.

**Bimbenet-Privat 2022**
Michèle Bimbenet-Privat, *Orfèvrerie de la Renaissance et des Temps modernes. XVIe, XVIIe et XVIIIe siècles. La collection du musée du Louvre*, Dijon, Faton, and Paris, Louvre éditions, 2022, 3 vols.

**Blanc-Riehl and Nielen 2019**
Clément Blanc-Riehl and Marie-Adélaïde Nielen, "Sigillum Iohannis filii regis et paris Francie," in Guyotjeannin and Mattéoni 2019, 59–83.

**Blanchet 1900**
Adrien Blanchet, *Les camées de Bourges*, Caen, H. Delesques, 1900.

**Boespflug and König 1998**
François Boespflug et Eberhard König, *Les "Très Belles Heures" de Jean de France, duc de Berry*, Paris, Les Éditions du Cerf, 1998.

**Bon 2011**
Philippe Bon (ed.), *Le Château et l'art: à la croisée des sources*, Mehun-sur-Yèvre, Groupe historique et archéologique de la région de Mehun-sur-Yèvre, 2011.

**Borchert 2019**
Till-Holger Borchert, "Pieter Bruegel the Elder and Book Illumination," in Alice Hoppe-Harnoncourt (ed.), *Pieter Bruegel the Elder: The Hand of the Master*, Veurne, Hannibal, 2019, 96–113.

**Borchert 2024**
Till-Holger Borchert, "Finding Michael: Tracing a Lost Image of an Archangel," *Colnaghi Studies Journal*, 14, 2024, 9–30.

**Bouquillard 2021**
Jocelyn Bouquillard, "Les fac-similés lithographiés d'enluminures publiés sous la Monarchie de Juillet par le comte Auguste de Bastard," *Histoire et civilisation du livre*, 17, November 2021, 111–25.

**Brix 2024**
Antoine Brix, *Devenir l'histoire de France: la fortune des "Grandes chroniques de France" au Moyen âge*, Paris, Éditions du Comité des travaux historiques et scientifiques, 2024.

**Broeckhuijsen 2002**
Klara H. Broeckhuijsen, "The Legend of the Grateful Dead: A Misinterpreted Miniature in the Très Riches Heures of Jean de Berry," in Bert Cardon, Jan Van der Stock, and Dominique Vanwijnsberghe (eds.), *"Als ich can," Liber Amicorum in Memory of Professor Dr. Maurits Smeyers*, Leuven, Uitgeverij Peeters, 2002, 212–30.

**Buettner 2001**
Brigitte Buettner, "Past's Presents: New Year's Gifts at the Valois Courts, ca. 1400," *The Art Bulletin*, 83, 2001, 598–625.

**Buettner 2004**
Brigitte Buettner, "Le système des objets dans le testament de Blanche de Navarre," *Clio*, online November 27, 2006, accessed January 25, 2025 [URL: http://journals.openedition.org/clio/644; DOI: https://doi.org/10.4000/clio.644].

**Bukowski 2018**
Beniamin M. Bukowski, *Les extraordinaires frères Limbourg*, Montpellier, Éditions Deuxième époque, 2018.

**Calkins 1981**
Robert G. Calkins, "An Italian in Paris: The Master of the Brussels Initials and His Participation in the French Book Industry," *Gesta*, 20, 1981, 223–32.

**Camille 1990**
Michael Camille, "The 'Très Riches Heures': An Illuminated Manuscript in the Age of Mechanical Reproduction," *Critical Inquiry*, 17, 1990, 72–107.

**Camille 2001**
Michael Camille, "'For Our Devotion and Pleasure': The Sexual Objects of Jean, Duc de Berry," *Art History*, 24, 2, April 2001, 169–94.

**Campbell 1981**
Lorne Campbell, "Notes on Netherlandish Painting in the Veneto in the 15th and 16th Centuries," *The Burlington Magazine*, vol. 123, no. 941, August 1981, 467–73.

**Campbell and Foister 1986**
Lorne Campbell and Susan Foister, "Gerard, Susanna and Lucas Horenbout," *The Burlington Magazine*, vol. 128, no. 1003, October 1986, 719–27.

**Camps 2018**
Rob Camps, "New Insights into the Maelwael Family in Nijmegen," in *Maelwael Van Lymborch Studies*, I, 2018, 149–59.

**Carné 1975**
Marcel Carné, *La Vie à belles dents: souvenirs*, Paris, J.-P. Ollivier, 1975.

**Cazelles 1988a**
Raymond Cazelles, *Les Très Riches Heures du duc de Berry*, foreword by Umberto Eco, Paris, Seghers, 1988.

**Cazelles 1988b**
Raymond Cazelles, "Problèmes soulevés par les Très Riches Heures," in Cazelles 1988a, 226–31.

**Cazelles 2013**
Raymond Cazelles, *Le duc d'Aumale, prince, chef de guerre, mécène*, Paris, Tallandier, 2013.

**Cazelles and Rathofer 1984**
Raymond Cazelles and Johannes Rathofer, *Les Très Riches Heures du Duc de Berry*, Lucerne, Faksimile Verlag, 1984.

**Cazelles and Rathofer 1988**
Raymond Cazelles and Johannes Rathofer, foreword by Umberto Eco, *Illuminations of Heaven and Earth: The Glories of the Très Riches Heures du Duc De Berry*, New York, Harry N. Abrams, 1988.

**Chahine 2013**
Claire Chahine, *Cuir et parchemin ou la métamorphose de la peau*, Paris, CNRS éditions, 2013.

**Champeaux and Gauchery 1894**
Alfred de Champeaux and Paul Gauchery, Les travaux d'art exécutés pour Jean de France duc de Berry avec une étude biographique sur les artistes employés par ce prince, Paris, H. Champion, 1894.

**Châtelet 1998**
Albert Châtelet, "Pour en finir avec Barthélemy d'Eyck," *Gazette des beaux-arts*, 131, May–June 1998, 199–220.

**Châtelet 1999**
Albert Châtelet, "Le tombeau d'un commensal du duc de Berry," in Fabienne Joubert and Dany Sandron (eds.), *Pierre, lumière, couleur. Études d'histoire de l'art du Moyen Âge en l'honneur d'Anne Prache*, Paris, Presses de l'Université Paris-Sorbonne, 1999, 405–11.

**Châtelet 2000**
Albert Châtelet, *L'Âge d'or du manuscrit à peintures en France au temps de Charles VI et les Heures du Maréchal Boucicaut*, Dijon, Faton, 2000.

**Châtelet 2008**
Albert Châtelet, "Les Heures de Dunois conservées à la British Library," *Art de l'enluminure*, 25, June–August 2008, 12–73.

**Châtelet 2010**
Albert Châtelet, *Les Très Riches Heures du duc de Berry*, *Art de l'enluminure*, special issue no. 1, 2010.

**Checa Cremades 2010**
Fernando Checa Cremades (ed.), *Los inventarios de Carlos V y la familia Imperial / The Inventories of Charles V and the Imperial Family*, vol. 3, Madrid, Villaverde, 2010, 2391–94, 2425–78.

**Cherry 2010**
John Cherry, *The Holy Thorn Reliquary*, London, British Museum Press (British Museum Objects in Focus), 2010.

**Clark 2003**
Gregory T. Clark, *The Spitz Master: A Parisian Book of Hours*, Los Angeles, J. Paul Getty Museum, 2003.

**Clark 2004**
Gregory T. Clark, "Le Maître des Heures Spitz, un artiste du cercle des Limbourg," *Art de l'enluminure*, 8, 2004, 32–60.

**Clark 2005**
Gregory T. Clark, "The Influence of the Limbourg Brothers in France and the Southern Netherlands, 1400–1460," in Nijmegen 2005, 208–35.

**Clark 2016**
Gregory T. Clark, *Art in a Time of War: The Master of the Morgan 453 and Manuscript Illumination in Paris during the English Eccupation (1419–1435)*, Toronto, Pontifical Institute of Mediaeval Studies, 2016.

**Clarke 2011**
Mark Clarke, *Mediaeval Painters' Materials and Techniques: The Montpellier Liber Diversarum Arcium*, London, Archetype Publications, 2011.

**Cohen et al. 2023**
Zina Cohen et al., "Black Inks under Examination: Part I and II," *Technè*, 55, 2023, 90–95, and 56, 105–13.

**Coilly 2001**
Nathalie Coilly, "La reliure d'étoffe à l'époque de Charles V: l'exemple de Jean de Berry (1340–1416)," *Bulletin du bibliophile*, 1, 2001, 7–35.

**Colenbrander 2006**
Herman Theodoor Colenbrander, *Op zoek naar de gebroeders Limburg: de Très Riches Heures in het Musée Condé in Chantilly, Het Wapenboek Gelre in de Koninklijke Bibliotheek Albert I in Brussel en Jan Maelwael en zijn neefjes Polequin, Jehannequin en Herman van Limburg*, PhD diss., University of Amsterdam, 2006, [s. l.], H. Th. Colenbrander, 2006.

**Courteault et al. 1979**
Henri Courteault et al. (eds.), *Les Chroniques du roi Charles VII par Gilles le Bouvier, dit le Héraut Berry*, Paris, Klincksieck, 1979.

**Dacos, Giuliano, and Pannuti 1980**
Nicole Dacos, Antonio Giuliano and Ulrico Pannuti, *Il tesoro di Lorenzo il Magnifico. Repertorio delle gemme e dei vasi*, Florence, Sansoni editore, 1980.

**De Bruijn Kops 2022**
David de Bruijn Kops, "Pseudo-Arabic Inscriptions in the Work of Claus Sluter, Johan Maelwael, Henry Bellechose, and the Van Lymborch Brothers during the Post-Nicopolis Reign of Philip the Bold and John the Fearless, 1398–1419," in *Maelwael Van Lymborch Studies*, II, 2022, 47–77.

**[De Hamel] 1999**
[Christopher De Hamel], *Book of Hours Illuminated by the Master of the Breviary of Jean sans Peur*, London, Sotheby's, 1999.

**De Hamel 2004**
Christopher De Hamel, *Les Rothschild collectionneurs de manuscrits*, Paris, Bibliothèque nationale de France, 2004 (Conférences Léopold Delisle).

**De Hamel 2016**
Christopher De Hamel, *Meetings with Remarkable Manuscripts*, London, Allen Lane, and New York, Penguin Books, 2016.

**Debae 1995**
Marguerite Debae, *La bibliothèque de Marguerite d'Autriche: essai de reconstitution d'après l'inventaire de 1523–1524*, Leuven and Paris, Peeters, 1995.

**Dehaisnes 1886**
C. Dehaisnes, *Documents et extraits divers concernant histoire de l'art dans la Flandre, l'Artois, et le Hainaut avant le XVe siècle*, I-II, Lille, 1886

**Dekeyzer 2004**
Brigitte Dekeyzer, *Layers of Illusion: The Mayer van den Bergh Breviary*, Ghent, Ludion, 2004.

**Deldicque 2024a**
Mathieu Deldicque, "La commande artistique de l'entourage de Charles le Bien Servi," in Paris 2024, 74–79.

**Deldicque 2024b**
Mathieu Deldicque, "La diffusion de l'Ars nova sous le règne de Charles VII," in Paris 2024, 204–07.

**Delisle 1868–81**
Léopold Delisle, *Le cabinet des Manuscrits de la Bibliothèque impériale nationale*, Paris, Imprimerie nationale, 1868–1881, 4 vols.

**Delisle 1884**
Léopold Delisle, "Les livres d'heures du duc de Berry," *Gazette des beaux-arts*, no. 29, 1884, 97–110, 281–92, 391–405.

**Delisle 1885**
Léopold Delisle (ed.), *Testament de Blanche de Navarre, reine de France, publié d'après les documents des archives des Basses-Pyrénées*, Paris, s. n., 1885 (Extrait des Mémoires de la Société de l'histoire de Paris et de l'Île-de-France, XII).

**Delisle 1905**
Léopold Delisle, *Chantilly. Le Cabinet des livres. Imprimés antérieurs au milieu du xvi^e^ siècle*, Paris, Plon-Nourrit, 1905.

**Delisle 1907**
Léopold Delisle, *Recherches sur la Librairie de Charles V*, Paris, H. Champion, 1907, 2 vols.

**Dion 2025**
Marie-Pierre Dion, "La reconstruction d'une bibliothèque princière au xix^e^ siècle: le Cabinet des livres du château de Chantilly," in *La Nef des livres : mélanges offerts à Frédéric Barbier*, Geneva, Droz, Paris, École Pratique des Hautes Études, 2025 [forthcoming].

***DLF* 1994**
Geneviève Hasenohr and Michel Zink (eds.), *Dictionnaire des lettres françaises. Le Moyen Âge*, new ed., Paris, Fayard, 1994.

**Dodgson 1935**
Campbell Dodgson, *The Vasari Society, Second Series*, XVI, Oxford, Oxford University Press, 1935.

**Dogaer 1967**
Georges Dogaer, "Petrus Gilberti, een vroeg-vijftiende-eeuws Frans verluchter," *Archives et Bibliothèques de Belgique*, vol. 38, 1967, 117–19.

**Dückers 2005**
Rob Dückers, "De gebroeders Van Limburg en de Noordelijke Nederlanden. Boekverluchting en paneelschilderkunst in het hertogdom Gelre en omstreken, circa 1380–1435," in Nijmegen 2005, 65–83.

**Dückers 2009**
Rob Dückers, "A Close Encounter? The Limbourg Brothers and Illumination in the Northern Netherlands in the First Half of the Fifteenth Century," in Dückers and Roelofs 2009, 149–89.

**Dückers 2017**
Rob Dückers, "Johan Maelwael en de boekverluchting in het Ile-de-France en in de Noordelijke Nederlanden," in Amsterdam 2017–18, 60–67.

**Dückers and Roelofs 2009**
Rob Dückers and Pieter Roelofs (eds.), *The Limbourg Brothers: Reflections on the Origins and the Legacy of three Illuminators from Nijmegen*, Leyde, Brill, 2009.

**Ducrocq 1942**
Pierre Ducrocq, "Les Visiteurs du soir," *L'Appel*, December 10, 1942.

**Dufour and Rabut 1870**
Auguste Dufour and François Rabut, "Les peintres et les peintures en Savoie du xiv^e^ au xix^e^ siècle," *Mémoires et documents publiés par la Société savoisienne d'histoire et d'archéologie*, XII, 1870, 3–304.

**Durrieu 1903**
Paul Durrieu, "Les Très Riches Heures du duc de Berry conservées à Chantilly, au Musée Condé, et le bréviaire Grimani," *Bibliothèque de l'École des Chartes*, vol. 64, 1903, 321–28.

**Durrieu 1904**
Paul Durrieu, *Les Très Riches Heures de Jean de France, duc de Berry*, Paris, Plon, 1904.

**Durrieu 1909**
Paul Durrieu, "Les petits chiens du duc de Berry," *Comptes rendus des séances de l'Académie des Inscriptions et Belles-Lettres*, 53, no. 9, 1909, 866–875.

**Eichberger 2002**
Dagmar Eichberger, *Leben mit Kunst. Wirken durch Kunst: Sammelwesen und Hofkunst unter Margarete von Österreich, Regentin der Niederlande*, Turnhout, Brepols, 2002.

**Eichberger 2018**
Dagmar Eichberger, "A Widow of Intellect and Artistic Discernment: Archduchess Margaret of Austria (1480–1530)," in Sabine Haag et al. (eds.), *Women: The Art of Power*, Vienna, KHM-Museumsverband, 2018, 25–35.

**Eisler 1995**
Colin Eisler (ed.), *The Prayer Book of Michelino da Besozzo*, New York, George Braziller Inc., 1995.

**Evans and Brinkmann 1995**
Mark L. Evans and Bodo Brinkmann, *Das Stundenbuch der Sforza – Kommentarband*, Lucerne, Faksimile Verlag, 1995.

**Farber 1993**
Allen S. Farber, "Considering a Marginal Master: The Work of an Early Fifteenth Century Parisian Manuscript Decorator," *Gesta*, vol. 32, 1993, 21–39.

**Favière 1996**
Jean Favière, "Histoires d'Orange: de Jean de Berry à Jacques Cœur," *Mélanges Jean-Yves Ribault, Cahiers d'archéologie et d'histoire du Berry*, November 1996, 149–53.

**Ferré 2009**
Rose-Marie Ferré, "Barthélemy d'Eyck," in Angers 2009–10, 123–31.

**Ferri 2020**
Laurent Ferri, "Un conservateur atypique à Chantilly: Philippe Pétain," in Florence Descamps, Frédéric Chappey, and Philippe Plagnieux (eds.), *Mélanges en l'honneur de Jean-Michel Leniaud: un bretteur au service du patrimoine*, Le Kremlin-Bicêtre, Mare & Martin, 2020, 617–34.

**Ferri and Jacquemard 2018**
Laurent Ferri and Hélène Jacquemard, *Les Très Riches Heures du Duc de Berry*, Paris, Skira, 2018.

**Flokstra and Jahn 2003**
Marinus Flokstra and Ralf G. Jahn, "Heraut Gelre, de rol van de middeleeuwse heraut en de Gelderse ridderschap in de 'Codex Gelre'," in Johannes Stinner and Karl-Heinz Tekath (eds.), *Het hertogdom Gelre*, Utrecht, Historischer Verein für Geldern und Umgebung, 2003, 315–22.

**Frezzato 1994**
Fabio Frezzato (ed.), *Cennino Cennini: Il libro dell'arte*, Vicenza, [s.n.], 1994.

**Frimmel 1886 [1974]**
Theodor Frimmel, *Der Anonimo Morelliano (Marcantonio Michiel's Notizia d'opera del disegno)*, Vienna, Graeser, 1886 [Hildesheim, Olms, 1974].

**Gaborit-Chopin 1978**
Danielle Gaborit-Chopin, *Elfenbeinkunst im Mittelalter*, Berlin, Mann, 1978.

**Gaborit-Chopin, Alcouffe, and Bardoz 2003**
Danielle Gaborit-Chopin, Daniel Alcouffe, and Marie-Cécile Bardoz, *Ivoires médiévaux, v^e^–xv^e^ siècle: catalogue, musée du Louvre, département des Objets d'art*, Paris, Réunion des musées nationaux, 2003.

**Gandilhon 1933**
René Gandilhon, *Inventaire des sceaux du Berry antérieurs à 1515, précédé d'une étude de sigillographie et de diplomatique*, Bourges, Impr. A. Tardy, 1933.

**Garnier 2023**
Nicole Garnier, "Le duc d'Aumale et le Risorgimento," in *Regarder l'Histoire en face: l'Italie au xix^e^ siècle au musée Condé* (Chantilly, Musée Condé, June 3–October 1, 2023), Baptiste Roelly (ed.), Dijon, Faton, and Chantilly, Château de Chantilly, 2023, 92–99.

**Gasiglia-Laster 1995**
Danièle Gasiglia-Laster, "*Les Visiteurs du soir. Une date peut en cacher une autre,*" *Cahiers de l'Association internationale des études françaises*, no. 47, 1995, 79–98.

**Gautier and Hermant 2024**
Marc-Édouard Gautier and Maxence Hermant, *Le livre des tournois du roi René illustré par Barthélemy d'Eyck*, *Art de l'enluminure*, 88, March–May 2024.

**Gibbs and Karczewska 2001**
Stephanie Viereck Gibbs and Kathryn Karczewska (eds.), René of Anjou, *The Book of the Love-Smitten Heart*, New York, Routledge, 2001.

**Giuliano 2003**
Antonio Giuliano (ed.), *Studi normanni e federiciani*, Rome, "L'Erma" di Bretschneider, 2003.

**Gnecchi 1912**
Francesco Gnecchi, *I Medaglioni Romani. II. Bronzo*, Milan, U. Hoepli, 1912.

**Gonzalez 2016**
Victor Gonzalez, *Caractérisation micro-structurale et luminescence des carbonates de plomb: apport à la discrimination des pigments blancs de plomb des œuvres peintes*, PhD diss., Université Pierre-et-Marie-Curie – Paris VI, 2016.

**Gonzalez et al. 2017**
Victor Gonzalez, Gilles Wallez, Thomas Calligaro, Marine Cotte, Wout de Nolf, Myriam Eveno, Élisabeth Ravaud, and Michel Menu, "Synchrotron-Based High Angle Resolution and High Lateral Resolution X-Ray Diffraction: Revealing Lead White Pigment Qualities in Old Masters Paintings," *Analytical Chemistry*, 2017 [DOI:https://doi.org/10.1021/acs.analchem.7b02949].

**Gorissen 1954**
Friedrich Gorissen, "Jan Maelwael und die Brüder Limburg. Eine Nimweger Künstlerfamilie um die Wende des 14. Jhs," Bijdragen en Mededelingen Gelre, 54, 1954, 153–221.

**Gorissen 1957**
Friedrich Gorissen, "Jan Maelwael, die Brüder Limburg und der Herold Gelre. Nachträge und Berichtigungen," Bijdragen en Mededelingen Gelre, 57, 1957, 166–78.

**Gras 2016**
Samuel Gras, *La vallée de la Loire à l'époque de Jean Fouquet: la carrière de trois enlumineurs actifs entre 1460 et 1480*, PhD diss., Université Charles de Gaulle – Lille III, 2016, 4 vols. [unpublished].

**Guenée 1992**
Bernard Guenée, *Un meurtre, une société. L'assassinat du duc d'Orléans, 23 novembre 1407*, Paris, Gallimard, 1992.

**Guenée 2004**
Bernard Guenée, *La folie de Charles VI, roi bien-aimé*, Paris, Perrin, 2004.

**Guérin 1893**
Paul Guérin, *Recueil des documents concernant le Poitou contenus dans les registres de la Chancellerie de France. VI. 1390–1403*, Poitiers, 1893.

**Guiffrey 1878**
Jules Guiffrey, "Peintres, ymagiers, verriers, maçons, enlumineurs, écrivains et libraires du XIVe et du XVe siècle," *Nouvelles archives de l'art français. Recueil de documents inédits publiés par la Société de l'histoire de l'art français*, Paris, J. Baur, 1878, 158–60, 167–68.

**Guiffrey 1894–96**
Jules Guiffrey (ed.), *Inventaires de Jean, duc de Berry (1401–1416)*, Paris, E. Leroux, 1894–96, 2 vols.

**Guillebert de Metz [1434] 1855**
Guillebert de Metz, *Description de la ville de Paris au XVe siècle*, Paris, Auguste Aubry, 1855 [manuscript Le Roux de Lincy, 1434].

**Guineau and Villela-Petit 2002**
Bernard Guineau and Inès Villela-Petit, "Couleurs et technique picturale du Maître de Boucicaut," *Revue de l'art*, 135, 2002, 23–42.

**Guineau and Villela-Petit 2003**
Bernard Guineau and Inès Villela-Petit, "Le Maître de Boucicaut revisité: palette et technique d'un enlumineur parisien au début du XVe siècle," *Art de l'enluminure*, 6, 2003, 3–33.

**Guyotjeannin and Mattéoni 2019**
Olivier Guyotjeannin and Olivier Mattéoni (eds.), *Jean de Berry et l'écrit: les pratiques documentaires d'un fils de roi de France*, Paris, Éditions de la Sorbonne, Publications de l'École nationale des Chartes, 2019.

**Hablot 2000**
Laurent Hablot, "La 'mise en signes' du livre princier à la fin du Moyen Âge. Emblématique, histoire politique et codicologie," *Gazette du livre médiéval*, vol. 36, 2000, 25–35.

**Hablot 2018**
Laurent Hablot, "The Van Lymborch Brothers: Heraldic Painters? The Role of Heraldic and Emblematic Motifs in the Art of the Van Lymborch Brothers," in *Maelwael Van Lymborch Studies*, I, 2018, 112–29.

**Hahnloser and Brugger-Koch 1985**
Hans R. Hahnloser and Susanne Brugger-Koch, *Corpus des Hartsteinschliffe des 12.–15 Jahrhunderts*, Berlin, Deutscher Verlag für Kunstwissenschaft, 1985.

**Hansen 1984**
Wilhelm Hansen, *Kalenderminiaturen der Stundenbücher. Mittelalterliches Leben im Jahreslauf*, Munich, Callwey, 1984.

**Hedeman 1991**
Anne D. Hedeman, *The Royal Image: Illustration of the Grandes Chroniques de France, 1274–1422*, Berkeley, Los Angeles, and Oxford, University of California Press, 1991.

**Hedeman 2011**
Anne D. Hedeman, "Advising France Through the Example of England: Visual Narrative in the *Livre de la prinse et mort du roy Richart* (Harl. MS. 1319)," *Journal électronique de la British Library*, London, 2011.

**Hedeman 2022**
Anne D. Hedeman, *Visual Translation: Illuminated Manuscripts and the First French Humanists*, Notre Dame, University of Notre Dame Press, 2022.

**Henryot 2022**
Fabienne Henryot, *De l'oratoire privé à la bibliothèque publique. L'autre histoire des livres d'heures*, Turnhout, Brepols, 2022.

**Hermant 2022**
Maxence Hermant, "Les princes de Condé et leurs manuscrits: collections, confiscations révolutionnaires et restitutions," *Le Musée Condé*, 79, 2022, 4–10.

**Hirschbiegel 2003**
Jan Hirschbiegel, *Étrennes. Untersuchungen zum höfischen Geschenkverkehr im spätmittelalterlichen Frankreich der Zeit König Karls VI. (1380–1422)*, Munich, Oldenbourg, 2003.

**Hofmann 2007**
Mara Hofmann, "Haincelin de Haguenau et l'acanthe à Paris," in Hofman, König, and Zöhl 2007, 99–109.

**Hofmann 2014**
Mara Hofmann, "La décoration secondaire dans les manuscrits français: Paris entre 1380 et 1420–1430," in Claudia Rabel (ed.), *Le manuscrit enluminé. Études réunies en hommage à Patricia Stirnemann*, Paris, Le Léopard d'or, 2014, 75–99.

**Hofmann, König, and Zöhl 2007**
Mara Hofmann, Eberhard König, and Caroline Zöhl (eds.), *Quand la peinture était dans les livres. Mélanges en l'honneur de François Avril*, Turnhout, Brepols/Paris, Bibliothèque nationale de France, 2007 (Ars Nova, 15).

**Howard and Najorka 2017**
Helen Howard and Jens Najorka, "An Unusual Gilding Technique on Two Panels by Pietro Lorenzetti," in Janet Bridgland (ed.), *ICOM-CC 18th Triennial Conference Preprints, Copenhagen, 4–8 September 2017*, Paris, International Council of Museums, 2017, art. 1307.

**Hulin de Loo 1903**
Georges Hulin de Loo, "Les Très Riches Heures de Jean de France, duc de Berry, par Pol de Limbourc et ses frères," *Bulletin de la Société d'histoire et d'archéologie de Gand*, 11, 1903, 178–204.

**Husband 2008**
Timothy B. Husband, *The Art of Illumination: The Limbourg Brothers and the "Belles Heures" of Jean de France, Duc de Berry*, New York and New Haven, Yale University Press, 2008.

**Husband 2012a**
Timothy B. Husband, "Les frères de Limbourg," in Paris 2012, 21–37.

**Husband 2012b**
Timothy B. Husband, "Sources et influences," in Paris 2012, 39–79.

**Inglis 2011**
Erik Inglis, *Jean Fouquet and the Invention of France: Art and Nation after the Hundred Years War*, New Haven, Yale University Press, 2011.

**Jacob 2012**
Marie Jacob, *Dans l'atelier des Colombe (Bourges 1470–1500). La représentation de l'Antiquité en France à la fin du XVe siècle*, Rennes, Presses universitaires de Rennes, 2012.

**Jacob 2013**
Marie Jacob, "Jean Colombe," in Stirnemann and Villela-Petit 2013, 152–70.

**Jacquemard 2021**
Hélène Jacquemard, "Les manuscrits enluminés de la collection du duc d'Aumale: l'héritage et le goût," *Histoire et civilisation du livre*, 17, November 2021, 173–84.

**Jarry 1890**
Louis Jarry, *Testaments, inventaire et compte des obsèques de Jean, bâtard d'Orléans*, Orléans, H. Herluison, 1890.

**Jeannot 2012**
Delphine Jeannot, *Le mécénat bibliophilique de Jean sans Peur et de Marguerite de Bavière (1404–1424)*, Turnhout, Brepols, 2012.

**Ker 1983**
Neil Ripley Ker, *Medieval Manuscripts in British Libraries*, Lampeter and Oxford, Clarendon Press, 1983.

**Kolokytha 2014**
Chara Kolokytha, "'L'amour de l'art en France est toujours aussi fécond': la Maison d'éditions Verve et la reproduction de manuscrits à peintures conservés dans les Bibliothèques de France pendant les années noires (1939–1944)," *French Cultural Studies 2*, 25, 2014, 121–139.

**König 1976**
Eberhard König, "Un grand miniaturiste inconnu du XVe siècle français: le peintre de l'Octobre des 'Très Riches Heures du duc de Berry'," *Les Dossiers de l'archéologie*, 16, May–June 1976, 96–123.

**König 1991**
Eberhard König, *Les Heures de Marguerite d'Orléans*, Paris, Les Éditions du Cerf, 1991.

**König 1996**
Eberhard König, *Das liebentbrannte Herz: Der Wiener Codex und der Maler Barthélemy d'Eyck*, Graz, Akademische Druck- und Verlagsanstalt, 1996.

**König 2003a**
Eberhard König, *Les Belles Heures du Duc de Berry, Acc. No. 54.1.1, Metropolitan Museum of Art, The Cloisters Collection, New York*, Lucerne, Faksimile Verlag, 2003.

**König 2003b**
Eberhard König, *Les Belles Heures du Duc de Berry. Begleitband zur Faksimile-Edition*, Lucerne, Faksimile Verlag, 2003.

**König 2006**
Eberhard König, "Innovation et tradition dans les livres d'heures du duc de Berry," in Taburet-Delahaye 2006, 25–44.

**König 2007**
Eberhard König, *The Bedford Hours: The Making of a Medieval Masterpiece*, London, British Library, 2007.

**König 2016**
Eberhard König, *Das Genie der Zeichnung. Ein unbekanntes Manuskript mit 30 großen Darstellungen von einem der Brüder Limburg*, Ramsen, Antiquariat Bibermühle, Heribert Tenschert, 2016.

**König 2018**
Eberhard König, "The Master of St. Jerome: One of the Van Lymborch Brothers," in *Maelwael Van Lymborch Studies*, I, 2018, 41–63.

**König and Heyder 2016**
Eberhard König and Joris Corin Heyder (eds.), *Das Breviarium Grimani*, Simbach am Inn, Buchhandlung Anton Pfeiler Junior, 2016.

**Korteweg 2005**
Anne S. Korteweg, "The Form and Content of Jean de Berry's Books of Hours," in Nijmegen 2005, 135–41.

**Kovács 2004**
Éva Kovács, *L'Âge d'or de l'orfèvrerie parisienne au temps des premiers Valois*, Dijon, Faton, 2004.

**Kren 1988**
Thomas Kren, "Simon Bening et le développement de la peinture de paysage dans l'enluminure flamande," in Kren and Rathofer 1988, 349–401.

**Kren and Rathofer 1988**
*Simon Bening: Flämischer Kalender – Flemish Calendar – Calendrier flamand. Clm 23638, Bayerische Staatsbibliothek, München. Kommentar – Commentary – Commentaire: Thomas Kren et Johannes Rathofer*, Lucerne, Faksimile Verlag, 1988.

**Krieger 2012**
Michaele Krieger, *Gerard Horenbout und der Meister Jakobs IV. von Schottland: Stilkritische Überlegungen zur flämischen Buchmalerei*, Vienna, Böhlau, 2012.

**Laborde 1872**
Léon de Laborde, *Glossaire français du Moyen Âge à l'usage de l'archéologue et de l'amateur des arts*, Paris, A. Labitte, 1872.

**Laffitte 2007**
Marie-Pierre Laffitte, "Quelques exemples de serpentes anciennes dans les manuscrits à peintures," in Hofmann, König, and Zöhl 2007, 139–44.

**Lasko 1962**
Peter Lasko, "The Thorn Reliquary," *Apollo*, 76, 2, 1962, 258–64.

**Lawson 2005**
Margaret Lawson, "The 'Belles Heures' of Jean, Duc de Berry: The Materials and Techniques of the Limbourg Brothers," in Nijmegen 2005, 148–63.

**Lawson 2008**
Margaret Lawson, "Technical Observations: Materials, Techniques, and Conservation of the 'Belles Heures' Manuscript," in Los Angeles and New York 2008–10, 325–41.

**Lawson 2012**
Margaret Lawson, "Observations techniques sur le manuscrit des 'Belles Heures'. Matières, procédés de fabrication et mesures de conservation," in Paris 2012, 346–62.

**Lebailly 2005**
Émilie Lebailly, "Le dauphin Louis, duc de Guyenne, et les arts précieux," *Bulletin monumental*, vol. 163–4, 2005, 357–74.

**Lebigue 2014**
Jean-Baptiste Lebigue, "Jean de Berry à l'heure de l'Union. Les *Très Riches Heures* et la réforme du calendrier à la fin du Grand Schisme," in Christine Barralis et al. (eds.), *Église et État, Église ou État? Les clercs et la genèse de l'État moderne*, Paris, Éditions de la Sorbonne/Rome, Publications de l'École française de Rome, 2014, 367–89.

**Legaré 2005**
Anne-Marie Legaré, "'La librairye de Madame': Twee prinsessen en hun bibliotheken," in Dagmar Eichberg (ed.), *Dames met klasse: Margareta van York/Margareta van Oostenrijk*, Leuven, Davidsfonds, 2005, 207–19.

**Lehoux 1956a**
Françoise Lehoux, "Mort et funérailles de Jean de Berry (June 1416)," *Bibliothèque de l'École des Chartes*, vol. 114, 1956, 76–96.

**Lehoux 1956b**
Françoise Lehoux, "Le duc de Berri, les juifs et les Lombards," *Revue historique*, vol. 215, 1, 1956, 38–57.

**Lehoux 1966–68**
Françoise Lehoux, *Jean de France, duc de Berri, sa vie, son action politique (1340–1416)*, Paris, A. et J. Picard, 1966–68, 4 vols.

**Lemmens 2005a**
Gerard Lemmens, "Nijmegen During the Limbourgs' Youth, 1380–1400," in Nijmegen 2005, 28–33.

**Lemmens 2005b**
Gerard Lemmens, "Architectuur en beeldende kunst in de Middeleeuwen," in Jan Kuys and Hans Bots (eds.), *Nijmegen. Geschiedenis van de oudste stad van Nederland*, Wormer, Immerc, 2005, II, 200–25.

**Letort 2022**
Ella Letort, "Plagues and Processions: Re-Examining the Drawings of Ms. Douce 144," in *Maelwael Van Lymborch Studies*, II, 2022, 160–79.

**Lewis 1987**
Paul Lewis, "Preservation Takes Rare Manuscripts from the Public," *New York Times*, January 25, 1987.

**Longnon and Cazelles 1969a**
*Les Très Riches Heures du duc de Berry, Musée Condé, Chantilly*, foreword by Charles Samaran, introduction and captions by Jean Longnon and Raymond Cazelles, Vilo, 1969.

**Longnon and Cazelles 1969b**
*The Très Riches Heures of Jean, Duke of Berry, Musée Condé, Chantilly*, foreword by Millard Meiss, introduction and captions by Jean Longnon and Raymond Cazelles, trans. from the French by Victoria Benedict, New York, Braziller, 1969.

**Lorentz 2004a**
Philippe Lorentz, "Jean Malouel et les frères de Limbourg," in Paris 2004b, 292–93.

**Lorentz 2004b**
Philippe Lorentz, "Les carnets de dessins, 'laboratoires' de la création artistique," in Paris 2004b, 304–06.

**Macon 1926**
Gustave Macon, "Les trésors des bibliothèques françaises: la bibliothèque de Chantilly," *Bulletin du bibliophile et du bibliothécaire*, January 1926, 68–69.

***Maelwael Van Lymborch Studies*, I, 2018**
*Maelwael Van Lymborch Studies*, I, Johan Oosterman and Jos Koldeweij (eds.), Turnhout, Brepols, 2018.

***Maelwael Van Lymborch Studies*, II, 2022**
*Maelwael Van Lymborch Studies*, II, André Stufkens (ed.), Turnhout, Brepols, 2022.

**Malgouyres 2022**
Philippe Malgouyres, *Camées et intailles. L'art des pierres gravées*, Paris, Gallimard, 2022.

**Malgouyres 2023a**
Philippe Malgouyres, "La Renaissance, l'âge de cristal," in Paris 2023–24, 244–57.

**Malgouyres 2023b**
Philippe Malgouyres, "À propos des camées antiques des collections de Charles V et de Jean, duc de Berry," *Bulletin de la Société nationale des Antiquaires de France*, 2023 (session of October 25).

**Malgouyres [forthcoming]**
Philippe Malgouyres "Camées gothiques: quelques fausses antiquités dans la collection de Jean, duc de Berry (1340–1416)," *Gemmae* [forthcoming].

**Manion [1991] 2020**
Margaret M. Manion, "Art and Devotion: The Prayer-books of Jean de Berry," in Margaret M. Manion and Bernard J. Muir (eds.), *Medieval Texts and Images: Studies of Manuscripts from the Middle Ages*, London and New York, Routledge, 2020 [1991], 177–200.

**Manion 1995**
Margaret M. Manion, "Psalter illustration in the 'Très Riches Heures' of Jean de Berry," *Gesta*, XXXIV-2, 1995, 147–61.

**Marette 1961**
Jacqueline Marette, *Connaissance des primitifs par l'étude du bois, du* xii*e au* xvi*e siècle*, Paris, Éditions A. et J. Picard, 1961.

**Marrow 1985**
James H. Marrow, "Miniatures inédites de Jean Fouquet: Les Heures de Simon de Varie," *Revue de l'art*, 67, 1985, 3–28.

**Mattéoni 2022**
Olivier Mattéoni (ed.), *Les Bourbons en leur bibliothèque (*xiii*e–*xiv*e siècle)*, Paris, Éditions de la Sorbonne, 2022.

**Mayer and Puglia 2016**
Debora D. Mayer and A. Puglia, "The Challenge of Scale: Treatment of 160 Illuminated Manuscripts for Exhibition," *The Book and Paper Group Annual*, 35, 2016, 61–69.

**Mazzone 2018**
Marie Mazzone, "Le Maître du Romuleon: Philibert Colombe?," in Frédéric Elsig (ed.), *Peindre à Bourges aux* xv*e–*xvi*e siècles*, Cinisello Balsamo (Milan), Silvana editoriale, 2018, 115–25.

**McKitterick 2019**
David McKitterick, *The Philobiblon Society: Sociability & Book Collecting in Mid-Victorian Britain*, London, The Roxburghe Club, 2019.

**Medica 2010–11**
Massimo Medica, "Un nome per il 'Maestro delle Iniziali di Bruxelles': Giovanni di fra' Silvestro," *Arte a Bologna, Bollettino dei Musei Civici d'Arte Antica*, vols. 7–8, 2010–11, 11–22.

**Medica 2012**
Massimo Medica, "Un précieux missel bolonais de l'époque du Grand Schisme. Los Angeles, Musée J. Paul Getty, ms. 71," *Art de l'enluminure*, 41, 2012, 2–71.

**Meiss 1956**
Millard Meiss, "The Exhibition of French Manuscripts of the XIII–XVI Centuries at the Bibliothèque Nationale," *The Art Bulletin*, 38, 1956, 187–96.

**Meiss 1963**
Millard Meiss, "A Lost Portrait of Jean de Berry by the Limbourgs," *The Burlington Magazine*,. 105, no. 719, February 1963, 49–53.

**Meiss 1967**
Millard Meiss, *French Painting in the Time of Jean de Berry. The Late Fourteenth Century and the Patronage of the Duke*, London and New York, Phaidon, 1967, 2 vols.

**Meiss 1968**
Millard Meiss, *French Painting in the Time of Jean de Berry. The Boucicaut Master*, London and New York, Phaidon, 1968.

**Meiss 1969**
Millard Meiss, *French Painting in the Time of Jean de Berry. The Late Fourteenth Century and the Patronage of the Duke*, London and New York, Phaidon, 2nd ed., 1969, 2 vols.

**Meiss 1974a**
Millard Meiss, *French Painting in the Time of Jean de Berry. The Limbourgs and Their Contemporaries*, London, Thames & Hudson/New York, Pierpont Morgan Library, 1974, 2 vols.

**Meiss 1974b**
Millard Meiss, "The Rohan Master and the Twenties," in Meiss 1974a, I, 256–77.

**Meiss and Beatson 1977**
Millard Meiss and Elizabeth H. Beatson (eds.), *La Vie de Nostre Benoit Sauveur Ihesuscrist & La Saincte Vie de Nostre Dame...*, New York, New York University Press, 1977.

**Meiss and Off 1971**
Millard Meiss and Sharon Off, "The Bookkeeping of Robinet d'Estampes and the Chronology of Jean de Berry's Manuscripts," *The Art Bulletin*, 53, June 1971, 225–35.

**Merlet and Mély 1886**
Lucien Merlet and Fernand de Mély (eds.), *Inventaire des reliques et joyaux de l'Église Notre-Dame de Chartres publié d'après le manuscrit original*, Chartres, Imprimerie de Garnier, 1886.

**Merrifield 1849**
Mary Ph. Merrifield, *Original Treatises Dating from the XIIth to XVIIIth Centuries on the Arts of Painting, in Oil, Miniature, Mosaic, and on Glass; of Gilding, Dyeing, and the Preparation of Colours and Artificial Gems*, London, J. Murray, 1849, 2 vols.

**Merrifield 1999**
Mary Ph. Merrifield, *Medieval and Renaissance Treatises on the Arts of Painting*, New York, Dover Publications, new ed., 1999.

**Meunier 2006**
Florian Meunier, "Le renouveau de l'architecture civile sous Charles VI, de Bicêtre à l'hôtel de Bourbon," in Taburet-Delahaye 2006, 219–46.

**Meurgey 1930**
Jacques Meurgey, *Chantilly. Les principaux manuscrits à peintures du Musée Condé à Chantilly*, Paris, Société française de reproductions de manuscrits à peintures, 1930.

**Miller 1988**
Edward Miller, *Prince of Librarians: The Life and Times of Antonio Panizzi of the British Museum*, London, British Library, 1988.

**Mognetti 2018**
Élisabeth Mognetti, "Quelques emprunts ponctuels au Maître des Anges rebelles dans la miniature française de la première moitié du xv^e^ siècle," in Michel Laclotte (ed.), *Regards sur les primitifs. Mélanges en l'honneur de Dominique Thiébaut*, Paris, Hazan and Louvre éditions, 2018, 128–35.

**Monnier [1940] 1976**
Adrienne Monnier, "La Nature de la France," *Verve*, 8, 1940; in Richard McDougall (ed.), *The Very Rich Hours of Adrienne Monnier*, London, Millington, 1976, 421.

**Montesquiou-Fezensac and Gaborit 1973–77**
Blaise de Montesquiou-Fezensac and Danièle Gaborit-Chopin, *Le Trésor de Saint-Denis*, Paris, Picard, 1973–77, 3 vols.

**Morgan 1992**
Nigel Morgan, "Texts of Devotion and Religious Instruction Associated with Margaret of York," in Thomas Kres (ed.), *Margaret of York, Simon Marmion, and "The Visions of Tondal,"* Los Angeles, J. Paul Getty Museum, 1992, 63–76.

**Morrison 2006**
Elizabeth Morrison, "Iconographic Originality in the Oeuvre of the Master of the David Scenes," in Elizabeth Morrison and Thomas Kren (eds.), *Flemish Manuscript Painting in Context: Recent Research*, Los Angeles, J. Paul Getty Museum, 2006, 149–64.

**Mulas, Visioli, and Zaggia 2015**
Pier Luigi Mulas, Monica Visioli, and Massimo Zaggia, "Michelino da Besozzo. Un maître italien du gothique international," *Art de l'enluminure*, 55, 2015, 2–49.

**Munby 1972**
Alan Noel Latimer Munby, *Connoisseurs and Medieval Miniatures, 1750–1850*, Oxford, Clarendon Press, 1972.

**Nash 2008**
Susie Nash, "Claus Sluter's 'Well of Moses' for the Chartreuse de Champmol Reconsidered: Part III," *The Burlington Magazine*, vol. 150, no. 1268, November 2008, 724–41.

**Nash 2010**
Susie Nash, "'Pour couleurs et autres choses prise de lui': The Supply, Acquisition, Cost and Employment of Painters' Materials at the Burgundian Court, c. 1375–1419," in Jo Kirby, Susie Nash, and Joanna Cannon, *Trade in Artist's Materials: Markets and Commerce in Europe to 1700*, London, Archetype Publications, 2010, 97–182.

**Nash 2022**
Susie Nash, "The 'Martyrdom of St Denis', the Chartreuse de Champmol and the Battle of Nicopolis," in *Maelwael Van Lymborch Studies*, II, 2022, 13–45.

**Nash 2024a**
Susie Nash, "The de Limbourg Brothers and Simone Martini's Orsini Polyptych," in *Siena: The Rise of Painting 1300–1350* (New York, The Metropolitan Museum of Art, October 13, 2024–January 26, 2025; London, The National Gallery, March 8–June 22, 2025), Joanna Cannon (ed.), London, National Gallery, 2024, 240–53.

**Nash 2024b**
Susie Nash, "No sorrow like unto my sorrow: Philip the Bold, The Great Cross and the Battle of Nicopolis," *The Burlington Magazine*, vol. 166, no. 1459, October 2024, 997–1027.

**Niessen, Roelofs, and van Veen-Liefrink 2005**
Willy Niessen, Pieter Roelofs, and Mieke van Veen-Liefrink, "The Limbourg Brothers in Nijmegen, Bourges, and Paris," in Nijmegen 2005, 13–27.

**Nijsten 1992**
Gerard Nijsten, *Het hof van Gelre. Cultuur ten tijde van de hertogen uit het Gulikse en Egmondse huis (1371–1473)*, Kampen, Kok Agora, 1992.

**Padberg Evenboer 2023a**
Klaas Padberg Evenboer, "Unieke Zutphense wandschildering na 60 jaar ontsleuteld," *Blazoen. Kwartaalblad voor heraldiek en zegelkunde*, 9, 2, 2023, 70–76.

**Padberg Evenboer 2023b**
Klaas Padberg Evenboer, "Keizer en krijgsman zijn ook helden," *Blazoen. Kwartaalblad voor heraldiek en zegelkunde*, 9, 2, 2023, 77–78.

**Panayotova 2014**
Stella Panayotova, "The Rohan Masters: Collaboration and Experimentation in the Hours of Isabella Stuart," in Colum P. Hourihane (ed.), *Manuscripta Illuminata: Approaches to Understanding Medieval and Renaissance Manuscripts*, Princeton, Princeton University, 2014, 14–46.

**Panofsky 1953**
Erwin Panofsky, *Early Netherlandish Painting: Its Origins and Character*, Cambridge, MA, Harvard University Press, 1953.

**Paul-Marcetteau 1991**
Agnès Paul-Marcetteau, "Les bibliothèques des princes d'Orléans, princes de sang," in Dominique Varry (ed.), *Histoire des bibliothèques françaises. III. Les bibliothèques de la Révolution et du xix^e^ siècle*, Paris, Promodis, 1991, 94–97.

**Pearsall and Salter 1973**
Derek Pearsall and Elizabeth Salter, *Landscapes and Seasons of the Medieval World*, London, Elek, 1973.

**Perkinson 2009**
Stephen Perkinson, "Likeness, Loyalty, and the Life of the Court Artist: Portraiture in the Calendar Scenes of the 'Très Riches Heures'," in Dückers and Roelofs 2009, 51–83.

**Petrucci Nardelli 1989**
Franca Petrucci Nardelli, *La Legatura italiana*, Rome, La nuova Italia scientifica, 1989.

**Pons 2005**
Nicolas Pons, "La dévotion du duc Jean de Berry d'après ses inventaires mobiliers," *Revue historique du Centre-Ouest. IV. Autour de Jean de Berry*, 2005, 273–89.

**Porcher 1953a**
Jean Porcher (ed.), *Les Belles Heures de Jean de France, duc de Berry. Reproduction intégrale des enluminures*, Paris, Bibliothèque nationale, 1953.

**Prochno 2002a**
Renate Prochno, *Die Kartause von Champmol. Grablege der burgundischen Herzöge (1364–1477)*, Berlin, Akademie Verlag, 2002.

**Prochno 2002b**
Renate Prochno, "Jean Malouel, Altarbilder 1398–1403," in Prochno 2002a, 204–06.

**Quignard 2023**
Pascal Quignard, *Les Heures heureuses: Dernier royaume XII*, Paris, Albin Michel, 2023.

**Rabel 2004**
Claudia Rabel, "Les livres de la Sainte-Chapelle de Bourges," in Bourges 2004, 154–71.

**Rapin 2006**
Thomas Rapin, "La maîtrise d'ouvrage de Jean de France, duc de Berry (1340–1416). Reconstitution et analyse critique d'une documentation dispersée," *Tabularia – Sources écrites de la Normandie médiévale* (online review), vol. 6, 2006, 33–73.

**Rapin 2010**
Thomas Rapin, *Les chantiers de Jean de France, duc de Berry: maîtrise d'ouvrage et architecture à la fin du Moyen Âge*, PhD diss., Université de Poitiers, 2010.

**Rapin 2012**
Thomas Rapin, "Les demeures parisiennes du duc de Berry," in *La Demeure médiévale à Paris* (Paris, Archives nationales, October 17, 2012–January 13, 2013), Valentine Weiss and Étienne Hamon (eds.), Paris, Somogy and Archives nationales, 2012, 160–62.

**Rapin 2018**
Thomas Rapin, "Les relations entre les artistes de Jean de Berry et les tuiliers mudéjars du royaume d'Aragon," *Bulletin monumental*, vol. 176-1, 2018, 21–23.

**Rapin 2019**
Thomas Rapin, "Écritures de chantier. La chambre des comptes de Bourges et la politique monumentale de Jean de Berry," in Guyotjeannin and Mattéoni 2019, 85–112.

**Raynaud 2006a**
Clémence Raynaud, "Jean de France, duc de Berry: enquête sur un maître d'ouvrage à la fin du Moyen Âge," in Agnès Bos et al. (eds.), *Materiam superabat opus. Hommage à Alain Erlande-Brandenburg*, Paris, École nationale des Chartes and Réunion des musées nationaux, 2006, 236–43.

**Raynaud 2006b**
Clémence Raynaud, "Construction et maîtrise d'œuvre: le cas des chantiers du duc de Berry," in Taburet-Delahaye 2006, 261–78.

**Reynaud 1989**
Nicole Reynaud, "Barthélemy d'Eyck avant 1450," *Revue de l'art*, 84, 1989, 22–43.

**Reynaud 2006a**
Nicole Reynaud, *Jean Fouquet. Les Heures d'Étienne Chevalier*, Dijon, Faton, 2006.

**Reynaud 2006b**
Nicole Reynaud, "I. Fouquet peintre et enlumineur," in Reynaud 2006a, 242–43.

**Reynaud 2007**
Nicole Reynaud, "Petite note à propos des Très Riches Heures du duc de Berry et de leur entrée à la cour de Savoie," in Hofmann, König, and Zöhl 2007, 273–77.

**Reynolds 2005**
Catherine Reynolds, "The 'Très Riches Heures', the Bedford Workshop and Barthélemy d'Eyck," *The Burlington Magazine*, vol. 147, no. 1229, August 2005, 526–33.

**Ribault 1990a**
Jean-Yves Ribault, "Enlumineurs et financiers: Documents berrichons inédits sur les frères de Limbourg," *Revue de l'art*, 88, 1990, 48–52.

**Ribault 1990b**
Jean-Yves Ribault, "Les carrières d'ocre de Saint-Georges-sur-la-Prée (Cher). État des connaissances documentaires," in *Pigments et colorants de l'Antiquité et du Moyen Âge*, Paris, Éditions du CNRS, 1990, 207–15

**Ribault 1999**
Jean-Yves Ribault, "'Pour nostre dévocion et plaisance', l'amour de l'art selon le duc Jean de Berry," in Jean-Yves Ribault (ed.), *Mécènes et collectionneurs. Les variantes d'une passion*, Paris, Éditions du CTHS, 1999, I, 11–26.

**Ribault 2001**
Jean-Yves Ribault, "Les Colombe, une famille d'artistes à Bourges au XV^e^ siècle," in Jean-René Gaborit (ed.), *Michel Colombe et son temps*, Paris, Éditions du CTHS, 2001, 13–26.

**Rickert 1957**
Margaret Rickert, *The Art Bulletin*, 39, 1, 1957, 73–77.

**Rivière Ciavaldini 2018**
Laurence Rivière Ciavaldini, "'Fortune infortunte fort une': De l'infortune à la fortune dans quelques manuscrits de Marguerite d'Autriche," in Bourg-en-Bresse 2018, 94–105.

**Robin 1985**
Françoise Robin, *La Cour d'Anjou-Provence. La vie artistique sous le règne de René*, Paris, Picard, 1985.

**Robin 2008**
Françoise Robin, "Le luxe des collections aux XIV^e^ et XV^e^ siècles," in André Vernet (ed.), *Histoire des bibliothèques françaises. I. Les bibliothèques médiévales, du VI^e^ siècle à 1530*, Paris, Édtions du Cercle de la librairie, 2008, 248–64.

**Roelofs 2005**
Pieter Roelofs, "Johan Maelwael, Court Painter in Guelders and Burgundy," in Nijmegen 2005, 35–54.

**Roelofs 2017a**
Pieter Roelofs, "Johan Maelwael: Painter at the Court of Burgundy," in Amsterdam 2017–18, 13–23

**Roelofs 2017b**
Pieter Roelofs, "Johan Maelwael and the Ducal Painting Workshop in Burgundy," in Amsterdam 2017–18, 24–33.

**Roelofs 2018**
Pieter Roelofs, "Johan Maelwael & the Van Lymborch Brothers: A Proposal for a Standardized Form of their Name," in *Maelwael Van Lymborch Studies*, I, 2018, 6–9.

**Roman 2021**
Nathalie Roman, "Paul Durrieu (1855–1925), l'œil d'un historien," *Histoire et civilisation du livre*, 17, 2021, 139–54.

**Roques 1963**
Marguerite Roques, *Les Apports néerlandais dans la peinture du sud-est de la France, XIV^e^, XV^e^ et XVI^e^ siècles*, Bordeaux, Union française d'impression, 1963.

**Rouse and Rouse 2000**
Richard H. Rouse and Mary A. Rouse, *Manuscripts and their Makers: Commercial Book Producers in Medieval Paris, 1200–1500*, Turnhout, Harvey Miller Publishers, 2000, 2 vols.

**Rubin 2011**
Patricia Rubin, "Understanding Renaissance Portraiture," in *The Renaissance Portrait from Donatello to Bellini* (Berlin, Bode-Museum, August 25– November 20, 2011; New York, The Metropolitan Museum of Art, December 21 2011– March 18, 2012), Keith Christiansen and Stefan Weppelmann (eds.), New York, The Metropolitan Museum of Art, 2011, 2–26.

**Salamagne 2010**
Alain Salamagne, *Le palais et son décor au temps de Jean de Berry*, Tours, Presses de l'Université François-Rabelais, 2010.

**Salmon 2012**
Dimitri Salmon, "Redécouverte et histoire récente du Christ de pitié attribué à Jean Malouel," in Thiébaut 2012, 27–31.

**Saroni 2004**
Giovanna Saroni, *La biblioteca di Amadeo VIII di Savoia (1391–1451)*, Turin, Allemandi, 2004.

**Schellart 1952**
F.J. Schellart (ed.), *Volksboek van Margarieta van Lymborch (1516)*, Amsterdam, 1952.

**Scheller 1995**
Robert W. Scheller, *Exemplum: Model-Book Drawings and the Practice of Artistic Transmission in the Middle Ages (ca. 900–ca. 1470)*, Amsterdam, Amsterdam University Press, 1995.

**Schmid 2018**
Vanessa I. Schmid (ed.), *The Orléans Collection*, New Orleans Museum of Art, 2018.

**Schmidt 2005**
Victor M. Schmidt, "The Limbourgs and Italian Art," in Nijmegen 2005, 179–89.

**Schmidt and Ramirez-Weaver 2005**
Gerhard Schmidt and Eric Ramirez-Weaver, "Wenceslas IV's Books and Their Illuminators," in *Prague: The Crown of Bohemia, 1347–1437* (New York, The Metropolitan Museum of Art, September 20, 2005–January 3, 2006; Prague, Château de Prague, February 16–May 21, 2006), Barbara Drake Boehm and Jiri Fajt (eds.), New York, The Metropolitan Museum of Art, 2005, 220–24.

**Schnerb 2008**
Bertrand Schnerb, "La croix de Saint-André, ensaigne congnoissable des Bourguignons," in Denise Turrel et al. (eds.), *Signes et couleurs des identités politiques du Moyen Âge à nos jours*, Rennes, Presses universitaires de Rennes, 2008, 45–55.

**Seidel 2011**
Christine Seidel, "Jean Colombe am Hof der Herzöge von Savoyen," in Gabriele Bartz and Christine Seidel, *Die Apokalypse der Herzöge von Savoyen*, Simbach am Inn, Anton Pfeiler, 2011, 148–79.

**Seidel 2017**
Christine Seidel, *Zwischen Tradition und Innovation: die Anfänge des Buchmalers Jean Colombe und die Kunst in Bourges zur Zeit Karls VII. von Frankreich*, Simbach am Inn, Anton Pfeiler, 2017.

**Seidel 2018**
Christine Seidel, "Images in Pen and Ink: Technical Remarks on the 'Drawn Van Lymborch Hours'," in *Maelwael Van Lymborch Studies*, I, 2018, 88–103.

**Slanicka 2002**
Simona Slanicka, *Krieg der Zeichen. Die visuelle Politik Johanns ohne Furcht und der armagnakische-burgundische Bürgerkrieg*, Göttingen, Vandenhoeck und Ruprecht Verlag, 2002.

**Solan Bethmale 2016**
Olivier de Solan Bethmale, *La réforme du calendrier aux conciles de Constance et de Bâle… Corpus édité, traduit et commenté*, Paris, Éditions du CNRS, 2016.

**Sricchia Santoro 2017**
Fiorella Sricchio Santoro, *Antonello, i suoi mondi, il suo seguito*, Florence, Centro Di, 2017.

**Stammers 2023**
Tom Stammers, "Materializing France in Exile: Henri, Duc d'Aumale, the Orléans Family and the Transnational Politics of Collecting c. 1848–80," *Histoire française*, 37, 2023, 442–67.

**Stange 1938**
Alfred Stange, *Deutsche Malerei der Gotik. III. Norddeutschland in der Zeit von 1400 bis 1450*, Berlin, Deutscher Kunstverlag, 1938.

**Sterligov 1980**
Andrej B. Sterligov, *Das Stundenbuch Ludwigs von Orleans*, Frankfurt, Insel-Verlag, 1980, 2 vols.

**Sterling 1983**
Charles Sterling, *Enguerrand Quarton. Le peintre de la Pietà d'Avignon*, Paris, Réunion des musées nationaux, 1983.

**Sterling 1987–90**
Charles Sterling, *La Peinture médiévale à Paris, 1300–1500*, Paris, La Bibliothèque des Arts, 1987–90, 2 vols.

**Stirnemann 2006**
Patricia Stirnemann, "Combien de copistes et artistes ont contribué aux *Très Riches Heures?*," in Taburet-Delahaye 2006, 365–80.

**Stirnemann 2009**
Patricia Stirnemann, "Les 'Très Riches Heures' et les Heures Bedford," *Revista de História da Arte*, vol. 7, 2009, 138–51.

**Stirnemann 2018**
Patricia Stirnemann, "Johan Maelwael, the Van Lymborch Brothers and the 'Très Riches Heures du duc de Berry'," in *Maelwael Van Lymborch Studies*, I, 2018, 19–37.

**Stirnemann 2021**
Patricia Stirnemann, "Barthélemy d'Eyck et les Très Riches Heures," in Claudia Rabel et al. (eds.), *Dans l'atelier de Michel Pastoureau*, Tours, Presses universitaires François-Rabelais, 2021, 290–93.

**Stirnemann and Rabel 2005**
Patricia Stirnemann and Claudia Rabel, "The 'Très Riches Heures' and the Two Artists Associated with the Bedford Workshop," *The Burlington Magazine*, vol. 147, no. 1229, August 2005, 534–38.

**Stirnemann and Villela-Petit 2013**
Patricia Stirnemann and Inès Villela-Petit (eds.), *Les Très Riches Heures. Das Meisterwerk für den Herzog von Berry*, Lucerne, Faksimile Verlag, 2013.

**Stratford 2022**
Neil Stratford, *La Coupe de sainte Agnès (France – Espagne – Angleterre)*, Paris, Académie des Inscriptions et Belles-Lettres, 2022.

**Studničková 2006**
Milada Studničková, "Courant tchèque dans l'art de la miniature," in *Sigismundus rex et imperator. Art et culture au temps de Sigismond de Luxembourg, 1387–1437* (Budapest, Szépművészeti Múzeum, March 18–June 18, 2006; Luxembourg, Musée national d'histoire et d'art, July 13–October 15, 2006), Imre Takács (ed.), Mayence, Ph. von Zabern, 2006, 529–35.

**Stufkens 2020**
André Stufkens, *Nieuwe horizonten in de kunst van de Maelwael-Van Lymborchs*, Nijmegen, Stichting Maelwael van Lymborch Studies, 2020.

**Stufkens and Verhoeven 2018**
André Stufkens and Clemens Verhoeven, "Pulse & Impulse. Mission Statement about Patience and Fluid Exchange," in *Maelwael Van Lymborch Studies*, I, 2018, 15–17.

**Stumpel 2016**
J. Stumpel, 'Modelboeken', in M. Haveman & A. Overbeek, *Het reizende detail in de kunst van 1400 tot 1500*, Amsterdam, 2016.

**Taburet-Delahaye 2006**
Élisabeth Taburet-Delahaye (ed.), *La Création artistique en France autour de 1400*, Paris, École du Louvre, 2006.

**Tait 1986**
Hugh Tait, *Catalogue of the Waddesdon Bequest in the British Museum. I. The Jewels*, London, British Museum Publications, 1986.

**Tesnière 2000**
Marie-Hélène Tesnière, "À propos de la traduction de Tite-Live par Pierre Bersuire. Le *manuscrit Oxford, Bibliothèque Bodléienne, Rawlinson C 447," Romania, vol. 118, no. 471–72, 2000, 449–98.*

**Thiébaut 2004**
Dominique Thiébaut, "Barthélemy d'Eyck," in Paris 2004a, 123–41.

**Thiébaut 2006**
Dominique Thiébaut, "Antonello, Barthélemy d'Eyck, Enguerrand Quarton e altri: contatti, influenze reciproche o coincidenze artistiche?," in *Antonello da Messina: l'opera completa* (Rome, Scuderie del Quirinale, March 18–June 25, 2006), Mauro Lucco (ed.), Cinisello Balsamo (Milan), Silvana editoriale, 2006, 36–57.

**Thiébaut 2012**
Dominique Thiébaut, with the collaboration of Dimitri Salmon, *Attribué à Jean Malouel. Le Christ de Pitié*, Paris, Hazan and Louvre éditions, 2012.

**Thiébaut 2015**
Dominique Thiébaut, "Enquête sur un chef-d'œuvre," *Grande Galerie*, 34, December 2015–January/February 2016, 66–68.

**Thompson 1926**
Daniel V. Thompson, "'Liber de Coloribus Illuminatorum Siue Pictorum' from Sloane Ms. No. 1754," *Speculum*, 1, 1926, 251–360.

**Thompson 1935**
Daniel V. Thompson, "'De Coloribus, Naturalia exscripta et collecta', from Ehrfurt, Stadtbücherеї, Ms. Amplonius Quarto 189 (XIII–XIV century)," *Technical Studies in the Field of the Fine Arts*, 3, 1935, 133–45.

**Tomasi 2005**
Michele Tomasi, "Le retable des Embriachi du musée du Louvre: datation, fonction, destination, iconographie," *Revue du Louvre et des musées de France*, 3, 2005, 47–55.

**Toscano 2024**
Gennaro Toscano, "Voyages des hommes, circulation des œuvres en France et Italie," in Paris 2024, 248–53.

**Toulet 2001**
Emmanuelle Toulet, "Le Cabinet des livres du duc d'Aumale," *Bulletin du bibliophile*, 2001, 1, 3.

**Toulet 2005**
Emmanuelle Toulet, "Les expositions de manuscrits: l'exploration progressive d'une collection," *Bulletin du bibliophile*, 2005, 1, 11–29.

**Toulet 2010**
Emmanuelle Toulet, "*Voulant conserver à la France…*: la donation de la bibliothèque de Chantilly à l'Institut de France," *in Dons et legs dans les bibliothèques publiques: "Je lègue ma bibliothèque à…,"* Gap, Atelier Perrousseaux, 2010, 241–55.

**Toulet 2013**
Emmanuelle Toulet, "Von der 'Genueser Handschrift' zu den Très Riches Heures des Herzogs von Berry," in *Les Très Riches Heures: das Meisterwerk für den Herzog von Berry*, Lucerne, Quaternio Verlag Lucern, 2013, 31–36.

**Ubl 2017**
Matthias Ubl, "'He who paints well': Herman, Willem, and Johan Maelwael and Heraldic Painting around 1400," in Amsterdam 2017–18, 42–53.

**Urso and Mulas 2014**
Teresa d'Urso and Pier Luigi Mulas, *La passion du prince pour les belles occupations de l'esprit: enluminures italiennes dans la collection du duc d'Aumale*, Chantilly, Domaine de Chantilly, 2014.

**Van Bergen 2016**
Saskia van Bergen, "Illuminated Books of Hours and the hHeritage of L.M.J. Delaissé: The Archaeology of the Book in Recent Publications," *Jaarboek voor Nederlandse Boekgeschiedenis. Jaargang*, vol. 23, 2016 [online].

**Van Buren, Marrow, and Pettenati 1996**
Anne H. van Buren, James H. Marrow and Silvana Pettenati, *Heures de Turin-Milan: Inv. no 47. Museo Civico d'Arte Antica. Torino, Commentaire*, Lucerne, Faksimile Verlag, 1996.

**Van den Bergen-Pantens 1983**
Christiane Van den Bergen-Pantens, "Portraits troyens et héraldique imaginaire. Les exemples d'Hector et de Penthésilée," in *Comunicaciones al XV Congreso Internacional de las Ciencias Genealogica y Heráldica, Madrid, 19–25 septiembre 1982*, Madrid, Instituto Salazar y Castro, 1983, I, 219–30.

**Van Dyke 2015**
Yana van Dyke, "Conservation Concerns: The Care of Medieval Manuscripts," January 27, 2015; (accessed November 2, 2024 [https://www.metmuseum.org/fr/exhibitions/listings/2014/winchester-bible/blog/posts/conservation-concerns].

**Van Rijen 2005**
Jean-Pierre van Rijen, "Precious Metalwork in Gold Leaf: Everyday Lustre at the Court of Jean de Berry, as Depicted by the Limbourg Brothers," in Nijmegen 2005, 165–78.

**Van Schevichaven 1914**
Herman D. J. van Schevichaven, "Johan Maelwael," in Petrus J. Blok and Philip C. Molhuysen (eds.), *Nieuw Nederlandsch biografisch woordenboek*, III, Leyde, Sijthoff, 1914.

**Van Spaen 1808**
Willem Anne van Spaen, *Proeven van historie en oudheidkunde*, Cleves, W. Möller, 1808.

**Vial 2019**
Charles-Éloi Vial, "Louis-Philippe et les livres: de la collection familiale à la bibliothèque du musée de l'Histoire de France," in *Histoire et civilisation du livre*, 15, 2019, 319–40.

**Villela-Petit 2003**
Inès Villela-Petit, *Le Bréviaire de Châteauroux*, Paris, Somogy, 2003.

**Villela-Petit 2004a**
Inès Villela-Petit, *Le Gothique international. L'art en France au temps de Charles VI*, Paris, Hazan and Louvre éditions, 2004.

**Villela-Petit 2004b**
Inès Villela-Petit, "Création, imitation, transposition," in Villela-Petit 2004a, 36–43.

**Villela-Petit 2004c**
Inès Villela-Petit, "Béraud III, dauphin d'Auvergne ou Guichard II Dauphin? Un cas d'homonymie héraldique," *Revue française d'héraldique et de sigillographie*, 71–72, 2004, 53–72.

**Villela-Petit 2004d**
Inès Villela-Petit, "La petite clef d'harmonie," in Chantilly 2004, 64–75.

**Villela-Petit 2006a**
Inès Villela-Petit, "Deux visions de la Cité de Dieu: le Maître de Virgile et le Maître de Boèce," *Art de l'enluminure*, 17, 2006, 2–65.

**Villela-Petit 2006b**
Inès Villela-Petit, "Copies, Reworkings and Renewals in Late Medieval Recipe Books," in Jilleen Nadolny (ed.), *Medieval Painting in Northern Europe: Techniques, Analysis, Art History*, London, Archetype Publications, 2006, 167–81.

**Villela-Petit 2007**
Inès Villela-Petit, "Dévotion et culte des reliques chez Jean de Berry," *Bulletin monumental*, vol. 165–4, 2007, 393–94.

**Villela-Petit 2008**
Inès Villela-Petit, "À la recherche d'Anastaise," *Cahiers de recherches médiévales*, vol. 16, 2008, 301–16.

**Villela-Petit 2010a**
Inès Villela-Petit, "La France et le gothique international (1360–1430)," in Philippe Plagnieux (ed.), *L'art du Moyen Âge en France*, Paris, Citadelles & Mazenod, 2010, 382–441.

**Villela-Petit 2010b**
Inès Villela-Petit, "Les Heures de Jeanne du Peschin, dame de Giac. Aux origines du Maître de Rohan," *Art de l'enluminure*, 34, 2010, 2–63.

**Villela-Petit 2010c**
Inès Villela-Petit, *The Très Riches Heures of the Duke of Berry: Chantilly, Musée Condé, ms. 65: Reader's Guide*, Modena, Franco Cosimo Panini Editore, 2010.

**Villela-Petit 2011a**
Inès Villela-Petit, "Quatre feuillets des *Très Belles Heures de Notre Dame* de Jean de Berry," in Avril, Reynaud, and Cordellier 2011, nos. 77–80, 140–56.

**Villela-Petit 2011b**
Inès Villela-Petit, "Portement de Croix de Jacquemart de Hesdin," in Avril, Reynaud, and Cordellier 2011, no. 81, 157–59.

**Villela-Petit 2012a**
Inès Villela-Petit, "Historié de blanc et de noir: la tradition du 'portrait d'encre' in l'enluminure parisienne des XIVe et XVe siècles," in Marion Boudon-Machuel, Maurice Brock, and Pascale Charron (eds.), *Aux limites de la couleur: monochromie & polychromie dans les arts (1300–1600)*, Turnhout, Brepols, 2012, 25–34.

**Villela-Petit 2012b**
Inès Villela-Petit, "La banque Limbourg Frères," *Bulletin de la Société française de numismatique*, 2012, 172–77.

**Villela-Petit 2012c**
Inès Villela-Petit, "Introduction sur les enlumineurs ornemanistes," in Gilbert Ouy, Christine Reno and Inès Villela-Petit, *Album Christine de Pizan*, Turnhout, Brepols, 2012, 39–88.

**Villela-Petit 2013a**
Inès Villela-Petit, "Der Fürst und sein Spiegel – Jean de Berry und sein berühmtes Buch," in Stirnemann and Villela-Petit 2013, 43–67.

**Villela-Petit 2013b**
Inès Villela-Petit, "Die Brüder Limburg," in Stirnemann and Villela-Petit 2013, 73–117.

**Villela-Petit 2013c**
Inès Villela-Petit, "Der Meister zwischen den Kampagnen: Barthélemy d'Eyck," in Stirnemann and Villela-Petit 2013, 125–43.

**Villela-Petit 2018a**
Inès Villela-Petit, "The Drawn Hours: A New Masterpiece by the Van Lymborch Brothers?," in *Maelwael Van Lymborch Studies*, I, 2018, 64–83.

**Villela-Petit 2018b**
Inès Villela-Petit, "Les Très Riches Heures, de Jean de Berry à Marguerite d'Autriche," in Bourg-en-Bresse 2018, 106–09.

**Villela-Petit 2019**
Inès Villela-Petit, "Le Livre de la chasse et ses enlumineurs," in *Gaston Fébus, Livre de chasse*, Barcelona, M. Moleiro, 2019, 76–109.

**Villela-Petit 2021**
Inès Villela-Petit, "Le Maître des Textes romains," *Bulletin de la Société nationale des Antiquaires de France*, 2018, 2021, 43–76.

**Villela-Petit 2022**
Inès Villela-Petit, "Painter versus Illuminator: Looking for Paul van Lymborch," in *Maelwael Van Lymborch Studies*, II, 2022, 129–59.

**Villela-Petit 2023**
Inès Villela-Petit, "Un livre d'heures pour la duchesse? Collaborations et rivalités à la cour de Jean de Berry," *Art de l'enluminure*, 85, 2023, 4–60.

**Villela-Petit [forthcoming]**
Inès Villela-Petit, "Les enluminures du Salluste Guidi di Bagno: analyse stylistique" [forthcoming].

**Waagen 1857**
Gustav Waagen, *Galleries and Cabinets of Art in Great Britain: Being an Account of More than Forty Collections of Paintings, Drawings, Sculptures, Mss., etc. etc. Visited in 1854 and 1856, and Now for the First Time Described*, London, John Murray, 1857.

**Warnke [1985] 1989**
Martin Warnke, *L'artiste et la cour. Aux origines de l'artiste moderne*, Paris, Éditions de la Maison des sciences de l'homme, 1989 [1985].

**Watteeuw and Reynolds 2013**
Lieve Watteeuw and Catherine Reynolds, *Catalogue of Illuminated Manuscripts, Museum Plantin-Moretus, Antwerp*, Leuven, Peeters, 2013.

**Watteeuw and Van der Stock 2010**
Lieve Watteeuw and Jan Van der Stock (eds.), *The Anjou Bible: A Royal Manuscript Revealed (Naples 1340)*, Paris and Leuven, Walpole, 2010.

**Wentzel 1954**
Hans Wentzel, "Die grosse Kamee mit Poseidon und Athena in Paris," *Wallraf-Richartz-Jahrbuch*, 16, 1954, 53–76.

**Wieck 1991**
Roger S. Wieck, "The Savoy Hours and Its Impact on Jean, Duc de Berry," *The Yale University Library Gazette*, 66, 1991, 159–80.

**Wieck 2005**
Roger S. Wieck, "Bibliophilic Jealousy and the Manuscripts Patronage of Jean, Duc de Berry," in Nijmegen 2005, 121–34.

**Winckler 1930**
Friedrich Winckler, "Paul de Limbourg in Florence," *The Burlington Magazine*, vol. 56, no. 323, February 1930, 95–96.

**Zimmermann 1883**
Heinrich Zimmermann, "Inventoire des bagues, joyaulx, vaisselles d'or et d'argent et pluseurs autres choses appartenens a madame Marguerite d'Autriche, lesquelles bagues ont esté delivrées par monseignuer et madame de segret en la ville de Valenciennes le 14 jour de juing l'an 1493," *Jahrbuch der kunsthistorischen des allerhöchsten Kaiserhauses*, 1, 1883, XXVIII–XXX.

## EXHIBITION CATALOGUES


**Amsterdam 2017–18**
*Johan Maelwael* (Amsterdam, Rijksmuseum, October 6, 2017–January 7, 2018), Pieter Roelofs (ed.), Amsterdam, Rijksmuseum, 2017.

**Angers 2009–10**
*Splendeur de l'enluminure: le roi René et les livres* (Angers, Château d'Angers, Galerie de l'Apocalypse, October 3, 2009–January 3, 2010), Marc-Édouard Gautier (ed.), Arles, Actes Sud, 2009.

**Berne, Bruges, and Vienna 2008–10**
*Charles le Téméraire (1433–1477): splendeurs de la cour de Bourgogne* (Berne, Musée historique de Berne, April 25–August 24, 2008; Bruges, Bruggemuseum and Groeningemuseum, March 27–July 21, 2009; Vienna, Kunsthistorisches Museum, September 15, 2009–January 10, 2010), Susan Marti, Till-Holger Borchert and Gabriele Keck (eds.), Brussels, Fonds Mercator, 2009.

**Bourg-en-Bresse 2018**
*Primitifs flamands. Trésors de Marguerite d'Autriche, de Jan Van Eyck à Jérôme Bosch* (Bourg-en-Bresse, monastère royal de Brou, May 8–August 26, 2018), Pierre Gilles Girault and Magalie Briat-Philippe (eds.), Rennes, Presses universitaires de Rennes, 2018.

**Bourges 2004**
*La Sainte-Chapelle de Bourges, une fondation disparue de Jean de France, duc de Berry* (Bourges, Musée du Berry, June 26–October 31, 2004), Béatrice de Chancel-Bardelot and Clémence Raynaud (eds.), Paris, Somogy, 2004.

**Châlons-en-Champagne, Troyes, and Reims 2007–08**
*Très riches heures de Champagne. L'enluminure en Champagne à la fin du Moyen Âge* (municipal libraries of Châlons-en-Champagne, Troyes, and Reims, 2007–08), François Avril, Maxence Hermant, and Françoise Bibolet (eds.), Paris, Hazan, 2007.

**Chantilly 1956**
*Les plus beaux manuscrits à peintures du Musée Condé* (Chantilly, Musée Condé, March 4–November 1, 1956), Chantilly, Institut de France, 1956.

**Chantilly 2004**
*Les Très Riches Heures du duc de Berry et l'enluminure en France au début du XVe siècle* (Chantilly, Musée Condé, March 31–August 2, 2004), Patricia Stirnemann et al., Paris, Somogy/Chantilly, Musée Condé, 2004.

**Chantilly 2019–20**
*La collection Chourses-Coëtivy. Une librairie médiévale à l'aube de la Renaissance* (Chantilly, Château de Chantilly, October 12, 2019–January 6, 2020), Roseline Claerr and Marie-Pierre Dion (eds.), Chantilly, Domaine de Chantilly, 2019.

**Chicago, Paris, and London 2016–17**
*La peinture américaine des années 1930. The Age of Anxiety* (Chicago, The Art Institute of Chicago, June 5–September 18, 2016; Paris, Musée de l'Orangerie, October 12, 2016–January 30, 2017; London, Royal Academy of Arts, February 25–June 4, 2017), Judith A. Barter and Laurence des Cars (eds.), Malakoff, Hazan/Paris, Musée de l'Orangerie, 2016.

**Cleveland 1967–68**
*Treasures from Medieval France* (Cleveland Museum of Art, November 16, 1967–January 29, 1968), William D. Wixom (ed.), Cleveland, Cleveland Museum of Art, 1967.

**Cleves and Düsseldorf 1984–85**
*Land im Mittelpunkt der Mächte. Die Herzogtümer Jülich, Kleve, Berg* (Cleves, Museum Haus Koekkoek, September 15–November 11, 1984; Düsseldorf, Stadtmuseum Düsseldorf, November 25, 1984–February 25, 1985), Guido de Werd and Wieland Koenig (eds.), Cleves, Boss-Verlag, 1984

**Dijon and Cleveland 2004–05**
*L'Art à la cour de Bourgogne: le mécénat de Philippe le Hardi et de Jean sans Peur (1364–1419): les princes des fleurs de lis* (Dijon, Musée des Beaux-Arts, May 28–September 13, 2004; Cleveland, The Cleveland Museum of Art, October 24, 2004–January 9, 2005), Stephen N. Fliegel and Sophie Jugie (eds.), Paris, Réunion des musées nationaux, 2004.

**Fontevraud 2024**
*Bernard Buffet médiéval et pop* (Fontevraud, Musée d'art moderne de Fontevraud, June 8–September 29, 2024), Dominique Gagneux, Gatien Du Bois, and Aude Le Mercier (eds.), Paris, Glénat/Fontevraud, FAM, 2024.

**Kevelaer et al. 2001–02**
*De Gouden Eeuw van Gelre. Kunst en cultuur in het oude hertogdom* (Kevelaer, Niederrheinisches Museum für Volkskunde und Kulturgeschichte, March 24–June 24, 2001; Nijmegen, Museum Het Valkhof; Zutphen, Stedelijk Museum Zutphen; Roermond, Stedelijk Museum Roermond, March 2–April 28, 2002), Peter van der Coelen (ed.), Geldern, Historischer Verein für Geldern und Umgebung, 2001.

**London 2002–03**
*Art in the Making: Underdrawing in the Renaissance Paintings* (London, The National Gallery, October 30, 2002–February 13, 2003), David Bomford (ed.), London, The National Gallery, 2002.

**Los Angeles and London 2003–04**
*Illuminating the Renaissance: The Triumph of Flemish Manuscript Painting in Europe* (Los Angeles, J. Paul Getty Museum, June 17–September 7, 2003; London, Royal Academy of Arts, November 29, 2003–February 22, 2004), Scot McKendrick and Thomas Kren (eds.), Los Angeles, J. Paul Getty Museum, 2003.

**Los Angeles and New York 2008–10**
*The Art of Illumination: The Limbourg Brothers and the Belles Heures of Jean de France, Duc de Berry* (Los Angeles, J. Paul Getty Museum, November 18, 2008–February 8, 2009; New York, The Metropolitan Museum of Art, September 22, 2009–January 3, 2010), New Haven and London, Yale University Press, 2008.

**Magdebourg 2006**
*Heiliges Römisches Reich Deutscher Nation, 962 bis 1806. Von Otto dem Grossen bis zum Ausgang des Mittelalters* (Magdebourg, Kunsthistorisches Museum, August 28–December 10, 2006), Matthias Puhle and Claus-Peter Hasse (eds.), Dresde, Sandstein Verlag, 2006.

**New York 1982–83**
*The Last Flowering: French Painting in Manuscripts, 1420–1530, from American Collections* (New York, Pierpont Morgan Library, November 18, 1982–January 30, 1983), John Plummer and Gregory Clark (eds.), New York, Pierpont Morgan Library, 1982.

**New York, London, and San Marino 2021–22**
*Inspiring Walt Disney: The Animation of French Decorative Arts* (New York, The Metropolitan Museum of Art, December 6, 2021–March 6, 2022; London, The Wallace Collection; San Marino, The Huntington Library, Art Museum and Botanical Gardens, 2022), Wolf Burchard (ed.), New York, The Metropolitan Museum of Art, 2021.

**Nijmegen 2005**
*The Limbourg Brothers: Nijmegen Masters at the French Court, 1400–1416* (Nijmegen, Museum Het Valkhof, August 28–November 20, 2005), Rob Dückers and Pieter Roelofs (eds.), Stuttgart, Belser, 2005.

**Nijmegen 2018–19**
*Ik, Maria van Gelre. De hertogin en haar uitzonderlijke gebedenboek (1380–1429)* (Nijmegen, Museum Het Valkhof, October 13, 2018–January 6, 2019), Johan Oosterman (ed.), Nijmegen, Museum Het Valkhof, 2018.

**Paris 1955–56**
*Les manuscrits à peintures en France du XIIIe au XVIe siècle* (Paris, Bibliothèque nationale, September 17, 1955–December 30, 1956), Jean Porcher (ed.), Paris, Bibliothèque nationale, 1955.

**Paris 1981–82**
*Les fastes du gothique. Le siècle de Charles V* (Paris, Galeries nationales du Grand Palais, October 9, 1981–February 1, 1982), Françoise Baron (ed.), Paris, Réunion des musées nationaux, 1981.

**Paris 1993–94**
*Les manuscrits à peintures en France, 1440–1520* (Paris, Bibliothèque nationale, October 16, 1993–January 16, 1994), François Avril and Nicole Reynaud (eds.), Paris, Flammarion, 1993.

**Paris 2003**
*Jean Fouquet, peintre et enlumineur du XVe siècle* (Paris, Bibliothèque nationale de France, March 25–June 22, 2003), François Avril (ed.), Paris, Hazan, 2003.

**Paris 2004a**
*Primitifs français. Découvertes et redécouvertes* (Paris, Musée du Louvre, February 27–May 17, 2004), Dominique Thiébaut et al. (eds.), Paris, Réunion des musées nationaux, 2004.

**Paris 2004b**
*Paris 1400. Les arts sous Charles VI* (Paris, musée du Louvre, March 22–July 12, 2004), Élisabeth Taburet-Delahaye (ed.), Paris, Réunion des musées nationaux and Fayard, 2004.

**Paris 2012**
*Les Belles Heures du duc de Berry* (Paris, Musée du Louvre, April 5–June 25, 2012), Hélène Grollemund and Pascal Torres (eds.), Paris, Somogy, 2012.

**Paris 2021–22**
*Venus d'ailleurs: matériaux et objets voyageurs* (Paris, Musée du Louvre, September 22, 2021–July 4, 2022), Philippe Malgouyres (ed.), Paris, Seuil, 2021.

**Paris 2023–24**
*Voyage dans le cristal* (Paris, Musée national du Moyen Âge – Thermes et hôtel de Cluny, September 26, 2023–January 14, 2024), Isabelle Bardiès-Fronty and Stéphane Pennec (eds.), Paris, Réunion des musées nationaux – Grand Palais, 2023.

**Paris 2024**
*Les arts en France sous Charles VII* (Paris, Musée national du Moyen Âge – Thermes et hôtel de Cluny, March 12–June 16, 2024), Mathieu Deldicque et al. (eds.), Paris, Réunion des musées nationaux – Grand Palais, 2024.

oculis tue maiestatis
offerimus subsidium
nobis tue pietatis im
pende. Per dominum
nostrum ihm xpm fi
lium tuum qui tecu.
Sanctus. sanctus sanct.
Dominus deus sabbaoth.
pleni sunt celi et terra gloria
tua osanna in excelsis.
Benedictus qui venit
in nomine osanna in excelsis.
Agnus dei qui tollis pec
cata mundi miserere nobis.
Agnus dei qui tollis pec
cata mundi miserere nobis.
Agnus dei qui tollis peccata
mundi dona nobis pacem. co.
Responsum accepit symeon
a spiritu sancto non visurum
se mortem nisi videret xpm
domini. postcommunio

Quesumus domine
deus noster: ut sacro
sancta misteria que p
reparacionis nostre mu
nimine contulisti: in
tercedente beata semper
virgine dei genitrice
maria: et presens nob
remedium esse facias
et futurum. Per xpm
dominum nostrum. Amen.

Fols. 204v–205

Fols. 205v–206

Fol. 208v – Inside back cover

## LIST OF ABBREVIATIONS

BAV (Vatican City): Biblioteca Apostolica Vaticana
BGE (Geneva): Bibliothèque publique de Genève
Bibl. du musée Condé (Chantilly): Bibliothèque du musée Condé
Bibl. Mazarine (Paris): Bibliothèque Mazarine
BL (London): British Library
BnF, Ms. (Paris): Bibliothèque nationale de France, département des Manuscrits
BM (Angers): Bibliothèque municipale
BM (Bourges): Sainte-Chapelle
BM (Metz): Bibliothèques-Médiathèques de Metz
BMI (Epinal): Bibliothèque multimédia intercommunale d'Épinal,
Bodl. Library (Oxford): Bodleian Library
BSB (Munich): Bayerische Staatsbibliothek
BSG (Paris): Bibliothèque Sainte-Geneviève
KBR (Brussels): Royal Library of Belgium
KHM (Vienna): Kunsthistoriches Museum
KMSKA (Antwerp): Royal Museums of Fine Arts
KU (Louvain) : Katholieke Universiteit Leuven
Met (New York): The Metropolitan Museum
NGA (Washington): National Gallery of Art
ÖNB (Vienna): Österreichische Nationalbibliothek
SBB (Berlin): Staatsbibliothek zu Berlin
UCB (Berkeley): University of California, Berkeley, Bancroft Library
V&A (London): Victoria and Albert Museum

# COLOPHON

**This book is published on the occasion of the exhibition *Les Très Riches Heures du duc de Berry* organized by the Musée Condé at the Jeu de Paume, Château de Chantilly, from June 7 to October 5, 2025.**


**Commissioner**
Mathieu Deldicque
*Chief heritage curator, Director of the Musée Condé and the Musée vivant du Cheval*

**In collaboration with**
Marie-Pierre Dion
*General libraries curator, Head of the Musée Condé library and archives*

**Exhibition manager**
Camille Olivier
*Head of documentary resources at the Musée Condé*


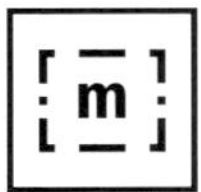


**The exhibition has benefited from the exceptional partnership of the Bibliothèque nationale de France and the Musée du Berry in Bourges.**

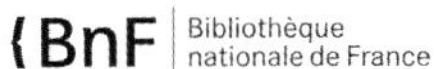


The scientific analyses of *the Très Riches Heures du duc de Berry* were carried out at the Centre de recherche et de restauration des Musées de France (C2RMF).

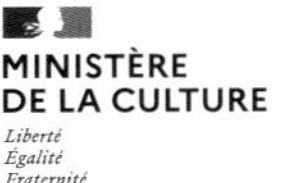


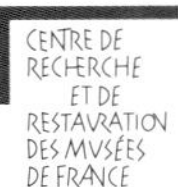


**The exhibition has been awarded the label "Exhibition of national interest" by the Ministry of Culture.**

Exposition d'intérêt national
RÉPUBLIQUE FRANÇAISE


**SCENOGRAPHY**
JAAMS (Claudine Dreyfus and Isabelle Devin)

*Construction*
MPI

*Graphic design*
Lawrence Bitterly

*Lighting*
Stéphanie Daniel and MDA

*Multimedia*
Ludwik Pruszkowski

*Digital application design*
Mosquito (Emmanuel Rouillier)

*Digital application development*
23FORWARD (Arnaud Martin)

**CATALOGUE**

First published in the United States of America in 2025 by Rizzoli Electa, a Division of Rizzoli International Publications, Inc.
49 West 27th Street
New York, NY 10001
rizzoliusa.com


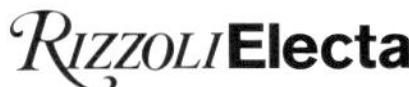



Originally published in Belgium in 2025 by Hannibal Books
Appelmarkt 8
8630 Veurne, Belgium
hannibalbooks.be


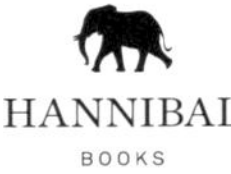





ISBN: 978-0-8478-7597-9
Library of Congress Control Number: 2025933677

Printed in Italy
2025 2026 2027 / 10 9 8 7 6 5 4 3 2 1

**For Rizzoli Electa**

*Publisher*
Charles Miers

*Associate Publisher*
Margaret Rennolds Chace

*Editor*
Klaus Kirschbaum

*Assistant Editor*
Emily Ligniti

**For Hannibal Books**

*Publisher*
Gautier Platteau

*Project Manager*
Sara Colson

*Designer*
Tim Bisschop

*Art Director*
Natacha Hofman

*Image Editing*
Séverine Lacante

*Copyeditor*
Cath Phillips

*Illustrations*
Marina Rouyer, Assistant Curator at the Musée Condé

*Translator*
Patrick Lennon

The authorized representative in the EU for product safety and compliance is Mondadori Libri S.p.A., via Gian Battista Vico 42, Milan, Italy, 20123
mondadori.it

*Visit us online*
Facebook.com/RizzoliNewYork
Instagram.com/RizzoliBooks
Youtube.com/user/RizzoliNY

Front cover: Van Lymborch brothers, *Très Riches Heures*, fol. 4v: April

Back cover: Van Lymborch brothers, *Très Riches Heures*, fol. 14v: Zodiacal Man

## LENDERS

The Musée Condé extends its sincere thanks to the institutions whose generous loans provided crucial support for this project:

Berlin, Gemäldegalerie: Anja Deller, Stephan Kemperdick

Besançon, Bibliothèque municipale: Henry Ferreira-Lopes, Pierre-Emmanuel Guilleray

Bourges, Bibliothèque municipale: Caroline Laurent, Yann Galut

Bourges, Cathedral of Saint-Étienne (Direction régionale des Affaires Culturelles DRAC Centre-Val de Loire): Anne Embs, Irène Jourdheuil

Bourges, Musée du Berry: Florence Margo-Schwoebel, Florent Allemand, Íris Coelho, Laure Mazoyer

Brussels, Royal Library of Belgium: Michiel Verweij, Benoît Labarre

Cambrai, Bibliothèque municipale: Sara Pretto, Laurent Dierckens

Geneva, Bibliothèque de Genève: Frédérique Sardet, Luz Esperanza Lopez

Lyon, Bibliothèque municipale: Delphine Guedra, Jérôme Sirdey

Lyon, Musée historique des tissus: Aziza Gril-Mariotte, Marion Falaise, Charlotte Maday

Marcoussis, Church of Sainte-Marie-Madeleine: Colette Aymard, Philippe Dress, Laurent Olivier, Guy Kremer, Caroline Mege, Patrick Bourgueil

Mehun-sur-Yèvre, Musée du Château Charles VII: Philippe Bon

New York, The Metropolitan Museum of Art: Max Hollein, Griffith Mann, Christine Brennan, Emily Foss, Marci King

New York, Morgan Library & Museum: Colin Bailey, Roger S. Wieck, Anne Reilly Manalo, Rose Durand

New York, The New York Public Library: Alexander Garcia

Oxford, Bodleian Library: Craig McPhedran, Sallyanne Gilchrist, Madeline Slaven

Oxford, Keble College: Fiona Wilson

Paris, Archives nationales: Bruno Ricard, Natacha Villeroy

Paris, Bibliothèque nationale de France: Gilles Pécout, Marie de Laubier, Emmanuel Coquery, Gennaro Toscano, Guillaume Fau, Charlotte Denoël, Maxence Hermant, Paul Froment, Mathilde Avisseau-Broustet, Frédérique Duyrat, Olivier Bosc, Delphine Minotti, Brigitte Robin-Loiseau

Paris, Bibliothèque Sainte-Geneviève: François Michaud, Nathalie Rollet-Bricklin

Paris, bibliothèques de l'Institut de France: Yann Sordet, Patrick Latour, Sabrina Castandet-Le Bris, Marianne Besseyre, Agnès Rico

Paris, Cinémathèque Robert-Lynen: Laure Leroyer, Aurélie Champ

Paris, Conservatoire national des arts et métiers (CNAM): Michèle Antoine, Mélanie Drappier, Cyrille Foasso, Olivier Labat

Paris, Musée du Louvre: Laurence Des Cars, Olivier Gabet, Sébastien Allard, Xavier Salmon, Aline François-Colin, Philippe Malgouyres

Paris, Musée Jacquemart-André: Pierre Curie, Hélène Echifre

Rodez, Société des Lettres, Sciences et Arts de l'Aveyron: Bruno Ginisty, Jacques Frayssenge, Pierre Lançon

Troyes, Musée des Beaux-Arts: Éric Blanchegorge, Céline Chazaud, Mélanie Kaspesczyk

Washington, National Gallery of Art: Rebecca Myles

## PATRONS

Such an extensive project would not have been possible without all the patrons, donors, friends, and partners who contributed in various ways to making it a reality. I wish to express my deepest gratitude to them all for their trust and loyalty.

The restoration of the *Très Riches Heures du duc de Berry* and its exhibition benefited from the support of, among others, the Fondation Etrillard, the Friends of the Domaine de Chantilly, the TEFAF Museum Restoration Fund, the Académie des Beaux-Arts, and Sotheby's.

**Key donors**
Académie des Beaux-Arts
Jean-Marie and Betty Eveillard
Fondation Etrillard
Fondation La Marck
Friends of the Domaine de Chantilly
Hubert and Mireille Goldschmidt
Sotheby's
TEFAF Museum Restoration Fund Daniel Thierry

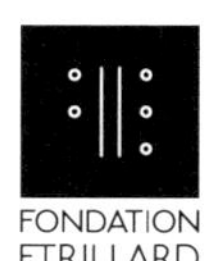


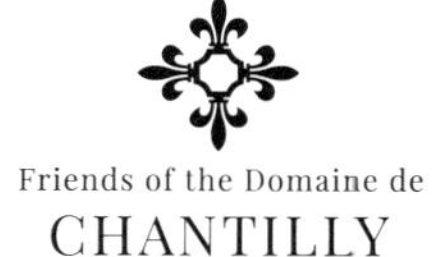


TEFAF

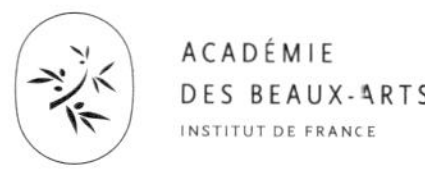


Sotheby's EST. 1744

**Sponsors of the calendar months**
Amis du Musée Condé (January)
Lionel and Ariane Sauvage (February)
BSIP – Lydie Naneix (March)
Charlotte Kramer (April)
Kazumi Mashita (May)
City of Nijmegen (June)
Kate Agius (July)
Panhard International (August)
participatory campaign (September)
Les Enluminures (October)
Alice Goldet (November)
Caroline Guerrand (December)

**Sponsors of other illuminations in the manuscript**
BSIP – Lydie Naneix (Zodiacal Man)
Valentine Denjoy (Three Magi)

**Major donors**
Louis de Bayser, René Botto, Adrien Brus, Compagnie des bibliophiles de l'Automobile Club de France, Raymond Dion, Sébastien Farin, Baudouin de Grave, Benjamin Jarry, Jean-Daniel Large, Thierry Lassabatere, Marie des Neiges de L'Eprevier, Annaëlle Marchand, Mr and Mrs Ludovic de Montille, Nicolas Suspene

**Donors**
Richard Armand, Amaury de Belleville, Adrien Breiman, Antoine de Broglie, Michel Brunet, Michel and Béatrice Brus, Michèle Carles, Cercle Amical du Berry, Charles Chatelin, Corinne Coudert, Paulette Decottignies, Catherine Duru, Alix Floquet, Dominique Gommery, Romain Goumy Arcouet, François Gueant, Camille Hatty, Jean-François Homassel, Jean-Yves Lardeux, Aurélie Le Caer, Librairie Vignes, Cédric Marc, Anne Miller, Monique Pascal, Philippe Paszkiewicz, Lionel Pernot, Béatrice Pichon, Claire Poirier, Frédéric Sailland, Julien Serey, The Crosby Fund, Samuel Valcke, Émilie Vallet, Philippe Vauclin

and all those who lent their support.

The tactile display making it possible to discover the month of September of the *Très Riches Heures* was supported by the Ministry of Culture and the Fondation Banque Populaire.

## ACKNOWLEDGMENTS

Such an ambitious project, and one launched so long ago (in 2012!), is not the work of a single person. Analyzing, restoring, studying, and exhibiting the *Très Riches Heures du duc de Berry* requires working with the finest talents.

I first wish to thank Marie-Pierre Dion, General libraries curator, and Head of the Musée Condé library and archives, who with great care used all her expertise to ensure the restoration of this iconic manuscript. Camille Olivier, Head of documentary resources at the Musée Condé, valiantly took on the management of the ambitious exhibition accompanying this restoration; and Marina Rouyer, assistant curator at the Musée Condé, compiled the many illustrations for this catalogue.

I am grateful to the members of the board of curators of the Musée Condé, Stéphanie Baratte, Camille Godon, Sylvie Hallot, Ulysse Jardat, Sabine Jardon, Florent Picouleau, as well as Anne Miller, Béatrice Pichon, Émeric d'Arcimoles, Sophie Bienaimé, Laetitia de Monicault, and to all the teams at the Château de Chantilly, including general administration, patronage, outreach, building, public contracts, support functions, security, communications and marketing, ticketing and gift shop, tourist development, reservations, security systems, and many other departments: this exhibition is the fruit of a collective ambition, that of Domaine de Chantilly of which the *Très Riches Heures* is in a sense the most sacred heart.

The Domaine de Chantilly is fortunate to have the support of societies of friends and benefactors who help to safeguard and promote its treasures.

Thank you to the Friends of the Domaine de Chantilly and their chair, Prince Amyn Aga Khan, and their director, Patricia Kim, as well as to the friends of Musée Condé and their president Claude Charpentier. I also wish to thank the Institut de France, its chancellor and its departments. Thank you to the Direction régionale des Affaires Culturelles (DRAC) Hauts-de-France, Hilaire Multon, Christine Lancestremère, Juliette Guépratte, and Florence Bord.

At the very beginning of this project, many years ago, I was fortunate to benefit from the advice and expertise of François Avril, Marie Jacob, Pierre-Yves Le Pogam, Philippe Lorentz, Patricia Stirnemann, Dominique Thiébaut, and Inès Villela-Petit; without them, this exhibition would not have become what it is today.

Thanks are also due to all those who, in one way or another, contributed to the success of this project, in particular Marie Akar, Cyril Barthalois and Béatrice Beaufils, Oriane Beaufils for her careful rereadings, Anne-Sophie Bermonville, Nathalie Brunel, Ghislain Brunel, Fleur Callegari, Sophie Caron, Sophie Fady Cayrel, Aurélie Champ, Philippe Champy, Claude Charpentier, Julien De Vos, Odile Dharcourt, Émilie Diné, Léa Ferrez-Lenhard, Laurent Ferri, Ingeborg Formann, Nicole Garnier, Maxence Hermant, Sandra Hindman, Hélène Jacquemard, Stéphane Jacques, Susan Kendall, Maria Kröpfl, Guy Ladrière, Sophie Le Flamanc, Pascale Legueu, Isabelle le Masne de Chermont, Séverine Lepape, Pierre Emmanuel Marty, Ève Menei, Sabine Maffre, Michel Mondet, Maria Adalgisa Ottaviani, Graziella Pastore, Miguel Perez de Guzman, Laurent Petitgirard, Xavier Ploix, Jim Poncelet, Simon Prunet-Foch, Emmanuel Rouillier, Xavier S. Salomon, Romain Siegenfuhr, Pierre Sissmann, Claire Turkovics, Michel Urtado, Jean-Jacques Vandewalle, Pierre Vigneron, and the Maelwael-Van Lymborch Foundation and all its members, in particular Pieter Roelofs, André Stufkens, Peter van der Heijden, and Lieke Kamphuis.

A whole team of researchers and curators were kind enough to share the fruit of their studies here, and we wish to thank them for doing so.

The manuscript was the subject of unprecedented scientific analyses carried out over many months at the Centre de recherche et de restoration des Musées de France (C2RMF), whose teams we here acknowledge: Jean-Michel Loyer-Hascouët, Élisabeth Ravaud, Nacer Berri, Martina Lange-Bréjon de Lavergnée, Hugo Plumel, Marie Lionnet-de Loitière. Its meticulous and necessary restoration was carried out by a team of experts led by Coralie Barbe, with Florence Malo and Emmanuelle Hincelin.

In Fine éditions d'art have outdone themselves in producing the most ambitious exhibition catalogue ever produced by the Condé Museum. Thank you to Véronique Balmelle, Marc-Alexis Baranes, Marine Bezou, Anne Chapoutot, Lore Gauterie, Clara Koumyoumdjian, Luc Martin, Stéphanie Méséguer, Denis Richerol, and Charlotte Villain Chevolleau. Thanks also to Gautier Platteau and Sara Colson for the English and German versions of this catalogue.

The exhibition benefited from the scenographic expertise of a seasoned team including Claudine Dreyfus and Isabelle Devin (JAAMS, scenographers), Lawrence Bitterly (graphic design), Stéphanie Daniel (lighting), Patrick Mandron (miniature boxes), MPI, and Version Bronze.

## AUTHORS

Edited by

**Mathieu Deldicque**
*Chief heritage curator, Director of the Musée Condé and the Musée vivant du Cheval*

In collaboration with

**Marie-Pierre Dion**
*General libraries curator, Head of the Musée Condé library and archives*

**Coralie Barbe and Florence Malo**
*Heritage restorers*

**Véronique de Becdelièvre**
*Paleographic archivist*

**Till-Holger Borchert**
*Director, Suermondt-Ludwig Museum, Aachen*

**Laurent Hablot**
*Director of studies, École Pratique des Hautes Études*

**Marie Jacob-Yapi**
*Senior lecturer in the History of Medieval Art, University of Rennes 2*

**Philippe Malgouyres**
*General heritage curator, Musée du Louvre, Department of Objets d'art*

**Élisabeth Ravaud, Anne Michelin, Kilian Laclavetine, Éric Laval, and Laurence Clivet**
*Centre de recherche et de restauration des musées de France (C2RMF)*

**Pieter Roelofs**
*Chief curator, Fine Arts and Decorative Arts Department, Rijksmuseum*

**Dominique Thiébaut**
*Honorary general curator of heritage*

**Inès Villela-Petit**
*Curator of heritage*

## PHOTO CREDITS

© ADGAP Courtesy Michael Werner Gallery, New York: 321

© Alamy: 316, 320 (bottom)

© Archives départementale du Cher: 98 bottom, 177

© Archivia di Stato, Turin: 288

© Atelier Coralie Barbe: 350 (top), 352–59

© Bibliothèque de Genève: 113

© Bibliothèque Mazarine, Paris: 312

© Bibliothèque du musée Condé, Chantilly: 303, 304 (bottom), 310 (top), 311 (top), 315, 320 (top), 338 (fig. 20, right)

© Bibliothèque municipale de Bourges: 110–11

© Bibliothèque nationale de France, Paris: 76 (left), 106 (right), 107, 108, 115–16, 123–24, 126, 128, 148 (left), 149 (left), 157 (left), 224 (bottom), 226, 236 (right), 249 (bottom), 268

© Bibliothèque royale de Belgique, Brussels: 109, 201 (right)

© Bibliothèque Sainte-Geneviève, Paris: 106 (left)

© BKP Berlin / Distribution GrandPalaisRmn / Jörg P. Anders: 182

© Bridgeman Images: 109, 160–61, 164 (bottom), 248 (right), 252 (bottom), 276, 278, 302 (right)

© Bridgeman Images / Bodleian Libraries, University of Oxford: 223 (right), 224 (top)

© Bridgeman Images / The British library archives: 223 (left), 232, 266 (right), 284–85

© Bridgeman Images / photo: Luisa Ricciarini / Osterreichische Nationalbibliothek, Vienna: 250, 251 (bottom)

© Bridgeman Images / The Fitzwilliam Museum: 236 (left)

© British Museum, London: 76 (right), 78

© C2RMF, photo: L. Clivet: 333 (bottom), 334, 336 (bottom), 338 (bottom), 341–43, 344 (top)

© C2RMF, photo: E. Lambert- J.L Bellec: 191–92

© C2RMF, photo: E. Ravaud: 333 (top), 335, 337, 338 (figs. 18, 19, 20 left), 339–40, 344 (figs. 42, 43)

© Cathedral of Toledo: 77 (left)

© Château-musée Charles VII, Mehun-sur-Yèvre : 75 (bottom)

© Chester Beatty Library, Dublin: 286

© Cinémathèque Robert-Lynen, Paris: 311 (bottom)

© Conseil départemental du Cher : 91

© DRAC Centre-Val de Loire, photo : François Lauginie: 85

© GrandPalaisRmn / Domaine de Chantilly / Adrien Didierjean: 310 (bottom), 313, 314, 315, 358 (bottom, right)

© GrandPalaisRmn / Domaine de Chantilly / Michel Urtado: 4–5, 10, 47–48, 50–52, 53–55, 57, 60–62, 64, 65 (bottom), 68–73, 75, 80, 81 (top), 82–83, 88–89, 92–93, 102–105,118–122, 129–34, 144–47, 148 (right), 149 (right), 150 (right), 151 (right), 152–55, 159, 162–63, 165–168, 170, 171–74, 187–190, 194–95, 210–21, 228–231, 256–63, 266 (left), 267, 270–71, 298–99, 306–09, 330–31, 346–49, 362–63, 374–78

© GrandPalaisRmn / Musée du Louvre / Image GrandPalaisRmn: 97 (top)

© GrandPalaisRmn / Musée du Louvre / Daniel Arnaudet: 99

© GrandPalaisRmn / Musée du Louvre / Gérard Blot: 222

© GrandPalaisRmn / Musée du Louvre / Adrien Didierjean: 183

© GrandPalaisRmn / Musée du Louvre / Tony Querrec: 178

© GrandPalaisRmn / Musée du Louvre / Hervé Lewandowski: 99

© GrandpalaisRmn / Musée du Louvre / Stéphane Maréchalle: 84, 94–95, 99–100, 164

© GrandPalaisRmn / Musée du Louvre / Franck Raux: 176

© IRHT-CNRS / Domaine de Chantilly: 16–39, 45–46, 58–59, 65 (top), 66–67, 136–141, 180–81, 184–85, 196–97, 204–05, 238–243, 246–47, 248 (left), 249 (top), 252 (top), 254–55, 272–73, 280–81, 290–95, 322–27

© KHM-Museumsverband, Vienna: 79

© Musée Condé, Chantilly: 300, 302 (left), 304 (top)

© Musées et Patrimoine Historique de la Ville de Bourges, photo : François Lauginie: 97 (bottom)

© Museo Archeologico Nazionale di Napoli, Raffaello Bencini / Bridgeman Images: 98 (top)

© Museum national d'Histoire naturelle, photo: Anne Michelin: 336 (top)

© Patrimonio Nacional de España: 77 (right)

© Real Biblioteca de El Escorial : 274 (bottom)

© Rijksmuseum, Amsterdam: 200

© Staatsbibliothek, Berlin: 202 (bottom)

© Stedelijk Museum, Zutphen: 201 (left)

© The J. Paul Getty Museum, Los Angeles: 234–35

© The Metropolitan Museum of Art, New York: 274 (top)

© The Metropolitan Museum of Art, The Cloisters Collection, New York: 86, 125, 127, 150 (left), 151 (left), 177, 186, 208

© The Morgan Library & Museum, New York: 209, 251 (top)

© The National Gallery of Art, Washington: 156 (right), 179

© The Victoria and Albert Museum, London / Dist. GrandPalaisRmn-image Victoria and Albert Museum: 96

© The Walters Art Museum, Baltimore: 81 (bottom)

© Uppsala University Library: 202 (top)

© All rights reserved: 77, 157 (right), 169, 233, 317–19, 350 (top)

### Economic Rights

© Marcel Broodthaers/ADAGP, Paris, 2025: 321

Appendix

# The Complete *Très Riches Heures*

Inside front cover – Flyleaf

Flyleaf v – Flyleaf

Flyleaf v – fol. 1

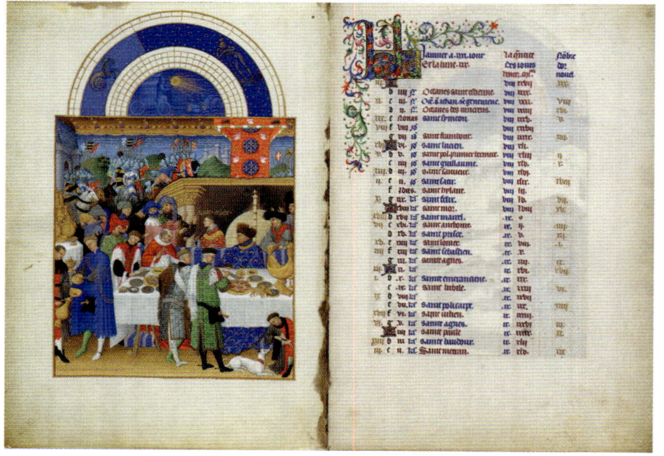

fol. 1v–2

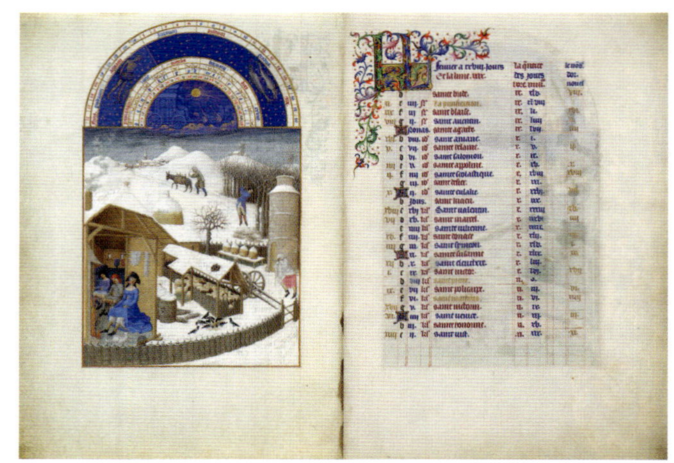

fol. 2v–3

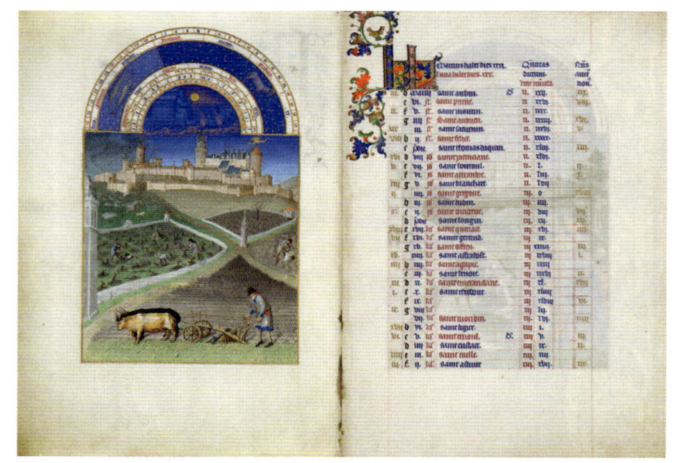

fol. 3v–4

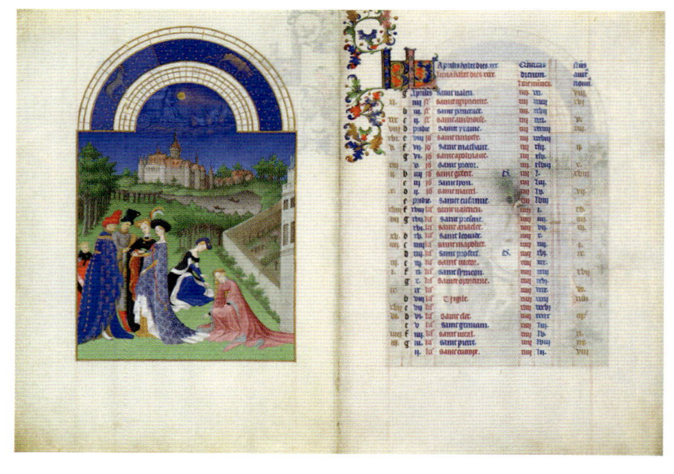

fol. 4v–5

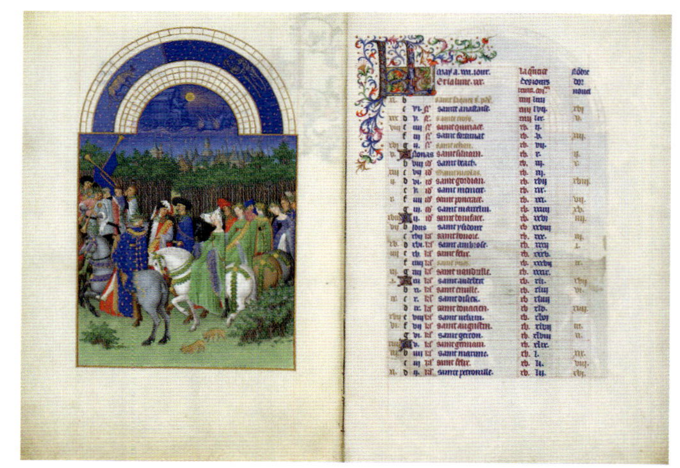

fol. 5v–6

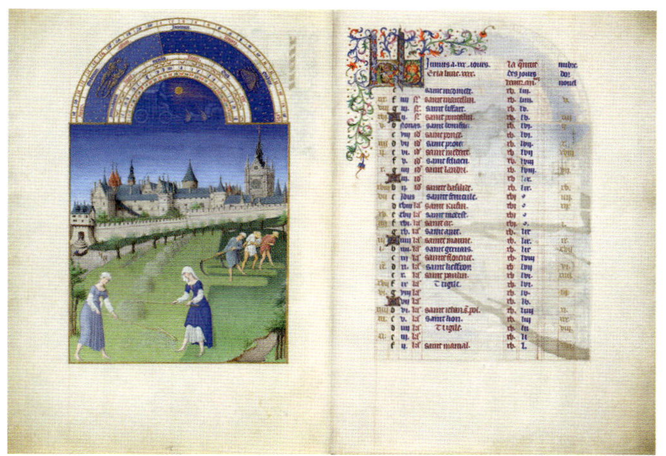
fol. 6v–7

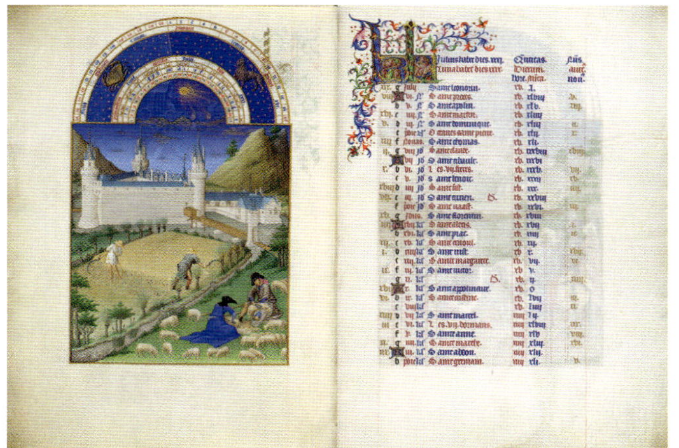
fol. 7v–8

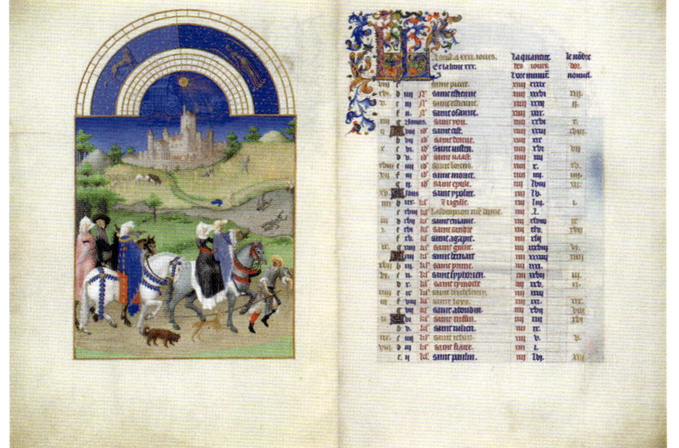
fol. 8v–9

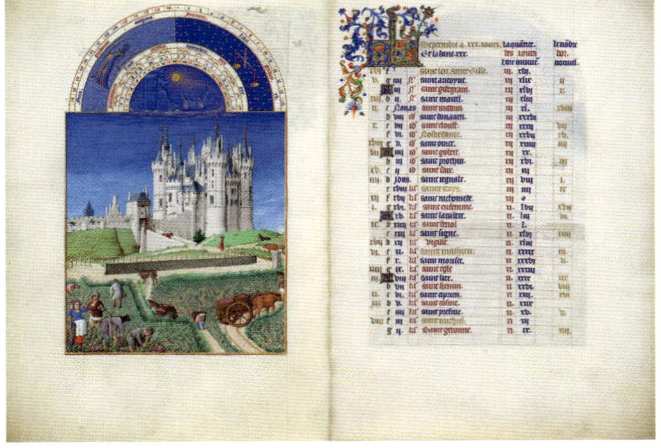
fol. 9v–10

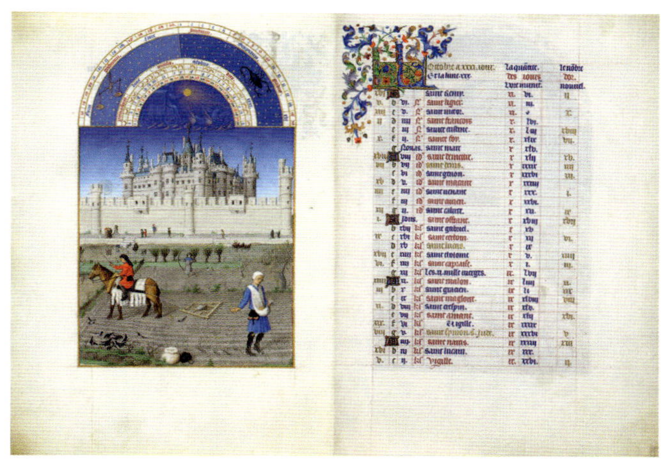
fol. 10v–11

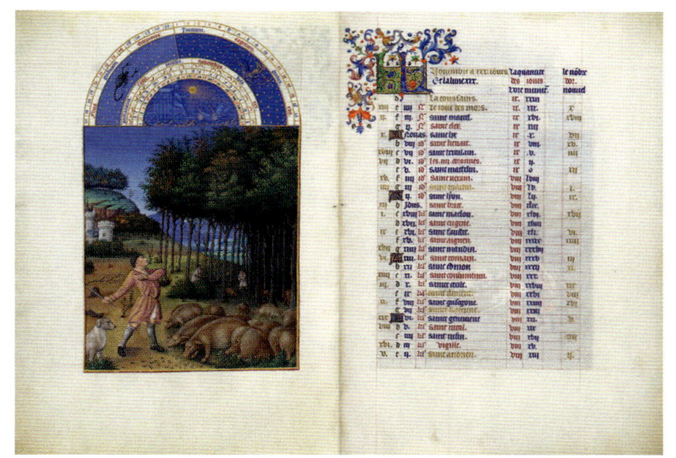
fol. 11v–12

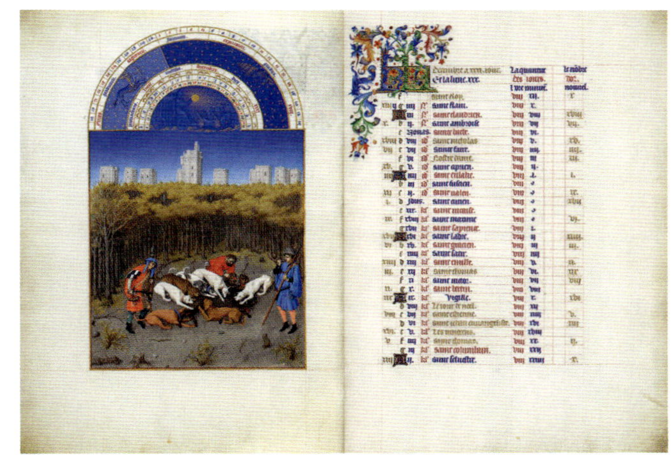
fol. 12v–13

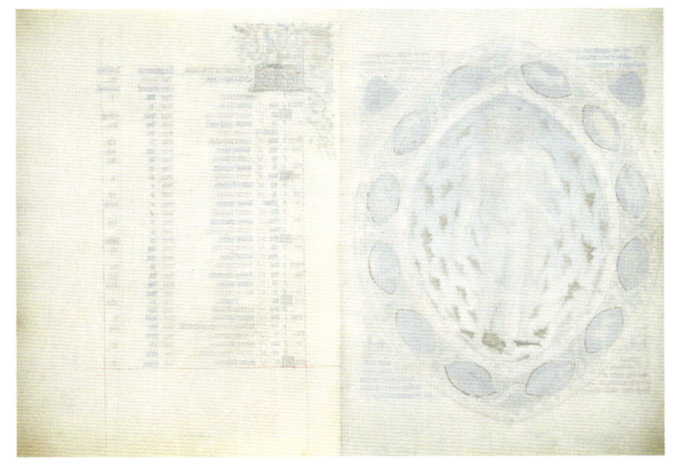
fol. 13v–14

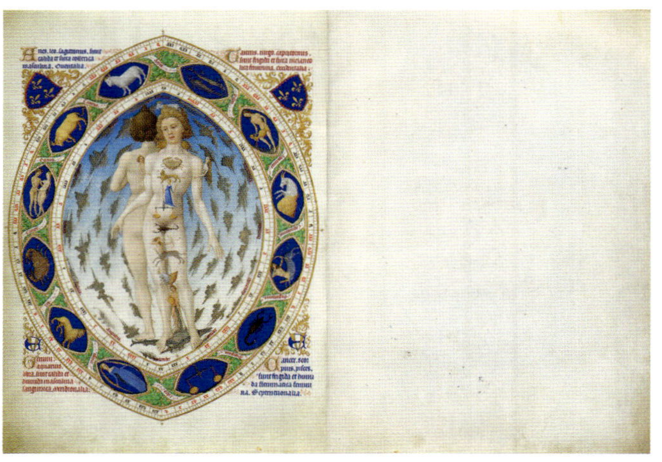

fol. 14v–15

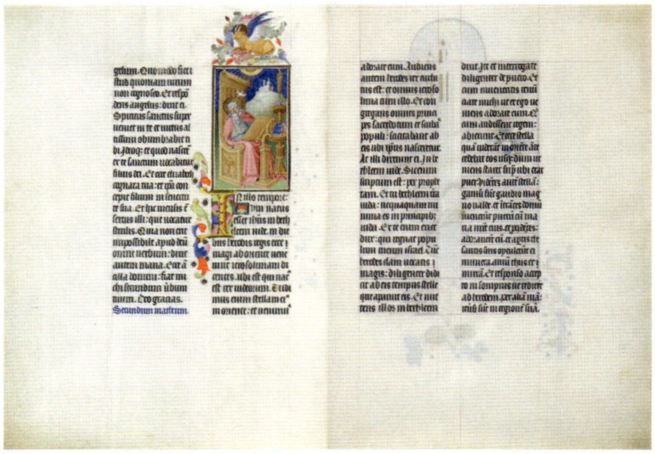

fol. 18v–19

fol. 15v–16

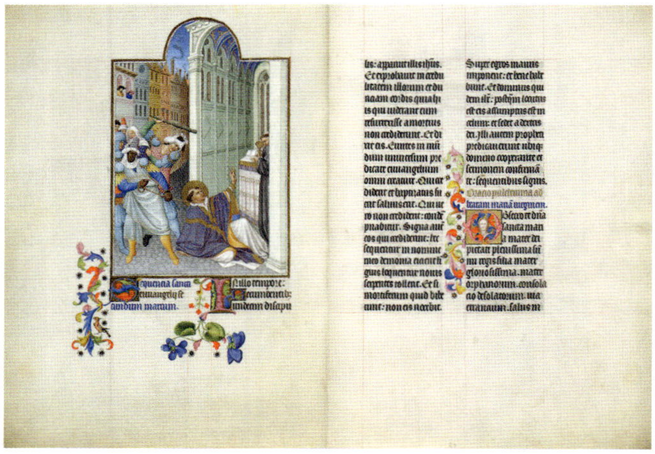

fol. 19v–20

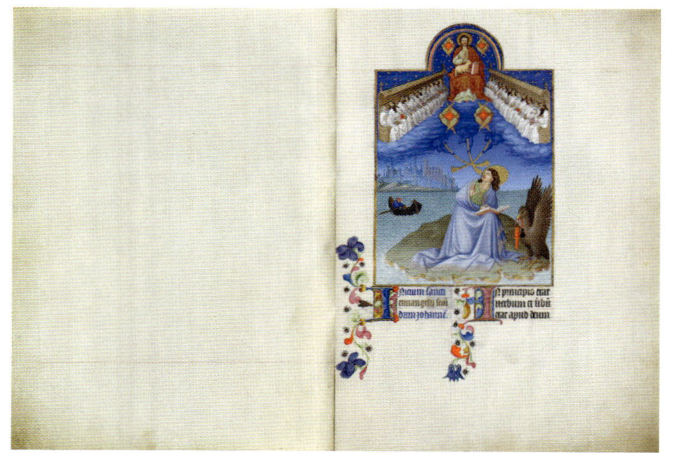

fol. 16v–17

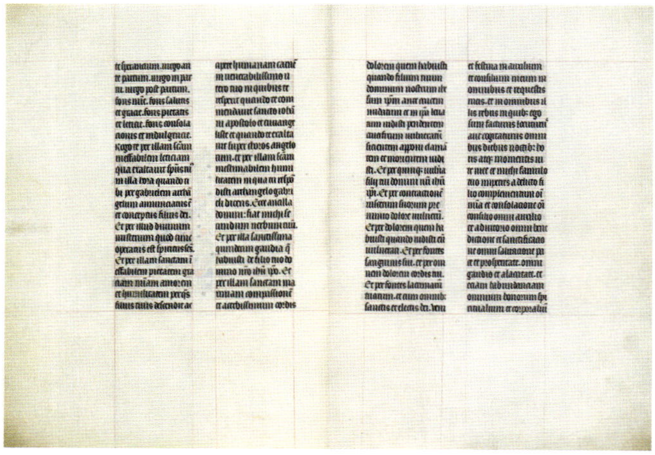

fol. 20v–21

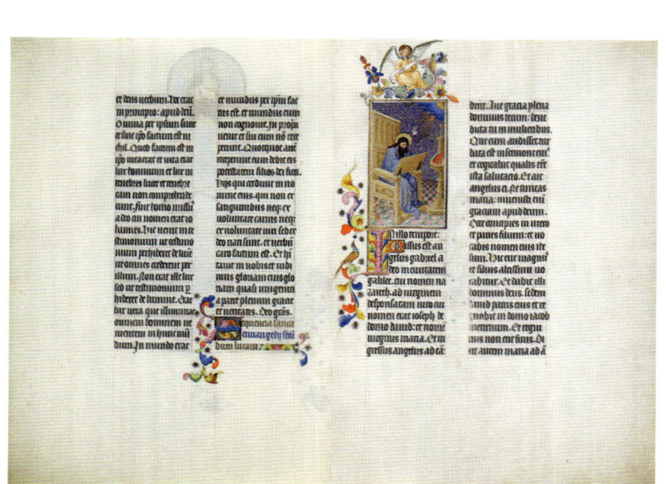

fol. 17v–18

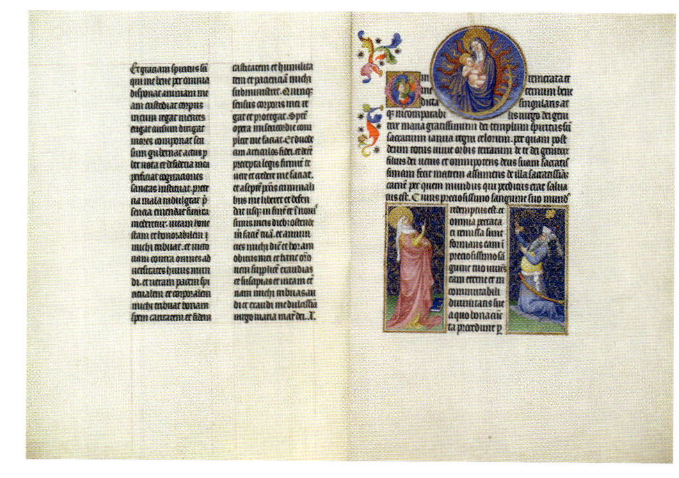

fol. 21v–22

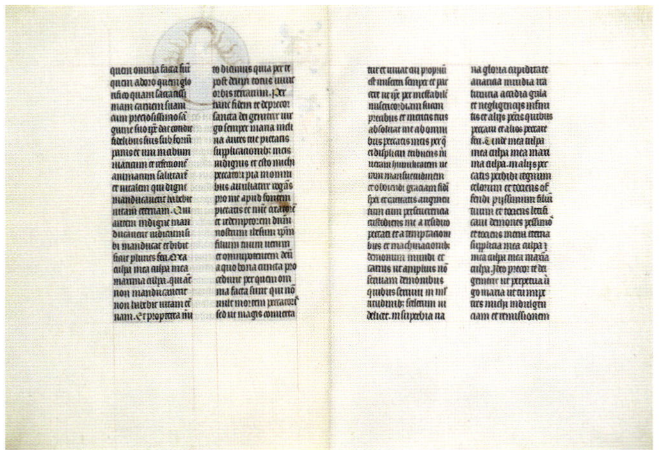

fol. 22v–23

fol. 26v–27

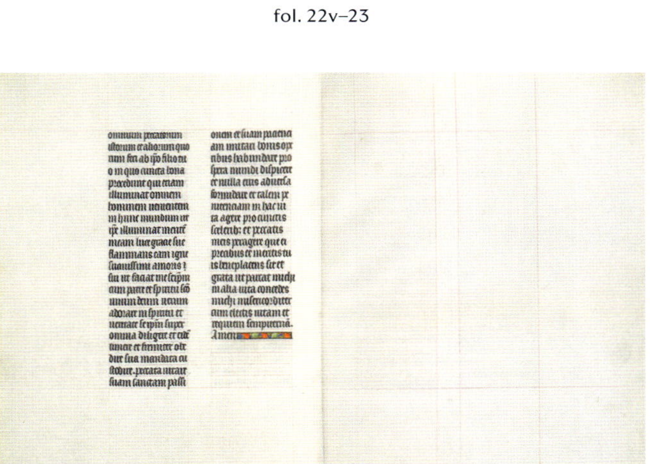

fol. 23v–24

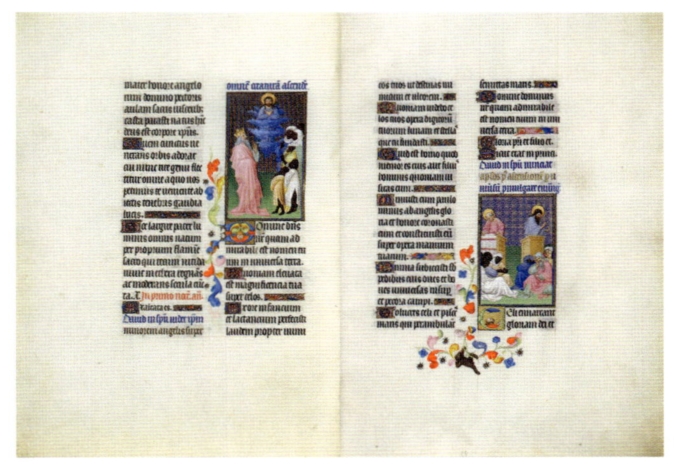

fol. 27v–28

fol. 24v–25

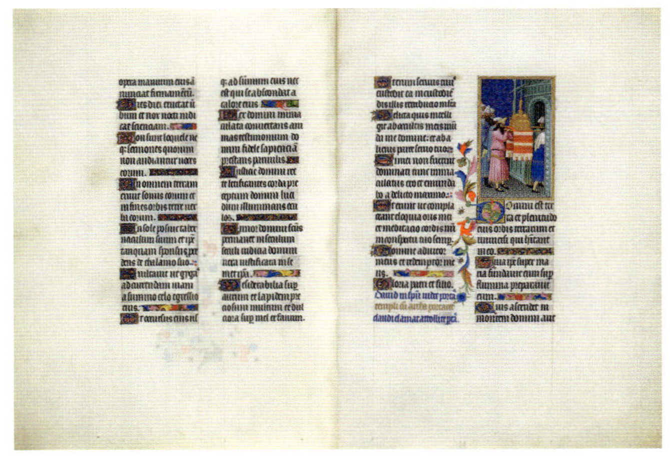

fol. 28v–29

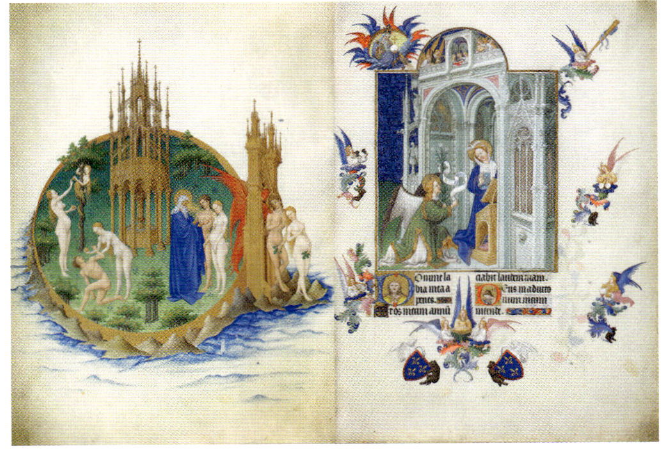

fol. 25v–26

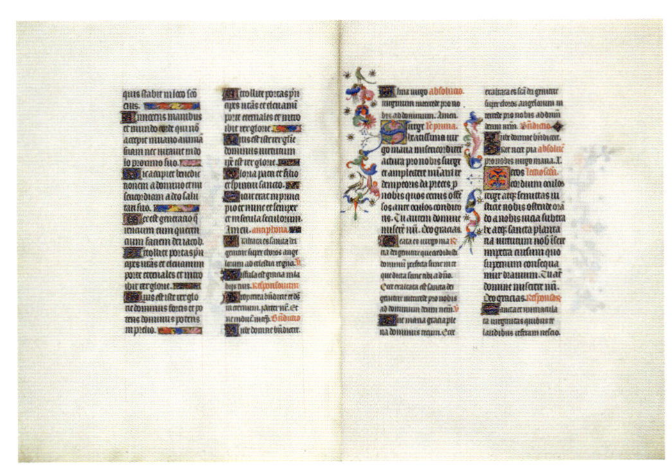

fol. 29v–30

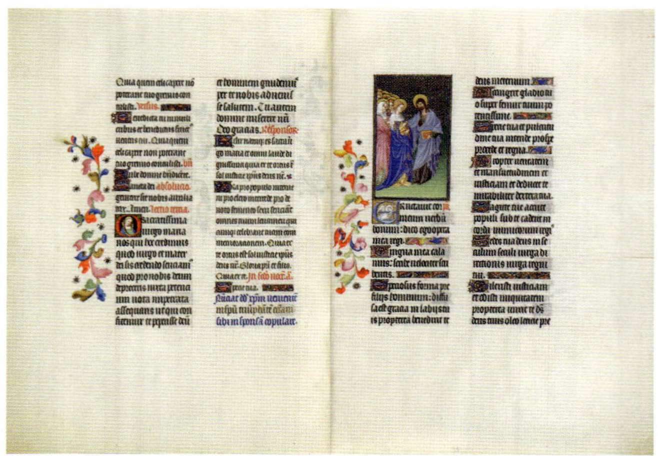

fol. 30v–31

fol. 34v–35

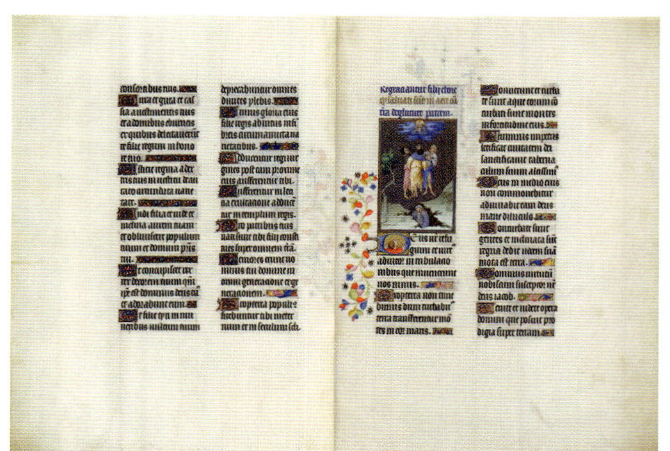

fol. 31v–32

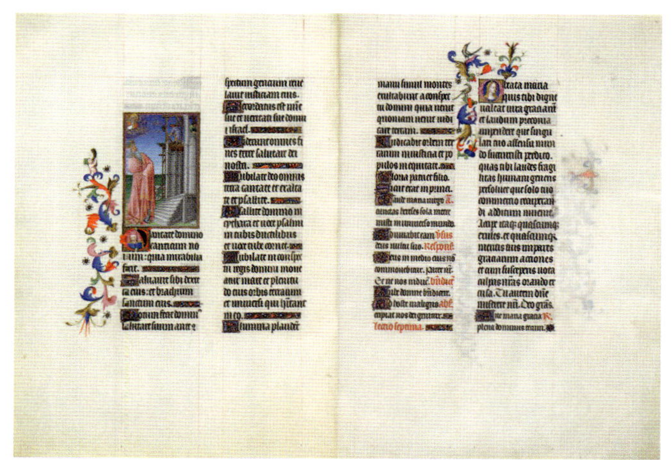

fol. 35v–36

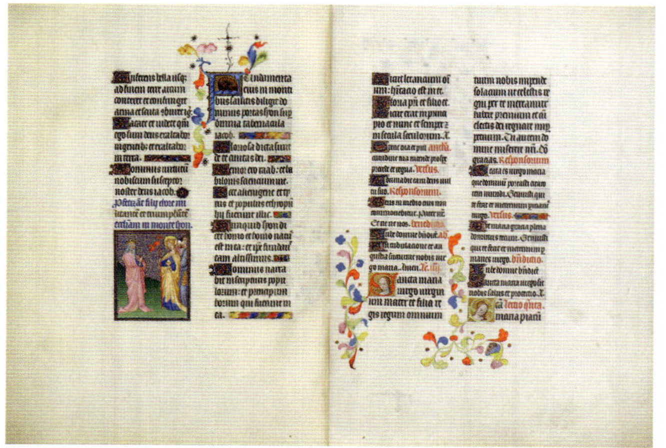

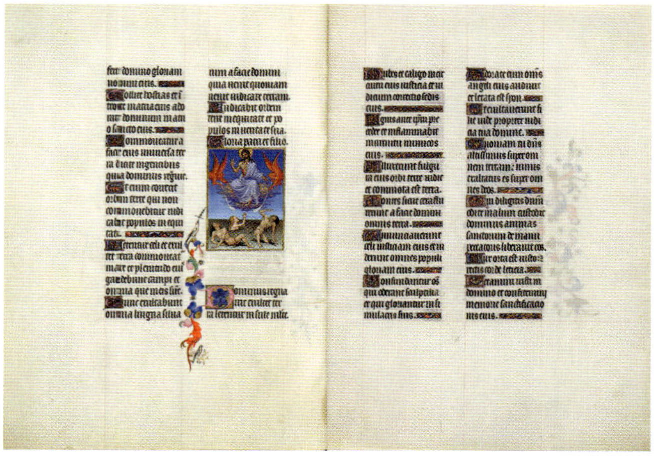

fol. 32v–33

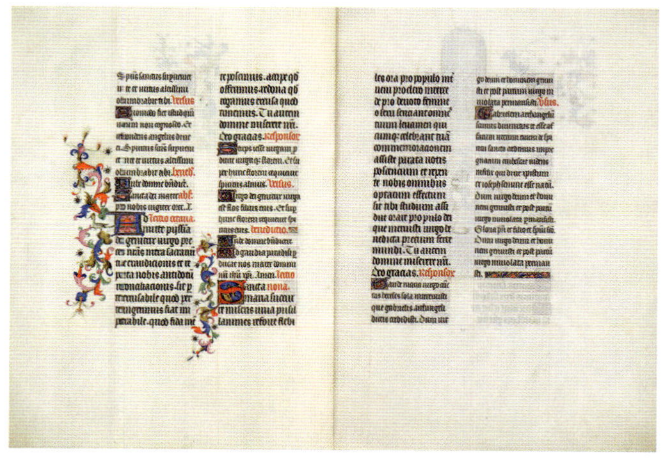

fol. 36v–37

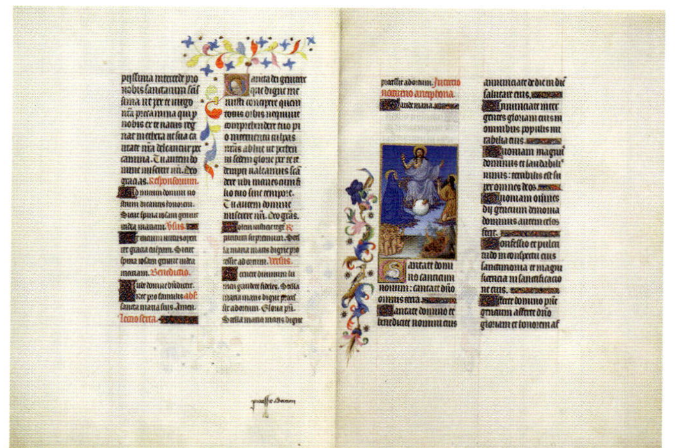

fol. 33v–34

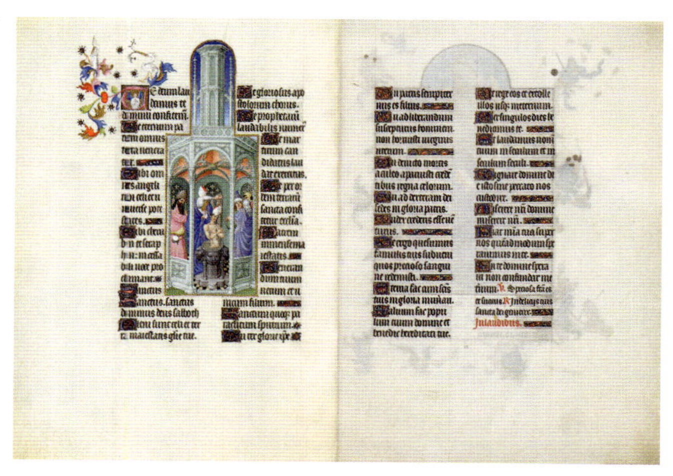

fol. 37v–38

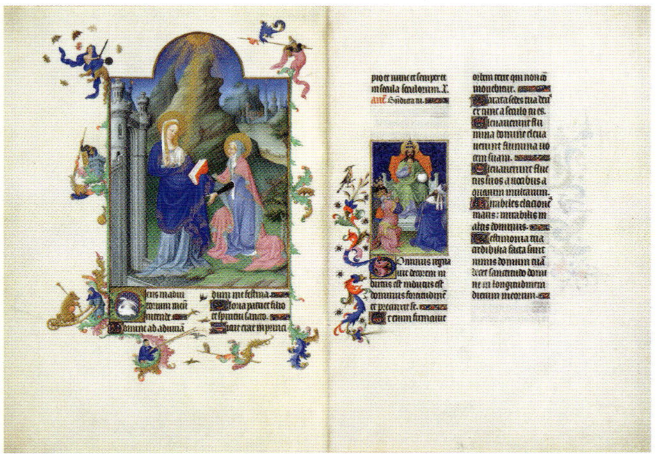

fol. 38v–39

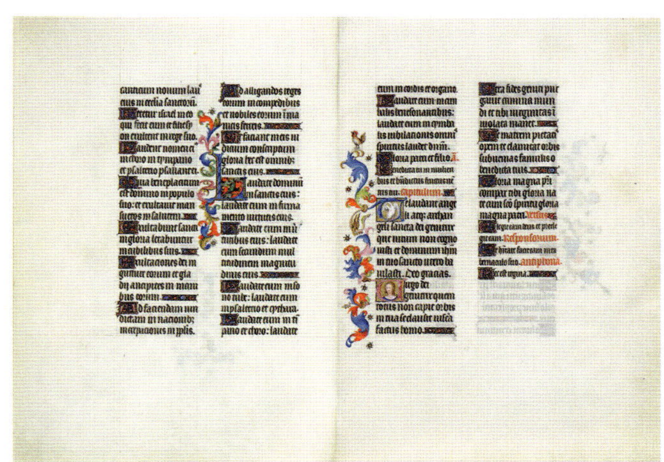

fol. 42v–43

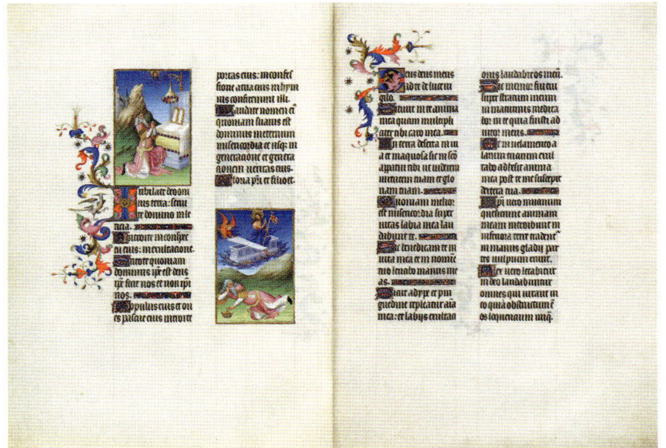

fol. 39v–40

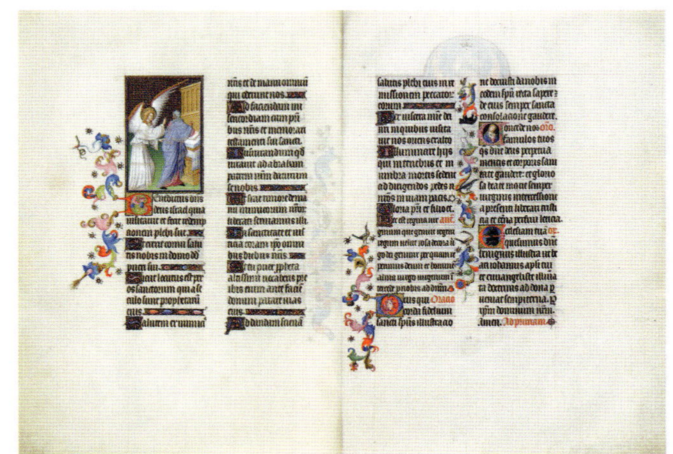

fol. 43v–44

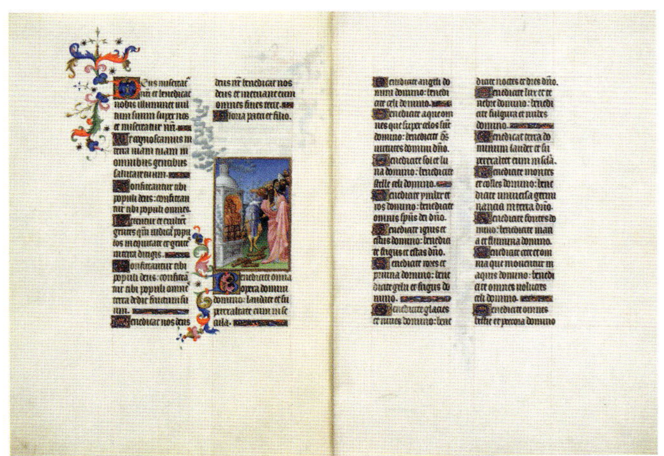

fol. 40v–41

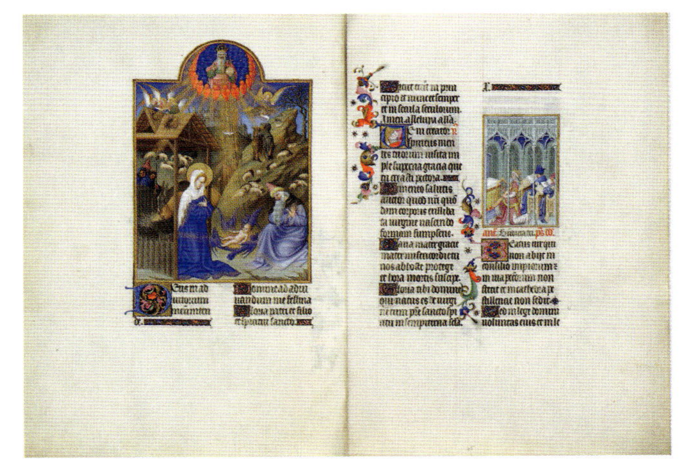

fol. 44v–45

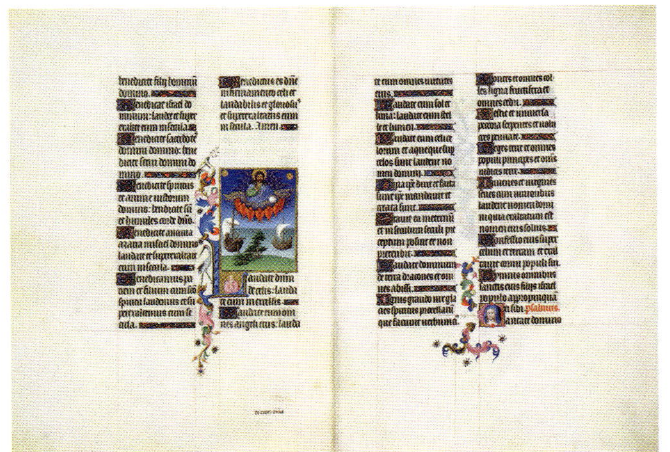

fol. 41v–42

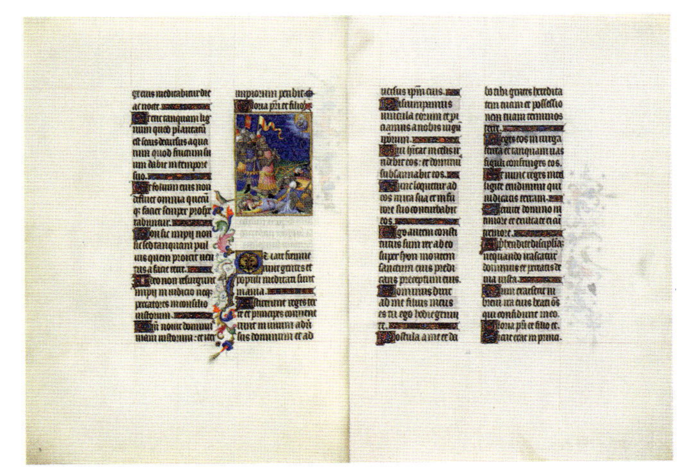

fol. 45v–46

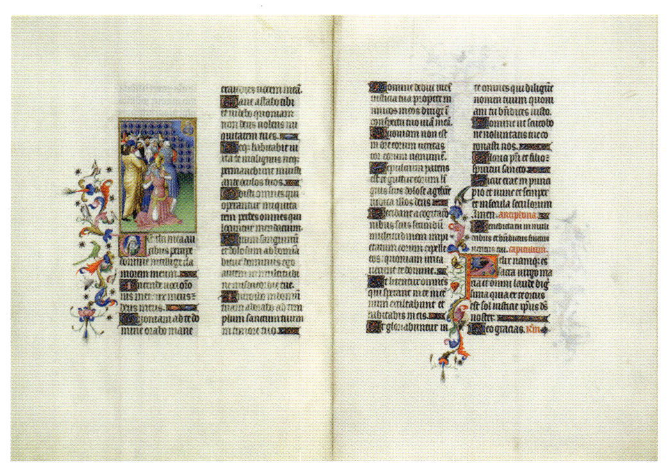

fol. 46v–47

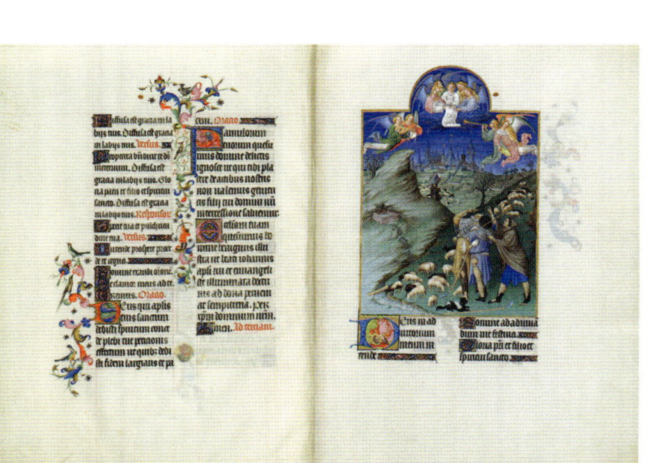

fol. 47v–48

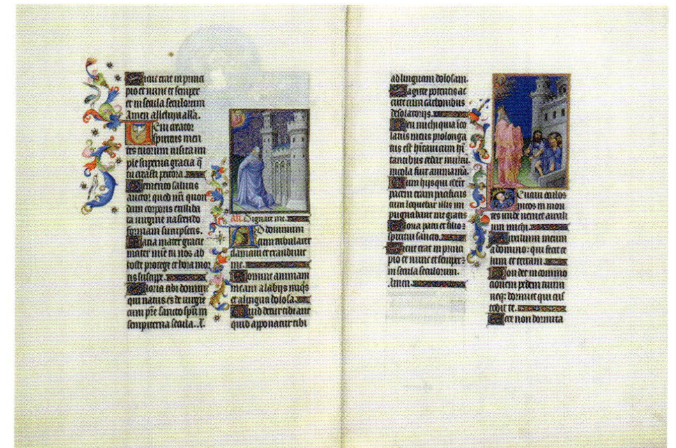

fol. 48v–49

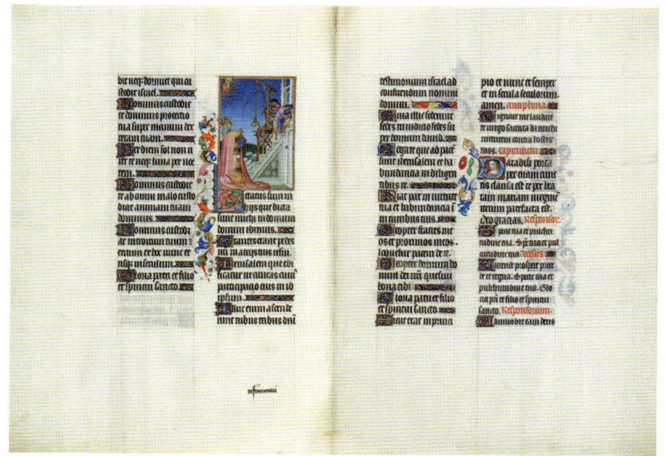

fol. 49v–50

fol. 50v–51

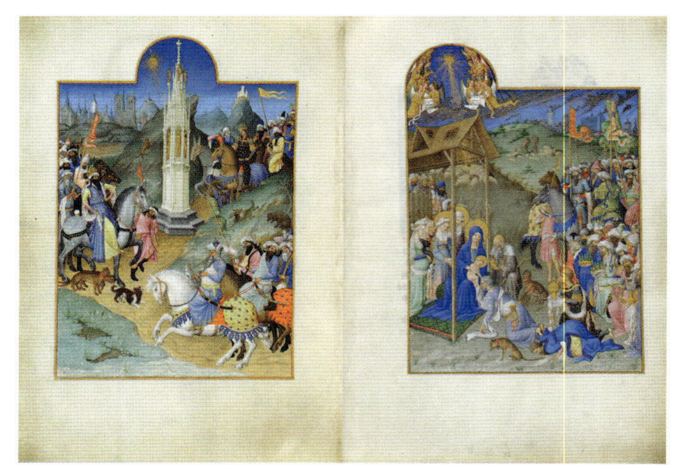

fol. 51v–52

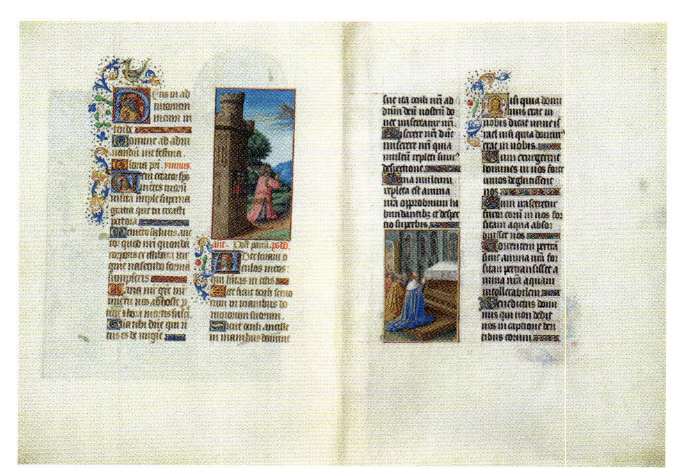

fol. 52v–53

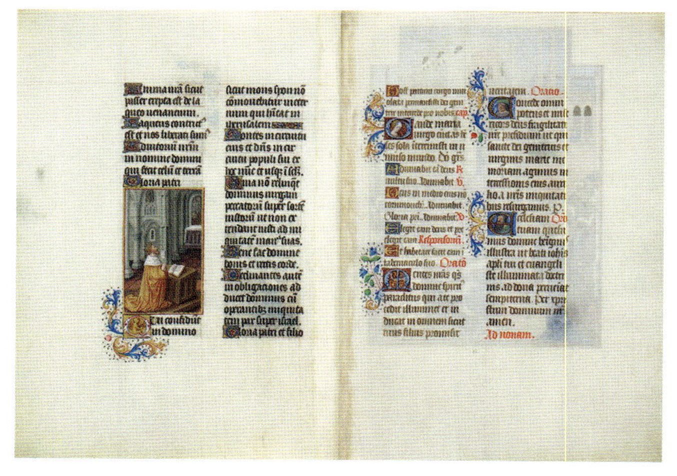

fol. 53v–54

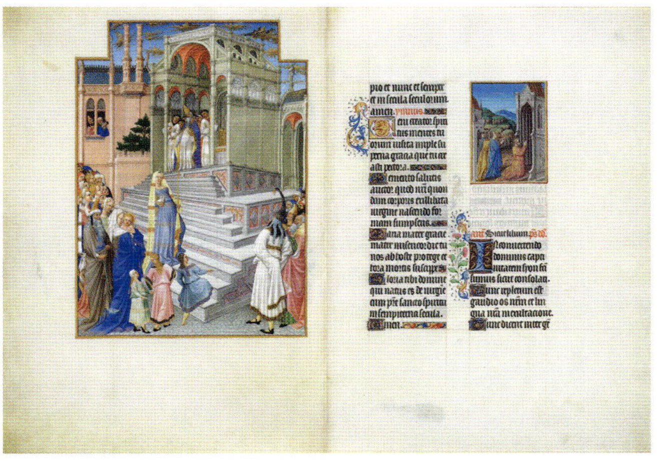

fol. 54v–55

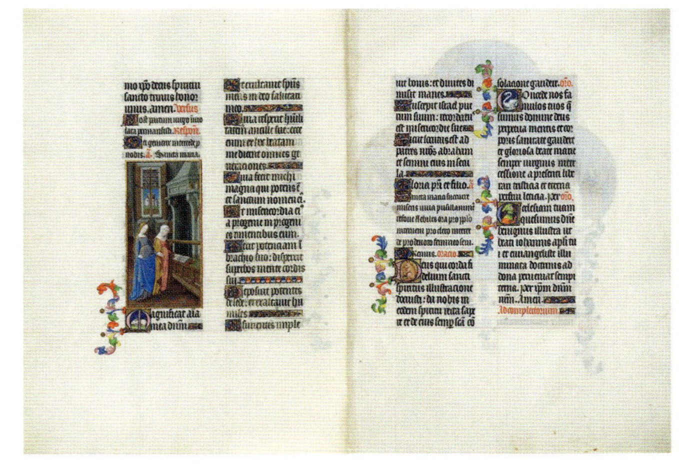

fol. 58v–59

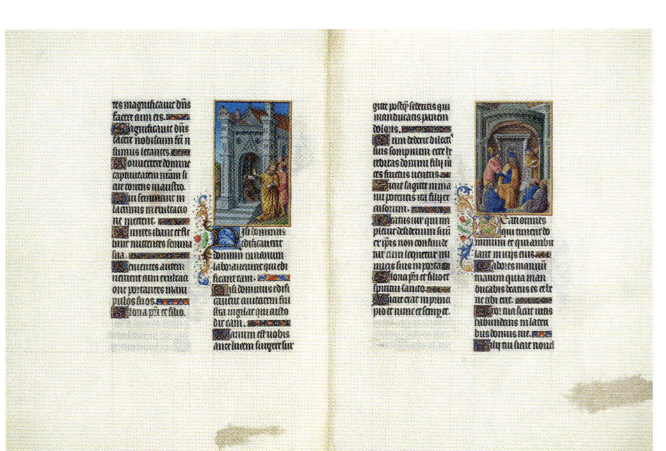

fol. 55v–56

fol. 59v–60

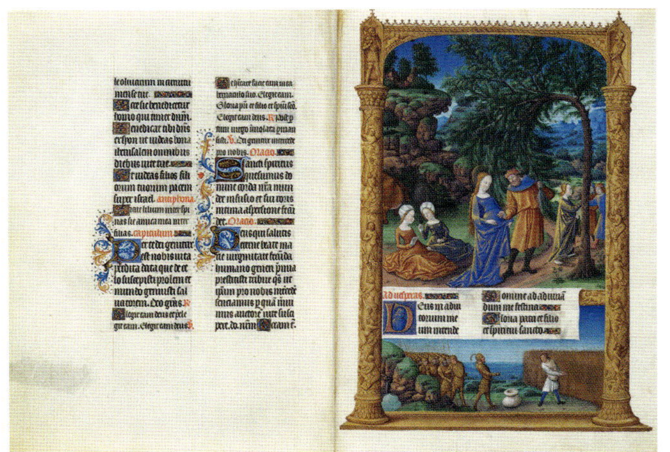

fol. 56v–57

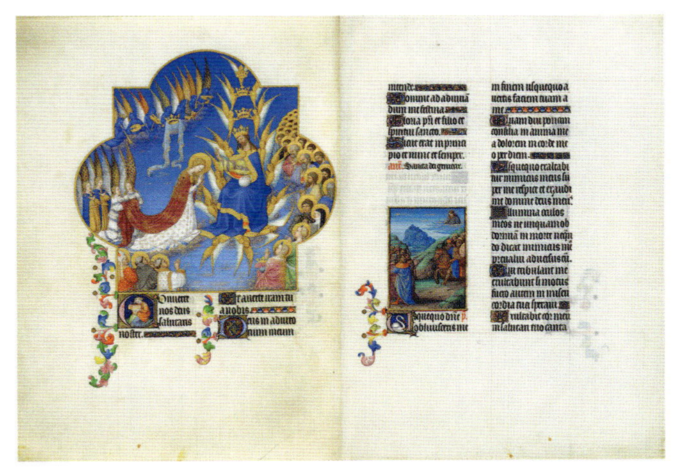

fol. 60v–61

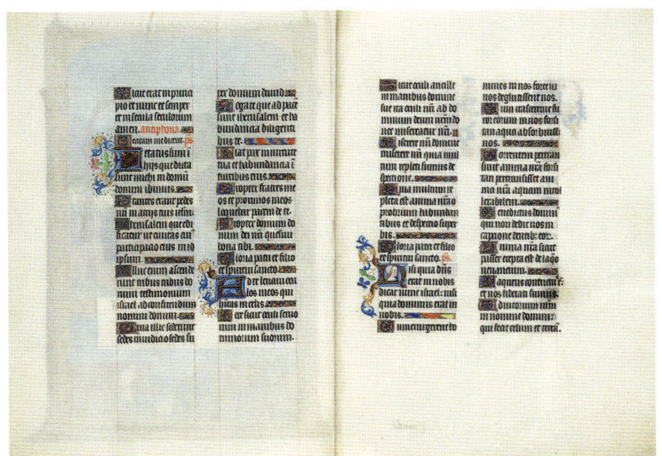

fol. 57v–58

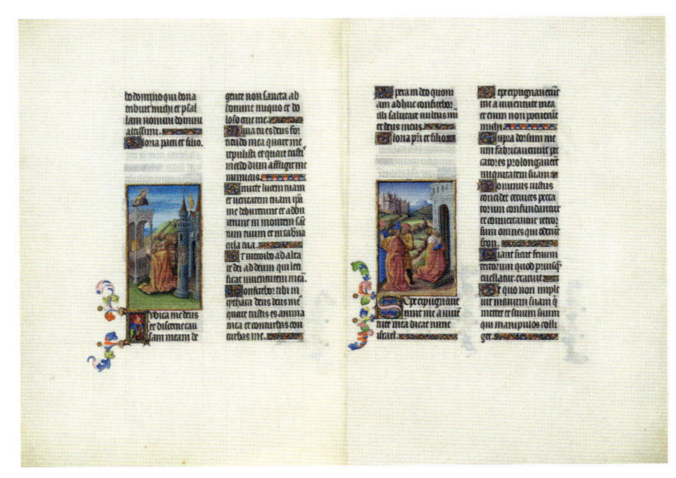

fol. 61v–62

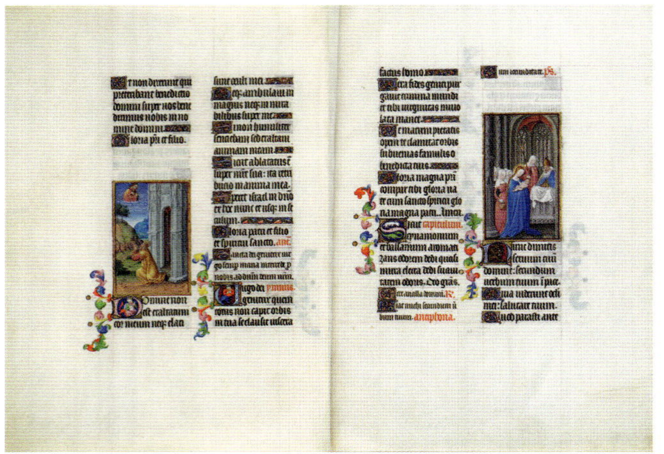

fol. 62v–63

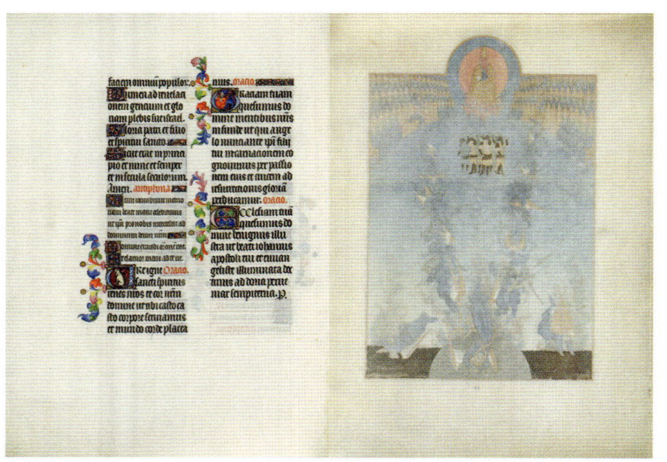

fol. 63v–64

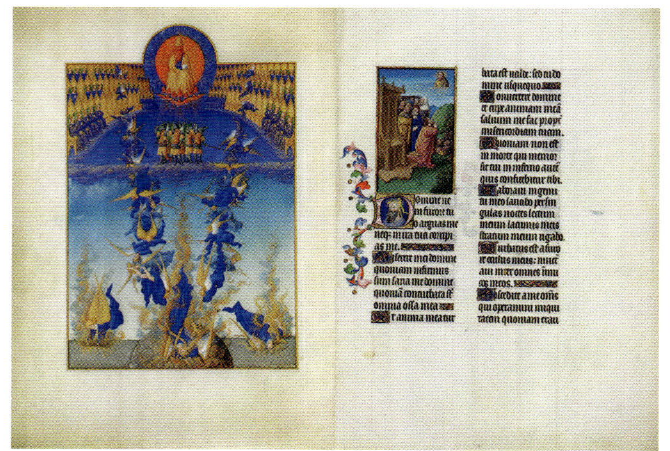

fol. 64v–65

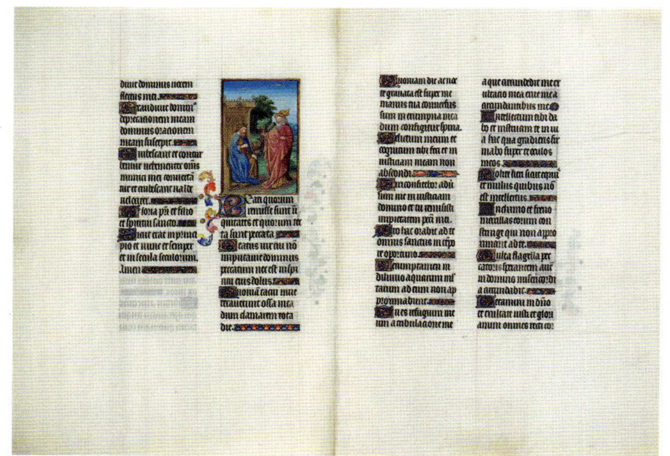

fol. 65v–66

fol. 66v–67

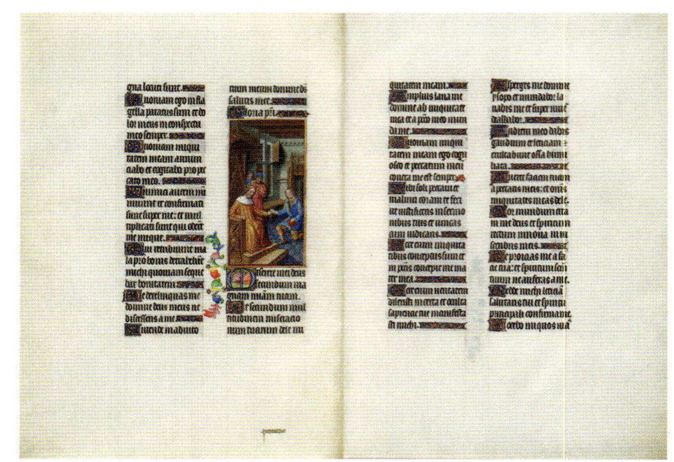

fol. 67v–68

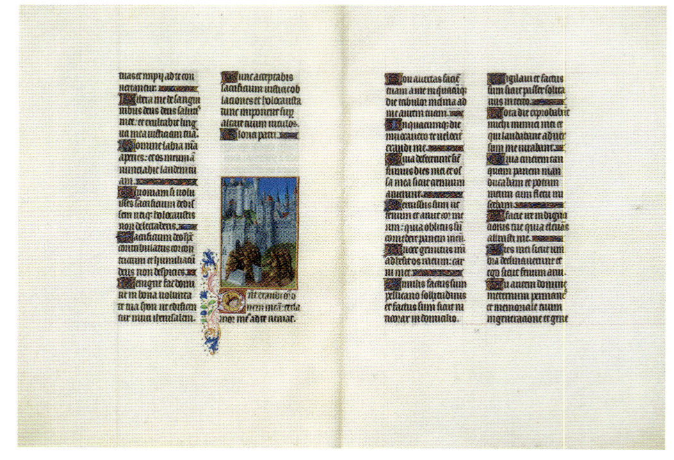

fol. 68v–69

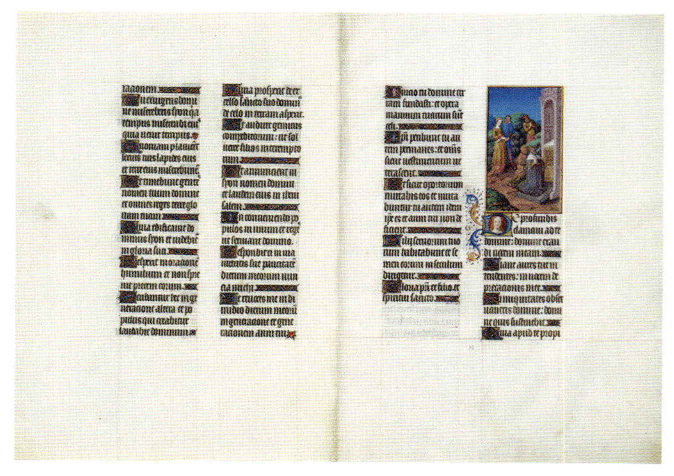

fol. 69v–70

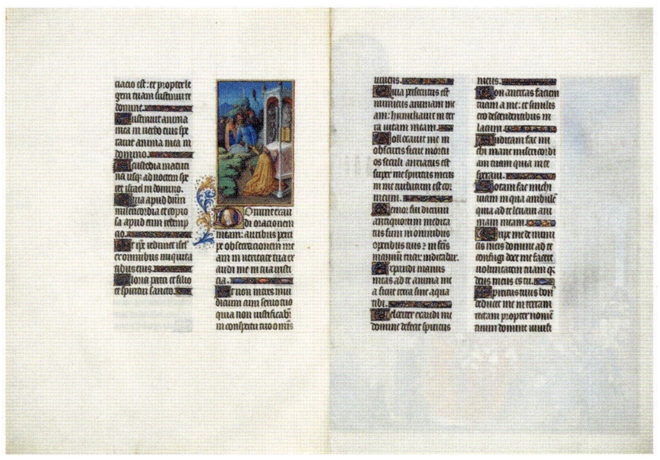

fol. 70v–71

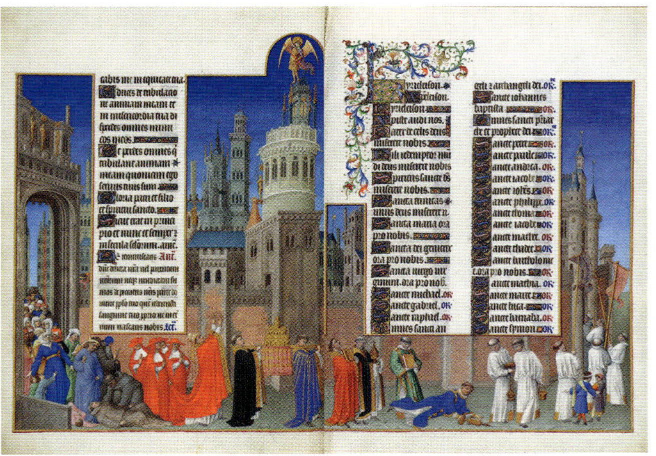

fol. 71v–72

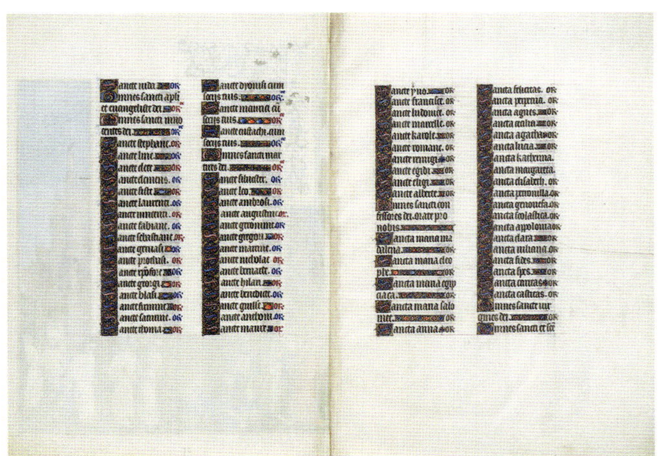

fol. 72v–73

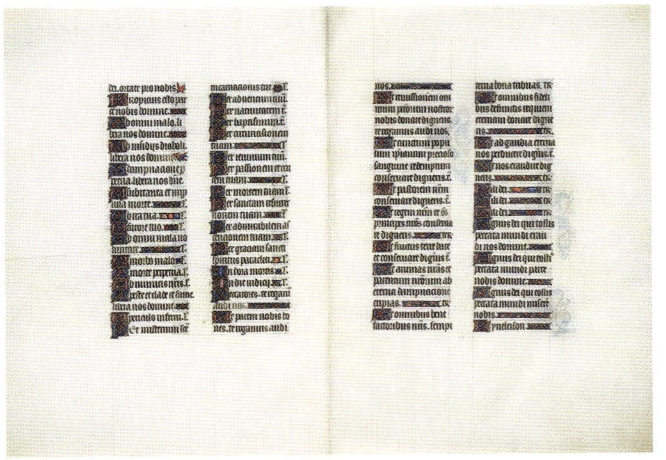

fol. 73v–74

fol. 74v–75

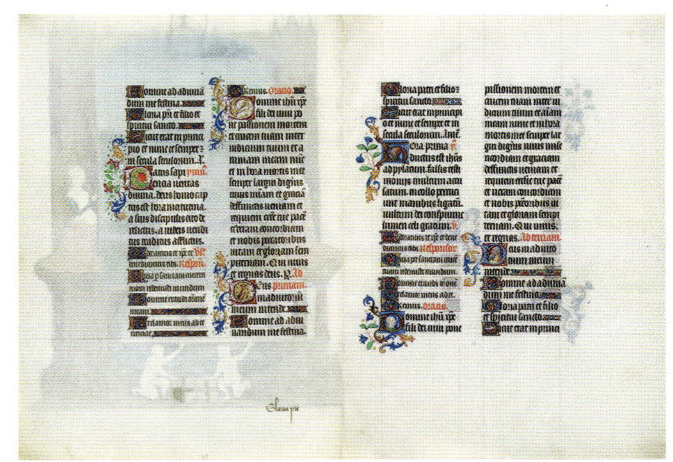

fol. 75v–76

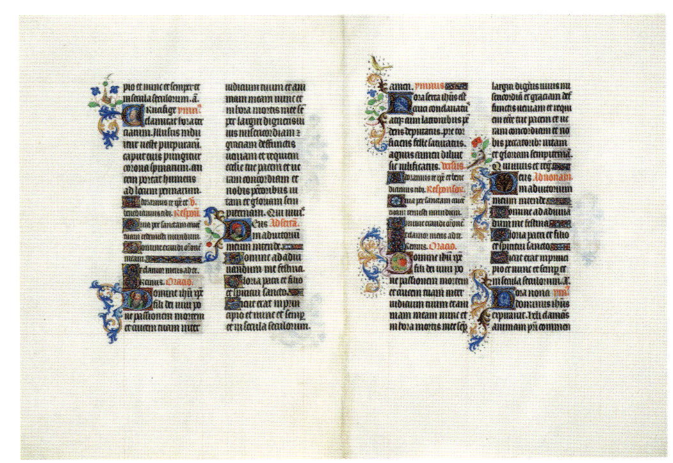

fol. 76v–77

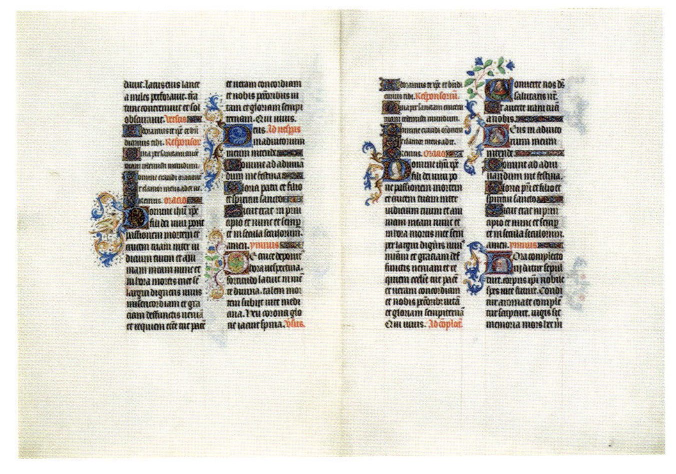

fol. 77v–78

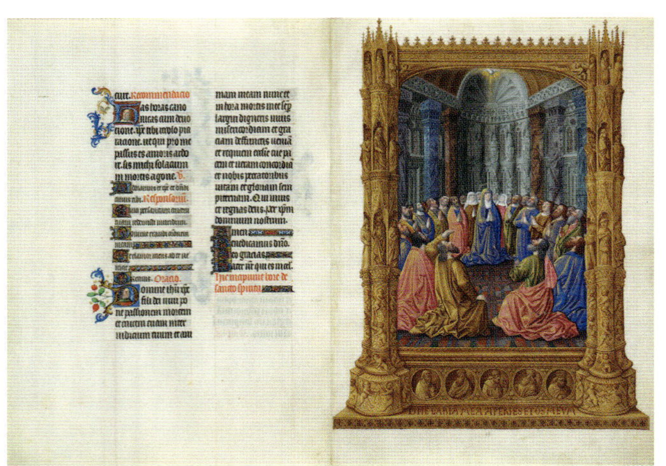

fol. 78v–79

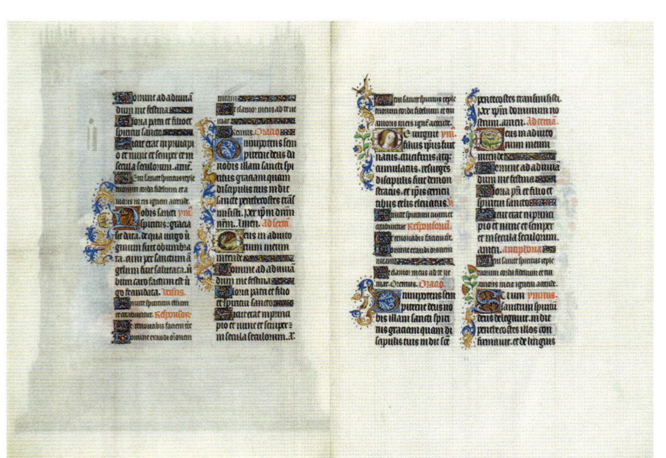

fol. 79v–80

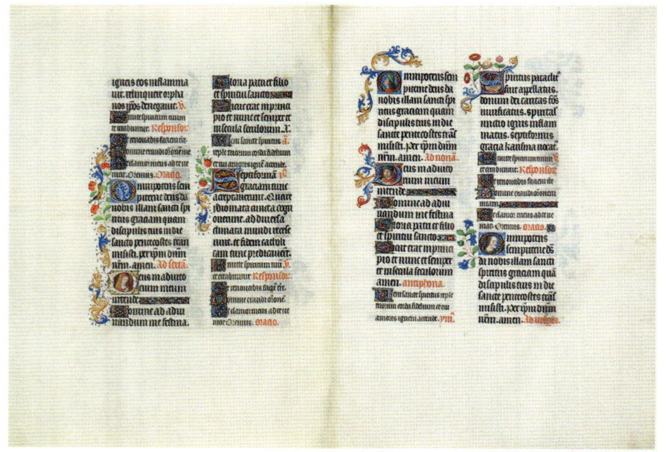

fol. 80v–81

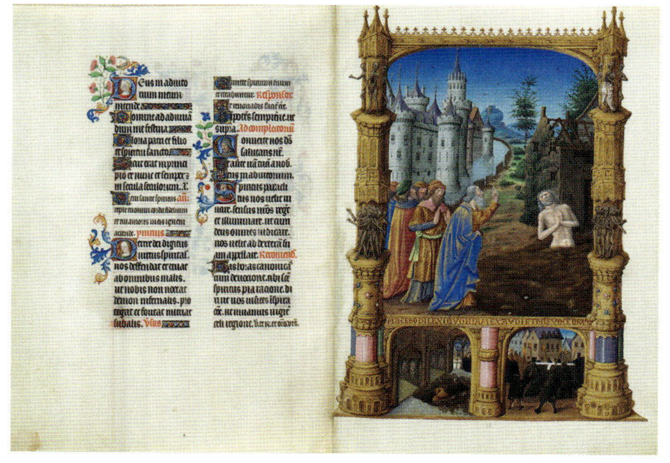

fol. 81v–82

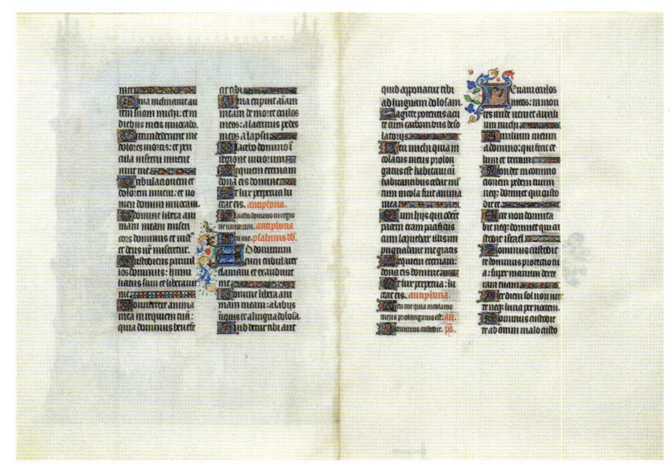

fol. 82v–83

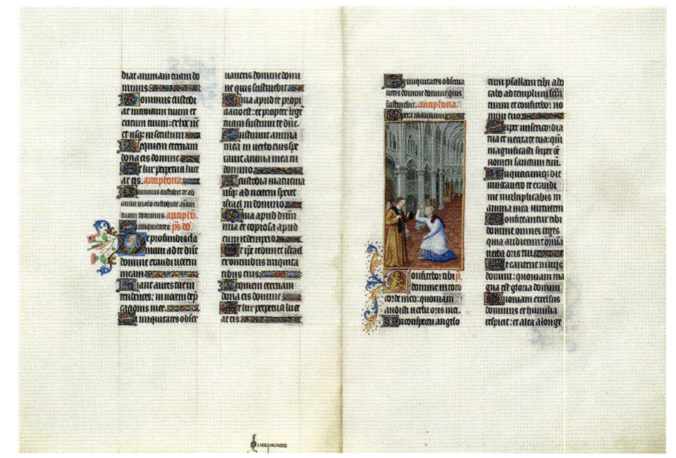

fol. 83v–84

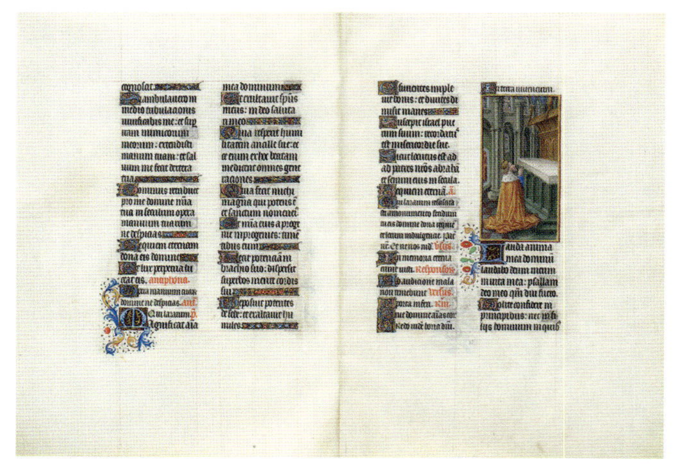

fol. 84v–85

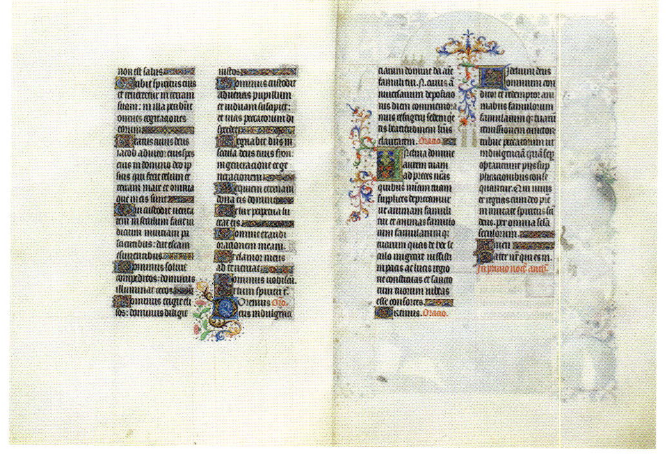

fol. 85v–86

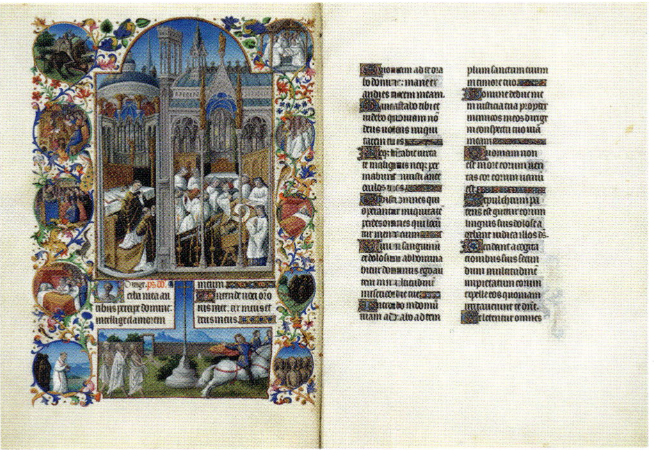

fol. 86v–87

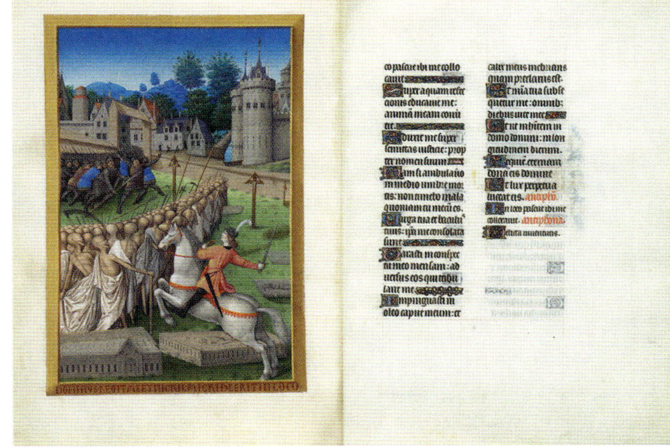

fol. 90v–91

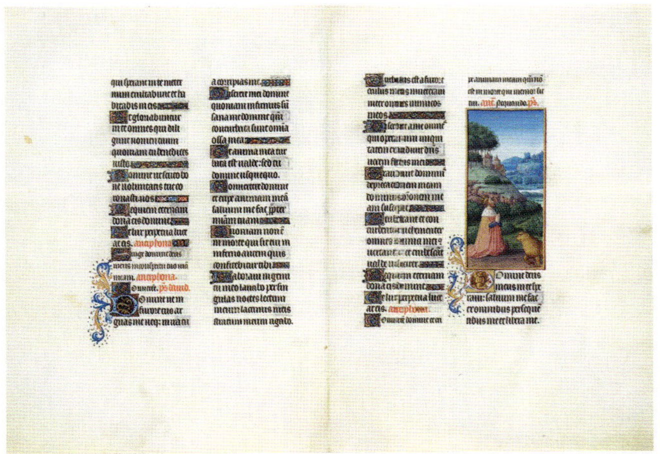

fol. 87v–88

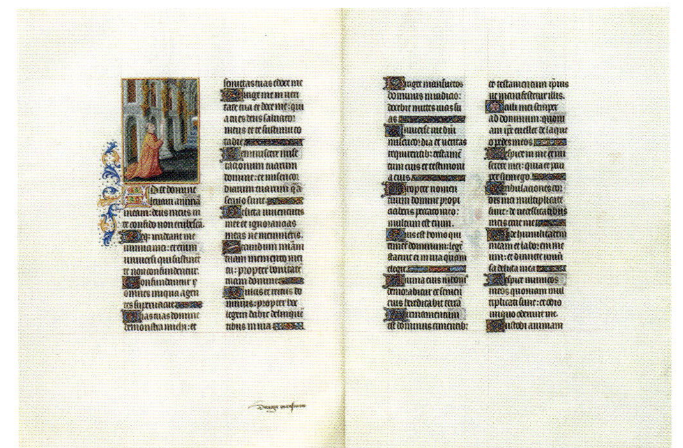

fol. 91v–92

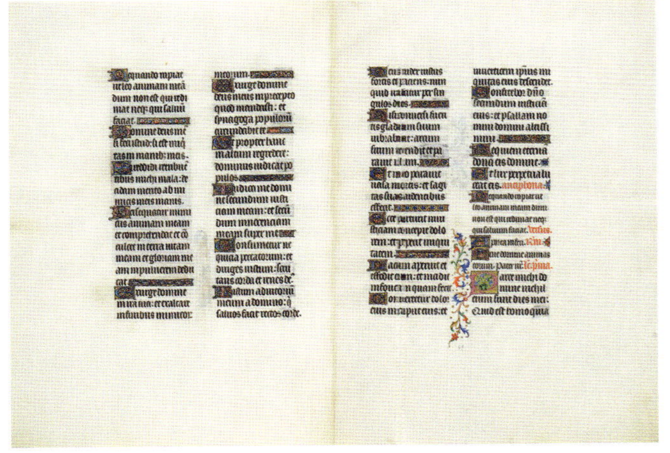

fol. 88v–89

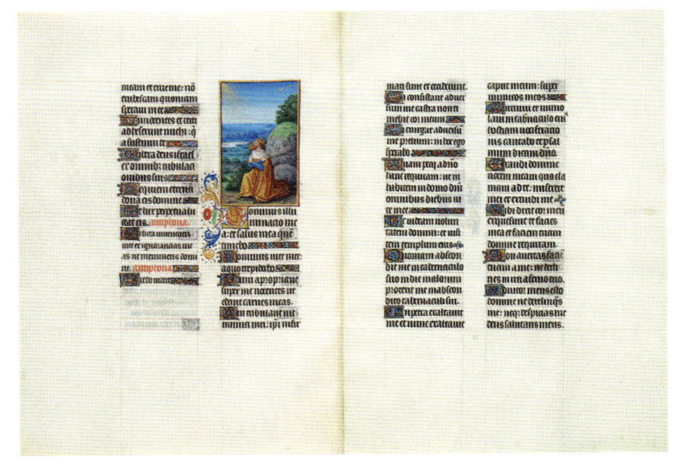

fol. 92v–93

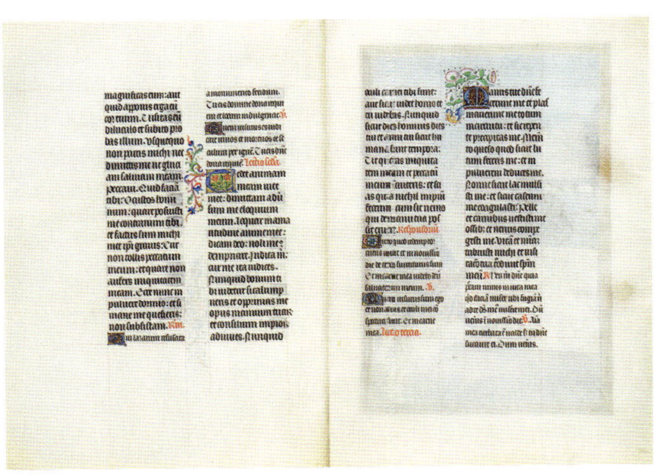

fol. 89v–90

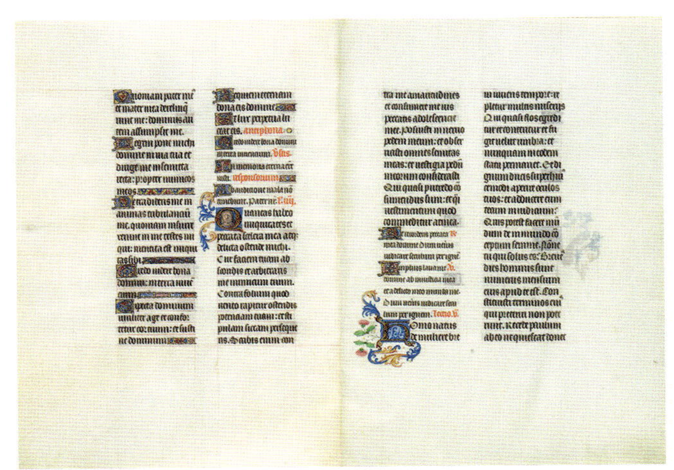

fol. 93v–94

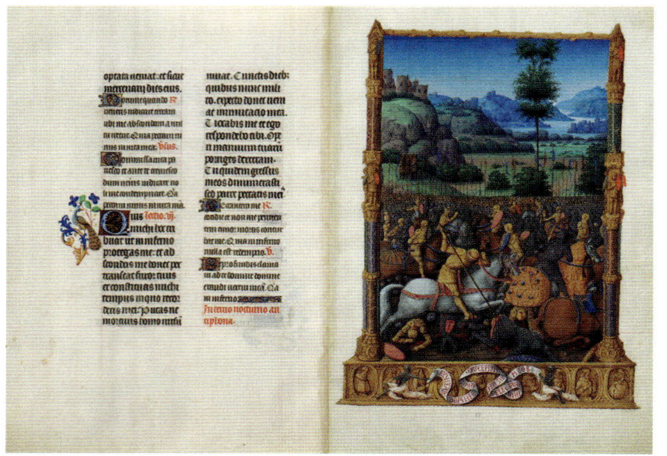
fol. 94v–95

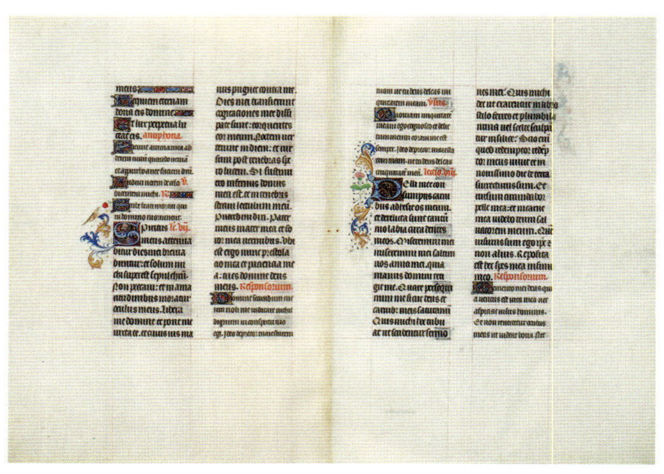
fol. 98v–99

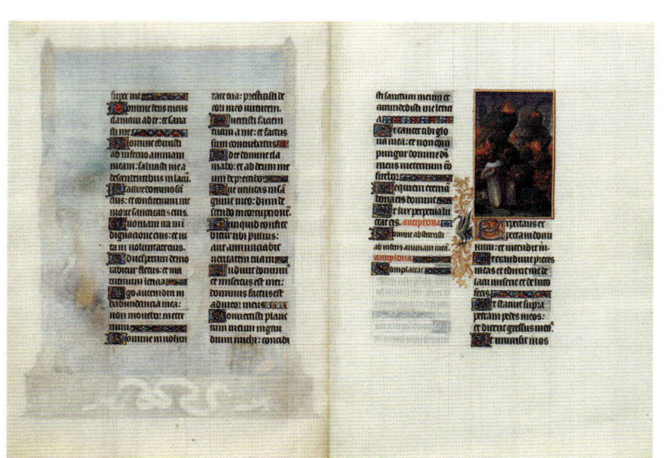
fol. 95v–96

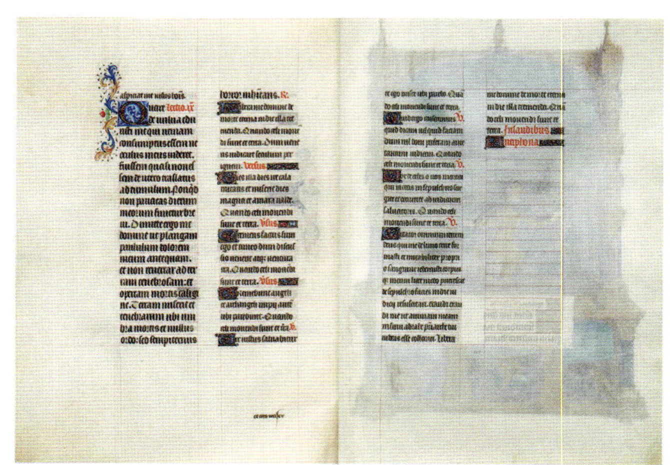
fol. 99v–100

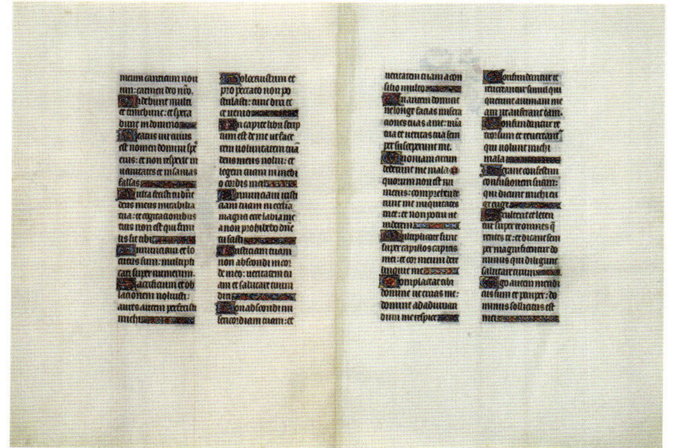
fol. 96v–97

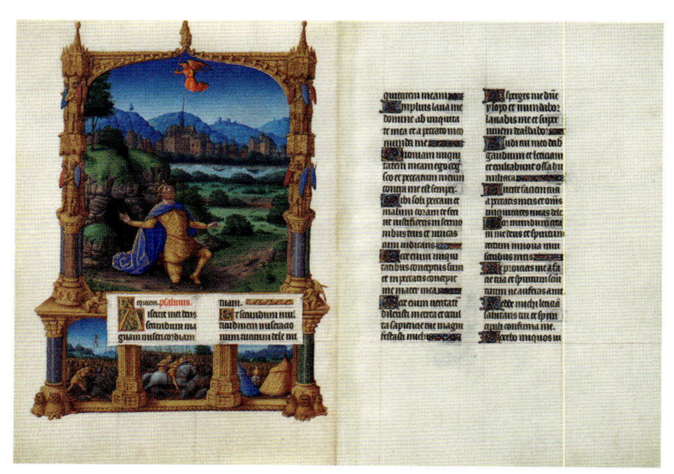
fol. 100v–101

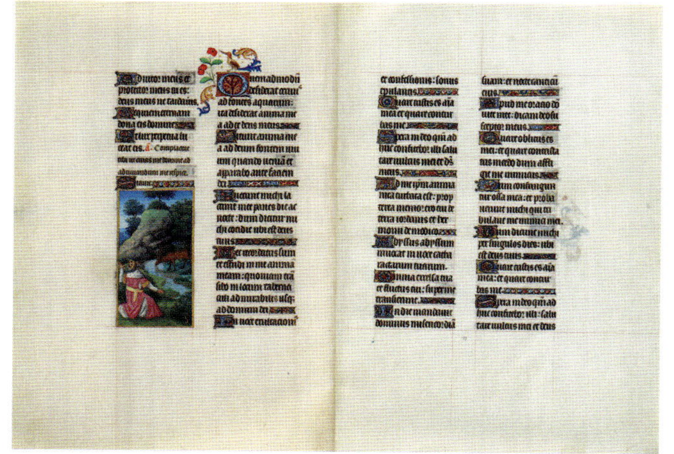
fol. 97v–98

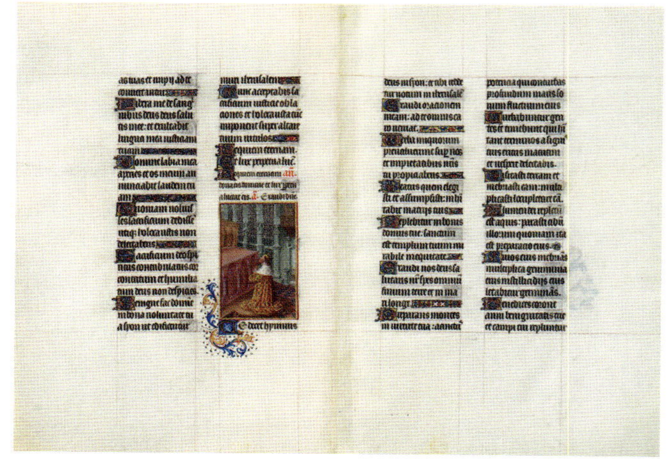
fol. 101v–102

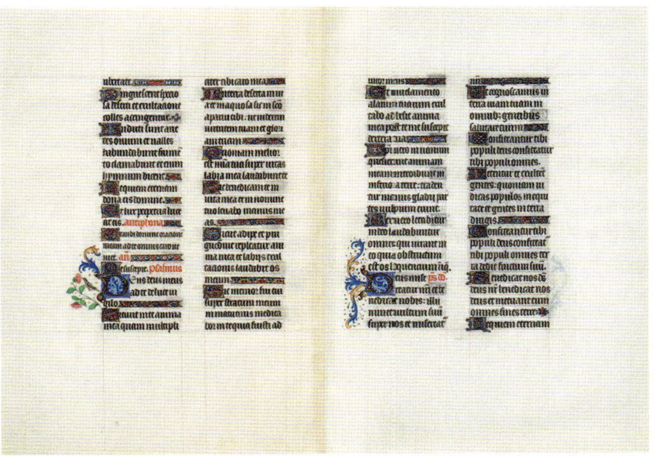
fol. 102v–103

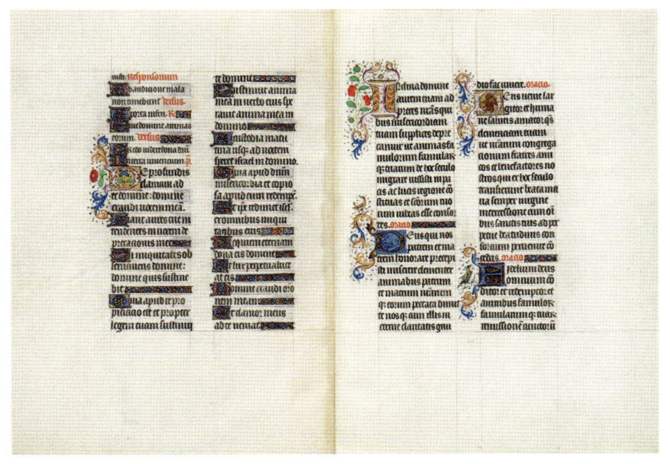
fol. 106v–107

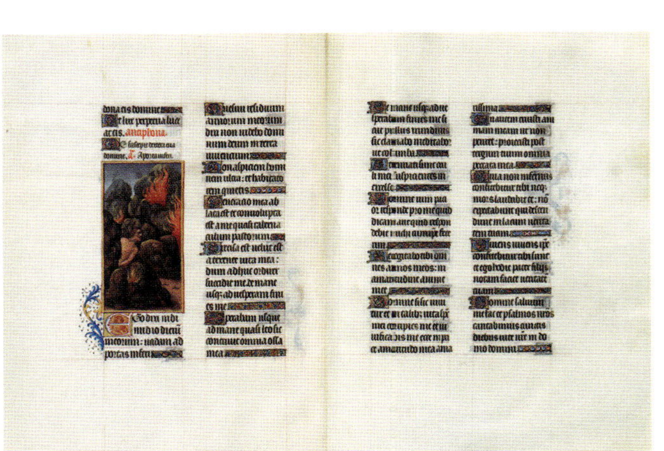
fol. 103v–104

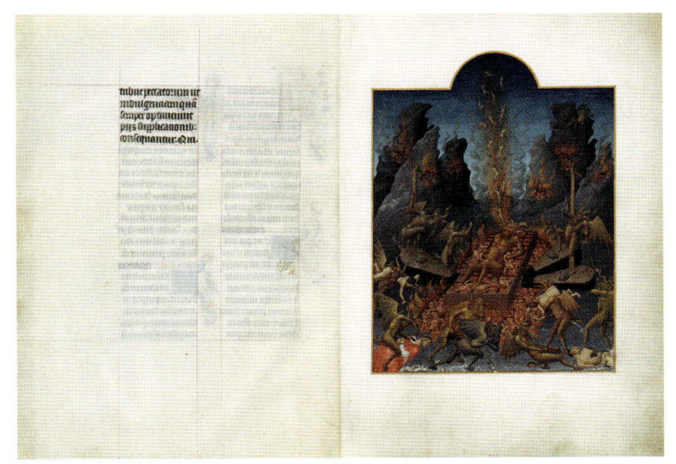
fol. 107v–108

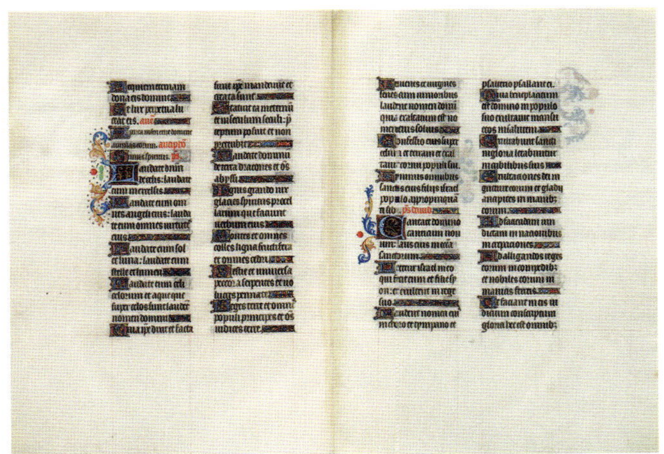
fol. 104v–105

fol. 108v–109

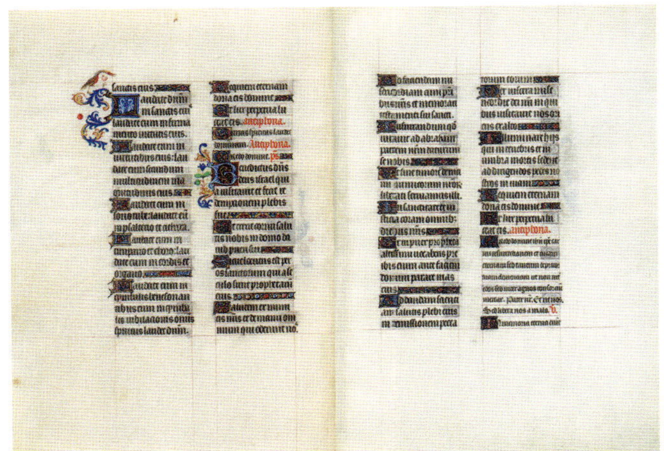
fol. 105v–106

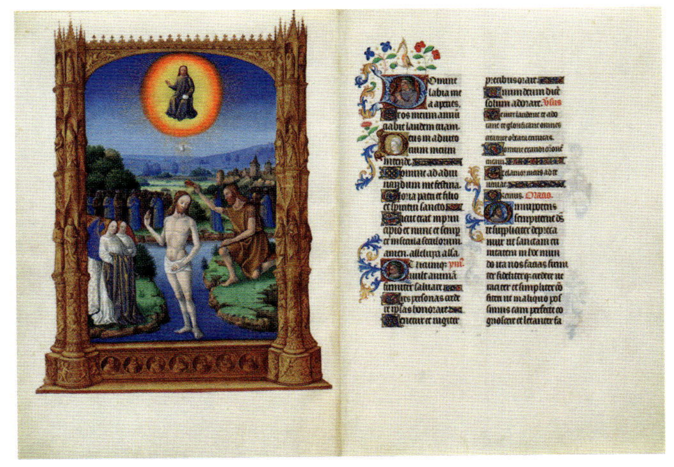
fol. 109v–110

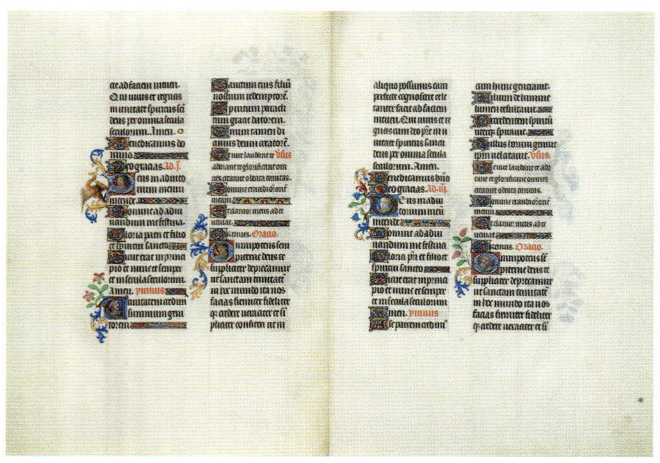

fol. 110v–111

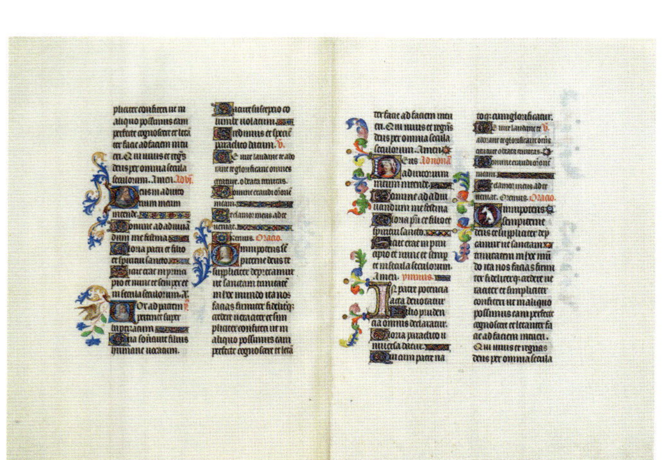

fol. 111v–112

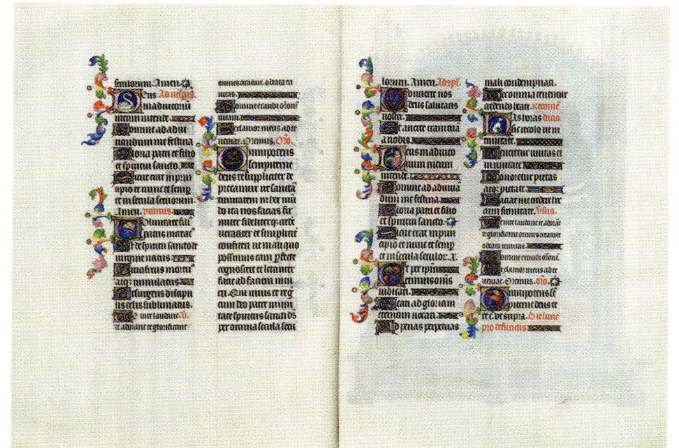

fol. 112v–113

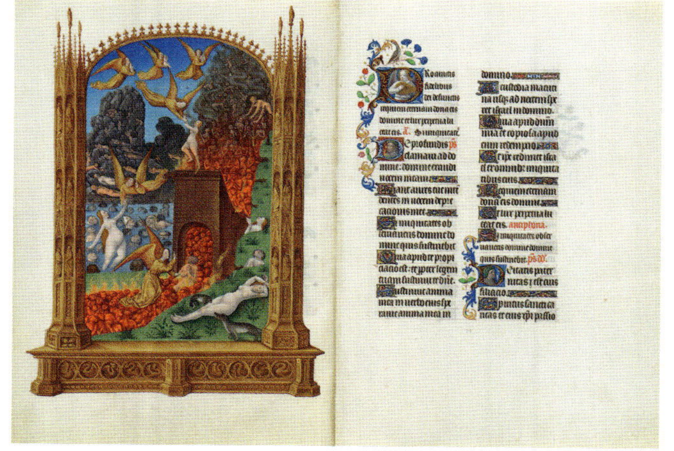

fol. 113v–114

fol. 114v–115

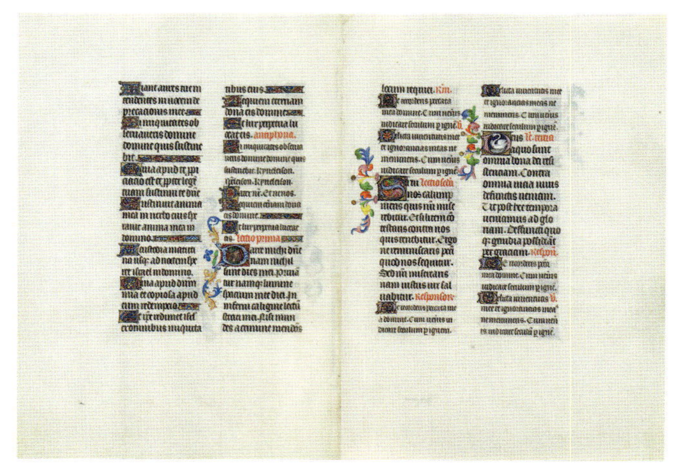

fol. 115v–116

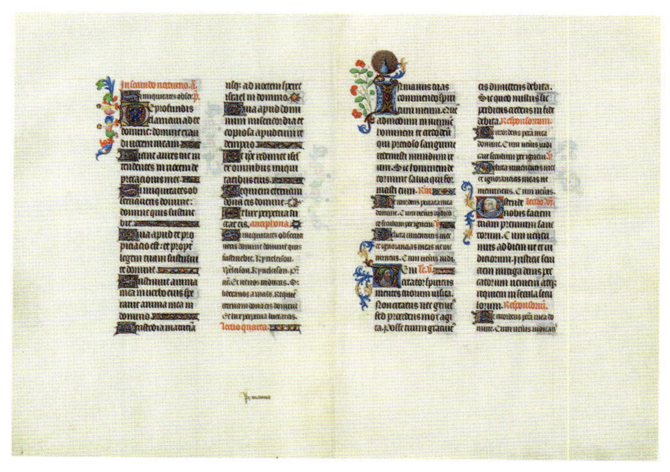

fol. 116v–117

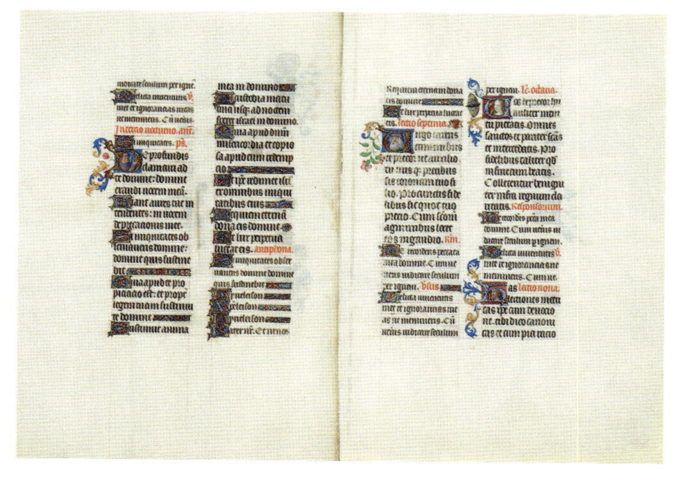

fol. 117v–118

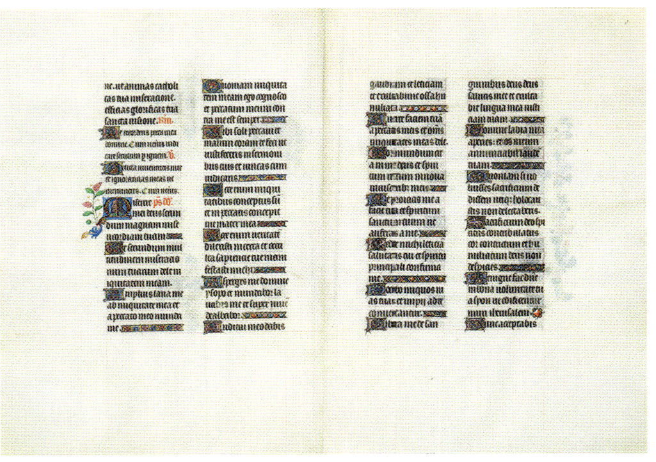
fol. 118v–119

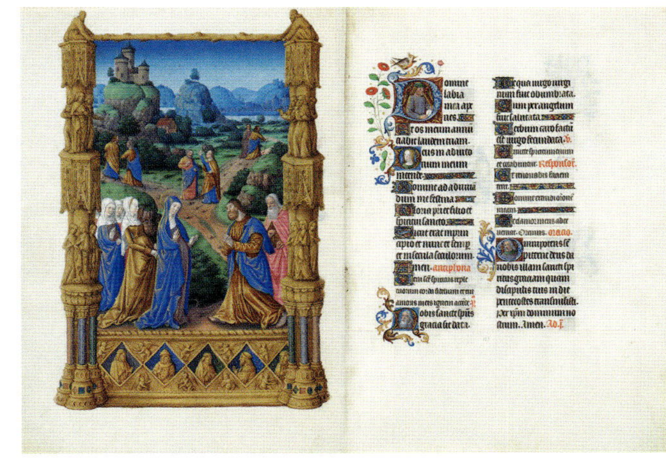
fol. 122v–123

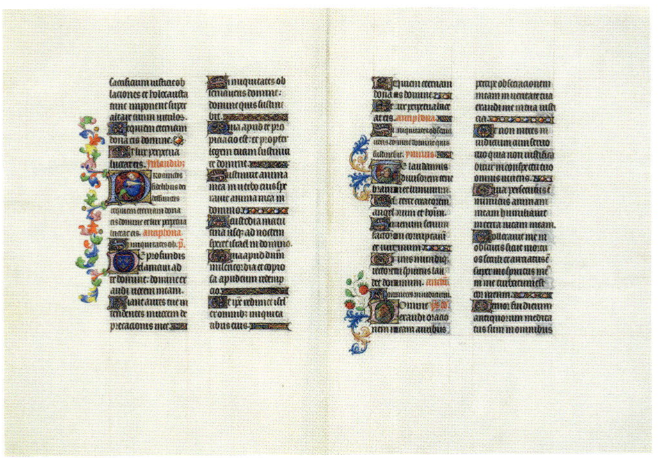
fol. 119v–120

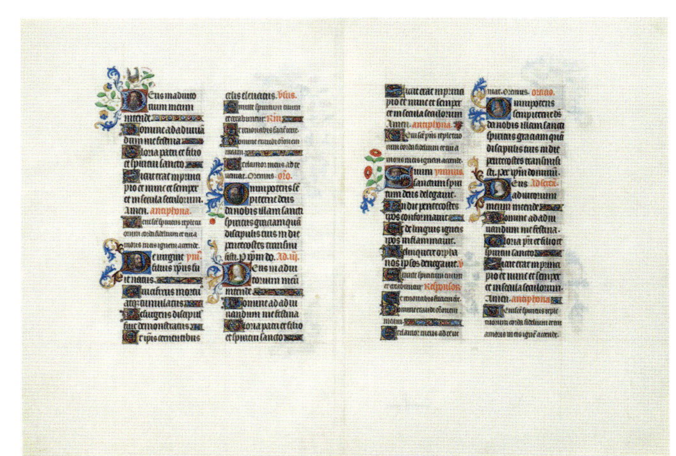
fol. 123v–124

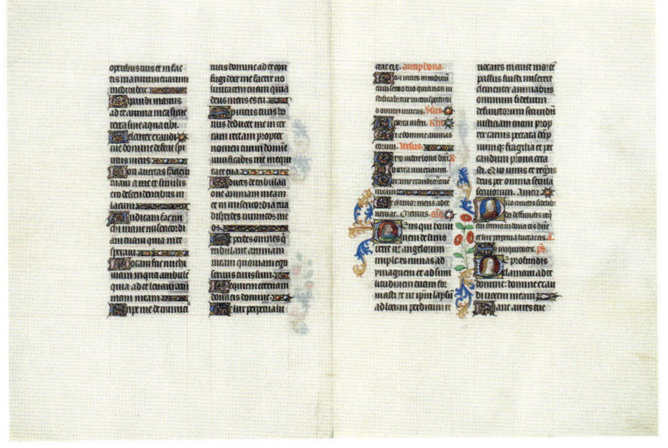
fol. 120v–121

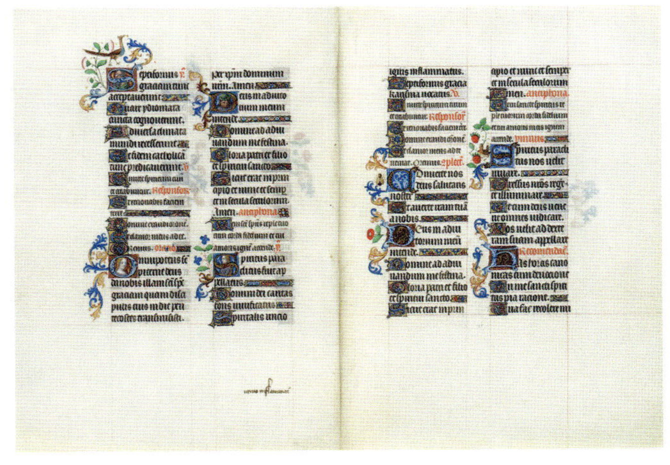
fol. 124v–125

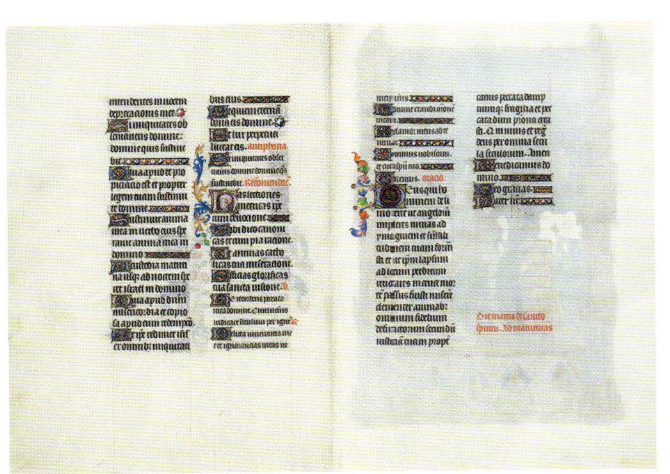
fol. 121v–122

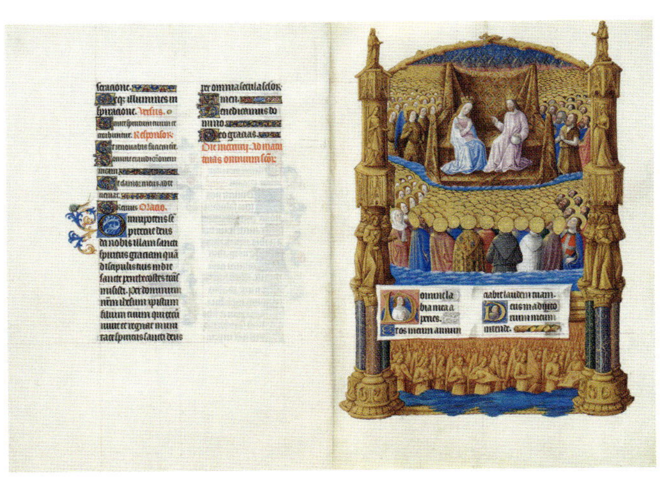
fol. 125v–126

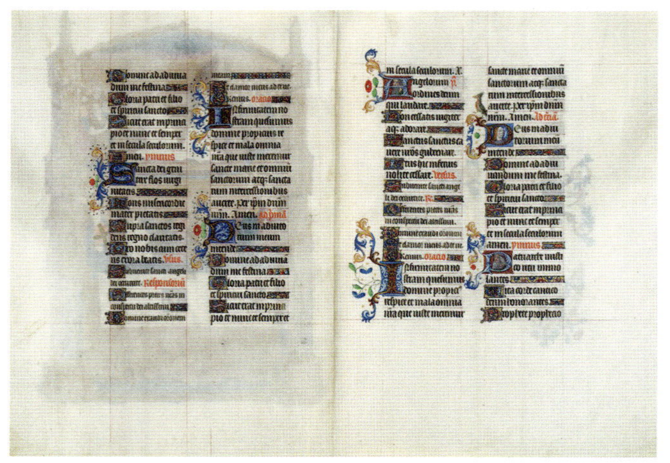

fol. 126v–127

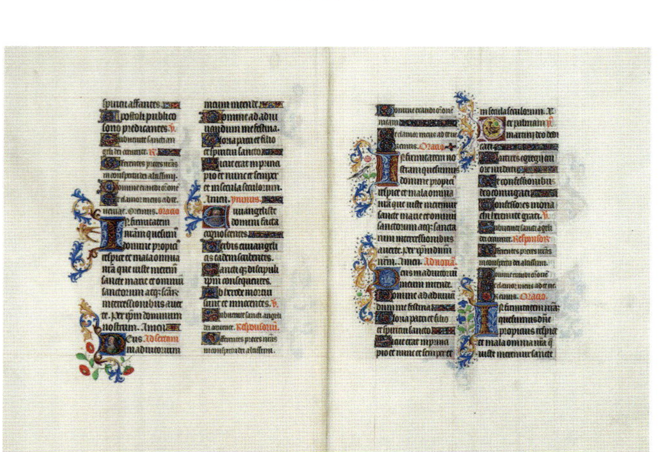

fol. 127v–128

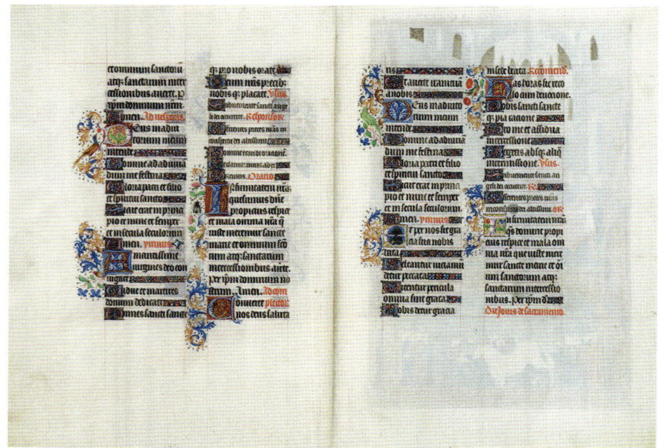

fol. 128v–129

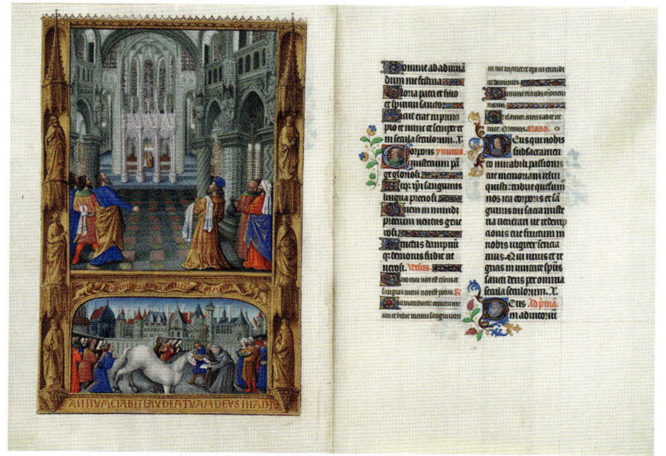

fol. 129v–130

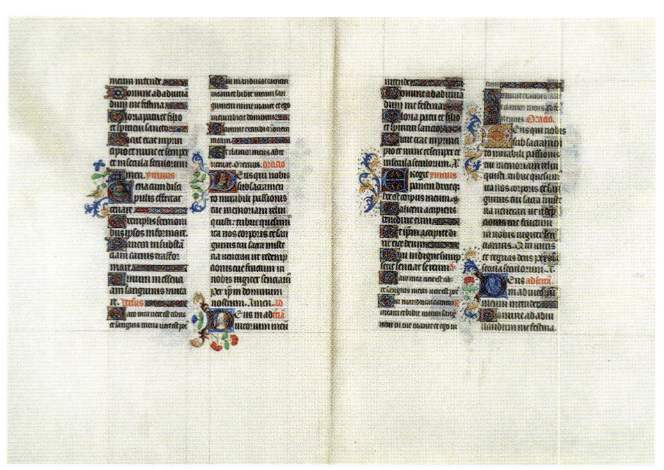

fol. 130v–131

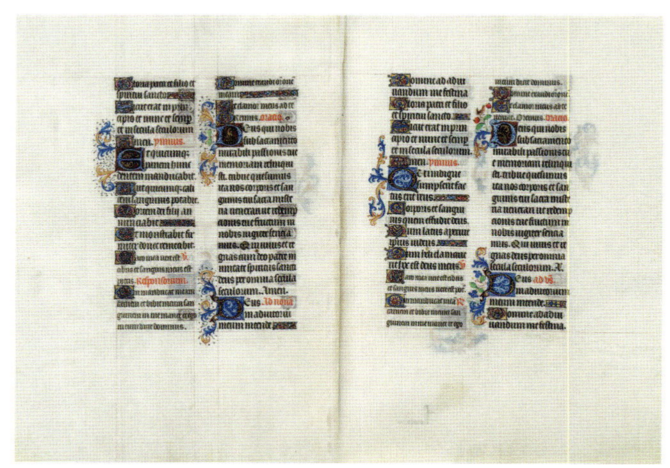

fol. 131v–132

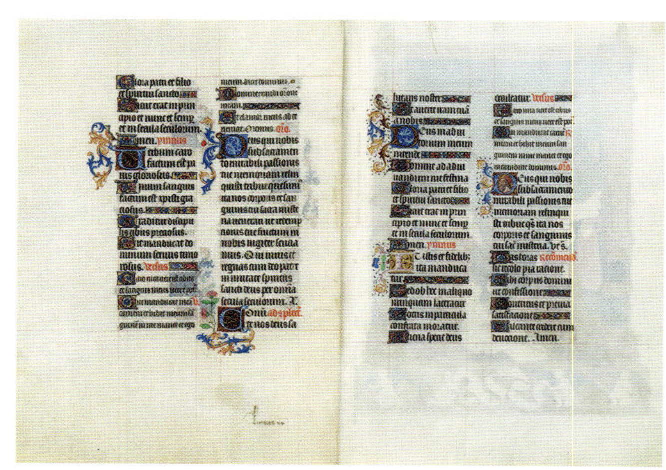

fol. 132v–133

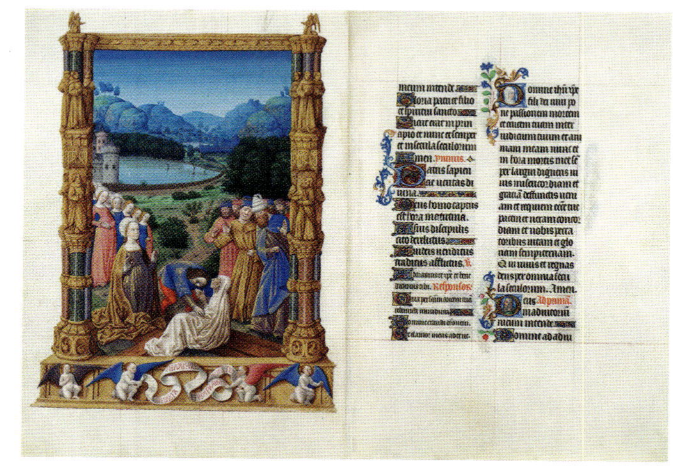

fol. 133v–134

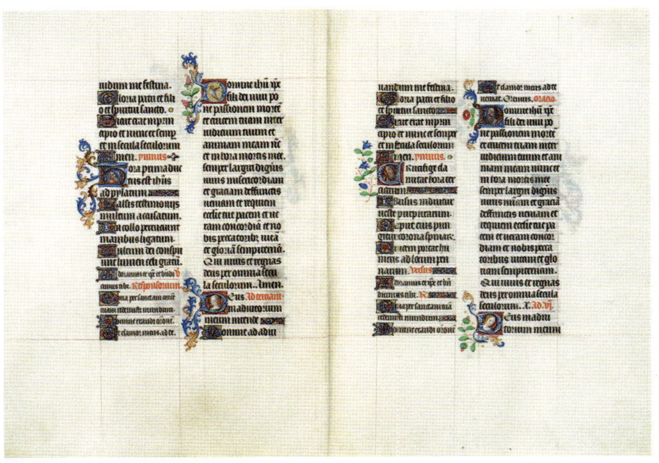

fol. 134v–135

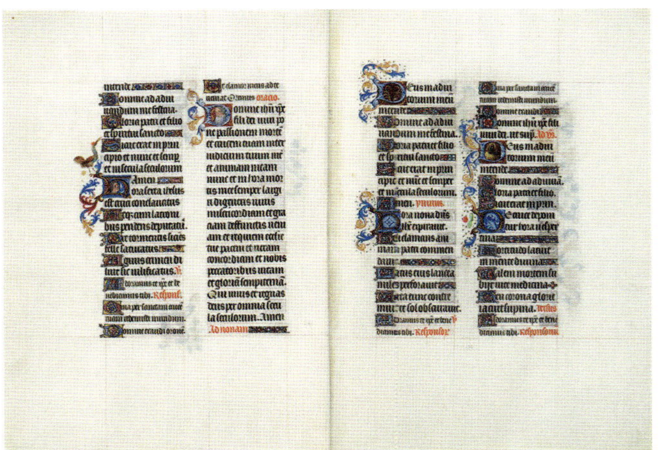

fol. 135v–136

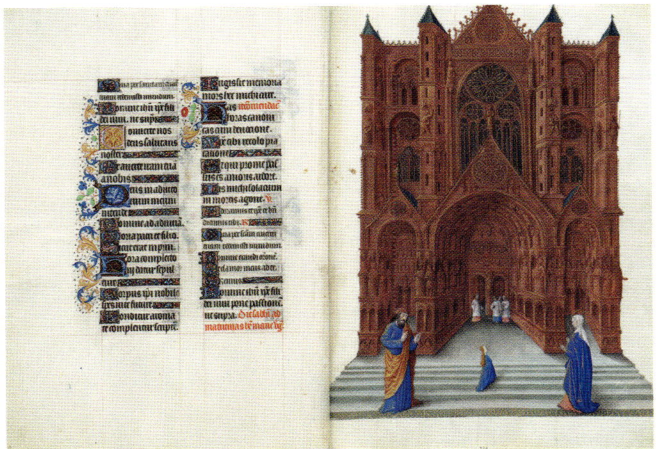

fol. 136v–137

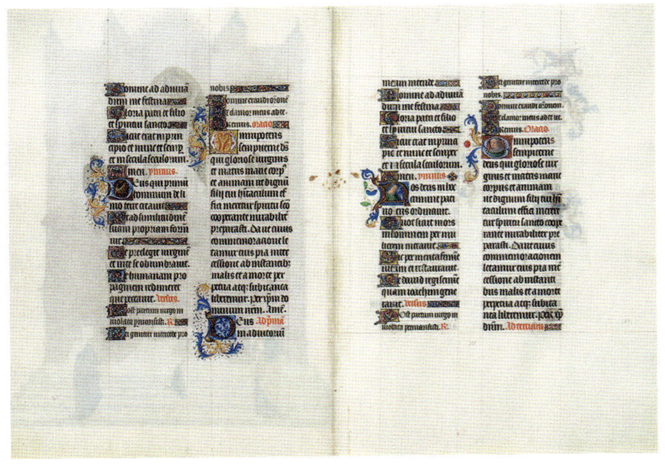

fol. 137v–138

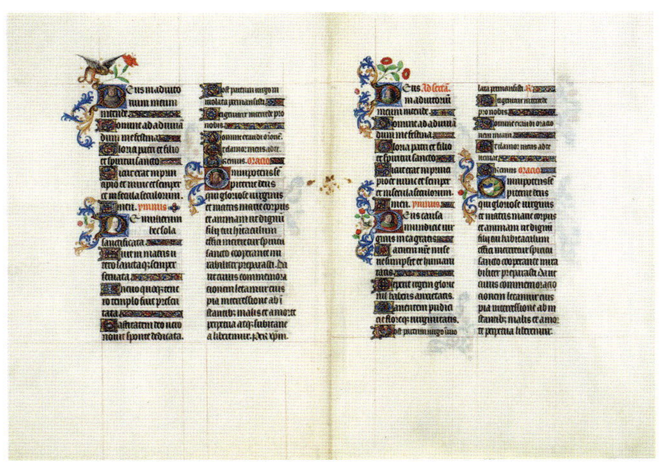

fol. 138v–139

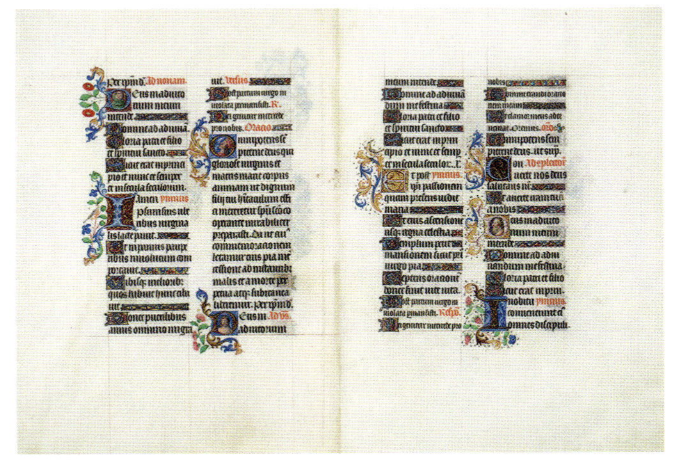

fol. 139v–140

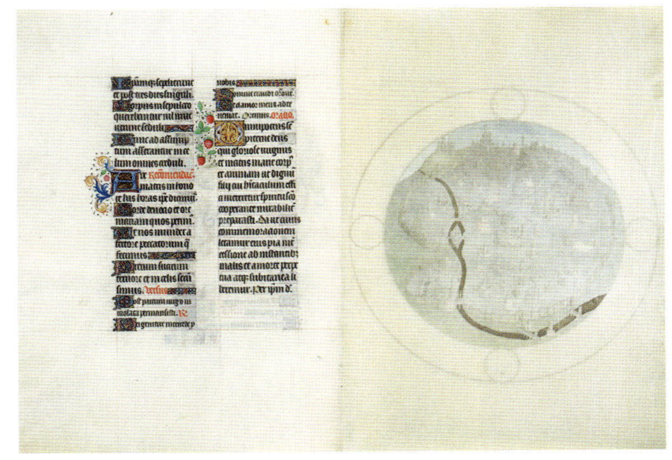

fol. 140v–141

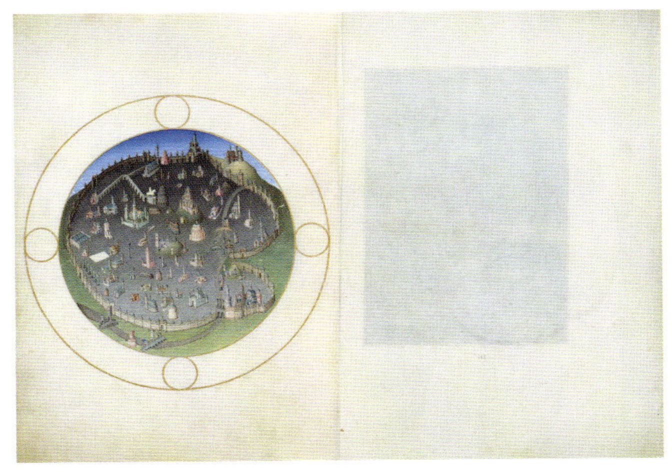

fol. 141v–142

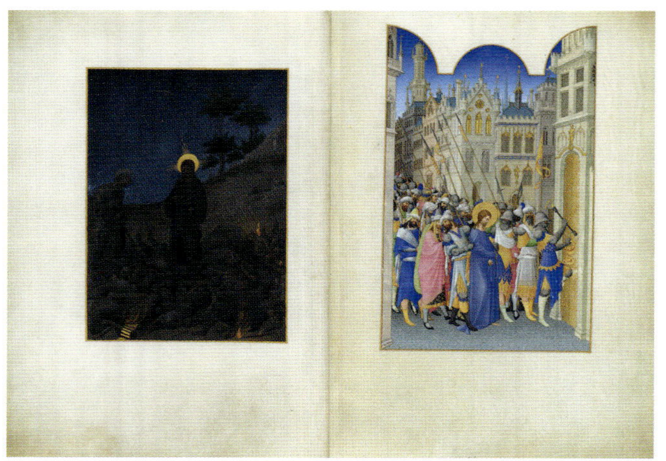

fol. 142v–143

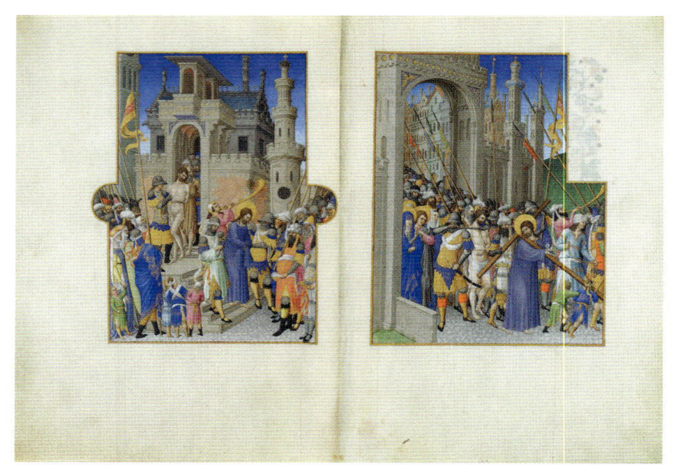

fol. 146v–147

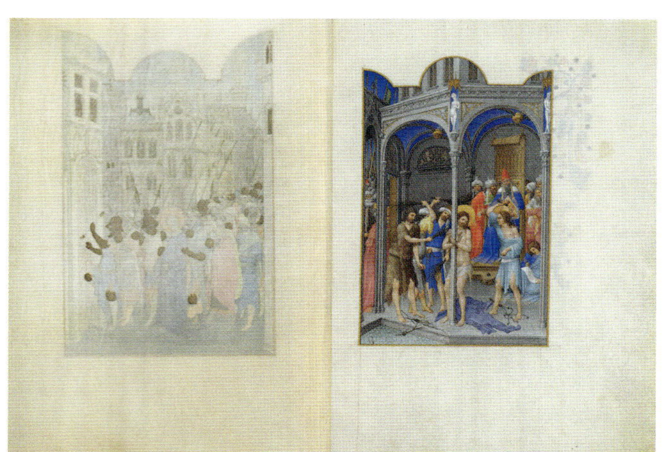

fol. 143v–144

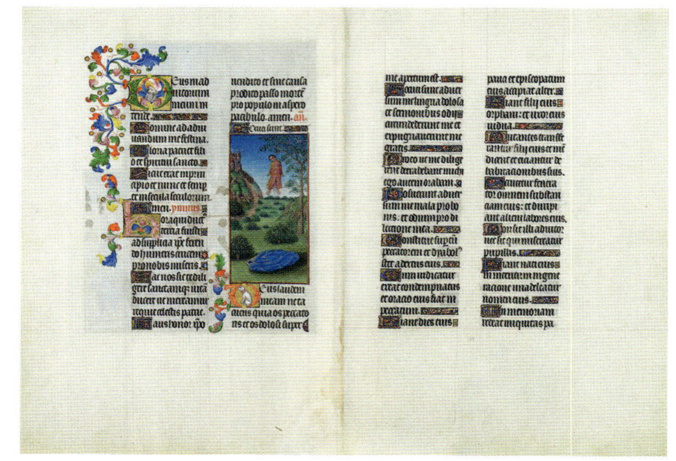

fol. 147v–148

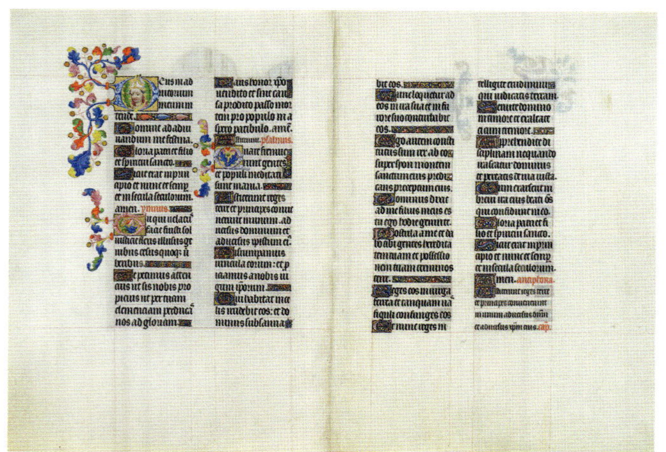

fol. 144v–145

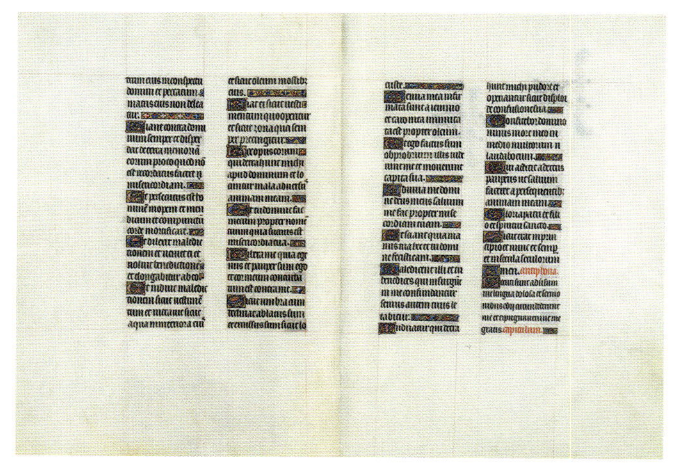

fol. 148v–149

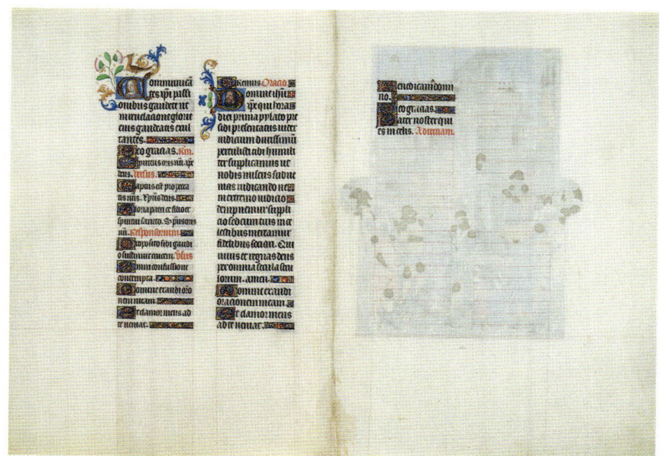

fol. 145v–146

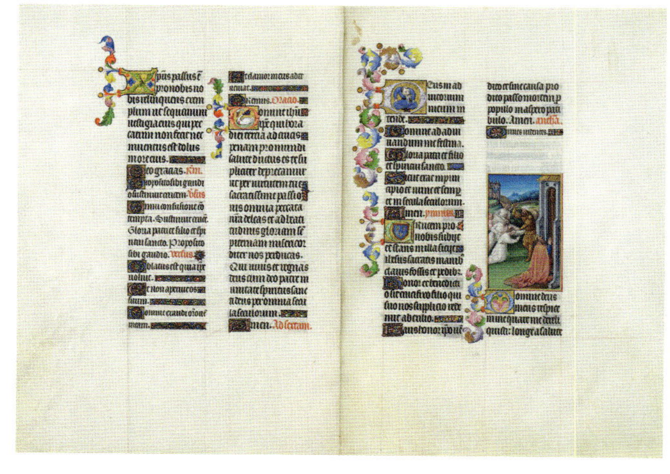

fol. 149v–150

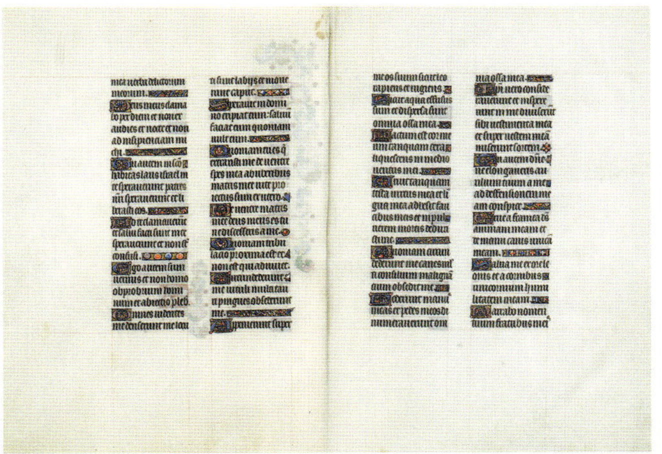

fol. 150v–151

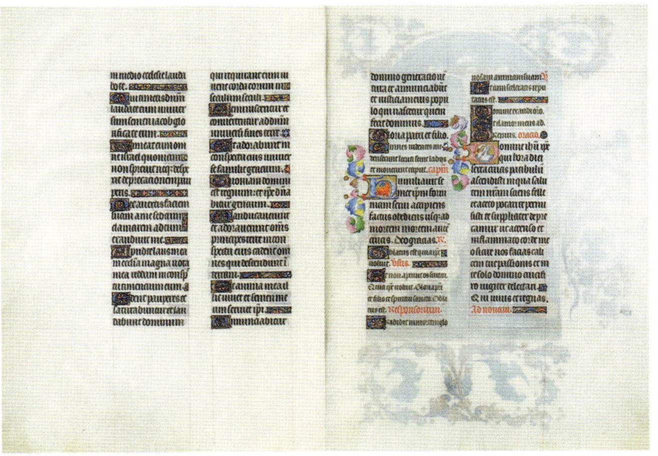

fol. 151v–152

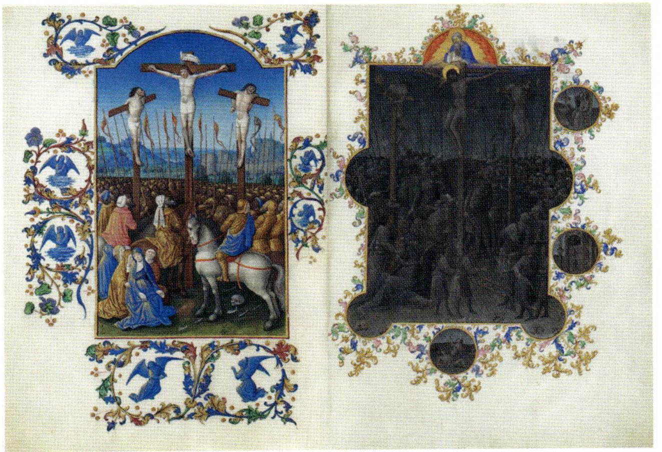

fol. 152v–153

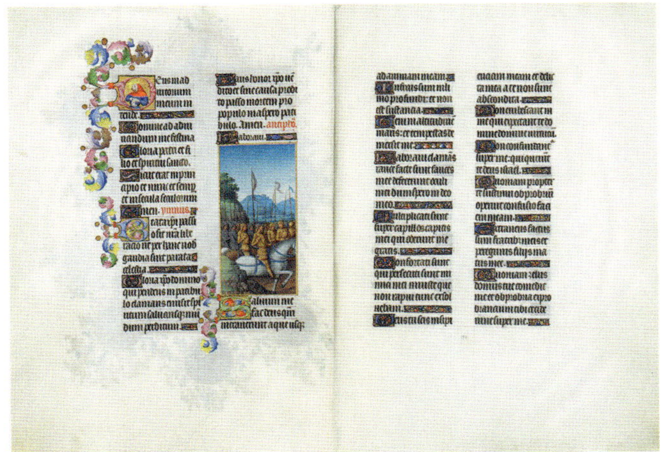

fol. 153v–154

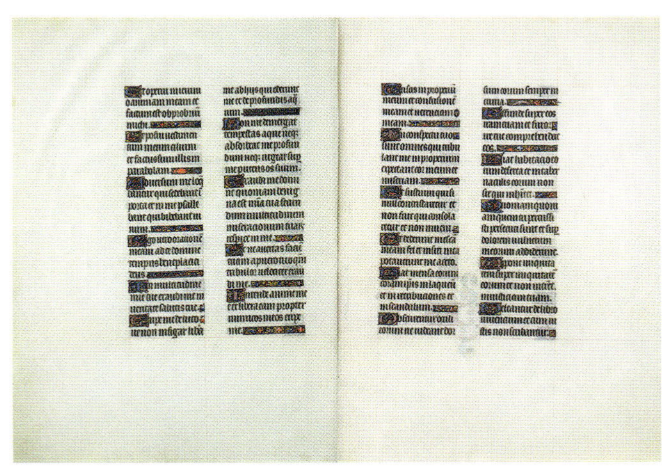

fol. 154v–155

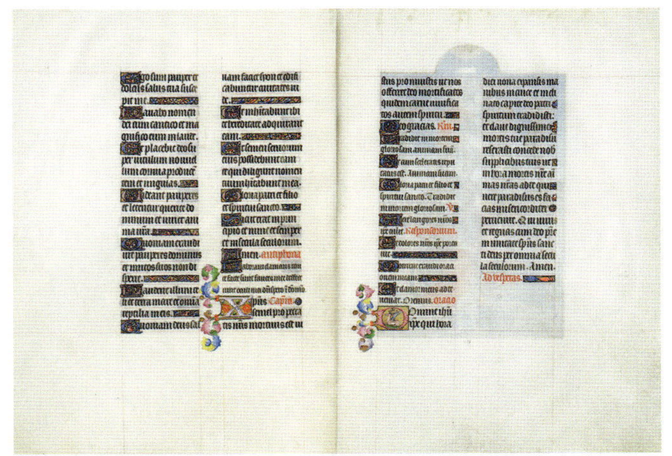

fol. 155v–156

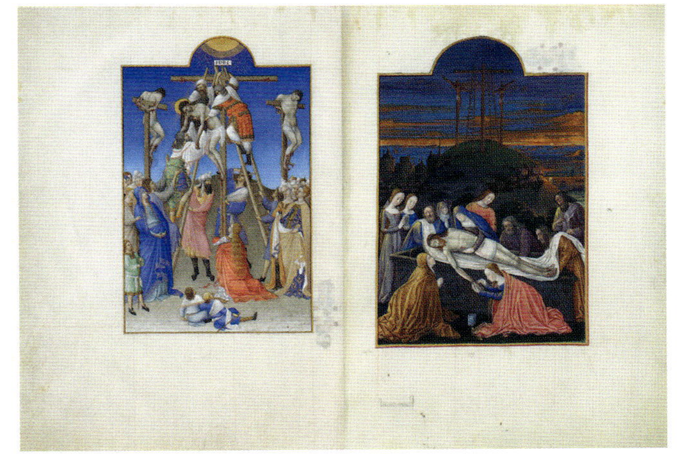

fol. 156v–157

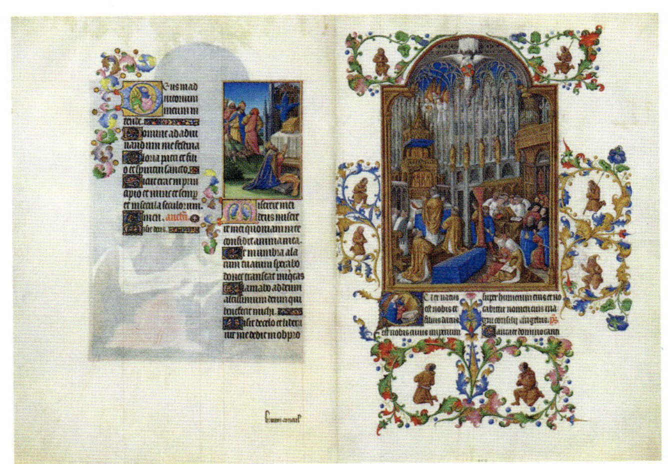

fol. 157v–158

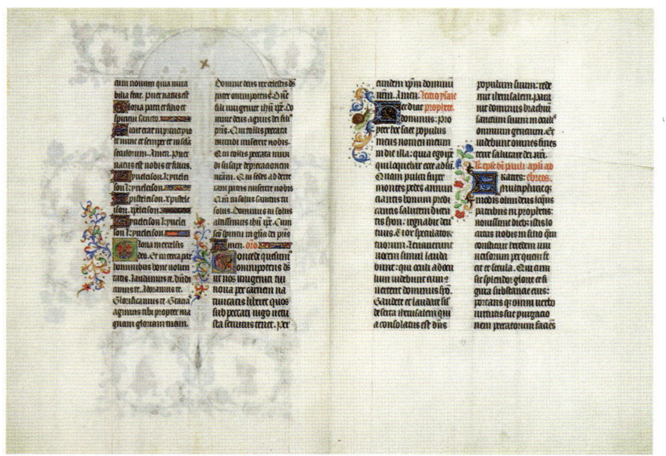

fol. 158v–159

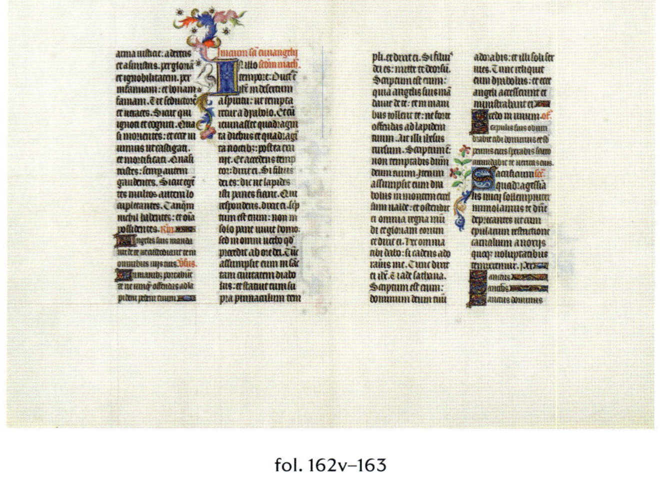

fol. 162v–163

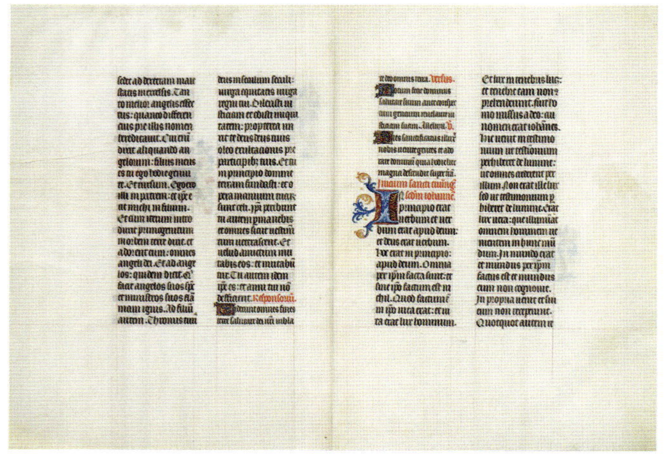

fol. 159v–160

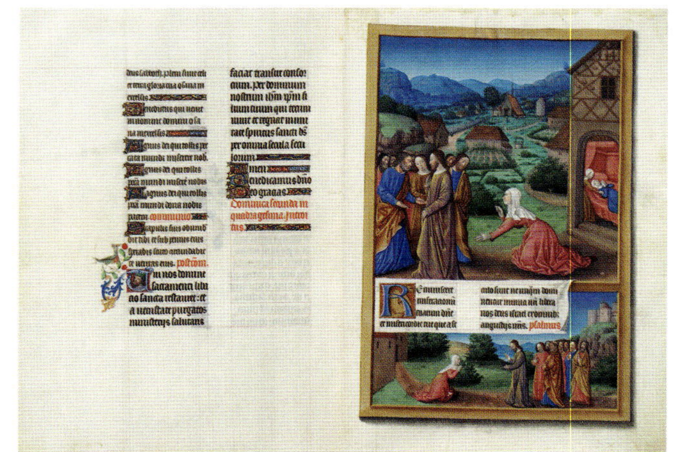

fol. 163v–164

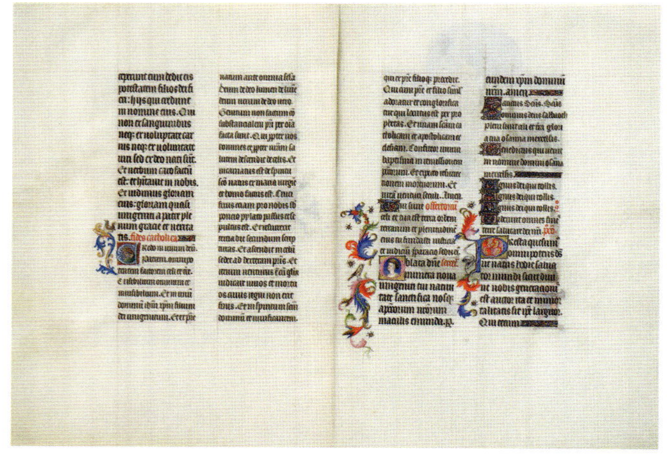

fol. 160v–161

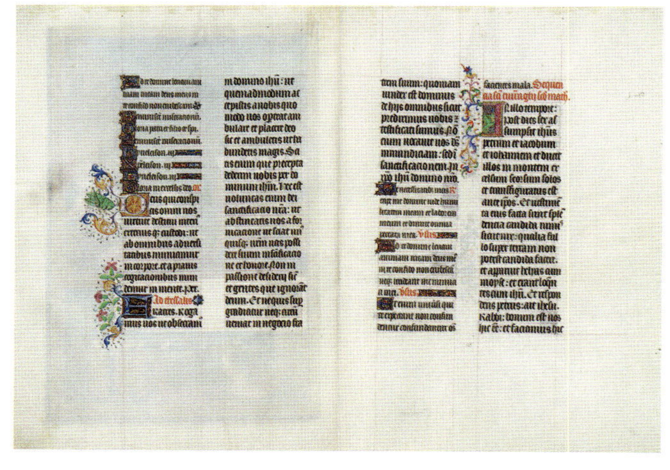

fol. 164v–165

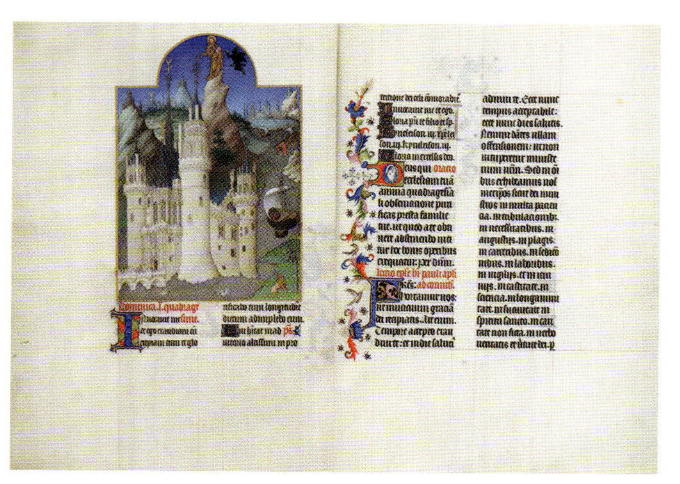

fol. 161v–162

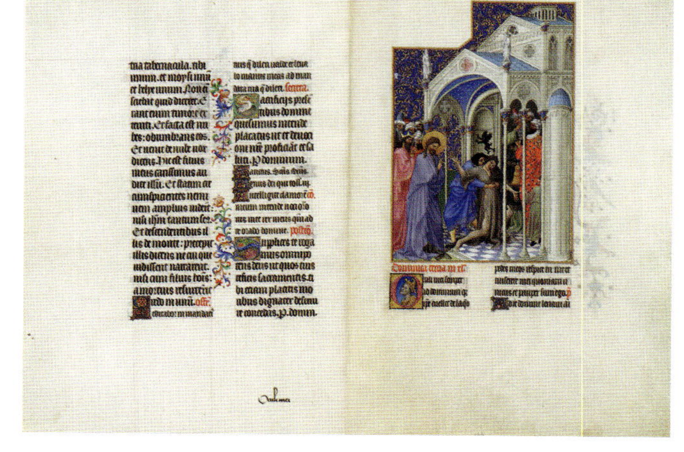

fol. 165v–166

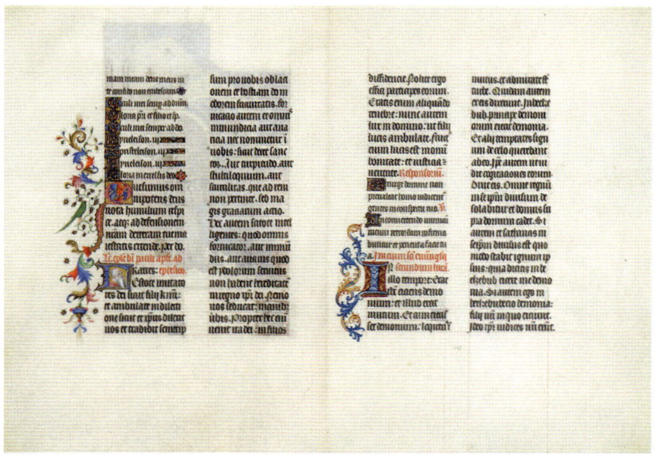
fol. 166v–167

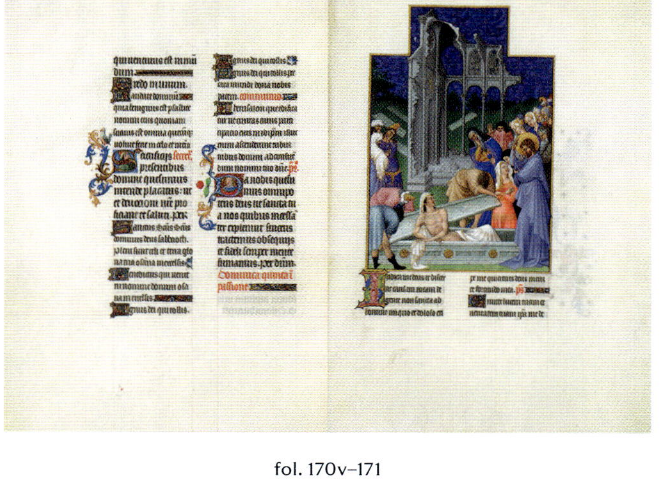
fol. 170v–171

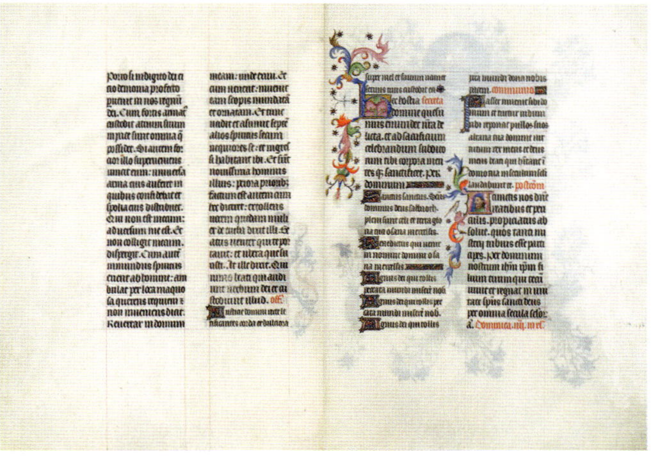
fol. 167v–168

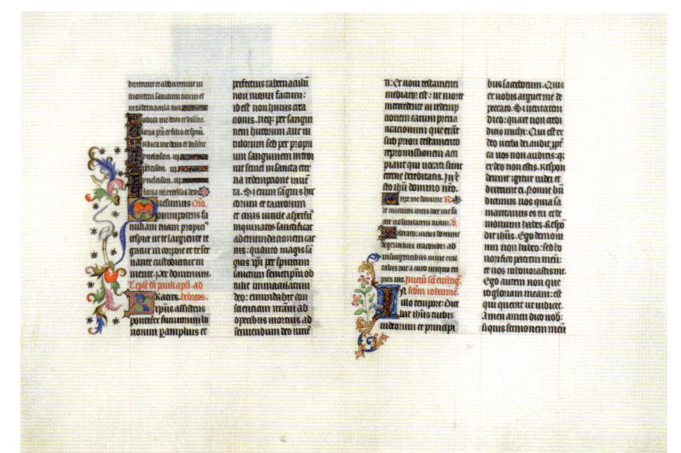
fol. 171v–172

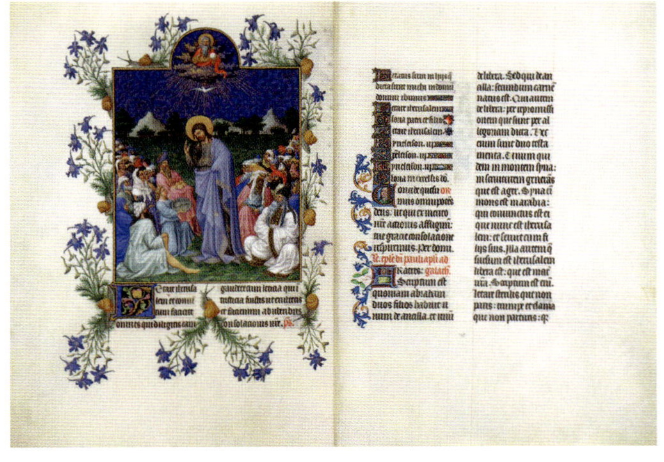
fol. 168v–169

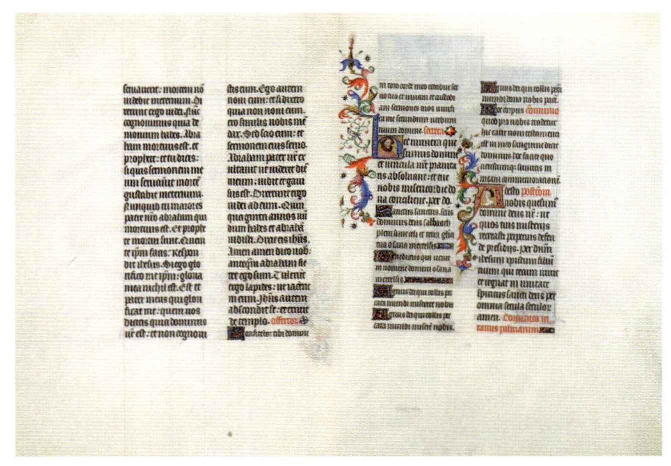
fol. 172v–173

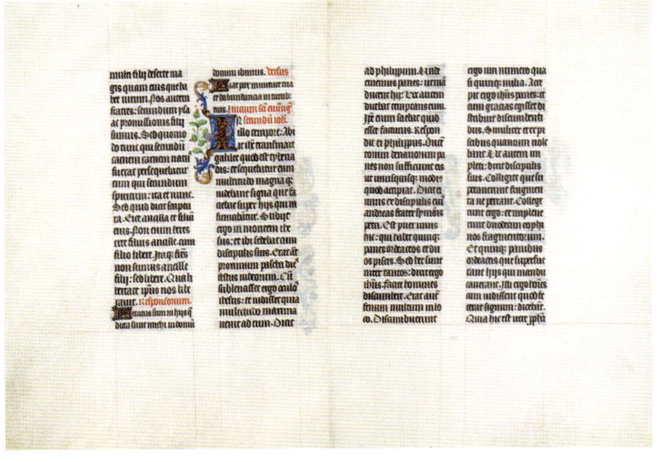
fol. 169v–170

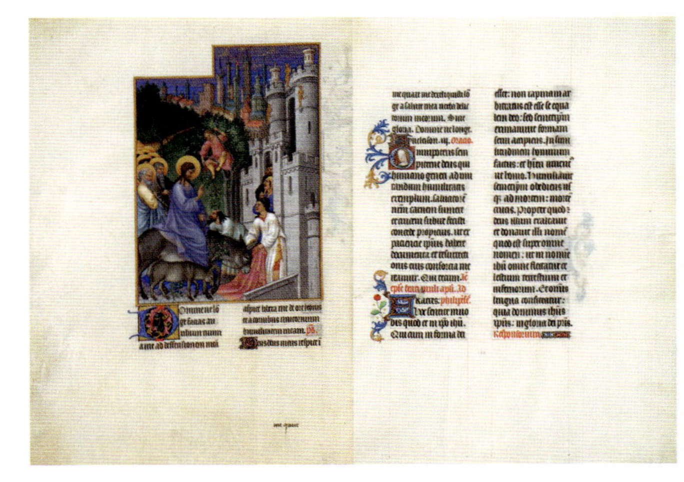
fol. 173v–174

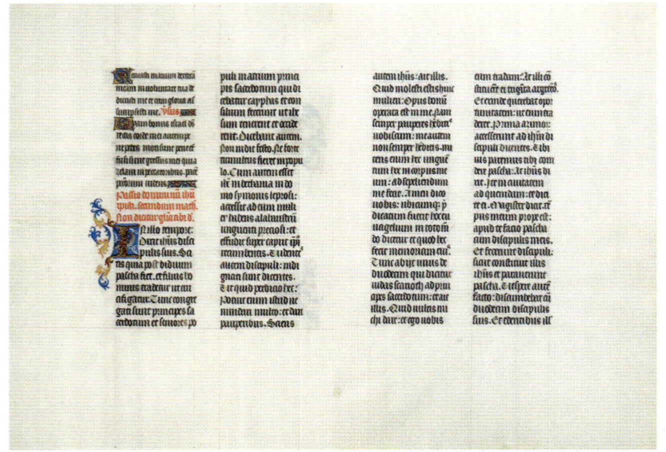

fol. 174v–175

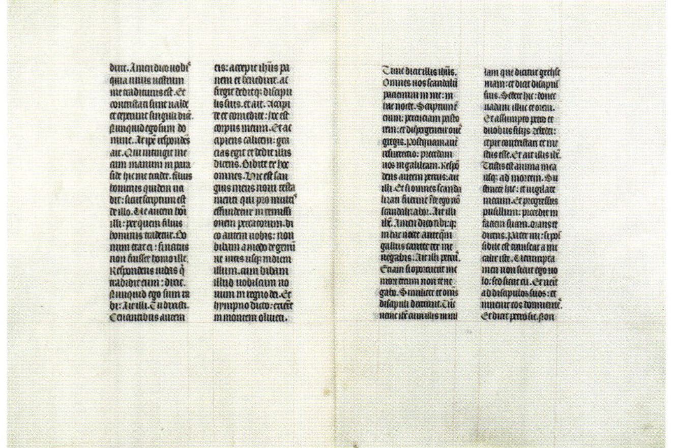

fol. 175v–176

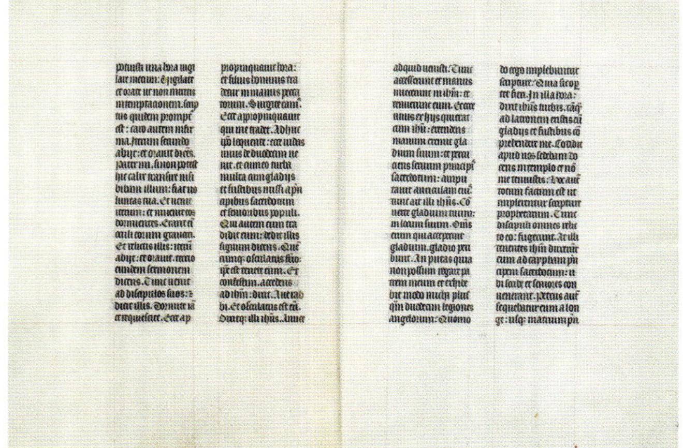

fol. 176v–177

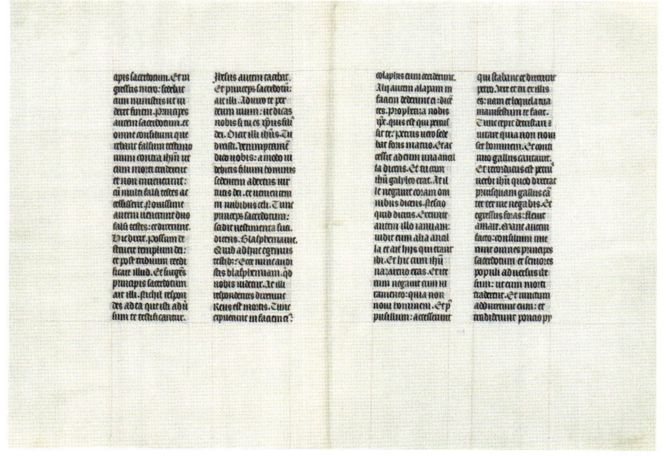

fol. 177v–178

fol. 178v–179

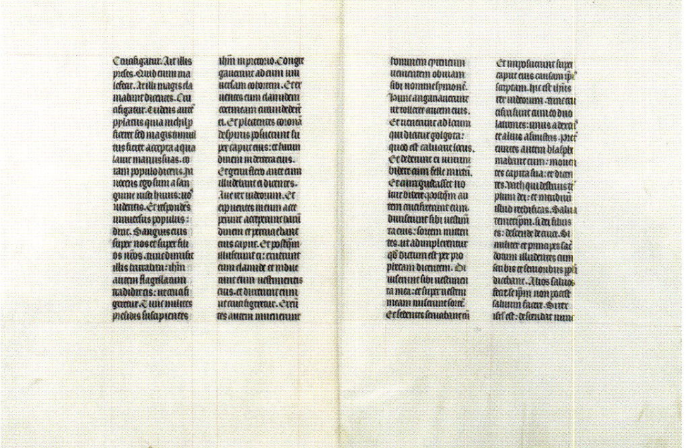

fol. 179v–180

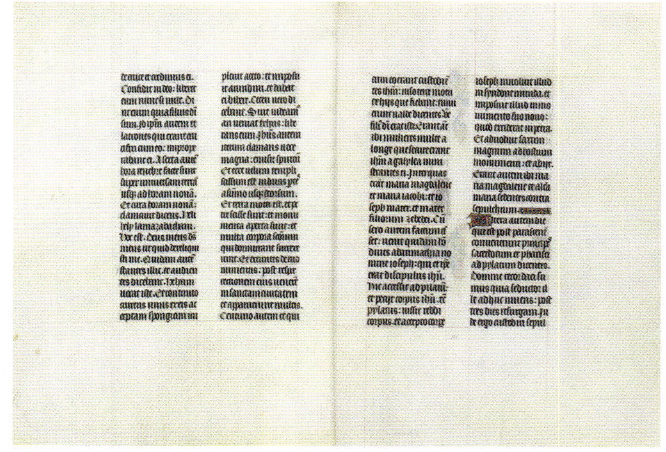

fol. 180v–181

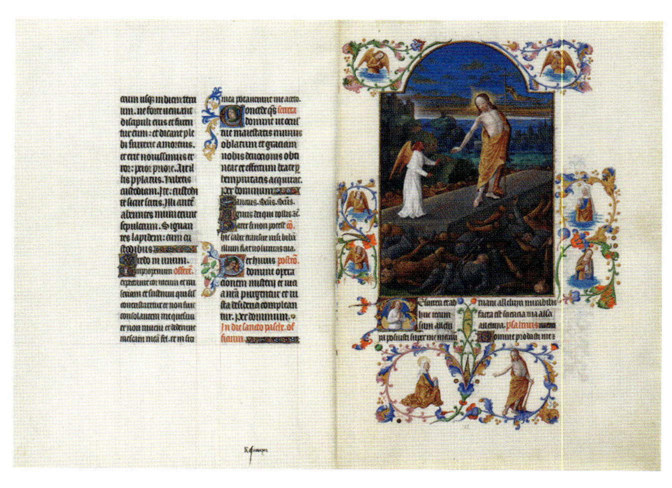

fol. 181v–182

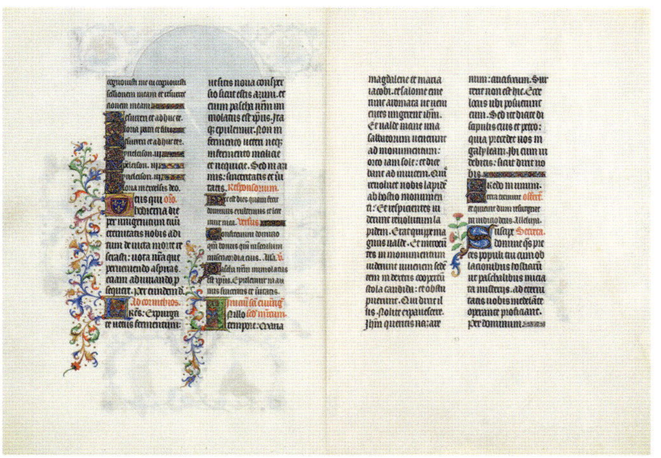

fol. 182v–183

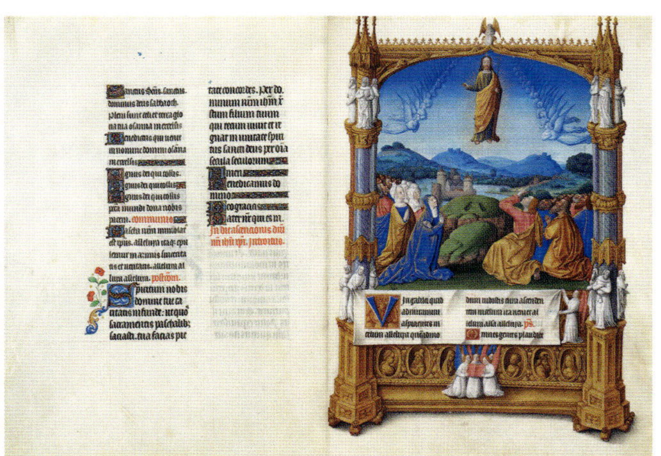

fol. 183v–184

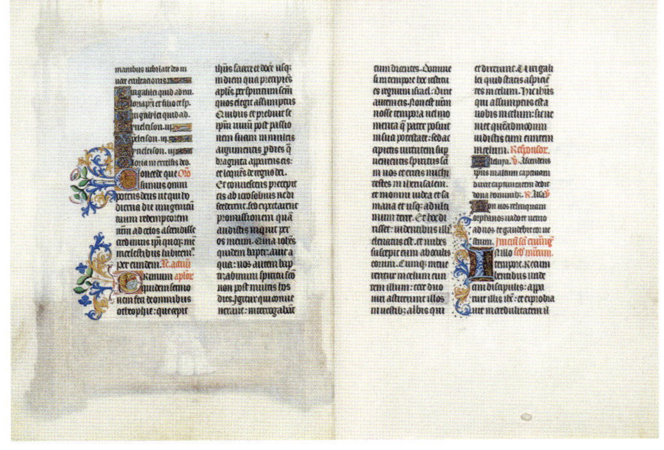

fol. 184v–185

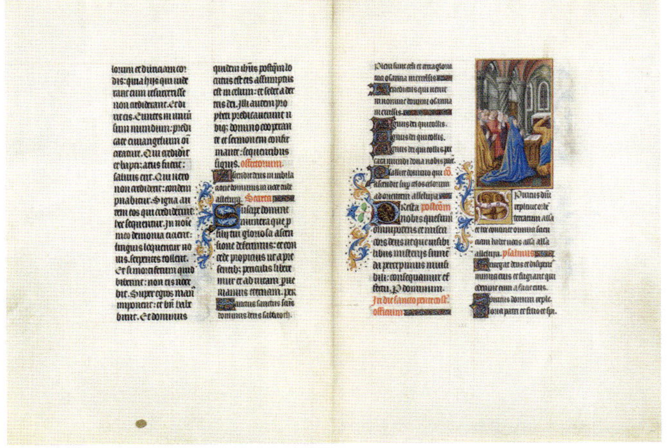

fol. 185v–186

fol. 186v–187

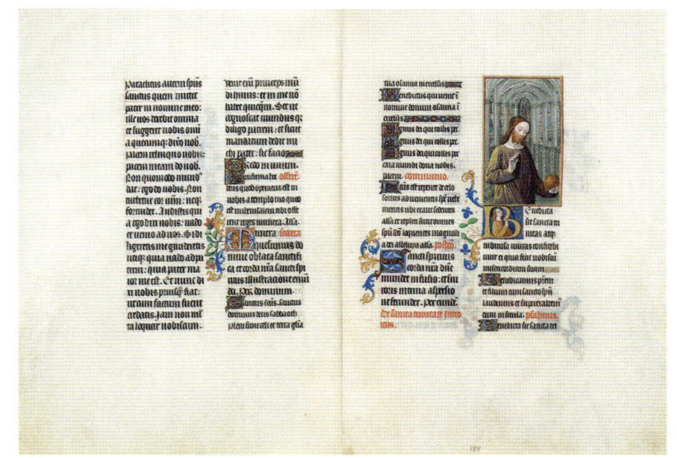

fol. 187v–188

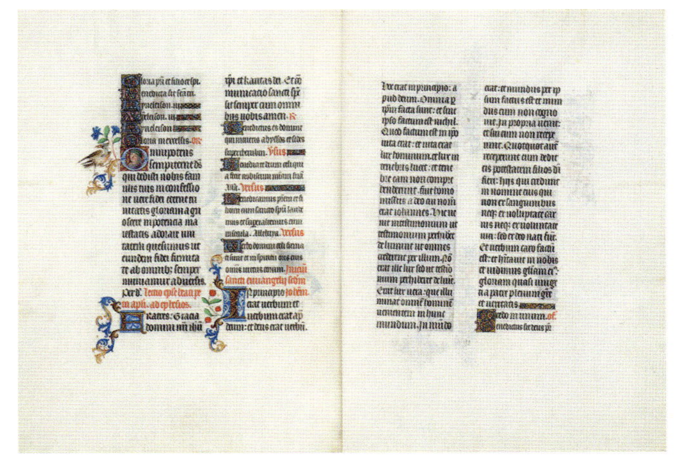

fol. 188v–189

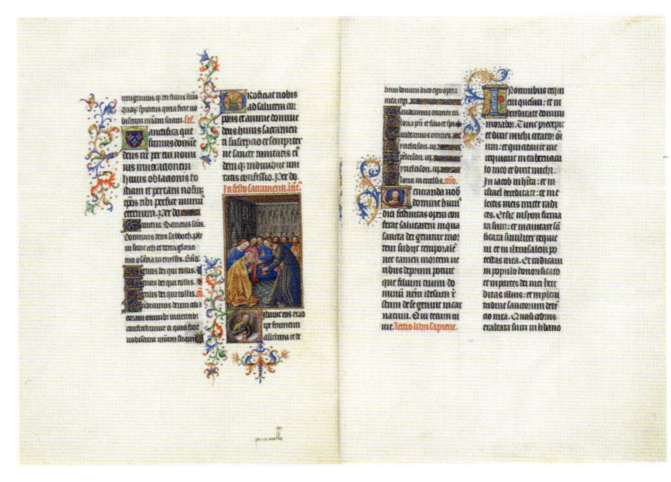

fol. 189v–190

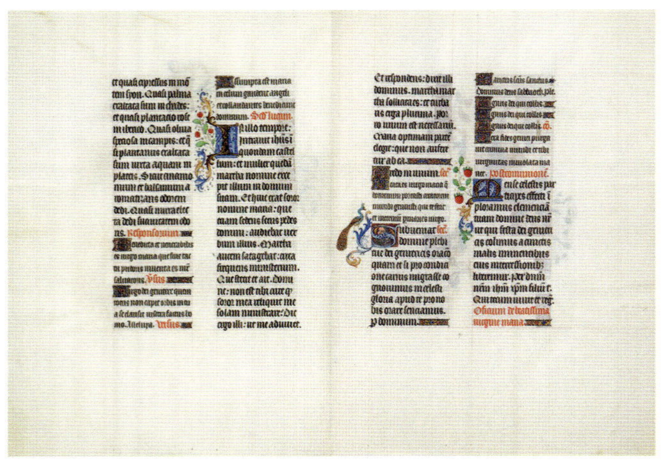

fol. 190v–191

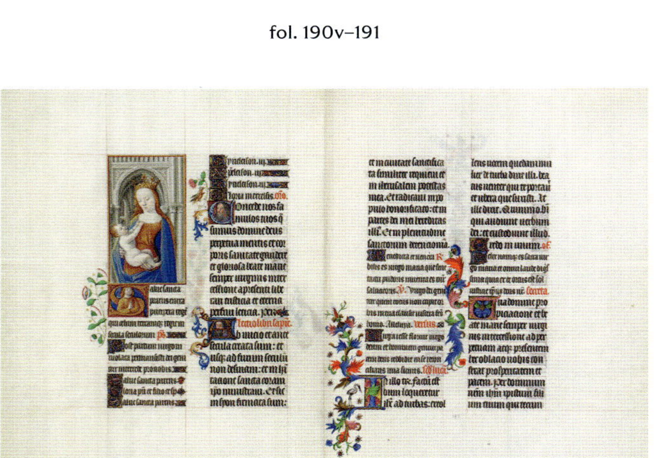

fol. 191v–192

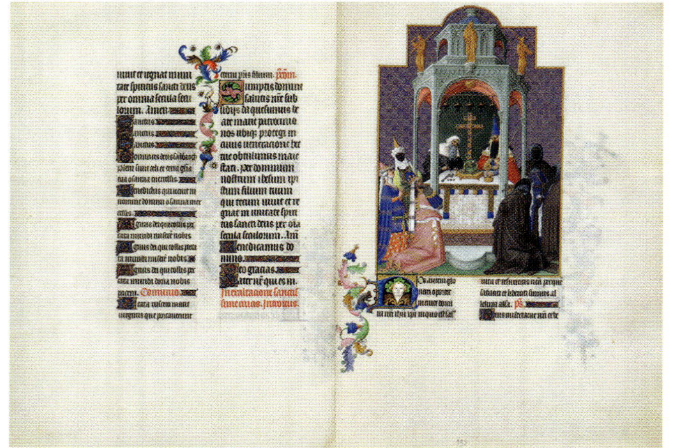

fol. 192v–193

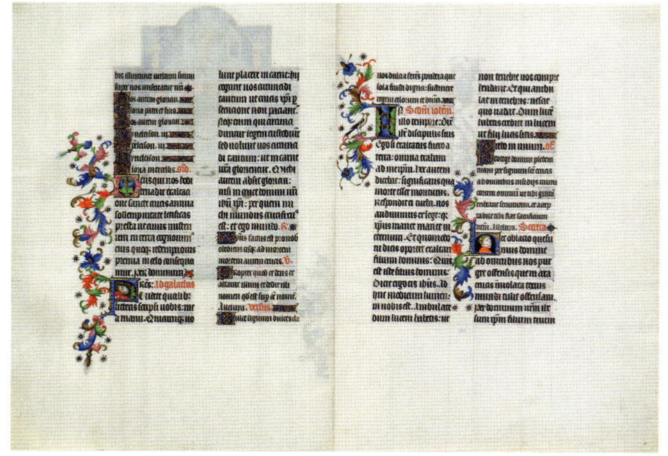

fol. 193v–194

fol. 194v–195

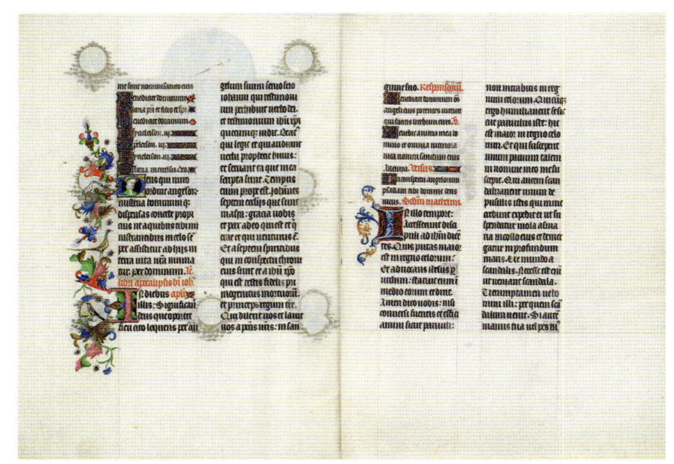

fol. 195v–196

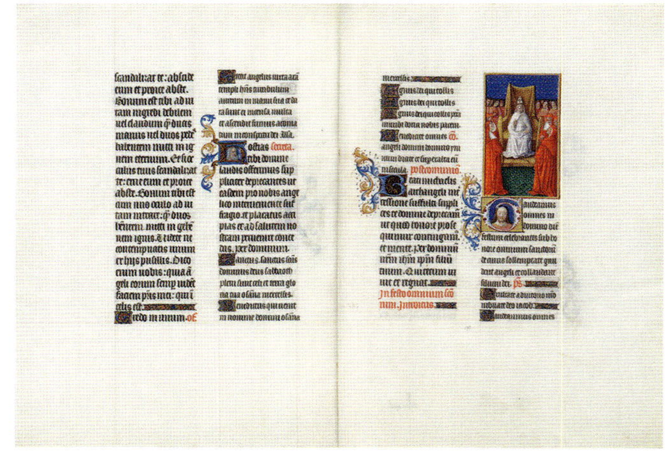

fol. 196v–197

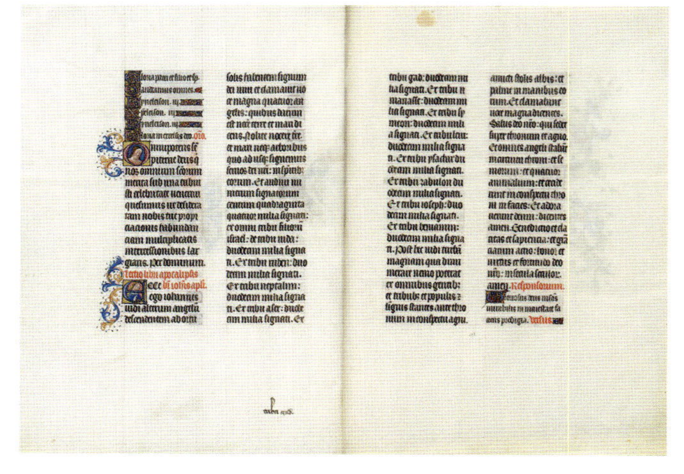

fol. 197v–198

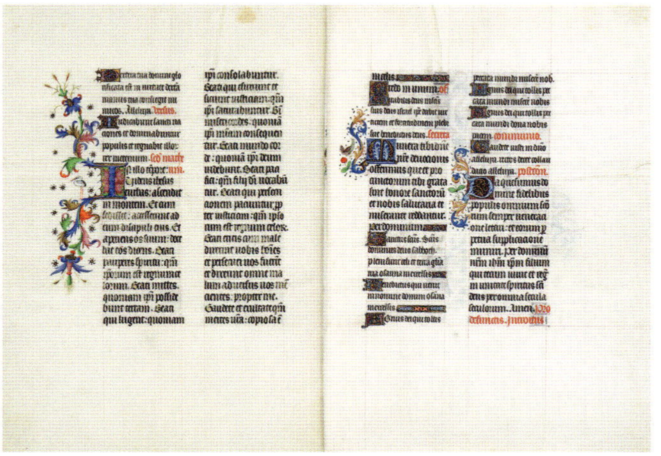

fol. 198v–199

fol. 202v–203

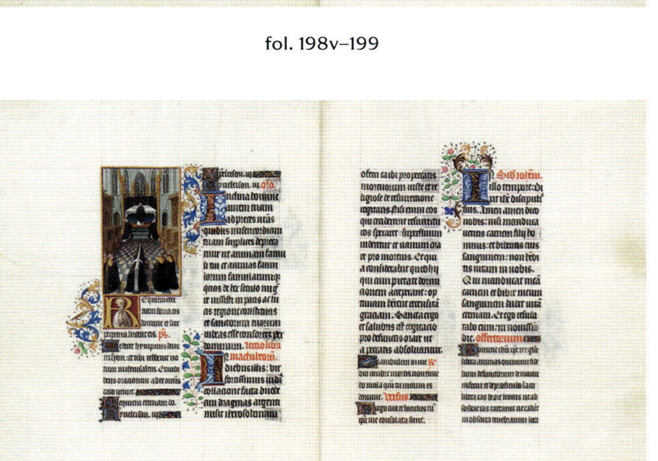

fol. 199v–200

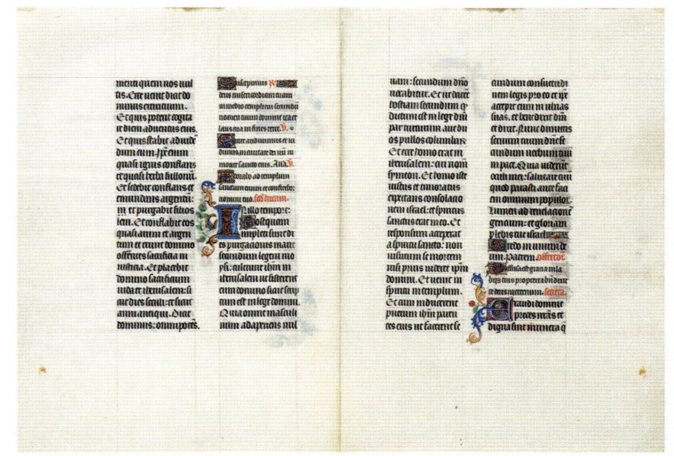

fol. 203v–204

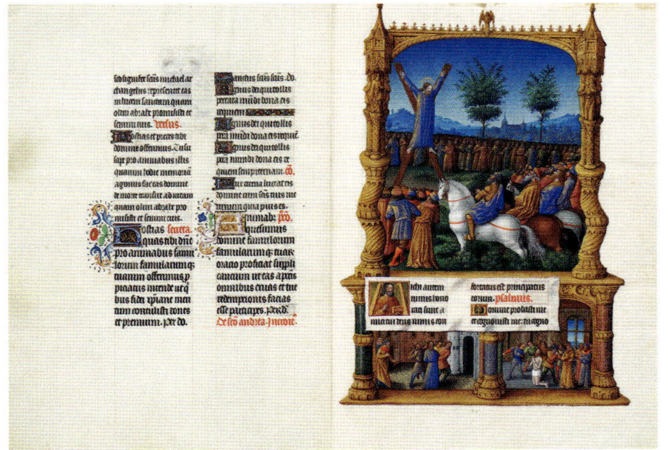

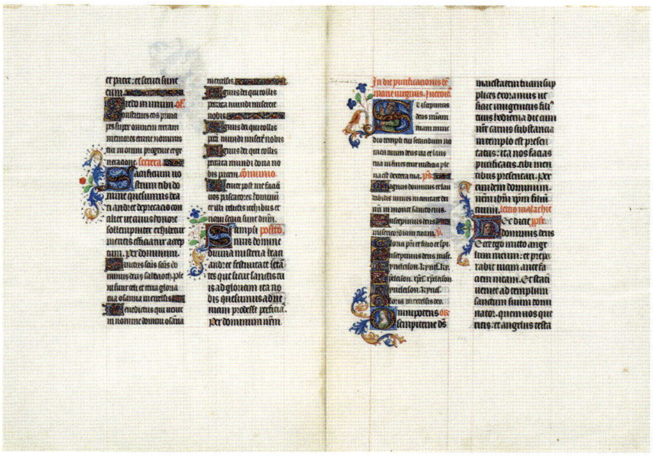

fol. 200v–201

fol. 204v–205

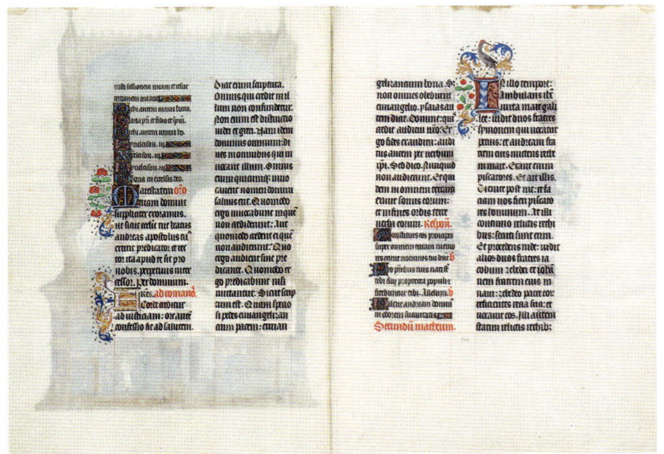

fol. 201v–202

fol. 205v–206

fol. 206v–207

fol. 207v–208

fol. 208v – Inside back cover

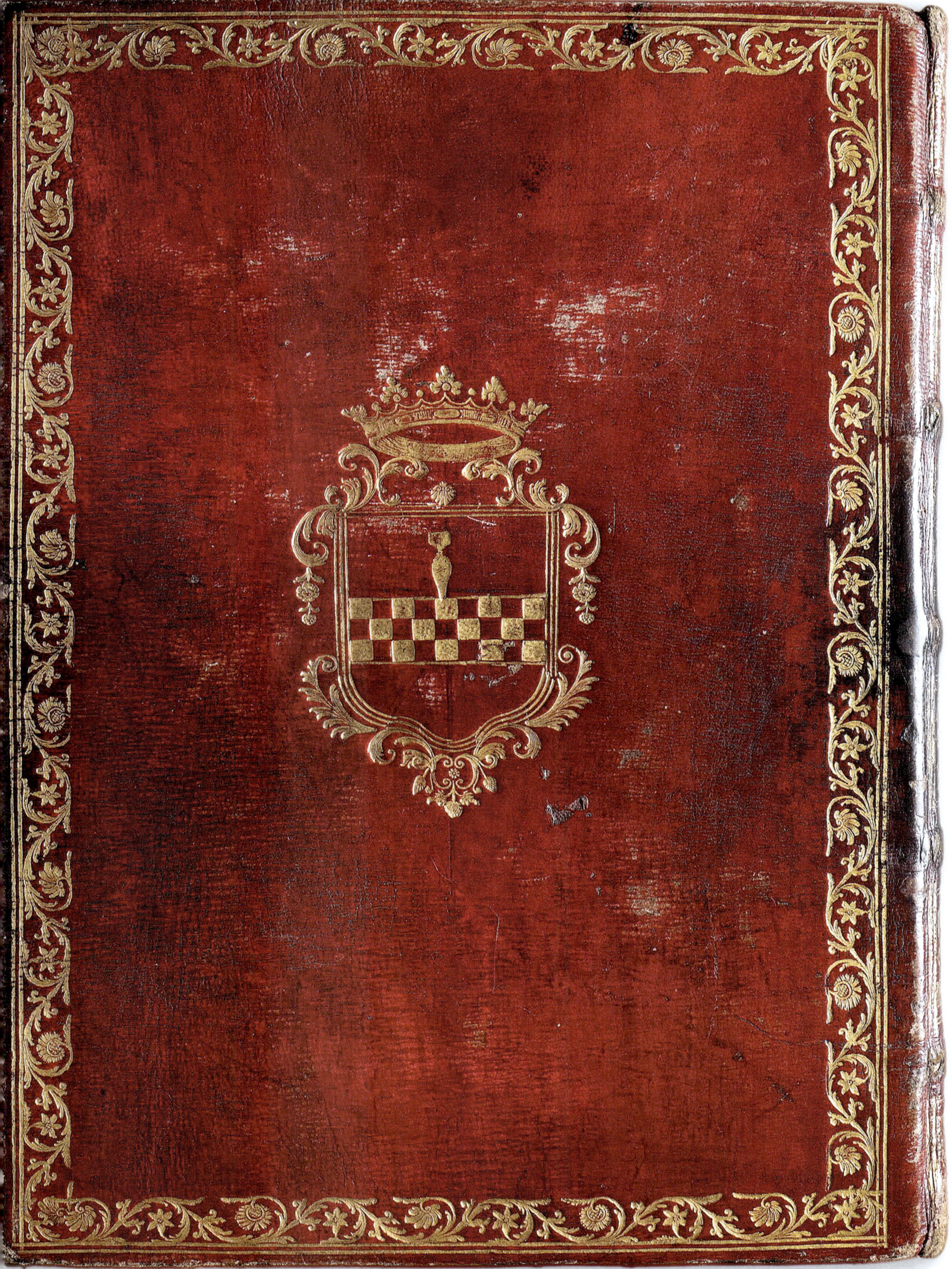